The IEBM Handbook of International Business

**Titles from the International Encyclopedia of
Business and Management series**

International Encyclopedia of Business and Management
6 volume set, hardback, 0-415-07399-5

Concise International Encyclopedia of Business and Management
1 volume edition, hardback, 1-86152-114-6

Pocket International Encyclopedia of Business and Management
Paperback, 1-86152-113-8

The IEBM Encyclopedia of Marketing
Edited by Michael J Baker
Hardback, 1-86152-304-1

The IEBM Regional Encyclopedia of Business and Management
4 volume set, hardback 1-86152-403-X

IEBM Handbook Series

The IEBM Handbook of Human Resource Management
Edited by Michael Poole and Malcolm Warner
Hardback, 1-86152-166-9

The IEBM Handbook of Information Technology in Business
Edited by Milan Zeleny
Hardback, 1-86152-308-4

The IEBM Handbook of Management Thinking
Edited by Malcolm Warner
Hardback, 1-86152-162-6

The IEBM Handbook of Organizational Behaviour
Edited by Arndt Sorge and Malcolm Warner
Hardback, 1-86152-157-X

The IEBM Handbook of International Business

Edited by
Rosalie L. Tung

INTERNATIONAL THOMSON BUSINESS PRESS

I(T)P® An International Thomson Publishing Company

London • Bonn • Boston • Johannesburg • Madrid • Melbourne • Mexico City • New York • Paris •
Singapore • Tokyo • Toronto • Albany, NY • Belmont, CA • Cincinnati, OH • Detroit, MI

The IEBM Handbook of International Business

Copyright ©1999 International Thomson Business Press

First published by International Thomson Business Press

I(T)P®   A division of International Thomson Publishing Inc.
The ITP logo is a trademark under licence

British Library Cataloguing-in-Publication Data
A catalogue record for this book is available from the British Library

First edition 1998

Typeset by Hodgson Williams Associates, Cambridge
Printed in the UK by T J International, Cornwall

ISBN 1-86152-216-9

International Thomson Business Press
Berkshire House
168–173 High Holborn
London WC1V 7AA
UK

http://www.itbp.com

Contents

To my daughter, Michele,
hoping she will thrive in this brave new world

List of Contributors

Professor Etsuo Abe
School of Business Administration
Meiji University
Tokyo
Japan

Mohi Ahmed
PhD Candidate, School of Communication
Faculty of Applied Science
Simon Fraser University
Burnaby
British Colombia
Canada

Mr Michael Backman
AEMC Fellow
Australia

Professor Greg J. Bamber
Director, Graduate School of Management
(GSM)
Griffith University
Brisbane
Australia

Professor Paul W. Beamish
Director, Asian Management Institute
Ivey Business School
University of Western Ontario
London
Canada

Dr John Cathie
Department of Land Economy
University of Cambridge
England

Kellie Caught
Australian Centre in Strategic Management
Queensland University of Technology
Brisbane
Australia

Professor Min Chen
Associate Professor
Thunderbird – The American Graduate
School of International Management
Glendale
Arizona
USA

Professor Dong-Sung Cho
College of Business Administration
Seoul National University
Korea

Professor Farok Contractor
Graduate School of Business
Rutgers University
Newark
New Jersey
USA

Dr John D. Daniels
E. Claiborne Robins Dintiguished Professor
E. Claiborne Robins School of Business
University of Richmond
USA

Professor Arnoud De Meyer
Professor of Technology Management
INSEAD
Fontainebleau
France

Dr P. Candace Deans
Associate Professor of Information
Management
Thunderbird – The American Graduate
School of International Management
Glendale
Arizona
USA

Dr Gunter Dufey
Professor of International Business and
Finance
School of Business Administration
University of Michigan
Ann Arbor
USA

Professor Thomas Dunfee
The Wharton School
University of Pennsylvania
Philadelphia
USA

Vincent Edwards
Head of Research
Buckinghamshire Business School
Buckinghamshire Chilterns University
Chalfont St. Giles
England

Professor Ellen Fagenson-Eland
Associate Professor
School of Management
George Mason University
Virginia
USA

Dr Robert S. Frank
President
R. Shelby Frank and Associates
Highlands Ranch
Colorado
USA

Michelle Gittelman
Department of Management
The Wharton School
University of Pennsylvania
Philadelphia
USA

Dr Ian Glover
Management and Organization Department
School of Management
University of Stirling
Scotland

Dr Greg Harris
City University Business School
City University
London
England

Dr Stephen J. Havlovic
Associate Professor, Industrial Relations
and Human Resource Management
Faculty of Business Administration
Simon Fraser University
Burnaby
British Columbia
Canada

Dr Geert Hofstede
Emeritus Professor of Organizational
Anthropology and International
Management
University of Maastricht
The Netherlands

Professor Takatoshi Ito
Institute of Economic Research
Hitotsubashi University
Tokyo
Japan
and Senior Advisor, Research Department
International Monetary Fund
Washington, DC, USA

Professor Jane H. Ives
Bentley College
Massachusetts
USA

Professor Laurent L. Jacque
Fletcher School of Law and Diplomacy
Tufts University
Medford
Massachusetts
USA
and Professor of Economics and
International Finance
Groupe HEC School of Management
Jouy-en-Josas
France

Professor Arvind K. Jain
Associate Professor
Concordia University
Montreal
Canada

Anne Jenkins
Senior Research Associate
Durham University Business School
University of Durham
England

Dr Johny K. Johansson
McCrane/Shaker Professor of International
Business and Marketing
Georgetown School of Business
Georgetown University
Washington DC
USA

Professor Pat Joynt
PowerGen Professor of Management
Development
Henley Management College
Henley-on-Thames
England
and Norway School of Management
Sandvika
Norway

Professor Peter J. Killing
Visiting Professor of Strategy
IMD
Lausanne
Switzerland

Professor Bruce Kogut
The Wharton School
University of Pennsylvania
Philadelphia
USA

Professor Christopher M. Korth
Haworth College of Business
Western Michigan Unversity
Kalamazoo
Michigan
USA

Professor Nagesh Kumar
INTECH
United Nations University
Maastricht
The Netherlands

C.H. Kwan
Senior Economist
Center for Policy Research
Nomura Research Institute
Tokyo
Japan

Professor Ernest R. Larkins
E. Harold Stokes/KPMG Peat Marwick
Professor of Accountancy
Georgia State University
Atlanta, Georgia
USA

Dr Chung-Ming Lau
Associate Professor
Department of Management
Chinese University of Hong Kong
Hong Kong

Dr Kevin McCormick
School of Social Sciences
Sussex University
Falmer, Brighton
England

Professor Dr Rainer Marr
Instutut für Personal- und
Organisationsforschung
Fakultät für Wirtschafts und
Organisationswissenschaften
Universität der Bundeswehr München
Munich
Germany

Dr Debra Meyerson
Scholar
Institute for Research on Women and
Gender
Stanford University
California
USA

Professor Edwin L. Miller
University of Michigan Business School
University of Michigan
Ann Arbor
USA

Professor Rolf Mirus
Eric Geddes Professor of Business
Faculty of Business Administration
University of Alberta
Edmonton
Canada

Dr Michael H. Moffett
Associate Professor of Finance
Thunderbird –The American Graduate
School of International Management
Glendale
Arizona
USA

Professor Robert T. Moran
Professor of International Studies; Director,
Program in Cross-Cultural Communication
Thunderbird –The American Graduate
School of International Management
Glendale
Arizona
USA

Elizabeth Moran de Longeaux
Master of International Management (MIM)
Candidate
Thunderbird –The American Graduate
School of International Management
Glendale
Arizona
USA

Professor Jonathan Morris
Cardiff Business School
University of Wales, Cardiff
Wales

Dr Stanley J. Paliwoda
Professor and Chair of Marketing
Fellow of the Chartered Insitute of
Marketing of the UK
Faculty of Management
University of Calgary
Alberta
Canada

Professor Michael Poole
Professor of Human Resource Management
Cardiff Business School
University of Wales, Cardiff
Wales

Professor Betty Jane Punnett
Mona Institute of Business
University of the West Indies
Kingston
Jamaica

Professor Lee H. Radebaugh
KPMG Peat Marwick Professor
Director, Center for International Business,
Education and Research
Brigham Young University
Provo
Utah
USA

Robert J. Radway
Adjunct Professor of International Business
Pace University
and President, Vector International (a
consulting firm for planning and execution
of international business strategy)
New York
USA

Collin C. Randlesome
Senior Lecturer
Cranfield School of Management
Cranfield University
Bedford
England

Professor Neil R. Richardson
Department of Political Science
University of Wisconsin - Madison
USA

Professor David A. Ricks
Distinguished Professor of International
Business
Thunderbird –The American Graduate
School of International Management
Glendale
Arizona
USA

Dr Franklin R. Root
Professor Emeritus of International
Management
The Wharton School
University of Pennsylvania
Philadelphia
USA

Dr Alan M. Rugman
Thames Water Fellow in Strategic
Management
Templeton College
University of Oxford
England

Professor Naoto Sasaki
Professor of International Management
Department of Business
Hamamatsu University
Hamamatsu-shi
Japan

Professor Richard Scase
Faculty of Social Science
University of Kent at Canterbury
England

Professor Hans Schollhammer
Chairman, International Management
Program
Anderson Graduate School of Management
University of California
Los Angeles
USA

Dr James A. Schweikart
Associate Professor of Accounting
E. Claiborne Robins School of Business
University of Richmond
USA

Professor Brian Scott-Quinn
Director, ISMA Centre
The Business School for Financial Markets
University of Reading
Berkshire
England

Professor Daniel P. Sullivan
Department of Business Administration
University of Delaware
Newark
USA

Professor Dennis Swann
Department of Economics
Loughborough University
Leicestershire
England

Dr Joseph Szarka
Senior Lecturer
School of European Studies
University of Bath
England

Dr Joo-Seng Tan
Nanyang Business School
Nanyang Technological University
Singapore

Professor Rosalie L. Tung
Ming and Stella Wong Professor of
International Business
Faculty of Business Administration
Simon Fraser University
Burnaby
British Columbia
Canada

Ann Vereecke
Assistant Professor
The Vlerick School of Management
University of Ghent
Belgium

Professor Heidi Vernon
Northeastern University
Boston
Massachusetts
USA

Professor Zhong-Ming Wang
School of Management
Hangzhou University
Zhejiang Province
China

Professor Lawrence H. Wortzel
before his death, Boston University
Massachusetts
USA

Professor Ryh-song Yeh
Associate Professor
Department of Management
Chinese University of Hong Kong
Hong Kong

Dr Bernard M. Yeung
Associate Professor of International
Business
Business School
University of Michigan
Ann Arbor

Acknowledgements

The publishers would like to thank the following for permission to use copyright material:

Culture, cross-national
Country clusters
S.Ronen and O. Shenkar (1985) 'Clustering countries on attitudinal dimensions: a review and synthesis', *Academy of Management Review*.

Cultural values: levels of individualism in alpha and beta. Reproduced from M. Mendenhall, B.J. Punnett and D.A. Ricks (1995) *Global Management*, by permission of Blackwell Publishers.

Economics of developing countries
Real non-oil commodity prices: long term developments
Reproduced by permission of the International Monetary Fund.

Financial management, international
Exchange rate quotations: pound spot - forward against the pound; Exchange rate quotations: dollar spot - forward against the dollar; Eurocurrency interest rates (loan rate, deposit rate, per cent per annum) Copyright © *Financial Times* 1993.

Globalization
Costs of air transportation, telephone calls, and computers in 1990 dollars, 1930-90 Reproduced from R.J. Herring and R.E. Litan (1995) *Financial Regulation in the Global Economy*, by permission of The Brookings Institution.

Human resource management, international
Flow chart of the selection-decision process
Permission granted by Columbia University, New York City.

International operations
The strategic role of plants
Reproduced by permission of K. Ferdows

International trade and foreign direct investment
Principal explanations of comparative advantage in international trade
Reproduced from F.G. Root (1994) *International Trade and Investment,* 7th edn, by permission of South-Western College Publishing.
Credit to the US Small Business Administration, Office of Advocacy.

Management in Japan
The P-D-C-A cycle/quality circle
Reproduced from J.M. Juran (1988) *Quality in Japan, Juran's Quality Control Handbook,* by permission of The McGraw-Hill Companies.

Management in South Korea
Growth strategies of *chaebols*
K.H. Chung and H.C. Lee (1989) *Korean Managerial Dynamics,* reprinted with permission of Greenwood Publishing Group, Inc., Westport, CT. © 1989.

Backgrounds of *chaebol* executives
Reproduced by permission of JAI Press Inc.

Originally published in Min Chen (1995) *Asian Management Systems: Chinese, Japanese and Korean Styles of Business,* London: International Thomson Business Press.

Multinational corporations
The top fifteen multinational corporations UNCTAD Division on Transnational Corporations and Development, *World Investment Report 1994: Transnational Corporations, Employment and the Workplace* (New York, United Nations, 1994).

Toyoda family
The Toyoda family: members in director positions with Toyota
Permission granted by Elsevier Science.

Critical differences between Fordism , neo-Fordism and lean production in 'Towards Lean Management? International Transferability of Japanese Management Studies to Australia', Shadur, M. A. and Bamber, G. J., from *The International Executive*, 36 (3) Copyright © 1994 John Wiley & Sons, Inc. Reprinted by permission of John Wiley & Sons, Inc. USA

Introduction

Undoubtedly, one of the most significant developments in the last quarter of the twentieth century is the globalization of industries. While international commerce has been around since the time of the ancient Phoenicians, until the 1970s, trade between and among nations has been rather limited and highly regulated. With the dismantling of the Cold War and quantum advances in telecommunications and technology, which render instantaneous access to information from around the world a virtual reality, the era of the global village is truly upon us. Many aspects of our work and non-work lives are affected by what takes place in other countries, far and near. To survive in this new economic world order, it is increasingly difficult for corporations (and the people that work within these entities) to wear ethnocentric blinders to screen out developments in other countries, regardless of how distant they are, both geographically and culturally.

To reflect the realities of this new economic world order, new terms and concepts have been coined. These include: world class organizations, knowledge society, learning organizations, boundarylessness, stateless organizations, cosmopolitans, and corporate diplomats. These new terms and concepts all point to the need for the emergence and/or development of organizations that can span geographic and cultural boundaries in all aspects of their activities, including the acquisition, manufacture and provision of products and services. To operate effectively in this new economic world order, it is imperative that people possess knowledge on a broad spectrum of issues and concepts that affect business transactions around the globe.

This *Handbook* is developed with that objective in mind, namely, to provide a handy source of reference to those who have to or who seek to operate within this new economic world order. While countless books and articles have been written on international business (including international management), many people may not have the time or the resources to sift through this voluminous amount of information and material in order to gain an adequate understanding of some pressing issues/concepts that pertain to this broad and rapidly changing field of inquiry. To address this situation, this *Handbook* offers, within one single volume, a ready and up-to-date source of information on a comprehensive range of topics, issues and concepts that pertain to the field of international business.

The entries in this volume are written by leading experts in their respective fields from around the world. While the majority of the authors are academics, the entries are written in a language which appeals to both practitioners and theoreticians who want quick access to an authoritative guide on the major topics that arise in the area of international business. This book is also essential reading for students of international business who seek to prepare themselves for the opportunities and challenges of doing business in the twenty-first century. Even students who wish to pursue careers in a domestic context can benefit from this *Handbook* because in an era of global interdependence, the country of domicile of the manager is increasingly becoming inconsequential since the person becomes part of an international team.

The essays in this volume are organized around four major areas:
1 general principles, concepts and issues in international business;
2 management concepts and issues with a country/region focus;
3 profiles of leading business firms; and
4 biographies of international business leaders.

All the entries that appear in this *Handbook* were written specifically for this volume and/or its related six-volume *International Encyclopedia of Business and Management*

(*IEBM*, in short) (1996). Where the entries first appeared in the IEBM, they have been updated to incorporate the latest changes and developments on that specific topic. To ensure consistency throughout, each entry in the 'General principles' and 'Country/region focus' categories begins with an 'Overview' section which introduces the reader to the issue/concept under discussion and provides a summary of the major topics to be addressed in that essay. The main body of the text contains an analysis and synthesis of the major topics pertaining to the concept/issue in question. Each entry ends with a 'Conclusion' section which goes beyond a mere summary of the ideas and issues raised in the piece to include a projection of future trends and directions in that subject. This is followed by a 'Further readings' section which contains an annotated bibliography of readings on that subject. Given the rapid changes that occur within some subject areas, such as the European Union, World Trade Organization, and Asian Pacific Economic Cooperation, the relevant website addresses are included to enable the reader to check up on the latest developments on that topic.

Due to space limitations, it is obviously impossible to include all countries in the world in the 'Country/region focus' segment. Only the major industrialized and developing countries which are key players in the international economic arena are included.

The third section of the *Handbook* contains short profiles of a select sample of transnational companies. Depending upon definition, while the number of companies that can be characterized as transnationals run into the hundreds, if not thousands, only thirty-four companies were selected for inclusion here. The criteria for inclusion were one or more of the following:

1 size as measured in assets, annual revenues or number of employees worldwide;
2 global reach;

3 dominance in a given industry worldwide; and significant contributions to the industry (including technological innovations and/or innovative management practices/systems).

Every attempt has been made to include companies from diverse countries and industries. As with all other lists, there are bound to be omissions due to space constraints. The profile on each international company contains an overview of the company/group, followed by a brief history, a summary of major innovations and significant contributions, and concludes with an identification of major challenges and opportunities that lie ahead.

The last section of the *Handbook* contains biographies of international business leaders. Twenty-five individuals/families are selected for inclusion here. These individuals/families have made significant contributions to their respective companies, industries, and the promotion/advancement of international business, in general. In certain cases, some of these people have actually created a new field. Furthermore, many of the people included in this segment have revolutionized management thought and practices. Again, every attempt has been made to include people from around the world and from a diversity of industries. The format of the biographies parallels that for company profiles.

A project of this magnitude can only be carried to fruition through the hard work and dedication of many people. It is impossible to identify all of them by name here. I would like to thank all the authors, the in-house publishing team, Professor Malcolm Warner and others who have been instrumental to the successful development of the IEBM project. I would also like to thank my husband, Byron, and daughter, Michele, for their understanding as to why I spent endless hours during my sabbatical year writing, editing and communicating with contributors from around the world.

Rosalie L. Tung, FRSC
May 1998

General principles, issues and concepts

Accounting, international

Overview

Managers cannot make good decisions without the availability of adequate and timely financial information. Although accounting and information systems specialists provide this information, all managers need to understand which data are needed and the problems specialists face in gathering those data from around the world. The accounting and finance functions are very closely related. Each relies on the other in fulfilling its own responsibilities. The financial manager of any company, whether domestic or international, is responsible for procuring and managing the company's financial resources. That manager relies on the accountant to provide the information necessary to manage financial resources.

The actual and potential flow of assets across national boundaries complicates the finance and accounting functions. The multinational corporation (MNC) must learn to cope with differing inflation rates, exchange rate changes, currency controls, expropriation risks, customs duties, levels of sophistication and local requirements.

A company's accounting or controllership function is responsible for collecting and analysing data for internal and external users. Foreign managers and subsidiaries are usually evaluated based on data provided by the controller's office. Reports must be generated for internal consideration, local governmental needs, creditors, employees, shareholders and prospective investors. The controller must be concerned about the impact of many different currencies and inflation rates on the statements as well as being familiar with different countries' accounting systems.

1 The development of accounting around the world

One problem which a multinational corporation (MNC) faces is that accounting standards and practices vary around the world; for example, financial statements in Germany do not look the same as those in the USA (see MULTINATIONAL CORPORATIONS). Some observers argue that this is a minor matter, a problem of form rather than substance. In fact, however, the substance also differs, in that assets are measured differently and income is determined differently in different countries.

A good example of this situation involves SmithKline Beecham plc, a UK firm that is the product of a merger between a US firm (SmithKline) and a UK firm (Beecham). When the new merged company tried to raise funds in the United States, it had to disclose its income according to both UK and US accounting standards and also to reconcile the difference. Because of differences in accounting policies, SmithKline Beecham reported a net income of £130 million according to UK standards but a net income of only £87 million according to US standards. There were several reasons for this difference; the major one was the different ways in which UK and US companies are allowed to account for mergers.

These variations put the MNC in a difficult position because it needs to prepare and understand reports generated according to the local accounting standards as well as prepare financial statements consistent with generally accepted accounting principles (GAAP) in the home country in order to provide information for home country users of financial statements. Each country develops its own GAAP, which are the accounting standards recognized by the profession as being required in the preparation of financial statements for external users. Each country's GAAP is a function of the factors discussed in the following sections. The more the GAAP differs from country to country, the more costly and difficult it is for an MNC to generate financial statements.

Accounting objectives

Accounting is basically a process of identifying, recording and interpreting economic events, and its goals and purposes should be clearly stated in the objectives of any accounting system. According to the Financial Accounting Standards Board (FASB), the private sector body that establishes accounting standards in the USA, financial reporting should provide information useful in the following areas:

- investment and credit decisions
- assessments of cash-flow prospects
- evaluation of enterprise resources, claims to those resources, and changes in them

The users of these data identified by the board are primarily investors and creditors, although other users might be considered important. The International Accounting Standards Committee (IASC), a standard-setting organization composed of professional accounting organizations from over eighty countries, includes employees as well as investors and creditors as the critical users. Also named as users of this information are suppliers, customers, regulatory and taxing authorities, and many others.

Although the question of whether there should be a uniform set of accounting standards and practices for all classes of users worldwide, or even for one class of users, has been discussed widely, no consensus has been reached. To understand the different accounting principles and how they affect the MNC's operations, one must be aware of some of the forces leading to the development of accounting principles internationally (see Figure 1).

Similar to business in general, corporate accounting and information disclosure practices are influenced by a variety of economic, social and political factors. A model of the environmental factors involved is presented in Figure 1 from which we can see many influences at work. These include the nature of enterprise ownership, the business activities of the enterprise, sources of finance and the stage of development of capital markets, the nature of the taxation system, the existence and significance of the accounting profession, the state of accounting education and research, the nature of the political system, the social climate, the stage of economic growth and development, the rate of inflation, the nature of the legal system, and the nature of accounting

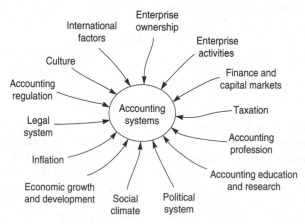

Figure 1 Environmental influences on accounting
Source: Radebaugh and Gray (1993: 44)

regulation. The nature of accounting systems at the country level will vary according to the relative influence of these environmental factors and such systems will, in turn, tend to reinforce established patterns of behaviour.

Relative to enterprise ownership, the need for public accountability and disclosure will be greater where there is a broad ownership of shares compared to family ownership. Where there is state ownership, the influence of centralized control on the nature of accounting systems will tend to be overriding in terms of serving macroeconomic objectives. The activities of enterprises will also be influential on the nature of the accounting system depending on whether the business is agricultural, extractive, manufacturing, and so on; whether it is diversified; whether it is multinational; and whether it is a large group of companies or a small business.

The source of finance is another important influence. Clearly, there will be more pressure for public accountability and information disclosure where finance is raised from external shareholders as opposed to banks or family sources when information will be available more directly.

Taxation is a very important factor in situations where accounting systems are strongly influenced by state objectives; that is, public accounting reports are used as a basis for determining tax liabilities such as in France and Germany, in contrast to the USA and UK, where the published accounts are adjusted for tax purposes and submitted separately from the reports to shareholders.

Where there is a more developed accounting profession there are likely to be more developed, judgmentally based public accounting systems as opposed to more centralized and uniform systems. Furthermore, the development of professional accounting will depend on the existence of a sound infrastructure of accounting education and research which is often lacking, for example, in developing countries.

The political system is obviously a very important influence on accounting in that the nature of the accounting system will reflect political philosophies and objectives (for example, central planning versus private enterprise). The social climate in terms of attitudes to informing and consulting employees and with respect to environmental concerns will also be influential. In Europe, for example, there is a much more positive approach to information disclosure relating to such matters than in the USA.

The nature and extent of economic growth and development will also be influential in so far as change from an agricultural to a manufacturing economy will pose new accounting problems such as the depreciation of machinery, leasing, and so on. In many countries, services are now becoming more important and thus the problems of how to account for intangible assets such as brand names, goodwill and human resources have become significant. Inflation is often associated with economic growth and is a major influence on accounting where hyperinflation is rife (for example, in South America) to the extent that alternative systems to the traditional historic cost approach are preferred.

The legal system is also important in determining the extent to which company law governs the regulation of accounting (see INTERNATIONAL BUSINESS, LEGAL DIMENSIONS OF). In countries with a tradition of codified Roman law (or civil codes) – as in France and Germany, compared to common law as in the UK and USA – accounting regulations tend to be detailed and comprehensive. Furthermore, the influence of the accounting profession in setting accounting standards tends to be much less in such countries compared to situations where company law is supplemented by professional regulation as in the UK and USA.

In addition, the influence of culture (societal or national values) needs to be taken into account in terms of its underlying impact on accounting traditions and practices. International factors are also bringing about changes in the environment and to some extent providing forces for international accounting harmonization as opposed to the constraining influences operating at national levels.

Naturally, the influence of these factors is dynamic and will vary both between and within countries over time. Moreover, it

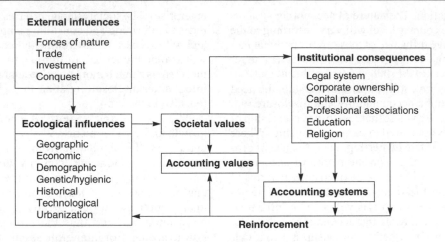

Figure 2 Culture, societal values and the accounting subculture
Source: Gray (1988: 7)

appears that there is an evolutionary process of some complexity at work with special reference to the growing number of international and regional influences such as those arising from the activities of MNCs and intergovernmental organizations such as the United Nations (UN), the Organization for Economic Cooperation and Development (OECD), and the European Union (EU; see EUROPEAN UNION). In the European context, the EU is an especially significant influence in that any agreement on the harmonization of accounting and information disclosure eventually becomes legally enforceable through a process of implementation in the national laws of the member countries.

Cultural differences

A major source of influence on accounting standards and practices is culture. National differences in culture have emerged over long periods of time and have often maintained their stability over many generations (see CULTURE, CROSS-NATIONAL). How does this happen and how does change occur?

The origins of culture, or societal values, can be found in a variety of factors affecting the ecological or physical environment. Societal values lead to the development and maintenance of institutions in society, which include family systems, social class

structures, the political system, the legal system, the financial system, the nature of business ownership, the education system, and so on. These institutions, once developed, tend to reinforce societal values and the factors giving rise to such values. However, when change at the national level occurs, it is mainly as a result of external forces, through the forces of nature or the forces of people. Such external forces affect societal values via the physical environment and may impact on the functioning of institutions. Culture, or societal values, at the national level may be expected to permeate through to organizational and occupational subcultures, though with varying degrees of integration. Accounting and accountants thus can be incorporated in this framework with accounting systems and practices influenced and reinforcing societal values. In this way we can obtain possibly more fundamental insights into why there are differences between national systems of accounting and reporting, both internal and external. Figure 2 provides a model of the process whereby societal values are expressed at the level of the accounting subculture. Accordingly, the value system or attitudes of accountants are shown as being related to and derived from societal values with special reference to work-related values. Accounting 'values' will, in time, impact on accounting systems including public reporting and disclosure.

Of special interest to international investors are the differences in measurement and disclosure practices from among countries. Measurement refers to such issues as how to value assets, including inventory and fixed assets. Disclosure refers to the presentation of information and discussion of results in documents that are prepared for external users of financial data, such as the annual report. Figure 3 depicts the possible locations of the accounting practices of various groupings of countries in a matrix of the cultural values of secrecy/transparency and optimism/conservatism. With respect to accounting, secrecy and transparency refer to the degree to which corporations disclose information to the public. Countries such as Germany, Switzerland and Japan tend to have less disclosure (illustrating the cultural value of secrecy) than the USA and the UK – the Anglo-Saxon countries – which are more transparent or open with respect to disclosure. This is illustrated in more extensive footnotes in reports of the Anglo-Saxon countries than is the case elsewhere.

Optimism and conservatism (in an accounting, not a political, sense) refer to the degree of caution companies exhibit in valuing assets and recognizing income – an illustration of the measurement issues mentioned above. More conservative countries from an accounting point of view tend to understate assets and income, whereas optimistic countries tend to be more liberal in their recognition of income. The problem with comparing this cultural value is that accounting is inherently conservative, so we are really looking at the degree of conservatism. For example, German companies are funded largely by banks, and banks are concerned with liquidity. Therefore, German companies tend to be very conservative in recording profits – which keeps them from paying taxes and declaring dividends – while piling up cash reserves that can be used to service their bank debt. In contrast, US companies want to show optimistic earnings in order to attract investors. Generally, UK companies tend to be more optimistic in earnings recognition than US companies, but US companies are significantly more optimistic than other European companies and Japanese ones. Thus there are significant differences in accounting standards and practices worldwide that affect earnings measures (see MANAGEMENT IN GERMANY; MANAGEMENT IN THE UNITED KINGDOM).

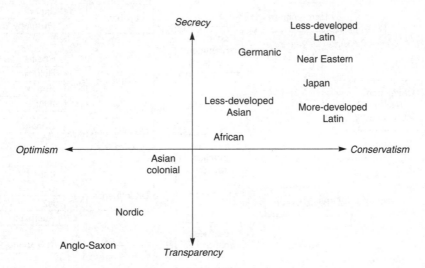

Figure 3 Accounting systems: measurement and disclosure
Source: Radebaugh and Gray (1993: 76)

Classification of accounting systems

While there are many differences in national environments, with corresponding different effects on accounting systems, there are also many similarities. Attempts to classify countries and identify patterns or groupings are still very much at the early stages, but such efforts would seem to be useful in gaining a better understanding of the key factors influencing the development of accounting systems with consequent benefit in terms of predicting likely changes and their impact.

Accounting systems in socialist economies such as The People's Republic of China are, of course, quite different from those in developed market economies such as the USA, Japan and the EU countries (see MANAGEMENT IN CHINA). In the former socialist economies of Russia and eastern Europe, for example, accounting is in a state of transition to a market approach. As far as public accounting and reporting in the market economies are concerned, however, it seems that a number of distinct models of accounting may be identified including, at the very least, the Anglo-American and continental European traditions. But given the change factors at work, it is not an easy task to make accurate assessments or predictions of future evolution. The current situation is highly dynamic in the context of the activities of a wide range of national and international organizations, as well as the changing nature of business and especially multinational operations. It may well be that new models or patterns of accounting and reporting are in the process of being formed. The UK and continental European traditions, for example, are now in the process of coordination and some fusion following EU developments in accounting harmonization.

Although accounting standards and practices differ worldwide, systems used in various countries can be grouped according to common characteristics. Figure 4 illustrates one approach to classifying accounting systems. This scheme does not attempt to classify

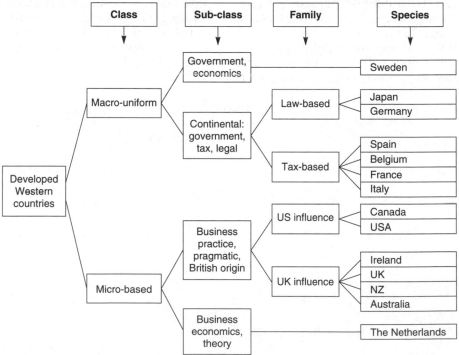

Figure 4 A hypothetical classification of financial reporting measurement practices in developed Western countries
Source: Nobes (1983: 7)

all countries but simply illustrates the concept using several developed Western countries.

In Figure 4, accounting systems are initially divided into macro-uniform and micro-based systems. Macro-uniform systems are shaped more by governmental influence than are microsystems. Except for Sweden's system, macro-uniform systems are influenced by tax law or just a strong legal system. These systems also tend to be more conservative and secretive about disclosure. Micro-based systems, except for that of The Netherlands, include features that support pragmatic business practice and have evolved from the UK system. The US system is closer to the macro-uniform systems, however, because of the strong influence of the Securities and Exchange Commission (SEC), a federal government agency that regulates securities offerings within the USA.

The bottom line is that MNCs need to adjust to different accounting systems around the world. Thus the accounting function is made more complex and costly to perform. An MNC's parent company must gather data from far-flung subsidiaries and affiliates and convert those data into a format consistent with the home country's preferred accounting system.

An MNC expected to provide its annual report or at least its financial statements to foreign users has five major alternatives regarding presentation of financial data:

1 Provide accounting information according to home country GAAP and hope that foreign investors are willing to accept those numbers. This is known as the principle of mutual recognition. In other words, if a German company provides financial information according to German GAAP and a US company provides financial information according to US GAAP, mutual recognition requires that the USA accept the German statements and Germany accept the US statements.
2 Provide accounting information according to international GAAP (IASC standards) and hope that the host country accepts those numbers.
3 Provide accounting information according to host country GAAP, which is what Japanese companies tend to do when they list securities in the USA. They provide financial information according to US GAAP rather than Japanese GAAP.
4 Provide accounting information according to home country GAAP that is reconciled to host-country GAAP. This is how most foreign companies that list on the US exchanges provide financial information. The US SEC requires that foreign companies provide information according to US GAAP or reconciled to US GAAP.

An example of the reconciliation approach is found in Table 1, which is the reconciliation of consolidated net income and shareholders' equity from German GAAP to US GAAP for Daimler–Benz in 1993 and 1994. The reconciliation highlights significant differences in results and the major sources of difference. Similar reconciliation statements can be found in Form 20–F of most foreign corporations who list or trade securities on any of the US stock exchanges. These reconciliations spotlight the significant differences between US and foreign GAAP.

2 Harmonization of differences

Despite the many differences in accounting standards and practices, a number of forces are leading to harmonization:

1 a movement to provide information compatible with the needs of investors;
2 the global integration of capital markets, which means that investors have easier and faster access to investment opportunities around the world and therefore need financial information that is more comparable;
3 the need of MNCs to raise capital outside their own national capital markets while generating as few different financial statements as possible;
4 regional political and economic harmonization, such as the efforts of the EU, which affects accounting as well as trade and investment issues;
5 pressure from MNCs for more uniform standards to allow greater ease and reduced

Table 1 Daimler–Benz reconciliation of consolidated net income and stockholders' equity to US GAAP

– in millions of DM –	1994	1993
Consolidated net income in accordance with Bgerman HGB (Commercial Code)	**895**	615
+/– Minority interest	**159**	(13)
Adjusted net income under German GAAP	**1,054**	602
+/– Changes in appropriated retained earnings: provisions, reserves and valuation differences	**409**	(4,262)
	1,463	(3,660)
Additional adjustments		
+/– Long-term contracts	**53**	78
Goodwill and business acquisitions	**(350)**	(287)
Deconsolidation of MBL Fahrzeug-Leasing GmbH & company KG, effective 30 June 1994	**(652)**	–
Pensions and other post-retirement benefits	**(432)**	(624)
Foreign-currency translation	**(22)**	(40)
Financial instruments	**633**	(225)
Securities	**(388)**	–
Other valuation differences	**73**	292
Deferred taxes	**496**	2,627
Consolidated net income/loss in accordance with US GAAP before cumulative effect of a change in accounting principle	**874**	(1,839)
Cumulative effect of change in accounting for certain investments in debt and equity securities as of 1 January 1994, net of tax of DM 235 million	**178**	–
Consolidated net income/loss in accordance with US GAAP	**1,052**	(1,839)
Earnings/loss per share in accordance with US GAAP	**DM 21.53**	DM (39.47)
Earnings/loss per American Depositary Share[1] in accordance with US GAAP	**DM 2.15**	DM (3.95)
Stockholders' equity in accordance with German HGB	**20,251**	18,145
./. Minority interest	**(151)**	(561)
Adjusted stockholders' equity under German GAAP	**20,100**	17,584
+ Appropriated retained earnings: provisions, reserves and valuation differences	**6,205**	5,770
	26,305	23,354
Additional adjustments		
+/– Long-term contracts	**262**	207
Goodwill and business acquisition	**1,978**	2,284
Deconsolidation of MBL Fahrzeug-Leasing GmbH & company KG, effective 30 June 1994	**(652)**	–
Pensions and other post-retirement benefits	**(2,250)**	(1,821)
Foreign-currency translation	**63**	85
Financial instruments	**1,013**	381
Securities	**27**	–
Other valuation differences	**(185)**	(698)
Deferred taxes	**2,874**	2,489
Stockholders' equity in accordance with US GAAP	**29,435**	26,281

1 Corresponds to one-tenth of a share of stock of DM50 par value
Source: Daimler-Benz (1994: 67)

costs in general reporting in each country and in reporting to be used by investors in the parent company's country.

Impelled by these developments, some countries and organizations are working to harmonize accounting standards on a regional as well as an international level. Regionally, the most ambitious and potentially most effective efforts are taking place in the EU. The European Commission is empowered to set directives, which are orders to member countries to bring their laws into line with EU requirements within a certain transition period. The initial accounting directives addressed the type and format of financial statements, the measurement bases on which the financial statements should be prepared, the importance of consolidated financial statements, and the requirement that auditors must ensure that the financial statements reflect a true and fair view of the operations of the company being audited.

The EU's influence is being felt beyond the borders of its members. The European Free Trade Association (EFTA) and eastern European countries are attempting to adopt EU accounting directives in preparation for becoming members. In addition, eastern European countries and those of the former Soviet Union are moving from centrally planned to market economies, and they need an accounting system that will aid in the transition. The EU directives provide some guidance in this area.

The International Accounting Standards Committee (IASC), organized in 1973 by the professional accounting bodies of Mexico and several primarily industrial countries, has worked towards harmonizing accounting standards. The organization comprises over a hundred professional accounting organizations representing more than eighty countries and 900,000 accountants. Initially, the IASC wanted to develop standards that would have rapid and broad acceptance; thus it seemed to focus mostly on improved disclosure. More recently, it has been interested in tackling some more substantive issues.

The IASC has no legislative mandate like that of the EU, so it must rely on goodwill for acceptance of its standards. However, a number of countries have used the standards as models for their own. For example, Singapore has successfully adopted IASC standards. Other countries have modified the standards as appropriate for their own national settings. In addition, the International Organization of Securities Commissions (IOSCO) is working with the IASC to ensure that the standards being developed can be adopted by companies that want to list securities on a variety of national stock exchanges.

3 Transactions in foreign currency

A major accounting problem for international business arises from operating in different currencies (see FOREIGN EXCHANGE RISK, MANAGEMENT OF). In addition to eliminating or minimizing foreign-exchange risk, a company must concern itself with the proper recording and subsequent accounting of assets, liabilities, revenues and expenses that are measured or denominated in foreign currencies. These transactions can result from the purchase and sale of goods and services as well as the borrowing and lending of foreign currency. Accounting for foreign currency transactions and the translation of foreign currency financial statements varies from country to country, but we will use IAS 21 of the IASC for the basic discussion here, and then present major differences that exist from country to country.

Recording of transactions

Any time an importer is required to pay for equipment or merchandise in a foreign currency, it must trade its own currency for that of the exporter in order to make the payment. Likewise, an exporter that denominates its sale in the currency of the importer must convert the receipts into its own currency. Assume that a US company sells inventory to a UK importer with the sale denominated in pounds sterling rather than in dollars. According to IAS 21, the foreign currency transaction should be recorded at the spot rate on the date of the transaction. At subsequent balance sheet dates, the foreign currency monetary items should be reported using the closing rate; non-monetary items carried at historical cost should be reported using the exchange rate at the date of the transaction; and non-monetary items carried at fair market values should be reported using the exchange rate at the time the values were determined. Exchange differences arising on the settlement of monetary items or on reporting the enterprise's monetary items at rates different from those on which they were initially recorded during the period, or reported in previous financial statements, should be recognized as income or expenses in the period in which they arise.

If the US exporter sells goods or services for £100,000 when the exchange rate is $1.5700, the exporter would record the following entries:

Cash   157,00
    Sales   157,000
    £100,000 @ $1.5700

If the importer pays immediately, there is no problem. But what happens if the exporter extends thirty days' credit to the importer? The original entry would be the same as the above, except that cash would be replaced with accounts receivable.

Accounts Receivable   157,000
    Sales   157,000

If the rate stays the same over the next thirty days, the exporter will receive £100,000 at the end of the month and will convert the sterling into $157,000 at the rate of $1.5700. However, if the rate changes to $1.5850, the exporter would record the final settlement as follows:

Cash   158,500
    Accounts Receivable   157,000
    Foreign exchange gain   1,500

The sale stays recorded at the original value of $157,000, but there is a difference between the dollar value of the accounts receivable ($157,000) and the actual cash received when the pounds sterling are converted into dollars ($158,500). The difference of $1,500 is a foreign-exchange gain that must be recognized in that period. These gains and losses arising from foreign currency transactions must be recognized at the end of each accounting period even if the receivable (or payable in the case of a purchase) has not been settled. Typically, this adjustment is made monthly. For the example above, assume the end of the month has arrived and the exporter has still not been paid. The sale is still valued at $157,000, but the receivable has to be updated to the new exchange rate of $1.5850.

The IASC has an allowed alternative treatment for foreign currency transactions in addition to the benchmark treatment described above. There is a different treatment for exchange differences resulting from a severe devaluation or depreciation of a currency against which there is no practical means of hedging and which affect liabilities that cannot be settled and arise directly on the recent acquisition of an asset invoiced in a foreign currency. In these cases, the exchange differences are not taken directly to income but may be included in the carrying amount of the related asset.

National treatments

FASB Statement No. 52 in the USA agrees with the benchmark treatment of IAS 21. However, the US Internal Revenue Service requires that companies defer gains and losses until the receivables or payables are actually liquidated. Then the net gains or losses can be taken to income. The Canadian approach is similar to the benchmark treatment except that gains or losses on long-term items are deferred and amortized over the term of the underlying transaction, similar to the allowed alternative treatment. In Japan, gains or losses on long-term items are deferred until the settlement date. In France, losses are recognized but gains are deferred until the settlement date. This is also the approach followed by the Germans.

4 Translation of foreign currency financial statements

Even though MNCs receive reports originally developed in a variety of different currencies, they eventually must end up with one set of financial statements in their parent currency in order to help management and investors get an aggregate view of worldwide activities in a common currency. The process of restating foreign currency financial statements into the parent currency is known as translation. The combination of all of these translated financial statements into one is known as consolidation.

Translation is a two-step process:

1 The foreign currency financial statements are recast into statements consistent with parent GAAP.
2 All foreign currency amounts are translated or remeasured into the parent's currency.

Translation methods

IAS 21 allows either of two methods to be used to translate financial statements: the current-rate method or the temporal method. The method the company chooses depends on the functional currency of the foreign operation, which is the currency of the primary economic environment in which that entity operates. For example, one of AT&T's largest subsidiaries outside the USA is in England. The primary economic environment of the subsidiary is England, and the functional currency is the British pound sterling. Several factors must be considered to determine whether the parent's currency or the foreign operation's currency is the functional currency. Among the major factors are cash flows, sales prices, sales market data, expenses, financing and intercompany transactions. For example, if the cash flows and/or expenses are primarily in the foreign operation's currency, that is the functional currency. If they are in the parent's currency, that is the functional currency. In the language of IAS 21, the method used to translate financial statements depends on whether the foreign operations are integral to the operations of the reporting enterprise (the functional currency is the parent currency) or foreign entities (the functional currency is the local currency).

If the functional currency is that of the local operating environment, the company must use the current-rate method. The current-rate method provides that all assets and liabilities are translated at the closing exchange rate (known as the current rate according to FASB Statement No. 52), which is the spot exchange rate on the balance sheet date. All income statement items are translated at the average exchange rate, and owners' equity is translated at the rate in effect when capital stock was issued and retained earnings were accumulated. For example, Coca-Cola states in its *Annual Report* that it distributes its products in more than 195 countries and uses approximately forty-two functional currencies. In Japan and Mexico, the functional currency would be the yen and the peso, respectively, because Coca-Cola's primary operating environments would be the local environments. Thus Coca-Cola would use the current-rate method to translate the financial statements of operations in Japan and Mexico from yen and pesos to dollars.

Although the spot rate is used for translation purposes, which spot rate does a company select when multiple exchange rates exist? In general, the exchange rate used to translate foreign currency financial statements is the rate that must be used for dividends sent back to the parent company. In some countries, this exchange rate is also called the financial rate.

If the functional currency is the parent's currency, the MNC must use the temporal method. The temporal method provides that only monetary assets (cash, marketable securities, and receivables) and liabilities are translated at the closing (current) exchange rate. Inventory and property, plant and equipment are translated at the historical rate, that is, the exchange rate in effect when the assets were acquired. In general, net income also is translated at the average exchange rate, but cost of goods sold and depreciation expenses are translated at the appropriate historical exchange rate.

Tables 2 and 3 show a balance sheet and income statement developed under both approaches in order to compare the differences in translation methodologies. Some of the key assumptions are as follows:

Table 2 Balance sheet, 31 December 1994

	Pounds	Temporal method		Current-rate method	
		Rate	Dollars	Rate	Dollars
Cash	20000	1.49	29800	1.49	29800
Accounts receivable	40000	1.49	59600	1.49	59600
Inventories	40000	1.51	60400	1.49	59600
Fixed assets	100000	1.8	180000	1.49	149000
Accumulated dep.	(20000)		(36000)	1.49	(29800)
Total	180000		293800	1.49	268200
Accounts payable	30000	1.49	44700	1.49	44700
Long-term debt	44000	1.49	65560	1.49	65560
Capital sock	60000	1.8	108000	1.8	108000
Retained earnings	46000	*	75540	*	76480
Accum. trans. Adj.					(26540)
Total	180000		293800		268200

* Retained earnings is the sum of all income earned in prior years and translated into dollars and this year's income. There is no single exchange rate used to translate retained earnings into dollars.

Source: Daniels and Radeburgh (1995: 690)

- $1.8000 historical exchange rate when fixed assets were acquired and capital stock was issued
- $1.4900 closing (current) exchange rate on 31 December 1994
- $1.5200 average exchange rate during 1994
- $1.5100 exchange rate during which ending inventory was acquired
- $1.5150 historical exchange rate for cost of goods sold

Also, the beginning balance in retained earnings for both methods is assumed to be $40,000. The UK pound was falling in value between the time when the fixed assets were acquired and the end of the year, so the balance sheet reflects a negative accumulated translation adjustment under the current-rate method. This is consistent with the idea that assets were losing value in a weak currency.

Disclosure of foreign-exchange gains and losses

A major difference between the two translation methods is the recognition of foreign-exchange gains and losses. Under the current-rate method, the gain or loss is called an accumulated translation adjustment and is taken directly to the balance sheet as a separate line item in owners' equity. Under the temporal method, the gain or loss is taken directly to the income statement and thus affects earnings per share. For example, Colgate–Palmolive recorded a negative accumulated translation adjustment balance of $372.9 million on 31 December 1993 and a negative balance of $439.3 million on 31 December 1994. This is illustrated in Table 4, which is the owners' equity portion of the balance sheet for Colgate–Palmolive for 1994.

IAS 21 also requires that companies with subsidiaries in hyperinflationary economies (those with a cumulative rate of inflation of

Table 3 Income statement, 1994

		Temporal method		Current-rate method	
	Pounds	*Rate*	*Dollars*	*Rate*	*Dollars*
Sales		1.5200	349600	1.5200	349600
Expenses					
Cost of goods sold	(110000)	1.5150	(166650)	1.5200	(167200)
Depreciation	(10000)	1.8000	(18000)	1.5200	(15200)
Other	(80000)	1.5200	(121600)	1.5200	(121600)
Taxes	(6000)	1.5200	(9120)	1.5200	(9120)
	24000		34230		36480
Trans. Gain (Loss)			1310		
Net income	24000		35540		36480

about 100 per cent over a three-year period) should adjust financial statements for price level changes according to IAS 29 and then translate the financial statements using the current-rate method.

National practices

Most countries use either the temporal or the current-rate method. The British pioneered the current-rate method, so UK companies rarely use the temporal method. Even though the temporal method or some variation thereof was used in the USA until Statement 52 permitted the use of the current-rate method, few companies use the temporal method today, except in the case of hyperinflationary economies. This is a major departure from IAS 21 as described above.

5 Performance evaluation and control

Table 5 identifies the major financial measures these companies use to evaluate foreign subsidiaries and their managers. Budgets, profits, and return on investment (ROI) dominate the list.

There are national differences in the way these measures are employed. In a study of UK subsidiaries of Japanese companies, it was determined that Japanese companies focus more on strategic planning as a control instrument, with special emphasis on sales and market-share growth, whereas UK companies tend to focus more on financial control systems to increase short-term profits at the expense of longer-term benefits in areas like R&D and management training. The Japanese parent company placed significant emphasis on overall corporate performance, with profitability measures becoming more important over time. Profit budgets, sales budgets and cash flow potential from the subsidiary to the parent company were also found to be important measures. Significantly, ROI was not ranked as a useful measure in any of the companies surveyed. Given the importance attached to product cost and quality, the companies often used several performance measures related to product costs, such as break-even point, fixed and variable cost, personnel cost, sales per head, and profit and loss per head. The companies also compared results with other similar manufacturing units of the company in different countries and with prior-period results.

Table 4 Statement of shareholders' equity, Colgate–Palmolive Company, 31 December 1993 and 1994 (dollars in millions)

	1994	1993
Preferred stock	**408.4**	414.3
Common stock, $1 par value (500000000 shares authorized, 181213295 issued)	**183.2**	183.2
Additional paid-in capital	**1,020.4**	1000.9
Retained earnings	**2,496.7**	2163.4
Cumulative translation adjustments	**(439.3)**	(372.9)
	3,669.4	3388.9
Unearned compensation	**(384.1)**	(389.9)
Treasury stock, at cost	**(1462.4)**	(1124.0)
Total shareholders' equity	**1,822.9**	1875.0
	$6142.4	$5761.2

Source: Colgate–Palmolive (1994)

It is interesting to note how currency translation can affect the financial ratios identified in Table 5. Using the information in Tables 2 and 3, it is possible to compute the ROI (net income/total assets) in UK pounds, US dollars under the current-rate method, and US dollars under the temporal method. The ROI is 13.3 per cent in pounds. However, in dollars it is 13.6 per cent using the current-rate method but only 8.7 per cent using the temporal method. Net income is lower and total assets are higher under the temporal method than under the current-rate method in this example. When evaluating subsidiaries' results, managers need to be sure to compare like measures.

Budgets

The most important financial measure is the budget. MNCs must determine the appropriate currency in which the budget should be

Table 5 Measures used to evaluate foreign subsidiaries and their managers

Financial measure	Percentage of thr sixty-four multinational enterprises using each measure	
	Foreign subsidiary	*Foreign subsidiary managers*
Return on investment (ROI)	74	67
Profits	78	66
Budgeted ROI compared to actual ROI	66	64
Budgeted profit comapred to actual profit	86	87
Other measures	36	36

Source: Abdallah and Keller (1985)

prepared: the local currency of the country in which the subsidiary is established or the reporting currency of the parent company (the parent currency). Using the local currency is advantageous because the subsidiary's management operates in that currency and it is more indicative of the overall operating environment than is the parent currency. Another argument for using the local currency is that the exchange rate is something over which local management has no control, so it would not be wise to have a key uncontrollable item as part of the budgeting and evaluation process.

On the other hand, it is often difficult for top management in the parent's country to understand budgets generated in different currencies. This is especially true for a geographically diverse company such as the UK company Cadbury–Schweppes. Translating the budget into the parent currency enables top management to compare the performance of subsidiaries from all over the world and forces subsidiaries' managers to think in terms of the parent currency.

Generally, the budget is translated into the parent currency and then compared with final results. However, there are many different exchange rates that can be used for establishing the budget and monitoring results. Table 6 identifies nine different combinations for establishing the budget and monitoring results using three different exchange rates: (1) the actual exchange rate in effect when the budget was established; (2) a projected, or forecasted, rate that is a prediction of what the exchange

rate is expected to be during the period being budgeted; and (3) the exchange rate actually in effect when performance takes place.

Of the possibilities identified in Table 6, the ones most likely to be used are A-3, P-2, and P-3. The advantage of P-2 and P-3 is that management is forced to forecast the exchange rate for budget purposes. Although this is very difficult to do, it is helpful for management in attempting to determine where the company might be at the end of the forecasting period. The difference between P-2 and P-3 is that under P-2, there is no foreign-exchange variance, only an operating variance, whereas under P-3, the foreign-exchange variance is the difference between the forecasted and actual exchange rates. For A-3, the foreign-exchange variance is the difference between the rate in effect when the budget was made and the actual rate at the end of the period. For both A-3 and P-3, performance is measured at the actual exchange rate at the end of the period.

6 Conclusion

Companies conduct business overseas at different levels. Some domestic companies engage in international business solely through exporting and importing, and there are unique accounting issues regarding the recording of transactions denominated in a foreign currency. Gains and losses related to foreign currency receivables and payables may result as the exchange rate changes between accounting periods, and companies

Table 6 Possible combinations of exchange rates for the budget process

	Rate used to track performance relative to budget		
Rate used for determining budget	*Actual at time of budget*	*Projected at time of budget*	*Actual at end of period*
Actual at time of budget	A-1	A-2	A-3
Projected at time of budget	P-1	P-2	P-3
Actual at end of period (through updating)	E-1	E-2	E-3

Source: Lessard and Lorange (1977: 630)

must recognize those gains and losses in income.

Many companies also go beyond their national borders to raise capital, and they must deal with differences in accounting and listing requirements. Given that GAAP differ from country to country, companies may be forced to recast or reconcile their financial statements to the GAAP. Given the significant differences in GAAP, this may not be an easy thing to do.

As multinational enterprises (MNEs) invest overseas, their foreign subsidiaries must generate financial statements compatible with parent country GAAP and translate those financial statements into the reporting currency of the parent country before they can be consolidated with parent company results. In addition, the MNE must deal with performance evaluation and control issues, including the establishment of the budget and monitoring of results.

LEE H. RADEBAUGH
BRIGHAM YOUNG UNIVERSITY

Further reading

(References cited in the text marked *)

* Abdallah, W.M. and Keller, D.E. (1985) 'Measures used to evaluate foreign subsidiaries and foreign subsidiary managers', *Management Accounting* October: 27. (Provides the results of a survey of sixty-four MNEs to identify the methods that they used to evaluate the performance of foreign subsidiaries and their managers.)

Choi, Frederick D.S. (1991) *Handbook of International Accounting*, New York: Wiley. (Advanced reference work which covers topics such as accounting function, practices and standards, currency transactions, pricing, pensions and auditing.)

Choi, Frederick D.S. and Mueller, Gerhard G. (1992) *International Accounting*, 2nd edn, Englewood Cliffs, NJ: Prentice Hall. (Explores problems and issues from the accounting perspective and includes discussion questions and exercises.)

* Colgate–Palmolive (1994) *Annual Report*. (Contains narrative about the company's product lines and geographic areas, with financial information in US dollars and according to US GAAP.)

Coopers & Lybrand (1993) *International Accounting Summaries*, 2nd edn, New York: Wiley. (An authoritative reference work on international accounting standards, standards in the EU, and national standards and practices in central and eastern Europe, along with detailed information about twenty-three countries.)

* Daimler–Benz (1994) *Annual Report*. (Contains narrative in English and financial information in German marks and according to German GAAP; also provides a reconciliation to US GAAP income and shareholders' equity.)

* Daniels, John D. and Radebaugh, Lee H. (1995) *International Business: Environments and Operations*, 7th edn, Reading, MA: Addison-Wesley. (Addresses issues of culture, the environment, small businesses and import/export, and offers 'ethical dilemma' exercises. Chapter 19 is particularly relevant.)

* Gray, S.J. (1988) 'Towards a theory of cultural influence on the development of accounting systems internationally', *Abacus* March: 7. (Discusses how national culture or societal values affect accounting values and accounting systems.)

International Accounting Standards Committee (1995) *International Accounting Standards, 1995*, London: IASC. (The full text of all International Accounting Standards extant at 1 January 1995 (and issued each year), the Revised International Accounting Standards effective for financial statements covering periods beginning on or after 1 January 1996, and current Exposure Drafts.)

* Lessard, D.R. and Lorange, P. (1977) 'Currency changes in management control: resolving the centralization/decentralization dilemma', *The Accounting Review* 52 (July): 630. (Discusses the use of different exchange rates in establishing budgets and tracking performance, and the pros and cons of methods that result in foreign exchange variances versus those that do not.)

* Nobes, C.W. (1983) 'A judgemental international classification of financial reporting practices', *Journal of Business Finance and Accounting* Spring: 7. (Discusses how accounting systems can be classified according to macro-uniform and micro-based systems, then identifies characteristics of these approaches and how countries can be classified.)

Nobes, C. and Parker, R. (eds) (1991) *Comparative International Accounting*, 3rd edn, New York and London: Prentice Hall. (An authoritative work which includes individual country studies and offers a perspective on topics such as international auditing.)

* Radebaugh, L.H. and Gray, S.J. (1993) *International Accounting and Multinational Enterprises*, 3rd edn, New York: Wiley. (Focuses on the business strategies and accounting applications of multinational enterprises, with international case studies.)

See also: CULTURE, CROSS-NATIONAL; ECONOMIC INTEGRATION, INTERNATIONAL; EUROPEAN UNION; FOREIGN EXCHANGE RISK, MANAGEMENT OF; GLOBALIZATION; INTERNATIONAL BUSINESS, LEGAL DIMENSIONS OF; INTERNATIONAL TRADE AND FOREIGN DIRECT INVESTMENT; MANAGEMENT IN CHINA; MANAGEMENT IN GERMANY; MANAGEMENT IN THE UK; MULTINATIONAL CORPORATIONS

Related topics in the IEBM: ACCOUNTING; HARMONIZATION; INFLATION

Advertising strategy, international

Overview

Advertising is an important form of promotion used by companies to communicate with their existing and potential customers. In most instances advertising consists of messages conveyed in paid media such as television, radio, newspapers and magazines, cinemas and posters, but advertising messages can also be transmitted by means such as painting slogans on company vans. Advertising is a key element in the marketing mix and for many companies constitutes a major source of expenditure.

The principal purpose of advertising is to influence consumer behaviour, stimulating consumers towards actions such as product trial, purchase, repeat purchase or retention. As such, when designing an advertising campaign the company must ensure that it understands consumer behaviour and the variables which can affect it. This problem is compounded when marketing internationally, as behaviour varies between cultures and responses to advertising stimuli are also subject to change.

It has recently been argued that global consumer convergence, that is, an increasing similarity in tastes and consumption patterns, compounded with the advent of global media such as satellite television, has made it possible for companies to develop global advertising campaigns which would be more effective at achieving these goals. A number of large multinationals have tried such campaigns, with mixed success. Others have argued that localized campaigns, where advertisements are adapted to local tastes and conditions, are more likely to be successful. The importance of this issue lies in the fact that large companies spend many millions on advertising each year, and failure to target advertising successfully can have a serious effect not only on product or brand performance but on overall company performance itself. The entry concludes by looking briefly at international advertising strategic options, in particular at how companies deal with the twin issues of globalization and localization.

1 The goals of advertising

All companies need to communicate with their customers or other designated target groups, in order both to make customers aware of the products and services on offer and to detail the benefits or advantages of these products and services relative to competitive offerings. Perhaps the ideal way of communicating with customers is to send sales representatives to talk to each one face to face, but in most instances this is neither economically viable nor physically possible. Companies in sophisticated industrial goods companies, such as makers of oil drilling equipment or aerospace components, may have only a handful of customers making very high value purchases, and in these cases it is possible for the selling company to use direct sales representatives. At the other end of the scale, however, companies which manufacture consumer products often have millions of customers spread across different countries and continents; the sheer impossibility of personal communication makes some form of alternate communications channel necessary. One of the most commonly adopted channels is advertising.

Advertising campaigns can range from small local campaigns using local television and newspapers or even a single billboard or poster advertisement, up to global advertising campaigns aimed at scores of different markets and with budgets in the millions. Often the same product can be advertised in different ways by both manufacturers and retailers; in the USA, for example, cars are often advertised for sale in local media by local dealers, while the manufacturers place complementary advertisements in the national media.

Companies may choose to advertise their products and services for several reasons. These may include:

1   the need or desire to increase sales or market share;
2   the need to protect current sales or market share position;
3   the need to slow sales decline;
4   justification for a price premium (by branding the product/service and adding value, a price premium can be commanded).

Advertising and consumer behaviour

Advertising attempts to achieve these goals by influencing consumer behaviour. The role of advertising can perhaps best be conceptualized by relating it to the consumer decision-making process and determining the stages of that process where advertising can exert influence. One common model of this process is the AIDA model, in which consumers move through four stages: *awareness*, *interest*, *desire* and *action*.

Advertising can focus on any one of these stages in order to achieve different results. Awareness, for example, is an important objective because people tend to buy products or services with which they are familiar; research shows that in most situations customers tend to prefer products of which they have some previous knowledge (Lavridge and Steiner 1961). If two similar or identical products are available, most customers will tend to favour the product that they know in order to reduce perceived risk (always assuming, of course, that previous experience with the product has been satisfactory). The correlation between familiarity and propensity to purchase has been demonstrated in research

which shows that there is an apparent relationship between awareness and brand share.

In theory, at least, advertising can help establish awareness by providing consumers with information about the product or brand and making the consumer aware of its existence. By extending the process further and focusing on particular types of information or particular product features, advertising can also create interest; and, by focusing further upon those product features which are most closely related to key consumer needs, produce desire and stimulate action. For example, a soft drink advertisement which emphasizes the product name could be used to establish awareness; an advertisement for the same product which shows it being drunk by a number of fashionably dressed young people might stimulate interest (at least in that particular consumer segment), while the addition of a voiceover message emphasizing the drink's taste and thirst-quenching qualities might stimulate desire, particularly on a hot day.

Advertising is thus intended to differentiate a product in the eyes of the consumer and give it a unique positioning. There remains considerable debate as to how effective advertising is in achieving this goal. One problem is clutter, the sheer volume of advertising messages to which consumers are subjected. Consumers see and hear so many advertisements for so many products and services that it becomes increasingly impossible to distinguish between them; and if the advertisement makes no impact on the consumer then the message it is attempting to send is lost.

More critical is the debate as to whether advertising actually has the power to create attitudes that will lead the consumer to purchase the product (through stimulating interest and desire), or whether its role is in most instances confined to simply establishing awareness. Central to this discussion is the relationship between attitudes and behaviour. Until relatively recently, conventional marketing wisdom stated that attitudes determined behaviour and that the role of marketing was thus to create favourable attitudes towards products. In most instances, it was assumed that the role of advertising was to convey information that would lead the target group to believe that the given product was superior to that of the competition (Joyce 1967).

However, subsequent research has found that there is rarely a direct relationship between attitudes and behaviour. Purchasing behaviour cannot be explained by attitudes alone; in other words, positive attitudes toward a product do not necessarily translate into sales. At the same time, rational models of consumer behaviour have become increasingly suspect (Palda 1966). These models stated that consumer choice was based on purposive goal-seeking and that consumers conducted an information search to obtain the facts that would enable them to compare the performance and physical attributes of the various products on offer. However, research has demonstrated that consumer preferences can be more accurately explained by their personal feelings towards the competing products, and by their perceptions of the images of these products (Murray 1986). It is for this reason that many consumers buy brands rather than products; their perceptions are influenced by brand reputation and image as well as product attributes.

Instead of merely focusing on creating positive attitudes regarding the product's performance and price, therefore, advertising has a role to play in building brand identities and images. Certainly there are still situations where the central role of advertising is to convey information, particularly if the consumers are highly involved with the product in question. But for products where there is no or little perceived risk, advertising can provide added value by helping to differentiate the brand at an emotional level as well as an intellectual level. For example, advertising can be used to link products to consumer lifestyles by associating the product or brand with a particular fashion or status. Advertisements for soft drinks might show the product as being part of a fashionable healthy lifestyle; advertisements of luxury cars may suggest that ownership of such a car adds to the owner's personal prestige; advertisements for running shoes might associate them with youth culture. All this suggests that advertising can be used to stimulate interest without having to create, let alone change, consumer attitudes (Ehrenberg 1974).

It should be stressed that AIDA is just one possible model, and the role of advertising will vary according to the model being followed. For instance, many products are repeat purchases and the Awareness–Trial–Repeat model is probably a more accurate description of the customer decision-making process. In this case the primary objective of advertising is to remind customers about the brand and ensure they remember it next time they go to make a purchase. Careful analysis is required at the planning stage to determine what decision-making process is being used by the target customers; such analysis provides an essential framework for investigating the potential role of advertising and setting coherent objectives.

2 Advertising effectiveness

While it seems possible that advertising can create interest and possibly desire by branding products rather than changing attitudes, advertising's ability to actually influence sales and contribute to the bottom line remains open to question. The relationship between advertising and profitability is difficult to work out, primarily because it is almost impossible to isolate the impact of advertising from all the other variables that affect purchasing decisions. It is unlikely that many consumers, upon exposure to an advertisement, immediately go out and make a purchase; equally, it cannot be said that advertising has no effect at all, as firms which do not advertise while competitors do frequently see these competitors win market share. Reality lies somewhere between these two positions.

Certainly advertising cannot create sales unaided. Advertising campaigns must be supported by other marketing efforts such as the creation of effective distribution channels; the advertising 'pull' must be backed by a distribution 'push'. An airline could spend millions on building a strong brand image, but unless tickets are widely available through outlets such as travel agents, this effort will be wasted; however strong a reputation a model of car may have, this will not translate into sales unless there is also an effective dealer network. Another critical consideration is time scale; in many instances advertising is designed not to produce immediate sales but to help establish long-term branding. In these cases it is irrelevant whether there is an immediate correlation between advertising and sales.

Key factors

It is thus virtually impossible to come to any general conclusions about the effectiveness of advertising, and analysis of effectiveness has to focus on specific campaigns and establish whether the campaign met its goals. As noted above, these goals can be set in terms of creating awareness or establishing brand image as well as generating immediate sales. However, there are some key variables which will influence the impact of any advertising campaign. These include:

(1)The size of the advertising budget. A company spending very small amounts of money on advertising cannot realistically expect substantial returns. Budget usually has an effect on the quality of the advertisement; more importantly, it determines reach. Companies advertising locally may be able to get away with paying low media fees; companies advertising globally must be prepared to pay for media access. In general, the higher the budget the greater the potential audience for the message. Larger budgets also ensure greater frequency of advertising, which can be important in ensuring that the message is received by the target audience.

(2)The creative strategy on which the campaign is based. If this strategy is badly thought out or based on false information and targets an inappropriate target group, then the advertising is unlikely to have much effect. Advertising must be backed up by research and strategic planning (see below).

(3)The media strategy. What media will be most effective in reaching the target audience? In the West, television is a widely accessible medium capable of reaching mass audiences; in developing countries television is seen by rather fewer people. In any case, there may be specialist media capable of reaching audiences with more effect; advertisements for golf clubs may be more likely to be noticed by golfers if placed in golfing magazines than on television or in daily newspapers.

(4)The quality of the advertising itself. It may seem like a truism, but bad ads will not sell. An advertisement which fails to put across the message, or worse, repels or offends some portion of the target audience will harm rather than help the brand. International advertising is full of examples of misplaced or poorly designed advertisements causing offence in target audiences (see MARKETING, CULTURAL DIFFERENCES IN); more commonly, advertisements simply do not press their message home and fail to engage the consumer's attention.

(5)The advertising budgets of the competition and the quality of their advertising. This point is particularly important. Advertising does not takes place in a vacuum, with consumers avidly waiting to consume it; in western countries especially, consumers are exposed to hundreds, if not thousands, of advertisements each week. Most do not pay attention to more than a small percentage of the many messages directed at them. This massive volume of advertising, including advertisements from direct and indirect competitors and those from companies and organizations with completely different messages, can be seen as 'noise' against which any advertisement must compete for the consumer's attention. This adds another dimension to the need for large budgets, which are necessary to ensure frequency; advertisements from organizations with small budgets, such as museums, often get 'lost' in the clutter and are overlooked by their potential audience. Even then, attention is not guaranteed; hence the importance of creativity and quality. In the midst of large volumes of advertising it tends to be the more original and creative advertisements which break through the screening process and are registered by the consumer. Humour and other emotional devices that would on the surface appear to have little to do with the product being advertised are frequently employed in this context; the most famous and extreme examples are probably those employed by the Italian firm Benetton, which sometimes use deliberately shocking or provoking images in order to attract attention.

3 Advertising development and planning

As noted above, creativity and quality are essential. However, unless the advertisement is part of a carefully planned and researched strategy, it will have little hope of reaching its objectives. The planning stage is probably the most critical step in advertising development. The first step is to gather information on the market or markets in which the brand is competing. It is important to first define this market and identify the brand's actual competitors. For instance, does a muesli product compete only with other muesli products, or with all breakfast cereals, or alternatively with all health foods? There are also important variations between markets; the three scenarios mentioned above might apply an identical product in different geographical markets or even market segments. Products are often at different stages of their life cycle in different markets, which can have a further effect on positioning and competition. Market analysis should also focus on identifying emerging trends in the market including future competition, new product preferences, etc.

The second step is to analyse the competition, focusing in particular on competitor advertising strategies and campaigns and analysing their effectiveness, seeking to understand as far as possible the particular factors that determine effectiveness. If possible, past advertising campaigns should be included in the review. Examining other campaigns, both successful and unsuccessful, and determining the reasons for success or failure can greatly assist the advertiser to understand what kinds of messages work in a particular market.

The final and possibly the most important stage of the planning process is to analyse actual and potential customers. The techniques used for this sort of research are similar to those used in more general marketing research and include the definition and analysis of market segments, understanding the consumer decision-making process in each segment, and the role played by advertising in the choice process. If for instance it has been decided to target non-users, it is essential to establish how advertising can convince them to try the brand and what the conversion costs will be. Research is particularly important in international marketing as it is possible that all of these factors will vary from market to market or even from segment to segment within each market; economic, social and cultural differences will all have an impact on consumer behaviour (see MARKETING, CULTURAL DIFFERENCES IN).

The quality of the research programme which precedes the development of an advertising strategy is thus critical to the effectiveness of that strategy. In many instances the difference between success and failure in an advertising campaign can be attributed more to the quality of the research than the execution of the campaign itself. Research rarely provides categorical answers and the results must be interpreted with skill.

4 International advertising standardization

One of the major strategic issues facing companies planning to advertise in international markets is whether international advertising should be standardized across markets or adapted to local market conditions. The growth of global markets in international advertising in recent years means that the standardization debate is of increasing importance.

International advertising campaigns grew naturally out of the growth and expansion of multinational companies which could market their products and brands into many worldwide markets (see MARKETING MANAGEMENT, INTERNATIONAL; MULTINATIONAL CORPORATIONS). Originally, the national or regional subsidiaries of the multinationals operated more or less independently and advertising along with other marketing strategies was left up to the discretion of local managers. Since the early 1960s, however, multinationals (particularly those based in the USA) have been deploying *standardized* international advertising campaigns, in other words a single advertising campaign which is replicated in all the company's markets. In most instances, these campaigns consisted simply of exporting advertising campaigns developed in the USA to overseas markets. However, as these companies have become more experienced at managing international advertising coordination, campaigns have been developed specifically for international use. Some of the earliest users of standardized international advertising campaigns were Coca-Cola, Pepsi-Cola, Marlboro and Levis. These four campaigns in particular have been widely perceived as being very successful.

What has made standardization possible is the communications revolution, which (in theory at least) allows the headquarters of multinational companies much greater ability to monitor and control the marketing policies of their subsidiaries. New communications technologies have improved both the ability to design and coordinate standardized campaigns, drawing on feedback from many markets in order to ensure that campaigns are as up to date as possible, and the ability to deploy campaigns through media such as global satellite television. Advertising agencies have responded to these new opportunities by expanding into global operations themselves, and in the 1980s agencies such as DMB&B and Saatchi & Saatchi became multinationals in their own right.

This having been said, there is considerable debate as to whether standardized advertising is truly effective. It is worth noting that some multinationals such as Coca-Cola have since dropped their standardized campaigns and moved to a policy of local development.

Definition of standardization

In its pure form, standardization means that the advertiser uses the same advertisement, with identical copy (either written or voice-over) and visuals, in all its country markets. This definition of standardization is commonly encountered, either implicitly or explicitly, in the literature on this subject.

However, while examples of this kind of total standardization do exist, they are relatively rare. Studies of the advertising practices of multinationals have found that most companies, even those which start out by developing standardized global campaigns, finish up by adapting or modifying at least some elements for some markets. There are considerable variations in the actual degree of modification or adaptation; in some instances a standardized campaign might be in general use with occasional modifications in national markets to copy or visuals, while in other cases 'standardization' might mean nothing more than the standardized use of a brand logo. It is therefore difficult to accurately define standardization; although many companies operate a policy of advertising standardization, in practice they frequently depart from this policy and undertake adaptations on a pragmatic basis. The reasons for this variance will be discussed below (Peebles *et al.* 1977; Harris 1994).

Pressures towards standardization

The initial argument put forward in favour of standardizing international advertising was that the same communications revolution that enabled companies to control their national subsidiaries was also creating international consumer convergence. It was proposed that exposure to international media had harmonized consumer attitudes and expectations, to such an extent that international advertising was both feasible and necessary (Elinder 1965; Fatt 1967). The convergence case was argued most forcibly by Levitt (1983) who contends that we now lived in a global village inhabited by global consumers, and that national markets had in effect merged into a global market.

Other arguments presented in favour of standardized international advertising campaigns include:

1 there are economies of scale that can be realized, especially in terms of reduced media production costs (Killough 1978);
2 even if complete convergence has not yet occurred, there is evidence pointing to the

existence of international consumer segments (Martenson 1987);

3 in areas of media overlap (such as Switzerland, for example) the presence of several national advertising campaigns could result in conflicting messages and consumer confusion (Sorenson and Weichmann 1975);

4 standardization can help to create an international image for brands such as Martini (Hite and Fraser 1988);

5 standardized campaigns work, and brands such as Coca-Cola which have been backed up by standardized international advertising have been very successful (Levitt 1983);

6 good ideas should be exploited, and campaigns that have proved successful in national markets should be used in other markets (Quelch and Hoff 1986; Riesenbeck and Freeling 1991);

7 conversely, much national or local advertising is sub-optimal, primarily because local subsidiaries lack the skills and resources to develop effective advertising (Weichmann and Pringle 1979).

More recently, the argument has also been put forward that standardized advertising is an essential part of a global strategy and that companies which fail to standardize are ignoring powerful international trends (Levitt 1983). However, the primary thrust of the case for standardization remains based on the concept of convergence, namely that national cultures are no longer a powerful force and that there is instead a global culture in which consumers everywhere are receptive to the same kinds of messages.

Arguments against standardization

There are also many opponents of advertising standardization. One of the most frequently used arguments attacks the concept of convergence (Onkvisit and Shaw 1987). Contrary to Levitt, many authors believe that in many situations national culture still influences the way consumers react to advertisements. It is further argued that, regardless of whether convergence exists or not, local market conditions will vary too much for standardization to be the optimal policy. Differences in relative market shares, stages in the product life cycle, local (rather than multinational) competition, marketing and media infrastructures and local government regulations on advertising claims will all vary from country to country, and all will have an effect on advertising effectiveness (Downham 1982; Hill and Still 1984).

The economies of scale argument has also been attacked on the grounds that the economies achievable are small by comparison to the actual total advertising budgets (Sorenson and Weichmann 1975). On more detailed implementational issues, several writers have contended that international advertising campaigns tend to be bland because they must appeal to such a wide and diverse audience; in other words they are based on the lowest common denominator. Further, no detailed econometric analysis has ever been presented which indicates that standardization has indeed increased the international sales performances of relevant brands (Walters 1986). While the performance of brands such as Coca-Cola is frequently cited as evidence concerning what can be achieved by standardization, critics of standardization have noted that in none of these instances was the international campaign ever tested against the local option; in other words, there is no evidence that standardized campaigns achieve significantly higher sales or profitability than localized campaigns (although it should be added that neither is there evidence to the contrary) (Onkvisit and Shaw 1987).

Neither has the contention that standardization is a necessary component of a global strategy (see GLOBALIZATION) received much support. Critics of this view contend that this is too simplistic and represents a triumph of an accounting perspective over a marketing perspective. Rather, it is argued, contingency factors or situational variables should be analysed to determine whether advertising standardization is an appropriate strategy. The focus to date has been on two factors, product type and the stage of economic development of the markets concerned. For instance, standardization might be an appropriate strategy in national markets at a high stage of economic development, where consumer convergence is more likely to have taken place; in developing markets, however, it might be seen as inappropriate.

5 Strategic issues

As was noted above, however, much of the debate on standardization and localization has had limited effect on international advertising in practice. Companies have responded to the changing needs of the global advertising market with a pragmatic mix combining elements of both strategies.

To ascertain why this is the case, one need only look at the goals and effects of advertising as described earlier in this entry. The fundamental goal of all advertising is to reach consumers and influence their behaviour, usually in a way that will make them react more positively towards the brand in question. Advertising is thus different from other marketing strategies in that it is both more visible and more subtle; it influences demand without creating it, and its effects are often unmeasurable. New products or brands have the potential to actually create demand (as in the case of Sony and the Walkman); a new advertising campaign merely influences demand.

Total standardization, though perhaps ideal in theory, ignores variations in consumer behaviour between countries and between markets. There is enough evidence to suggest that although global consumer segments have converged to a degree, that convergence is not total (see MARKETING, CULTURAL DIFFERENCES IN); indeed, factors such as nationalism and environmentalism may even be driving segments in some markets further apart. The point is that the picture is not simply black and white, and total standardization is simply not a practical option.

For many companies, however, total localization is equally impractical, and the reasons for this are often found not in the marketplace but within the company itself. Studies of the rationales behind the advertising policies of multinationals, particularly those which have a policy of standardization (even if this policy is often modified in practice) note that when

setting an advertising strategy, these companies are not solely influenced by their analysis of external market conditions and the degree to which consumer segments in that market have converged. Indeed, there are few indications that any real analysis is carried out on the economic efficacy of standardization, particularly on the relative impacts of standardized and local advertising on sales (Harris 1996).

This is not to say that the companies concerned behave irrationally, but rather that their managers bring a wide agenda to the decision-making process. In many companies, decisions on advertising policy are driven by internal factors relating to international organization and process issues as well as by analysis of the external environment; in some cases, the former even predominate. External needs, such as sales maximization, are sometimes seen as less important.

The key internal issues are primarily organizational efficiency and cost savings. The major concern of many companies is the perceived need to exploit the size and international structure of the company, so as to avoid unnecessary duplication and the consequent waste of resources; in one study, a number of respondents stated that they considered it wasteful for national markets to develop different advertising campaigns for the same brand. There is also a desire to use standardized advertising as a means of unifying the company and making it greater than the sum of its parts.

Another factor which concerns managers in many companies is the scarcity of good ideas. In the study mentioned above, a number of respondents expressed concern about the poor quality of much locally-developed advertising; national subsidiaries simply did not have access to the talent or resources necessary to produce effective advertising. As such, standardized advertising, whatever faults it might have, was perceived as being more likely to be effective, on the grounds that bad ads do not sell. Conversely, the view was expressed that companies could achieve competitive advantage by exploiting their leverage as multinationals, and by coordinating and harmonizing various national advertising campaigns. Leverage could be achieved by utilizing the advertising skills possessed by the corporate headquarters, and by exploiting good ideas originally developed in certain national markets and transferring them to other national markets. By taking advantage of the company's collective experience, it was felt that more effective advertising campaigns could be produced.

These issues affect international advertising strategy in a number of ways, and result in three principal strategic options. In cases where the primary concern is to exploit good ideas, companies which allow national markets to produce their own advertising (with consequent lower levels of standardization) in effect have a strategy of *cross-fertilization*; when national campaigns are particularly successful, the attempt is then made to replicate these in other markets so as to make best use of the limited supply of good ideas. Other companies use a *lead market* system in order to avoid duplication; here, an idea which may be developed by corporate headquarters is tried out in one market first, the results are observed and adjustments or adaptations made before the campaign is launched on a wider basis. In these cases, standardizing some or all elements of advertising can be seen as a means to an end, a way of exploiting creativity and improving efficiency, rather than as a goal in itself.

In other companies, standardization is part of an overall policy of central development and can thus be considered a corporate goal in its own right. In these companies, the decision as to whether or not to introduce standardized advertising campaigns is frequently influenced by much more than just the relative merits of standardization and localization. Here the broader organizational and strategic considerations mentioned earlier often intervene. These companies are probably more likely to use *central development* as the source of most advertising, with headquarters providing the resources and input for campaigns which are then imposed on subsidiary markets.

6 Conclusion

Any description of advertising and advertising strategy must at best be generalized. Advertising itself can range from simple actions such as putting up a poster to coordinated print and broadcast media campaigns which may well be interlinked with other marketing strategies such as sales promotions or public relations efforts. A similar diversity applies to the advertising strategies of multinationals. Despite the debate on standardization and localization, it appears that most companies design their own strategies which use elements of both interchangeably.

Many multinationals recognize the value and importance of standardization, if for no other reason than to take advantage of economies of scale and exploit creative resources more effectively. The global advertising campaigns of the last two decades, backed by the full resources of the multinationals and often produced on a global basis by advertising agencies who are themselves multinationals, have been of obvious high quality. However, the very level of the resources involved makes these campaigns risky. A standardized campaign by its very nature assumes a high degree of consumer convergence, and if research fails to show the existence of such convergence then the campaign will be limited in effectiveness and the company may not see a return on its expenditure.

What therefore happens is that many companies adopt an overall policy of standardization and then adapt their advertising strategies in certain markets where market conditions require it. Voiceovers and/or visuals can be changed on a market by market basis if the original seems likely to be effective or might cause offence in that market. Adaptation thus reduces the risks associated with standardization. The wholly pragmatic nature of these changes can be seen by the fact that companies which practise product adaptation will sometimes use almost completely standardized global advertising (such as Pepsi-Cola) while companies which sell virtually identical products around the world will develop strongly localized advertising (such as Nescafé).

There is little consensus on the best form of advertising strategy, just as there is little consensus on the best form of international product strategy. Multinationals are often forced to balance the economic and organizational demands for standardization against the market imperatives of consumer demand and divergence; the result is often a compromise somewhere between the two positions. Currently, companies developing international advertising campaigns rely on three alternative methods, central development, cross-fertilization and a lead market system, as described above.

No detailed analysis has yet been undertaken concerning the respective merits of these alternative processes; likewise, little attention has been paid to the question of what types of advertising executions lend themselves best to international transfer. As in all advertising, and indeed all marketing, the key to a successful international advertising strategy remains good research and analysis. The ultimate goal of advertising remains to communicate with and influence consumers. The strategy chosen must ultimately reflect those goals.

GREG HARRIS
CITY UNIVERSITY BUSINESS SCHOOL
LONDON

Further reading

(References cited in the text marked *)

* Downham, J.S. (1982) 'Presentation to the AMA Annual Marketing Conference', May. (Conference presentation which argued strongly for the effects of local market conditions on advertising effectiveness.)
* Ehrenberg, A. (1974) 'Repetitive advertising and the consumer', *Journal of Advertising Research* (2): 25–33. (Examines advertising effectiveness, particularly with reference to repeated messages.)
* Elinder, E. (1965) 'How international can European advertising be?', *Journal of Marketing* 29 (2): 7–11. (Argues the case for international advertising standardization, especially in a European context.)
* Fatt, A.C. (1967) 'The danger of local international advertising', *Journal of Marketing* (1): 60–2. (This article also argues the case for advertising

standardization, positing a number of potential problems with localized advertising.)
Harris, G. (1987) 'The implications of low-involvement theory for advertising effectiveness', *International Journal of Advertising* 6: 207–21. (A more detailed examination of the effects of low involvement.)
* Harris, G. (1994) 'International advertising standardization: what do the multinationals actually standardize?', *Journal of International Marketing* 2 (4): 13–30. (Reports on a survey of advertising standardization in practice among multinational companies.)
* Harris, G. (1996) 'Study of international advertising standardization', *Journal of Marketing Management* (2). (Forthcoming article which looks at the rationales behind standardization and non-standardization in greater detail.)
* Hill, J.S. and Still, R.R. (1984) 'Adapting products to LDC tastes', *Harvard Business Review* (March–April): 92–101. (Useful article on product adaptation, with implications for advertising.)
* Hite, R.E. and Fraser, C. (1988) 'International advertising strategies of multinational corporations', *Journal of Advertising Research* 28 (3): 9–17. (Good article reporting on a survey of multinational practice.)
* Joyce, T. (1967) 'What do we know about how advertising works?', in C. Weinburg *et al.* (eds), *Analytical Marketing Management*, London: Harper & Row. (This chapter details some of the current knowledge about advertising effectiveness.)
* Killough, J. (1978) 'Improved payoffs from transnational advertising', *Harvard Business Review* (July–August): 102–10. (Argues the case for standardized advertising, with particular emphasis on the benefits of economies of scale.)
* Lavridge, R.C. and Steiner, G.A. (1961) 'A model for predictive measurements of advertising effectiveness', *Journal of Marketing* (4): 59–62. (An examination of advertising effectiveness, with some particularly useful descriptions of consumer involvement and awareness.)
* Levitt, T. (1983) 'The globalization of markets', *Harvard Business Review* (May–June): 92–102. (A classic article on globalization.)
* Martenson, R. (1987) 'Advertising strategies in the USA and Sweden', *International Journal of Advertising* 6: 133–44. (An interesting cross-national comparison of effectiveness.)
* Murray, H. (1986) 'Advertising's effect on sales: proven or just assumed?', *International Journal of Advertising* 5: 15–36. (Article on adver-

tising effectiveness, which grapples with the problem of understanding the effectiveness of advertising.)

* Onkvisit, S. and Shaw, J. (1987) 'Standardized international advertising: a review and critical evaluation of the theoretical and empirical evidence', *Columbia Journal of World Business* (3): 43–55. (A useful review of the debate on standardization.)

* Palda, K.S. (1966) 'The hypothesis of a hierarchy of effects: a partial evaluation', *Journal of Marketing Research* (2): 102–7. (Valuable article on the theory of hierarchy of effects.)

* Peebles, D.M., Ryans, J.K. and Vernon, I.R. (1977) 'A new perspective on advertising standardization', *European Journal of Advertising* 2: 567–76. (An examination of advertising practices among multinationals, which concludes that most companies take a pragmatic view of the standardization debate.)

* Quelch, J.A. and Hoff, E.J. (1986) 'Customizing global marketing', *Harvard Business Review* (May–June): 59–68. (Describes how good ideas developed in one market can be successfully transferred to others.)

* Riesenbeck, H. and Freeling, A. (1991) 'How global are global brands?', *The McKinsey Quarterly* 4: 3–18. (A critical examination of global brands, with strong implications for advertising.)

* Sorenson, R.Z. and Weichmann, U.E. (1975) 'How multinationals view marketing standardization', *Harvard Business Review* (May–June):

38–54. (An early study of attitudes towards standardization.)

* Walters, P.G. (1986) 'International marketing policy: a discussion of the standardization construct and its relevance for corporate policy', *Journal of International Business Studies* (2): 55–69. (Argues that there is no evidence that standardization of advertising has increased brand performance.)

* Weichmann, U.E. and Pringle, L.G. (1979) 'Problems that plague multinational marketers', *Harvard Business Review* (July–August): 118–24. (Argues in favour of standardization as a means of improving international advertising quality and exploiting rare good ideas.)

See also: GLOBALIZATION; INTERNATIONAL MARKETING; MARKETING, CULTURAL DIFFERENCES IN; MARKETING MANAGEMENT, INTERNATIONAL; MULTINATIONAL CORPORATIONS

Related topics in the IEBM: ADVERTISING CAMPAIGNS; BRANDS; BUSINESS-TO-BUSINESS MARKETING; CHANNEL MARKETING; CONSUMER BEHAVIOUR; MCLUHAN, H.M.; MARKETING; MARKETING PLANNING; MARKETING; MARKETING STRATEGY; MARKETING RESEARCH; PRODUCT POLICY CONCEPTS IN MARKETING; PUBLIC RELATIONS; SALES PROMOTION; SEGMENTATION

Asia-Pacific Economic Cooperation (APEC)

1 History and background
2 The Action Agenda and Plan
3 Conclusion

Overview

APEC was formed as an informal dialogue group in 1989 in response to the growing importance of Asia-Pacific economies and an increasing protectionist sentiment worldwide. Since 1993 APEC has become an important organization embodying the vision of Asia-Pacific free trade and investment, and a sense of community. It has developed specific action agendas to achieve this vision by 2010 for developed members and by 2020 for developing members. APEC is not a trade bloc, but a loosely coupled economic community of twenty-one member economies (hereafter referred to as the members). It has been criticized, however, for ignoring the various social and political issues in the region. (Note: the members are referred to as economies as opposed to countries.)

1 History and background

APEC was initiated by the then Australian prime minister, R. J. Hawke, in January 1989 in response to the growing interdependence among Asia-Pacific countries and the emerging threat to the General Agreement on Tariffs and Trade (GATT) from the protectionist tendencies in the development of the European Union (EU; see EUROPEAN UNION) and NAFTA (see NORTH AMERICAN FREE-TRADE AGREEMENT). The idea was to create a forum for high-ranking officials in economic affairs from Asia-Pacific economies to meet periodically to discuss common concerns. The first meeting was held in Canberra, Australia, in 1989, and the twelve participating countries were Australia, Canada, Japan, New Zealand, South Korea, the United States, Brunei, Indonesia, Malaysia, the Philippines, Singapore

and Thailand. The last six countries are the members of ASEAN (see ASSOCIATION OF SOUTH-EAST ASIAN NATIONS). China, Hong Kong and Taiwan were admitted in 1991, followed by Papua New Guinea and Mexico in 1993, and Chile in 1994. APEC then became the largest economic community in the world and its combined gross domestic product (GDP) and trade accounted for more than half of total world income and global trade.

The objectives of APEC are clearly stated in the 1991 Seoul Declaration:

- to sustain the growth and development of the region for the common good of its people;
- to enhance the positive gains resulting from increasing economic interdependence, and to encourage the flow of goods, services, capital, and technology;
- to develop and strengthen the open multilateral trading system in the interests of not only the Asia Pacific but also the rest of world;
- to reduce barriers to trade in goods and services among participants in a manner consistent with GATT principles.

The declaration also recognized the importance of the private sector for the dynamism of APEC economies and thus encouraged it to participate in APEC activities. These vague objectives, however, reflected the fact that APEC was initially an open and non-formal consultative forum for member countries to explore various possibilities of economic cooperation.

Under the influence of the United States, the 1993 Seattle summit of the leaders from member countries changed the role of APEC. This summit, led by the US president, Bill Clinton, envisioned free trade, free investment and economic cooperation, and encouraged the development of a sense of community in the Asia-Pacific region. The summit also decided to hold annual summits of the leaders of member economies, which increased the importance of APEC and energized the ministers and officials to carry out the resolutions made in the summits. The 1995 summit, held in Bogor, Indonesia, was an important milestone. It passed the Bogor Declaration, which embodied a historical commitment that member economies should eliminate all trade and investment barriers in the Asia-Pacific region by 2010 for developed members and by 2020 for developing members. The declaration called for members to develop an Action Agenda to achieve this vision. APEC has thus evolved into an institutionalized organization with the goal of free trade and investment among member economies in the next 25 years. This has changed the image of APEC from that of a low-level social club to that of a high-level organization aimed at specific action agendas, although its resolutions are still not binding.

In order to have consistent action plans developed by member economies, the Osaka Action Agenda was developed in 1995 after various meetings and consultations. The Osaka Action Agenda confirmed the guiding principles of open trade and investment, and required each member country to develop individual action plans for consultation. These individual action plans are known as Manila Action Plans and were approved in 1996.

The 1997 summit, held in Vancouver, Canada, after a currency crisis in the region, reconfirmed the aims of the Manila Declaration to enhance financial stability in the region, to speed up tariff reductions in nine industries (environmental products and services, fisheries, wood products, jewellery and precious stones, energy, chemicals, telecommunications, toys, and medical equipment) by 1999, to facilitate the simplification of customs procedures by 2000, and to complete the negotiations in liberating the financial sector under the WTO (see WORLD TRADE ORGANIZATION). The Vancouver summit was further committed to strengthening women's role in economic development, and to accepting Peru, Russia and Vietnam as new members in 1998.

With regard to organizational structure, the highest level and the most prominent activity for APEC are the annual leaders' summit, which, although symbolic, signifies commitment to trade and investment liberalization and economic cooperation. The most important decision-making body is the annual ministerial meeting, comprising the ministers of economic and foreign affairs from every member economy. The senior officials meeting is at the operational core of APEC. The Eminent Persons Group, comprising one eminent academic expert or business leader from each member economy, is an important group which makes recommendations on how to facilitate regional trade and investment. A small secretariat and three permanent committees – the Budget Administration Committee, the Committee on Trade and Investment and the Economic Committee – provide logistic support and policy analyses.

2 The Action Agenda and Plan

The Osaka Action Agenda is a blueprint for implementing the free trade and investment envisioned in the Bogor Declaration. It specifies fifteen specific areas for liberalization and facilitation, including tariffs, nontariff measures, services, investment, standards and conformance, customs procedures, intellectual property rights, competition policy, government procurement, deregulation, dispute mediation, mobility of business people, implementation of the Uruguay Round outcomes, and information gathering and analysis. Some areas are market access issues and some – such as intellectual property rights, investment, competition and deregulation – are new sources of contention, especially between the US and other members.

In each of these areas the Action Agenda spells out the overall liberalization and facilitation objectives, and the guidelines for actions and steps to be taken individually and collectively. A set of general principles was applied to the agenda to ensure that liberalization and facilitation measures incorporate comprehensiveness (i.e. they cover all sectors and all barriers), WTO consistency, overall comparability, non-discrimination, transparency, standstill (i.e. no increase in protection), simultaneous start, continuous process and differentiated timetables, flexibility and cooperation. Differentiated timetables and flexibility are available to member economies according to their different levels of economic development and diverse circumstances in each economy. Yet the long-term goal of free trade and investment is to be achieved no later than 2010 for industrialized economies and 2020 for developing economies.

The action agendas have also developed policies and steps to be undertaken collectively by APEC's ten working groups, which cover areas in human resource development, industrial science and technology, small and medium-sized enterprises, economic infrastructure, energy, transportation, telecommunications and information, tourism, trade and investment data, trade promotion, marine resource conservation, fisheries and agricultural technology. These activities are to advance the economic and technical cooperation of the region, as well as cross-cultural ties.

3 Conclusion

APEC is not a trade bloc but a super-regional trade arrangement of several trade blocs and some non-trade-bloc economies. Unlike trade blocs such as the European Union, APEC includes three trade blocs and one emerging economy. The three trade blocs are NAFTA (Canada, the United States and Mexico), the Australian–New Zealand Free-Trade Area and the ASEAN Free-Trade Area (Brunei, Indonesia, Malaysia, the Philippines, Singapore, Thailand and other non-APEC members); the emerging trade area is the Great China Economy, the increasingly integrated economy of China, Hong Kong and Taiwan. APEC is a unique trade arrangement. It adopts 'open regionalism', advocating non-exclusive and non-discriminatory principles to avoid the regional mentality prevailing in current trade blocs. These principles are consistent with GATT and WTO principles. With some exceptions, such as

the agricultural sector, it opens APEC trade arrangements to non-members as long as they provide corresponding concessions. This practice avoids preferential treatment and 'free ride'.

Undoubtedly, free trade in the Asia-Pacific region has brought benefits to all member economies. However, 'open regionalism' is based on a unilateral and voluntary principle, which prevent members from initiating tariff reductions and trade-barrier elimination. Everyone wants to enjoy a free ride. The pressure from domestic interest groups frequently forces member economies to exclude their industries from action agendas or include them on 'exception lists' (e.g. Japan claims that the fisheries, toys and jewellery industries are sensitive). Many members still lack the political will to show their commitment to free trade and investment. The United States and Australia are the principle advocates of trade liberalization, whereas Malaysia is quite opposed to it. Japan falls somewhere in between, claiming that the US demands are extreme. The objective of being an Asia-Pacific community still appears to be an aspiration rather than a reality.

APEC is characterized by its diversity in terms of geographical location, income levels, stages of economic development, and economic and political systems among the members. Despite the different attitudes of the United States, China, Japan and ASEAN towards APEC, APEC provides an important forum for its members to resolve potential conflicts. While it is hard to estimate the performance of APEC in helping to promote free trade and investment and economic cooperation, it does provide a mechanism to facilitate bilateral trade negotiations among members, and between APEC and other trade blocs, to promote global trade.

The importance of APEC, at least symbolically, draws the attention of various interest groups to member economies. These groups criticize APEC for overemphasizing economic issues and ignoring the many social and political issues in the region, such as the poor treatment of labour, environmental protection and human rights. The commitment to strengthening women's role in economic development in the 1997 Vancouver summit was a response to such pressure from interest groups.

RYH-SONG YEH
THE CHINESE UNIVERSITY OF HONG KONG

Further reading

Alt.Apec (1977) (A home page set up by an interest group called Alternative APEC, which contains documents, feature articles on APEC and a news-clipping archive on anti-APEC campaigns.)

APEC secretariat (1997) Asia-Pacific Economic Co-operation, http://www.apecsec.org.sg/. (The APEC home page, which includes an introduction to APEC, latest updates, publications and Web sites, the Osaka Action Agenda, the Manila Action Plan and other documents.)

Elek, A. (1995) 'APEC beyond Bogor: an open economic association in Asian-Pacific region', *Asian-Pacific Economic Literature* 9(1): 1–15. (Discusses the evolutionary nature of open regionalism as a strategy moving toward free trade in responding to the realities in the region.)

Frankel, J., Stein, E. and Wei, S. (1994) *APEC and Regional Trading Arrangements in the Pacific*, Washington, DC: Institute for International Economics, Working Paper on Asian Pacific Economic Co-operation, 94–1. (Demonstrates statistically that APEC countries already form a regional trading bloc even though it is not one.)

Guillermo, A. (1997) 'Velvet revolution', *Features*: Alt.Apec. (Presents the argument that APEC would cause developing economies to be more dependent on and to be dominated by developed nations.)

Hou, J.W., Ichimur, S., Nya, S., Werin, L. and Young, L. (1995) 'Pacific Rim trade and development: historical environment and future prospects', *Contemporary Economic Policy* 13(4): 1–25. (A panel discussion by the authors on how cultural heritage and historical background set the tone for the region's success in trade and development.)

Kim, S.H. (1996) 'APEC: a superregional trading bloc', *Multinational Business Review*, spring: 63–7. (A short note describing the history, features and organizational structure of APEC.)

Manning, R.A. and Stern, P. (1994) 'The myth of the Pacific community', *Foreign Affairs*, November/December: 79–93. (Suggests that the Pacific community idea appears more aspiration than reality, and that the US should play a more active role.)

Polak, J.J. (1996) 'Is APEC a natural regional trading bloc? A critique of the "gravity model" of international trade', *World Economy* 19(5): 533–43. (Argues that Frankel, Stein and Wei's conclusion in their article is wrong, due to a mis-specification inherent in the traditional gravity model.)

See also: ASSOCIATION OF SOUTH-EAST ASIAN NATIONS; EUROPEAN UNION; NORTH AMERICAN FREE-TRADE AGREEMENT; WANG, YUNG CHING; WORLD TRADE ORGANIZATION

Related topics in the IEBM: ECONOMIC INTEGRATION, INTERNATIONAL

Association of South-East Asian Nations (ASEAN)

Overview

ASEAN was formed in 1967 as a dialogue for regional cooperation. Since then the five-member organization has expanded to include ten members, the five founding nations of Indonesia, Malaysia, the Philippines, Singapore and Thailand, and five new members, Brunei, Burma, Cambodia, Laos and Vietnam. No specific progress was made in economic cooperation until the formation of the ASEAN Free-Trade Area (AFTA) in 1992, which occurred after most of the founding nations had experienced rapid economic growth in the 1980s. Not only has ASEAN become an important trade bloc in the world, but it has also played a politically important balancing role among the major powers in dealing with the United States, Japan and China in southeast Asia.

1 History and background

ASEAN was formed in Bangkok by Indonesia, Malaysia, the Philippines, Thailand and Singapore in 1967. Although the five members were not specific about goals, steps and organization, they did emphasize the necessity of periodic meetings of the members to discuss regional cooperation. Many attempts at regional economic cooperation were made, but these were not very successful until the launch of AFTA in 1992. AFTA is one of most significant developments in southeast Asia, and ASEAN as a whole has finally made a specific commitment to the idea of a free-trade area. Since 1967 ASEAN has expanded its membership, admitting Brunei in 1984,

Vietnam in 1995, and Cambodia, Laos and Burma (Myanmar) in 1997.

The major motivation behind forming ASEAN was to prevent the spread of communism to southeast Asia. In 1967 the Americans were still fighting in Vietnam, and the domino effect was a real and vivid scenario to southeast Asian nations. The relations among the members were also tense. Singapore had separated from Malaysia two years earlier; the territorial conflict between Indonesia and Malaysia had ended a year previously; and the dispute over Sabah between Malaysia and the Philippines had not yet been settled. However, this common threat of communism pushed these five countries – with their many differences in history, culture, religion, race, language and socioeconomic systems – to get together to form something akin to a social club. Although few real effects were expected, the cooperation among the five nations helped create a peaceful atmosphere for stability and an opportunity for each member to pursue economic development.

No further actions were taken until the collapse of Vietnam and Cambodia in 1975. An emerging sense of crisis galvanized the five members into concrete cooperation. The first leaders' summit, held in Bali, Indonesia, in 1976, declared some specific goals and plans for action. A permanent secretariat was established in Jakarta. An organizational structure – the heads of government meeting – was formed as the highest decision-making body, with the ministers' meeting as the second most important. Some regular committees were set up to coordinate various issues at various governmental levels.

After the Bali Declaration ASEAN committed itself to economic cooperation in three areas:

- preferential trade arrangement (PTA);
- ASEAN industrial projects (AIP);

- ASEAN industrial complementation (AIC).

PTA was designed to change the existing trade structure among member countries, while AIP and AIC were intended to create new areas of trade (e.g. the production of automotive parts and components). Although ASEAN was not successful in free-trade and economic cooperation, individual member countries did make rapid economic progress in the 1980s.

The unsuccessful progress can be demonstrated by looking at the proportion of total trade that was intra-regional. The ratio declined from 21 per cent in 1970 to 20 per cent in 1985, dropping even further, to 18 per cent, in 1990, although the total volume of intra-regional trade had increased fortyfold. This decline is attributable to three interrelated factors:

- the low income level and the lack of complementation in industrial structure among members (except Singapore, most members export agricultural and labour-intensive products);
- the competition for export markets and foreign investments from non-member countries;
- strong nationalistic attitudes of some member countries towards free trade and joint projects (e.g. there has been rivalry over the location of high value-added processes for the automotive project; Indonesia opted not to join the programme out of concern to protect its own automotive industry and market, while Singapore and Brunei are not participating because they do not have an automotive sector).

The rapid economic growth of some member countries has been attributed to such economic liberalization as export-oriented economic policy and promotions of foreign direct investment (FDI) from the USA, Japan, European countries, Taiwan and Korea. Although multilateral free trade was not easy to achieve in ASEAN, some bilateral agreements were able to move forward. The most well-known example was the Singapore–Johore–Riau Islands growth triangle, which was created by the two bilateral agreements signed by Singapore with Indonesia and Malaysia, respectively.

2 ASEAN Free-Trade Area (AFTA)

The end of the Cold War at the beginning of 1990 and the threats of protectionism from European and NAFTA (see NORTH AMERICAN FREE-TRADE AGREEMENT) blocs eroded the free-trade principles of the General Agreement on Tariffs and Trade (GATT). This change created a challenge for ASEAN. In order to adapt to the changes in the international environment, to promote regional competitiveness of industrial products in the world markets and to further attract foreign investment into the region, ASEAN leaders felt a strong need to speed up regional trade liberalization by eliminating regional tariff and non-tariff barriers. A summit of six government heads was held in Singapore in 1992 to declare that ASEAN was committed to achieving an ASEAN Free-Trade Area within fifteen years.

One specific measure was the agreement on Common Effective Preferential Tariff (CEPT), signed by six members. This declared that, starting from 1 January 1993, the import tariffs on regional non-agricultural products would be lowered to the range between 0 and 5 per cent within fifteen years. A regional product is defined as a product of which the amount of value added created in the region accounts for more than 40 per cent of the total value. Non-agricultural products are manufacturing and processed agricultural products. The term 'common' means that import tariffs of the products listed in CEPT should be reduced to 5 per cent or less. This is different from past concessions in PTA, in which a proportion of tariff, rather than the absolute level of tariff, was reduced. Finally, the term 'effective' means that the nominal rate is equal to the real rate; that is, non-tariff trade barriers should be eliminated. All members should also comply with the 'tariff-concession timetable' proposed by one member to other members. ASEAN entered a new era.

This commitment was further strengthened in the Bangkok Declaration of 1995, in which members agreed that AFTA should be established before 2003, and regional tariff reduced to 5 per cent in 2000, with the exception of some 'sensitive items' like sugar and rice. Other important decisions included in the Bangkok Declaration requested that each member:

- provide a timetable for eliminating non-tariff barriers like customs surcharges, technical regulations, product characteristic requirement and single channel for imports;
- adopt the Harmonized System (H-S) classification at the eight-digit level and implement the GATT Transaction Value system of custom valuation by 2000;
- strengthen and enhance existing cooperation efforts in trade in services by establishing or improving infrastructural facilities, joint production, marketing and purchasing agreements, research and development, and exchange information;
- strengthen cooperation in intellectual property rights and cooperation with the WTO (see WORLD TRADE ORGANIZATION) and APEC (see ASIA-PACIFIC ECONOMIC COOPERATION).

Vietnam, which joined ASEAN in 1995, was not required to comply with the tariff-reduction schedule until 2006. The other three new members, Burma, Cambodia and Laos, were given ten years from January 1988 to comply with the schedule. The inclusion of the four new members may result in tensions for the cohesion of ASEAN because of their lesser economic development and their different economic and political systems.

3 ASEAN and the major powers

In the area of political and security cooperation ASEAN has made some progress. ASEAN has signed several accords and treaties declaring southeast Asia a zone of peace, freedom, neutrality and a nuclear-free zone. ASEAN as a whole has increased its stature among major powers such as the US, China,

Japan and the European Community (EC; see EUROPEAN UNION). The ASEAN Regional Forum (ARF) was established in 1994 to involve the United States, Japan and China in multilateral dialogue. Although the Cold War is over, the United States still has huge economic and political interests in the region for containing or engaging with China, an emerging Asian superpower. The United States has strengthened security pacts with Japan and Australia and maintained special military cooperation with the Philippines, Malaysia, Singapore and Indonesia. ASEAN is Japan's most important export market and destination for direct investment; and Japan needs ASEAN's support in seeking permanent membership in the United Nations (UN) Security Council. To China, ASEAN is in a vital position controlling the route of China's future energy and food supplies from Australia, the Middle East and Europe. The increasing economic and military power of China seems not to pose an imminent threat to ASEAN, although China has territorial disputes with the Philippines, Malaysia, Indonesia, Brunei and Vietnam over a potentially huge oil reserve in the South China Seas. In addition, there is the Five Power Defence Arrangement linking Britain, Australia and New Zealand with Singapore and Malaysia.

In this complicated international environment ASEAN uses ARF to play a balancing act to reduce tensions and conflicts that may jeopardize ASEAN interests. Between the United States and China, it avoids automatic alignments with either Washington or Beijing. On the one hand, it defends China on human rights and assures China that there is no anti-Chinese coalition, and, on the other hand, it sides quietly with Washington on China's threats to use force against Taiwan and puts pressure on China to settle territorial disputes through multilateral dialogues over islands in the South China Seas.

4 Conclusion

ASEAN has made significant progress in economic growth but not in intra-regional trade, which accounted for around 21 per cent of total trade in 1996, which is similar to the percentage achieved in 1970. The vision of AFTA is a very important milestone in the history of ASEAN, but how successful it will be remains to be seen. ASEAN has played an important role in balancing the politics of the major powers – most notably the United States, China and Japan – and in facilitating negotiations with other trade blocs and international organizations. This role is expected to continue in the era of global economic competition and integration.

The currency crisis that began in Thailand in mid-1997 and then spread to the rest of the ASEAN members and other Asian countries posed a serious threat to the economic development of ASEAN members. However, with the help and prescriptions of the International Monetary Fund (IMF), ASEAN members have undertaken further fundamental institutional reforms in reducing the protective relationships between government and business, balancing corporate balance sheets, and opening and liberalizing domestic markets. Even though Malaysia did not accept the IMF's assistance, the country has introduced the same reforms. These reforms have strengthened the need for further financial and economic cooperation among ASEAN members and enhanced the opportunity of achieving the free trade envisioned by 2003.

RYH-SONG YEH
THE CHINESE UNIVERSITY OF HONG KONG

Further reading

Acharya, A. and Stubbs, R. (eds) (1995) *New Challenge for ASEAN: Emerging Policy Issues*, Vancouver: University of British Columbia Press. (Presents essays on economic policy, social conditions and environmental conditions in ASEAN, and relations between Canada and ASEAN countries.)

ASEAN secretariat (1977) http://www.asean-sec.org/. (The ASEAN home page, which has various documents, including an overview and others pertaining to political and security issues, economics, trade statistics, dialogue relations and functional cooperation.)

Cunha, Derek da (1996) *The Evolving Pacific Power Structure*, Singapore: Institute of Southeast Asian Studies. (Presents essays on the great powers in the region, national security, defences in Asia and southeast Asia, the balance of power and the ASEAN regional forum.)

DeRosa, D.A. (1995) *Regional Trading Arrangements Among Developing Countries: The ASEAN Example*, Washington DC: International Food Policy Institute. (A research report on free trade, tariff, trade blocs, commerce, commercial policy, economic integration and econometric models in southeast Asia.)

Goyer, J.F. (1996) 'ASEAN Free Trade Area: making the region more investment competitive', *East Asian Executive Reports* 18(4): 9–13. (Gives a brief introduction to trade agreements before and after AFTA, including PTA, AIP, AIC/BBC, AIJV, CEPT, exclusions and other areas of cooperation.).

Whiting, A. (1997) 'Asean pressures China', *Far Eastern Economic Review* 160(17): 28. (A short note on a personal observation of how ASEAN plays a balancing political role between the United States and China.)

Yue, C.S. and Tan, J.L.H. (eds) (1996) *ASEAN in the WTO: Challenge and Responses*, Singapore: Institute of Southeast Asian Studies. (Presents essays on the WTO, capital movement, trade, labour policy, service industries and foreign economic relations in ASEAN countries.)

See also: ASIA-PACIFIC ECONOMIC COOPERATION; EUROPEAN UNION; NORTH AMERICAN FREE-TRADE AGREEMENT; WANG, YUNG CHING; WORLD TRADE ORGANIZATION

Related topics in the IEBM: INTERNATIONAL ECONOMIC INTEGRATION

Countertrade

Overview

Countertrade (CT) is a broad term which refers to any form of trade involving partial or total payment with goods or services, instead of with money alone. Other terms that are frequently used are 'barter', 'non-monetary trade' and 'reciprocal trade'.

The traditional, and most familiar, form of countertrade is simple barter. This is the direct exchange of a small number of goods and/or services, usually between just two parties. Such simple exchange is inefficient and cumbersome, and is therefore rare in wholesale business (either corporate or government) today. However, strong motivation for managers to find creative means of finance and marketing has stimulated the development of many other forms of barter which are much more creative and more responsive to modern business needs. Some of these modern variations on barter are widely used in wholesale business today. Collectively, they are all called countertrade.

Since entities are not required to file data on countertrade, no good statistics exist in this regard. Most experts have estimated that approximately 10–20 per cent of world trade involves some form of countertrade. However, some less reliable estimates have suggested that the share could go as high as 50 per cent within a few years.

1 Varieties of countertrade

Simple barter (also called traditional barter, straight barter or pure barter)

This is the traditional, generally informal, variety of barter – the type with which most people are familiar. It involves few parties, few products, and there is a direct exchange between the parties (i.e. there are no intermediaries). No money is exchanged. A single contract is involved, and that is often only an oral contract.

Before the advent of money all trade was done in this manner. Yet even in today's monetary economies such simple barter is very common: collectors exchange coins, stamps or whatever else they are collecting; small businesses exchange services (e.g. the family doctor and the dentist exchange their services); farmers agree to help each other bring in their crops; newspapers and radio stations offer advertising space in exchange for restaurant meals or hotel rooms.

Although such exchanges of goods or services are common, they have severe limitations. Comparable pricing can be a problem. It is usually difficult to trade more than two or three products on each side of the transaction. Likewise it becomes cumbersome if more than two or three parties are involved. Also, obtaining the financing to produce goods to be bartered can be very difficult.

Such simple barter has obvious limitations for large companies, and even for most small companies. It is basically limited by what economists refer to as the need for a 'simultaneous coincidence of wants': the buyer must have a need to acquire goods and/or services from the seller at approximately the same time that the seller wishes to sell. This is a severe limitation on the prospects for the expansion of simple barter.

Clearing-account barter

For many companies, the second countertrade category, clearing-account barter, overcomes the limitations of simple barter of few products and few participants. With clearing-account barter, each party agrees in a specific contract to purchase a specified value of goods and services over a period of time. In exchange, of course, each party receives the right to purchase the same value of goods and services. The array of products involved may also be specified.

Clearing-account barter thus allows for a much wider range of products and for settlement over a much longer period of time than is normally the case with simple barter. In one instance the former Soviet Union acquired hundreds of millions of dollars worth of phosphates from Morocco in exchange for an equal value of Soviet-made machine tools and other specified manufactured goods. The Soviets acquired the phosphates that they needed very soon after the initiation of the clearing-account arrangement. The Moroccans drew down their barter line of credit over several years.

Clearing accounts also lend themselves to the development of barter exchanges, where hundreds or even thousands of members can enter into barter commitments in exchange for barter credits. Since barter exchanges have numerous members and even more numerous goods and services, a member may enter into a barter commitment not knowing what will be acquired from other members of the exchange. Barter exchanges most commonly involve retail and other small businesses, such as electricians, appliance stores, motels, radio stations, grocers, restaurants, attorneys, doctors, etc.

Because of the size and diversity of the membership of many of the exchanges, members often do not know the parties with whom they will eventually spend their credits. This gives rise to problems similar to those of futures and options exchanges. The foundation for the barter exchange is similar to that of the latter: the exchange itself guarantees all credits and serves as an arbiter of disputes.

Since barter exchanges rely on confidence in credits that are guaranteed by the exchange, the barter credits themselves often become a tradeable form of credit. In many exchanges members are able to trade the credits among themselves, or even with non-members: the credits can be used to acquire goods and services or even to settle debts.

Parallel barter (often called counter-purchase barter or simply counter-purchase)

One of the greatest shortcomings of simple barter, and often of clearing-account barter as well, is that it can be difficult or almost impossible for either party to obtain pre-production or trade financing. Lenders and their regulators are seldom comfortable with a simple barter contract or barter credits, since there is no payment with money and the lender may have questions about valuing offsetting shipments – unless the goods have prices that can be readily confirmed. Also, government reporting requirements, accounting practices, tax laws, import customs requirements or simply corporate policy often require separate sales contracts.

The third type of countertrade, parallel barter, avoids these problems. The parties to the counter-purchase agreement sign separate contracts agreeing to purchase specified goods and/or services from the other and to make payment in money. Thus each party has its own distinct sales contract, as with any non-barter sale. It involves at least two contracts, each of which clearly values the shipment, and each party pays for what it receives in the trade. Each seller can use its sales contract to obtain financing or to satisfy governmental, tax, customs or accounting requirements.

The reason that this trading arrangement is a form of barter is because neither sale will occur without the other sale also occurring. In order to tie the two sales irrevocably together, a third contract is often signed which ties the two sales contracts together and guarantees that each party must fulfil both of the sales contracts.

Parallel barter has many of the advantages of clearing-account barter. It is easier to accommodate both more products and many parties than with simple barter. Also, the contracts may cover long periods. And, since money is paid by each party, the two contracts do not necessarily need to be of equal magnitude – one party might end up with a net receipt of money over and above the receipt of goods. Because of its flexibility, parallel barter is the predominant form of countertrade in use today.

Offset

The flexibility of parallel barter has led to the extensive use of this special variety for certain types of large-scale contract. Offset barter is used in such 'large-ticket' contracts as commercial aircraft, communications infrastructure and defence-contract sales to foreign countries. The name derives from the demand of purchasers of these huge orders – some of which exceed $1 billion – that the seller 'offset' some or all of the large foreign-exchange costs. This is to be done by requiring sellers to purchase goods or services from the buyer sufficient to cover a significant portion or even all of the contract. Offsets have become the norm for large aircraft, both commercial and military, and other large defence contracts, such as tanks, ships and missiles.

There are two major varieties of offset. The most obvious, called direct offset, involves the seller acquiring from the purchasing country some of the components used in its own sale to that country, or some of the assembly might even be done in that country. In either case the desire of the purchaser is to minimize its foreign-exchange costs. For example, Boeing has agreed to build component parts in China as part of commercial aircraft that it sold to China.

Indirect offset also involves an obligation by the seller to acquire goods and services from the purchaser. However, the purchases are unrelated to the goods sold. Sometimes indirect offsets can be very complicated. A very diversified company may be in a position to commit to a very wide range of indirect offset commitments. For example, in 1997 Saab Military Aircraft of Sweden signed a protocol with the Government of Hungary to make investments and technology transfers into Hungary, expand exports from Hungary and help it to develop expanded industrial contacts in other countries. Saab is part of the Wallenberg industrial group. It has proposed involving many other parts of the Wallenberg group in satisfying its Hungarian offset obligations. To be included are Ericsson (mobile telephone equipment), Electrolux (household appliances), SKF (ball bearings), ABB (engineering) and Scania (trucks). Obviously, offset greatly complicates the sale, but it is often the only way in which the sale can be made.

Buyback barter (also called compensation-agreement barter)

This is a common practice in the creation and development of industrial and mineral-extraction projects, especially in developing countries. These contracts arise when the owner of the project offers part of the production from the development as partial or total compensation to the developer (who may also have financed the entire project). For example, the government of a developing country that wishes to develop its oil reserves but lacks the funds, technology and expertise might demand that the foreign company take oil produced by the new facility for its compensation.

Thus buyback involves a commitment by the seller to advance assets to the purchaser, including technology, equipment, construction or development expertise, and much or even all of the cost of construction. The compensation to the seller (i.e. the buyback) may be years after the initiation of the project. For example, copper-development projects in both Latin America and Africa have occurred involving buyback barter, with the developers taking copper as compensation. Similarly, Levi Strauss built a factory for manufacturing blue jeans in Romania; the company was compensated with a share of the jeans produced. For governments that lack the hard currency, technology and expertise, this arrangement provides not only a valuable industry but ownership of the assets as well.

Since the country or company that is having the project developed on its behalf is generally not well established in that industry, the buyback agreement sometimes involves a commitment by the developer of the project to market the product abroad. Oil companies, for example, might refine and market not only their own share of the oil, but that of the producing country as well. Gulf Oil did this with an oil and gas development in Bolivia.

These are the five principal forms of countertrade: simple barter, clearing-account barter, parallel barter, offset and buyback barter. Table 1 compares the five types of countertrade. Generally, only a single contract is involved in countertrade, but parallel barter involves two and often three contracts (column 1). Financial compensation is seldom used with simple barter or clearing-account barter, but is sometimes used with buyback and is always used with parallel barter (column 2). Credit is sometimes used with simple barter and is always used with the other four varieties (column 3). Simultaneous exchange may occur, but is not required, with simple and parallel barters. However, because of the very nature of clearing-account and buyback barter it does not occur (column 4). Simple barter is rare on the wholesale level. Clearing-account barter is fairly common, especially that involving small and medium-sized companies via barter exchanges. Parallel barter is very common – indeed, it is the most common variety. Offset and buyback barter are both fairly common (column 5).

2 Reasons for countertrade

The many variations of countertrade have made the basic notion of barter both more flexible and more acceptable than simple barter. However, at best, any variation of barter is more difficult than monetary commerce. Why, then, is barter not only surviving but even thriving in the modern world?

Buyers' motivations for countertrade

Buyers have many reasons for being interested in countertrade. The most obvious is the availability of money. If funds are short and credit lines are difficult or expensive (to either a company or a country) the possibility of exchanging goods or services for what it needs, instead of using money or getting in debt, can be very attractive.

A related motivation in many developing countries is balance-of-payments problems and an excess of foreign debts, coupled with a national shortage of foreign exchange. In such a situation governments may ration foreign exchange. The government may also be motivated by a desire for job creation. Some governments even mandate that a portion or all of an import must be matched by countertrade. Here again, a buyer has a strong incentive to seek 'non-monetary trade'.

Table 1 The basic characteristics of the various forms of barter

	Number of contracts	Is money used?	Is credit extended?	Is exchange simultaneous?	Predominance today
Simple barter	1*	No	Possibly	Not necessarily	Relatively rare**
Clearing-account barter	1	No	Yes	No	Common
Parallel barter	2 or 3	Yes	Yes	Not necessarily	Very common
Offset	2 or 3	Yes	Yes	No	Common
Buyback barter	1	Sometimes	Yes	No	Fairly common

Note:
* Either written or oral
** Except on the retail level

Sellers' motivations for countertrade

Marketers can also have strong incentives to offer countertrade. Intense competition is a strong inducement. Even dominant companies such as Boeing and Philips offer countertrade as a competitive financing tool – offering customers the opportunity to pay part of an order with reciprocal trade. For companies that are not dominant in an industry and are trying to establish themselves or to grow, countertrade can provide an entrée.

Sellers can be especially creative when they have excess inventory or even excess capacity. In order to move inventory or to increase capacity utilization, companies may be prepared to employ a technique that they would not use under other circumstances.

As these examples show, countertrade can be treated as either a standard tool of business (e.g. aircraft, weapons, construction) or as an occasional tool.

The costing incentive for countertrade

The two sections above illustrate how both buyers and sellers can be attracted to countertrade. However, different industries, and even different companies within the same industry, can vary greatly in their potential interest in employing countertrade and their ability to do so flexibly. A key factor is marginal cost of production. Low marginal-cost products, whether goods or services, have much greater incentive and flexibility in employing countertrade.

The cost for a magazine to add an additional page of advertising or for a radio station to add more commercial messages is very low. Similarly, it is very cheap for software companies or video-production companies to produce additional copies of their software programs or videos (which is why companies in both industries can afford sometimes to give their product away free, hoping to attract users who will purchase later versions). Some oil producers (e.g. Saudi Arabia) have production costs that are just a fraction of the market price. And airlines and hotels have very low marginal prices. All of these are industries and producers in which there is high potential for countertrade, since they are offering products which have low marginal costs. Therefore there is a high degree of flexible countertrade pricing, which can bring those producers an attractive return. Companies with high marginal costs have less pricing flexibility but can also find countertrade attractive. Boeing is an example.

3 Conclusion

We are living in an era of creative business practices (e.g. forwards, options, swaps). Managers are often very open to exploring the potential benefits of new (or, in the case of barter, very old) techniques. In all of these areas, and many more, some companies at some times may find very attractive tools. Managers should be open-minded, but very cautious – new techniques may bring either profits or pitfalls. New techniques are almost always riskier than the 'tried and true'. However, new tools may bring unusual opportunities. Countertrade is one of those areas.

CHRISTOPHER M. KORTH
WESTERN MICHIGAN UNIVERSITY

Further reading

Brown, Christopher (1994) *Countertrade: Paying in Goods & Services*, London: Longman. (Gives an introduction to corporate countertrade.)

Francis, Dick (1987) *Countertrade Handbook*, Cambridge: Woodhead-Faulkner. (Provides a broad introductory overview of many of the major aspects of countertrade.)

Hammond, Grant T. (1990) *Countertrade, Offsets & Barter in the International Political Economy*, London: Pinter Publishing Company. (Focuses on the political aspects of international countertrade.)

Korth, Christopher M. (1981) 'Barter: an old practice yields new profits', *Business*, September–October: 2–8. (A concise discussion of the modern use of barter, how and where it is used, and cautions about its risks.)

Korth, Christopher M. (ed.) (1987) *International Countertrade*, New York: Quorum Books. (Presents twenty-three essays by corporate practitioners, government officials and academics with a wide range of experience and attitudes toward many different varieties of countertrade.)

Korth, Christopher M. (1987) 'An overview of countertrade' in *International Countertrade*, New York: Quorum Books. (Provides a detailed discussion of conditions under which countertrade is most likely to appear and prosper.)

Liesch, Peter W. (1991) *Government-Mandated Countertrade*, Brookfield, VT: Gower Publishing Company. (Examines some of the many government requirements for countertrade – not just for government contracts but also for corporate ones.)

Nockles, Gilbert (1987) *Offset: Securing a Competitive Advantage & Economic Development in the 1990s*, London: FT Business Information. (Focuses specifically on one of the most significant of the government-mandated forms of countertrade.)

Martin, Stephen (ed.) (1996) *Economics of Offsets*, Amsterdam: Harwood Academic Publishers. (A collection of articles which examine the impact of offset in several different countries.)

Rowe, Michael (1989) *Countertrade*, London: Euromoney. (Presents a broad corporate overview of countertrade from the publishers of *Euromoney* magazine.)

Verzariu, Pompiliu (1985) *Countertrade, Barter & Offsets*, New York: McGraw-Hill. (A US Government official's view of the principal forms of countertrade.)

Zurawicki, Leon and Suichmezian, Louis (1991) *Global Countertrade: An Annotated Bibliography*, New York: Garland Publishing Company. (An annotated listing of journal articles, books and doctoral dissertations since 1965.)

Communication, cross-cultural

Overview

In the literature on cross-cultural communication, the terms 'cross-cultural communication', 'intercultural communication' and 'international communication' are frequently used interchangeably. Although 'crosscultural communication' and 'intercultural communication' can be treated synonymously, an important distinction needs to be made between 'cross-cultural communication' and 'international communication'. 'International communication' takes place across political or national borders while 'cross-cultural communication' takes place across cultures. Both terms have their usefulness. If one is talking about communications between a multinational organization and its subsidiaries located in other countries, either 'international communication' or 'crosscultural communication' can be used. However, if one is speaking of communications between colleagues working in a multicultural organization but in the same country, the term 'cross-cultural communication' is obviously more appropriate. In this study, the term 'cross-cultural communication' is used.

Two words need to be defined: 'culture' and 'communication'. As both have various meanings, depending on one's intention and persuasion, for present purposes their definitions are as follows.

Culture can be defined as a community's shared values, attitudes, behaviour and acts of communicating which are passed from one generation to the next. Communication means a goal-directed and context-bound exchange of meaning between two or more parties. In other words, communication takes place between people for a specific reason in a particular medium and environment. An American meets a Japanese to negotiate a business deal. The context in which the purpose of communication takes place can be either within the same culture or across different cultures. In the example given, the business negotiation takes place across different cultures. Communication is therefore a culture-bound activity. To communicate means expressing the uniqueness of one's cultural heritage, and this includes not only the verbal and non-verbal peculiarities but also the preferred medium and context of communication.

The scope for cross-cultural communication is extremely wide. It is a multidisciplinary field of study with roots in anthropology, sociology, psychology, cognition and linguistics, among other disciplines. For the purposes of this study, the focus will be on cross-cultural communication in business and management.

1 Culturally sensitive communication

As a field of study, cross-cultural communication can be characterized as the unceasing quest for a culturally sensitive model of communication. Underlying this quest is the dissatisfaction with the early linear-based and culturally impoverished models of communication such as those in Shannon and Weaver (1949). Such communication models fail to account for the role and impact of culture in communication. The growing realization of the importance of culture in communication has led more scholars to modify the earlier models as well as to construct new models that are able to capture the complexity and dynamics of cross-cultural communication.

In the 1990s, a rapidly changing world propelled by technological advances in communications compels its people to communicate across many cultural and geographical boundaries. In Britain, Europe, America, Asia and other parts of the world, the workplace is seeing greater interaction and communication among peoples of different cultures and experiences. The multicultural communication environment of business organizations is an indisputable thriving reality.

With more businesspeople needing to communicate with others from different cultures, more businesses are concerned about the importance and impact of cross-cultural communication. This is because the way in which businesses manage cross-cultural communication will determine their economic survival and competitiveness in the global marketplace.

Multinational and multicultural managers increasingly realize how vital it is to have a better understanding of the social system, the organizational as well as technological environment in which their businesses function. Insights from cross-cultural communication are increasingly important to management who wish to improve their understanding of organizational behaviour as well as the multicultural nature of business communication. Managers who have a systematic understanding of the cultural and organizational dynamics of cross-cultural communication will enhance organizational effectiveness and business performance.

2 Some cultural contrasts

Eastern and Western cultures

Many scholars have written about the cultural differences between the West and the East (see ORGANIZATION CULTURE). Among them, three are highlighted here: cognition, relationship with nature, and the concept of truth. Western culture is said to incline to think in a linear fashion. A cause leads to an effect. In Eastern culture, a cause can be an effect as well as that which leads to an effect. The past, present and future are interconnected and therefore they can affect one another. Western culture tends to be orientated towards mastery over nature while Eastern culture seeks

harmony with nature. Regarding the concept of truth, the view of Western culture of ultimate truth or reality is based more on scientific and empirical explanation while that of Eastern culture is based more on revealed truth. Cultural differences between East and West have a significant impact on the communication behaviour and pattern.

Perceptions of cultural differences between East and West are insufficient to help business people get by when communicating across cultures. These perceptions have to be backed up by a clear understanding of the context of communication. According to Hall and Hall (1990), context refers to the information that circumscribes communication. One needs to understand that the informational context, that is, the kind of information (whether verbal or non-verbal) and the degree of background data (whether required or assumed) that has to be transmitted, varies from culture to culture.

High-context and low-context cultures

One fundamental area that concerns cross-cultural communication scholars is the communication differences between high-context cultures and low-context cultures. According to Hall (1976), any cultural transaction can basically be divided into two communication systems: high-context and low-context. In high-context cultures, the transactions feature preprogrammed information which is in the receiver and in the setting, with only minimal information in the transmitted message (implicit code). By contrast, in low-context cultures, transactions are the reverse, with most of the information in the transmitted message (explicit code).

Although no one culture exists exclusively at either extreme, in general, low-context cultures refer to groups of cultures that value individual orientation and overt communication codes and maintain a heterogeneous normative structure with low cultural demand characteristics. Conversely, high-context cultures refer to groups of cultures that value group-identity orientation and covert communication codes and maintain a homogeneous normative structure with high cultural demand characteristics. For Hall, Germany, Scandinavia and the USA are situated at the low-context end of the continuum; Chinese, Japanese and Korean cultures are located at the high-context end. It is obvious that philosophy can influence communication – Confucianism, for example, has permeated the culture of all three east Asian countries.

In high-context cultures, that of Japan, for example, a larger portion of the message is left unspecified and accessed through the context, non-verbal cues and between-the-lines interpretation of what is actually said or written. The Japanese also prefer oral communication to written communication. In contrast, in North America, which is labelled as a low-context culture, messages are expected to be explicit and specific. More is spelt out than left for the receiver to deduce from the context. Thus it can be concluded that relative emphasis either on written or oral communication is a function of whether the country has a high- or low-context culture.

Polychronic and monochronic cultures

Another area of concern in cross-cultural communication is how temporal conception contributes to cultural differences in communication. Hall (1983) distinguished two patterns of time that govern the individualistic and collectivistic cultures: monochronic time schedule (M-time) and polychronic time schedule (P-time). According to Hall, P-time stresses the involvement of people and completion of transactions rather than adherence to preset schedules. Appointments are not taken as seriously and, as a consequence, are frequently broken. P-time is treated as less tangible than M-time. For Hall, Latin American, Middle Eastern, African, Asian, French and Greek cultures are representatives of P-time patterns, while North American and German cultures are representatives of M-time patterns.

M-time patterns appear to predominate in individualistic, low-context cultures while P-time patterns appear to predominate in group-based, high-context cultures. M-time cultures tend to have a linear and compartmentalized view of time while P-time cultures generally have a more flexible one. In P-time cultures, time is seen as more contextually based and relationally orientated. Differences in time conception affect the management and resolution of conflicts in cross-cultural communication.

People in monochronic cultures tend to be direct when communicating good news or neutral news. Very little 'contexting', that is, the process of filling in background information, is needed, as people usually come to the point very quickly. Also, people in monochronic cultures tend to value quick responses in discussions with little introductory phrasing or politeness. Owing to the linear conception of time, communication tasks are segmented into predetermined units of time which can circumscribe the time span of business communication.

By contrast, oral and written communication in polychronic cultures can be more indirect or circular. A business talk can go off at tangents as business people view all information as having its proper place and function in the whole context of communication. Conflicts may arise when a business person from a monochronic culture interacts with another from a polychronic culture as the latter may consider the direct approach preferred by the other party as being rude.

3 Managing cultural differences in communication

An understanding of cultural differences will not only assist business people to bridge the communication gap between cultures but also multinational or multicultural managers to manage cultural differences more effectively. Studies on managing cultural differences in communication have grown both in number and popularity. They now form the basis of multicultural training and cultural diversity training of multinational companies operating in various cultural environments.

Courses and seminars offering participants 'new skills for global success' inevitably focus on the development and sharpening of cultural competence for cross-cultural business communication, including written communication, negotiations and conducting meetings. For instance, businesspeople from Britain are taught how to deal with the negotiating styles of the Japanese and Koreans. French salespeople learn how to make an effective sales presentation to a Japanese, Indonesian or Chinese prospect. Banking employees in mainland China are taught how to communicate with American and European clients.

One practical application of the insights obtained from studies on the East–West cultural divide is cross-cultural conflict management, an important area in cross-cultural communication studies. An example of such a study is Ting-Toomey's attempt at formulating a theory of culture and conflict (1994). In her analysis of factors that may lead to cross-cultural conflict, she explains how communication clashes can arise from such cultural differences as that between high-context cultures and low-context cultures, collectivistic cultures and individualistic cultures, and polychronic cultures and monochronic cultures. For instance, the maintenance of 'face' or self-respect in a conflict situation differs between a high-context culture and a low-context culture. Ting-Toomey also offers specific suggestions on how to deal with such conflicts. In resolving conflicts in cross-cultural communication, all parties involved must not only know about their own cultures but also demonstrate a willingness to accept differences in other cultures.

4 Communicating across national cultures

If communication is culture-bound and culture-specific, then the communication policies, patterns and preferences vary according to national cultures. Communication is therefore as individual as every culture because every culture has its own set of values. And these values have an impact on management and organizational behaviour. In his landmark study on the consequences of culture on management, Hofstede (1980) contended that each culture provides 'value sets' or 'mental programmes' which are culture-specific. These programmes affect the way

people in each culture perceive and interpret the world, influencing their expectations, goals, beliefs and ultimately behaviour in everyday life, including their work experiences and communication (see ORGANIZATION CULTURE).

Hofstede identified four major attitudes or value dimensions which differentiate national cultures: power distance, uncertainty avoidance, individualism–collectivism and masculinity–femininity. Power distance refers to the extent to which members of a culture accept the distribution of power in institutions and organizations. Uncertainty avoidance refers to the degree to which members of a culture feel uncomfortable with uncertainty and ambiguity, which leads them to support beliefs promising certainty and to maintain institutions protecting conformity. Individualism refers to a preference for a loosely knit social framework to take care of themselves and their immediate families only, as opposed to collectivism, which stands for preference for a tightly knit social framework in which individuals can expect their relatives, clan or other in-group members to look after them in exchange for unquestioning loyalty. Masculinity refers to a preference for achievement, heroism, assertiveness and material success, as opposed to femininity, which stands for a preference for relationships, modesty, caring for the weak, and the quality of life.

Hofstede's major conclusion is that different cultures have different value systems. Consequently, management and organizational theories and practices appropriate to some countries may be wholly inappropriate to other countries with different value systems. Ethnocentric US solutions do not always solve the management dilemmas of other nations. For instance, Peter Drucker's management by objectives works well in the USA and other individualistic cultures but not in collectivistic cultures which regard the performance of individuals as part of the relationship with the boss.

Cross-cultural communication, like organizational behaviour and management practices, is affected by the manifestation of national values or beliefs in corporate communication, including the four identified by Hofstede: power distance, uncertainty avoidance, individualism (or collectivism), and masculinity (or femininity). The implication is that business people and managers have to be sensitive to the peculiar cultural mind-set of nations, especially when they have to deal with people from other countries.

5 Meeting the challenges ahead

In looking ahead, researchers and scholars in cross-cultural communication will have to contend with two kinds of challenge. The first is in improving the theory and model of cross-cultural communication. Distinguishing communication along cultural parameters such as individualism versus collectivism, high-context versus low-context, and polychronic versus monochronic, or even along value dimensions as identified by Hofstede, may have useful but limited applications in cross-cultural communication: useful because they serve as reference points of comparison; limited because as soon as they are identified, they tend to highlight only those that are distinguishable by those parameters. Culture is difficult to pin down. Anyone who is seriously interested in studying cross-cultural communication must guard against the temptation to oversimplify cultural differences and differences between national cultures. Scholars of cross-cultural communication should be alert to the dangers of stereotyping cultural or national characteristics. Further research on the differences between national cultures, for instance between macroculture and microculture, dominant culture and subcultures, is required.

In their review of existing work on cross-cultural business communication, Limaye and Victor (1995) identified major weaknesses in the existing corpus. One of their main criticisms is that most of the studies conducted so far have been too culture-specific or have examined only narrow slices of those cultures, and therefore its findings may not apply across cultures. Future research has to focus on developing a culturally sensitive theory and model of cross-cultural

communication as well as establishing a stronger empirical foundation.

The building of that foundation can be brought about by fostering greater collaboration among scholars from various cultures. An immediate benefit of such cooperation is the chance of overcoming potential cultural biases among researchers. Another is the possibility of obtaining greater insights into the multidimensional, multilayered, and multifaceted nature of cross-cultural communication. Given that cross-cultural communication is a multidisciplinary field of study, scholars and researchers from various related disciplines also need to come together to bring to bear their various forms of expertise and training.

The second challenge is to cope with changes in communications technology. The world today is experiencing rapid advancements in communications technology with the advent of the fax, e-mail, teleconferencing, video-conferencing and multimedia communication. Truly, cross-cultural communication has become borderless communication with people surfing on the global information superhighway anywhere and anytime. Virtual communication is the next frontier in cross-cultural communication. Business people have to learn to cope with the demands and changes wrought by the information revolution and face new problems of communication brought about by the swift pace of communication and information explosion.

The growing interdependence of nations in the global economy has resulted in the formation of regional trading zones and groups which promote economic cooperation among many nations, for instance the European Union (EU), the North America Free Trade Agreement (NAFTA), the Asia Pacific Economic Cooperation (APEC), and the ASEAN Free Trade Area (AFTA – 'ASEAN' is the Association of Southeast Asian Nations). When nations come together, their cultures will also come into contact. Cultural differences exist among member countries of multicultural APEC (which consists of the USA, Japan, Korea, China and the dynamic economies of southeast Asia) as well as within member countries of the EU. Inevitably, cross-cultural communication will be pivotal in the arena of international business collaboration and multi-national management.

JOO-SENG TAN
NANYANG TECHNOLOGICAL UNIVERSITY
SINGAPORE

Further reading

(References cited in the text marked *)

* Hall, E.T. (1976) *Beyond Culture*, New York: Doubleday/Currency. (A classic text on the contexts of culture, high context versus low context.)
* Hall, E.T. (1983) *The Dance of Life*, New York: Doubleday/Currency. (Another classic text on how time conception, monochronic versus polychronic, leads to cultural differences.)
* Hall, E.T. and Hall, M.R. (1990) *Understanding Cultural Differences*, Yarmouth, ME: Intercultural Press. (Illuminating cross-cultural comparisons of the Germans, French and Americans.)
  Harris, P.R. and Moran, R.T. (1991) *Managing Cultural Differences*, 3rd edn, Houston, TX: Gulf Publishing. (Discussions and practical pointers on how to manage for cross-cultural effectiveness.)
* Hofstede, G. (1980) *Culture's Consequences: International Differences in Work-Related Values*, London: Sage Publications. (A classic text on how national cultures can affect organizational behaviour and management policies.)
  Jackson, T. (ed.) (1995) *Cross-cultural Management*, Oxford: Butterworth Heinemann. (A helpful anthology of articles on various aspects of cross-cultural management, including managing cultural differences.)
* Limaye, M.R. and Victor, D.A. (1995) 'Crosscultural business communication research: state of the art and hypotheses for the 1990s', in T.

Jackson (ed.), *Cross-cultural Management*, Oxford: Butterworth Heinemann. (Presents ten useful and illuminating hypotheses on cross-cultural business communication.)
  Samovar, L.A. and Porter, R.E. (eds) (1994) *Intercultural Communication: A Reader*, 7th edn, Belmont, CA: Wadsworth Inc. (A useful introduction to the theories and practice of intercultural communication.)
* Shannon, C.E. and Weaver, W. (1949) *The Mathematical Theory of Communication*, Urbana, IL: University of Illinois Press. (A classic text on the linear model of communication.)
  Terpstra, V. (1985) *The Cultural Environment of International Business*, Cincinnati, OH: South-Western Publishing Co. (Analyses how multinational corporations adapt to the multicultural environment.)
* Ting-Toomey, S. (1994) 'Managing intercultural conflicts effectively', in L.A. Samovar and R.E. Porter (eds), *Intercultural Communication: A Reader*, 7th edn, Belmont, CA: Wadsworth Inc. (Examines the issue of cross-cultural conflict management.)
  Trompenaars, F. (1994) *Riding the Waves of Culture: Understanding Cultural Diversity in Business*, London: Nicholas Brealey Publishing. (Explores four types of corporate culture and the cultural differences between them.)
  Victor, D.A. (1992) *International Business Communication*, New York: HarperCollins. (Textbook for students of cross-cultural business communication with detailed review of literature and direct business applications.)

See also: CULTURE, CROSS-NATIONAL; GLOBALIZATION; INTERNATIONAL BUSINESS NEGOTIATIONS; ORGANIZATION CULTURE

Related topics in the IEBM: COMMUNICATION; CULTURE; HOFSTEDE, G.; INFORMATION TECHNOLOGY; ORGANIZATION BEHAVIOUR

Culture, cross-national

1 **The importance of cultural values for international managers**
2 **The meaning of culture**
3 **Ethnocentrism and parochialism**
4 **Defining and understanding cultural values**
5 **Cultural value models**
6 **Variation within cultures**
7 **Going beyond national culture**
8 **Conclusion**

Overview

This entry discusses firms doing business across national borders, and the role of culture in effective management of these firms. Figure 1 outlines relationships between a variety of variables and organizational effectiveness. The major focus here are the four central items identified as *cross-national culture* (national culture, for short), *cultural values*, *individual and group needs, attitudes, norms*, and *organizational effectiveness*.

Figure 1 identifies national culture as emanating from *societal* variables (not necessarily restricted by national boundaries) such as language, religion and history, as well as *national* variables (which are clearly associated with national boundaries) such as government, laws and regulations, geography and economic conditions. This national culture is also seen as being influenced by current events both within the country and in the world at large. National culture is, thus, relatively stable but does change in response to circumstances.

National culture is depicted as playing a fundamental role in forming cultural values. In turn, these values interact with the needs, attitudes and norms of individuals and groups and result in behaviours which contribute to organizational effectiveness, or lack thereof. Additional influences are the values derived from the corporate culture and the individual's professional culture; thus individuals and groups within an organization can be

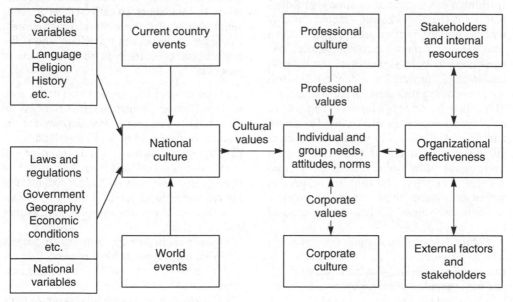

Figure 1 Culture and international management

expected to share some values, but they can also be expected to differ with respect to others.

The organization's effectiveness will increase to the extent that the factors influencing behaviour are understood by managers. An international firm's performance is likely to be enhanced when systems are in place that are congruent with the various influences that determine behaviours. While it is clearly impossible to understand all of the factors influencing behaviour, national cultures and attendant values appear to be an important starting point. A focus on national culture has been questioned by some scholars. Their concern is that the idea that nations and cultures may be coterminous is incorrect and, thus, thinking in these terms is misleading. It is certainly the case that nations and cultures are not the same; nevertheless, it seems appropriate from an international organization's viewpoint to consider national cultures, as the following illustrates.

An organization's activities are legally constrained by national requirements, rather than cultural ones. This results in international firms identifying with national boundaries. Human resource considerations encourage firms to take a national perspective. The workforce in a particular location is predominantly a national workforce – labour mobility within a country is often greater than between countries. This means that management systems need to be designed with the national character of the workforce in mind. Governments encourage this through legislation; usually, laws and regulations regarding employees encompass all citizens of a country and do not apply differentially to different cultural groups. In contrast, laws and regulations may differ quite dramatically from country to country. The firm has to function within this system; therefore, it is appropriate to begin its cultural analysis at the national culture level.

Figure 1 serves as a guide for this entry, which is divided into four main sections. The first considers the importance of cultural values for international managers and discusses why national cultures are expected to vary; it explores the relationship of societal culture and national culture to behaviour. The second section focuses on the meaning of cultural values; it defines various terms and looks at their associations. The third examines three cultural value models that can be applied at the national level and their impact on effective management and the last considers a variety of additional issues – stereotyping, variation within nations, overlapping cultures and environmental forces leading to convergence or divergence of cultures in different national locations.

I The importance of cultural values for international managers

Managers in international businesses need to understand and appreciate a variety of differences among nations. Among other differences, nations exhibit varying cultural profiles; thus, understanding the cultural environment is a component of the international manager's task. Managers who have worked in foreign locations acknowledge that understanding the culture in those locations is necessary if one is to manage effectively (see HUMAN RESOURCE MANAGEMENT, INTERNATIONAL). Virtually all of the activities undertaken by managers are affected, at least to some degree, by the cultural environment. Consider some examples which show the importance of culture in the management process:

(1) International firms need to negotiate with various foreign constituencies. Success in these negotiations rests on understanding the cultural background of the negotiators.
(2) Strategic alliances are becoming more and more common between firms with different strategies and objectives. To succeed, managers may need to understand the cultural factors that influence organizational strategies and objectives.
(3) Managers in foreign locations frequently find that employees behave in ways that are quite different from these managers' expectations.
(4) Expatriates (employees working outside their home country) find culture shock affects

their general ability to function well in foreign locations (see HUMAN RESOURCE MANAGEMENT, INTERNATIONAL). Cultural understanding and adaptability have been identified as contributing to better expatriation.

(5) Various functional aspects of organizations, such as accounting, finance, and marketing can differ markedly from one location to another. For an organization to be effective overseas, these functional aspects must fit the local culture.

2 The meaning of culture

Culture is a concept that is familiar to most people. It is difficult, however, to specify what is meant by the concept. For example, two anthropologists (Kroeber and Kluckhohn 1952) catalogued 164 separate and distinct definitions of the word 'culture'. This issue is further complicated by the fact that the word culture has several quite different meanings. Culture can refer to a shared, commonly-held body of general beliefs and values that define what is right for one group (Kluckhohn and Strodtbeck 1961; Lane and DiStefano 1988), or to socially elitist concepts, including refinement of mind, tastes and manners (Heller 1988).

The word apparently originates with the Latin *cultura*, which is related to *cultus*, which can be translated as cult or worship. Members of a cult believe in specific ways of doing things, and thus develop a culture which enshrines those beliefs. Culture here is used in this sense. The following definition, proposed by Terpstra and David, delineates what is meant by the word culture in the international management context:

> Culture is a learned, shared, compelling, interrelated set of symbols whose meaning provides a set of orientations for members of a society. These orientations, taken together, provide solutions to problems that all societies must solve if they are to remain viable.
>
> (Terpstra and David 1985: 5)

There are several elements of this definition which are important to gain an understanding of the relationship of cultural issues and international management (Punnett and Ricks 1992):

(1) Culture is learned – this means that it is not innate; people are socialized from childhood to learn the rules and norms of their culture. It also means that when one goes to another culture, it is possible to learn the new culture.

(2) Culture is shared – this means that the focus is on those things that are shared by members of a particular group rather than on individual differences; as such, it means that it is possible to study and identify group patterns.

(3) Culture is compelling – this means that specific behaviour is determined by culture without individuals being aware of the influence of their culture; as such, it means that it is important to understand culture in order to understand behaviour.

(4) Culture is interrelated – this means that while various facets of culture can be examined in isolation, these should be understood in context of the whole; as such, it means that a culture needs to be studied as a complete entity.

(5) Culture provides orientation to people – this means that a particular group reacts in general in the same way to a given stimulus; as such, it means that understanding a culture can help in determining how group members might react in various situations.

Because culture is so fundamental to society, it influences people's behaviours in critical ways. Effective management depends, at least in part, on ensuring that people behave in ways that are appropriate for the organization. This means that understanding culture is important for managers. Where cultural differences exist they should be accommodated to achieve desired behaviour and results. This is easier in theory than it is in reality. Each of us is influenced by our own culture, and people are inevitably somewhat ethnocentric as the following section explains.

3 Ethnocentrism and parochialism

Anthropologists believe that cultural attributes develop as a response to the environment and become a preferred way of behaving for a group of people because they help the people survive. It is not surprising, then, that cultural preferences are associated with right and correct ways of behaving. Consequently, different ways of behaving are seen as bad and incorrect. If 'our way' somehow contributed to our survival, it is hard to accept that 'their way' can also be acceptable. This view of the world is referred to as an ethnocentric view. Ethnocentric means that the view of our own and other cultures is centred on our own, and the belief that our own culture is superior to others.

Adler (1986) described a similar view of one's own culture as best in terms of parochialism. Parochial people also assume that the home culture is superior but the assumption arises for different reasons. The assumption of superiority arises not because cultures are compared but because differences are not recognized. This often arises where someone simply lacks knowledge about other cultures.

Ethnocentrism implies that the belief in the home culture's superiority is conscious, while parochialism implies only that the home culture is believed to be superior because little is known of other cultures. Both ethnocentrism and parochialism are common among managers who have to deal with people in foreign locations. Managers need not feel guilty about ethnocentrism or parochialism, given its frequent occurrence. Managers do need, however, to recognize that they are likely to exhibit either or both of these attitudes, and that these attitudes will inhibit their ability to work effectively in other cultures. The first step is to recognize the prevalence of these attitudes. Once recognized, one can begin to change them. Changing these attitudes begins with developing a better understanding of one's home culture.

4 Defining and understanding cultural values

Values are useful in explaining and understanding cultural similarities and differences in behaviour; thus, understanding values and their cultural basis is helpful to international managers. If international managers understand how values can vary from culture to culture, they are more likely to accept and interpret correctly behavioural differences. This acceptance and correct interpretation, in turn, enable managers to interact effectively with others whose values and behaviours are unfamiliar.

It is helpful to define the concept as well as to distinguish it from, and relate it to, others. This serves to delineate the domain of cultural values, and to underscore their importance to international managers. The following discussion begins with cultural values, then examines needs, attitudes and norms. These latter concepts are all similar to that of cultural values, but each contributes somewhat differently to behaviour.

Values

Values have been described as enduring beliefs that specific modes of conduct or end states of existence are socially preferable to their opposites (Rokeach 1973); a value system is seen as a relatively permanent perceptual framework which influences an individual's behaviour (England 1978). Values establish the standards by which the importance of everything in society is judged. Throughout these definitions, the important issue for international management appears to be the role of social values in behaviour.

In a general sense, values and norms are societal, while needs and attitudes are individual. Values interact with needs, attributes and norms as the following discussion explains.

Needs

Needs are described as forces motivating an individual to act in a certain way; once satisfied, needs no longer have an impact on behaviour. For example, a need for food motivates people to seek food; once people have eaten, they normally no longer seek food (unless motivated by other needs). Cultural values interact with individual needs because they influence how people choose to satisfy their needs.

It is generally accepted that two of the most basic and universal human needs are the need for food and the need for sex, yet satisfaction of these needs differs because of societal values. In most societies a value of human life precludes cannibalism to satisfy a need for food. Societies often have accepted times for eating, and even when people are hungry, they observe these timeframes. Similarly, social customs regarding sexual partners limit satisfaction of sexual needs.

Many societies practice restrictions regarding food, often associated with religious rituals. During Lent, Christians may forgo favourite foods or limit their intake of meat. During the month of Ramadan, Muslims fast completely during daylight hours. Some sects eat no meat, some do not allow beef, others prohibit shellfish or pork, and still others do not allow certain combinations of foods. Individual needs are put aside to observe these restrictions.

Many societies also have customs regarding the timing and selection of sexual partners. Some societies allow men to have multiple wives, others have group marriages where any partner may have sex with any other. In some locations marriages are arranged for girls at birth and they must remain virgins until marriage, in others men and women select their own sexual and marriage partners. As with food, individual needs are put aside to observe these restrictions.

Attitudes

Attitudes are described as a tendency to respond favourably or unfavourably to objects or situations, based on beliefs about them. Societal values influence what we respond favourably to and what we view with disfavour.

In a business setting dress can mean quite different things depending on what the society values, and how different types of dress are interpreted. If wearing a suit and tie indicates a conservative business perspective and conservatism is valued, this would result in a favourable attitude to someone in this attire. Elsewhere, if innovation in business was more highly valued, and wearing a brightly coloured T-shirt and jeans was seen as indicating an innovative perspective, this might be viewed positively. Similarly, in some societies males with long hair are seen negatively, while in others long hair represents virtue.

Norms

Norms prescribe or proscribe specific behaviours in specific situations and result in standardized, distinctive ways of behaving. They are seen as normal (thus the word 'norms') and appropriate behaviour. A typical US norm involves eating with the fork in the right hand and this seems acceptable and normal to people who have lived in the USA for extended periods. People in many other countries hold their forks in the left hand, and in other places forks are not used at all. For those accustomed to using the right hand for a fork, the reverse can be quite uncomfortable and using chopsticks in place of a fork almost impossible. Similarly, for those used to a fork in the left hand or chopsticks, the US norm is uncomfortable.

Norms probably originated from values but they no longer clearly represent these. The US norm of eating with the fork in the right hand would not be described as a 'societal value'; it is simply the accepted way of behaving in the USA.

5 Cultural value models

There are a variety of cultural value models that have been developed by scholars in different fields. Three have been selected to give a sense of the models available for managers. These particular models were identified because they have been presented widely in the international management literature. Each model is described and its limitations noted, then the model is related to some aspect of management. This discussion is very simplistic and in no way comprehensive. It is intended only to illustrate the potential for practical applications of cultural models in the international business setting.

Country clusters

Examining clusters of countries that share similar values can be a useful approach for international managers. One of the most extensive studies resulting in country clusters was carried out by Ronen and Shenkar (1985). This was a synthesis of previous research and identified eight clusters of countries. A number of countries which did not fall into one of the clusters were identified as independent. These clusters are illustrated in Figure 2.

The countries included in the diagram in Figure 2 reflected the available research. The clusters can be helpful to managers who have to decide on the degree to which cultural adaptation is needed when moving cross-culturally. A manager interacting with colleagues from within the home cluster can expect relatively similar values and easy adaptation – Australians interacting with Canadians will be on somewhat familiar territory. Moving outside the home cluster can be relatively more difficult because of the likely diversity of values and greater need for adaptation – a Mexican going to Saudi Arabia is likely to be faced with more cultural adaptation than the Australian working in Canada.

The countries included in the list are only those where appropriate research has occurred. Sometimes it is possible to make informed judgements regarding the likely

---

Cluster 1 - Anglo
  Australia, Canada, New Zealand, UK, USA

Cluster 2 - Germanic
  Austria, Germany, Switzerland

Cluster 3 - Latin European
  Belgium, France, Italy, Portugal, Spain

Cluster 4 - Nordic
  Denmark, Finland, Norway, Sweden

Cluster 5 - Latin American
  Argentina, Chile, Columbia, Mexico, Peru, Venezuela

Cluster 6 - Near Eastern
  Greece, Iran, Turkey

Cluster 7 - Far Eastern
  Hong Kong, Indonesia, Malaysia, Philippines, Singapore, South Vietnam, Taiwan

Cluster 8 - Arab
  Bahrain, Kuwait, Saudi Arabia, United Arab Emirates

Independent (not closely related to other countries)
  Japan, India, Israel

Note Countries within a cluster are considered similar with regard to their cultural values. Clusters are arranged in an approximate order of cluster similarity; that is, the Anglo cluster is more similar to the European clusters (Germanic, Latin European and Nordic) than it is to the Latin American, Near Eastern, Far Eastern and Arab clusters. A major limitation of these clusters is that they are based on empirical studies which, at that time, did not include Africa, much of Asia, and eastern Europe. Asia has received more attention recently (see Hofstede 1991), but Africa and eastern Europe still have not been studied extensively.

Figure 2 Country clusters
Source: Punnett (1989: 17)

position of countries which are not represented, based on information about their cultural antecedents and neighbours.

Limitations of country cluster information

These clusters can help international managers but there are some limitations to consider. For example:

1 Geographic regions such as Africa and eastern Europe are not represented, and within clusters, major countries are missing (for example, Brazil in Latin America and the People's Republic of China in the Far East). Managers may be particularly interested in one of these countries or regions.
2 The clusters are based on variables studied in the past; it is possible that different clusters would emerge if studying different variables.
3 These clusters do not identify the relative similarity among clusters; this may be an important consideration for international managers.
4 The clusters may overemphasize similarity within a cluster or dissimilarity among clusters. Countries within a cluster do differ and those in different clusters can exhibit some similarities.

The role of country clusters in international decisions

Grouping countries into culturally similar clusters is helpful to international managers in a number of ways. If we consider some typical concerns of international managers we can see how country clusters might be used. The following examples are by no means inclusive, there are many additional ways in which country cluster information can be used by international managers. These examples should, however, give a sense of how this information may be factored into international management decisions.

(1) Members of a cluster can be expected to share basic cultural values, and people in all the countries in a cluster are likely to behave in relatively similar ways. Managers with experience in one country (say, Norway) can then move relatively easily to another country

in the same cluster (say, Finland). This does not mean that everything in Finland will be the same as in Norway. Rather, it means that the experience gained in Norway is likely to be helpful in adjusting to Finland.

(2) Managers in one country in a cluster can move to others in the same cluster with a minimum of culture shock and with relatively little need for adaptation. Movement from one cultural cluster to another can be expected to be somewhat difficult. Managers in one cluster moving to another cluster need to be particularly aware of the effect of cultural differences. They need to expect culture shock and be prepared to adapt to the new cultural experience.

(3) Countries in different clusters are likely to exhibit different cultural values and the people to behave in relatively dissimilar ways. Managers moving from a country in one cluster (say, Singapore) to a country in a different cluster (say, Argentina) can expect to encounter substantial differences. They can be prepared for this and adapt their management style as needed.

(4) Decisions regarding locations for international subsidiaries can take advantage of information provided by country clusters. A firm seeking to expand internationally might initially want to gain experience in culturally similar locations. For example, a Canadian firm might expand to other countries in the Anglo cluster. Alternatively an international firm with substantial experience may feel there is potential benefit in expanding to countries that are culturally different. In this case, the Canadian firm could consider places like Saudi Arabia, Portugal or Indonesia.

(5) International staffing decisions can benefit from a consideration of country clusters. Allocating personnel to relatively similar cultures (for example, moving French personnel to Belgium) minimizes the culture shock they should experience. Such a move can be relatively easy, and extensive cross-cultural training and support are not needed. In contrast, a move to a country in a different cluster (for example, French personnel to the USA) may present a greater challenge. In this move a greater degree of culture shock is likely and, therefore, appropriate training and support

have to be provided (see HUMAN RESOURCE MANAGEMENT, INTERNATIONAL).

(6) International managers can consider country clusters in relation to joint ventures and strategic alliances. Many alliances fail because of the differing objectives of the parties involved, and to some extent these objectives reflect the national culture (for example, Japanese managers are generally believed to take a longer-term view than US managers). Firms entering alliances within a familiar cluster may be able to reach agreement on objectives more easily than in an unfamiliar cluster. When entering an alliance in an unfamiliar cluster, it is important to allow adequate time to discuss objectives in detail and it may be necessary to consider innovative proposals.

(7) Managers may find negotiations follow similar procedures within clusters but can change quite dramatically between clusters. Managers who are aware of this are likely to be better negotiators because they will prepare for and use the similarities and differences that exist.

(8) Managers need to consider whether management practices and approaches can be transferred from one country to another. Management practices are more likely to be generalizable within cultural clusters. Managers who have successfully worked in one country can have some confidence that they can be effective in other countries in the same cluster.

(9) International managers often have to make decisions about expanding to new locations. Given a choice of expanding to two locations which are equally attractive in other ways, cultural similarities and differences may be a deciding factor. Expansion to new locations within a familiar cluster is likely to involve fewer unexpected occurrences than expanding to an unfamiliar cluster. In contrast, the differences that are inherent in a new cluster may provide opportunities that do not exist in culturally similar locations.

(10) Subsidiaries of international firms are often grouped based on similarities of activities, and regional groupings are fairly common. Country clusters provide one basis for deciding on regional groupings. Countries within a cluster can be expected to share some characteristics such as language, religion, etc. and to express relatively similar values. These similarities suggest that taking a common approach to countries within a cluster may be appropriate.

(11) Marketing in different countries can be a major challenge for international managers. A major concern for marketers is taking advantage of efficiencies offered by standardized marketing approaches while adapting to cultural differences. Country clusters provide input into decisions regarding marketing standardization and adaptation. The relative similarity of countries within a cluster suggests that greater standardization may be appropriate while differences between clusters highlight the need for adaptation.

Kluckhohn and Strodtbeck's value orientation model

The anthropologists Kluckhohn and Strodtbeck (1961) explained cultural similarities and differences in terms of basic problems which all human societies face. Cultural differences are explained by varying ways of coping with these problems – different societies adopt different solutions. This model has been used by a number of international management authors and provides a means of assessing national culture that many people find helpful.

Consider the various solutions that societies have developed for the five problem areas identified by these two anthropologists.

Relationship to nature – subjugation, harmony and mastery
Societies which view themselves as subjugated to nature view life as essentially preordained; people are not masters of their own destinies, and trying to change the inevitable is futile. Societies which view themselves as living in harmony with nature believe that people must alter their behaviour to accommodate nature. Societies that view themselves as able to master nature think in terms of the supremacy of the human race, and harnessing the forces of nature.

Time orientation – past, present and future
Societies which are orientated towards the past look for solutions in the past; what would our forefathers have done? Societies which are present-orientated consider the immediate effects of their actions; what will happen if I do this? Societies which are future-orientated look to the long-term results of today's events; what will happen to future generations if we do these things today?

Basic human nature – evil, good, mixed
Societies which believe that people are primarily evil focus on controlling the behaviour of people through specified codes of conduct and sanctions for wrongdoing. Societies that believe that people are essentially good would exhibit trust and rely on verbal agreements. Societies that see people as mixed probably also see people as changeable and would focus on means to modify behaviour, to encourage desired behaviour and discourage behaviours that are not desirable.

Activity orientation – being, containing and controlling, doing
Societies which are primarily 'being'-orientated are emotional; people react spontaneously based on what they feel at the time. Those which are 'doing'-orientated are constantly striving to achieve; people are driven by a need to accomplish difficult tasks. Those concerned with containing and controlling focus on moderation and orderliness; people seek to achieve a balance in life and in society.

Human relationships – individual, lineal, co-lineal
Societies which are primarily individual believe that individuals should be independent, and take responsibility for their own actions. Those that are lineal are concerned with the family line and the power structure that underlies a hierarchy. Those that are co-lineal are group-orientated and emphasize group interactions and actions.

The Kluckhohn and Strodtbeck model in international management

These value orientations can be related to effective management practices in different locations. The following suggestions illustrate how these orientations may be related to management.

1 In a society that believes humans are subjugated by nature, planning would be futile, because the future is preordained.
2 In a society that is present-orientated, rewards would be closely tied to current performance.
3 In a society that believes in the basic goodness of humans, participative management is likely to be the normal approach.
4 In a society that is primarily being-orientated, decisions are likely to be intuitive with less concern for logic.
5 In a society that is hierarchical, the organization structure might reflect this in a formal, authority-based hierarchy.

Understanding these dimensions of culture can provide international managers with insights into people's behaviour in foreign locations, and allow these managers to adapt their own style and adjust their organization's practices to accommodate the differences. Consider the following possibilities:
(1) In a society that thinks in terms of mastery over nature, technology is likely to be admired and people willing to work towards production goals and objectives set by management. In a society that emphasizes harmony with nature, technology may be accepted but there will be concern over the impact of technology on nature, and goals and objectives will be acceptable if they relate both to productivity and the environment. In a society that sees itself as subject to nature, mastery of technology may be viewed with caution and specific goals and objectives disliked.
(2) In a past-orientated society, market research would focus on the past and customer tastes would not be expected to change dramatically or quickly. Sales efforts would emphasize past quality, performance, etc., and would use familiar approaches. In a present-orientated society, market research

would focus on what is current, and identify products and services with immediate practical benefits. Sales efforts would emphasize these immediate benefits and use topical references and up-to-date approaches. In a future-orientated society, market research would be concerned with expectations of the future and would try to identify tomorrow's tastes and needs. Sales efforts will emphasize the long-term benefits of products and services and use futuristic references and images.

(3) If the society believes that all people are basically good then managers will expect that people working for a firm intend to do their best and contribute to the organization's effectiveness. If errors occur they will be explained as occurring in spite of people's efforts. If people are believed to be basically evil, managers will not expect people to work hard on their own. Errors will be explained in terms of individual human error and disassociated from the firm. If people are seen as mixed, the selection of the best people to work in the firm might be emphasized. Errors can be admitted readily and the actions taken to correct and avoid them in the future explained.

(4) In a being-orientated society people are spontaneous and react emotionally. Accounting and financial systems would need to be relatively flexible allowing for alternative ways of carrying out necessary activities. Policies and procedures would be general and provide guidelines rather than specific and detailed instructions. In a containing and controlling society the emphasis would be on logic. Systems would be rationally designed and explained assuming that people will comply with logical systems. Policies and procedures will be complex and include both qualitative and quantitative guidelines and instructions. In a doing-orientated society the concern is for activity and accomplishment. Systems will be pragmatic, emphasizing expected results. Policies and procedures will be relatively simple and described in operational, active terms.

(5) In a society that is primarily individual the individual person will be the focus of management activities. This will be true of decision making, leadership, work design, rewards,

etc. In a society that is lineal, the hierarchy of power and authority will be important in all management activities. Leadership is associated with level in the organization which is accompanied by power and authority. Vertical differentiation will be stressed, and decisions, work design and rewards will conform to the hierarchical structure. In a society that is co-lineal, group activities are normal and preferred. The group becomes the focus in terms of decisions, leadership, work design and rewards.

Hofstede's value survey model

The value survey model (VSM) has been widely discussed in international management literature and it appears to provide information of relevance from a managerial point of view. The Hofstede (1980) model proposed four dimensions of culture (a fifth dimension was added based on research in the Far East – Chinese Culture Connection, 1987 – but is not discussed here).

Individualism
Individualism (IDV) is the degree to which individual decision making and action is accepted and encouraged by the society. Where IDV is high, the society emphasizes the role of the individual; where IDV is low, the society emphasizes the role of the group. Some societies view individualism positively and see it as the basis for creativity and achievement; others view it with disapproval and see it as disruptive to group harmony and cooperation.

Uncertainty avoidance
Uncertainty avoidance (UAI) is the degree to which the society is willing to accept and deal with uncertainty. Where UAI is high, the society is concerned with certainty and security, and seeks to avoid uncertainty; where UAI is low, the society is comfortable with a high degree of uncertainty and is open to the unknown. Some societies view certainty as necessary, so that people can function without worrying about the consequences of uncertainty; others view uncertainty as providing

excitement and opportunities for innovation and change.

Power distance

Power distance (PDI) is the degree to which power differences are accepted and sanctioned by society. Where PDI is high, the society believes that there should be a well-defined order of inequality in which everyone has a rightful place; where PDI is low, the prevalent belief is that all people should have equal rights and the opportunity to change their position in the society. Some societies view a well-ordered distribution of power as contributing to a well-managed society because each person knows what their position is, and people are, in fact, protected by this order. Others view power as corrupting, and believe that those with less power will inevitably suffer at the hands of those with more.

Masculinity

Masculinity (MAS) is the degree to which traditional male values are important to a society. Traditional male values incorporate assertiveness, performance, ambition, achievement and material possessions, while traditional female values focus on the quality of life, the environment, nurturing and concern for the less fortunate. In societies that are high on MAS, sex roles are clearly differentiated and men are dominant; if MAS is low, sex roles are more fluid and feminine values predominate throughout. Some societies see the traditional male values as being necessary for survival; that is, men must be aggressive and women must be protected. Others view both sexes as equal contributors to society and believe that a dominance by traditional male values is destructive. The extremes of each of these indices have been described. Most countries are not at the extreme, but may be moderately high or moderately low; thus, effective management practices will not usually reflect an extreme tendency. An examination of profiles of different countries shows the variety that is possible considering these four dimensions. Some examples illustrate how these might influence management practices.

(1) New Zealand as a society is individualistic, does not avoid uncertainty and believes in equality and traditional male values. This would suggest that organizational structures will be relatively flat, with individuals making decisions on their own and competing for scarce resources.

(2) Italy as a society is individualistic, avoids uncertainty and believes in equality (within the confines of sex distinctions) and traditional male values. This would suggest a similar structure, but a reliance on gathering information for decisions and an emphasis on job security and seniority are important components of the management system.

(3) Singapore as a society is collectivist, does not avoid uncertainty, believes in power distinctions and is relatively low on masculinity. This suggests a paternalistic leadership system, with the leader expressing concern for subordinates and the quality of life, but without undue concern for job security.

(4) Japan as a society is collectivist but also high on uncertainty avoidance as well as masculinity, and relatively high on power distance. This would suggest a system that seeks consensus among group members but is competitive and has clear distinctions in terms of power; job security would be stressed and jobs allocated on the basis of sex.

Limitations of the value survey model

The scores reported by Hofstede are based on employees within one organization, a large US multinational company. Certain types of individuals will be attracted to such an organization, and this will be reflected in these scores. These scores should not, therefore, be interpreted as an accurate description of the national culture as a whole; rather, they should be seen as an indication of the similarities and differences that one might expect to find among employees in this type of organization in different countries.

In addition, these scores represent a central tendency in a particular population, but there is likely to be a wide array of values in any country; organizations and industries will attract and retain individuals with value systems that fit into the organizational culture. For example, a study of fast food restaurant managers in Canada and the USA revealed a very low level of individualism, combined with no uncertainty avoidance and high power distance and masculinity (Punnett and Withane 1990). This is quite dissimilar from the Canadian and US value profile presented by Hofstede; but, it appears to match the needs of an industry where people must work in close coordination, where there is little job security and where there are clear distinctions of power and a great deal of competition.

Researchers have also expressed concerns regarding the survey instrument used in Hofstede's research, and the validity of the measure has been questioned. Researchers question whether the country scores provided are representative of the normal population and whether the important cultural variables are the ones being measured. These concerns should all be kept in mind when interpreting the results of Hofstede's study. From a practical perspective, the cultural variables described by the model are intuitively appealing because of their apparent relationship to the management process.

Using the value survey model in international management

The management process is often described as consisting of planning, organizing, staffing, directing and controlling. These aspects of the management process probably occur in some form in all businesses, but the form may differ depending on the environment. In particular, the cultural values that are typical of a particular society can influence what is effective in terms of the management process. Consider some extremes of the Hofstede dimensions as they might relate to aspects of the management process.

Where individualism is high, individual input is sought from those individuals who have particular knowledge or expertise. Superiors are expected to make day-to-day decisions and communicate these to subordinates who are expected to carry them out. Input may be sought from subordinates, or others, who will be affected by decisions, or who have particular knowledge or expertise. Individuals may

disagree with particular decisions, but will generally go along with them if the majority agree, or if the decision has been made by a person in a position of power.

Individuals are given specific responsibility for completing tasks and achieving goals and objectives. The individual is expected to make the necessary decisions to carry through a given assignment. Management by objectives (MBO) is a popular approach, because MBO incorporates the idea of top management setting strategic directions, lower levels developing action plans to achieve these, and individuals accepting and working towards individual goals.

Where collectivism is high, organizational plans are formulated on the basis of the larger societal direction, and with input from all organizational members. The overall direction of the organization is discussed and agreed to throughout the organization. Decisions are made collectively, with all affected participating in the process. Disagreements are dealt with throughout the process, and consensus from all members is sought. Tasks and assignments are carried out by groups. There is pressure from the group for conformance to acceptable standards. When decisions need to be made, they are made by the group as a whole. The quality circle approach is popular, because it incorporates the idea of bottom-up decision making, consensus among members and group involvement.

Where uncertainty avoidance is high, uncertainty can be avoided by having group members share responsibility for planning and decisions, or, alternatively, by having one person in a position of power take responsibility. The advice of experts is likely to be important in formulating plans and making decisions. Planning provides security and is well accepted. Plans are likely to be detailed and complex, incorporating priorities and contingencies. Specific plans provide direction and little ambiguity. Strategic planning is as long-term as it is practical. Checks and balances ensure that performance is at the planned level, and allow for correction before a major departure occurs. Decisions are reached slowly. If responsibility is shared, then group agreement is important to the planning process. If a powerful individual makes the decisions, then these are imparted to subordinates as absolutes. In any case, disagreement is discouraged.

Where uncertainty avoidance is low, planning is flexible and relatively short-term. Uncertainty is seen as inevitable, and therefore the organization must be able to change direction quickly. Planning is accepted as providing guidance but not constraints. Formal planning is most likely to take place at top levels and be, at least partially, based on a subjective evaluation of opportunities. Personal preferences are likely to be evident in strategic directions. A certain amount of risk taking will be encouraged. Individuals are likely to accept the risk of individual decision making, and the need for making quick decisions will be stressed.

Where power distance is high, planning and decision making is done at the top. Input is accepted from those in powerful positions, but no input is expected from those at lower levels. Long-term plans are kept secret. Operational decisions are made on a daily basis by superiors, and work assigned to subordinates. All decisions are referred to the superior, and subordinates are discouraged from taking the initiative and making decisions. Subordinates accept assigned work and carry out tasks as instructed. Those in positions of power are respected; those in inferior positions expect that more powerful individuals will take responsibility for decision making.

Where power distance is low, everyone is seen as being capable of contributing to the planning process, and input from a variety of organizational levels is sought in developing strategic plans. Decision making in general is participative, and long-term plans are likely to be shared among organizational members. Operational decisions incorporate the views of those who must carry them out. The people involved in particular tasks are expected to make the routine decisions necessary to complete the task, and decisions are only referred to the superior when they involve unusual circumstances. Power differences exist, but are minimized, and friendly relationships between superiors and subordinates are normal.

Where traditional masculine values predominate, strategic plans emphasize specific, measurable advances by the organization (for example, increases in market share, profitability, etc.); these are difficult but believed to be achievable, and results are observable. Strategic choices are made at the top level. Operational decisions will focus on task accomplishment and tasks will be undertaken by those people most likely to perform at the desired level. Certain tasks will be seen as more suitable for males, others as more suitable for females. In some cases, responsibility for different types of decisions will be on the basis of sex. Outside of their traditional decision making roles, each sex will tend to emulate the other.

Where traditional feminine values predominate, strategic plans will take into account the environment, the quality of working life, and concern for the less fortunate. Profitability and market share, for example, will be defined within this context. Operational decisions will focus on satisfaction with work and development of a congenial and nurturing work environment. Task accomplishment will be within this framework. Work will be seen as generally suitable for either sex, with more concern for assigning work according to individual abilities and preferences. Decision making will be shared between the sexes. Decision making responsibility will depend on ability and preferences rather than sex. Male values of achievement, money and performance will rank equally with female values of nurturing, quality of life and caring for the less fortunate.

6 Variation within cultures

Models of cultural values are helpful in understanding cultural similarities and differences. In essence, however, they are stereotypes. Any culture is far more complex than such models would suggest, and it is important that this complexity is recognized. One can think of these cultural stereotypes as describing the values of a typical member of a particular culture, but must acknowledge that any culture is made up of individuals, many of whom will not share the typical values. In working with people from other cultures, both of these aspects need to be considered (Mendenhall *et al.* 1995). To illustrate both cultural preference and individual variation, consider two cultures, Alpha and Beta; Alpha might be a culture described as valuing personal initiative, and Beta as valuing group harmony (the USA and Japan, respectively, would fit these descriptions to some degree). These values are measured on an individualism scale.

If these preferences are considered as describing the average in these two societies, these cultural values can be pictured graphically as normal curves. In Figure 3, the y axis represents the relative frequency of occurrence of individualism in society, and the x

axis represents a continuum from low individualism to high individualism. The individualism preferences of the two cultures, Alpha and Beta, are pictured on the graph. As Graph A illustrates, there are some Alphans who are quite concerned with group harmony (contrary to their average) and there are some Betans who are quite concerned with personal initiative (contrary to their average). It is possible to talk of the Alphans as generally being high on individualism and concerned with personal initiative, and the Betans as generally being low on individualism and concerned with group harmony. At the same time, individuals within both the Alpha and Beta cultures can vary from this general preference. In contrast, it is possible, although unlikely, that there could be virtually no overlap between two cultures as in Graph B. Two cultures can also be very similar and yet reflect a subtle difference in preferences. This would be the case in Canada and the USA, two countries often seen as holding similar values, yet with some differences in their cultural values. This is illustrated in Graph C; here, there is a great deal of overlap between the cultures, yet the norm structures for each country are slightly different.

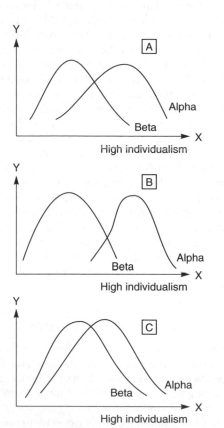

Figure 3 Cultural values: levels of individualism in Alpha and Beta
Source: Mendenhall *et al.* (1995: 292)

7 Going beyond national culture

A focus simply on national culture can be somewhat misleading if one limits consideration to this level. There are clear cases where cultures transcend national boundaries (for example, the British culture in many former colonies) and other cases where several cultures are evident in one nation (for example, multiculturalism in Canada). Equally, because cultures change in response to the environment, they may become more similar or more different over time. On the whole, as discussed earlier, from the organization's viewpoint, a focus on national cultures is an appropriate beginning. Within this framework, subcultures, overlapping cultures, and forces for convergence and divergence need to be considered.

Understanding subcultures

Identifying subcultures and their values is necessary in some situations and can be particularly useful to international managers; for example:

(1) A subculture may hold values which are in sharp contrast to those of the broader national culture. If a manager is interacting substantially with members of such a subculture, he or she will need to appreciate and accommodate these differences. Sikh immigrants to Canada still maintain their cultural heritage and believe in the importance of wearing turbans. The Royal Canadian Mounted Police – Canada's famed Mounties – found it was necessary to accommodate this cultural custom in order to attract and retain Sikhs in the force.

(2) The values of a subculture can be more similar to a foreign manager's own cultural values than those of the broader national culture. A manager might want to seek out members of this subculture in situations where similar values are desired. A manager from a largely Christian country such as the United Kingdom might find some similarity of values with the Christian minority in Japan, and might seek out this group at certain times, particularly in times of grief.

(3) Members of a subculture whose values are in conflict with the broader national culture may not be integrated into the workforce easily. Contrasting values may cause personal conflicts among employees from different groups. A manager must be sensitive to these potential conflicts and identify ways of dealing with them. The indigenous Malays and the Chinese in Malaysia have been described as exhibiting sometimes radically different values that can lead to conflicts at work. These are partially due to conflicting religious practices – the Malays, for the most part, are Muslims while the Chinese are Confucian and Buddhists – and partially due to attitudes towards work – the Malays are seen as easygoing and working to live, while the Chinese are described as concerned with getting ahead and work is more central to their lives.

(4) Synergy can develop where employees with different values work together because they may view the same situation from varying perspectives. Managers who can effectively control interactions among employees with different values can benefit from the development of new and innovative ways of thinking. The Bata Shoe Company has subsidiaries throughout the world and finds that by bringing its diverse marketing managers together in Canada, new ideas for products and marketing approaches can be developed.

(5) Working with a variety of subcultures within one national location provides many of the same experiences as working in a new national culture. Managers can increase their cross-cultural sensitivity by seeking out members of different cultural minorities and interacting and working with them on an ongoing basis. The USA is made up of many groups which maintain their cultural heritage in spite of being Americans. Some companies have made a virtue of this cultural diversity; for example, Monsanto is reported to have developed programmes to ensure that all employees are culturally aware.

Understanding overlapping cultures

Subcultures are often encountered and cannot be ignored by international managers. The same is true of cultures that overlap national boundaries. There are many situations where groups in different countries share similar values. In fact, the subcultures identified previously (for example, the Sikhs) can be found in many countries and their values will be somewhat similar in each location. The similarities in values are often attributable to shared ethnicity or religion; some examples illustrate this potential overlap:

(1) Rastafarians (members of a religious sect originating in Jamaica) can be found throughout the Caribbean and in Canada, the UK and the USA. Those values and customs associated with their religious beliefs remain similar even when they have been integrated into societies outside Jamaica.

(2) The Jewish people often exhibit similar values no matter where in the world they have settled. To some extent this is because of shared religious beliefs, but even non-practising Jews feel a kinship with other Jews

in different parts of the world, and many Jews see this as a shared cultural heritage, not simply a religious similarity.

(3) The British left a clear mark on many of their colonies, and the governing class in former British colonies retain many British characteristics.

(4) The boundaries of many nations have been identified so that cultural groups have been divided. These groups often share more culture with their counterparts in other countries than with the nation in which they live. The Kurdish people of Iran, Iraq and Turkey provide a good example of this division of a culture. Ethnic Russians living in many of the new states formed from the USSR are in a similar situation.

It can also be helpful for international managers to identify overlapping cultural values that may be found in different locations. Familiarity with the cultural values of a group in one location can then be useful in identifying values of a counterpart group elsewhere.

Forces for convergence and divergence

Whether cultures are converging or diverging is a further issue of interest to international managers. Some people argue that there are many forces in the world which encourage countries to become more alike and to share common values. For example, the ease of global communication and travel means that people are often exposed to foreigners and foreign media. People in the USA can watch French television, listen to radio broadcasts from the People's Republic of China and attend Indian movies. Without ever leaving home, they can meet Japanese tourists, talk with Saudi business people, and have dinner with African students in Balinese restaurants. Similarly, around the world, products that originated in the USA are sought – Levi's jeans, Coca-Cola, Elvis Presley records and Rambo movies, among other things. The British rock group 'the Beatles' have been popular in countries as diverse as the USA, Russia and Japan. Over time, it would seem that if people are exposed to similar experiences, and interact with others from different cultures, there might be a convergence of values.

The current worldwide concern with the environment also suggests a potential converging of values. If cultural values develop in response to perceived survival needs, then global concerns that are not defined by national boundaries may lead to global solutions and shared values. Similarly, regional economic integration, as exemplified by the European Union, is also a force for convergence of values. These regions seek to standardize a variety of practices, and this standardization, in turn, is likely to influence cultural values.

In addition, the existence of multinational and global companies has been seen as contributing to the convergence of cultures. These organizations inevitably take aspects of the home culture with them to foreign locations, and subsidiaries will share, to some extent, a corporate culture and perhaps a professional culture. At the same time, as the firm draws its leaders from around the world there is a sharing of values. Over time, this would suggest an increasing importance of the corporate influence and some convergence of values.

In contrast, there are arguments that cultural values are not converging, but may be diverging. The ease of communication and travel may have this latter effect. Extensive exposure to foreigners and foreign media may increase awareness of the home values, which may be seen as particularly 'good' in contrast to foreign values. A sense of domination by foreigners can result in a determination to maintain one's own value system. Canadians, for example, feel that they are very influenced by the USA and react by being more Canadian; some people in the USA are concerned about the Japanese influence and react by perceiving Japanese ways as negative.

Events in the late 1980s and early 1990s, such as the collapse of the Soviet Union, suggest that strong cultural value differences have been maintained by groups within the union in spite of efforts to eliminate these differences. Similarly, French Canadians wish to be recognized as a distinct society and native American groups' arguments for self-government focus around cultural uniqueness and suggest divergence rather than convergence.

It could also be argued that the activities of multinational and global companies can contribute to divergence. Some of these companies provide products or services specifically developed for particular countries or regions and they adapt their decisions to fit the needs of different locations. This sensitivity to cultural differences can in effect perpetuate the differences.

Arguments for both convergence and divergence are quite reasonable. Perhaps one can conclude that convergence will occur in some aspects of culture and divergence in others. International managers should be aware of the forces leading to both, and in specific situations consider their likely impact.

8 Conclusion

The relationship of national culture and international management is an extremely complex one. The discussion in this entry is necessarily limited in scope and depth. It should, however, provide the reader with a basic understanding of the issues associated with developing and using cultural understanding to enhance international operations.

There are western biases inherent in these discussions of culture and management. For example, the management process – consisting of planning, organizing, staffing, directing and controlling – is familiar to most readers because that is how business and management is usually approached in North America and Europe, but consider the following.

1 Is planning a necessary part of management? If events are pre-determined, planning may at best be a waste of time, and at worst a questioning of a higher power.
2 Should firms be formally organized? If personal influence is important in day-to-day activities, it may not be appropriate to identify positions within the firm.
3 Can people be allocated to fill positions within the firm? If people prefer to work at

tasks as they arise, it may not be helpful to allocate them to specific slots.
4 Does management actively seek to direct and motivate subordinates? If people believe that they should work hard only for personal achievement, it may be counterproductive for management actively to direct and motivate them.

This inherent western bias to thinking about management illustrates a major challenge for international cross-cultural management. Effective managers should not take anything for granted. Openness to the possibility that the world is not the world you know and accept is constantly necessary.

BETTY JANE PUNNETT
UNIVERSITY OF THE WEST INDIES

Further reading

(References cited in the text marked *)

* Adler, N.J. (1986) *International Dimensions of Organizational Behavior*, Boston, MA: PWS-KENT Publishing Company. (An excellent overview of the topic intended as a companion text for courses in organizational behaviour.)

Bhagat, R. and McQuaid, S.J. (1982) 'The role of subjective culture in organizations: a review and direction for future research', *Journal of Applied Psychology – Monograph* 67 (5): 61–74. (A comprehensive, scholarly review of the relationship between culture and organizations.)

* England, G. (1978) 'Managers and their value systems: A five country comparative study', *Columbia Journal of World Business*, 13 (2): 35–44. (A relatively early study of differences in national culture as they relate to managers, which identifies both similarities and differences in managerial values across national boundaries.)

* Heller, F.A. (1988) 'Cost benefits of multinational research on organizations', *International Studies of Management and Organization* 18 (3): 5–18. A discussion of the need for international management research, including a better understanding of the role of culture in international management.)

* Hofstede, G. (1980) *Culture's Consequences*, Beverley Hills, CA: Sage Publications. (An extensive study of the differences in values across cultures around the world, which gives substan-

tial insight into the relationship of culture, values and behaviour.)

* Hofstede, G. (1991) *Cultures and Organizations – Software of the Mind*, London: McGraw-Hill. (An extension of the 1980 work, incorporating Confucian dynamism to the model, and further discussing the role of culture in organizations.)

* Kluckhohn, A. and Strodtbeck, F. (1961) *Variations in Value Orientations*, Westport, CT: Greenwood Press. (A well-recognized anthropological assessment of variations in values that has been adopted by some management scholars.)

* Kroeber, A. and Kluckhohn, C. (1952) *Culture: A Critical Review of Concepts and Definitions*, Cambridge, MA: Papers of the Peabody Museum, Harvard University. (A classic discussion of the meaning of culture, its development and its implications.)

* Lane, H. and DiStefano, J. (1988) *International Management Behavior – From Policy to Practice*, Scarborough, Ont: Nelson Canada. (A text of cases, readings and conceptual discussion which examines behaviour in the context of international management.)

* Mendenhall, M., Punnett, B.J. and Ricks, D.A. (1995) *Global Management*, Boston, MA: Blackwell. (A comprehensive text on all aspects of international management.)

* Punnett, B.J. (1989) *Experiencing International Business and Management*, Boston, MA: PWS-KENT Publishing Company. (A unique collection of experiential exercises, projects and profiles pertaining to international business and management.)

Punnett, B.J. (1997) 'Towards effective management of expatriate spouses', *Journal of World Business*. (A discussion of the challenges faced by expatriate spouses with suggestions for managing these challenges.)

* Punnett, B.J. and Ricks, D.A. (1992) *International Business*, Boston, MA: PWS-KENT Publishing Company. (A comprehensive introduction to the field of international business.)

* Punnett, B.J. and Withane, S. (1990) 'Hofstede's value survey model: to embrace or abandon?', in S.B. Prasad (ed.), *Advances in International Comparative Management*, vol. 5: 69–90. (An application of Hofstede's model in different industries and with different ethnic groups.)

Ricks, D.A. (1983) *Big Business Blunders – Mistakes in Multinational Marketing*, Homewood, IL: Dow-Jones Irwin. (A wonderful and humorous compilation of mistakes that companies have made around the world.)

* Rokeach, J. (1973) *The Nature of Human Values*, New York: Free Press. (Fundamental to the understanding of values and their impact on human behaviour.)

* Ronen, S. and Shenkar, O. (1985) 'Clustering countries on attitudinal dimensions: A review and synthesis', *Academy of Management Review* 10 (3): 435–54. (A comprehensive review of previous studies to identify clusters of countries exhibiting similar national cultures.)

* Terpstra, V. and David, K. (1985) *The Cultural Environment of International Business*, Cincinnati, OH: Southwestern Publishing. (An excellent text reviewing many aspects of culture and their relationship to international business.)

See also: GLOBAL STRATEGIC ALLIANCES; GLOBALIZATION; HUMAN RESOURCE MANAGEMENT, INTERNATIONAL; INTERNATIONAL BUSINESS NEGOTIATIONS; INTERNATIONAL MARKETING; MANAGEMENT IN ITALY; MANAGEMENT IN JAPAN; MARKETING MANAGEMENT, INTERNATIONAL; MULTINATIONAL CORPORATIONS; ORGANIZATION CULTURE

Related topics in the IEBM: BATA SYSTEM OF MANAGEMENT; DECISION MAKING; GLOBALIZATION AND CORPORATE NATIONALITY; GLOBALIZATION AND SOCIETY; HERZBERG, F.; INTERNATIONAL BUSINESS ELITES; LEADERSHIP; MANAGEMENT IN AUSTRALIA; MANAGEMENT IN MEXICO; MANAGEMENT IN NORTH AMERICA; MANAGEMENT IN SCANDINAVIA; MANAGEMENT IN SINGAPORE; MANAGEMENT IN THE ARAB WORLD; MARKETING RESEARCH; MIGRANT MANAGERS; MOTIVATION AND SATISFACTION; ORGANIZATION STRUCTURE; ORGANIZING, PROCESS OF; POWER; WOMEN IN MANAGEMENT AND BUSINESS

Economic integration, international

Overview

Regional economic integration can be viewed in terms of a hierarchy of arrangements which extend from the preferential tariff agreement to the free trade area, the customs union, the common market and, in the extreme case, the economic union. The latter is now frequently described as economic and monetary union.

Various economic benefits are said to arise from the removal of internal tariff and quota barriers to trade in goods between the partner economies, although some protection from import competition from third countries will remain. Further integration benefits arise from the removal of protective devices generally referred to as non-tariff barriers. Higher beneficial forms of integration would depend on the removal of internal obstacles to trade between the partners in services. A common market involves an attack on mainly government-inspired regulations which impede the free cross-frontier flow of services of production, that is, labour, professional persons, capital and business enterprise.

The highest form of economic integration is economic and monetary union. This does not just involve the removal of inter-state barriers to the free movement of goods and services, but also extends the integration process to monetary and fiscal matters. At a minimum such additional macroeconomic arrangements involve a system of fixed exchange rates between participating national currencies; at a maximum they imply the introduction of a single unified currency and national fiscal systems. Such an extension of integration carries with it additional economic benefits, as well as a further erosion of national economic sovereignty. The decision-making structures associated with the specific economic integration policies now in place in various parts of the world economy vary widely from highly centralized and administratively well-supported systems to those which exhibit considerable decentralization and minimal bureaucracy. Theorists of integration speculate that economic integration can spill over into political integration; the European Union is a classic case of the latter process at work.

1 Introduction

While international economic integration is not a new phenomenon, as witnessed by the German *Zollverein* in the nineteenth century, there is no evidence of the term being used in economic analysis prior to 1942. International economic integration denotes a state of affairs, or a process, involving the combination of previously separate national economies into larger economic arrangements. A distinction needs to be made between overall international economic integration via the General Agreement on Tariffs and Trade (GATT) and regional integration. It is the regional variety, with its attendant element of discrimination against third countries, which is the focus of this analysis.

One way of achieving the integration of previously separate national economies is to eliminate barriers to the flow of goods, services, factors of production (that is, labour, the professions, capital and business enterprise) and money between the constituent states. International economic integration goes beyond the conclusion of mere international cooperation agreements, although such acts of cooperation may be part of a larger scheme of economic unification.

2 Specific forms of international economic integration

The least demanding form of international economic integration is the preferential tariff agreement. In such an arrangement, the countries involved reduce but do not undertake to eliminate totally their import tariffs (customs duties) on the trade in goods flowing between them; meanwhile, they retain tariff protection on goods entering their economies from outside (see INTERNATIONAL TRADE AND FOREIGN DIRECT INVESTMENT).

In a free-trade area arrangement the participants agree to remove totally their tariff (and quota) protection on the trade in goods flowing between them but remain free to determine the level of external tariff protection on goods entering their economies from third countries. Notably, in a free-trade area rules of origin have to be devised. These prevent what is called trade deflection. This is defined as the import of goods from third countries into the free-trade area by member state A, which has a lower external tariff than member state B, in order to re-export them to member state B.

In a customs union the member states agree to remove tariffs and quotas on intra-bloc trade but agree to introduce a common level of tariff protection on goods entering the union from third countries. This uniform protective arrangement is usually called the common external tariff (CET), although in the Rome Treaty which created the European Community (EC, part of the European Union, or EU – see Table 1; EUROPEAN UNION) it is referred to as the common customs tariff (CCT). Arrangements of this kind are clearly discriminatory, since they represent free trade within the bloc but discrimination against the rest of the world. Post-war arrangements appear at first sight to have contravened GATT rules, since the latter called for non-discrimination in tariff arrangements. However, in practice, GATT rules provided an escape route. Provided the level of the CET was no higher than the average of the previous national tariffs, it satisfied GATT principles. Since the CCT of the EC was based on a straight arithmetical average of the previous national tariffs, it was deemed to be acceptable.

In a common market a customs union is supplemented by arrangements which permit the free flow of factors of production. Thus an individual can offer himself or herself for employment in any member state of the common market; capital can flow to where it can earn the highest remuneration; business executives can set up subsidiaries, branches, etc. in any of the participating states.

Finally, there is a concept of economic union or economic and monetary union. The 'economic' aspect of the union refers to the existence of a common market. The 'monetary' aspect relates to the associated monetary and fiscal arrangements, and may involve the introduction of a common currency together with highly unified fiscal arrangements. In effect, the member states become mere regions of the larger economic area. The variety of possible monetary and fiscal scenarios in such a union is detailed below.

3 Particular features of the integration process

It is important to emphasize that actual integration exercises may not fit neatly into any of the aforementioned scenarios. Thus, as we have seen, a customs union involves a CET combined with the total elimination of internal tariffs. However, the parties to an integration arrangement may reduce the internal barriers only partially, in which case the resulting arrangement is, in effect, a partial customs union.

It is equally essential to recognize that, while integration arrangements may be overall in character, they may also be only partial in coverage. For example, the European Coal and Steel Community (see Table 1) related purely to free trade between the partners in respect of iron, steel and coal. The European Free-Trade Association (EFTA – see Table 1) was essentially concerned with free trade in industrial goods and services – agricultural trade was largely excluded from the arrangement.

Integration exercises may also overlap. Thus when in 1973 the United Kingdom (UK)

Table 1 Exercises in international economic integration

Integration exercise	Members	Nature of exercise
Association of South East Asian Nations	Brunei, Darussalan, Inodonesia, Malaysia, Philippines, Singapore, Thailand	Preferential tariff agreement accompanied by programmes of economic cooperation over a wide field, including joint production projects
Caribbean Community	Antigua, Barbados, Guyana, Jamaica, Trinidad and Tobago, Grenada, St Lucia, St Vincent, Montserrat, St Kitts-Nevis-Anguilla, Belize	Customs union which envisages possibility of full economic union by 2000
Central African Customs and Economic Union	Cameroon, Central African Republic, Chad, Congo, Equitorial Guinea, Gabon	Customs union
Central African Monetary Union	Same members as Central African Customs and Economic Union	Monetary union with common currency and union central bank
Central American Common Market	Costa Rica, El Salvador, Guatamala, Honduras, Nicaragua	Originally conceived as a free-trade area which would progressively develop into a customs union and then a common market
Council for Mutual Economic Cooperation	USSR, Bulgaria, Cuba, Czechoslovakia, East Germany, Hungary, Mongolia, Poland, Romania, Vietnam	Aim was not free trade but rather to plan production on a joint basis and to seek a bilateral trade balance between partners
Economic Community of West African States	Benin, Burkina Faso, Cape Verde, Cote d'Ivoire, Gambia, Ghana, Guinea, Guinea-Bissau, Liberia, Mali, Mauritania, Niger, Nigeria, Senegal, Sierra Leone, Togo	Customs union
European Coal and Steel Community	Same members as European Union	Originally a free-trade area arrangement in respect of trade in coal, iron and steel products. A common external tariff for iron and steel introduced at a later stage
European Free-Trade Association	Norway, Sweden, Switzerland, Austria, Finland, Iceland, Liechtenstein, Portugal, UK	Free-trade area with reciprocal free-trade agreement (excluding agriculture) with European Union. Also closely tied in to European Community via European Economic Area agreement (but see below)
European Community	Germany, France, UK, Italy, Spain, Belgium, the Netherlands, Luxembourg, Portugal, Denmark, Irish Republic, Greece, Austria, Sweden, Finland	Originally called the European Economic Community and latterly the European Community. Initial aim was to create a common market. Masstricht Treaty on European Union envisages ultimate state of Economic and Monetary Union as part of the all-embracing European Union
North American Free-Trade Agreement	USA, Canada and Mexico	Free-trade area. Successor to US/Canada Free-Trade Agreement

and Denmark deserted EFTA in favour of the EC the two trading blocs concluded a reciprocal free-trade arrangement. However, this applied only to the industrial and service sectors, since the EC had introduced extremely protective arrangements in relation to its farming sector, which would have been jeopardized by free trade in agricultural produce. Subsequently, most of the EFTA countries and the EC concluded the European Economic Area agreement, which integrated the majority of EFTA states into the EC single market. Most EFTA states are, however, now full members of the EC.

A distinction needs to be made between negative and positive integration. A good deal of the process of economic integration, certainly in the context of a free-enterprise economy, is indeed negative. It consists of removing barriers to the free and undistorted flow of goods, services, factors, etc. However, integration activity can also be positive – it can take the form of the development of common policies. An example would be the introduction of joint industrial development programmes. Thus a key feature of the activities of the Association of South-East Asian Nations (ASEAN – see Table 1; ASSOCIATION OF SOUTH-EAST ASIAN NATIONS) has been cooperation in industry. This has taken the form of joint production of basic industrial goods, the achievement of complementarity in national industrial development programmes and other joint industrial ventures. Joint industrial ventures have also been a key feature of the Central African Customs and Economic Union (CACEU – see Table 1). Specific projects have included joint industrial investments in the production of cotton textiles, insecticides, fertilizers, petrochemicals, pharmaceuticals and cement. Even the famous (or infamous) EC Common Agricultural Policy has had its positive aspect, since alongside the dismantling of barriers to internal trade in agricultural produce and the elimination of different national systems of agricultural price support there has been the positive aim of raising the level of farmers' incomes nearer to those of their industrial counterparts.

Mention must also be made of the concept of spill-over. Theorists of the economic integration process – referred to as neo-functionalists – have pointed to what has been called the expansive logic of integration. Functional spill-over emphasizes the idea that when a group of countries embarks on a scheme of limited economic integration spill-over effects are likely to arise which will drive them on to higher levels of integration. The following is an example of a spill-over effect. Assume that a group of countries has indeed embarked on a limited economic integration exercise which involves the free movement of goods, services and factors but excludes monetary matters. Because of the latter, exchange rates are free to rise and fall as market forces dictate. Subsequent experience may suggest that flexible exchange rates inhibit the flow of goods, services and factors. This tendency arises from the uncertainties associated with exchange-rate volatility. It may therefore be argued that flexible exchange rates should be replaced by fixed rates. Exchange rates, however, cannot remain fixed unless the monetary conditions in the member states are harmonized so as to give rise to uniform rates of inflation (or deflation). Such harmonization would require that national sovereignty over monetary matters would have to be given up in favour of centralized monetary coordination. It might indeed be concluded that stability would be better achieved by having a common currency. In short, although the member states may embark on a limited integration exercise, they may be driven remorselessly down the path to greater and greater economic integration. That at least was the expectation of the neo-functionalists.

The neo-functionalists also expected that economic integration would give rise to a political spill-over. Their theorizing was somewhat obscure, but the general proposition was very credible. In the first place, it was not unreasonable to expect that the process of economic integration could have a confidence-building effect. Successful efforts in the economic sphere could suggest the possibility of successful outcomes in policy areas that were not economic in character. Not only that, but pooled efforts could be expected to carry more weight than individual ones. Equally important was the point that the distinction between economic and non-economic issues is often difficult to draw.

In large measure, economic integration proceeds through the agency of free trade and competition. It has therefore assumed the existence of a substantial free-enterprise sector within the integrating partners. However, economic integration has also occurred in a state-enterprise context. This was so in the case of the Council for Mutual Economic Co-operation (CMEA or Comecon – see Table 1). The members of Comecon, which was founded in 1949, were those communist states which, until the reforms in eastern Europe, looked to the Soviet Union for political leadership. The aim was not to trade freely – which was neither possible nor desired, given that trade was a state monopoly in each of the member countries – but rather to plan production on a joint basis and seek to ensure that the resulting trade flows balanced. However, the economic reforms in eastern Europe, together with the reunification of Germany, meant that this particular exercise in economic integration was doomed to extinction.

4 The process of economic integration

A distinction can be made between stage one and stage two of the integration process. Stage one covers the process up to and including the formation of a common market. It is therefore concerned with external protective arrangements coupled with the removal of barriers to the internal free movement of goods and services, and in the case of a common market this would extend to the establishment of conditions which enabled factors of production to move freely across frontiers. Stage two covers the further process of monetary integration, which would transform a common market into an economic union (economic and monetary union). It is therefore concerned with the unifying of policy in respect of the money supply, interest rates, exchange rates and fiscal matters.

The stage-one process

Preferential tariff arrangements and free-trade areas leave the participating states free in respect of their external trading relationships, and there is nothing that needs to be added, other than to recollect that rules of origin may be introduced (see discussion above and below). However, as has been noted, in a customs union (and a common market) a CET is established. In practice, a CET may be subject to exceptions – that is, not all countries may pay the tariff. For example, in the case of the EC the ex-colonial dependencies of the original members (and many of those of members who joined later) were allowed tariff-free access (for manufactured goods) to the EC internal market. Subsequently, the EC concluded a whole series of trade agreements that exempted individual countries and groups of countries from the CET. At a later stage the EC introduced the general system of preferences, which granted tariff-free quotas to developing countries in respect of their manufactured exports to the EC – that is, up to a specified quantitative level, imports into the EC were exempted from the CET (without reciprocity).

A CET may be accompanied by other protective devices. These include collectively negotiated import quotas (for example the multi-fibre arrangements concerning imports of textiles and clothing into the EC), collectively negotiated voluntary export restraints and collectively operated anti-dumping duties. In 1984 the EC adopted what has come to be called the new commercial policy instrument. It can be invoked against illicit practices that affect Community exports to the rest of the world, as well as Community imports. When such illicit practices are proved to exist, various retaliatory actions can be introduced by the Council of Ministers, including increasing the level of import duties and the application of quotas.

The removal of internal protection poses major problems. Quite clearly, it involves the abolition of tariffs on internal trade. Such liberalization may, however, be accompanied by rules concerning the degree of local content. For example, in the case of the North American Free Trade Agreement (NAFTA – see Table 1; NORTH AMERICAN FREE-TRADE AGREEMENT) textiles and apparel will be free of duty within NAFTA only if they are made from yarn or fibre also coming from within NAFTA, a provision likely to encourage firms using overseas supplies of yarn to switch to local suppliers. Another such rule is that cars require 62.5 per cent North American content to qualify for duty-free status within NAFTA, significantly higher than the 50 per cent provision in the existing pre-NAFTA agreement between Canada and the USA. Equally, tariff liberalization requires the removal of charges that are equivalent to tariffs. For example, in the case of the EC the Italian government was in the habit of applying what it called a 'statistical levy' to imports and exports. The EC Commission pointed out that this was the equivalent of a customs duty and should be eliminated. When the Italian government refused to comply, the matter was referred to the European Court of Justice, which upheld the Commission's action. Additionally, the removal of internal protection requires the abolition of quantitative restrictions on imports (and exports). Such quantitative restrictions can arise indirectly. A particularly good illustration is provided by the celebrated EC Cassis de Dijon case.

Cassis de Dijon is a French liqueur manufactured from blackcurrants. The German company Rewe-Zentral AG sought to import the French liqueur and requested an authorization from the West German Federal Monopoly Administration for Spirits. The latter body informed Rewe that West German law forbade the sale of liqueurs with less than 32 per cent alcohol content, although for liqueurs of the Cassis type a minimum of 25 per cent was allowed. This was no help to the Cassis importer as Cassis has an alcoholic content of only 15–20 per cent, and thus it was illegal to import it. Rewe contested the ban in the German courts and the matter was referred to the European Court of Justice for a preliminary ruling. The court declared that the German law in question was in these specific circumstances a measure equivalent to a quota and was therefore prohibited under Article 30 of the Rome Treaty. The minimum alcoholic content rule had in this particular case the effect of a zero import quota. Clearly, measures of this kind have to be rooted out if internal free trade is to be established in a free-trade area.

Tariff (and quota) barriers may be removed, but a host of non-tariff barriers (NTBs; see NON-TARIFF BARRIERS) remain to be dealt with. These are associated with public procurement, state subsidies, product standards, taxation arrangements, state monopolies, anti-competitive business practices and border formalities.

Public procurement poses a major NTB problem. In the EC government spending represents about 45 per cent of total spending.

However, some of this is spending on wages and salaries, etc., whereas the problem from the point of view of internal trade liberalization is public spending on goods and services. This latter category amounts to approximately 15 per cent of total spending. Typically, such spending is carried out on a 'buy-national' basis, in which central, regional and local governments tend to support national champions rather than buying the best or the cheapest. Naturally, such behaviour negates the effectiveness of internal tariff disarmament. It therefore requires the institution of rules that require public authorities, at whatever level, to act in a non-discriminatory way. The EC approached this problem by requiring that public invitations to tender should be widely publicized within the Community, prescribing rules that favour open, as opposed to negotiated, tendering (the latter could involve only one firm being considered). Such measures require that decisions to purchase are based on the selection of the cheapest or the best and provide methods of redress where these principles are ignored. Interestingly, NAFTA included a modest agreement to open central government procurement to competition. Apparently, however, this provision need not bind lower layers of government.

State subsidies, too, can distort the competitive process, and can mean that domestic but inefficient sources of supply are able to survive while more efficient but unaided sources within the rest of the integrated area are put at a competitive disadvantage. Such subsidies may take the form of grants to bail out relatively inefficient and possibly loss-making domestic firms or industries (sectoral aids). Alternatively, subsidies may take the form of regional development grants (subsidies to capital or labour) – that is, regional aids. These may be justifiable as a means of compensating for some locational disadvantage, thus helping to raise depressed living standards, but the level of assistance may be excessive; in other words, the aid may more than compensate for locational disadvantages and become a disguised means of granting unfair competitive advantages. Aids may take the form of grants designed to cheapen the price of exports – that is, pure export aids.

Since the late 1980s governments within the EC have tended to favour subsidies for research and less development (R&D) activity. Particularly difficult problems arise in connection with the public enterprise sector, since it is quite possible that in one state an industry may be in public ownership and in receipt of (possibly concealed) subsidies, whereas the same industry in another member state may be privately owned and be required to stand on its own. Individual states may also distort competition by advancing capital to their privately owned industries at less than commercial rates.

A system of surveillance, with powers to ban unfair and unjustified state subsidies, is essential if cross-frontier competition is to be fair. This approach has been adopted by the EC, with the enforcement task being devolved to the EC Commission. Distortion of competition can also arise as a result of differential fiscal concessions. This has been a major problem in the Caribbean Community (CARICOM – see Table 1) and led to the introduction of a scheme for the harmonization of fiscal assistance to industry. Distortions of competition and unfair competitive advantages may also arise if member states deliberately lower environmental, health and safety, minimum-wage and child-labour standards as a means of attracting footloose investment. NAFTA has led to the establishment of two commissions with powers to impose fines and remove trade privileges where such standards are lowered deliberately.

The role of product standards as an NTB has already been illustrated by the Cassis de Dijon case. Modern governments tend to intervene on a considerable scale in setting standards which cover the description, contents and design of goods, in order to prevent consumer deception. Standards also aim to protect consumers from injury, and can also lead to greater efficiency by providing for longer production runs and equipment compatibility. While such interventions in the marketplace are entirely legitimate, standards may differ between partner states and cross-frontier trade may therefore be prevented. This leads to a loss of beneficial competition and choice. Alternatively, goods may have to be modified to meet the standards of each member-state market, with a consequent loss of the economies of large-volume production. Two approaches to this problem are possible. One is mutual recognition of national standards – this is feasible where differences do not pose a threat to, for example, life and limb. However, where health, efficiency or compatibility issues are clearly involved, the only solution is to devise common or harmonized standards. Goods conforming to them will then be readily marketable throughout the integrated area. The EC has adopted both approaches – mutual recognition in some instances has been paralleled by action under Article 100 of the Rome Treaty, which provides for the adoption (by means of directives) of a legally based system of harmonized standards. These supersede national laws. CARICOM is also notable for the special attention it has given to this problem. A specially created Caribbean Common Market Council has been established to advise the Common Market Council of Ministers on this issue and to promote the development of uniform standards in the member states.

Taxation can also pose problems. Since the focus at this point is on the trade in goods and services, the taxation in question is indirect. The experience of the EC in this area is particularly instructive. Two issues arose, the preferred structure of indirect taxation and the rates to be imposed. The Community chose to adopt two main types of indirect tax – excise duties, together with some form of turnover tax. The major area of debate arose in connection with the actual form of turnover tax to be adopted. Two alternative models were on offer, the German cascade system and the French value-added tax (VAT). Ultimately VAT was chosen, since it did not bias industrial structures towards vertical integration, whereas (in order to minimize tax) the cascade system did.

VAT had another advantage, which is connected with the treatment of indirect taxes in international trade. Since tax rates are likely to differ from country to country, competitive distortions may arise because imports from countries with high tax rates can be undercut by domestic production in countries with low rates. In order to avoid this state of affairs the destination system has traditionally been employed in international trade. This means that goods for export are zero-rated and importing countries impose the same rate of indirect tax on imports as they apply to their own products. The perceived advantage of VAT was that it was relatively transparent – that is, it was easy for the EC Commission to verify that the tax remitted on exports was not excessive and did not give rise to a concealed export subsidy. However, one of the longer-term aims of the European single-market programme is to adopt the origin system, whereby goods are exported bearing VAT, but this will only be possible when national VAT rates have been approximated. In the meantime some distortions continue as shoppers cross borders to obtain goods in countries with lower VAT rates; this problem also arises in respect of unharmonized excise rates.

NTBs also arise in connection with monopoly. Here, two kinds need to be identified. On the one hand, there are state fiscal monopolies and, on the other, for the most part there is the problem of private market power. The former kind of NTB is a revenue-raising device – for example, an enterprise, probably state owned, is given a monopoly of the supply of some particular good. Alcohol and tobacco products are typical cases in Europe. Having a monopoly, the enterprise can restrict output, raise prices and earn monopoly profits. The profits can be claimed by the state as part of its tax revenues. To be effective, such monopolies have to be able to restrict and, if necessary, prohibit competing imports. Inevitably, therefore, an NTB arises and has to be addressed.

Market power – which is not exclusively private in origin, since state enterprises may be involved – can also arise through the agency of cartels, dominant (possibly monopoly) firms and mergers. All of these can give rise to NTBs that prevent or distort beneficial cross-frontier competition within the integrated area. Cartels may, for example, establish cross-frontier market-sharing agreements in which the producers in member state A agree not to sell in the market of member state B and vice versa. Dominant or monopoly firms may, by virtue of their control over the supply of a product in a particular domestic market, be able to induce dealers to deal with them exclusively, thus effectively sealing the market off from import competition. Mergers may also be a method by which the inconvenient competition of outside suppliers can be taken over and suppressed.

The EC has an outstanding record in dealing with NTBs arising through the agency of cartels, dominant firms and mergers. Article 85 of the Rome Treaty bans cartels that restrict competition, provided that there is an effect on inter-state trade. However, exemptions are possible where benefits arise and consumers share in them. In practice, naked price-fixing, output-restricting and market-sharing agreements, which offer no counterbalancing advantage, will be struck down automatically. The European Commission possesses impressive powers of enforcement and can impose severe fines. The abusive behaviour of dominant firms can also be attacked, providing there is evidence to show that the flow of trade between the member states is affected. Since 1989 large-scale mergers which create or strengthen a dominant market position and significantly impede competition can be banned. Public enterprises are also subject to these rules of competition.

The question of border formalities must also be mentioned briefly. These can significantly add to the cost of goods being traded in the integrated area and this detracts from the advantages deriving from economic integration.

Trade liberalization within an integrated area also requires that action should be taken to create free trade in services. The removal of internal tariffs is normally only relevant to trade in goods but not to trade in services. However, the elimination of NTBs is relevant to the liberalization of service trade. Apart from the kinds of NTBs discussed above, obstacles in this sector are often associated with governmental regulatory systems – as in insurance, banking and transport. These often restrict entry into particular sectors of economic activity.

When economic integration extends to the stage of a common market there is a need to create conditions in which factors of production are also free to move from state to state. To a large extent, integration requires the modification of various forms of state intervention. In the case of labour it requires liberalization of work-permit systems, transmission of information on job opportunities, making social security rights transferable, etc. In the field of professional services it involves in particular the harmonization of training requirements and the mutual recognition of diplomas, degrees, etc. In the case of capital it calls for the removal of exchange controls, the harmonization of corporation taxation (so that the allocation of capital is not distorted by differences in national rates, etc.) and the conclusion of double-taxation agreements. The liberalization of business enterprise involves the harmonization of regulatory systems (in order that enterprises licensed in one member state can set up subsidiaries or branches in another member state) and the harmonization of national legal systems to facilitate cross-frontier business integration (mergers, joint ventures, etc.).

The advantages of the stage-one process

The advantages of the stage-one process are discussed most conveniently by focusing on the stage of integration immediately preceding the formation of a customs union. The advantages of liberalizing factor movements will be considered thereafter.

Although a customs union is an exercise in free trade, it is not a substitute for universal free trade, which economists have always regarded as beneficial. A customs union represents free trade within the bloc but discrimination against the rest of the world. For this reason, the effects may be beneficial or disbeneficial. In other words, a customs union may give rise to trade creation or trade diversion and therefore is not unambiguously beneficial. In Table 2, in the case of good A, country I initially applies a non-discriminatory 50 per cent tariff in respect of imports from country II and country III. The most efficient producer of the good is country II, but it is excluded by the tariff. If country I and country II form a customs union but leave country III facing the tariff, there will then be a beneficial switch of production from the less efficient country I to the more efficient

Table 2 Trade creation and trade diversion

Good	Cost or cost plus duty per unit	Country III exporting to country I	Flow of trade	Goods produced by country I	Flow of trade	Country II exporting to country I	Results
A	Cost	14		17		12	Trade creation
	Cost plus duty prior to customs union	21	No trade: country I produces A	17	No trade: country I produces A	18	
	Cost plus duty after customs union	21	No trade	17		12	
B	Cost	12		20		14	Trade diversion
	Cost plus duty prior to customs union	18		20	No trade	21	
	Cost plus duty after customs union	18	No trade	20		14	

country II. This is *trade creation*. In the case of good B the most efficient supplier is country III, which supplies the good to country I prior to formation of the union. After the formation of the union, however, country II can undercut country III. There will be a switch of production from the more efficient country III to the less efficient country II that is not beneficial. This is *trade diversion*.

Whether a customs union is on balance beneficial depends partly on the relative magnitude of the types of conflicting effects outlined in the preceding paragraph. However, this static analysis does not take account of two further benefits, namely the possibility that the enlarged market will provide greater scope for economies of scale and that it is likely to give rise to a more intensely competitive environment. The latter could lead to a lowering of costs, and increased levels of investment and R&D spending. The customs union is also likely to confer greater bargaining power in international trade negotiations than would be enjoyed if the union states acted independently. A common market also involves the free movement of factors. Here, the major benefit is that factors are free to flow to the locations where they earn the highest return and produce the greatest economic welfare.

The stage-two process

The stage-two process consists of the transformation of a common market into an economic union, or economic and monetary union. This implies that the partners in the integration process embark on a programme of monetary integration. Monetary integration can itself be broken down into its monetary and fiscal components. These can be based, in turn, on either minimalist or maximalist models.

The monetary component
The monetary component of monetary integration may consist of an arrangement in which the participating states fix the rate of exchange between their separate national currencies. An arrangement of this kind can take the form of a fairly loose arrangement in which margins of fluctuation are allowed around fixed central exchange-rate parities, with the central parities being adjusted from time to time. This mode of operation was adopted in the Exchange Rate Mechanism (ERM) of the EC's European Monetary System (the latter was established in 1979). The monetary arrangement might, however, be stiffened by agreeing to fix exchange-rate parities irrevocably, with no margins of fluctuation. This measure could be combined with full convertibility of the member-state currencies. The term 'full convertibility' refers to a situation in which individuals or enterprises can change one member-state currency into another in whatever quantity they wish whenever they wish. Such an arrangement is referred to as an exchange-rate union and is a minimalist monetary arrangement. However, such exchange rates would not be viable in the longer term unless national macroeconomic policies were coordinated so as to achieve a convergence of economic performance in matters such as national rates of inflation.

If a fixed quantity of one national currency can always be exchanged for a fixed quantity of another, in whatever quantity required, then one is, in effect, a substitute for the other. It could then be argued that, for convenience and economy, it would be logical to take the further but considerable step of replacing the separate national currencies with one union currency. This arrangement is referred to as a currency union and represents a maximalist monetary arrangement.

If the latter path is followed there is a need to establish a union central bank system to control the supply of the common currency and to determine the union interest-rate structure. An analysis of the ingredients of monetary union does not suggest that there is any unique formula governing the organization, political relationship and aims of such a central bank. It could be monolithic or it could be part of a federal arrangement in which the union central bank operated in conjunction with the pre-existing national central banks. The union central bank could be independent of political influence or, at the other extreme, it could take instructions from the political authorities. In practice, a dependent union central bank would be likely to be pulled in various directions by conflicting national interests. That being so, a significant degree of independence seems to be a more practical option. The objective set for a union central bank could be the achievement of price stability within the union, although some other overriding objective, such as the maintenance of a high level of employment or the achievement of more rapid economic development – or a combination of all of these – might be specified.

The union bank would be charged with managing the exchange rate of the union currency *vis-à-vis* outside currencies. To this end, it would be reasonable to assume that the member states would transfer their foreign-exchange reserves to the central bank. The union central bank might have total discretion with respect to the exchange rate. Alternatively, it might be allowed full control of day-to-day support operations but be subject to the general supervision of exchange-rate policy by the political authorities. The union central bank would take on the role of lender of last resort. It would presumably play some role in the prudential regulation of commercial banks.

The fiscal component

Monetary union, as already noted, also has a fiscal dimension. In short, member states could not be allowed to run budget deficits of unlimited size, since one way of financing them would be to borrow. Large-scale borrowing would tend to drive interest rates up, not only in the deficit state, but in the union as a whole, since national monetary systems would be fully unified, with one set of interest rates. A *minimalist* fiscal model therefore presumes that some central authority exists which can set limits to national budget deficits. Tax rates (and structures) might still be determined at national level, although if the model was similar to that envisaged by the EC, then while taxes would still be imposed and collected by each member state, their structure and rates would in the main be harmonized in line with the needs of the customs union and common market. A *maximalist* fiscal model would require that the imposition of

taxes and the collection of revenues should be placed in the hands of some central authority. It might then pass some revenue back to the constituent states for local discretionary purposes. The central authority would also determine the appropriate level of the union budget deficit or surplus. In a democratic setting such a system would presumably be accompanied by a significant and parallel degree of political unification on the principle of no taxation without representation. The maximalist model outlined here, in respect of both its monetary and fiscal aspects, is that which was adopted by the USA.

A monetary union clearly involves the giving up of substantial amounts of economic sovereignty. For example, the powers to manipulate the supply of the currency, interest rates and exchange rates are surrendered. This prospect leaves individual members in a potentially vulnerable position. The possibility that they could suffer an asymmetric shock, and that income and employment levels could therefore fall cannot be ruled out. In the absence of self-correcting mechanisms of wage-price flexibility or labour migration, considerable political tensions could build up. For this reason, a system of resource transfers to less prosperous states could be the price demanded by some states for agreeing to monetary unification. It is perhaps worth noting that significant resource transfers from richer to poorer constituent parts of the union are a feature of many federal arrangements.

While preferential tariff agreements, free-trade areas and customs unions are relatively common and a number of common markets or incipient common markets exist, exercises that have already advanced to the stage of monetary integration or propose advancing to it are relatively rare. One example is the Central African Customs and Economic Union (CACEU), to which has been added the Central African Monetary Union (see Table 1). It has a common currency, the Central African Financial Cooperation Franc, which is issued by the Bank of the Central African States. The EC, following the Maastricht Treaty on European Union, aims to turn its common market into an economic and monetary union with a common currency in the shape of the euro.

The supply of euros would be in the hands of an independent European System of Central Banks. A high degree of fiscal integration would also exist; key features of the system would be harmonization of the structure and rates of indirect, and possibly direct, taxes, together with central control over national budget deficits. The Caribbean Community (CARICOM) also envisages a move towards monetary integration by the year 2000.

The advantages of the stage-two process

A minimalist monetary arrangement, particularly with irrevocably fixed exchange rates, removes the uncertainty which floating exchange rates give rise to. This facilitates intra-union trade exchanges of both goods and services, and thus enables the integrating states to enjoy more fully the advantages of specialization according to comparative advantage, economies of scale, greater competition and wider choice. The removal of exchange-rate uncertainty also facilitates the intra-union flow of factors of production. Thus, for example, it enables further advantage to be taken of the ability of capital to flow to those locations where it will earn the highest return. If a maximalist arrangement is introduced in which a common currency emerges, two further advantages arise, namely the elimination of the transactions costs that arise when differing currencies have to be exchanged, and the greater transparency which arises when economic transactions can be evaluated in terms of one currency.

The pool of reserves that are required when a common currency emerges will be less than the sum of the national reserves held prior to union. The member states will therefore enjoy a temporary gain in that an external trade deficit can be financed by allowing reserves to fall to the lower required level. If the common currency becomes an international currency an element of seigniorage will arise. In other words, countries outside the union will be willing to hold the union currency as an asset; thus imports of goods and services into the union can be financed by increased outside holdings of the union currency rather than by exports. The seigniorage advantage can be exaggerated, since there will also be an outflow of interest payments. Finally, a common currency greatly increases the bargaining power of the participating states when engaging in international monetary negotiations. Individually, the members may carry little or no weight, but collectively they can exert an influence that reflects their regional interests.

5 Other aspects of integration

Economic integration exercises require a decision-making structure. Typically, this tends to take the form of a supreme body consisting of heads of state and government, who make key strategic decisions, and a council (or councils) of ministers, who meet more frequently to deal with specific policy issues. For example, in the case of the Economic Community of West African States (ECOWAS – see Table 1) the heads of state meet once a year and the council of ministers meets twice. They are supported by an executive presided over by an executive secretary. A similar arrangement exists in the EC, with the European Council at the top and the law-making EC Council of Ministers below. They are supported by an executive in the form of the European Commission.

Not all integration exercises incorporate a permanent central executive body. Thus CARICOM delegates the execution of policy to a series of committees consisting of the relevant ministers from each member state. Ministerial decision making varies. The EC has moved increasingly to majority voting, whereas in ASEAN unanimity is the invariable rule. Integration exercises usually involve some arbitration body. ECOWAS has a community tribunal which interprets the founding treaty. The founding treaties of the EC delegate this task to the European Court of Justice.

Integration arrangements often give rise to a supporting development bank. Thus in the Central American Common Market (see Table 1) the Central American Bank for Economic Integration finances regional development projects. In the case of the EC, the European Investment Bank has for many years channelled vast amounts of loan-based assistance into the backward regions of the union. In addition, the EC established a community budget which, apart from bearing the administrative cost of the union, also awards grants for such purposes as regional and social improvement.

DENNIS SWANN
LOUGHBOROUGH UNIVERSITY

Further reading

Bainbridge, T. and Teasdale, A. (1995) *The Penguin Companion Policy*, London: Penguin. (A glossary of European Community institutions, policies and definitions.)

Baldwin, R.E. (1994) *Towards an Integrated Europe*, London: CEPR. (A discussion of the consequences of enlarging the European Community to include eastern Europe.)

Gros, D. and Thygesen, N. (1992) *European Monetary Integration*, London: Longman. (An analysis of monetary integration in the EC context which includes a discussion of early attempts at monetary union.)

Healey, N.M. (ed.) (1995) *The Economics of the New Europe*, London: Routledge. (A survey of European Community economic policy.)

Henderson, R. (1993) *European Finance*, London: McGraw-Hill. (A survey of the financial and monetary aspects of the European Community.)

Jovanovic, M.N. (1992) *International Economic Integration*, London: Routledge. (An introduction to the various forms of economic integration which includes an account of Comecon and ASEAN.)

Montagnon, P. (ed.) (1990) *European Competition*, London: RIJA. (A survey of European Community competition policy.)

Nielsen, J., Heinrich, U. and Hansen, J.D. (1991) *An Economic Analysis of the EC*, London: McGraw-Hill. (A highly theoretical treatment of economic integration in the EC context, covering microeconomic and macroeconomic aspects of the process.)

Swann, D. (ed.) (1992) *The Single European Market and Beyond*, London: Routledge. (An account of the Single European Act of 1986, its emergence and its impact on the integration process.)

Swann, D. (1995) *The Economics of the Common Market*, 8th edn, London: Penguin. (Presents an overall view of the European economic integration process, including the Single Market and the Maastricht Treaty.)

Swann, D. (1996) *European Economic Integration*, Cheltenham: Edward Elgar. (A review of the European Community economic policy following the Maastricht Treaty.)

See also: ASSOCIATION OF SOUTH-EAST ASIAN NATIONS; EUROPEAN UNION; INTERNATIONAL PAYMENTS; INTERNATIONAL TRADE AND FOREIGN DIRECT INVESTMENT; NORTH-AMERICAN FREE-TRADE AGREEMENT; NON-TARIFF BARRIERS

Related topics in the IEBM: GENERAL AGREEMENT ON TARIFFS AND TRADE; GOVERNMENT, INDUSTRY AND THE PUBLIC SECTOR; HUMAN RESOURCE FLOWS; MANAGEMENT IN EASTERN EUROPE; MANAGEMENT IN EUROPE; MANAGEMENT IN PACIFIC ASIA; MANAGEMENT IN RUSSIA; MONETARISM

European Union (EU)

Overview

The European Union (EU), currently comprising fifteen member countries, is an ever evolving entity whose fundamental and consistent aim is the complete economic integration and a high degree of political unification of European nations that accept this vision. From an historical perspective, the EU is the outgrowth of the formation of the European Economic Community (EEC) through the Treaty of Rome (signed 25 March 1957), which committed Belgium, Germany, France, Italy, Luxembourg and the Netherlands to the creation of a common market for goods, services and freedom of movement for people and capital among the member countries. The Treaty of Rome reflects a vision of an ever closer economic and monetary union among the member countries, culminating eventually in a political union as well, the federated United States of Europe.

The vision of the founding members of the European Common Market was not shared by all European countries, although they recognized the benefits resulting from economic integration and the removal of trade barriers. The United Kingdom, in particular, was ambivalent about the aim of an ever closer economic and political union, and the creation of supranational institutions. Under the leadership of the United Kingdom, Austria, Denmark, Norway, Portugal, Sweden and Switzerland formed the European Free-Trade Area (EFTA) in 1960, with the aim of removing trading barriers among the member countries but retaining national autonomy with regard to economic policies, and without contemplating a political union. Thus two competing visions of European integration have come to co-exist and have affected European integrative endeavours ever since. However, the achievements and initial success of the EEC led the United Kingdom to apply for membership. The United Kingdom, Denmark and Ireland became part of the first wave of enlargement of the membership of the EEC in 1973; Greece joined in 1981, followed by Portugal and Spain in 1986. Austria, Finland and Sweden became members of the EU in 1995, thus bringing its membership to fifteen countries, with a total population of more than 370 million people (see Table 1). A further enlargement of EU membership is due to take place around 2005. The Czech Republic, Estonia, Hungary, Poland, Slovenia and possibly Cyprus have been identified as the earliest likely candidates for the next round of EU expansion, with Bulgaria, Lithuania, Latvia, Romania and Slovakia to be considered for eventual conclusion later on.

1 Milestones in the development of the EU

The evolution of the EU is marked by some extraordinary and significant achievements. The major milestones include:

- 1963: Yaounde Agreement, in which former colonies of EEC members were granted trade advantages and financial aid
- 1968: all tariffs among the six member countries were eliminated
- 1969: establishment of a common agricultural policy that involved free trade in agricultural products among the member countries, the institution of common target price levels for major agricultural products (e.g. grain, meat, milk) and a price-support system with benefits to relatively inefficient producers
- 1973: Denmark, Ireland and the United Kingdom became members

Table 1 Member countries of the European Union

Country	Member since	1996 Population (millions)	1996 GDP (US$ billions)
Belgium	1958	10.2	258.8
France	1958	58.4	1,406.9
Germany	1958	82.0	2,276.8
Italy	1958	57.4	1,235.9
Luxembourg	1958	0.4	17.8
Netherlands	1958	15.6	380.4
Denmark	1973	5.3	170.0
Irelandv	1973	3.6	70.8
United Kingdom	1973	58.3	1,210.0
Greece	1981	10.5	111.6
Portugal	1986	9.9	105.7
Spain	1986	39.3	561.1
Austria	19865	8.1	236.9
Finland	1995	5.1	122.7
Sweden	1995	8.9	244.3
European Union		372.0	8,409.7

- 1981: Greece became a member
- 1986: adoption of the Single European Act; promulgation of over 300 Directives designed to guide the harmonization of thousands of laws and regulations, and to achieve a single, integrated market among EU members by 1992; Portugal and Spain became members
- 1992: Maastricht Treaty to attain monetary union; EU members which plan to adopt the single currency must meet specified convergence criteria
- 1995: Austria, Finland and Sweden became members
- 1999: a common currency, the euro, to be introduced; it will replace the various national currencies no later than 1 January 2002; Denmark, Sweden and the United Kingdom will not adopt the euro when it is first introduced

European economic integration, political unification and social cohesion constitute an ongoing process which has been remarkably successful in spite of the many disagreements and conflicts that had to be dealt with. The impetus for reconciling conflicting interests among EU member countries has most frequently been provided by the vision enshrined in the founding document, the 1957 Treaty of Rome, and by some of the supranational institutions created as guardians of an envisaged united Europe. A central role in this regard has been played by the European Commission and its staff, headquartered in Brussels (Belgium), which is sometimes derisively referred to as the Brussels bureaucracy. An understanding of the process of European integration requires an appreciation of the institutional structures and of the decision-making framework as a driving force of the EU.

2 The institutional framework of the EU

Just as the objectives and policies of European integration evolved over time, so did the supranational institutions that were devised to give expression to the vision of an ever closer economic and political union among the member countries. The EU has nine major

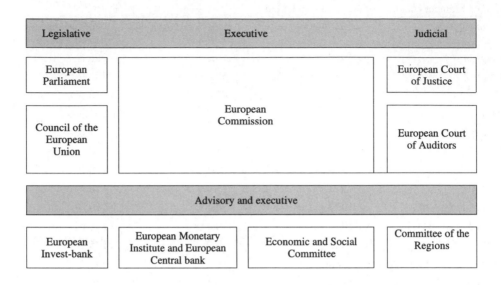

Legislative	Executive	Judicial
European Parliament	European Commission	European Court of Justice
Council of the European Union		European Court of Auditors

Advisory and executive

European Invest-bank	European Monetary Institute and European Central bank	Economic and Social Committee	Committee of the Regions

Figure 1 The institutions of the European Union

supranational institutional entities, which interact in a dynamic political process (see Figure 1).

The European Parliament, whose 626 members are directly elected for five-year terms and which meets in Strasbourg (France), represents the citizens of the European Union. As a result of the Single European Act of 1986 and the Treaty on the European Union of 1992, the European Parliament has legislative power on a broad range of issues involving, for example, social programmes, economic policies, consumer affairs and international agreements. In addition, the Parliament approves the Union's budget and exercises political supervision over executive institutions such as the European Commission, whose members are appointed by the Parliament.

The Council of the European Union, also known as the Council of Ministers, is another legislative institution representing the governments of the member states. Council meetings involve either the heads of member governments or the heads of various ministries such as foreign affairs, finance or agriculture. The Council issues directives, regulations or decisions that are binding with regard to the aspects that are being addressed. The presidency of the Council rotates among the member countries and changes every six months.

At the centre of the institutional structure of the EU is the European Commission as its major initiating and executive force. The Commission has twenty members with France, Germany, Italy, Spain and the United Kingdom having two representatives each, and the other EU countries having one representative each. The Commission is supported by an administrative staff of about 20,000 people divided among some thirty directorates and departments. The Commission, as the Union's executive body, has the right to initiate legislation, and it exerts its influence at every stage of implementing policy decisions and in administering the Union's budget appropriations. The Commission members, appointed for five-year terms, are required to be independent of their national governments and to act only in the interest of the Union. The president of the Commission is selected by the heads of government of the EU members in consultation with the European Parliament.

The Court of Justice of the European Union, located in Luxembourg, consists of fifteen judges who are appointed for six-year terms. Their responsibility is to ensure that European treaties, legislation and Directives are interpreted in accordance with European law and carried out in an appropriate manner. The European Court of Auditors, also located in Luxembourg, is required to check on the appropriate collection and disposal of the Union's funds.

Among the major institutional integrative devices of the EU are two important consultative committees: the Economic and Social Committee and the Committee on the Regions, each with 222 members. The major role of these committees is to provide a forum for the discussion of economic, social and regional issues, to find common ground on these issues and to resolve possible conflicts of interest among national, economic or social groupings.

Two additional institutions will gain in importance over time. The European Investment Bank, whose primary purpose is to provide long-term funds for capital projects that serve the Union's balanced economic development and its integration through infrastructure facilities and communication networks. With the advent of European monetary union (EMU) and the introduction of the euro as the single currency, the European Monetary Institute and the European Central Bank (ECB) will have the enormous responsibilities of safeguarding the stability of the euro and of creating conditions for a prosperous economic development of the Union.

3 Major challenges facing the EU

Since its inception the EU has been faced with numerous conflicts and even crises concerning a wide range of decision issues, most frequently agricultural policies, the member countries' contribution to the Union's budget and budget allocations. However, the most persistent controversy has centred on conflicting visions of the speed and intensity of European integration. For some, the paramount concern has consistently been the speedy realization of a politically and economically integrated Europe where purely national interests and the maintenance of a high degree of national sovereignty are subordinated to the supranational interests of the Union as a whole. For those holding this view, a 'deepening' of the union is more important than its territorial extension through the admission of new member countries. A contrasting vision of Europe emphasizes the economic benefits of an enlarged market area and the removal of restrictions to economic exchanges while maintaining a high degree of national autonomy in economic and political decision-making – unencumbered by supranational interference. For those holding this vision of a more limited European integration, an enlargement of the market area by admitting additional member countries is more important than 'deepening' the union. Over time the EU has made significant progress towards the realization of both visions. However, the fundamental differences in outlook persist and will continue to pose a challenge for the future development of the Union.

In addition to the challenges resulting from competing visions of European integration, the most significant issues the Union is facing are those outlined below.

The successful introduction of a single currency

The conversion to a common currency involving ten or more industrialized countries whose combined gross domestic product (GDP) accounts for more than 25 per cent of the global output in goods and services is an historic, unprecedented undertaking with enormous challenges as well as economic, social and political consequences. For example, the required fiscal discipline of holding governmental budget deficits below 3.0 per cent of a country's GDP in order to ensure a high degree of monetary stability is stifling economic growth and is a major contributing factor in the high-unemployment situation that plagues most EU countries. With the creation of the ECB and the imposition of uniform monetary policies that largely pre-empt independent national economic policies, competing national interests may create tensions and thus lead to serious challenges in the political realm. In addition, conflicts between those countries of the EU that adopt the common currency and those countries that stay outside EMU will almost certainly become more pronounced.

The accession of new member countries

The envisaged further enlargement of the Union creates significant new challenges, mostly on two accounts:

- There exists a rather wide gap in the level of economic achievement between the prospective members and the member countries of the EU. Effective and full membership requires that this gap be bridged to an extent that necessitates, however, a significant resource transfer, particularly from the richer Union countries. In view of their own economic difficulties, as reflected in high unemployment rates, and given the constraints imposed by the introduction of the common currency, large-scale economic assistance to prospective new members is likely to lead to tensions within the Union, as well as between the Union and the countries seeking accession.
- In a democratic context, all the member countries are participating in decision processes affecting the Union. The larger the membership and the more disparate their interests, the more difficult is it to reach decisions, particularly in those areas that require a consensus. Further enlarging Union membership will pose a challenge for the Union's cohesion and its decision-making effectiveness.

Other challenges

In spite of the unremitting efforts to achieve a truly integrated, federalist United States of Europe, it must be recognized that for historic, cultural and geographical reasons there exist significant disparities which give rise to conflicting national demands that are not easily reconcilable. For example, the financial contributions to the European budget are a continuous source of tension, particularly for those member countries that are net contributors. Agricultural policies and subsidies to inefficient sectors are another enduring source of contention, as are a wide range of core activities, many of them single-market related, such as features of social and labour policies, and environmental and regional policies aimed at reducing disparities among member countries. Reducing these disparities is essential for EU cohesion, and it is a responsibility that is often quite readily accepted by the European Commission and its staff. This has led to the perception of a remote, centralized bureaucracy in Brussels that readily intervenes in local or regional affairs without sufficient sensitivity to local conditions or preferences. The EU's relationships with the rest of the world are also a source of concerns and a challenge. Non-member countries frequently view the union as too inward-looking, and the term 'fortress Europe' is used to describe it as a protectionist bloc. The development of the EU as a cohesive economic and political power with a single currency and a common defence policy is likely to exacerbate existing tensions and rivalries with other national or regional interests.

HANS SCHOLLHAMMER
UNIVERSITY OF CALIFORNIA
LOS ANGELES

Further reading

Basic Statistics of the European Union, Luxembourg: Office for Official Publications of the European Communities.

Bright, Christopher (1995) *The European Union: Understanding the Brussels Process*, New York: Wiley. (Covers the evolution of the EU, institutional roles and decision processes.)

Calingaert, Michael (1996) *European Integration Revisited: Progress, Prospects and U.S. Interests*, Boulder, CO: Westview Press. (Reviews recent EU developments and their implications for the United States.)

Coffey, Peter (1996) *Europe: Toward 2001*, Boston, MA: Kluwer Academic Publishing. (Presents current issues and prospective developments.)

The European Union: Annual Review of Activities, Oxford: Blackwell Publishers.

European Union Database Directory, Brussels: Office for Official Publications of the European Communities.

George, Stephen (1996) *Politics and Policy in the European Union*, Oxford and New York: Oxford University Press. (Presents different political views on European integration.)

Henig, Stanley (1997) *The Uniting of Europe: From Discord to Concord*, London and New York: Routledge. (Analyses the reasons for differing viewpoints among EU members and emerging consensus.)

Kenen, Peter (1995) *Economic and Monetary Union in Europe*, Cambridge and New York: Cambridge University Press. (Presents the conceptual foundations for economic and monetary integration.)

McAllister, Richard (1997) *From EC to EU*, London and New York: Routledge. (Analyses European integration in an historic context.)

Overturf, Stephen (1997) *Money and European Union*, New York: St Martin's Press. (Presents the rationale for and the challenges of European monetary union.)

Piening, Christopher (1997) *Global Europe: The European Union in World Affairs*, Boulder, CO: L. Rienner Publishing. (Discusses the role of the European Union in a global context.)

Pinder, John (1995) *European Community: The Building of a Union*, 2nd edition, Oxford and New York: Oxford University Press. (Excellent review of fluctuating economic and political forces for and against unification.)

Preston, Christopher (1997) *Enlargement and Integration in the European Union*, London and New York: Routledge. (Focuses on the impact of the accession of eastern European countries as EU members.)

Taylor, Paul (1996) *The European Union in the 1990s*, Oxford and New York: Oxford University Press. (Analyses current issues, controversies and prospective resolutions.)

Ungerer, Horst (1997) *A Concise History of European Monetary Integration*, Westport: Quorum Books. (Traces the evolution of European monetary union.)

Futher resources

http://europa.eu.int

See also: ASSOCIATION OF SOUTH-EAST ASIAN NATIONS; ECONOMIC INTEGRATION, INTERNATIONAL; INTERNATIONAL BUSINESS, LEGAL DIMENSIONS OF; NORTH AMERICAN FREE TRADE AREA

Related topics in the IEBM: BANKING IN WESTERN EUROPE; CONFLICT AND POLITICS; ECONOMIES OF CENTRAL AND EASTERN EUROPE, TRANSITION OF

Exporting

1 Strategic aspects of exporting
2 Tactical aspects of exporting

Overview

The adoption of an international strategy may be a response to industry change in regulation, market demand, product and process technology, suppliers, competition, or the firms growth objectives. Exporting is one strategic option for international market development. After brief discussion of the strategic decisions involved in exporting, this entry gives an overview of the principal tactical elements.

Exporting, as one method for internationalizing a firm's scope of activity, is distinct from locating marketing, distribution or manufacturing operations or subsidiaries in foreign markets or entering into alliances and partnerships. It may be used as a lower risk entry strategy to test a new market or to develop experience of international trade.

Exporting is taken here to mean the sale of goods/services across national boundaries to an independent organization. Exporting may be either direct or indirect. Direct exports are those goods sold to an independent organization outside the domestic market. Indirect exports are those goods sold to an intermediary based in the domestic market for onward sale in international markets. These two exporting routes have very different levels of commitment and risk for the company.

Associated with the decision to use exporting as the chosen method of foreign market entry are the major decisions of market selection, where markets need not necessarily be countries but customers or regions with appropriate characteristics (sophisticated consumers with high disposable income might suggest a target of major cities), channel selection, and the development of an international marketing plan.

The strategic circumstances of the company will influence the objectives to be achieved through exporting and the way in which these objectives will be achieved – including decisions about how many markets to enter, the degree of product development, the time horizon for seeing returns, channel choice and methods of selling – and affect company capability.

1 Strategic aspects of exporting

The decision to choose exporting over other forms of market entry may be as a result of internal factors, including strategic objectives, resource limitations, product nature, etc., or may be attributable to target market characteristics (size and attractiveness of market, regulatory constraints). Thus, depending on the decision process adopted in a company, the choice to export may follow from the identification of the target market, or markets may be selected as a result of the company deciding that exporting is the most appropriate mode for internationalization (see FOREIGN MARKET ENTRY STRATEGIES).

Market selection is also affected by the global structure of the industry. Competitive risk arises where the configuration of manufacturing plants and sales operations of competitors presents a potential advantage in terms of differing political and foreign exchange risk. This is related to the risk posed by the portfolio of markets the firm operates within, if the majority of sales are to one export market then the firm will suffer losses or falling demand as the imported prices rise.

The criteria for market selection are based on goals for the target market, such as the level of sales and profit sought. The selection of markets is an iterating process of researching target markets to assess them against specific criteria and the extent to which they are compatible with the current nature of the product and company. Markets are successively eliminated until the final set contains no more than a handful which best fulfil the criteria and can therefore be considered the best target markets for detailed investigation.

Additional criteria based on situational factors (previous experience of, or sales to, certain markets, major customers relocating or setting up a new division, common language and family connections) are common and valid criteria for initial market selection and thus influence those markets that enter into the initial set. Selecting target countries may not be an issue for companies operating in a specialized global niche, where customers are scattered around the world.

Channel selection

The choice of how to distribute and promote products to the customer is governed by the nature of the product and the preferences/habits of customers' buying behaviour. The range of distribution channels for international markets is wide. The choice of distribution channel often moves from the low risk indirect exporting, through direct selling, appointed agents, distributors, to a higher risk company-owned sales office, or a subsidiary, as the firm grows and gains export experience.

With a decision to export, part of the channel decision has already been taken. Further decisions have then to be made about the specific direct and indirect methods. Indirect exporting channels include 'piggybacking' (where the goods are sold to a company selling complementary goods for sale through their established distribution network abroad), group sales arrangements, domestic buying offices (of say, US department stores), export houses and consortia.

The advantages of indirect exporting are that little knowledge about the destination markets is required, the transaction is much less complicated with prices in domestic currency and simpler transportation requirements. Technically it is a domestic sale, and unless it is an OEM (original equipment manufacturer) deal, the company is building some awareness of their product in the overseas/foreign market. The disadvantages are the complete lack of control of the way the product is marketed, the brand image, to whom goods are sold and at what price. An important drawback is the lack of information gained from the market, the most a company is likely to learn is that their product is acceptable in certain regions or industries. The company would have no access to detailed data on customers or their needs, thus not allowing any learning to take place about the market or the end user, and so enable the development of market strategy.

The direct mechanisms for exporting include direct contact with the customers (sales reps, mail order, etc.), or via intermediaries like agents or distributors. Agents are organizations who promote the goods and receive a commission for the sales they generate. Distributors buy the goods from the company and sell them on. The principal difference is that agents do not take title to the goods. Firms need to make decisions about the benefits of appointing sole or exclusive intermediaries. Sole intermediaries are the only organization appointed by the company to act on their behalf within a particular region, exclusive intermediaries, however, handle all sales within the region, even those generated by the principal.

At first glance it might appear that distributors are lower risk as they buy the goods from the company, the company would get paid sooner and would only be exposed to a single credit risk. However, in terms of administration it is easier to sell to a single distributor compared with individual accounts generated by an agent, sales may be constrained by the strategic objectives and financial limitations of the distributor. There are no such expansion limits with an agent, and the company will have access to the data on customers and end prices, but there is a greater credit risk. The choice of channel is influenced by industry practice, and whether there are many small or few large customers. It is important to recognize that channel choice may be difficult or costly to reverse in the short term. For example, agents, under EU law, are well protected and unilateral termination of their contract may involve compensation payments to agents, for the goodwill generated for the company.

2 Tactical aspects of exporting

The many different tasks involved in exporting are associated with marketing, the physical distribution and regulatory/legal aspects of the process. Export marketing involves specific product and pricing decisions, the recruitment and management of channels of distribution and promotions. Market research is an integral part of these activities.

Market research

Market research informs all parts of the exporting process, from early market selection, channel selection, understanding consumer needs/behaviour to transaction regulations. Consequently, it is an ongoing process that involves developing an information system and a network of contacts and sources of information. Important areas to research might include:

1 Size of market value/volume/approximate number of customers;
2 Nature of market, that is, customer needs and buyer behaviour, distribution channels and promotion channels, major players;
3 Competition domestic and otherwise, standard terms of business (agent support etc.) and debt recovery;
4 Regulations on product standards, packaging, pollution/emissions; on import duties, quotas, import licences, local competition, inter-company agreements;
5 Legal issues – contract law, patent infringement, legal procedures;
6 Distribution companies/regulations (loads/driver hours), documentation and certification/testing of products by government departments/independent authorities (and your rights – to attend, appeal).

Both formal (that is, official and verifiable) and informal (opinion) information is required in the assessment and understanding of markets, and different methods and sources are needed for these. As ever, the information gathered needs to be interpreted with care, data can be misleading and an assessment of the reliability of sources is useful.

Many different organizations and directories are available to assist in market research. Trade associations, international trade press, exhibitions, sponsored trade missions, bilateral chambers of commerce and embassies are all useful sources of factual information and advice. Libraries and the Internet hold many collections of statistics covering general economic indicators and general country information. Credit agencies assess risk, international banks and the professional market research organizations publish market and country profiles. There are several comprehensive directories (for example, EuroPages) and guides (for example, Croner's Guide for Exporting) for exporters that are invaluable references, for significant details as well as the regulatory requirements of every country.

Product adaptation

In deciding whether to adapt the product, the company may look for markets that will accept the existing product, maybe where current products are less sophisticated. The two motivations for modifying the product are to suit customer preferences and to comply with regulations and standards operating in the market.

The range of sizes/quantities and models/varieties may need to be altered, as may the ingredients or components themselves. Labelling (including instructions) and packaging laws vary widely in accordance with consumer protection and environmental legislation. Products may need to undergo rigorous testing to gain approval and certification in new markets (the exacting standards of the US Food and Drug Administration, for example). In some cases the standards may not be obligatory but may be beneficial in that they offer guidelines to market expectations. Finally, the branding and image of the product needs to be transferable to different cultures.

Modifications may extend to spares and consumables. The design of after-sales service for example may result in the development of 'black box' replacement parts to facilitate repairs. It will also have implications for the distribution channels in terms of the types of spares that must be carried in stock. There may be a need to modify consumables in response to regulations and/or customer preferences.

Pricing

The pricing of goods for foreign markets is complex and is one of the crucial elements for success in exporting. The factors important in international pricing are the market share objectives, customers' ability to buy, the firm's costs and profit goals, product life cycle stage, differing regulatory conditions, foreign exchange, structure of market distribution channels and competition. Pricing is also affected by the terms of sale agreed upon, such as the stage of transportation at which the buyer takes title and responsibility for freight and insurance.

The two most commonly used approaches are cost-orientated and market-orientated pricing. Market orientation starts with an assessment of demand, an estimation of the price range that the product would sell at and an assessment of the competition. The next stage is to subtract the various intermediary margins, taxes and transport from the market price to determine whether the company can afford to sell at that price. The lack of market information about margins is a difficulty with this approach.

From a cost orientation, the increased costs of exporting are added on to the cost of the product. These include the cost of transport, packaging, tariffs, documentation and the increased time that goods are in transit. In certain markets extra costs may be incurred by the need for longer credit periods and the cost of hedging against exchange rate movements. This approach to pricing does not take market characteristics into account.

Exporters may sell goods at what would be a loss-making price in the domestic market, on the basis that these are additional sales and using marginal costing. However, companies for whom exporting contributes significantly to overall turnover will find this difficult to sustain in the long run.

Export pricing policy needs to address the relationship between export and domestic prices. Many companies have moved to a single pricing policy in their overseas markets to eliminate parallel importing (where goods are bought in a neighbouring market at the lower price and resold below the official market price). The resultant negotiating power exerted by purchasers or loss of purchasers' confidence as a consequence of awareness of price differences across neighbouring markets can be damaging to the exporting company. Sophisticated discounting structures may get round the single pricing policy but bring back the danger of parallel importing.

A major question is that of which currency to quote in; the importer would prefer quotations in their local currency – to facilitate comparisons with local supply – but that passes on the risk of adverse exchange rate fluctuations to the exporter. The decision to some extent depends on the norms of the market and the industry.

Export finance, banks and methods of payment

Payment terms are part of the pricing decision and have implications for financing export activity. Payment terms include the method of payment, the credit terms and the currency chosen. These carry certain risks: the method of payment will affect the risk of non-payment; credit terms will affect profitability and amount of working capital needed; the currency chosen will carry an exchange risk (see FOREIGN EXCHANGE RISK, MANAGEMENT OF).

The methods of payment vary in terms of risk to the exporter, and carry a progressively higher risk of non-payment: cash with order, letters of credit (confirmed, unconfirmed), bills of exchange, open account. Consignment trade carries the highest risk to the exporter as he retains title to the goods until the importer has sold them. Assessing the creditworthiness of the customer is key to deciding upon which payment terms to use. Commercial organizations (Export Credit Guarantees Department and Trade Indemnity PLC in the UK) assist the exporter both by assessing and insuring the credit risk of individuals and the political risk of countries (see POLITICAL RISK). Credit terms may vary from market to market, added to which there is the difficulty of implementing an effective credit control policy internationally. In addition to which transaction times for exporting are longer, consequently there is an increase in the working capital required. There are various bank schemes that address this need for working capital, such as factoring and discounting. The choice of currency carries a transaction risk associated with foreign exchange movements where the value of payment may decrease over the credit period (the concern of the exporter) or increase (the concern of the importer). Banks can assist with decisions about whether and how to hedge against this risk.

Legislation and legal issues

Transactions between organizations governed by differing legal systems can be problematic (see INTERNATIONAL BUSINESS, LEGAL DIMENSIONS OF). The legal issues surrounding contracts can be complicated and it is advisable that contracts are based on one system of law, and indicate which law governs in case of dispute. In all cases it is better that the rights and duties of each party are clearly set out beforehand as seeking redress in foreign markets is difficult. However, some clauses may be legally unenforceable in certain countries even if they were technically agreed to when signing the contract. The International Chamber of Commerce can assist in a number of ways, for example by providing specimen contracts and by acting as arbitrator in the case of disputes.

There is no international law as such, although elements of international trade are facilitated by bodies such as the United Nations Conference on Trade and Development and the World Trade Organization (see WORLD TRADE ORGANIZATION), and there are international conventions governing the carriage of goods. Another area of international trade that is increasingly subjected to regulation is competition law (covering, for example, restrictive agreements, monopoly situations in exports, and horizontal and vertical price maintenance).

The internationally accepted trade terms ('Incoterms') were established by the International Chamber of Commerce as part of their role in facilitating international trade. When incoterms are specified in the sales contract, they ensure a clear definition of the buyer's and seller's responsibilities, and avoid misinterpretation and disputes. There are four main categories of incoterms: (1) those where the seller makes the goods available at their premises, (EXW (ex works)); (2) those where the seller delivers the goods to the carrier, but the carriage is arranged and paid for by the buyer (FAS (free alongside ship), FOB (free on board), etc.); (3) the seller is responsible for the main carriage (CFR (cost and freight), CIF (cost, insurance, freight), etc.); and (4) where the seller is responsible for all costs and risks incurred to bring the goods into the country of destination (DAF (delivered at frontier), DEQ (delivered ex quay), etc.).

Exporters often prefer to quote terms that give them the least liability such as FOB, similarly the importer would usually prefer terms such as CIF or DDP (delivered duty paid) to the point of entry into the country, which again facilitates cost comparison with domestic suppliers. However, the importer may prefer to make his own arrangements. For example, he may have access to the means of transportation, wish to use his regular freight forwarder because he can secure better terms or he may not wish to spend scarce foreign exchange on transportation.

Transport, documentation and insurance

In arranging for the transportation of goods, the exporter needs to deal with three key areas: mode of transport, documentation required, and insuring the goods in transit.

The range of options for transport to the destination country includes air (direct or consolidated), sea (regular or chartered), rail, road and multimodal. The decision should take into account the total distribution cost as well as the nature of the product, frequency of delivery and distance of the destination country. The total cost of distribution includes the amount of time the goods are in transit (which determines the amount of interest charged on capital employed), as well as differing insurance rates which vary according to the mode of transport chosen.

Much documentation is required to accompany the export order throughout the stages of the transaction. Principally, the documents relate to transportation, regulatory requirements (inspections and licences, statistical tracking of trade), finance and insurance.

Transport documents serve to facilitate the movement of goods. The requirements vary significantly depending on the country of export, the destination country, mode of transport and the nature of the goods. Examples include export cargo shipping instructions, shipping notes, bills of lading, sea waybills, air waybills and consignment notes. In addition, regulatory requirements in some countries will stipulate the need for additional documents, such as certificates of origin, import or export licences, etc. Transport documents are important to the financial transaction when payment is by letter of credit, as the exporter will only receive payment if the documents match the requirements of the letter of credit.

A number of additional documents relate to the financial transaction, including invoices, bills of exchange and letters of credit. Insurance documents (either an insurance policy or certificate) may also be required. Marine insurance covers goods in transit and is essential to guard against loss, damage or pilfering of goods. Incoterms make it clear when risk passes and who is therefore responsible for the insurance of goods. However, even when insurance is technically the responsibility of the buyer, the exporter may be asked to take out an insurance policy on behalf of the buyer. It may also be appropriate for sellers to take out contingency insurance to safeguard their interests, for example if the buyer fails to insure goods and they are lost they may refuse to pay for the goods.

The freight forwarder's role is that of intermediary between the company and the transport firm. At the simplest level they would book space with the carrier, but they have the capability to handle the export documentation, advise on the mode, route and best deals and may even assist with customs procedures.

Organization for exporting

In order to manage the organization for the activities involved in exporting, a strong management function is needed. The export office/manager will coordinate both the strategic and tactical aspects of exporting in conjunction with the different functions in the firm. Their responsibility for the profitability of export activity will include setting sales targets and measuring effectiveness in addition to managing and supporting remote staff and intermediaries. The common problems associated with exporting are those of managerial and production capacity limitations, inadequate information systems resulting in poor foreign communication skills and personal contacts and difficulties in transaction creation (De Noble *et al.* 1989).

Managing intermediaries

Getting the most from the firm's intermediaries is a major contributor to success in exporting. Time should be spent in recruiting the right firm. The intermediary should be selected after careful consideration of what is required from him. The relative size of the intermediary may affect the degree of influence the principal has on the nature of the relationship. Negotiating the agreement, important though this is, is not as important as managing the relationship between the companies. Good communication channels, regular attention and assistance with promotions and sales literature are essential to develop an effective partnership. To reduce the likelihood of conflict firms would be well advised to investigate the market independently rather than rely solely on information from the intermediary and work in partnership with the intermediary.

ANNE JENKINS
DURHAM UNIVERSITY BUSINESS SCHOOL

Further reading

(References cited in the text marked *)

Branch, A. (1994) *Export Practice and Management*, London: Chapman and Hall. (Definitive text on how to go about the practicalities of exporting. Accessible, well written and detailed.)

* Buckley, P.J. and Ghauri, P. (Eds) (1993) *The Internationalisation of the Firm: A Reader*, London: Academic Press, Harcourt Brace Jovanich. (Sets exporting in its wider context, reviewing major theories of internationalization; provides cases of the processes and decisions involved in exporting.)

* De Noble, A.F., Castaldi, R.M. and Moliver, D.M. (1989) 'Export intermediaries: small business perceptions of services and performance', *Journal of Small Business Management* April: 33–41. (Highlights the common problems facing smaller firms in exporting and gives results of a survey examining the effectiveness of organizations providing assistance with these.)

Hodgetts, R.M. and Luthans, F. (1991) *International Management*, Singapore: McGraw-Hill. (Comprehensively addresses the many facets of international management. Provides useful illustrative cases.)

International Chamber of Commerce (1990) *Incoterms 1990*, Paris: ICC Publishing S.A. (Essential explanations of international trading terms.)

Piercy, N. (1982) *Export Strategy: Markets and Competition*, London: Allen & Unwin. (Useful discussion of the sources of competitive advantage in terms of export strategies.)

Rugman, A.M., Lecraw, D.J. and Booth, L.D. (1985) *International Business: Firm and Environment*, Singapore: McGraw-Hill. (Examines the financial and regulatory environments of international trade in addition to the different issues surrounding the management of international business.)

Sullivan, K., Orr, F. and Reis, D. (1994) 'Going international? Here's how', *International Management* January–February: 22–25. (Sets out a critical path method to assist in the management of the initial steps of international trade.)

Terpstra, V. and Sarathy, R. (1994) *International Marketing*, 6th edn, Fort Worth, TX: Dryden. (Good textbook covering all aspects of international marketing, with a strong section on exporting.)

See also: FINANCIAL MANAGEMENT, INTERNATIONAL; FOREIGN EXCHANGE RISK, MANAGEMENT OF; FOREIGN MARKET ENTRY STRATEGIES; GLOBAL STRATEGIC ALLIANCES; GLOBAL STRATEGIC PLANNING; INTERNATIONAL BUSINESS, LEGAL DIMENSIONS OF; INTERNATIONAL MARKETING; POLITICAL RISK; WORLD TRADE ORGANIZATION

Related topics in the IEBM: BRANDS; CHANNEL MANAGEMENT; COUNTRY RISK ANALYSIS; CREDIT MANAGEMENT; PRICING ISSUES IN MARKETING

Financial management, international

Overview

International financial management is not a separate set of issues from domestic or traditional financial management, but does involve a number of risks and complexities not confronted domestically. International financial management means that all the standard financial activities and decisions within a firm (capital budgeting, capital structure, raising long-term capital, working capital and cash flow management, etc.) will be complicated by the differences in markets, laws and especially currencies of conducting business internationally. This management requires many different activities from those of traditional domestic financial management practices. An added distinction in this area of management is that between a firm which only imports and exports, an *international* firm, and a firm which not only conducts direct import/export business but also possesses foreign affiliate and subsidiary operations, a *multinational* firm (sometimes referred to as multi-domestic and transnational).

This entry provides an overview of contemporary international financial management practices. Our emphasis is on the managerial dimensions – the theories, expectations and perspectives which the decision maker must utilize in the conduct of international business. The entry is composed of two parts. The first part provides an overview of foreign exchange rates and international financial markets. The second section details the financial management activities which an international or multinational firm must undertake in its normal course of business, including international capital budgeting, managing international capital structure, working capital management and performance evaluation and control.

1 Exchange rate fundamentals

Currency markets

The price of one country's monetary units, its currency, in terms of another country's currency is called a foreign currency *exchange rate*. For example, the exchange rate between the US dollar (US$) and the German mark (deutschmark, or DM) may be 1.5 marks per dollar, or simply abbreviated DM1.5000/US$. This is the same exchange rate as when it is stated US$1.00 – DM1.50. Since most international business activities require at least one of the two parties to first purchase the other country's currency before purchasing any good, service or asset, a proper understanding of exchange rates and exchange rate markets is very important to the conduct of international business (see GLOBALIZATION; INTERNATIONAL PAYMENTS; MULTINATIONAL CORPORATIONS).

Exchange rate quotations and terminology

Table 1 illustrates common currency quotations as listed in one of the world's leading financial newspapers, the *Financial Times* for 1 September 1993. The first set of exchange rates listed in Table 1 are foreign currency quotations versus the British pound sterling (C$/£, BF/£, DM/£, etc.). Quotes are sampled at the close of trading in the London

Table 1 Exchange rate quotations: pound spot–forward against the pound

1 Sept	Close (bid/offer)	One month	% pa	Three months	% pa
US	1.5070 – 1.5080	0.37 – 0.35 cpm	2.87	1.02 – 0.99 pm	2.67
Canada	1.9855 – 1.9865	0.28 – 0.19 cpm	1.42	0.67 – 0.54 pm	1.22
Belgium	53.75 – 53.85	21 – 29 cdis	–5.58	53 – 62 dis	–4.28
Germany	2.5000 – 2.5050	$\frac{1}{8} - \frac{1}{4}$ pfdis	–0.90	$\frac{3}{8} - \frac{1}{2}$ dis	–0.70
Italy	2402.75 – 2403.75	6 – 8 lire dis	–3.50	18 – 21 dis	–3.25
Norway	10.8875 – 10.8975	$\frac{1}{8} - \frac{5}{8}$ dis	–0.41	$\frac{1}{4} - 1$ sid	–0.23
France	8.7725 – 8.7825	$1\frac{1}{8} - 1\frac{1}{2}$ dis	–1.79	$2\frac{7}{8} - 3\frac{3}{8}$ sid	–1.42
Sweden	12.2975 – 12.3075	$2 - 2\frac{3}{4}$ ore dis	–2.32	$5\frac{5}{8} - 6\frac{3}{8}$ dis	–1.91
Japan	158.75 – 159.75	$\frac{1}{2} - \frac{3}{8}$ ypm	3.30	$1\frac{1}{4} - 1\frac{1}{8}$ pm	2.98
Switzerland	2.1950 – 2.2050	$\frac{1}{4} - \frac{1}{8}$ cpm	1.02	$\frac{3}{4} - \frac{1}{2}$ pm	1.14
Ecu	1.3090 – 1.3100	0.22 – 0.27 cdis	–2.25	0.55 – 0.63 dis	–1.80

Source: Adpated from the *Financial Times*, September 2 1993: 28
Note: Commercial rates taken towards the end of London Trading

financial markets. A spot transaction is the exchange of currencies for immediate delivery. Although it is defined as immediate, in practice, settlement actually occurs one to two business days following the agreed upon exchange, depending on the specific currency. The pound sterling is quoted at $1.5070/£ bid (the rate at which a commercial buyer can buy US dollars or sell sterling) and $1.5080/£ offer (the rate at which a commercial customer can sell dollars or buy sterling) at the close of trading on 1 September. Table 2 quotes spot and forward foreign currencies per US dollar in the London market on the same date.

The other currency quotations listed in Tables 1 and 2 are forward rates. Forward exchange rates are contracts which provide for two parties to exchange currencies on a future date at an agreed upon exchange rate. Forwards are typically traded for the major volume currencies for maturities of 30, 90, 120, 180 and 360 days (from the present date). The forward, like the basic spot exchange, can be for any amount of currency the two parties wish. Forward contracts serve a variety of purposes but their primary purpose is to allow a firm to lock in a future rate of exchange. This is a valuable tool in a world in which exchange rates are continually changing.

Once again using the pound sterling, the one-month forward bid rate is quoted in Table 1 as currency basis points added to the existing spot rate (US$/£):

	Bid	Offer
Spot rate	1.5070	1.5080
One-month points	–0.0037	–0.0035
Forward rate	1.5033	1.5045

Because the US dollar is selling forward at a premium (cpm is cents premium), the forward points are subtracted from the US dollar per pound spot rate to calculate the one-month forward bid offer outright rates. The one-month forward rate indicates a stronger US dollar versus the pound sterling (requiring fewer dollars per pound). The per cent per annum (% pa) premium on the $/£ forward rate is calculated from the annualized average of the forward points over the initial spot rates:

Table 2 Exchange rate quotations: dollar spot–forward against the dollar

1 Sept	Close (bid/offer)	One month	% pa	Three months	% pa
UK	1.5070 – 1.5080	0.37 – 0.35 cpm	2.87	1.02 – 0.99 pm	2.67
Canada	1.3210 – 1.3220	0.14 – 0.18 cpm	–1.45	0.46 – 0.51 pm	–1.47
Belgium	35.65 – 35.75	24 – 31 cdis	–9.24	64 – 73 dis	–7.68
Germany	1.6590 – 1.6600	0.54 – 0.55 pfdis	–3.94	1.44 – 1.46 dis	–3.50
Italy	1594.00 – 1594.50	8.40 – 9.00 lire dis	–6.55	23.50 – 24.50 dis	–6.02
Norway	7.2225 – 7.2275	1.75 – 2.30 dis	–3.36	4.95 – 5.75 sid	–2.96
France	5.8200 – 5.8250	2.23 – 2.33 dis	–4.70	6.05 – 6.25 sid	–4.22
Sweden	8.1575 – 8.1625	3.25 – 3.85 ore dis	–5.22	9.00 – 10.00 dis	–4.66
Japan	105.65 – 105.75	0.03 – 0.01 ypm	0.23	0.13 – 0.10 pm	0.44
Switzerland	1,4585 – 1.4595	0.22 – 0.25 cpm	–1.93	0.58 – 0.63 pm	–1.66
Ecu	1.1455 – 1.1465	0.50– 0.48 cdis	5.13	1.30 – 1.26 dis	4.47

Source: Adpated from the *Financial Times*, 2 September 1993: 28
Note: Commercial rates taken towards the end of London trading. The UK and ECU are quoted in US dollars per pound and ECU. Forward premiums and discounts apply to the US dollar and not to the individual currency. Forward rates are quoted on the basis of premium (pm) or discount (dis) versus the spot rate

$$\text{premium} = \frac{\left[\dfrac{0.0037+0.0035}{2}\right]}{\left[\dfrac{0.0037+0.0035}{2}\right]}$$

$$\times \frac{12 \text{ months}}{1 \text{ month}} \times 100$$

$$= +2.87\%$$

As the following section on eurocurrency interest rate details, the forward points (and therefore the forward premium) reflect interest differentials (in this case, US\$ and £ interest rates).

The quotations listed may also differentiate between rates applicable to business trade, commercial rates or, for financial asset purchases or sales, financial rates. Those countries which have government regulations regarding the exchange of their currency may post official rates, while the markets operating outside their jurisdiction will list a floating rate. In this case any exchange of currency which is not under the control of that government is interpreted to be a better indication of the currency's true market value.

The *Financial Times* quotations list the rates of exchange between major national currencies. The exchange rate for the deutschmark versus the US dollar is DM1.6600/US\$. This is a *direct* quote on the deutschmark or an *indirect* quote on the US dollar. The inverse of this spot rate is the indirect quote on the deutschmark or direct quote on the US dollar, US\$0.6024/DM. The two forms of the exchange rate are of course equal (to the number of decimal places commonly quoted as shown), one being the inverse of the other.

Luckily, the world foreign currency markets do follow some conventions so that confusion is minimized. With only a few exceptions, most currencies are quoted in direct form quotes versus the US dollar (DM/US\$, ¥/US\$, FF/US\$, etc.). The major exceptions are those currencies at one time or another associated with the British

Commonwealth, including the Australian dollar and of course the British pound sterling, which are customarily quoted as US$ per pound sterling or US$ per Australian dollar. Once again, it makes no real difference whether one quotes US$/¥, or ¥/US$, as long as one knows which is being used for the transaction (Buckley 1992; Eiteman *et al.* 1995).

Exchange rate determination

If currency values remained fixed, many of the basic management issues in multinational financial management would be solved. The contemporary international monetary system is, however, not fixed, and is in reality an eclectic combination of freely floating, managed floating, adjustable fixed and fixed exchange rate systems. Currency fluctuations – whether the movements are government-decreed (devaluation or revaluation) or market-determined (depreciation or appreciation) – change the profitability of individual business transactions. These very value changes can threaten the value of a multinational business. It is therefore useful to understand what determines exchange rates, and to then understand what changes exchange rate values.

An exchange rate is the relative price of two currencies. Let us assume that we have a unit of count to measure the price of DM and US$. The price of one US dollar may then be 1.6600 deutschmarks, or simultaneously, the price of one deutschmark may be 1/1.6600 or $0.6024. If these are nothing but prices, then the forces which set the prices, supply and demand, set exchange rates. The absolute price of a currency increases as the demand for that currency expands and/or the supply of it contracts. For example, if the supply of US dollars (US$) grows much more rapidly on world markets than the supply of deutschmarks (DM) offered in exchange for dollars, the market price of the US$ will fall and the market price of the DM will rise. Or, if the demand for deutschmarks grows faster than the dollar because of the stronger performance of the German economy, the mark will rise in price relative to the dollar.

Since governments influence (or dictate in some countries) the supply of currency, the behaviour of exchange rates depends on the exchange rate regime governments choose. Under a fixed exchange rate regime, the government sets the official exchange rate and stands by to take whatever action is necessary to maintain the 'fix'. This fixed exchange rate system, characteristic of the international monetary system among Western countries under the Bretton Woods Agreement, 1944–71, is *dependent* on the government's ability to set and maintain the exchange rate at a value near that which a floating rate market would actually achieve (see ECONOMIC INTEGRATION, INTERNATIONAL). In this case, the relative demand and supply of currencies adjust to conform to officially pegged exchange rates. For instance, if the DM/US$ exchange rate is set too high by the monetary authorities (the US dollar is overvalued), the supply of dollars must shrink over time relative to the supply of DM so as to justify the overpriced dollar. When the market adjustment cannot be carried out fast enough, and governments run out of the will and the ability (foreign currency reserves) to defend pegged exchange rates, speculative attacks develop and the pegged rate may collapse. Indeed, speculative attacks often hasten the collapse of pegged exchange rate systems.

When governments allow currency values to be determined by the market it is referred to as a floating or flexible exchange rate system. Experience with flexible exchange rate systems to date indicates current relative demand for and supply of currencies are not as important as expected *future* relative demand and supply of currencies in determining exchange rates. The result is understandable because money is a storage of value and hence a form of asset. The price of an asset rightly reflects investors' expectations on the asset's future value. Market participants will expect the dollar's value to fall versus the mark when they think that the future supply of US dollars will increase relatively faster than the Deutschemark. Because investors are unwilling to hold on to assets which are expected to fall in value, these expectations may become self-fulfilling. The expectation is reflected immediately and the DM/US$ exchange rate (the relative price of US$ measured by DM) drops immediately.

Because expectations are incorporated in currency markets, changes in exchange rates are largely due to changes in expectations. Hence, whenever new information about future changes in currency value arrives, exchange rates fluctuate. By definition, new information is not expected. Thus, exchange rate changes are often unpredictable, just as we would expect in asset prices.

2 International money and capital markets

A money market is traditionally defined as a market for deposits, accounts or securities which have maturities of one year or less. The international money markets, often termed the *eurocurrency* markets, constitute an enormous financial market which is in many ways outside the jurisdiction and supervision of world financial and governmental authorities.

A eurocurrency is any foreign currency denominated deposit or account at a financial institution outside the country of the currency's issuance. For example, US dollars which are held on account in a bank in London are termed *eurodollars*. Similarly, Japanese yen held on account in a Parisian financial institution would be classified as euro-yen. The 'euro' prefix does not mean these currencies or accounts are only European, as deutschmarks on account in Singapore would also be classified as eurocurrency, a euro-mark account.

Eurocurrency interest rates

What is the significance of these foreign currency denominated accounts? Simply put, the purity of value which comes from no governmental interference or restrictions with their use. Because eurocurrency accounts are not controlled or managed by governments (for example, the Bank of England has no control over eurodollar accounts), the financial institutions pay no deposit insurance, hold no reserve requirements and are normally not subject to any interest rate setting restriction

with respect to these accounts. Eurocurrencies are one of the purest indicators of what these currencies should yield in terms of interest.

There are literally hundreds of different major interest rates around the globe, but the international financial markets focus on a very few eurocurrency deposit/loan rates and inter-bank interest rates. Inter-bank rates charged by banks to banks in the major international financial centres such as London, Frankfurt, Paris, New York, Tokyo, Singapore and Hong Kong, are generally regarded as the central interest rate in the respective market. The interest rate which is used most often in international loan agreements is the eurocurrency interest rate on US dollars in London between banks: LIBOR, the London Inter-Bank Offer Rate. Because it is a eurocurrency rate, it floats freely without regard to any governmental restrictions on reserves or deposit insurance or any other regulation or restriction which would add expense to transactions using this capital. (The inter-bank rates for other currencies in other markets are often named similarly, PIBOR – Paris inter-bank offer rate, MIBOR – Madrid inter-bank offer rate, HIBOR – Hong Kong inter-bank offer rate and so on) While LIBOR is the offer rate, the cost of funds offered to those acquiring a loan, the London Inter-Bank Bid Rate (LIBID) is the rate of interest other banks can earn on eurocurrency deposits.

The relationship between domestic interest rates, international eurocurrency interest rates and international eurocurrency inter-bank interest rates is illustrated in Figure 1. First, in

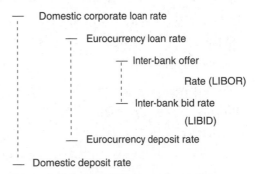

Figure 1 Relationship between domestic interest rates and eurocurrency interest rates

principle, deposit rates are lowest in domestic markets and loan rates are highest. Second, because of the deregulated structure and highly competitive nature of the international eurocurrency markets, the spreads between deposit and loan rates (bid and offer) are smaller. The inter-bank rates, LIBID–LIBOR, are deposit/loan rates applicable to transactions between the highest quality multinational banks.

The eurocurrency market is, however, only a big player market. Only well-known international firms, financial or non-financial, have access to the quantities of capital necessary to operate in the euromarkets. However, as described in the following sections on international debt and equity markets, more and more firms are gaining access to the euromarkets.

These eurocurrency interest rates also play a large role in the foreign exchange markets themselves. They are, in fact, the interest rates used in the calculation of the forward rates noted earlier in Tables 1 and 2. Forward rates are calculated from the spot rate in effect on the contract date and adjusted by the respective eurocurrency interest rates. Table 3 displays the eurocurrency interest rates for various currencies.

3 International debt and equity markets

A firm which is initially purely domestic in structure and activity services its capital needs from its home country financial markets. As the firm expands internationally, however, it requires access to larger and more diverse sources of capital (Brigham and Gapenski 1994; Eiteman *et al.* 1995). Diversification of the firm's financing can potentially lower the firm's overall weighted average cost of capital if the debt markets which it accesses are not perfectly integrated and the currencies of denomination and interest rate structures are not perfectly positively correlated in their movements. The cost of capital for the multinational firm, like differential material and wage costs, is a potential source of competitive advantage.

The international financial manager has a variety of alternatives for funding the firm. The standard financial dimensions of pricing (fixed versus variable rates), maturity, coupon payment frequency (annual, semi-annual, quarterly, etc.) are expanded by one critical characteristic: currency of denomination. Table 4 lists the primary instrument alternatives available at present on the international financial markets. This 'menu' of international financial instruments is, however, generally available only to those firms which are large enough and creditworthy enough to establish a name for themselves both in their own home

Table 3 Eurocurrency interest rates (loan rate, deposit rate, per cent per annum)

1 Sept	Short term	7 days notice	One month	Three months
Sterling	$6\frac{5}{8} - 6\frac{3}{8}$	$6\frac{1}{4} - 6$	$5\frac{15}{16} - 5\frac{13}{16}$	$5\frac{15}{16} - 5\frac{13}{16}$
US dollar	$3\frac{1}{4} - 3\frac{1}{8}$	$3\frac{1}{8} - 3$	$3\frac{3}{16} - 3\frac{1}{16}$	$3\frac{1}{4} - 3\frac{1}{8}$
Canadian dollar	$4\frac{1}{4} - 4$	$4\frac{7}{16} - 4\frac{3}{16}$	$4\frac{11}{16} - 4\frac{7}{16}$	$4\frac{7}{8} - 4\frac{5}{8}$
Dutch guilder	$6\frac{13}{16} - 6\frac{11}{16}$	$6\frac{13}{16} - 6\frac{11}{16}$	$6\frac{13}{16} - 6\frac{11}{16}$	$6\frac{1}{2} - 6\frac{3}{8}$
D-Mark	$7\frac{5}{16} - 7\frac{3}{16}$	$7 - 6\frac{7}{8}$	$6\frac{15}{16} - 6\frac{13}{16}$	$6\frac{11}{16} - 6\frac{9}{16}$
French franc	$7\frac{7}{8} - 7\frac{5}{8}$	$7\frac{7}{8} - 7\frac{5}{8}$	$7\frac{11}{16} - 7\frac{9}{16}$	$7\frac{1}{2} - 7\frac{1}{4}$
Italian lira	$11 - 9$	$9\frac{3}{4} - 9\frac{1}{4}$	$9\frac{5}{8} - 9\frac{1}{8}$	$9\frac{1}{2} - 9\frac{1}{8}$

Source: Adapted from the *Financial Times*, 2 September 1993: 28
Note: Short-term rates are call for US dollar and Japanese yen; others, two days notice

Table 4 Raising debt capital on the international financial markets

Market and instruments	Form	Pricing
Commercial bank loans		
1 Short- to medium-term bank loans	not securitized	fixed rate, floating rate
2 Syndicated Credits (Eurocredits)	not securitized	floating rate
Euronote market		
1 Euronotes	securitized	floating rate, short-term
2 Euro-Commercial Paper (ECP)	securitized	fixed rate, short-term
3 Euro-Medium-Term Notes (EMTN)	securitized	fixed rate, short-term
International bond markets		
1 Straight fixed rate issues	securitized	fixed rate
2 Floating rate notes (FRNs)	securitized	floating rate
3 Equity-related Issues	securitized	fixed rate, equity dependent

country financial market and the international markets (Giddy 1994).

The euronote market

The euronote market is a collective term for a variety of short- to medium-term types of financing. Euronotes are actually arrangements or 'facilities' for acquiring capital; the two primary types being note issuance facilities (NIFs) and revolving underwriting facilities (RUFs). These facilities allow a firm to borrow capital as needed, but at a predetermined rate of interest through notes which were guaranteed to be purchased by a group of financial institutions.

A second major source of sustained financing in the euronote market came from a financial export of the USA, commercial paper (CP). Commercial paper is a short-term note, typically 30, 60, 90 or 180 days in maturity, sold directly into the financial markets by large corporations. The market originated in the USA in the 1970s when major firms began raising capital directly from the financial markets without going through banks. The international version, euro-commercial paper (ECP), arrived in the European markets with a splash in the early 1980s.

One of the primary reasons for the success of the ECP market is the lack of a similar market in most national financial markets. Domestic commercial paper markets were legalized in many major countries only in the mid to late 1980s: France, 1985; the UK, 1986; Japan, 1987; Belgium, 1990; and Germany, 1991. But before the domestic markets arose, the ECP market served most of the large industrial borrowers. Although the growth of domestic commercial paper markets has taken a little steam out of the ECP market of late, it has continued to provide the majority of the financing in the general euronote market since the mid-1980s.

The third type of financing available from the euronote market is the euro-medium-term note (EMTN). Another export of the rapidly innovating financial markets in the USA, the EMTN is the euromarket version of a method of selling short- to medium-maturity bonds when needed. Unlike a bond issue which is the sale of a large quantity of long-term debt all at one time, medium-term notes can be sold gradually into the market as the firm decides it needs additional debt financing. This is the result of having a 'shelf-registration', in which the government authorities allow a large quantity of debt – the notes – to be registered but to be held 'on the shelf' and sold as needed by the firm. The medium-term note has filled a maturity gap in debt security issuance between the short-term commercial paper and the traditional longer maturities of bonds. The euromarket version, the EMTN, has been just as successful for the very same reasons.

International bond market

The international bond market is the dominant source of capital outside of national capital markets. Amounting to only $50 billion in 1981, the international bond markets grew to over $300 billion in new gross financing in 1991. The markets have shown little hesitation in their growth, pausing only briefly with the international debt crises and doubts of the early 1980s. This rapid growth is a result of the recognition of many multinational firms that they can acquire the capital in both amounts and prices outside their own home country market (markets often quite small) which will allow them to grow and compete on global markets.

Foreign borrowers have been using the large, well-developed capital markets of countries like the USA and the UK for many years. These markets have shown their willingness to lend to borrowers from all over the world, not just domestic corporations, enabling multinational firms from small countries to acquire badly needed capital at reasonable prices.

An issue in a domestic market by a foreign borrower is classified as a 'foreign bond'. For example, a bond issue in London, denominated in sterling by a Japanese corporation is a foreign bond, and is locally called a *bulldog*. Other foreign bond nicknames include *Yankee bonds* (foreign issues in the USA), *Rembrandts* (foreign issues in The Netherlands) and *Samurai bonds* (foreign issues in Japan). When bonds are issued by foreign borrowers in these markets, they are subject to the same laws and regulations and restrictions which apply to all domestic borrowers. For example, if a Japanese firm issues a bond in the USA, it still must comply with all of the rules as stated by the US Securities and Exchange Commission, including the fact that they must be dollar-denominated.

Bonds which are issued outside the country of the borrower and are denominated in a currency other than that of the local currency where issued, are termed *eurobonds*. For example, many US firms may issue euro-yen bonds on world markets. These bonds are sold in international financial centres such as London or Frankfurt, but are denominated in Japanese yen. Because these bonds are scattered about the global markets, most are a type of bond known as a *bearer bond*. A bearer bond is legally owned by whoever physically holds it, with no master registration list being held by government authorities. Without registration, a government possesses no record of interest income from bond investments.

Bearer bonds have a series of small coupons which border the bond itself. On an annual basis, one of the coupons is cut or 'clipped' from the bond and taken to a banking institution which is one of the listed paying agents. The bank will pay the holder of the coupon the interest payment due and no official records of payment are normally kept. As one might predict, these bonds have historically been a very attractive investment for individuals wishing to keep interest earnings to a minimum in the eyes of tax authorities!

Aside from the foreign bond/eurobond distinction, international bonds are also classified by the way in which the buyer is repaid: (1) straight or fixed-rate bonds; (2) floating-rate bonds; and (3) bonds with equity links. As in any domestic market, the type of bond issued reflects what the firm issuing the bond feels is the type which will be both most acceptable to the market and most easily repaid by the firm.

The majority of bonds issued internationally are, however, still the traditional fixed-rate bond. This is a debt issuance of typically between four and ten years in maturity, with a fixed coupon payment (interest payment) to the buyer of the bond annually. Because the timing and amount of all interest and principal repayments is known at the time of sale, the fixed-rate issue is always considered a solid and attractive investment. The growth of the international bond market is in large dependent on the continued success of the fixed-rate issue.

International equity markets

Firms are financed with both debt and equity. Although the debt markets have been the centre of activity in the international financial markets over the past three decades, there are signs that interest in international equity capital is rising. Foreign firms often issue new shares in foreign markets and list their stock on major stock exchanges such as those in New York, Tokyo or London. The purpose of foreign issues and listings is to expand the investor base and hopefully to gain access to capital markets in which the demand for shares of equity ownership is strong. The larger the investor base, the cheaper, potentially, the cost of equity capital – a potential source of competitive advantage.

For example, a foreign firm wishing to list its shares on the New York Stock Exchange in the USA does so through American depositary receipts (ADRs). These are the receipts to bank accounts which hold shares of the foreign firm's stock in its home country. Because the equities are actually denominated in a foreign currency, by holding them in a bank account and the receipt on the account in turn being listed on the US exchange, the shares can be 'revalued' in dollars and redivided so that the price per share is more typical of that of the US equity markets ($20 to $60 per share being the frequently desired per share price range).

Although listing on a multitude of foreign exchanges is quite common with the world's largest multinational corporations, the degree of success achieved to date is debatable. There is evidence that most foreign listings do little more than react to price movements of the stock on its home exchange and with little additional investor appeal other than simple international diversification reasons. In fact, a number of large US-based multinationals delisted their stock on exchanges in Europe and Tokyo in the early 1990s. For these firms, the added costs of multiple equity listings were not justified by the limited benefits accruing to the firm. But the increasing interest in international equities in many large capital markets such as the USA will most likely eventually result in improved equity performance.

There has been considerable growth, however, in what is termed the *euro-equity markets*. A euro-equity issue is the simultaneous sale of a firm's shares in several different countries, with or without listing the shares on an exchange in the firm's home country. Once issued, most euro-equities are listed at least on the computer screen-based quoting system of the International Stock Exchange in London (over 700 such firms today).

There is, however, continued debate regarding the future of euro-equities and international equities in general. The sale of equities outside the country of the firm's home country operations and denominated in non-domestic currencies is argued to constitute little more than a mail order form of stock ownership. Since the market is still in its infancy, it is too early to conclude anything about its long-term prospects as a sustainable source of equity capital for the world's corporations. When Daimler-Benz of Germany chose to list its shares on the New York Stock Exchange in the early 1990s, it may have signalled a new trend in equity capital acquisition worldwide. Daimler-Benz, like many firms, wished to raise equity capital in the same markets and currencies of its major affiliate operations. Few firms prior to this have been willing to incur the costs and potential risks of such foreign listings.

Private placements

One of the largest and largely unpublicized capital markets is the private placement market. A private placement is the sale of debt or equity to a large investor. The sale is normally a one-time only transaction in which the buyer of the bond or stock shares purchases the investment and intends to hold it until maturity (if debt) or until repurchased by the firm (if equity). Once private placements are made, there is no re-sale or secondary market for these securities (like the stock and bond market exchanges around the world). If the security was intended to be publicly traded, the issuing firm would have to meet a number of disclosure and registration requirements with the regulatory authorities, a time- and resource-consuming process. For example, when Daimler-Benz of Germany chose to list its shares publicly in the USA, the firm incurred millions of dollars in expenses in adapting its financial statements and meeting the disclosure requirements required by the US Securities and Exchange Commission. Firms which use private placements avoid most of these listing expenses.

Traditionally, much of the volume of private placements of securities occurred in Europe, with a sizeable amount being placed with large Swiss financial institutions and private investors. Beginning in the late 1980s, the private placement market has grown substantially across all countries as the world's financial markets have grown and the role that large institutional investors such as pension funds and insurance firms have gained control over increasing shares of investment capital.

Accessing the international financial markets

Although these international markets are large and growing larger, this does not mean they are for everyone. For many years only the largest of the world's multinational firms could enter another country's capital markets and find acceptance. There are two reasons for this limited access historically: information and reputation.

Financial markets are by definition risk-averse. This means they are very reluctant to make loans to or buy debt issued by firms which they know little about. Therefore, the ability to access the international markets is one which is dependent on a firm's reputation, its ability to educate the markets in what it does and how successful it has been in its line of business. This requires the firm to have patience, however, as this educational and informational dissemination stage may take considerable time.

The firm must in the end be willing to expend the resources and effort required to build a credit reputation in the international markets. If successful, the firm may enjoy the benefits of new and larger and more diversified sources of the capital it needs for its continued growth and competitiveness.

4 International financial management

International Capital Budgeting

Any investment, whether the acquisition of real estate or the construction of a manufacturing facility in another country, is financially justified if the present value of expected cash inflows is greater than the present value of expected cash outflows – in other words, a positive net present value (NPV). The construction of a capital budget is the process of projecting the net operating cash flows of the potential investment in order to determine if it is indeed a good investment or not.

Capital budget components

All capital budgets, either domestic or international, are only as good as the accuracy of the cost and revenue assumptions. Adequately anticipating all of the incremental expenses that the individual project imposes on the firm is critical to a proper analysis. If the undertaking of a new project in a foreign country requires the establishment of a new office in the parent firm for handling shipments of people and materials, this needs to be added in to the incremental cash flows of the project. A capital budget is composed of three primary cash flow components: (1) initial expenses and capital outlays; (2) operating cash flows; and (3) terminal cash flows. All three components are altered in an international capital budget.

The decision criteria for an individual investment is whether the NPV of the project is positive or negative. Traditional capital budgeting exercises, when conducted domestically, discount expected future net cash flows by the weighted average cost of capital for the firm if the project is of the same risk as the firm.

The financial analyst undertaking an international capital budget, however, must also systematically address a number of issues unique to an international investment. These concerns include exchange rate risks, international taxation and tax differences across countries, political risks, transfer pricing, repatriation of income from foreign operations

Table 5 Preliminary capital budget: Singapore manufacturing facility

		1994	1995	1996	1997
1	Net cash flow in S$	(1,660,000)	400,000	700,000	1,600,000
2	Exchange rate, S$/US$	1.6600	1.7430	1.8302	1.9217
3	Net cash flow in US$	(1,000,000)	229,489	382,472	832,596
4	Preset value factor	1.0000	.8475	.7182	.6086
5	Present value in US$	(1,000,000)	194,492	274,691	506,718
6	Net present value from parent viewpoint	US$(24,098)			
7	Present value in S$	(1,660,000)	339,00	502,740	973,760
8	Net present value from project viewpoint	S$ 155,500			

and interdependence of domestic and foreign operations. All of these issues must be incorporated by financial analysts in their assessment of the viability of the proposed investment.

The issue of whether the added risk introduced by cross-border investments, including the risk components of currency values, potential government restrictions on the movements of capital, or even the potential political stability of the country in which the investment is to take place, should be captured in the analysis by adding a risk premium to the discount rate used. Although there are those who believe that the added risk should result in a higher discount factor, there are also those who believe that the additional risk of international projects should be captured in the estimation of the net cash flows themselves, and through added sensitivity analysis in the conduct of the capital budgeting exercise.

A sample capital budgeting analysis

The capital budget for a hypothetical manufacturing plant in Singapore can serve as a basic example. Raffles, a US manufacturer of household consumer products is considering the construction of a plant in Singapore in 1994. It will cost US$1,660,000 to build, and would be ready for operation on 1 January 1995. Raffles will operate the plant for three years, at the end of which it will sell the plant to the Singapore government.

To analyse the proposed investment Raffles must estimate what the sales revenues would be per year, the costs of production, the overhead expenses of operating the plant per year, the depreciation allowances for the new plant and equipment and the Singapore tax rate on corporate income. The estimation of all net operating cash flows is very important to the analysis of the project. Often the entire acceptability of a foreign investment may depend on the sales forecast for the foreign project.

However, Raffles needs US dollars, not Singapore dollars. The only way the stockholders of Raffles would be willing to undertake this investment is if it would be profitable in terms of their own currency, the US dollar. This is the primary theoretical distinction between a domestic capital budget and a multinational capital budget. The evaluation of the project in the viewpoint of the parent will focus on whatever cash flows, either operational or financial, find their way back to the parent firm in US dollars.

Raffles must therefore forecast the movement of the Singapore dollar (S$) over the four-year period as well. The spot rate on 1 January 1994 is S$1.6600/US$. Raffles concludes that the rate of inflation will be roughly 5 per cent higher per year in Singapore than in the USA. If the theory of purchasing power parity (PPP) holds, it should take roughly 5 per cent more Singapore dollars to buy a US dollar per year. Using this assumption, Raffles forecasts the exchange rate from 1994–7 (see Table 5).

After considerable study and analysis, Raffles estimates that the net cash flows of the Singapore project, in Singapore dollars, would be those shown on line 1 in Table 5. These net cash flow impacts are not, however, easily determined. If done properly, the marginal impacts on cash flows must include factors net savings on firm-wide tax liabilities and profits arising from intra-divisional sales (transfers), which are true marginal impacts. Once net cash flow impacts are isolated, the firm must also determine if there is any potential risk that the cash flows arising from the foreign project itself would be in any way prevented by governments from being repatriated to the parent. In the example of Singapore there are no such restrictions or risks to cash flow repatriation.

Line 2 lists the expected exchange rate between Singapore dollars and US dollars over the four-year period, assuming it takes 5 per cent more Singapore dollars per US dollar each year (the Singapore dollar is therefore expected to depreciate versus the US dollar). Combining the net cash flow forecast in Singapore dollars with the expected exchange rates, Raffles can now calculate the net cash flow per year in US dollars. Raffles notes that, although the initial expense is sizeable, S$1,660,000 or US$1,000,000, the project produces net positive cash flows in its first year of operations of US$229,489.

Raffles estimates that its cost of capital, both debt and equity combined (the weighted average cost of capital), is about 18 per cent per year. Using this as the rate of discount, the discount factor for each of the future years is found. Finally, the net cash flow in US dollars multiplied by the present value factor yields the present values of each net cash flow. The net present value of the Singapore project to the US parent firm is negative ($24,098) and Raffles may decide not to proceed with the investment.

Risks in international investments

How is this capital budget different from a similar project undertaken within the investor's home country? It is riskier, at least from the standpoint of cross-border risk. The risk of international investment is considered greater because the proposed investment will lie within the jurisdiction of a different government. Governments have the ability to pass new laws, including the potential nationalization of the entire project. The typical problems which may arise from operating in a different country are changes in foreign tax laws, restrictions placed on when or how much in profits may be repatriated to the parent company and other types of restrictions which hinder the free movement of merchandise and capital between the proposed project, the parent and any other country relevant to its material inputs or sales.

The other major distinction between a domestic investment and a foreign investment is that the viewpoint or perspective of the parent and the project are no longer the same. The two perspectives differ because the parent only values cash flows it derives from the project. So, for example, in Table 5, the project generates sufficient net cash flows in Singapore dollars that the project is acceptable from the project's viewpoint, a positive NPV of S$155,500. A Singapore-based investor would therefore find the project acceptable. However, from the US parent's viewpoint, the NPV of the US dollar cash flows to be generated and returned to the US firm are negative and therefore unacceptable.

But what if the spot exchange rate were not to deteriorate, remaining the same over the four-year period or possibly the Singapore dollar even appreciating versus the US dollar? Or what if the Singapore government were to restrict the payment of dividends back to the US parent firm, or somehow prohibit the Singapore subsidiary from exchanging Singapore dollars for US dollars (capital controls)? Without cash flows in US dollars, the parent would have no way of justifying the investment; and all of this occurs while the project itself is sufficiently profitable when measured in its own local currency. This split between project and parent viewpoint is a distinct feature of international investment analysis. The standard principle of financial decision making must always apply: any individual investment can be judged only on the basis of the future cash flows which it returns – in the investor's own currency – to the investor.

Capital structure of foreign affiliates

The determination of the capital structure of a firm is the first of financial management decisions. The relative proportions of debt and equity (and even the total capitalization of the firm) is fundamental to the firm's cost of capital. The multinational firm's weighted average cost of capital (WACC) – the weights being the proportions of debt and equity, respectively – is expressed as follows:

$$\text{WACC} = \frac{\text{Debt}}{\text{Total Assets}}$$
$$= k_d(1-t) + \frac{\text{Equity}}{\text{Total Assets}} k_e$$

In this equation, debt + equity = total assets, k_d is the cost of debt, k_e is the cost of equity (common or preferred stock) and t is the marginal corporate tax rate. Note that because interest expenses on debt are deductible expenses of the firm (this is true with few exceptions worldwide), the cost of debt is reduced by the tax rate. The managerial decision for the firm is to determine the proportions of debt and equity in the firm's structure which provide adequate funding for the firm's global operations and result in the lowest weighted average cost of capital.

Although simple in theory, the determination of the optimal capital structure in practice is quite difficult (Brigham and Gapenski 1994). As the proportion of debt increases – initially lowering the weighted average cost of capital because debt is cheaper at this stage – more of the firm's cash flows will be required for debt-service. Because stockholders will only reap direct income in the form of dividends after all debt-service is complete, the fundamental trade-off between the interests of stockholders and debt-holders is an uneasy one for financial management.

The financial management of the multinational firm must address the following questions in the process of funding foreign operations and investments:

1 What is the necessary level of funding for foreign operations to be adequately financed and to assure competitiveness?
2 What proportions of debt and equity are to be used?
3 What sources of debt-capital are preferable for foreign operations?
4 What currency of denomination is preferable for this debt?

First, the adequate funding of foreign operations is critical. A firm which is underfunded cannot compete effectively in today's global marketplace. It is the responsibility of financial management to assure foreign affiliates and subsidiaries of adequate access to funding, whatever the debt/equity proportions and costs.

Second, the choice of what proportions of debt and equity to use in foreign offices, branches, affiliates and subsidiaries is usually dictated by either the debt–equity structure of the parent firm, or the debt–equity structure of competitive firms in the foreign country – host country to the investment. The parent firm sees equity investment as capital at risk and would ideally prefer to risk little of its own capital and instead fund the foreign subsidiary with large quantities of debt. Although this would still be putting the parent's capital at risk, debt-service provides a strict schedule for cash flow repatriation to the lender with regular principal and interest payments according to the debt agreement.

Dividends are returned to the parent (assuming positive net income) through managerial discretion. It is this discretion, the proportion of profits which are to be returned to the parent versus profits which are to be retained, which often leads to conflict between host country authorities and the multinational firm's parent. The parent firm wishes a real cash flow return on its investment, while host-country authorities generally wish to see a large proportion of profit reinvested in the country. The overriding principle is, however, still the same: the parent must assure adequate funding for foreign operations in order for those operations to compete effectively in the global marketplace.

Third, the sources of debt for a foreign subsidiary are theoretically quite large, but in reality are frequently quite limited. The alternatives listed in Table 6 are often reduced radically in practice because many countries possess relatively small capital markets of their own. These countries may either officially restrict the borrowing by foreign-owned firms in their countries, or simply do not have affordable capital available for the foreign firm's use. The parent firm is then forced to provide not only the equity, but also a large proportion of the debt to its own foreign subsidiaries. If the project or subsidiary is a new project, it has no existing line of business or credit standing. The parent must then represent the subsidiary's credit worth and provide the debt capital at least until the project is operating and showing (hopefully) positive net cash flows. Ultimately, all multinational parents – much in the same vein as a human parent – wish for their offspring to grow sufficiently to eventually provide their own funding!

The larger international firms will often have their own financial subsidiaries/companies established purely for the purpose of acquiring the capital needed for the entire company's continuing growth needs. These financial subsidiaries will in many cases be the actual unit extending the debt or equity capital to the foreign project or subsidiary. Hopefully, with time and success, the foreign operation will grow sufficiently to establish its own credit standing and acquire more and more of its capital needs from the local markets in which it operates, or even from the international markets which become aware of its growth.

The fourth and final question, what currency should debt capital be denominated in, depends on which currency dominates the cash flows of the foreign operations. The currency which dominates the cost and revenue structure of the foreign subsidiary (and this is not necessarily the currency of the country in which it is located), termed the *functional currency* of operations, is the preferable currency for debt-denomination. Financial management of foreign operations is complex enough without foreign affiliates struggling with the payment of foreign currency denominated interest and principal payments.

5 International cash flow management

Working capital management is the financing of short-term or current assets, but is used here to generally describe all short-term financing and financial management of the firm. Even a relatively small multinational firm will have a number of different cash flows moving throughout its system at one time. The maintenance of proper liquidity, the monitoring of payments and the acquisition of additional capital when needed, requires a great degree of organization and planning in international operations today.

Operational and financial cash flows

Firms possess both operational cash flows and financial cash flows. Operating cash flows are those which arise from the everyday business activities of the firm, such as paying for

Table 6 Financing alternatives for foreign affiliates

Foreign affiliate can raise equity capital:	*Foreign affiliate can raise debt capital:*
1 from the parent	1 from the parent
2 from a joint venture partner in the parent's country, a joint venture partner in the host country, or a share issue in the host country	2 from the parent firm's home market through a bank loan or bond issue, or a bank loan or bond issue in the host country market
3 from a third country market such as a share issue in the euro-equity market	3 from a third country bank loan, Bond issue, euro-syndicated credit or eurobond issue

materials or resources (accounts payable) or receiving payments for items sold (accounts receivable). In addition to the direct cost and revenue cash flows from operations, there are a number of indirect cash flows. These indirect cash flows are primarily licence fees paid to the owners of particular technological processes and royalties to the holders of patents or copyrights. Many multinational firms also spread their overhead and management expenses incurred by the parent company over their foreign affiliates and subsidiaries who are utilizing the parent's administrative services.

The second category of cash flows, financial cash flows, arise from the funding activities of the firm. The servicing of existing funding sources, interest on existing debt and dividend payments to existing shareholders, are obviously fundamental to the financing of the firm. Periodic additions to debt or equity through new bank loans, bond issuances or supplemental stock sales may constitute additional financial cash flows in the international firm.

Sample cash flow mapping

Figure 2 provides an overview of how these cash flows may appear for a UK-based multinational firm. In addition to having some export sales in Canada, it may import some materials from Spain. The firm accesses several different European markets by first selling its product to its German subsidiary, which then provides the final touches necessary for sales in Germany, France and Switzerland. Sales and purchases by the parent with Canada and Spain give rise to a continuing series of accounts receivable and accounts payable, many of which may be denominated in Canadian dollars, Spanish pesetas or its own currency, sterling.

Cash flows between the UK parent and the German subsidiary will be both operational and financial in nature. The sale of the major product line to the German subsidiary creates intra-firm account receivables and payables. Many of these intra-firm sales may be two-way if the German subsidiary is actually producing products not made in the UK but needed there. The German subsidiary may also be utilizing techniques, machinery or processes which are owned by the parent, so

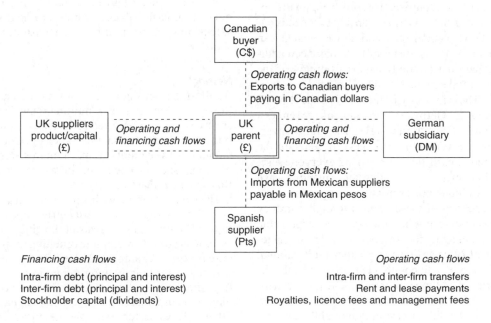

Figure 2 Cash flows of a UK-based multinational firm with a German subsidiary

royalties and license fees must also be paid to the parent. These cash flows are usually calculated as a percentage of the sales price.

There are also a number of financial cash flows between the UK parent and the German subsidiary. If the subsidiary is partially financed by loans extended by the parent, principal and interest payments will need to be made on a regular basis by the subsidiary to the parent. If the German subsidiary is successful in its operations and generates a profit, that portion of the profits not re-invested in the subsidiary will be repatriated to the parent as dividends.

One of the most difficult pricing decisions many multinational firms must make is the price at which they sell their own products to their own subsidiaries and affiliates. These prices, *transfer prices*, are theoretically equivalent to what the same product would cost if purchased on the open market. However, it is often impossible to find such a product on the open market; it is unique to this firm and this firm's product line. The result is a price which is set internally and may result in the subsidiary being more or less profitable. This, in turn, has impacts on taxes paid in host and home countries. If at some point in the operations of the German subsidiary it needs additional capital over and above what it can retain from its own profits, it may need additional debt or equity capital from any of the potential sources listed in Table 6.

The subsidiary in turn is dependent on its sales in Germany (deutschmark revenues), France (French franc revenues) and Switzerland (Swiss franc revenues) to generate the needed cash flows for paying everyone else. This 'map' of operating and financial cash flows does not even attempt to describe the frequency of these various foreign currency cash flows or specify who will be responsible for managing the currency risks. The management of cash flows in a larger multinational firm, one with possibly ten or twenty subsidiaries, is obviously complex. The proper management of these cash flows is, however, critical to the success or failure of the international business.

Cash flow management

The structure of the firm dictates the ways in which cash flows and financial resources can be managed. The trend in the last decade has been for the increasing centralization of most financial and treasury operations. The centralized treasury is often responsible for both funding operations and cash flow management. The centralized treasury may often enjoy significant economies of scale, offering more services and expertise to the various units of the firm worldwide than the individual units themselves could support. However, regardless of whether the firm follows a centralized or decentralized approach, there are a number of operating structures which aid the multinational firm in managing its cash flows.

Cash pooling

A large firm with a number of units operating both within an individual country and across countries may be able to economize on the amount of firm assets needed in cash if operated through one central pool. With one pool of capital and up-to-date information on the cash flows in and out of the various units, the firm spends much less in terms of forgone interest on cash balances which are held in safekeeping against unforeseen cash flow shortfalls.

Netting

As illustrated in Figure 2, many of the cash flows between units of a multinational firm are two-way and may result in unnecessary transfer costs and transaction expenses. Coordination between units simply requires some planning and budgeting of intra-firm cash flows in order that two-way flows are 'netted' against one another, with only one smaller cash flow having to be undertaken as opposed to two. Many countries restrict the ability of firms to net cash flows, limiting netting to specific types (for example transfers between the parent and subsidiary) and time periods (netting often allowed only on cash flows scheduled to occur within ten or thirty days of each other). Taiwan, for example, requires the application and approval for all cash flow netting arrangements by foreign firms operating in Taiwan.

Leads and lags

The timing of payments between units of a multinational is somewhat flexible. This flexibility in when which currencies are paid to which units allows the firm to not only position cash flows where they are needed most, but may actually aid in currency risk management. A foreign subsidiary unit that must obtain US dollars to pay the parent for intra-firm shipments, who is expecting its own local currency of business to fall in value relative to the US dollar, may wish to try and speed up or 'lead' its payments to the parent. Similarly, if the local currency was expected to rise versus the dollar, it may wish to wait or 'lag' payments until exchange rates are more favourable.

Re-invoicing

Multinational firms with a variety of manufacturing and distribution subsidiaries scattered over a number of countries within a region may often find it more economical to have one office or subsidiary taking ownership of all payments between units. This subsidiary literally buys from one unit and sells to a second unit, therefore taking ownership of the goods and re-invoicing the sale to the next unit. Once ownership is changed, the sale/purchase can be redenominated in a different currency, netted against other payments, hedged against specific currency exposures or repriced in accordance with the tax benefits of the re-invoicing centre's host country. The additional flexibility achievable in cash management, product pricing and profit placement may be substantial.

Internal banks

Some multinational firms have found that their financial resources and needs are becoming either too large or too sophisticated for the financial services which are available in many of their local subsidiary markets. One solution to this has been the establishment of an internal bank within the firm. This bank actually buys and sells payables and receivables from the various units. This frees the units of the firm from struggling for continual working capital financing and allows them to focus on their primary business activities. Hewlett Packard (USA) and Asea Brown Boveri (Switzerland) are two high-profile examples of firms using internal banks for cash flow management.

These structures and procedures are often used in different combinations to fit the needs of the individual multinational firm. Some techniques are encouraged or prohibited by laws and regulations, depending on the host country's government and stage of capital market liberalization. In fact, it is not uncommon to find one type of system at work in one hemisphere of a firm's operations, but with a very different system in use in the other hemisphere. Multinational cash flow management requires a good deal of flexibility in thinking on the part of management.

6 Performance evaluation and control

Proper periodic performance evaluation is necessary to guide management, both at the parent firm and at the foreign affiliate level, for four basic reasons:

1 to ensure adequate profitability;
2 to act as an early warning device;
3 to serve as an operating basis for allocating the firm's resources;
4 to evaluate individual managers.

This final reason, evaluation of managers, is critical to the future success of a multinational firm; managers of affiliates must be given unambiguous objectives against which they will be judged. Only then can they work with confidence to improve the profitability of the firm as a whole through their management of the affiliate as a part.

A number of studies have examined the criteria used to evaluate foreign affiliate performance. Although there is a wide range of different evaluation systems utilized in practice, a few conclusions can be drawn. First, financial criteria are by far the most common and generally dominate all other criteria. Second, systems which utilize budgets – where the manager or affiliate is compared in actual performance to budgeted performance – is also used with regularity. Third, return on investment (ROI) is the most common specific indicator of performance relative to budget.

Performance evaluation is particularly difficult in an international context. First, changes in currency values alter the profitability of foreign investments completely independently of the actual performance of the foreign affiliate or its management. A foreign affiliate could attain levels of record profitability, yet when the foreign currency is repatriated to the parent firm, exchange rate changes could result in the foreign earnings being appreciably less. It is therefore important to utilize criteria which separate out the local currency performance from the home currency performance, the transitory from the permanent.

A second issue is whether foreign affiliates should be evaluated in isolation, or as the components of a multinational network or 'team'. The value and performance of one affiliate's activities may often accrue to another affiliate. Not only does the parent firm in a multinational framework frequently dictate policies and resource allocations which may benefit the parent at the expense of the affiliate, but many of these same decisions may artificially reallocate 'success' among the affiliates as well.

Finally, it should be recognized that many international investments are undertaken for strategic purposes, the value of which is often difficult or impossible to determine with short-run financial ratios or criteria. These strategic goals include the need to penetrate foreign markets in early stages of market development, securing costly footholds in emerging markets and even entering areas or countries in which returns will not be realized for many years to come.

7 Conclusion

The future of international financial management is in many ways likely to parallel and grow around the trends dominating international business itself. The movement towards ever larger regional trading blocks, for example the expansion of the European Union and the signing of the North American Free Trade Agreement (NAFTA), will allow more free and frequent financial interactions between firms and between operating units of the same firm across countries. This will also probably create an environment for increasingly centralized financial decision making, once again requiring more knowledge among all participants of how the part is connected to the whole. Combined with the globalization of industry itself, management's responsibility for the timely and efficient management of the firm's cash flows will only increase in significance and complexity in the decade to come.

MICHAEL H. MOFFETT
THUNDERBIRD-AMERICAN GRADUATE
SCHOOL OF INTERNATIONAL MANAGEMENT

BERNARD YEUNG
UNIVERSITY OF MICHIGAN

Further reading

(References cited in the text marked *)

* Brigham, E.F. and Gapenski, L.C. (1994) *Financial Management: Theory and Practice*, 7th edn, Chicago, IL: Dryden Press. (This is an excellent overview of all traditional areas of financial management in a domestic context.)
* Buckley, A. (1992) *Multinational Finance*, 2nd edn, New York: Prentice Hall. (One of the only international financial management texts which takes an expressly British perspective to emerging issues in corporate finance.)
* Eiteman, D.K., Stonehill, A.I. and Moffett, M.H. (1995) *Multinational Business Finance*, 7th edn, Reading, MA: Addison-Wesley. (The leading text in the multiple dimensions of multinational financial management for nearly two decades.)
* *Financial Times*, 2 September 1993: 28.
* Giddy, I.H. (1994) *Global Financial Markets*, Lexington, MA: D.C. Heath & Company. (The single most informative textbook on the theory and practices of global financial markets.)
 Shapiro, A.C. (1992) *Multinational Financial Management*, 4th edn, Boston, MA: Allyn & Bacon. (A popular text which explains many of the international financial issues in the context of traditional domestic financial management.)

Smith, C.W., Smithson, C.W. and Sykes Wilford, D. (1995) *Managing Financial Risk*, New York: Irwin Professional Publishing. (An excellent overview of the developing field of financial risk management.)

Smith, R.C. and Walter, I. (1990) *Global Financial Services*, New York: Harper & Row. (A comprehensive treatment of the international markets and systems which comprise the framework of international business and financial activity.)

See also: ACCOUNTING, INTERNATIONAL; ECONOMIC INTEGRATION, INTERNATIONAL; FOREIGN EXCHANGE RISK, MANAGEMENT OF; GLOBALIZATION; INTERNATIONAL PAYMENTS; INTERNATIONAL TRADE AND FOREIGN DIRECT INVESTMENT; MULTINATIONAL CORPORATIONS

Related topics in the IEBM: ACCOUNTING; APPRAISAL METHODS; BUSINESS ECONOMICS; CAPITAL, COST OF; CORPORATE PENSION FUND; COUNTRY RISK ANALYSIS; CREATIVE ACCOUNTING; EXCHANGE RATE ECONOMICS; EXCHANGE RATE MANAGEMENT; FINANCE, INTERNATIONAL; FINANCIAL MARKETS, INTERNATIONAL; FORWARD AND FUTURES CONTRACTS; ORGANIZATIONAL PERFORMANCE

Foreign currency derivatives

1 **The market for derivative products**
2 **Forward and futures contracts**
3 **Options**
4 **Foreign currency swaps**
5 **Conclusion: the future of derivatives**

Overview

Derivatives, as the name implies, are derived from some other financial asset, known as the underlying asset. The fundamental purpose of a derivative product is to transfer the risks associated with the underlying asset between contracting parties. The most commonly managed risk is the price risk – the risk that the price of the underlying asset can change. Derivatives can, however, also shift other risks associated with the underlying asset, for example the credit risk. Foreign currency derivatives deal with contracts for the exchange of two currencies. The purpose of a foreign currency derivative is to shift the consequences of changes in exchange rates between the buyers and the sellers. Investors who purchase derivatives have one of two objectives: either hedging or speculation. Appropriate use of derivatives for hedging requires that the user understand the nature of the underlying risk that has to be managed, objectives of risk management and the characteristics of various derivatives that will be considered as risk-management tools. This entry explains the characteristics of three types of derivatives: forwards and futures, options and swaps. For each type of derivative, we will explain how the derivative is used, how its value changes with fluctuations in the relevant exchange rate, and provide an introduction to the pricing of these derivatives.

1 The market for derivative products

Growth of financial derivative products has been one of the major developments in the financial markets in the 1980s and 1990s.

Although some derivative products, such as futures and options, have existed for a very long time, recent changes in the financial environment have created new kinds of risks and hence demand for innovative ways to manage these risks. The response of financial institutions has been to offer an increasing array of complex combinations and extensions of existing and new assets to investors, such as range forwards, swaptions, look-back options and path-dependent options.

Derivative products are offered through two channels: organized exchanges and the over-the-counter (OTC) market. Organized exchanges – for example the London International Financial Futures Exchange (LIFFE) or the Chicago Mercantile Exchange – have expanded their menu of derivative products in the 1990s. Banks and other financial institutions offer – and are willing to tailor make – derivative products in what is known as the OTC market. Due to the flexibility of this market it is much bigger than the exchange-traded segment of the derivatives market. Derivatives on foreign currencies constitute only a small part of the total derivatives market. According to the Bank for International Settlements (BIS), foreign currency futures accounted for only about 0.81 per cent of all futures contracts outstanding at the organized exchanges at the end of 1996. Foreign currency options had a slightly higher share, 1.3 per cent, of all the options contracts.

2 Forward and futures contracts

A forward contract is a contract that will be fulfilled at some future date. A foreign currency forward contract calls for an exchange of two currencies at a designated point in time in the future. The two parties to the contract decide the amounts of the two currencies that will be exchanged – and hence the exchange rate at which the conversion will take place – and the date at which the exchange will take place. Cancellation of a forward contract requires either a payment of a fee or a search for a third party that needs exactly the same amount of the currency on the same date as contracted in the original forward contract.

A currency futures contract is an agreement to buy or sell a predetermined amount of a foreign currency at the market price at fixed maturities, known as delivery dates. The International Money Market of the Chicago Mercantile Exchange, for example, offers a futures contracts in Deutschmarks (DM) in terms of US dollars. The size of the contract in this case has been fixed at 125,000 DM and the exchange is ready to buy or sell any number of contracts maturing in any eight of the twelve months of the year which have been chosen by the exchange as maturity months. In each of these months, the contract expires on the third Wednesday of the month. Suppose that on 10 March 1998 an investor buys one Deutschmark contract which

matures in December of the same year. The investor is said to be taking a long position in Deutschmarks, which, in this case, is a short position in dollars. Suppose the investor buys the contract at a time when its price is $0.62/DM. This means that the investor has agreed to acquire 125,000 DM at a price of 125,000 × 0.62, or $ 77,500, on 16 December 1998. This contract is guaranteed by the exchange and the investor does not have to worry about the credit risk of the seller of the Deutschmarks.

Investors acquire a forward or a futures contract either to hedge or to speculate. A hedger wishes to fix the price at which he or she will acquire the foreign currency at the future date. A speculator takes a long position in a currency which he or she expects will rise in value. Although both these instruments, a forward as well as a futures, allow investors either to hedge or to speculate, a forward contract is more commonly used by

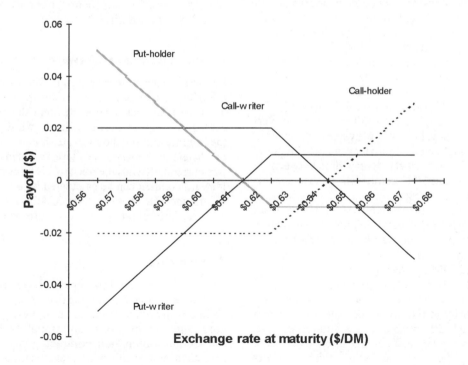

Figure 1 Pay offs from a call or put option
Options: Call option at a strike price of $0.62/DM with a fee of $0.02/DM
           Put option at a strike price of $0.62/DM with a fee of $0.01/DM

hedgers and a futures contract is preferred by speculators. This preference is due to the different settlements mechanisms used for these two contracts.

On the day a forward contract is purchased its value is zero. This is because on the purchase date the contracted rate, $0.62/DM in the example above, is the same as the exchange rate in the market. Hence the contract has no market value. Over the subsequent days a forward contract acquires positive (or negative) value if the currency that the investor purchased rises (falls) in value. On the maturity date the investor acquires the foreign currency at the contracted rate regardless of the market price of the currency. The hedger has achieved his or her purpose – he or she obtains the currency at the initial forward rate. The speculator gains (loses) the difference between the contracted forward rate and the current spot rate in the market.

A future contract achieves the same result for the investor – although the mechanics are slightly different. In the example above, the value of the contract held by our investor will change – at least till the end of the day – as the market price of the futures contract for December changes in the days following the purchase. If the market price goes up, say to $0.63/DM, the contract will be worth (0.63 – 0.62) × 125,000, or $1250. At the end of every trading day, however, the value of the contract is brought back to zero by a practice known as 'mark to market'. Every day between 10 March and 16 December the exchange either pays the investor the amount by which the value has increased ($1250 if the price changes to $0.63/DM) or requires the investor to pay the amount by which the value has gone down (if the price had fallen below $0.62/DM). After the contract has been marked to market, it is understood that the investor will acquire the foreign currency at the maturity at the new price. The investor now has $1250 in cash and a futures contract whose value, after being marked to market, is zero. The exchange follows this practice of marking the contract to market to minimize the credit risk; if the investor fails to fulfil the contract the maximum loss that the exchange can suffer is due to the price movement during the day. In practice, however, even that loss is reduced because the exchange requires the investors to deposit a margin, usually 10 per cent of the value of the contract, with the exchange. When the contract is marked to market it is really the margin that is made current – that is, brought back to its original level of 10 per cent.

Differences between forwards and futures

Although the futures and the forward contracts differ from each other in a number of minor details, the main difference between them arises from the standardized nature of the futures contract. Standardization of the futures contract makes it more suitable for trading on an exchange and allows a liquid market to develop. The two contracts also differ in the nature of cash flows; a futures contract can have a cash flow every day over its life, whereas a forward contract has only one cash flow – at maturity.

Pricing of futures and forward contracts

Foreign currency forwards and futures are relatively easy to price. A relationship known as interest-rate parity stipulates that the percentage difference between the forward (or the futures) rate and the spot rate should equal the difference between the interest rates in the two currencies. Thus the price of a futures or a forward contract can be calculated by adjusting the spot rate by the difference between the risk-free interest rates in the two currencies.

3 Options

One of the most useful concepts in developing derivative products is the idea of an option. Unlike many other contracts, an option does not *require* an investor to go through with a transaction. An option contract gives the investor a choice: either complete the transaction or, if the price of the underlying asset has changed such that he or she will lose if he or she completes the transaction, ignore the transaction.

To understand how an option works, consider the investor who purchased a Deutschmark futures contract for 125,000 DM at $0.62/DM. This investor would lose money if the Deutschmark were to depreciate, say, to $0.60/DM. The investor would like to have the possibility of forgetting about the contract if the exchange rate for Deutschmarks moves in a direction that would cause him or her to lose money. An option offers such flexibility for a price.

A foreign currency option provides the *holder* of a *call option* with the choice of buying the foreign currency at a fixed price, called the *exercise price*, till the maturity date. (A European option allows the choice to the investor only *on* the maturity date; an American option, on the other hand, can be exercised on *any* date before maturity). The choice is provided by a *writer* of the option. The choice exists only for the holder of the option; the writer of the option is required to fulfil the contract if the holder chooses to exercise the option. During the life of the contract the holder of the call option can exercise the option if the price of the foreign currency rises above the exercise price, thus profiting from the difference between the market price and the exercise price, less a premium that is discussed below. Similarly, a *put option* allows the holder of the option to sell the foreign currency at a fixed exercise price. As in the case of a call option, only the holder of the option has the choice.

The writer of an option cannot expect to gain from a change in the exchange rate. If the exchange rate moves in a direction favourable to the holder of the option the option will be exercised; if it moves in a direction favourable to the writer, the contract will expire without being exercised. In return for taking the risk of having to pay the holder, the writer receives a premium that is charged at the time the contract is sold. This premium, also known as the price or the fee for an option, is kept by the writer whether the option is exercised or not.

The profit or loss from an option contract depends upon whether it is a call option or a put option, and whether the investor is the writer of the option or the holder of the option. Figure 1 shows the payoff from each option position on the vertical axis, given the exchange rate at the maturity on the horizontal axis. Both the call and the put options are assumed to have an exercise price of $0.62/DM and we assume a premium of 2¢/DM for the call option and of 1¢/DM for the put option.

Pricing of options

Option prices assume that both the holder and the writer are rational investors, and hence the price is set such that the expected gain from holding or writing the option is comparable to that from holding other assets in the economy, after adjustments for risk. The following variables affect the returns of an option, and hence the price of an option:

Volatility of the exchange rate: the holder gains only if the exchange rate moves above the exercise price. The more volatile the exchange rate, the higher the chance that the exchange rate for the foreign currency will move into the zone where the option will have to be exercised. The writer of the option will take this into account, and hence options for currencies with high volatility will require high premiums.

Time: the longer that an option holder has to exercise the option, the higher the chance that the exchange rate will have time to move into the profitable zone. Thus options with long maturities will cost more than options with short maturities, *ceteris paribus*.

Exercise price relative to the spot price: how far the exchange rate has to move before an option enters the 'in-the-money' zone will also influence the premium or the price of the option.

Risk-free interest rate: the option price also depends on the risk associated with the contract. The risk-free interest rate provides the base from which the cost of risk is calculated.

4 Foreign currency swaps

In its simplest form, a swap is an exchange of two very similar assets which differ in some important dimension. Two bonds, for example, may be issued by the same borrower for the same maturity but may be denominated in different currencies. By swapping these assets, the two parties which originally owned these assets are changing the characteristic of the asset they own along that dimension. By swapping the assets, each party takes over the rights and the obligations associated with the asset previously owned by the counter-party. A foreign currency swap involves the exchange, or swap, of assets in two different currencies. Each party to the swap takes on all the responsibilities of the asset owned by the counter-party, including the risk associated with changes in exchange rates. A typical currency swap may result in two companies exchanging their debts denominated in two different currencies. One company may, for example, swap its fixed-rate dollar-denominated debt for another company's floating-rate yen-denominated debt. Each company will assume payments for the debt that the other company had initially negotiated in the financial market.

Swaps are motivated by imperfections in financial markets or by changes in firms' circumstances. In the example above, one in which the two firms swapped their debt obligations, the swap would have been motivated by the fact that each company is better known in its home market. The dollar debt would have been acquired initially by a US company that really needs a yen loan, and the yen debt would have been acquired by a Japanese firm that really would rather have a dollar loan on its books. Each company realizes that it will pay a higher price for a debt in its desired currency of debt than a domestic firm of equal credit risk. The solution in this case is that each company borrows in the market where it is relatively well known and then swaps the debt with the foreign company. In a swap transaction both parties end up saving on their interest costs or avoiding exchange-rate-related risks.

Swaps are arranged by commercial or investment banks, which, in addition to finding the parties whose needs match each other, also assume some credit risk. Banks usually guarantee that as long as each party to the swap meets its part of the swap payments the bank will complete the transaction. The banks charge a fee for this guarantee and the service, thus dividing the gains from a swap three ways between the three parties.

5 Conclusion: the future of derivatives

A wide variety of complex derivatives has been created by combining the characteristics of three types of basic derivative products: forwards or futures, options and swaps. In the 1990s derivative products developed a negative image with the public because of highly publicized débâcles attributed to derivatives, the most famous of which have been the losses incurred by Orange County, California, and by Metalgesellschaft, and the bankruptcy of Barings Bank in the UK. The award of the Noble Prize in Economics in 1997 to two economists for their contributions in the field of derivatives may restore some deserved respectability to these instruments, especially given the role that they can play in helping firms fine-tune their financial strategies and minimize the cost of their liabilities. In view of the potential usefulness of derivatives, most large banks continue to develop their pool of expertise devoted to identifying the needs of corporate customers and designing special products that would satisfy these needs. In the future the largest demand will be for tailor-made products that combine selected features of the basic derivatives in order to help firms and investors that have very specific needs. The availability and the use of these products by the most aggressive firms will increase the pressures on their competitors to learn about these derivatives and make these products an essential element of their financial strategy.

ARVIND K. JAIN
CONCORDIA UNIVERSITY

Further reading

Benninga, Simon (1997) *Financial Modeling*, Cambridge, MA: MIT Press. (Explains calculations associated with financial problems, including those for options.)

Daigler, Robert T. (1993) *Financial Futures Markets*, New York: Harper Collins. (Starting from simple description, the author explains in detail the use and operations of futures contracts.)

Federal Reserve Bank of Atlanta (1993) *Financial Derivatives: New Instruments and Their Uses*. (A book of readings that introduces some innovations, especially swaps, interest-rate derivatives and complex options.)

Hull, John C. (1993) *Options, Futures, and Other Derivative Securities*, 2nd edition, Englewood Cliffs, NJ: Prentice-Hall. (An excellent book dealing with complex issues regarding trading strategies and the pricing of options.)

Kapner, Kenneth P. and Marshall, John F. (1990) *The Swaps Handbook: Swaps and Related Risk Management Instruments*, New York: New York Institute of Finance. (Gives a comprehensive description of swaps – what they are, how they are traded, priced and used; also gives a description of futures and options.)

Kolb, Robert W. (1991) *Options: An Introduction*, London: Basil Blackwell. (Introduces the basics of how options work and of option pricing.)

Kolb, Robert W. (1992) *The Financial Derivative Reader*, London: Basil Blackwell. (A book of readings dealing with the applications of derivatives in a wide variety of areas.)

See also: FINANCIAL MANAGEMENT, INTERNATIONAL; FOREIGN EXCHANGE RISK, MANAGEMENT OF

Related topics in the IEBM: EXCHANGE RATE MANAGEMENT; INTEREST RATE RISK

Foreign exchange risk, management of

Overview

Since the demise of the Bretton Woods system of quasi-fixed exchange rates in 1973, the international monetary system has experienced an ever-increasing degree of exchange rate volatility coupled with periods of prolonged over- or under-shooting in currency values. This metamorphosis of the foreign exchange market has spurred the creation of new hedging instruments/techniques, whose proliferation (see Figure 1 for a chronological illustration of their introduction) – although welcomed by players in the currency market – has confounded many a would-be treasurer as to the appropriate instrument to be used in resolving their elusive foreign exchange risk management conundrum.

When exchange rate volatility is coupled with the ever-growing integration of the world economy, it is easy to understand why foreign exchange risk management is increasingly woven into global strategic management. This entry will define what is 'at risk' by identifying three basic foreign exchange risk exposure concepts: transaction, translation and economic exposure – discussing for each of them available hedging instruments and techniques. First, however, we review in some depth the 'state of the art' in foreign exchange rate forecasting. Our pessimistic conclusion with respect to forecasters' ability to generate reliable forecasts is the very foundation for foreign exchange risk management. To the extent that we cannot forecast exchange rates with great accuracy, it becomes imperative to manage exposure to foreign exchange risk.

1 The currency forecasting conundrum

The current international monetary system is comprised of four major categories of exchange rate relationships. Major industrialized countries such as the USA, Japan and the UK allow the price of their currency to be freely determined by market forces with very minimal central bank intervention. This is the so-called system of floating exchange rates, in the context of which forecasting is the most daunting.

Other major industrialized countries or newly industrialized countries such as France, Germany, Taiwan, Mexico, South Korea and others continue to stabilize their exchange rates within prescribed bands of fluctuations (as is the case of the European Monetary System which binds twelve currencies in a well defined grid of par values), or peg them against the US dollar ($) or an artificial currency unit such as the European Currency Unit (ECU) or the special drawing right (SDR). Such a system requires a militant central bank willing and ready to intervene at a moment's notice to correct underlying market forces which may have pushed the exchange rate astray (see ECONOMIC INTEGRATION, INTERNATIONAL). Forecasting will then focus more carefully on balance of payments disequilibria (over/undervaluation in the value of the currency) and on the staying power of the central bank.

Most other currencies – usually found in less-developed countries – are tightly controlled, with foreign exchange transactions channelled through the central bank which typically overvalues its currency. Forecasting in this case focuses on the timing of the inevitable exchange rate adjustment. Last but not least, are the many countries which suffer from hyperinflation (inflation in excess of 25 per cent per annum), whose currencies continuously depreciate more or less in line with

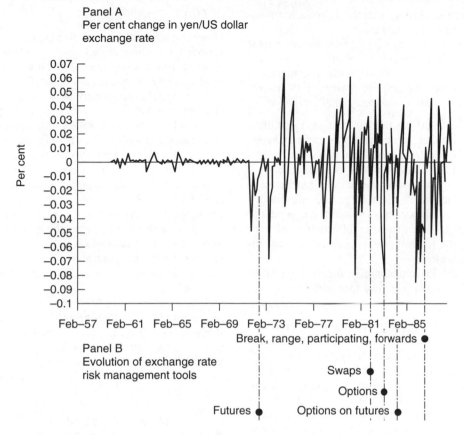

Panel A
Per cent change in yen/US dollar
exchange rate

Figure 1 Genesis of Forex hedging products
Source: Waite *et al.* 1989

the underlying rate of inflation according to the theory of purchasing power parity. This is the case of countries such as Brazil, Turkey or Russia, which practice frequent mini-devaluations until they are forced to a maxi-devaluation to close the overvaluation gap. In such cases, the forecasting game revolves around anticipating the magnitude of the lag between the nominal (as quoted by the central bank) and the underlying equilibrium exchange rate as predicted by the purchasing power parity theory.

Forecasting floating exchange rates

Exchange rate behaviour under the floating rate system is characterized by relatively small exchange rate changes that occur continuously as new information is received. This section opens by first questioning the general validity of generating exchange rate forecasts. This is based on the notion that market determined exchange rates – that is *spot* and *forward* exchange rates – incorporate all currently available information. Thus, it might be redundant to attempt to forecast exchange rates, since whatever information the forecasting model would use has already been fully incorporated in the spot and forward rate.

The market efficiency hypothesis
The return in early 1973 to floating exchange rates by a number of major currencies generated considerable interest as to whether

foreign exchange markets do indeed constitute 'efficient' markets.

By definition, a foreign exchange market in which exchange rates would fully and immediately reflect all available information is said to be *efficient*. Three degrees of market efficiency are customarily distinguished:

1 The *weakly* efficient market hypothesis holds that a time series of historical change rates contains no information which can be used to forecast future spot exchange rates.
2 The *semi-strong* version of market efficiency holds that a large and competitive group of market participants has access to all publicly available information relevant to the formation of expectations about future rates.
3 If the set of available information also includes private or insiders' information, the market is said to be *strongly* efficient.

Conversely, an inefficient foreign exchange market (in the 'weak' form sense) would indicate that past exchange rates contain useful information in forecasting future exchange rates, as information only disseminates itself slowly among market participants. This explains the existence of a successful technical forecasting industry which relies on trends analysis.

Forward exchange rates as predictors of future spot exchange rates

The semi-strong version of market efficiency is consistent with the notion that all publicly available information is fully and immediately incorporated in the forward rate. Thus, speculators who think that the forward rate, $F(d)$, is above their expectation (expected value) of the future spot exchange rate, $E[S(t)]$, will sell the foreign currency forward, thus bidding down the forward rate until it equals the expected future spot rate. Conversely, speculators who see the forward rate undervaluing the expected future spot rate will buy the foreign currency thus bidding the forward rate up until both forward and expected future spot exchange rates become equal. In statistical terms, the current forward rate would be an 'unbiased predictor' of the future spot exchange rates:

$$F(d) = E[S(t)]$$

However, it should be emphasized that this simple forecasting model does not claim to offer a point estimate of a future spot exchange rate; rather, it asserts that if the forecasting model is repeatedly used, on average and only on average, the forward exchange rate will be equal to the future spot exchange rate. Thus, if a trading firm is only occasionally involved in international business, it should not rely on this forecasting model; conversely, a multinational corporation, repeatedly involved in thousands of foreign exchange transactions could argue that such a model is helpful because over the long term it will break even, that is, exchange gains/losses arising from the forward exchange rate over/undervaluing the exchange rate would even out.

Empirical evidence for or against this simple hypothesis has been provided by several studies. The general consensus emerging from empirical studies is that testing the market efficiency hypothesis is questionable from a methodological point of view (expectations – an *ex ante* concept – are measured with historical *ex-post* data and if it is verified, the market may not really be efficient). Indeed, the continuing success of econometric forecasting services proves that international treasurers are willing to pay a hefty price for forecasts when they could rely on a free market based forecast provided by forward rates.

Econometric forecasting

Econometric forecasting models are a systematic effort to uncover a functional relationship between a set of *explanatory* (exogenous) variables, such as prices, interest rates, or rates of growth in money supplies, and a *dependent* (endogenous) variable – namely, the exchange rate. The functional relationship may involve only the current period values of the exogenous variables or may be of a lagged nature, that is, it may incorporate past periods' values taken on by the exogenous variables. In this latter case econometric modelling is clearly inconsistent with the 'market efficiency' hypothesis, whereas in the former case it is not necessarily so.

As an illustration, a simple forecasting model could express the percentage change in the US dollar price of one deutschmark $[S(t+1) - S(t)]/S(t)$, over the time interval $(t, t + 1)$, as a linear function of the expected differential in inflation rates and of the known differential in short-term interest rates:

$$\frac{S(t+1) - S(t)}{S(t)} = a\left[r_{us}(t, t+1) - r_g(t, t+1) \right]$$
$$+ b\left[i_{us}(t, t+1) - i_g(t, t+1) \right] + e(t)$$

where a and b are positive linear coefficients arrived at through multi-regression analysis and $r_{us}(t,t+1)$, $r_g(t,t+1)$, $i_{us}(t,t+1)$, $i_g(t,t+1)$, are US and German inflation and interest rates respectively over the period $[t, t + 1]$.

The specification of the model itself, that is, the nature of the functional relationship (not necessarily linear) as well as the choice of exogenous variables included, is generally a blend of economic theory (in this case a combination of the purchasing power parity theory and international Fisher effect) together with the model builder's experience and intuition. In that sense, econometric building is as much an art as a science.

An in-depth discussion of the econometric methodology underlying multi-variate regression analysis (that would, for instance, be used in deriving numerical values for coefficients a and b in the above equation) is beyond the scope of this entry and will not be attempted here. Suffice it to say, at this point, that structural equations (usually one for each currency forecast) are extracted from time series of exogenous and endogenous variables, that is, from past observations. This means that if a drastic change in the structural relationship between independent and dependent variables were to occur and be disregarded in specifying functional relationships, the econometric model forecasting value would be adversely affected.

One last additional feature of econometric forecasting models worth commenting upon is the random error $e(t)$ in the above equation that is always incorporated in this type of model. The inclusion of such a 'stochastic'

element allows probability statements to be made about the forecasted variable – for example, under a given set of conditions one might say that there is a 95 per cent chance that the future (ninety days later) dollar price of one deutschmark will be bounded between 0.5112 and 0.5205. This is indeed an attractive feature compared with a point estimate (as provided, for instance, by forward exchange rates), especially when it is recalled that the information is to be used in a risk management context.

Assessing econometric forecasting models' track records

International treasurers have to decide, first, whether it is worth the subscription fee (as high as $100,000 per annum) to purchase such forecasting services and, second, which forecasting service to subscribe to. Before we attempt to answer either question the reader should be reminded that at any single time the forward exchange market provides unconditional point estimates of future spot exchange rates (forecasting horizon is naturally given by maturities of forward exchange contracts – thirty, sixty, ninety, one hundred and eighty, and three hundred and sixty days) and that the forecasting service is free. Econometric forecasting services generally provide monthly, quarterly, biannual and annual average exchange rates rather than end-of-period point estimates. Such point estimates come usually as unconditional forecasts but provisions for conditional forecasts can easily be made.

Traditionally, the performance of currency forecasting services is assessed against the forward exchange rate, that is, whether the forecast surpasses the forward exchange rate in predicting the actual future spot exchange rate. Levich (1980) offers a methodological framework for conducting such performance analysis by focusing on the forecast error e defined as exchange rate forecast minus the actual future spot exchange rate. One obvious desirable property of such a forecast error is that it be small in absolute value; however, this simple criterion needs to be qualified according to the sign of the forecast error. Consider the example of the quarterly forward rate (forecast I) for the pound sterling $F(90)^I = 1.48$ and a second forecast $S(90)^{II} = 1.58$. If the actual spot exchange rate turns out to be $S(90) = 1.52$, the forecast error associated with the first forecast (based on the forward rate): $e_I = -\$0.04$ is smaller than the one associated with the second: $e_{II} = +0.06$. However, the second forecast, $S(90)_{II}$, is superior because it would lead investigators to the correct decision, that is, not to hedge any asset position in sterling resulting from exporting or foreign investing.

Therefore, if the magnitude of forecast errors is ignored, one can evaluate a forecaster's performance by calculating the fraction of periods where the forecast correctly predicts only the direction of exchange rate movements *vis-à-vis* the current forward exchange rate – the critical information input for hedging.

Design of composite forecasts

The above methodological framework – dubbed 'the right side of the market approach' by Bilson (1983) – has clear limitations in the sense that it provides a currency-by-currency evaluation which compares each service against the forward rate, but not against other forecasting services. More importantly, there is no way of knowing whether some combination of two or more services would be superior to a single service – hence the idea of a composite forecast.

To correct the above deficiencies, Bilson proposed to construct a composite portfolio forecast by formulating an exchange rate forecasting equation as a weighted average of single forecasting services $S(t)^k$. For example, for maturity t and currency i the composite forecast $S(t)^C$ would be written as:

$$S(t)^C = (1 - w_i^1 - w_i^2)F(t) + w_i^1 S(t)^1 + w_1^2 S(t)^2 + e_i(t)$$

where w_i^k ($k=1,2$) is the estimate of the weight given to forecast $S(t)^k$ and derived through econometric techniques. Interestingly, a composite forecast could include (and weigh heavily) the forward exchange rate for a particular currency and maturity combination.

Forecasting pegged yet adjustable exchange rates

The challenge faced here by the international treasurer is different from the problem of forecasting floating exchange rates since they deal almost exclusively with currencies which are mispriced/overvalued, and often subject to partial exchange controls. This section develops a simple four step forecasting framework. First, through a review of selected economic indicators, the forecaster can identify which countries have a balance of payments that is in fundamental disequilibrium. In the case of controlled exchange rates, the balance of payments is by definition in equilibrium and controls are simply implemented to suppress it. Second, for such countries, the forecaster can measure the pressure that market forces exercise on prevailing exchange rates. Third, the level of central banks' foreign exchange reserves gives an indication of the future point in time at which the central bank will no longer be in a position to defend the prevailing exchange rate and may be forced to take corrective measures such as devaluation. The fourth and crucial step is to predict the type of corrective policies that political decision makers are likely to implement: will the country under pressure adjust through a manipulation of its exchange rate (devaluation or revaluation) or instead initiate, perhaps for political reasons, deflationary or inflationary policies combined with exchange controls and extensive international borrowing?

Step one: assessing balance of payments outlook

What is needed here is an 'early warning' system which will assist the international treasurer in pinpointing countries whose currencies are becoming potential candidates for adjustment. Like any early warning system, it should be carefully monitored for the early detection of meaningful variances from established patterns. Of most importance to the forecaster is evidence of a yawning deficit or surplus in a country's balance of payments, provided by two 'quick' and 'dirty' indicators, respectively measuring the rate of depletion or growth in international reserves and the coverage of import spending by export earnings (see INTERNATIONAL PAYMENTS).

Rate of change in international reserves

A country experiencing a widening deficit (surplus) in its balance of payments, resulting from an overall imbalance in its current and capital account, must ultimately settle it by drawing down (accumulating) its central bank's liquid external assets of convertible foreign currencies (essentially US dollars, gold and SDRs). These liquid assets, generally called international reserves, are analogous to the cash account of a firm's balance sheet and therefore disregard short-term liabilities that the country may have incurred through its public and/or private sector. Through depletion of its international reserves, a country will be able to finance a deficit on its balance of payments. Conversely, a country experiencing a surplus on its balance of payments will accumulate international reserves.

Indeed, a rate of growth/depletion significantly at variance from zero clearly points to a disturbance in the country's balance of payments equilibrium. It generally reflects systematic central bank intervention, as the value of its currency is being defended against downward (or upward) market pressures. A persisting trend away from zero will indicate that the disturbance is not of a random nature; that is, the disturbance is structural and likely to translate itself into fundamental disequilibrium.

Indicator of trade performance

Evidence of a deteriorating balance of trade is signalled by a lower coverage of import expenditures by export earnings; instead of focusing on the absolute size of the ratio itself, the international treasurer should closely watch downward or upward trends in this indicator of trade performance (see INTERNATIONAL TRADE AND FOREIGN DIRECT INVESTMENT).

These indicators provide good *ex-post* evidence of a fully fledged disequilibrium in the balance of payments of the country under scrutiny. Of better forecasting value are indicators capturing underlying economic trends

likely to reduce a lagged disequilibrium in the balance of payments under study.

A deterioration in a country's balance of trade usually lags by as much as three to six months (depending on the nature of the country's foreign trade) a build-up of inflationary pressures; thus the international treasurer should refine their assessment of a country's balance of payments outlook by probing underlying trends in relative prices.

Higher domestic prices usually undermine the competitiveness of a country's export products in the world marketplace; more specifically, if domestic inflation entrenches itself at a rate exceeding that of the country's major trading partners, foreign demand for domestically produced goods will seek lower-priced alternatives; conversely, domestic buyers will shift to the purchase of foreign (imported) goods. The resulting deterioration of the balance of trade (higher imports and lower exports) will put pressure on the prevailing exchange rate and devaluation will become necessary in order for the country to re-establish its trade position.

Step two: measuring magnitude of required adjustment

Once a currency has been singled out for adjustment, the currency forecaster should carry out the second step of the forecasting procedure – assessing the magnitude of the change in the exchange rate required to bring the balance of payments back into equilibrium. Essentially, this can be done in two ways.

Generalized application of the purchasing power parity hypothesis

The percentage change in the exchange rate between country i's currency and country j's currency is approximated by a trade-weighted average of inflation rate differentials:

$$\frac{S_{i,j}(t)^* - S_{i,j}(t)}{S_{i,j}(t)} = r_i(t) - \sum_{j=1}^{n} w(t)_i^j r_j(t)$$

where $S_{i,j}(t)$ is the currency i price of one unit of currency j before devaluation or revaluation (that is, in the disequilibrium situation), whereas $S_{i,j}(t)^*$ would simply be the equilibrium exchange rate as predicted by the purchasing power parity hypothesis: $r_i(t)$ and $r_j(t)$ measure the rate of inflation experienced by countries i and j over the period starting with the last parity adjustment up to time t and the $w(t)_i^j$ are the weights associated with each of the n trading partners of country i. This is in essence a trade-weighted generalization of the well-known purchasing power parity formula and gives a very reliable measure of a currency over/under valuation *vis-à-vis* its benchmark equilibrium value.

Forward rates of exchange as predictors of future spot exchange rate

Under a system of stabilized exchange rates, the estimate of the equilibrium exchange rate $S_{i,j}(t)^*$ provided by a generalized application of the purchasing power parity theory will be usefully supplemented by the forward market anticipation of the future spot exchange rate. In the case of newly industrialized countries, such as India, Mexico and Turkey, the forward exchange rates may not be readily available from market sources; however, 'home-made' forward exchange rates can always be computed with the help of the interest rate parity theorem: denoting by i_i and i_j the respective interest rates on short-term government securities, the corresponding forward exchange rate $F_{i,j}(d)$ can be expressed as:

$$F_{i,j}(d) = S_{i,j}(0)\frac{1 + i_i}{1 + i_j}$$

where d measures the forecasting horizon.

Free market–black market rates as an indicator of the future spot exchange rate

Under a system of tightly controlled exchange rates (absence of a forward exchange market) a proxy estimate of what the equilibrium exchange rate should be is provided by the black market rate. It should be pointed out, however, that the black market rates often overestimate the extent of the needed devaluation to bring back the balance of payments into fundamental equilibrium, and should be used in combination with the equilibrium rate provided by a trade-weighted application of the purchasing power parity doctrine.

Step three: timing of adjustment policies

Once the pressure on a given currency has been estimated as the discrepancy between the forecasted (equilibrium) rate $S_{i,j}(t)^*$ and the actual prevailing rate of exchange $S_{i,j}(t)$, the currency forecaster can probe the resistance capacity of the country under pressure to adjust. The ability to resist or to delay the implementation of corrective policies is very much dependent on the overall amount of international reserves that can be spent to finance the deficit resulting from the fundamental balance of the payments disequilibrium. An index $\phi_i(t)$ measuring the 'grace' period can be computed as follows:

$$\varphi_i(t) = \frac{R_i(t) + R_i(t)^*}{D_i(t)}$$

where $\phi_i(t)$ measures the number of periods t (usually monthly or quarterly) during which country i can afford to sustain a deficit of $D_i(t)$ per period, and $R_i(t)$ is the amount of total reserves (both owned and borrowed) available to country i. Such reserves are made up of owned reserves of foreign exchange, gold and SDRs. $R_i(t)^*$ is the estimated amount of international liquidity that can be readily obtained from international sources (standby agreements), from other central banks (swap agreements), or simply borrowed from international money and capital markets such as the Eurobond market. As time runs out, the index $\phi_i(t)$ decreases and the 'grace' period, by the end of which adjustment policies can no longer be postponed, shortens dangerously.

Step four: nature of adjustment policies

Whether a country whose balance of payments is in fundamental disequilibrium will actually devalue (revalue) its currency or let it float downward (or upward) to adjust is ultimately a political decision (see INTERNATIONAL PAYMENTS). No matter how necessary a devaluation (or revaluation) may be from an economic point of view, political factors have the final word in deciding between the implementation of inflationary (or deflationary) policies and/or the imposition of exchange controls versus a change in the par value of the currency. This discussion proceeds on the assumption that the nature of the balance of payments disequilibrium is of a deficit type; symmetrical conclusions would be obtained in the case of a balance of payments surplus.

Deflating or tightening exchange controls
In the case of a structural balance of payments deficit, policy makers will first consider the implementation of a deflationary (contractionary) policy as a way of bringing the balance of payments back into fundamental equilibrium. An appropriate combination of restrictive fiscal and monetary policies (often dictated by the International Monetary Fund when large foreign debt liabilities have to be refinanced) should presumably induce a reduction of aggregate domestic demand for both domestic and foreign-produced goods so that the demand for imports falls and the supply of exports rises. Such results may be easier to obtain if deflationary policies are combined with internal controls on wages and prices. Furthermore, external controls, essentially on capital account transactions, should further reinforce the improvement in the balance of trade that should follow a deflationary policy combined with internal controls.

Clearly, deflation will work best when the income elasticity of demand for imports is large, for example, if a cut of 1 per cent in national income reduces the volume of imports by 3 per cent (income elasticity is 3), only half as much deflation is needed to secure a given improvement in the balance of trade (lower imports resulting from lower national income) as when the income elasticity is 1.5. The effect of domestic deflation on exports is less clear; much will depend on the *modus operandi* of deflationary policies and on the state of world trade. When world trade is buoyant, it is important to have supplies available and to be competitive in delivery dates; deflation will definitely help by making additional manufactured goods readily available for export. Conversely, when world trade slumps there is no shortage of supply, and additional exports will be primarily achieved through reduced prices; deflation will prove of little help.

The cost of such remedial action for external disequilibrium (deficit in the balance of payments) is predictable enough: unemployment, which, to say the least, is unlikely to arouse popular enthusiasm.

Devaluation
If a combination of deflation and controls does not work out the way it was intended, if the expected political cost of unemployment cannot be afforded by the decision makers in power, or if a policy of large-scale borrowing has reached its limits, the weapon of last resort will have to be used: devaluation.

At this point, political factors such as proximity of elections or political credos of policy makers will have to be reviewed in a qualitative manner by the currency analyst. In so doing they should be able to determine how much longer a devaluation can be postponed for purely political reasons, or whether a devaluation is totally ruled out on *a priori* grounds by responsible decision makers.

In summary, currency forecasting remains a treacherous exercise whose outcome is at best uncertain: this clearly motivates the careful design of foreign exchange rate management policies.

2 Covering transaction exposure

Foreign exchange risk exposure for independent exporters and importers results from contracts which provide for deferred payments (accounts receivable in the case of exports and accounts payable in the case of imports) in a currency that is usually foreign to one of the parties involved. Hence, the party that signs the contract in a foreign currency is exposed to the risk that the prevailing exchange rate when the contract is signed may have changed when the payment becomes due, thereby exposing itself to foreign exchange loss or gain.

So called hedging techniques for the elimination (or reduction) of such transaction risks are introduced in this section; specifically, the mechanics of covering transaction exposures with forward contracts versus money market hedges as well as currency options are discussed for short-term exposures, which are typical of most international trade and financing transactions. The different and somewhat more complex case of long-dated exposures hedged through tailor-made invoicing or currency swaps as well as the case of contingent exposures characteristic of international bidding and transnational mergers and acquisitions is discussed second.

Short-term transaction exposure in international trade

Consider the case of Lufthansa, the German Airline, which, in early 1985, after hard negotiations, had closed a deal for the purchase of twenty Boeing 737 aircraft for approximately $500 million; the contract called for delivery and payment one year hence (see MANAGEMENT IN GERMANY).

Nature of exposure

Lufthansa is facing a dollar-denominated liability exposure in the amount of $500 million to be paid in full upon the delivery of the aircrafts. At the time of contracting, the dollar ($) cost of one deutschmark (DM) stood at 3.2, and any appreciation of the US currency over the exposure horizon (time period elapsing between the signing of the purchase agreement and the actual payment – approximately one year) would result in a significantly higher DM cost than initially budgeted.

Figure 2 sketches the DM import cost as a function of the actual exchange rate

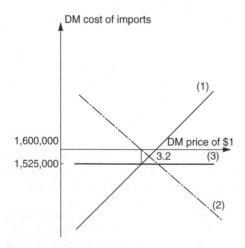

Figure 2 Hedging with forward contracts

prevailing at the time of payment. Clearly, any scenario to the right of DM3.2 = $1 (exchange rate at the outset of the exposure horizon) is of great concern to Lufthansa, whereas any scenario to the left of 3.2 would result in significant cost savings due to the appreciation of the DM *vis-à-vis* the US dollar. Optimally, Lufthansa wants to avoid the DM depreciation scenario while staying flexible, were the DM to revalue. In the next several sections we review the different hedging strategies available to Lufthansa, pointing out the costs and benefits associated with each of them – in particular as they relate to Lufthansa's hedging objectives.

Hedging with forward contracts

By entering into a forward purchase contract for US dollars (forward sale of DM) Lufthansa is locking in the DM cost of buying dollars for delivery at payment time, which in this case was DM3.05 = $1. Thus, on 15 February 1986 Lufthansa would tender DM3.05 500,000,000 = DM1,525,000,000 and receive $500,000,000 – the exact amount owed to Boeing Aircraft Corporation in order to take delivery of the twenty aircraft. Forward contracts are irrevocable commitments to be honoured by both parties regardless of what may happen to the future spot exchange rate. This essential property of forward contracts is depicted in Figure 2 by the horizontal line (3) which is the sum of Lufthansa's 'naked' (before hedging) US dollar position (1) and the purchase of forward dollar position – which in isolation is a speculative position sketched by line (2). Alternatively, Lufthansa may want to consider the use of money markets to construct a synthetic forward contract whose cost should be carefully compared to a forward contract offered by the bank.

Hedging through the money market

Lufthansa can borrow an amount – yet to be determined – x of DM at the annual interest rate of 6 per cent to be exchanged immediately through a spot transaction into $x/3.2$ dollar. The dollar cash balance would then accrue interest earnings at the interest rate of 12 per cent so that at delivery time Lufthansa will have the necessary dollar cash balance to meet its payment obligation in full. Since Lufthansa will be earning interest on its dollar balance, it needs to borrow only the present value of its dollar liability discounted at the US interest rate:

$$x = \left(\frac{500,000,000}{1+0.12} \right) 3.2$$

=DM 1,429,000

However, to complete the full costing of the money market hedge, Lufthansa should take into account the interest due to the German bank in the amount of:

1,429,000 (1 + 0.06) = DM 1,514,000

which turns out to be slightly cheaper than the direct forward contract offered by the bank (see line 4 on Figure 3). Indeed, any discrepancy between the two options will tend to be arbitraged away by the vigilant dealers of money market desks at large commercial banks; this is the well-known interest rate parity theorem which binds money markets so closely (in this instance the DM and US dollar) to the spot and forward exchange markets.

Hedging with currency options
As can be observed from Figures 2 and 3 neither hedge strategy will allow Lufthansa to benefit from a possible appreciation in the value of the DM against the US dollar.

Granted Lufthansa is well protected against the possible devaluation of the DM but to be well prepared against both eventualities, Lufthansa needs a different hedging instrument called a currency option. Currency options – unlike forward and future contracts – give you the right without the obligation to buy (call) or sell (put) a certain quantity of foreign currency at an agreed price called the strike price. For this flexibility the option purchaser has to pay an upfront cash premium which is a sunk cost. Currency options can be obtained at different strike prices with the corresponding premium higher (lower) the more (less) favourable the strike price for the option buyer. In this particular instance, Lufthansa was considering buying a dollar call option (DM put option) at a strike price of DM3.18 = $1 for an upfront cash premium of DM0.04 per dollar (total premium of DM20 million).

Figure 4 sketches the risk profile of buying a dollar call option: Lufthansa would exercise the option if the DM were to weaken below DM3.18 = $1 and conversely abandon the currency option if the DM were to appreciate beyond the strike price as it would be cheaper for Lufthansa to purchase dollars on the spot exchange market at a cheaper rate; of course, the option premium paid upfront has to be taken into account and the effective break even rate is the strike price adjusted for the future value of the premium which, in this case, would be equal to

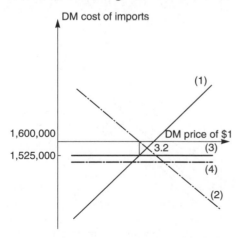

Figure 3 Hedging through the money market

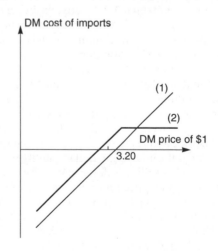

Figure 4 Hedging with currency options

DM [3.18 - 0.04 (1 + 0.06)] = 3.12.

It is this flexibility to exercise or not to exercise the option which uniquely differentiates this hedging instrument from a forward contract. This flexibility, however, comes at a considerable cost which, more often than not, deters would-be corporate hedgers from resorting to the use of options. It is in this spirit that financial engineering has purported to introduce a new generation of forex products providing the corporate hedger with downside protection or upside potential, at a reduced or zero upfront premium expense. This family of products includes forward range and forward participation contracts to name only a very few; they are often referred to as derivatives as they turn out to be simple combinations/derivations of options and forward contracts.

Hedging with forex derivatives

Lufthansa presumably liked the idea of a call option on the dollar but baulked at the idea of spending close to DM20 million just to hedge currency risk when protection could be purchased seemingly at a zero cost with a forward contract. Missing from this analysis is, of course, the opportunity cost of any saving arising from a DM revaluation. Here financial innovation could help and Lufthansa would be well advised to consider the use of a forward participation contract which would offer downside protection while allowing Lufthansa to participate (less than fully) in the DM upside potential. Practically, the buyer of a forward participation agreement would normally decide the maximum (ceiling) strike price for the call option component whereas the bank selling the forward participation contract will set the corresponding participation rate resulting in a zero upfront premium. Thus, such contracts are the combination of (1) the purchase of a dollar call option at a strike price above the forward rate for the full amount of the underlying dollar liability position; and (2) selling a dollar put option with the same strike price for only a fraction of the underlying exposure, so that the call option premium will be fully financed by the writing of the put option. In this case Lufthansa could set a ceiling on the DM cost of purchasing dollars at DM3.40 = $1 while participating to the

tune of 70 per cent of any cost saving which would result from a DM appreciation (see Figure 5 for a comparison of a call option with a forward participation agreement). It would certainly be a lot easier for Lufthansa's international treasurer to convince the company board of directors to proceed with this strategy than to buy a call option for the modest cost of DM 20 million!

Alternatively, if Lufthansa were somewhat less bullish on the DM potential appreciation, it could consider entering into a forward range agreement which would also provide a ceiling to the cost of buying dollars while allowing full participation in the upside DM potential but only within a pre-agreed range. Specifically, entering into a forward range agreement is tantamount to (1) buying a dollar call option at a strike price above the forward exchange rate; and (2) selling a put option with a strike price below the forward exchange rate, so that the premium cost of the call option is indeed fully financed by the revenue generated by writing the put option. For example, Lufthansa could have locked into a forward range contract its dollar liability position by guaranteeing a ceiling DM cost for buying dollars of DM3.28 = $1 , and, conversely, limiting its upside potential on the DM appreciation at DM3.00 = $1. Within the range of 3.00 to 3.28, Lufthansa will have to buy dollars at

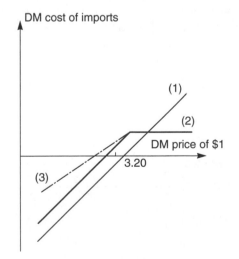

Figure 5 Hedging with forward participation agreements

whatever spot rate prevails at the maturity of the contract.

Figure 6 compares the risk profile of buying a call option versus entering into a forward range agreement. Both forward participation agreements and forward range contracts are similar to forward contracts in the sense that they require full delivery regardless of exchange rate outcomes; even though they happen to be a combination of option contracts they do not allow the contract holder to abandon the contract under any circumstances.

Postscript: Lufthansa's unfriendly currency skies

The reader may be interested to know what the outcome of Lufthansa's real life forex predicament was. Conscious of the dollar gross overvaluation (DM undervaluation) Herr Ruhnan, Lufthansa's CEO, decided to hedge through a forward contract only 50 per cent of its dollar exposure, thus leaving the other 50 per cent of the dollar exposure open to potential cost savings, were the dollar to depreciate over the next twelve months. As it turned out, the dollar did depreciate to DM2.30 = $1, but Lufthansa benefited on only 50 per cent of its exposure, while the other 50 per cent had been locked at the forward rate which turned out to be less than favourable. Herr Ruhnan was blamed for costing his employer DM80 million (in an opportunity sense) and nearly lost his job. Had he purchased a dollar call option

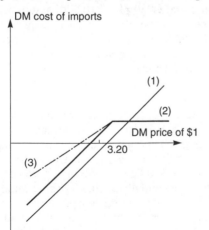

Figure 6 Hedging with forward range agreements

(which could have been negotiated with a bank) he would have been hailed a hero!

Hedging 'stochastic' exposures

So far our discussion has proceeded on the assumption that the transaction was immediately materialized by a contract; this is undoubtedly the case of an export order received on a particular date, filled out of existing inventory and delivered within a fixed period of time with, of course, credit extended to the buyer in the form of an account receivable invoiced/denominated in the buyer's currency; this is also the case of an importer such as Lufthansa who commits to purchasing foreign goods to be paid at a future point in time in the (foreign) currency of the seller. However, consider the situation in which it is necessary to quote prices in another currency contingent upon the customer's acceptance. This is often the case of exporters tendering bids on 'big ticket items' such as aircrafts, weapons systems, power plants, etc. Similarly for manufacturers issuing price lists denominated in foreign currencies there may be no fixed starting date as far as the seller's quotation is concerned, and it is therefore impossible to enter into a contractual hedge whose maturity and amount would exactly match the projected transaction that has yet to materialize. Here again the introduction in the 1980s of currency options on spot as well as futures has considerably simplified the forex challenge confronted by international bidders as illustrated above. Let us turn now to a real life situation to show how such fancy forex hedging products can be put to good use.

Consider the case of Marcel Dassault SA, the French defence contractor tendering on the sale of twenty Mirage fighters to the Kingdom of Thailand. The bid is entered on 1 April 1992 – along with competing tenders from Israel, Sweden and the USA – in the amount of $500 million. The result of this bidding contest will be announced on 1 June 1992 and delivery-cum-payment will take place on 1 September 1992. Thus Marcel Dassault SA may find itself with an asset exposure denominated in US dollars for the amount of half a billion dollars but it will not know with any certainty until three months from bidding time whether indeed it should concern itself with this transaction exposure. Over that period Marcel Dassault SA knows that it may be exposed to a dollar transaction exposure but any traditional hedging through a forward contract or a money market hedge may turn out to be embarrassingly expensive if the bid were not awarded and the dollar had appreciated.

However, Marcel Dassault SA could purchase a three month dollar put option to buy September French franc (FF) futures (to sell dollar futures) for a cash premium of FF0.20 per dollar sold forward at the guaranteed future exchange rate of FF5.27 = $1. If the bid were awarded to Marcel Dassault SA and the dollar had – for example – appreciated to FF5.88 = $1 by 1 June, the option would be simply abandoned and Marcel Dassault SA would contract to sell dollar forward at the rate of FF5.88 = $1 for an effective yield of FF5.88 - 0.20 = FF5.68 per $1. Had the dollar depreciated (rather than appreciated), the option would have been exercised and Marcel Dassault would have taken delivery of the FF future contract. Conversely, had Marcel Dassault not been awarded the bid, it would have the flexibility of simply abandoning the option (dollar has appreciated, the option is worthless and its cash premium should be construed as a sunk cost of bidding and Marcel Dassault may recoup part or totality of the option premium) or selling the option for its residual value (dollar has depreciated).

Long dated exposures in international trade

As mentioned earlier, foreign exchange risks can always be eliminated by invoicing in your own currency; however, this is clearly not necessarily good for relationships between customers and suppliers. Furthermore, the fact that the other party is made to bear the exchange risk will normally be reflected in the price at which the transaction will be concluded, so that the trader who insists on invoicing in his own currency as a passive 'no-trouble' policy is in fact paying for shifting the foreign exchange risk to the other party. The trader may be paying more than

they might have to, had they been prepared to be more flexible in the choice of currency denomination. Compromise solutions are available in the nature of contracts denominated in currency units that allow for the parties to share the burden of a change in the exchange rate between contracting time and payment time. We consider next some of the most widely used invoicing techniques in international trade (see INTERNATIONAL TRADE AND FOREIGN DIRECT INVESTMENT).

Contracts denominated in both parties' currencies

Consider the case of Mitsubishi Heavy Industries sourcing iron ore from Canadian Pacific Ltd, the transportation-cum-mining conglomerate. To ensure consistency of supply, the Japanese company signs a five-year contract, fixing both price and quantity to be purchased by the Japanese party (see MANAGEMENT IN JAPAN). If the contract is denominated in Canadian dollars (C$), at C$100 per metric ton, a depreciation of the Japanese yen (¥) over the next five years will be totally supported by the Japanese importer. Conversely, had the contract been denominated in Japanese yen at ¥10,000 per metric ton, a depreciation of the Japanese yen would, in this case, be fully supported by the Canadian exporter.

Under the circumstances of a purely bilateral contract (50:50 per cent basis), it is conceptually appealing to price a metric ton of iron ore at C$50 plus ¥10,000, assuming, as above, that the prevailing exchange rate of ¥100 to C$1 is in existence. Consider the two following occurrences under alternative contracting schemes.

Scenario 1

Japanese yen depreciates over the first year from ¥100 to ¥125 = C$1 under the first contracting scheme (contract fully denominated in Canadian dollars): the Canadian firm receives C$100 per metric ton of iron ore as anticipated initially but the Japanese importer pays ¥12,500 per metric ton of iron ore, which is ¥2,500 per unit more than initially anticipated; the Japanese importer fully supports the exchange loss. Had the contract been denominated in Japanese yen, at ¥10,000 per metric ton, the Canadian firm would only receive C$92.307, which is C$7.693 less per unit than was anticipated. In the case of a contract pricing the metric ton of iron ore at C$50 plus ¥5,000, the Japanese importer would pay ¥6,250 plus ¥5,000, which is still an exchange loss of ¥1,250 per metric ton of iron ore as compared to the price that was envisioned initially, but an improvement over the ¥2,500 loss that would have been incurred had the contract been denominated in Canadian dollars. Conversely, the Canadian exporter receives C$50 plus C$46.153 which is still a loss of C$3.847 per unit as compared with the price envisioned initially. Under this last contracting scheme both parties have shared equally in the exchange loss.

Scenario 2

Japanese yen appreciates over the first year from ¥100 to ¥90 = C$1. The exchange gain reaped by each party can be worked out under the same three alternative contracting schemes. The result will be found to be entirely symmetrical with those reached in the case of a depreciation of the Japanese yen.

A related invoicing method often used in this case of bilateral trade relationships is to establish a neutral brand around the original exchange rate of an arbitrary width of, say, ¥5 within which the exchange gains/losses are fully assumed by the importer. All three

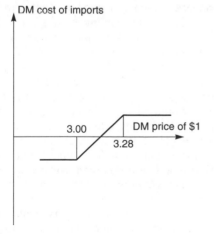

Figure 7 Split currency invoicing

invoicing methods are depicted graphically in Figure 7.

The idea, however, of a 50:50 split of foreign exchange risk is clearly unsuitable for such products or services as air fares or shipping rates that are actually or potentially traded multilaterally. In such cases, two compromise solutions can be envisioned, involving the use of a third country's currency or of an artificial currency unit as a basis for contract denomination.

Contract denominated in a third country's currency

For non-US trading parties, denominating longer-term contracts in US dollars may have attractive properties. Although the burden of foreign exchange risk is neither eliminated nor even shared, it may be compensated by 'convenience returns' that trading companies exporting to and importing from a great many countries will derive from a uniform dollar invoicing. Such 'convenience returns' are in the nature of the netting of accounts receivable and accounts payable denominated in dollars, resulting in substantially smaller transaction costs, because only the algebraic balance of accounts receivable and accounts payable is eventually converted from the dollar into the domestic reference currency, or vice versa. Furthermore, by transacting in only one foreign currency, the trading firm will be able to develop a significant expertise in exchange rate forecasting that a multiplicity of foreign exchange dealings would preclude. Using only one foreign currency should also allow the firm to get much better rates because the scale of its exchange transactions will be significantly larger than if it were fragmenting exchange transactions in several currencies. Finally, the exchange market of dollars against any simple currency is usually much deeper and less volatile than between currencies of nations that are only insignificant or minor economic partners.

Contract denominated in an artificial currency unit

This is another compromise solution that has been gaining momentum ever since the heyday of the Bretton system was over. The idea is to apportion the foreign exchange risk in a somewhat indeterminate sense between the two transacting parties by denominating the contract in a unit of account that is based on several currencies, such as the European Currency Unit (ECU) or the special drawing right (SDR), rather than on the currency of one of the transacting parties or on a third currency such as the US dollar. In so doing, the value of the contract is pegged to the value of a standard that remains reasonably stable over time, thereby accurately reflecting the intentions of the buyer and seller as expressed in the original agreement.

Because of the geographical diversification resulting from the inclusion of several currencies, the value of a long-term contract denominated in artificial currency units should be less susceptible to pronounced fluctuations in the event of exchange rate changes than in the case of single currency contract denomination. Artificial currency units are proving increasingly popular in long-term debt financing, as illustrated by the steady growth of ECU denominated debentures.

3 Hedging translation exposure

Publicly held multinational companies are required to disclose quarterly earnings to their shareholders and the financial community at large; such earnings will typically include a significant foreign component generated by foreign branches and subsidiaries domiciled in different currency habitats whose financial accounts are prepared in the local currency (see GLOBALIZATION; MULTINATIONAL CORPORATIONS). Thus, prior to worldwide consolidation of foreign currency denominated balance sheets and income statements, the US based multinational has information about its earning performance as measured in the currency of each country in which it operates, for example, the Malaysian ringgit, Indonesian rupiah, Mexican peso, etc., not quite the magic dollar denominated earning-per-share so eagerly awaited by shareholders and financial analysts on Wall Street. Therefore, the multinational corporation needs to aggregate earnings from each of its foreign operations after it has skilfully restated or translated each foreign

currency denominated financial statement into its *reference currency* in which worldwide earnings should be ultimately disclosed. This requires the corporate comptroller to expend considerable efforts in applying accounting rules as they pertain to the translation process (Financial Accounting Standard Board Statement no. 52 in the USA, SSAP #20 in the UK and similar rules in other industrialized countries) in order to prepare consolidated financial statements for the multinational corporation, from which earnings per share can be readily extracted. It should be emphasized that this periodic exercise of remeasuring accounting performance does not involve any conversion of currencies nor any cash flow even though the parent company may report foreign exchange losses (gains) of a translation nature, as such losses (or possibly gains) are of an unrealized nature, an important point to which we will return later.

Indeed the reader may wonder why, if such losses (gains) are in fact of a non-cash flow nature, they are worth discussing: the answer has much to do with how efficient the financial markets are in distinguishing between accounting numbers (a combination of realized and unrealized cash flows) and truly realized cash flows available for dividends distribution, capital expenditures, friendly or unfriendly corporate acquisitions, etc. The empirical evidence would indicate that capital markets are generally less 'gullible' than in former years, that is, paying more attention to value than to accounting earnings but not quite as efficient as economic theory would have them be; in other words financial markets do pay attention to the gimmickry of translation gains/losses and publicly-held corporations do have to concern themselves with the smooth stream of earnings that they report periodically. Otherwise they may be penalized by skittish shareholders overreacting to seemingly volatile earnings – that is, requiring a higher return for perceived heightened volatility which in turn depresses the price–earnings ratio – admittedly a crude measure of the firm cost of equity capital. We next turn to the mechanics of translation exposure measurement and management.

Measuring translation exposure

Gauging the extent of translation exposure in a particular foreign currency is inextricably linked to the question of which exchange rate should be used in restating financial statements from the local currency into the reference currency. The controversy has centred around whether it should be the current or closing exchange rate prevailing at the time of consolidation or the historical exchange rate which prevailed when assets were first acquired or liabilities first incurred.

When foreign currency denominated balance sheets are translated into reference currency terms at the current closing rate, the net translation exposure is simply the net worth of the foreign subsidiary since all assets and liabilities (but not equity nor retained earnings) are uniformly translated at the exchange rate prevailing at the time of consolidation/translation. This is the method currently used by US and UK multinationals, except for the case of US translation rules for hyperinflationary countries which have to rely on the monetary/non-monetary method of translation.

Consider the case of Pax Americana whose French subsidiary's pro forma balance sheet as of 1 October 1993 is given in Table 1.

Note that long-term debt to Pax Americana's parent and accounts payable denominated in US dollars are not exposed items nor are they relevant to the computation of the translation exposure.

Thus, if the French franc were to depreciate over the next reporting cycle, from $0.20 to $0.18 = FF1 Pax Americana–USA would incur an unrealized translation loss of

$$FF200,000,00 \ (0.20 - 0.18) = \$4,000,000$$

which would be reported in the sub-equity account of its balance sheet. The translation loss would not flow through the income statement until such time as Pax Americana–France is sold and an accounting loss is reported by the parent company. If translation losses were repeatedly incurred by Pax Americana–USA, its debt–equity ratio would deteriorate which may result in higher cost of capital with bank creditors and generally lower credit ratings.

Hedging translation exposure

There are two methods for hedging translation exposure based on: (1) a forward contract; and (2) local borrowing. Both involve creating a cash flow gain (hopefully) which will neutralize the projected translation loss.

Returning to the pro forma 31 December 1993 balance sheet of the French subsidiary of Pax Americana prepared on 1 October 1993 and detailed in Table 1, assume that accounts receivable can be discounted at an annual rate of 12 per cent. Dollar denominated accounts payable can be prepaid with a saving of 10 per cent. Six month treasury bills denominated in US dollars yield 7.5 per cent annually, FF can be borrowed at an annual rate of 11 per cent and finally, spot and ninety day forward FF are available at $0.20 and $0.185 respectively.

Contractual hedging

Contractual hedging can be carried out by selling ninety days forward the FF amount corresponding to Pax Americana's net pro forma translation exposure. The cost thus incurred is:

$$FF200,000,000 \ [0.185 - 0.20] = -\$3,000,000$$

and is the algebraic sum of the unknown speculative cash gain/loss on the forward contract and the unknown, unrealized non-cash flow translation loss/gain. Both functions are depicted on Figure 8 and the reader will note how they add to the net contractual hedging function – a horizontal line independent from the unknown, end of the period exchange rate.

Financial hedging

Contractual hedging should now be compared with the cost of financial hedging which is based on borrowing in the currency of the translation exposure and immediately transferring the proceeds into a reference currency (unexposed) asset. Specifically, Pax Americana can essentially borrow from two sources and would presumably choose the least costly one. By discounting accounts receivable the French affiliate of Pax Americana is borrowing from its customers at an annual rate of $i^{l}_{f} = 0.12$ which is slightly more expensive than the French banking system

Table 1 Pro forma balance sheet of Pax Americana–France (31 December 1993)

Assets (in thousands of FF)		Liabilities (in thousands of FF)	
Fixed assets	1000000	Long-term debt to parent (denominated in $)	1000000
Amounts receivable [1] (denominated in FF)	500000	Long-term debt (denominated in FF)	500000
Inventory of imported raw materials	300000	Accounts payable (denominated in $)[1]	500000
Inventory of finished goods	300000		
Marketable securities (denominated in FF)	300000	Net worth	500000
Cash	100000		
Total	2500000		2500000

Its translation exposure under current or closing rate accounting method can be readily measured as:

Exposed assets (+)	= Inventory of finished goods (300,000) + Marketable securities (300,000) + Cash (100,000)
	= 700,000
Exposed liabilities	= FF-denominated long-term debt (500,000)
	= 500,000
Net translation exposure	= 700,000,000 − 500,000,000 = 200,000,000

[1] Six-month maturity

$(i^2_f = 0.11)$. The offsetting increase in non-exposed assets (investment in US treasury bills at $i^1_d = 0.075$) or decrease in non-exposed liabilities (prepayment of dollar denominated accounts payable at $i^2_d = 0.10$ should be tailored to maximize return (or to

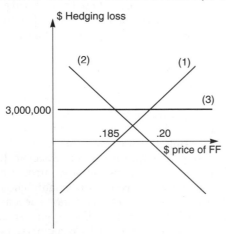

Figure 8 Hedging translation exposure through forward contracts

minimize costs). Accordingly, Pax Americana––France should borrow the present value of its net FF translation exposure from the French banking system and use it to prepay its dollar denominated accounts payable. The net cost of financial hedging amounts to:

$$200,000,000 \times 0.20\left(\frac{1+0.10/4}{1+0.11/4}\right) - 1$$

$$= -\$97,320$$

In summary, financial hedging should be implemented as long as the cash flow component of either approach is not taken into account in the comparison.

Arbitraging exposed versus non-exposed balance sheet items

At this point it might be useful to examine the accounting significance of hedging through interest rate arbitrage. First, borrowing in local (devaluation-prone) currency the present value of the projected translation exposure creates an exposed liability that would offset the translation exposure, provided that the equivalent exposed asset (cash resulting from the loan proceeds) is immediately converted into a non-exposed asset – for example, by investing in devaluation-safe reference currency. Local borrowing as such is a necessary, but not a sufficient, condition for financial hedging to succeed. That is, creating an offsetting exposed liability has to be matched by transforming the exposed asset item into a non-exposed asset item.

The principle is perfectly general and can be readily extended to any financial or commercial transactions that would allow the affiliate operating in a devaluation-prone currency to either:

1 Decrease exposed assets and increase non-exposed assets. (For example, sell marketable securities denominated in the local currency and invest them in marketable securities denominated in devaluation-safe currencies.)
2 Increase exposed liabilities and increase non-exposed assets. (For example, borrow locally and invest proceeds in marketable securities denominated in devaluation-safe currencies.)
3 Decrease exposed assets and decrease non-exposed liabilities. (For example, use up cash or discount accounts receivable denominated in devaluation-prone currencies, to prepay accounts payable denominated in devaluation-safe currencies, or to prepay dividends to the parent company.)
4 Increase exposed liabilities and decrease non-exposed liabilities. (For example, borrow locally to retire medium- or long-term debt denominated in devaluation-safe currencies, to prepay accounts payable denominated in devaluation-safe currencies, or to prepay dividends to the parent company.)

Whatever the technical device used, the hedging entity will incur costs (not necessarily positive) in adjusting the segmentation of the exposed affiliate's balance sheet into exposed versus non-exposed items. Regardless of the technique used, the formulation of the net cost of financial hedging remains valid provided that the following substitutions are carried out:

i_f = Cost of increasing exposed liabilities or opportunity cost of reducing exposed assets.

i_d = Return from increasing non-exposed assets or cost savings from reducing non-exposed liabilities.

4 Economic exposure

The concept of economic exposure links exchange rates to the value of the firm as it attempts to capture the impact of exchange rate movements on the net present value of its worldwide future cash flows. To understand this relationship one needs to probe how future corporate cash flows – that is, revenue and cost streams – will be cumulatively impacted upwards or downwards by movements in the exchange rate. Once such understanding has been achieved, the multinational firm will be in a position to design guidelines which should mitigate undue economic exposure to the vagaries of exchange rate fluctuations.

Whereas transaction exposure focused on short-term – readily measurable – cash flow effects of exchange rate fluctuations, economic exposure (sometimes called operating exposure because it focuses on operating cash flows) takes a longer view of how future cash flows – and ultimately value – will respond to changing exchange rate relationships. It is similar to an *elasticity* concept which would capture the percentage change in the value of the firm (possibly proxied by its market capitalization) to a one per cent change in the weighted average value of the US dollar against foreign currencies. Unlike transaction and translation exposure concepts which can be readily extracted from financial statements, economic exposure does not lend itself to easy quantification. At best the international treasurer will analyse qualitatively how cash flows will directly or indirectly respond to changing exchange rates before any economic hedge can be articulated.

Consider the case of Whirlpool, the US leader in 'white goods', which in the early 1980s was facing up to very strong competition from Italian imports. As a private label manufacturer which held a dominant position in the US market, Whirlpool was a typical domestic firm sourcing primarily from US suppliers (costs are denominated in US dollars) and selling exclusively to US retailers (revenues are denominated in US dollars). Thus a superficial analysis of its economic exposure to exchange risk would conclude that Whirlpool should be sheltered or unexposed to adverse movements in the value of the dollar on foreign exchange markets; yet in the early 1980s the fortunes of the company were harshly buffeted by the relentless rise in the value of the dollar *vis-à-vis* other major currencies.

Measuring Whirlpool's economic exposure

A closer look at Whirlpool's net cash flow sensitivity to the appreciation of the dollar reveals that imports of comparable but lower priced products were quickly encroaching into the firm's dominant market share. Indeed as the US dollar kept appreciating/overshooting against the Italian lira, Whirlpool's products were progressively becoming overpriced, leaving Whirlpool with a difficult strategic quandary: should it allow cheaper imports to win market share (Whirlpool would price its products in line with US inflation) or should it hold onto its market share by pricing in line with imports, that is in line with the dollar value of the Italian lira? The second option would presumably result in deteriorating operating margins and eventually outright losses, even though it would allow Whirlpool to block off imports. In effect Whirlpool's economic exposure to the value of the dollar was directly linked to its overvaluation *vis-à-vis* the Italian lira. The case of Whirlpool is easily generalizable: a firm's economic exposure to exchange risk is derived from the extent to which its key competitors' cost structure is itself impacted by that same exchange rate; this assumes that output markets to which the various competitors sell are closely integrated or the same (no tariff barriers or excessive transportation costs preventing smooth arbitrage). See Figure 9 for a taxonomy of economic exposures.

Costs	Revenues	
	Export market	Domestic market (import competition present)
Imported inputs		
Domestically sourced inputs (import competition)		
Domestically sourced inputs (no import competition)		

Costs	Revenues	
	Export market	Domestic market (absence of import competition)
Imported inputs		
Domestically sourced inputs (import competition)		
Domestically sourced inputs (no import competition)		

Figure 9 Taxonomy of economic exposures

Hedging Whirlpool's economic exposure

In order to maintain market share in its own domestic market Whirlpool had to be able to peg its prices to the value of the lira rather than to US inflation. By procuring compressors from Italian suppliers Whirlpool was able to match for about 35 per cent of its cost base the competitive advantage of its key rivals. As the dollar continued to overshoot until late 1985, Whirlpool neutralized the cost advantage of its import competitors by aligning its cost structure with its Italian exporters. Another approach could have been to borrow Italian lira so as to capitalize on exchange gains which would have in turn subsidized Whirlpool's domestic sales allowing it to remain price competitive. Either way Whirlpool would have matched imports prices by linking its cash outflows to the value of the lira. Thus, managing economic exposure far exceeds the realm of traditional hedging products and techniques to encompass pricing, procurement and financing policies.

5 Conclusion

In summary, this entry has argued that corporate need for hedging foreign exchange risk was largely predicated on our less than stellar performance as currency forecasters. Of course, the verdict has to be qualified by the nature of the exchange rate determination system: in section 1 forecasters' trials and tribulations were detailed in the context of floating exchange rates – the truly inscrutable and most treacherous specie – versus stabilized or controlled exchange rates, which are somewhat better behaved (that is, easier to forecast), courtesy of central bankers' heroic interventions in the foreign exchange market. However, the International Monetary System is heading toward more currencies priced by relatively unhampered supply and demand forces in the forex market. This also means that central banks are increasingly recognizing how really impotent they are in the face of private market participants. Any international discussion of returning to some form of stabilized exchange rates builds more on nostalgia than on sound economic analysis!

Once humbled by less than successful currency forecasting, the international treasurer will take inventory of the firm's exposure to currency risk; in section 2, transaction exposure measurement and management was reviewed at great length, and hedging tools – old and new – were matched to deterministic and stochastic exposures. Section 3 dealt with translation exposures – the mystifying byproduct of periodic consolidation of foreign with domestic operations which results in unrealized non-cash flow exchange loss/gain. Manufacturing firms and financial institutions are increasingly broadening their concept of exposure to forex risk and integrating it with interest rate risk, commodity price risk and insurance purchasing. Risk management thus entails the design of corporate guidelines which allow for consistent hedging policies both across different risk situations and over time; financial engineers are still in the infancy stage of developing such concepts and tools, however.

In the final section we sketched the meaning of economic/operating exposure to currency risk by linking the firm's value to exchange rates. Needless to say, the currency hedger – equipped with an ever fancier tool kit of forex products and derivatives – will be well inspired to focus its attention on managing strategically its economic exposure through appropriate sourcing, financing and pricing policies which will maximize the value of the firm over the long term. Obsession with exhaustive hedging of transaction exposures and excessive attention to the 'cosmetic' impact of translation risk should be de-emphasized as they deflect firms' attention away from directing their best effort to the creation of value through sound management of their economic exposure – admittedly more of a global strategic management challenge than a financial management conundrum.

LAURENT L. JACQUE
TUFTS UNIVERSITY, USA
GROUPE HEC, FRANCE

Further reading

(References cited in the text marked *)

Ahn, M. and Falloon, W.D. (1991) *Strategic Risk Management*, Chicago, IL: Probus Publishing Company. (A full-length treatment of the economic exposure concept of foreign exchange risk management accompanied by several real-life case studies.)

* Bilson, J.F.O. (1983) 'The evaluation and use of foreign exchange rate forecasting services', in R.H. Herring (ed.), *Management of Foreign Exchange Risk*, Cambridge: Cambridge University Press. (Operationalizes the concept of performance-weighted composite forecasts for the foreign exchange market.)

De Rosa, D.F. (1991a) *Managing Foreign Exchange Risk*, Chicago, IL: Probus Publishing Company. (Foreign exchange risk management in international stock portfolio managers. Excellent discussion of currency options for hedging purposes.)

De Rosa, D.F. (1991b) *Options on Foreign Exchange*, Chicago, IL: Probus Publishing Company. (Treatise on valuation and strategies for using currency options for foreign exchange risk management. Everything you ever wanted to know about currency options and more.)

Jacque, L.L. (1996) *Management and Control of Foreign Exchange Risk*, Norwell, MA: Kluwer Academic Publishers. (Advanced treatment of the subject matter which introduces algebraic valuation and decision rules for major hedging decisions.)

Kenyon, A. (1990) *Currency Risk and Business Management*, Cambridge, MA: Blackwell. (A British practitioner's perspective on the subject written with illuminating corporate illustrations.)

* Levich, R.M. (1980) 'Analyzing the accuracy of foreign exchange advisory services: theory and evidence', in R.M. Levich and C. Wihlborg (eds), *Exchange Risk and Exposure*, Lexington, MA: D.C. Heath. (Develops a statistical framework for comparing the accuracy of a given forecast *vis-à-vis* the forward exchange rate.)

Shapiro, A.C. (1989) *Multinational Financial Management*, 3rd Edn, Boston, MA: Allyn & Bacon. (An intermediate level international corporate finance text which devotes several chapters to foreign exchange risk management. The next level up in depth and sophistication for the reader of this entry.)

Smith, C.W., Smithson, C.W. and Wilford, D.S. (1990) *Managing Financial Risk*, New York: Harper & Row. (The classical treatise on products and techniques for managing currency, interest rate and commodity price risks.)

* Waite et al. (1989) 'The evolution of risk management products', *Journal of Applied Corporate Finance*, Winter.

Wunnicke, D., Wilson D. and Wunnicke, B. (1992) *Corporate Financial Risk Management*, New York: Wiley. (Legal and tax aspects of foreign exchange risk management are discussed in great detail by practicing experts.)

See also: ECONOMIC INTEGRATION, INTERNATIONAL; FINANCIAL MANAGEMENT, INTERNATIONAL; INTERNATIONAL PAYMENTS; INTERNATIONAL TRADE AND FOREIGN DIRECT INVESTMENT; MANAGEMENT IN GERMANY; MANAGEMENT IN JAPAN; MULTINATIONAL CORPORATIONS

Related topics in the IEBM: AIRLINE MANAGEMENT; ECONOMICS OF DEVELOPING COUNTRIES; EFFICIENT MARKET HYPOTHESIS; FORWARD AND FUTURES CONTRACTS; MODELLING AND FORECASTING; INFLATION; MONETARISM

Foreign market entry strategies

Overview

Entering foreign markets presents several strategic choices to the manager. Let us suppose the objective is to deliver a product or service to customers in a new market abroad. The first choice is whether to produce inside that country, or whether to produce the good or service in the company's existing plants and ship the item to the new market. The first decision, then, is between local production and exports. Several economic and strategy criteria affect this choice. To export the item to a foreign market means additional costs of freight, customs duties, insurance, special packing and other taxes which may be avoided if the item were to be produced in the country itself. On the other hand, setting up production in the foreign nation involves additional capital investment, and might make for higher production costs compared to the company's existing facilities (especially when we take exports from the latter on a variable cost basis). The manager also has to consider the risks and organizational issues associated with a new foreign investment, such as political instability, currency fluctuations and training a new management and staff to fit in with the company's existing procedures, hierarchy and operating specifications.

Licensing the company's expertise, patents or brands to another firm in the foreign market, and to have this firm produce the good or service for customers there, is another option. The licensee company receives training and the rights to intellectual property, and in turn pays fees and royalties to the company as licensor. This is sometimes a 'hands-off' approach to international expansion, involving less control over the foreign operation than an equity investment. Since it is the licensee company that makes the investment and assumes the risk of developing the market in their country, the royalties and technical fees they are willing to pay the licensor are often inferior to the dividends and growth in equity value the company could have earned if it had made the foreign investment by itself.

Each option involves different levels of investment, expected return, control, risk, duration, competitive threat, tax and strategy implications. There is no single optimal choice. The decision depends on the product and market in question, on the company's financial and managerial resources, its risk averseness and overall global strategy. First, the 'classic' foreign market entry choices of exporting, licensing and foreign direct investment as strategy alternatives are presented, and how a firm may choose a particular mode in developing a particular country market is shown. Reality, however, is often far more complicated. For one thing, tax, risk and strategy often call for combining some of the options rather than treating them as substitutes for each other. Second, globalization trends call for treating a foreign market not as a compartmentalized operation, but as one that is integrated with the rest of the global firm's activities. When the actual actions of mature global companies are examined, foreign affiliates (equity investment) which have received technology or intellectual property from the parent (under license) are often found, while at the same time their inputs are supplied by an affiliate in another nation (intra-firm exports).

In the second part of this entry, situations under which direct investment, licensing and exports are not viewed as substitutes but are treated as complementary strategies are examined. Firms beginning their international expansion are more likely to view them as substitutes. The mature globalizing firm is also likely to view them as concurrent strategies.

1 The classic strategy options

The three classic international expansion options are shown in Table 1 which indicates that cash returns under each type are likely to be very different in magnitude, timing, duration, risk and tax liability. In exporting, profit margins are earned immediately, shipment by shipment, under control of the company; risks are those associated with the exporting location, and the profits are immediately taxable in the exporting nation.

In foreign direct investment (FDI) a new company is acquired or created abroad with a substantial investment, and the investing company owns all or part of its shares (see GLOBALIZATION). In the term 'foreign direct investment' the word 'direct' reminds us that the investor directly controls, or has some influence over, the management of the foreign company. A shareholding under 10 per cent is generally considered passive or portfolio investment. Shareholding above 10 per cent is considered 'direct investment'. The degree of control is, of course, only very loosely correlated with the percentage of shares held. By value, most international direct investment takes the form of fully-owned subsidiaries or majority (over 50 per cent shares) affiliates. When the equity investment is less than 100 per cent, the remaining shares may be owned by a local investor who is called a joint venture partner. The cash returns under a capital investment are usually considerably delayed compared to exporting or licensing, but all in all, they are likely to be far bigger and lead to eventual growth in equity value as well. Unlike licensing, for instance, there is usually no time limited agreement, although capital investments do, of course, face the risk of failure and eventual termination. The investment is also subject to political and foreign exchange risk in the foreign country. Dividend returns are a partial distribution after the corporate tax bite in the country, and remittances are subject to an additional withholding tax in several nations (see GLOBAL STRATEGIC ALLIANCES; INTERNATIONAL TRADE AND FOREIGN DIRECT INVESTMENT).

In licensing the returns are under an agreement (between two independent or arm's-length firms, in the first part of this entry). Agreements usually have a limited life, of between three and ten years generally, unless renewed. The agreement often calls for a significant lump sum payment at the inception, plus running royalties, usually expressed as a percentage of the sales value of the licensed item in the licensee's market. Most governments (within limits) allow licensing fees and royalties to be counted as deductible expenses to the payer, that is, the licensee. This means that, unlike dividends, remittance of licensing payments legally escapes the foreign country's corporate income tax altogether. This

Table 1 Classic strategy options and type of income from each

Strategy	Type of return
1 Exporting the product, that is, trading	Immediate direct profit mark-up on item sold; taxable in exporting country
2 Foreign direct investment	Eventual profits and equity growth declared by foreign subsidiary; taxable in foreign nation
3 Licensing to independent party	Technical fees and royalties over life of the agreement; tax deductible to licensee firm

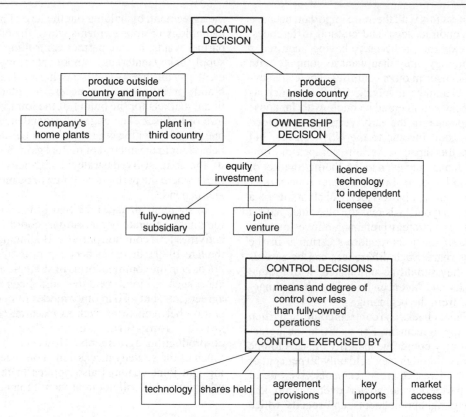

Figure 1 The three key decision domains: location, ownership and control

confers a marginal to significant advantage to the licensing option.

Key decisions in international expansion

Among the key variables in choosing a foreign market entry mode are location, ownership and control, as shown in Figure 1. The location question regards where the product is to be made, or the service created. Do production and transport costs, tariffs, non-tariff barriers and other factors favour producing inside the foreign market, or justify importing from the company's other plants? Cost comparisons are to be tempered by long-run forecasts of relative exchange rates when calculating import costs, just as local production cost estimates are to be tempered by forecasts of input costs of local labour, materials and finance. Costs are sometimes not the crucial factor because marketing success may be predicated on delivery and quality, rather than on price.

Non-economic criteria may dominate the location decision (see INTERNATIONAL TRADE AND FOREIGN DIRECT INVESTMENT).

If the decision is made to produce inside the foreign market, this can be done by a foreign direct investment, either fully-owned, or a joint venture, or by a licensing arrangement. In the latter two cases a partner firm is involved, and designing the arrangement to exercise 'control' over the operation becomes important. In a fully-owned subsidiary, or a majority foreign affiliate, managers obey the wishes of the parent firm, even if they are local nationals. But when other interests are involved, such as joint venture partners or licensees, their aims, methods and behaviour may not conform to the investor company's objectives. The term 'control' should not appear sinister or manipulative. In any good business arrangement involving two or more parties, mutual checks and balances should be built in. In international business this is all the more important because of economic, legal and cultural differences. For example, a licensee, having acquired a technology, may then want to compete with the licensor in other countries. There are several examples involving US firms, such as RCA, which licensed technology to Japanese companies. In the early years they provided very good income to the US licensors, but later, the Japanese became competitors outside Japan, and even in the 'home' market of the US licensors. In a joint venture one partner may want a high dividend declaration or a quick 'payout', whereas the other may have a long-term strategy preferring reinvestment of most of the joint venture's earnings in the early years. Such differences can be serious and they should be anticipated, with mutual checks and balances built into the arrangement from the beginning.

These checks and controls could be written into the agreement. For example, an agreement may confer the majority of seats to one partner although they hold only 50 per cent or fewer shares. Some agreements give one of the partners veto power over certain key managerial appointments, and specify which production method will be used, maximum and minimum dividend payouts in each year, and so on. Control can also be wielded outside the agreement, by holding out the lure of new technology or improvements which the other partner wants; by one partner controlling the supply of key materials, components or ingredients; by the threat of withdrawing a valuable brand; or by controlling access to international markets for the output of the joint venture or licensee. The ongoing dependence of one partner over the other would temper their behaviour in the interest of mutual gain. Some of the longest-lived strategic alliances are those where the partners continue to be mutually dependent.

In strategic alliances the two firms, while remaining separate organizations, coordinate activities for a common purpose. Beginning in the late 1980s, there has been a proliferation, not only in the common forms of strategic alliance such as joint ventures and licensing agreements, but also in other modes of cooperation between firms such as research consortia, long-term contracting and co-production agreements. However since much of the strategy discussion about licensing and joint ventures also applies to these other forms we will not treat them separately here.

Table 2 Pros and cons of an export strategy

Pros	Cons
• No new investment (for small export orders)	• Exisiting slack production capacity may be used up by domestic demand
• Very profitable on variable cost basis	• Can face formidable non-tariff, transport, tariff and other barriers
• Economies of large-scale production	• High exposure to foreign exchange risk (in long-term strategic sense)
• Utilizes existing capacity and employees	• Just-in-time delivery and customer relations difficult
• Familiar production environment	
• Very low foreign exchange risk exposure (short-term)	

2 Exporting as an international strategy

Advantages of exporting

Exporting is a logical means of serving a foreign market when the exporting location has a comparative advantage, or when the foreign market is small (see EXPORTING). For an initial expansion into a foreign market, exporting from existing plants means no new investment is needed with its capital investment and risk (see POLITICAL RISK). The company merely uses its slack capacity by increasing plant running hours or adding shifts. Plant managers love export orders, especially if domestic demand is slack, as they utilize existing equipment and employees. (See Table 2 for a summary of the advantages.)

Assuming that the fixed costs of the plant are covered by existing domestic sales, any incremental order adds handsomely to profit, since any revenue above variable cost goes directly to profits. An export order at a price less than the domestic price can still be profitable. The domestic price may cover all costs – fixed and variable. The export price can be higher if the foreign customers can pay more, or it can be lower than the domestic price if the foreign market is price sensitive.

Drawbacks of exporting

The drawbacks of an export strategy are also indicated in Table 2. The additional costs of freight, insurance, special packing and customs tariffs often make the delivered or landed cost in the foreign market prohibitively high, even with costing near to the variable cost floor.

International freight costs, on average, are 5 per cent of value or below. However this is an average with huge variation, depending on location and the ratio of transport cost to product value. Because of the country's location, Australian consumers pay a higher price for many goods. Being light in relation to value, a diamond may be mined in South Africa, cut in Israel, set in jewellery in Hong Kong, and the finished piece sold in the USA, without too much of a freight penalty. Other bulk goods, however, such as construction materials, are restricted by freight costs to a certain radius around their manufacturing location. Software is exported from India to the USA at the click of a key; but this is misleading if we ignore the huge outlays for satellites and transponders.

After forty years of the General Agreement on Tariffs and Trade (GATT) talks, customs duties in the major industrialized nations are down to an average of 5 or 6 per cent. Today, far more than tariffs, 'non-tariff barriers' (NTBs; see NON-TARIFF BARRIERS) remain a principal obstacle to trade. Non-tariff barriers impede trade, not by adding on an extra cost element, but by regulations, bureaucracy, tough or unreasonable inspection requirements and quantitative restrictions on imports. Restrictive quotas have been imposed on a wide range of items from clothing to cauliflowers to cars, and inspection rules and certification requirements for certain items have been made so tough as to preclude their import. A 'buy local' mentality in some nations may produce a similar *de facto* limitation on imports. Many markets simply cannot be served by exports because of such restrictions.

Another problem with exporting is that while utilizing existing spare capacity is desirable, that argument can only be carried up to the capacity limit. After that, how does the firm handle further growth or demand in the foreign market? Up to a point the company can handle foreign demand by adding second or third shifts. Even this approach is less efficient, since additional shift workers have to be paid higher wages, quality is often poorer and the reject rate higher. The time comes when the company will have to contemplate adding another factory or line, which requires additional capital investment. Then the firm can no longer treat its incremental export sales on a variable cost basis.

Exporting as an evolutionary stage

At this stage in the evolution of a company's international business, when another plant must be added, some companies conclude that they may as well build a plant inside the foreign market. This would save on transport costs, customs duties and logistics, shorten delivery times and improve customer contacts. This is how firms most often make their first overseas investment.

In some cases, companies may conclude that the foreign market is too small or uncertain, or the required capital investment too massive to justify such a step. Such companies must then restrict their international business to a level based on available capacity or consider the licensing option.

Foreign exchange risks in exporting

Each shipment can usually be hedged against foreign exchange risk (see FOREIGN EXCHANGE RISK, MANAGEMENT OF). It is easiest for exporters to ask for payment in their own currency. However this does not eliminate the exchange risk but transfers it to the importer. So this approach can work at the risk of annoying the buyer. It depends on whether it is the buyer or seller that holds the dominant position. At any rate, for major currencies (such as the US dollar, Japanese yen, deutschmark, French franc or sterling) in which most exports are denominated, forward cover is easily obtained, whereby a bank commits, in advance, the foreign exchange rate on shipment. Thus, each shipment can be hedged and the exchange rate made certain.

However, forward cover and options extend out only a year at most into the future. Moreover, while the exchange rate for each shipment can be fixed in advance, the forward rate itself will move over time with the spot rate for a currency (appreciation or devaluation). Hence in the long run there is no escape from foreign exchange risks associated with exporting. Plants dedicated to export markets are fundamentally exposed to shifts in the exchange rate over the long term. The most dramatic example of this was faced by Japanese companies. Consider a Minolta plant selling cameras to the USA. In 1986, 260 yen was equal to 1 US dollar (¥260 = $1). Three years later in 1989, ¥130 = $1. The best scenario for Minolta would have been to double the dollar price for their cameras, so that a camera priced at $100 in 1986 would be priced at $200 in 1989. However, because of intense competition in the US market for cameras (aided by the open market policies of the US government) the dollar unit price of cameras could not be raised significantly. As a result, the Japanese exporters of cameras saw, not their profits, but their gross yen revenues slashed in half. A calamitous situation for Japanese companies; a happy situation for the US consumer. Thus, while exporting has minimal exchange risk in the short term (shipment by shipment), this strategy leaves the company exposed in the long term.

A numerical example

The numerical example in Tables 3 and 4 illustrates the concepts of: (1) variable and average cost pricing; (2) economies of scale; (3) tariff barriers; and (4) transfer pricing and 'dumping', which enter into export decisions.

A US video game manufacturer sells 200,000 units of a video game to a mature domestic market. Variable cost per game is $9 each and fixed costs amount to $2,200,000 per year. The game is sold in the USA at a wholesale price of $22 each, involving a profit mark-up of 10 per cent, or $2, over the average cost of $20 per game. Maximum capacity of the factory is 250,000 video games per year. We see in Table 3 that there are strong economies of scale – from a prohibitively high cost of $229 per unit for a volume of 10,000 units, to a reasonable $20 per unit at a volume of 200,000 games.

Let us suppose that the company receives a letter one day, indicating that there may be a nascent demand for the video game in a foreign market. Would the company please quote for a trial export shipment of 10,000 units, on a 'landed cost' basis (meaning that the exporter bears all costs including freight, insurance and import tariff), to the foreign market? Investigation reveals freight and insurance costs to be $1 per game, and the tariff will be 50 per cent on 'free on board' (FOB) value. (FOB in international trade refers to the cost of goods delivered on board a vessel or aircraft in the exporter's port.)

The most common reaction of small US exporters is to reason thus: 'we charge $22 to our domestic customers. Why should we

Table 3 Scale economies in video game production

Quantity	Variable cost total	Fixed cost	Total costs	Average cost
10000	90000	2200000	2290000	$ 229
100000	900000	2200000	3100000	$ 31
200000	1800000	2200000	4000000	$ 20
210000	1890000	2200000	4090000	$ 19.48
250000	2250000	2200000	4450000	$ 17.8

Variable cost per unit	= $9
Domestic sakes Q	= 200000 games per year
Trial export order	= 10000 games
Domestic wholesale price	= $22 (10 per cent above average cost)
Maximum factory capacity	= 250000 games per year

treat our foreign clients any better or worse? We will charge them the same $22 plus whatever freight and tariff costs are incurred – that is their responsibility'. This is quote 3 in Table 4, which amounts to a landed cost of $34 in the foreign market. Quote 2 is similar, with only a slight difference. Since the export order adds to domestic volume, making the total 210,000 units, this lowers average cost to $19.48 (in Table 3). Add to $19.48 the customary $2 profit margin, and we get $21.48 as the FOB value. This makes for a landed cost of $33.22 in the foreign market, as shown in Table 4.

However, both quotes 2 and 3 may be wildly off the mark. Foreign markets are likely to be very different from the domestic market in tastes, income, product cycle maturity, competition and price elasticity. To make an export quote based on the domestic price is nothing more than a shot in the dark. Unfortunately, this is what many exporters do (particularly small ones), either because of ignorance, or because the costs of overseas market research are too high. The foreign market may be able to sustain a price much higher than the domestic price. Customers there might be affluent, or the video game, being new, might attract a coterie of fanatics willing to pay a high price. Alternatively, the foreign market may only be able to sustain a price much lower than the domestic US price. What the manager needs to do is to calculate a minimum and a maximum.

What is the minimum? If fixed costs are said to be covered by domestic sales, any quote above the $9 variable cost floor would make some contribution towards profit. Quote 1 in Table 4 constitutes the absolute minimum price. It corresponds to a landed

Table 4 Possible export quotations for video game (delivered to foreign market)

Quote	FOB US Port	Freight and insurance	Customs Duty at 50% on FOB	Total landed cost in foreign market
1	$9.00	+ 1	+ 0.50(9)	= $14.5
2	$21.48	+ 1	+ 0.50(21.48)	= $33.22
3	$22.00	+ 1	+ 0.50(22)	= $34
4	$38.00	+ 1	+ 0.50(38)	= $58

cost of $14.50 in the foreign nation – useful if the market is poor or competitive.

What is the maximum? Here we cannot work upwards from FOB cost, but must work downwards from whatever price the market can bear. Let us suppose in this scenario that the market is affluent, and competition is weak, and that 10,000 video games can be sold at a wholesale price of $58 each (quote 4 in Table 4). The export executive, working backwards from the expression:

$$X + 1 + 0.50X = 58.00$$

derives an FOB value of $38, which is much higher than the US price of $22.

The essential point is that the price charged in one territory (domestic), often has little bearing on the price to be charged in another territory (export). This is especially true in international business when the territories are separated by borders, oceans, cultural and income differences. The exceptions to this statement occur only when the item is easily moved, and encounters low tariffs. Then, unauthorized parties may buy the item in the cheaper price location and ship it to a higher price nation, thus undercutting the company's own distribution channels and undermining its price discrimination policy. Companies respond to this 'grey market' by attempting to differentiate products, using different designs, packaging or warranties for different nations. However, this is costly to the company and may not work the closer the product is to a commodity. Thus, there are such things as globally standard prices for copper, wheat and oil. The price variation across countries for small, easily transported items like watch batteries tends to be lower. Pan-European regulatory scrutiny of drug prices have reduced price disparities for drugs in the European Union (EU). However, the vast majority of manufactured goods and services are not standardized, but remain differentiated – by design, technology, brand names and the uses they are put to in different nations.

There is therefore no need, and it is globally sub-optimal, for a company to charge identical prices in the different countries it sells in. The very attempt is foolish and doomed in a world of floating exchange rates; for even if prices were set equal in two different countries, they would soon drift apart as the rate of exchange varied.

Dumping and international trade

The Japanese were the first to digest this important lesson and apply its potential fully. In competitive markets they showed flexibility by setting prices low (a bit above variable cost – quote 1 in Table 4), but below global average cost (quote 2). A company cannot do this in all countries, because it would go bankrupt if average costs were not covered over all territories taken together. However, the 'below-global-average-cost' price in competitive territories can be made up by an international firm by charging 'above--global-average-cost' prices in other countries where the market can sustain a high price (quote 4).

The Japanese have been accused of 'dumping' products in the USA. The USA is one of the most price competitive markets in the world for many industries. Foreign producers exporting a product to the USA are often forced to accept very low prices. They make up for this by charging higher prices for the same item in other countries. For Japanese producers, the 'other country' is often Japan itself. Japanese consumers indeed pay higher prices than their US counterparts for a wide range of items. The same 'boom box' (an AM/FM stereo radio, plus cassette recorder) sold in Manhattan for $150, may cost a Japanese teenager the yen equivalent of $250. There are thousands of similar examples.

The explanation is that the USA is an open, low-tariff, fiercely competitive market for consumer electronics. Companies from all over the world try and sell their products. Other countries, by contrast, may have a sheltered market and the competition is generally among fewer companies who then set a higher price.

The US public at large does not understand this aspect of dumping. Most consider it nasty and predatory. Looking at it one way, the teenager in Tokyo is subsidizing the teenager in Manhattan. If the Manhattan buyer understood this fact of international business they would probably say, 'if this is dumping, then dump more products on me at a low price'. Unfortunately, things are not so simple or neat. The US consumer's gain is offset by the loss of jobs, in perhaps Ohio or Michigan, if not in Manhattan itself.

Transfer pricing in exporting

The observant reader may have found something curious going on in Table 4. Notice that the customs duty is not constant. It varies depending on the FOB price. Who sets the FOB price? The exporting company, of course. The customs official will look at the FOB figure typed on the manufacturer's invoice and compute the duty owed, at 50 per cent of the FOB figure. In quote 1, it would amount to 0.50(9) = $14.50. If quote 4 were used instead, the duty would be 0.50(38) = $19.00. This is a huge variation.

Let us change our story a little, just to make a point. Instead of an independent US exporter and an independent foreign importer at 'arm's-length' to each other, let us consider:

1 scenario A, where the importer and exporter collude with each other;
2 scenario B, where the US company exports to its own sales office abroad – the importer and exporter are one company.

In the above two scenarios, there is a strong temptation to declare a lower FOB price on the invoice, in order to pay less duty. Remember that the landed cost abroad is a wholesale price. The ultimate retail customer would pay the same price, regardless. The gain from a lower customs duty would be pocketed by the company in scenario B or shared between the importer and exporter in scenario A.

This can be illegal! If the customs authorities can prove an intent to defraud by 'under-invoicing', that is, deliberately putting a lower price on the invoice, that is clearly illegal. Regrettably, this is a widespread practice, especially in some developing nations. There are countries whose total figure as reported in International Monetary Fund (IMF) statistics is suspect.

Alas, things are not always so clear-cut. Suppose the foreign market for the video games was very competitive and our company set a low FOB price for that reason, merely to penetrate the market. If customs authorities investigated, they would find the company selling the game for $22 in the USA, but at a lower price in their country. They may accuse the company of under-invoicing and cheating, even although the FOB price was not set low in order to cheat. International company executives have to be vigilant about the possibility that even although their motives are honest, their company could be accused of under-invoicing, dumping and price discrimination.

The evolution from exporting to foreign direct investment

In our example, the US factory has a maximum production capacity of 250,000 video games. With US sales of 200,000 units, the most that can be produced for exports is 50,000. Although the foreign demand for this particular video game is only 10,000 units at present, in time it could be as great as the US sales of 200,000 units. Another factory will be needed to serve mature foreign demand. If so, it may as well be established there. This will avoid the cost of freight and the tariff. For these reasons many companies decide to make a foreign direct investment near their foreign customers, despite the uncertainties of operating in a strange environment. Thus exporting may evolve, over time, to a foreign direct investment strategy.

3 Foreign direct investment

As a mode of international business, direct investment made by US firms abroad is far more important than exports from US plants or the licensing of technology and intangible assets. For example, in 1990, the sales made by the foreign affiliates of US-based multinationals were worth approximately $1,400 billion. By contrast, US exports totalled only about $400 billion (United Nations 1992; US Department of Commerce 1993).

Market-seeking investments

The reasons for investing abroad and the advantages which accrue to a multinational firm are shown in Table 5. By far the most common motivation for foreign investment is to exploit an untapped potential market. Through its past research, product development and advertising expenditures, the firm may possess a distinctive technology, product and brand equity which local companies in the country may not have. US and Japanese computer companies' international dominance is based on proprietary high technology. But there are humbler products than computers that have led their firms to develop untapped foreign markets. Kellogg's corn flakes and

Table 5 Strategy motivations for investing abroad

Market driven investment

- to develop a ripe or untapped foreign market based on differentiated product or proprietary firm technology
- Oliogopolistic or defensive counter-moves
- Overcoming trade barriers

Natural resource-seeking investment

- multinational company efficiency in:
- exploration
- extraction
- refining
- global distribution

Global rationalization and cost reduction

- access to cheapest sources of inputs and resources
- vertically-integrated investments
- production-sharing
- economies of global scale

Risk diversification

- taking advantage of non-synchronous business cycles
- reduction in foreign exchange risk
- reduction in total political risk exposure

other breakfast cereals are not high technology products, but the company has made several investments in Europe, Japan, Australia, South Africa and some developing countries. Dietary habits among the middle and upper classes in those countries were changing, or could be changed by advertising. Attractively packaged cereal boxes and the internationally recognized Kellogg brand name meant that buyers were enjoying not just the cereal but also identifying themselves with new ideas.

Natural resource investments

In natural resource investments, global firms are most sensitive to criticism that they are exploiting the country's natural 'patrimony'. However, large multinational firms often offer proprietary expertise in all stages from exploration to extraction to distribution. These advantages cannot be easily replicated by local companies in one nation.

An example of the global network advantage that the major oil companies possess is found in their quantitative production scheduling models. Crude oil, being an organic substance, is found in an astonishing variety of specific gravities, hydrocarbon mixes, impurities, etc. No two wells produce the same crude. Refineries have different capabilities. Some can handle light crudes, others heavy. Some can tolerate a sulphur content, others not, and so on. Furthermore, within each refinery, the company can take the same crude oil and decide what kind of refined petroleum product it needs, depending on market demand, price and inventory. In some cases, they may want more aviation fuel, or heating oil or kerosene. The operating cost, scale and capacities of refineries vary, of course. The final set of variables relate to transport and tariff costs. They arise from the location of the wells in n countries, with oil tankers going to p refineries, from which the finished products are shipped to m markets. Additionally, the price paid by the company for the crude, and the price it gets for each refined product vary over time and have a bearing on the optimal plant allocation decision. This makes for a gigantic, global optimization problem.

The problem is insoluble in its detailed form, even using the best analysts and computers. But algorithms exist inside the large companies, and are used. The fact that the major oil companies have this flexibility to route their crude from many sources to refineries worldwide gives them a considerable cost advantage over purely national or smaller oil firms. On some occasions a global oil company may have scores of vessels in mid-ocean which can be redirected to different ports, as prices, inventories and demand change in different markets. This global network advantage cannot be replicated by one-nation firms.

Global rationalization

In fact, the oil companies are using some of the concepts listed in Table 5 under global rationalization and cost reduction. Compared to purely national firms, the global firm has access to the cheapest sources, not just for resources like oil, but also for capital and personnel (see HUMAN RESOURCE MANAGEMENT, INTERNATIONAL). There is widespread borrowing by companies in international financial markets. (Even a domestic company can do the same, but it is less likely to do so, and its information is likely to be poorer.) Some international hotel chains make it a point to recruit in nations like Egypt or India, where skilled, French- and English-speaking managers and staff are available at modest salaries. Immigration laws do not easily allow foreign personnel to enter other nations to work. However, several nations do allow such skilled workers, especially when there is a labour shortage in their countries. Global firms are constantly asking governments to permit the entry of specialist managerial and technical personnel. Regional integration, such as the EU, necessarily involves the relaxation of barriers to expatriate employment.

The concepts of vertical integration, 'production rationalization' and scale economies are separate, but intertwined in many global operations. If an automobile company designs a car for sale in many countries, it need not then produce all the components in each market. By combining duplicative facilities – for example, by producing the transmission/axle sub-assembly in only three locations instead of ten, the company gains in two ways. First, there is a saving in moving production to the lower cost global locations and eliminating the more expensive locations. Second, there is an additional cost saving because the scale of operation in the remaining locations is now larger. The plants are vertically integrated with the assembly operations and the markets. However, this means that the company must now undertake a far larger volume of shipments of components and sub-assemblies across national borders. This increases transport cost and risk since the plants are now more dependent on each other. If something went wrong in the transmission plant, it would affect assembly in many countries. However, such risks and the extra movement costs must be outweighed by the overall cost savings in the automobile industry which is moving towards a greater degree of global integration.

Risk-reducing investments

There are obvious political and foreign exchange risks in making direct investments abroad. How can an investment *reduce* the company's risk? One method is to channel investment into product areas and countries where the business cycle is 'out-of-phase' with the company's existing operations – the principle underlying diversification, in short. While Europe may still be in a recession, North America may be in an expansionary stage.

The concept is also applicable in currencies. For several years, the deutschmark and Swiss franc have appreciated against the Italian lira or Greek drachma. If a company believes this trend will continue, then it should try and locate its European operations in both sets of countries, since the net exposure in their cash flows and accounts can be greatly reduced by carefully structuring their liabilities and assets in the two currencies. This is not to say that investments are made purely for risk-reduction reasons, but these could be important secondary considerations.

When it comes to reducing so-called 'political' risk, Honda, Toyota and other Japanese companies provide a good illustration (see

MANAGEMENT IN JAPAN). Giving an industry protection by imposing quotas or tariffs has economic consequences, but it is essentially a political act. After many years there still remains an uncertainty as to the policy of the USA on importing cars from Japan versus curtailing that import, or imposing a 'local-value-added' requirement which would mandate some local production. Honda and Toyota hedge their bets by having assembly operations in the USA as well as importing. They are less vulnerable to future shifts in US policy compared to other firms which do not yet have this dual source capability. This also gives them the flexibility to switch output from one side of the Pacific to another as the yen goes up or down against the dollar. With ships specially designed to bulk carry cars, the cost of shipping an automobile across the Pacific is no higher than sending a car from Detroit to California.

4 Licensing

The third 'classic' foreign market strategy is licensing to an independent local firm in the other country. Instead of undertaking to manufacture or sell on its own, it transfers that capability to another firm which pays it lump sum fees and royalties. Usually the licensee has exclusive rights to their market for the duration of the agreement.

How does licensing compare with the other two international strategy options? In choosing any option, the manager must balance its advantages and drawbacks *vis-à-vis* the alternatives. This balance is described in Table 6.

Of the strategy alternatives, licensing has unquestionably the highest return on incremental investment (ROI), if we consider the research and development (R&D) costs of a particular product as 'sunk' or already expended. Then the incremental costs of negotiating an agreement, transferring blueprints and specifications, and training the licensee's personnel can be very small – in the region of

Table 6 Licensing compared with other strategies

Advantages	Drawbacks
• Very high ROI (if R&D costs neglected)	• Often lower NPV compared with other strategies
• No new capital investment	• Royalties alone may be a poor income source (unless other income types included in agreement)
• Low negotiation/implementation costs	• Agreements may have a limited life (unless renewed)
• Most income goes directly to profits	• Lack of control over licensee's quality may hurt licensor's reputation
• Low cyclical fluctutation in income (compared to dividends)	• Licensee can become a competitor after agreement expires, or even before
• Very low political risk	
• Could have lower tax rate to licensor if licensing income treated as return on capital	
• Company can license in many worthwhile markets closed to exports or investment	
• Quicker way to enter foreign market compared to investment	
• Licensee may be used as a guinea pig to test market	
• Return of technical information from licensee	

a few hundred thousand dollars at the most – compared with the millions needed for a capital investment in factories, buildings and personnel. This investment and its risks are borne by the licensee. Once the agreement is signed and the licensee trained, subsequent licensing income is pure profit to the licensor. One study shows that over the life of international agreements, more than 90 per cent of licensing income earned by US companies goes directly to the 'bottom line' – that is to say, costs of executing the agreement average well below 10 per cent of revenues, a fabulous ROI indeed. Moreover, if the product is patented and foreign markets can be segmented by strong patents in each nation, or hard to ship from one country to another, in theory the company could sign separate agreements in each worthwhile foreign market, thus increasing total global licensing income.

While ROI from licensing is very high, net present value (NPV) is usually lower compared with the other strategies of direct investment or exporting. After all, companies are not in the business of maximizing ROI, but NPV. This is perhaps the main drawback to licensing – inadequate *total* income from royalties. By tradition, if not theory, most royalty rates are less than 8 or 10 per cent of the licensee's sales, and the average is perhaps 4 per cent. Considering how little was spent to implement the agreement and transfer the technology this is attractive, but if the company invested in the foreign nation and sold the product itself, the total income could be much higher (except in mature or very competitive industries where return on capital investment is low already).

When comparing licensing with other alternatives, one cannot overlook the fact that agreements have a limited life, ranging from three to twelve years typically, although they are frequently renewed because the licensee still depends on, and benefits from, the link. By contrast an investment has a theoretically unlimited life, and the company at least hopes that it will continue to earn dividends on its foreign investment indefinitely.

Another possible advantage accruing to licensing is that whereas dividends declared by foreign direct investment affiliates are subject to tax in the parent nation at the regular corporate income tax rate, royalty income may attract a lower, capital returns rate of tax. Although licensing (to independent foreign parties) runs a distant third as an overseas strategy in the minds of many executives, in recent years its use has been growing somewhat. Of course, for smaller companies, for many multinational firms based outside the USA and for mature industries, licensing can be an important global strategy.

Another factor that powerfully affects any strategy choice is the relative risk of the two options. The lower the risk, the lower the discount rate, and the higher the net present value. Licensing has inherently lower risks compared to a company's own investment because:

1   Royalties are usually a percentage of sales. Sales fluctuate over a business cycle or recession much less than dividends, which are declared out of profits, if any. In a bad year there may be no dividends, however, a licensee still pays the royalty.
2   There is no 'political' risk in licensing. Agreements are almost always honoured by all governments.
3   The licensee is the guinea pig, making the investment and testing the waters of the marketplace. (There have been instances where a successful licensee has been brushed aside by a more powerful licensor, once the agreement has expired.)

On the other hand, licensees may become so successful and entrenched that they may become competitors with the original licensor not only in that country, but other countries as well. In the worst scenario the foreign licensee comes back to compete in the licensor's home market. Several Japanese licensees of US firms have done exactly that. A classic example involves RCA which, in the 1970s, licensed colour television technology to Japanese companies, only to find them competing with RCA in the US market itself. However, in the majority of cases, the licensee remains, to some degree, technologically and organizationally inferior, and sometimes dependent on the licensor for materials or trademarks. In most cases the licensee is bound under the purview of the agreement to the assigned territory. On average, executives today do not show an excessive concern with the issue of licensee competitiveness in third markets. In specific industries, however, such as semiconductors, biosciences and some chemical processes, the consideration is so dominant as to preclude licensing to non-affiliated firms.

In an increasingly risky environment for direct investment, firms can no longer afford a policy which ignores the option of licensing. That licensing in many selected situations is not only very profitable, but superior in a net risk-adjusted comparison with alternatives, is an idea gaining ground. Some of the largest companies already have far more global licensees than subsidiaries; and cases exist where the more stable licensing income from royalties related to licensee sales has helped to smooth out the greater volatility of dividend income, since profits are, by definition, more variable than output volume.

5 Comparing the three classic strategy options

Table 7 and Figure 2 list the principal factors affecting the choice of strategy. Although such generalizations cannot possibly apply to all companies or all countries, however, these concepts are useful for a manager to consider when choosing an appropriate strategy for their firm.

Direct investment in majority controlled or fully-owned investment generally yields the highest total net returns despite the high investment of capital and personnel. This is because the firm internalizes its advantages in technology, organizational learning, intangible proprietary assets such as patents or trademarks, and an international scope of operation. These give it control of strategy, as opposed to sharing decisions with other parties who may later become competitors. However, the risks are also greatest in such a strategy. Besides ordinary commercial risk of business failure, there is political risk in that the host nation government policies may go against the interests of foreign investors.

Exporting can be highly profitable at very low risk, but this is only true if the company uses existing plants' slack capacity for exports. Assuming domestic or existing sales cover fixed costs, the incremental contribution of exports, over the variable costs thereof, is substantial. Risks and costs are much higher, however, if a factory is built especially for exports.

Table 7 Factors involved in choosing a strategy

	Majority/fully-owned investment	Exporting	Licensing
Total returns	high	moderate	moderate to low
Financial resource costs	high	low	negligible
Managerial resource costs	high	moderate	small
Control over foreign operation	high	high	low
Ordinary commercial risk	high	low	almost zero
Political risk	high (depends on country)	low	zero
Foreign exchange or convertability risk	high (depends on country	low	lowest
Effective tax rate	high	highest	lower
Threat of creating competition	very low	low	can be high

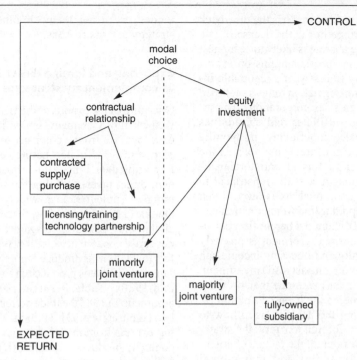

Control versus return mapping of modal choices

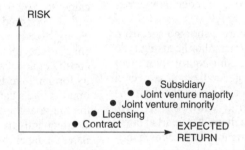

Risk versus return map of alternatives

Figure 2 Levels of control, risk and return
Source: Contractor and Narayanan (1990)

Licensing involves negligible costs of execution compared with the revenues earned from agreements. Over 90 per cent of licensing revenues are pure profit (in an incremental sense, ignoring sunk R&D costs). However, the absolute profit from licensing is generally, although not necessarily, smaller than profit which could be earned from direct investment or export sales, but then the risks are generally far lower also. There is little investment of financial or managerial resources, and commercial risk is borne by the licensee. Assuming that the global market is segmented by patents or tariffs, so that each country is a separate territory, then a licensing agreement can be signed in every viable market. This would make global revenue from licensing worthwhile. By comparison, even the largest of companies find it impossible to make an investment in each worthwhile foreign market.

In selected cases, licensing has the drawback of creating a competitor in the licensee.

The effective tax rate is likely to be highest in exporting since profit margins on export sales go directly to that year's reportable income in the exporting nation (unless sheltered through a foreign sales corporation). The income of foreign affiliates and subsidiaries may be reinvested indefinitely, postponing the parent nation tax bite, if not taxes in the country of operation. It is not until foreign affiliates' dividends are actually repatriated to the parent that additional tax is owed. Even then, the taxes paid to the foreign nation can be used as a credit against parent firm tax liability. If a licensing agreement is properly structured, royalty and licensing income can be treated as a return on past R&D investment. This is taxed at a far lower rate than ordinary corporate income, in the licensor's nation.

Before making the decision as to how to earn income in a foreign territory, the strategist needs to consider all the factors of potential income, financial and managerial resource cost, commercial, political and foreign exchange risk, the effective tax rate and the potential for creating or reducing international competition.

In conclusion, Figure 2 shows a spectrum of choices, from contractual or licensing type arrangements to increasing equity investment at the other end. As a generalization, expected return and control increase as the firm increases its equity strike. However, the risk also increases. For each product/market combination, the strategist must decide which modal choice provides the optimum combination of return, control and risk in the foreign market.

6 Combining international strategies

So far in this entry we have examined how contractual methods such as licensing versus exporting or direct investment in the foreign market may be looked upon as substitute methods for serving the foreign customer. We next look at what some mature global companies are actually doing, which is combining the benefits of the foreign market entry modes, by using them simultaneously for strategy and tax reasons.

Exporting and foreign direct investment as complementary strategies

One-third of the exports of the US economy, as well as those of many major industrialized countries, are from a company to its own foreign equity affiliates acting as importers. Exporting then, is not a pure substitute for foreign direct investment, but the two are intermingled strategies. In a widely-read article, Ohmae (1987) tried to show that the trade deficit that the USA suffered against Japan should not cause concern because it was offset by the fact that US firms produced more in Japan than Japanese affiliates produced in the USA in the mid-1980s. Table 8 summarizes Ohmae's argument. In 1984 the trade deficit between the two countries was $31.2 billion. However adding exports from the USA to Japan (A) to US company production in Japan (B), the total of $69.5 billion was almost exactly equal to exports from Japan to the USA (C), plus Japanese company production in the US (D) which came to $69.6 billion. Thus, what Ohmae called US 'product presence' in Japan, was almost exactly equal to Japanese 'product presence' in the USA. Ohmae's point is correct in considerable measure, in that local production by foreign investment affiliates substitutes for imports into a nation. However, he overlooked the fact that the two are also complementary. Consequently there is a lot of double counting. Sales in Japan by US affiliates have components imported from their US parents. Consequently part of A is double counted in B. Similarly, part of the value of Japanese company production in the USA (D), is accounted for by part of C, which is the exports from Japan to the USA. To compound the statistical spaghetti-mix, on the output side, part of B shows up in C. That is to say, some US company production in Japan is exported back to the USA, just as Japanese affiliates may export part of their production in the USA (D), back to Japan (A).

Because of the complementary way in which global companies use exports and direct investment simultaneously, Ohmae's

Table 8 'Lies, damn lies & statistics': trade and investment balances

1984   1984

• Exports from USA to Japan – Exports from Japan to USA = Trade DEFICIT

      25.6   56.8   = 31.2

• The consumer's perspective (Kenichi Ohmae)

The Japanese market for US items   *vs*   The US Market for Japanese items

$$\left(\begin{array}{c} \text{Exports from} \\ \text{USA to Japan} \end{array} + \begin{array}{c} \text{US company} \\ \text{production in} \\ \text{Japan} \end{array} \right) vs \left(\begin{array}{c} \text{Exports from} \\ \text{Japan to USA} \end{array} + \begin{array}{c} \text{Japanese} \\ \text{company} \\ \text{production in} \\ \text{USA} \end{array} \right)$$

	A		B	*vs*		C		D
1984	(25.6	+	43.9)			(56.8	+	12.8)

         69.5   *vs*   69.6

Comments

1   Job balance: [43.9 + 56.8] vs [25.6 + 12.8]

2   *Some double counting*

    (i)   Some sales in Japan by US affiliates have inputs from US exports, that is, some value added in B with A inputs

    (ii)   Similarly, some value added in D from C inputs

    (iii)   Part of B shows up in C , that is, Japanese production of US affiliates exported to the USA

    (iv)   Part of D is similarly exported from USA to Japan and shows up in A

• The picture in 1989: Ohmae's balance is upset

$$\left(\begin{array}{c} \text{Exports from} + \\ \text{USA to Japan} \end{array} \begin{array}{c} \text{US company} \\ \text{production in} \\ \text{Japan} \end{array} \right) vs \left(\begin{array}{c} \text{Exports from} + \\ \text{Japan to USA} \end{array} \begin{array}{c} \text{Japanese} \\ \text{company} \\ \text{production in} \\ \text{USA} \end{array} \right)$$

	A		B	<<		C		D
1989	(49	+	55)			(94	+	270)

**   Ohmae suggests one could add to this side of the ledger the $60 billion of items produced in Japan under license from US firms but this is stretching too far since the Japanese firms make products which substitute for and compete with US firm production.

Source: adapted from Ohmae (1987)

statistics did not give the complete picture even for the mid-1980s. Since then, there has been a surge in both Japanese direct investment in the USA as well as in exports from Japan to the USA, while US-based firms' investments and exports to Japan grew at only a respectable rate. Consequently, even using Ohmae's accounting, the balance was upset as shown at the bottom of Table 8.

Finally, even the labels 'US firm' or 'Japanese firm' will become inaccurate in the future. A large part of the global sales of companies like Honda already take place in the US market, with over 60 per cent value-added locally for some models. A significant part of Honda's R&D and design operations are in the USA. In the 1990s, the company is exporting cars back to Japan, some components in the cars having made a ten thousand mile round trip back to Japan, while many of the other parts are US or Mexican. Already, a small fraction of the shares of many Japanese companies are owned by US and European portfolio investors, a fraction that will grow in the future.

Direct investment and licensing in combination

Most governments allow licensing fees and royalties to be considered a deductible expense, even when a fully-owned subsidiary is paying its own parent. Governments offer this tax concession (illustrated in Table 9) in order to induce the transfer of technology and intellectual property to their countries. From the point of view of foreign investors, many of them would have transferred the expertise and intellectual property to their majority equity affiliates anyway, even without this concession, but governments have no way of distinguishing those that would have transferred the technology without the tax incentive, from companies that would not have done so. Hence the concession is offered to all. As illustrated in Table 9 the remittance of royalty to the foreign (Japanese) parent escapes US corporate income tax altogether. The total tax liability is lowered. Therefore, there is a temptation to channel more of the remittance via the royalty channel, even if that means less is remitted under the 'profit after local tax' category, because the total of the two cash flow channels is higher than after-tax profits alone. Some companies may indeed divert 'too much' of their intra-corporate funds via the royalty and intellectual property payments categories in order to minimize tax liability in a nation. Then tax authorities' audits ask the company to justify the intra-corporate charge; but who is to say whether a 10 per cent royalty is unreasonable, or where a 5 per cent royalty is reasonable? That depends on the value of the technology, the market, the R&D cost and several complicated factors.

Table 9 Tax effect on intra-firm royalty payment

	$		$
• Sales by Japanese subsidiary in USA	100	• • Sales by Japanese subsidiary in USA	100
• Total costs (excluding royalties)	700	• • Royalty (at 5% on sales)	50
• Profit before tax	300	• • Total costs (including royalties)	700
• US tax (at 30%)	90	• • Profit before tax	250
• Profit after tax	210	• • US tax (at 30%)	75
		• • Profit after US tax	175
		• • Royalty remittance to Japanese parent	50
		• • Total remittance to parent	225

Table 10 What if the above affiliate was a joint venture?

Scenario 1: shareholding	Scenario 2: shareholding	Scenario 3: shareholding

60%	40%	60%	40%	52%	48%
Japanese	US	Japanese	US	Japanese	US
(No license)		(With license)		(With license)	

- Profit after tax

- Profit after tax

- Profit after tax

Scenario 1:
210
(60%) 126 — Remittance to Japanese parent
(40%) 84 — For US partner

Scenario 2:
175
(60%) 50 + 105
(40%) 70 — For US partner
155 — Remittance to Japanese parent

Scenario 3:
175
(52%) 50 + 91
(48%) 84 — For US partner
141 — Remittance to Japanese parent

What is an appropriate charge for global overheads levied against a subsidiary in another nation? What fee should a parent charge an affiliate for introducing a brand into the country? These remain the burning issues of our day.

The fact remains however, that as a consequence of the deductibility of such intracorporate payments, two-thirds to three-quarters of the royalty and licensing fees remitted across national borders are between foreign majority affiliates and parents. Only a third or less are between unrelated or quasi-arm's-length licensors and licensees.

Table 10 indicates the effects of a licensing agreement cum joint venture. This is a very common arrangement. Let us suppose that the joint venture has 60 per cent of shares held by a Japanese partner and 40 per cent held by a US partner. Distribution of the $210 after-tax profit proportional to the shareholding would earn $126 for the Japanese and $84 for the US partner in scenario 1. With the introduction of 5 per cent royalties payable to the Japanese partner by the joint venture corporation in scenario 2, the Japanese partner's take (legally) jumps to $155. The US partner's after-tax distribution declines somewhat to $70. As a

negotiating demand therefore, the US partner may demand an increased 48 per cent shareholding in scenario 3 in order to accommodate the Japanese partner's desire for a licensing agreement. The 48 per cent shareholding of the US partner restores their share to $84 in scenario 3, while still leaving the Japanese partner better off than in scenario 1 with a total take of $141.

Why companies should consider combining strategies for global integration

It has been shown in this entry that licensing, foreign direct investment and exporting are used in many cases as substitute methods for serving foreign markets. But if the company's intention is to have an integrated global strategy and make a foreign equity investment, then it should consider combining the methods to achieve higher income and control and to reduce risk. Table 11 summarizes the advantages.

Agreement-defined fees and royalties have the tax advantage described above, as well as tax advantages in the home country over receipts of foreign affiliate dividends. A critical

Table 11

Lump sum fees and royalties	Dividends/equity sake	Margins on components or product traded with affiliate or licensee
• Lump sum fee provides immediate cash return	• Direct share in future success and profits of affiliate	• Margins can be very high on proprietary, high technology, or branded
• Royalties earned even if affiliate/licensee's profits are zero	• More valuable as years pass than fixed royalties	• Less affected by cyclical fluctutations as dividends are
• Licensing income is a distribution before local tax in a foreign nation	• No expiration	• Profit margin can be earned outside affiliate/licensee country jurisdiction that is, no convertibility risk; no local taxes
• Possible lower tax in home nation		
• More easily convertible than dividends		
• All royalties kept by licensor (dividends may have to be shared in a joint venture)		

factor in joint ventures is that while profits are shared, one of the partners, as licensor, gets *all* of the royalties and fees. Lump sum fees paid on signing the agreement provide immediate and certain returns, in contrast with distant and uncertain dividends. Royalties are payable even if the venture's profits are zero. Moreover, a royalty linked to sales is axiomatically more stable over the business cycle than dividends. In recessions, many firms have found that royalties come in at almost the normal level, even when profits on their equity investment have disappeared.

On the other hand there is no denying the fact that an equity stake is a direct claim on the future success and profits of a venture, and this is likely to be far more valuable, in the long run, than royalties which are usually capped at a fixed percentage and eventually expire. (Licensing agreements should be continued indefinitely to take advantage of legal tax concessions. However, in the case of a joint venture, the local partners may be unwilling to renew the joint venture's licensing

agreement with the international company, because it reduces their share of dividends.)

Finally, there are significant advantages in setting up an intra-corporate trading relationship for the purchase of components or sale of finished products between the global firm and its affiliates in each nation. There are, of course, strategic imperatives in many businesses for this type of global integration. In addition, there are other advantages. Margins on the supply of components, being linked to production, are a more stable profit flow to a global firm, compared to volatile dividends. Moreover, mark-ups can be high on proprietary, high-technology or branded items, and these mark-ups are earned outside the tax jurisdiction of the country. (There is often a very thin line between the above strategy prescription and conscious tax evasion by transfer pricing abuses. The latter is illegal and immoral).

Figure 3 provides a simple example of transfer pricing. An affiliate A supplies 1,000 widgets per year to affiliate B, initially at $1 each, in scenario 1. The tax rate in A is 30 per

S C E N A R I O 1	1,000 widgets per year at $1 each		

A ← $1,000 payment → B

S C E N A R I O 1			
(tax rate: 30%)		(tax rate: 50%)		total profit
pretax profit	10,000	pretax profit	4,000	after taxes
tax (30%)	3,000	tax (50%)	2,000	7,000 + 2,000
aftertax profit	7,000	aftertax profit	2,000	= 9,000

S C E N A R I O 2	1,000 widgets per year at $1.50 each		

A ← $1,500 payment → B

(tax rate: 30%)		(tax rate: 50%)		total profit
pretax profit	10,500	pretax profit	3,500	after taxes
tax (30%)	3,150	tax (50%)	1,750	7,350 + 1,750
aftertax profit	7,350	aftertax profit	1,750	= 9,100

Figure 3

cent, and in country B it is 50 per cent, with pre-tax profit levels in each affiliate as shown in Figure 3. There is therefore an obvious temptation to declare less profit in the high-tax location B, and to declare more profit in the lower-tax country A. This is done in scenario 2 by raising the unit transfer price to, say, $1.50 per widget. In scenario 2 (compared with scenario 1) after-tax profits in B decline less than the amount by which after-tax profits in A increase. Consequently the global total, after-tax profit of the global company as a whole increases from $9,000 in scenario 1, to $9,100 in scenario 2.

However, this results in paying $250 less tax to country B, which is illegal if the intent was to evade taxes. In the long run, no company or individual can survive or prosper on such a basis without being discovered. An honest company will attempt to follow 'arm's-length pricing', based on an estimation of what the transfer price would be if companies A and B were independent, arm's-length firms. Alas, things are not always so clear-cut, since there are no 'arm's--length equivalents' for much of the intra-corporate trade within global firms which is based on products and services which are highly differentiated, partially assembled or even unique. In many cases there is no similar item on the market. Consider another scenario. What if affiliate A has undertaken costly R&D to develop a new model,

and for that legitimate reason wishes to raise the transfer price to $1.50 per unit? This illustrates how, even with honest motives, a company can be accused of cheating.

This form of transfer pricing manipulation is not likely to be widespread. Notice how, in Figure 3, even with a fairly wide differential in tax rates between the nations, and although the unit transfer price was raised by as much as 50 per cent, the total after-tax profit of the global firm increased by a measly $100 or 1.1 per cent. With converging tax rates in the major Organization for Economic Cooperation and Development nations the incentive is even less. Far more important is the fact that the intra-corporate trade was set up between affiliates A and B in the first place. Suppose that in years past B was sourcing this widget locally. Now A supplies B, in scenario 1. That means that as much as $1,000 is being transferred to a lower tax jurisdiction – and perfectly legally. Unit price manipulation therefore is of far less consequence than the fact that after-tax global rationalization calls for (legally) setting up internal intra-corporate trade in components and finished products.

7 Conclusion

For many companies beginning their international expansion into a foreign market, the strategy options include exporting, foreign direct investment and contractual arrangements (of which the most notable is the licensing of expertise and intellectual property to a firm in the foreign market). This entry discussed the pros and cons of each, and enumerated several criteria whereby a firm may choose between the foreign market entry methods. The choice of method will depend on the firm, the product and the foreign market in question. There is no one optimum. Some of the important criteria influencing the choice include expected returns, intended duration of the strategy and product cycle, required degree of managerial control, the risk appetite of the company, availability of financial and managerial resources, applicable tax rules, political and foreign exchange risk, and the risk of future competition from former licensees and strategic allies.

In the second part of this entry it was shown that as firms mature, and integrate globally, they will not treat foreign market entry methods as merely separate options, but consider combining these methods, and have a trading and a licensing relationship with their affiliates and equity partners abroad. Exports, licensing and foreign direct investment, in this view, are alternate channels for income extraction, as much as they are market-serving strategies. Moreover, this combined approach lowers volatility and risk, increases control and strengthens ties with partners (if any) in the other nation. With increased globalization of business this trend will become even more important in the future.

FAROK J CONTRACTOR
RUTGERS UNIVERSITY

Further reading

(References cited in the text marked *)

Andersen, E. and Gatignon, H. (1986) 'Modes of foreign entry: a transaction cost analysis and propositions', *Journal of International Business Studies* Fall: 1–26. (An analysis of how transaction costs affect the market entry choice.)

Contractor, F.J. (1986) *Licensing In International Strategy: A Guide for Planning and Negotiations*, Westport, CT: Quorum Books. (A comprehensive volume on the role of licensing in the international strategies of companies. The book contains considerable empirical data drawn from firms directly, as well as from secondary sources. Several cases illustrate what companies are doing.)

Contractor, F.J. (1990) 'Ownership patterns of US joint ventures abroad and the liberalization of foreign government regulations in the 1980s: evidence from the benchmark surveys', *Journal of International Business Studies* (1): 55–74. (An empirical analysis of the variation across countries in equity ownership by US companies in foreign joint ventures. The paper also traces the liberalization in foreign investment rules in forty-six nations.)

* Contractor, F.J. and Narayanan, V. (1990) 'Technology development in the multinational firm: a framework for planning and strategy',*R&D Management* 20 (4). (Article describing how new technology can be integrated into multinational strategy.)

DiLullo, A. and Whichard, O. (1991) 'US international sales and purchases of services', *Survey of Current Business* (September): 66–79. (International transactions by US companies in the services sector are analysed.)

Gomes-Casseres, B. (1989) 'Ownership structures of foreign subsidiaries: theory and evidence', *Journal of Economic Behavior and Organization* 11: 1–25. (This paper traces the percentage equity of foreign affiliates held by parent firms in global companies. Ownership and strategic control are contrasted.)

Hill, C., Hwang, P. and Kim, W.-C. (1990) 'An eclectic theory of the choice of international entry mode', *Strategic Management Journal* 11: 117–28. (An analysis of the choice between licensing, joint ventures and wholly-owned subsidiaries as a function of strategy factors.)

Kim, W.-C. and Hwang, P. (1992) 'Global strategy and multinationals' entry mode choice', *Journal of International Business Studies* (1): 29–53. (An empirical analysis of the choice between licensing, joint ventures and wholly-owned subsidiaries as a function of factors such as industry concentration, transnational synergies, country risk, competition and firm-specific know-how.)

Lowe, J. and Mataloni, R. (1991) 'US direct investment abroad: 1989 benchmark survey results', *Survey of Current Business* October: 29–55. (A summary of results from the monumental survey of 2,300 US-based multinationals.)

* Ohmae, K. (1987) 'Companies without countries', *The McKinsey Quarterly* Autumn: 49–63. (The

author questions conventional wisdom about global companies.)

Reich, R. (1990) 'Who is us?', *Harvard Business Review* (January–February): 53–64. (The author describes how the affiliation of companies with their national or home base is becoming weaker.)

UNCTAD (1993) *World Investment Report 1993: Transnational Corporations and Integrated International Production*, New York: United Nations. (The 1993 annual report issued by the United Nations Conference on Trade and Development focuses on integration of economic activity across national borders.)

* United Nations (1992) *World Investment Report 1992*, New York: United Nations. (Digest of information gleaned from UN sources.)

* US Department of Commerce (1993) *US Direct Investment Abroad: 1989 Benchmark Survey Final Results*, Washington, DC: US Government Printing Office. (Official statistics from US government sources.)

See also: EXPORTING; FOREIGN EXCHANGE RISK, MANAGEMENT OF; GLOBAL STRATEGIC ALLIANCES; GLOBALIZATION; HUMAN RESOURCE MANAGEMENT, INTERNATIONAL; INTERNATIONAL BUSINESS, FUTURE TRENDS; INTERNATIONAL MARKETING; INTERNATIONAL TRADE AND FOREIGN DIRECT INVESTMENT; MANAGEMENT IN JAPAN; NON-TARIFF BARRIERS; POLITICAL RISK

Related topics in the IEBM: BUSINESS STRATEGY, JAPANESE; GENERAL AGREEMENT ON TARIFFS AND TRADE; HUMAN RESOURCE FLOWS; INTELLECTUAL PROPERTY; MANAGEMENT IN NORTH AMERICA; MARKETING STRATEGY

Global strategic alliances

Overview

International alliances are cooperative arrangements formed by organizations from two or more countries. An international alliance is considered strategic when it involves the allocation of the resources that the general manager of the firm deems important to the organization's future success.

An international alliance may be established as a greenfield operation, or may be the result of several companies deciding to combine existing resources. The purpose of most international strategic alliances is to allow partners to pool resources and coordinate their efforts to achieve results that neither could obtain acting alone.

In recent years international strategic alliances have become increasingly popular. They have moved from being a way to enter foreign markets of peripheral interest, or of gaining some returns from peripheral technologies, to become a part of the mainstream of corporate activity. Major firms from all over the world are using global strategic alliances as a key element of their corporate strategies. Even firms such as IBM that have traditionally operated independently around

Table 1 A typology of international industrial alliance modes

Form of cooperation	Equity or non-equity	Length of agreement	Transfer of resources and rights
Joint ventures	Equity	Unlimited	Whole range?
Foreign minority holdings	Equity	Unlimited	Whole range?
'Fade-out' agreements	Equity	Limited	Whole range? (for limited period)
Licensing	Non-equity	Limited by contract	Limited range
Franchising	Non-equity	Limited by contract	Limited + support
Management contracts	Non-equity	Limited by contract	Limited
Technical training	Non-equity	Limited	Small
Turnkey ventures	Non-equity	Limited	Limited in time
Contractual joint ventures	Non-equity	Limited	Specified by contract
International subcontracting	Non-equity	Limited	Small
Strategic buyer-supplier coalitions	Non-equity	Limited by contract but long-term	Limited + support

Source: Adapted in part from Buckley and Casson (1985)

the world, are increasingly turning to alliances.

1 Introduction

An infinite number of alliance forms exist. Alliances can vary according to: (1) whether they involve equity investment or not; (2) the length of the agreement, that is, focused project alliances versus major alliances expected to continue indefinitely; and (3) whether a whole range of resources and rights is transferred, or whether only a single function or task is involved. Table 1 provides a typology of the major global strategic alliance modes.

Some organizations use a variety of alliance modes simultaneously and extensively. For example, Toshiba, Japan's oldest and third largest electronics company, has used strategic alliances as part of its strategy to complement innovation and manufacturing skills. In 1993, Toshiba was involved in over twenty alliances with firms such as Apple Computer, IBM, Motorola and Siemens. Similarly, Takuma Yamamoto, Chairman of Fujitsu Ltd, the world's second largest computer company, noted that alliances are the centrepiece of their global strategy. As Figure 1 illustrates, alliances are an integral part of the computer industry.

The rising popularity of alliances has come despite their reputation for being difficult to manage. Failures are common and usually widely publicized. Beijing Jeep, for example, was reportedly losing millions after disputes between its Chinese and US joint venture partners. Only intervention from the highest political levels in both China and the USA was able to get this venture back on track. Even at time of writing, this venture is still not reaching its original target production levels (see MANAGEMENT IN CHINA).

Surveys suggest that as many as half the companies with international joint ventures in high-income countries are dissatisfied with their ventures' performance, and that the dissatisfaction rate for ventures in low income countries is even higher. Why do managers keep creating new joint ventures in the face of such widespread dissatisfaction and the potentially high costs of failure? The reasons are presented in the remainder of this entry, as are some guidelines for global alliance success. We pay particular attention to equity joint ventures because these are the most difficult form of alliance to design and manage.

2 Why do companies create global strategic alliances?

Alliances can be used to achieve one of four basic purposes (see Table 2). These are: (1) to strengthen the firm's existing business; (2) to take the firm's existing products into new markets; (3) to obtain new products which can be sold in the firm's existing markets; and (4) to diversify into a new business.

Companies using alliances for each of these purposes will have different concerns, and will be looking for partners with different characteristics. Firms wanting to strengthen their existing business, for example, will most likely be looking for partners among their current competitors, while those wanting to enter new geographic markets will be looking for overseas firms in related businesses with good local market knowledge. Although often treated as a single category of business activity, global alliances are remarkably diverse, as the following descriptions indicate.

Table 2 Motives for international joint venture formation

New markets	To take existing products to foreign markets	To diversify into a new business
Existing markets	To strengthen the existing business	To bring foreign products to local markets
	Existing products	New products

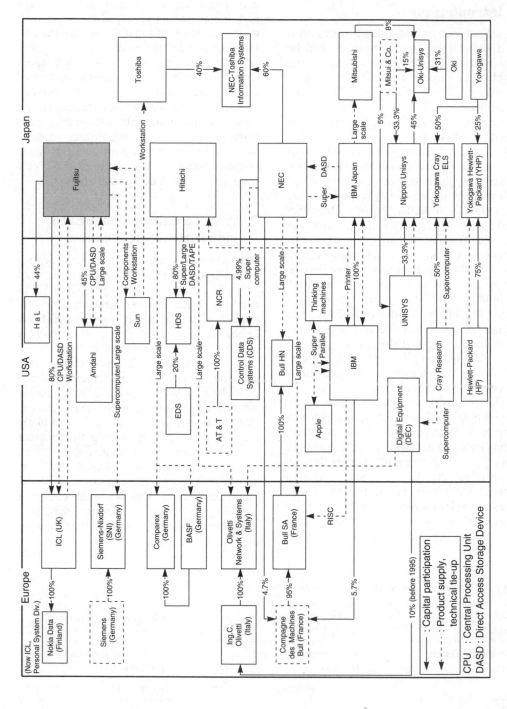

Figure 1 Alliances of world leading computer suppliers

3 Strengthening the existing business

Global alliances are used in a variety of ways by firms wishing to strengthen or protect their existing businesses. Among the most important are those formed to achieve economies of scale, those which allow the firm to acquire needed technology and know-how, and those which reduce the financial risk of major projects. Alliances formed for the latter two reasons may have the added benefit of eliminating a potential competitor from a particular product or market area.

Achieving economies of scale

Small and medium-sized firms often use alliances to attempt to match the economies of scale achieved by their larger competitors. Alliances have been used to give their partners economies of scale in raw material and component supply, research and development, and marketing and distribution. Alliances have also been used as a vehicle for carrying out divisional mergers, which yield economies across the full spectrum of business activity.

A mature world market prompted Ingersoll-Rand and Dresser Industries to merge their pump business in a joint venture called Ingersoll-Dresser Pumps (IDP). Formed in 1992, the global joint venture had sales of almost $900 million, 7,000 employees and factories around the world. Facing excess industry capacity and a need for higher levels of customer service, the venture allowed the companies to reach a scale and scope equal to any other company in the world. In addition to providing critical mass, the joint venture allowed for capacity, technology and sales force consolidation.

Raw material and component supply

In many industries, smaller firms create alliances to obtain raw materials or manufacture components jointly. Automobile assemblers, for instance, frequently have jointly owned engine plants which supply certain low volume engines to different companies. By producing engines for several partners, the plant is able to obtain economies of scale and each company receives engines at a lower cost than it could obtain if it were to produce them itself.

The managers involved in such ventures are quick to point out that these financial savings do not come without a cost. Design changes in jointly produced engines, for example, tend to be slow because all partners have to agree on them. In fact, one joint venture which produced computer printers fell seriously behind the state of the art in printer design because the parents could not agree on the features they wanted in the jointly designed printer. Because all of the venture's output was sold to the parents, the joint venture personnel had no direct contact with end customers and could not resolve the dispute.

Transfer pricing is another headache which arises in joint ventures which supply their parents. A low transfer price on products shipped from the venture to the parents, for instance, means that whichever parent buys the most product obtains the most benefit. Parents taking a higher volume claim that this is fair, as it is their volume which plays an important role in making the joint venture viable. On the other hand, some parents argue for a higher transfer price, which means that the economic benefits are captured in the venture and will flow, most likely via dividends, to the parents in proportion to their shareholdings in the venture. As the shareholdings generally reflect the original asset contributions to the venture and not the volumes taken out every year, this means the parents fare differently under this arrangement. Clearly, the potential for transfer price disputes is significant.

Research and development

Shared research and development efforts are common in Japan and Europe, but have only recently begun to be allowed in the USA, under its relatively strict anti-trust laws. The rationale for such programmes is that participating firms can save both time and money by collaborating, and may, by combining the efforts of the participating companies' scientists, come up with results that would otherwise have been impossible.

The choice facing firms wishing to carry out collaborative research is whether to simply coordinate their efforts and share costs, or to actually set up a jointly owned company. There are hundreds of multi-company research programmes in Europe which are not joint ventures. Typically, scientists from the participating companies agree on the research objectives and the most likely avenues of exploration to achieve those objectives. For example, if there are four promising ways to attack a particular problem, each of four participating companies would be assigned one route and told to pursue it. Meetings would be held perhaps quarterly to share results and approaches taken, and when (hopefully) one route proved to be successful, all firms would be fully informed on the new techniques and technology.

The alternative way to carry out collaborative research is to establish a jointly owned company and provide it with staff, budget and a physical location. For example, in 1984, three European computer firms – ICL, Groupe Bull and Siemens – established a joint research company in Munich known as the European Computer Research Centre (ECRC). This company, funded at a level of approximately $10 million per year, comprised a staff of fifty researchers working on artificial intelligence projects. Using a joint venture for such work offered the advantage that all the staff were in the same place, making it easier to discuss ideas and results, and to alter research priorities. By 1992, the ECRC had grown to seventy researchers involved in new and advanced computer languages and databases. In 1993, two US computer firms, Hewlett-Packard and Digital Equipment Corporation (DEC), became equal partners in ECRC. ECRC, which has close links with European Commission policy makers, will help to formulate, specify and implement plans for the multi-billion pound (SYMBOL) Europe-wide computer networks.

Similar efforts have taken place in the USA. Among these are Micro Electronics and Computer Technology Corporation, Semiconductor Research Corporation and SEMATECH. SEMATECH is a government–industry cooperative alliance formed from fourteen high-technology companies representing 80 per cent of the US national capacity for semi-conductor manufacturing. It helps assist its members with continuous improvements, compressing product cycles, establishing supplier relationships and strengthening core competencies while emphasizing work leading to process and product improvements.

The disadvantage of using a common site is that many researchers may not want to move there. In the case of ECRC, only one-third of the research staff in Munich came from the parent companies, which were located in France, the UK and Germany. In the USA a somewhat different problem arose when the president of a joint research company established by a dozen US computer firms discovered that the participating companies were not sending their best people to the new company. Many of these firms were apparently hoping the others would send their best people, which would allow them to save their own key people for the home firm. Eventually 200 of the joint company's 330 scientists had to be hired from the outside.

A sensitive issue for firms engaging in collaborative research, whether through joint ventures or not, is how far the collaboration should extend. Because the partners are usually competitors, the often expressed ideal is that the joint effort will focus only on 'pre-competitive' basic research, and not, for example, on product development work. This is often a difficult line to draw. In the case of ECRC, the decision was made to license any technology developed by the venture on a royalty-free basis to the parents, who then adapted it for their own purposes.

Marketing and distribution

Many international joint ventures involve shared research, development and production, but stop short of joint marketing (see MARKETING MANAGEMENT, INTERNATIONAL). The cars coming out of the widely publicized joint venture between Toyota and General Motors in California, for instance, are clearly branded as GM or Toyota products and are sold competitively through each parent's distribution network. The same is true of the Fords and Mazdas rolling off an assembly line in Michigan. Antitrust plays a role in the decision to keep marketing activities separate, but so does the partners' intrinsic desire to maintain separate brand identities and increase their own market share. These cooperating firms have not forgotten that they are competitors.

There are, nevertheless, some ventures which are formed for the express purpose of achieving economies in marketing and distribution. General Mills used such an alliance strategy in the European market. In 1992, General Mills and PepsiCo won approval to merge their European snack-food businesses, making the combined company the largest in the $17 billion market. PepsiCo's well known brands and marketing and distribution strength gave immediate market strength to General Mills. The latter had used a similar alliance with Nestlé to create Cereal Partners Worldwide (CPWO) to gain a foothold in Europe. With sales of $250 million in 1992, CPWO hoped to achieve $1 billion in sales and 20 per cent market share by the year 2000.

In marketing and distribution alliances each firm is hoping for wider market coverage at a lower cost. The trade-off is a loss of direct control over the sales force, potentially slower decision making, and a possible loss of direct contact with the customer.

Somewhat similar in intent are cooperative marketing agreements, which are not joint ventures, but agreements by two firms with related product lines to sell one another's products. When Control Data pulled out of the supercomputer business in 1989, for example, it established an agreement with Cray Research, the world's leading supercomputer manufacturer, that allowed Control Data to sell Cray supercomputers, while Cray would sell Control Data's mainframes and workstations. Both companies ended up with a more complete line to sell, without the managerial complications of a joint venture.

Divisional mergers

Multinational companies with subsidiaries that they have concluded are too small to be economic have sometimes chosen to create a joint venture by combining their 'too small' operations with those of a competitor (see MULTINATIONAL CORPORATIONS). Fiat and Peugeot, for example, merged their automobile operations in Argentina, where both companies were doing poorly. The new joint venture started life with a market share of 35 per cent and a chance for greatly improved economies in design, production and marketing. Faced with similar pressures, Ford and Volkswagen have done the same thing in Brazil, creating a jointly-owned company called Auto Latina.

Elsewhere, Dresser Industries of the USA and Komatsu of Japan combined existing businesses in 1988 to create an equally owned joint venture to compete in the construction and mining equipment business in the western hemisphere. Komatsu's motivation for entering the venture was to establish a manufacturing source for its products in North America, as a rapidly rising yen made sourcing from Japan ever more expensive. Explaining Dresser's desire for the joint venture, a vice president stated that the equipment business was becoming ever more capital intensive, and the only routes to success were to be a very narrow niche player, or a major full line producer. The Komatsu deal created the latter, a strong full-line company with first year sales in excess of $1.5 billion, which ranked number two in the Americas.

A divisional merger can also allow a firm a graceful exit from a business in which it is no longer interested. General Motors appeared to be taking this route when it merged its heavy truck business with that of Volvo, forming a new company in which GM maintained only a 24 per cent interest. In a similar move Honeywell gave up trying to continue alone in the computer industry, when it folded its business into a venture with Groupe Bull of France and NEC of Japan. Honeywell held a 40 per cent stake in the resulting joint venture.

4 Acquiring technology in the core business

Firms that have wanted to acquire technology in their core business area have traditionally done so through licence agreements or by developing the technology themselves. Increasingly, however, companies are turning to joint ventures for this purpose because developing technology in-house is seen as taking too long, and license agreements, while giving the firm access to patent rights and engineers' ideas, may not provide much in the way of shop floor know-how. The power of an alliance is that a firm may be able to have its employees working shoulder to shoulder with those of its partner, trying to solve the same problems. This is where real learning can take place.

The General Motors joint venture with Toyota provided an opportunity for GM to obtain a source of low cost small cars, and to watch first hand how Toyota managers, who were in operational control of the venture, were able to produce high quality automobiles at low cost. Most observers have concluded that the opportunity for General Motors to learn new production techniques was more significant than the supply of cars coming from the venture. Some have even suggested that if GM can apply the lessons of the joint venture to its other US plants, the venture will have been worthwhile – even if every car the venture produced were driven into the Pacific Ocean!

5 Reducing financial risk

Some projects are too big or too risky for firms to tackle alone. This is why oil companies use joint ventures to split the costs of searching for new oilfields, and why the aircraft industry is increasingly using joint ventures and 'risk sharing subcontractors' to put up some of the funds required to develop new aircraft and engines. The actions of the leading aerospace companies illustrate these concerns. A group of Japanese firms developed and built approximately 15 per cent of the airframe of the Boeing 767, under an arrangement that allows the Japanese firms to benefit if the plane sells well or to suffer if it does not. Boeing's next airliner, the 777, is being developed in collaboration with a consortium made up of Mitsubishi Heavy Industries, Kawasaki Heavy Industries and Fuji Heavy Industries. On the 777 project, the Japanese share has increased to 21 per cent. Similarly, Airbus Industrie, itself an alliance of British, French, German and Spanish aerospace companies, looked to Asia for a proposed 600–800 seat jumbo airliner.

Do such joint ventures make sense? For the oil companies, the answer is clearly yes. In these ventures one partner takes a lead role and manages the venture on a day-to-day basis. Management complexity, one of the major potential drawbacks of joint ventures, is kept to a minimum. If the venture finds oil, transfer prices are not a problem: the rewards of the venture are easy to divide between the partners. In situations like this, forming a joint venture is an efficient and sensible way of sharing risk.

It is not as obvious that the aircraft industry ventures are a good idea, at least, not for industry leaders such as Boeing. The Japanese are not entering these ventures simply in the hopes of earning an attractive return on their investment; they are gearing up to produce, sooner or later, their own aircraft. When asked why Boeing was willing to train potential competitors in aircraft design and manufacture, the president replied that he would rather have the Japanese in a venture with him than in one with his competitors.

Other organizations, such as the multinational furniture retailer IKEA, have formed a multitude of non-equity alliances with component suppliers around the world. IKEA provided its suppliers with some or all of: raw material procurement, packaging materials, storage, specialized equipment and machinery, and engineering. In return, it received low-cost, good-quality customized products from committed and (usually) loyal suppliers, while retaining the right to walk away if quality or cost standards were not achieved. All this was achieved without incurring the financial risks associated with the purchase of such firms.

6 Taking products to foreign markets

Firms with domestic products that they believe will be successful in foreign markets face a choice. They can produce the product at home and export it, license the technology to local firms around the world, establish wholly owned subsidiaries in foreign countries, or form joint ventures with local partners. Many firms conclude that exporting is unlikely to lead to significant market penetration, building wholly owned subsidiaries is too slow and requires too many resources, and licensing does not offer an adequate financial return. The result is that an international joint venture, while seldom seen as an ideal choice, is often the most attractive compromise.

Moving into foreign markets entails a degree of risk, and most firms that decide to form an alliance with a local firm are doing so in order to reduce the risk associated with their new market entry. Very often, they look for a partner which deals with a related product line, and thus has a good feel for the local market. As a further risk reducing measure, the alliance may begin life as simply a sales and marketing operation, until the product or service begins to sell well and volumes rise. In the case of a manufactured product, 'screwdriver' assembly plants may be set up to assemble components shipped from the foreign parent. Eventually, the venture may modify or redesign the product to suit the local market better, and establish complete local manufacturing, sourcing raw material and components locally. The objective is to withhold major investment until the market uncertainty is reduced.

Following customers to foreign markets

Another way to reduce the risk of a foreign market entry is to follow firms or individuals who are already customers at home. At the individual customer level, major airlines around the world have formed global networks in order to serve their home-based clients who are travelling to locations they do not serve. In 1990, European (Swissair), Asian (Singapore Airlines) and North American (Delta Airlines) carriers joined together in an alliance they called Global Excellence. In 1993, this alliance provided passenger and cargo transport on major routes around the globe. The alliance partners complement each other in terms of route network and logistics, reservation systems, through check-in, connecting flights and frequent flyer programmes.

At the firm customer level, in recent years many Japanese automobile suppliers have followed Honda, Toyota and Nissan as they set up new plants in North America and Europe. Very often these suppliers, uncertain of their ability to operate in a foreign environment, decide to form a joint venture with a local partner. There are, for example, a great many automobile supplier joint ventures in the USA formed between Japanese and US auto suppliers, to supply the Japanese 'transplant' automobile manufacturers. For the Americans, such ventures are a way to learn Japanese manufacturing techniques and to tap into a growing market (Inkpen 1992). Such ventures are often not very satisfactory for the US partners, for reasons to be discussed subsequently.

Investing in 'markets of the future'

Some of the riskiest joint ventures are those established by firms taking an early position in what they see as their 'markets of the future'. Attracting the most attention in recent years have been ventures in China, eastern Europe and the former Soviet Union. Each of these areas offers very large untapped markets, as well as a possible source of low cost raw materials and labour. The major problems faced by Western firms in penetrating such markets are their unfamiliarity with the local culture, establishing Western attitudes towards quality, and in some areas, repatriating earnings in hard currency. The solution (sometimes imposed by local government) has often been the creation of joint ventures with local partners who 'know the ropes' and can deal with the local bureaucracy.

Knowledge of the local economy, politics and culture is the key contribution of many local partners in global alliances. Interestingly,

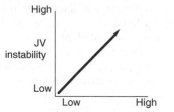

Figure 2 Joint venture stability
Source: Beamish and Inkpen (1995)

their foreign partners' attitudes tend to fall into one of two camps with regard to this local partner contribution. Some foreign partners are quite content with access to this local partner contribution. These alliances tend to be stable – having no unplanned equity changes or major reorganizations. Other foreign partners are not content with access, and to acquire this local market knowledge themselves. These tend to be unstable. In fact, as Figure 2 suggests, the greater the acquisition of local knowledge by the foreign partner, the more likely it is that instability will result.

Acquisition of local knowledge may not be an objective of the foreign partner if the foreign partner believes: (1) the local partner will always know the local market better; (2) the cost of obtaining this knowledge exceeds the pay-off; and (3) it lacks the necessary skills.

Because the environments differ between market and planned economies, and between developed and developing countries, it should come as no surprise that joint ventures often have different characteristics in these locales. As Table 3 illustrates, the characteristics of joint ventures often differ widely according to:

- reasons for creating them
- frequency of association with government partners
- their use versus other modes of foreign involvement
- the origin of the foreign partner
- duration
- ownership level
- ownership–control relationship
- control–performance relationship
- stability

- overall performance

A local partner is no guarantee of success, as the regulatory environment can change quickly in some locations. Xerox Shanghai is a good example of a joint venture which has had to adapt to major changes. Formed in 1987 after three years of negotiation, Xerox Shanghai's first shock came in 1988 when the government introduced purchase controls which state that before purchasing a copier, a potential customer must obtain permission from several government agencies. The net result, in Xerox's estimation, is that the market is only 20 per cent of what it would be without such controls. The joint venture's other problem stemmed from a devaluation of the local currency, which dramatically raised the cost of imported components. The good news, however, is that Xerox is the market share leader in the Chinese market, due in part to the fact that competitors such as Ricoh, Canon and Toshiba have not formed local joint ventures, and are thus not seen as such good corporate citizens. The company also obtained tax concessions, and the net result is that profits are on target.

7 Bringing foreign products to local markets

For every firm that uses an international joint venture to take its product to a foreign market, there is a local company that sees the joint venture as an attractive way to bring a foreign product to its existing market. It is, of course, this complementarity of interest that makes the joint venture possible.

Local partners enter joint ventures to get better utilization of existing plants or distribution channels, to protect themselves against threatening new technology or simply as an impetus for new growth. Typically, the financial rewards that the local partner receives from a venture are different from those accruing to the foreign partner. For example:

1 Many foreign partners make a profit shipping finished products and components to their joint ventures. These profits are particularly attractive because they are in hard

currency, which may not be true of the venture's profits, and because the foreign partner captures 100 per cent of them, not just a share.

2 Many foreign partners receive a technology fee, which is a fixed percentage of the sales volume of the joint venture. The local partner may or may not receive a management fee of like amount.

3 Foreign partners typically pay a withholding tax on dividends remitted to them from the venture. Local firms do not.

As a result of these differences, the local partner is often far more concerned with the venture's bottom line earnings and dividend payout than the foreign partner. This means that the foreign partner is likely to be happier to keep the venture as simply a marketing operation or a 'screwdriver' assembly operation, than to develop it to the point where it buys less imported material.

Although this logic is understandable, it can be shortsighted. The best example of the benefits that can come back to a parent from a powerful joint venture (JV) is Toppan Moore,

Table 3 Summary of differences of joint venture characteristics

Characteristics	Developed country market economy	Developing country market economy	Developing country planned economy (China)
Major reason for creating venture	Skill required	Government pressure	Government pressure
Frequency of association with government partners	Low	Moderate	Very high
Overall use of joint ventures versus other modes of foreign involvement	Significant	High (but contingent on country, industry and technology level)	Very high (regardless of country, industry or technology level)
Origin of foreign partner	Other developed countries	Developed countries	Ethnic related countries (that is, Hong Kong)
Proportion of intended joint ventures actually implemented	High	Relatively high	Low (under 50%)
Use of joint ventures with a predetermined duration	Low (excpt in certain industries)	Low	High
Most common level of ownership for multinational enterprise	Equal	Minority	Minority
Number of autonomously managed ventures	Small	Negligible	Negligible
Ownership control relationship	Direct (dominant control with majority ownership; shared control with equal ownership)	Difficult to discern because most multinational enterprises have a minority ownership position	Indirect
Control–performance realtionship in successful joint ventures	Inconclusive	Shared or split	Split control
Instability rate	30%	45%	Low
Multinational enterprise managerial enterprise managerial assessment of dissatisfaction with performance	37%	61%	High

Source: Beamish (1993)

a venture begun in Japan in the early 1960s between Moore Business Forms of Toronto and Toppan Printing of Tokyo. The underlying logic of the original agreement was to enable Toppan Printing to introduce new products into an existing market, while Moore would be able to create a new market with its existing products. What evolved was an arrangement whereby the sales method and production planning would be independent of both parent companies, while cost and pricing principles would generally follow Moore's methods.

Over the next two decades, the JV firm evolved from one which was heavily dependent on Moore for technological developments, to one which now had the capability to alter products to meet the specific requirements of Japanese customers, develop its own production know-how and bring new products to market. The culmination of this evolution was a 1990s new product innovation developed in cooperation with Moore of a hand-held intelligent data entry terminal that had been highly successful in eliminating paperwork in the North American parcel delivery market.

8 Using joint ventures for diversification

As the previous examples illustrate, many joint ventures take products which one parent knows well into a market which the other knows well. Some however, break new ground, and move one or both parents into products and markets that are new to them.

Learning *from* your partner

One of the most interesting stories surrounding the rise of Japanese companies since the Second World War is that of their attempt to move into the commercial aircraft market. In 1962, with the backing of the Japanese government, Mitsubishi, Fuji and Kawasaki Heavy Industries introduced a medium sized short-haul aircraft called the YX-11. It was a commercial disaster because, according to a later government study, the participants lacked basic knowledge and experience in design, production and marketing of aircraft. The best solution, it was decided, was to form alliances with firms in the industry that knew what they were doing.

Since then these three Japanese companies have joined with Boeing in the manufacture of the 767, and with a number of major engine manufacturers to develop a new jet engine. The most recent step has been their 21 per cent involvement in the Boeing 777. This was a very significant move for the Japanese, as they now have 200 engineers at Boeing's operations in Seattle, involved in design, testing and development work. The Japanese are also involved in manufacturing and sales financing.

Using such arrangements to acquire the skills necessary to compete in a new business is a long-term proposition, but clearly one that the Japanese are willing to live with. Given the fact that most acquisitions of unrelated business do not succeed, and that trying to enter a new business without help is extremely difficult, choosing partners who will help you learn the business does not look like a bad strategy.

Learning *with* your partner

Very occasionally, two firms form a joint venture to take them into a business which is new to both of them. Usually the new business is somewhat related to an existing business of one partner or the other, but the joint venture is nevertheless a significant step into the unknown.

When moving into a new field in which the pay-off is seen as being a long way in the future, a joint venture offers several advantages. The most obvious is that costs are shared. The other important factor is that it may be more difficult for a firm to drop the project because of commitments made to its partner. An in-house project can be quietly folded up, but a decision to pull out of a joint venture is more public, and generally more difficult. Thus, if perseverance is a key to success, the extra staying power that a joint venture can provide may be crucial.

Table 4 Joint venture checklist

1 Understanding your capabilities and needs

- Do you really need a partner? For how long?

- How big is the pay-off? How likely is success?

- Is a joint venture the best option?

2 Choosing an appropriate partner

- Does the partner share your objectives for the venture?

- Does the partner have the necessary skills and resources? Will you get access to them?

- Will you be compatible?

- Can you arrange an 'engagement period'?

3 Designing the joint venture

- Define the venture's scope of activity, and its strategic freedom vis-à-vis its parents.

- Lay out each parent's duties and pay-offs, to create a 'win-win' situation.

- Establish the managerial role of each partner.

4 Doing the deal

- How much paperwork is enough? Trust versus legal considerations.

- Agree on an end game.

5 Making the venture work

- Give the venture continuing top management attention.

- Manage cultural differences.

- Watch out for inequities.

- Be flexible.

9 Requirements for international joint venture success

The checklist in Table 4 presents many of the items that a manager should consider when establishing an international joint venture. Each of these is discussed in the following sections.

Understanding your capabilities and needs

The decision to enter an alliance should not be taken lightly. As mentioned earlier, alliances require a great deal of management attention and in spite of the care and attention they receive, many prove unsatisfactory to their parents.

Firms considering entering an alliance should satisfy themselves that they have selected the most appropriate form of collaboration to get what they need. They should also carefully consider the time period for which they are likely to need help. Some alliances such as equity joint ventures have been labelled 'permanent solutions to temporary problems' by firms who entered a venture to get help on some aspect of their business, but were stuck with the venture structure when they no longer needed help.

As noted earlier, General Mills formed a joint venture with Nestlé of Switzerland to try and catch up with Kellogg in the breakfast cereal markets outside North America, where Kellogg has long been dominant. Part of the deal was that Nestlé's brand name would appear on all of the joint venture's products, even those like Cheerios, which were brought to the venture by General Mills. In return, Nestlé is providing distribution to markets in which General Mills has never been present. The immediate pay-offs for each firm are evident, but will both still be happy with the arrangement in ten years? Only time will tell, but to some outsiders it looks like the venture is building markets for Nestlé.

Choosing an appropriate partner

It is not easy, before a venture begins, to determine many of the things a manager would most like to know about a potential partner, such as the true extent of its capabilities, what its objectives are in forming the venture, and whether or not it will be easy to work with. A hasty answer to such questions may lead a firm into a bad relationship, or cause it to pass up a good opportunity.

For these reasons it is often best if companies begin a relationship in a small way, with a simple agreement that is important, but not a matter of life and death to either parent. As confidence between the firms grows, the scope of the business activities can broaden. Take, for example, the Ford-Mazda alliance, one of the most successful in automotive history. It began in 1971 when Ford bought Mazda trucks to sell in Asia. In 1979, Ford bought a 25 per cent stake in Mazda to rescue the struggling Japanese auto maker and to gain access to a small car manufacturer. Today, the two cooperate on new vehicle design and production, and exchange expertise. Ford brings skills in international marketing and finance, while Mazda offers manufacturing and product development expertise. In Japan, they jointly own Autorama, a chain of import car dealerships. Ford and Mazda have worked jointly on ten current auto models. Most often, Ford focuses on styling and Mazda attends to key engineering contributions. In 1992, one out of every four Ford cars sold in the USA benefited from Mazda involvement, while two out of every five Mazdas were influenced by Ford.

Another good example is provided by Corning Glass, which in 1970 made a major breakthrough in the development of optical fibres which could be used for telecommunication applications, replacing traditional copper wire or co-axial cable. The most likely customers of this fibre outside the USA were the European national telecoms, who were well known to be very nationalistic purchasers. To gain access to these customers Corning set up development agreements in 1973 and 1974 with companies in the UK, France, Germany and Italy, who were already suppliers to the telecoms. These agreements called for the European firms to develop the technology necessary to combine the fibres into cables, while Corning continued to develop the optical fibres themselves. Soon the partners began to import fibre from Corning and cable it locally. Then, when the partners were comfortable with each other and each market was ready, Corning and the partners set up joint ventures to produce optical fibre locally. These ventures have worked extremely well, and their continuing success became particularly important in the late 1980s, as growth in

the US market levelled off. Corning is widely acknowledged as one of the world's most successful users of joint ventures.

Managers are constantly told that they should choose a joint venture partner that they trust. As these examples suggest, however, trust between partners is something that can only be developed over time, as a result of shared experiences. You cannot start with trust. Moreover, national cultural differences can sometimes get in the way of the development of trust. Nodding of the head can be viewed as 'I agree and will follow through', or elsewhere simply as polite acknowledgement that 'I hear you'. Misinterpretation of perceived commitment can impede the creation of trust.

Designing the joint venture

In the excitement of setting up a new operation in a foreign country, or getting access to technology provided by an overseas partner, it is important not to lose sight of the basic strategic requirements that must be met if a joint venture is to be successful. The questions that must be addressed are the same when any new business is proposed. Is the market attractive? How strong is the competition? How will the new company compete? Will it have the required resources? And so on.

In addition to these concerns there are three others which are particularly relevant to joint venture design. One is the question of *strategic freedom*. This has to do with the relationship between the venture and its parents. How much freedom will the venture be given to do as it wishes with respect to choosing suppliers, a product line and customers? In the Dow Chemical venture in Korea a dispute between the partners centred around the requirement that the venture buy materials, at what the Koreans believed to be an inflated price, from Dow's new wholly owned Korean plant. Clearly the US and Korean vision of the amount of strategic freedom open to the venture was rather different.

The second issue of importance is that the joint venture be a *win–win* situation. This means that the pay-off to each parent if the venture is successful should be a big one, as this will keep both parents working for the success of the venture when times are tough. If the strategic analysis suggests that the return to either parent will be marginal, the venture should be restructured or abandoned.

Finally, it is critical to decide on the *management roles* that each parent company will play. The venture will be easier to manage if one parent plays a *dominant* role and has a lot of influence over both strategic and day-to-day operations of the venture, or if one parent plays a lead role in the day-to-day operation of the joint venture. Most difficult to manage are *shared management* ventures in which both parents have a significant input into both strategic decisions and the everyday operations of the venture. Despite their associated management problems, shared management ventures are frequently used. A possible middle ground between shared and dominant control is *split control*, where each partner dominates decision making in certain issues. Figures 3, 4 and 5 illustrate the various forms.

In spite of the fact that dominant parent ventures are easier to manage than shared management ventures they are not always the appropriate type of venture to establish. Dominant parent ventures are most likely to be effective when one partner has the knowledge and skill to make the venture a success and the other party is contributing simply money, a trademark, or perhaps a one-time transfer of technology. Research has indicated, for instance, that ventures in developing countries in which the foreign parent is dominant do not tend to be successful. Shared management ventures are necessary when the venture needs active consultation between members of each parent company, as when deciding how to modify a product supplied by one parent for the local market which is well known by the other, or to modify a production process designed by one parent to be suitable for a workforce and working conditions well known by the other.

A joint venture is headed for trouble when a parent tries to take a larger role in its management than makes sense. A US company with a joint venture in Japan, for instance, insisted that one of its people be the executive vice president of the venture. This was not

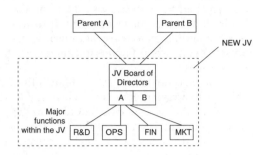

Figure 3 Dominant control

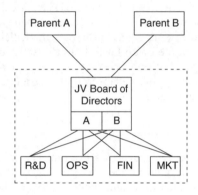

Figure 4 Split control

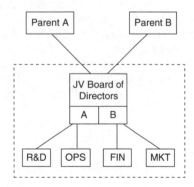

Figure 5 Shared control

reasonable, because the man had nothing to bring to the management of the venture. He simply served as a constant reminder to the Japanese that the US partner did not trust them. The Americans were pushing for a shared management venture, when it was more logical to allow the Japanese, who certainly had all the necessary skills, to be the dominant or at least the leading firm. The major US contribution to the venture was to allow it to use its world-famous trademarks and brand names.

A second example involves a French firm which was bringing complex technology to the venture that needed to be modified for the Japanese market. It was clear that the French firm required a significant say in the management of the venture. On the other hand, the French had no knowledge of the Japanese market, and thus the Japanese also needed a significant role in the venture. The logical solution would have been a shared management venture, and equal influence in decisions made at the board level. Unfortunately, both companies wanted to play a dominant role, and the venture collapsed in a decision making stalemate.

Doing the deal

Experienced managers argue that it is the relationship between the partners that is of key importance in a joint venture, not the legal agreement that binds them together. Nevertheless, most are careful to ensure that they have a good agreement in place, one that they understand, and are comfortable with.

The principal elements of an abbreviated joint venture agreement are listed in Table 5. Most of these are straightforward, and relate to topics discussed in this entry. One item on the list which has not been discussed is the termination of the venture.

Some managers baulk at discussing divorce during the marriage ceremony on the grounds that it suggests a lack of commitment to the alliance. Others argue that it is a pointless exercise because the necessary legal infrastructure to enforce the dissolution is not in place in some jurisdictions. On balance however, it is important to work out a method of terminating the venture in the event of a serious disagreement, and to do this at a time when heads are cool and goodwill abounds. The usual technique is to use a *shotgun clause* which allows either party to name a price at which it will buy the other's shares in the venture. However, once this provision is activated and the first company has named a price, the second firm has the option of selling at this price or buying the first company's shares at the same price. This ensures that only fair offers are made, at least as long as both parents are large enough to be capable of buying each other out.

Table 5 Abbreviated joint ventures implementation checklist

- Define scope and purpose
- Assess and evaluate contributions of parties
- Evaluate alternative forms for joint venture
  Equity
  Non-equity
- Allocate proportionate equity shares
- Control
  Overall strategy
  Ongoing management
- Use of technology and technical assistance
- Prepare non-bonding letter of agreement as basis for formal documents
- Prepare agreement for incorporated joint venture
- Clarify decisions requiring unanimity
  Rights of access to plant records
  Marketing
  Duration
  Provisions for termination
  Transfer of interest
  Rights on termination
  Governing law
  Arbitration
  Force majeure
- Prepare or amend articles of incorporation
- Prepare bylaws for joint venture cooperation
- Fiscal year

Source: Stitt and Baker (1985)

Making the venture work

Strategic alliances and joint ventures are successfully managed through three sets of activities and a special type of performance evaluation (see CULTURE, CROSS-NATIONAL). These activities are initiation actions, maintenance actions and building actions (Neupert 1994). Initiation actions are activities that lay the groundwork for beginning the alliance. These actions help to define for the partners where the alliance is headed, what is expected of each partner, and what is ultimately expected from the alliance. Defining obligations and expectations up-front helps reduce problems later. Maintenance actions address the day-to-day operational tasks of the alliance. They get to the heart of the alliance, since it is only through the successful completion of the tasks that the alliance will be continued. These actions are the necessary, but not sufficient actions that facilitate moving the relationship from a transactional and operational level to a long-term, mutually beneficial alliance. Through building actions, the partners prove they are worthy of trust and deserving of the effort required to overcome differences.

Joint ventures need close and continuing attention, particularly in their early months. In addition to establishing a healthy working relationship between the parents and the venture general manager, managers should be on the lookout for the impact that cultural differences may be having on the venture, and for the emergence of unforeseen inequities.

International alliances, like any type of international activity, require that managers of different national cultures work together. Unless managers have been sensitized to the characteristics of the culture that they are dealing with, this can lead to misunderstandings and serious problems. Many Western managers, for instance, are frustrated by the slow, consensus-orientated decision making style of the Japanese. Equally, the Japanese find US individualistic decision making to be surprising, as the decisions are made so quickly, but the implementation is often so slow. Firms that are sophisticated in the use of international alliances are well aware of such

problems and have taken action to minimize them. Ford, for example, has put more than 1500 managers through courses to improve their ability to work with Japanese and Korean managers. Similarly, Swissair routinely provides in-house seminars for its employees to gain insight into its partners' cultures in the Global Excellence alliance. This helps Swissair not only provide better service to its own customers, but also understand better their partners' strengths.

It is important to remember that cultural differences do not just arise from differences in nationality. Corporate and professional cultures may vary as well. For example:

1 Small firms working with large partners are often surprised and dismayed by the fact that it can take months rather than days to get approval of a new project. In some cases the cultural differences appear to be greater between small and large firms of the same nationality than, say, between multinationals of different nationality, particularly if the multinationals are in the same industry.

2 Firms working with two partners from the same country have been surprised to find how different the companies are in cultural habits. A Japanese automobile firm headquartered in rural Japan is a very different company from one run from Tokyo.

3 Cultural differences between managers working in different functional areas may be greater than those between managers in the same function in different firms. European engineers, for example, discovered when discussing a potential joint venture with a US partner, that they had more in common with the US engineers than with the marketing people in their own company.

A very common alliance problem is that the objectives of the parents, which coincided when the venture was formed, diverge over time. Such divergences can be brought on by changes in the fortunes of the partners. This was the case in the breakup of the General Motors–Daewoo joint venture in Korea in 1992. Relations between the partners were already strained due to GM's unwillingness to put further equity into the venture, in spite of a debt–equity ratio of more than 8:1, when in 1991, faced with rapidly declining market share, the Korean parent decided that the venture should go for growth and maximize market share, whereas General Motors, itself in a poor financial position, insisted that the emphasis be on current profitability. When Daewoo, without telling General Motors, introduced a concessionary financing programme for the joint venture's customers, the relationship was on the rocks, never to recover (see MANAGEMENT IN SOUTH KOREA).

A final note concerns the unintended inequities which may arise during the life of a venture. Due to an unforeseen circumstance, one parent may be winning from the venture while the other is losing. A venture established in the mid-1980s between Japanese and US parents, for instance, was buying components from the Japanese parent at prices based in dollars. As the yen rose in value, the Japanese partner was receiving fewer and fewer yen for each shipment. The advice of many experienced venture managers is that in such a situation a change in the original agreement should be made, so that the hardship is shared between the parents. That was done in this case, and the venture is performing extremely well, although it is not as profitable as originally anticipated.

10 Conclusion

For the reasons outlined in this piece, global alliances are an increasingly important part of the strategy of many firms. They are, however, difficult to design and manage well, and so far many are performing below their management's expectations. This should not, however, be an excuse for firms to avoid them. In many industries, the winners are going to be the companies that most quickly learn to manage alliances effectively, and are willing to use them in core areas.

Some observers of the global alliance phenomenon believe that the risk of technological loss to one's partner is so great with alliances that they should be avoided in core areas (see Figure 6). Certainly, such a risk exists particularly if your firm is not moving forward technologically, or if your partner is both inclined and capable of absorbing your technology. Yet this begs the question: is it better to try and learn to manage the risk – while capturing the contributions of a partner – or to avoid the risk altogether, but not benefit from any partner's contribution? It is a judgement call, but in our view often a risk worth taking.

In the future, global strategic alliances will continue to be used both with core technologies and in core markets. Yet new challenges in alliance management are ahead, and new frontiers need to be crossed (see Figure 7).

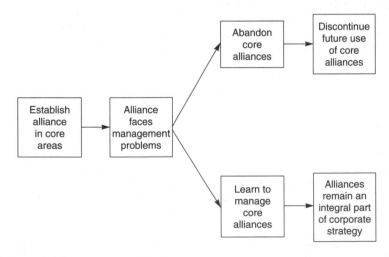

Figure 6 Should alliances be used in core areas?

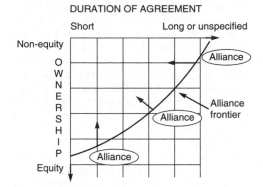

DURATION OF AGREEMENT

Figure 7 Future challenges with global strategic alliances

There is much to learn about the management of non-equity alliances: how to balance control/influence when ownership is not present; determining the appropriate range of resources to be devoted to the alliance; and so forth. A second challenge will be the need to manage alliances which are formed for a predetermined, shorter duration. This will require an ability to choose an appropriate partner, design and implement the alliance, and attain the intended benefits – all within a condensed timeframe. It will not be easy, but as the experiences of some of the firms we have noted can attest to, it is possible. As the pace of change continues to accelerate, continued emphasis will be needed on how to effectively enter, manage and, where appropriate, exit international alliances.

PAUL W. BEAMISH
UNIVERSITY OF WESTERN ONTARIO

J. PETER KILLING
IMD

Note

The authors would like to acknowledge the assistance of Kent Neupert in the preparation of this entry. Portions of this entry are taken from Killing (1994).

Further reading

(References cited in the text marked *)

Beamish, P.W. (1988) *Multinational Joint Ventures in Developing Countries*, London: Rout-ledge. (This book examines JV characteristics, issues of partner selection, and partner need and commitment, and provides guidelines for both parent company and JV general managers.)

* Beamish, P.W. (1993) 'The characteristics of joint ventures in the People's Republic of China', *Journal of International Marketing* 1 (2): 29–48. (A meta-analysis of twelve characteristics of JVs in a developing country with a planned economy – China – with JVs in developed countries with market economies and developing countries with market economies.)

* Beamish, P.W. and Inkpen, A. (1995) 'Keeping international joint ventures stable and profitable', *Long Range Planning* 28(3). (A practitioner article which argues why some joint ventures will be inherently more stable, or unstable, than others.)

Beamish, P.W., Delios, A. and Lecraw, D.J. (1997) *Japanese Multinationals in the Global Economy*, Cheltenham: Edward Elgar. (Presents some of the key data regarding Japanese foreign direct investment, including the use of alliances, from a subsidiary perspective.)

* Buckley, P.J. and Casson, M. (1985) *The Economic Theory of the Multinational Enterprise*, New York: St Martin's Press. (An early and important contribution to MNR theory.)

Contractor, F. and Lorange, P. (eds) (1988) *Cooperative Strategies in International Business*, Lexington, NY: Lexington Books. (This collection of twenty-eight articles resulted from a 1986 conference, and is still a useful book on alliances. Three conferences on the same theme were hosted by Beamish and Killing in March 1996 in Europe, Asia and North America, and the proceedings were published as the Cooperative Strategies series by the New Lexington Press in 1997; the results can be also found in a special issue of *Journal of International Business Studies*, 1996, 27(5).)

Dunning, J.H. (1995) 'Reappraising the eclectic paradigm in an age of alliance capitalism', *Journal of International Business Studies* 26 (3). (This article discusses the implications of alliance capitalism for our theorizing about the determinants of multinational enterprise activity.)

* Inkpen, A. (1992) 'Learning and collaboration: an examination of North American–Japanese joint ventures', PhD thesis, University of Western Ontario. (An investigation of the organizational learning opportunities provided to parent firms in international joint ventures.)

Killing, J.P. (1983) *Strategies for Joint Venture Success*, New York: Praeger. (Written expressly for managers, this book focuses on international joint ventures formed between firms from industrialized countries.)

* Killing, J.P. (1994) 'The design and management of international joint ventures', in P. Beamish, P. Killing, D. Lecraw and A. Morrison (eds), *International Management: Text and Cases*, Burr Ridge, IL: Irwin. (A practitioner-orientated chapter on equity joint ventures which served in part as the basis for the present entry.)

McLellan, K. and Beamish, P. (1994) 'The new frontier for information technology outsourcing: international banking', *European Management Journal*: 210–15. (This study illustrates how firms that are using an outside party to deliver a critical component of their strategy can transform the relationship from a buyer–supplier contract to a non-equity alliance.)

* Neupert, K. (1994) 'Implementing strategic buyer–supplier alliances for product development', PhD thesis, University of Western Ontario. (The thesis developed and tested a model of strategic alliance management using thirty-eight non-equity product development alliances.)

Schaan, J.-L. (1988) 'How to control a joint venture even as a minority partner', *Journal of General Management* 14 (1): 4–16. (An illuminating empirical study of the positive and negative control mechanisms available to multinational enterprises when they do business in locales where they prefer, or are forced, to take a minority equity position.)

* Stitt, H.J. and Baker, S.R. (1985) *The Licensing and Joint Venture Guide*, 3rd edn, Ontario: Ministry of Industry, Trade and Technology. (A useful series of checklists for establishing and managing licensing and joint venture agreements.)

Woodcock, P., Beamish, P. and Makino, S. (1994) 'Ownership-based entry strategies and international performance', *Journal of International Business Studies* 25 (2): 253–73. (An empirical and theoretical study which suggests that different entry modes have different performance outcomes based upon their resource and organizational control demands. The supporting evidence suggests wholly owned new ventures will outperform joint ventures, which will outperform acquisitions.)

Zeira, Y. and Shenkar, O. (eds) (1990) *Human Resource Management in International Joint Ventures*, special issue of *Mangement International Review* 30. (A collection of eight articles about human resource management in international joint ventures.)

See also: CULTURE, CROSS-NATIONAL; EXPORTING; GLOBAL STRATEGIC PLANNING; GLOBALIZATION; INTERNATIONAL MARKETING; INTERNATIONAL TRADE AND FOREIGN DIRECT INVESTMENT; MANAGEMENT IN CHINA; MANAGEMENT IN SOUTH KOREA; MARKETING MANAGEMENT, INTERNATIONAL; MULTINATIONAL CORPORATIONS

Related topics in the IEBM: AIRLINE MANAGEMENT; BRANDS; BUSINESS ECONOMICS; BUSINESS STRATEGY, JAPANESE; CHANNEL MANAGEMENT; GLOBALIZATION AND CORPORATE NATIONALITY; INFORMATION TECHNOLOGY; INNOVATION MANAGEMENT; JAPANIZATION; MANUFACTURING STRATEGY; ORGANIZATIONAL PERFORMANCE; STRATEGIC CHOICE; STRATEGY, CONCEPT OF

Global strategic planning

Overview

Strategic planning in today's dynamic global environment is the most difficult, complex task managers face. No book, whatever its length could cover all the nuances and contingencies managers should take into account in formulating their strategic plans. In this entry we focus on the essentials. We examine the role of strategic planning and analyse the key factors managers should consider as they develop their strategic plans.

In many industries the dynamic nature of the global environment creates a constant pull towards domination by global business units and a simultaneous opposing push towards domination by domestic units. Business units displaying a wide variety of configurations and resource deployment characteristics exist and even thrive in this turbulent environment. In many industries, domestic, multi-market and global participants all thrive; however the determinants of success do not remain constant.

We present and explain a customer focused definition of competitive advantage. We analyse the four key determinants of industry structure: industry characteristics; consumer behaviour; competitor behaviour; and the political and regulatory environment in which businesses operate. Our unit of analysis is the business unit or industry rather than the firm

because competition takes place at the business unit level within industries rather than the firm level.

Next we present and discuss a simple conceptual scheme, the Four Cs model. Managers can use this model to formulate strategic plans in the light of their industry's structure. This model encompasses four dimensions managers must consider in developing strategic plans. Analysis of customers and competitors identifies the potential of a particular strategy. Analysis of industry climate and one's own business unit's capabilities identifies the business unit's ability to realize the potential of a given strategy.

1 The role and content of strategic planning

A corporation is an entity devoted to achieving its stakeholders' goals. Typically, many stakeholders' goals are financial, centring on achieving high levels of profits or cash flow, or a high market value for the firm. Certain stakeholders may also concern themselves with social goals such as providing employment opportunities or finding a cure for a previously non-curable disease. Whether their goals are financial or non-financial, managers achieve them by making or buying and then selling products or services at a price greater than their cost to the firm. Firms require profits and cash flow to achieve non-financial as well as financial goals.

Strategic planning is the road map or prescription for achieving these goals. It identifies the products or services the firm will offer and the customers to whom it will offer them. It describes all the activities in which the firm must engage in order to accomplish the strategic plan. Managers should engage in and then integrate strategic planning at two levels, the corporate or firm level and the product line or strategic business unit (SBU) level. In this entry, we shall identify this latter level simply as the business unit.

Product line or business unit level planning is critical because consumers buy products, not firms. Firms compete in, and consumers make product choices from, specific industries; for this reason the basic unit of a strategic analysis should be a distinct business or industry (Porter 1991). Analysts generally define an industry as a group of closely substitutable products with a more or less common set of buyers. The goal of business unit level strategic planning is to answer the question: how and where should we compete in this industry?

The goal of firm or corporate level strategic planning is to answer the question: in which industries should we compete? In a one-industry and business unit firm, of course, corporate or firm level strategic planning would be redundant. Planning at this level is, however, critical for the product or geographically diversified firm. Planning can help the firm identify and take advantage of any synergism that may result from competing in more than one industry, or in more than one market. It can make optimum use of the firm's cash flow and other resources.

Firm level planning is also critical to identifying new product opportunities that may fall outside the industries in which the firm already participates. It also helps to identify the total financial and other resources the firm needs to accomplish its plan. The effectiveness of firm level planning depends on the quality of the business unit planning that provides the input on which corporate level planning is based.

In this entry we will concentrate mainly on business level planning. We will first look at planning that starts from the business unit's existing product line and focuses on the industry in which the unit competes. Most business units compete in well defined industries. They depend on their present industries and those industries' customers for the bulk of their future sales and profits. Most such industries are either mature or racing towards maturity; business units in them face fierce competition for sales and profits. Thorough understanding of competitive advantage and how to obtain it is a necessity for survival in these industries.

It is useful to view strategic planning as a system of interrelated decisions, as shown in Figure 1. As this figure shows, a business unit faces three core planning decisions. It must decide what products to offer, which consumers to target and where to produce or source the products it will market. Most planners must make these decisions in light of the firm's existing product lines; therefore its present product line conditions a unit's choices of target consumers and production strategy. The firm's present product lines may also influence the direction of its new product development activities.

To support the three core decisions, the business unit must decide on a research and development (R&D) and technology strategy and a marketing strategy. It must also decide on an organization structure and must secure appropriate financing. As we shall discuss later, to make these decisions the business unit must analyse a number of factors both external and internal to its firm.

Figure 1 Global strategy dimensions

2 The impact of the global marketplace on strategic planning

Beginning in the 1950s, international trade has burgeoned and regulations governing foreign investment have become increasingly more liberal (see INTERNATIONAL TRADE AND FOREIGN DIRECT INVESTMENT). As a result, most business units, regardless of the geographical scope of their activities, operate in a global, rather than a national marketplace. Market interpenetration, the presence of foreign firms in each other's home markets, has become common. When a business unit, even in a purely domestic firm, makes its strategic plans, it must take into account threats and examine opportunities emanating from beyond its country's borders.

Strategic planning in the global marketplace is a matter of finding one's proper place in the world, rather than merely in one's home country. It is therefore considerably more complex than planning only for the domestic market. In the global marketplace, the planning unit must still make all the decisions shown in Figure 1, but the alternatives are considerably broader. The business unit has a much wider variety of choices, especially of market and manufacturing alternatives. Configuration, the deployment of activities and resources across countries, becomes a pivotal consideration in formulating a strategic plan.

Business units that want to market in more than one country face a more diverse set of potential customers; therefore they must decide not only what to produce but whether to modify their domestic products for particular foreign markets. If they export, they must manage more complicated logistics and perform all of the special procedures required for shipping merchandise across national borders (see INTERNATIONAL MARKETING).

Firms operating in more than one country must inevitably deal with foreign currencies, which adds another complication and an additional source of risk. This point was brought home with a vengence during the east Asian monetary crisis of 1997–8. Regardless of their home country, firms are subject to the laws of every country in which they operate. In addition, they must still adhere to a variety of their home country's laws even with respect to their foreign operations. US firms, for example, must obey US anti-trust laws and the US Foreign Corrupt Practices Act worldwide.

Every business unit, whether domestic or global in scope, faces a wide range of competitors that may have different skills, goals and modes of operation. These competitors' responses may be different from those expected from home country competitors. The actions of such foreign competitors can represent a new kind of threat to a business unit's domestic market position. Xerox, for example, steadily upgraded the performance and raised the cost of its photocopiers. In doing so, they ignored a potential market for simple, low-cost machines. Xerox believed it could earn higher margins on higher priced photocopiers and was confident no US or European firm would challenge the company at the lower end of the market. Japanese firms saw Xerox's strategy as an opportunity and vigorously attacked the low-priced end of the market. The Japanese firms were willing to accept thin margins in the short run to gain a foothold in the photocopier market. They filled the void Xerox had left and then began to move up-market. Japanese photocopier manufacturers now compete along a broad spectrum of copier sizes and capabilities.

Entering foreign markets inevitably changes the firm's deployment of its manufacturing facilities (see EXPORTING; FOREIGN MARKET ENTRY STRATEGIES). The history of multinational enterprise is that firms cannot sustain forever a large presence in foreign markets solely by exporting. Either regulatory forces or cost pressures force firms, however reluctantly, to manufacture in at least some of the countries in which they market. This means that a commitment to foreign markets also becomes a commitment to substantial future capital expenditures.

3 Competitive advantage: the cornerstone of business success

It is a widely accepted tenet of business strategy that, to succeed in the marketplace, a business unit must have a competitive advantage. Competitive advantage results when a business unit chooses wisely the particular activities it will perform and then performs those activities well. The marketplace is the guidepost for selecting activities, for it is the marketplace and the consumers and competitors in it that govern a business unit's opportunities to gain competitive advantage.

In this regard, the marketplace is local, not global. It is local because conditions from market to market are likely to be different in many aspects. To be successful in any market, a business unit must have a competitive advantage in that market. It may gain in ability to perform certain potentially advantage-gaining activities because it covers a good part of the global marketplace. However, it will realize that potential only in those markets in which it can deliver superior value to consumers.

The basis of a business unit's competitive advantage is its ability to provide superior perceived value to potential customers. Competing successfully means providing a product or service or some combination thereof that customers will perceive as offering more value than the offerings of competitors. Superior value is not simply low price. It is product content in relation to price. It is usual to call each offering in the marketplace a value proposition.

Product content encompasses more than the product's physical characteristics. It can include augmentations such as services bundled with a product that add to its perceived value. A respected brand name can also add to a product's perceived value. Consumers view a brand name as a guarantee that a particular product includes the expected or promised content. For products purchased primarily for their functional or utilitarian content, brand name serves as a guarantee of performance. In product categories where symbolic value is important, brand names guarantee conveyance of the product's symbolic value.

The competitive battle is a battle of value propositions. Because consumers have different preferences, both low- and high-priced products can offer superior perceived value. Some consumers will prefer a low-priced product and will accept fewer features or less durability, for example. Others will want more features and will be willing to pay a higher price to receive them. Thus, a variety of value propositions can be successful in a single industry.

Typically, business units compete to provide superior perceived value within market segments consisting of relatively similar offerings. Mid-priced cars compete primarily against other mid-priced cars. Personal computers compete primarily against each other rather than against minicomputers. Providing superior perceived value is a matter of offering more perceived product content at the same price as competitors, or of offering similar perceived product content at a lower price than competitors. Essentially, these choices are variants of the generic cost leadership and differentiation strategies.

In every case, the customer, not the manufacturer, is the arbiter of consumer value. Perceived value is the value the consumer, not the producer, assigns to the product. Adding cost to a product by adding features does not necessarily increase its value to the consumer, nor does removing costs by eliminating features necessarily decrease its perceived value. Business units must develop a deep understanding of their customers to ensure that they provide a superior proposition.

A key task in strategic planning is to identify the specific elements of product content that create perceived value. Once the business unit understands the product elements that are the value creators, it can identify the specific activities that create the value. This is the point at which the value chain comes into play. The value chain is a useful tool for visualizing the flow of activities in a firm, and their associated costs. Correctly applied, it helps in mapping, organizing and integrating the identified value creating activities. Incorrectly applied, it focuses only on cost, and not on value.

The strategic challenge for most business units is to gain a sustainable competitive advantage by offering perceived value that competitors cannot duplicate. Traditionally, managers have considered superior or newer products, superior manufacturing skills and well-known brand names to be sources of sustainable competitive advantage. Unfortunately, each of these sources of competitive advantage is contestable, rather than sustainable, especially in the global environment.

The temptation of a large global market encourages firms to contest the advantages of others; the intense competition in the global market forces them to do so. Market leaders must engage in innovation, manufacturing improvement and brand building if they want to sustain their competitive advantages. Market followers, of whom there are more and more every year, must work diligently to erode whatever advantages leaders enjoy and to build new advantages of their own.

Innovation may make existing products obsolete so that a competitive advantage in an existing product can become meaningless as consumers learn a new value calculus. For example, the compact disc player made valueless a consumer electronic firm's advantage in record playing equipment. Innovations however, are an increasingly less sustainable source of competitive advantage for the innovator. Reverse engineering has become a high art and competitors more and more quickly duplicate or even improve upon their rivals' innovations.

Manufacturing processes are in a constant state of refinement, if not change, and are more and more difficult to keep proprietary. Increasingly, the sources of manufacturing advantage are in capital equipment rather than in low-cost, or even highly skilled labour. New machinery is more and more readily available to all; the ability to improve manufacturing processes is therefore more broadly available. New techniques such as flexible manufacturing and lean manufacturing diffuse more and more quickly. The Korean auto manufacturers, for example, quickly adopt Japanese producers' manufacturing innovations.

Brand names, traditionally perceived by consumers as guarantees of superior value, seem less permanent. New brands, often promoted by recent entrants, appear and displace traditional leaders thought to have sustainable positions. Proctor & Gamble's entrant to the detergent market, Ariel, has displaced Unilever's Omo as the leading detergent brand throughout most of western Europe. In both Europe and the USA, more recent entries by Japanese firms replaced many of the traditional leading domestic consumer electronics brands. Consumers appear more and more willing to forgo tradition.

In the global environment which most business units face, a cost advantage, or at the very least, cost parity with competitors is a requirement for survival. Price competition appears earlier and earlier in the product life cycle, and price is becoming the dominant component in many business units' value propositions. No matter how fast the growth rate in any new product, the number of competitors offering the product seems to increase faster than the rate of growth. Products such as personal computers have become virtual commodities while markets for them are still growing.

In summary, there are fewer and fewer opportunities, extending for shorter and shorter periods of time, in which any firm can maintain a product lead over its competition. With a larger number of firms offering similar or competing products earlier and earlier in a product's life cycle, the business unit looking for volume must become a low cost producer. Even the firm that develops a new-to-the-world innovation must worry about manufacturing costs from the very beginning.

4 Competing in the global marketplace does not always require global reach

The reality of the global marketplace, however, does not mean every business unit must market or manufacture globally or, for that matter, market or manufacture outside its own country. There is still room in the world for domestic as well as global business units. In fact, many industries include a variety of business units ranging from purely domestic to global, along with many regional or multi-market competitors in between.

Some business units focus their international efforts on a single continent. Zenith, a US TV manufacturer, markets only in the other North American countries Canada and Mexico, in addition to the USA. Others concentrate their efforts on the advanced industrialized countries, including the so-called triad of western Europe, North America and Japan.

Still others, such as the Daewoo corporation from South Korea pay particular attention to markets in the developing countries. Each of these strategies can be successful under the right circumstances.

There is also variety in business units' manufacturing configurations. Some of the domestic-only marketers, such as Zenith, may manufacture or source outside their home markets. While global marketing usually requires multiple and dispersed manufacturing sites, certain business units that market regionally or even globally may export to the world from a single manufacturing site. These are exceptional cases, however.

In the past the Boeing Corporation (see BOEING COMPANY) manufactured all its aeroplanes in the USA but sold them worldwide. Boeing is facing increasing pressure to source aeroplane parts and sub-assemblies, and even to manufacture whole aeroplanes, in some of the countries to which it sells its planes. The Japanese automobile manufacturers exported to every overseas market in which they sold until forced by protectionist pressure to start manufacturing abroad.

Every business unit's goal should be to select the configuration or resource deployment pattern that offers it the best chance to gain and maintain a competitive advantage. Even in industries apparently dominated by global business units, business units with more modest configurations can prosper. The variety of marketing and manufacturing configurations within, as well as across, many industries can be quite broad. Moreover, an industry presently dominated by global players is not necessarily a permanent phenomenon nor does such domination preclude new firms from entering the industry.

While there may be conditions or circumstances that are driving a particular industry towards domination by global firms, there are also countervailing conditions that may drive the industry in the other direction. The entry of Korean firms into consumer electronics, automobile and lately chip manufacturing, weakened US and Japanese firms' hold on the global market for these products. These dynamics occur for a variety of reasons, all of which affect the ability of a business unit to gain and maintain a competitive advantage.

In every industry, however, some configurations may offer better opportunities for a specific business unit. Therefore, strategic planners must be able to identify the best alternatives for their own business units. Planners must understand the factors that determine the shape of an industry and the sources of tension that drive it towards domination either by global or by domestic firms.

A business unit's resource deployment and market choices are contingent on the activities that produce its competitive advantage and the economics of those activities. It is critical that planners understand fully the economics of their own industries and the relationship between industry economics and market coverage.

5 Determinants of industry domination

Global business units are likely to dominate an industry when the sources of their competitive advantage come from a multi-market or global presence. Global business units dominate when their global presence enables them to perform better or more efficiently the activities that produce superior customer value. Domestic-only business units can compete successfully where they can provide superior perceived value in their domestic markets without a multi-market or global presence.

In most industries, four interacting factors, or tensions, determine the configuration or resource deployment that is most likely to produce a competitive advantage. They are shown in Figure 2 and are (1) the intrinsic characteristics of the industry; (2) the behaviour of consumers; (3) the behaviour of business units in the industry; and (4) the political and regulatory environment in which these business units operate.

None of these factors is immutable. They are in a constant state of flux, pulling towards domination by global business units and pushing towards domination by domestic business units. They are not always independent. Two or more factors pushing or pulling in the same

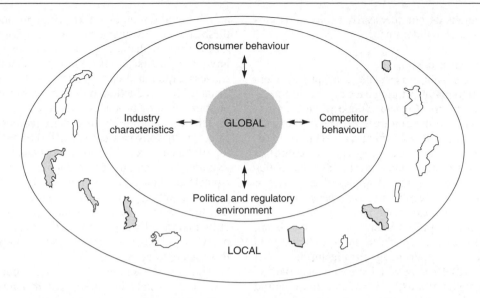

Figure 2 Determinants of industry domination

direction can have a multiplicative effect in determining the business unit types that will dominate an industry. When there is conflict among the factors, the result can be an industry with a wide range of configurations, none of which dominates.

Intrinsic characteristics of the industry

In value chain terms, if the important value producing activities lie to the right of the value chain, there will be a push towards domination by domestic business units. When the important activities lie to the left of the value chain or in supporting activities such as R&D, there is a pull towards domination by multi-market or global business units. The reasons are clear: business units must perform the activities to the right of the value chain in each market and therefore must duplicate in each market the resources and infrastructure necessary to perform them.

Other considerations aside, the smaller the proportion of shipping cost in relation to manufacturing cost, the more likely the industry is to feel the pull towards global domination. Similarly, the less perishable the

product, either because of physical deterioration or the vagaries of fashion, the more likely the industry is to feel that same pull.

In product life cycle terms, domination by global firms tends to be strongest at the growth and early mature stages of the cycle. Mature industries, in fact, may provide opportunities for new non-global entrants. This is especially true in industries with low rates of innovation, standardized products and simple or well understood and easily imitated manufacturing processes. As we shall see, however, there are significant exceptions to both the value chain and product life cycle generalizations.

We can group global pull determinants into two classes, manufacturing cost-based and innovation-based. There are three principal manufacturing cost effects: (1) economies of scale; (2) experience curve; and (3) economies of scope. They all exert global pull in the same manner, by producing lower costs as volumes increase, but the situations in which each exerts its pull is different. The global pull that innovation intensive industries exert is somewhat more complex, as is the case of industries characterized by standardized products. Industries producing standardized products do not necessarily exhibit a pull towards global domination.

Economies of scale

Scale economy is a static concept and refers only to manufacturing capacity. Scale economies are most usually found when the fixed costs of production are high in relation to variable costs. Process industries such as petrochemicals and highly automated manufacturing industries such as automobiles and TVs are prime examples of industries in which scale economies have been important determinants of manufacturing costs.

Global pull is strong when a significant proportion of a business unit's total costs: (1) accrue in performing manufacturing activities; (2) decrease with increasing manufacturing volume; and (3) when the volume required to achieve a low cost position in an industry requires a multi-market presence. In such industries, business units based in countries with large domestic markets have a natural advantage over their small market-based competitors.

In some manufacturing industries scale economies may not result from high finished goods production volumes. They may result instead from the ability to integrate backwards the high rates of finished goods production volume make possible. Again, the automobile industry provides an example. An automobile producer can achieve low costs at relatively low vehicle assembly volumes. High assembly volumes may not result in lower assembly costs. Cost savings associated with increased volume will occur because the producer can afford to make, rather than buy parts. In many industries, achieving scale economies in parts or components requires higher production volumes than assembling finished goods.

Experience curve effects

In contrast, experience curve effects are longitudinal rather than cross-sectional. The experience curve doctrine, as applied to manufacturing costs, posits that a firm's costs of producing a particular product are a function of the total number of such products it has produced over time. Organizational learning and innovation in manufacturing produce these effects. Obviously, if the doctrine is correct, the firm with the largest total volume will have the lowest costs. Analysts usually express experience curve effects as the percentage cost reduction obtained with each doubling of total production volume.

The key assumption of experience curve effects is that any new entrant will start at the top of the curve and will not be cost competitive until its accumulated production volume equals that of the highest volume competitors. Since marketing globally can provide a business unit with more volume than marketing only domestically, global marketing is an imperative for both early and late entrants under this assumption.

The key assumption of experience curve effects holds only in certain circumstances. Experience curve effects are most likely to be observed in industries in which the manufacturing technology is both new and fast changing, closely held rather than widely available, and can be learned only through doing. In the microchip industry, for example, the only way to bring manufacturing costs down is to manufacture them oneself. Moreover, experience curve effects in such industries come partly from increased capacity and a higher rate of capacity utilization.

In many heavy as well as light manufacturing industries, experience curve effects are much less apparent. We see in industry after industry that inexperienced late entrants are competing successfully with much more experienced earlier entrants. Part of the explanation may lie in factor cost differentials that overcome inexperience; the latest entrants in many industries locate in low wage areas. A more powerful explanation is that these are industries with well known manufacturing technologies and widely available production machinery and components. In such circumstances, a new entrant does not have to start at the top of the experience curve.

In both scale and experience generated volume and cost relationships, the strategist must understand the exact source of the business unit's cost advantage to maintain its competitive value. In a significant number of cases, a cost advantage is not the result of increased volume in the finished product. The cost advantage is in one or more components of the finished product. For many years Texas Instruments (TI) dominated the calculator market. TI's domination did not result from its calculator volume; but rather from its dominant position in manufacturing the chip that was the costliest component in the calculator. TI's control of the chip market enabled it to offer a better value proposition than competitors. TI also took advantage of scope economies to produce a broad product line, offering at each price level more performance than competitors' calculators.

A more recent case is Matsushita's domination of the global video recorder (VCR) market (see MATSUSHITA, K.). A significant contributor to its position in VCRs is its volume in recording heads and related subassemblies, key modules in a VCR. Matsushita produces 42 per cent of the world's VCRs, but 65 per cent of its recording heads (Lorenz 1993). Brand differentiation has become increasingly difficult to maintain in VCRs. Matsushita's cost advantage has allowed the firm to compete intensively while still generating some profits.

Specialist suppliers of key modules have begun to dominate some other industries globally. These include suppliers of products as diverse as components for personal computers and automobile piston assemblies. The success these suppliers enjoy adds additional credence to the importance of identifying exactly where in the value chain the key producers of customer value lie.

Events in the 1990s, however, point out the risks as well as the advantages of being a dominant player in a global industry in which costs are volume related. Maintaining one's position in such a market requires continued growth in capacity that at least equals market growth, lest a competitor catch up. The market for VCRs has become almost stagnant and Matsushita now finds itself with high fixed costs and idle capacity. As difficult as this situation may be for a highly diversified Matsushita, it will be even more difficult for a business unit that supplies only components.

Economies of scope

Economy of scope in manufacturing is the ability to produce a wide range of products more efficiently than producing each separately. Scope economies are becoming an increasingly important source of competitive advantage in a wide range of industries. Automobile manufacturers assemble right- and left-hand drive vehicles on the same production line. Photocopier manufacturers assemble several models on the same line, using as many common parts as possible. Manufacturers of consumer electronics products strive to offer the broadest product lines they can, sharing facilities wherever possible.

Scope economies in manufacturing enable business units to tailor their products to the specific demands of particular markets with minimum cost penalty. It allows them to offer products for which demand might be small in any one country. Economies of scope also contribute significantly to competitive advantages on the right side of the value chain. The business unit with a wide selection of models and related product lines can spread its marketing and distribution costs over a wider number of products. At the same time, it can offer consumers a wider choice. Japanese manufacturers of consumer electronics have used scope economies to great advantage in becoming global players.

Innovation intensive industries

Global or multi-market firms tend to dominate industries with high rates of innovation (see INTERNATIONAL TRADE AND FOREIGN DIRECT INVESTMENT). This is especially true of industries with short product life cycles, where new products displace old, and where developing new products requires extensive research with uncertain results. One such industry is ethical pharmaceuticals. Newer and better drug treatments regularly replace old ones. Competitors try to improve on any new drug that a rival introduces.

To ensure future profitability pharmaceutical companies must spend heavily on research. However, R&D has not produced enough new products to sustain high growth levels into the new millennium. In 1998

Smith-Kline PLC and Glaxo Wellcome PLC proposed merging to create the world's biggest drug company. Potentially, this combination would allow a new pharmaceutical giant to dominate global market share in a variety of products and greatly enhance its ability to market globally.

Firms that do not have global marketing infrastructures enter into joint venture or licensing agreements in order to gain global market coverage. Many biotechnology firms in the USA, which typically do not have global market coverage are entering into these arrangements.

The automobile industry is another example. Competitive rivalry requires a steady stream of new cars. The principal costs of innovation in the automobile industry are product design and testing and subsequent tooling for the new model. Once again, global market coverage offers opportunities for greater sales. The large firm can spread its R&D costs over a larger volume of cars and thus introduce new models more frequently.

Not every innovation prone industry, however, must be dominated by global business units. Consumer packaged goods industries typically develop great numbers of new products. In most cases, their R&D costs are modest; their major research cost may be marketing research, which they must conduct locally. They can produce many of their new products in existing facilities and do so efficiently at relatively modest volumes. In consumer packaged goods industries the major advantage a global business unit gains is the additional innovation stimuli provided by their presence in many diverse markets.

Industries producing standardized products

Industries amenable to product standardization are likely to be dominated by global firms only under certain circumstances. The pull towards global domination in these industries is strongest when the product is either protected by a strong enforceable patent or requires proprietary know-how that is either difficult to learn or can be kept secret. In a very few situations, a powerful brand name

will permit a business unit to dominate its industry globally.

Without such conditions, the push towards domination by domestic firms will be strong, and moderated only by the ability of global firms to maintain a cost advantage. When economies of scale in manufacturing are the source of the cost advantage, the business unit need enter only enough markets to be sure of reaching scale. Ideally, these should be markets that will also pre-empt competitors' abilities to reach scale. Given the choice, a small number of large markets may be preferable to a large number of smaller markets.

If competition in large markets is intense, however, the business unit can, with impunity, spread its efforts to include smaller markets. The German auto makers, Mercedes-Benz and BMW both follow this strategy; they spread their sales worldwide, including small as well as large markets. In this example, the cost of increasing share in a large market is higher than the cost of obtaining equivalent volume spread among several small markets.

If the source of competitive advantage is experience curve, the business unit must concern itself with its production volume relative to competitors. Simply reaching an economic scale is not sufficient; it must also be a higher volume producer than its competitors. The safest strategy for achieving a higher relative volume is to enter as many markets as possible, being especially sure to penetrate large markets deeply. This strategy offers the best chance of blocking competitors from gaining large market shares in large markets. The business unit competing on experience curve must expand production rapidly and market aggressively everywhere it can.

The behaviour of consumers

The characteristics of the industries in which global pull is strongest are those in which consumers' preference is for the same value proposition worldwide. A prime example is industries with a substantial proportion of customers that are themselves global business units that purchase the product to use locally in several countries. The pull is strongest when the product purchased is complex and must be identical wherever customers purchase it.

The automobile parts industry has become global, as its customers, the automobile companies, broadened the number of countries in which they produce cars. Suppliers of telecommunications equipment, especially equipment used in corporate data transmission networks, must be able to supply products and services locally everywhere their global customers require it. Capital goods industries have become global as global manufacturers have standardized their products and processes worldwide.

Global pull from customers that are themselves global occurs in service industries such as banking and accounting as well as in manufacturing industries. Many global business units prefer to use one bank worldwide for services such as lock box, which collects and collates deposits from any number of sites. Dealing with one bank facilitates keeping track of money and maintaining the desired basket of currencies. Similarly, many global firms prefer to use the same auditing firm worldwide. Global customers are globalizing investment banking as well; global firms want to distribute their securities throughout the world.

For household, as opposed to business, consumers the picture is more mixed. Industries composed of branded goods with high symbolic value can support some global business units. Coca-Cola and Pepsi have demonstrated that global business units can dominate the market for low priced products. Both the Ralph Lauren Polo and the Levi's jeans brands have become global but certainly do not dominate their industry. The same is true for certain brands in product categories such as Scotch whisky brands that many world travellers may favour. In both these examples, however, the market shares of global units are small.

In most cases, the idiosyncratic preferences of consumers around the globe mitigate against standardization and therefore against domination by global business units (Douglas and Wind 1987). The exception is when the cost savings made possible by standardization provide more value to consumers than the customized features that would otherwise be included. The ever wider adoption of production techniques that make possible low costs at low volumes are reducing the cost of adding customized features to products.

Global businesses do exist in many packaged goods categories and in fast foods. These businesses may operate worldwide using a single brand name and offering a core of standardized products. They operate, however, much like a portfolio of domestic businesses. They are self-contained units in most of the countries in which they operate, and their product lines, usually quite wide, typically contain some country specific products in addition to a global core product line. For example, most McDonald's in western Europe serve wine and beer; those in Japan offer special items tailored to Japanese taste.

Consumers can change the balance between global and domestic firms in an industry when there are changes in the elements of product content that create perceived value for them. In the clothing industry, the key consumers are the retail stores that determine what assortments to offer their customers. During the 1970s and 1980s, low delivered cost was critically important to these customers. They would purchase far in advance, accept long delivery times, and maintain large inventories to obtain the lowest possible price. However, in the 1990s, fashion cycles have become shorter. For the retailer, showing new merchandise more frequently and minimizing possession costs have become more important than minimizing product cost. Retailers demand short lead times and fast, fast delivery; they all want to minimize their inventories. As a result, geographical proximity to the market has become more important than low cost for fashion intensive items. Low cost remains the paramount consideration for slowly changing merchandise categories such as men's white shirts.

The political and regulatory environment

The political and regulatory environment demonstrates the same push and pull exhibited by the other factors affecting industry domination. The interest of an individual country is in a strong domestic economy. While paying lip service to the benefits provided by international trade, most countries would rather export more and import less.

The business and agricultural communities in many countries pressure their governments to restrict imports, and governments may respond with any number of actions. There are a wide variety of barriers countries can erect to minimize imports, extending well beyond simply raising tariffs. Countries can restrict foreign investment, institute onerous inspection techniques, strictly regulate product labelling and content or impose restrictions on advertising. These are examples of non-tariff barriers to trade.

On the export side, countries can also take actions to increase their firms' presence in the global marketplace. They can try to create national champions by creating domestic demand for products of a certain industry. France has attempted to create such champions in the telecommunications industry through its Minitel programme. Countries can encourage industry wide research programmes as the USA has done with Sematech in the microchip field. They can subsidize exports to make exporting a more attractive option for their country's businesses.

Trading blocs such as the North American Free Trade Agreement (NAFTA), the European Union (EU) and the Asean Free Trade Area (AFTA) are emerging and strengthening (see ASSOCIATION OF SOUTH-EAST ASIAN NATIONS; NORTH AMERICAN FREE-TRADE AGREEMENT). These blocs minimize or eliminate tariffs and other restrictions on the movement of goods, services and capital within the bloc. They may, however, impose high tariffs or other restrictions on goods coming from outside and therefore have the potential to impede as well as facilitate trade. Trading blocs, of course, push industries towards domination by domestic business units.

The World Trade Organization (WTO; see WORLD TRADE ORGANIZATION) is the global body charged with devising a uniform set of regulations that encourage and facilitate international trade. The function of the WTO and its predecessor the General Agreement on Tariffs and Trade (GATT) is to eliminate trade restrictions. It has been a powerful force in removing tariff barriers and increasing the volume of international trade. In carrying out its mandate it has facilitated the creation of global business units.

6 The strategies firms employ

As we pointed out earlier, industry characteristics, volume related economies and innovation rates primarily determine the strength of the pull towards domination by global business units. There are some circumstances in which business units can take the actions that change the characteristics of an industry and in doing so change the direction of an industry. There are other circumstances in which a business unit can develop and exploit an advantage that is not based on industry characteristics.

Changing the characteristics of an industry

It may be less difficult than it seems to change the characteristics of an industry. There are some circumstances in which significant changes are possible. Change is possible in industries in which sales volume affects product costs. In such industries, business units will vie either to magnify or diminish these volume effects. The business unit that belongs to a large firm with extensive financial resources should take actions that magnify the effects of volume, while the less financial resource rich business unit should act to diminish these effects.

The trend is towards diminution of the effects of volume on manufacturing cost and thus towards diminished global pull. In the auto industry, for example, manufacturing scale has always been critical, and the large vertically integrated firm has had a manufacturing cost advantage. Over the last few years the development of flexible production methods has made it possible for firms to achieve low costs at smaller production volumes.

Smaller producers are also attacking the costs of product development by involving their suppliers more intensively in the product development process. They use their small size to advantage in shortening the time between product conception and market introduction. For example, Chrysler managed to bring two new series of cars, the LH and Neon models, to market in a fraction of the time and at a fraction of the cost of Ford's new Mondeo.

The rise of specialist supplier firms and the willingness of some automobile manufacturers to sell parts to others has lessened the advantage of vertical integration; some even claim that vertical integration is now a handicap rather than an advantage. When an automobile manufacturer becomes a parts seller, advantages accrue to it as well as to the buyer. Mitsubishi, an automobile manufacturer with a small market share, is a major producer of engines. It supplies Chrysler, Korea's Hyundai (see CHUNG FAMILY OF HYUNDAI) and Malaysia's Proton Saga, among others. These engine sales help Mitsubishi keep its own cars competitive despite its small market share.

In the future, it may become increasingly difficult to maintain the pull towards global domination in industries in which costs are volume related. The combination of independent specialist parts suppliers, flexible production techniques and fast product development can overcome the cost disadvantage that formerly accompanied small volume finished goods production. A freer international trade environment will also benefit the smaller business unit. Through exporting, it will be able to increase its sales volume without investing in overseas manufacturing facilities.

Shifting costs from one side of the value chain to the other can also change the industry balance between global and domestic business units. Right side costs include marketing, domestic distribution and service, which business units must incur on a country by country basis. The higher these costs in relation to total product costs, the more ably a domestic business unit can compete. Xerox based its

advantage in photocopiers partly on an extensive after sales service capability. Canon, on the other hand, tried to design and manufacture copiers requiring a minimum of service and maintenance.

The foregoing discussion presents only a sampling of the ways in which a business unit can potentially change the shape of an industry through its actions. Not all choices are equally valuable. The value of a particular choice depends on its potential to produce a sustainable competitive advantage and the ability of the business unit to realize the advantage. Truly sustainable competitive advantages are fast becoming a rare commodity.

Exploiting a unique location, capability or asset

In certain circumstances a business unit can become a strong global competitor even when its competitive advantage does not result from building a multi-market or global presence. In these circumstances, the firm's existing geographic location, capabilities or business specific assets provide a basis for the business unit to become a multi-market or global competitor. These are cases of exploiting an advantage gained in the domestic market.

A business unit's geographic location can endow it with a factor cost-based competitive advantage the unit can use to export to world markets. Labour intensive industries such as clothing manufacture provide an example. Location-based competitive advantages derived from low labour costs have proven sustainable only in the short term. Business units that base their value propositions on low prices made possible by low labour costs must expect to move their production sites regularly as wages increase at their present sites.

Many Hong Kong and South Korean producers of clothing and athletic shoes, for example, have moved their export manufacturing sites to lower labour cost countries such as Indonesia, Thailand and Bangladesh. It is worth noting that even traditional labour intensive industries are becoming significantly more automated. Computer guided lasers now cut cloth assembled by computer controlled sewing machines. In the future, the principal areas of cost saving may be in supervisory and middle management personnel rather than in direct manufacturing labour.

A cost advantage in raw materials or facilities can be more permanent than a labour cost advantage. Indonesia has become a global marketer of plywood by taking advantage of the low cost logs made available to plywood manufacturers there. The USA can competitively market agricultural products such as wheat and chickens despite high salaries and wages. Low land costs, huge farms and highly mechanized growing and processing methods more than offset high labour costs. Countries that produce oil or natural gas have a basis for developing a competitively advantaged petrochemicals industry.

Location can also be a source of competitive advantage even when it does not directly produce a factor cost advantage. Porter (1990) has identified four characteristics of countries that can aid business units' efforts to develop a competitive advantage. These are:

- the availability of skilled labour and appropriate infrastructure
- demand conditions
- the presence of related and supporting industries
- the strategy, structure and rivalry among firms competing in that nation

In technology-intensive industries, scientific establishments, usually university-based, that conduct basic research and train new researchers are a critical component of infrastructure. For example, the absence of such establishments has limited Japanese firms' ability to invent brand new technologies, while the presence of scientific establishments has fostered US firms' invention capability in industries such as biotechnology.

The capability to invent does not by itself ensure success in the marketplace. This capability must be coupled with the ability to commercialize the invention, to transform a laboratory idea or expensive prototype into a mass-marketable product. For commercialization to occur, the presence of supporting industries may be much more critical than the presence of a scientific establishment dedicated to basic research.

Supporting industries are particularly critical for new product lines that use or adapt technologies, components or manufacturing techniques from existing product lines. The evolution of the consumer electronics industry in Japan provides an illustration. Japanese firms' lead in television, audio receivers and tape recorders made virtually inevitable its lead in VCRs. Its experience in cameras coupled with its electronics capabilities ensured its position in camcorders. Its lead in electronics, coupled with a high level of domestic demand, facilitated its global position in fax machines. Domestic rivalry encouraged innovation and then globalization in order to build volume (see MANAGEMENT IN JAPAN).

The absence of supporting industries also helps explain why VCRs, although invented in the USA, were commercialized in Japan. US firms' manufacturing capacity in consumer electronics had already moved offshore. Their offshore manufacturing depended on low labour costs rather than on improving productivity through automation and development of better components. Japanese firms, on the other hand, were busily developing larger and larger integrated circuits and manufacturing techniques that took maximum advantage of these circuits' potential to improve productivity. Taiwan emerged in the 1990s as a world leader in personal computer manufacture based on a combination of speed, flexibility and the presence of supporting industries.

In industries in which costs are volume related, a high level of domestic demand clearly facilitates a business unit's ability to gain competitive advantage. In industries with high rates of innovation, the character of demand may be even more important than its level. Proximity to lead users is a critical innovation stimulus. Japanese manufacturing firms lead the world in their use of robots. These firms provided the stimulus for Japan's lead in robot manufacture.

Global business units may dominate an industry even when they do not have a factor cost advantage and when global presence is not the key source of their competitive advantage. This can occur when the business unit brings to foreign markets a unique ability to perform activities that produce superior customer value. The success of the US fast food firms and convenience stores in world markets is an example. Their principal value creating activities are in management systems. The fast food marketers designed systems to cook and serve food of invariant quality quickly and efficiently. The convenience stores developed transferable management systems. In both cases, the systems work with a variety of product offerings and are easily transferable across borders.

The global spread of fast food and convenience stores is not the source of their advantage in the global market. Their ability to spread globally came from the systems they developed at home. As we pointed out in our earlier discussion of fast foods, systems were not enough to guarantee success; both the fast food marketers and the convenience store operators had to modify their product offerings to satisfy the consumers in each country they entered.

While the competitive value of brand names has diminished, there are some circumstances in which a brand name still provides a basis for a multi-market or global business. These are circumstances in which consumers perceive that a particular brand name guarantees superior or unique value as compared to competitors' offerings. As we pointed out earlier, the best opportunities are likely to be in product categories with potentially high symbolic value. In these cases, it is the brand name itself that provides the additional value consumers perceive in the generic product. The ephemeral nature of the images the brand may convey can insulate it from competition at least for a time.

7 Identifying the best opportunities

Despite the great difficulty in developing a long-term, sustainable competitive advantage, firms can pursue actions that lead to competitive advantages sustainable for a period of time. Ghemawat (1991) labels sources of such advantage sticky factors

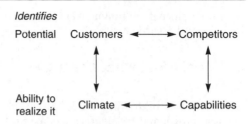

Figure 3 The four C's analysis

because they resist erosion by competitors. He recommends that business units conduct a sustainability analysis to determine the speed with which a particular source of competitive advantage is likely to erode.

The Four Cs Analysis (Wortzel and Vernon-Wortzel 1995) shown in Figure 3 is a useful organizing concept for conducting a sustainability analysis. The Four Cs studies customers and competitors to identify the potentially promising value propositions. It studies the legal and regulatory climate and the business unit's capabilities to assess which of the promising value propositions it is in the best position to deliver.

The purpose of the customer and competitor analyses is to determine the best value propositions and the actions necessary to achieve them. These analyses should consider both present and potential customers and both present and potential competitors. The climate analysis should anticipate changes as well as identify the portions of the present political and regulatory environment that most affect the business unit's ability to deliver the desired value propositions.

The critical element in determining a business unit's ability to realize an opportunity is the unit's own capabilities. Capabilities are the business processes and activities that build perceived value into the business unit's products and services (Stalk *et al.* 1992). Capabilities go beyond the activities covered in the value chain. They include activities such as fast product design time and the ability to anticipate competitors' responses, for example. A capability analysis should consider the business unit's present capabilities as well as its ability to develop needed capabilities in the future. The business unit that understands all four Cs will be well along the path to finding its proper place in the global environment.

8 Conclusion: what the future holds

Unless powerful trading blocs with high external tariffs and restrictions become predominant, existing trends towards freer international trade and foreign direct investment should continue. Further market interpenetration will mean ever tougher competition. In existing industries, more competitors from more countries will vie for market share in every country.

In most such industries, it will be increasingly difficult for business units to maintain a degree of product differentiation that is meaningful to customers. Low price will be ever more critical to maintaining a superior value proposition. Clearly, a business unit must be a low cost producer in order to offer low prices and remain profitable. Achieving a low cost position is not always contingent on global reach, as we pointed out earlier.

Speciality producers that are sources of key components have emerged and facilitated new business units' entry into product lines that use these components. Through careful sourcing, in an increasing number of industries, smaller domestic or regional business units may be able to compete successfully with much larger global firms. Global firms, because of their higher overheads, and the inertia that often accompanies large size will face many challenges from smaller, less global business units.

The history of multinational firms tells us, in fact, that these firms do best when they can pursue a product differentiation strategy that allows them to command higher prices for their offerings. Product differentiation strategies will be less and less durable in the future. Specialist suppliers, the diffusion of manufacturing process technology, reverse engineering and a host of other factors decrease the time it takes and the risks involved for followers to bringing new products to market.

All in all, the competitive environment will be such that existing industries will offer only limited growth and profit potential. Hamel and Prahalad (1991) argue convincingly that the big profits of the future will come not from well-defined positions in well-defined industries but rather from as yet undefined new products in as yet undefined new industries. These new products may not simply be extensions of the firm's present offerings.

Hamel and Prahalad believe the most successful firms of the future will be the creators of new competitive space. Developing and successfully commercializing such new products requires a unique combination of capabilities. The business unit that wants to create such new competitive space must understand customers well enough to anticipate their needs even before the customers themselves can express them. It must be able to translate quickly unrecognized needs into products. This requires a combination of development, engineering, sourcing and manufacturing skills.

A would-be creator of new competitive space must also have a global marketing and distribution network. In a world in which competitors quickly imitate any potentially successful new product, the first mover has an advantage only when it can fill the distribution channels everywhere, leaving as little as possible of that new competitive space for its rivals.

HEIDI VERNON
NORTHEASTERN UNIVERSITY

LAWRENCE H. WORTZEL (DECD)
FORMERLY OF BOSTON UNIVERSITY

Further reading

(References cited in the text marked *)

Bartlett, C. and Ghoshal, S. (eds) (1991) *Global Strategy*, special issue of *Strategic Management Journal* 12. (A collection of conceptual and empirical articles on various aspects of global strategy.)

* Douglas, S.P. and Wind, Y. (1987) 'The myth of globalization', *Columbia Journal of World Business* (Winter): 19–29. (Discusses in some detail the pitfalls of global product and market standardization.)

* Ghemawat, P. (1991) *Commitment*, New York: The Free Press. (A discussion of value, how to

identify and create opportunities, and how to sustain them.)

* Hamel, G. and Prahalad, C.K. (1991) 'Corporate imagination and expeditionary marketing', *Harvard Business Review* (July–August): 81–92. (An explication of the authors' thesis about the importance of creating new products and the vision required to capitalize on the opportunities.)

* Lorenz, C. (1993) 'Conventional strategic wisdom takes a knock', *Financial Times* (17 December): 9. (A report of a speech by C.K. Prahalad that explicates some new theories about strategy and questions some old ones.)

Porter, M. (ed.) (1986) *Competition in Global Industries*, Boston, MA: Harvard Business School Press. (A collection of papers which, taken together, offer a broad perspective on global strategy.)

* Porter, M. (1990) *The Competitive Advantage of Nations*, New York: The Free Press. (This book presents and analyses the results of a study of the process by which firms gained competitive advantage, and the role of their home country environment in the process. The study was conducted in ten countries and encompassed several industries.)

* Porter, M. (1991) 'Towards a dynamic theory of strategy', *Strategic Management Journal* 12: 95–117. (An explication of the theory underlying a competitive advantage perspective on strategic planning.)

* Stalk, G., Evans, P. and Shulman, L.E. (1992) 'Competing on capabilities: the new rules of corporate strategy', *Harvard Business Review* (March–April): 57–69. (An argument that the ability to conduct value creating business processes is a critical component of strategy.)

Vernon, R. and Wells, L.T. (1991) *The Manager in the International Economy*, Englewood Cliffs, NJ: Prentice Hall. (A discussion of the national and international environments in which global firms must operate, together with a discussion of the firm viewed from within.)

Vernon-Wortzel, H. and Wortzel, L. (eds) (1991) *Global Strategic Management*, New York: Wiley. (A managerially focused collection of readings encompassing global strategy and all the business functional areas.)

* Wortzel, L.H. and Vernon-Wortzel, H. (1995) *Strategic Marketing in the Global Economy*, New York: Oxford University Press. (Discusses marketing strategies for firms that must compete with global marketers, both worldwide and in their domestic markets.)

See also: ASSOCIATION OF SOUTH-EAST ASIAN NATIONS; BOEING COMPANY; CHUNG FAMILY OF HYUNDAI; EXPORTING; FOREIGN MARKET ENTRY STRATEGIES; GLOBAL STRATEGIC ALLIANCES; GLOBALIZATION; INTERNATIONAL BUSINESS, FUTURE TRENDS; INTERNATIONAL MARKETING; INTERNATIONAL OPERATIONS; INTERNATIONAL TRADE AND FOREIGN DIRECT INVESTMENT; MANAGEMENT IN JAPAN; MATSUSHITA, K.; MULTINATIONAL CORPORATIONS; NORTH AMERICAN FREE TRADE AGREEMENT; WORLD TARDE ORGANIZATION

Related topics of IEBM: GENERAL AGREEMENT ON TARIFFS AND TRADE; MARKETING STRATEGY; MANUFACTURING STRATEGY; ORGANIZATION BEHAVIOUR; ORGANIZATIONAL LEARNING; PORTER, M.E.; STRATEGIC MARKETING PLANNING; STRATEGY, CONCEPT OF

Globalization

Overview

Globalization is the process of increasing integration in world civilization. The transformation of its definition reveals the extent to which globalization has proceeded in the last decades. In the 1970s, globalization was seen in terms of the increasing interdependence among states. In today's economy, interdependence among nations is of less central interest, as powerful global actors (for example, multinational corporations and financial institutions) have created a world in which borders are less consequential.

The extent of globalization can be captured through a number of descriptive indicators: parity in prices – prices and interest rates should converge with globalization; effect on behaviours – nation states, firms, and other actors consider their actions and others' actions in one state as influencing their interests in another; world culture – the sharing of cultural values across countries; ideological – the convergence in beliefs about what constitutes a desirable polity. Each of these indicators hides the distinction between *interdependence* and *integration*. Financial markets may converge to price parity, as long as investors can move money from one country to the other. They need not be integrated in the form of a world market for equities. Governments and firms may respond to the actions of their counterparts in other countries, and yet the political and economic significance of borders

may be preserved. National cultures and ideologies can respond to foreign ideas in a reactionary way. Austrian churches are topped by onion-shaped cupolas and the French croissant is derived from the Islamic crescent. Yet both of these cultural artefacts are symbolic of the clash between competing and interdependent cultures, not their integration.

The transition from interdependence to integration is seen in the many regional economic groupings that have been spawned over the last forty years. The period immediately after the Second World War saw the creation of international institutions to manage interdependence, although under the tutelage of a few powerful countries. The success of these institutions has varied, but the ones created in the economic sphere have unquestionably increased in membership and importance. The International Monetary Fund has grown from 29 in 1945 to 182 members. The World Bank Group has expanded into project financing in developing countries. In the area of trade, the failed attempt to create an international institution in the 1940s has recently been rectified through the establishment of the World Trade Organization.

Unnoticed in the discussion over interdependence were the forces that have led to a growing integration in the world economy. At the regional level, the results of integration are the most obvious. The European Union is clearly the most prominent example of interdependent states seeking to resolve conflict and to enjoy the benefits of a wider market through economic and political integration. Yet their example is reflected in the less ambitious efforts of other countries. The North American Free-Trade Agreement (NAFTA; see NORTH AMERICAN FREE-TRADE AGREEMENT) is a case of low-level integration in so far as the elimination of tariffs and some harmonization of environmental and labour laws are involved. But the world trend is towards more integration, albeit at the regional level, with agreements in Latin America (for example, Mercosur) and in east Asia (for example, ASEAN; see ASSOCIATION OF SOUTH-EAST ASIAN NATIONS), and increasing *de facto* integration in southern Africa occurring only in the past decade.

Interdependence and integration are not unilateral trends in world history. There are counterbalancing factors, particularly those unleashed through the actions of threatened groups or governments. Because globalization influences power and social standing among groups, it is a process that lies at the heart of social change and political policy in all countries. Extreme examples are the responses of countries (for example, Iran) undergoing rapid change which incur a reversal in their openness to the world economy. The debate is not only economic, but ideological and religious. Less extreme examples are no doubt the more modal cases, such as the decision of France in the early 1980s to impose constraints on capital movements.

It is misleading to believe that globalization is determined simply by the development of new technologies in communication and transportation. Since groups and governments can influence the extent and pace of globalization, world integration and interdependence are not simply exogenous and given factors in the course of history. They are both the cause and effect of social and political change. Globalization constrains governments and other actors, such as firms, in their capability to carry out domestic policies. But since governments and firms are also powerful actors, they can influence the process of globalization. Decisions to deregulate or to lower tariffs influence the degree of commerce. In this regard, globalization is both an endogenous and exogenous factor determined in its pace and development by the actions of governments, firms, and other social actors, but influencing also in its turn the behaviour of these same actors.

From the perspective of economics, integration appears as inevitable because of the gains to eliminating institutional imperfections in the movement of goods, services and capital. There is in other words a powerful dynamic unleashed through the creation of positive feedback to integration. Larger markets should increase a more efficient allocation of world resources. Yet, not only is this dynamic sensitive to the process by which integration occurs (for example, by regions or by world agreement), it also results in the dislocation of workers and important social groups and institutions. Even if one were to accept that integration improves world welfare in some global assessment of the costs and benefits, the distributional consequences are substantial, as are the effects on the relative power of nation-states.

Globalization, by the very definition of its expansiveness, covers a wide geographic and conceptual terrain. In the following entry, a short historical prelude and concise presentation of indicators of globalization are presented. The analysis of globalization as cause and effect in an historical process is illustrated through two applications. The first concerns the growth of the multinational corporation through foreign direct investment (see INTERNATIONAL TRADE AND FOREIGN DIRECT INVESTMENT); the second summarizes some of the research on the political economy of globalization. By way of conclusion, the question as to whether globalization is, given its current progress, an irreversible process is examined in detail.

1 Historical prelude

Increased interdependence and integration are forces that have marked world history. To a non-trivial extent, the expansion of early humans to new terrains is the emblematic example of globalization through massive migrations of people across long distances. The diffusion of myths and rituals through these migrations is evident in the common heritage of Indo-European civilization and, more broadly, among civilizations that have enjoyed contact and communication.

Nor is this interdependence a characteristic of modern economies. Semitic traders – Syrians, Jews and Aramaeans – played an important role in the last centuries of the Roman Empire. Custom duties were low, with only 2 to 2.5 per cent of value levied at the borders of each province. Raw materials were sent to the empire: gold and ivory from Africa, silk from China, spices from Arabia. But only high value to weight items could be transported, and there was a strong tendency for areas away from coastal areas and cities to resort to self-sufficiency. Since Rome had few luxury goods to offer in return, its trade with Asia was paid in gold and other specie, encouraging the debasing of its coinage. The breakup of Rome placed further taxes on the movement of goods, a situation that in many respects is only today being remedied.

Trade and commerce were also hampered by the absence of formalized international law and institutions, in addition to the costs of commerce and taxation. The role of particular ethnic groups, such as Armenians, Gujarati, Fijian Chinese, and Jews, in world trade has historically been of great importance not only for the transport and sales of goods, but also of ideas. These groups played the role of cross-cultural brokers, who succeeded in establishing cosmopolitan communities across long distances. Trade was possible because of strict rules of enforcement and the possibility of detection within these groups.

It is a perennially debated issue when the start of a world capitalist order can be said to have begun. Fernand Braudel (1979), whose studies are certainly the best-known statements on the origins of the world economy, places its emergence between the fifteenth and eighteenth centuries. No doubt there was still tremendous variation not only at the lowest levels of production, but also in the emergent markets for valuable goods and financial credit. Variations in prices for gold and silver caused large movements of the species in opposite directions. Europe generally placed a higher value on gold. With the importation of silver from the Americas, Europe was able to finance its deficit with Russia and Asia better than Rome. France demurred from the policy of hoarding gold, and silver fetched a higher price there. Nevertheless, prices among the major European states were already interdependent by the end of this period.

The period of rapid convergence in prices among regional and national markets was only realized in the 1800s with the fall in communication and transportation costs. News took about three weeks to travel from Venice to London in 1500; no improvement had been made by 1765. The famous story of the Rothschild family learning of the outcome of the battle of Waterloo through its own emissaries obscures the fact that this practice did not originate with them and was hardly new. By the end of the century, with the creation of the telegraph, such practices were harder to put into effect. Transportation also was agonizingly slow. The slow pace of transport by road led to massive canal-building in the 1700s in England, France and elsewhere. By the end of the 1800s, low tariff rates and the massive outflow of capital – particularly from Great Britain and France – resulted in only minor differentials in traded goods and interest rates. Indeed, financial indices were more related across a few select industrial countries during the *belle époque* and the inter-war years than since 1945.

In the course of history, the interlude from 1914 to 1989 may appear politically as a departure from a long-term trend towards the globalization of world markets and world culture. But the period prior to 1914 was primarily a period of interdependence among a small number of states. The aftermath of the Second World War has seen, instead, the creation of world institutions. The effects of these institutions, and the secular growth in world trade and investment have caused far-reaching changes in the world economy. Some of these changes are examined below.

2 Indicators of increasing integration

The recent pace of technological advance has allowed for a deeper integration of the classic factors of production of land, labour and capital. The world economy, as we have stated, is not simply technologically determined, and the degree and pace of integration of these factors have been shaped by institutional and political influences. Table 1 illustrates how the costs of international integration as represented by transportation, communication, and information processing, have declined very sharply, particularly after the 1970s.

Table 1 Costs of air transportation, telephone calls and computers in 1990 dollars, 1930–90

Year	Average air transportation revenue per passenger mile	Cost of a three-minute call, New York to London	Department of Commerce computer price deflator (1990=1000)
1930	0.68	244.65	n.a
1940	0.46	188.51	n.a
1950	0.30	53.20	n.a
1960	0.24	45.86	125000
1970	0.16	31.58	19474
1980	0.10	4.80	3620
1990	0.11	3.32	1000

Source: Herring and Litan (1995)

In the post-war period, falling tariffs and advances in air and freight transport allowed for a great expansion of world trade, leading to greater interdependence of national markets for goods (see INTERNATIONAL TRADE AND FOREIGN DIRECT INVESTMENT). An expanded role for trade in national economies also brought with it greater interdependence at the level of macroeconomic and fiscal policies.

In recent years, the most far-reaching degree of integration has occurred in the area of capital. Both technological as well as political and economic developments have hastened the process of financial integration. Until very recently, financial markets remained relatively fragmented and national governments retained close control of domestic financial flows. Firms had little choice but to raise funds from domestic sources.

During the 1980s, a confluence of supply and demand factors made possible the rapid globalization and integration of financial market flows. On the supply side these included the deregulation of currency controls, innovations in financial instruments, and advances in communications and information technologies that allowed transactions to be executed rapidly across long distances. On the demand side were a wave of corporate restructurings that increased the need for new sources of financing, rapid growth in foreign investment and trade, and the adoption of free-market principles by a number of previously regulated economies.

Growth and internationalization have been particularly pronounced in equity, bond and foreign exchange markets, where capitalization exploded in the 1980s. Banks operate trading rooms that essentially represent globalized distribution systems for financial products such as equity, debt, foreign exchange and more exotic instruments such as derivatives. Global turnover in the world's foreign exchange markets reached $1 trillion per day in 1992. In 1981, about $200 billion worth of international bonds was issued; by 1992, the figure had reached nearly $1.8 trillion (Herring and Litan 1995). The market value of foreign equities traded on the London Stock Exchange grew from $738 billion in 1982 to $3.2 trillion in 1993. These figures illustrate how financial market integration has made possible the instantaneous mobility of massive amounts of capital on a global basis.

While the markets themselves have become globalized, financial *systems* remain nationally bounded, highly interdependent but not integrated. Corporate debt–equity ratios remain highly differentiated among major Organization for Economic Cooperation and Development (OECD) countries, and national governments continue to pursue divergent macroeconomic strategies. The bulk of national investment is sourced from domestic savings in the form of retained earnings – that is, funds that are not traded on any market. An important difference also lies in corporate governance: not only are there wide differences in how corporate governance is exercised, there is also little internationalization of boards of directors. An important measure of how far the globalization of markets has led to integration is the degree of convergence of rates of return in different financial markets. Herring and Litan (1995) find that although rates have converged at the lowest levels of financial integration, real interest rates – the most important index of integration – have not reached parity.

At the same time as capital markets, if not financial systems, have become globally integrated, labour markets have remained fragmented (see Ehrenberg 1994). In the European Union, efforts to harmonize labour practices were resisted by unions in northern countries, particularly Germany, which hoped to protect the gains they had won domestically. In the UK, employers feared that they would lose flexibility if they had to adopt the stringent rules governing treatment of employees prevalent in France and Germany. Trade unions in North America opposed the North American Free Trade Agreement (NAFTA) in anticipation of capital flight and loss of jobs. As barriers to trade and investment fall, multinational corporations are encouraged to rationalize production by configuring their activities efficiently across national borders; such moves may be perceived as 'social dumping' by labour organizations.

Worldwide, workers from areas of political instability and economic hardship continue to emigrate to countries that offer them greater opportunities. From a long-term perspective, however, labour markets are now less integrated than they were before the First World War. Migration of workers accounts for only a small proportion of the global workforce, and is dwarfed by population growth. The number of immigrants to the USA over the 1980s was lower than it was in the first decade of the century. Unlike the period before the First World War, immigrant workers are now less likely to become integrated into the national labour force by becoming permanent residents, as labour laws become tighter in the face of slower economic growth (United Nations 1994). Unlike domestic markets for capital, labour has remained relatively segmented and immobile in this phase of international integration. In so far as national labour markets are integrated through the activities of multinational corporations, however, they have been affected by a surge in foreign investment in recent years (see HUMAN RESOURCE MANAGEMENT, INTERNATIONAL). This phenomenon and its implications are explored below.

3 The surge in foreign direct investment

Neither the increased internationalization of economic activity nor the rapid improvement in cross-border communication and transport links is a new phenomenon. However, what sets the recent phase of internationalization apart from past waves is that it is primarily being driven by foreign direct investment (FDI) rather than by arm's-length trade. International capital flows have been quite large in the past, particularly in the last decades of the nineteenth century and prior to the First World War. Only the US stood out as unusual in having more outward flows of direct investment than portfolio flows (Wilkins 1974). Though a net debtor, the USA was the origin of many of the first multinational corporations, for example, Kodak, Singer and International Harvester. But the UK remained a vastly more important source of international capital overall, and dominated even direct investment flows until the Second World War.

The period after the Second World War showed a rapid increase in the US position overseas. Vaupel and Curhan (1973) found that in the period from 1939 to the mid-1970s, US multinationals accounted for about two-thirds of the increase in foreign direct stock and the growth in the number of overseas affiliates. In the 1960s, the largest 180 American multinational corporations were adding on average about six foreign subsidiaries per year to their growing overseas networks. This extraordinary dominance led to deep concerns in many countries over their dependence on the USA. Virtually all major OECD countries commissioned studies in the 1960s on the implications of direct investment, which for some countries, such as the UK, Canada and Belgium, had risen to remarkably high percentages of production in many industries. Important conflicts between nation-states occurred as a result; an example is the refusal of the French government to acknowledge that the American embargo against exports to China applied to the French subsidiaries of American multinational corporations. This concern over multinational corporations culminated in a series of non-binding policy statements by international institutions (for example, OECD guidelines on multinational corporations) and in the creation of new international agencies (such as the United Nations Centre on Transnational Corporations) (see MULTINATIONAL CORPORATIONS).

The concern over multinational corporations waned in many countries, a trend that is correlated with the diminished role of the USA in direct investment flows. With the gradual devaluation of the dollar – particularly after the collapse of the Bretton Woods system in the early 1970s – the USA became a more attractive location for investment and by the late 1980s, inflows to the USA exceeded outflows more than twice. European investment in particular increased. In the early 1980s, Japanese direct investment increased dramatically in the USA, rising to new highs in the mid- to late 1980s.

The second half of the 1980s witnessed a sharp increase in foreign investment flows in the world overall. Between 1981 and 1985, yearly outflows of FDI averaged $48 billion; by 1986–90, world outflows more than quadrupled to reach an annual average of $168 billion (United Nations 1994). Worldwide outflows of foreign investment grew three times faster than both exports and gross domestic product, lending support to the claim that foreign investment had replaced trade as the engine of international economic integration.

The surge in FDI was overwhelmingly concentrated among developed countries, which accounted for about 95 per cent of the outflows and 84 per cent of the inflows of total flows in the latter part of the 1980s. Among the most notable changes over this period was the decline of the USA as a net investor and the corresponding rise of Japan as a home country; the USA and Japan switched places as number one and number three respectively in terms of their shares of worldwide FDI outflows (the UK remained in the number two position). Much of the new Japanese investment was motivated by perceptions of rising protectionism in the US market (see Kogut and Chang 1991), the rising value of the yen, which favoured local production over exports, and the desire on the part of Japanese multinationals to access technologies embedded in US firms. Similar forces were at work in Europe, where the European Community (EC) programme of unification threatened to cause substantial trade diversion, particularly from Japan.

Within Europe, the programme to eliminate non-tariff barriers to trade and open national markets to greater competition caused intra-European investment and merger and acquisition activity to rise rapidly. The early phase of European integration, which eliminated tariff barriers to trade, expanded interdependence among countries, particularly in terms of currency movements, but stopped short of political and economic integration. As of the mid-1980s, the EC remained a collection of relatively fragmented national markets, which was considered to be an important factor in the lagging productivity and technological performance of European firms. The 1992 programme, by proposing that economic, social and monetary policies be harmonized, implied a major restructuring of industry within the EC, potentially allowing a far greater division of labour across member countries. While efforts towards monetary integration fell short of expectations, significant progress was made at achieving greater economic integration, spurred both by harmonization of policies relating to business practices, as well as by a rapid increase in intra-EC FDI. Much of this investment was aimed at rationalizing production, both in anticipation of as much as in response to declining barriers to trade. Even as they were increasing investment in the EC, European multinationals increased their presence in the US market.

Perhaps the most spectacular rise in FDI came from Japan, particularly after 1985. Between 1988 and 1990, Japanese investment flows to the EC were 13 per cent higher than the total flows over the previous thirty-six years combined; flows to the USA, where Japanese firms already had a much larger stake, were 8 per cent higher in the same period than in the previous thirty-six years combined (United Nations 1991). In both locations, Japanese firms responded to diversification opportunities that were unique to those markets (Mason and Encarnation 1994). Japanese investment also grew rapidly in east Asia, as Japanese firms upgraded their domestic facilities and shifted more mature production to lower-cost locations. Whereas US multinationals had dominated east Asian countries as a home country for FDI in the 1970s, Japan became the dominant investor in the region by the 1980s (United Nations 1991). At the same time, foreign investment in Japan itself remained disproportionately low, even after controls on inward investment were relaxed. The persistence of low investment levels in Japan has been partly attributed to structural features of the Japanese economy, such as extensive cross-shareholding among business partners, that remain highly differentiated from its main economic partners (see MANAGEMENT IN JAPAN).

By the early 1990s, the phenomenal growth in FDI had waned, and indeed net flows were negative in 1991 and 1992, with the sharpest declines in outflows from Japan, the UK and Germany. The drop has been attributed to recession (in Japan, domestic investment fell along with foreign investment); divestment following a wave of speculative investment in such sectors as real estate; and the beginning of a period in which firms focused their attentions on managing their overseas assets rather than acquiring new ones. For the time being, the wave of foreign investment that washed over the world economy in the latter part of the 1980s had subsided.

The impact of the surge of new investment, and the major shifts in country positions that it left in its wake, continues to be felt in the 1990s. For one, it changed the landscape of key industries among major recipient countries. In a study of the US affiliates of non-US multinationals, Kogut and Gittelman (1994) found that 105 affiliates qualified for inclusion in the 1994 *Fortune* 500 list of the largest US industrial corporations. Over the 1980s, the contribution of foreign affiliates to US manufacturing gross product more than doubled, reaching $258 billion in 1991, or 8.4 per cent of total manufacturing gross product in the US economy. The presence of multinationals is particularly strong in technology-intensive, oligopolistic industries: in the chemicals and computer industries, multinational corporations operating in the USA doubled their share of US assets over the 1980s, accounting for 40 per cent and 20 per cent of industry assets, respectively, in 1991. By the end of the 1980s there was not a single UK-owned large-volume car manufacturer, although the UK automobile industry remained important, with companies such as Honda and Nissan exporting to the rest of Europe from their UK subsidiaries.

4 Global corporations and integration

The implications of the expansion of the multinational corporation were not well anticipated by economic theory. The earlier literature focused on 'push' explanations for direct investment, namely those factors in the industry of the country of origin that motivated the outward investment. The dominant school of thought reflected the attention paid to the large portfolio flows prior to the Second World War and held that the multinational corporation resulted from the arbitrage of international differences in rates of return to capital. Hymer (1976) showed that this theory failed to explain why FDI was mainly concentrated among countries with similar rates of return and did not co-vary with other forms of capital flows, such as portfolio investment. His work developed an industrial organization foundation for the study of the multinational, which rested on the assumptions that: (1) multinational firms had to possess some advantage over host-country firms, such as superior marketing skills or technology, in order to justify the added costs of foreign production; and (2) that multinational firms had to be more efficient to internalize that advantage by controlling the foreign production rather than exporting or licensing (see MULTI-NATIONAL CORPORATIONS, ORGANIZATION STRUCTURES IN). Hymer's explanation of multinational activity rested on the Bain structure–conduct–performance model, in which barriers to entry such as product differentiation and scale economies allowed firms to enjoy monopolistic advantages which could be profitably exploited in overseas markets. It is not surprising that many, including Hymer himself, came to be critical of multinational corporations because of their potential monopolistic abuse.

Hymer's work provided the basis for studies that hypothesized that the overseas activities of multinational corporations were aimed at extending oligopolistic rivalry from the home country to foreign locations. Indeed, most FDI has historically been, and continues to be, concentrated in industries characterized by high seller concentration, research and development (R&D) intensity and product differentiation – the hallmarks of oligopolistic industries (Caves 1982). The push factors isolated by Hymer have proven to be robust predictors of outward direct investment.

There has been, however, a gradual change in thinking about the multinational corporation, moving from intra-national interdependence to international interdependence to eventual recognition of the implications of integrated multinational networks. Intranational interdependence was the presumption in the early studies, which conceptualized outward investment as an extension of home-based activities. One of the most important studies on international investment was Vernon's (1966) analysis of FDI as an outcome of rivalry among oligopolists from one nation who extend their rivalry overseas only when their home market begins to mature. Firms invest abroad in order either to pre-empt or retaliate against the moves of domestic rivals. Indeed, analysis of the timing of foreign investments of US multinationals prior to 1970

reveals a pattern of bunching in oligopolistic industries, which supports the thesis of inter-firm rivalry as a determinant of overseas investment.

The recognition that oligopolistic reaction might occur at an international level was developed a decade after Vernon's early work. Graham (1978) demonstrated that oligopolistic interdependence was carried out across national borders. In an analysis of cross-investments by US and European multinational enterprises over the period 1950–70, he showed that European investments in the USA were associated with earlier incursions into Europe by US multinationals.

Oligopolistic models of multinational activity thus stressed the notion of national firms pushed abroad by the forces of international interdependence. As such, they carry a home-country bias, in which firms exploit advantages acquired in one country in the market of another. If models of oligopolistic interdependence and the advantages stemming from cross-border corporate networks can explain the factors pushing firms to become multinationals, what are the 'pull' factors that also account for the location of FDI? An obvious answer is that direct investment flows to locations where materials are found, or wages are relatively cheap. Certainly, investments of a vertical nature, that is for sourcing inputs, respond to differences in factor costs. But there was also a recognition of glaring anomalies, such as the very significant flows of direct investment concentrated among high-wage countries.

In a landmark study, Cantwell (1989) pointed out that the technological capabilities of the host country attract multinationals to invest in those locations. In this way, the multinational may acquire the knowledge and technologies that are embedded in particular locations. Here, Hymer's paradigm of the multinational being advantaged over host-country rivals is turned around, and it is the pull of location-specific country capabilities that attracts foreign investment. This thesis was tested by Kogut and Chang (1991), who found that Japanese investments are principally motivated by technological rivalry, except for some indication that Japanese joint ventures are associated with sourcing US technological capabilities.

The growing interdependence of the world in technology flows is deeply affected by the bridges built by multinational corporations between high-technology regions, in part to arbitrage differences in technological regulatory regimes. Although most R&D is still performed domestically, large multinational corporations perform a significant proportion of their research activities internationally. Kobrin (1991) finds that technological intensity in an industry is a significant determinant of cross-border integration of US multinationals. The 1980s have witnessed a proliferation of these strategic alliances in high-technology industries, such that the notion of 'national' technologies is losing meaning.

Push and pull theories fail to take account of the advantages of multinationality *per se*, in which the ability to coordinate a network of overseas affiliates provides opportunities that go beyond those in standard models of oligopolistic competition. Kogut (1983) noted that theories of direct investment were preoccupied with explaining the initial investment overseas and neglected to understand the implications of a multinational network. He proposes a model of foreign investment as a sequential process, in which the multinational network can be used to exploit international differences in institutional frameworks, provide learning and externalities and allow for joint economies of production on an international scale. That is, there are opportunities that can only be exploited by the multinational corporation; here, multinationality itself has become a source of advantage possessed by the firm.

The proposition that multinationality *per se* provides unique advantages raises the intriguing notion that lack of integration in the public sector provides opportunities for private gains from integration. In a completely integrated market, prices would be equalized and the market conditions determining profitability would move together uniformly, such that there would be no advantage to having the option to shift operations from one part of the market to another. Where markets are less than completely integrated, however, it pays

to buy the option to respond to changing relative conditions among locations. The option takes the form of a network of foreign affiliates that are jointly coordinated to maximize network-wide returns. In other words, it is the ability of multinationals to integrate their activities across markets that are not fully integrated that provides for profitable opportunities. Over time, it would be expected that the increased integration of multinational networks would drive increasing integration at the country level, as the process of deepening integrated corporate networks runs into political and institutional barriers.

The formation and growth of regional networks by multinationals has acted as a push factor in regional integration arrangements such as NAFTA and the European Union. It is instructive to note that in 1989, four years before NAFTA was put in place, US multinationals accounted for 27 per cent of Mexican exports to the USA and 42 per cent of Mexican imports from the USA; virtually all of which was in the form of intra-firm trade (United Nations 1992). The existence of intra-firm production networks spanning countries in a region shines a light on discrepancies between national regimes, putting pressure on governments to take actions that will shape the integration process in a mutually beneficial way. Arrangements at the policy level, in turn, can improve the profit performance of multinationals and encourage further integration by lowering some of the transaction costs associated with international arbitrage by, for instance, harmonizing product requirements and lowering barriers to trade. In such a scenario, integration at the firm level and integration at the policy level are self-reinforcing processes.

What is often hidden in these theories of push, pull, and the multinational network is the role of the multinational corporation in diffusing work practices. Many work practices are embodied in a complexity of organizational relationships; disentangling the grain from the chaff is difficult by observation only. As such, the multinational corporation can act to transfer best-practice knowledge and superior methods of organizing production to different locations in its overseas network. Wilkins (1974) has shown how these practices are often the basis of the initial investment overseas, but in turn, inspire competition. Indeed, the history by Chandler (1990), which compares large corporations in the USA, UK and Germany, has many examples of the initial success but eventual failure of overseas investment as foreign competitors learned how to do it better. The first Hymer condition, that a foreign firm must have an advantage to compete, can be satisfied initially but eradicated over time.

The early rise of American multinationals can be explained partly by their possession of the new organizing principles of standardization and mass production. Similarly, the wave of Japanese investments is a reflection, in part, of the transfer of organizing principles to new markets. There is evidence of the transfer of Japanese production *keiretsu* to US and European locations. These principles sometimes face important problems of adaptation, such as seen in the joint venture between Toyota and General Motors located in California (see GLOBAL STRATEGIC ALLIANCES).

No matter what the degree of adaptation, there is little doubt that speed of diffusion has been unalterably influenced by the existence of large multinational corporations. The slow speed of the diffusion of new technologies – such as the kilometre per year speed of agricultural innovations in the early industrial period – belongs to a distant age. Not only does money move rapidly, but so do ideas and new organizing practices, because the world is now far more integrated through organizations that span across national borders.

5 The global organization of multinationals

The role of multinational corporations in the globalization of production, and the diffusion of ideas, is seen in the evolution of their international organization. In a seminal article, Perlmutter (1969) provided a basis for thinking about the relationship of structure to levels of international integration by setting out three orientations a multinational could adopt towards its foreign affiliates: ethnocentric, polycentric and geocentric, each progressively less culturally biased towards the home country. In the ethnocentric firm, affiliates are dependent upon the parent, which takes full responsibility for decision making and strategic activities such as research and development. The structure is highly centralized; overseas affiliates serve as little more than foreign points of entry for the outputs that emanate from the home-based parent. The polycentric organization introduces interdependence into the structure: although managed under a single umbrella, international affiliates are allowed to become somewhat independent of the parent in order to conform to the needs of their individual markets. Some decisions, such as marketing strategies, might be decentralized to the affiliate level, although overall resource allocation decisions remain with the parent. A geocentric organization is one which is highly decentralized, where responsibilities are delegated according to functional requirements rather than by home and host country distinctions.

Stopford and Wells (1972) traced the evolution of multinational structure as a function of multinational strategy. They found empirical support for the hypothesis that the more diversified a firm's international product mix and the greater the degree of internationalization, the more likely the firm was to move from an international division structure to a more rationalized international configuration. In the former case, overseas subsidiaries replicated the operations of the parent in the host country and operated relatively independently of the latter, resembling Perlmutter's polycentric organizations. To cope with rising complexity of product mix and growing internationalization, managers implemented structures that allowed for greater integration and coordination of activities. These included worldwide product divisions, which allowed for a high degree of integration and operating efficiency but weakened local responsiveness, area divisions, which carried the reverse properties, and matrix structures, which were intended to address the weaknesses of the first two but posed problems of managerial and coordination complexity.

Stopford and Wells' study demonstrated the evolution of structures to fit strategy, as US firms, which were competitive leaders in international markets, engaged in a learning process about the optimal mix between integration, responsiveness and complexity. Franko (1976) shows that late-moving European multinational enterprises skipped the international division phase and moved directly to global structures (area divisions, matrix and worldwide product). Moreover, whereas US firms tended to reorganize their structures in the home market first, European firms, which were far more internationalized and diversified, undertook domestic and foreign reorganization simultaneously, forgoing the learning, trial-and-error process of US firms. For US firms, domestic competitive strategy drove structural change, while for European firms it was primarily international competitive conditions that triggered a re-alignment of structure with strategy.

Recent additions to the structure literature have stressed the multinational as an integrated network of cooperative relationships, among affiliates as well as with firms outside the multinational corporation's organizational boundaries. Hedlund (1986) proposes a heterarchical model of the multinational firm. Such a firm employs a mix of organizing principles (ownership, joint ventures, subcontracting) to maximize flexibility in response to contingencies. Distinctions between headquarters and subsidiaries, home and host countries disappear: normative control replaces bureaucratic regulation and coercion and horizontal communication and coordination replace a hierarchical control structure. Others argue that multinational structures will evolve into differentiated organizations to reflect their external environments. Where barriers across countries and regions are high, intra-organizational coordination and integration will be relatively underdeveloped, while in regions of high integration, multinationals will evolve into dense network structures.

6 The political economy of globalization

The gradual emergence of multinational networks integrated by large organizations is the outcome of the co-evolution between the structure of international organizations and opportunities of the international environment. Governments have hardly faded away amidst these changes, and attempts to regulate the entry and behaviour of multinational corporations have posed, and continue to pose, a threat of conflict between the firm and the host nation-state. But as the world has moved from interdependence to integration, the challenge to government policy has shifted from regulation of the firm to a more fundamental problem, as to whether broader political and social agendas can be realized in an environment of mobile capital and integrated world production.

An important line of work has concerned the influence of liberalization on the ability of governments to pursue domestic policies. This issue of independence from world markets has been at the heart of international monetary and trade economics for almost fifty years. Interest has focused on the tendency of trade to equalize prices of goods and factors among countries. The Stolper and Samuelson theorems (1941) clarified the implications for distributional costs within a country: nations may gain by trade, but the less abundant factor will be hurt.

The models by Fleming (1962) and Mundell (1962) extended these kinds of concerns to monetary policy. Their work posed the dilemma of a government trying to pursue two policies of internal and external stabilization with one control variable: the money supply. Under fixed exchange rates, monetary policy is rendered less effective by capital mobility; money seeks the haven with the highest risk-adjusted return. Flexible exchange rates obviate the effectiveness of fiscal policy, as interest rates and exchange rates counterbalance any stimulus.

These fundamental results, all formalized in the 1950s, did not percolate into the thinking on the political economy of government policies until the 1980s. Rogowski (1989) expanded the traditional literature on customs policy and distributional politics to consider how trade expansion and contraction influence domestic political alignments. His analysis proposes a counter-intuitive result: that expansion weakens the exposed group politically, but contraction strengthens it. The work of Rogowski, which can be taken as exemplifying a broader literature, is primarily a study of interdependence: how trade influences domestic political arrangements.

An important related issue concerns the effect of globalization on the ability of a government to pursue its national objectives. The constraint of the world economy would seem particularly severe for left-wing governments wishing to pursue social welfare policies. Budget deficits, high taxation depressing the return on capital, or financing by inflationary policies should, in theory, be constrained by international economic pressures in an environment in which capital is mobile.

The evidence has not shown this. Garrett (1995) found a fairly subtle relationship between leftist politics and globalization. At low levels, leftist governments pursued policies with few consequences for overall government spending and budget deficits but at higher rates of capital taxation. As internationalization increased, fiscal expansion increased for countries with leftist governments. Left-labour governments have pursued, in other words, a social welfare agenda despite increased internationalization.

All these studies point to a complex relationship between political policy and internationalization. The silver lining is that governments may be able to pursue activist policy agendas if markets perceive that the long-term productivity of the economy may be improved. If such a possibility is not to be admitted, then it becomes difficult to imagine how the success of a high tax, social welfare economy of a Germany can be explained.

However, in light of the currency crises of the early 1990s, there is strong evidence that bad macroeconomic policy leads to substantial penalties in conditions of high capital mobility. Eichengreen and Wyplosz (1991) have analysed the currency crisis in the efforts to achieve European monetary union. The shock

to the system stemmed from the reunification of the two Germanies and the massive excess demand created by the collapse of the East German economy. Under a Mundell–Fleming model of adjustment under fixed exchange rates, such a crisis would be remedied by three alternatives: decreasing real wages, an inflationary policy to increase German prices and to satisfy demand through imports of relatively less expensive goods, or a revaluation of the currency to achieve the same effect as an inflationary policy. The policy of cutting real wages is constrained by the difficulties of coordinating and implementing such a policy. Inflationary policies are counter to the stated stance of the independent Bundesbank. Revaluing the Deutschmark – the preferred policy of the Bundesbank – was constrained by the public affirmations of political leaders in other European countries about maintaining the prevailing exchange rates. However, the strategy taken to maintain external stability was a resort to high real domestic interest rates. Financial markets did not find these policies credible given the high levels of unemployment. One by one, governments caved in to international pressures by devaluing their currency relative to the Deutschmark. But underneath these basic economic pressures was a dissatisfied Bundesbank that suggested publicly that exchange rates were out of alignment.

To some, the forces of globalization have effectively eradicated government control. Trade talks on liberalization are often stumped over such issues as how to tax the flow of information, when its origins cannot be determined. Currently, the absence of strong countervailing international agreements and institutions suggests that world integration has rendered national deviations, be it social or tax policy, more costly. But a more cautious estimate is that the very strength of these changes may be the cause for institutional responses.

7 Conclusion

The force of economic globalization is not simply the domination of political action by world financial and real goods markets.

Certainly, domestic policy freedom is more curtailed as interdependence increases. But there are three alternatives for achieving political ends that may fly in the face of short-term economic priorities. One is simply autarky; yet this policy path is ever exacting a higher opportunity cost due to the expansion and attractiveness of world trade and investment. The other is the pursuit of political and social objectives that lead to long-term growth in productivity. There is increasing evidence that nations that succeed in building institutions that support economic coordination and human capital formation can enjoy persisting high levels of productivity and income, despite the simultaneous pursuit of social policies that entail high levels of taxation and government-sponsored employment. Finally, there is the belief that countervailing measures may be enacted to regain political control. Eichengreen and Wyplosz (1991), for example, propose a Tobin-tax to throw sand in the gears of capital mobility in order to slow capital flight. But international coordination requires, still, the agreement of interdependent actors. In here lies the irony that the increasing integration of the world economy stands in sharp contrast to the uneasy division of the political landscape into independent, though interdependent, nation states.

BRUCE KOGUT

MICHELLE GITTELMAN

WHARTON SCHOOL AT THE UNIVERSITY OF PENNSYLVANIA

Further reading

(References cited in the text marked *)

Bartlett, C.A., Doz, Y. and Hedlund, G. (eds) (1990) *Managing the Global Firm*, London: Routledge. (A collection of essays by noted researchers in international strategy, containing early statements exploring the multinational corporation as a network of subsidiaries.)

* Braudel, F. (1979) *The Structures of Everyday Life: The Limits of the Possible*, vols 1–3, New York: Harper & Row. (A vast three-volume work that details the history and evolution of modern social and economic life, from the Middle Ages to the Industrial Revolution.)

* Cantwell, J. (1989) *Technological Innovation and Multinational Corporations*, Oxford: Blackwell. (A landmark study on how knowledge accumulates in particular countries and provides competitive advantages to local firms and pulls direct investment from the outside.)

* Caves, R.E. (1982) *Multinational Enterprise and Economic Analysis*, Cambridge: Cambridge University Press. (This research textbook is the primary handbook on studies of foreign direct investment and includes a vast bibliography.)

* Chandler, A. (1990) *Scale and Scope*, New York: The Free Press. (Sweeping study of the varieties of capitalism and the role of big business that will remain an important and controversial work for some time.)

Dunning, J. (1993) *Multinational Enterprises and the Global Economy*, Addison-Wesley. (Comprehensive text covering research about the multinational corporation, from economics to cross-cultural studies.)

* Ehrenberg, R. (1994) *Labor Markets and Integrating National Economies*, Washington: The Brookings Institution. (One of a series of books published by US think-tank the Brookings Institution on the topic of world integration.)

* Eichengreen, B. and Wyplosz, C. (1991) 'The unstable EMS', *Brookings Papers on Economic Activity* 1: 51–124. (An exploration of the dynamics of the breakdown of the European monetary system in 1992 and 1993.)

* Fleming, J.M. (1962) 'Domestic financial policies under fixed and under floating exchange rates', *IMF Staff Papers* 9: 369–79. (The original contribution to the Mundell–Fleming model of the effects of monetary and fiscal policy.)

* Franko, L. (1976) *The European Multinationals*, New York: Harper. (An early study on the growth and organizational evolution of European multinationals.)

Froot, K. (1992) *Foreign Direct Investment*, Chicago, IL: University of Chicago Press. (Papers by leading scholars examining patterns of foreign direct investment in the 1980s and the history of multinational corporations' activities.)

* Garrett, G. (1995) 'Capital mobility, trade and the domestic politics of economic policy', *International Organization* 49 (4): 657–87. (Empirical investigation into the domestic political effects of increasing economic integration, showing that left-labour governments are not necessarily undermined by increased internationalization.)

* Graham, E.M. (1978) 'Transatlantic investment by multinational firms: a rivalistic phenomenon', *Journal of Post-Keynesian Economics* 1: 82–99. (Shows that multinational investments

are motivated by international oligopolistic competition.)

* Hedlund, G. (1986) 'The hypermodern MNC – heterarchy', *Human Resource Management* 25 (Spring): 9–35. (Sets out a view of the firm as a complex system tending towards multiple centres of competence as opposed to a hierarchical control structure.)

* Herring, R.J. and Litan, R.E. (1995) *Financial Regulation in the Global Economy*, Washington, DC: The Brookings Institution. (One of the Brookings series, a detailed analysis of international integration of financial markets.)

* Hymer, S. (1976) *International Operations of the National Firms: A Study of the Foreign Direct Investment*, Cambridge, MA: MIT Press. (The classic statement that moved the study of foreign direct investment out of the arena of international capital flows and into the arena of industry structure and competition and the transfer of technology.)

Keohane, R.O. and Nye, J.S. (1977) *Power and Interdependence: World Politics in Transition*, Boston, MA: Little, Brown. (A landmark study that moved international relations away from the study of the high politics of state strategy and into the realm of economics, resources and political will.)

* Kobrin, S.J. (1991) 'An empirical analysis of the determinants of global integration', *Strategic Management Journal* 12: 17–31. (Examines the relative importance of numerous factors, including technology and economies of scale, in determining the extent of overseas activities by US multinationals.)

* Kogut, B. (1983) 'Foreign direct investment as a sequential process', in C.P. Kindleberger and D. Audretsch (eds), *The Multinational Corporation in the 1980s*, Cambridge, MA: MIT Press. (Proposes a model of the multinational corporation which stresses the advantages of controlling an international network of affiliates.)

* Kogut, B. and Chang, S.J. (1991) 'Technological capabilities and Japanese direct investment in the United States', *Review of Economics and Statistics* 73: 401–413. (Gives empirical support to the hypothesis that US–Japanese technological rivalry is a determinant of Japanese foreign direct investment in the USA.)

* Kogut, B. and Gittelman, M. (1994) 'The largest foreign multinationals in the United States and their contribution to the American economy', Reginald Jones Center Working Paper, Philadelphia, PA: The Wharton School at the University of Pennsylvania. (Analyses the US-based operations of over 100 multinational corporations and compares the performance of foreign companies to domestic firms from the late 1970s to the present.)

* Mason, M. and Encarnation, D. (1994) *Does Ownership Matter: Japanese Investment in a Unifying Europe*, Oxford: Clarendon Press. (A collection of papers exploring various facets of one of the most prominent expressions of increasing integration, the expansion of Japanese multinationals into Europe.)

* Mundell, R.A. (1962) 'The appropriate use of monetary and fiscal policy for internal and external balance', *IMF Staff Papers* 9: 70–9. (The original contribution to the Mundell–Fleming model.)

* Perlmutter, H. (1969) 'The tortuous evolution of the multinational enterprise', *Columbia Journal of World Business* 4 (1): 9–18. (Classic essay linking the cultural orientation of a multinational corporation to its corporate strategy and the structure of its overseas network.)

* Rogowski, R. (1989) *Commerce and Coalitions: How Trade Affects Domestic Political Alignments*, Princeton, NJ: Princeton University Press. (Explores the domestic political consequences of the Stolper–Samuelson theorem that trade hurts those factors that are scarce and aids those that are abundant.)

* Stolper, W. and Samuelson, P. (1941) 'Protection and real wages', *Review of Economic Studies* 9: 58–73. (An important analysis of the consequences of trade.)

* Stopford, J.M. and Wells, L.T. (1972) *Managing the Multinational Enterprise: Organization of the Firm and Ownership of the Subsidiaries*, New York: Basic Books. (Comprehensive study of the multinational corporation that documents the evolution of the organizational structures and strategies of international companies within the political context of host governments.)

* United Nations (1991; 1992; 1994) *World Investment Report*, Geneva: United Nations. (A series of annual reports, starting in 1991, that present statistics on the activities of multinational corporations and worldwide foreign direct investment trends, as well as focusing on specific themes relating to multinational corporations in the world economy.)

* Vaupel, J.W. and Curhan, J.P. (1973) *The World's Largest Multinational Enterprises*, Cambridge, MA: Harvard University Press. (A sourcebook of tables showing detailed information on more than 25,000 overseas subsidiaries of US and

non-US multinational corporations from 1900 to the mid-1970s.)

* Vernon, R. (1966) 'International investment and international trade in the product cycle', *Quarterly Journal of Economics* 80: 190–207. (Classic essay laying the theoretical groundwork for a life-cycle model of international business.)
* Wilkins, M. (1974) *The Maturing of Multinational Enterprise: American Business Abroad from 1914 to 1970*, Cambridge, MA: Harvard University Press. (A well-documented study of the historical expansion of US firms overseas.)

See also: ASSOCIATION OF SOUTH-EAST ASIAN NATIONS; ECONOMIC INTEGRATION, INTERNATIONAL; GLOBAL STRATEGIC ALLIANCES; HUMAN RESOURCE MANAGEMENT, INTERNATIONAL; INTERNATIONAL TRADE AND FOREIGN DIRECT INVESTMENT; MANAGEMENT IN JAPAN; MULTINATIONAL CORPORATIONS; MULTINATIONAL CORPORATIONS, ORGANIZATION STRUCTURES IN; NORTH AMERICAN FREE-TRADE AGREEMENT

Related topics in the IEBM: BANKING IN JAPAN; CHANDLER, A.D.; FINANCE, INTERNATIONAL; FINANCIAL MARKETS, INTERNATIONAL; HUMAN RESOURCE FLOWS; JAPANIZATION; LABOUR MARKETS; MANAGEMENT IN PACIFIC ASIA; MULTINATIONAL CORPORATIONS, HISTORY OF; PORTER, M.E.

Human resource management, international

Overview

The successful operation of a multinational firm is contingent upon the availability of technology, technological know-how, capital and human resources. Without a highly developed pool of human resources (including managerial and technical talent), technology, technological know-how and capital cannot be effectively and efficiently allocated or transferred from corporate headquarters to the scattered subsidiaries. Developing and managing this managerial and technical talent is the function of international human resource management.

International human resource management has five main dimensions: first, the selection and recruitment of qualified individuals capable of furthering organizational goals; second, the training and development of personnel at all levels to maximize organizational performance; third, the assessment of employee performance to ensure that organizational goals are met; fourth, the retention of competent corporate personnel who can continue to facilitate the attainment of organizational goals; and fifth, the management of the interface between labour and management to ensure smooth organizational functioning.

This entry examines the international dimension of these five aspects of human resource management. Where relevant, the international human resource management policies and practices of a sample of US, European, Japanese and Australian multinationals will be discussed and compared.

1 Selection and recruitment

An assumption is often made that an effective manager at home will also be an effective manager abroad. Moreover, many companies continue to focus primarily on the technical competence criterion for expatriate assignments. There are two reasons for this: (1) task requirements are usually more easily identifiable; and (2) since technical competence almost always prevents immediate failure on the job, particularly in high pressure situations, the selectors play safe by placing a heavy emphasis on technical qualifications and little on the individual's ability to adapt to a foreign environment. Both these assumptions are suspect, however, when one examines the rate of expatriate failure and the reasons for such failure.

Some US multinationals experienced expatriate failure rates as high as 30–40 per cent; in contrast, European, Japanese, and Australian multinationals experienced significantly lower rates of expatriate failure (Tung 1990). Nevertheless, these casualties of selection not only represent substantial lost investment, they also constitute a human resource waste since most of those who fail seem to have a noteworthy home track record. Failures often constitute a heavy personal blow to the expatriates' self-esteem. Hence, even if they are accepted back by corporate headquarters, it may take some time before they regain confidence in their own abilities. The unsettling experience for the person's family, both emotionally and physically, represents yet another consequence.

What are the causes of expatriate failure? In the US sample the most important reasons for expatriate failure, in descending order of importance, were:

1 inability of the manager's spouse to adjust to a different physical or cultural environment;
2 the manager's inability to adapt to a different physical or cultural environment;
3 other family-related problems;
4 the manager's personality or emotional immaturity;
5 the manager's inability to cope with the responsibilities posed by overseas work;
6 the manager's lack of technical competence;
7 the manager's lack of motivation to work overseas.

These findings are consistent with other studies which show that the family situation and an inability to relate are factors usually responsible for failure or poor performance abroad. The family situation is also the principal cause of failure among European and Australian multinationals. For Japanese multinationals the most important reasons for failure were significantly different. In this sample the reasons for failure, given in descending order of importance, were:

1 the manager's inability to cope with the larger responsibilities posed by the overseas work;
2 the manager's inability to adapt to a different physical or cultural environment;
3 the manager's personality or emotional immaturity;
4 the manager's lack of technical competence;
5 inability of the manager's spouse to adjust to a different physical or cultural environment;
6 lack of motivation to work overseas;
7 other family-related problems.

In Japan status shock, not culture shock, is a primary cause of failure. The Japanese, who are more used to working as a team, suddenly take on the burden of overseeing a diverse range of responsibilities and functions, in isolation, in a foreign subsidiary.

The principal causes of failure among US, European and Australian multinationals are the family situation and lack of human relation skills of the manager, rather than technical incompetence. This brings us to the question of what should be the selection criteria for overseas assignments.

Selection criteria

Overseas managerial assignments can be classified into four major categories: (1) the chief executive officer (CEO), whose responsibility is to oversee and direct the entire foreign operation; (2) the functional head, whose job is to establish functional departments in a foreign subsidiary; (3) the troubleshooter, whose function is to analyse and solve specific operational problems; and (4) the operative, or rank and file.

Jobs in each of these categories involve varying degrees of contact with the host culture and varying assignment lengths. For example, one would expect a CEO to have more extensive contact with members of the local community than a troubleshooter, and the troubleshooter's job in a certain country to be of shorter duration than the CEO's.

It is possible to create an eighteen-point criteria list for expatriate assignments across these four job types:

* experience within the company
* technical knowledge of the business
* knowledge of the language of the host country
* overall experience and education
* managerial talent
* interest in overseas work
* initiative and creativity
* independence
* previous overseas experience
* respect for the culture of the host country
* sex/gender of candidate
* age
* stability of marital relationship
* spouse's and family's adaptability
* adaptability and flexibility in a new environmental setting
* maturity and emotional stability
* communicative ability
* same criteria as for other comparable jobs at home

For US multinationals, for each job category certain criteria were considered more important than others. Attributes like 'adaptability and flexibility in a new environmental setting' and 'communicative ability' were more frequently identified as very important for jobs requiring more extensive contact with the local community (CEO and functional head) than for jobs that were more technically orientated (troubleshooter). Despite this recognition of the need to select candidates who are adaptable and flexible in new environmental settings, only 5 per cent of the US companies surveyed administered any test to assess these attributes. However, nearly half of the companies did interview both the candidate and spouse to gauge their interest in living and working overseas. This latter practice may reflect the growing awareness that the spouse's attitude towards an overseas posting can be pivotal to success. A potential problem is where the candidate and spouse feign enthusiasm for fear that a negative attitude towards an overseas posting may adversely affect the candidate's career within the company.

For the west European sample the most important criterion for selecting candidates in the CEO category was 'managerial talent'. The most important criterion for selecting candidates in the functional head, troubleshooter and operative categories was 'technical knowledge of business'. 'Adaptability and flexibility in a new environmental setting' was also considered very important for all job categories except operatives. 'Interest in overseas work' was cited as a very important criterion for each of the four job categories by a majority of the firms, although this was not cited as frequently as the other aforementioned criteria. While 'adaptability and flexibility' was not mentioned as the most important criterion, 21 per cent of the European firms used tests to assess the candidate's relational abilities. In common with the US multinationals, many of the European firms conducted interviews with both the candidate and spouse to determine their interest in working abroad.

In the Japanese sample, like their European counterparts, the most important criterion for selecting candidates in the CEO category was 'managerial talent', and the most important criterion for selecting candidates in the functional head, troubleshooter and operative categories was 'technical knowledge of business'. Most of the Japanese companies considered 'experience within the company' a very important criterion for jobs in three of the four job categories (CEO, functional head and troubleshooter). This perhaps reflects the system of employment in Japanese society which emphasizes length of service in the company and experience acquired over that time. 'Adaptability and flexibility in a new environmental setting' was also cited as a very important criterion for each of the four categories by a majority of the firms, although this was not cited as frequently as the other criteria. None of the Japanese firms used any psychological test to determine the candidate's relational abilities. While the majority of companies interviewed the candidate about the overseas position, none of them included the spouse in such meetings. This was very different from the practice in US and European multinationals and could be attributed to the fact that Japanese culture has a different view of the spouse's (in this case, the wife's) role and status in the family.

While Japanese multinationals may not administer a specific test or include the spouse in the interview, the characteristics of the Japanese employment system are such that it permits ample opportunity for the supervisor to determine a candidate's suitability for an overseas assignment. Given the intense socialization during the after-hours sessions in drinking bars (*karaoke*) and restaurants, a supervisor often has detailed knowledge of an employee's background and family situation. Most Japanese companies also keep very detailed personnel inventories on their career staff. These are compiled from the annual or semi-annual performance evaluations completed by the individual, his or her immediate supervisor and the chief of the division. In addition, candidates who are considered for an overseas assignment (excluding those who have been selected to study abroad) typically have been with the company for ten years. Hence, the company has ample time to assess capabilities and qualifications, including adaptability to a new environmental setting.

In Australian multinationals, while the criteria used for selecting candidates for international assignments varied, two dimensions stood out. One pertained to the willingness of the individual to undertake the overseas assignment. In fact, several of the multinationals relied exclusively on volunteers. Given the present emphasis on international experience in most Australian corporations and the desire of many Australians to travel to foreign lands, there appears to be no shortage of highly qualified individuals who would volunteer for an overseas assignment. A second major criterion was the potential of the candidate for senior management positions. In other words, an overseas assignment is used as part of the overall career development strategy of high flyers in the company. Some of the Australian multinationals surveyed tried to select those who had demonstrated a certain resilience in their character and who were tolerant of things foreign. Several of the Australian executives indicated that they look for a 'Paul Hogan' mentality: in the Australian hit movie, Crocodile Dundee, the hero (played by actor Paul Hogan) typified the Australian spirit and mentality – adventurous, friendly and adaptable. A number of Australian executives perceived this trait as critical to success in living and working abroad. Even those Australian companies which did not use the adaptability criterion in their selection decision believed that it would be important to incorporate this dimension in the future.

A question can be raised as to whether the gender of the candidate should be taken into consideration in identifying appropriateness for an international assignment. Over one-half of the west European and Japanese multinationals used 'sex/gender of a candidate' as a criterion in all four job categories. Gender was not mentioned as a criterion by any of the US multinationals. This is probably due to differences in equal employment legislation. Despite the assertion by US multinationals that the gender of the candidate is not a consideration in the selection decision, the low percentage of women who are sent on expatriate assignments may suggest that there is a discrepancy between officially stated policy and actual practice. In the late 1990s about 17 per cent of US expatriates were female, an increase from 5 per cent a decade ago (Tung and Arthur Andersen 1997).

What are the reasons for such limited use of women expatriates? Sixty-nine per cent of the nearly 5,000 respondents in US multinationals surveyed by the firm of Moran, Stahl & Boyer (1988) did not perceive any advantage in expatriating a woman over a man, citing the following barriers to the use of women in overseas postings:

1 cultural prejudices and limitations;
2 male-dominated management group in the company;
3 employment of the accompanying male spouse;
4 inflexibility and resentment of male peers, subordinates and superiors;
5 lack of support groups for working expatriate females;
6 lack of access to local male networks;
7 pregnancy;
8 acceptance of working women in the expatriate community;
9 militant feminism of some US female employees;
10 unwillingness of women to accept foreign assignments.

Despite their limited use in overseas assignments, how have women expatriates fared? The same study showed that 93 per cent of the respondents who had expatriated women abroad were extremely satisfied with their performance overseas. Similarly, in another study of women expatriates in Pacific Asia it was found that women were accepted by Asian businesses (Adler 1987).

A barrier to the use of women as expatriates was employment of the accompanying male spouse. According to another survey of twenty chief executives of US multinationals, the majority of respondents believed that the issue of dual-career families will become a major problem confronting their companies in the next decade (Tung 1988). Because most Japanese wives do not work outside their home, the issue of dual-career couples is not a concern among Japanese multinationals. In both European and Australian multinationals this problem was less prominent because of the lower percentage of women who were employed as professionals in these countries.

Selection of parent-, host- and third-country nationals

Multinationals have three sources of human power supply available to them: (1) parent-country nationals (PCNs), or those who are citizens of the home country of the multinational corporation; (2) host-country nationals (HCNs), or citizens of the country of foreign operation; and (3) third-country nationals (TCNs), or nationals who are neither citizens of the home country of the multinational nor of the country in which the foreign operation is located.

Analysis thus far has focused on the use of PCNs. The reasons for using PCNs, HCNs and TCNs are multiple and varied, and the selection criteria may be summarized as in Figure 1.

It is noteworthy that west European multinationals seem to use expatriate assignments as a mechanism for developing an international orientation among their management personnel. In the 1990s, US multinationals are also following this trend (Tung and Arthur Andersen 1997). In order to compete effectively in a world characterized by the globalization of industries, European multinationals recognize the need to develop this orientation among its management personnel.

The extent to which PCNs, HCNs and TCNs are used at various levels of management in different geographic regions of the world varies. For the US and west European samples, HCNs are used to a much greater extent at all levels of management in developed regions of the world compared to less-developed countries. This is logical as one

	US			EUROPE			JAPAN		
	PCN	HCN	TCN	PCN	HCN	TCN	PCN	HCN	TCN
Start-up foreign enterprise	X			X					
Technical expertise	X	X		X					
Familiarity with culture	X				X				
Knowledge of language	X				X				
Reduced costs	X								
Good public relations	X								
TCN best person for the job			X			X			
Development of an international orientation for headquarters' management				X					
PCN best person for the job							X		
HCN best person for the job								X	

(TCN for Japan: Not applicable. None of Jap. MNCs used TCNs, except for Africa)

Figure 1 Reasons for using parent-country nationals (PCNs), host-country nationals (HCNs) and third-country nationals (TCNs)
Source: Tung (1982)

would expect the more developed nations to have a larger pool of personnel that would possess the necessary human power and technical skills to staff management-level positions. Unfortunately, the countries staffed by a smaller percentage of HCNs at management levels of US and European subsidiaries tend to be ones whose culture, values and business practices differ substantially from those at home. Consequently, the issue of selecting a candidate who would be able to live and work in a very dissimilar cultural environment still constitutes a pressing problem.

Japanese multinationals, on the other hand, employ considerably more PCNs in their overseas operations at the senior and middle-management levels. This phenomenon may be attributed, in part at least, to the significant differences that exist between Japanese and non-Japanese styles of management which can create problems of integration, particularly at the senior management level. One problem pertains to language differences. Virtually all communication between corporate headquarters in Japan and the foreign subsidiary is in Japanese. There are very few non-Japanese who are thoroughly proficient in the Japanese language. The more extensive use of PCNs at the senior and middle management levels in Japanese multinationals may also be a function of the stage of internationalization of Japanese firms. Compared with their US and European counterparts, Japanese companies are more recent entrants into the multinational scene. Aside from the large general trading companies, the majority of Japanese firms only began overseas expansion in the 1960s. In start-up phases there is a greater tendency for multinationals to use PCNs.

Another characteristic of international human resource management practices in Japanese multinationals is the limited use of TCNs. Except for Africa, the Japanese multinationals studied did not use TCNs at all. When asked why, the Japanese multinationals indicated that since they already experience difficulties in trying to integrate a local workforce with their expatriate staff, they do not wish to confound the situation by adding a third dimension, namely TCNs.

The trend towards the increased use of HCNs at various levels of management in overseas operations has continued for US multinationals. While acknowledging the obvious advantages associated with the use of HCNs, such as reduced costs and greater familiarity with the local environment, there can be limitations associated with relying exclusively on HCNs. Because of geographic distance and cultural differences, corporate control becomes more tenuous.

Duration of overseas assignment

Most overseas assignments of US multinationals are for two or three years. Such short stints are not conducive to high performance because the expatriate barely has time to adjust before transfer home or to another overseas location. Research has shown that when expatriates are exempted from active managerial responsibilities in the first several months of foreign assignment, particularly to countries where the cultural distance is great, it can facilitate acculturation. However, extending the overseas assignment can lead to concern by the employee about repatriation.

Japanese multinationals tend to have a longer duration of overseas assignment, with an average of five years, except for assignments to the Middle East, which are generally of two years' duration. This latter policy stems from the perceived harsh living conditions in that geographic region. The longer duration of overseas assignments means that the Japanese expatriate has more time to adjust. Many Japanese multinationals do not expect the expatriate to perform to full capacity until the third year of assignment, as the first two years abroad are viewed as part of the basic period of adjustment.

Except for overseas assignments that are strictly for career development purposes, expatriate assignments in European multinationals average five years or more. Some of the European multinationals allow an adjustment period of up to one year. Besides allowing more time to adjust, the longer duration of overseas assignment also provides a greater incentive for the expatriate to learn more about the host country, including its language.

2 Training for cross-cultural encounters

The focus here is on training programmes that are designed to improve the relational skills crucial to effective performance in expatriate job assignments. Training programmes or procedures employed typically fall into the five categories below, presented in ascending order of rigour. They constitute a continuum ranging from low rigour (area studies) to highly rigorous training programmes (field experiences). Depending upon the type of job and the country of foreign assignment the individual should be exposed to one or several of these programmes (see CULTURE, CROSS-NATIONAL; ORGANIZATION CULTURE).

Area studies programmes. These include environmental briefing and cultural orientation programmes designed to provide the trainee with information about a particular country's sociopolitical history, geography, stage of economic development and cultural institutions. The content is factual in nature.

The basic assumption behind this approach is that knowledge will lead to increased empathy, thus modifying behavioural patterns and facilitating intercultural relationships. Although there is some indication that increased knowledge will remove some of the fear and aggression that tend to be aroused by the unknown, evidence that knowledge will invariably result in increased empathy is sparse and usually not the result of rigorous experimental control. When used alone area studies programmes are inadequate for preparing trainees for assignments which require extensive contact with the local community overseas. Furthermore, since cultural differences between any two countries could be innumerable, training programmes of an area studies nature could not possibly pass on to the trainee all the knowledge that would be required over the duration of the overseas assignment.

Culture assimilator. This consists of a series of seventy-five to one hundred short episodes briefly describing an intercultural encounter. Encounters which are judged (by a panel of experts, including returned expatriates) to be critical to the interaction situations

between members of two different cultures are included.

Studies have shown that this training device can be effective preparation for cross-cultural encounters. Culture assimilators, however, are designed specifically for people who have to be assigned overseas on short notice. Consequently, where time is not a critical factor, and in assignments which require extensive contact with members of the local community, this technique should be supplemented by the more rigorous training programmes.

Language training. The candidate is taught the language, usually verbal only, of the host country. While knowledge of the host country's language can facilitate cross-cultural interaction, it often involves months, or sometimes years, before a candidate can master the foreign language.

Sensitivity training. These programmes focus upon learning at the affective level and are designed to develop an attitudinal flexibility within the trainees so that they can become aware of and acclimatize to unfamiliar modes of behaviour and value systems. Although the effectiveness of sensitivity training sessions has been questioned, there is some indication that sensitivity training can reduce racial/ethnic prejudice.

Field experiences. These involve sending the candidate to the country of assignment or microcultures in the home country (for example, Indian reservations, urban black ghettos) where the trainees may undergo some of the emotional stress that can be expected while living and working with people from a different culture or subculture. Research indicates that even though differences in cultural content exist between these microcultures and the country to which the trainee is ultimately assigned, trainees seem to benefit from an encounter with people whose way of life is different from their own, since the process of adaptation can be similar. The US Peace Corps has used this technique successfully with their volunteers.

These programmes vary in their focus upon cognitive and affective learning and in the medium of instruction, information content, time and resources required. They are by no means mutually exclusive and should be complementary. Japanese multinationals by far provide the most rigorous training to prepare their expatriates for cross-cultural encounters. While the type and nature of programmes provided by the Japanese multinationals vary, a typical programme would include the following components.

(1) *Language training*. Most Japanese companies sponsor intensive language training programmes, ranging from three months to one year in duration. To promote fluency in a foreign language, many Japanese companies invite Caucasians to share the same dormitories in order to provide their trainees with ample opportunity to practise their language skills and to gain a better understanding of the foreign country.

(2) *Field experience*. Many Japanese multinationals select members of their staff to serve as trainees in their overseas offices for one year. As trainees their primary mission is to observe closely and, hence, learn about the company's foreign operations. The trainees also try to acquire as much information as possible about the foreign country, including non-economic variables. This kind of training prepares them for an eventual offshore assignment, which is viewed as part of one's career development.

(3) *Graduate programmes abroad*. Every year many Japanese multinationals send between ten and twenty career staff members to attend graduate business, law and engineering programmes abroad. The company pays tuition and all expenses in addition to the employee's regular salary. While attending graduate school the Japanese employee is exposed to foreign principles of management which would prepare him for an eventual overseas assignment. Furthermore, the two years abroad would allow the Japanese employee to experience first hand the problems of living in and adapting to a foreign society.

(4) *In-house training programmes*. Besides language training the expatriates take courses in international finance and international economics and are exposed to environmental briefings about the country of assignment.

(5) *Outside agencies*. Besides in-house training programmes there are several institutes in Japan that prepare expatriates for overseas assignments. The Institute for International Studies and Training, for example, was established under the auspices of the Japanese Ministry of International Trade and Industry in 1967. It offers three-month and one-year residential programmes.

3 A contingency framework for selection and training

In light of the different categories of overseas job assignments and the contributions of various factors to success on the job, any comprehensive selection and training paradigm has to incorporate a complex set of variables and allow for their interaction. The selection criteria and training programmes that should be used for different categories of overseas assignments can be summarized in a contingency framework of selection and training shown in Figure 2.

Due to the variability of each situation in terms of the country of foreign assignment and the task to be performed, constant weights applicable to all instances could not be assigned to each of these factors. A more feasible strategy is to adopt a contingency approach to the selection and training of personnel for overseas assignment.

This approach requires a clear identification of task, environment and the psychological characteristics of the individual under consideration. Before headquarters launches a search (at home) for an appropriate individual to fill an overseas job, it should consider if the job in question can be filled by an HCN. If the answer is yes, this alternative source should certainly be considered. If the position cannot be filled by an HCN then a search must be conducted among those who are already with domestic operations or within competing industries (either PCNs or TCNs).

An indication should always be obtained as to whether a candidate is willing to serve abroad. If the individual is averse to serving abroad then no training programme is capable of changing this basic attitude. If the individual is willing to live and work in a foreign environment an indication of the extent to which he/she is tolerant of cultural differences and

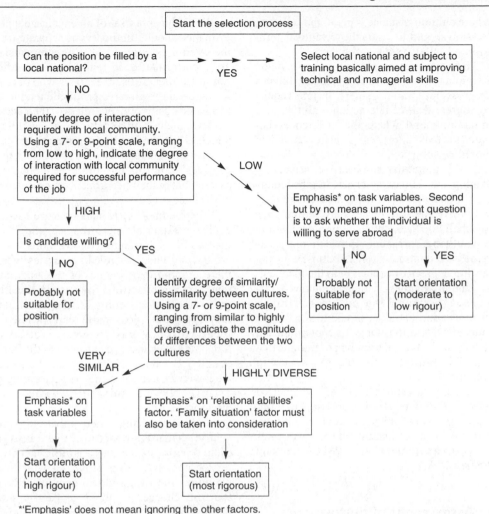

Start the selection process

Can the position be filled by a local national?

YES → Select local national and subject to training basically aimed at improving technical and managerial skills

NO

Identify degree of interaction required with local community. Using a 7- or 9-point scale, ranging from low to high, indicate the degree of interaction with local community required for successful performance of the job

LOW → Emphasis* on task variables. Second but by no means unimportant question is to ask whether the individual is willing to serve abroad

HIGH

Is candidate willing?

YES

NO → Probably not suitable for position

Identify degree of similarity/dissimilarity between cultures. Using a 7- or 9-point scale, ranging from similar to highly diverse, indicate the magnitude of differences between the two cultures

NO → Probably not suitable for position

YES → Start orientation (moderate to low rigour)

VERY SIMILAR

HIGHLY DIVERSE

Emphasis* on task variables

Emphasis* on 'relational abilities' factor. 'Family situation' factor must also be taken into consideration

Start orientation (moderate to high rigour)

Start orientation (most rigorous)

*'Emphasis' does not mean ignoring the other factors. It only means that it should be the dominant factor.

Figure 2 Flow chart of the selection–decision process
Source: Tung (1981)

his/her ability to work towards intercultural cooperation should be obtained. Several psychometric instruments are available for assessing a candidate's suitability for an overseas assignment.

Another step in the decision process is the identification of the degree of interaction with the local community that is required by the job. In positions involving extensive contact with the culture and an understanding of the local value system (such as CEOs and functional heads), 'relational abilities' and 'environmental variables' become more critical and should become dominant factors in the selection decision. The selector should then proceed to examine the degree to which the foreign environment differs from the home situation. This is referred to as the cultural distance. If the cultural distance is low, that is, differences are insignificant (such as those between the USA and Canada), the selection should focus primarily on task variables.

Where cultural distance is great, the selection decision should focus on the 'relational abilities' and 'family situation' factors.

The subsequent step involves the provision of training programmes to prepare candidates for cross-cultural encounters. In jobs requiring a great deal of interaction with the local community and where the differences between the two cultures are great, the candidate should be subjected to all five types of training, with particular emphasis on sensitivity training and field experiences. In jobs requiring minimal contact with the local community and where the differences between cultures are small, the area studies programme would probably be sufficient. Between these extremes is a continuum of situations requiring varying degrees of contact with the local culture and involving varying magnitudes of difference between the cultures. Human resource administrators should locate the job under consideration along this continuum and determine the type of training programme that would be suitable for the expatriate in question.

Research has shown that firms which used more appropriate selection criteria and training programmes for each of the four job categories experienced significantly lower rates of expatriate failure (Tung 1981; Arthur and Bennett 1995).

4 Assessment of performance

The international aspect of performance assessment raises three basic questions: (1) what standards should be used in assessing performance abroad?; (2) who should perform the evaluation?; and (3) what time horizon should be used in assessing performance?

Standards in assessing performance

There are four basic approaches to assessing performance in the multinational context: (1) ethnocentric (home country standards); (2) polycentric (host country standards); (3) regiocentric (standards within a given geographic region); and (4) geocentric (global standards) (Heenan and Perlmutter 1979).

While the appraisal of an expatriate's performance should, in theory, be separate from the overall assessment of a foreign subsidiary's performance, in reality, the two often run in parallel. Thus, executives who operate in a subsidiary which is profitable tend to be evaluated positively, regardless of their actual performance. Conversely, in a subsidiary which is not profitable, even though the factors responsible for the loss are beyond the executives' control, corporate headquarters' assessment of their performance would generally be negative.

Where ethnocentric standards are used to evaluate expatriate performance, the latter may be liable for factors or situations which are beyond their control. In countries where there is rapid depreciation of the local currency, and/or hyperinflation accompanied by government price controls, the subsidiary may operate at a loss, particularly where the local currency has to be converted or translated back into the currency of the home country. For this, expatriates may be penalized even though they may be performing as efficiently as possible under the circumstances.

On the other hand, where poly- and regiocentric standards are used to evaluate an expatriate's performance, there is little incentive for the person to adopt strategies which can maximize the firm's global position. Where the firm chooses to adopt geocentric standards, which may entail, for example, the rationalization of production activities around the world, leading to plant closures or worker layoffs in some locations, host governments may not view such policies favourably. This dilemma epitomizes the classic tension between a national/local responsiveness strategy and a global rationalization strategy.

To overcome some of the problems associated with the use of ethnocentric standards, it has been suggested that a 'difficulty level' index should be incorporated into the assessment of an expatriate's performance (Oddou and Mendenhall 1991). This index would take into consideration three factors: (1) the operational language used in the subsidiary (operational language refers to the language used in the day-to-day operations of the subsidiary);

(2) cultural distance; and (3) the stability of factors which affect the expatriate's performance.

If expatriates are not proficient in the operational language it may take them longer to communicate with others both within and outside the context of the work situation. The higher the cultural distance, the higher the index. Similarly, the more unstable the factors, such as volatile exchange rates, the higher the index. Thus, for a 'somewhat more difficult' country, performance appraisal would be multiplied by an index factor of 1.2, whereas for a country which is 'much more difficult' the index factor would be 1.6.

Who should perform the evaluation?

A related issue is who has the necessary perspective to assess the expatriate's performance. If, for example, corporate headquarters were to perform the assessment, they may not have a full and accurate understanding of the circumstances and situations affecting the employee's performance. On the other hand, if the assessment were to be performed by the local management, the latter may not have the perspective necessary to evaluate performance within the broader context of the firm's global strategy. To obtain a more accurate picture of the expatriate's performance, both corporate headquarters and local management should be involved.

Time horizon to be used in assessing performance

US multinationals generally possess a short-term orientation with regard to planning and assessment of performance. This overemphasis on short-term results may be detrimental to the attainment of the long-term goals of the company. In contrast, European, Japanese and Australian multinationals espouse a longer term orientation in their human resource management practices. In these areas employers are generally more tolerant of circumstances that may temporarily affect a person's performance. Consequently, they tend to make allowances for

performance that is below average in the initial period of assignment abroad.

5 Retention of personnel

Two factors which can affect a firm's ability to retain competent corporate personnel to meet their international human resource management needs are: (1) compensation – is there adequate compensation for service abroad? and (2) repatriation – does the overseas assignment have a positive impact upon the expatriate's subsequent career advancement within the organization on repatriation?

Compensation

The typical cost of expatriating a family abroad is three to four times base salary. A compensation package is comprised of base salary and one or more of the following allowances/premiums.
(1) *Cost-of-living differential*. This takes into consideration the differences in costs in various parts of the world so that expatriates can enjoy the same, if not better, standard of living they were accustomed to at home.
(2) *Foreign service premium*. Besides cost-of-living differentials, some multinationals pay a foreign service premium to induce an employee to accept a foreign assignment.
(3) *Relocation allowance*. Some multinationals pay a lump sum outright to offset nonrecurring incidental costs necessitated by relocation.
(4) *Hardship and danger premiums*. Danger pay applies to specific emergency situations such as war, revolution or political unrest, and is discontinued once the emergency situation ceases. Hardship premiums, on the other hand, represent an ongoing allowance for assignments to countries with harsh living conditions, such as climate or inadequate amenities.

Besides monetary incentives many multinationals adopt other measures to make assignments to hardship locations more bearable, such as shorter durations of overseas assignments and more frequent vacations to seaside resorts or home leave.

Repatriation

Although companies make an effort to facilitate adaptation to the foreign environment – such as providing pre-departure training and other types of relocation assistance, including finding accommodation – most do little for the individual upon repatriation because they assume that the problems of re-entry to the home country and home operation are minimal. Unfortunately, this is not always true: the process of re-entry after several years of absence – including settling into a new position, a new home and the spouse's searching for a job – may be traumatic. Research has shown that repatriates and their families often experience a reverse culture shock upon re-entry (Harvey 1989).

The re-entry process can be particularly painful when expectations of upward career advancement are not realized. Frustration sets in when repatriates find they are not able to use immediately the skills and experience acquired abroad. This phenomenon is relatively common among US multinationals where international experience is not considered a very important criterion for promotion to senior management positions (Tung and Miller 1990). This practice stands in sharp contrast to the policies and practices in many leading European, Japanese and Australian multinationals. Worse yet, according to Tung and Arthur Andersen (1997), almost 60 per cent of US expatriates were not guaranteed a position at home upon successful completion of an international assignment. Another one third were guaranteed a position at the same level at which they were expatriated.

Two factors account for this difference in attitude towards an international assignment among US, European, Japanese and Australian multinationals. First, the majority of European, Japanese and Australian companies derive a significantly larger proportion of their corporate revenues from abroad. Thus, overseas positions are often viewed as exciting and challenging. Second, because of the heavier emphasis on domestic operations in US multinationals, many fear that if they are removed from corporate headquarters for an extended period of time, they will be out of the mainstream and, hence, bypassed for promotion. The ease or difficulty of reabsorption is influenced by three factors: (1) the duration of the overseas assignment; (2) the overall qualification of the expatriate; and (3) the attitude of top management towards international experience.

In general, the longer the duration of an offshore assignment, the more difficult reabsorption is. The problem is generally magnified when the repatriate has only mediocre skills and talents. Now that most European firms have phased out career expatriation, expatriate assignments are primarily used for career development purposes. An international assignment is viewed as an expedient means to acquire broad management experience and so only those individuals with high potential for senior management positions are sent abroad. An overwhelming majority of the companies in Japan and Australia, and now Europe, will refuse to send people on international assignments unless they are identified as having senior management potential.

To minimize the downside risks associated with repatriation, multinational firms should provide a better support system to allay expatriate concerns about career issues while serving abroad. A comprehensive support system should entail one or more of the components listed below.

A mentor–mentee programme should be instituted, where there is a one-on-one pairing of an expatriate with a member of senior management in the home organization. The latter has responsibility for monitoring the career path of the expatriate while abroad. This allays expatriates' concern about career opportunities back home and lets them devote full attention to the duties and responsibilities of the overseas assignment.

Where one-on-one pairing is not possible, a separate organizational unit should be established with primary responsibility for the specific needs of expatriates, such as career planning with the individual prior to departure, continuing guidance and/or counselling to help expatriates keep their career path on track while abroad, and career planning about their next assignment at the home office or another foreign location six to eight months prior to their return.

Constant contact between the home office and expatriates should be maintained to make them feel that they are still an important part of the home organization. In many Japanese multinationals there are special courier services for delivering newspapers, mail and gifts from the home office. According to a Japanese bank executive, his company provides both moral and financial support to its expatriates. An executive of an Australian natural resources company suggests the use of teleconferencing to provide that 'personal touch' to mitigate the isolation expatriates often experience overseas.

6 Managing the labour and management interface

There are two major issues in this area: (1) the extent to which industrial relations and practices around the world can constrain the activities of multinational firms; and (2) the labour unions' perspective of multinational corporations.

Labour's constraints upon multinationals

There is a diversity of industrial relations practices across countries in terms of the strength of unions, difference in wages and other compensation packages. The extent of worker participation in management also differs.

Strength of the unions. Some multinationals are concerned about locating manufacturing plants in places which are heavily unionized because they associate strong unionization with frequent work disruptions. Japanese automobile makers avoid 'union territory' in locating sites for their manufacturing plants in the USA. For example, Nissan chose to locate in Smyrna, Tennessee and Toyota in Georgetown, Kentucky.

Difference in wages. Other aspects of industrial/labour relations policies which can affect the operations of the international firm, particularly from the cost standpoint, are minimum wage rates, average number of hours worked per week and per year, and number of days of annual vacation plus other holidays.

Worker participation in management. Another salient way in which labour unions can affect and/or constrain the activities of international firms is the extent to which they are involved in management. This is referred to as industrial democracy. Another variation is co-determination, where labour participates in the economic management of the firm.

The heterogeneity of labour policies and practices poses problems of adjustment for the international firm. In particular it frustrates attempts at central coordination from headquarters and the rationalization of manufacturing facilities worldwide.

The organic solution to this dilemma would be multinational unionization. At present multinational unions do not exist even though the term 'international' is used by some national unions. National unions can be affiliated with International Trade Secretariats; these are autonomous entities which are organized on the basis of trade or industry and which have working relations with the International Confederation of Free Trade Unions (ICFTU). Some national unions have also entered into international confederations across industry lines. The ICFTU, for example, which has its headquarters in Brussels, Belgium, has a membership including most European national unions. It is a less powerful force in developing countries, however.

There are two major impediments to the formation of multinational unions. First, in some countries unions are heavily involved in the political process of their country and may constitute the backbone of a political party. Hence these unions have a strong national identity which is not conducive to multinationalization. Second, the ideological differences across unions can be significant. Some have a strong political or religious orientation, while others may subscribe to the principles of co-determination or corporate ownership. Even in the EC pan-EC worker rights have yet to be realized. The diluted version of the Social Charter, adopted by the EC heads of states (with Margaret Thatcher dissenting) in December 1989, is a non-binding agreement which provides rather vague and incomplete guidelines on social and labour policies.

Multinational unionization which can harmonize standards for multinational corporations and which can also increase the bargaining power of unions does not seem attainable in the 1990s. Labour unions have attempted, however, to establish a set of labour relations standards which could guide the activities of multinational corporations around the world. One such standard has been adopted by the International Labour Organization (ILO) and by the Organization of Economic Cooperation and Development (OECD). This set of standards is generally referred to as the OECD Guidelines and is non-mandatory. The Guidelines, first adopted in 1976 and subsequently revised, established standards on disclosure of information, competition, financing, taxation, employment and industrial relations, and science and technology. They call on international companies to: 'within the framework of law, regulations, and prevailing labour relations and employment practices . . . respect the right of organizations of employees, and engage in constructive negotiations'.

Unions' perspective of multinational corporations

Unions also view multinationals as a threat. They perceive the growing might of the geographically dispersed empire of multinationals as reducing their bargaining position with management, which resides in corporate head office somewhere offshore.

From the unions' perspective, multinationals can constrain the bargaining power of labour unions in four significant ways (Gladwyn and Walter 1980).

(1) *Employment displacement/transfer of production*. In attempts to reduce costs and to rationalize their production activities around the world, multinationals can relocate their manufacturing facilities from one region of the world to another, thus leading to plant closures and downsizing of some existing operations. These result in displacement of workers in some countries.

(2) *Reduced strike vulnerability*. In the event of a strike, a multinational firm can source from plants abroad to continue servicing the needs of the local market. This diffuses the effectiveness of local strike actions.

(3) *Reduced negotiating authority*. Many unions believe that local subsidiaries of foreign-based multinationals are not vested with genuine authority to make decisions on collective bargaining. Thus, they feel that their concerns may not be adequately represented to and/or understood by decision makers in corporate headquarters, who may be less attuned to local social, economic and cultural conditions.

(4) *Lack of information on ability to pay*. Many unions allege that they have limited access to financial data on the multinational corporation. They argue, for example, that profit and loss figures on the subsidiary may be distorted through intra-firm transfer pricing. Furthermore, many multinationals, in pursuing a global strategy, may deliberately sacrifice the profits of a local subsidiary to maximize worldwide performance. Thus, relying upon financial data on the local operation alone, instead of utilizing financial data for the multinational as a whole, may distort pay criterion often used in collective bargaining.

7 Conclusion

Each of the five salient aspects of international human resource management (selection, training, evaluation of performance, retention and labour–management relations) can affect organizational functioning. In the future international human resource management will take on even greater significance in the overall strategic management and planning of multinational firms for several reasons: (1) the globalization of the world economy; (2) the globalization of the workforce; and (3) regional economic integration.

The globalization of the world economy has resulted in an unprecedented demand for managers who can adopt an international perspective in decision making, strategic planning and management. Such international orientation, among other things, can be developed over one or two stints of overseas assignments. Thus the primary objective of expatriation will increasingly shift from one of filling a job opening overseas to serving as a mechanism for the overall career development of employees with high potentials for senior management positions.

Johnston (1991) coined the term 'Global workforce 2000' to refer to the increasing mobility of the workforce across international boundaries. There is a growing trend towards the emigration of younger workers from developing countries to industrialized nations. Several factors have contributed to this development. First, many governments have been lowering barriers to immigration and emigration. Second, low birth-rates and an ageing workforce in many developed economies have resulted in labour shortages. Younger, mobile workers from developing nations can fill such a void. The emergence of regional trading blocs (such as the EC and the North American Free Trade Agreement) has contributed to the growing mobility of workers and harmonization of labour policies and practices among countries within a trading bloc.

These developments necessitate that international human resource management, in addition to the five main dimensions discussed in this piece, devote more attention to the issues of dual-career couples, managing diversity and the development of an international orientation. As more women enter into professional and managerial positions, multinational corporations have to deal with the relocation of dual-career couples. So far, US multinationals have not addressed this issue adequately. The problem of dual-career couples will also pose an increasing challenge to European multinationals in the future.

Thus far, the focus of managing diversity has been primarily on cross-national differences, such as selection criteria for effective performance abroad and training for cross-cultural encounters. With the increasing participation of women and ethnic minorities in the labour force at various levels, including managerial and professional positions, corporations have to devote greater attention to managing and valuing intra-national diversity. There are many similarities, as well as differences, in the dynamics and processes of managing cross-national versus intra-national diversity (Tung 1993). Research findings and experiences acquired in the field of managing cross-national diversity can be fruitfully applied and/or adapted to managing intra-national diversity.

With respect to developing an international orientation, three issues are noteworthy. First, the development of a global mentality requires a fundamental reorientation in all dimensions of human resource management policies and practices, in particular, the design of a reward structure to encourage employees to think and act globally. Second, in some countries with large domestic markets, and thus a more ethnocentric orientation (such as the USA), the successful development of a global mentality also necessitates fundamental changes to the education system in elementary and secondary schools. For example, requiring proficiency in a second language and the study of world geography and history can help raise young people's awareness and consciousness of other cultures and their *modus operandi*. Third, while stressing the need to develop a global mentality, a delicate balance must be struck between a local/national responsiveness strategy and a global rationalization strategy. In general, host governments are suspicious of global rationalization strategies which may result in plant closures and/or worker layoffs in their respective countries.

The challenges which lie ahead in the international human resource management arena can be daunting. However, if organizations seek to gain and/or maintain their global competitiveness in the decades ahead, these issues must be addressed.

ROSALIE L. TUNG
FACULTY OF BUSINESS
SIMON FRASER UNIVERSITY
CANADA

Further reading

(References cited in the text marked *)

* Adler, N.J. (1987) 'Pacific basin managers: a *gaijin*, not a woman', *Human Resource Management* 26 (2): 169–91. (Interviews with North

American female expatriates on their experiences of living and working in the Asia Pacific region.)

* Arthur, W. and Bennett, L. (1995) 'The international assignee: the relative importance of factors perceived to contribute to success', *Personnel Psychology* 48: 99–114. (An empirical investigation of factors important for expatriate success, along with their relative importance.)

Dowling, P.J., Schuler, R.S. and Welch, D.E. (1994) *International Dimensions of Human Resource Management*, Boston, MA: PWS-KENT Publishing Company. (A text in international human resource development, including selection, training, development and compensation.)

* Gladwyn, T. and Walter, I. (1980) *Multinationals under Fire*, New York: Wiley. (A survey and analysis of the dangers and challenges confronting multinationals in their worldwide operations.)

* Harvey, M.C. (1989) 'Repatriation of corporate executives: an empirical study', *Journal of International Business Studies* 20 (1): 131–44. (A survey of the problems and issues faced by repatriates upon returning home.)

* Heenan, D.A. and Perlmutter, H.V. (1979) *Multinational Organization Development*, Reading, MA: Addison-Wesley. (An analysis of how companies can develop an international perspective to take advantage of global opportunities.)

* Johnston, W.B. (1991) 'Global work force 2000: the new world labor market', *Harvard Business Review* 69 (1): 115–27. (A discussion of changes in the international labour market and their implications for management.)

* Moran, Stahl & Boyer (1988) *Status of American Female Expatriate Employees: Survey Results*, Boulder, CO: Moran, Stahl & Boyer. (A survey of the deployment of women in expatriate assignments and reasons for their underutilization.)

* Oddou, G. and Mendenhall, M. (1991) 'Expatriate performance appraisal: problems and solutions', in M. Mendenhall and G. Oddou (eds), *Readings and Cases in International Human Resource Management*, Boston, MA: PWS-KENT Publishing Company. (A discussion of the problems associated with the performance appraisal of expatriates, and their solutions.)

* Tung, R.L. (1981) 'Selection and training of personnel for overseas assignments', *Columbia Journal of World Business* 16 (1): 68–78. (A theoretical framework for the selection and training of personnel for international assignments.)

* Tung, R.L. (1982) 'Selection and training of U.S., European and Japanese multinationals', *California Management Review* 25 (1): 57–71. (A survey of the policies and practices on expatriate assignments among US, Japanese and western European multinationals.)

* Tung, R.L. (1988) 'Career issues in international assignments', *Academy of Management Executive* 2 (3): 241–4. (A discussion of two key issues associated with international assignments, dual-career couples and repatriation.)

* Tung, R.L. (1990) 'International human resource management policies and practices: a comparative analysis', in G.R. Ferris and K.M. Rowland (eds), *Research in Personnel and Human Resources Management*, suppl. 2, Greenwich, CT: JAI Press Inc. (A comparative analysis of international human resource management practices among US, western European, Japanese and Australian multinationals.)

* Tung, R.L. (1993) 'Managing cross-national and intra-national diversity', *Human Resource Management Journal* 23 (4): 461–77. (An analysis of the similarities and differences in dynamics of managing cross-cultural versus intranational diversity.)

* Tung, R.L. and Arthur Andersen (1997) *Exploring International Assignees' Viewpoints: A Study of the Expatriation/Repatriation Process*, Chicago, IL: Arthur Andersen Inc. (A study of 409 international assignees' attitudes to and experience with expatriation and repatriation.)

* Tung, R.L. and Miller, E.L. (1990) 'Managing in the twenty-first century: the need for global orientation', *Management International Review* 30 (1): 5–18. (A survey of career development of senior management personnel in US companies.)

See also: CULTURE, CROSS-NATIONAL; ECONOMIC INTEGRATION, INTERNATIONAL; GLOBALIZATION; MANAGEMENT EDUCATION AND DEVELOPMENT, INTERNATIONAL; MANAGEMENT IN JAPAN; MULTINATIONAL CORPORATIONS, ORGANIZATION STRUCTURE IN; ORGANIZATION CULTURE

Related topics in the IEBM: APPRAISAL METHODS; GLOBALIZATION AND CORPORATE NATIONALITY; GLOBALIZATION AND SOCIETY; HUMAN RESOURCE MAANGEMENT; INDUSTRIAL AND ALABOUR RELA-

TIONS; INDUSTRIAL DEMOCRACY; INTERNATIONAL BUSINESS ELITES; MANAGEMENT IN AUSTRALIA; MANAGEMENT IN EUROPE; MANAGEMENT IN NORTH AMERICA; MIGRANT MANAGERS; ORGANIZATION BEHAVIOUR; ORGANIZATIONAL PERFORMANCE; TRADE UNIONS; WOMEN MANAGERS IN ORGANIZATIONS

International business, future trends

Overview

Major forces are in operation today that are transforming both the manner in which international business is conducted and the environments in which the firm operates. Managing in this evolving global business environment requires a new kind of leadership response that reflects sensitivity to the challenges of continuous change. Competition has become increasingly global in scope and more fierce in nature. Business executives are being forced to re-evaluate the very assumptions and values upon which their organizations were founded. These assessments are providing the impetus for new managerial strategies that are reshaping the structure and processes of the business enterprise.

The challenges and opportunities of international management will become more integrated and interdependent as technological advances bring the world closer together and information becomes more readily available and instantly accessible. The unique cultural, political, legal, economic and technological challenges of international management will be addressed between topic areas and across functional dimensions. The traditional functions of marketing, finance, manufacturing and human resource management will become more interdependent and less distinct as separate entities. Information will provide the

interdisciplinary link and integrating force that makes this possible.

As organizations integrate around information and become more dependent on global information networks, management layers will continue to dissolve. More flexible organizational structures will evolve that are no longer dependent on the hierarchical management assumptions of the past. The challenge for future leaders is to integrate and manage across these forces of change.

Information will play a key role in this transformation process. Tomorrow's leaders will manage organizations in which the creation of wealth will depend on how well the information asset is managed. The success or failure of the global organization will increasingly be evaluated in terms of its ability to leverage and manage information.

In this entry, we examine major forces transforming the global enterprise and its international environment. The dynamic environmental setting of international business and the role of information technology as a driving force set the stage for new paradigm shifts in international management. Information has evolved as a central core asset that is essential to the effective management of all corporate initiatives. We focus on quality management and the emerging global workforce as two prominent areas in which information will play an important role. These paradigm shifts are examined in the context of their impact on the global enterprise and implications for future international business leaders.

1 The dynamic environment of international management

International managers face unprecedented change both inside the organization as well as from external forces that impact corporate strategy. Companies are re-engineering their business processes, downsizing, empowering employees, focusing on customer satisfaction and quality initiatives, fostering teamwork, creating strategic alliances worldwide and promoting information technology solutions to meet these managerial challenges. Without doubt, we are living in a period that will be viewed as a revolution in business. As companies strive to survive in this new and changing business world, flexibility, spontaneity and new approaches to business management will be the key to success.

The information age

The shift from an industrial age to an information age represents a major turning point not only for corporations but for society as a whole. The impacts will radiate to all corners of the globe. Just as social and economic structures underwent radical change as a result of the industrial revolution, the same shift is occurring as we move from the industrial era to the new information age. The product of this information age is knowledge. Knowledge has become the critical resource to manage as opposed to land, labour and capital. As stressed by Drucker (1993), the shift to knowledge as the key resource creates new social structures, economic dynamics and new political forces.

As familiarity with the industrial age is replaced with an emerging information age, organizational power shifts to information and knowledge. Information technology is playing a major role in this transformation process. In fact, information technology is the creator of this new information economy. As companies become more comfortable with the technology, the focus shifts to developing applications that support corporate strategies and ways in which to harness the power of information. Information management will be a key to the success of tomorrow's global enterprise. The challenges will be matched by the opportunities of managing in an evolving knowledge-based world of business.

A paradigm shift for international business management

An emerging paradigm shift in management practice is occurring as global companies respond to changes reshaping business strategies, structures and processes (see GLOBALIZATION). The very nature of work is being redefined as information technology provides the means to empower workers with sophisticated resources to enhance productivity and the manner in which work is accomplished. The breakdown of management hierarchies, due to more effective and efficient information flows, will impact the organization in ways not yet realized. Future executives will encounter unprecedented organizational demands and challenges unfamiliar to their predecessors.

Global business drivers

Drucker (1992) postulates five important areas that are bringing change to social and economic foundations as well as change in the strategies, structures and management of business. First, economic relationships will increasingly take place between trading blocs rather than countries. In this environment, bilateral and trilateral deals will become commonplace. Second, businesses will turn to strategic alliances as the means to integrate themselves into the world economy. These alliances will probably be extended to include not only business ventures but also other forms of partnerships with non-business enterprises such as universities and government entities. Third, the restructuring of businesses will continue as companies respond to the changing management requirements of information-based organizations. Fourth, the governance of companies is being debated as the trend towards private ownership of large companies continues. Finally, changes in international politics and policies as opposed to concerns of domestic economies will dominate in the next decade. Global business leaders will be forced to respond to these changing trends and identify the effects for their own organizations.

The transnational solution

Without question, companies are recognizing the need for new approaches to meet the challenges of international business management. Changing business forces spurred along by innovations in information technology have resulted in new strategies that are no longer one-dimensional. As Bartlett and Ghoshal (1989) emphasize, successful companies today and in the future will be those that can meet diverse local needs, increase global efficiency and increase the pace of innovation and worldwide learning simultaneously. Companies that exercise these skills fit the evolving distinction of the transnational firm.

The transnational solution represents a changing managerial paradigm. The Bartlett and Ghoshal model is not a specific strategic posture or organizational structure. The transnational is appropriately described as a managerial mentality. This mindset is an essential component of the transnational solution. Wendt (1993) argues that the transnational solution may not be the best approach for all companies, but it is particularly essential for large companies operating in high technology dependent, and knowledge and information-intensive industries. These companies are more readily faced with the challenges of survival in a constantly changing global environment.

The difficulties that are part of the transnational solution cannot be understated. Thriving as a transnational requires hard work, faster responsiveness and intelligent strategies (Wendt 1993). The emergence of the transnational will change business as we know it today and out of its roots will emerge a new paradigm of international business management.

2 The role of information technology in international business

Information technology (IT) is an integrating theme, a catalyst and a solution to many of the challenges facing global managers today. Information technology provides the tools that enable us to operate in a 'borderless' and shrinking world (see GLOBAL STRATEGIC ALLIANCES). Advancements in information technology provide the means by which to communicate electronically and access information more efficiently across national borders. Applications of these technologies are changing the nature of work, decision-making processes and organizational coordination, control and structure. The global enterprise of the future will face new managerial challenges that reflect the role of information as an asset in meeting the demands of its global environment.

Information technology is not only a major force driving the global marketplace, but also an important strategic resource to the corporation. The firm's information technology infrastructure provides the communication base for the flow of international data and information. Designing and maintaining the information technology infrastructure to respond to change and future technological breakthroughs will represent a major investment for companies in the future. The managerial challenges for global companies are immense since they encounter increased complexities, more intricate cost structures, and political, cultural, economic and legal barriers.

The potential power of information technology as a means for gaining global competitive advantage is a given today (see GLOBAL STRATEGIC PLANNING). Companies that cannot compete technologically will be at a competitive disadvantage. Technology has become a cost of doing business, not an option to be evaluated. Countries are, likewise, recognizing the importance of a well-developed technological infrastructure as a necessity for remaining competitive and attracting business opportunities.

Deans and Ricks (1992) describe the role of information technology in a global context from three perspectives:

1 As a means for establishing a worldwide communication infrastructure for international business activity.
2 As a facilitator of international information flows.
3 As a competitive weapon to be utilized for competitive advantage.

Information technology is increasingly being recognized as a central component of corporate business strategy. Information technology provides the mechanisms by which vital information can be captured, analysed and transmitted efficiently. Companies that are innovative in tapping the power of this resource will be likely to retain competitive advantage. In an international context, sensitivity to cultural diversity, careful planning for foreign environments and responsiveness to local characteristics will be of paramount importance (Deans and Ricks 1992).

Emerging technologies to support international information flows

International communication is becoming much less difficult as technologies such as fax, voicemail, electronic mail and video-conferencing are perfected to meet the growing needs of the international business world. The growth of notebook computers and personal digital assistants will make information more readily available and accessible throughout the world. These devices are being supported by new types of interfaces such as voice and pen point that make utilization of the technology easier and more efficient. In addition, these emerging technologies support independence from factors such as location, wires and language that present barriers to global coordination (Hald and Konsynski 1993).

Multimedia technology has tremendous potential for providing enhanced communication for international operations and overcoming the obstacles of distance and cultural diversity. Multimedia applications combine data, sound, video and graphics in innovative ways that appeal to more than one of the senses simultaneously. The decreased cost of compact disc technology will speed the availability of multimedia access (Hald and Konsynski 1993).

Mobile communication in the form of cellular phones and beepers allows employees to take advantage of time zone differences and make better use of otherwise unproductive spans of time. These technologies are transforming the way work is accomplished. The use of mobile technologies in conjunction with laptop computers provides the means by which to improve efficiency and respond more readily to customer needs. These technologies are changing the very nature of international business transactions.

Wireless communication is fast becoming the wave of the future. Although wireless communication is only now beginning to emerge as a viable alternative, it is expected to have a considerable impact on the international business world. Easy access to information regardless of time and location will transform power relationships and decision making activities throughout the organization. The end-user can tap into information as readily as corporate executives forcing increased decision making at the locus of control.

Establishing communication networks globally, however, is not as easy as setting up similar systems within one country. Incompatible standards, poor links for voice, data and video, as well as language, cultural and regulatory differences make global networks a challenge, especially in some parts of the world. As countries continue to improve their technological infrastructures to support the technological demands of global companies these issues will become less significant.

These new emerging technologies are also making international business opportunities more feasible for smaller companies. As prices for fax machines, video-conferencing systems, cellular phones and online databases come down, the benefits to small and medium-sized companies in international markets increase immensely. Technology is a driving force enabling more companies worldwide to participate in global commerce.

The evolving virtual corporation

The concept of the virtual corporation is emerging as a consequence of the readily available technology linking businesses around the world. The virtual corporation represents a temporary network of independent companies linked by information technology for the purpose of sharing skills, costs and market access. It will exist without the traditional organizational chart and central headquarters. This evolving corporate concept consists of a group of collaborators which quickly unite to exploit a specific opportunity. The venture may end once this opportunity has been met. Each company involved in the venture contributes its unique core capabilities to the effort. In essence, each partner will provide what it does best to be integrated with the best of other companies (Byrne 1993).

Rosenbluth Travel, one of the five largest travel agencies in the USA, exemplifies the concept of what might be described as a global virtual corporation (Miller *et al.* 1993). Rather than expand through foreign direct investment, the company chose to work with the best foreign partners it could find through a cooperative alliance that comprises thirty-two partners spanning thirty-seven countries. This virtual arrangement relies on information technology to structure and restructure itself. The information technology infrastructure provides the coordinating link that makes information available to clients and travellers worldwide. The flexibility of this arrangement allows the company to evolve as global travel support needs change.

Currently, most of these ventures are primarily alliances and outsourcing agreements. Although companies have long come together for specific projects and then dissolved once the task has been accomplished, today's larger corporations are using this virtual concept to gain access to new technologies and new markets. The virtual model is being recognized as an important organizational innovation.

3 The emergence of the information-based multinational corporation

The global company of the future will be characterized as an information-intensive organization (see MULTINATIONAL CORPORATIONS). A shift from paper-based to electronic-based information flow will be inevitable. Greater information intensity and availability of information on demand will force a re-evaluation of traditional corporate functions such as planning and marketing. The contribution and positioning of these functions and the impact of this change in the context of organizational strategies is yet to be seen (Hald and Konsynski 1993).

Information management will be important to the future success of the global enterprise. Information technology provides the basic infrastructure, applications capabilities and means by which to facilitate the flow of information. Accessing and managing vast amounts of information in a manner that provides the firm competitive advantage will be a major challenge. Sharing information across organizational functions, departments and management structures eliminates layers of management, thus facilitating faster decision making and increased efficiencies. At the same time, trade-offs in the form of increased job stress and redefined job functions will place added burdens on management. Developing information management strategies that can tap the right information for the appropriate people will be an important challenge for corporations.

Information as an asset

Information has become the glue that holds business entities together and provides linkages with the external world. Managing information as an asset with strategic value is a concept few organizations have seriously integrated into their strategic plans (McGee and Prusak 1993). This is probably due in part to the fact that information has unique characteristics not common to other forms of assets. Its value is difficult to measure and its intangible nature adds to this complexity.

The implementation of a system by Price Waterhouse exemplifies an example of a planning effort to link information technology with the organization's strategic goals. The company developed a proprietary system that links all their staff together on a global network that provides vast amounts of information in real time, allows employees to work together on projects in different locations, and updates the network that continually captures information to be used in subsequent projects. This system has afforded the company substantial gains in efficiency and responsiveness.

In an international business setting the value of information as a resource becomes crucial as more variables come into play and decision-making processes become more complex (Deans and Ricks 1992). Managing international information effectively will play a key role in the firm's competitive position. Adequate and up-to-date information about foreign business environments will become increasingly important as more companies compete for global markets. Accessible, cost-effective information may provide the competitive edge that makes the difference between success or failure.

The information economy fosters an environment in which information drives the creation of wealth. Companies that are more effective in their use of information are moving ahead as winners in the new business world. It has clearly become essential that companies become information rich as a means of leading the competition (McGee and Prusak 1993).

Knowledge as a resource

The raw material of the information-intensive organization is knowledge. As emphasized by Drucker (1993), there is currently no economic theory to explain how knowledge behaves as an economic resource. There is a need for a theory that recognizes knowledge as a key component of wealth production. Drucker predicts that a new theory of a knowledge-based economy will be different from that of existing economic theory. Since it is not currently possible to quantify knowledge, these economic relationships are difficult to obtain and explain.

Knowledge and information will continue to provide the greater returns on wealth as opposed to traditional resources (Drucker 1993). By its very nature, knowledge changes very rapidly, making it necessary to periodically acquire new knowledge in order to remain competitive. The dynamics of knowledge management require that corporations build change management into their existing structures. The change from a capitalist society to a knowledge-based society will clearly yield new managerial challenges and evolving opportunities (Drucker 1993).

4 Global quality initiatives

Global quality initiatives represent still another response of corporations to increased competition and the changing business climate. Dobyns and Crawford-Mason (1991) refer to this era as the quality revolution. Quality is fast becoming the international standard for trade and a dimension of management that must be addressed by companies competing on a global scale.

The quality management vision represents a major change in the way companies are organized and operate. Implementing quality initiatives for global operations that mesh with organizational changes currently in progress make the task at hand even more difficult. Large global companies that have implemented quality programmes advocate the necessity of these programmes for future competitive advantage, both in terms of financial benefits and rewards to the organization as a whole (Dobyns and Crawford-Mason 1991).

Quality in a customer-driven business world

Quality is the corporate response to a customer-driven economy. In today's business world, power has clearly shifted to the consumer. The consumer has more choices, more companies competing for their attention, and international access to products. Businesses must meet customer needs by providing quality products and services that are superior to those of their competitors worldwide. The result has been a new management paradigm that requires continuous emphasis on quality management.

Quality is also a natural consequence of the changes and competitive challenges facing corporate leaders worldwide. Information technology is playing a critical role in efforts to improve product and service quality, enhance the availability of crucial information that focuses on the individuality of the customer base, and speed up the product cycle time. Information will be the essential resource enabling more effective quality management.

ISO 9000: an international standard for trade

A prominent example of the importance being placed on global quality initiatives is the European Union's (EU; see EUROPEAN UNION) push towards ISO 9000, a series of quality standards that originated as part of the EU's efforts to become a single market. The purpose of the standards is to harmonize the large number of existing quality standards in order to establish consistency and a common language that ensures quality products crossing boundaries of the EU countries. The ISO 9000 set of standards has been adopted by the EU and over fifty-five nations as their voluntary national quality standard and the number of companies registered to an ISO 9000 standard continues to grow (Byrnes 1992).

As the importance of the standard is recognized by more companies and its advantage as a competitive marketing tool is realized, pressure to become certified will increase. In fact, ISO 9000 certification is rapidly becoming a requirement for companies doing business in Europe. Furthermore, many companies are beginning to require ISO 9000 certification of their suppliers as well. Certification, therefore, is fast becoming a cost of doing business internationally, rather than an option to be evaluated.

These trends clearly indicate that quality and quality management will continue to play a major role as competitive determinants for global companies. A concept that at one time was limited to technical issues is now a continuous improvement process involving every aspect of the business. It is a fundamental business strategy that will be essential for survival in the global arena of the future.

5 The evolving global workforce

The changing global management environment is further complicated by an increasingly diverse and international workforce.

This workforce will play a significant role in how companies respond to current changes in the global business environment (see HUMAN RESOURCE MANAGEMENT, INTERNATIONAL). We are seeing the emergence of a global workforce with talents and capabilities for accomplishing anything, anywhere. Executives from around the globe confirm that increasingly sophisticated work is being done in nations whose workforces are highly capable (O'Rielly 1992). Just as with products, companies will look for quality labour anywhere in the world. The essence of the information age makes it possible for managers to evaluate where work can best be done. It is clear that work will flow to the places best able to perform economically and efficiently (O'Reilly 1992). The pressures of foreign competition are providing the impetus for this shift in how and where the world's work is done.

Major characteristics of the world's workforce

Johnston (1991) describes the following major trends as characterizing the world's changing workforce:

1   The world's workforce will become more mobile and employers will increasingly search anywhere in the world for the skills they need.
2   Industrialized nations will reconsider their protectionist immigration policies.
3   Women will enter the workforce in growing numbers, especially in developing countries.
4   Gradual standardization of labour practices will occur among industrialized countries.
5   Developing countries will produce a growing share of the world's high school and college graduates.

These trends clearly indicate a shift from a labour market that has evolved from local, regional and national to one that is truly international. A more diverse workforce will require new training programmes as employees with diverse cultural backgrounds, values and established norms are forced to work together in team-orientated assignments. An understanding of cultural diversity will become paramount in all business settings, not just for those being assigned to foreign locations. Companies that embrace the opportunities and encourage ethnic minorities, women and foreign nationals to contribute to the organizational goals will be in a better position to obtain competitive advantage.

A work environment that is free of the traditional management hierarchies will result in new expectations for advancement and new meanings for traditional titles. New reward structures will evolve that value employee performance and worth in ways that replace traditional promotion patterns and reflect new organizational needs. Individuals will also be forced to take more responsibility for their own career paths (Drucker 1993).

A natural consequence of the information age will be a more empowered workforce. Greater responsibility will be passed to those most capable and knowledgeable. Jobs will require more complex skill levels, information access will transfer decision-making activities to the end-user, and the typical firm's most essential asset will become knowledge.

Knowledge workers

Not only are changes occurring in the geographical domain that defines the new labour market, but also in the fundamental concepts that characterize this new and evolving workforce. Organizations will compete more fiercely for qualified, knowledgeable people, a resource that is becoming paramount in importance to the success of the organization. Drucker (1993) describes the transformation to knowledge workers and service workers as the new challenge of the post-capitalist society.

Knowledge workers will assume greater responsibility and the potential to become self-managed. This will create an organizational chart that is non-hierarchical with a vast number of decision makers at traditionally lower management levels. These shifts in responsibility will continue to erode middle management positions.

Knowledge workers will be in a position to command good incomes because they will be in demand. At the same time, knowledge workers must be part of an organization. From this perspective, there is interdependence between the two. Organizations will no longer earn loyalty through a pay-packet, but by providing opportunities for knowledge workers to put their knowledge to work (Drucker 1993).

6 Leadership challenges and opportunities

The competitive pressures that are changing the structures of organizations and the manner in which firms are managed require new forms of leadership (Hax 1989). Tomorrow's global leader will of necessity be a manager of change. Leaders must respond to the forces of an increasingly diverse workforce, quality management at the core of organizational objectives, unpredictable technological breakthroughs, and the increasing power of information and knowledge. In short, tomorrow's leaders must provide vision and exercise power in new ways that respond to the paradigm shifts of tomorrow's corporation.

Fundamental shifts are occurring in the nature of the responsibilities imposed on managers. First, managing from an authority and control position is being replaced by situations in which the manager is neither controlling nor controlled. Future executives will no longer gain recognition based on the number of people reporting to them. As businesses continue to grow through alliances and outsourcing activities, management control and authority will take on new meanings. For example, it may be necessary to outsource activities that have their own senior management. These types of arrangements tend to upset managers who have traditionally operated under high degrees of control and ownership (Drucker 1993). Second, the role of managers is being transformed to one of leader status. As workers assume greater decision-making power, the role of the traditional manager shifts to one of providing vision and guidance for the organization. Third, information and intellectual assets are becoming increasingly more important. Managing intangible assets requires new approaches and a new managerial mindset. Managers of organizations that are inflexible and resistant to change will find this transition more difficult than those that embrace change and experiment with new management approaches. Finally, it will be necessary to develop new strategies and approaches because future problems will probably not be solved with yesterday's techniques.

In short, managers of the future will participate in an international business environment much different from that of the past. This evolution will be accompanied by new management practices that better match the needs of the organization. Advancements in technology will continue to force re-evaluations of organizational practices and strategies. Global managers will continue to face greater complexity, uncertainty and dynamic forces both external and internal to the organization. Adjusting and adapting to these changes, and at the same time taking advantage of the opportunities, will be the managerial challenge of future global leaders.

P. CANDACE DEANS

DAVID A. RICKS

THUNDERBIRD – THE AMERICAN GRADUATE
SCHOOL OF INTERNATIONAL MANAGEMENT

Further reading

(References cited in the text marked *)

* Bartlett, C.A. and Ghoshal, S. (1989) *Managing Across Borders*, Boston, MA: Harvard Business School Press. (Provides research findings and guidance for companies operating in today's global environment.)

* Byrne, J.A. (1993) 'The virtual corporation', *Business Week* 8 February: 99–103. (Describes the concept of the virtual corporation and its future role in business.)

* Byrnes, D. (1992) 'Exploring the world of ISO 9000', *Quality* 31 (10): 19–31. (An examination of key issues relating to the ISO 9000 worldwide standards and the resulting implications for companies.)

* Deans, P.C. and Ricks, D.A. (1992) 'Achieving global competitive advantage through information technology', *Competitiveness Review* 2 (2): 2–6. (A discussion of the role of information technology as a means for achieving global competitive advantage.)

* Dobyns, L. and Crawford-Mason, C. (1991) *Quality or Else*, Boston, MA: Houghton Mifflin. (The authors describe the quality revolution that is reshaping the way businesses think and operate.)

* Drucker, P.F. (1992) *Managing for the Future*, New York: Truman Talley Books. (Drucker's enlightening views on world business and management imperatives for the 1990s and beyond.)

* Drucker, P.F. (1993) *Post-Capitalist Society*, New York: HarperBusiness. (An insightful analysis of the transformation from the age of capitalism to the knowledge society.)

* Hald, A. and Konsynski, B.R. (1993) 'Seven technologies to watch in globalization', in S. Bradley, J. Hausman and R. Nolan (eds), *Globalization, Technology and Competition*, Boston, MA: Harvard Business School Press. (An analysis of technological trends of significance to global corporations in the future.)

* Hax, A.C. (1989) 'Building the firm of the future', *Sloan Management Review* 31 (2): 75–82. (Enlightening discussion of the USA's future competitiveness in the context of globalization, technology and leadership.)

* Johnston, W.B. (1991) 'Global workforce 2000: the new world labor market', *Harvard Business Review* 69 (2): 115–27. (A statistical analysis of the increasingly mobile future global workforce.)

* McGee, J.V. and Prusak, L. (1993) *Managing Information Strategically*, New York: Wiley. (Describes the transition of the corporate world to an information economy and the value of information in the creation of wealth.)

* Miller, D., Clemons, E. and Row, M. (1993) 'Information technology and the global virtual corporation', in S. Bradley, J. Hausman and R. Nolan (eds), *Globalization, Technology and Competition*, Boston, MA: Harvard Business School Press. (A case study of a global virtual corporation.)

* O'Reilly, B. (1992) 'Your new global workforce', *Fortune* 14 December: 52–66. (A description of the fundamental shifts currently shaping how and where the world's work is accomplished.)

* Wendt, H. (1993) *Global Embrace*, New York: HarperBusiness. (This book describes the nature of the transnational company and resulting

managerial challenges posed by the transnational corporate form.)

See also: EUROPEAN UNION; GLOBAL STRATEGIC ALLIANCES; GLOBAL STRATEGIC PLANNING; GLOBALIZATION; HUMAN RESOURCE MANAGEMENT, INTERNATIONAL; MULTINATIONAL CORPORATIONS;

Related topics in the IEBM: COMMUNICATION; DRUCKER, P.F.; HUMAN RESOURCE MANAGEMENT; INFORMATION REVOLUTION; ORGANIZATION STRUCTURE; STRATEGY, CONCEPT OF; TOTAL QUALITY MANAGEMENT

International business, legal dimensions of

Overview

The international executive crossing national boundaries must necessarily be concerned about the legal context for activities planned abroad. Such concerns may best be satisfied by asking a series of questions: Do home-country laws apply extra-territorially to all firms when they go abroad? Do all countries use the same rules of taxation and accounting systems? Are such firms free to undertake any activity not specifically prohibited by law, as they generally would be in the USA, UK and other common law countries, or must activities abroad be specifically authorized by enabling legislation? Are the financing documents and commercial paper commonly used in the home market also valid and enforceable abroad? Do laws governing a company's trademarks and technology vary from country to country? When exporting to different countries in the European Union (EU), for example, can the firm control its French, German, Dutch and Italian distributors territorially to preclude unfair competition by price cutting and selling across borders at prices lower than the neighbouring distributor? Is the firm free to send home-country nationals to run sales offices or manage production and distribution in any foreign country?

If, in fact, the global marketer must deal with the national laws of each country, does some kind of 'international federal system' exist, much like the federal system in the USA which overlays different legal structures in each of the fifty US states? Further, are home-country 'common law-trained' lawyers familiar with laws in the major foreign countries, or does the marketer have to select and deal with foreign lawyers in each jurisdiction? If the latter will be the case, are legal systems similar or different around the world? If different, how many differing types of legal systems exist? How are lawyers trained in different systems or countries, and is their role in business transactions similar to that of lawyers or solicitors at home? Indeed, how many home-country business strategies were formulated based on assumptions which were, in turn, based upon legal rights and remedies in home courts under known conditions? These are just some of the issues covered under the broad title of 'the legal dimensions of international business'.

1 Nation-states and sovereignty

Sovereignty means, *inter alia*, that nation-states exercise control over economic activities within their borders. This generality should be placed in context according to two important criteria: (1) the stage of development of the country and (2) the political and economic system in place in the country (see POLITICAL RISK). Nations thus exercise control over their industrial development, including the establishment of protectionist practices or barriers (policies, laws, regulations, etc.), to promote pioneer industries or protect non-competitive sectors from cheap imports (see INTERNATIONAL TRADE AND FOREIGN DIRECT INVESTMENT).

Conversely, when market-driven nations evolve to advanced stages of development, they establish laws to promote fair competition (anti-trust or anti-monopoly laws and regulations) and declare that contracts, combinations or conspiracies in restraint of (free) trade are illegal. In some cases the policy may provide that abuse of dominant market positions is also illegal, as well as predatory or discriminatory pricing practices. Laws are passed to define and preserve the social order of a nation, and extend to political, cultural and even intellectual activities and social conduct, with balancing limitations to prevent over-regulation. Examples of such protection include laws to protect against invasion of privacy which may affect credit bureaux, transborder data flow between divisions of any multinational company (MNC), restrictions on advertising, and telemarketing activities (see MULTINATIONAL CORPORATIONS).

Property and property rights

Some laws define respective interests in property, both tangible (real and personal property) and intangible (intellectual property such as patents, trademarks, copyrights and computer software). In every society the laws defining and governing these are national laws. But what about the doctrine inherent in socialist policies that the means of production belong to the State? In the past this translated into state ownership of property including perhaps land, buildings and capital equipment. If productive property did not belong to the State in some socialist countries, it belonged to the workers, or a workers cooperative, or even to the ruling communist party.

What is important in such contexts is that such property does not belong to the individual, and corporations (if they exist) do not belong to individual shareholders. This means that landowners may not collect rents, shareholders may not collect dividends and lessors may not collect lease rentals on equipment or software leased to users. In fact no leasing companies or facilities could exist since the concept itself traditionally did not exist under such systems. These considerations become important when looking at countries in transition from centrally planned (socialist) command economies to market-driven (capitalist) free enterprise economies.

Constitutional systems and 'pre-emption'

In the USA, the Federal Constitution and federal system establish the doctrine of pre-emption by those federal laws affecting interstate or foreign commerce over state laws which may not. In defining the separation of powers between the Executive, Legislative and Judicial branches of government the United States Constitution states that 'Congress shall have the power to regulate commerce with foreign nations and among the several states' (US Constitution, Art. I, Sec. 8). Furthermore, it subordinates state law to federal law by stating that 'all treaties made... under the authority of the United States shall be the supreme law of the land; and the judges in every state shall be bound thereby' (US Constitution, Art. VI).

Thus, in the USA, when two individuals or corporations enter into a contract, such contract is normally governed by the contract law of either the state in which the contract was entered, or perhaps the state in which performance is to be rendered. But if the contract is for distribution of products across interstate commerce, federal antitrust laws also apply. Contracts involving patents, trademarks and copyrights, such as a licence agreement to make, use and sell throughout the USA and its territories, a patented and branded (trademarked) product with copyrighted instruction manual, would also be subject to federal laws applicable to patents, trademarks and copyrights. Since the UK does not have a written constitution or a federalist system, this principle is inapplicable. Not all countries are constitutional democracies, however, and many lack the underlying document or doctrine supporting this pre-emption concept.

Colonial and hybrid legal systems

Many other (especially developing) countries were former colonies of Britain, France, Portugal, Holland or Germany, and operate under legal structures imposed by the former colonial powers or copied from other countries (often Italy) and modified by post-independence changes. The result in many developing countries is a hybrid system, unlike that found in the USA, England, France, Germany or other industrialized countries. For example, when the People's Republic of China entered the 'post-Mao' era in the late 1970s with its modernization programme, Chinese officials determined the need to attract Western capital and technology (see MANAGEMENT IN CHINA). After considerable research and investigations around socialist, Asian and Western markets, they embarked on a programme to enact a modern legal framework and proceeded to enact laws governing foreign economic contracts, joint ventures, labour relations, taxation, technology transfer and other subjects familiar to Western and other foreign investors (Pearson 1991). Since the system lacked the underlying legal concepts and traditions necessary to fully interpret such laws however, it was necessary for foreign investors to include an inordinate amount of assumptions and details in their contracts to gain and maintain such management rights as the right to hire and fire employees and to liquidate the business (Birden 1994). Under Western systems these rights traditionally existed in the commercial law and had been taken for granted, although modern trends in western Europe have limited these rights.

2 The exchange of goods and services

What is marketed or transferred across national boundaries includes goods and services, capital, persons, technology and property rights. Intangibles such as rights to repayment of debt (debt instruments) or shares of stock (equity instruments) are frequently transferred and sometimes monetized or securitized. In recent decades, Western societies have increasingly progressed towards freer movement of goods, services, technology, capital and persons across national boundaries. Regional economic groupings including free trade areas such as the Latin American Free Trade Agreement (LAFTA), North American Free-Trade Agreement (NAFTA; see NORTH AMERICAN FREE-TRADE AGREEMENT), Association of South-East Asian Nations (ASEAN; see ASSOCIATION OF SOUTH-EAST ASIAN NATIONS) and European Free Trade Association (EFTA), and common markets such as the European Union (EU; see EUROPEAN UNION), the Caribbean Community (CARICOM), the East African Common Market and the Andean Common Market (ANCOM) have incorporated these types of policy objectives into their charters or mission statements (see ECONOMIC INTEGRATION, INTERNATIONAL). The World Trade Organization (WTO, formerly General Agreement on Tariffs and Trade or GATT; see WORLD TRADE ORGANIZATION) is an attempt to reduce tariff and non-tariff barriers to trade in goods and services among an increasingly large number of countries. Formed by treaties, these arrangements contribute to the formation of international law.

Conflict of laws

Normally all economic activities within national territory are governed by national laws. But which nation's laws apply to a transaction which crosses boundaries? If the national laws applicable to a simple export transaction of country Q differ from those of country P, which country's law applies to the export contract? And which apply to the letter of credit opened to finance the export transaction? The answer is that the parties must agree and specify in the contract which law applies to that contract and all acts or omissions arising thereunder. If a dispute arises under a contract which must be heard and determined by a disinterested party such as a court or an arbitration panel, such applicable law designated by the parties will be honoured, provided it bears any reasonable relationship to the transaction. This means it should be either the law of the domicile or principal place of business of one of the parties, the place where the contract was entered, or the place of performance of the contract.

If the parties fail to specify the applicable law, a fairly complex set of rules governing the 'conflict of laws' will be applied by the court or arbitration tribunal, taking into account roughly the criteria defined above (domiciles and place of execution or perform-ance) (Delaume 1972). Sometimes the result will be determined by weighing the relative criteria and determining to apply the law of the place of most significant contacts (picture the scales of justice with these criteria stacked on either scale). Since this outcome is not al-ways predictable, it is prudent to agree on the applicable law during negotiations and in-clude it expressly in the contract. This, of course, assumes that freedom of contract pre-vails in the country where business is being conducted.

Freedom of contract

Freedom of contract principles are taken for granted by managers and professionals trained in common-law countries. Common lawyers in the USA, UK and elsewhere have usually advised their clients that for a contract to be binding and enforceable, there must be an offer and acceptance, consideration, defi-niteness and lawful subject matter. What they normally have not explained is that many for-eign governments have, from time to time, interfered with commercial contracts. This has resulted from differences in political doc-trines involving the respective roles of the State and private enterprise. The rules of the game can differ from place to place, and these do not relate merely to differences in legal systems (for example Common, Civil, Islamic, Hindu law). Rather, and particularly in many developing and socialist countries, the host government has frequently become a third party in the negotiations. Indeed, the concept of renegotiation of contracts has at times been presumed and automatically applied in some developing and socialist countries, while unheard of in the USA, UK and traditional market economies with either common or civil law traditions.

When, where and why these nation-states intervene depends on the level of industrial development, political and economic sys-tems, traditions and often the current political winds. When governments change, contracts made with the former government may not necessarily be enforced or enforceable against successor governments. The concept of what

may be consistent with or contrary to public policy of a successor host government may depend on current priorities for attracting technology or capital, balance of payments, or even on a hotly contested political election campaign.

Foreign companies have often served as convenient scapegoats to be expropriated or nationalized *despite previous contractual guarantees*. Thus, whenever possible, con-tracts in countries with such histories must be drafted and negotiated by experienced inter-national business managers and lawyers aware of that history, and such contracts must consider exit strategies and commercial lever-age available to anticipate such occurrences (see POLITICAL RISK).

Examples of expropriation or nationalization

When Fidel Castro's Cuban Revolutionary Government nationalized the Cuban subsidi-aries of many US companies in the early 1960s, it devised a novel compensation for-mula which considered back taxes computed on a basis which was totally different from the agreements previously negotiated with the dictatorial Batista regime which it replaced (Banco Nacional de Cuba v. Sabbatino 1964). Similarly novel formulae were followed in the subsequent expropriation of copper mines in Peru and Chile, iron ore and oil properties in Venezuela, and selected manufacturing, banking and public utility investments throughout Latin America and other regions in the 1960s and 1970s (Radway 1981). Crea-tive calculations under these formulae when applied would have resulted in foreign MNCs owing considerable sums to the government which nationalized or expropriated their prop-erties. Successor governments in these devel-oping countries often approached the former owners of such nationalized properties at the point in time when that local government was in financial trouble, and proceeded to repri-vatize these firms both to raise money (to reduce foreign debt) and eliminate subsidies to inefficient enterprises. These cycles will doubtless continue.

The Islamic Fundamentalist (Khomeini) revolution in Iran in 1979, which included the holding of fifty-two Americans hostage for 444 days, resulted in a freeze on Iranian assets by the US government, and non-payment of hundreds of claims to American, European and Asian companies working in Iran. The special international tribunal established at the Hague to resolve the resulting disputes continued throughout the 1980s and into the 1990s (Aldrich 1994).

Other examples include the nationalizations which arose from communist revolutions in the USSR in 1917 and China in 1949, the Mexican nationalization of its oil properties in 1938, Peronist nationalization of banks and public utilities in Argentina in the 1950s, and Mitterand's Socialist Party election in France in 1982.

Creeping expropriation

Short of outright nationalization, the phrase 'creeping expropriation' was coined to refer to severe limitations placed on economic activities of foreign firms by host governments in certain developing countries (Weston 1975). These limitations have included restrictions on profit remittances, dividends, royalties or technical assistance fees from local investments or technology arrangements, coupled with increased local content requirements, price controls and other requirements which serve to reduce return on investment. Multinational firms have also suffered discriminatory tariffs and non-tariff barriers with the practical effects of keeping out certain producer and consumer goods from those countries, and discriminatory laws on patents and trademarks. The intellectual property restrictions had the practical effect of eliminating or drastically reducing protection of, among others, pharmaceutical substances, compounds or products (Radway 1983a).

Other restrictions have required international producers and marketers of certain consumer products (especially beverages, packaged food and cereals, cigarettes, cosmetics and toiletries) to invest huge sums of money to repackage all products to *link* their internationally recognized trademarks with newly devised local trademarks belonging to unaffiliated distributors. In some countries the MNCs were ultimately advised to *fade out* their international trademarks altogether. These colossal barriers were generally renegotiated but not until enormously expensive education and lobbying campaigns were mounted by industry associations and governments of the OECD countries.

By the late 1980s, after part of a 'lost decade' in a Latin America replete with debt crisis and low or negative GNP growth, many of these restrictive and discriminatory laws were reversed in order to again attract foreign direct investment and badly needed foreign technology (Zahler 1994). The end of the cold war and restructuring of political allegiances contributed significantly to these changes.

In spite of contracts and guarantees negotiated in India prior to enactment of the Foreign Exchange Reserve Act (1974), Johnson & Johnson (a major US pharmaceutical multinational) and other foreign investors subsequently had to submit to a host of regulations to retain majority equity positions in established companies. These restrictions included: (1) an agreement to limit production to the original product line (no expansion or modifications beyond the baby products originally introduced); (2) limitations on importing equipment even when the parent company agreed to donate the equipment to its Indian subsidiary instead of gaining credit for the equipment as a registered capital contribution; (3) limitations on compensation of expatriate executives, reducing pay to the drastically lower level of nationals, and sometimes even limits on compensation to Indians; (4) unrealistic export commitments with no regard to competitiveness on global markets; and (5) strict transfer-of-technology rules resulting in such companies withholding new technology from their Indian affiliate due to lack of adequate protection and compensation. During the 1970s many of these rules were copied in whole or in part by Malaysia, Indonesia, the Philippines, Nigeria, Brazil and other developing countries (Radway 1983b). During the 1980s the same countries began to reverse these discriminatory rules in order once again to attract capital and open their markets.

It has been suggested that Union Carbide's 1984 plant disaster in Bhopal, India, was one of many potential disasters waiting to happen. The rationale for this relates to the adoption by some governments of less-developed countries (LDCs) of confrontational and discriminatory rules against foreign companies and their contracts in the stormy late 1960s and 1970s. This argument posits that these rules deprived the MNCs of private property rights (constitutionally or otherwise guaranteed in the UK and USA) without due process of law, and simply placed them in untenable positions. IBM and Coca-Cola, for instance, withdrew from India after unsuccessful negotiations to protect their absolute control over proprietary technology, previously guaranteed by signed contracts (Encarnation and Vachini 1985). Due to such events, renegotiation of signed contracts at LDC governments' insistence became commonplace during the 1970s.

It is clear from these examples that the international playing field differs from its domestic counterpart. Contract agreements must, therefore, be prepared and negotiated in a totally different context, each with reference to local law (an example of the adage 'think global, act local'). To avoid being locked into a commitment which a firm feels obliged to honour but which may be viewed differently by the other party or its government, business factors as well as cultural or environmental factors must be considered.

Agents, representatives and employees

Commonly in the USA, if a firm has properly researched the contract with its local distributor or agent, and such agent fails to sell the agreed quota of product to justify exclusivity rights granted for the territory, the firm may terminate and replace the agent with another in that territory, or convert to non-exclusive arrangements. However, in a majority of countries around the world, the laws provide that if firms neglect their homework, they may be stuck with the non-performing agent *and* obliged to pay a huge indemnity for protecting

their own marketing interests in that territory. Laws may also interfere with the right to dismiss employees or control the labour force in many countries in Europe, especially Belgium, Holland, Germany and Sweden. Management rights often taken for granted elsewhere are limited or altogether denied in these as well as in remaining socialist countries and certain LDCs.

3 International contracts

A contract in international business is not merely a document setting forth quantity, price and delivery schedule of the products. It must take into consideration the legal system and political and currency risks in the country involved. Contracts make provisions regarding how and where disputes should be resolved out of court, by whom (arbitrators), in what language, under what rules, and in which currency any award should be denominated. Such contracts also usually clarify which substantive and procedural laws should be applied to interpret the contract, and both where and how an arbitral award will be enforced (Perillo 1994). In some cases it should provide that the arbitral award must be submitted to a specified law court to obtain a confirming judgment, which may then be enforced under international conventions or treaties. An increasing number of such treaties now address some of these important technical issues, but the parties involved must verify in advance whether the respective countries have signed and ratified such treaties.

The possibilities of denial of what the multinational firm considers its essential rights or privileges by the host sovereign must be considered, and rights to terminate the agreement under such conditions are included when appropriate. When termination of certain agreements (such as a distributorship) may be against local public policy, other provisions should be considered such as payment of fixed sums of (liquidated) damages in the event of material breach of contract, and escrow accounts to safeguard such funds.

Most importantly, however, the commercial objectives of the international manager are always kept in mind when such agreements are prepared. Although common law lawyers advise clients on their legal remedies in event of non-performance, many UK and US companies do not want to be a plaintiff in the courts of most foreign countries for a variety of historical reasons, both legal and socio-political. For example, entrepreneurs and individuals in many countries believe that UK and US companies are exploitative *per se*, attitudes which often seem to be shared by officers of many legal systems. Thus, as part of a firm's regional strategy, commercial leverage (retaining something the other party will continue to need) is usually evaluated and incorporated into foreign contract agreements, considering the local social and business culture, the company's international reputation and the drain on corporate resources arising from litigation in a foreign court.

Warranties and guarantees

The warranties or guarantees a company offers with its products should be carefully designed and limited to conditions under its control, and not those which can be changed by local governments when power shifts. In the direct foreign investment situation, the firm's presence is normally dependent on agreements with the host government on import duties, taxes, export commitments, local content, price controls, availability of hard currency, supply of utilities to the plant, and a plethora of other items (including severe indemnities for terminating local employees, even in the event of liquidation).

The international manager usually takes time to identify each of these assumptions and to anticipate alternatives if and when the host government's permission is revoked or invalidated. If the firm is prevented from including such provisions in an agreement, it will often hedge its exposure up front or shortly thereafter, and should develop contingency plans.

Evaluation of country risk

Major distinctions, then, are made in planning for foreign contract agreements. Degree of country or environmental risk (including political, currency and project risk) differ sharply in agreements, for example, in Germany or Sweden contrasted with Iran, Algeria, North Korea or perhaps Vietnam (Radway 1983b; Salbu and Brahn 1992) (see FOREIGN EXCHANGE RISK, MANAGEMENT OF; POLITICAL RISK).

Most managers make long-term investment contracts to extend as long as possible. Conventional wisdom may suggest that joint ventures, for example, should last for ninety-nine years or indefinitely. This is not always a good idea. Although not usually considered, certain types of agreements can be made for shorter terms with defined performance criteria. These can always be extended, but termination of longer agreements without incurring huge penalties may be more difficult than expected, if not impossible. Joint venture agreements may also be entered into for short durations, perhaps five or eight years. If the relationship deteriorates, honour or face can be saved on both sides by adhering to a preset termination schedule rather than cancelling a charter scheduled for ninety-nine years. These issues are interpreted more literally in some countries than others.

So-called 'boilerplate' (standard-form contract language) should almost never be used in international contracts. Such language was invariably developed for domestic contracts in a totally different legal and cultural system which both parties understood (Salbu 1993). The indiscriminate transplant of such language often has unintended and disastrous consequences. Since many international agreements are translated into local language, the vocabulary employed in the agreement should be simple and easily translatable rather than jargon or 'legalese' which may confuse domestic agreements, is impossible to translate and does not achieve desired objectives. This is due both to language and to differing legal systems.

Exporting products or services

Exporting home-country products abroad helps to create more jobs at home, generating funds to pay for imports and keeping home economies competitive (see INTERNATIONAL TRADE AND FOREIGN DIRECT INVESTMENT).

For first-time exporters, three important considerations distinguish exporting from selling in the home market: (1) financing through letters of credit; (2) export documentation and packaging; and (3) selecting and dealing with foreign agents and distributors (Stewart 1994). The latter subject is distinctly different from using manufacturer's representatives or distributors in the domestic market, and introduces critical legal dimensions to the global picture (see FOREIGN MARKET ENTRY STRATEGIES).

With new-to-market exporters, language alone has often been the sole determinant of who is selected as its agent for selling products in a foreign market. Historically, few US or British business executives could speak foreign languages, and since many US firms were large enough to aggressively seek out foreign markets after the Second World War, English became the universal language of business. Thus, if an agent spoke English, he could land the account. Without a thorough investigation of alternatives, the English-speaking local was often engaged without question: the global countryside is littered with the (Anglo-American) economic corpses of such naiveté (see CULTURE, CROSS-NATIONAL).

Next came the situation where the local agent developed the market to the point where the foreign firm decided to establish its own sales office in a country. The agent often got sacked in these cases. Such agents in Europe, Latin America, the Middle East and elsewhere complained to their governments. The result was the emergence of laws regulating relationships between foreign companies coming to sell in local markets, and their local agents. The laws relating to termination of agents in Belgium, Puerto Rico and some Middle Eastern countries are well known by exporters and international lawyers for these reasons. Belgium, like other countries in western Europe, has been traditionally paternalistic in its treatment of employees. Because these independent contractors were not employees, they fell outside the labour laws and were vulnerable. Such agents were among those who loudly complained when sacked, and laws were subsequently passed to treat them more like employees, entitling them to severance benefits: usually lost anticipated profits for up to five years.

Common law corporate lawyers without specialized knowledge inserted 'normal' provisions in these agency contracts which provided for termination 'for cause'. Although valid and appropriate in the company's home country, they were worthless when it came time to terminate abroad. The laws in many of these countries provided that such agreements could only be terminated for such behaviour as criminal activity or total refusal to perform the contract. After time passed and the companies learned more about local market and distribution channels, they often met someone better connected (perhaps actually engaged in the mainstream of their business). Convinced that sales should be higher, they could thus be persuaded that the existing agent was underperforming. A deal was then reached with the new person, the foreign entrepreneur assuring the new agent that no difficulty existed to terminate the old one. The new agent would start bringing in orders, and before long the foreign firm was paying double commissions (naturally both agents received an 'exclusive' in the territory). The existing agent refused to quit, with the support of the local legal system. (In 1995 Costa Rica revoked such a law.)

In addition to the termination problem, exporters traditionally faced several other legal problems in arrangements with local distributors or representatives. For example, many companies lost trademark rights by not checking local law before telling their agent to register the USA or UK trademark. Trademark law in the common law countries is generally based on the principle of 'first usage', meaning the first party to use the mark commercially acquires some legal rights. Registration in the USA, for example, is notice of ownership of the mark but the system still grants the user legal rights before registration. In many (perhaps most) other countries, however, the system is different. The first to register a mark owns it, whether or not they have used it (Samuels and Samuels 1993). All the rights belong to the registered owner. Thus, if the local agent registers the mark in their own name, it is theirs. Worse, when some unscrupulous local company or individual read about new products in trade publications, many registered those marks immediately in their own country, then awaited the arrival of RCA, Coca-Cola, Goodyear, DuPont or other unsuspecting multinational firms intending to sell in the local market. The lawsuit usually resulted in a disproportionately large licence fee being paid to the local party for the use of his local rights to the foreign trademark. This sport proved popular in post-communist Russia.

Anti-bribery laws

There are also what have become the infamous payments arrangements, including over- and under-billing arrangements. In one of the oldest international games going, the distributor manages to persuade the company to allow him to escalate his invoices above stated distributor prices, the difference being deposited in the distributor's personal dollar account abroad. This is a clear violation of local exchange control laws. Underbilling works on similar principles, except that the objective is to defraud local customs departments, since the distributor complains that duties are so high they impede sales of the product. In both the former and latter cases the international company is aiding and abetting the local distributor in violating local currency control laws. Since such laws do not exist in the USA or UK, inexperienced exporters are unfamiliar with them and are often easily persuaded that they are unfair and repressive tools of a corrupt local regime. Indeed the integrity of the local regime is quite irrelevant. Local laws apply to economic activities within local borders: that is precisely what sovereignty means.

Under the US Foreign Corrupt Practices Act, even though the practices described above did not previously violate USA currency or customs laws, aiding or abetting the violation of foreign laws became illegal *in the USA*, not for the local distributor or representative, but for the US firm. The main thrusts of the FCPA however were its anti-bribery provisions and the so-called 'books and records' provisions. The former made it illegal for any US company termed an 'issuer' under the Securities and Exchange Commission (SEC) statutes, or *any* citizen or resident, to make any payment, gift, contribution or anything comparable, to certain classes of people (or political parties) in foreign countries with intent to *obtain or retain* business. That simple summary has been carefully analysed and many questions exist about what constitutes a violation, but penalties are enormous and *they cannot be paid or reimbursed by the company*, the theory being that only individuals commit such crimes. Jail sentences in excess of one to five years and fines in excess of $1 million have been levied on those convicted. It is also clear that the law will not permit indirectly (through an 'agent', joint venture partner or other third party) that which it prohibits directly.

The accounting or 'books and records' provisions were directed at slush funds allegedly kept by foreign subsidiaries of US multinationals to disguise such unlawful payments but, when refined and expanded, these provisions basically reach all types of financial activities or entries in accounts and records which produce the same consequences, plus violations of such local statutes mentioned above. The USA may be the only country with such provisions on its books, and recent US administrations have tended to relax enforcement of this statute, although most US multinationals have incorporated the policy into their internal codes of conduct (Levy 1985).

Anti-boycott regulations

Anti-boycott systems tend to be in effect from time to time with respect to certain countries or groups of countries. When Arab countries implemented a massive boycott of Israel, part of their procedure was a refusal to deal with US firms exporting to or manufacturing in Israel. Lists of such companies were produced and maintained by boycott offices in major Arab countries. Questionnaires which investigated dealings with Israel were sent to US companies wishing to sell to large Arab markets. Many US executives were summoned to Washington by the Federal Government, since anti-boycott regulations issued by the

US Department of Commerce required the reporting of merely receiving such a questionnaire or other inquiry, which were often answered while ignoring or winking at federal regulations (Gantz 1995). Firms caught doing this were violating Federal Law and punished. Reduction of political tensions in such regions generally results in reduced enforcement of such policy.

Export control laws

Since 1917, the USA has enacted laws dealing with some aspects of export controls, particularly exports to countries classified as an enemy or in a group with which the USA was not on friendly terms (these laws are organized under Title 22 USC, Foreign Relations and Intercourse: Chapter 39 deals specifically with arms export control). The export control laws and regulations are complex and often confusing, but aggressive enforcement and prosecution of domestic and foreign violators resulted in well publicized convictions, fines and jail sentences in the second half of the 1980s and into the 1990s, resulting primarily from activities in Iraq, Libya and Iran. Though often overly broad in the definition of product classes, and vague enough to allow the apparently random denial of export licences to US firms, experts agree that violations of these laws (intentionally or otherwise) by foreigners operating in and through Europe saved the Russians and their allies billions of dollars in research and countless years in weapons development. Exports of nuclear-related weaponry technology by US, German and other Western firms to Iraq and former Soviet satellites, and the Toshiba Machine Co. case (Arjay Associates Inc. v. Bush 1989) concerning multiple-blade submarine propeller technology, are among the most high-visibility and best-publicized examples. Ground-to-air missile technology leakage through sieves existing in NATO countries is another vivid and recent example. Re-exporting to controlled country locations by foreign distributors or customers is equally prohibited. Although these laws were revised after the Cold War ended, permitting several dual-use items to be exported and revising the list of controlled countries, one can imagine the US government acting to permanently deny export privileges to US companies violating serious provisions of these federal statutes.

In addition to maintaining export privileges, understanding the many concepts outlined is basic to improving the home firm's ability to do business abroad. These concepts reach further than merely dealing with foreign agents and distributors. With respect to penetrating foreign markets effectively, more homework is in order. Careful investigation of home and local laws applicable to these transactions, and a thorough selection and evaluation of foreign distributors and representatives greatly improves a firm's knowledge of the rules of the game and how the score is kept. The exporter can then concentrate on price, quality and delivery, and adaptation to local markets and competition (see EXPORTING).

4 Licensing technology abroad

A normal progression after exporting has been to license the firm's technology to a manufacturer or service provider located in the foreign country once the market has been developed. Licensing is a marketing strategy which has earned large profits for small companies. At the same time it creates competitors, against which protection must be planned.

Since intellectual property (patents, trademarks, service marks, copyrights, software) are corporate assets, licensors should know whether these assets can be protected in a foreign country (Stanback 1989). Important legal dimensions to be considered include local intellectual property laws, the confidentiality (also called 'secrecy' or non-disclosure) protection available, and whether the host country has adopted laws regulating transfer of technology, very popular during the 1970s (Radway 1983a). Common laws afford strong protection for industrial (trade) secrets or 'know-how' if adequately documented, since the UK, USA and Canada are technology developers and exporters, and their laws provide rapid and inexpensive injunctive relief against industrial pirates attempting to infringe patents or trademarks or steal know-how or trade secrets.

Other countries, however, are different. As a generalization, intellectual property protection is better in industrialized, market economies, but this does not always apply to trade secrets, which are never covered under intellectual property laws but are subject to normal contract law. Thus, the relationship with a licensee must be planned and developed carefully to provide incentives for the licensor and the licensee to remain together for mutual benefit. Since trade secrets are treated differently, licensing unpatented know-how under trade secret protection is generally tied to local criminal or penal laws, and tightly linked to employment agreements with each employee or professional who may be exposed to the protected technical or commercial information.

What can be licensed and how

Important licensing considerations include analysis of what properties the firm may license, how to price the licensable assets, whether to limit the grant to the right to 'make' the product or add the rights to 'use' and 'sell' the product as well, and whether to include a right to sub-license. As with distribution agreements, decisions must also be made on exclusivity, the size of the licensee's 'territory', the field of use of the licenced products or processes, and other elements.

Before being acquired by General Electric (GE), for example, RCA was one of the few major industrial MNCs with a licensing division which was a profit centre (many firms in entertainment and in the apparel, toy and cosmetics industries have profitably licensed trademarks for some time). With picture tubes, for example, RCA made a strategic determination to license all qualified applicants on a non-exclusive basis, based on a projected growth curve for the global market. It maintained research laboratories in the USA, Europe and Japan to support this worldwide licensing programme, and a staff of licensing executives, attorneys and support personnel to negotiate and administer the highly profitable programme. Today, communications and commercial electronics companies like AT&T, GE, Alcatel, Toshiba, Olivetti, Fujitsu, Siemens, Matsushita and Philips are cross-licensing laser, optical fibre and other technologies to develop new generations of products without infringing basic or blocking patents.

Many chemical companies, especially specialty chemical producers, license technology as an afterthought to gain marginal returns on sunken capital invested for products initially produced for the domestic market, then exported. The biotechnology field is exploding, with licensing in and out of new properties such as monoclonal antibodies, due to the enormous costs of developing, testing and gaining regulatory approval. Genetically engineered products have also raised other sets of legal and ethical issues worldwide.

Character licensing is another active area. Walt Disney Enterprises exploits cartoon characters such as Donald Duck and Mickey Mouse, created initially by animators for film and subsequently applied to comic books, T-shirts, toys, games and other products. This field broadened to utilize western film heroes like Roy Rogers and others, then sports stars (Diego Maradona, Michael Jordan, Andre Agassi *et al.*), and newer animated characters such as the Lion King, and today one sees a national fast food franchise bearing Roy Rogers' name in the USA, and the faces of Madonna and Michael Jackson around the globe.

Copyright licensing traditionally involved record companies (Columbia), book and magazine publishers (McGraw-Hill), radio and television broadcasters, music publishers, composers and producers of stage and screen productions. Today copyright licensing is also mushrooming in software for personal computers by IBM, Apple, Microsoft, Lotus, Novell and a host of other new companies.

Law and regulation of licensing

Neither US nor British laws regulate the licensing process *per se* as is the case in other countries of the EU, Australia, Japan and many developing countries under technology transfer laws. Protection of patent and trademark rights under common law in the UK and USA is strong, and common law relies on precedent of prior court cases to provide certainty and guidance on the do's and don'ts. There are no legal limits on the duration of the agreement or the amount of royalties paid, which are subject to commercial negotiation between licensor and licensee, nor restrictions on remittances of royalties abroad. In addition to the US requirement to register patents, trademarks and copyrights with the Federal Patent Office, legal regulations applicable to licensing are the anti-trust/anti-monopoly laws and of course taxation laws and regulations. These guidelines cannot be relied upon when licensing abroad.

Patent, trademark infringement, piracy and other problems

A patent is granted by the government and is a limited monopoly which includes the right to prevent others from making, using or selling the invention in the sovereign territory of that government (Goldstein 1993). A patent, therefore, is territorial in scope. The requirements for granting of patents differ by country and must be checked in advance. The life of the patent also differs by country. The International (Paris) Convention for the Protection of Industrial Property was signed in 1883, but this international treaty, amended several times since, does not standardize such elements. As with all treaties, lawyers must verify both execution and ratification of the treaty by the market country.

More recently, a 1978 Patent Cooperation Treaty (PCT) in the USA and a 1977 European Patent Treaty (EPT) became effective. These essentially make it less difficult and less expensive to file corresponding applications in member countries (Murashige 1994). These treaties also help firms to buy between twelve (EPT) and thirty months (PCT) from the original filing date to the date of filing in foreign locations, thereby delaying payment of corresponding costs and fees (including translation costs) which can be substantial. One of the major controversies between industrialized and developing countries in the

past related to mandatory licensing of patents which were not being 'worked' or exploited by registered owners or patentees. These discussions were conducted under the auspices of the World Intellectual Property Organization (WIPO), a specialized agency of the United Nations.

Totally different systems exist for trademark registration globally, and the common law system is not the most common. A trademark is used by a manufacturer, merchant or licensee to identify their goods and distinguish them from those of others (Murashige 1994). In the USA, trademark differs from both patent and copyright in that the latter two derive their legal status from a statutory grant, while trademark rights arise through use of the mark on the goods or services in commerce. The licence is the agreement whereby the trademark owner permits their mark to be used by the licensee under specified conditions. However, as has been pointed out, US and UK firms have repeatedly made the mistake in other countries of authorizing the local agent or distributor to register the mark, resulting in ownership of the mark accruing to the locals. Being unaware of the legal differences, these firms have made costly assumptions without validating them.

Know-how and trade secrets

In addition to licensing patents and trademarks, it is common in the UK and the USA to license unpatented know-how or trade secrets (see TECHNOLOGY STRATEGY, INTERNATIONAL). These are considered a form of industrial property which are protected by contract rather than by statute. As defined by the American Law Institute:

A trade secret may consist of any formula, pattern, device or compilation of information which is used in one's business and which gives an opportunity to obtain an advantage over competitors who do not know or use it. It may be a formula for a chemical compound, a process of manufacturing, treating or preserving materials, a pattern for a machine or other device, or a list of customers.

(Restatement of Torts 1939: 757)

Generally, a trade secret relates to the production of goods such as a machine, or a formula for the production of an article, but it may also relate to trade or other business operations such as a schedule for determining discounts, rebates or other concessions in a price list or catalogue, a list of specialized customers, or a method of book-keeping or office management.

Know-how is commonly a selected blend of individual non-secret elements wherein the blend, rather than any individual element, is the secret. Someone who owns know-how has commonly distilled from the sea of public knowledge a unique set of parameters of process and plant which, for example, will produce X tons of Y product of Z quality at XX cost with YY personnel who can be trained in ZZ man hours to operate the plant. If that package of know-how is preserved in confidence through non-disclosure or secrecy agreements, the package (the compilation or combination of the parameters) is both confidential know-how and also a trade secret. It is, therefore, proprietary information. Many countries have not traditionally developed technology, so their laws have not been concerned about protection, especially the protection of unpatented technology. In such cases, protection must be sought through careful drafting, linking the non-disclosure and non-competition agreements (whereby the licensee agrees not to compete with the supplier for a limited term) with local criminal or penal law provisions, and also binding each employee carefully to those restrictions in their employment agreements.

Protecting computer software

Computer software falls into its own category. Although protectable by copyright, it is generally not patentable in most countries (Goodman 1984). Trade secret protection is available and commonly invoked to protect software. Many software licensors employ a combination of copyright and trade secret protection, and take great care about both copyright protection on the software itself and revealing source codes, particularly with software for micros, sold in quite a different manner to traditional mainframe or mini-computer software (Marsland 1994). Due to the microcomputer revolution, licensing or leasing of software has grown rapidly in North America, the UK and Europe, requiring more research into local laws and patterns for protecting software. Asia has been notoriously lax in this protection.

5 Foreign direct investment

When addressing foreign direct investment (FDI) in particular, the marketer must consider country or environmental risks involved, including laws, policies and regulations that may vitiate assumptions underlying the investment (see FOREIGN MARKET ENTRY STRATEGIES; INTERNATIONAL TRADE AND FOREIGN DIRECT INVESTMENT). Such basic assumptions include return on the investment, payback period, and ability to import essential materials, components, compounds or software into that market to produce products and services. These assumptions also include repatriation of capital and remittance of profits and dividends back home (Chew 1994). As has already been described, these activities are not always permitted as freely in some markets as in others. Restrictions may be contained in specific laws regulating direct foreign investment and exchange controls, or they may be scattered throughout the legal system, and especially in local decrees, regulations and administrative practices. Where countries are in transition from one political and economic system to another, it may be uncommonly difficult to identify exactly what are the rules of the game (Qingjiang 1987).

Exchange controls limit the process by which one can obtain convertible currency to remit dividends in dollars or sterling, pay interest on loans to headquarters or foreign lenders, and pay royalties to the technology licensor.

Foreign investment and technology transfer laws

To examine FDI around the world one must look beyond quantity of foreign equity holdings to carefully examine regulatory structures and intervention systems whereby foreign capital and technology is screened, evaluated and controlled before entry is approved. Japan, for instance, has gone through several major liberalizations since the Second World War, when foreign investment was initially limited to a maximum of 50 per cent and was absolutely prohibited in most sectors. The US Occupation Authorities were instrumental in the 1949 adoption by the Japanese Diet of the Foreign Exchange and Foreign Trade Control Law. This gave the government (through the Ministry of International Trade and Industry (MITI), Ministry of Finance and Bank of Japan) authority to control inflow and outflow of goods and services, while the foreign investment law similarly allowed them to control the flow of capital and technology. These agencies determined which industries were approved to take licences of foreign technology and how much they could pay in royalties. During the early 1960s after Japan acceded to the IMF, the World Bank and GATT, it began the process of liberalization of its tariff and non-tariff barriers. Although Japan could not be termed a developing country, its unique rebuilding programme and remarkable success caused many developing country and United Nations technocrats to study the 'Japanese Model' of economic development and to adopt some laws and other regulations deemed suitable or appropriate to their national development objectives.

India, by its Foreign Exchange Reserve Act of 1974, was one of the first and possibly the most restrictive country in applying prohibitions, and was later copied in part by Indonesia, Malaysia, Nigeria, and the Philippines (Radway 1983b). Some aspects of India's regulations applicable to industry have also been copied by several other LDCs. India's rules established three tiers of maximum foreign equity at 60 per cent, 40 per cent and 0 per cent, depending on certain criteria. Indian

nationals were to hold certain key positions, and restrictions were placed on imports, royalties for foreign technology and the lines of business in which foreign MNCs could engage, which generally made it difficult for MNCs to operate as they would elsewhere. (IBM – see INTERNATIONAL BUSINESS MACHINES CORPORATION – and Coca-Cola withdrew in the 1970s after failure to negotiate acceptable compromises with Indian governments.) Many foreign joint ventures in India involve unusual percentage equity splits, such as Union Carbide Corporation's (UCC) joint venture which received publicity in the wake of the tragedy at its chemical facility at Bhopal. UCC owned 50.1 per cent, with 49.9 per cent owned by Indians. However, even if equity appeared to favour the foreigner, due to stringent laws of the type mentioned above, effective control of the joint venture was generally in local hands, allowing Indian technicians and managers to reject any operational proposals from UCC. The shadow of government control looms large over these joint ventures in real life. India, like many other countries, has liberalized these restrictions in recent years to attract capital and technology required for growth.

Since its effective date in 1973, the Mexican Foreign Investment Law has generally limited foreign investors to 49 per cent equity in newly established Mexican companies, as well as pre-existing Mexican companies through share acquisition (Radway 1983a). In three specific industries (automotive parts, secondary petrochemical and mining) that percentage was lower. In industries deemed to be strategic or essential to the national security or patrimony of the country, foreign participation was totally prohibited. However, depending on prevailing economic conditions, exceptions were often made when the foreign proposal contained the right combination of benefits to the developing country. After Mexico joined GATT in 1987 it liberalized many of these policies, permitting 100 per cent FDI in certain sectors. The Mexican government further liberalized foreign investment and related policies prior to their entry into NAFTA. Economic reforms of many countries have radically changed such restrictions. They may change again in the future.

In the Agreement of Cartagena signed in 1969 in Colombia by five South American countries (Bolivia, Chile, Colombia, Ecuador and Peru; Venezuela joined in 1973 and Chile withdrew), a joint commission was established to coordinate policy decisions relating to economic activity among the member countries and with outside sources of capital and technology. Some broad principles were extracted from the European Common Market (Treaty of Rome) as these five countries established the Andean Pact and attempted to become a customs union. Many administrative decisions were issued including Decision 24 in 1971 which regulated foreign investment, technology transfer and related subjects. Decision 24 limited new foreign investment to 49 per cent in those sectors where it was permitted at all, and its most striking provision declared that existing foreign investment must be divested (faded out) over a fifteen year period for the three more advanced countries (Colombia, Chile and Peru) and twenty years for Bolivia and Ecuador (Radway 1982). Decision 24 classified investors into three categories: foreign (80 per cent or more foreign owned), mixed (between 79 per cent and 50 per cent foreign owned) and national (49 per cent or less foreign owned) and established a system of economic consequences for participation in the subregional market. In the late 1980s and early 1990s many of these restrictions were dropped to encourage investment and legal reform.

South Korean policy was patterned after earlier rules in Japan, and its Foreign Capital Inducement Law and related rules limited foreign investors generally to 50 per cent, resulting in hundreds of foreign joint ventures with Korean partners. South Korea, like many other examples listed, has liberalized somewhat. Former socialist countries of eastern Europe, plus North Korea, the People's Republic of China, Vietnam, Cuba and others with similar economic and political systems formerly prohibited any foreign equity ownership, consistent with socialist political doctrines (Radway 1983b). Major economic reforms in the 1980s and 1990s opened up privatization and possibilities of different levels of equity ownership for foreign investors, both in China with its market socialism and in eastern European countries in transition. Attempts to balance market principles with traditional political concepts sometimes resulted in occasionally unusual and unworkable arrangements in transition countries.

Tension between host governments and international, multinational or global corporations are unlikely ever to disappear, and it is important that marketers should investigate national contexts carefully before approving FDI projects.

International guidelines on FDI

During the confrontational period (roughly 1974–85), developing countries were mobilized as a group using the United Nations as a forum. More specifically the United Nations Conference on Trade and Development (UNCTAD), which first met during the 1960s (the 'First Development Decade'), became a permanent specialized agency of the UN, and the most vocal forum in which developing countries manifested demands to limit activities of international companies. Studies of foreign investment in developing countries were conducted during the 1960s using UN grants, from which arose the seeds of the dependency theory, especially in Latin America. By the early 1970s, many Latin American countries had enacted strict laws controlling foreign investment and technology transfer (Radway 1981). Four different groups of countries had emerged in the early UNCTAD meetings, casually referred to as Groups A, B, C and D. Groups A and C were combined and became the 'Group of 77' (G-77) or the developing countries. Group B was essentially the OECD countries, and Group D the Socialist Bloc. G-77 initiated negotiations on a code of conduct for transnational enterprises, which was later shifted from UNCTAD to the commission on transnational enterprises (TNE). They also initiated codes of conduct on technology transfer and restrictive business practices, both of which remained in UNCTAD. The Group B countries resisted many of these restrictions, and the Group D countries, following a political rather than a technical agenda, manipulated both Group B and G-77. In a changing world these distinctions have now faded.

The International Chamber of Commerce (ICC) initiated an effort to preempt the TNE Code, which was eventually adopted as four separate sets of voluntary guidelines by the OECD. One of these was a set of guidelines for multinational corporations to observe in relation to FDI in developing countries, adopted in 1976. The UN Commission on Transnationals conducted meetings and negotiations for one and a half decades, and appeared to abandon the effort in the early 1990s as agreement on all points was impossible, and many had lost interest.

In 1992 the World Bank's Development Committee, in conjunction with the International Finance Corporation (IFC) and the Multilateral Investment Guarantee Agency (MIGA), produced a set of 'Guidelines on the Treatment of Foreign Direct Investment', which were directed at both host and home governments. Significantly, these guidelines included recommendations that FDI should be given essentially *national treatment*, and that any expropriation or nationalization should be followed by *prompt, adequate and effective compensation*, the position industrialized countries had traditionally maintained.

Conflict resolution, settlement and litigation

The USA is the most litigious nation on earth, and US business executives developed management styles, management systems and strategies based partly on rights and remedies available under US law and practice. Conflicts inevitably arise in business anywhere, and more so when different cultures come together to buy, sell, compete and cooperate in global markets. In the USA, UK and Canada most of these disputes are settled either by negotiations among the parties or by their lawyers in court.

Litigation in foreign courts, however, becomes vastly more complex due not only to differences in language, legal systems, currencies, and traditional customs and patterns, but also due to differences in procedures involved in the messy process of producing evidence to prove claims, and learning which evidence may be admissible in which countries under which conditions (Salbu 1993; Smit 1994). In addition, judgments earned in foreign courts may not always be enforceable at home due to a different, complex set of rules.

Alternatives to litigation in courts, in order to provide a faster and less expensive means to resolve commercial (trade) and investment disputes, sprout from a centuries old tradition. Chambers of trade and commerce first began to hear and resolve such disputes when trade first occurred between different tribes or nations. One of the basic sources of international law is called the 'Law Merchant', referred to in many legal texts and histories, much of which was built centuries ago through disputes arising from trade and shipping, and mostly resolved in places like London, Paris, Rotterdam and the Jedda (Saudi Arabia) chambers of commerce.

Settlement of modern disputes in international business takes various forms and is realized in many locations. The most widely discussed form of extra-judicial settlement of disputes is arbitration. But there are other means, the most common of which include fact-finding, conciliation, mediation and, of course, negotiations between the parties. Arbitration has traditionally been promoted mostly through the best known international business organization, the International Chamber of Commerce (ICC), situated in Paris. Arbitration became so common that courts of arbitration have long existed in London, Zurich, Vienna and elsewhere. The London court of arbitration has periodically updated its laws and procedures and constantly hears such conflicts.

In the period following the Second World War, as the USA became more involved in international commerce, the American Arbitration Association (AAA) became recognized throughout North America as an efficient institution with its own rules and facilities for this purpose. The AAA entered into agreements with the ICC and other international organizations to promote the use of alternative dispute resolution methods, and serves as the agent to administer ICC arbitrations in America, as well as those of the Inter-American Commercial Arbitration Commission (IACAC) and others.

Trade or commercial disputes are quite different from investment disputes involving FDI, and by treaty in 1965 the World Bank established its International Centre for Settlement of Investment Disputes (ICSID) to resolve disputes between World Bank members which ratified the ICSID treaty (Hirsch 1993). ICSID activity was minimal in its early years, but has increased slowly. Since the 1992 World Bank guidelines called for ICSID arbitration, its use has been expected to increase (Morrison 1991).

The ICC was the first administering agency, remains the best known, and recently modernized some of its older rules. It has gained a reputation for being slower (biggest backlog) and more expensive and cumbersome than some alternatives. And the alternatives have proliferated in recent years. The Swedish arbitration institute of the Stockholm chamber of commerce became a neutral location and agency to administer disputes between Western and socialist countries, and gained credibility as a result of even-handed administration. Others have emerged in recent years in many regions of the world.

The United Nations Conference on International Trade Law (UNCITRAL) has helped significantly. UNCITRAL met during several years and produced rules for international commercial arbitration which have become more or less standard, and many of the organizations adopted essentially UNCITRAL rules, modified as appropriate (Franchini 1994). Many developing countries, for example, have long held prejudices against ICC, AAA and other developed country organizations which they assumed were biased in favour of multinational companies. They insisted on settlement in national courts, which was unacceptable to international firms and banks. This was especially true in Latin America under the Calvo Doctrine, effective since 1890, which required disputes arising with foreign investors to be resolved in national courts under national laws. (Carlos Calvo, a nineteenth century Argentine jurist, believed that foreigners doing business in a country are entitled only to nondiscriminatory treatment. Additionally, by doing business in a country, a foreigner gives implied consent to be treated equally with nationals under national law and in national courts. This doctrine was adopted across Latin America.) The UNCITRAL rules and the proliferation of regional centres around the world have changed these attitudes somewhat and increased the use of arbitration.

Critical elements of arbitration

Obviously arbitration can be a minefield for the unwary. Many firms and lawyers, inexperienced in international arbitration practice, have relied on a 'standard boilerplate' arbitration clause in contracts, which called for ICC arbitration in Paris (Salbu and Brahn 1992). While Paris has its attractions, the parties were not always prepared for all the relevant issues. These include, among other important factors: selection of arbitrators, power of the arbitrators, situs of the arbitration, substantive law to be applied, procedural and arbitration law to be applied (which can differ), administering institution or agency, length of time to render decisions, currency in which award must be issued, *language of the proceedings and evidence*, and enforcement of the arbitral award. Regarding enforcement, two international treaties are extremely important: the New York Convention on Enforcement of Foreign Arbitral Awards (1958), and the International (Panama) Convention on International Commercial Arbitration (1976). (The former provided a clearly defined procedure for enforcement of arbitral awards rendered in foreign jurisdictions; the latter has been signed by most Latin American countries, breaking down a traditional resistance to arbitration.) As with all matters involving treaties, execution and ratification by the country in question must be verified before drafting the clause.

International law and treaties

National law has always been the principal law applicable to international transactions. However, the concept of international law does exist and is growing in importance. Traditional sources of international law include custom and usage of the trade, and treaty law. There are various texts on 'the law of nations' which discuss origins and evolution of international law, originally applied only to relations between nations (Brierly 1963). The leading professional society in the USA in this field is the American Society of International Law (ASIL), comprised of scholars from around the world, judges and leading international law practitioners, including many from the UK. The ASIL publishes the quarterly *American Journal of International Law* (AJIL), *International Legal Materials* (ILM), and various special publications. ILM is an authoritative collection of international, bilateral and multilateral treaties, containing cases decided in national courts, arbitral tribunals and the International Court of Justice (ICJ), and other documents contributing heavily to the increasing body of 'international law', including international business law.

The Charter of the United Nations, which established the International Court of Justice at the Hague, also established the International Law Commission expressly to pursue the codification and development of international law. Today there exists a plethora of high quality publications in the UK, Canada, Europe and elsewhere covering virtually all aspects of commonwealth law, community law, international law, comparative law, and other regional and national law topics (some are included in Further reading in this entry).

6 Treaties and conventions

International marketers were formerly referred to bilateral treaties between their home State and the country in which they intended to do business in order to identify basic protections extended to foreigners. These treaties of friendship, commerce and navigation (FCN treaties) mostly extended basic rights of engagement in commerce to foreigners, including rights to establish a business without discrimination. While the UK and USA entered into FCN treaties with several dozen of the more important trading nations, these FCN treaties have proven unsatisfactory in relation to more complex issues arising under international business, such as 'national treatment', dispute settlement, expropriation (including compensation) and non-tariff barriers to FDI.

Double taxation and bilateral investment treaties

National systems of taxation are complex and differ sharply, often resulting in effective double taxation for international trade and investment transactions. The UK, USA, Holland and other nations have entered into treaties for the avoidance of double taxation with an increasing number of important trading countries. Such treaties deal with levels of withholding and other important economic issues affecting foreign companies and the taxation of their income, property and activities.

Bilateral investment treaties (BITs) are the most recent set of treaties affecting international companies. They aim at levelling the playing field for FDI (for example, by providing for national treatment and prompt, adequate and effective compensation in the event of expropriation), thereby addressing issues which the more general FCN treaties could not. The USA and UK are engaged in active programmes to negotiate BITs.

UNCITRAL conventions

UNCITRAL has actively convened legal scholars from representative countries to produce conventions or treaties on different aspects of commerce. One of its recent successes is the UN Convention on Contracts for the International Sales of Goods (CISG), signed in 1980 and effective in most of the members of WTO/GATT, including Canada, the UK and the USA. The CISG attempts to do what the Uniform Commercial Code did in the USA, essentially to standardize rules applicable to sale of goods in international trade. The CISG also provides that, without

259

specific reservations or express language to the contrary, any contract among private parties from member States will be subject to the UNCITRAL rules for dispute settlement.

The fundamental principle with respect to treaties, however, is that to be applied they must be signed and ratified by the countries involved. This is especially important with multilateral treaties such as the New York Convention on Enforcement of Foreign Arbitral Awards and the ICSID Convention. By October 1993, the International Electronics Association had recommended that its members utilize electronic data interchange (EDI) for structured format communications relating to international commerce. UN/EDIFACT is the UN's set of rules for EDI in administration, commerce and transport. They comprise a set of internationally agreed standards, directories and guidelines for the electronic interchange of structured data related to trade in goods and services, between independent computerized information systems.

Regional organizations

The Treaty of Rome establishing the EEC (known as the EU since the Maastricht Treaty of 1991) contains hundreds of articles pertinent to the legal dimensions of international business. Articles 30–6, for instance, establish the general policy referred to as 'free movement of goods, people, capital and technology' among the member States. Articles 85–6 contain the competition rules, as amended by various directives of the Commission. These and other regulations and directives constitute Community Law (still referred to by that name since Maastricht), somewhat analogous to Federal Law in the USA, which preempts national laws in most cases, providing at least minimum standards. Marketers must be aware, however, that national laws of some member States (for example, Germany) may be more restrictive in the area of competition or anti-trust law, and always should be consulted. Community law is intended to harmonize national laws to promote the purposes defined in Articles 30–6, and bring to minimum standards laws of

some member States which were previously more lax. This does not preclude more restrictive positions in national laws.

The Single European Act, effective in 1987, amended the Treaty of Rome and provided strong impetus to completion of a Single Market by 31 December 1992. While technically the target was not completely met, some 90 per cent of the new recommendations were implemented into national laws by most member States by that date, resulting in effective harmonization in many areas. Much work remained to be done after that date, but the process moved forward significantly with respect to laws and standards. The Maastricht Treaty further amended the original treaty, and provided further impetus for the accession of EFTA and eastern European countries upon meeting specified requirements. Austria, Finland and Sweden joined the EU after national referenda, and Norway declined.

Other regional organizations equally deserve comment, although none has achieved the same level of legal cooperation and harmony as the EU. NAFTA and Mercosur are the most recent regional developments in the western hemisphere, and the possible merger of these two with other Latin American nations to form the Free Trade Area of the Americas (FTAA) was envisioned at the December 1994 Summit of the American Presidents in Miami.

Anti-bribery treaty signed

For more than 20 years the USA waged a solitary war on corruption in international business transactions through its Foreign Corrupt Practices Act (FCPA), effective in 1976. On 17 December 1997, 29 members of the Organisation for Economic Cooperation and Development (OECD), including the USA and five non-memeber observers (Argentina, Brazil, Bulgaria, Chile and the Slovak Republic) signed the Convention on Combating Bribery of Foreign Public Officials in International Business Transactions (Low and Burton 1998). This means the home countries of the majority of large international competitors (i.e. the UK, USA, Germany, France and Japan). The principal provision prohibits bribery of foreign public officials to secure improper business advantages, including officials of international organizations like the World Bank and its affiliates and the International Monetary Fund (IMF). Furthermore, prior to this important international treaty, 21 of the 34 members of the Organisation of American States (OAS) on 29 March 1996 signed the Inter-American Convention Against Corruption (Low *et al.* 1998), which contained similar objectives, and the USA and Canada signed the convention later that year. That Convention is now in effect following the requisite number of ratifications having been deposited.

7 Conclusion

To the uninitiated, legal dimensions of international business may appear to be an impenetrable maze of irreconcilable treaties, decrees, laws, regulations, tariffs, policies, ordinances, administrative actions, cases and other unfamiliar restrictions. In practice, this is clearly not the case. Multinational companies such as Shell, BP, ICI, Unilever, IBM, Nestlé, Exxon, General Motors, and dozens of other UK and North American firms have navigated these choppy waters for decades. Multinationals from Sweden have done so for a century.

The process of understanding and rationalizing the legal dimensions is much like exporting successfully and establishing global operations. Like market research, preliminary legal research is essential and must include investigation for competent local counsel. Thinking global and acting local applies to the legal function as much as to other areas.

Looking to the future, globalization and increased cooperation across borders will undoubtedly facilitate convergence of legal systems, policies and standards affecting economic activities. The great civil and common law traditions have long since begun this process, and UNCITRAL negotiations for international commercial treaties have resulted in compromises and harmonization which is bound to find its way back to national laws. At the same time, restrictions on local advertising (for example tobacco and alcohol advertising, as well as advertising directed at children) will depend more on local cultural standards and patterns of morals, and may remain diffuse, hindering attempts at global branding.

In addition, some form of international law of competition (anti-trust or anti-monopoly) may be necessary to regulate strategic alliances among behemoths from different legal systems who are clever enough and strategic enough to design their arrangements around national and regional anti-monopoly policies.

Finally, alternative forms of dispute resolution will continue to grow and achieve greater acceptance, as regional centres establish traditions of fairness to all parties, and binational, trinational and regional panels like those established in NAFTA will be called upon with greater frequency to resolve trade, investment, environmental and labour disputes.

ROBERT J. RADWAY
PACE UNIVERSITY

Note
The author expresses his appreciation to Angelo N. Chaclas for research assistance.

List of cases cited

Arjay Assocs, Inc. v. Bush, 8 Fed. Cir. (T) 16, 891 F.2d 894, 1989 U.S. App. LEXIS 18481 (1989).

Banco Nacional de Cuba v. Sabbatino, 376 U.S. 398, 11 L. Ed. 2d 804, 84 S. Ct. 923 (1964).

Further reading

(References cited in the text marked *)

* Aldrich, G. (1994) 'What constitutes a compensable taking of property? The decisions of the Iran–United States claims tribunal', *American Journal of International Law* 88 (4): 585–610. (This carefully crafted article by a judge of the Iranian claims tribunal analyses the decisions of the tribunal and the distinctions of the different types of 'taking' of property. Includes a reference to Weston's classic article.)
* Birden, P. (1994) 'Technology transfers to China: an outline of Chinese law', *Loyola Los Angeles International and Comparative Law Journal* 16

(2): 413–53. (Reviews the Foreign Economic Contract Law and other laws relating to various methods of transferring technology to China.)

* Brierly, J.L. (1963) *The Law of Nations*, 6th edn, ed. Sir Humphrey Waldock, London: Oxford University Press. (Classic treatment of the nature and sources of public international law.)

* Chew, P. (1994) 'Political risk and U.S. investments in China: chimera of protection and predictability?', *Virginia Journal of International Law* 34: 615–24. (Describes how restrictive repatriation policies can be as operationally devastating to an investor as outright expropriation.)

* Delaume, G. (1972) 'Choice of law and forum clauses in Eurobonds', *Columbia Journal of Transnational Law* 11 (1): 240–66. (Uses Eurobonds as a practical application to discuss the complex topics of conflicts (choice) of law and choice of forum.)

* Encarnation, D. and Vachini, S. (1985) 'Foreign ownership: when hosts change the rules', *Harvard Business Review* 63 (5): 152–8. (Explores the range of responses by MNCs when host governments change the rules of FDI.)

* Franchini, J. (1994) 'International arbitration under the UNCITRAL rules: a contractual provision for improvement, *Fordham Law Review* 62 (7): 2223–44. (Discusses the creation of UNCITRAL arbitration rules and the weaknesses of those rules emerging from Iran claims tribunal proceedings.)

* Gantz, D. (1995) 'A post-Uruguay round introduction to international trade law in the United States', *Arizona Journal of International and Comparative Law* 12: 7–16. (Comments on the Israel/Arab boycott conflict as affecting USA corporations.)

* Goldstein, P. (1993) *Copyright, Patent, Trademark and Related State Doctrines*, 3rd edn, Westbury, NY: Foundation Press. (Classic law school case book on federal intellectual property laws and related doctrines in the states of the USA.)

* Goodman, J. (1984) 'The policy implications of granting patent protection to computer software: an economic analysis', *Vanderbilt Law Review* 37 (1): 147–81. (Looks at some of the problems associated with patenting and protecting software.)

* Hirsch, M. (1993) *The Arbitration Mechanism of the International Centre for the Settlement of Investment Disputes*, Dordrecht: Martinus Nijhoff. (Comprehensive history of policy behind the ICSID, its regulations, cases and general doctrines of arbitration.)

* Levy, R. (1985) 'The anti-bribery provisions of the foreign corrupt practices act of 1977: are they really as valuable as we think they are?', *Delaware Journal of Corporate Law* 10 (1): 71–95. (Examines inconsistencies in the FCPA and the impracticality of its enforcement.)

* Low, L.A. And Burton, M.A. (1988) 'Corruption is target of multilateral efforts', *National Law Journal*, Washington, DC 4 May.

* Low, L.A., Bjorklund, A.K. And Atkinson K.C. (1988) 'The Inter-American convention against corruption', 38 *Vancouver Journal of International Law*, 243–92.

* Marsland, V. (1994) 'Copyright protection and reverse engineering of software – an EC/UK perspective', *University of Dayton Law Review* 19 (3): 1021–62. (Addresses aspects of EC and UK law relating to copyright protection and reverse-engineering of software, and discusses important policy issues.)

* Morrison, F.L. (1991) 'The future of international adjudication', *Minnesota Law Review* 75 (3): 827–47. (Analysis of the interpretation and construction of litigation practice in courts in different jurisdictions.)

* Murashige, K.H. (1994) 'Symposium on intellectual property: article – harmonization of patent laws', *Houston Journal of International Law* 16 (3): 591–614. (Discusses various international treaties directed towards reconciling differences among national patent laws and procedures.)

* Pearson, M.M. (1991) 'The erosion of controls over foreign capital in China, 1979–1988: having their cake and eating it too?', *Modern China* 17 (1): 112–50. (Examines two problems emerging in China's dual-edged strategy towards FDI from 1979–88: poor implementation and the need to liberalize formal controls.)

* Perillo, J.M. (1994) 'UNIDROIT principles of international commercial contracts: the black letter text and a review', *Fordham Law Review* 63 (2): 281–344. (Discusses UNIDROIT principles of international contracts and the CISG on which it was partly based, and how legal scholars have brought differing legal systems closer together on many legal issues.)

* Qingjiang, G. (1987) 'Restrictive business practices bar technology flow to developing countries', *Columbia Business and Law Review* 1987 (1): 117–38. (Reviews antitrust and patent policies and effects on developing countries and argues how negotiations for international codes of conduct for technology transfer should maximize global growth.)

* Radway, R.J. (1981) 'The next decade in Latin America: anticipating the future from the past', *Case Western Reserve Journal of International Law* 13 (1): 3–36. (Comprehensive review of development policies in Latin America emerging from UN-sponsored studies and 'dependency theory' which predicts difficulty in shifting from equity to debt-financing of development.)
* Radway, R.J. (1982) 'Venezuela revisited: foreign investment, technology, and related issues', *Vanderbilt Journal of Transnational Law* 15 (1): 1–45. (Second article on fast-changing Venezuelan laws on FDI, TOT and others affecting MNCs.)
* Radway, R.J. (1983a) 'Antitrust, technology transfers and joint ventures in Latin American developments', *Lawyer of the Americas, University of Miami Journal of International Law* 15 (1): 47–70. (Evaluates the regulatory and control structure in Latin America affecting capital and technology flows from an antitrust perspective, including joint ventures.)
* Radway, R.J. (1983b) 'Overview of foreign joint ventures', *The Business Lawyer* (American Bar Association) 38 (3): 1033–1106. (Comprehensive review of laws regulating joint ventures (including FDI) around the developing world.)
* Salbu, S.R. (1993) 'Parental coordination and conflict in international joint ventures: the use of contract to address legal, linguistic and cultural concerns', *Case Western Reserve Law Review* 43 (4): 1221–67. (Addresses problems peculiar to international joint ventures including dispute resolution, linguistics and cultural factors.)
* Salbu, S.R. and Brahn, R.A. (1992) 'Strategic considerations in designing joint venture contracts', *Columbia Business and Law Review* 1992 (2): 253–307. (An examination of strategic contracting issues associated with using the JV form.)
* Samuels, J.M. and Samuels, L.B. (1993) 'The changing landscape of international trademark law', *George Washington Journal of International Law and Economics* 27 (2&3): 433–55. (Explains the trademark provisions in the GATT and Nafta agreements, the Madrid Protocol and the draft WIPO treaty.)
* Smit, H. (1994) 'Recent developments in international litigation', *South Texas Law Review* 35 (2): 215–42. (Evaluation of a complex body of laws and protocol rules affecting litigation in foreign jurisdictions.)
* Stanback, G. (1989) 'International intellectual property protection: an integrated solution to the inadequate protection problem', *Virginia Journal of International Law* 29 (2): 517–60. (Compares developing and developed country views on protection of intellectual property (control versus trade) and proposes his new view.)
* Stewart, T.P. (ed.) (1994) *Export Practice: Customs and International Trade Law*, New York: Practising Law Institute. (Comprehensive and practical guide for the practitioner to the private and public laws applicable to this complex field.)
* Weston, B.H. (1975) 'Constructive takings under international law: a modern foray into the problem of "creeping expropriation"', *Virginia Journal of International Law* 16 (4): 103–75. (Classic review of subtle and non-obvious methods by which host governments deprive foreign investors of property rights without nationalizing or expropriating entire investment.)
* Zahler, R. (1994) 'The background, rationale and success of the Chilean economic policy', *Loyola Los Angeles International and Comparative Law Journal* 16 (2): 275–89. (Describes the ills of the 1980s for Chile and Latin America generally and the subsequent economic reforms.)

See also: ACCOUNTING, INTERNATIONAL; ASSOCIATION OF SOUTH-EAST ASIAN NATIONS; CULTURE, CROSS-NATIONAL; ECONOMIC INTEGRATION, INTERNATIONAL; EUROPEAN UNION; EXPORTING; FOREIGN EXCHANGE RISK, MANAGEMENT OF; FOREIGN MARKET ENTRY STRATEGIES; GLOBALIZATION; INTERNATIONAL BUSINESS MACHINES CORPORATION; INTERNATIONAL BUSINESS NEGOTIATIONS; INTERNATIONAL TRADE AND FOREIGN DIRECT INVESTMENT; MANAGEMENT IN CHINA; MULTINATIONAL CORPORATIONS; NORTH AMERICAN FREE-TRADE AGREEMENT; POLITICAL RISK; TECHNOLOGY STRATEGY, INTERNATIONAL; WORLD TRADE ORGANIZATION

Related topics in the IEBM: BUSINESS ETHICS; COMPETITIVE STRATEGIES, DEVELOPMENT OF; COUNTRY RISK ANALYSIS; ECONOMICS OF DEVELOPING COUNTRIES; ENVIRONMENTAL MANAGEMENT; GENERAL AGREEMENT ON TARIFFS AND TRADE; INTELLECTUAL PROPERTY; LAW, COMMERCIAL; MANAGEMENT IN PACIFIC ASIA

International business ethics

Overview

International business ethics encompasses organizational and individual obligations pertaining to actions affecting others in a global context. Much of the focus is on global corporations and the responsibilities they face when they do business in countries that have customs and norms at a variance with those in the firm's home country. International business ethics, by its very nature, invokes fundamental and weighty philosophical issues. These include such core questions as the degree of respect that should be given to local traditions and customs when doing business in a host country. Or do universal human values exist, and, if they do, how can they be accurately identified? There has been recent recognition of the importance of international business ethics, particularly in the context of ubiquitous, seemingly insoluble issues such as bribery and the piracy of intellectual property.

In seeking answers to the thorny questions of international ethics, some advocate a one-size-fits-all universalistic approach to ethical standards. Others support various forms of relativism emphasizing respect for and compliance with local norms and customs. The most common approach to international business ethics, however, is to seek some workable middle ground between universalism and relativism. A wealth of approaches are being developed and debated. They range from Milton Friedmanesque approaches that would allow businesses to act to maximize profits subject only to the constraints of a viable international law, to the specification of lengthy lists of positive ethical obligations for global corporations. These academic debates are shadowed in public policy forums where the focus is on whether trade organizations and regional government authorities should incorporate considerations of ethical standards into their operations. Recently several global non-governmental organizations have been created to deal with specific issues such as bribery or to provide general benchmarks for international business ethics.

1 Introduction

A French firm operates in Saudi Arabia and is told that it may not employ women, even French nationals working for the firm, as drivers. A Nigerian firm doing business in Italy is told that most foreign firms in Italy report only about 25 per cent of their earnings and that certain personal payments are to be made directly to the Italian tax assessor. A US firm builds a plant in Korea and finds that in order to compete with local firms it must modify its safety standards; Korean workers at the plant refuse to wear hard hats or to comply with certain of the firm's other employee safety practices. A Canadian firm wishing to do business in China is told that it must expect to pay bribes. An Italian clothing firm contracting out the manufacture of its merchandise realizes that it does not know the conditions in the plants used by its supplier. A Japanese firm enters into a contract to dispose of highly toxic chemicals in Mozambique. It provides the relevant Mozambique officials with extensive scientific reports detailing the dangers associated with the products.

	Approach	
Level	*Descriptive*	*Normative*
Global		
National/societal		
Organizational		
Individual		

Figure 1 The context of business ethics

Each example portrays a realistic decision faced daily by managers of global firms. Beyond such specific decisions lie broader questions such as whether global firms have any sort of practice obligations. Do, for example, global corporations have an obligation to generate employment within the developing world? Or do firms have an obligation willingly to pay taxes to the governments of developing countries, even when they could escape the payments through transfer arrangements easily within their power? Do firms have an obligation to pay above market wages in countries where the market wage falls below what would be considered a minimum standard in the firm's home country?

At the organization level lies the important task of finding the best way to provide ethical guidance for managers. Are codes of ethics essential, or just a phenomenon relevant primarily to North America? If firms do decide to use a code of ethics, is it better to have a single unified code that applies to all subsidiaries and all transactions wherever they occur; or, instead, should firms design specialized, targeted codes for their foreign subsidiaries that take into consideration the local customs and cultures? Similarly, should the ethics function be centralized at headquarters or should it be regionalized through the allocation of ethics practice officers to each subsidiary?

These issues define the broad scope of international issues and pose difficult questions for business ethics theorists. Before describing proffered solutions, it is first necessary to step back and consider these issues in a broader context.

2 Origins/context

Figure 1 demonstrates the context of business ethics.

Approaches to business ethics may be divided into two major categories. The descriptive approach merely seeks to identify and describe behaviour as it exists. Descriptive ethics involves surveys of standard practices or attitudes about correct behaviour and so on. Normative ethics, in contrast, is concerned with determining what constitutes correct or right behaviour. The tools of normative ethics are logic and analysis. The well-known ethical theories of utilitarianism and Kantianism are examples of normative ethics.

Business ethics begins with individuals. Individual managers and professionals make decisions that have an impact on the welfare and interests of others. Those making decisions are influenced by the manner in which they reason about ethical obligations, their level of psychological moral development, the organizational and societal environment in which they act, and their own personality, values and experiences. There is also evidence that the nature of the decision itself is an important influence.

Economic enterprise, by its very nature, involves group activity. People naturally form organizations of varying sizes to carry out tasks that would be impossible for one or a few to accomplish. All market systems produce some large economic organizations, which may be comprised of hundreds of thousands of people all directed toward common objectives. The nature of those organizations will affect the ethical attitudes and behaviours of their members. A social group possesses a unique moral status – it is far more than a mere aggregation of the moral beings who make up the organization.

All economic systems with significant open markets are dependent on participants respecting basic conventions of proper marketplace behaviour. Honesty, acting in good faith and trustworthiness are necessary to support the efficient exchange of goods and services. Without sufficient levels of trust and promise-keeping, economic transactions become costly and cumbersome, even impossible. Because of these and similar consequences, ethical behaviour is essential to the operation of a dynamic economy.

The same dynamics hold true at the global level. In the arena of international trade it is essential that individuals honour promises and act with integrity. Realistically, at the global level the pressures weighing against ethical behaviour are often quite severe. There is often no sovereign authority equivalent to the court systems of developed countries to provide institutional support for ethical behaviour. Further, the clash of cultures may make it difficult even to know what is the right thing to do. Compelling reasons may seem to justify an act that would be considered wrong if committed at home. The next section focuses on the normative ethical approaches available to help identify correct behaviour in a global context.

3 Analysis

'When in Rome do as the Romans do.' This well-known aphorism captures an idea that some believe is the only viable strategy for international business dealings. When faced with strong local customs, the astute manager is advised to go along with them – pay the bribe, accede to the local standards on plant safety, follow a local practice of gender discrimination. A variety of pragmatic and ethical arguments can be advanced in support of relativism. Relativism is seen as respecting diversity and the moral autonomy of other humans. The relativist will argue: 'Who am I to judge what is correct behaviour for another?' or 'One should respect the values of other cultures; it is ethical imperialism and

therefore wrong for one society to try to impose its values on other societies.' The pragmatist adds that one has no choice but to go along with it when one's competitors are engaging in a practice, or when the demand for what might be considered unethical behaviour in other venues is backed up by the coercive power of a corrupt local government.

But there are very powerful arguments against relativism. It is counter-intuitive to most people. There are some things, such as killing for economic gain or cannibalism, that are considered wrong by almost everyone. James Q. Wilson (1993) attributes this to an innate moral sense possessed by almost all humans. It helps explain, among other things, why lie detectors work on most people. Perhaps influenced by an innate moral conscience, many people appear to be unwilling to accept relativism as a generally applicable principle. Instead, they draw a line. It is hard to imagine a firm accepting a requirement that it literally sacrifice the life of one of its managers in order to obtain a license to do business in another culture.

Relativism is also criticized as an illogical ethical theory. Relativism appears to deny individuals and groups the opportunity to be universalists by believing in and acting consistently with conceptions of universal values. It also fails to provide any basis for resolving conflicts between social groups when there is an interaction among them, as in trade among cultures with mutually exclusive values.

Perhaps the greatest problem with relativism comes from what it represents. It constitutes moral abdication, the surrendering of the ability to make any moral judgements concerning the actions of others. The true relativist must accept slavery, human sacrifice, cannibalism or any other practice that represents a genuine norm within a social group. So long as the practice is established as a generally accepted norm within a culture, it must be accepted under relativism. That is why very few modern philosophers support the strong form of relativism.

If relativism is seen as unsatisfactory by many, what are the other options? The polar opposite to relativism is absolutism or universalism. In its strong form, absolutism holds that there is only one truth, only one answer, which must be followed in all contexts. Such a view is commonly held by religious fundamentalists. It is also reflected in the view that DeGeorge (1993) has described as the Righteous American, which holds that North American values are superior to those found elsewhere on the globe and should therefore be preferred in all cases of conflict. Traces of this idea are also found among those who believe that a certain form of political organization (popular democracy) or economic system (shareholder capitalism) is the only viable system.

Universalism also has significant drawbacks. The idea that there is a single truth immediately leads to questions of the identity and source of such a truth. Where many do not agree with or understand such a truth, the result of universalism is to hold people to standards with which they disagree. It thus appears to involve an implicit coerciveness. Universalism may also be criticized for failing to respect diversity among cultures.

Recognizing the many problems associated with the polar extremes of unmitigated relativism and universalism, scholars of business ethics have sought to identify some acceptable middle ground with room for fundamental human rights and values while also respecting local diversity. Examples of some of the major attempts are provided below.

4 Social-contract-based approaches

A social-contract-based approach to business ethics involves the use of implied contracts or understandings to establish ethical rights and obligations for business firms, professionals and managers. The authority or legitimacy of these ethical rights and obligations is based upon assumed rational, self-interested consent to the terms of a hypothetical social contract. Specific ethical obligations and rights are then deduced from this imaginary contract. The device of a social contract has been used in business ethics since the early 1980s and has been particularly important in the area of international business ethics.

To some, the idea of a hypothetical social contract is too abstract or speculative. They question how specific standards for business conduct can be derived from an imaginary agreement. However, there is evidence that the concept does influence decision-making and that some people do believe in the existence of actual social contracts. Thus, as Donaldson argues, people may behave as though an actual agreement exists. For example, recent studies indicate that US managers sometimes explain their projected behaviours and attitudes by reference to the existence of 'unwritten contracts' or 'unspoken promises', or by reference to whether actions are 'traditionally acceptable' or 'culturally acceptable.'

Uses of the term include commonplace references to a 'social contract' between a firm and its employees, or to general understandings among members of professional groups or societies concerning standards for ethical behaviour. Emphasis on social norms and their role in moderating the relationship between individuals and society is also an important part of Eastern approaches to business ethics. For example, a traditional Japanese approach to business ethics, Moralogy, which is briefly described below, encourages 'moral agents to respect existing social norms and behaviors which have become the basis of social life ... and which are indispensable for the maintenance and progress of a sound society'. A social-contract-based approach to business ethics is not limited to any particular type of economic system. It is fully compatible not only with any of the so-called seven cultures of capitalism (Hampden-Turner and Trompenaars 1993), but also with socialist economies of varying degrees of market freedom and property ownership.

Tom Donaldson (1989, 1982) was the first to apply the concept of social contract to the arena of business ethics and then to extend it to explicit consideration of ethical obligations in international business. Donaldson develops a special social contract theory for business ethics in his book *Corporations and Morality* (1982). In this seminal effort Donaldson focuses on the issue of corporate rights and obligations. Following the classical social contract tradition of using a hypothetical agreement as a device for parsing specific rights and obligations, Donaldson imagines the terms of an agreement that could be rationally entered into between all productive cooperative enterprises (firms) and the members of a given society prior to the beginnings of their economic system. The original contractors are imagined as existing in a state of prehistory in which they know the characteristics of the organizations they wish to create, but have control in the sense that they have complete flexibility in designing the surrounding legal and social environment.

Donaldson assumes that the parties would want the benefits of specialization of labour, output and distribution, increased wages and the ability to pay for injuries that would result from having corporations. On the other hand, all parties would want to limit corporation-generated harms such as pollution, depletion of natural resources, destruction of personal accountability and worker alienation. Representatives of productive organizations want the members of society to agree to establish an environment conducive to the organizations providing needed goods and services, resulting, in turn, in reasonable profits. The terms of the resulting social contract require that the harms be minimized and that when the inevitable trade-offs are made, they be made consistently with 'the general canons of justice' (Donaldson 1982: 53).

Donaldson broadens his theory in *The Ethics of International Business* (1989), where he considers all economic actors, not just corporations, employees and consumers. He also extends his focus beyond a single society to consider explicitly issues of cultural relativism. Donaldson envisions a global social contract setting a minimum floor of responsibility for all business firms. Specifically, global firms have an obligation to enhance the long-term welfare of employees and consumers, minimize the drawbacks of large productive organizations, and refrain from violating minimum standards of justice and human rights. These obligations are defined in terms of ten fundamental rights (freedom of physical movement, property ownership, freedom from torture, fair trial, non-discriminatory

treatment, physical security, freedom of speech and association, minimum education, political participation and subsistence) which global firms should avoid depriving their employees of and, in some very limited circumstances, should protect against deprivation by others. Donaldson is unwilling to extend a duty to global corporations to aid those deprived of any of the ten fundamental rights. Donaldson also recognizes that variances in standards among nations may sometimes be due to differing levels of economic development, and he is willing to accept some lowering of ethical standards on that ground so long as core human rights are not violated.

Donaldson's (1996) basic approach to cases of cultural conflict is to distinguish between two different contexts. One is a case of conflict of relative development where a culture has accepted 'lower' standards due to a relatively deprived level of economic development. In that case Donaldson suggests that the acceptability of the practice to a global corporation depends on whether its home culture would have accepted the lower standards, giving as an example paying lower wages to oil-rig workers off Angola than to workers in the Gulf of Mexico. Donaldson concludes that the US would have accepted lower wages to get investment and jobs in similar circumstances, thus justifying the payment of the lower wages to the Angolans.

The second context is the case of a conflict of cultural tradition, for example differing attitudes between the US and Saudi Arabia concerning female managers. In the case of a conflict of cultural tradition a global firm should follow a 'lower' standard only when it is impossible to conduct business successfully without undertaking the practice and when the practice does not violate a core human value. Donaldson suggests that the Japanese practice of gift-giving satisfies this criteria and therefore is a permissible local practice to adopt.

Donaldson and Dunfee (1994) have developed a globally oriented contractarian approach, called integrative social contracts theory (ISCT), which relies upon real, contextual microsocial contract norms within an overall framework based on a classical, hypothetical macro social contract. The term 'integrative' reflects the two very different types of social contracts encompassed by the theory: a hypothetical macro social contract used as an heuristic device and actual microsocial contracts based within living communities. The plural term 'contracts' refers not only to the two types of contracts, but also to the literally millions of community-based microsocial contracts whose norms are important in rendering normative judgements in business ethics.

ISCT is grounded in the familiar idea that social norms serve as a foundation for rules of behaviour within communities. Donaldson and Dunfee hypothesize that rational global contractors would seek to provide for the need for a moral background essential to sustain productive business, while at the same time retaining the ability to select their own values and moral rules to the maximum extent possible. The key terms of this global macro social contract are developed in some detail. The first two terms of the macro social contract are as follows:

1 Local economic communities may specify ethical norms for their members through micro social contracts (i.e. the 'moral free space' term).
2 Norm-generating microsocial contracts must be grounded in informed consent buttressed by rights of exit and voice (i.e. the 'protected informed consent' term).

Communities are at the core of the macro social contract. A community is defined in ISCT as 'a self-defined, self-circumscribed group of people who interact in the context of shared tasks, values, or goals and who are capable of establishing norms of ethical behavior for themselves' (Donaldson and Dunfee 1994: 262). Corporations, subsidiaries, even departments or informal units within an organization, along with partnerships, professional groups, trade associations and nation-states, may all be ISCT communities in the context of a given ethical decision. In focusing on communities, ISCT recognizes that norm-governed group activity is a critical component of economic life.

The parameters of ethical behaviour in advertising may vary among Japan, France and the United States. Acting within their own moral free space, each of these communities should be able to establish indigenous 'authentic' ethical norms supported by the attitudes and behaviour of a substantial majority of their citizens.

A major impact of ISCT is to establish that norms are obligatory for dissenting members of communities when an authentic norm has been identified and it satisfies the other requirements of ISCT given below. The obligation stems from the consent given when one acts as a member of a community, perhaps by accepting the benefits of the community environment. However, ISCT imposes some additional requirements on the operation of the community. The community must respect the right of members to withdraw from or exit group membership. Thus a dissenting member of a community who is quite distressed about a particular authentic norm may elect to leave the community. Employees may, and generally should, leave a corporation whose values are significantly at odds with their important personal values. Similarly, an individual should have the opportunity to exercise his or her voice within the community. This is consistent with much of the organizational justice literature documenting employee attitudes concerned with procedural justice. Often some form of voice – e.g. the right to a 'hearing' to present one's side of the case or to confront an accuser – is critical to judgements that a firm has acted justly.

To avoid excessive relativism, and with the recognition that communities do indeed develop authentic norms supporting racial and gender discrimination as well as other problematic practices, it is assumed in ISCT that the original contractors would wish to recognize a thin set of universal principles that would constrain the relativism of community moral free space. Accordingly, the third term of the macro social contract states:

3 In order to be obligatory, a microsocial contract norm must be compatible with hypernorms (i.e. the 'hypernorms' term).

Hypernorms are defined as 'principles so fundamental to human existence that ... we would expect them to be reflected in a convergence of religious, philosophical, and cultural beliefs' (Donaldson and Dunfee 1994: 265). As expressed by Walzer, they would be a thin 'set of standards to which all societies can be held – negative injunctions, most likely, rules against murder, deceit, torture, oppression, and tyranny' (Walzer 1994: 10).

An obvious question is how to ascertain the existence of particular hypernorms. Donaldson and Dunfee (1994) describe the efforts of anthropologists, political scientists and philosophers, among others, who are searching for a convergence of beliefs and values at the global level. Scholars from many cultures and academic disciplines are asking similar questions concerning what humans commonly believe. An appropriate starting point would be an attempt to identify the extent of convergence among the convergence scholars.

Frederick (1991) studied six intergovernmental compacts (including the Organization for Economic Cooperation and Development's (OECD) Guidelines for Multinational Enterprises, the Helsinki Final Act and the International Labour Organization's (ILO) Tripartite Declaration of Principles Concerning Multinational Enterprises) to identify principles common to the set. Similarly, one could look to the statements of global organizations as potential sources of hypernorms. The Caux Principles developed by the Caux Round Table, a group of senior executives from Asia, Europe and North America who meet annually in Caux, Switzerland, are a prime example; so too is the document *Towards a Global Ethic*, produced by the Council for a Parliament of the World's Religions. From these, some samples can be pulled which seem correct as examples of hypernorms. Here are three candidates:

- Firms should adopt adequate health and safety standards for employees and grant employees the right to know about job-related health hazards (Frederick 1991: 166).
- You should not lie; speak and act truthfully (Parliament of the World's Religions 1993: 11).
- Businesses (should be expected to) honour their obligations in a spirit of honesty and

fairness (Caux Round Table Principles for Business 1994: s. 2, Principle One).

Finally, there are short cuts that managers can use to identify hypernorms for the purpose of making ethical decisions. As a first step a manager could look to the type of general references cited above. The explicit purpose of the Caux Principles is to provide guidance in such matters and they have been widely disseminated. Second, one could try to imagine the likely public response if the action being contemplated were to appear as the lead story on the international edition of CNN, or on the front page of *The Financial Times*. This global version of the traditional local newspaper test may serve to encourage one to think in terms of whether actions might violate widespread understandings of right and wrong. A similar approach would be to ask oneself or others whether or not the proposed action might be seen as violating an important tenet of one of the major world religions. Finally, a manager could enquire of a diverse set of peers whether a proposed course of action might be considered to violate a global ethical principle.

Hypernorms thus bound the moral free space of communities. If, for example, a hypernorm prohibiting coarse bribery exists, then any authentic norm recognizing bribery among, say, a community of corrupt government officials in Russia is not legitimate *ipso facto*. However, hypernorms do not provide a complete bounding of the moral free space of communities. There may still be a conflict between two or more norms that are legitimate. The final term of the macro social contract is as follows:

4 In the case of conflicts among norms satisfying terms 1–3, priority must be established through the application of rules consistent with the spirit and letter of the macro social contract (i.e. the 'priority rules' term).

It will often be the case that multiple legitimate norms applicable to the same ethical judgement come into conflict. This may happen when a transaction crosses two distinctly different communities, as is often the case in global business transactions. Cultures may have quite different norms concerning what constitutes appropriate gifts or entertainment in a particular business context. An American firm doing business in Beijing must decide whether it will follow the local practice of mutual exchange of favours, a mechanism for building connections in China (*guanxi*). A Chinese official wants his son hired for a job at a US plant before he will grant a necessary licence. The action, acceptable within certain circles in China, violates norms of fairness in the US. Here, both norms are clearly established and authentic and both may be considered legitimate, because neither violates a hypernorm. To resolve problems of this type ISCT specifies a loose set of six priority rules which are influenced by the concepts behind principles of international conflicts of law and dispute resolution (Donaldson and Dunfee 1994: 169–70). They are derived from the basic assumptions and terms of the macro social contract and are as follows:

- Transactions solely within a single community which do not have significant adverse effects on other humans or communities should be governed by the host community's norms.
- Community norms for resolving priority should be applied, so long as they do not have significant adverse effects on other humans or communities.
- The more extensive the community which is the source of the norm, the greater the priority which should be given to the norm.
- Norms essential to the maintenance of the economic environment in which the transaction occurs should have priority over norms potentially damaging to that environment.
- Where multiple conflicting norms are involved, patterns of consistency among the alternative norms provide a basis for prioritization.
- Well-defined norms should ordinarily have priority over more general, less precise norms.

Thus the recent social-contract-based approaches differ from more theoretical approaches by relying upon the actual changing norms of business and society.

5 Stakeholder approaches

An important concept in Western business ethics is that of stakeholders. The term stakeholder identifies those who have a 'stake' or an interest in the decision of an organization. Definitions vary but the essence of the idea is that those who may be significantly affected by an organization's action or who are at risk as a result of the decision have a 'stake' in that decision. Typical listings of stakeholders include, among others, consumers, users, bystanders, government agencies at the federal, state and local levels, suppliers, creditors and distributors. More recent writings also include those internal to the firm, including employees, shareholders and even senior managers. Controversial issues include whether the media, the environment or terrorists can be stakeholders. An important task for business ethicists is to define the extent and nature of the obligations of organizations to consider the interests of stakeholders in their decisions. Many business ethics scholars argue that organizations do have fiduciary-type obligations to stakeholders who have significant legitimate interests affected by organizational actions. Their writings comprise what may be thought of as normative stakeholder theory – a conceptual framework of what constitutes right behaviour for dealing with stakeholders.

Application of normative stakeholder theory to a global context produces an additional set of thorny questions. Does the scope of stakeholder obligations vary among nation-states? That is, does the locus of the decision or the home of the corporate actor, by itself, have an impact on the definition of responsibilities to stakeholders? For example, can there be different stakeholder expectations for business decisions made in Korea than in the United States? Do Korean and US organizations have different stakeholder obligations independent of the locus of the decision? If so, what factors influence or control the definition of stakeholder interests that might allow this to be possible?

Consider the important issue of plant safety. Might stakeholder interests in Korea be genuinely defined to allow lower levels of plant safety than would be the case for operations within France or the US? If so, *all* firms operating plants within Korea would have lower levels of stakeholder obligation to employees and local communities than would firms conducting comparable operations in France or the US. This question contains important implications for global business practice. If it is legitimate to define stakeholder obligations in relation to the country in which the decision is made one might conclude that Union Carbide is entitled to follow lower standards for plant safety in Bhopal, India, than in Kanawha, West Virginia. Because the focus is solely on the locus country, the same would be true for Tata Steel, an Indian company, which would have a higher level of stakeholder obligations for operations in the US than for domestic operations within India.

The stakeholder concept is taking on increasing importance in global ethics. It entered the political arena when Tony Blair, the British prime minister, called for stakeholder capitalism as part of his successful election campaign in the UK. The concept is emphasized in the Caux Principles, which reflect the input of senior executives from Asia, Europe and North America. Much of the thinking about stakeholders has been limited by national conceptions of corporate governance, and more work needs to be done to develop a genuinely global stakeholder theory.

6 Kantian approaches

Kantian ethics emphasize duty. Kant presented several formulations of the categorical imperative (an unconditional obligation for all humans). Two statements are particularly well known: 'I ought never act in such a way that I could not will that my maxim should be a universal law'; 'Act so that you treat humanity, whether in your own person or in that of another, always as an end and never as a means only.' A resolute Kantian, Norman Bowie (1993) argues that Kant's arguments transcend culture. Therefore in an open competitive global marketplace Kantian managers will come to realize that deception, promise-breaking and discrimination are actions that cannot be 'consistently universalized' (Bowie 1993: 97). Once global managers come to that realization, Bowie predicts that honesty will rise while bribery and discrimination will decrease within competitive global markets. Specifically, Bowie puts forth the following upbeat propositions (Bowie 1993: 99–102):

- P1: As international business increases, employee honesty will tend to rise.
- P2: As international business among countries increases, bribery will decrease.
- P4: As international business increases, discrimination based on sex, race, religion or national origin will decrease when that discrimination is based on tastes or misinformation about those discriminated against.

Critics of Kantian ethics argue that Kant's approach is too general for useful application by managers. Further, the nature of competition may require that one take advantage of informational asymmetries or other practices difficult to square with the categorical imperative. Finally, one can easily conceive of rules which satisfy the categorical imperative and yet come into conflict with one another, for example 'never use animals to test non-essential products for humans' and 'always test adequately for safety any product for human consumption, even if its requires the use of animals'. A manager for a global cosmetics company may be at a loss as to how to apply Kantian ethics to the case of facial cosmetics.

Even so, Kantian ethics offers considerable promise for providing guidance to managers seeking to do the right thing in global transactions.

7 Realism/neo-Hobbesianism

Velasquez (1992) takes a revised realist or neo-Hobbesian approach to international business ethics. He argues that powerful global corporations are often subject neither to a global sovereign authority nor to the effective limiting power of nation-states. Their actions are beyond the reach of the legal systems of nation-states and often the effective jurisdiction of any effective international authority. In that environment it is often difficult for one business actor to signal reliability to another, so that those who breach ethical conventions such as promise-keeping or honesty may escape any negative reputation effects. In such a circumstance the desire to maximize profit and the intense pressures of competition may spur firms to unethical behaviour. Velasquez argues that there is little hope for an effective common morality for global business in the absence of some Leviathan who can enforce its terms. Velasquez states the following premise:

> In the absence of an international sovereign, all rational agents will chose not to comply with the tenets of ordinary morality, when doing so will put one at a serious competitive disadvantage, provided that interactions are not repeated and that agents are not able to signal their reliability to each other.
>
> (Velasquez 1992)

This view is representative of those who take a legalistic view of morality. Morality is thought of as the product of external social control. The only viable solution is the establishment of a powerful international authority. This is in contrast to the Kantian and social contractarian views which assume that people try to do the right thing and are concerned about the respect of their peers. Under these views, most positive ethical behaviour is thought to be the product of internalized norms and methods of moral reasoning rather than the result of external coercion.

8 Moralogy

One aspect of international business ethics is the study of comparative approaches to business ethics. For an overview, see the special issue of the *Journal of Business Ethics* introduced by Enderle (1997), which features reports on local approaches to business ethics from scholars from many regions of the globe. Moralogy, an indigenous Japanese approach primarily influential among medium-sized firms, is described in this section as an example of a non-Western approach. The term 'moralogy', a coined word, may be thought of as corresponding to a system of moral science.

Under moralogy, morality is classified into two types: ordinary morality and supreme morality. Ordinary morality is equivalent to conventional morality, and represents the combination of daily practices and standards with personal virtues. Rules concerning confidentiality between accountants and clients or general norms concerning gift-giving and entertainment in business relationships would be considered part of ordinary morality. The relevant personal virtues would include temperance, diligence and self-control.

Ordinary morality is viewed as a necessary though not sufficient condition for achieving universal justice. The core principle of universal justice is 'omnidirectional fairness', fairness for every stakeholder. Moralogy identifies five principles of supreme morality which if followed in all decisions would guide managers and their firms toward the goal of omnidirectional fairness. The first principle is 'self-renunciation', which encourages managers to consider their motives. Self-centred motives and arrogance are to be guarded against. The second principle is 'benevolence'. This involves treating people fairly and with empathy. The third principle is 'precedence of duty'. This requires a manager to consider the stakes and interests of other people in decision processes. The fourth principle is 'respect for ortholinons'. Ortholinons are those who have gone before and have contributed to current society through their practice of morality. They include ancestors, national figures, spiritual figures and so on. Managers should act so as to repay their spiritual and material debts to their ortholinons. Finally, there is the principle of 'enlightenment and salvation'. Under this principle work is understood to be connected to all aspects of life. Further, there should be emphasis on continual learning and education.

Although the term is difficult to translate into the existing approaches to business ethics in the United States and Europe, the closest analogy may be to think of moralogy as a virtue-based stakeholder theory.

9 Ecumenical approaches

An approach of growing popularity is to identify middle-level rules which may serve as guideposts for multinational corporations (MNCs; see MULTINATIONAL CORPORATIONS). These may be based in a single theory or, more commonly, in a variety of generally recognized ethical theories. Richard DeGeorge (1993) has provided one of the most elaborate of the ecumenically grounded middle-level approaches. His guidelines are directed particularly at United States-based multinationals and their dealings within the less developed countries. DeGeorge seeks a realistic middle ground between the absolutist Righteous American who inflexibly always follows his or her home country norms and the Naive Immoralist who is willing to accept any type of practice so long as there is evidence that 'everyone is doing it'. In response, DeGeorge offers seven illustrative rules for behaviour. DeGeorge bases the principles on an ecumenical foundation, using several ethical theories – something that is apparent from even a cursory glance at the principles.

- Do no intentional direct harm.
- Produce more good than harm for the host country.
- Contribute to the host country's development.
- Respect the human rights of employees.
- To the extent that local culture does not violate ethical norms, MNCs should respect the local culture and work with and not against it.
- MNCs should pay their fair share of taxes.
- Cooperate with local governments in developing and enforcing just background institutions.

10 Corporate strategies

What, then, are the options for how firms might manage across cultures? For example, should all firms adopt the US practice of having formal ethics programmes and detailed corporate codes of ethics? Although empirical evidence indicates that the use of codes is increasing in Europe (Langlois and Schlegelmilch 1990) and in Japan (1997 survey in *Diamond Weekly*), there is also evidence that country and industry type have significant effects, both on identification of ethical problems and the nature and comprehensiveness of written ethics policies and ethics training (Schlegelmilch and Robertson 1996).

Dunfee (1996) has suggested a framework of alternative strategies available to firms to deal with cultural conflicts in global transactions. Four basic categories of firms, classified on the basis of the strategies they tend to employ when confronted with conflicting norms across cultures, are as follows: the corporate imperialist, the corporate chameleon, the corporate nationalist and the corporate pragmatist.

The corporate imperialist is a firm which tends to be admired by business ethicists. Corporate imperialists operate on the basis of a very strong and clear set of organizational values. The values are internally derived and focused, and often will have been developed with primary reference to the history and culture of the firm. For US firms, these values are likely to be reflected in a unified or single headquarters-level code. A unified code is involved when a firm has a single code which is used for all subsidiaries wherever they are located. The fundamental decision principle employed by the corporate imperialist is to apply its own values and principles everywhere the company does business. The company's values dominate and trump all conflicting customs and norms.

The second alternative is the corporate chameleon. Such a firm would follow local norms and customs, which will generally be considered to dominate or trump home-office policies or any universal standards. Chameleons do not merely respect local customs and traditions; they fully adopt and internalize them. If they operate subsidiaries they tend to see these as local firms within the host environment. Thus a European corporate chameleon would view its Japanese subsidiary as a Japanese firm. The corporate chameleons can be recognized by the fact that they tend to have subcodes for regional or national subsidiaries. They may also have corporate practice officers assigned to each subsidiary, with full responsibility for matters involving ethical standards and practices.

The third category of firm is the corporate nationalist. Its approach may be thought of as a global version of what Lynn Paine has described as the compliance-oriented firm. In an article in the *Harvard Business Review* Paine made an important distinction between firms that follow a compliance-oriented approach to business ethics and firms that emphasize integrity by instilling 'a sense of shared accountability among employees' (Paine 1994: 11) keyed to the organization's own values. Firms following a compliance strategy focus on standards imposed by laws, industry codes and other outside sources. Such programmes are often lawyer-driven. In contrast, an integrity strategy is based upon self-chosen standards reflecting the company's values and aspirations, and is typically led by senior management. Corporate nationalists would tend to be global versions of Paine's compliance-oriented firms which look particularly to the laws and customs of their home country as the primary reference point for resolving cross-cultural issues. On close analysis, such firms do not have a strong individualized culture or customized set of organizational values, but instead adopt the values and customs of their home country. Wherever possible they will seek to mould the local environment in which they operate into patterns consistent with their home culture. Certain US and Japanese firms seem to take this approach.

The final alternative, and probably by far the most common, is the corporate pragmatist. Such firms are the business equivalent of the pragmatic politician. All decisions are focused towards achieving a particular immediate or short-term goal. There is no anchor of a core set of values designed to be a first point of reference in a given circumstance. Instead of taking an a priori approach to ethics, its managers pick and choose among local customs and practices, organizational norms and home-country values, depending on the circumstances and which strategy will lead to an economic advantage. The approach will often be egoistic, prudential and instrumental. Like pirate ships of old, they may carry a wide array of flags, any one of which they may run up the pole to gain advantage or to surprise.

These four alternatives represent a simple framework for assessing the basic alternative strategies for managing across cultures. They do not involve subtle distinctions and it may be that few companies can be classified as a pure version of one of the types.

11 Non-governmental organizations

The increasing prominence of the field of international business ethics is reflected in the recent appearance of prominent non-governmental organizations that support the development of ethical practices and standards. Transparency International (TI) is a prime example. A Berlin-based organization with offices around the world, TI's mission is to 'curb corruption through international and national coalitions encouraging governments to establish and implement effective laws, policies and anti-corruption programs. Strengthen public support and understanding for anti-corruption programs ... Encourage all parties to international business transactions to operate at the highest levels of integrity.' TI publishes a Corruption Perception Index on an annual basis which ranks countries of the world on the basis of perceived corruption on the part of those doing business there. The index and other information about TI can be found at their Web site (http://www.transparency.de). TI was a major player in getting the OECD to act against bribery within its member states.

The Caux Round Table (CRT) was founded in 1986 as an independent organization made up of business leaders from around the world. The organization 'focuses attention on the balance between economic performance, social responsibility and environmental protection, necessary to achieve the goal of sustainable development. From time to time the organization publishes principles and position papers. The CRT Principles for Business, which were published in 1994, have been widely disseminated in many languages, to favourable comment in the financial press. To view the principles and any recent working papers of the organization, visit its Web site at http://www.cauxroundtable.org.

12 Conclusion/the future

Increasingly, managers and even ordinary citizens are coming to realize the vital importance of ethics in international business. A safe prediction is that there will be more emphasis on the topic within firms, global financial organizations such as the International Monetary Fund (IMF) and the World Bank, and a wide variety of global organizations such as the ILO and the OECD. Theorists are struggling to catch up with these developments. Specific focus by ethical theorists on international issues is a relatively recent phenomenon. The theories that are just starting to emerge have potential, but they require a great deal of work before a satisfactory theory of global business ethics can emerge.

THOMAS W. DUNFEE
THE WHARTON SCHOOL

Further reading

* Bowie, N. (1993) 'International business, a universal morality and the challenge of nationalism', in T.W. Dunfee and Y. Nagayasu (eds) *Business Ethics: Japan and the Global Economy*, Dordrecht: Kluwer Academic Publishers. (Describes the general implications of a Kantian-based approach to international business ethics.)
* DeGeorge, R.T. (1993) *Competing with Integrity in International Business*, Oxford: Oxford University Press. (Provides a justification for and a discussion of seven fundamental guidelines for competing with integrity in international business; discusses specific issues related to doing business in Japan, China and the former USSR; deals at length with issues such as bribery, financial manipulation and plant safety.)
* Donaldson, T. (1982) *Corporations and Morality*, Englewood Cliffs, NJ: Prentice Hall. (Presents the initial development of a social-contracts-based approach to business ethics.)
* Donaldson, T. (1989) *The Ethics of International Business*, New York: Oxford University Press. (Describes the social-contract-derived approach to developing standards for international business firms; describes and justifies an

algorithm for resolving issues based in cultural conflicts; provides an elaborate parsing out of a set of ten fundamental human rights, with a discussion of their implications for decisions made by international firms.)
* Donaldson, T. (1996) 'Values in tension: ethics away from home', *Harvard Business Review*, September–October: 48–62. (Presents a pragmatic discussion of an approach for dealing with ethical conflicts based in differing cultural values; discusses bribery and software piracy.)
* Donaldson T. and Dunfee T.W. (1994) 'Towards a unified conception of business ethics: integrative social contracts theory', *Academy of Management Review* 19(2): 252–84. (Lays out the basic ideas of integrative social contracts theory for management scholars.)
* Dunfee, T.W. (1996) 'Ethical challenges of managing across cultures', Invited Plenary Paper presented at the Ninth Annual European Business Ethics Network Conference, Seeheim, Germany, September; available as *Working Paper 96–9–032* from the Department of Legal Studies, the Wharton School, University of Pennsylvania, Philadelphia, PA 19104, USA.
  Dunfee, T.W. and Nagayasu, Y. (eds) (1993) *Business Ethics: Japan and the Global Economy*, Dordrecht: Kluwer Academic Publishers. (An example of an in-depth analysis of ethics in a particular country; ten Asian scholars join several business ethicists to describe the nature and history of business ethics in Japan.)
* Enderle, G. (1997) 'A worldwide survey of business ethics in the 1990s', *Journal of Business Ethics* 16(14): 1475–83. (Introduction to a special issue of the journal which contains reports on the status of business ethics in most regions of the world; an excellent source for local perspectives on business ethics.)
* Frederick, W.C. (1991) 'The moral authority of transnational corporate codes', *Journal of Business Ethics* 10(3): 165–77.
* Hampden-Turner, C. and Trompenaars (1993) *The Seven Cultures of Capitalism*, New York: Doubleday. (Presents a comparative analysis of different forms of capitalism, based in part on a massive survey of senior managers from the US, Europe and Japan.)
* Langlois, C.C. and Schlegelmilch, B.B. (1990) 'Do corporate codes of ethics reflect national character? Evidence from Europe and the United States', *Journal of International Business Studies* 21(4): 519–39. (Presents a comparative empirical survey of codes in Europe and the US.)
* Paine, L.S. (1994) 'Managing for organizational integrity', *Harvard Business Review*,

March–April: 106–17. (Gives a useful description of and clarifies the distinction between integrity-based and compliance-based corporate ethics programmes.)

* Schlegelmilch, B.B. and Robertson, D.C. (1996) 'The influence of country and industry on ethical perceptions of senior executives in the U.S. and Europe', *Journal of International Business Studies*, 4th quarter: 859–81. (Presents a large-scale survey of the ethical perceptions of senior mangers in the US, the UK, Austria and Germany.)

Taka, I. and Dunfee, T.W. (1997) 'Japanese moralogy as business ethics', *Journal of Business Ethics* 16(5): 507–19. (Summarizes an indigenous Japanese approach to business ethics called moralogy.)

* Velasquez, M. (1992) 'International business, morality, and the common good', *Business Ethics Quarterly* 2(2): 27–40. (Describes a neo-Hobbesian approach to international business ethics; emphasizes the limits of reputational constraints and the need for sovereign authority at the global level.)

* Walzer, M. (1994) *Thick and Thin: Moral Argument at Home and Abroad*, Notre Dame, IN, University of Notre Dame Press.

* Wilson, J.Q. (1993) *The Moral Sense*, New York: Free Press. (Presents evidence for the existence of an innate moral sense among humans and suggests some elements of natural morality.)

Further resources
* http://www.cauxroundtable.org
* http://www.transparency.de

See also: MULTINATIONAL CORPORATIONS

International business negotiations

Overview

The growing interdependence in the world economic arena has led to the formation of collaborative agreements between entities from different nations. A major requisite to the formation of such agreements is the successful negotiation of the terms and conditions for their establishment. Depending upon the type and nature of the investment, these negotiations take place with one or both of the following entities: (1) the various governmental ministries and agencies which have jurisdiction over different aspects of inward foreign direct investment, such as the extent of foreign participation permitted in the venture, the raising of capital in the local money market, the remittance of profits and dividends, and matters pertaining to technology transfer; and (2) the local partner or partners, in the event of a cooperative venture, over the terms and conditions of the agreement, such as percentage of equity ownership to be divided between the foreign and local investors, who assumes management control, pricing of output/services, staffing of key managerial positions, the nature of products and/or services to be provided by the venture, and the life of the venture. Even after the establishment of the collaborative agreement, the partners need to negotiate on issues that may arise in the relationship, and thus maintain peaceful co-existence between them. Should relations between the partners deteriorate to the point of irreconcilable differences,

that is, one or both partners see termination of the contractual agreement as the only viable option, the parties still need to negotiate with each other on the terms of dissolution. In short, international business negotiations are crucial at entry, exit and throughout the relationships between the host and home country partners.

This entry examines the major approaches to the study of negotiations, particularly international business negotiations. To understand better the dynamics and process of such negotiations, it is necessary to have a conceptual framework which can facilitate the analysis and, hence, selection of strategies to be pursued under a given set of conditions. Research findings pertaining to cross-national business negotiations are reviewed. A checklist of factors which can enhance the probability of successful outcomes in cross-national business negotiations is then presented.

1 Major approaches to the study of negotiations

There are seven schools of thought, or approaches to the study of negotiations (Zartman 1976):

1 The descriptive approach traces the history and outcome of particular negotiation situations.
2 The contextual approach examines the process and outcome of negotiations in light of the history of the negotiation itself and/or the broader historical context into which the specific negotiation fits.
3 The structural approach identifies and examines the situations and conditions, such as patterns of relationships, which can enhance the successful outcome of a given negotiation.
4 The strategic approach reviews strategic decisions and choices in the context of the

values at stake and the pattern of selection of the respective parties.

5 The use of personality types to explain for outcomes of negotiations.

6 The behavioural approach studies outcomes in the context of behavioural skills of the participants.

7 The process approach that studies negotiations in the context of challenge-and-response encounters.

A cursory review of these seven approaches to the study of negotiations reminds one of the fable of the six blind men and the elephant. While each approach can facilitate our understanding of a selected aspect or facet of negotiations, no approach alone is capable of capturing, and thus explaining and accounting for, the phenomenon of negotiations in its true complexity, with its multitude of interactions and interrelationships. A conceptual paradigm which attempts to integrate several of these approaches into the context of international business negotiations is presented below.

2 A conceptual paradigm of international business negotiations

A comprehensive paradigm of international business negotiations has to encompass at least the following five dimensions: contextual environment, negotiation context, negotiator characteristics, strategy selection and process/progress, and negotiation outcomes. The interrelationships among these five dimensions are presented in Figure 1.

Contextual environments

The contextual environment can be divided into four general categories: political, economic, institutional–legal and cultural (Fayerweather and Kapoor 1976). The significance of each contextual environment in influencing the progress and outcome of negotiations is identified below.

Political environment

Any cooperative agreement between economic entities from two nations must be examined within the context of the political relations that prevail between the countries, such as whether there are diplomatic relations between the two countries, whether 'most favoured nation' (MFN) trading status is extended, whether dual-use technology can be exported to the country and whether there are unresolved issues between the countries, such as frozen assets, and so on. Concerns about political instability may deter prospective foreign investors from entering or expanding their existing operations in the host country (see INTERNATIONAL TRADE AND FOREIGN DIRECT INVESTMENT).

Business negotiations between entities from two countries must also be viewed within the context of the political philosophies that govern the respective countries. So-called pure economic transactions are often dictated by political considerations. For example, after the Tiananmen Square incident in the People's Republic of China on 4 June 1989, the USA threatened to withdraw MFN status to Chinese exports if the latter did not make positive and significant improvements in its domestic policy on human rights.

Economic environment

Since political and economic considerations are often inextricably intertwined, the distinctions between the political and economic environments may often be fuzzy. Under economic considerations, the focus is on three sets of variables:

1 The type of economic system in a country, such as market, centrally-planned or mixed economies. This determines the nature and form of economic cooperation that can take place. For example, wholly-owned foreign investment from abroad was not permitted under the former USSR.

2 The level of economic development in the country. In general, many lesser developed countries (LDCs) are chronically short of capital (especially foreign exchange), technological know-how and skilled labour. Given these circumstances, the partner

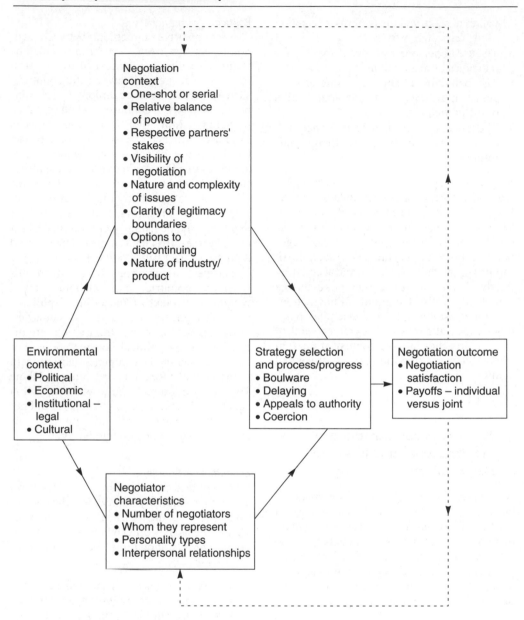

Figure 1 Conceptual framework of international business negotiations

from the advanced nation must assume much of the responsibility in financing and providing technology and technological know-how.

3 The national objectives or priorities of the host country, such as five- and ten-year plans and industrial policies. These deter-

mine the type and nature of projects that are encouraged in the country at the time. Foreign firms seeking investment in projects which fall outside the priority industries, as identified in the host country's economic plans, will meet with limited success.

Institutional–legal environment

The institutional–legal environment influences the progress and outcome of business negotiations in three primary ways. It provides legislation (such as investment, labour-management and tax laws) that affects the nature and form of collaborative agreement in the host country. It influences the partner's attitude toward law and litigation. In the USA, for instance, contracts are viewed in legalistic terms; whereas in Japan, contracts are viewed more in the context of the social relationship that exists between the partners. This difference in attitude towards law implies that a firm may have to rely upon alternative methods of conflict resolution with Japanese partners. Finally, it reflects the diversity of institutional settings across countries. In Japan, for example, the relationship between business and government is a cosy one. Foreign firms which seek to negotiate with Japanese entities have to understand this peculiar aspect of the institutional environment in Japan and its implications in terms of who to include in the negotiation team, what is possible and probable, and what strategies to pursue in the course of the negotiations (see MANAGEMENT IN JAPAN).

Cultural environment

Culture can affect negotiations in three important ways (see CULTURE, CROSS-NATIONAL). It affects how people process and interpret information. In Japan, for example, there are two types of logic: linear (akin to Greek Aristotelian logic) and indirection. Indirection can be illustrated by the Japanese saying: 'when the wind blows, it is good for the makers of wooden tubs'. The logic runs something like this: when it is windy, people become sad. To overcome their melancholy, they play a stringed instrument (*shamisen*), the strings of which are made of catgut. To make the *shamisen*, people kill cats which result in a depletion of the feline population, thus leading to a proliferation in mice. The mice gnaw at the wooden tubs which store grain, damaging them, and ultimately resulting in an increased demand for wooden tubs. Hence, the saying. While the logic may seem convoluted and incomprehensible from the Western

perspective, it highlights two significant points: first, the Japanese preoccupation with long-term implications of actions; and second, their ability to perceive relationships between apparently unrelated systems, the wind blowing and the demand for wooden tubs (Hall and Hall 1987). Differences in logical systems explain how two people from different cultures can view the same situation, an objective reality, and come up with completely different interpretations of what had occurred.

Culture influences people's perception of what is reasonable, right and acceptable, thus affecting the choice of strategies to be pursued in the negotiation process and the resolution of conflicts. In the west, for example, the concept of 'right' is fundamental and paramount to most types of relationships. Each party insists upon its rights – the right to fire, the right to strike, the right to higher wages, and so on. In Japan, in contrast, the notion of 'right' is a foreign one. When Japan tried to adopt a modern constitution after 1868, it had a difficult time in incorporating the term 'right' into the text. Until then, all relationships had been defined in terms of duties and responsibilities. Consequently, despite the incorporation of the term 'right' into the constitution, relationships between two or more entities in the country continued to operate on the traditional basis of mutual obligations. Thus, management has the obligation to take care of the workforce, while the workforce has the duty to work hard to fulfil organizational goals (Ballon 1986).

Cultural differences result in dissimilarities in decision making and negotiating styles, and choice of methods of conflict resolution. In studies of business negotiations between US firms, on the one hand, and Japanese, Chinese and Korean firms, on the other, there were major differences in decision-making and negotiating styles and choice of methods of conflict resolution between Americans, Japanese, Chinese and Koreans (Tung 1989).

Negotiation context

Negotiation context refers to the structural properties specific to a given negotiation situation (Strauss 1978). These can fall into nine categories, as follows.

Motives and criteria

An accurate assessment of the motives will assist in the projection of how accommodating or non-conceding a particular party to the negotiation will be. If one partner needs the agreement badly enough, it will bend over backwards to meet the terms and demands of the other party.

In the negotiations between Boeing Commercial Airplane Company (see BOEING COMPANY) and Civil Transport Development Corporation (CTDC – an entity created under the sponsorship of the Japanese government with three working entities: Mitsubishi Heavy Industries, Kawasaki Heavy Industries and Fuji Heavy Industries – see MITSUBISHI HEAVY INDUSTRIES, LTD) for a joint programme to manufacture Boeing's 767 aeroplanes, the Japanese were very accommodating and acquiesced to most of Boeing's terms, including the mode of cooperation (joint programme as opposed to joint venture), absorption of fixed costs related to the items they manufacture, and assumption of market, foreign exchange and performance risks. Why were the Japanese, astute negotiators and businessmen, so accommodating? The answer lies in an analysis of CTDC's motives. In the early 1980s, the Japanese government identified aircraft, both military and commercial, as a potential growth industry. Moreover, the US government had pressured the Japanese to assume greater responsibility for its own defence. Since there is much complementarity between the production of military and civilian aircrafts in terms of technological know-how and equipment, the production of commercial aircraft represents a viable route for recouping or recovering the costs of research and development on military defence (see MANAGEMENT IN JAPAN).

Besides analysing the motives, the criteria used by the parties to assess the feasibility of a project should also be examined. For example, US partners are generally more concerned about short-term profitability. Consequently, the return on investment (ROI) and payback period constitute important criteria. Japanese partners, on the other hand, focus more on the criteria of market share and growth. Other criteria include the percentage of equity ownership and the ability to exercise management control. Some firms will not accept a minority equity position nor will they relinquish management control over the venture.

Information on a partner's motives and criteria can be obtained through meticulous fact finding, including intelligence gathering using various means. Knowledge of motives and criteria can facilitate the selection of the most appropriate strategies during the course of negotiations.

Common interests

The two parties to a negotiation must have something in common, such as a common desire to develop a new product or to increase production and sales in a given market (see INTERNATIONAL MARKETING). During the course of negotiations, however, the two parties may become so engrossed with differences and conflicts that they tend to lose sight of the commonalities and mutual interests that exist between them. If and when this occurs, the negotiations often break down because both sides see little incentive to continuing the negotiations. Consequently, while attempting to resolve the conflicts between the parties, the partners should always try to emphasize the commonalities that exist between them to spur both parties to an amicable resolution of the differences.

Conflicting interests

These refer to the differences between the parties, and there are four matters which can often be found as the cause of conflict: equity share, management control, evaluation of each partner's contribution and level of technology to be transferred to the venture.

In many studies of business negotiations between Americans, on the one hand, and Japanese, Koreans and Chinese, on the other, equity share emerged as one of the most sensitive issues in the negotiations. For the purpose of consolidating their worldwide profit-and-loss statements, US firms generally insist on a minimum equity ownership of 51 per cent.

The east Asian partners, however, often also desire majority equity ownership. In Japan, while there is virtually no legal restriction on the percentage of foreign equity ownership, the issue of equity is still sensitive. Since Korea had been invaded and conquered by foreigners on several occasions in its past history, they are very concerned about foreigners exercising undue control. The same situation applies in China (see MANAGEMENT IN CHINA; MANAGEMENT IN JAPAN).

Management control is generally reflected in two areas: representation on the board and staffing of senior management positions. Representation on the board is generally commensurate with the percentage of equity ownership, although in ventures with a 51:49 split, there is usually an equal number of directors from either side. In most collaborative agreements with east Asian partners, most decisions in 51:49 ventures are made through mutual discussion rather than by vote. The more contentious issue in terms of management control is the staffing of senior management positions. In many east–west ventures, the Western partner feels that it is imperative to use expatriates to staff certain key positions to maintain adequate control over the technology being transferred and to prevent the eastern partner from coordinating its joint-venture activities, particularly in the areas of finance and personnel, with the rest of the industrial group to which it belongs. In terms of financing, this coordination can be in the form of intracompany loans and borrowing. In the area of personnel, the joint-venture company can become a dumping ground for excess personnel from the eastern partner. Nationalistic reasons aside, the eastern partners, in general, feel that they should exercise management control because they are more familiar with the unique aspects of managing and operating in the local environment.

A primary motive for entering into a cooperative agreement with a foreign entity is to complement one's own resources, such as capital, technology, know-how and market access. In the 50:50 joint venture formed between General Motors and Toyota Motor to manufacture small cars in Fremont,

California, Toyota's contribution was $100 million cash. General Motors's contributions were $11 million cash and the Fremont manufacturing plant. Where non-cash contributions are involved, such as General Motors' Fremont manufacturing plant, a dollar value has to be assigned to such fixed assets. The cash value of such properties is, of course, subject to negotiation.

In many cases, a major motive for entering into a cooperative agreement with a foreign entity from an industrialized country is to acquire advanced technology. In fact, when China first promulgated its joint venture law in 1979, foreign investors were required to supply technology that was 'truly advanced'; otherwise, the investors had to indemnify the Chinese partner for 'losses caused by deception through the intentional provision of outdated equipment or technology' (Article 4). The Chinese soon realized that in light of deficiencies in the country's infrastructure, 'truly advanced' technology may not necessarily be the most appropriate at that stage of the country's development. For every US dollar's worth of imported equipment, China has to spend another three dollars on ancillary equipment before the imported technology can be put into operation. Consequently, that provision of the Chinese joint venture law was subsequently revised to read: 'truly advanced and appropriate to China's needs' (see MANAGEMENT IN CHINA).

Nature and complexity of issues to be negotiated

Where the issues under negotiation are numerous and complex, each party has to make constant trade-offs by assessing its priorities and the utility functions of each trade-off. Where the negotiation is serially-linked with other problems, one party may make more concessions in a given negotiation so as to maximize outcomes in other related situations.

In general, negotiators tend to be more accommodating, cooperative, and honest in repetitive bargaining situations as compared to one-shot transactions because of the prospects of future encounters. In other words, there is a need to maintain a smooth and ongoing relationship between the parties. Consequently, where the negotiations are serially-linked or repetitive, the issue of reciprocity or repercussion becomes a major consideration. Furthermore, where the negotiation is serially-linked, negotiators tend to tread more cautiously because of the implications that a particular decision may have on subsequent and related occurrences (Raiffa 1982). These linkages may extend to companies which are not presently a party to the negotiation. A partner to a negotiation may be concerned about establishing a precedent to which it could be bound later. For example, prior to Boeing's joint program with CTDC, it had only worked with other manufacturers on a contracting or sub-contracting basis. Consequently, Boeing was concerned about the precedent this joint programme may set for its future dealings with other domestic or foreign entities. Hence the reason for the detailed and long drawn-out negotiations about the nature and form of the working arrangement between the parties.

Relative balance of power
This determines the extent to which each partner will accommodate or concede to the demands of the other. In the case of the joint production programme between Boeing and CTDC, since Boeing possessed the technological know-how, it was able to bargain from a position of strength. Consequently, the Japanese partner had to make many concessions, including adapting to the US style of negotiation.

Visibility of negotiations
This refers to the extent to which the transaction will attract the general public's interest, thereby influencing the negotiator's selection of strategy in the negotiation situation. If the project under negotiation is perceived to be in the public interest, the negotiator may deliberately make public statements and/or leaks to the press, sometimes with the objective of pressuring the other party to come to agreement. Where the project may be perceived adversely by the public, the negotiators will try to keep the talks secret.

Clarity of legitimacy boundaries
This is determined, to a large extent, by the contextual environment. What may be perceived as legitimate in one country may not be so considered in another. In the USA, for example, the giving and receiving of bribes violates the 1977 Foreign Corrupt Practices Act. In many countries in Asia, Latin America and the Middle East, however, the use of bribes is considered a normal part of business transactions.

Options to discontinuing negotiations
Where there are available options to discontinuing negotiations, either party may be less motivated to work towards an agreement, thus affecting the selection of strategies and hence the progress and outcome of the negotiation. Where one or both parties perceive the cessation of negotiations as detrimental to their interests, then either or both parties would become more compromising and hence more willing to explore alternative modes of conflict resolution.

Nature of industry/product
Given the nationalistic sentiments in many LDCs, a major incentive to collaboration with foreign partners is to acquire much needed technology and technological know-how to advance economic development at home. Where the foreign partner can supply the needed technology, its relative balance of power in the negotiation situation will be bolstered, thus influencing the progress and outcome of the negotiations.

Negotiator characteristics

Negotiator characteristics have a direct bearing on the progress and outcome of negotiations because negotiations are, after all, conducted by and between individuals. Negotiator characteristics fall into five general categories.

Number of negotiators
Where there are several negotiators on a team, differences in values and hence opinions may exist within the group. To resolve such intragroup differences, trade-offs and

compromises have to be made, thus affecting the selection of strategies to be pursued, and hence the progress and outcome of the negotiation. Even when there is only one negotiator, the person may still experience internal conflicts (Raiffa 1982).

Whom they represent

The issue of whom the negotiators represent can influence the selection of strategy, and hence the progress and outcome of negotiations in at least two major ways. First, a negotiator who represents the public or quasi-public sector has a very different set of concerns as compared to a representative from private industry. A negotiator for the public or quasi-public sector, in general, has to consider the implications that their decision has on society at large, and how they can represent effectively the interests of the public, or at least impart such an impression. A representative of the private sector, on the other hand, is responsible to a narrower constituency, and hence can pursue strategies that maximize organizational rather than societal outcomes.

A second way in which the issue of whom the negotiator represents can influence the progress and outcome of the negotiations pertains to the options available to discontinuing negotiations. In negotiations with the private sector, in case of disagreement, there are more options to discontinuing negotiations. A party can simply cease negotiations and seek another more compatible partner. For example, Toyota had negotiated unsuccessfully with Ford Motors for thirteen months before it turned to General Motors for the possible formation of a joint venture in the USA. The latter talks were successful and resulted in the 50:50 joint venture in Fremont, California. This alternative is generally not available in the case of negotiations with the public sector.

Personality types

Some personality types which may influence the progress and outcome of negotiations are listed below (Graham and Allerheiligen 1983).

1 Introversion versus extroversion. (In general, extroversion is positively related to performance.)
2 Experience as measured by age, years of work experience and extent of inter-organizational contacts. (In general, the more experienced individuals, up to a certain threshold level, should meet with greater success in the negotiation situation.)
3 Internationalism versus isolationism. (In general, internationalists tend to be more cooperative than isolationists in negotiation situations.)
4 Self-esteem: both task specific and generalized self-esteem. (In general, the higher the self-esteem, the more positive the outcome.)

Interpersonal relationships

Besides personality attributes of the negotiators, the choice of strategies is also influenced by the interpersonal relationships that exist between members of the negotiating teams. Where the negotiators trust and respect their counterparts on the opposing team, the issues under negotiation can be more easily defined and narrowed down, thus facilitating a meeting of the minds on the negotiating table. Trust, for example, is essential to the successful operation of joint ventures formed between US and Japanese entities (Peterson and Shimada 1978).

Bilingual team member

Where the parties to a negotiation do not speak a common language, the services of an interpreter are generally required. Thus, negotiator characteristics can be confounded by the use of interpreters. Interpreters have been described as 'gatekeepers' because they can filter the information that is received by the target audience and can affect the target audience's perception of the situation through the manner in which the information is conveyed.

In light of this problem, it is advisable to include a bilingual member on one's negotiating team. A bilingual member, while not actively involved in the translations, can correct mistakes as they occur. Misunderstandings due to inadequate interpretation services impede the progress of negotiations and may completely disrupt them because the perspectives of both sides cannot be presented accurately. Besides mere interpretation, a bilingual person familiar with the partner's culture can also interpret the non-verbal messages for the rest of the team. Moreover, a bilingual member can make suggestions about the best way to present certain issues where there are cultural differences in discussing various viewpoints.

Strategy selection and process/progress

The negotiation context and negotiator characteristics jointly influence the strategies that are selected by both parties, first, in approaching the negotiation situation, and second, in resolving conflicts and/or differences. Strategies for approaching the negotiation situation and resolving differences include the following:

1 Strategic misrepresentation. Under this approach, one side deliberately magnifies the significance of the issue(s) conceded to in order to bargain for better terms in other areas (Raiffa 1982). Strategic misrepresentation is a form of deception and is widely used in military warfare. In 1983, when the USA invaded Grenada, it deliberately leaked information to the press that an aircraft carrier and warships were being dispatched to the Middle East to assist peace-keeping efforts in Lebanon. Actually, the fleet and troops were on their way to Grenada. This diversionary tactic worked and accounted for the swift invasion of the island.
2 Linkage with other problems. This approach is used where the negotiations are serially-linked.
3 Boulware strategy. Under this approach, one party makes an offer at the beginning and remains firm on it throughout. This strategy is only possible when one is negotiating from a position of strength, as in Boeing's case with CTDC.
4 Delaying strategy. Under this strategy, one party uses time to its advantage. The objective is to wear down one's opponents.

5 Appeals to authority. This approach includes arbitration and mediation. The ploy is to select an intermediary whose motivations and outlooks most closely resemble one's own, thus maximizing the probability of favourable outcome.
6 Coercion or threats of coercion. This strategy is possible where one team enjoys a relative balance of power over the other.
7 Litigation. This is the most drastic approach and occurs where one party initiates legal action against another to enforce an agreement and/or to recover certain damages/losses resulting from a breach of contract.
8 Compromise. This occurs when the partners to the negotiation are willing to make trade-offs or concessions.
9 Mediation. Mediation or conciliation occurs when a go-between (usually a mutual friend of both parties to the dispute) is brought in to help resolve the differences between the two partners. Mediation is less formal than arbitration.
10 Arbitration. Arbitration involves the appointment of a third party who makes an award (that is, decides on the outcomes) after listening to the perspectives of both sides to the dispute. Arbitration, which is widely used in the resolution of labour disputes, has become a popular mechanism for resolving international commercial disputes for several reasons:
(a) Certainty. The arbitration clause states in advance who will arbitrate, where it will be held, and how it will proceed.
(b) If the parties to the agreement so desire, the proceedings are private and confidential.
(c) The arbitrator's award in most international commercial disputes is binding, final and usually enforceable in most countries. By virtue of the New York Convention on the Recognition and Enforcement of Foreign Arbitral Awards, signed and adhered to by over 70 countries worldwide, it is usually easier to enforce an arbitration award, as compared to a court judgment, in a third country.
(d) In disputes involving a government or government party, a claim of sovereign immunity can always be made. If this occurs, any

attempt to sue a government in a third country court becomes almost futile. By agreeing to arbitration, the host government has waived its right to claim sovereign immunity (McClendon 1985).

11 Mutual discussion. This involves lengthy sessions where both sides talk and listen to each other in an attempt to clarify, and thus resolve the issues under dispute. If the dispute can be attributed to misunderstandings between the parties, sessions which seek to unravel the rationale behind contentious issues can clarify such misunderstandings, and restore harmony between the parties.

Negotiation outcomes

The outcomes of a given negotiation situation can be assessed along several dimensions. In the event of agreement, the outcome can be measured in terms of negotiator satisfaction, and payoffs in the form of joint or individual profits. In the event of a stalemate or deadlock, one has to examine whether alternative strategies can be devised to help unblock the stalemate. In the event of a complete breakdown between the parties, both partners can withdraw and dissolve the negotiations.

In Figure 1, there is a feedback loop from 'negotiation outcomes' to 'negotiation context' and 'negotiator characteristics' because the outcomes of a particular negotiation may be combined with other negotiation situations, and thus have a cumulative impact on the context in which a future negotiation is conducted, and/or the way in which the negotiator perceives and behaves in similar or related negotiations.

3 Research findings on cross-national business negotiations

Research findings pertaining to cross-national business negotiations are presented here, with focus on the following: cross-cultural differences in decision-making and negotiating styles; factors which account for the success and failure of cross-national business

negotiations; and relationships between incidence of success and practices for the conduct of cross-national negotiations (see CULTURE, CROSS-NATIONAL; ORGANIZATION CULTURE).

Findings of several studies of business negotiations between American firms, on the one hand, and Japanese, Chinese and South Korean entities, on the other, are presented here. The reasons for focusing on research findings pertaining to east Asian samples are threefold: first, in light of the phenomenal economic growth in many east Asian countries, business leaders believe that economic opportunities in the next century will emanate from the Pacific Rim countries. Second, significant differences exist between the west and east Asians. Thus, in order to bargain from a position of strength, or at least equality, one has to be knowledgeable about such differences. Third, most of the available empirical research on cross-national negotiations has utilized east Asian samples (see ECONOMIES OF EAST ASIA).

Differences in decision-making and negotiating styles

Most Americans perceive major and significant differences in decision-making and negotiating styles between themselves and their east Asian partners. The most salient differences are presented here.

Delays in decision making

In east Asia, matters do not progress as rapidly as they typically do in the West. Protracted negotiations which extend to several years are fairly common in China and Japan. Most Westerners who have negotiated with the Japanese and Chinese will readily acknowledge that patience is a paramount virtue in doing business in Asia. Westerners who seek to do business in these countries have to abandon their usual time frame and allow matters to proceed at their own pace, which is characteristically unhurried. Five factors have contributed to the general slowness in the progress of negotiations:

1 The east Asian emphasis on relationships which are pivotal to all aspects of societal

functioning. Relationships are usually developed over years of personal association. The east Asian partner needs time to observe a prospective partner because a business agreement, like a marriage, once entered into is generally viewed as inviolate, and not to be easily discontinued according to the whims of the partners.

2 The use of consensus in decision making in the case of Japan. It takes time to arrive at a consensus.

3 The longer-term orientation in planning. East Asians tend to look at what will happen ten or twenty years in the future. Hence delays of a few months, or sometimes even years, may appear inconsequential from their perspective.

4 Language barriers usually result in the use of interpreters. This means that the negotiations may take twice as long with all the translations to and from a given language.

5 The inertia of a massive bureaucracy, in the case of China.

In Korea, in contrast, since many companies are still run by the owner/founder of the company or his family, decision making tends to be more centralized. Consequently, decisions can generally be made more quickly in Korean companies. Despite the relative speed with which decisions can be made, relationships are also emphasized in the Korean context. Furthermore, Korean partners, similar to their Japanese counterparts, may often use a delaying strategy in an attempt to arrive at a desired outcome. The use of this stalling technique may stem from a perception that Westerners, particularly Americans, are generally more eager than Koreans to reach closure within a relatively short period of time. By stalling, the Koreans hope to wear down their Western partners and thereby gain more and better concessions.

Personal considerations versus Western logic

Since relationships are pivotal to success in business transactions in east Asia, an east Asian partner may not always make decisions on the basis of logic alone; rather, these may often be influenced by personal considerations. Moreover, the types of logic espoused in these countries may be different from Western linear logic, as presented earlier.

The Koreans acknowledge that Western logic or reasoning, by itself, may not be adequate to persuade a Korean to adopt a particular course of action. Personal considerations can be equally as important, if not more so. The Koreans may often respond to *kibun*, which can be defined as the personal feeling, the attitude and mood, the mental state which is an extremely important factor in ego fulfilment (Jang 1988).

Lack of decision-making authority

Most east Asian negotiating teams do not appear to be vested with decision-making authority and have to defer to higher authority in their respective organizational hierarchies. While this is usually true, sometimes it may be an excuse to bide for more time. This apparent lack of decision making authority on the part of the negotiation team members has two major implications: first, it will result in delays in decision-making; and second, the need to socialize with decision makers to facilitate the process.

Avoidance of direct confrontation

Given the emphasis on face saving in east Asia, direct confrontation of issues is generally avoided, with the exception of Korea. While face saving is important in any culture, in east Asia it takes on heightened sensitivity. Confrontative techniques which back an opponent into a corner thus allowing little room for manoeuvre should be avoided. The Japanese and Chinese are generally very polite and do not openly voice or show their displeasure with the manner in which certain things are said and handled. They prefer to hint at issues or be vague in their responses, so that if these do not work out, no party will be particularly embarrassed. The Japanese are indirect even in their compliments.

Along with this aversion towards direct confrontation is a tendency among the Japanese and Chinese to avoid extremes. Because of the overriding concern with maintaining harmony, the Japanese tend to avoid extremes and prefer to adopt a middle-of-the-road attitude. The avoidance of extremes, combined with the desire to save face, often translate into an aversion to use the word 'no' in conversations. This trait has led some prominent Japanese leaders, such as Sony Corporation's Akio Morita, to argue that in light of Japan's ascendancy in the global economic arena and heightened 'Japanese bashing' in other industrialized nations, this tradition is outdated (see MORITA, AKIO).

This avoidance of direct confrontation also translates into an aversion for litigation. The USA is one of the most litigious societies in the world. It has 70 per cent of the world's lawyers with nearly 18 million new lawsuits every year. This amounts to an annual outlay of $80 billion in direct litigation costs and $300 billion in indirect costs. This litigious mentality does not carry over well into other countries. In a study of business negotiations between US and Japanese entities, it was found that only 4 per cent of the disputes between the parties were resolved through the combined mechanisms of litigation and arbitration, while 74 per cent of the disputes were resolved by mutual discussion (Tung 1984).

Use of silence
In Japan, vagueness in responses in negotiations is sometimes accompanied by prolonged periods of silence (see MANAGEMENT IN JAPAN). In Japan the maxim that 'silence is golden' still holds good, and may stem from the Japanese desire to avoid confrontation, which is deeply imbued in individuals from childhood. Studies which compared children's quarrels in various European countries with those in Japan found that while prompt retort, in general, was expected in the European countries, Japanese children generally remained quiet even if they felt they were right (Van Zandt 1970). When an impasse is reached in a negotiation, the typical Japanese response is either silence, withdrawal or a change of subject. To the Japanese, a period of silence may allow matters to cool off and give both sides an opportunity to rethink the issue. Westerners, in particular Americans, on the other hand, may feel uncomfortable and have the urge to say something. At these crucial junctures, Americans are most susceptible to committing tactical errors.

Factors for success in cross-national business negotiations

There are six factors responsible for the success of business negotiations with Japanese firms, which are detailed below.

Attitude of US firm
This factor includes items pertaining to the preparation of the US firm, patience on the part of the US team, and the latter's sincerity. All these items are related to the willingness of the US firm to devote time and effort to cultivate a business relationship with the Japanese partner, perceived to be most critical to success in negotiations. This finding points to the need for US firms to exercise patience and develop a longer-range perspective when investing and doing business in Japan.

Cultural awareness
This factor includes items such as familiarity with Japanese customs and business practices. The item 'uniqueness of product/service that Japanese firm could offer', also loaded highly on this factor. A possible explanation is that where a Japanese product or service is unique, the US firm would tend to be more accommodating and hence exhibit a greater willingness to adapt to cultural differences in order to obtain access to the product and/or service. This factor was perceived by most US firms as less important than the previous factor, attitude of US firm. In the Japanese sample, familiarity with a foreign culture is a necessary but insufficient condition for success. There must be a genuine willingness on the part of both sides to work towards some common ground – that is, to accommodate the needs of the other party.

Attitude of Japanese firm
This factor includes a single item pertaining to the sincerity, honesty and good faith exhibited by the Japanese partner in the negotiations. Since it takes two to tango, by definition, negotiations require the mutual cooperation and efforts of both parties.

Product characteristics

This factor consists of the uniqueness of the product or service offered by the US firm. Given the difficulties encountered by foreign investors in establishing operations in Japan, and the general competitiveness of Japanese producers, the product or service offered by the US firm has to be truly unique. Otherwise, the chances of a US firm's gaining successful entry and penetration into the Japanese market may be severely hampered.

Personal relationships

This factor includes the friendly ties built up between the parties over a number of years. This again points to the need for patience and the importance of cultivating and developing personal ties to ensure the successful operation of joint cooperative arrangements between the parties.

Technical expertise

Technical expertise provided by the US firm to the Japanese partner in the past reflects a combination of the previous two factors, 'product characteristics' and 'personal relationships'. In the early post-war years of US–Japan bilateral relations, Japan imported a lot of technology in the form of licensing agreements and was a major recipient of US technical-assistance programmes. Although the Japanese have made remarkable strides in technological development since then, many remain grateful for the initial assistance provided them after the war; yet others concede that the USA still has a technological edge in certain areas. Consequently, technical expertise provided by US firms to their Japanese partners in the past is viewed as a contributing factor to the success of business negotiations.

In negotiations with the Chinese, there are, by contrast, only three factors to consider to reach a successful outcome:

- familiarity with Chinese culture/systems
- attitude of US firm
- technical/product characteristics.

This last factor includes items such as uniqueness of the product supplied by the US investor and China's need for the product. The item, 'meticulous preparation on the part of the US negotiation team', also loaded on this factor because a primary motive for China's open-door policy is to attract advanced technology to facilitate its modernization efforts; hence, the willingness of foreign entities to invest time and effort to explain technical specifications to China is crucial to success. The provision of technical seminars and exchanges generally facilitate the attainment of positive outcomes.

Factors for failure in cross-national business negotiations

In the Japanese sample, there are two factors responsible for the failure of business negotiations. These are cultural differences and product characteristics.

'Cultural differences' includes items pertaining to communication breakdown and differences in business practices, negotiating styles and social norms. The item, 'lack of sincerity on the part of the Japanese', also loaded highly on this factor. A possible explanation for this finding is that perceived insincerity on the part of the Japanese negotiators can be attributed, in part, to cultural differences. For example, in the west, eye contact during handshaking and conversation is considered a sign of honesty and sincerity. In Japan, on the other hand, eye contact is not common during the exchange of greetings nor in the course of conversations. Hence behaviour patterns that are specific to a given cultural environment may be misconstrued by members of other cultures as indications of insincerity and dishonesty.

Two points with regard to cultural differences deserve attention. First, although cultural differences may be viewed as less important than 'attitude of US firms' in the success of business negotiations, ignoring such differences may be detrimental to the outcome of negotiations. Unfamiliarity with cultural differences and an inability to bridge the cultural gap can lead to the collapse of business negotiations. Second, the specific item, 'insurmountable cultural differences', which loaded on this factor was perceived by approximately half the respondents as either irrelevant or responsible 'to a very little extent' for the failure of business negotiations. This suggests that although differences in social customs, negotiating styles and business practices may pose tremendous obstacles to the progress of negotiations, most respondents perceive these barriers as surmountable. Western firms should take heart that with careful preparation and proper understanding, cultural differences need not impede progress or negatively affect the outcome of business negotiations.

Product characteristics includes two items (a) Japanese did not need products/services offered by the US firm, and (b) too many competitors all offering the same products/services that US company supplies. This finding again points to the extreme competitiveness of the Japanese market and the need for Western firms to offer unique products or services in order to make significant inroads into the Japanese economy.

In the Chinese sample, there are four factors responsible for failure:

1 Cultural differences, including items pertaining to differences in ideology and social customs.
2 Differences in business systems, including items relating specifically to differences in business and negotiation styles.
3 Chinese negotiation characteristics, containing the items 'Chinese insincerity' and 'communication breakdown'. Perceived insincerity on the part of the Chinese and communication breakdown, similar to the Japanese situation, are attributable, by and large, to misunderstandings between the Americans and Chinese.
4 Technical/product characteristics, including the two items of 'Chinese did not need product/service' and 'too many competitors all offering the same products/services'.

The first three factors pertain to differences in societal and business practices between the two countries and highlight the fact that unfamiliarity with cultural differences and failure to bridge the cultural gap can very often lead to the collapse of business negotiations. In the Chinese sample, cultural awareness emerges as the most important factor responsible for both the success and failure of a venture. In other words, familiarity with cultural differences can enhance the chances of success in doing business with the Chinese (see MANAGEMENT IN CHINA).

Relationships between success and negotiation practices

The relationships between incidence of success and certain negotiation practices are examined. Negotiation practices include:

1 Number of previous negotiations with the east Asian partner.
2 Type of industry.
3 Type of trade relationship.
4 Assets of US firm.
5 Types of programmes used in preparing for the negotiations, such as reading books on the host country's business practices and social customs.
6 Hired experts to train negotiators.
7 Use of simulated negotiations.

In the Japanese sample, having had previous negotiations with the Japanese and reading books on Japanese business practices and social customs were significantly associated with success rates. Other explanatory variables, such as type of trade relationship, assets of US firm, hiring of experts to train negotiators and the use of simulated negotiations were not significantly related to success. A marginally significant difference was found for those firms that were engaged in high-technology industries such as engineering, aerospace and electronics.

These findings on the Japanese sample have several implications: first, those firms that plan to enter into trade would benefit from learning about other companies' experiences and thereby avoid pitfalls. Second, certain preparatory procedures designed to familiarize Western negotiators with cultural differences, such as reading books on Japanese business practices, can enhance the incidence of favourable outcomes. Third, firms in various industries and of different sizes can be successful in doing business in Japan. Fourth, in view of the extreme competitiveness of the Japanese market, firms in high technology industries tend to meet with greater incidence of success.

In the Chinese sample, only two independent variables were found to be statistically significant. These were exports and joint ventures with China. All the other independent variables had no significant relationship to the incidence of success. The findings suggest that in light of China's desire to generate and conserve foreign exchange, projects that can facilitate this goal, such as exporting and joint-venture operations which produce items for export or as import substitution, do meet with higher incidence of success. This points to the need to fully understand the contextual environment which governs a negotiation situation.

4 Enhancing success in cross-national negotiations – a checklist

A twenty-point checklist for enhancing success in cross-national negotiations can be developed along the following lines:

1 Study the contextual environments, namely the political, economic, institutional-legal and cultural systems that can affect the process and outcome of negotiations.
2 Study the negotiation context specific to the negotiation situation at hand.
3 Engage in meticulous fact finding and information gathering about one's partner, including their motives and criteria.
4 Understand the market, including the nature and degree of competition, and make an assessment of whether one's products/services are needed in the target market.
5 Be flexible, explore alternative modes of conflict resolution.
6 Respect cultural differences.
7 Include a bilingual member on the negotiation team, where possible.
8 Build and nurture relationships with one's partner, particularly the key decision makers.

9 Be consistent, that is, follow precedents set in earlier negotiations. At the same time, be cognizant of the fact that one may be setting new precedents.
10 Make sure the respective areas of expertise are represented on the negotiation team.
11 In protracted negotiations, provide continuity as far as composition of negotiation team members are concerned.
12 Be patient, allow matters to progress at their own pace.
13 Listen, and ask probing questions.
14 Determine who the negotiation team members of the opposing side are. Do they represent the private or the public sectors? Are they vested with decision-making authority? Cultivate contacts with key decision makers.
15 Assess the options to discontinuing negotiations.
16 Identify common interests.
17 Be well rested – international business negotiations are gruelling, physically and mentally.
18 Pay attention to minute details.
19 Be prepared for the unexpected.
20 Above all else, know yourself.

5 Conclusion

In light of the growing interdependence in the global economic arena, it is imperative that business practitioners develop a greater expertise in negotiation skills, particularly on a cross-cultural basis. According to a survey of 1500 top executives in twenty countries, negotiation and conflict resolution skills ranked four out of ten in terms of requisite skills to be possessed by executives in the twenty-first century (Korn/Ferry International and Columbia University Graduate School of Business 1989).

In addition, various developments are likely to impose greater challenges on negotiation skills. For example, the formation of many and varied forms of cooperative agreements, economic and non-economic, among entities from disparate parts of the world. These include co-production, joint research and development, and co-marketing, many of which are on a project basis. Thus, negotiators must be adept at these new forms of collaborative arrangements. Also, fundamental and rapid changes in the political and economic systems in many countries around the world, such as the dismantling of communism in eastern Europe and the instalment of the first Black president in South Africa, pose new challenges and opportunities for doing business in these countries. Negotiators have to understand the full implications of these developments and operate within these evolving political, economic and societal frameworks.

Additionally, the growing participation of ethnic minorities and women in professional and managerial ranks in many industrialized nations may offer new challenges to negotiations. The approach to business by ethnic minorities may be significantly different from that of the traditional white male majority since the former may still espouse values and attitudes which are part of their ancestors' cultural heritage. Research has shown that there are substantial differences in communication patterns between males and females in North America. Tannen (1990) has coined the term 'genderlect' to characterize such differences. In general, men seek independence over interdependence, prefer conflict over preservation of harmony, engage in report rather than rapport talk, adopt a lecturing rather than listening mode, and use 'yeah' to indicate concurrence rather than 'I am with you' or 'I follow'. Negotiators have to be cognizant of such differences and adjust their styles accordingly.

Good negotiation skills are necessary at almost every phase of a firm's operation in the international arena. Before a firm can enter into a foreign market and begin manufacture and marketing of its products and/or services, it has to negotiate with the host government and/or host country partner (in the event of a cooperative agreement) for the terms and conditions of the entry and/or collaboration. Negotiations are necessary to resolve differences that may arise between the partners throughout the relationship to maintain peaceful coexistence. Should relations deteriorate to the point where one or both partners wish to terminate the agreement, the parties still need to negotiate with each other regarding the terms of dissolution.

The conceptual paradigm of international business negotiations presented in this entry provides an understanding of the dynamics and complexities associated with cross-national negotiations. Practical suggestions, including a checklist of factors to enhance success, are offered to help managers better prepare for managing and operating in an international context.

ROSALIE L. TUNG
SIMON FRASER UNIVERSITY

Further reading

(References cited in the text marked *)

Adler, N.J., Graham, J.L. and Schwarz Gehrke, T. (1987) 'Business negotiations in Canada, Mexico and the United States', *Journal of Business Research* 15: 411–29. (A comparative analysis of styles and patterns of business negotiations among Americans, Canadians and Mexicans.)

* Ballon, R.J. (1986) 'Japan: the government–business relationship', in R.L. Tung (ed.), *Strategic Management in the United States and Japan: A Comparative Analysis*, Cambridge, MA: Ballinger. (An analysis of the relationships between government and business in Japan and how they compare and contrast with those in the West.)

* Fayerweather, J. and Kapoor, A. (1976) *Strategy and Negotiation for the International Corporation*, Cambridge, MA: Ballinger. (Using in-depth case analysis, this book illustrates the complexities and dynamics associated with cross-national business negotiations.)

* Graham, J.L. and Allerheiligen, R. (1983) 'Bargainer characteristics and international business negotiations', paper presented at the National Meeting of the Academy of International Business, San Francisco, 27–30 December. (An investigation of how specific negotiator characteristics relate to negotiation outcome.)

* Hall, E.T. and Hall, M. (1987) *Hidden Differences: Doing Business with the Japanese*, Garden City, NY: Anchor Press. (An insightful analysis of the similarities and differences between Americans and Japanese in their approach to and conduct of business.)

* Jang, S.H. (1988) 'Managing joint venture partnership in Korea', paper presented at the Korean–American Business Institute, Annual Seminar on Doing Business in Korea, Seoul,

3–4 May. (A practical guide to successful cooperation between US and Korean partners in joint-venture relationships.)

* Korn/Ferry International and Columbia University Graduate School of Business (1989) *Twenty-first Century Report: Reinventing the CEO*, New York: Korn/Ferry International & Columbia University Graduate School of Business. (A survey of senior executives of large companies on the requisites for becoming CEOs in the twenty-first century.)

Lewicki, R.J., Weiss, S.E. and Lewin, D. (1992) 'Models of conflict, negotiation and third party processes: a review and synthesis', *Journal of Organizational Behavior* 13: 209–52. (A literature review of models of negotiation and conflict resolution.)

* McClendon, J.S. (1985) 'Dispute resolution: a critical part of the international business negotiation process', paper presented at the National Meetings of the Academy of International Business, New York, 19 October. (A discussion of the alternative methods of conflict resolution in the international business context, with a specific focus on arbitration.)

* Peterson, R.B. and Shimada, J.Y. (1978) 'Sources of management problems in Japanese–American joint ventures', *Academy of Management Review* 3 (4): 796–804. (An examination of the problems associated with US–Japanese cooperative agreements.)

* Raiffa, H. (1982) *The Art and Science of Negotiation*, Cambridge, MA: Harvard University Press. (A comprehensive analysis of the salient issues and dynamics associated with negotiations.)

Rubin, J.Z. and Brown, B.R. (1975) *The Social Psychology of Bargaining and Negotiation*, New York: Academic Press. (A socio-psychological approach to negotiations and bargaining behaviour.)

* Strauss, A.L. (1978) *Negotiations, Varieties, Contexts, Process, and Social Order*, San Francisco, CA: Jossey Bass. (An insightful analysis of the different types of negotiations and the contexts in which they occur.)

* Tannen, D. (1990) *You Just Don't Understand: Men and Women in Conversation*, New York: Ballantine. (An analysis of the gap in communication patterns between men and women.)

* Tung, R.L. (1984) *Business Negotiations with the Japanese*, Lexington, MA: D.C. Heath. (A survey and case studies of business negotiations between US and Japanese companies.)

* Tung, R.L. (1988) 'Toward a conceptual paradigm of international business negotiations', in R.D.

Farmer (ed.), *Advances in International Comparative Management*, vol. 3, Greenwich, CT: JAI Press. (A conceptual paradigm of international business negotiations is posited, based on a literature review of existing approaches to negotiations.)

* Tung, R.L. (1989) 'A longitudinal study of United States–China business negotiations', *China Economic Review* 1 (1): 57–71. (A longitudinal study tracking the outcome of business negotiations between US and Chinese firms from 1979 to 1987.)

* Tung, R.L. (1991) 'Handshakes across the sea: cross-cultural negotiating for success', *Organizational Dynamics* 14 (3): 30–40. (A study of business negotiations between US and South Korean firms, including key factors for success.)

* Van Zandt, H.F. (1970) 'How to negotiate in Japan?', *Harvard Business Review*, November–December: 45–56. (A guide to successful negotiations with the Japanese.)

Wall, J.A., Jr (1985) *Negotiation: Theory and Practice*, Glenview, IL: Scott, Foresman. (An analysis of negotiations with implications for theory and practice.)

Weiss, S.E. (1993) 'Analysis of complex negotiations in international business: the RBC perspective', *Organization Science* 4 (2): 269–300. (A literature review and development of a new paradigm of international business negotiations.)

* Zartman, I.W. (ed.) (1976) *The 50% Solution*, New York: Anchor Press. (A collection of articles on salient issues pertaining to negotiations and conflict resolution.)

See also: BOEING COMPANY; BUSINESS STRATEGIES, EAST ASIAN; CULTURE, CROSS-NATIONAL; ECONOMIES OF EAST ASIA; GLOBAL STRATEGIC ALLIANCES; GLOBAL STRATEGIC PLANNING; GLOBALIZATION; INTERNATIONAL BUSINESS, LEGAL DIMENSIONS OF; INTERNATIONAL MARKETING; INTERNATIONAL TRADE AND FOREIGN DIRECT INVESTMENT; MANAGEMENT IN CHINA; MANAGEMENT IN JAPAN; MITSUBISHI HEAVY INDUSTRIES, LTD; MORITA, AKIO; ORGANIZATION CULTURE

Related topics in the IEBM: BUSINESS CULTURE, JAPANESE; BUSINESS CULTURE, NORTH AMERICAN; DECISION-MAKING; GLOBALIZATION AND SOCIETY; MANAGEMENT IN CHINA; MANAGEMENT IN JAPAN; MITSUBISHI HEAVY INDUSTRIES, LTD; MORITA, AKIO; ORGANIZATION CULTURE; MANAGEMENT IN NORTH AMERICA; MANAGEMENT

IN PACIFIC ASIA; MANAGEMENT IN SOUTH
AFRICA; ORGANIZATION BEHAVIOUR; OR-
GANIZATION STRUCTURE; STRATEGY-
MAKING, POLITICS OF; TECHNOLOGY
STRATEGY, INTERNATIONAL

International marketing

1 **Definitional issues**
2 **Behavioural and economic theories of internationalization**
3 **Modes of foreign market entry**
4 **Factors in market success**

Overview

This entry takes an overview of international marketing, beginning with definitional issues concerning the nature of the subject. Behavioural and economic theories of international marketing are discussed, including stages theories, the random approach and networks. The entry then proceeds to discuss modes of foreign market entry, looking at standard marketing elements such as product, price, promotion and distribution in an international perspective. As well, issues specific to international marketing are examined, such as standardization and customization. The entry concludes with a discussion of the key factors necessary for success in international marketing.

1 Definitional issues

The literature on international marketing, while continuing to evolve, has now reached a critical mass. From around 1980 onwards, there have been a number of different attempts to review the international marketing literature as a body. Cavusgil and Nevin (1981, 1983) and Li and Cavusgil (1991) attempted to summarize and classify research streams and development. Bradley (1986) focused on developments in the systems-exchange paradigm looking at the structure in which developments are taking place, while Douglas and Craig (1992) undertook a study of advances in international marketing from the purely descriptive to the managerial and strategic, and tied this into a framework of three key phases: initial foreign market entry, local national market expansion and global

rationalization. Ford and Leonidou (1992) reviewed research developments in international marketing from a European perspective, while Gemunden (1992) reviewed success factors of export marketing in a meta-analytic critique of empirical studies.

It is generally agreed that competition now takes place on a global scale (see GLOBALIZATION). However, international marketing has suffered from a definitional problem, in much the same way that marketing itself has had difficulty in finding a suitable definition. Marketing has often been used simply as a preferred term for 'selling'. In international marketing, however, the essential tasks tend to be more managerial and strategic in focus. There are four key characteristics of international marketing:

1 International marketing is about the development of foreign markets for the longer term. In this context, closeness to the customer and the ability and willingness to allocate scarce resources to modify products and promotion is often what separates success from failure.
2 International marketing is a later stage of internationalization involving direct investment in a foreign presence, that is accompanied by experience gained through simple exporting (see EXPORTING).
3 Standardization becomes an important issue, although the focus must still be on the customer; international marketing offers possible benefits and economies of scale, but these can only be realized provided customers continue to buy. International offerings which have been standardized to the point of blandness may fail for that reason alone. There is little difference between a production orientation, which marketing students are taught is wrong, and an international or global standardization strategy which fails to recognize individuals as customers. Where products or

technologies are new, such a strategy may succeed, but not in growing or mature markets where competitors are keen to develop differential advantages.

4 International segmentation strategies make international marketing possible. Instead of fixating on what makes people different, it is more effective and profitable to determine common wants and needs. The category of needs is more easily discernible than the category of wants, particularly when applied across international markets. However, groups of people with similar outlooks and wants can be identified and pinpointed more easily than ever before, due to the advent of computerization and the ability to profile consumers according to socio-economic, geographic and lifestyle data. The result is a powerful marketing tool that allows companies to test market and produce infinite versions of standard products so as to meet accurately the wants of a particular market segment.

2 Behavioural and economic theories of internationalization

There are a number of prominent theories of internationalization which are relevant to international marketing. The 'stages theory' of the Uppsala School (Turnbull and Valla 1986; Rao and Naider 1992) posits an incremental and sequential pattern, suggesting that companies begin by using agents and steadily increasing their investment until they acquire or create a wholly-owned subsidiary. Eclectic theory, advanced by Dunning (1981, 1988), brought together three strands of economic theory: *internalization advantages*, which account for why it is more profitable for the firm to market its products itself rather than sell them or the right to use them to a foreign firm; *locational advantages*, which make it more profitable to have resources based in the foreign market rather than service it with exports; and *ownership advantages*, which may comprise intangible assets such as know-how and patents, which nevertheless constitute an advantage relative to firms of

other nationalities in the same foreign market. Internalization theory was further developed by Rugman (1983), but has so far failed to explain the scope of international marketing relative to production. Another early theory of foreign direct investment and internationalization was the product life cycle for international trade as developed by Wells (1968) and Vernon (1966, 1979); however, this theory has now been largely discredited and set aside as irrelevant to contemporary trading conditions.

There has also been a great deal of research on exporting in recent years, beginning with the work of Johanson and Weidersheim-Paul (1975) and including Bilkey and Tesar (1977) and Cavusgil and Nevin (1980). These studies examined the behaviour of exporters (rather than marketers) and established that there were stages in their development as well. One of the most significant findings was the discovery of psychic or psychological distance, whereby exporters feel more comfortable in exporting (initially, at least) to markets which are psychologically close to their own. This led then to the concept of an extended domestic market or regional market prior to full internationalization (see EXPORTING).

Cavusgil and Li (1991), in their summary of international marketing literature, identified seven broad types of study:

1 environmental studies of international marketing;
2 comparative studies of market systems;
3 international marketing management;
4 internationalization process perspectives;
5 buyer behaviour studies;
6 interaction approach;
7 market globalization perspectives.

The issue in international marketing now is not why companies go abroad but, given that they seek to do so, is there a pattern or patterns which they can follow which would allow them to trace their progress and perhaps see ahead to what the next steps might involve. In the past the main theories in this area stemmed directly from economics and so describe test tube conditions, rather than volatile market conditions where human beings are the key focus. Today, however, a great deal of attention is now being paid to relationship marketing and network marketing as an explanation for international marketing expansion.

A staged approach or random action?

Cavusgil and Li (1991) suggest that there are two different processes at work, a *sequential* process and a *random* process. In the former, firms go through different stages in a sequential order, while in the latter process firms bypass or leap over certain stages.

The choice of the word random, however, can lead to misinterpretation in that it may unintentionally convey the impression that firms lack a strategy if they do not pursue sequential stages of internationalization. This in turn gives a false impression that there is a right way and a wrong way to pursue internationalization. In fact, the mode of foreign market entry must always be contingent upon the specific situation of the target market, including projections of market potential and the resources that the company is willing and able to devote to that market, given a certain level of risk and assumed payback period. This may in turn suggest that some market stages can and should be skipped.

Cavusgil and Li also discuss the interaction approach, which was developed in Sweden the 1970s and later reinvented in North America in the 1990s. The interaction approach, devised by the IMP Group of researchers, challenges existing marketing thinking which is strongly based on the principle of the four Ps. From their empirical research, the IMP Group have shown convincingly that the four Ps model is too simple to reflect reality, as it assumes there is no serious competition in the market and that buyers are passive. The reality of the situation is that markets are dynamic and that buyers are astute and knowledgeable. This has been established in various published studies, notably Håkansson (1982).

Networks as an explanation

Johanson and Mattson (1986) view the industrial system composed of firms engaged in the production, distribution and use of goods and services as a network of relationships, where firms are free to choose their counterparts and market forces are at play. Each firm in the network has relationships first with customers, distributors and suppliers, and then with the suppliers' suppliers, customers' customers and so on. Networks are stable but not static, and most exchange takes place within the framework of established relationships. Efforts therefore should be made to maintain, develop and change the relationships. This implies that the firm's activities in industrial markets are cumulative processes where relationships are constantly established, maintained, developed and broken in order both to give satisfactory short-term economic return and to create positions in the network, thus securing the long-term survival and development of the firm. The internationalization of the firm means that the firm establishes and develops positions in relation to counterparts in foreign networks.

3 Modes of foreign market entry

In international marketing no two markets are the same, just as within particular domestic markets, no two consumers are exactly alike. One of the most common mistakes in international marketing is to assume that market segments within the same geographical region will exhibit the same characteristics. Even where this may be broadly true, the generalizations may serve to conceal real and existing differences. Further, while it may be easy to identify market segments across countries, it is often considerably more difficult to justify their viability in terms of size, measurability, access, ability and willingness to buy. For example, Bulgaria has a population of around nine million and a Turkish minority of around one million. This does not necessarily mean that the Turkish community can be isolated as a segment; not unless the firm in question can provide a product that will appeal to all members of the community irrespective of individual characteristics such as age, socio-economic class and personal disposable earnings.

Where viable segments can be identified, the strategies required to meet those markets will vary depending on a variety of geographical and cultural factors. Distribution is one obvious example of variance; different countries with similar market segments may well have very different distribution systems, necessitating strategic changes. There is no one correct mode of foreign market entry; instead, firms should adopt a contingency approach to international markets and to being prepared to accept a portfolio of market entry methods best suited to the particular market in question. Over time, markets and market segments may change radically or even disappear altogether. There must be a readiness to always challenge the status quo and ensure that the firm achieves the best possible fit with the market in question (see FOREIGN MARKET ENTRY STRATEGIES).

Logistical decisions

In international marketing, it is particularly important to know how products are brought to market. The crucial logistical questions are those which concern speed to market and enduring corporate policy. Technology can create new opportunities as well as threats. An example can be found in the management education market for MBA degrees, which were for many years the premier business qualification. Recently, however, the market has changed and students who might have chosen full-time MBA programmes are increasingly looking for qualifications that can be achieved through part-time study, creating a growing market for executive, modular and distance learning programmes. In the past this market opportunity might well have been passed over. However, technology now provides academic institutions with the means of communication for delivering programmes in a variety of ways. Teleconferencing, audio and video cassette tapes as well as study guides and work books facilitate a new type of distance learning that is becoming increasingly accepted. Competition, consumer pull and technology push have helped bring these realities to market.

Another example can be found in retail banking. Banks now find that, in Western countries, only about 30 per cent or fewer of their customers actually go into a branch; the remainder use automated teller machines (ATMs) outside the bank or conduct their business over the telephone, giving instructions for deposits and withdrawals without ever making face-to-face human contact. Added service, and therefore value to the customer, lies in the number of machines which the bank has and the services which these machines are able to provide. There is thus a constant relationship between investment and technology. Speed, reliability, dependability and customer access are important criteria.

Segmentation and mass customization

As well as customer service, information technology provides firms with access to databanks and the computing power to analyse data and pinpoint likely marketing prospects. From the mass marketing of the Model T Ford of the 1920s to the present day, many significant changes have taken place. Marketers are able to break market demand down into component parts and identify segments within a market. The danger lies in analysing a market so that it becomes fragmented rather than segmented. Without the ability to measure a market segment, access it and establish an ability and willingness to buy, there is in effect no viable market segment in existence. Again, it is worth noting the limitations of geographical segmentation; segments cross over national frontiers and the same marketing strategy may work in different countries. Skiers are one example of an international market segment.

Continuous improvement and mass customization, compared with market fragmentation, require very different organizational value management roles and systems. This was discovered by Toyota, which reduced its range of models by one-fifth when it was discovered that 20 per cent of the range accounted for 80 per cent of sales (Pine *et al.* 1993). In mass customization, the basic design of the product is assumed to be what customers want; technically elegant features that add to manufacturing cost are valueless if customers do not want them. Continuous improvement can be a subset of mass customization, but it does not work the other way round. Continuous improvement may be subsumed under mass customization, but the latter cannot serve as an overall guiding strategy for an organization.

Distribution channel selection

How and where a product is presented and at what price is crucial to market success. Positioning is all-important. When intermediaries are used in foreign markets, whether they are agents or direct distributors, it is important to recognize that these intermediaries hold the company name in trust. Accordingly, firms must give the kind of support that will enable intermediaries to compete effectively in their local market. Responsibility for market representation and customer handling is a shared activity except where there is desire to allocate blame.

When choosing a distribution strategy, firms have three basic options:

1 use the same distribution channels that they themselves use in other markets;
2 use the same distribution channels as other competitors in the target market;
3 innovate and develop a distribution channel that is completely new to both the target market and the firm.

Distribution strategy must reflect product positioning and the implied relationship between price and quality, and a particular distribution strategy will clearly have an impact on other marketing mix variables. Distribution channels must be responsive to the customer needs, and will undergo greater change through the product life cycle than will the products themselves. Personal computers provide a good example of a distribution evolution from specialist retail outlets to department stores and general retailers. The needs of the consumer become less as the product matures, and the customer is better informed and therefore better able to make a judgement. Information and technical support become less important, although they may

still influence individual sales. Internationally, distribution channels are changing and there is a clear trend emerging of shorter distribution channels between manufacturers and customers.

Branding and country of origin

As product specifications become widely disseminated, they assume a certain threshold knowledge level, customers become less reliant on the need for specialist knowledge and information and instead assume responsibility for their own product decisions. Price now becomes a decision criteria. Branding has taken over from country of origin in terms of importance as a product feature. The multinational corporation has displaced the nation-state in terms of consumer acceptance of products, reliability and dependability from one batch to another and assurance of quality implicit in the brand name; the maker's name now carries more weight as a consumer choice criterion than the country in which the product is made. This has given rise to a variety of activities both legal and illegal, such as parallel importing and counterfeiting.

However, branding is still affected to some degree by country of origin associations, which can be negative as well as positive. Common examples include US-manufactured consumer products such as Coca-Cola, which can suffer when local feeling turns against the USA. Coca-Cola is a quintessentially American product, though there are not very many products with such global portability. Fast moving consumer goods are the favourites; next come computers, cars and durables, purchased less often but with a cachet related to the manufacturer and the manufacturer's perceived country of origin (see MARKETING MANAGEMENT, INTERNATIONAL).

Pricing

Pricing is not a variable that can be standardized internationally except within a fixed percentage band, as currencies are subject to exchange rate fluctuations. Differences in taxation structure and in general and specific duties further complicate the situation and can render a competitive product uncompetitive. One of the most dangerous factors in this regard is the countervailing duty, whereby the government of the target market, responding to local market pressure, decides to act to protect local industry. In this case the price of the imported goods is brought up to the level of the nearest domestic competitor; the gap between the two is filled by the countervailing duty.

Costs of importing, duties and tariffs payable upon entry, plus the costs of the distribution channel and its expectations of discounts and rebates together with expected level of service, all serve to set pricing parameters. Analysis of all these factors will reveal the necessary target price that has to be set at the factory gate in order to make exports to a particular market competitive. On the other hand, pricing can be used as a strategic tool just as in domestic markets for buying market share; pricing is also an effective means of product positioning and enhancing the prestige and exclusivity of a brand.

Promotion

Being able to handle the different and unusual is a requirement of international marketing, and nowhere does this apply more strongly than in the field of promotions. Personal reactions to promotional strategies are extremely varied. Free samples from manufacturers, for example, are often regarded with annoyance by people in western Europe or North America; in Poland, on the other hand, the people who receive free samples write 'thank you' letters to the manufacturers.

In international as in domestic markets, technology is changing the face of promotion. The shift from advertising to direct mail is continuing, and new media such as interactive diskettes and multimedia computer shopping via modem or television are in development. Satellite television is broadening the scope of promotion as it terminates national control over television broadcasting.

All this does not mean that micro issues can be ignored, and care has to be taken to ensure promotions are effective in each local marketplace. For example, even countries with small populations, such as Canada and Belgium, may have more than one official language plus several unofficial ones; failure to recognize these languages may lead to alienation of one consumer group or the other, as people like to be spoken to in their own language. Further, local advertising and packaging regulations may require local language content or bilingual labelling.

Language is particularly important in advertising in that spoken or written text is, along with visual imagery, one of the two key elements of any advertising campaign. It assumes that the company is at the same stage of market development in all markets and targeting essentially similar customers; BMW is an excellent example of a company which superbly positions its product line internationally with claims such as 'the ultimate driving machine'. The challenge of language is less in the direct translation than in rendering meaningful all the more subtle nuances of the original text. Compared with English, Latin languages require 20 to 25 per cent more space, and German and Scandinavian languages 25 to 30 per cent more (Gruber 1984).

What translates most easily is a simple concept which lends itself to visual imagery. Institutional advertising is particularly successful in this regard, following a strategy of promoting the company and cultivating customer loyalty with less concentration on the product itself; this is a strategy which has been followed for some years by oil companies, in particular. The latter have sought to differentiate themselves by adding extra service or value, such as free car washes or weekly price specials, in order to encourage customer loyalty. Portrayal of social responsibility and care for customer concerns are also frequent themes of institutional advertising, which can be seen as a form of 'topping up' the advertising activities of local outlets, hopefully providing further good reasons for customers to continue being loyal to that company (see AD-VERTISING STRATEGY, INTERNATIONAL).

4 Factors in market success

Market success is ultimately dependent on brand awareness, brand availability, quality, value and customer service support as perceived by the customer, and quality of sales representation as perceived by the distribution channel. In order to market overseas the company must be able not only to match the best of local foreign market competition but also to maintain sufficient competitive advantage in what the company is able to offer as to stay ahead of the local competitors. Good communication is therefore essential with the foreign target market; the firm must know its foreign customers and create unique value for them. Checklists of factors of which the international marketing executive should be aware and should build into market planning are to be found under each separate component of the marketing mix as detailed in Paliwoda (1994).

There is strength in seeking to replicate market success gained elsewhere. To that extent, success in international marketing may be seen as an extension of what is done domestically. However, the issue is more complicated than this, and it may be useful to consider what is required in terms of the 'nine Ps', as developed by Paliwoda (1994):

1 People. The service element in any transaction is becoming increasingly important. Consider the people who are representing your company abroad as carefully as you consider your customers. Investigate and get to know them well, know their dislikes and likes and how they like to be treated (including issues of language). This will heighten your competitive advantage and may reveal needs in training or infrastructural investment.

2 Process. The means by which a company goes abroad vary, as does the rationale. The process requires planning, commitment and motivation for success to ensue. Consider the cost factors involved in servicing the chosen foreign target market, and build the extra costs of servicing that market relative to the home market into all projections of returns from that market. Determine what is to be the level of pres-

ence necessary for effective representation given all available data on what the company can afford and how it views the strategic importance of that particular market, now and for the future. Internationalization as a process goes beyond exporting to involve investment in resources overseas, and customers overseas.

3 Power. Domestic competitive advantage is not automatically transferable with any given degree of success. Many domestic companies have taken a strong home market product and moved it overseas hoping for similar success, but this success has eluded them. This may be due to a number of factors, ranging from not reading the market correctly (including non-tariff barriers, lack of supporting infrastructure overseas relative to home and thence weakness in product support and information) to inability of the local consumers to afford or accept the product in question. Power extends to issues related to power over intermediaries, including agents and licensees, and ability to gain control over branded product counterfeits. Opportunity analysis can only be conducted from within a market to form a proper assessment of the market, its size, dynamism and whether or not it is traditional, which will help establish salient operation environment factors as well as opportunities for corporate return on investment and options for public relations, publicity and lobbying activities.

4 Product/service. The service element is now often indistinguishable from the product offering. Branding encapsulates the importance of this form of competitive advantage in a physical form. Standardization and adaptation are the two polar extremes, but research investigation may reveal customer segments across nations which are broadly similar. Adaptation of promotional messages may then create the important local identity or reassurance that local needs are being met. This is not to say that with mass customization there is no genuine attempt to produce an effective variant of a successful product that has been fine-tuned for the market in question.

Perceptions are every bit as important as reality. What the customer receives and what he or she perceives they receive from a product or service may reveal a shortfall that needs to be examined. Therein lies the danger of corporate marketing disasters: branding, packaging, labelling and language are as important as technical specifications.

5 Promotion and publicity. In the last five years there have developed tremendous opportunities for satellite and cable television and database marketing. Print media are also buoyant, but new embryonic media forms such as the Internet have yet to achieve anything significant (though there is no doubt that they have great future potential). Different media availability and local cultural norms and infrastructure explain the impossibility of truly standardizing international promotion. Sales promotion internationally is catching up with other forms of media promotion with the advent of computer database marketing and the immediacy of direct marketing compensation for the lower costs and long lead times of more traditional forms of media promotion.

6 Pricing has many facets. It may be the price at which the product is available and sold on shelves overseas, or it may relate to contract pricing within the distribution channel and the agreement to offer goods on consignment on a sale or return basis, or even perhaps the acceptance of countertrade as a means of payment. These factors greatly influence the price at which goods then enter any given point in the distribution channel. Additional foreign costs are the norm, and so any delays in receiving payment or restrictions on currency or profit repatriation must be investigated ahead of time. Pricing in terms of low price is a disastrous strategy. Instead, companies should seek to offer higher value added; this strategy allows companies of all sizes to compete effectively in the longer term.

7 Place of sale or distribution relates to how goods enter the distribution channel and the basis on which the producer or foreign principal has agreed to supply goods to that particular market. Analysis should be undertaken as to the compatibility of motivations of all parties within the distribution channel to compare expectations ahead of shortfalls occurring in practice. Customer service levels pursued by each member in the distribution channel are perhaps the most obvious and clearly have resource, and therefore cost, implications as well. It is important to identify where the added value is being created for the customer; only where added value is perceived is it real. Otherwise, it is simply an addition to total overhead.

8 Planning and control is usually taken to mean head office control and centralization, whereas there is perhaps more relaxation of controls and more autonomy now being given to subsidiaries overseas. None the less, planning and control require the creation of strategies, and careful monitoring by local experts as well as by head office administration. How and where profits are created and reaped can have significant benefits not just for the tax exposure of the company overall, but also for employee morale. Generally, this can be planned and controlled.

9 Precedents. In the legal sense, we are all aware of landmark judgements which have created change, whether political, legal or social, in marketing. Good practice can be borrowed. This very idea of benchmarking best practice within an industry can give rise to new strategies in foreign markets that are not practised at home. A company may therefore be able to behave abroad as the competitor does in the home market. Learned behaviour can be highly advantageous; for example, learning organizational responses to issues such as environmental backlash to the use of fossil fuels or non-renewable resources can help the company address its critics across markets. It creates focus and so engenders commitment, a key factor for long-term success.

STANLEY J. PALIWODA
UNIVERSITY OF CALGARY

Further reading

(References cited in the text marked *)

* Bilkey, W.J. and Tesar, G. (1977) 'The export behaviour of smaller Wisconsin manufacturing firms', *Journal of International Business Studies* 10 (1): 93–8. (A seminal article on export behaviour.)
* Bradley, F.M. (1986) 'Inquiry and decision in international marketing', *Irish Marketing Review* 1: 131–47. (Study of decision making in international marketing.)
* Cavusgil, S.T. and Li, T. (1991) *International Marketing: An Annotated Bibliography*, Chicago, IL: American Marketing Association. (Fairly wide ranging, but limited to those journals available in the USA.)
* Cavusgil, S.T. and Nevin, J.R. (1980) 'A conceptualisation of the initial involvement in international marketing', in C.W. Lamb, Jr and P.M. Dunne (eds), *Theoretical Development in Marketing*, Chicago, IL: American Marketing Association. (This work arose out of research by Cavusgil into exporter behavioural stages.)
* Cavusgil, S.T. and Nevin, J.R. (1981) 'State of the art in international marketing', in B.M. Enis and K.J. Roering (eds), *Review of Marketing*, Chicago, IL: American Marketing Association. (The first attempt by Cavusgil to bring together the international marketing literature as a body.)
* Cavusgil, S.T. and Nevin, J.R. (1983) *International Marketing: An Annotated Bibliography*, Chicago, IL: American Marketing Association. (An earlier version of Cavusgil and Li (1991); fairly wide-ranging.)
* Douglas, S.P. and Craig, C.S. (1992) 'Advances in international marketing', *International Journal of Research in Marketing* 9: 291–318. (Very well-written overview summarizing the field.)
* Dunning, J.H. (1981) *International Production and the Multinational Enterprise*, London: Allen & Unwin. (This is a landmark in the international business literature.)
* Dunning, J.H. (1988) 'The eclectic paradigm of international production: a restatement and some possible extensions', *Journal of International Business Studies* 19 (1): 1–32. (An elaboration or update of Dunning (1981).)
* Ford, D. and Leonidou, L. (1992) 'Research developments in international marketing: a European perspective', in S.J. Paliwoda (ed.), *New Perspectives on International Marketing*, London: Routledge. (A good summary of research pursued in Europe, and not widely acknowledged.)
* Gemunden, H.G. (1992) 'Success factors of export marketing: a meta-analytic critique of the empirical studies', in S.J. Paliwoda (ed.), *New Perspectives on International Marketing*, London: Routledge. (An excellent and comprehensive analytical review of the literature.)
* Gruber, U. (1984) 'The role of multilingual copy adaptation in international advertising', in S.J. Paliwoda and J.K. Ryans, Jr (eds), *International Marketing Reader*, London: Routledge. (Focuses on the transferability of meaning across languages.)
* Håkansson, H. (1982) *International Marketing and Purchasing of Industrial Goods: An Interaction Approach*, New York: Wiley. (A now famous work in which the author lays many of the foundations of relationship marketing.)
* Johanson, J. and Mattson, L.G. (1986) 'International marketing and internationalization processes – a network approach', in P.W. Turnbull and S.J. Paliwoda (eds), *Research in International Marketing*, London: Croom Helm. (An alternative explanation of internationalization.)
* Johanson, J. and Weidersheim-Paul, F. (1975) 'The internationalization of the firm: four Swedish case studies', *Journal of Management Studies* 12 (3): 305–22. (A very early seminal article on exporter behavioural profiles.)
* Li, T. and Cavusgil, S.T. (1991) 'International marketing: a classification of research streams and assessment on their development since 1982', in *Enhancing Knowledge Development in Marketing*, vol. 2, AMA Educators' Proceedings, Chicago, IL: American Marketing Association. (An attempt to classify different research streams in the literature.)
* Paliwoda, S.J. (1993) *International Marketing*, 2nd edn, Oxford: Butterworth Heinemann. (Textbook with cases, examining individual aspects of the international marketing mix and some trading regions.)
* Paliwoda, S.J. (1994) *Essence of International Marketing*, Hemel Hempstead: Prentice Hall. (A short and concise practitioner-orientated book with useful checklists.)
* Pine, B.J., II, Victor, B. and Boynton, A.C. (1993) 'Making mass customization work', *Harvard Business Review* 71 (September–October): 108–22. (While some advocate segmentation to the nth degree, this study advocates successful standardization.)
* Rao, T.R. and Naider, G.M. (1992) 'Are the stages of internationalization empirically supportable?', *Journal of Global Marketing* 6 (1): 147–70. (The theoretical stages of international marketing are tested in this article.)

* Rugman, A.M. (1983) *New Theories of the Multinational Enterprise*, London: Croom Helm. (Focuses chiefly on internalization, which derives from Dunning.)
* Turnbull, P.W. and Valla, J. (1986) *Strategies for International Industrial Marketing*, London: Croom Helm. (A six-country approach to international marketing at the micro level, focusing on buyers and suppliers.)
* Vernon, R. (1966) 'International investment and international trade in the product cycle', *Quarterly Journal of Economics* (May): 190–207. (The original article on product life cycle theory and international trade.)
* Vernon, R. (1979) 'Product cycle hypothesis in a new international environment', *Oxford Statistical and Economic Papers* (November): 255–67. (A revision of the 1966 product cycle theory of international trade.)
* Wells, L.T., Jr (1968) 'A product life cycle for international trade?', *Journal of Marketing* 32: 1–6. (A Harvard colleague of Vernon, Wells noted how discretionary and luxury items would be influenced by environmental factors.)

See also: ADVERTISING STRATEGY, INTERNATIONAL; EXPORTING; FOREIGN MARKET ENTRY STRATEGIES; GLOBAL STRATEGIC PLANNING; GLOBALIZATION; MARKETING MANAGEMENT, INTERNATIONAL

Related topics in the IEBM: BRANDS; CHANNEL MANAGEMENT; LOGISTICS; MARKETING; MARKETING ENVIRONMENT; MARKETING, FOUNDATIONS OF; MARKETING STRATEGY; NETWORKS AND ORGANIZATIONS; PRICING ISSUES IN MARKETING; RELATIONSHIP MARKETING; SEGMENTATION

International operations

1 **Introduction**
2 **Rethinking the manufacturing strategy**
3 **Key decisions of the international manufacturing strategy**
4 **Major managerial concerns**
5 **Conclusion**

Overview

In the literature on production and operations management, little has been written about the international aspects of the field. How a company with operations in several countries should structure its operations is a question which still, to a large extent, remains unanswered in literature. It is nevertheless an important question nowadays, as many companies become more global in their operations and as even domestic companies are faced with global competitors.

Managers have identified the lack of an adequate manufacturing strategy as one of the main barriers to the effective management of their international manufacturing operations. How to set up and manage an effective and efficient network of plants is a key issue here.

This entry will first explore the main elements of the international network of plants. The benefits of having one or more plants abroad will be analysed and the number of plants in the international network and their optimal size will be discussed. The selection of the plant location is a key decision in the process of building a network of international operations and will also be explored in this entry. Attention will be paid to the allocation of manufacturing competence to the distinct plants in the network and more specifically to the advantages and disadvantages of centralizing the manufacturing functions in the company.

Each plant is just a building block which has to fit in the overall 'architecture' of the international network. Therefore, two theoretical models will be described that provide insights for designing this network 'architecture' of the multinational company.

Next, some of the managerial issues that arise in the operations of such an international plant network will be explored: how to improve the overall productivity of the network; how to optimize the flow of information and the flow of goods within the network; and finally how to transform each plant in the network into a 'virtual' plant.

1 Introduction

Several models have been developed which describe the internationalization strategy options for a company. The model developed by Bartlett and Ghoshal is adopted as the frame of reference for this entry. This model describes how, since the 1980s, many companies have been faced with a growing complexity of their businesses. Whereas traditionally companies had to respond to pressures for global integration or local differentiation, increasingly now they have to respond to both (Bartlett and Ghoshal 1989). Consequently, today many multinational companies develop capabilities to respond to diverse national demands, while at the same time they integrate and coordinate their activities to reduce costs and improve productivity (see MULTINATIONAL CORPORATIONS). Examples are the car or the telecommunication industry. This trend is clearly visible in Europe: the evolution towards a single market has increased the benefits that can be gained from global or at least Pan-European integration (see GLOBALIZATION). The food industry, for example, will probably always have to be responsive to differences in taste across Europe. Preferences for sweet or sour, mild or spicy, vary considerably from north to south and from east to west.

2 Rethinking the manufacturing strategy

These changes force multinational companies to rethink their global strategy in general and to rethink their manufacturing strategy more specifically (see GLOBAL STRATEGIC PLANNING). The same task is challenging domestic companies, as they may face global competitors in the near future. In order to effectively compete with those giant global companies, a small domestic company may decide to go for foreign markets and eventually to establish plants abroad to obtain a cost reduction through economies of scale.

Designing a global manufacturing strategy is not an easy task as there are no straightforward answers that fit any business context. At the same time it is a critical task, as has been shown in a study by Klassen and Whybark in which they identified the barriers to the effective management of international manufacturing operations (Klassen and Whybark 1993). Lack of a global view and manufacturing strategy appeared to be the two most important barriers to effective international operations. The lack of a global view refers to the difficulties managers face when exploring and evaluating opportunities in global markets, and assessing their global competitors. The second barrier, the manufacturing strategy, is directly related to the international operations. This entry will focus on this second barrier and highlight some ideas that will help companies to reformulate their manufacturing strategy in the light of the international operations.

Some of the manufacturing issues discussed are similar to the ones that arise in companies with multiple plants within a single country. As such, the framework which will be developed is to some extent also valid for these domestic companies. Some of these issues become more important in the international context, such as the inter-plant distance. Others are uniquely applicable in companies operating in multiple countries, such as the importance of government incentives and differences in tax systems for the selection of a plant location.

3 Key decisions of the international manufacturing strategy

Whether a multinational company in expansion is in search of new opportunities to operate abroad or it faces a rationalization and restructuring of its foreign operations, the key decisions that have to be made are of the same nature. In both cases a manufacturing strategy plan is needed which focuses on the plant configuration. This plan should answer questions such as: How many plants should the company have ideally? Why should the company operate abroad? Where should these plants be located? What level of competence should each plant have? Which strategic role should be attributed to each plant? Which products should be produced in which plant?

For each of these questions some concepts and models will be described that will be helpful to the managers who are responsible for setting up the plant configuration. It is obvious though that these topics are interdependent and should be discussed jointly on the strategic level of the company. This strategic exercise will result in a coherent set of plants, in which each plant will contribute to the corporate strategy of the company.

Why should the company exploit plants abroad?

Multi-site companies may theoretically consist of several plants, located in a single region or country. There are, however, benefits to be gained from locating the plants on a larger distance, abroad. It is therefore useful to examine in detail what drives a company to locate a plant abroad.

Usually, a company will have a combination of several good reasons for setting up or acquiring a plant abroad. The primary reason to go abroad, which is the main factor that convinces management to go for it, basically falls into one of the following three classes (Ferdows 1989):

1 Access to low cost production input factors (labour, materials, energy and capital). The exploitation of production facilities in

countries in which wages are low can be an important cost advantage, especially for labour intensive industries. There are many examples of companies which for this reason have plants in the Far East or in eastern Europe. The proximity of cheaper raw materials or energy may also be a reason for going abroad. This factor explains, for example, the location of production plants in Saudi Arabia close to the oil fields, or the location of food processors near the agricultural suppliers of fresh fruits or vegetables. The next production factor, capital, may be a factor in choosing among alternative plant locations. A company may, for example, obtain a cheaper loan for capital invested in a certain country. This will, however, seldom be a primary reason or driver to go abroad, but may become important in subsequent iterations for determining the location of the plant.

2 Proximity to the market. The establishment of a production plant in an important market or close to an important customer may have a direct cost influence through a reduction in transport costs. But even more important than these cost effects are the less tangible effects of this decision. Proximity to the customers allows for more rapid and more reliable delivery, which obviously has a positive impact on the service level towards the customers. Plants producing perishable goods, for example, may have to be located near their market. Being close to the customer also facilitates the establishment of a just-in-time relation, which enhances the competitive position of both the producer and the customer. It also encourages customer involvement in product design and development, which is especially important for products that require a high degree of customization. This is, for example, the case for Bekaert, a Belgian steel cord producer, which has established plants close to some of its large customers, mainly multinational producers of tyres, in order to allow for cooperation in technological developments.

3 The proximity to sources of technological knowledge. Proximity to universities, research centres or sophisticated suppliers, competitors and customers makes it possible for the company to absorb know-how and to learn from the experts in these places. This factor explains to a large extent the location of subcontractors near IBM plants, or the location of LEGO plants in Denmark, Switzerland and Japan, three countries with a sophisticated knowledge base on plastics. Apart from technological product or process know-how, a plant may also learn about sophisticated administrative systems of suppliers, customers or competitors. Plants located in Japan, for example, may have the opportunity to learn about the concepts and the philosophy of just-in-time applied in the Japanese plants (see MANAGEMENT IN JAPAN). The exploitation of a plant in a region with qualified engineers, scientists or technicians, or with highly skilled workers also makes it easier to attract these talented people into the company, thus incorporating knowledge into the company through these people. Plants established in the proximity of technological know-how are an important source of knowledge for the company as a whole. They are at the basis of the learning capability of the company. As will be seen later in this entry, it is important to link these plants tightly with the other plants of the company to allow for the diffusion of knowledge across the whole network of plants (De Meyer 1993).

How many plants should the company have ideally?

Theoretically, it is possible to calculate the economically optimal number of plants a company should have. If one can estimate the aggregate capacity required to meet market demand and calculate the optimal plant size, the optimal number of plants is found by dividing the required capacity by the optimal plant size. But how to calculate the optimal plant size?

As its size increases, the plant can exploit more 'economies of scale': the fixed costs are spread over a larger production volume, which makes the cost per unit go down. But at the same time the plant may be subject to 'diseconomies of scale'. As the production output grows, the plant usually has to distribute its products over a larger geographic area, which affects the distribution costs. There may also be a tendency to increase the level of coordination and control more than proportionally, by creating a more bureaucratic organization. Managerial costs per unit of production will, therefore, go up as well. These few examples of diseconomies of scale illustrate that there clearly may be disadvantages to the increase of plant size. If the economies and diseconomies of scale can be identified and quantified, it becomes possible to calculate the optimal plant size (Hayes and Wheelwright 1984).

In practice, however, it may be extremely difficult to estimate the parameters required to calculate the optimal plant size. Moreover, as described in the previous section, a company may have several reasons for exploiting a plant, other than the purely economical, quantifiable reasons. A plant with an economically sub-optimal size may, therefore, very well be justified. The European market, for example, traditionally was a fragmented market, which may have forced companies to produce locally with relatively small plants in multiple countries. The removal of trade barriers, however, has decreased the need for some companies to produce locally in a certain country. This change favours the concentration of production in larger plants, thus allowing the company to approach the optimal plant size.

As the calculated plant size can only be a rough estimate of the optimal size, and as many qualitative factors should also be taken into account, it may be concluded that the calculated size only gives an indication of the ideal plant size and correspondingly of the number of plants a company should establish. It should not be considered as a strict guideline. The economically optimal plant size may change over time. The growing degree of automation, for example, which has taken place in many plants, has changed the cost structure of these production facilities: the proportion of direct labour cost decreases, whereas the proportion of indirect labour and capital cost increases. As a result, the optimal plant size increases. In stagnating or declining markets, this trend towards larger plants inevitably implies a reduction in the number of plants.

A possible disadvantage of an increase in the production volume of the plant might be a loss of flexibility. Traditional production systems often call for a trade-off between production volume on the one hand and product variety on the other hand (Hayes and Wheelwright 1984). The more recent, automated production systems, however, such as flexible manufacturing systems (FMS), computer-aided design or manufacturing (CAD/CAM) or computer-integrated manufacturing (CIM), combine speed and flexibility, thus allowing the company to produce a high variety of products in high volumes (Lei and Goldhar 1991).

Where should these plants be located?

The decision to exploit a plant abroad is only a starting point. Where exactly to locate the plant is the next question. Although the primary reason to go abroad, as described above, gives some direction, it usually leaves several alternatives open. A company may, for example, decide to locate a plant in the USA, in order to reduce transport costs by being closer to the US market. Or it may want to invest in eastern Europe to take advantage of low cost labour. But it may still be undecided about which US state or eastern European country would be most appropriate. Although some location criteria will be strongly linked with the drive to locate the plant abroad, some others can as well become important now, such as environmental issues, expatriate issues, etc.

The main issues that may be important in determining the plant location are listed in Table 1; three of them will be discussed in more detail: access to markets, government incentives and the environment.

Access to markets
Peripherality, which means that the plant is located at a large distance from the important markets, can be a serious disadvantage, as has already been discussed. 'Distance' should not be viewed strictly in terms of miles or kilometres only. The time to transfer goods from producer to customer is in some circumstances more meaningful to define the distance. If, for

example, goods can be transported economically by aeroplane, the 'distance' between Japan and Europe may be fairly short. Customs are another element of 'distance' in this broader sense.

The idea of time rather than mileage as a measure of distance is nicely illustrated in an analogy described by Friberg:

> If, for example, a commercial truck driver who left New York and drove the 5000 or so kilometres to Los Angeles respected all the applicable work and rest rules, he could drive that entire distance at an average speed of 60 kilometres per hour. If that same rule-obeying driver in the same lorry were to leave the Midlands in the United Kingdom, pass by London, and drive down to Athens, also a distance of some 5000 kilometres, he would be able to average only 12 kilometres per hour. It is worth noting that 12 kilometres per hour happens to be the speed of a horse and cart.
>
> (Friberg 1988: 28):

The elimination of customs in the unified Europe has definitely shortened this 'time distance' between the Midlands and Athens.

Government incentives

Especially in the case of developing regions or regions with high unemployment, national government sometimes offers financial incentives to encourage manufacturing investment in the region. Within Europe, incentives are also provided by the EU for some of its regions. Among the criteria which are regularly used to decide upon the attribution of a government grant are: the number of jobs created in the region; the degree of export orientation; the technological content of the product or process; and the degree of use of local suppliers and local raw material (Ernst & Young 1992).

The environment

Since the late 1980s there has been a growing awareness about the impact of industrial activities on the environment (Ernst & Young 1992). There is severe pressure on business to invest in the protection, and even improvement, of the environment. Research has shown that within Europe the nature and the size of the environmental problems vary from one country to the next and so does the country's capability to solve these problems. This shows that the environment is clearly an issue which should be taken into account when choosing a plant location.

Many aspects of the environment may influence the working conditions and the productivity of the workers. Poor air quality, for example, appears to reduce human and plant activity. Perhaps even more important is the fact that environmental regulations restrict the location choice of the company. If, for example, regulations concerning waste disposal vary across countries – as is the case in Europe – it may happen that a plant would get an exploitation permission in one country but not in another.

What level of competence should each plant have?

The previous discussions have brought us now to the point where we have a set of plants in different countries, which have been chosen on a rational basis. The question remains how to organize and coordinate this set of plants.

In order to manage the manufacturing function in the company, some level of competence is required in several managerial tasks, such as planning, procurement, product and process development, maintenance and production. One possible option is to centralize these tasks in headquarters or in a central plant. This clearly has the advantage that corporate management has full control over the operations in the plants. Centralization also avoids duplication of effort. With decentralized product development for example there is a risk of having multiple development teams working on a similar product. Another advantage of the centralized approach is that it creates more uniformity among the plants. Finally, centralization makes it easier to obtain a critical mass in the manufacturing function, such as product and process development, or procurement, where centralization increases the bargaining power of the company as larger

Table 1 Location criteria

Labour	labour cost
	productivity
	absenteeism
	labour availability (the possibility to find skilled workers)
	social regulations
	strength of the unions
Raw materials	cost of raw materials
	availability of raw materials
	quality of raw materials
	reliability of raw materials
Access to the market	distance (time) to customer
	customs
	tariff barriers
Property costs	property or rental costs of land, plants and offices
Transport	cost of transport
	availability and quality of transport infrastructure (air, road, rail or ship transport)
	availability and quality of transport organizations
Telecommunication	telecommunication cost
	availability and quality of the communication network
Energy	cost of energy
	availability of electricity, gas, oil or coal
Government incentives	financial incentives to encourage manufacturing investment
Taxes	structure of the tax system
	tax rates
Environment	state of the environment (water, air, noise, land, climate)
	environmental regulations
Expatriate issues	personal tax systems
	cost of accommodation, cost of living
	work permit requirements
	availability and quality of international schools
	crime rate
	quality of life

Source: Haigh (1990); Ernst and Young (1992)

volumes may be purchased from a single supplier.

But the loss of control and efficiency which is inherent in decentralization may be counterbalanced by the advantages of decentralizing managerial tasks. Decentralized planning, procurement and product development, for example, increase the ability of the plants to respond to market needs more flexibly and rapidly. It allows the plants to be innovative and to develop new or improved products in cooperation with the customers.

It is clear that each company should attempt to achieve the delicate balance of centralization and decentralization of the manufacturing tasks. This balance should not necessarily be the same for each manufacturing function, nor should it be the same for each plant in the company. A company may have good reasons to limit the investment in managerial competence in one plant, which will then produce products developed elsewhere, according to a plan imposed on the plant. At the same time the company may provide room for an ample manufacturing staff in another plant, which will then be the designer plant for new products or which will take the lead in, for example, quality management or just-in-time for the company as a whole.

The four key decisions which have been described up to this point are to some extent decisions concerning each plant separately. They provide the building blocks, the components, of the company's plant network. In order to make sure that 'the whole is more than the sum of its parts' these building blocks must be assembled into a well-considered architecture. In the following two sections two theoretical models will be described which provide insights for designing the network architecture of the multinational company.

Network architecture: the strategic role of the plants

The two characteristics of a plant which have been described above – the primary reason for its existence and exploitation, and the extent of manufacturing tasks allocated to the plant – in combination determine the 'strategic role' or 'charter' of the plant. This strategic role in fact gives an idea of how and to what extent the plant may contribute to the strategic mission of the company as a whole, ranging from plants that merely act as implementors of plans developed outside of the plant to plants that are key players in the attempt of the company to outperform its competitors.

The model describing the strategic roles of plants has been developed by Ferdows (1989) and is shown in Figure 1. Ferdows distinguishes six different types of plants:

1 The offshore plant. The plant has been established essentially to utilize local cheap production input factors. Managerial investment in the plant is kept to the minimum essential to run the production efficiently.

2 The source plant. As the offshore plant, the source plant has been established essentially to utilize local cheap production input factors, but it has more managerial assets and a lot more autonomy than the offshore plant. The strategic role of the source plant is more substantial, as it may become a focal point for the development and/or production of specific components or products and for the design or improvement of specific production processes.

3 The server plant. The server plant is established for serving a national or regional market, with a minimum level of managerial investment, sufficient to run the production efficiently. Its role is essentially limited to the manufacturing of the products for the market.

4 The contributor plant. As the server plant, the contributor also serves a specific national or regional market, but its strategic role goes beyond just supplying products. It is comparable to the source plant in that it develops know-how for the company and as such contributes to the competitive advantage of the company.

5 The outpost plant. The outpost collects useful information from universities or research centres, or from technologically advanced competitors, suppliers or customers and it transfers this information to headquarters or other plants in the company. It has been set up though with relatively little local competence. Empirical studies have yielded very few examples of outpost plants. Presumably, it is extremely difficult for a plant to tap into local technological know-how without giving any know-how in return to the technologically advanced partners in the region. It may, therefore, be unrealistic to collect information through a plant without investing in the expertise within the plant.

6 The lead plant. The lead plant is located in a technologically advanced region and has developed a large competence base in manufacturing. Its role is to tap into local technological resources but, unlike the outpost plant, the lead plant has the ability to use this information effectively. The lead plant acts as a partner of headquarters in developing manufacturing capabilities within the company. It is often the 'centre of excellence',

where products are developed and produced for the global market.

The advantage of this model is that it allows the management team of a company to 'map' the set of plants according to their strategic roles. This map clearly shows eventual imbalances in the set of plants and highlights opportunities for further development of plants. A possible conclusion may be, for example, that a company is not as customer oriented as it claims to be, if the classification shows a lack of contributor or server plants. Or vice versa, if the classification shows a relatively large number of servers and contributors, one may realize that cutting costs may require a restructuring and reorientation of the set of plants of the company.

As Figure 1 shows, this model is not static. There seems to be an evolution of the plants 'upward' in the model. Plants abroad usually start as offshore or server plants. But over the years, if these plants stay in their original role, which implies that there will be relatively little local competence, the plant may fall behind in productivity, as there are few manufacturing managers capable of maintaining a high rate of improvement. Second, those plants contribute very little to the company as a whole or, otherwise stated, the company as a whole might be missing an opportunity to benefit from local expertise and market know-how. And third, by treating the plant merely as a supplier of products, the company certainly does not create a challenging environment for the local management team. In the long run, this may demotivate the local managers and at the same time make it more difficult to convince talented people to join the plant.

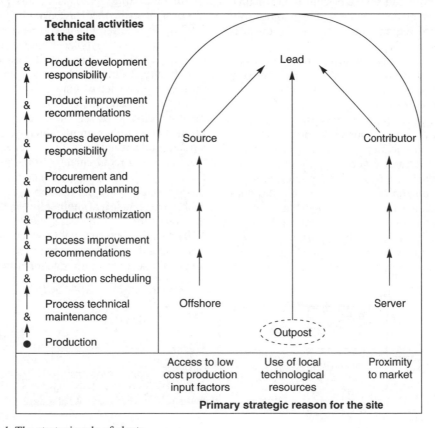

Figure 1 The strategic role of plants
Source: Ferdows (1989)

These observations explain why it is desirable for a company to invest in its plants' competence, in order to allow the plants to fulfil a more substantial strategic role. It is striking that world-class manufacturers have proportionally more source, contributor or lead plants in their network than the average global companies (Ferdows 1997). But even without an explicit, top-down decision to develop local competence, some plants seem to follow a natural way upwards in the model. The pressure to reduce time-to-market or to increase customer service, for example, may stimulate local management to develop the local competence base. Similarly, one may argue that managers will spontaneously seek the control of a growing amount of competencies and assets, as this increases their status and prestige within the company. So there is a bottom-up pressure of the plants as well, which makes them grow into source or contributor plants. For those plants located in a technologically advanced region a move further up towards the lead role is possible.

Other, usually less successful, plants may disappear from the 'map' as the company closes down the plant or sells it to another company. Reasons for this can be the competitive pressure to reduce costs, which may call for a concentration of the production in a smaller number of plants, as described earlier, or the appearance of new opportunities. The fall of the Iron Curtain, for example, has made many companies move part of their production facilities to eastern Europe, thus decreasing their production in western Europe: eastern Europe offers the opportunity to benefit from low wages; at the same time, the distance between the plant and the mother company is small compared to a plant in the Far East, so that transportation costs are reasonable and communication with the local management team is not hampered.

Network architecture: the focus of the plants

The fact that a plant is located in a certain region mainly for reasons of cost, market or technology has been discussed. It has been argued that some manufacturing functions may be run on a centralized basis, whereas others may better be delegated to the plants. But up to now we have no criterion that may help us decide which products or components to produce in which plant. From the point of view of the company, there is a whole portfolio of products which have to be allocated to the plants.

An interesting approach to this problem has been described by Hayes and Schmenner (1978). They argue that a company has the choice between two – polar – organizing principles: the product focus and the process focus. Figure 2 clarifies the two approaches through a simplified example.

In the product-focused company each plant is responsible for the production of a product or a product group which consists of similar products in terms of market needs and manufacturing requirements. In the process-focused company each plant concentrates on a distinct stage of the production process. As such, each plant is just another link in the production chain.

The choice between the product and process focus has strong implications for the range of tasks of the corporate manufacturing

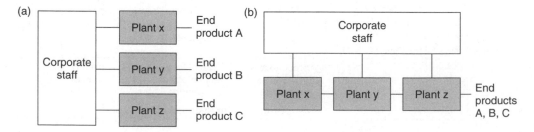

Figure 2 Two forms of organizing principle: (a) the product focus and (b) the process focus

staff and the plant management. The plants in a process-focused company in general operate less autonomously than the plants in a product-focused company. The reason is obvious: by spreading the distinct stages of a production process over more than one production unit, coordination is required to get a product out of the process-focused organization. Usually decisions concerning capital, technology and product development will be made locally in the product-focused company, whereas they will be centralized in corporate staff for the process-focused company. The production plan of the process-focused company is usually more complicated as it should be an integrated plan for the plants, whereas the production plan for a product-focused plant is relatively independent of the plan for other plants in the company. The higher level of coordination required in the process-focused company implies that, in general, this type of company has a lower degree of flexibility: it is more difficult to introduce new products rapidly or to change the output level of the plants. On the other hand, it offers opportunities for cost reduction through economies of scale (Hayes and Schmenner 1978).

Up to here, the product/process focus issue has been presented as if any company can go for either one or the other. In reality it is not that simple. The factors influencing the choice between the two options may be different for distinct product lines or business segments of one company. The message here is not that the two options should not co-exist within one company, but rather that if they co-exist, they should be separated managerially as much as possible. We have argued before that the two options place different demands on the corporate staff and the plant managers. Adopting the two approaches within the same organization, under the same managerial structure, will create confusion and conflicts of interest. This implies that the transfer of products between a plant in the process-focused part of the company and a plant in the product-focused part should not be coordinated by the corporate staff, but should rather happen through negotiation between the plants (Hayes and Schmenner 1978).

Research has shown that within Europe many multinational companies, anticipating the shift of the European market from a fragmented towards a more integrated market, have moved towards a clear product or process focus (Collins *et al.* 1989) (see ECONOMIC INTEGRATION, INTERNATIONAL). Their plants have been specialized in a more limited number of product lines or in a more limited stage of the production process. As a result of this plant focus, the number of technologies to be mastered by the manufacturing staff of the plant has decreased, and the planning and control task has been simplified.

Both models – the strategic roles model and the product/process focus model – approach the issue of designing the architecture of the multinational network of plants from a different angle. As such, they will provide complementary insights to the manager who is in charge of the international operations of the company. These models are, however, not fully independent. We expect that a process-focused company will locate its plants – each of them dedicated to a particular stage of the production process – in a country or region either which has a considerable knowledge base in this particular process stage or which provides low cost production input factors to the process. We have argued that the process focus requires a relatively high level of coordination and, therefore, we expect a relatively high degree of centralization of manufacturing tasks. It may be concluded that the process-focused company is more likely to have a network of predominantly offshore and outpost plants, and to some extent source and lead plants.

In the product-focused company on the other hand, each plant is dedicated to a limited number of products or product lines. It is therefore reasonable to expect a relatively high degree of autonomy in these plants for manufacturing tasks such as product and process design, and production planning. We expect that the product-focused company is more likely to have a network of predominantly source, lead or contributor plants.

4 Major managerial concerns

In this final section some of the major managerial issues that arise in the operations of a multinational plant network will be explored, namely improving the overall network productivity, optimizing the flow of information and flow of goods within the network and transforming each network plant into a 'virtual' plant.

Managing the network productivity

The overall productivity of the network is determined by the productivity of the individual plants. A study carried out by Chew *et al.* (1990) has shown that the productivity of a plant within a multinational company may vary substantially among the distinct plants. Performance differences between the best and the worst plant were shown to be on the order of magnitude of 2:1. Although these performance differences may occur in any multi-plant network, they are probably more pronounced in a multinational network because of the longer inter-plant distances and the possibility of cultural differences and of differences in the performance measurement systems.

We may wonder why it is that some plants perform considerably less well than their colleague plants within the same company. The researchers have concluded that these companies have missed the opportunity to increase the productivity of the weakest plants, especially because they fail to optimize the transfer of know-how from the more productive plants to the weaker ones. As such, the overall company performance remains below the level which could be obtained.

In order to create the possibility of transferring know-how, we believe that three conditions should be fulfilled. First, some plants in the network must have the capability to transfer and therefore to develop know-how valuable for the other plants. By definition this implies that there must be a number of source plants, contributors and/or lead plants in the set of plants.

Second, the managers in these plants must be motivated to share their know-how with other plants. The transfer will not happen unless the corporate culture and the performance measurement system stress the importance of sharing know-how. If the corporate culture is characterized, for example, by the belief that each plant is unique and that each plant has a unique set of customers, it is more likely that managers are not motivated to learn from one another. This type of culture breeds the 'not-invented-here' attitude, rather than an openness to the new ideas developed in other plants. The performance measurement system should provide uniform productivity measures for all the plants in the network. Differences in the age and size of the plants, their technologies and their location, for example, are factors which may influence the productivity of the plant. As these factors are beyond the control of plant management, they should be filtered out of the productivity measure used for plant comparison. We refer to Chew *et al.* (1990) for details on the construction of a uniform plant productivity measure. The performance measurement system should be the basis for the incentives awarded to the plant managers in order to motivate them to transfer their know-how to other plants and, vice versa, to adopt know-how developed at other plants.

A final condition is that the manufacturing staff in the plants must be trained to recognize opportunities to transfer know-how. First of all, the staff must become well aware of the know-how developed in one or more plants. Second, they must become aware of the possibility to apply this know-how in another plant.

Managing the communication network

In the previous section the importance of the transfer of know-how between plants was discussed. The effectiveness and efficiency of this transfer of information depends heavily on the quality of the communication between the plants. Research on R&D (research and development) centres has highlighted several elements that have an important impact on the communication between the centres (De Meyer 1993). The conclusions from this study may be helpful to understand the communication efforts between production plants as well:

1 An important element is the 'socialization' effort; companies may attempt to create a 'family' atmosphere, which may favour formal and informal exchange of information. Socialization can be accomplished by temporary assignments of managers to a foreign plant or by the stimulation of travelling between the plants.

2 Many companies use rules and procedures to stimulate formal communication. There may be a policy that innovations must be carefully reported and documented, and there may be a formal channel to distribute these documents to all the plants. Or a strict planning process may force the plants to exchange information.

3 The plants may have a 'gatekeeper', a person who is very familiar with the internal organization of the plant and who – at the same time – has many contacts with people in other plants.

4 The organizational mechanisms are another element which came up in the study. Several advantages and disadvantages of centralization have already been discussed. An issue which in this respect has not been discussed yet is the centralization of information. It is clear that having central staff who collect and distribute relevant information has its advantages. On the other hand, direct communication between the plants may be faster and more reliable than this rather bureaucratic centralized mechanism.

5 A further element is the importance of electronic communication media such as computer networks, electronic mail systems and video conferencing. But although electronic communication facilitates communication all over the world, it cannot be the sole source of communication a company relies upon: it appears that the level of confidence between people decreases continuously if they communicate solely through electronic media without any direct contact. This has been described as the 'half-life effect of electronic communication' in analogy with the decay of, for example, nuclear radiation. However, a certain amount of confidence between people is crucial if these people have to work together effectively. As such, periodic face-to-face contact seems necessary to re-establish the confidence required for effective cooperation (De Meyer 1991).

Managing the flow of goods

The choice between the product and process focus has major logistical implications for the company as it determines to a large extent the flow of goods in the network. The process focus by definition implies the transportation of semi-finished products from one plant to another. The inter-plant distance is therefore an important decision parameter, as well as the quality of the available transportation infrastructure. Some characteristics of the product may have important logistical consequences which must be taken into account when deciding to adopt a product or process focus. It is for instance more appropriate to adopt a product focus for products which would be very costly or haphazard to transport between two production stages. The case of a soft drink company illustrates this point. One of the bottling plants in the company has vertically integrated into the business of blowing plastic bottles. Instead of having two production stages – blowing and filling bottles – spread over two plants, the company has now integrated the process under one roof. This new approach eliminates the transportation of the empty bottles, which is predominantly a (costly) transportation of air!

Another characteristic of the product which comes into play is the perishability of the raw materials or the semi-finished products. Food processors may have to locate a plant near the suppliers of raw material and adopt a product focus, if the raw material and the semi-finished product would perish during transport to a distant plant. On the other hand, the company may adopt a process focus if the raw material is perishable, but the semi-finished product is not. Fruit juice, for example, may be squeezed near the supplier of fruit, transported in bulk and packaged anywhere else in the world. This example illustrates at the same time the importance of the location of the supplier(s) of raw materials or components in the choice of the plant configuration.

Having established a tight network of plants which support the strategy of the company as a whole, with clear strategic roles and a clear-cut focus, the manager now has to re-think the allocation of products so that the combination of total logistical cost, delivery reliability and customer service is optimized. This task is of course extremely difficult as multiple factors have to be taken into account, such as the number of distribution centres, the transportation costs and transportation facilities and infrastructure, the capacity and capabilities of the plants, the distance between the plants and suppliers, the distance between the plants and distribution centres, and the inter-plant distances. Another important aspect of this task is the make-or-buy decision: it may be more desirable to outsource part of the logistical chain, rather than to own the whole transportation and distribution network. It is also a task which asks for frequent revision. As the parameters of the decision change, the decision should be re-evaluated.

Creating the virtual plant

Is it sufficient that a company has established a clear and rational network of its international plant configuration, and then optimized the allocation of manufacturing tasks to compete effectively in tomorrow's market? The answer is probably no!

Its next challenge is to integrate manufacturing with the other functions, rather than to maintain manufacturing as a separate and isolated function (De Meyer and Wittenberg-Cox 1992). Manufacturing is more than just the physical process of building a product on the basis of some components and materials; it is an integral part of one long value-creating chain which finally leads to a product that will satisfy the customer needs.

Manufacturing should, therefore, be integrated with other functions within the company such as marketing, product development and process development. 'Quality function deployment' and 'design for manufacturing' are two examples that stress precisely the need for this integration. But these two examples go beyond the mere internal integration of functions. The plant of the future will also integrate externally with its customers, suppliers and environment. Companies profit by treating suppliers as long-term partners: delivery reliability of raw materials or components may increase; inventories can be reduced; quality inspection of incoming goods can be eliminated; and cooperation in product development becomes feasible. A partnership with the customer may be just as valuable. Information about customer needs is an important input for the product design process, and integration with the customer's planning system provides useful information for the company's own production planning. The environment has also become an important player in the competitive game. A company that does not produce environmentally friendly products or use an environmentally friendly production process may very well be the losing company tomorrow.

This interaction with external partners enables the company to transform raw materials and components into value, rather than mere products, for the customer. We would call this future plant a 'virtual' plant (De Meyer 1992). The process of internal integration with the other functions and external integration with the suppliers, customers and environment is more complex for the multinational than for the domestic company as it requires a coordination of several partners across national borders.

5 Conclusion

In this entry it has been argued that the effective management of the international operations of a company requires first of all a clear-cut manufacturing strategy. The multinational company should be viewed as a network of plants, each with a clear strategic role and a clear focus, that support the strategy of the company as a whole. The number and size of the plants, their location and the level of competence in each plant are issues that require thorough analysis.

Second, it has been shown that the management of an international network of plants is in fact the management of flows: flows of know-how between the plants; flows of information between the managers in the network;

flows of goods between the plants. Managing these flows should lead to a productive network of 'virtual' plants.

ARNOUD DE MEYER
INSEAD

ANN VEREECKE
THE VLERICK SCHOOL OF MANAGEMENT,
UNIVERSITY OF GHENT

Further reading

(References cited in the text marked *)

Baden-Fuller, C.W.F. and Stopford, J.M. (1991) 'Globalization frustrated: the case of white goods', *Strategic Management Journal* 12: 493–507. (Argues that even in a mature industry a national strategy may be more profitable than a global strategy.)
* Bartlett, C.A. and Ghoshal, S. (1989) *Managing Across Borders: The Transnational Solution*, London: Hutchinson Business Books. (Describes the strategic and organizational options of multinational enterprises.)
* Chew, B.W., Bresnahan, T.F., Clark, K.B. (1990) 'Measurement, coordination and learning in a multiplant network', in R.S. Kaplan (ed.), *Measures for Manufacturing Excellence*, Harvard Business School Press. (Explores the reasons behind the differences in performance between distinct plants within the same company.)
* Collins, R.S., Schmenner, R.W., Whybark, D.C. (1989) 'Pan-European manufacturing: the road to 1992', *European Business Journal* 1 (4): 43–51. (Describes the evolution of the manufacturing strategy of European multinationals at the end of the 1980s.)
* De Meyer, A. (1991) 'Tech talk: how managers are stimulating global R&D communication', *Sloan Management Review* (Spring): 49–58. (Reports on the activities of large multinational companies that try to improve communication among and within their R&D laboratories.)
* De Meyer, A. (1992) 'Creating the virtual factory: report on the 1992 European Manufacturing Futures Survey', INSEAD. (A rigorous report of the results of a survey sent to European manufacturing companies concerning their manufacturing strategy and their performance.)
* De Meyer, A. (1993) 'Management of an international network of industrial R&D laboratories', *R&D Management* 23 (2): 109–20. (This paper explores why and how companies manage an international network of R&D laboratories.)
* De Meyer, A. and Wittenberg-Cox, A. (1992) *Creating Product Value: Putting Manufacturing on the Strategic Agenda*, London: Pitman. (Provides the general manager with a quick overview of the relevant issues in manufacturing strategy.)
* Ernst & Young (1992) *Regions of the New Europe: A Comparative Assessment of Key Factors in Choosing Your Location*, London: Ernst & Young. (A structured analysis of plant location issues in sixteen European countries.)
* Ferdows, K. (1989) 'Mapping international factory networks', in K. Ferdows (ed.), *Managing International Manufacturing*, Elsevier. (Describes the different types of plants and the evolution of their strategic roles within the company.)
* Ferdows, K. (1997) 'Making the most of foreign factories', *Harvard Business Review* (March–April): 73–88. (Discusses the structure and evolution of global plant networks and illustrates this through a couple of case studies.)
* Friberg, E.G. (1988) 'The challenge of 1992', *The McKinsey Quarterly* (Autumn): 27–40. (Provides a framework to analyse the impact the European integration has had on the industry level.)
Haigh, R. (1990) 'Selecting a US plant location: the management decision process in foreign companies', *Columbia Journal of World Business* (Autumn): 22–31. (Describes the selection process of plant location in twenty US companies.)
* Hayes, R.H. and Schmenner, R.W. (1978) 'How should you organize manufacturing?', *Harvard Business Review* (January–February): 105–18. (An important paper, which describes how to link the manufacturing strategy to the corporate strategy of the company.)
* Hayes, R.H. and Wheelwright, S.C. (1984) *Restoring Our Competitive Edge: Competing Through Manufacturing*, Chichester: Wiley. (Describes how the manufacturing strategy can support the company's competitive strategy.)
* Klassen, R.D. and Whybark, D.C. (1993) 'Key barriers to the effective management of international manufacturing operations', Kenan-Flagler Business School. (Identifies and ranks the key barriers to the effective management of international manufacturing operations.)
* Lei, D. and Goldhar, J.D. (1991) 'Computer-integrated manufacturing (CIM): redefining the manufacturing firm into a global service business', *International Journal of Production and Operations Management* 11 (1): 5–18. (Ex-

amines the impact of CIM on the company's competitive advantages.)

Prahalad, C.K. and Doz, Y.L. (1987) *The Multinational Mission: Balancing Local Demands and Global Vision*, New York: The Free Press. (Shows how to formulate strategic decisions in the global marketplace.)

See also: ECONOMIC INTEGRATION, INTERNATIONAL; GLOBAL STRATEGIC PLANNING; GLOBALIZATION; INTERNATIONAL MARKETING; MULTINATIONAL CORPORATIONS

Related topics in the IEBM: ENVIRONMENTAL AND RESOURCE ECONOMICS; ENVIRONMENTAL MANAGEMENT; GOVERNMENT, INDUSTRY AND THE PUBLIC SECTOR; JUST-IN-TIME PHILOSOPHIES; INNOVATION AND TECHNICAL CHANGE; MANAGEMENT IN EASTERN EUROPE; MANAGEMENT IN PACIFIC ASIA; MANUFACTURING STRATEGY; OPERATIONS MANAGEMENT; STRATEGY, CONCEPT OF; STRATEGY, IMPLEMENTATION OF

International payments

Overview

Statistics on international payment flows were compiled long before gross national product data were gathered. Since governments historically have controlled foreign trade by imposing taxes and/or quantitative restrictions, and these controls require bureaucratic record keeping, data on international transactions, both real and financial, actually precede data on domestic output.

Because the balance of payments (BOP) represents the most comprehensive information available on the involvement of the domestic economy with the rest of the world, BOP data are used widely for policy decisions and for predicting trends in credit and foreign exchange markets, and in the course of the economy itself (hence the likelihood of specific government actions). For this reason, it is important that the concepts on which data collection is based are clearly understood, otherwise no meaningful information can be extracted.

Accordingly, this entry will start with a working definition of the balance of payments and describe the logic behind the mechanics of BOP accounting before addressing the nature and interpretation of BOP statements. In the concluding section the balance of payments will be linked to the international investment position of a country.

1 Balance of payments accounting: the logic behind the mechanics

The most authoritative source on balance of payments (BOP) matters is the International Monetary Fund's *Balance of Payments Manual*. It lays out in detail how nations should compile their BOP tables, thus creating desirable conformity in data collection and presentation, and it also provides a useful definition:

> A balance of payments statement can be broadly described as the record of an economy's international economic transactions, that is, of the goods and services that an economy has received from and provided to the rest of the world and of the changes in the economy's claims on and liabilities to the rest of the world. Such a record can be put to a variety of uses, beyond the basic one of appraising the effects of the transactions on the domestic affairs of the economy itself. As an economy's balance of payments mirrors the rest of the world's dealings with that economy, the international community is directly concerned with the statements for its individual members. Interpretation of such statements from that viewpoint is obviously made easier when all countries' statistics are based on the same concepts and are compiled in a uniform way.
>
> (International Monetary Fund 1977: 1)

Balance of payments accounting is based on the principle of double-entry book-keeping, that is, every transaction gives rise to equal and offsetting debit and credit entries (see FINANCIAL MANAGEMENT, INTERNATIONAL). Double-entry book-keeping for balance of payments purposes involves a 'real' account and a 'money' account for each transaction. Three kinds of 'real' items can be transferred across national boundaries: goods, services and claims. Taking the home country perspective, an example of the first transaction would be the shipment of a machine overseas; of the second, providing airline seats to non-residents on a domestic airline; and of the third, granting a loan to a foreign borrower. In each case the 'real' account records the value of the transaction, while the 'money' account registers the *payment* as the counter-entry: the crediting of the domestic exporter's bank account at home or abroad, the receipt of funds by the domestic air carrier, and the transfer of the loan proceeds to the foreign borrower's account (see ECONOMIC INTEGRATION, INTERNATIONAL).

It is sometimes difficult to distinguish between claims transactions and the corresponding payments or receipts. It may be helpful to think of the claim as represented by a tangible document such as an executed note, a debt contract or a security; the payment (or receipt), on the other hand, is reflected simply in a decrease (or increase) in a demand deposit account at a commercial bank. While demand deposits are, in a very strict sense, also claims, they are so highly liquid that they should be viewed, in this context, as unique monetary assets.

In mercantilist days, the explicit national goal was the piling up of export receipts. This is the reason why today's BOP accounts define those transactions that give rise to receipts of funds as credit (+) items. Obviously, the export of a machine gives rise to the receipt of funds. Airline seats for non-residents give rise to receipts for the home country if the seats are provided by a domestic airline; but when they are provided by a foreign airline to home country residents, a debit (–) item results, because payments for the service are made to a non-resident company.

Granting a loan to a non-resident means the importing of a claim (the borrower's IOU). Payment is made to a non-resident; hence, it is a debit (–) item. On the other hand, when a foreign investor places his funds in a bank in the home country, the bank is receiving payment – a credit (+) item – while 'exporting' its promise to pay a claim. On the basis of these simple examples, the following generalizations are useful:

Exports of goods, services and claims are credit (+) entries in the BOP.
Imports of goods, services and claims are debit (–) entries in the BOP.

International business transaction	Real transaction	'Money' transaction
1 Merchandise export	**a** Delivery **b** Increase foreign stockpile Decrease domestic stockpile **c** Credit	**a** Payment **b** Increase domestically-owned monetary assets Decrease foreign-owned assets (or reduced domestic liabilities) **c** Debit
2 Sales of services abroad	**a** Provision of service **b** Not applicable **c** Credit	**a** Payment **b** (as above) **c** Debit
3 Lending (capital 'export')	**a** Accept claim or financial instrument **b** Increase in domestic investments abroad Increase in foreign liabilities **c** Debit	**a** Payment of loan proceeds **b** Increase of foreign-owned monetary assets (= increase in domestic monetary liabilities) **c** Credit

a denotes activities
b reflects change in asset or liability position
c represents accounting entry

Figure 1 Balance of payments accounting (home country perspective)

The payments corresponding to these trade transactions give rise to debit and credit items, respectively. When monetary assets (at home or abroad) owned by residents increase (or liabilities decrease), they are *debits*; when the monetary assets of residents decrease (or liabilities increase), they are treated as *credit* items. In this context it is worth pointing out that the economics literature commonly refers to claims imports as capital exports or outflows, a practice which is potentially confusing inasmuch as capital exports are debit items and goods exports are credit items.

Figure 1 summarizes these accounting principles, relating the 'real' and 'money' component of each international business transaction to the specific action or activity, the change in the specific asset or liability position, and its respective accounting treatment.

One of the most confusing aspects of BOP accounting is the conventional identification of an individual transaction as being a credit (+) or a debit (–) item. This seems to go against the rule of double-entry bookkeeping. It is important to note that for BOP purposes, a credit (+) or debit (–) item refers only to the entry in the real account; the entry in the money account is ignored for all practical purposes, a fact reflected in Figure 2.

As a result of this double-entry feature of the accounting framework, international payments always balance, in the sense that for every credit there will be a corresponding debit. However, this accounting balance must be distinguished from the economic notion of a disequilibrium or imbalance in a particular subset of real accounts. For example, the merchandise trade balance may show imports significantly higher than exports, that is, a net debit (see INTERNATIONAL TRADE AND FOREIGN DIRECT INVESTMENT). In accounting terms the offsetting 'money' transaction is a corresponding increase in liabilities to non-residents. Yet the resulting debt levels may not be sustainable economically. Therefore an adjustment in imports and exports will have to occur in order to address such a disequilibrium in the trade balance.

There are other, more complicated, issues. For instance, how are the interest payments on a loan to a non-resident treated? When the loan is made, it is recorded as an import of claims. The subsequent interest payments are then entered as *payments* for the *services* of the funds lent – in other words, as credit (+) items for the 'export' of a service.

How should the acquisition of domestic stock by a foreign investor be treated if they obtained the funds from the sale of, say, a basic raw material to this country? BOP accounting conventions view this transaction as two separate events, which are reported accordingly. The raw material import is a debit (–) item in the goods category of the domestic BOP; the sale of domestic shares is a claims export, and hence a credit (+) item in the claims category; and the investor now has a claim against the equity of a domestic company. The corresponding entries in the 'money' account cancel out; the funds paid to the foreign investor for the raw material import (a debit item) are used to pay for the securities (a credit item) (see FINANCIAL MANAGEMENT, INTERNATIONAL).

Gifts pose special problems because they involve a receipt (a payment) of funds without a corresponding, immediate real transaction such as an export (or import) shipment. In this case, an entry into an account called 'unilateral transfers' (or gifts) substitutes for the real transaction. It is akin to the sending (or receipt) of a 'thank-you note', the 'export' (or import) of which gives rise to a credit (or debit) item.

Up to now transactions have been classified into credit or debit items, a horizontal classification. Another aspect of the BOP organization is the division into groups of transactions, a vertical classification. Five categories can be distinguished: (1) traditional merchandise trade involving goods only; (2) service transactions, including payments and receipts of interest, royalties and dividends; (3) unilateral transactions such as gifts, grants and remittances; (4) transactions involving financial claims; and (5) official reserve transactions.

Using these distinctions, a BOP table for the home country can be constructed for the illustrative transactions listed below:

Transaction	Debit	Credit	Cumulative Net
I Merchandise transactions:			
1		20	+20
2	16		+ 4
II Service transactions:			
3		2	+ 6
4	1		+ 5
5	3		+ 2
III Unilateral transactions:			
6	4		– 2
IV Claims transactions:			
7	8		–10
8		13	+ 3
9	10		– 7
10		12	+ 5
V Official transactions:			
11	5		0
	47	47	0.0

Figure 2 A hypothetical BOP table

1 export of machines: 20
2 import of foreign cars: 16
3 receipt of interest on loans to non-residents: 2
4 payments of royalties to non-residents: 1
5 shipping costs of domestic machines on foreign carriers: 3
6 domestic government grant to a less developed country: 4
7 domestic residents' purchases of foreign bonds: 8
8 non-residents' purchases of domestic stock: 13
9 acquisition of plants abroad (direct investment): 10
10 new deposits of non-residents in domestic banks: 12
11 sale of domestic government debt securities by foreign central banks back to domestic securities dealers: 5

On the basis of our definition of debits and credits so far, the BOP statement shown in Figure 2 is the result. To minimize confusion about official transactions, in particular, keep in mind that an increase (decrease) in foreign official claims against the domestic country would be booked just like a decrease (increase) in domestic official holdings of financial claims against foreign entities (see ACCOUNTING, INTERNATIONAL). Note also that the transactions listed may not be as independent of each other as appears at first glance, a point that will be discussed below.

2 The balance of payments: its nature and interpretation

The basic financial statements of a firm are the *balance sheet*, the *income statement* and the *funds statement*. The BOP cannot be compared to a balance sheet because the BOP

	Uses	Sources
Income from sales		100
Other income		50
Operating expenditures	90	
Total funds from operations*		60
Investment in fixed assets (net)	20	
Decrease of long-term liabilities (net)	10	
Dividends paid	5	
Total funds used	35	
Net increase in working capital	25	
Memo: increase in cash balances	5	

* Funds are classified as: Allowances for depreciation and amortization
plus net income

Figure 3 Funds statement for any year: typical company

covers a period of time, while the balance sheet gives the financial position of the firm at a given point in time. Similarly, there is nothing resembling costs, revenues or periodic earnings in a BOP which would allow one to draw parallels between the income statement and the balance of payments. This leaves the funds statement: it is this particular statement of a firm that corresponds to the balance of payments; therefore, it deserves closer scrutiny.

The nature of the funds statement

In general, the funds statement of a firm identifies the changes in the items contained in the balance sheet between the beginning and the end of a reporting period. Sources and uses of funds (the meaning of the term 'funds' is probably best given by 'purchasing power') can be classified as follows:

1 Sources:
  (a) net decrease in any asset (other than cash)
  (b) net increase in any liability
  (c) proceeds from sale of equity

  (d) funds from operations (this is frequently given as net income plus depreciation; however, the alternative method used here avoids the confusing treatment of depreciation as a 'source' of funds)
2 Uses:
  (a) net increases in any asset (other than cash)
  (b) net decreases in any liability
  (c) a retirement or purchase of stock
  (d) cash dividends

Figure 3 shows a simplified funds statement of a company, typically found in any annual report, while Figure 4 shows the same funds statement, slightly expanded and rearranged. Note that some of the excessive netting has been abandoned, which means the sole purpose of the totals is to check that debits equal credits. Furthermore, at the bottom of the statement, a special cash account, increases of cash balances, focuses attention on changes that took place in this item.

Figure 5 shows a balance of payments scheme that is very simplified but contains all items necessary to illustrate BOP accounting.

	Uses (debit)	Sources (credit)
Income from sales products		100
Expenditures for operations (wages, materials, taxes)	90	
Receipts of interest and dividends from securities held		50
Interest and dividends paid	5	
Contributions and gifts received		–
Contributions and gifts made	–	
Reductions of receivables and other non-cash current assets		–
Increases of payables and other current liabilities except notes due on call		20
Increases of receivables and other non-cash current assets	30	
Decreases of payables and other current liabilities except notes due on call	10	
Reductions of long-term assets		20
Increases of long-term liabilities		–
Increases of long-term assets	40	
Decreases of long-term liabilities	10	–
Reductions of cash balances		
Increases of notes due on call		–
Increases of cash balances	5	
Repayments of notes due on call	–	
Total (to check debits equal credits)	190	190

Figure 4 Funds statement for any year: typical company

Figure 5 is the BOP format followed by most countries. The USA, to avoid possible difficulties in interpretation, has decided to use a format that de-emphasizes partial balances, that is, netting of particular subsets of transactions.

Analogy between funds statement and balance of payments

The BOP shares a critical feature with the corporate funds statement. Both convey the effect of funds *movements*; this is the most useful aspect of such an accounting statement. However, it is virtually impossible to make

I Current account	Debits	Credits	Cumulative Net
1 Merchandise trade	90	100	
Trade balance			+10
2 Services (military, net investment income, travel, transportation, etc.)	5	50	
3 Unilateral transfers (private and government)			
Current account balance			+55
II Capital account			
4a Direct investment	20		
4b Portfolio investment	10		
5 Short-term private capital (liquid claims and liabilities)	25	5	
6 Errors and omissions			
Official settlements balance (or official reserve transactions balance)			+5
7 Official capital (short-term liquid and marketable liabilities to foreign governments)	5		
8 Reserve assets (gold, foreign exchange, SDRs)			
Totals (to check debits equal to credits)	155	155	0

Figure 5 Balance of payments for any year: Home Country Inc.

qualitative interpretations on the basis of the quantitative data alone. In other words, without information beyond the data in the statement, it is impossible to say whether a change represents an improvement or a deterioration in the situation of the firm or country. As with any corporate statement, it is even more important in the context of a funds statement to ask the questions, 'good for what?', or 'bad in what respect?'.

Returning for a moment to the comparison between the BOP and the income statement, a clear objective is implicit in the latter: the greater the amount of net income, the better. In other words, more is considered 'good'; less is considered 'bad'. This emphatically is not true with respect to the funds statement, or the BOP. It is true that in the case of a firm, bankruptcy can occur because of illiquidity, which would show up in a series of funds statements. However, a series of funds statements indicating increased financial liquidity does not lead to the conclusion that this trend is good for the firm. In fact, the presence of excess cash and working capital usually indicates that the firm is poorly managed – management lacks ideas about good investment projects and may be tempted to squander the excess cash on poor investments. Thus, the analysis of a funds statement requires additional knowledge about a firm's circumstances. For example, one would look at such factors as the variability of its cash flow, the liquidity of its assets, the maturity structure of its liabilities, and, above all, the quality of its management. The analysis of a country's BOP involves similar considerations, such as the amount of official liquid assets (reserves), exchange rate movements, structure of exports and imports, and especially the stability of the political system in times of economic stress.

It should be remembered that BOP data are the only source of information on a nation's involvement in the international economy and the international financial system. When relying on such data for insights into the inter-action between the domestic economy and the rest of the world, it is important not only to have a grasp of the accounting framework but also to explain the underlying forces reflected in the data. The following section pinpoints the two types of problems in analysing and in-terpreting BOP data. The first are fundamen-tal in nature, while the second are more technical.

Fundamental problems in interpreting balance of payments data

Interrelationships between balance of payments accounts

One feature of any BOP statement is the clas-sification of transactions into merchandise trade, services, various capital transactions, etc. Such a classification gives the erroneous impression that each class of transactions is independent. Actually, these accounts are often causally interrelated in a very complex manner. The relationships are complex because they are sometimes 'complementary' and sometimes 'competing'. Moreover, the strength of these relationships can vary.

A complementary relationship exists when a debit or credit transaction in one account category leads to a debit or credit transaction in another account. An example of this phe-nomenon would be a direct investment trans-action that involves portfolio capital or a trade transaction in the same direction. Assume that a domestic firm purchases the controlling shares of a foreign enterprise. This acquisition could lead to the injection of additional work-ing capital in the form of intra-company loans, or to imports of merchandise when the foreign affiliate begins to produce goods for export back to the parent.

Typically, however, the relationship among transactions tends to be 'competing'. The obvious case is an increase in foreign aid that leads to an increase in exports, especially when the aid is 'tied' to purchases from the donor country. In this case the foreign aid (debit item) is directly related to the credit item in the export account.

The problem of interrelationships is par-ticularly vexing for the analyst dealing with short-term capital transactions (see FOREIGN EXCHANGE RISK, MANAGEMENT OF). Techni-cally, an international capital transaction – that is, the purchase of an interest-bearing time deposit, a so-called CD, from a foreign bank – represents merely an exchange of fi-nancial claims: the purchaser acquires a for-eign currency denominated asset by giving up ownership of, say, a demand deposit in his country of residence. Thus, the bank will very likely sell that currency on the foreign ex-change market, causing a decrease (deprecia-tion) in the price of the currency of the investor.

From this simple example, there are two important implications. First, government policies aimed at influencing the external ac-counts must consider such interrelationships in order to be successful. Second, the underly-ing intent in any transaction largely deter-mines the ultimate effect on both the balance of payments and the exchange rate.

The concepts of deficits and surpluses

Since the accounting framework of the BOP implies overall balance of debits and credits, imbalances such as deficits (net debits) and surpluses (net credits) can occur only in com-ponent accounts of a country's BOP. Recall from Figure 5 that the simple overall balance identity is composed of:

Current Account (CA) + Capital Account (KA) + Official Reserve Transactions (ORT) $\equiv 0$

It is possible, however, to focus attention on individual accounts. For example, to study what has been happening to imports of oil, the balance between oil exports and imports could be computed. As already noted, a net debit is a deficit, a net credit a surplus.

The 'balance on goods and services' is of interest because it represents the net external contribution to the gross national product (GNP), thus linking the BOP to the national income accounts. A deficit means that a country spends more on goods and services than it produces, by going into debt or reducing a net asset position *vis-à-vis* non-residents. Or, if one is interested in the concept of gross domestic product (GDP), the focus would be on the 'balance on goods and non-interest services', as this excludes from consideration the income from a net foreign asset or liability position.

Commonly, the 'balance on current account' is drawn. A deficit on current account means that spending for goods, services and transfers exceeds the national means and is financed by incurring a debt to the rest of the world or reducing a previously established net creditor position. The USA, for example, changed from being the largest creditor nation to the largest debtor country in the world in the mid-1980s.

This can be seen by manipulating the overall balance constraint:

$$CA + KA + ORT \equiv 0$$

$$CA < 0 \Rightarrow KA + ORT > 0$$

Fast-growing developing countries, whose firms import goods and services to build a modern infrastructure and production base, borrow mostly from international capital markets, and probably have current account deficits. Domestic savings, even when relatively abundant, are often inadequate in these countries given the level of investment. However, international lenders see the countries' future production potential and are willing to provide funds, tempted by the promise of high returns. South Korea and Malaysia are recent examples of such current account deficits (see ECONOMIES OF EAST ASIA).

By contrast, in mature economies, with ageing populations who have high income and savings, such as Japan or until recently Germany, one may find current account surpluses coupled with the build-up of a net foreign asset position from lending to non-residents. Two cases can be distinguished:

$$CA = -KA, \qquad ORT = 0 \qquad (1)$$

This is the definition of a freely floating exchange rate if there are no indirect attempts to influence its course. When official reserve transactions are zero, or close to it, the government and its agencies refrain from direct buying and selling of reserve assets, such as convertible foreign exchange, gold, or special drawing right (SDR) allocations. If the government also refrains from using deliberate interest rate and tax policies, or tariffs, quotas and moral suasion to influence the exchange rate, then private markets truly determine that rate. However, in practice, the exchange rate is viewed as too important a variable to leave completely to market forces. In consequence governments or central banks often attempt to influence the exchange rate, either directly by sales or purchases of foreign currencies (official reserve transactions), or indirectly by setting short-term interest rates so as to attract or discourage investment in assets denominated in the national currency. Such actions are referred to as 'managed float'.

$$CA + KA = -ORT \neq 0 \qquad (2)$$

When official reserves are sold to prevent a decline in the international value of the local currency, this represents an overall, or basic balance of payments deficit. When reserves are accumulated, to prevent appreciation of the exchange rate, we speak of an overall balance of payments surplus.

It is important to understand that in the course of the year that the BOP covers, all entries must be viewed as simultaneous, so there is no presumption of causality between the current and the capital account balances. It is not possible to determine whether a current account deficit caused a capital account surplus or whether the latter caused the former.

However, it is worth recalling that the benefits of international specialization and trade are measured by the *volume*, not the balance of trade. Bilateral trade and current account imbalances may be the sign of efficient international division of labour, or they may be transitional, for example, a bad harvest necessitating wheat imports, or structural, for example, a country with a strong preference for current spending on goods and services (see INTERNATIONAL TRADE AND FOREIGN DIRECT INVESTMENT). For these reasons, plus the fact that the statistics are often subject to revisions later, it is almost impossible to put an interpretation on a deficit or surplus in the BOP, regardless of whether the current account, the overall or another deficit concept is used, unless additional economic data are also relied upon. These issues are addressed in the following section.

Informational content of balance of payments data

If we try to reconstruct what happened to a country by studying BOP data, we need to use the latter in conjunction with information on developments in the (effective) exchange rate. Since BOP data are *ex post* in nature, they merely indicate that total purchases of foreign exchange were equal to total sales. However, if the effective exchange rate depreciated during the period, it is permissible to infer that an *ex ante* excess demand for foreign currency was eliminated through adjustment of the exchange rate. Exchange rate changes affecting transactions that enter both the current and the capital account bring about the *ex post* balance of debits and credits.

To illustrate this point, let us pursue a particular international payments transaction, the purchase of a foreign currency CD by a private investor who is attracted by a high expected return. When the investor pays for the CD with a demand deposit, the issuing bank ends up with undesired demand balances in the investor's currency. As the bank attempts to sell them (and there is no central bank intervention), the investor's currency will depreciate. This depreciation, in turn, will result in additional exports from and fewer imports into the investor's country. In addition, since the depreciation will change the expected yield on financial assets in that currency, it will induce purchases of such claims.

When a country experiences a series of current account deficits, then the accounting mechanics imply that the additional goods and services are paid for by a capital account surplus. If the (effective) exchange rate is taken into consideration, a series of current account deficits may reveal useful information about that country's economic performance. For example, if the holders of the accumulating claims on the deficit country are willing to hold financial assets in that currency, no change in the (effective) exchange rate will be observed with the series of current account deficits. On the other hand, a depreciating (effective) exchange rate would indicate that this was necessary to bring into balance the volume of desired purchases and sales of that country's currency. Therefore a series of current account deficits which persist over a business cycle and which are not just related to a boom at home or a recession abroad reflect deteriorating competitiveness of the country which, in turn, is remedied by depreciation of its currency.

Even in combination with the actual exchange rate, however, BOP data are difficult to interpret. It could be that private investors sold the currency because they expected a current account deficit, or a deterioration in it. This would suggest that interpretation of BOP data must be relative to the *expected* BOP position.

The major reason, then, that new data, for example, the merchandise trade balance for the USA, receives so much attention, is that it gives information about the performance of the US economy relative to expectations. When the dollar rises in response to the new merchandise trade balance, then there is good news in the published data, that is, there are more exports or fewer imports or both, suggesting unexpected underlying strength which warrants buying the dollar. In this sense the balance of trade can be used as an information variable in the assessment of the performance of an economy. The foreign exchange markets use this information to make buy and sell decisions. This is despite the fact that revisions are likely and that the increasingly significant service transactions are not included in the merchandise trade balance. Of course, other variables, such as a government's reputation with respect to monetary stability, will also be considered.

Technical problems

Actual collection and accuracy of balance of payments data

In order to understand and properly interpret BOP data it helps to know something about

1985	1986	1987	1988	1989	1990	1991
−80.2	−66.2	−48.2	−59.5	−75.9	−112.5	−91.1

Figure 6 Global current account discrepancy, 1985–91 ($ billion)

the actual collection process and the accuracy of the data. Given the large number of international transactions, it is clear that government agencies do not keep records of every one of them, so the data are in part based on estimation, in part based on reports from 'intermediaries', and in part relying on reports by individual transactors.

Examples of a transactor-based reporting system are the data on merchandise trade and foreign direct investment. As regards merchandise trade, transactors provide the information on customs documents which then form the basis of the reported statistics. In the case of foreign direct investment, the information is obtained by partial or complete surveys of multinational enterprises resident in the jurisdiction and so form the basis of the statistics on direct investment and income derived from it.

Data based on reports from 'intermediaries' are widely used in ascertaining the foreign assets and liabilities of residents. Typically, banks and security dealers are such 'intermediaries' who report positions held on behalf of resident customers, as well as their own positions.

Estimates are made when too many individuals would have to be surveyed to obtain information quickly and cost-effectively, for example, for travel and tourism and some parts of portfolio income. Administrative records, such as tax files, accounts of official agencies or international banking statistics may be used in these estimations.

In view of the increasing internationalization of production and the integration of financial markets, it is not surprising that BOP compilation systems encounter significant challenges which show up as 'errors and omissions' in national data, and as global

discrepancies in the current and capital account. While in theory the current account balance for the whole world should be zero, as one country's imports would be another's exports, etc., inconsistencies in reporting cause it to deviate considerably from zero. The inconsistencies derive from the amounts actually reported by different countries for the same transaction, for example, either of both countries reporting incorrectly or one not at all. Thus we actually observe the net debits (deficits) in Figure 6.

Figure 7 shows that a cumulative net credit balance (surplus) in the capital account offsets a good part of the cumulative current account deficit, the remainder representing errors and omissions.

The data in Figure 7 suggest that asymmetric treatment by two or more countries of the same transactions may be one cause of the current account discrepancy. The difficulties of collecting the balance of payments statistics are compounded by the phenomenal growth of international capital transfers. These are the consequence of the deregulation of financial markets in many countries, enabling investors to choose more freely the currency, nature and location of their investments. Breakthroughs in telecommunications have greatly facilitated funds transfer across borders, and reduced transactions costs due to increased trading volumes have also been major contributing forces to this development.

There is, moreover, a natural tendency to report cross-border debts and their necessary servicing costs more accurately than cross-border assets and the income derived from them: high tax rates and political tensions encourage concealing the latter. In addition, larger current account deficits have occurred

Current account	407 (of which 170 investment income)
Capital account	297
Errors and omissions	110

Figure 7 Cumulative global discrepancy, 1977–93 ($ billion)
Source: International Monetary Fund (1987: 7)

in recent decades, and they have been financed increasingly in capital markets rather than by official reserves. The reason for this development can be found in the pursuit of diversification by asset holders and the spread of international banking.

A complicating factor for the compilation of exact BOP statistics is the growth in offshore financial centres and the attendant innovative activity. By stimulating international financial flows to and from such centres, they make the tracing of funds flow more difficult. On the one hand, foreign-owned banks and financial service companies in such centres receive income on investments and for shipping, insurance and banking services. On the other hand, they pay interest on borrowed funds to a broad range of lenders, and they pay dividends/profits to their home bases. To capture the resulting debits and credits for BOP purposes requires that the foreign-owned banks and service companies be treated as residents of the financial centre. Yet because most of their activities are purely international from the local government's point of view, offshore financial centres such as Hong Kong and The Netherlands Antilles view them as non-residents, hence report little or nothing on their activities in their BOP. The result is that international transactions, especially the interest received on international bonds and bank deposits owned abroad, cannot be accurately captured by the data compilation agencies.

The country of residence of the ultimate creditor is therefore difficult to determine. Similarly, Swiss banks do not break down by country of residence their deposits from cross-border locations. Thus while the outgoing interest payments are in fact recorded as Swiss debits, it is estimated that only 20 per cent of these payments are captured as credits by the recipient countries.

Financial innovation and the advance of international bond and equity markets have increased these difficulties. The emergence of currency swaps in the last decade can serve as an illustration. With existing reporting systems relying on banks' asset and liability positions, and with swaps not reported on balance sheets, data collected are less accurate. For instance, when company A in country X borrows dollars from company B in country X, and exchanges these dollars for yen with company C in country Z, an international credit/liability position is created without being reflected in the reported data. As new financial instruments are introduced and traded, and put through currency and ownership transformation as in the above swap, it becomes much more difficult to identify the actual cross-border asset ownership. This shrouds the payments of interest and principal between 'resident' and 'non-resident' in greater ambiguity.

So it has been hard for the BOP account systems to keep pace with the innovation and increased volume of transaction in international capital markets, making for poorer overall statistical quality and implying that caution is needed when using BOP information, whether for business decisions or public policy. In fact, the possibility exists that a particular country has a surplus when a deficit is reported. When investment income and foreign assets are under-recorded, it is then also possible that statistics on indebtedness are seriously flawed.

National compilers of BOP data, on the other hand, are hard at work to adapt their methods to the evolving financial environment, partly by closer cooperation with each other. Also, the current account discrepancy for the world is small when put into the context of total world current account payments (1.6 per cent in 1991). Nevertheless, it must concern national compilers that investment income is particularly poorly captured. As mentioned earlier, cross-border financial transactions have grown especially fast in response to new technology, innovation and deregulation. During the 1980s international bank lending was rising more than ten times as fast as GDP, and international sales of bonds and stocks were growing at average annual rates approaching 30 per cent. Interest and dividend flows should therefore have grown correspondingly. Since the capital account of the BOP captures only the net movement of claims the data do not reveal the phenomenal underlying growth.

The definition of resident for balance of payments purposes

The resident/non-resident distinction is one of the basic features of BOP accounting. It should be clearly understood because it implies potentially different economic behaviour. Experts, however, are frequently at odds over where to draw the line between residents and non-residents.

These conflicts arise especially when the business operations of residents of one country are effectively conducted through affiliates established in another. We have already seen that the offshore financial centres of Hong Kong and The Netherlands Antilles treat the foreign banks and finance companies resident in their territories as non-residents for BOP purposes because the bulk of their activities is international, that is, with other non-residents. Moreover, the decision-making power can be assumed to rest with their head offices abroad. Consequently, the location of assets and liabilities is harder to determine, and the ultimate recipients of international investment income flows are more difficult to trace.

On the other hand, it may not be economically sound to consider the agencies of foreign banks residents for BOP purposes, as is the case in the USA. The US BOP omits all involvement such agencies have with US residents because, in fact, the agencies' foreign head offices make most of the decisions regarding these transactions.

The task of defining a foreign affiliate as resident or non-resident on the basis of its decision-making structure may prove insurmountable. It must be recognized, however, that giving resident status to these firms is based on the possibly inaccurate premise that, like other residents, their participation in the US economy makes them subject to all the factors and policies that influence it.

Effect of exchange rate changes on values

One of the major technical difficulties in the collection of BOP data involves the valuation of transactions. Because time lags exist between the recording and the settling of transactions, this problem is especially acute in a system of fluctuating exchange rates. For example, an export transaction is recorded at the time the exports leave the country, but settlement might take place later. As long as there is a time lag, the potential for a change in exchange rates exists. Methods of converting foreign currencies to domestic currency may be based on the exchange rates prevailing on the day the transaction was recorded, the day the transaction was settled, or on the rates at which the transactors buy or sell the foreign currencies. Each method may yield a different value for each transaction, resulting in a distortion of the figures ultimately reported.

Another complication arises from the derivation of some of the data on capital transactions. Typically, the changes in the values between points in time are used as measures of transactions. The computation of transaction values from data on positions, therefore, leads to problems similar to those in estimating inventory changes from data on the stock value of inventories when prices change between successive dates.

Transactions not involving the foreign exchange market

While most international transactions go through the foreign exchange market, and therefore involve a supply of or demand for foreign currency, some significant exceptions do exist. Important examples are the contributions countries make to or receive from the International Monetary Fund, the World Bank, the European Union or other international organizations. In these cases, official exchange reserves change without any foreign exchange market transactions. Another exception is the interest earned on foreign bank accounts that is reinvested rather than remitted. As international portfolio diversification continues, this exception is likely to increase in importance. This should be kept in mind, because it has been the working assumption throughout this discussion that BOP transactions involve the foreign exchange markets.

3 The international investment position

Given the nature of balance of payments data, it is apparent that more information is required to supplement this data and to gain insights into government policy, exchange rate trends and the structure of international capital flows. The international investment position (IIP) statement of a country provides such information, and has the additional advantage that its data are directly related to the balance of payments. The IIP is essentially a balance sheet type of statement, depicting a country's assets abroad and its liabilities to non-residents. The link with the balance of payments is based on the fact that balance of payments flows give rise to changes in assets and liabilities, that are then captured in the IIP with its underlying stock concept.

Data from the IIP *per se* are of interest because they depict the net investment position, an important measure of the indebtedness of a country. The size of this indebtedness, together with its trend, provides important information on the debt capacity and the associated credit standing, or 'country risk', of a nation. In addition, the net indebtedness of a country may contribute to a risk premium in the foreign exchange market.

Data from the IIP also provide important details about the nature of foreign assets and liabilities, as well as their maturity structure. Here it is possible to draw some tentative generalizations. First, a net debt position of a country is indicative of a history of high preferences for current goods. This is typical for many rapidly growing less developed countries, but also for countries like the USA that tend to use up resources beyond their present output. By corollary, many mature economies tend to have a net asset position, as saving exceeds domestic investment.

Furthermore, if indebtedness is concentrated in the hands (or vaults) of central banks ('official holders'), it indicates that the currency has achieved reserve currency status. Likewise, the maintenance of large holdings of liquid assets (for example, deposits in the banking system) by private non-residents reflects the use of the currency in international commercial transactions, that is, the nation's money plays the role of an international vehicle currency.

Large holdings of bonds and equities by non-residents suggest efficiency and depth in the country's securities markets. The geographical distribution of assets and liabilities, by definition, provides a picture of international investment. Finally, the nature of the assets and liabilities provides clues about portfolio preferences and institutional barriers and incentives that affect international capital flows, and therefore the extent of integration of international markets for financial claims.

One of the major conclusions of this entry on international payments transactions is that it is very difficult to use such data to forecast the future. On the other hand, knowledge about the structure of a country's international relations, including its international debt position, increases awareness and sensitivity in all who make decisions in an international financial environment. These include portfolio managers who have to decide in which country returns are less likely to be affected by exchange rate depreciation and future taxes; bankers who must appraise the competitiveness of firms from a particular country; credit rating agencies who through their appraisals have an impact on the cost of borrowing; and government officials who increasingly negotiate and intervene on behalf of domestic firms with assets deployed abroad. Apart from reminding decision makers of the many international transactions that are possible, data from the balance of payments and the international investment position lead to better appreciation and anticipation of government policies at home and abroad.

4 Conclusion

The purpose of interpreting BOP data is to analyse the size and trend of the economic effects on a country of its exports and imports of goods, services and claims. Inferences are drawn from a nation's trade and current account balance about its international competitiveness and the sustainability of the present pattern of trade.

World trade and payments have undergone significant structural change since the liberalization of trade and capital flows in the 1950s. Not only has international production, the result of foreign direct investment, grown much faster than cross-border trade, international financial transactions have grown even faster, so that today one can speak of global financial markets (see GLOBALIZATION).

These developments have implications for how BOP statistics should be compiled and interpreted. First, with respect to trade, the focus on cross-border exports and imports masks the fact that much trade now is intra-firm in nature, as multinational corporations supply and source from their overseas affiliates. At present, BOP data tell us little about the extent of trade among related parties.

Second, one must learn to distinguish between a country's competitiveness as a location of production on the one hand, and the competitiveness of firms owned by residents of that country on the other. For example, a country may have developed a trade or current account deficit. If this deficit is not a reflection of a cyclical weakness abroad causing a temporary decline in exports, one may conclude that the country's competitive position has deteriorated. Yet if one looked at that nation's share of world export markets, including the sales of foreign affiliates, one might find that the firms owned by the country's residents have actually increased their share of the world market. This holds true for the USA which ran a trade deficit of $28 billion in 1991 but which would have recorded a surplus of $24.3 billion if the sales of its foreign affiliates (net of the sales in the USA of local affiliates of foreign firms) had been included (Landefeld *et al.* 1993).

The increasing internationalization of production and finance thus forces us to reassess the way in which we should collect and interpret data on international payments. While present BOP data represent important raw material for analysis and forecasting, they need to be supplemented by data on indebtedness, exchange rates, and sales of foreign affiliates in order to provide the basis for judging the present and future economic performance of a country.

GUNTER DUFEY
UNIVERSITY OF MICHIGAN BUSINESS SCHOOL

ROLF MIRUS
UNIVERSITY OF ALBERTA

Further reading

(References cited in the text marked *)

* International Monetary Fund (1977) *Balance of Payments Manual*, 4th edn, Washington, DC: International Monetary Fund. (A discussion of the concepts and principles which are germane to the systems of BOP accounting; intended specifically as a practical guide that provides recommendations on matters such as statistical compilation and reporting.)

* International Monetary Fund (1987) *Report on the World Current Account Discrepancy*, Washington, DC: International Monetary Fund. (The actually observed sizeable discrepancy of the world current account is the subject of this inquiry. Its findings point to capital flows as a major possible source.)

International Monetary Fund (1992a) *Balance of Payments Statistics – Yearbook*, part 2, Washington, DC: International Monetary Fund. (A primary source for global financial data, part 2 of the IMF yearbook contains tables of area and world totals of balance of payments components, and aggregate data.)

* International Monetary Fund (1992b) *Report on the Measurement of International Capital Flows*, Washington, DC: International Monetary Fund. (This volume covers three topics: the sources and the methodology employed by those compiling capital account data; problems in obtaining data on foreign direct investment; and the difficulties of measuring portfolio investment.)

Kester, A.Y. (1992) *Behind the Numbers: US Trade in the World Economy*, Washington, DC: National Academy Press. (This book represents a thorough review of the adequacy of the reported data on trade in goods and services for the USA.)

* Landefeld, J.S., Whichard, O.G. and Lowe, J.H. (1993) 'Alternative frameworks for US international transactions', *Survey of Current Business* (December): 50–61. (This article presents alternative measures of international sales of goods

and services for the USA and compares them to standard BOP measurements.)

See also: ACCOUNTING, INTERNATIONAL; ECONOMIC INTEGRATION, INTERNATIONAL; ECONOMICS OF DEVELOPING COUNTRIES; ECONOMIES OF EAST ASIA; FINANCIAL MANAGEMENT, INTERNATIONAL; FOREIGN EXCHANGE RISK, MANAGEMENT OF; GLOBALIZATION; INTERNATIONAL TRADE AND FOREIGN DIRECT INVESTMENT

Related topics in the IEBM: FINANCE, INTERNATIONAL; PRICING ISSUES IN MARKETING

International protection of intellectual property

Overview

International trade disputes in recent years have increasingly involved intellectual property rights (IPRs) and their protection and enforcement. Just what are intellectual property rights? How important are they in international trade and investment? How do they fit in with trends in globalization, deregulation, privatization, opening of markets and economic reforms generally? This entry will address these and the following set of issues.

What relation, if any, do IPRs bear to economic development? If, as some economists assert, gaps between rich and poor countries (and between the rich and poor within countries) are a function of the rate of absorption of technology, what correlation exists between levels of protection of IPRs and rates of absorption of technology or levels of technology being transferred?

Indeed, is protection of IPRs the key question? Or is enforcement of such rights the more important question? These questions will also be addressed.

And what is the relationship, if any, between international protection of IPRs and the information superhighway? Can information downloaded from the Internet be protected? In a related question, if Internet content (copyrighted material) is 'infringed' by unauthorized copying and distribution, who is liable? Is it the user, the Internet service provider (ISP), the administrator of a bulletin board (BBS) or chat room? What about protection of valuable databases? And what correlation or any kind of relation exists between privacy and the level of IPR protection, especially for firms involved in transborder data flow?

Then there is the revolution in biotechnology. Cloning of animals is now a reality. Plant varieties have been altered for several years, not only by hybrid selection, but now by manipulation of the individual genes. Can new plant varieties be protected? If so, how? And what about genetic sequences? Indeed, can genes themselves be patented?

Finally, in view of the new Trade-Related Intellectual Property System (TRIPS) negotiated in the Uruguay Round of the General Agreement on Tariffs and Trade (GATT) negotiations, which created the World Trade Organization (WTO; see WORLD TRADE ORGANIZATION), this entry will address those changes which will be brought about by TRIPS. Will TRIPS become the new standard for protection of IPRs? For enforcement? And if industrialized countries put pressure on developing countries to comply with TRIPS standards, engendering an increasing number of conflicts or disputes, what kind of dispute-settlement provisions does TRIPS contain? And are they compatible with WTO dispute-settlement procedures?

1 Intellectual property: definitions

First, what is intellectual property, how is it protected and how does the system of protection work? Intellectual property essentially comprises assets, both tangible and intangible. These assets are the product of innovation and creativity. They are the product of ideas. Societies, in the form of governments, have made a social contract to grant a certain status to those expressions and inventions, the status of property. Owners of property possess various types of rights. For our purposes, we are concerned with those rights traditionally protected by law.

The categories of intellectual property most commonly recognized are the trade secret, the patent, the copyright or right of authors, the trademark (and its companion service mark) and industrial designs. An important type of industrial design more recently recognized is the mask work, the expression of a design for a semiconductor chip which is exclusive to the creator of the same.

Trade secrets

Trade secrets are perhaps the most misunderstood. To be protectable at all they must be secret or not in the public domain. They commonly consist of a formula (e.g. for the treatment of fabric or other materials), compounds (e.g. pharmaceutical), processes (such as chemical processes) or compilations of information (such as a customer list by zip code or an employee list, which can be contained in a database). Trade secrets generally relate to the production of machinery or goods, or to the provision of unique services which provide commercial advantage to the owner. Computer software is protected by trade secret law only in some countries, and the length and degree of protection of trade secrets varies significantly, with the US, UK, Canada and other common-law countries being the most heedful, followed by western Europe (most European Union (EU) members; see EUROPEAN UNION). But trade secrets are embodied in contracts, and protected and enforced to the degree contract law is respected and enforced, since trade secrets are normally not included in patent, trademark or copyright laws, which require disclosure in return for protection.

Patents

Patents, on the other hand, are in the nature of a conditional monopoly granted by the sovereign to an individual inventor for a specific duration in return for disclosure in the form of publication. A patent is a temporary right to exclude others from using a novel, non-obvious and useful invention. Patents have been granted and protected since at least the Middle Ages, but the exclusions and durations have been troublesome. Patents, like trademarks (see below) must be registered to be protected (enforceable), normally at a national office maintained by the sovereign. In order for a patent to be issued, the invention had to be new and novel, including not reported or disclosed elsewhere in the world. This and other technical issues engendered a need for international cooperation, leading to the International Convention for the Protection of Industrial Property of 1883, commonly referred to as the Paris Convention. That which was earlier commonly referred to as industrial property has gradually become characterized today as intellectual property, as 'non-industrial' applications have multiplied. The principal feature of the Paris Convention is 'national treatment', a phrase essential to virtually all international treaties and agreements (e.g. GATT/WTO), which means only that a member country must accord the same treatment to foreigners as it accords to its own nationals. Another feature is a one-year priority for first filing under the Paris Convention. There is no requirement in the Paris Convention, amended several times (most recently 1967), that features such as term or duration of the patent be standardized, nor even for commonality of the categories of subject matter for which a sovereign will issue a patent (i.e. exclusions).

Trademarks

A trademark is a word, logo or design affixed to a product which denotes or identifies the source or origin of the product. It has evolved into an indication of quality and, like a patent, must be registered with an office normally maintained by the sovereign in order to be protected. According to Sherwood (1990), 'trademarks evolved into protectable rights from the understanding that it is unfair to present one's goods as the goods of another. This thought developed as part of the law of unfair competition.' Over time, the mark itself gained the appropriate legal standing independent of the body of unfair competition law. A registered trademark remains valid for a period of ten years and may be renewed for one or more additional ten-year terms, as long is it is in continuous use, and continues to identify and distinguish the owner's products or services. Protection may be eroded and even lost if the word or term for the goods becomes generic (e.g. sanka, kleenex, xerox). The Paris Convention covers both patents and trademarks. The convention provides for trademarks a feature in addition to that of national treatment (enjoyed by patents), which is the guarantee to the owner of trademark rights in one country a right of priority to file an application for the same mark in other member countries within six months of the date of the first application.

Copyright

The next important category is copyright, sometimes referred to as author's rights. The feature being protected here is the creative expression of the author, including books, musical compositions and virtually anything publishable in a medium which can be circulated. France was an early pioneer in extending rights to foreign authors, but issues like translations and state controls led to the Berne Convention for the Protection of Literary and Artistic Works (1886). Like the Paris Convention, the Berne Convention established the principle of national treatment for copyright, and also protected the rights of translation. Originally that right extended to print translations, but today it also includes film, audio, video and multimedia rights, among others. The public policy applicable to patents and trademarks results in limited durations of validity, while copyright extends to a period of fifty years beyond the life of the author. The term 'computer software' includes computer programs, databases and documentation of various sorts (Bender 1996). This category is complex, and various types of software are protected by copyright, trade secret law, trademark (documentation), and even patents, but software is also protected by commercial means, including source and object codes, accompanying software support and

maintenance, and sophisticated forms of encryption (Bender 1996). Rights protected under copyright law include not only the right to reproduce, but also rights to distribute and publicly display the copyrighted work. A person who violates any of the exclusive rights is a direct infringer (subject to the 'fair use' exceptions such as educational, religious and other non-commercial uses which promote public awareness, knowledge and the progress of science.)

Mask works

The category of industrial designs and utility models has long been protected, but in recent years the mask work is the latest and most commercially important expression of industrial design to be protected. Several countries which produce semiconductor 'chips' have enacted laws specifically covering mask works, protection for which is rather unique and falls between that of patent and copyright in concept. The USA enacted a statute in 1984 called the Semiconductor Chip Protection Act, granting protection for ten years from the earlier of date of registration or first commercial use, and including a provision intended to influence other countries to address this type of property, by extending protection only to foreign nationals whose countries offered reciprocity, a concept increasingly being used in international trade agreements.

Finally, as a result of the biotechnology and genetic engineering revolution a form of protection has evolved for varieties of plants bred through the use of newly developed techniques. This led to the enactment of the International Union for the Protection of New Varieties of Plants (UPOV) in 1987. Although this agreement has not yet been as broadly accepted as the Paris or Berne Conventions, this subject is important for a small but important block of countries, and research in this area is known to be active in a large number of countries. It should be noted that it took the USA 100 years to accede to the Berne Convention, although it participated in the Universal Copyright Convention as an alternative (Sherwood 1990).

2 Conflict between industrialized and developing nations

Because most inventions, trademarks and copyrights had been generated in industrialized countries, protection of IPRs was stronger, albeit uneven, in those countries. Developing countries were suspicious of and sceptical about the value of royalties paid on the licences of foreign-owned IPRs. The systems of protection (laws and regulations) in developing countries was not a high legislative priority and was therefore found lacking by IPR owners from industrialized countries, who were also the source of foreign direct investment (FDI) (see FOREIGN MARKET ENTRY STRATEGIES; INTERNATIONAL TRADE AND FOREIGN DIRECT INVESTMENT) and technology transfer (TT) (see INTERNATIONAL TECHNOLOGY TRANSFER) to the former. Suppliers of FDI and TT frequently asserted that they withheld the most advanced and latest technology from their own subsidiaries in developing countries, as well as unrelated joint-venture partners, licensees and other types of alliances. The reason given for this was lack of adequate protection of IPRs. Developing-country government officials, however, did not agree. They did not view a strong level of IPR protection as part of the infrastructure of development. In fact, they did not generally see the relationship between a strong IPR system and development; nor did they see the trade implications of IPR protection.

The era of confrontation

This debate raged in developing countries during the 1970s as United Nations (UN) studies influenced developing-country governments to enact restrictive laws controlling FDI and TT, especially in Latin American countries and other important emerging markets (e.g. India, Nigeria and South Korea). However, high growth rates by Asian 'tigers' and a so-called 'lost decade' in Latin America coupled with the end of a protracted cold war have led to a re-examination of prior policies in many developing countries and new policies in countries in transition from centrally planned to market economies. This coincided with expanding world trade generally, globalization (see GLOBALIZATION) of financial markets, the formation of regional trading blocs, and a stronger world trading system of rights and obligations embodied in the GATT. The final and most important development leading to major change was the protracted Uruguay Round of trade negotiations under the GATT (see EUROPEAN UNION; NORTH AMERICAN FREE-TRADE AGREEMENT; ASSOCIATION OF SOUTH-EAST ASIAN NATIONS; ASIAN PACIFIC ECONOMIC COMMUNITY; ECONOMIC INTEGRATION, INTERNATIONAL)

The Uruguay Round and the WTO

In its final form, the Uruguay Round expanded previous discussions and reached agreement on trade in services (in the form of the Generalized Agreement on Trade in Services, or GATS), agreement on trade-related aspects of intellectual property rights (TRIPS), and agreement on trade-related investment measures (TRIMS), as well as the legal structure for a modernized and restructured administration (now called the World Trade Organization or WTO; see WORLD TRADE ORGANIZATION), and a sophisticated system of dispute settlement, which was highly successful in its first years of operation, finally including developing countries filing disputes against industrialized countries and vice versa, instead of disputes merely among industrialized countries. As more attention began to focus on the role of IPRs in an increasingly information-oriented, globalized world, the US International Trade Commission conducted various studies during the 1980s, and in 1991 the International Finance Corporation (IFC) of the World Bank initiated a study on *Intellectual Property Protection, Foreign Direct Investment and Technology Transfer* (Mansfield 1994).

The Mansfield studies

Professor Edwin Mansfield of the University of Pennsylvania conducted a study of 100 US firms in six different industries, of which 94 provided useable returns. The Mansfield study (the first of its kind), although limited to US firms, essentially confirmed what many suppliers of FDI and TT had asserted for many years, although with several important distinctions and qualifications. This World Bank/IFC study concluded that the strength or weakness of IPR protection has an important effect on some, but not all, FDI decisions, especially in R&D facilities, and most importantly in industries like chemicals and pharmaceuticals, food and, to a slightly lesser degree, machinery and electrical equipment. The study also found material influence on the metals and transportation industries, and significant differences between the types of establishments to which technology was transferred in developing countries (i.e. lower in distribution-type establishments and more important in R&D and manufacturing) (Mansfield 1994). The IFC sponsored Professor Mansfield in a second study to learn how German and Japanese firms perceived the issues, and he generally found a fairly high correlation with the American study, although with sharper differences appearing in the lower-technology sectors (Mansfield 1995).

3 The TRIPS agreement

Partly as a result of several studies, the continued rounds of trade negotiations beginning with the Tokyo Round and including the Uruguay Round, and endless conferences, meetings and discussions, developing countries began to appreciate the relation between IPR protection and development. Early discussions focused on the narrow issue of counterfeit trading, but the TRIPS agreement 'is the most comprehensive international agreement on IPRs ever negotiated' (Primo Braga 1995). In addition to national treatment and most-favoured nation (MFN), the TRIPS contained a strong commitment to transparency, and established minimum standards of protection and enforcement guidelines for the first time. Member countries which join WTO automatically adhere to TRIPS rules, as TRIPS forms one of the main pillars of the WTO. Members have some discretion on implementation of the standards, and industrialized-country

suppliers continue to complain about inadequate protection in certain developing countries, but several important developing countries have strengthened their intellectual property laws in anticipation of the TRIPS agreement being signed and afterwards (e.g. Mexico, Chile, South Korea, Taiwan, Slovenia and the Czech Republic). Disputes arising under TRIPS will be resolved under the sophisticated WTO dispute-settlement procedure.

Copyrights

The TRIPS agreement provides that member countries comply with the Berne Convention, as amended, with minor exceptions. Some thirty-three GATT contracting parties were not members of the Berne Convention prior to TRIPS. The main innovations of the agreement pertain to computer programs and databases, stipulating that they shall be protected as literary works under Berne.

Trademarks

TRIPS confirms and clarifies some aspects of the Paris Convention regarding trademarks and their registration, strengthening such protection and including a commitment to transparency. An important feature regarding trademarks gives owners of well-known trademarks the power to challenge marks which are confusingly similar and is designed to eliminate speculative trademark registration, which has been a common practice in many developing countries. Certain individuals would immediately register trademarks in developing countries as soon as notice is published of the application for such rights in the USA or the UK.

Patents

TRIPS expanded the definition of patentable subject matter to include processes as well as products in all fields of technology. This definition alone obliges many developing countries to revise their patent laws, as many did not grant patents for some food, pharmaceutical and chemical products and, especially, processes. It also included a provision for the protection of biotechnological inventions (including cell and gene manipulation) and requires members to provide protection for plant varieties through patents or some other effective method.

Mask works

TRIPS adopted many provisions from the Treaty on Intellectual Property in Respect of Integrated Circuits (Washington Treaty, 1989), but introduced changes strengthening the protection for layout designs, as all the chip producing countries were not satisfied with and none ratified the Washington Treaty.

Trade secrets

Although the TRIPS agreement did not use the specific term 'trade secrets', it includes a provision for the protection of undisclosed information, which is linked to unfair competition practice as defined in the Paris Convention. There was heated North–South debate on trade secrets and developing countries strongly opposed treating trade secrets as IPRs. This compromise strengthens the protection, including non-disclosure of test data submitted to governments for approvals of food, agricultural, chemical and pharmaceutical products, which has been a sore point with technology suppliers in these areas.

4 Enforcement of IPRs

Strengthening laws and regulations protecting these categories of property rights is an important step towards recognition of their value and importance, both as assets and as an indicator of the desirable climate for FDI and TT. However, it is only part of the question of international protection of IPRs. The companion issue is judicial enforcement. This includes the rule of law, the opportunity of those alleging infringement of their rights to sue the alleged infringers and obtain objective decisions on the merits, and the ability to collect actual damages and ensure

the cessation of those activities which constitute the alleged violations. Without enforceability of the rights, intellectual property assets are of little value.

Rating intellectual property systems in developing countries

As a result of the increased interest in IPR systems, their protection and enforcement, a study (Sherwood 1997a) was initiated to evaluate and rate the IPR systems in eighteen developing countries, mostly in the Western Hemisphere plus India, Pakistan and South Korea. The system rates overall national regimes on a base scale of 100. The author states that the system was not applied to the intellectual property systems of Europe, Japan or the USA, but estimates the results for those countries to be in the range 75–90 or higher, while the countries studied ranged from 12 to 83, Bahamas receiving the highest (83) rating in the group. The intellectual property systems were evaluated under eight major categories.

Enforceability

Judicial independence was the pivotal element of enforceability, along with the education and training of judges, the availability of legal tools (i.e. injunctive relief and seizures), familiarity with IPR concepts, and trained prosecutors, police and customs officials willing to act reliably. Transparency and corruption were also considered in this category.

Administration

Transparency – meaning rational decisions openly explained to the public – was a principal element of the administration of IPR enforcement systems. Efficiency was the second pillar, considered to be completion of actions within reasonable time periods (compared with administrative practice in industrialized countries). The third important consideration was low-cost administration, relative to the wealth of the country examined and also in comparison with other countries. This included elimination of unnecessary bureaucratic procedures. Corruption was also examined here to the extent possible.

Substantive law

Next the study examined the substantive law covering the five major areas considered (copyrights, patents, trademarks, trade secrets and life forms – plant and animal varieties). As each of these categories has been defined above, this treatment addresses only some indicators in each category. For example, regarding copyrights the analysis considered whether the law extends full treatment to all forms of creative expression such as computer software, databases, sound recordings and rebroadcast transmissions. With respect to patents, important criteria included whether the period of protection was less than the twenty-year TRIPS duration, and whether the patent value was diminished by easy availability of compulsory licences and severe narrowing of patent claims. For trademarks the principal factors were whether the system discriminated against foreign marks (i.e. 'linking' provisions first found in Andean Pact Decision 24 in 1971, which required local licensed users of foreign marks to link the foreign mark with a new local mark within a time period; this provision was extraordinarily controversial and energetically contested, and was never enforced in most countries with such provisions), and discouraged speculative registrations (discussed above). Since the category of trade secrets engendered such raging debates between developing countries and industrialized countries, the principal consideration in this area was whether the country maintained an adequate legal basis for protection of trade secrets, especially including action against third parties, either those hiring away employees with secret knowledge, or otherwise appropriating non-public and valuable commercial information without permission. Finally, in the new area of life forms evaluation was primarily concerned with whether plant breeders rights were protected and whether higher life forms were patentable.

Treaties

All countries examined in the study were also rated on their adherence to or compliance with international treaties and conventions protecting IPRs, such as the Paris, Berne and Geneva (on phonograms) conventions, the Patent Cooperation Treaty (PCT, 1978) (see INTERNATIONAL BUSINESS, LEGAL DIMENSIONS OF) and other relevant international agreements, some of which are mentioned above.

Clearly, opinions differ from developing-country authorities to industrialized-country suppliers of technology on the importance of many of these factors. However, recent studies (by Mansfield, Primo Braga, Sherwood and others) underscore the importance of 'TRIPS plus' standards of protection and enforcement of IPRs as an important criteria in attracting FDI and TT and augmenting economic development programmes. More studies in this area are needed and are certain to appear.

5 The Internet and its implications for IPRs

The most important development as 2000 approaches is the extensive use of the Internet, which began to erupt in the 1990s. The substantive Internet issues involve mostly copyright law and procedural issues of jurisdiction. Copyright owners have the exclusive right to reproduce their original work in copies, distribute copies, perform and display the work publicly, and prepare derivative works based on their original work (Bender 1996). But the original work must be affixed to a tangible medium of expression, sufficiently permanent to be perceived, reproduced or otherwise communicated for more than a transitory duration (Bender 1995). A computer program encoded on a disk or CD-ROM qualifies for protection. But what about one written on to random access memory (RAM)? Early indications suggest that RAM attachment is too transitory, but the question is certain to be litigated on different factual situations, and early USA cases are already divided on this issue.

Liability for copyright infringement

Clearly a computer user who downloads copyrighted material from the Internet without permission is infringing the owner's copyright and may be liable under appropriate copyright laws. Is the Internet service provider (ISP) who provides access to the Internet for that user also liable? This would appear to be overreaching, but the question is not yet settled. Can the ISP control the activities of its numerous individual subscribers? Certainly it can make prudent attempts with notices and the like, but control is impossible. Similarly, a person or organization which sponsors a bulletin board service (BBS) has the intention of facilitating the exchange of communication among and between BBS users. If a user posts material which infringes some owner's copyright, presumably that user would be liable for infringement. Would the BBS provider also be liable? That question has not yet been resolved. Since copyright infringement can be direct, contributory and even vicarious, according to cases decided in the USA (Bender 1997), it is apparent that these issues are complex, and new laws will be developed to address these economic and social concerns.

Database protection

The World Intellectual Property Organization (WIPO) of the UN convened a diplomatic conference on Database Protection and other matters arising from new technology and new media in December 1996. Database protection has been characterized as a solution in search of a problem (Maxeiner 1997). This presents another complex issue, for which two contrasting approaches have emerged, but no consensus has yet been reached. Database is defined in the EU Directive, effective 11 March 1996, as 'a collection of independent works, data or other materials arranged in a systematic or methodical way and individually accessible by electronic or other means'. A delicate balance must be maintained between society's interest in the free flow of information and economic interests in the creation and maintenance of valuable databases. With the expanding use of the Internet, owners of IPRs can have adequate protection only if it is global protection. The EU approach would create a new *sui generis* property right in databases (e.g. irrespective of originality). This means a new, unique property right of its own. The text of the Directive indicates that the right shall be available when there has been a 'substantial investment in either the obtaining, verification or presentation of the contents to prevent extraction and/or reutilization of the whole or of a substantial part' of the contents of the database. This would be a new basis for the establishment or granting of an IPR, since originality and creativity are not even mentioned. The question arises of what protection is available to database owners against users of the Internet with unfettered access to the database who are not in EU member states.

The US approach is contained in a bill (HR2652) still pending in Congress, which is entitled 'Misappropriation of Collections of Information'. The basis is the traditional doctrine of unfair competition, rather than copyright principles. This law, if passed, would impose liability on anyone who extracts or uses in commerce all or a substantial part of a collection of information resulting in economic damage (to the market for the product or service containing the information). The policy clearly would not affect or enlarge copyright protection; nor would it limit the constraints imposed by existing antitrust (competition) laws.

Some have argued that existing copyright, trade secret and unfair competition laws, in addition to commercial methods such as encryption (by inserting a microprocessor chip in the computer to provide a deciphering function and placing codes in the program which can be deciphered only by the chip) or the use of 'copy protect' coding on the diskette (so that the diskette can be used but not copied) are adequate to protect databases. But these are useless for databases available through the Internet, and are more effective with copyrighted software programs.

6 Conclusion

With technology advancing at ever increasing speeds, both protection and enforcement of these and not yet discovered forms of intellectual property are evolving, and commercial uses will lead legal protection and enforcement measures. The Internet in particular dramatizes the need for standardized global protection, as the use of the Internet expands across countries which may not even be members of the WTO, and therefore do not adhere to the TRIPS agreement.

In areas of both copyright protection and database protection, rights of transmission and distribution are threatened, in addition to the rights of unauthorized copying. Early cases, decided on differing factual situations, have divided, and will continue to split as more technology is developed and absorbed, creating more uses.

Multimedia is a term increasingly in use, and refers to a product combining text, still and/or moving images and sound. Optical storage devices and digital video disks are recent advances that create newer problems. These are the areas that will become increasingly important, and where the law will continue to develop.

ROBERT J. RADWAY
PRESIDENT VECTOR INTERNATIONAL
PACE UNIVERSITY
NEW YORK

Further reading

(References cited in the text marked *)

Armstrong, John A. (1993) 'Trends in global science and technology and what they mean for intellectual property systems', in M.B Wallerstein, M.E. Mogee and R.A. Schoen (eds) *Global Dimensions of Intellectual Property Rights in Science and Technology*, Washington, DC: National Academy Press, National Research Council. (Provides a thoughtful context for consideration of the future role of intellectual property in developing countries, and was prepared for a major policy conference.)

* Bender, David (1995) 'Domestic and international software licensing', paper presented at the Practicing Law Institute Annual Seminar on Technology Licensing and Litigation, Practicing Law Institute, New York, March. (Prepared for the annual institute for specialized attorneys working in this area; provides clear definitions, cases and a thorough discussion of the relevant licensing issues by the author of a leading multi-volume reference book published by a major legal publisher.)

* Bender, David (1996) 'Software licensing', *Technology Licensing and Litigation*, New York: Practicing Law Institute, March. (An update on the previous paper, including more recent cases and a thorough discussion of the complex infringement issues arising from newer technology.)

* Bender, David (1997) 'U.S. copyright law and the Internet', paper presented at the Korea Association for Info Media Law, Seoul, Korea, June. (Provides a deeper analysis of troublesome questions posed by information technology under US law and offers thoughts on future directions.)

Dam, Kenneth W. (1994) 'The economic underpinnings of patent law', *Journal of Legal Studies* 23: 247–71. (Assesses the evolution of patent policy in the USA in the twentieth century, including detailed analysis of court opinions, providing a strong basis for criticism of the conventional wisdom that patents are monopolies and thus bad policy.)

* European Union (1996) *Database Directive*, Final Version, Brussels, 11 March. (Full text of the Directive of the European Union providing for a new *sui generis* approach to the protection of databases.)

* Mansfield, Edwin (1994) *Intellectual Property Protection, Foreign Direct Investment and Technology Transfer*, Discussion Paper 19, Washington, DC: International Finance Corporation. (This empirical study and the following one, commissioned by the World Bank, provide important contributions to the long-raging discussion on the importance of intellectual property protection to technological growth in developing countries, using data from US corporations.)

* Mansfield, Edwin (1995) *Intellectual Property Protection, Direct Investment and Technology Transfer: Germany, Japan and the United States*, Discussion Paper 27, Washington, DC: International Finance Corporation. (The second of the World Bank commissioned studies gathered data from German and Japanese firms and essentially confirmed the data from US firms.)

Maskus, Keith E. (1996) 'Intellectual property rights in the global information economy', in Thomas J. Courchene (ed.) *Policy Frameworks for a Knowledge Economy*, Kingston, Ontario: John Deutsch Institute. (Uses Lebanon as an example of a small, open economy to assess regional trade accords, the relation of intellectual property to competition rules and the relationship between intellectual property and FDI.)

* Maxeiner, James R. (1997) 'Some comments on the issue of database protection', paper submitted in connection with panel participation at Copyright, New Technology and New Media: The U.S. Copyright Office Speaks on Intellectual Property Protection in the New Era, Washington, DC, December. (Reflects the views of one of the largest database owners as one side of the debate raging on whether and how to protect databases in the USA and on the Internet.)

* Primo Braga, Carlos A. (1995) 'Trade-related intellectual property issues: the Uruguay Round agreement and its economic implications', in W. Martin and L.A. Winters (eds) *The Uruguay Round and the Developing Economies*, World Bank Discussion Paper 307, Washington, DC: World Bank. (Lays out a history of the debate on the role of intellectual property in international trade in previous GATT negotiations, and evaluates the economics of IPRs and their implications for developing countries.)

* Sherwood, Robert M. (1990) *Intellectual Property and Economic Development*, Boulder, CO: Westview Press. (Now out of print, this book based on the author's extensive interviews with Brazilian and Mexican firms regarding the effect of the national intellectual property regimes on business patterns challenges conventional myths concerning the benefits produced by weak intellectual property protection through extensive case studies; attempts to show that weak protection frustrates local firms' decisions on innovation and puts forth the proposition that intellectual property should be viewed by developing countries as part of national infrastructure.)

* Sherwood, Robert M. (1997a) 'Intellectual property systems and investment stimulation: the rating of systems in eighteen developing countries', *IDEA: The Journal of Law and Technology* 37(2): 261–370, Franklin Pierce Law Center. (The second of two recent articles by the same author presents a novel methodology to assess and compare intellectual property systems from the perspective of private investors, both national and foreign. The study is based on extensive interviews in most of the countries described, and produces a numerical rating system comparing not only the laws and regulations, but also national policies and legal systems for enforcement of IPRs.)

* Sherwood, Robert M. (1997b) 'The TRIPS agreement: implications for developing countries', *IDEA: The Journal of Law and Technology* 37(3): 491–544, Franklin Pierce Law Center. (This study was commissioned by WIPO and examines the likely implications for developing countries arising out of the TRIPS agreement, including macroeconomic and judicial administrative implications).

US International Trade Commission (1988) *Foreign Protection of Intellectual Property Rights and the Effect on US Industry and Trade*, USITC Publication 2065, Washington, DC, February. (This largely statistical report was based on responses from nearly 400 US firms to a survey carried out in preparation for the Uruguay Round of Trade Negotiations, and was widely cited to support the assertion that US firms were losing billions of dollars annually to overseas piracy.)

US Patent and Trademark Office (1998) *Agreement on Trade-related Aspects of Intellectual Property Rights* (Contains a complete transcript of the TRIPS agreement signed on conclusion of the Uruguay Round of Trade Negotiations; at http://www.uspto.org.)

See also: ASIA-PACIFIC ECONOMIC COMMUNITY; ASSOCIATION OF SOUTH-EAST ASIAN NATIONS; EUROPEAN UNION; EXPORTING; FOREIGN MARKET ENTRY STRATEGIES; GLOBAL STRATEGIC ALLIANCES; GLOBAL STRATGIC PLANNING; GLOBALIZATION; INTERNATIONAL BUSINESS, LEGAL DIMENSIONS OF; INTERNATIONAL MARKETING; INTERNATIONAL TECHNOLOGY TRANSFER; INTERNATIONAL TRADE AND FOREIGN DIRECT INVESTMENT; MARKETING MANAGEMENT, INTERNATIONAL; NORTH AMERICAN FREE-TRADE AGREEMENT; NON-TARIFF BARRIERS; POLITICAL RISK; POLITICAL RISK, ASSESSMENT AND MANAGEMENT OF; TECHNOLOGY STRATEGY, INTERNATIONAL; WORLD TRADE ORGANIZATION

Related topics in the IEBM: ECONOMICS OF DEVELOPING COUNTRIES; GENERAL AGREEMENT ON TARIFFS AND TRADE (GATT)

International technology transfer (ITT)

Overview

International technology transfer (ITT) studies cover the economic relationship between a transferor and a transferee, as well as a whole series of related issues, such as the relevant national policies and legal framework of the nations in the world. For different environmental and developmental reasons, technological advances in different countries have always been uneven. The uneven nature of technological progress throughout the world provides the very basis for technology transfer. In the past few decades ITT has multiplied by leaps and bounds.

The concept of technology has been defined in many ways and from different angles. Simply put, it refers to a class of knowledge for making a specific product. The technical skills necessary to utilize a production technique and a product are often included in the definition of technology. In the arena of business, technology has a number of unique features. First, it does not have a fixed shape, consisting mainly of design, documents and prescriptions. It can also be diffused through oral dictation and illustration. Second, it can be used and transferred multiple times. Therefore its marginal cost is almost zero. Third, technology transfer often refers to the transfer of the right to use instead of to ownership. Therefore it has a public good nature. When knowledge is given to another party that knowledge usually remains available to the transferor. The benefits of using a technology can be seriously influenced by the number of people with the right to use it.

Technology has diverse forms, ranging from a fairly simple agricultural process to very complex computer systems. A distinction may be made between 'conventional technology' and 'high technology'. Conventional technology comprises, for example, the basic technology in the textile, paper and cement industries. In contrast, high-technology industries are characterized by heavy research and development (R&D) expenditure, rapid and continual technological change, the important role of complex patented or non-patented proprietary technology and large capital requirements.

There is also the distinction between open, semi-open and secret technologies. Open technology consists of various published and circulated technological theories, academic reports and open technology forums. Semi-open technologies are patented technologies. Inventors register their inventions for patent protection, under which nobody can use the invention without the permission of the patentee within the effective period of a patent, otherwise that person infringes on the right of the patentee. On the other hand, the patentee should publicize his or her technology so that the public can understand it and follow legitimate ways of using this technology. Inventors usually do not publicize all of the contents of their technology but keep at least some core parts secret. Therefore patented technology becomes semi-open. Secret technology refers to know-how, which consists of unpublicized core technologies and data, which are best protected by security measures and the laws on protecting commercial secrecy.

The term 'transfer' is more controversial in definition. People disagree on the factors that determine whether a transfer has really occurred. Some argue that technology is not transferred unless it is absorbed and actually used by the transferee. Others contend that how the transferee deals with the transferred technology should not be a determining factor in whether the technology is in fact transferred. However, unless technology transfer is contained in sales of technology-intensive equipment and products, it can be a more complicated concept than simple trade of physical goods. By transferring knowledge on how to make the product, the transferor has not automatically given up the knowledge but, rather, shares it with the transferee. Therefore it is not unreasonable to say that a transfer is not achieved until the transferee understands and can utilize the technology.

ITT is a complicated aspect of international business which is an organic part of a firm's international strategy, influenced by diverse factors, ranging from firm size, global strategy, cultural and geographical distance to receiving the country's development strategies and investment policies, and the recipient firm's absorptive capabilities. Technology can be transferred through licensing, franchising, foreign direct investment (FDI), sale of turnkey plants, subcontracting, co-production agreements, cooperative R&D programmes, export of high-technology products and capital goods, reverse engineering, exchange of scientific and technical personnel, international conferences and seminars, trade shows, education and training of foreigners, commercial visits, open literature, industrial espionage, government assistance programmes,

etc. Most of these transfers are difficult to monitor. Only when a technology is transferred via a market mechanism does it have an explicit value, though it may not reflect the 'true' value of the technology being transferred.

I International technology transfer

Unique business features

Every specific technology has a life cycle characterized by the S-curve, which describes the maturation and replacement of a technology, as well as the necessity of implementing different strategies for a technology at different stages of maturity, as shown in Figure 1. In the embryonic stage the technology, which has just passed experimental requirements, is not used for large-scale production and the value of transfer is not normally high. When a technology grows into the mature stage the value of transfer is climbing up to its climax, as it generates increasing economic benefits to the producers. But as a technology moves into its ageing stage it reaches its ceiling of performance. The marginal cost of developing an additional improvement grows, while the value of transferring this technology declines. The technology begins to

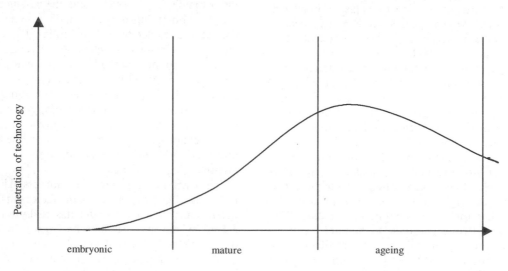

Figure 1 Technology life cycle

experience a downturn and degradation, and eventually it is abandoned.

There are a number of unique features in technology transfer. First, commercial technology transfer is highly monopolistic. The contemporary patent system has further reinforced such monopoly. In order to maintain the advantage of its technology and products, the owner of a technology does not normally transfer the technology, except in some specific situations, for example, when a transfer is necessary for occupying the market, when the transfer can bring huge profits, or when the transfer does not threaten its monopoly. In addition, as a result of unequal development of science and technology, developed countries tend to impose various restrictions on the transfer of advanced technology in order to maintain their monopolistic position.

Second, a single technology can be traded multiple times, as the transfer does not involve ownership but only the right to use. The number of transfers will have a direct impact on the value of the technology. When a technology is transferred to a variety of end-users the price the transferor charges will drop correspondingly. Only in specific situations is ownership transferred (such as subcontracted R&D), but the price is usually very high and conditions are very rigid. In contrast, ordinary merchandise trade involves the transfer of both ownership and the right to use.

Finally, technology transfer does not simply follow the basic market rule of exchange. The price of the transferred technology is *not* simply determined by its value (i.e. R&D costs plus margin) but, rather, is heavily influenced by the profits it can bring to the transferee. The price of the technology transferred is the 'licensor's share of licensee's profits'. When the transferor is in a monopolistic position he or she will tend to charge high prices. When the transferor is not in a monopolistic position he or she will tend to settle on a price for the technology that is far lower than the price needed to recapture the full cost of the technological effort, simply because the marginal costs associated with an additional sale are usually very low and the costs of generating the technology itself are sunk.

International product life-cycle theory (IPLC) and technology transfer

Products have life cycles encompassing initial innovations, incremental innovations and a declining process to the end. According to IPLC, the international participation of a business can be examined by following sequential stages in the life cycle of the product or process it develops. Owing to the restrictions in the flow of information across national borders and the growing demand for high-income consumer goods and labour-saving producer goods, innovation of new products is far more likely to be realized in highly developed and industrialized nations. These same innovations are more likely to be applied in less developed nations later, as these nations develop economies and consumer tastes similar to those of the highly industrialized nations.

This life-cycle roughly consists of six stages of development (see Figure 2). The first stage involves product development and domestic sales growth, in which the product undergoes test marketing, product redesign and re-engineering, and production scale-up. During the second stage, domestic sales continue to grow, but the growth rate may begin to decrease. Exports to other more developed countries may take place, with some of them entering the less developed countries, though all production still remains in the country where the product was originated. Heated domestic competition, better understanding of the product technology in other more developed countries and some host government's incentives usher in the third stage, the stage of FDI in more developed countries. When overseas markets grow to a substantial size manufacturers from more developed countries begin to enjoy scale of economies and may take away some markets in less developed countries (the fourth stage). In the fifth stage manufacturers from more developed countries are able to penetrate the home base of the original product-creating firm as they reach such a large scale in production that costs become low enough to offset the transportation and tariff protection of the home country. In the last stage manufacturers in less developed countries, with lower labour costs and improved skills, become exporters to the more developed countries and the home country.

One important implication of the product life-cycle theory of technology transfer is that the investment in R&D can be recovered over a much longer product life. This may also mean that a less developed country may find it cheaper to buy new technology rather than develop it locally, because a multinational corporation (MNC; see MULTINATIONAL CORPORATIONS) can spread the R&D costs across a worldwide market. Moreover, by the time a technology is transferred to less developed countries the company is likely to have recovered the major portion of the R&D costs and may therefore be willing to price the technology only on the basis of its much smaller marginal cost. Therefore both sides may benefit from technology transfer.

Key factors influencing the mode of technology transfer

Many factors can influence the mode of technology transfer. From the transferor's perspective, three groups of factors should be closely examined before it can decide on the mode of transfer and search for a suitable transferee: factors related to the technology to be transferred, the receiving country and the transferor itself.

The technology to be transferred
For the purpose of transfer, technology can be divided into two types: non-tacit and tacit. The former is reflected in designs, drawings and specifications, while the latter represents an individual's personal knowledge. Tacit technology is difficult to transfer in codified form alone and requires intensive human contacts. Age and level of sophistication have most direct influence on the proportion of tacit know-how in a technology.

The information contained in a mature technology is widely codified, while very few details are codified in a cutting-edge technology which has not been widely applied and is in a state of constant change. Therefore the latter has a substantial proportion of tacit information. In terms of the level of sophistication, simple technology which is easy to learn and use is in the category of non-tacit technology, while sophisticated technology, even though mature, cannot be completely codified, leaving many elements uncodified.

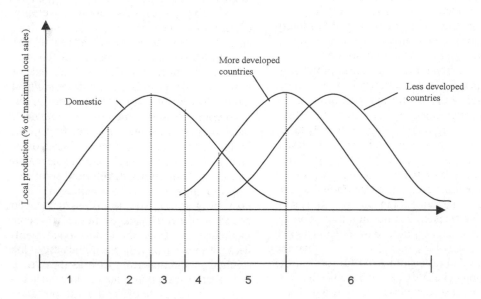

Figure 2 Product life-cycle phases
Source: Aggarwal 1991: 67.

The receiving country

The policies of the receiving country tend to have a major influence on the modes of transfer. Varying significantly in form and content, these policies range from supporting to restricting FDI and certain modes of technology transfer. Some governments show their preference for certain channels to acquire foreign technology (such as joint venture and turnkey project) by making other channels more difficult (such as licensing and wholly owned foreign enterprise). Few foreign companies can operate outside the realm set by the host government.

The capacity of the receiving country to absorb technology also has a considerable influence on the modes of technology transfer. The more developed the country is, the higher is the likelihood of licensing transactions as a channel to transfer technology. The rationale is that local firms in a developed country are better prepared to absorb foreign technology by licensing alone, while local firms in a developing country tend to need more commitment from transferors than licensing alone to assimilate the transferred technology successfully.

The transferor itself

Size probably has the most significant impact on the modes of transfer. A small firm has constantly to deal with serious financial constraints, which can easily cause it insolvency in a capital-intensive or time-consuming project. Lack of qualified personnel also restricts a small firm's capacity to internationalize its operations. The demands on senior executives at home also prevent them from devoting themselves to foreign projects. In short, a small firm is more likely to choose an option which makes fewer demands on its financial and human resources; licensing is obviously a more attractive option than wholly owned subsidiaries or joint ventures. Other factors include the nature of business, the structure of the company and the management style.

In contrast, a large MNC can afford to invest in an unprofitable project in a foreign country for such strategic considerations as establishing a pre-emptive market presence in that country. MNCs also have large pools of experienced international staff and can afford to involve themselves in projects in geographically and culturally remote countries. They can also participate in major projects that require considerable financial and human resource commitments. For the same reason, a wholly owned subsidiary may be a preferable means of technology transfer even though licensing is a much cheaper option, since the subsidiary may better serve its strategic purposes.

2 International technology licensing

International licensing

International licensing, defined broadly, comprises a variety of contractual arrangements whereby domestic firms (licensors) sell their intangible assets or property rights to foreign firms (licensees) in return for royalties and/or other forms of payment. The transfer of these intangible assets or property rights is the core of a licensing agreement. Under this arrangement the firms typically provide a limited right to produce and market the product in a specified geographical region. The transfer is usually supported by technical services to ensure the appropriate exploitation of the assets. Licensing agreements are normally long-term arrangements that may require significant investment by the licensee.

Licensing to foreign companies has long played an important role in business strategies in developed countries. With Japanese companies alone, American firms signed approximately 32,000 licensing agreements between 1952 and 1980. During the late 1980s licensing fees and royalty payments brought to US licensors more than $12 billion a year, roughly twice the rate earned a decade earlier. In the 1990s the pace of international licensing is accelerating, with more recent growth of international licensing led by smaller firms in industries protected by patents, such as biotechnology and pharmaceutical companies. International licensing is often conducted in the form of a cross-licensing agreement or technology swap between firms or as part of a larger, overall strategic partnership between firms.

Technology pricing principles and payment arrangements

International technology licensing is possible when both the licensor and the licensee of a particular technology perceive a reasonable chance of receiving net positive economic benefits from the transaction. The licensee becomes interested when he believes that the possession of a particular technology will strengthen his competitive position in the market, thereby bringing in higher profits. The licensor considers transferring the technology when the perceived compensation from the licensee surpasses the costs associated with the transfer.

The source of licensing revenue should be derived from the exploitation of the proprietary technology by the licensee. To determine licensing revenue one must estimate the incremental value added by the transferred technology to the licensee. Incremental value is embodied in one or all of the following:

- lowering production costs;
- raising quality and performance;
- increasing sales via better brand licensed in the transfer package.

One very important principle for pricing in technology transfer is that both the licensor and licensee share the incremental value generated by the technology. The price a licensee accepts normally constitutes only a part of the incremental value. Licensing revenue (which includes incremental value plus the licensee's production and marketing costs) should be allocated to the licensor and the licensee to cover their respective costs and to add to their respective economic rents to the deal. The economic rent of the licensing agreement refers to the licensee's total revenue from the use of the licensed technology minus the sum of the licensee's production and marketing costs and the licensor's transfer costs.

The United Nations Industrial Development Organization (UNIDO) interprets this idea of sharing as the principle of LSLP (or licensor's share of licensee's profit) and creates a formula to compute LSLP:

LSLP (%) = [The fee received by the supplier (technology price)/The profit of the recipient] × 100%.

There are two ways to decide LSLP. The first is LSLP based on the rate of return, which can be expressed as:

Rate of return
  = total profit/total technology fee

The second approach is LSLP based on commonly adopted figures. According to UNIDO's research, LSLP should be between 16 per cent and 26 per cent. Most cases in the United States put LSLP between 10 per cent and 30 per cent. Many countries, such as Japan, consider 25 per cent to be rational. Consider the following example of how to compute prices of licensing.

Air-conditioner manufacturer A plans to license to manufacturer B the technology to improve its air-conditioner manufacturing process and the right to use its own registered trademark for a period of five years. The discount rate is 14 per cent, while the negotiated LSLP is 25 per cent. In order to determine the price of this deal, B needs to forecast the incremental value which will be brought in the next five years due to the better reputation of A's trademark in the market. B projects that it will produce 200,000 units the first year, 250,000 units the second year, 300,000 units the third year, 350,000 units the fourth year and 400,000 units the fifth year. The incremental value for each unit is estimated at $10, thus the incremental values of the following five years should be as indicated in Table 1.

The total price of the 5 year right of using A's trademark should be:

$9,853,000 × 25% = $2,463,250

The pricing issue in technology licensing is inevitably complicated by the gaps in the pricing principles used by the licensor and the licensee, as shown in Figure 3.

Besides gaps in pricing principles, there are many other factors which influence the final price of a technology licensing agreement, and these can be classified into two categories

Table 1

Years	Annual incremental values of the next five years	Discount present-value coefficients	Present values
Year 1	$10 × 200,000 = $ 2,000,000	0.8772	$1,754,000
Year 2	$10 × 250,000 = $ 2,500,000	0.7695	$1,924,000
Year 3	$10 × 300,000 = $ 3,000,000	0.6750	$2,025,000
Year 4	$10 × 350,000 = $ 3,500,000	0.5921	$2,072,000
Year 5	$10 × 400,000 = $ 4,000,000	0.5194	$2,078,000
Total			$9,853,000

(Cho 1988: 74–5): 'agreement-specific factors', which comprise various agreement provisions such as market restrictions, exclusivity of the license, duration of the agreement, quantitative limits on product size, product quantity requirements, grant-back provisions, tie-in provisions and restrictions on the use of technology; and 'environment-specific factors', which include government regulations on agreement contents and provisions, level of competition in the licensee's product market, level of competition among alternative suppliers of the same or similar technology, political and business risk in the licensee country, and product and industry licensing norms.

Payment arrangements in technology licensing transactions can be broadly classified into three groups: one-time fees (front-end or lump-sum payments, technical service fees, other service fees); fees relating to licensing activity (total royalties, margins on components supplied or products purchased from licensee); other returns (grant-back values, tax savings, licensee equity).

Front-end or lump-sum fees are used for several reasons: to guarantee recovery of transfer costs; to provide basic compensation for disclosure of proprietary information; to allow the licensor to realize targeted returns in countries placing ceilings on royalty rates. Lump-sum fees are usually paid in instalments. A typical payment schedule in many developing countries (for example China) includes a first fee of 5–20 per cent of the total contract price, payable shortly after the contract is signed; a second fee of 35–50 per cent, payable after the basic engineering package is

completed and accepted by the licensee; a third fee of 20–30 per cent, payable after the plant starts up; and a final fee of 5–10 per cent, used as contractual 'risk' insurance and payable after qualified products are manufactured.

However, the licensees would like payments to be linked to their output to minimize their risks while keeping the licensor committed to helping them to produce and sell the products. Many developing countries have required royalties based on net selling price and placed the royalty rates in the range of 2–5 per cent. The royalty rate can also be determined by sales volume. If sales volume is small the royalty rate should be large; otherwise it should be small. In business practice a pure running royalty payment is rare. A common method is to combine initial fees paid after signing the contract or delivering technological documents with royalties. Initial fees should at least compensate for the costs incurred by the licensor in the transfer, such as the costs of preparing documents, quotations, project design, travel and technical assistance. For the protection of the licensee, initial fees are usually set at 10–20 per cent of the total technology price, while royalties account for the rest.

Owing to the relatively long period involved in a licensing agreement, the choice of currency for payment can also considerably distort negotiated prices. For this reason, the licensor would insist on using a hard currency, while the licensee prefers to use a soft currency in an international technology transaction. Therefore negotiations on the payment package can be very complicated and long-winded. The following is a simplified example of the impact of payment arrangement on overall pricing.

A Thai company has decided to acquire technology to manufacture a sophisticated telecom product, and two competing manufacturers (a German company and a French company) offer to sell the technology to the Thai company. According to the quotation offered by a German company, the Thais would pay DM 4.4 million right after the signing of the contract. Then the Thais would pay the Germans the remainder in royalty fees from the end of the third year to the end of the eighth year. The selling price of this product is DM 100 per piece. The planned annual output for this product is 845,000 pieces. The technology recipient's gross profits should be 30 per cent, and the supplier's LSLP is set at 16.7 per cent. (DM 1 = US$0.628 and discount rate = 10 per cent.) The French quotation is based on a front-end lump-sum payment schedule. The total quoted price is Ffr75 million. The Thais would pay a down payment of 20 per cent of the total, then pay 50 per cent by the end of the first year. The remaining 30 per cent would be paid by the end of the second year when the machinery begins to produce quality products. (Ffr1 = US$0.182 and discount rate = 10 per cent.)

Question: Given that the German and French technology is equally good for the Thai company, which quotation is more favourable to the Thai company?

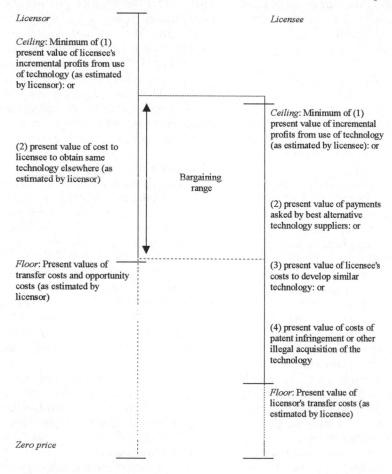

Figure 3 The normative model of licensing negotiations
Source: Root and Contractor 1981: 25.

German offer:

$4.4 + (16.7\% \times 30\% \times 100 \times 0.845)[(1 + 10\%)^6 - 1/10\%(1 + 10\%)^6] [1/(1 + 10\%)^2]$

$= DM\ 19.60\ million = US\$12.32\ million$

French offer:

$75 \times 20\% + 75 \times 50\%[1/(1 + 10\%)] + 75 \times 30\%[1/(1 + 10\%)^2]$

$= Ffr67.69\ million = US\$12.32\ million$

Answer: If other conditions are similar and exchange rates remain unchanged, the German quotation seems to be much more favourable, because the Thai licensee's risk and financial burden are significantly lower, even though there is hardly any differences in the present value of the two quotations.

Licensing agreement

The precise provisions of a licensing agreement depend on the objectives of the parties and their relative bargaining power, the nature of the intellectual property and the relevant national laws governing the relationship. Therefore technology licensing agreements may assume different forms, though a number of important provisions specific to licensing should be included in most licensing agreements.

Scope of licensing
The granting clause describes the precise scope of the licence. It addresses the very important question of what exactly is being delivered by the licensor to the licensee in return for payments and fees. In general, it involves a grant by the licensor to the licensee of the right to use the licensor's technology, normally in connection with the manufacture, use and/or sale of some desired products. It should clearly indicate whether the licence is exclusive or non-exclusive. Occasionally the granting clause may include a grantback provision that requires the licensee to transfer any improvements it has made on the licensed technology back to the licensor.

Restrictions on use
All licensing agreements include restrictions, with most of them containing some type of territorial restriction. Although the licensee may want to utilize the licensed technology as much as possible in the world, the licensor tends to reserve certain markets for itself or for other licensees by confining the licensee to a specific geographic territory or by imposing quantitative limits on the licensee's use of the technology. Whether the licensor can limit a licensee's right to sell outside its native country also depends on governmental regulations in that country and on laws governing restrictive business practices in the home country.

Performance requirements
The success of a licensing venture depends on the licensee's ability and commitment to manufacture the licensed product up to agreed quality standards and to exploit its sales potential in the target market fully. Besides suffering severe damage to its reputation, the licensor may forfeit its trademark rights in the target country if the licensee fails to meet the normal quality standards. To protect its interests, therefore, the licensor may insist on the inclusion of performance provisions in the agreement concerning both production and sales. Quality control may be executed by the licensor in the following two ways: the right of licensor to monitor the licensee's operations; and the right of the licensor to use its own engineers to supervise the licensee's production. Likewise, the licensee may insist on warranties to ensure that the intellectual property meets certain performance standards.

Intellectual property protection and confidentiality
To protect the licensed technology, licensors often clearly state the rights and privileges of the licensee in using it, how and within what scope it should be exploited, and what constitutes a misuse. When the licensed technology is a trade secret the agreement should contain a confidentiality clause that restricts the licensee's right to disclose the information. The licensor may also specify the licensee's responsibility to protect against infringement by competitors.

Duration
The length of the technology transfer agreement may depend on the perceived interests and the bargain position of the parties concerned. Licensees have frequently demanded long-term licences to ensure they can recover their investments. The duration of the licensing deal is also often subject to the governing national law. Some countries require minimum terms to ensure that local licensees recover their investments, while others impose a ceiling on the maximum term, at the end of which the technology should be awarded to the licensee. The term of the agreement can also be influenced by the nature of the intellectual property rights (IPRs), as an agreement transferring rights in patented equipment should not exceed the life of the patent.

3 Technology transfer via other major commercial channels

Major contractual arrangements

International franchising
Franchising is a variation of licensing in which a company (franchiser) licenses an entire business system and other property rights to an independent company or person (franchisee). The franchisee organizes its business under the franchiser's trade name and should follow the procedures and policies established by the franchiser. Under this form of business, therefore, the franchiser licenses the franchisee as a way of organizing and developing a business under its trade name in exchange for fees, running royalties and other compensation. The advantages and disadvantages of franchising are very similar to those of licensing.

International franchising is particularly enticing to a company when its product cannot be exported to a foreign target country, it is not interested in investing in that country as a producer and its production process (or business system) can be transferred to an independent company in that country without much difficulty. Therefore physical products whose manufacture entails significant capital investment and/or high levels of managerial or technical skills are usually not favourable candidates for franchising. The same logic is also applicable to service products that require sophisticated skills, such as accounting, advertising, banking, insurance and management consulting. This may be the main reason why international franchising is most popular in consumer service products that can be produced with relatively low levels of capital and skills. Fast-food chains such as Kentucky Fried Chicken have provided typical examples of international franchising.

International subcontracting
International subcontracting is a cross between licensing and investment, and is also known as outsourcing or contract manufacturing. In subcontracting, a company sources a product from an independent manufacturer in a foreign target country and subsequently markets that product in the target country or elsewhere. These contracts may be long term as part of a buyer–supplier relationship, or they may be temporary arrangements that terminate when the relevant contracts' activities come to an end.

Subcontracting encompasses agreements ranging from the purchase of components made overseas for assembly at the home base of the company to the complete production of specific products by foreign manufacturers. To acquire a product manufactured to its specifications the company is usually involved in the transfer of technology and technical assistance to the foreign manufacturer or the reverse transfer from the foreign manufacturer when it is eventually able to develop some new features related to the product. There are basically five major modes of technology transfer via subcontracting.

First, in an attempt to maintain and develop the subcontracting relationship, the MNC buyer may be obliged to make a sincere endeavour and resource commitments to transfer certain technology of its own to its suppliers. Second, where the MNC buyer does not transfer know-how in the operation of the process technology of the supplier its procedures to enforce its stringent quality/performance control system over the output supplied by the subcontractors may serve as useful feedback that may significantly enhance the technological learning of the latter. Third, when a subcontracting transaction is executed certain technological knowledge is informally transferred from the buyer to the seller. Fourth, when the supplier enters into the subcontracting relationship, it may be induced to make certain technological investments that it would otherwise not make without that relationship. Finally, as the technological level of the suppliers improves significantly, unilateral transfer may evolve into a bilateral exchange of technology, as evidenced in the relationship between Fuji and Xerox.

Subcontracting has traditionally been important in a number of industries, including aerospace, automobiles and construction. As global competition puts growing pressures on firms to cut their costs and shorten product development time subcontracting is becoming essential to many other industries, such as the electronic industry, because the development and production of new products involve such diverse technologies that a single company can hardly have competitive advantages in all of them. Heated competition has even driven rival firms into horizontal subcontracting agreements, each of which is capable of producing and marketing its products independently. Ford Motor Company, for instance, obtains axles for its passenger cars and manual transmissions for its smaller trucks from Mazda.

International subcontracting may have advantages and disadvantages. The advantages are that it enables the company to enter into the target country without having to use significant financial and management resources, avoids local ownership problems, and allows the company to maintain control over marketing, licensing and franchising. The major disadvantages are similar to those of licensing: it may be very difficult to find a suitable foreign manufacturer; even after an appropriate partner is located, significant technical assistance may be necessary to raise it up to the required quality and volume levels; the risk of creating a competitor is fairly high; and the company may develop an undesirable dependency on

foreign partners as a source of key components.

Turnkey projects

Turnkey projects are important in a variety of industries, typically involving the construction of large-scale capital works, such as the construction of water packaging plants, and pollution control, transportation, telecommunication and natural-resources exploration systems. In a typical turnkey project a company designs, builds and installs capital equipment with the intention of turning over control and operation to the purchasers after an agreed period. For example, in the 1980s Fiat successfully delivered automobile-producing plants to the former Soviet Union and Poland, rather than selling automobiles. The result has been a second generation of automobiles based on Fiat technology, but Fiat had no control over distribution and sale once the original agreement had expired.

As is shown in the above example, one primary motivation for the providers to participate in turnkey projects resembles those of licensing and subcontracting agreements in that they allow companies to penetrate foreign markets that would otherwise be closed to export and foreign manufacturing entry. But unless turnkey projects are combined with management contracts, the supplying company has hardly any control over the management of the facility or the marketing of the product. Furthermore, as many turnkey contracts are signed with host governments they are very vulnerable to the political risks of compulsory changes in key provisions, the unexpected calling of bank guarantees or even contract abrogation. These should be fully assessed before a company enters into a turnkey project in a foreign country.

Countertrade

Countertrade (see COUNTERTRADE) may be defined as a contractual arrangement that involves a combination of trade, licensing, investment and finance. Wherever necessary technology transfer is routinely required as a part of the package. For example, under a compensation or buyback agreement the selling company will sell industrial equipment, technology and/or an entire turnkey plant and agree to purchase a portion of the output manufactured from the use of the equipment. The offset transaction for F-16 sales between General Dynamics (GD) and Turkey is another good example. Faced with less costly competition from British Aerospace and the French aerospace companies, GD signed an offset arrangement with the Turkish government by offering to build a whole aircraft industry there and to invest in other projects as well.

Strategic alliances

Equity joint venture
An international joint venture is started when a foreign company shares in the ownership of a company in a target country with local private or public concerns. Technology is often transferred to the joint venture through an assignment or through a licensing arrangement. The technology-supplying partner may also be obliged to provide the necessary technical and management assistance. In view of the perishable nature of technology, it is hardly surprising that partners pay considerable attention to devising technology transfer schemes to protect their respective competitive advantages, particularly when the effective joint venture will entail ongoing technical relationships between owners and the venture. If the joint venture requires inventive activity the agreement will need to specify the respective financial, scientific and technological contributions of the parties to the joint venture, as well as the ownership rights of the partners in the industrial property rights and know-how which may be created.

As such, joint-venture agreements inevitably comprise provisions on a number of the restrictions typical in licensing agreements. For instance, the markets in which the product of the venture can be exploited may be designated on a discriminatory basis, or third-party competitors may be excluded from access to the products of the business, or they may be required to pay discriminatory prices. Transferring technology via joint venturing can also complicate formulas computing profits to both parties to the joint venture, thereby influencing relevant prices that may govern business deals for the proposed joint venture. As a joint-venture partner, the licensor can benefit not only from the dividend derived from the joint venture's profits, but also from licensing fees, royalties and/or components sales related to the technology transfer.

R&D cooperation and technology swaps
Parties to an R&D cooperative project may find it necessary to contribute technological skills, financing, management and equipment, while technology swaps resemble the licensing agreements discussed earlier, except that technology swaps normally refer only to trades of technology for technology. Technology-developing alliances are very common in fast-changing high-tech industries. For example, in the alliance between AT&T (see AT&T CORPORATION) and NEC (see NEC CORPORATION) AT&T provided some of its proprietary computer-aided-design technology in exchange for advanced logic chip designs developed by NEC. In spite of various benefits to the parties involved in such a deal, there is a high risk for both of them, which derives from three sources: first, there is a real chance that the R&D or cross-licensing efforts may not lead to desired products; second, the market demand may be highly uncertain, especially for the introduction of new products; third, the future action taken by partners, especially if a partner is a competitor, may also be uncertain.

Joint production agreements
Joint production agreements (or co-production agreements) share notable similarities with both subcontracting and equity joint ventures, because these three arrangements regularly require the licensing of specialized elements. The main difference between joint production arrangements and subcontracting lies in the fact that co-production partners are much more actively involved in the development of the product to be produced than is the case in typical subcontracting. In contrast to the case of equity joint ventures, the assets and management of each side are not incorporated into a joint business

	After-tax profit	
Case	Foreigner	Local investor
Foreign joint venture; royalties	$[(PQ - F - vQ - L - PQr)\alpha +$ $(L + PQr)] (1 - t_F)$	$(PQ - F - vQ - L - PQr)$ $(1 - \alpha) (1 - t_E)$
Arm's length licensing (no equity)	$(L + PQr) (1 - t_F)$	$(PQ - F - vQ - L - PQr) (1 - t_E)$
Only equity sharing	$(PQ - F - vQ) (\alpha) (1 - t_F)$	$(PQ - F - vQ) (1 - \alpha) (1 - t_E)$
Foreign joint venture; royalties not deductible	$[(PQ - F - vQ) (1 - t_E) - (L + Pqr)]$ $(1 - \alpha)$	$[(PQ - F - vQ) (1 - t_E) - (L + Pqr)]$ $(1 - \alpha)$

Notes:
P = unit selling price for the product made by the venture
Q = quantity sold
v = unit variable of production
F = total fixed costs
t_E = the effective tax rate on the local enterprise
t_F = the effective tax rate faced by the foreign company
L = initial lump sum payment
r = the rate of running royalty per unit sales
α = equity share (%)

Figure 4 After-tax profit expressions under different assumptions
Source: Adapted from Contractor 1985: 224.

entity when the relevant partners undertake to engage themselves in joint production or distribution operations.

Co-production is one of the most popular forms of interfirm cooperation between western companies and their counterparts in developing countries, as many of these countries place various restrictions on foreign ownership of local companies. This is especially true in the aerospace industry, where co-production is often a part of a countertrade arrangement. On the one hand, local governments often require co-production as a necessary precondition for the foreign aerospace industry to enter their markets. The transaction involving McDonnell-Douglas in China is built around such a co-production programme. On the other hand, the development and production of a new-model jet airline is so costly that even the largest companies in the industry may feel hard pressed for funds. In the case of Boeing's new 777 commercial jet liner, companies in six different countries were involved in sharing the financial burden and certain technologies for the development and production work.

Joint equity swaps

Unlike an equity joint venture, a joint equity swap, also known as a minority investment alliance, does not lead to the creation of a separate business entity. By forming an equity alliance the parties hope to secure long-term commitment to cooperation. IBM's (see INTERNATIONAL BUSINESS MACHINES CORPORATION) purchase of a minority stake in Groupe Bull, the French state-owned computer maker, illustrates the uniqueness of such equity alliances. Through this agreement IBM gained access to portable and notebook computer technologies while providing Bull with IBM's RISC-chip technologies.

Intrafirm transfers

Technology may be transferred to the target country within the context of transactions between an overseas parent company and a subsidiary established within that country. Relevant rights to intellectual property or know-how will be licensed to the subsidiary. Restrictions contained in these licenses will partly depend on the extent of ownership in the subsidiary held by the parent. The less ownership a parent has in a subsidiary, the less control it commands and the more restrictions it will impose on licensing. Usually, full ownership allows for the minimum restrictions. On the other hand, the subsidiary will be responsible for a designated activity within the corporate group. For example, it may be required to provide certain amounts of goods and services to be marketed by the parent. The extent and method of the transfer may also partly depend on the rules of the recipient country on foreign investment.

Since intrafirm transfers are usually less costly than interfirm transfers, a cost advantage can function as a bond. Several reasons for these lower costs exist: personnel in both countries share organizational and technological commonalities; time-consuming legal negotiations are not necessary between a parent and its wholly owned or predominantly controlled subsidiary; the risk of non-payment or a need for a performance bond is nearly non-existent; and concerns about a failure of the technology to work remain minimal. As such, an MNC often has a cost advantage in ITT over two separate firms operating at arm's length. Philips of Holland, for example, has regularly employed intrafirm transfers among electronic components manufactured in Europe, Asia and the United States to keep costs low.

4 Protecting intellectual property

The international dimension of intellectual property

What is handled by technology transfer – patent, trademark, know-how and copyright – can together be called intellectual property, which is generally divided into two major branches: industrial property and copyright. Intellectual property protection has been problematic in many countries. Technology transfer transactions are impossible without due protection of the intellectual property to be transferred, as potential transferees would have no interest in paying for the transfer. Intellectual property protection includes patent, trademark, trade secret (know-how) and copyright.

Patents

A patent can be defined as a statutory privilege granted by a government to an inventor and to other persons deriving their rights from the inventor, for a fixed period of years, to exclude other persons from utilizing a patented technology. Patents can also be divided into product and process patents: the former covers only technology related to a product itself, while the latter focuses on a unique way to make that product. Product patents are easier to obtain and are better protected than process patents.

Most countries grant patents only after the invention or product for which protection is sought has undergone three tests. Under the test of novelty, the invention must not have been made known in any place, domestically or abroad. The United States accepts a patent application at any time up to one year after publication, but most countries require that a patent application be filed before the invention has been publicly disclosed anywhere in the world, by any means, written or otherwise. The second test is that of non-obviousness to a person having an ordinary skill in the art. The third test is associated with commercial value; the invention qualified for a patent should have an industrial applicability.

There are various restrictions on the grant of patent and the transnational movement of patents. For reasons of national interest, some countries, such as Mexico, withhold patent protection from foreign inventions relating to agriculture, food, medical and pharmaceutical products, and nuclear technology. Many developing countries and countries from the British Commonwealth require the licensing of a patent if they are convinced that their own manufacturing cannot meet market demand. In some Latin American countries foreign patent holders are required to get a local company interested in taking a licence under a patent.

Trademark

A trademark represents a certification of origin, which tells the customer something about product quality. To be registered as a trademark a sign must be visible rather than audible or olfactory. Registrable signs include names, existing or invented words, letters, numbers, pictures and symbols. In contrast to the case of a patent, protection of a trademark may be indefinite as long as basic conditions are met.

Common-law countries, including the United States and members of the British Commonwealth, usually require continuous prior use in trade by the applicant as a precondition for issuing a valid trademark registration. Continuity of prior use, even if not registered, may provide adequate ground for protection. Civil-law countries (most other countries in the world) provide protection mainly on the basis of the act of registration. Consequently, a firm may lose its trademark if it fails to register it and to maintain its validity by paying an annual fee. Demonstrable prior use may not be sufficient for restoring ownership.

Trade secrets (know-how)
A trade secret is know-how that is kept secret within a business, offers a competitive advantage and is not generally known to the industry. Trade secrets cover manufacturing processes; methods and techniques; plans, designs and patterns; formulas; business information; and product.

Trade secrets do not enjoy statutory protection as patents and trademarks do, but the laws of many countries provide some sort of protection to ownership rights in trade secrets, conditional upon the maintenance of secrecy. It is not always possible to keep the secret, because a competitor can use a variety of channels to get the secrets, including hiring personnel and reverse engineering. Once a trade secret is publicly known anyone can use it freely. Trade secrets do not give the owner any right to prevent others from independently creating and using the same know-how.

Copyrights
Copyright protection covers the works of authors and artists by giving the copyright owner the right to control the reproduction and performance of the work. While the scope and length of copyright protection varies a great deal among countries, copyright generally provides protection for written works, films, music and performances. Most copyright laws protect works for a significant period of time, such as the life of the author plus fifty years. Because copyright laws vary considerably throughout the world, one must investigate each nation's laws individually to understand the level of legal protection available for copyrighted works.

Major conventions and treaties on intellectual property protection

Since the signing of the Paris Convention (1883), a number of international conventions, treaties and agreements have been promulgated to promote and harmonize the principle of reciprocity in the field of intellectual property. Although they do not pre-empt national law, they have provided general guidelines that have facilitated the international transfer of technology.

Paris Convention for the Protection of Industrial Property
The Paris Convention (1883) established an international union for the protection of industrial property. It has now been signed by over 100 countries. The two most important principles are the principle of national treatment and the principle of priority. The former requires the members to grant the same industrial property protection to nationals of other member nations as it grants to its own nationals. The latter grants innovators twelve months to apply for protection in other member countries.

Patent Cooperation Treaty (PCT)
The PCT was adopted in 1970 for the purpose of simplifying the process of securing international protection for patents. It provides an applicant from a member nation with the mechanism to file a single application for patent registration that designates the member nations in which the applicant seeks protection. After this filing, an international search is undertaken by a designated searching authority to determine the patentability of the applicant's invention in member nations. The

application and search report are then processed by the World Intellectual Property Organization (WIPO) for patent registration in the designated member nations.

Madrid Agreement

The Madrid Agreement, adopted in 1891, is designed to simplify procedures for companies wishing to secure trademark protection in a number of countries. Where a company has registered a trademark in a country which is a signatory to the Madrid Agreement, that company may, by filing a single application with the International Bureau of WIPO, receive protection for that mark in any other signatory country designated by the applicant. The applicant will enjoy protection for twenty years under the agreement on the same terms as the nationals of the country in which registration is obtained. By 1997 over forty countries had acceded to the Madrid Agreement.

The Berne Convention

The Berne Convention, created in 1886, requires member nations to give national treatment to authors publishing in any member country. An author who publishes a copyrighted book in Finland will have the same copyright protection in Argentina as any Argentinian author. The Berne Convention also prescribes some minimum copyright standards, such as the duration of copyright protection. Berne Convention members have to provide protection for at least the life of the author plus fifty years for most works, with minimum fifty-year protection for anonymous or pseudonymous works and cinematographical products, and twenty-five-year protection for photographic works and works of applied art. More than eighty countries are now parties to the convention.

The trade-related aspects of intellectual property rights (TRIPS)

With the growth of world trade in the 1980s, international differences in the protection of intellectual property have caused an increasing number of trade disputes. The Uruguay Round negotiations symbolized a watershed in international trade policy by including IPRs on the agenda. The TRIPS agreement in 1994 established a full range of protection on IPRs in the context of international trade, and provided for the effective enforcement of those standards both internally and internationally.

According to TRIPS, all countries were given one year from the date of TRIPS to implement the agreement. Developing countries are allowed an additional four years for implementation, except for provisions concerning patent protection for pharmaceutical and agricultural products, where they are given an additional nine years. At the end of the one-year transition period granted to all countries, however, developing countries must provide national treatment and most-favoured nation treatment, while allowing limited exceptions thereto for agreements administered by WIPO.

Enforcing intellectual property protection

Divergent views on intellectual property protection

Developing countries have often been accused of inefficiency in protecting the property rights of knowledge, including tolerance of piracy practices. The reactions of developed countries to such problems usually include threats and commercial retaliatory measures. For the advanced industrialized countries, IPRs such as patents provide compensation for risks incurred in the innovative process and therefore function as an incentive for such R&D activities. The company obtains its reward for technological leadership through the monopoly provided by the patent system.

Developing countries, on the other hand, have a very different point of view on the issue. Innovation there progresses along a path different from that in the developed countries, often beginning with a product's introduction and ending with control of the technology. The dynamics and standpoint of protecting innovative activities are entirely different. For many developing countries, the central concern of government has been with their own development to meet the basic needs of a rapidly growing population. IPRs, like patents, are often viewed as agents that build up the monopoly enjoyed by foreign MNCs. This poses difficult barriers for the development of indigenous firms.

By the mid-1980s developed countries had gained ground in the international debate on IPRs. Technological developments have greatly raised the economic value of knowledge appropriation as the world economy becomes more R&D-intensive, copying and imitating become easier, economic globalization continues and traditional jurisprudence on IPRs is challenged. It is not surprising to see an increasing concern with intellectual property among developed countries. The use of trade laws by the United States and the European Union (EU; see EUROPEAN UNION) in their fight against 'piracy' and the progress in the discussions on TRIPS in multilateral trade negotiations played an important role in this process.

During the same period the attitude of developing countries toward FDI and technology transfer has undergone major changes as a result of a number of changes in the course of their development and in international environments. The foreign debt crisis, counterproductive experiences of an inward-looking development strategy and highly regulatory policies, decreasing capital flows, and economic stagnation and hardships in many developing countries and former socialist countries are some of the reasons for the change in attitudes. There was also a renewed interest in assessing the potential benefits of improving protection of intellectual property among developing countries. The most notable changes in attitude are found in the newly industrialized countries, which have begun to feel the necessity to protect their own intellectual property in other developing countries. This is evidenced by an increasing number of cases in which companies from former piracy countries, such as Taiwan and South Korea, have filed law suits against infringement of their intellectual property in countries like China and Indonesia.

Business responses to IPR violations

While the overall environment of intellectual property protection has improved, a practical business strategy to enforce such protection is always indispensable. Adopting appropriate measures to ensure the protection of IPRs is essential for a number of reasons: it helps deter counterfeiters from manufacturing the product of the property rights owner; it contributes to continued R&D endeavours by preventing other companies from reproducing those endeavours at minimum cost; and it serves to guarantee the continued existence of an important source of international royalty income.

In order to protect their own IPRs effectively managers should, among others things, do the following:

- make an early assessment of the commercial value of a patent, because the first party to apply for a patent in one Paris Convention country has only one year of grace to apply for protection in other member states;
- establish a mechanism to ensure the continuation of a patent, trademark or copyright validity;
- establish a system to monitor important markets for infringement and to prosecute infringers;
- decide whether to develop a trademark protection strategy in targeted markets;
- determine who should own the property right – the parent or subsidiary;
- compare the suitability of either relying on patent protection or keeping secrecy;
- set up a subsidiary in one of the signatory countries to the Madrid Agreement through which to register the trademark.

Although serious problems exist in protecting IPRs abroad, hundreds of thousands of firms have found the transfer of such rights to be very profitable. The transfer of these rights has continually grown all over the world. With various bilateral and multilateral agreements, worldwide enforcement of protection is also improving significantly. However, to eliminate IPR violations is a long-term fight, if not impossible. In this fight, businesses should take on more responsibility by improving their own management. Robinson made the following comment in his classical book on ITT:

In the final analysis, the real protection of transferred technology lies in an untarnished corporate name, a high level of credibility in the eyes of consumers in all markets, superior technology supported by a record of ongoing innovation, a capability of effecting international technology transfer at a relatively low cost, a design-engineering sensitivity to the requirements peculiar to different markets, and sufficient organisational flexibility to select the most effective transfer vehicle and mount appropriate controls.

(Robinson 1988: 149)

5 Conclusion

ITT has significantly revolutionized international trade and greatly increased the involvement of different countries in the flow of goods and services across national boundaries. In addition to general economic benefits to their respective home societies in term of export promotion, increased job opportunities and technology advancement, technology transfer transactions also generate economic rents that both the transferor and transferee may share. In the post-Cold War era, technology transfer across national boundaries will be one of the most dynamic developments that contributes to closer and better interactions between countries from different economic levels and diverse political backgrounds.

With the growing globalization of international business, high-technology industries have become a major portion of international trade. Such industries as commercial aircraft and engines, semiconductor computer chips, telecommunications and pharmaceuticals are becoming a battlefield where companies fight to expand their market shares to survive and grow in ever fiercer international competition. Moreover, to penetrate emerging markets in eastern Europe, the former Soviet Union and Asia quicker than their competitors, western companies have found it indispensable to make direct investment in those countries in which technology transfer is inevitable. As Robert Kellar and Ravi Chinta have commented: 'To survive in the future a firm, especially a multinational corporation

(MNC), must be able to transfer technology to other countries better than the competition' (Keller and Chinta 1990: 33).

Finally, some of traditionally technology-net-importing countries, such as China and India, are becoming increasingly important sources of technology for not only developing countries but also western industrialized countries, as both of them own a large pool of well-trained scientists and engineers. For instance, Bangalore in India has become an increasingly important source of computer software for western companies, while China exports a wide variety of technologies ranging from nuclear power to high-yield crops. Into the next century, technology transfer will no longer be a one-way stream but, rather, will be characterized by mixture of transfers from developed to developing countries (still the main stream), from developing countries to other developing countries (growing very rapidly) and from less developed to more developed countries (emerging trickles).

MIN CHEN
THUNDERBIRD GRADUATE SCHOOL OF
MANAGEMENT

Further reading

(References cited in the text marked *)

* Aggarwal, Raj (1991) 'Technology transfer and economic growth: a historical perspective on current development', in Tamir Agmon and Mary Ann Von Glinow (eds) *Technology Transfer in International Business*, New York: Oxford University Press. (Discusses in detail the relationship between technology transfer and economic development.)

Bidault, Francis (1989) *Technology Pricing: From Principles to Strategy*, New York: St Martin's Press. (Discusses various aspects of pricing strategy for technology transfer projects.)

Chen, Min (1996) *Managing International Technology Transfer*, London/New York: International Thomson Business Press. (A comprehensive volume on the subject of managing ITT.)

* Cho, K.R. (1988) 'Issues of compensation in international technology licensing', *Management International Review* 28(2): 70–9.

* Contractor, Farok J. (1985) *Licensing in International Strategy: A Guide for Planning and Ne-*

gotiations, Westport, CT: Quorum Books. (A practical guide to technology licensing strategy and an expansion of the 1981 book.)

Harrigan, Kathryn R. (1986) *Managing for Joint Venture Success*, Lexington, MA: Lexington Books. (Describes various aspects of managing a joint venture).

Hennart, J.F. (1988) 'A transaction costs theory of equity joint ventures', *Strategic Management Journal* 9: 361–74. (Presents a theoretical exploration of transaction costs in the context of equity joint ventures.)

* Keller, Rober T. and Chinta, Ravi R. (1990) 'International technology transfer: strategies for success', *Academy of Management Executives* 4(2): 33–3.

* Robinson, Richard D. (1988) *The International Transfer of Technology: Theory, Issues, and Practice,* Cambridge, MA: Ballinger Publishing Co. (A comprehensive book on managing ITT.)

* Root, Franklin R. and Contractor, Farok J. (1981) 'Negotiating compensation in international licensing agreements', *Sloan Management Review*, winter: 23–52.

Samli, A.C. (1985) *Technology Transfer: Geographic, Economic, Cultural, and Technical Dimensions*, Westport, CT: Quorum Books. (Presents a collection of theoretical articles dealing with a wide range of topics on technology transfer across national boundaries.)

Smith, U. Gordon and Russell L. Parr (1993) *Intellectual Property: Licensing and Joint Venture Profit*, New York: John Wiley & Sons. (Presents a detailed discussion on how to evaluate such intangible assets as patents, trademarks, trade names and know-how in licensing and joint ventures.)

Watkin, William M. (1990) *Business Aspects of Technology Transfer: Marketing and Investment*, Park Ridge, NJ: Noyes Publications. (A business handbook on how to conduct technology transfer transactions.)

See also: AT&T CORPORATION; COUNTER-TRADE; EUROPEAN UNION; INTERNATIONAL BUSINESS MACHINES CORPORATION; MULTINATIONAL CORPORATIONS; NEC CORPORATION

International trade and foreign direct investment

Overview

During the past two centuries, the free trade paradigm based on the principle of comparative advantage has profoundly influenced national trade policies. This principle demonstrates that dissimilar national production possibilities are the basis of international trade that is gainful to both trading parties. Trade enables each country to specialize in making and exporting products in which it is comparatively efficient while importing products in which it is comparatively inefficient. As a consequence, the productivity of national economies is higher than it would be in the absence of trade.

The conventional explanation of comparative advantage is the existence of dissimilar factor endowments (broadly, land, labour and capital) across countries. But economists have now come forward with other explanations of comparative advantage deriving from international technology gaps, increasing returns and product differentiation. The old and new trade theories are complementary, offering collectively a better understanding of trade than the conventional theory.

Foreign direct investment (FDI) is an ownership interest (equity) in an enterprise located in one country that is held by residents (usually another enterprise) of another country. FDI is the distinctive feature of multinational enterprises (MNEs). Hence, a theory of FDI is also a theory of the MNE. Multinationals are the foremost agents in moving factors of production and technology from one country to another. In so doing, they strengthen the international economy by improving the allocation of resources worldwide. Also, MNEs are the key actors in international innovation, spreading new ideas and technology across countries.

A theory of FDI needs to explain how direct investing firms can compete with local firms in host countries, why firms choose to enter host countries as direct investors in production rather than as exporters or licensors, and why firms choose to invest in particular host countries. The traditional theory of international capital movements (portfolio investment theory) cannot give satisfactory answers to these questions; indeed, by assuming perfect competition it rules out the existence of FDI. New theories of FDI centred on monopolistic competition and transaction costs agree on the importance of market imperfections (departures from perfect competition) to explain direct investment.

It has become evident that we need a new paradigm that explains trade and direct investment at both national and enterprise levels. Prospects for creating such a paradigm over the next decade are good. Both trade and investment theories recognize the significance of market imperfections. Another contribution to constructing a new paradigm is Porter's 'diamond'. A single paradigm integrating trade and investment theories would offer better guidance to national policy makers and international managers than the current mix of seemingly unrelated theories.

I The principle of comparative advantage in international trade

Two paradigms have dominated explanations of international trade since the ending of the Middle Ages five centuries ago: mercantilism over the first three hundred years (1500–1800), and free trade since that time. Both paradigms have profoundly influenced the trade policies of nations. The free trade paradigm encompasses the principle of comparative advantage that animates the World Trade Organization (WTO; see WORLD TRADE ORGANIZATION) and remains the most potent rationale for the trade policies of industrialized countries, notably the USA, Japan and the European Union member countries. A logical starting point for an examination of international trade theory, therefore, is comparative advantage (see GLOBALIZATION).

The principle of comparative advantage has an impressive lineage in economic thought. Its great forerunner was Adam Smith's *The Wealth of Nations*, published in 1776. Attacking the mercantilists, who argued for the regulation of trade to secure a 'favourable balance of trade' (a surplus of exports over imports) that would bring in gold and silver in payment, Smith applied the doctrine of *laissez-faire* to international trade. All nations would benefit from unregulated, free trade that would allow individual countries to specialize in goods they were best suited to make, due to natural and acquired advantages. Smith's theory of trade is known as the theory of absolute advantage.

The next and decisive step in the development of trade theory was the publication in 1817 of Ricardo's *On the Principles of Political Economy and Taxation*, which introduced the principle of comparative advantage. Smith's theory of absolute advantage assumed that a country would always have a low-cost advantage in at least one product that it could export in exchange for other products. But suppose a country did not have an absolute cost advantage in any product? Ricardo answered that question with the principle of comparative advantage: even if England were less efficient than Portugal in the production of both cloth and wine (as measured by labour hours), it would still benefit England to specialize in cloth production and Portugal in wine production if England were comparatively more efficient (or less inefficient) in cloth than in wine production.

Since Ricardo, economists have added several refinements to the comparative advantage paradigm. For example, John Stuart Mill (1806–73) contributed the principle of reciprocal demand to explain the terms of trade between countries. Another refinement was the publication in 1933 of Bertil Ohlin's *Interregional and International Trade*. Drawing on the pioneer work of Eli Heckscher, Ohlin developed the proposition that a country exports those goods that use most intensively in their production the country's most abundant factors of production (land, labour and capital), and conversely. Ohlin replaced Ricardo's labour factor with multiple factors of production that operate in competitive markets to determine a country's comparative advantage. His theory, known as the Heckscher–Ohlin (H–O) model, remains the most widely accepted explanation of comparative advantage.

Dissimilar national production possibilities

A theory of international trade needs to answer three basic questions:

1 Why do countries export and import certain goods?
2 At which relative prices (terms of trade) do countries exchange goods?
3 What are the gains from international trade?

To demonstrate how comparative advantage answers these questions, we turn to a simple model. Assume there are only two countries in the world, Country A and Country B, and each produces only two commodities, cloth and wine. Assume also that if each country uses all of its productive factors (land, labour and capital) at a given level of technology, it can produce the alternative outputs of cloth and wine shown in the following list:

	Units of cloth	Units of wine
Country A	200	100
Country B	100	300

When translated into graphs, these output data appear as the production possibilities (or transformation) curves of the two countries, as shown in Figures 1 and 2 by the downward-sloping solid lines.

Country A's production possibilities curve (Figure 1) shows the various combinations of cloth and wine that its productive factors can produce when they are fully employed and used efficiently. For example, one possible output combination shown by point M on the curve represents 90 units of cloth and 55 units of wine. In contrast, point N represents a cloth–wine combination that is smaller than the possible output, because of factor unemployment or inefficient use. Point R to the right of the curve denotes a cloth–wine combination that is beyond the physical production capacity of Country A. Similar remarks can be made about Country B's production possibilities curve (Figure 2), where S represents 50 units of cloth and 150 units of wine.

To increase the output of wine by one unit in Country A, factors must be taken away from the production of cloth in such amounts as to lower the output of cloth by two units. In Country B, an increase in the output of wine by one unit lowers the output of cloth by one-third of a

unit. These production substitution ratios are shown by the slopes of the curves: two for Country A and one-third for Country B.

Under competitive conditions, the domestic terms of trade of cloth for wine equal the slope of the country's production possibilities curve. In Country A, one unit of cloth exchanges for one-half unit of wine while in Country B, one unit of cloth exchanges for three units of wine. Country A has a comparative advantage in cloth while Country B has a comparative advantage in wine.

The gains from trade

In the absence of international trade, each country can elect to consume only a cloth–wine combination that lies somewhere on its production possibilities curve, such as M in Figure 1 and S in Figure 2. The existence of different substitution ratios in the production of cloth and wine, however, offers both countries an opportunity to gain from mutual trade and to consume a cloth–wine combination that lies beyond their production possibilities frontiers. This happy outcome occurs when cloth and wine are traded at any international terms of trade that fall between the two domestic terms of trade (one cloth unit for one-half wine unit in Country A and one cloth unit for three wine units in Country B) which are equal to the domestic substitution ratios in the production of cloth and wine.

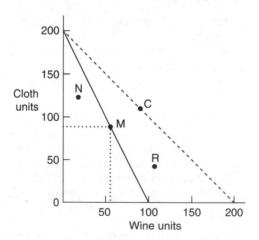

Figure 1 Production possibilities curve for Country A

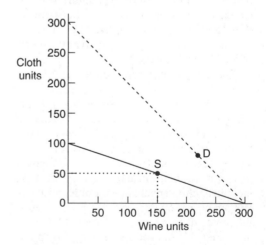

Figure 2 Production possibilities curve for Country B

When trade opens up between the two countries, reciprocal demand (that is, the demand of each country for the other's exports) determines international terms of trade that are depicted by the identical slopes of the dashed lines in Figures 1 and 2. At these international terms of trade (1 cloth unit = 1 wine unit), Country A specializes completely in cloth production, because it can obtain from Country B more wine for each unit of cloth than it can at home. Conversely, Country B specializes entirely in wine production, obtaining all its cloth from Country A. If Country A chooses to consume 80 units of wine, it will import them from Country B in exchange for 80 units of cloth. The converse is true for Country B. As a result of trade, then, Country A is able to consume a cloth–wine combination (120 units of cloth and 80 units of wine), indicated by point C on the international terms of trade line in Figure 1, that is superior to any combination Country A can produce in isolation. For Country B, point D in Figure 2 represents a cloth–wine combination (80 cloth units and 220 wine units) that is superior to any combination producible at home.

The international terms of trade of one cloth unit for one wine unit is an equilibrium rate in our example because it clears the market; that is, exports equal imports. A change in reciprocal demand, however, would establish a new equilibrium rate and thereby alter the division of gains. Gainful trade for both countries occurs at any international terms of trade that fall between the two domestic terms of trade. At any rate beyond the range set by the two domestic terms of trade, only one country gains, and trade does not occur because the other country is better off without trade. When the international terms of trade are the same as the domestic terms of trade of one country, then that country neither gains nor loses from trade and all the gain goes to the second country.

At the international terms of trade of one cloth unit for one wine unit, both countries gain from trade: with specialization their combined output of cloth and wine is higher than before, and the production increment is shared by consumers in both countries. An arithmetic recapitulation of the before- and after-trade situations is offered in Table 1.

2 Explanations of comparative advantage

Economists offer several complementary explanations of national comparative advantage: factor endowments, technology gaps, increasing returns and product differentiation.

Table 1 Comparison of before- and after-trade production, consumption and gains

	Before trade					
	Production		Consumption		Gains	
	Cloth	Wine	Cloth	Wine	Cloth	Wine
Country A	90	55	90	55	0	0
Country B	50	150	50	150	0	0
Combined	140	205	140	205	0	0
	After trade					
	Production		Consumption		Gains	
	Cloth	Wine	Cloth	Wine	Cloth	Wine
Country A	200	0	120	80	30	25
Country B	0	300	80	220	30	70
Combined	200	300	200	300	60	95

National factor endowments

The Heckscher–Ohlin (H–O) model attributes comparative advantage to different proportions of national factor endowments of land, labour and capital across countries. For that reason, it is also called the factor-proportions theory of trade. Comparative advantage arises when cost–price structures (the relative costs and prices of goods as illustrated in Figures 1 and 2) differ across countries, thereby providing a basis for gainful trade. But why should they differ? In a competitive market, the price of a good equals its marginal cost of production, which in turn reflects the prices of the marginal inputs of factors of production used to produce that good. Further, different goods are produced with different combinations of factor inputs. Hence if factor–price ratios (the ratios among rent, wages and interest) differ across countries, then goods–price ratios will also differ. In one country wages may be low relative to land rent, whereas in another country wages may be high relative to rent. Consequently, the first country can produce goods that require a great deal of labour and not much land more cheaply than goods that require a great deal of land but not much labour. In the second country, the opposite is true.

Why should factor–price ratios differ across countries? The H–O model traces such differences to relative factor endowments (supplies) that are dissimilar across countries. Countries differ greatly in their relative supplies of factors of production. A country like Australia has an abundant supply of natural resources (land) relative to its supplies of labour and capital. Therefore, rents in Australia are low relative to wages and interest. In contrast, Japan has a relatively scarce supply of natural resources so that rents are high relative to wages and interest. Such differences multiply because the three factors of production are heterogeneous with many subfactors. There are several kinds of land factors and many varieties of labour and capital. For example, one country has a temperate climate, another has a tropical climate; one country has oil but lacks iron ore, another has iron ore but lacks oil; one country has large supplies of educated skilled workers, another has a mostly illiterate, unskilled workforce; one country has steel plants, another has none; and so on. The number of specific factors is so large that any one country is certain to have factor–supply proportions that diverge in some respect from the proportions of other countries.

In summary, the H–O model postulates that a country has a comparative advantage in the production of goods that use relatively large amounts of its abundant factors of production and a comparative disadvantage in the production of goods that use relatively large amounts of its scarce factors of production. A country exports the former goods and imports the latter goods. Indirectly, then, a country exports the services of its abundant factors of production and imports the services of its scarce factors of production.

International technology gaps

According to the H–O model, the greatest share of international trade should be an exchange of manufactured goods for primary goods between industrial (capital-abundant) countries, on the one hand, and non-industrial (land- and labour-abundant) countries, on the other. However, the facts point to a contrary state of affairs. Statistical data reveal that: (1) the industrial countries (mainly the USA, Japan and western Europe) generate about two-thirds of total world exports; (2) two-thirds of these exports go to the industrial countries themselves, and this trade is primarily (although not exclusively) an exchange of manufactures for manufactures; (3) much (certainly over half) of the manufactures-for-manufactures trade is intra-industry trade, that is, a country's simultaneous export and import of products belonging to the same industry; (4) much intra-industry trade is also intra-firm trade between multinational enterprises and their own foreign subsidiaries; (5) trade between the industrial and non-industrial countries is less than a third of world trade, consisting mainly of an exchange of manufactures for primary products; and (6) the economic structures of the industrial countries are becoming more, not less, similar.

Why should two countries that have the same factor endowments and that produce and consume the same types of products trade at all? The answer to this question must be found in other explanations of comparative advantage. One explanation is international technology gaps.

Technology is the accumulated knowledge, skills and techniques that are applied to the production of goods and services. Technological innovations assume two basic forms: new and more economical ways of producing existing products (new production functions); and the production of wholly new products, both industrial and consumer (such as computers, televisions, plastics, synthetic fibres and jet aircraft, to name only a few of the more outstanding products innovated since the end of the Second World War), and improvements in existing products. These two forms are closely related; many new products, for example, are capital goods that make possible new production functions.

Technology theories postulate that certain countries have special advantages as innovators of new products. They also postulate that there is an 'imitation lag' that prevents other countries from immediately duplicating in production the new products of the innovating country. These two conditions give rise to technology gaps in particular products that afford the innovating country an export monopoly during the period of imitation lag.

International technology gaps in production functions and products have a dynamic impact on trade among nations as innovations open up new gaps and technological diffusion closes old gaps. There is ample evidence that both the opening and closing of technology gaps now occur much more rapidly than at any time in the past. For instance, the imitation lag for new semi-conductor designs has shrunk from eighteen months in the 1970s to six months in the 1990s. Diffusion occurs in several ways. Technical and other news media transmit knowledge of new discoveries from one country to another, as does trade in new products. Companies in advanced countries licence technical know-how and assistance to foreign companies in return for royalty payments and fees, or establish their own operations abroad using new technology. Diffusion is especially swift among the industrial countries because they have the capacity to use the new technical knowledge immediately. Therefore, technological leadership is constantly threatened by innovations elsewhere; nations must run hard to avoid falling behind. In the nineteenth century, comparative advantage changed slowly over a generation or more; in our own time, a country may enjoy a comparative advantage in a product for only a few years before technical diffusion and imitation or new technical discoveries wipe it out.

Increasing returns

Increasing returns are defined as a proportionate increase in the output of a good that is greater than the proportionate increase in all factor inputs that produce that output. Hence, a doubling of factor inputs more than doubles the output of a good, a tripling of inputs more than triples output, and so on. Consequently, unit costs of production fall as the scale of output increases. Increasing returns favour oligopolistic industries dominated by a small number of large firms.

Increasing returns provide a basis for international trade in addition to differences in factor endowments and technology gaps. Assume that two countries (A and B) have the same factor proportions and the same level of technology. In terms of the H–O model and technology-gap theory, no gainful trade is possible under these conditions. But suppose that Country A has a big domestic market that allows it to achieve increasing returns in manufacturing a product (say, automobiles) whereas Country B has only a small domestic market that limits it to high-cost, small-scale production of automobiles. It follows that Country A has a comparative advantage in automobiles based on increasing returns. When trade opens up, Country A will export automobiles to Country B. To eliminate Country A's comparative advantage in automobiles, producers in Country B would have to invest in new plants and equipment to achieve the increasing returns enjoyed by producers in Country A. But this would require both capital investment and time. And even if this investment were forthcoming, producers in Country B would have to absorb losses until the new plants were actually in operation. Without government assistance, these obstacles could prove insurmountable, even over the long term.

Increasing returns are associated with economies of scale, learning curve effects and economies of scope. Economies of scale occur when a higher volume of output enables a more productive use of specific factors of production. Giant machines, the assembly-line organization of production, high degrees of labour and managerial specialization, extensive research and development, and mass marketing are economical only for firms that have reached a substantial size.

The learning curve traces a decrease in the average total costs of a product as a firm's cumulative volume of output grows over the long term. Why should total unit costs fall with cumulative output? The explanation covers the entire firm, not only economies in the single plant. As the firm gains experience with a product over time, it can cut costs through a combination of effects, such as improving the performance of workers and managers through a growing familiarity with the product and related processes, and reducing inventory costs as production and marketing operations become more efficient. Hence, unit costs drop as experience leads to a smoother coordination of tasks and their performance.

A third explanation of increasing returns is economies of scope that may occur in a firm producing two or more different products. These economies appear when the unit costs of each of two or more products produced jointly by a firm are lower than the unit costs of the same products produced alone with the same level of inputs. Economies of scope can offer a competitive advantage to the diversified firm.

Product differentiation

Firms in the industrial countries develop and maintain differentiated products to obtain a competitive advantage in specific segments of their domestic markets. When these firms look abroad for markets, they find them mainly in foreign countries that have market segments matching the segments they are currently exploiting in their home markets. When they are successful, differentiated products give manufacturers a degree of monopoly power. The most prominent example of the pervasiveness of this strategy is the multitude of brands in the same consumer goods, but the strategy is also common for industrial products. A firm's products are distinguished from similar products of other firms in several ways, most commonly through style and design features, packaging, customer services, promotion and reputation. Less commonly, a firm makes a technological breakthrough with a new type of product that, for a time, has no close substitutes.

Most intra-industry trade is trade in differentiated products. The explanation of intra-industry trade, therefore, derives from factors that are specific to the individual firm. This firm-specific nature of intra-industry trade is highlighted when we recognize that about one-third of that trade occurs between multinational enterprises and their foreign subsidiaries.

The effect of product differentiation on international trade is expansive. Non-price competition stimulates demand by acquainting buyers with goods, by transforming latent demand into active demand, by introducing new products and new uses for old products, and by heightening the availability of products. In the long run, competition forces an identity between costs and prices as products lose their differentiation through imitation by competitors. Non-price competition, therefore, brings a dynamic, expansive element to international trade without the distortion of chronic monopoly profits.

Summary statement of international trade theories

The several theories of trade relate comparative advantage to certain attributes of trading countries: factor proportions, technology gaps, increasing returns and product differentiation. Each of these theories concentrates on a particular determinant that explains international trade under certain circumstances. Collectively, therefore, the theories offer a comprehensive understanding of international trade. In general, they provide complementary rather than conflicting explanations.

Table 2 indicates the principal explanations of comparative advantage depending on whether the product is (1) a primary or manufactured product; (2) a mineral or agricultural product (if a primary product); or (3) at an introductory, growth or mature phase of its life cycle (if a manufactured product).

Primary products are non-differentiated commodities whose prices are mainly set in commodity exchanges. Factor endowments are the main determinant of trade in such goods. However, a second-order distinction needs to be drawn between minerals and other (mostly agricultural) commodities. Big oligopolistic firms dominate the production and trade in minerals, such as petroleum, iron ore, bauxite and copper ore. These firms exploit mineral deposits through large-scale, capital-intensive operations in mining, processing, transportation and storage. Increasing returns, therefore, are an additional explanation of international trade in minerals. By and large, however, these firms share the same technology, and therefore technology gaps play only a modest role in minerals trade.

In contrast, agricultural production is spread among many producers who do not obtain increasing returns but who may be growing crops with dissimilar production functions. For instance, US agriculture uses a high level of mechanization, improved soil care, pest control, new varieties of seed, and so on. In contrast, agriculture in developing countries has remained labour-intensive. For that reason technology gaps, along with factor endowments, are a determinant of trade in agricultural goods.

The principal source of comparative advantage in manufactured goods depends on the phases of their life cycles. In the introductory phase, when the product is new, comparative advantage mainly derives from technology gaps. In the growth phase, when the innovating manufacturer's product has some imitators, product differentiation becomes the principal explanation of comparative advantage. In the mature phase, when the product loses differentiation, factor endowments and increasing returns emerge as the dominant influences on comparative advantage.

Only trade in agricultural commodities and commodity-like manufactures in the mature phase of their life cycles takes place in markets that approach the economist's model of perfect competition. In perfectly competitive markets, individual firms have no market power. In contrast, with technology gaps, increasing returns and product differentiation the individual firm exercises some degree of market power. An explanation of trade in new and differentiated manufactured products and in minerals, therefore, must pay attention to the market behaviour of individual firms, particularly multinational enterprises.

Table 2 Explanations of acomparative advantage in international trade

	Primary products		Manufactured products		
Explanations	Mineral	Agricultural	Introductory phase	Growth phase	Mature phase
Factor endowments	•	•			•
Technology gaps		•	•		
Increasing returns	•				•
Product differentiation				•	

Source: Adapted from Root (1994:129)

3 Theories of foreign direct investment and multinational enterprises

Foreign direct investment (FDI) is the full or partial ownership of an enterprise located in one country by investors located in another country (see MULTINATIONAL CORPORATIONS). Commonly, the direct investor has enough ownership of the foreign enterprise to exercise a degree of managerial control. The controlled enterprise becomes a foreign affiliate or subsidiary of the controlling enterprise (parent company).

FDI is the distinctive feature of the multinational enterprise (MNE). Hence, a theory of FDI is also a theory of the MNE. FDI is not only (or even primarily) an international transfer of capital; it is the extension of an enterprise from its home country into a foreign host country. The extension of enterprise involves flows of capital, technology and entrepreneurial skills to the host economy, where they are combined with local factors in the production of goods for local or export markets. This transfer of a 'bundle' of factor services remains under the control of the investing (parent) firm, as do the subsequent production and marketing activities of its subsidiary in the host country. Commonly, the transfer of factor services is accompanied by exports from the parent company of intermediate goods that are inputs in the subsidiary's production process or by exports of final goods channelled through the subsidiary's marketing facilities.

MNEs span the globe with their production, marketing and financial operations. These firms are responsible for a large share of international trade and almost all foreign direct investment. The MNE is the foremost agent in moving factors of production from one country to another. The intimate link between the trade and investment activities of MNEs calls for a synthesis of trade and investment theories.

MNEs are large firms in oligopolistic industries producing and selling mostly differentiated products. Strongly motivated by growth objectives and the maintenance of global market shares, and sensitive to each other's behaviour, MNEs prefer to compete with new and differentiated products rather than with price. These firms are also characterized by increasing returns in production and organization that support their oligopolistic power. Horizontally and vertically integrated across national boundaries, much of the international trade of MNEs is among their own national affiliates. For instance, more than one-third of US exports of manufactures consists of transfers from US parent companies to their foreign affiliates.

MNEs are more technologically intensive than their domestic counterparts. Such companies have a global capability to transfer technology through exports and licensing or through operations (FDI) in foreign countries. By both innovating and speeding up the international dispersion of technology, MNEs both create and destroy international technology gaps. In general, MNEs contribute to the world economy by improving the allocation of resources and promoting growth through innovation. This contribution has been compared with the earlier role of national corporations in building national economies by moving capital, technology and entrepreneurial skills from regions of factor abundance to regions of factor scarcity. MNEs today are building a world economy by integrating national economies.

Requirements of a foreign direct investment theory

A theory of FDI needs to answer three fundamental questions: (1) How can direct-investing firms compete successfully with local firms in a host country, given the inherent advantages of local firms operating in a familiar business environment? (2) Why do firms choose to enter host countries as direct investors in production rather than as exporters or licensers? (3) What determines where firms invest abroad? In answering these questions, an FDI theory would also explain why large firms in oligopolistic markets dominate FDI, why FDI occurs in some industries and not in others, why cross-investment occurs at both country and industry levels, and why only a few countries are the source of most FDI.

Unlike trade theory, which stretches back at least to Adam Smith, FDI theory is a new domain for economists and management scholars. The contemporary scope of FDI and MNEs is due mainly to developments starting in the 1960s. We look first at the failure of portfolio investment theory to explain FDI.

Theory of international portfolio investment

Conventional economic theory has relied on a model of portfolio investment to explain the international movement of capital as a factor of production. This theory postulates interest rate differences among countries as the cause of international capital movements. Capital moves from Country A to Country B because the long-term interest rate (return on capital) is higher in Country B than in Country A, reflecting the comparative abundance of capital in the latter country. Capital continues to move from Country A to Country B until interest rates become equal when the marginal product of capital in the two countries becomes the same.

We can depict portfolio theory in terms of the simple formula for capitalizing a stream of earnings, $C = Y/i$, where C is the value of a capital asset, Y is the stream of income produced by the asset, and i is the rate of interest. Then capital moves from Country A to Country B when the value of an asset is lower in Country B than in Country A for the same income stream. Investors in Country A will purchase the lower-priced asset in Country B. This theory offers a good explanation of international movements of portfolio capital (which does not carry managerial control) when account is taken of foreign exchange and other risks.

But is a difference in interest rates (cost of capital) between two countries a good explanation of FDI? Do MNEs establish foreign affiliates because they expect to earn higher rates of return on the same assets than they would at home? Or do they invest abroad because they expect to earn a higher income than

local companies do on the same assets, the cost of capital (i) being the same for both?

Statistical data fail to support the proposition that rates of return on FDI are higher than rates of return on home investment, particularly when the higher risks of foreign investment are taken into account. Sometimes rates are higher; sometimes they are not. Yield differences between investing (home) and host countries cannot explain the country distribution of FDI.

The second proposition, that MNEs expect to earn a higher income (Y) than local competitors, appears to be a better explanation of FDI. It is consistent with the observed fact that MNEs must assume many costs of international business that are not assumed by local companies. They must overcome barriers imposed by distance, time, information gaps, nationality, culture and other aspects of a foreign environment that are not experienced by local firms. These higher costs must be offset by higher incomes than are earned by local competitors. But to earn a higher income, the MNE must possess a competitive advantage over local competitors.

The proposition that FDI occurs because of differences in Y rather than differences in i is also consistent with the acquisition of local companies by MNEs. Why should the MNE be willing to pay more for a company than local investors? The most plausible answer is that the MNE expects to earn higher profits (a higher Y) from the acquired company than local investors would. Furthermore, this proposition is consistent with the observed fact that European and Japanese MNEs invest in the USA at the same time that US MNEs in the same industry are investing in Europe and Japan. Both sets of companies believe that they can compete effectively in each other's territory.

In summary, the theory of international portfolio investment cannot explain FDI. Indeed, by assuming perfectly competitive markets, this theory rules out FDI and the MNE. In such markets, local firms could buy the technology and other skills available to nonlocal firms. Hence, outside firms possessing no advantages over local firms would have no incentive to produce abroad. They would incur costs of doing business abroad (not incurred by local firms) that would not be offset by higher income. In that kind of world, capital would move through international capital markets rather than through the mediation of the international firm, as occurs with FDI. It follows that an explanation of FDI must be found in departures from perfect competition (what the economist calls 'market imperfections') that give the direct-investing firm competitive advantages over local firms.

We now turn to three FDI theories that agree on the importance of market imperfections but offer different approaches: monopolistic advantage theory, internalization theory and the eclectic paradigm.

Monopolistic advantage theory

Monopolistic advantage theory postulates that the investing firm possesses competitive advantages enabling it to operate subsidiaries abroad more profitably than local competing firms. These advantages are specific to the firm rather than to its national production locations. The advantages are owned by the firm and are not available to other firms on the open market. Hence, direct investment belongs more to the theory of industrial organization than to the theory of international capital movements. The monopolistic advantages of the investing firm fall into two broad categories: superior knowledge and oligopoly.

In discussing monopolistic advantage theory, it is desirable to distinguish between horizontal FDI and vertical FDI. Horizontal investment occurs when the investing company enters foreign countries to produce the same product or products that it produces at home. It represents, therefore, a geographical diversification in production of the company's product line. In contrast, vertical investment occurs when the investing company establishes operations in a foreign country to produce intermediate goods (such as raw materials or components) intended for use as inputs in the manufacture of its product line (backward vertical investment) or as inputs in the manufacture or distribution of products closer to the final buyer (forward vertical investment). One version of monopolistic advantage theory (superior knowledge) emphasizes horizontal investment; a second version (oligopoly) emphasizes vertical investment. (An MNE is usually an oligopolist with superior knowledge and therefore undertakes both vertical and horizontal investment.)

Superior knowledge includes all intangible skills possessed by the firm that give it a competitive advantage wherever it undertakes operations: technology, management and organization skills, marketing skills, and the like. Monopolistic advantage derives from the firm's control over the use of its knowledge assets, which can be transformed into differentiated products. All knowledge assets have the character of public goods in that the marginal cost of exploiting them through FDI is zero or very small relative to their returns. This is so because at any point the cost to the investing firm of acquiring its current knowledge assets has already been incurred sometime in the past (sunk cost) and also because the supply of its knowledge assets is highly elastic (approaching infinity in some instances), since their use in one country does not prevent their use in another country. Although the marginal cost of exploiting its knowledge assets in a foreign country is very low for the investing firm, local firms would need to invest the full cost to acquire similar assets.

Superior knowledge empowers a firm to create differentiated products with physical differences (deriving mainly from technology skills) or with psychological differences (deriving mainly from marketing skills) that distinguish them from competing products. In this way the firm gains a degree of control over product prices and sales, thereby obtaining an economic rent on its knowledge assets.

The monopolistic advantage theory postulates that horizontal FDI will be undertaken mainly by the more knowledge-intensive industries. This is confirmed by empirical data. Technology-intensive industries (such as petroleum refining, pharmaceuticals, industrial chemicals, farm machinery, electronics and transportation equipment) are the biggest source of FDI. Industries with high-level marketing skills (a proprietary knowledge asset), such as beverages, manufactured foods, soaps and cosmetics and fast-food restaurant chains, are also prominent foreign direct investors. Nestlé, Procter & Gamble, Coca-Cola and McDonald's illustrate this point.

Why are only a few industrial countries – the USA, Japan and some European countries – the source of most FDI in the world? Although knowledge assets are firm-specific and, once created, may be easily transferred by a firm to other countries, a firm cannot create knowledge assets out of thin air. In the first instance, it depends on its home country economy for the inputs necessary for their creation: scientists, engineers, managers, marketing specialists and other human factors. A firm also benefits from a high-income, sophisticated domestic market for the early exploitation of its knowledge assets. Because such human skills and markets are found in only a few industrial countries, firms with superior knowledge are concentrated in the same countries. As monopolistic advantage theory demonstrates, these firms are the principal source of FDI.

Foreign direct investors are, for the most part, big firms in oligopolistic industries characterized by only a few dominant members. Because rival firms are so few (usually not more than about ten even at the global level), each of them is very sensitive to the competitive moves of the others. This interdependence among oligopolistic firms in the same industry is the essence of oligopoly; it is the source of distinctive oligopolistic behaviour.

When an oligopolistic firm acts to obtain a competitive advantage by introducing a new product, entering a new market or acquiring a new source of raw materials, then rival firms are forced to respond with counteractions. To do otherwise would risk the loss of market position or growth to the advantage of the initiating firm. Indeed, the primary objective of oligopolistic firms appears to be growth (subject to a minimum profit constraint) rather than profit maximization. At the very least, each firm wants to grow as rapidly as rival firms; its relative rate of growth determines its relative size, which in turn determines its relative market power. For that reason, an oligopolistic firm is extremely sensitive to the actions of rival firms that threaten its market share. A fall in market share is viewed with alarm even when the total market is expanding so rapidly that the firm's absolute profits and sales are rising.

Oligopolistic firms obtain monopoly profits (economic rent) because entry barriers keep new firms out of the industry. Common entry barriers are increasing returns based on large, lump-sum investments of capital which would be very costly for outside firms to match; control over scarce or low-cost raw material supplies through vertical investment; differentiated products; and knowledge assets, such as patents, trademarks and brand names.

Vertical FDI is a prominent trait of oligopolies. Companies in steel, aluminium, copper and petroleum have invested abroad to acquire sources of raw materials. Why this backward integration into raw material sources? Why not obtain the needed raw materials from independent foreign producers? The general answer is that vertical backward FDI may be a more cost-effective way to build and sustain a competitive advantage. Specific answers include the avoidance of oligopolistic uncertainty and the erection of entry barriers to new rivals. For instance, when an oligopolist can obtain a critical raw material only from a second foreign oligopolist, the first oligopolist can remove the bargaining disadvantages and uncertainties of this bilateral oligopoly most directly through vertical FDI that creates its own source of supply. Thus, the avoidance of oligopolistic uncertainty is a motive for vertical foreign investment. Vertical foreign investments may also build barriers that prevent the entry of new firms into the industry. By denying to potential newcomers access to raw materials, the oligopolist is able to maintain market power. Vertical foreign investment is not confined to raw material extraction. Manufacturing companies may invest abroad to source components for transfer to production units in the home or third countries, or they may invest forward in distribution and marketing facilities.

Monopolistic advantage theory throws light on the phenomenon of cross-investment.

Because knowledge assets are firm-specific rather than country-specific, there is no contradiction in a US company investing in, say, Germany while at the same time a German company invests in the USA. As the two firms have differentiated products that appeal to different market segments, they may also belong to the same industry.

Although this theory also scores well in predicting the industrial composition of direct foreign investment, it does not explain why some knowledge-intensive industries, notably aerospace, are large exporters but only small foreign investors. It would appear that the possession of knowledge and other firm-specific assets is a necessary but not a sufficient condition for FDI. A second condition is that a firm with a monopolistic advantage can obtain the highest economic rent for its proprietary assets only by investing abroad in production under its control. That is, the return from foreign investment must be higher than the returns from exporting or licensing.

Internalization (transaction-cost) theory

The theory of internalization offers an explanation of why FDI may be a more effective way of exploiting foreign resources and markets than exporting or licensing.

Internalization theory postulates that: (1) markets can fail to allocate factor services and products efficiently due to risk and uncertainty, oligopoly, government interventions, externalities (the failure of market prices to capture all costs or revenues) and other departures from perfect competition; (2) markets and firms are alternative ways of organizing transactions of factor services and products; (3) transactions are internalized within a firm when their costs are less than the costs of external market transactions; and (4) the MNE is an institution that internalizes cross-national transactions through international production (FDI).

Transaction costs are the costs of organizing exchange: the costs of informing, monitoring and rewarding buyers and sellers. Markets depend mainly on prices to inform, monitor and reward participants, and they become inefficient when prices fail to capture all transaction values, thereby creating 'externalities'.

In contrast, firms organize exchange through central direction and control of their operations and employees, with arm's length market transactions giving way to intra-firm transfers. In organizing exchange, firms incur the cost of systems to inform, monitor and reward their employees. Internalization theory asserts that firms replace external markets with internal flows of factor services, technology and products when by doing so they can lower transaction costs. Putting the matter somewhat differently, firms internalize when they can capture more externalities through internal transfers than through sales and purchases in external markets.

Market failure is most evident in the exchange of knowledge. When a firm creates new knowledge, that knowledge becomes a public good. But a public good cannot be priced by a market because its marginal cost is zero: new users of the good can be supplied at no additional cost. Furthermore, at a zero price, there would be no incentive for firms to create knowledge. This externality can be partly overcome by the assignment of property rights (patents and trademarks) to the innovating firm, enabling it to restrict the use of the knowledge. However, only some of a firm's knowledge can be legally protected; other knowledge must be protected through the firm's own efforts to prevent disclosure to outsiders. The most direct way to prevent disclosure and thereby earn monopoly rent is for the firm to internalize its knowledge. Instead of selling (licensing) its knowledge to outsiders, the firm applies that knowledge only to production under its control. Internalization theory explains horizontal foreign investment, therefore, as a response to market failure in knowledge. Internalization enables a firm to 'appropriate' an economic rent for its knowledge that cannot be obtained in external markets.

Internalization theory also explains vertical integration as a replacement of inefficient external markets. Backward integration occurs when (1) there are high costs in coordinating successive production stages by market prices when buyers and sellers are few in number; (2) exchange extends over a lengthy period of time; and (3) buyers and sellers experience a high degree of uncertainty. Forward integration becomes an efficient way of organizing exchange when there is a high degree of interdependence between the manufacturing firm and marketing channel agencies, and it is costly to constrain that interdependence through market prices and contracts.

Eclectic paradigm of foreign direct investment

The theories of monopolistic advantage and internalization go a long way towards explaining FDI – but not all the way. These theories do not explain why the pattern of foreign involvement by MNEs (the mix of export, licensing and investment) differs across countries. The only plausible explanation of different country patterns is the influence of country-specific factors on foreign investment as well as on other forms of international involvement.

The FDI eclectic paradigm, associated with Dunning (1988), helps explain cross-country differences in the pattern of MNE involvement. To Dunning, FDI implies that location-specific advantages favour a particular host country while ownership-specific advantages favour the investing firm. International production, therefore, is attributable not only to the firm's monopolistic advantage and its ability to internalize that advantage but also to the presence of a foreign country in which production brings benefits to the firm that could not be obtained in another country. Because some market imperfections are related to country-specific endowments, the benefits of internalization for the MNE vary across countries. The eclectic paradigm draws, therefore, on the theories of international trade (comparative advantage) and location and also on the theories of monopolistic advantage and internalization. The principal contribution of the eclectic paradigm is an explanation of the distribution of international production by country.

4 Towards a new paradigm of international trade and investment

Theories of international trade, centred on national economies, and theories of FDI, centred on multinational enterprises, reflect their separate development by economists. Trade theories have ignored MNEs; FDI theories of monopolistic advantage and internalization have ignored national economies. Both sets of theories, therefore, fail to offer a full explanation of a global economy featured by massive flows of trade and direct investment involving national economies and MNEs. What is needed is a new paradigm that explains both trade and investment at both national and enterprise levels. Such a paradigm (which might be called international competitive advantage) would comprehend the behaviour of firms operating in imperfect factor and product markets within a global economy of dissimilar national factor and market endowments.

The prospects for a new paradigm are positive. Recent developments in trade theory attributing comparative advantage to technology gaps, increasing returns and product differentiation have enhanced the importance of firms, notably MNEs. On the side of investment theory, Dunning's eclectic paradigm includes national attributes explaining the geographical distribution of FDI. Both trade and investment theories now emphasize knowledge (technology) and both recognize the significance of imperfect markets.

A recent contribution to a new paradigm of international competitive advantage is Porter's (1990) model of national competitive advantage. Porter raises a key question: Why does a nation become the home base for successful international competitors in an industry engaging in both trade and investment? His answer to this question is a model consisting of four interdependent attributes of a nation that together determine a national environment that either promotes or inhibits the creation of competitive advantage in particular industries. Porter portrays this model as a figure shaped like a diamond. Hence, he refers to his model as the 'diamond'. The four broad national attributes making up Porter's diamond are:

- factor conditions
- demand conditions
- related and supporting industries
- firm strategy, structure and rivalry

Factor conditions

Factor conditions are a nation's factors of production – labour, natural resources, capital, knowledge resources and infrastructure – that provide inputs necessary to compete in any industry. A nation does not inherit but instead creates the most important factors, notably human resources and a scientific base.

Demand conditions

Demand conditions within a country determine national competitive advantage mainly through their composition (the mix and character of home buyer needs), size and pattern of growth, and their internationalization through multinational local buyers and other avenues. Home demand conditions help build competitive advantage when a particular industry segment is larger or more visible in the domestic market than in foreign markets.

Related and supporting industries

Related and supporting industries are a third broad determinant of national advantage in an industry. Related industries enable firms to coordinate or share activities and benefit from complementary products, such as computers and software. Supplier industries create advantages for downstream industries by giving them access to cost-effective inputs and their innovation and upgrading. A nation's firms benefit most when suppliers are themselves global competitors.

Firm strategy, structure and rivalry

Firm strategy, structure and rivalry shape national competitive advantage in several ways. A good match between strategies and organization (which are affected by national circumstances) and the sources of competitive advantage in a particular industry are critical for market effectiveness. Vigorous domestic rivalry is closely associated with the creation and persistence of competitive advantage in an industry. Indeed, rivalry is arguably the most important point on the diamond because it stimulates all of the others.

Porter postulates that nations succeed internationally in industries where the national diamond is most favourable. Two additional variables can influence the diamond: chance events (such as inventions, exchange rate shifts and wars) that create discontinuities allowing shifts in competitive positions, and government policies that influence the four determinants through financial support, regulation, procurement, taxation, and other means. Porter's model integrates trade and investment at the industry level where firms have a major role. However, by taking national and industry perspectives, he does not treat the autonomous role of the multinational enterprise.

It may be that a new paradigm of international competitive advantage cannot be based on any single theory of trade and investment. The outlook, however, is promising for a macro theory of national competitive advantage and a micro theory of enterprise competitive advantage. Both theories would treat the same phenomena but from different perspectives and both would belong to a single paradigm. Such a paradigm would greatly benefit national policy makers and international managers in making decisions relating to a global economy of trade and investment.

FRANKLIN R. ROOT
THE WHARTON SCHOOL
UNIVERSITY OF PENNSYLVANIA

Further reading

(References cited in the text marked *)

Buckley, P.J. (1988) 'The limits of explanation: testing the internalization theory of the multinational enterprise', *Journal of International Business Studies* 19 (2): 181–93. (This article explores the difficulties in testing the internalization approach to FDI theory.)

Casson, M. (1987) *The Firm and the Market*, Cambridge, MA: MIT Press. (This book extends internationalization theory to a wide range of applications, such as economic warfare.)

Caves, R.E. (1982) *Multinational Enterprise and Economic Analysis*, Cambridge: Cambridge University Press. (This book looks at the MNE in the light of economic theory.)

* Dunning, J.H. (1988) 'The theory of international production', *The International Trade Journal* 3 (1): 21–66. (This article traces the development of FDI theories with particular emphasis on the eclectic paradigm.)

Hennart, J.-F. (1982) *A Theory of Multinational Enterprise*, Ann Arbor, MI: University of Michigan Press. (An elaboration of the proposition that FDI occurs only when exchange is organized more efficiently within firms than in external markets.)

Kindleberger, C.P. and Andretch, D.B. (eds) (1983) *The Multinational Corporation in the 1980s*, Cambridge, MA: MIT Press. (Fourteen articles by economists on several aspects of the MNE, including FDI theory and new theories of trade.)

Krugman, P. (1990) *Rethinking International Trade*, Cambridge, MA: MIT Press. (Extensions of trade theory to encompass imperfectly competitive market structures.)

Pitelis, C.N. and Sugden, R. (eds) (1991) *The Nature of the Transnational Firm*, London: Routledge. (Nine articles on FDI theory and the multinational enterprise.)

* Porter, M.E. (1990) *The Competitive Advantage of Nations*, New York: The Free Press. (This study examines the national attributes determining international competitive advantage in specific industries.)

* Root, F.R. (1994) *International Trade and Investment*, 7th edn, Cincinnati, OH: South-Western Publishing Co. (This text offers a comprehensive treatment of international trade and investment theories in parts I and IV.)

Tharakan, P.K.M. and Kol, J. (eds) (1989) *Intraindustry Trade: Theory, Evidence and Extensions*, New York: St Martin's Press. (An examination of two-way trade between countries in products belonging to the same industry.)

United Nations (1988) *Transnational Corporations in World Development: Trends and Prospects*, New York: United Nations. (A survey of the role of transnational (multinational) corporations in the world economy, together with a statistical annex.)

United Nations (1991) *World Investment Report, The Triad in Foreign Direct Investment*, New York: United Nations. (An empirical study of the role of the triad – USA, Japan and the European Community – in FDI.)

See also: ECONOMIC INTEGRATION, INTERNATIONAL; EXPORTING; GLOBAL STRATEGIC PLANNING; GLOBALIZATION; MULTINATIONAL CORPORATIONS; WORLD TRADE ORGANIZATION

Related topics in the IEBM: GENERAL AGREEMENT ON TARIFFS AND TRADE; INNOVATION AND TECHNOLOGICAL CHANGE; MANUFACTURING STRATEGY; MILL, J.S.; NEO-CLASSICAL ECONOMICS; PORTER, M.E.; PRODUCT POLICY CONCEPTS IN MARKETING; RICARDO, D.; SMITH, A.; TRANSACTION COST ECONOMICS

Management education and development, international

Overview

International management development is a structured system for selecting, evaluating, tracking and training managers on a worldwide basis. Identifying and developing leaders is a key priority for globally-orientated firms, as there is a growing shortage of managerial personnel capable of meeting the requirements of these firms for technical competence, international expertise and global perspective. The development of global strategies, expansion into wider global markets and the need for international or global expertise through all levels of the managerial hierarchy have combined in such a way as to require greater attention to the development of a managerial and executive workforce which will be capable of meeting these organizational demands.

There comes a point in the development of the multinational firm when it becomes apparent that it is necessary for its management development programmes to become international in perspective and content (Marquardt and Engel 1993). Within those global and multinational companies already successfully competing in the world marketplace, new management development programmes are being launched to meet these needs. These programmes are designed to integrate an international perspective into managerial and executive development courses and content, to create a management cadre that possesses a deep understanding of the worldwide marketplace in which they compete, a sensitivity to the political, economic and social environment, and a commitment to organizational success (Odenwald 1993).

As multinational corporations broaden their perspectives to become globally competitive, the management development programmes will become global in orientation and composition. Sensitivity to multiple cultures, frequent foreign assignments, appreciation of the world as one marketplace and development of the firm's best human talent worldwide are hallmarks of globally oriented management development programmes.

The key to international management development is the human resource staffing cycle. Within this cycle, goals can be set for management development on the strategic, managerial and operational levels. Career planning is an important aspect of development; overseas assignments are a particularly useful way of enhancing managerial careers and developing international expertise. However, even sophisticated international management development programmes face problems, such as the potential 'cloning' of executives and the problems of relating performance to potential. However, international management development is and will remain an increasingly important aspect of corporate strategies as companies become more and more focused on the global marketplace.

1 Elements of the human resource staffing cycle

The development of managers who are prepared to lead the global multinational enterprise represents a critical organizational priority, and it is essential that firms understand and manage the human resource staffing cycle (see MULTINATIONAL CORPORATIONS; HUMAN RESOURCE MANAGEMENT, INTERNATIONAL). At the heart of the staffing cycle is management development, which can be defined as the process by which managers and executives increase their value to the firm through the acquisition of knowledge, skills and attitudes. Other elements in the staffing cycle include selection and tracking of personnel, evaluation of employee performance, identification of management potential and development, and training of the managerial and executive workforce.

Selection

The selection process has a direct relationship to management development because the better an organization's selection procedures are, the more likely the organization is to hire applicants and promote employees who already possess some of the skills and knowledge necessary to perform their jobs effectively.

Management succession planning is another activity that can be included under the rubric of selection because it is concerned with assuring that competent candidates are available for critical managerial and executive positions. One of the consequences of management succession planning is the continuous flow of highly qualified managerial and executive personnel who possess a deep understanding of the international or global marketplace environment, and the capability and desire to transfer that knowledge and skill into forceful action. Consequently, new ideas, new concepts and new plans are generated as a means of helping to avoid managerial obsolescence.

Training and development

The development of managers who have a global perspective and international expertise is the central feature of human resource management's international management development responsibilities. The successful development of the firm's managerial talent requires a continuous and coordinated set of activities which are generally considered to be integral elements of the staffing process. These include, to name a few, coordination of international assignments, administration of executive development programmes and supervision of management succession activities.

Performance appraisal

Performance appraisal is the cornerstone of an effective human resource staffing cycle because it provides information on both employee performance and employees' potential ability to handle increasingly important organizational assignments. The identification and evaluation of high-potential managers, regardless of where they are physically located in the worldwide operations of the company, is of essential importance to managerial development.

2 A framework for considering international management development

Figure 1 presents a framework for considering international management development. The nature and content of international management development can be analysed at three organizational levels, strategic, managerial and operational (see INTERNATIONAL BUSINESS, FUTURE TRENDS). The direction of analysis moves from the strategic level, which focuses on the future and is characterized by high uncertainty and ambiguity, through the managerial or intermediate level, which is viewed as being relatively more certain and less ambiguous, to the operational or immediate level, characterized by certainty and low ambiguity. This process can be seen in Figure 1. Human resource management's

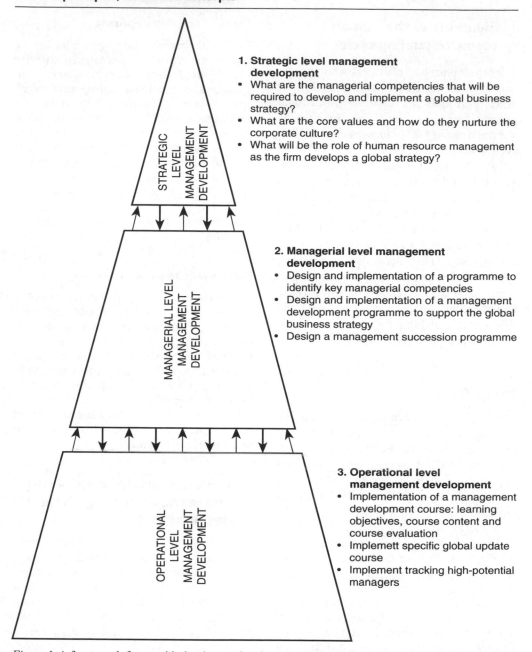

1. Strategic level management development
- What are the managerial competencies that will be required to develop and implement a global business strategy?
- What are the core values and how do they nurture the corporate culture?
- What will be the role of human resource management as the firm develops a global strategy?

2. Managerial level management development
- Design and implementation of a programme to identify key managerial competencies
- Design and implementation of a management development programme to support the global business strategy
- Design a management succession programme

3. Operational level management development
- Implementation of a management development course: learning objectives, course content and course evaluation
- Implemett specific global update course
- Implement tracking high-potential managers

Figure 1 A framework for considering international management development

participation in management development will occur at each level, but the nature of its involvement will vary by organizational level.

As Figure 1 shows, there are also feedback loops that allow for a high degree of

coordination and reforming of the goal or goals of international management development policy, programme design, practices and technique implementation, and ultimately the relationship between management development and organizational strategy. This conceptualization also shows the interdependencies between international management development and the other elements of the staffing cycle.

3 Levels of international management development

International management development at the strategic level

International management development at the strategic or long-term level is directed towards the establishment of linkages with the corporate mission and strategy. The objective of the strategic international management development plan is to build the managerial and executive competencies necessary for organizational success. This will require serious thought by management about future economic and geopolitical conditions, the nature of future competition and the firm's long-term strategy for dealing with these ambiguous conditions. Although the strategic level of analysis is ambiguous and highly futuristic, the goal of management development is to guarantee a continuous flow of managers and executives qualified to perform successfully in their present assignments and prepared to accept increasingly responsible assignments throughout the company's management structure.

Strategically-orientated international management development is multidimensional in its orientation. One dimension is represented by the identification of and agreement on the critical competencies needed in the key professional, managerial and executive positions in the organization, at present and in the future. Agreement on these competencies then becomes the basis for international management development at the managerial and operational levels. However, it should be emphasized that there will remain some measure of uncertainty associated with the development of the critical competencies, and these must be periodically reviewed in order to bring them into alignment with the firm's strategic plan and its assumptions about the future (Borucki and Lafley 1984).

Without continuous review, the critical competencies can become hopelessly outdated and potentially detrimental to the organization and its success in the global marketplace.

A second dimension focuses on the development and nurture of corporate culture. One aspect of the international management development mission is to plan for the development of professional, managerial and executive personnel who will approach problems from a similar orientation, and who will by their actions and common language reinforce the values and attitudes which are of critical importance to the corporation's way of conducting business.

A third dimension is futuristic in orientation, as the successful implementation of an organization's strategy is closely linked with the quality of its managerial talent. International management development is intended to provide a continuous flow of managerial and executive personnel who will be qualified and prepared to cope with a highly fluid and uncertain world. In other words, a management development programme should be judged by its success in developing a managerial workforce that will result in having 'the right people, at the right place, at the right time and doing the right things'.

International management development at the managerial level

Almost all private and public multinational and global companies have training and development programmes for their professional, managerial and executive personnel (see MULTINATIONAL CORPORATIONS). As pressure increases to develop a managerial workforce that will be professionally competent to manage the enterprise's international and global activities, executive and management training and development programmes will become even more critical to the goal of efficiently managing an organization's human resources and its overall leadership in the global marketplace. At the managerial or medium-term level, the objectives of international management development will be the development of profiles for successful performance at various managerial/professional levels, the development of an appraisal system that will measure job performance and evaluate managerial potential, and the establishment of an international management development programme. The challenge facing the enterprise's human resource management function is to develop training and development programmes that will prepare managers and executives to identify and resolve critical organizational issues, being managerially effective and cost efficient, while simultaneously thinking internationally.

Management development and training activities have been frequently viewed as 'nice to do' or even a 'necessary evil', and little attention has been devoted to the relationship between the strategic and the more pragmatic issues of international management and executive development. Given the heightened competition in the world marketplace and the expanding set of qualifications required of the managerial workforce, such an indifferent or negative attitude is no longer acceptable. More than ever before, there must be significant senior management endorsement and involvement in the enterprise's international management training and development activities, because new perspectives and commitments, new norms and new ways of thinking cannot flourish without such support. Active senior management interest in the development of the enterprise's managerial staff is necessary for ensuring an equally high level of commitment by the middle and lower-level managers responsible for developing their subordinates.

As a consequence of the aggressive growth strategies of multinational and global corporations, the demand for competent managers may well exceed the supply of such talent. Some firms failed to anticipate the need for managerial talent with the qualifications described above, and these have had to locate other sources and devise techniques for finding and hiring qualified managerial personnel. Some of the more traditional techniques include recruiting managers from other multinational companies, hiring qualified host-country or third-country nationals, hiring retired military personnel and government officials, or assigning less than qualified managerial personnel to newly-created or vacant jobs (see HUMAN RESOURCE MANAGEMENT, INTERNATIONAL). Such recruitment and selection techniques may be satisfactory in the short term, but they are likely to be ineffective over the long term because they are cost-ineffective and inappropriate for the resolution of the long-term demand and supply problem. The more successful multinational and global corporations have launched comprehensive international management development programmes that will, in the long term, remedy the supply and demand discrepancy and provide a continuous flow of well-qualified managers.

Identifying and developing the potential leadership of the global or multinational firm has become a priority human resource issue, and senior management and the human resource management function have come to recognize the need to be involved in the development of a strategy that meets long-term human resource needs. In many of the world's largest corporations, at least one day a month is devoted at board level to human resource issues and international executive development. At the managerial level, the human resource management department plays an active role in the development of management by establishing and administering the managerial succession programme and general management education programmes, engaging in formal classroom instruction, assisting in decisions about foreign assignments, fostering employee self-development programmes and providing career development services.

Critical competencies: a necessary first step

The integration of a global or international perspective into the development of managers and executives requires the firm to initiate several specific steps. The essential first step is to set out the critical competencies that will be needed in key professional, managerial and executive positions at the present and in the future. Research on the core qualities and competencies of managers suggests that these will vary by management level, by functional area and over time, and that there are some general managerial qualities which would

Table 1 Managerial competencies

Entry level	Management level	Executive level
technical qualifications	technical qualifications	technical qualifications
functional specialization	demonstrated functional specialization and competence	demonstrated accomplishments in strategy formulation and implementation
		knowledge of a particular functional area
Managerial qualifications	*Managerial qualifications*	*Executive administrative qualifications*
leadership potential	demonstrated managerial performance	demonstrated leadership and administrative skills
ability to communicate effectively	leadership skills	ability to develop and communicate a vision
	communication skills	
Personal qualifications	*Personal qualifications*	*Personal qualifications*
intellectual capabilites	creativity	integrity
achievement oriented	interpersonal skills	analytic
risk taker	loyal	risk-taking
	organized	intuitive
	responsible	diplomatic

seem to be appropriate for each managerial level. Table 1 provides an overall description of these competencies.

At each managerial and executive level, the career paths and descriptions of these critical competencies need to be set out, and these descriptions should then become integrated into other elements of the human resource staffing cycle. For example, a profile of the critical competencies at entry level positions provides the starting point for the recruitment and selection of entry level candidates. An awareness of the range of formal as well as informal management development opportunities at each management level enables managers to make intelligent personnel decisions with respect to a particular employee. The profile of critical competencies becomes the basis for evaluating the strengths and weaknesses of an employee's job performance and the organizational steps that can be undertaken to strengthen job performance; specifically, these could include participation in an executive education programme, transfer to a foreign subsidiary for a stated period

of time or involvement in task groups composed of managers of different nationalities.

Management succession

Management succession planning represents another management tool for identifying competent managerial candidates who are or will be available to play a critical role within a corporation's managerial hierarchy. Succession planning can be defined as the process which anticipates future managerial staffing requirements and the development of high-talent employees as managers to satisfy these needs. Implementation of the management succession process requires the introduction of policies and systems that will make succession planning part of the ongoing management process, and an expressed commitment by senior management to the support of international management development objectives and their implementation (Saklad 1978). Succession planning helps to ensure that the best available managers are used to fill key managerial positions, and it directs training and development activities towards the goal of meeting the technical and international requirements of high-potential managers and executives. The result is an investment in the development of managers, and the intentional movement of individuals among job assignments for development purposes.

International management and executive development programmes have different objectives; their orientations will vary, as will the means of providing the necessary information and knowledge. In some firms, executive and management education is limited to the task of locating and enroling members of the management team on programmes which provide necessary skills and help managers meet performance needs. In other firms, management and executive education is responsible for the overall development of the organization's management cadres; here, human resources managers will analyse the value added by external organizations who can provide training and development as opposed to the value added should the firm decide to develop its own internal training and development courses.

Among those taking an active role in executive education are likely to be training and development professionals, who will take responsibility for development of courses to meet employees' performance needs or participate in decisions about the type of programme that will best meet the needs of executives or managers. Typically, executive development courses focus on four major subject areas: promoting a manager's self-awareness of his or her leadership style, acquiring job skills, stimulating subordinate motivation and acquiring international knowledge. The overall intent of these development programmes is to develop effective internationally-orientated managers and executives.

Developing internationally or globally-orientated managers and executives is not always conducted exclusively by formal management trainers or corporate training and development staff. There is an argument for managerial development to be handled by other managers, and for making it the responsibility of senior managers to train and develop their own subordinates. This approach

means that management and executive training and development take place on the job, with the 'less experienced manager' assigned to a senior manager who becomes the junior's role model. The junior manager is expected to learn the necessary job requirements and skills by observing a more experienced manager and learning by doing.

The international assignment is one example of learning on the job. The benefits of this type of assignment can be great, as it combines on-the-job training with the development of the ability to manage across cultures. However, there is a great risk of failure as well; early return of an expatriate manager from an overseas assignment is one example of job and development failure. The reasons for such failure are many; they may include inadequate preparation for the overseas assignment, and the failure to cope successfully with the challenges of living and working in a foreign culture (Tung 1987). If a global or multinational firm adheres to the practice of using the international assignment as the only means for the development of its managerial and executive staff, then it is essential that an expatriate manager's superior be willing to commit time and effort to personal development; if there is managerial indifference or resistance to participation in the development of subordinates, then rates of failure and corresponding costs to the company will be exceedingly high.

Individual career development represents the third aspect of international management development, connecting the individual manager's needs with the organization's broader human resource needs. Individual career needs can include a wide range of issues, but the central focus is always on individuals and their development. The purpose of the process is the identification of common ground where the individual can promote the firm's goals while at the same time the organization can support the individual's professional development and growth.

International management development at the operational level

International management development at the operational level is orientated towards the day-to-day activities associated with administering international development programmes, including the design and implementation of specific courses. The general purposes of training and development include knowledge, skill acquisition and perspective. Any training and development course can have one or more of the following objectives: (1) to improve an individual's level of leadership skills; (2) to provide an individual with knowledge about how to perform a job more effectively and efficiently; (3) to increase an individual's skill in one or more areas of technical expertise; (4) to increase an individual's motivation to perform a job well; and (5) to develop skills and sensitivities for working effectively in internationally or globally oriented assignments.

The success of international management development at the operational level can be measured by using several different but related criteria. First, the programme must be driven by the organization's strategic plan and subsequent iterations from the strategic through the managerial to the operational levels of implementation. Second, the content of specific programmes must be relevant and timely for the development of the participants; as a corollary, the participants must view the content of the programme as relevant to their jobs and important for their professional development. Third, evaluation of the programme must be an integral part in any professional development activity.

The human resource management function has an important responsibility for the design of specific programmes. The technical elements required for developing training and development programmes that meet the needs of the organization and that will transfer positively from the classroom setting to job performance dominate the attention of the management training and development experts. They are responsible for such technical issues as defining the need for specific courses, developing course objectives and course design, deciding on course content and the procedures and exercises that will facilitate learning, developing the profile of eligible participants and establishing the criteria for course evaluation.

These programmes can include orientation sessions for managers and their families about to be posted overseas, along with information about the region and country and perhaps some elementary language instruction. Further, when the expatriate manager prepares to return home, some companies offer re-entry training which focuses on recent changes in the company and in the manager's home society. In general, at the operational (short-term) level international management development programmes are designed to provide for the short-term management needs that can be identified with a reasonably high degree of accuracy.

Acquisition of international expertise: managerial and operational level challenges

As firms become more actively involved in global competition, many jobs which were previously considered to be domestic in orientation now include international and global interactions, and cross-border contacts are becoming everyday experiences for many clerical, administrative and managerial personnel. These representatives of the company must feel comfortable when dealing with international contacts, and they must appreciate the impact that culture has on language, customs and behaviour. The training and development problem becomes one of presenting international or global information, knowledge and perspectives in such a way that they will be considered by the participants and their superiors to be both timely and important. The challenge facing the firm is therefore one of planning for the integration of an international or global perspective into the corporate culture and throughout the critical competencies of managerial, professional and administrative career paths.

When looking at firms currently engaged in international business, it becomes clear that international strategies and global strategies are not synonymous. In an excellent discussion of the distinction between international and global organizations, Bartlett and Ghoshal (1989) comment on multinational companies that have chosen to develop a strategy that allows them to be sensitive and responsive to national environments. These companies can be viewed as managing a 'portfolio of multiple national entities'; international expertise is defined as knowledge about a particular country, and the individual manager is grounded in the culture, language, history, economic system and business practices of that company. Other companies view their marketplace as global in composition and seamless in perspective and orientation, and have thus chosen to develop a global business strategy. These firms seek global efficiency, and the global operating environment and worldwide consumer demand, not the nation-state or the local market, are the dominant units of analysis. The global manager also approaches the firm's strategy and its operations from a global perspective, and the manager's behaviour will reflect that perspective because of the type of development that he or she has received.

4 Managing international job mobility: the overseas assignment

Specific decisions regarding international management development tend to be made at the operational level. The opportunities for gaining international expertise are almost limitless, but several in particular stand out. These options include foreign assignments, job rotation, task group assignments, special assignments, executive education programmes, or some combination of these options. Traditionally, multinational companies have relied on the international assignment as the most common method of gaining international experience, but more recently this practice has become less common due to the expense of supporting expatriates and their families, rising levels of national feeling in many foreign locations, the increasing number of qualified host country nationals available to fill managerial positions, and the general resistance by many managers to overseas assignments.

The international assignment

When a multinational company decides to post a manager to a foreign location, it generally assigns the expatriate to an overseas location for one of several reasons. These may include the need for qualified managers when the enterprise is launching its operations in a specific country and there are no qualified host country nationals available, or as a deliberate step in the manager's professional development or to assess his or her management skills. The decision in the latter case is based on consideration of data coming from several human resource management information sources including the critical competencies for each management level, data from the management succession planning process, evaluation of performance and identification of managerial potential.

Overseas assignments are also sometimes used as an opportunity to provide senior managers with exposure to the challenges of working in a foreign environment rather than an assignment designed to assess the executive's ability to manage effectively in an overseas setting. The objective in this case is simply to provide the manager or executive with some form of international experience, which is considered to be important for more responsible positions within the senior management hierarchy. These assignments are truly developmental in orientation.

Foreign nationals assigned to the parent company

International assignments have in the past been considered to be the domain of the parent company; in other words, it is the parent company that posts its own nationals to its overseas locations. However, inter-country mobility is becoming much more common, including foreign nationals being assigned to the headquarters of the parent company. The results of such assignments are manifold: (1) the expatriate is exposed to the values, norms and methods of the parent company, and the assignment is thus developmental for the foreign national working in the parent company; (2) the expatriate has an opportunity to develop networks among parent company managers/executives and technical personnel, and when expatriates return to their own countries they have a network that can be called upon when or if a problem arises; (3) the parent company has an opportunity to observe the expatriate's management skills and potential for future advancement in the enterprise; (4) the size and richness of the candidate pool for senior management positions are expanded; and (5) the management team becomes infused with a foreign perspective. It has become routine practice in many organizations to introduce foreign managers into the senior management hierarchy and thus challenge the company belief that the company way is the only way or the best way, or in other words, 'if it wasn't invented in the parent company, then it isn't worth much'.

International management education

Management education programmes represent another organizational response to the international development of the managers and executives. Such programmes can take many different directions to achieve their goals; one of the more traditional is the general orientation or management update. During these sessions, senior management discuss the firm's overall strategy and business plans for the coming year. Participants have an opportunity to learn more about the firm's overall strategy, what steps it plans to take to implement the strategy and how they themselves will be involved in the implementation of the strategy. The manager will be in a better position to make decisions that will be congruent with the firm's overall strategy, where he or she fits into the process and how individual performance can and will have an impact on organizational success.

The benefits to be derived from including foreign nationals in the firm's management development programmes are many, and they can help to ease some of the human resource management problems experienced by the firm. Management development programmes are an important tool for socializing a firm's management. One benefit is the transmission of corporate culture and core values and an awareness of the need to share a common language with other members of the firm's management; by including foreign nationals in the firm's management development programmes, it is likely that the content of class assignments, classroom discussions, participant interaction and involvement will become much more international in orientation.

Foreign language acquisition

There has been considerable discussion concerning the value of foreign language acquisition. Kobrin (1984) provides some important insights into the advantages and disadvantages. In general, there is value in speaking and knowing a second language because it will be valuable to the expatriate for representing his or her company, discharging the responsibilities of the job and participating in the day-to-day demands of interacting with host-country nationals. From an employment perspective, however, it is only under the most unusual circumstances that a firm would hire an applicant solely because of language abilities. Speaking a second language may be an important condition for employment, but the technical and managerial qualifications of the applicant will be much more critical.

There are several arguments in favour of managers speaking a second language. First, expatriate managers who speak a second language report that forcing others to speak in the expatriate's language or using a translator reduces their effectiveness when doing business. Second, fluency in the language of the country where expatriates are located enables them to move easily among host country employees and engage in conversations with customers, representatives of government and business leaders. The result is that expatriates can gather information that may be important to the success of the subsidiary. Third, as a corollary to the previous point, although the formal language of the firm is likely to be that of the parent company, subordinates may well talk among themselves in their own language; in this case, if expatriate managers are unable to speak the language of the host country then they may fail to understand important day-to-day information about their area of responsibility. Fourth, language fluency enables expatriates to have access to local society and the culture; failure to speak the language of the country can effectively isolate expatriates or limit them to those host country nationals who are fluent in the expatriate's own language.

However, there are also arguments against fluency in a second language. First, English is the international language of business and business people throughout the world are able to speak English; therefore there may be no need to become fluent in the language of the host country. Second, it may be unreasonable to devote much time to learning another language because one cannot acquire competency in a relatively short period of time. Third, some individuals simply do not possess the ability to learn to speak foreign languages; therefore it may not be worth the time or the anxiety to try to force them to learn. Fourth, international assignments are usually relatively short in duration and work demands may prevent the expatriate from devoting time to acquiring language fluency. Fifth, there are usually enough bilingual nationals available, and it is probably more efficient to hire the language skill than to learn the language. Sixth, senior level managers can discharge their managerial responsibilities without language fluency, although for those expatriates who are in middle managerial positions language fluency is more likely to be an important requirement.

Interest in learning to speak a foreign language is to some degree country-specific. In the USA there has never been an emphasis on learning a second or third language, and consequently managers have shown little interest in developing the fluency required to do business in a second language. European managers are much more likely to know a second or even a third language. Many Asian multinational companies require their expatriates to learn the language of the country to which they are being assigned; the basis of this requirement is essentially that the manager can then be much more effective if business is being conducted in the language of the host country.

One further argument in support of language fluency is that language becomes a surrogate measure of employees' ability to feel comfortable, and a demonstration of their interest, in a nation and a culture other than their own. For globally-orientated executives, language fluency suggests that they are interested in other cultures, and that interest will be important for other cross-cultural activities. It is not the language fluency in itself that is important; to the host country national, language fluency communicates considerable symbolic meaning about expatriates and their interest in the culture with which they must interact.

Repatriation

Repatriation from a foreign country assignment back to the home country represents a difficult transition both personally and professionally. Expatriates returning to their home organizations report experiencing serious re-entry problems (Gregerson and Black 1990). From the organization's perspective the international assignment should be important for management development, and managers consider it to be important for their careers; in practice, however, returning expatriates sometimes find the international assignment has a negative or neutral effect on their careers, and the home country organization often fails to appreciate the employees' knowledge and experience.

The returning expatriate has considerable experience which can be drawn upon in order to advance the firm's operations and enrich its international or global orientations. The challenge for the firm is to bring the returning manager's knowledge and skills into the ongoing management of worldwide operations, integrating the returnee back into the central organization and capitalizing on the wealth of information now available.

Steps can be taken to facilitate this process. Returning managers can be assigned to positions where their specific country knowledge and skills will be utilized. The repatriate represents a valuable resource for stimulating the globalization of the company, and frequent interactions between the repatriate and those who have had little opportunity to go abroad provide an excellent means of contributing to a more general understanding of the firm's global operations. As a result, the firm can increase its international sophistication and decrease the chance of parochialism among all personnel; integration of international perceptions and understandings of the individual repatriate manager will increase the global perspective of the entire organization. Parent company or home country managers can even be trained to understand and value the returning manager's foreign experience. The particular human resource problem is that of deciding where in the organization to place the returning manager in order to capitalize upon his or her skills and knowledge.

5 Career planning and international management development

Multinational and global companies are paying more attention to the careers of their employees. With rapidly changing economic conditions, a limited supply of competent managerial and professional/technical talent and changing job requirements, career development has become an important organizational challenge. As a result, in the 1990s retention, development and utilization of existing talent are receiving much attention from the management and human resource management functions of global enterprises. Individual career planning emphasizes an employee's career and work needs; the aim is to create a situation whereby the individual contributes to and enhances the institution while at the same time the institution helps the individual to grow and develop. Sound individual career planning seeks to optimize the fit between the individual's needs, strengths and weaknesses and the human resource requirements of the organization.

It is important to combine personal development strategies with the individual's vocational life stages, and an understanding of these stages provides a basis for designing job assignments that will meet both the individual employee's needs and the organization's human resource requirements. Miller and Form

(1951) have provided a classification of life stages based on job behaviours that is useful for discussing career planning. The most relevant vocational life stages are the exploration stage (age 15–24), the establishment stage (age 25–44), the maintenance stage (age 45–64) and the decline stage (age 65 or over).

The exploration stage is defined as that period during which the individual is gathering information about vocational interests and making preliminary decisions about an appropriate career field. A young employee who wants to change job functions would most likely be at the exploratory stage. It is at this stage that the company can help the employee become integrated into the organization and learn about the firm and job opportunities, as well as learn about his or her own career and vocational interests. The employee will be especially interested in gathering information about self, job opportunities and the company. Early assignments to foreign locations are an effective means of exposing young employees to the international dimensions of the firm, and the benefit to the organization will be the development of a pool of employees likely to accept future international assignments during their careers.

The establishment stage is the period when the individual attempts to find a permanent place in the field of work. As the individual's career desires and career pattern become clearer, effort will be made to stabilize or make secure a place in a particular field. For most people, this is the period of their most creative work. Development strategies are just beginning to emerge, and development of employees at this stage of their career can follow many different routes. International assignments, cross-national task forces and job rotation between the domestic and international spheres of the company's operations are powerful tools for stimulating employee motivation and development.

The maintenance stage is defined as that period when the employee has made a place in the world of work and personal effort is made to hold on to what has been accomplished. There will generally be little effort to break new ground. Cross-functional or cross-national task forces are assignments allowing the employee to move between functional areas, consulting and trouble-shooting assignments. These are examples of possible personnel decisions by the organization that will enable employees to re-energize their careers as well as helping to meet organizational needs.

The decline stage is the period when the employee's pace of work declines and interests turn from career advancement to other activities. For the older employee, career development needs are much less clear. Obviously the employee will have different career needs than will junior colleagues, and the challenge becomes one of finding ways of capitalizing upon the talents, skills and perspectives of these senior employees. Moving into new job assignments, training and developing junior level managers and acting as advisors to senior levels of management are examples of some ways in which the firm may capitalize on this rich resource of human capital.

6 Problem areas in international management development

The hallmark of management development is the careful planning and effective implementation of plans to ensure that employees will be developed in such a fashion as to acquire the necessary skills, experiences and perspective that will enable the firm to achieve its strategic goals. The key words are careful planning, effective implementation and acquisition of technical and managerial skills, as well as an international or global perspective. The overall objective of management development should be to develop managers and executives who understand the importance of the firm's involvement in the global marketplace and how international business can contribute to organizational success. Evans *et al.* (1990) have studied the human resource problems of European global and multinational corporations which have internationally-oriented management development programmes, and have identified several major concerns. Specifically, the successful development of managers and executives with an international or global perspective can lead to three potential

difficulties; the cloning or inbreeding of executives, the failure to differentiate between performance and potential, and the failure to manage international mobility.

Cloning executives

There is a danger that those firms which have most successfully articulated and implemented their management development programmes run the risk of shaping their managers so that they act in similar ways and accept the idea there is 'one best way' to approach or handle a problem. Given the dynamic geopolitical and economic world in which the multinational or global company exists, positive action must be taken to guarantee there will be a variety and diversity of ideas within the ranks of management. Vitality, change and dynamism must be fostered and nourished in the managerial development process. The pressures of corporate culture are generally towards a common approach to problems, and towards actions, common language and shared values which reinforce the corporation's way of doing business; these pressures may result in inflexibility and the discouragement of creativity and innovation. A major challenge is to find ways of avoiding or reducing this pressure.

Executive education programmes offered by business schools have become an important tool used by companies to cope with the problem of cloning and inbreeding, and firms use a variety of executive education programmes to develop their managers. The goals of executive education are to enrich the development of the participants, share ideas with other participants, develop a framework to reconsider standard approaches to corporate problems and to provide the participant with several 'big impact ideas'.

External executive programmes are valuable because they encourage managers and executives from different organizations to participate. The participants may represent a variety of different industries, nations and cultures. Such programmes are generally designed for executives who hold or are about to assume major responsibilities in their respective organizations; the benefit to the company and to the participants comes from a willingness to participate actively with others in case analysis, situational strategies, state-of-industry presentations and small group assignments. The fact that each participant works with a peer group of executives comparable in terms of background, level of responsibility and advancement goals helps place these learning experiences in a practical framework that adds a lasting impact to the programme material.

Some firms are also using customized executive education programmes to implement strategic change. The advantages of this type of programme include improved integration between the academic world of knowledge and the business world of results, a potentially greater impact on the participants than could be achieved by relying solely on the firm's human resource management function for designing the programme, deciding upon programme content and using only company instructors to present materials and lead discussions. The more desirable approach to the design and implementation of management development programmes is to combine the best of both the academic institution and the business enterprise for positive results in both organizations.

The trade-off between potential and performance

Any continuous process of international management development must include an assessment of the following: the organization's predicted future needs, the succession requirements necessary to meet future staffing needs, and the performance and potential of current management. In the past, emphasis has been placed on past performance as a predictor of future management success and an indicator of management potential. However, the assumption that past performance and future performance are connected has proven to be unreliable because of changing job requirements, dynamic organizational goals, fluid individual interests and changing employee capabilities.

One of the most chronic problems facing identification programmes is to define valid operational measures of 'high potential managers'. Without a working definition which measures the behaviours, qualifications and skills that should be evaluated, the most technically sophisticated identification programme will be unreliable. Sound performance in a particular job should not qualify an employee for advancement to a higher level of management; successful performance on a domestically-orientated assignment does not suggest that the employee has the managerial competence to occupy a position that requires international or global expertise and perspective. Unfortunately, many personnel decisions are made without examining job demands and critical competencies, and the employee is classified as 'high potential' solely on the basis of his or her current level of job performance; in such cases, little or no consideration has been given to the person's actual qualifications for higher-level positions. It may be necessary to assess what exactly each employee has the potential to do; measuring critical competencies can be of great help in developing this assessment more fully.

Another major organizational and human resource issue is that of separating potential from performance. Performance appraisal practices do a reasonably good job of evaluating current performance, but a system for identifying high potential remains elusive. It is an organizational fact of life in multinational and global corporations that talented people sometimes remain buried within the organization unless formal steps are taken to uncover them. Systematically providing opportunities for employees to demonstrate their qualities by placing them in a wide variety of different work-related situations assignments is one way of evaluating their suitability for promotion; by receiving evaluations from a number of other managers or evaluators, the firm can put together a broader picture of the employee and reduce the possibility of errors in judgement.

In this system, it is the individual manager who is the foundation of the international management development programme; it is the manager who plans and directs the activities of his or her subordinates, and it is the manager who evaluates the subordinate's job performance and suitability for promotion. Consequently it is the manager, not some elaborate and technically sophisticated programme, who plays the pivotal role in performance appraisal and assessment of potential.

Managing international mobility

A further ongoing problem associated with international management development is that of managing the mobility of managers and executives throughout the organization. Nothing creates managerial development and professional growth as effectively as a new job assignment. However, in many organizations there is no policy governing how long a person should remain in a particular job or the eligibility of foreign nationals to participate in the enterprise's management development programmes.

The human resource management function as well as senior management must make every effort to encourage local managers to identify and release employees who are considered to have potential for greater contributions within the firm. Managers have few incentives to nominate their outstanding subordinates for assignments in other parts of the organization, and policies, practices and procedures must be initiated to reward those managers who do nominate their subordinates in this fashion. Identifying the corporation's best talent and making sure that it is properly utilized is one of the most important long-range activities in any organization, especially in a multinational or global company. No matter how good the information systems are, no matter how good the production system, no matter how valid and thorough the organization's strategic planning, if the organization has the wrong person in a significant management position, organization performance will be diminished.

The firm has to develop ways to identify its most promising candidates and then move them into management positions that will be developmental in nature and important to the firm's success. The various elements of the human resource management staffing cycle come to play in this process. However, the most critical ingredient in the identification and movement of high-potential managerial candidates is senior management commitment. International management development programmes, management succession planning, career development and the supporting human resource management subsystems are only as important as top management makes them.

Corporations devote a great deal of time to the identification of high-potential personnel, the development of transfer policies and international management development activities. There is increasing individual resistance to international assignments, however, and it is becoming apparent that firms must be concerned about their transfer policies and motivating their employees to accept overseas assignments. Generally it is the individual who chooses to express an interest in serving overseas, who decides to accept or reject an offer to serve abroad, and who succeeds or fails in the overseas assignment. There may be multiple reasons for accepting or rejecting an overseas assignment, and it is becoming important to recognize that there are different perspectives on the desirability of accepting these assignments.

7 Conclusion

By the twenty-first century, those firms successfully competing in the world market will have adopted a corporate culture, a business strategy and a management orientation which is global in its perspective and implementation. The managers and executives leading these firms will be technically and managerially distinguished, and they will possess a global perspective. The appearance of such highly qualified middle and senior level managers will not be a chance event because their firm's management development programmes will have given them job assignments and experiences in order to enable them to acquire the necessary managerial and international expertise.

As firms commit themselves to participation in world markets, it is the human resource management function that is responsible for managing the staffing cycle, and especially management development, in such a way as to guarantee that the management cadres will possess the qualifications necessary for successful job performance. The implications for the human resource management function are especially demanding, and a twofold challenge needs to be met. First, the function needs to align its mission, programmes and services with the firm's overall business strategy and, consequently, respond to the human resource needs of the worldwide organization. From a human resource management perspective, a multinational firm will design its management development programmes in such a way as to guarantee that their managerial personnel will be grounded in the culture, language, history, economic system and business practices of particular countries, rather than developing managers to view the firm as operating in a global environment. Although the global firm will have subsidiaries in 'multiple national entities', its strategy and operations will reflect a global perspective rather than one which is solely sensitive and responsive to specific national environments. Consequently, the direction and substance of management development programmes in global organizations will be designed in such a way as to guarantee that their managers will have acquired an orientation that enables them to approach the firm's strategy and its operations from a global perspective.

Second, the human resources management function must initiate and manage its transition from a domestic or multinational-orientated staff function to one that is global in perspective, structure and responsibility. This will mean that human resource staff will be expected to effectively manage their own change process and, simultaneously, develop the international or global dimensions of their activities while at the same time contributing to the broader transition by the entire firm to a global organization.

In the future, international management development will continue to be an integral element within the human resource management system, and it will represent a strategic link between the firm's overall business strategy and the development of leaders who will be capable of coping with an intensely competitive world market. It is one thing for the firm to develop a global business strategy; it is another to have management cadres who are prepared technically and philosophically to carry out this strategy. By means of a well-planned and administered management development programme, the participating managers must become sensitive to the global demands influencing their behaviour and the importance of incorporating global concerns when they are relevant for business decisions. The challenge will be to weld a relationship that clearly binds international management development and the business strategy while simultaneously developing managers who will be qualified and committed to the implementation of that strategy.

The philosophy underpinning management development must be visionary in its perspective and pragmatic in its relationship to selection, placement, tracking, evaluation, training and development of personnel throughout the firm's worldwide operations. The outcome must be management development policies, programmes and practices that are designed to guarantee a continuous stream of managers who think and act globally in their managerial assignments.

The ultimate criterion by which to judge the effectiveness of management development programmes is whether the organization has the right people, at the right place, at the right time and doing the right things. However, to achieve that goal it is essential that each manager, wherever he or she is located within the firm's worldwide operations, must bear a twofold managerial responsibility, first for the development of the skills and abilities of subordinates, and second for bringing to the attention of senior level managers those subordinates who possess the potential to advance to higher levels of management. Identifying the corporation's best talent and making sure it is properly utilized is one of the most important long-range activities in any organization, and is especially important in a company that is global in perspective and business. The overall organizational outcomes will be an enriched managerial talent pool, increased intra-organizational mobility, redefinition of organizational culture and enhanced globalization of management practice.

As corporations become more global, more attention needs to be given to the design and enrichment of management development programmes in order to provide managers and executives with international job assignments, jobs requiring frequent international involvement, participation in cross-national task forces, involvement in executive education programmes and other elements of the staffing cycle. These will be translated into organizational policies and practices that will result in the globalization of the firm's management cadres, regardless of regional location. No one will be excluded because of national origin or regional assignment; diversity in national origin of participants in management development programmes and senior corporate management positions will be an important characteristic of the globalized firm. For some firms, this will mean a revolutionary new way of thinking about the development of their management and executive teams.

In summary, as business moves into the twenty-first century, those firms which gain competitive advantage in the global market will achieve that advantage through the development of an effective global business strategy, the design of globally-orientated policies, the realignment of staff and line activities in order to execute the global business strategy, and the acquisition of human resources prepared to execute that strategy. These corporations will have developed a corporate culture that is global in its values and perspective, and good ideas will know no national origin. Nationality will not be a discriminatory factor when staffing cycle decisions are made; corporations will hire increasing numbers of foreign nationals, assimilating them into the parent company, developing their management skills and qualifications and involving them in all aspects of corporate life.

Developing management programmes that consistently and systematically seek to capitalize on the diverse experiences and perspectives of their participants will be a pivotal

human resource management activity, because these will mean that managers will be more attuned to the vagaries of the global marketplace and the requirements for success in an arena with intense competition. Management development will occupy an increasingly important position within the human resource management system, and it will have evolved into a much more complex management activity that impacts on organizational performance in important ways.

EDWIN L. MILLER
UNIVERSITY OF MICHIGAN

Further reading

(References cited in the text marked *)

* Bartlett, C.A. and Ghoshal, S. (1989) *Managing Across Borders: The Transnational Solution*, Boston, MA: Harvard Business School Press. (A practical analysis of multinational corporate strategies and the importance of management development.)
* Borucki, C.C. and Lafley, A.F. (1984) 'Strategic human resource management', in C.J. Fombrun, N.M. Tichy and M.A. DeVanna (eds), *Strategic Human Resource Management*, New York: Wiley. (Provides a clear discussion of management development and staffing practices in Chase Manhattan Bank.)
* Evans, P., Lank, E. and Farquhar, A. (1990) 'Managing human resources in the international firm: Lessons from practice', in P. Evans, Y. Doz and A. Laurent (eds), *Human Resource Management in International Firms*, New York: St Martin's Press. (Summarizes research on the impact on human resource management and international executive development of globalization.)
* Gregerson, H.B. and Black, J.S. (1990) 'A multifaceted approach to expatriate retention in international assignments', *Group and Organizational Studies* 15: 461–85. (Provides in-depth views about the problems of retention, and on means of overcoming these problems.)
* Kobrin, S.J. (1984) *International Expertise in American Business: How to Play With the Kids On the Street*, New York: Institute of International Education. (A practical study of US multinational corporate practices for gaining international expertise. The results are provocative.)
* Marquardt, M.J. and Engel, D.E. (1993) *Global Human Resource Development*, Englewood

Cliffs, NJ: Prentice-Hall. (Presents a clear and thorough discussion of international and global management development programmes; a useful guide for students interested in the practical side of executive development.)

Mendenhall, M., Dunbar, E. and Oddou, G. (1987) 'Expatriate selection, training and career pathing: a review and critique', *Human Resource Management* 26 (3): 331–45. (This article is based on available research about international job assignments, and the authors additionally provide recommendations for policy changes.)

* Miller, D.C. and Form, W.H. (1951) *Industrial Sociology*, New York: Harper & Brothers. (A clear discussion of individual life stages and career development, which should be useful to students of management.)

Miller, E.L., Beechler, S., Bhatt, B. and Nath, R. (1986) 'The relationship between the global strategic planning process and human resource management function', *Human Resource Planning* 9 (1): 9–23. (Provides insights into the nature of the relationship between the strategic planning process of multinational firms and human resource management.)

* Odenwald, S.V. (1993) *Global Training: How to Design a Program for the Multinational Corporation*, Homewood, IL: Business One Irwin. (A practical 'how-to' guide for designing internationally oriented management development programmes; provides students with a comprehensive map for designing an executive development programme.)

Prahalad, C.K. and Doz, Y. (1987) *The Multinational Mission*, New York: The Free Press.

(Discusses the relationship between the human resource management staffing cycle and international management development.)

* Saklad, D. (1978) 'Manpower development and career development at Citicorp', *Human Resource Planning* 1 (4): 237–41. (Provides a clear picture of the mechanics of Citicorp's approach to management succession planning.)

* Tung, R. (1987) 'Expatriate assignments: enhancing success and minimizing failure', *Academy of Management Executive* 1 (2): 117–26. (Compares expatriate failure rates between the USA, Japan and Europe, and gives recommendations for expatriate success.)

Tung, R. (1988) 'Career issues in international assignments', *Academy of Management Executive* 2 (3): 241–4. (Based on field research, this article identifies and discusses several of the career issues encountered by expatriates.)

See also: HUMAN RESOURCE MANAGEMENT, INTERNATIONAL; INTERNATIONAL BUSINESS, FUTURE TRENDS; MULTINATIONAL CORPORATIONS

Related topics in the IEBM: BUSINESS SCHOOLS; CAREERS; EXECUTIVE TRAINING; HUMAN RESOURCE FLOWS; HUMAN RESOURCE MANAGEMENT; LEADERSHIP; MANAGEMENT DEVELOPMENT; MBA CONCEPT; MIGRANT MANAGERS; MOTIVATION AND SATISFACTION; RECRUITMENT AND SELECTION; STRATEGY, IMPLEMENTATION OF

Marketing, cultural differences in

Overview

The great French philosopher-mathematician Pascal once said that there are truths on one side of the Pyrenees that are falsehoods on the other. This metaphor for the effects of national boundaries on culture and perception aptly sums up the challenges facing managers who must undertake marketing on a global basis.

The rapid integration and growing interdependence of markets in the world economy has created a truly global marketplace, necessitating changes in marketing, market research, product development and distribution strategies. Not surprisingly, many companies have failed to adapt to these changes, and the literature on this subject contains many examples of marketing *faux pas*. The most common difficulties faced by global marketers relate to advertising in different cultural environments, as advertisements which were successful in one area fail to have any impact in another or fall foul of local restrictions on advertising media and content.

Another common problem relates to the differences in consumer tastes around the world. Companies which attempt to market globally must realize that not every product is going to be acceptable in every culture; an extreme example might be the marketing of shaving cream in countries where men do not customarily shave. Packaging, labelling, distribution and sales all raise their share of marketing problems.

Despite these formidable challenges and the many failures which have occurred, however, cross-cultural marketing can be effective and successful. In 1990 a survey of

Muscovites showed that McDonald's in Moscow had replaced Lenin's mausoleum as the most popular place to visit, by a ratio of three to one. By understanding local cultural preferences and finding ways to meet them, marketers can overcome cultural barriers and succeed on a global scale.

1 Culture and why it is important

Business literature and the curricula of undergraduate and graduate schools of management and business in most countries have for many years had a strong focus on marketing. However, the study of marketing tended to treat it as a fairly homogeneous series of concepts and universally applicable principles, and it is only recently that a similar focus has developed on the critical issue of managing cultural differences in marketing. Businesses have always needed to be aware of diversity, yet it is only since the 1970s that it has become a subject for serious study. One of the first books to be published on this subject was Harris and Moran (1979), and the body of relevant literature is still fairly small.

In the classical anthropological sense, 'culture' refers to the cumulative deposit of knowledge, beliefs, values, religion, customs and mores acquired by a group of people. This knowledge is passed on from generation to generation and becomes the unique lifestyle of a particular group. Culture gives people identity; it has many aspects, including language, dress and appearance, food and eating habits, time and time-consciousness, awards and recognition, roles and relationships, values and priorities, the sense of self and space, and mental processes and learning, as well as beliefs and attitudes that make people distinct. Hall (1959, 1966, 1983), Harris and Moran (1996), Moran and Reisenberger (1994) and Gardenswartz and Rowe (1993) have all stated that the study of cultures and the consideration of cultural differences are especially important for individuals who are intolerant of or judgemental towards others who may dress, act or behave differently, and who have a tendency to think that if something is different, it is inferior.

Hall, in his classic work (1959), stated that cultures can be either high-context or low-context cultures. This distinction is useful for the business person looking for meaning in verbal messages and communication. A high-context communication is one in which most of the information is either in the physical context or is internalized in the person; a low-context communication is one in which most of the information is contained in an explicit code. English, German and Swedish are low-context languages, while Japanese, Arabic, French and Spanish are high-context languages. In low-context communication, one is looking for meaning and understanding in what is said; the higher-context communicator may be looking for meaning and understanding in the position of the speaker, or the relationship between communicator and audience.

There are also different levels of culture. Three levels are commonly ascribed, the *technical level*, the *formal level* and the *informal level*. One analogy is between cultures and icebergs; most aspects of a culture are invisible from the surface. The technical level of culture refers to the parts that are visible. There is little emotion attached to the technical level and there are few inter-cultural misunderstandings at this level, as the reason for disagreement is usually quite easy to determine. For example, marketers discussing the advertising regulations imposed by various national governments are looking at the technical level.

The formal level of culture is partly visible and partly invisible, at the waterline of the 'iceberg'. People learn aspects of culture at the formal level usually by trial and error. They may be aware of the rules for a particular behaviour, such as a gesture, but they do not know why these rules exist. The emotion at the formal level of culture is high and violations result in negative feelings about the violator, even though the violation is often unintentional.

The informal level of culture lies below the surface, and actions and responses are usually automatic. The rules governing a behaviour or activity are usually not known, although it is usually apparent if something is wrong. Informal rules are learned through a process of modelling, in which the behaviour of others is expected to serve as the basis of one's own behaviour. One example of this process can be seen in the differing roles and expectations of males and females and how these vary from culture to culture. Both roles and variances in this case have a strong influence on marketing decisions.

2 Communication and advertising

The fact that 'culture' is a relative term and includes many variations in attitude and behaviour is of considerable importance to marketers operating in a global environment, yet all too often people fail to understand this fact. Communication is one area where cultural differences provide a continuing source of confusion and misunderstanding. Condon and Yousef (1975: 123) provide the following examples of common misconceptions in this field:

1 many people believe that the language of gestures is universal;
2 many people believe that one picture is worth a thousand words, the implication being that what is seen is much clearer than what is said;
3 many people believe that communication means speaking and that misunderstandings only occur with speaking;
4 many people believe that smiling, frowning and clapping are purely natural expressions.

Samovor and Porter (1985) identified several variables in the communication process whose values are determined to some extent by culture, specifically attitudes, social organization, forms of reasoning, social roles and expectations, and non-verbal communication. Each of these variables influences perceptions, which in turn influence meanings.

1 *Attitudes* are psychological states that predispose us to behave in certain ways. A common attitude, particularly undesirable for marketers working in a multi-cultural environment, is ethnocentrism, a tendency to judge others according to one's own personal or cultural standards. Ethnocentrism in marketing can lead to many problems. For example, an ethnocentric approach to marketing would assume that marketing strategies and tactics developed in the USA or the UK would work equally well in Brazil, instead of attempting to understand the cultural context in Brazil and then develop a marketing strategy which would fit that context. Marketing must attempt to understand other people in the context of their unique historical, political, economic, social and cultural backgrounds. Ricks (1993) cites an example of an international company which used the figure of an owl in its promotional efforts in India; to many Indians the owl is a symbol of bad luck.

2 The *social organization* of cultures is also a variable that influences our perceptions. Managers are members of a distinct social group, but at the same time they are also members of different geographically-based societies. Significant differences in values, approach, priorities and other factors within these groups can lead to problems in marketing. There may be conflicts between the manager's social group (of managers) and the society in which he or she is working. At one meeting between British and US managers working on a joint project, the US managers asked for certain proposals to be tabled (meaning to set a proposal aside and not discuss it), not realizing that in the UK 'tabled' means to directly bring up a subject for discussion. Inexact terminology and a lack of understanding of social organization led the US managers to ask for the exact opposite of what they wanted (Ricks 1993).

3 Thought patterns or *forms of reasoning* may differ from culture to culture. What is reasonable, logical and self-evident to a manager from one culture may be unreasonable, illogical and obscure to someone from another culture. One often-cited difference is that between Western cultures, which show a strong prejudice towards linear thinking, and Asiatic societies, where people exhibit much higher levels of spatial awareness. This can manifest itself in a variety of forms including attitudes to individuals and groups, attitudes to work and careers, and societal needs and wants.

4 The *social roles and expectations* of a culture also affect marketing, and marketers must avoid ascribing unrealistic forms of behaviour to persons in certain roles. The effects of this can be quite subtle. Television advertisements for Camay soap, which showed a man entering a bathroom while a woman was bathing, were very popular in Europe but were considered inappropriate and in poor taste in Japan.

5 *Non-verbal communication* also differs significantly across cultures and determines meanings in a variety of ways. For example, the North American hand gesture meaning 'okay' has obscene connotations in Brazil. Marketers working in foreign countries must endeavour to learn the body language as well as the spoken language of the cultures in which they are operating.

All of these variables are important in all forms of communication, including those between expatriate marketing managers and their own immediate subordinates in the local operation. Communication between managers and sales staff is as important as between marketers and customers. However, it is in the realm of advertising, the most immediate and visible form of communication, that cultural variables have their most dramatic effect. There are numerous stories of companies and advertising agencies which got their international advertising programmes wrong. United Airlines in the Far East used the slogan 'We know the Orient' in an advertisement in which the names of Asian countries were shown along with their coins, but in some cases used the wrong coins with the wrong names; Nike's television advertisements showing people from various cultures saying the company's slogan 'Just do it' in their native tongue ran into trouble when it transpired that one African tribesman was actually saying 'I don't want these'; Marlboro's advertisements which show a man riding a horse across open country had little meaning for consumers in densely crowded urban Hong Kong (Ricks 1993).

Equally, however, there are many companies which have mastered the art of successful international advertising, whether through carefully designed and implemented global campaigns targeted at perceived global customer segments, or through localized campaigns aimed at specific cultures (see ADVERTISING STRATEGY, INTERNATIONAL). They have been helped by the increasing strength and diversification of global advertising agencies, which now offer consulting advice on market research, product design and public relations as well as actual advertising.

It has also become increasingly imperative in multicultural societies for the marketer to take into account and address the various ethnic and religious sensibilities present (Rosen 1997). Over the last few decades the African-American, Hispanic and Asian-American populations have increased significantly within the United States. Communication and advertising to these groups, especially if they represent the target population, should focus on their relevant cultural characteristics in order to communicate in an effective manner. Most cultures are composed of diverse ethnic groups with preferences of colour, shape, style, values, and religious and other sensitivities. The challenge for today's marketer will be to develop a strategy targeting the unique aspects of each segment within a society through culturally sensitive messages.

3 Cross-cultural product strategy

Moran *et al.* (1993) describe three product philosophies exhibited by organizations when marketing their products in foreign markets:

1 *Standardization*, or 'We sell the same product to everyone, no matter where they live.' Organizations following this philosophy sell the same unchanged product in all markets and do not customize in order to account for local variations in taste or consumption. Blue Sky National Beverage Company of Santa Fe, NM, sells several flavours of soft drinks which are exactly the same in markets all around the world.

2 *Localization*, or 'We'll alter our products to sell them in other markets.' Organizations with this philosophy do alter their products to fit various markets, taking into account various legal, geographical, economic and cultural factors. The basic product and brand remain the same through all markets, but some product features are altered in accordance with local conditions. For example, Coca-Cola bottling plants around the world use the same basic concentrate but add slightly varying amounts of carbonation, sugar and colour in order to match the drink to local preferences.

3 *Customization*, or 'We find out what customers want, and then design products to meet their needs.' Organizations following this philosophy conduct extensive research to learn what foreign customers want and then design products to match their wants and preferences. The primary aim of these organizations is to establish good relationships and manufacture marketable products in each specific foreign market. The philosophy of Consumer Peripherals, a California-based disk drive manufacturer, is: 'Sell, design, build.'

Packaging and labelling

In some markets a product may be acceptable to consumers, but may still not sell because it is not packaged appropriately. Packages need to be attractive and enticing to the consumer, but they must also protect the product. Packages that are an appropriate size for one market may be either too large or too small for another; what fits into a US refrigerator might not fit into a Spanish one. Finally, products which are needed by one culture in large quantities may be used by another only in small measures; for example, large bottles of soft drinks may be unnecessary in a culture where wine is the standard drink.

Along with packaging, the labelling of a product must be culturally sensitive.

Marketers must be knowledgeable about what numbers are considered lucky or unlucky, what colours have significance or negative connotations, and what flowers or other objects have special significance in any particular culture. This knowledge can mean the difference between success and failure when labelling a product for multi-cultural use.

Word choice or translation on a label for global consumption must be given careful consideration. Product names and labels do not translate literally, and the omission of an accent mark can create difficulties. A translation error can ambush the intended message and prevent a wary consumer from purchasing the goods. The literacy rate of a country may also be a consideration when labelling a product; in a country where illiteracy is high, a label may need to be more of a graphic representation of the contents in order to sell the product.

4 Distribution and sales

Distribution is the path that products take between the manufacturer and the customer. Distribution channels are composed of buyers and sellers who bridge the gap between production and consumption. The components of a distribution channel can be classified as: (1) producers of products; (2) users of products; and (3) intermediary organizations at the retail or wholesale level. The intermediaries may or may not take title to the goods or handle them physically, but they do facilitate transfer of title.

In a global economy, producers must find suitable channels for distribution based on the local customs and culture in each market which can expedite the distribution of goods within that market. Distribution of goods in Europe will be quite different from distribution in Japan or in a developing country. The selection of intermediaries in a particular country, whether a local firm or individuals, can be critical to success.

Selling in another culture requires sensitivity and respect. Knowing the language of a country, its culture and customs, as well as its business culture, prepares an individual for success. Extensive product knowledge is a necessity, as is being able to adapt the product to local market requirements.

International selling also requires patience. Additional time is required to learn about one's customers as well as their markets and needs. Most importantly, developing trust cannot be hurried. If the seller can establish a good personal relationship with customers, then problems with quality, pricing or contracts can be negotiated.

5 Conclusion

Cultural differences represent formidable barriers in marketing, but they can also, if properly understood, be a source of advantage. Essentially, global marketing can be approached in two different ways. The first approach assumes a cultural-dominance model, wherein one cultural system strives to dominate the other. The second approach attempts to create a cultural synergy by understanding the similarities and differences between the two cultures and utilizing aspects of both.

Whichever approach is used, it is imperative that all the cultural factors involved are properly understood. The history of international marketing is full of costly mistakes stemming from lack of understanding of culture. The 'cultural variable' remains of key importance in all international marketing decisions.

ROBERT T. MORAN
ELIZABETH MORAN DE LONGEAUZ
THUNDERBIRD – THE AMERICAN GRADUATE
SCHOOL OF INTERNATIONAL MANAGEMENT

Further reading

(References cited in the text marked *)

* Condon, J.C. and Yousef, F. (1975) *Introduction to Intercultural Communication*, New York: Bobbs-Merrill. (This text covers aspects of inter-cultural communication from a theoretical perspective.)
* Gardenswartz, L. and Rowe, A. (1993) *Managing Diversity*, Homewood, IL: Irwin. (A guide through the unprecedented organizational challenges of a culturally expanding workforce.)

* Hall, E.T. (1959) *The Silent Language*, New York: Doubleday. (The author presents the paradox of culture, non-verbal communication, and the importance of understanding their joint impact.)

* Hall, E.T. (1966) *The Hidden Dimension*, New York: Doubleday. (This work considers the importance of space, colour and other variables in culture).

* Hall, E.T. (1983) *The Dance of Life*, New York: Doubleday. (This book deals with how people are connected and yet isolated by the hidden walls of time.)

* Harris, P. and Moran, R. (1979, 4th edn 1996) *Managing Cultural Differences*, Houston, TX: Gulf Publishing Company. (This foundation textbook identifies the need for new, cross-cultural perceptions and skills in the global environment. The original, referred to in the text of the entry, was published in 1979.)

Johansson, Johny K. (1997) *Global Marketing: Foreign Entry, Local Marketing and Global Management*, Irwin. (Focuses on marketing decisions and the environmental factors that affect them.)

Kashani, K. (1989) 'Beware of the pitfalls of global marketing', *Harvard Business Review* 67 (September–October): 91–8. (The author discusses the complexities and risks involved when attempting to globalize one's marketing.)

Martenson, R. (1987) 'Is standardisation of marketing feasible in culture-bound industries? A European case study', *International Marketing Review* 4 (Autumn): 7–16. (A case study showing how a global retailer coordinated its international marketing.)

* Moran, R., Harris, P. and Stripp, W. (1993) *Developing the Global Organization*, Houston, TX: Gulf Publishing Company. (A practical guide showing how to create a high-performance workforce to excel in an international environment.)

Norburn, D., Birley, S., Dunn, M. and Payne, A. (1989) 'A four nation study of the relationship between marketing effectiveness, corporate culture, corporate values, and market orientation', *Journal of International Business Studies* 20 (3): 451–68. (The article presents a study of four countries with a common language and their marketing effectiveness.)

* Ricks, D. (1993) *Blunders in International Business*, Cambridge, MA: Blackwell. (An excellent resource for identifying global business blunders in the areas of marketing, translation and product names.)

* Rosen, Martin B. (1997) 'Marketing to ethnically diverse populations', *National Underwriter* 101(31): 16–17. (This article covers the need for marketers to address specific ethnic groups within a society.)

Rosenbloom, B. (1990) 'Motivating your international channel partners', *Business Horizons* 33 (2): 53–6. (This article contains contributions on how to motivate partners in both international and domestic marketing channels.)

* Samovor, L.A. and Porter, R.E. (1985) *Intercultural Communication: A Reader*, Belmont, CA: Wadsworth. (This book includes forty essays covering the theoretical and practical aspects of the inter-cultural communication process.)

Terpstra, V. (1987) 'The evolution of international marketing', *International Marketing Review* 4 (2): 47–59. (Reviewing the past global environment, the author discusses the implications of change for international marketers.)

See also: ADVERTISING STRATEGY, INTERNATIONAL; COMMUNICATION, CROSS-CULTURAL; CULTURE, CROSS-NATIONAL; INTERNATIONAL MARKETING; MARKETING MANAGEMENT, INTERNATIONAL

Related topics in the IEBM: COMMUNICATION; CULTURE; MARKETING ENVIRONMENT

Marketing management, international

Overview

The term *international marketing* generally includes three separate but related marketing activities: foreign entry, local marketing and global coordination. In the foreign entry context, the marketer is usually seen as an exporter; marketing decisions include which countries to enter, and which modes of entry should be used. Questions of foreign market potential, identification of appropriate foreign representatives, tariff and non-tariff barriers and the use of trade facilitators are paramount.

Local marketing deals with the management of marketing in a foreign country. To some extent these marketing activities resemble those in any other country, and from this angle international marketing is often viewed as simply another application of standard marketing principles. However, the local marketer faces an environment which can be different in important respects from that at home. It thus becomes necessary to sensitize the local marketer to the basic assumptions on which marketing principles are founded, and to question these critically in the context of the foreign environment.

The global coordination aspect of international marketing deals with the problems a marketer faces when trying to generate cost savings and market synergies from the operations of a multinational corporation. Managerial problems include the identification of appropriate levels of standardization for various marketing activities, and the motivation of local subsidiaries in accepting globally standardized marketing programmes.

This three-part division has a correspondence in company growth. Smaller firms intent on international expansion will often begin by exporting, attempting to establish a market presence abroad with the help of independent agents and distributors. As involvement abroad grows, questions naturally arise as to whether the company should take greater control of the marketing effort in important countries and markets. Establishing a sales subsidiary and sending some expatriate managers abroad to manage it might facilitate greater control, but also creates a need to learn more about the foreign market. Finally, once the company has entered many markets and has some control over the marketing effort in each, the issue of better coordination of the global marketing effort becomes salient.

Historically speaking, global coordination is a fairly recent phenomenon. Multinational companies have traditionally treated each country as a free-standing profit centre. However, with the emergence of global communication facilities, the rapid diffusion and application of new technology and the success of global products and services in markets open to foreign competition, global coordination has become both possible and necessary. Strategic alliances and other collaborative efforts are making it possible for even smaller firms to consider global coordination of manufacturing and marketing.

1 Analysing foreign markets

As mentioned above, marketing a product or service in a foreign country is in many ways similar to marketing in the domestic market (see FOREIGN MARKET ENTRY STRATEGIES). The general principles of market segmentation and product positioning, and the strategic advantages of a customer orientation are still valid. On the other hand, because the environment differs, the implementation of these principles in terms of the so-called four Ps (product, price, place and promotion) and what it takes to stay close to the customer will often differ between country markets (see MARKETING, CULTURAL DIFFERENCES IN).

Market research

Before any decisions about how to manage local marketing in a foreign country can be reached, relevant information about that market has to be gathered. As a starting point, it is useful to review the data that led to entry in the first place. What information was used to screen the various countries? What was the assessed market potential? What particular features of the country were critical in the final choice? By using this information, and by adding to it from secondary sources and first-hand research within the country, the local manager can start to answer some basic questions about the local marketing environment.

The typical company moving into international markets has already developed the product or service it wants to sell. Thus, the typical marketing orientation which involves first finding out what the market wants is usually not applicable. This is quite logical: the firm should not consider doing business abroad unless it has something specific to offer. A European firm is unlikely to be successful in the Argentine market by first trying to anticipate what the market might want and then going on to develop a product or service; there must be some existing firm-specific advantage which overcomes the natural trade barriers which companies face when marketing abroad. In international marketing, unlike in domestic marketing, the firm will already have a product or service and then look for countries where a need can be filled (the 'internationalization' process of Johanson and Vahlne 1977).

Nevertheless, having an existing product means that the marketer needs to be doubly careful. The needs and wants that this product fills in the home market may not be filled by the same product in a new foreign market, or even may not exist at all. For example, disposable diapers are sold in the USA on the basis of convenience, but are attractive to Japanese

consumers for reasons of hygiene. Telephone answering machines are marketed in some countries as labour-saving devices while in others their appeal lies in the reliability of response. Automobiles bought for their fuel economy in a country such as Sweden may be bought because of styling in the USA (see CULTURE, CROSS-NATIONAL).

The marketer in a foreign country should take nothing for granted in assessing demand for a product. It is not just a matter of locating secondary data on economic indicators, population size and literacy levels, which are available through a variety of sources such as published United Nations statistics. What is important is to evaluate carefully where in the consumption pattern a particular product or service may fit in the new country market. While a newsletter service covering developments in alternative medicine might be of interest to body-builders in California, in a Third World country a similar newsletter could help provide basic education in nutrition. This is simply another way of saying that needs and wants are different. Golf has caught on in Europe primarily because it is a game well suited for leisure, of which the Europeans, who take long vacations, have plenty. In Japan, where working conditions are decidedly different, golf is attractive because it can be practised on inner-city golf ranges, offering lunchtime exercise and a respite from an overcrowded office.

The product life cycle

A prime consideration for the international marketer is the maturity level of the local market. The product life cycle, which distinguishes four stages in the life of a product (introduction, growth, maturity and decline) can be used to track the typical sales pattern of a product in a given market over time.

While a product may be at one stage of the life cycle in the home market, it may be in different stages in foreign markets. It is usually assumed that foreign markets are less mature than home markets, but this is not always true; neither is it true that the process towards maturity will take an equal length of time or be equally smooth everywhere. New markets will often be characterized by explosive growth spurts, followed by retrenchment as economic and political conditions change.

The stage of the life cycle directly affects the task that marketing has to perform. In the introductory stage, little is known about consumer reactions and a pro-active educational approach might be useful, suggesting usage situations for the prospective customer. In growth markets, the usage pattern is becoming established and the marketing task becomes one of guiding preferences towards features which represent competitive advantages for the firm. In the mature stage, product extensions can serve to develop new uses and extend the life cycle of the product.

A good illustration of this process is provided by Microsoft, the US software company. While foreign markets were still in their infancy, Microsoft provided business-orientated software including word processing and spreadsheet programmes. As more people began using computers at home, the firm developed the Works package which offered a combination of simpler versions of standard business packages. Finally, in mature markets the introduction of Microsoft Windows offered interactive mouse capability to compete with Apple's Macintosh, providing a viable alternative for users of IBM compatibles.

The timing of new product sequencing is important and demands considerable marketing flair, but it is helped by another life cycle factor. The speed of the movement along the life cycle curve depends to a great extent on the introduction of new products. Initial growth in the market attracts competition, including improved models and additional features; the firm which does not offer a competitive product will fall behind. For example, as Swatch, the Swiss watch maker, creates a new fashion market for watches, the company knows it has to remain competitive through future new product introductions. While domestic competitors may covertly agree to limit the speed of new product introductions, such agreements do not serve to keep out foreign competitors. Thus, in open markets without trade barriers, competitors and growing customer sophistication will

jointly determine the slope of the life cycle curve and thus the optimal timing sequence.

The level of maturity in the market directly influences the degree to which the firm-specific advantages of a product or service can be leveraged, as customer needs and sophistication will differ between maturity stages. The advantages of a mature home market, where competitive advantage exists in advanced product features, are of little value in introductory markets where basic function is the most important factor. Japanese telecommunications companies might have trouble competing in the US market, but do very well in Third World countries where their zero defect philosophy is highly attractive. The critical point is to identify imaginatively where there are gaps in the usage or consumption patterns of foreign customers, gaps which could be filled by existing products.

Consumer behaviour

Customers in different countries think and behave differently in important ways, and the salient product beliefs, attitudes and social norms may vary considerably between markets. The degree to which quality issues are important, attitudes towards foreign products and the degree to which individuals comply with social norms all affect consumer decision making in different ways. For example, where a Japanese supermarket shopper is fastidious and careful, an American consumer is often more impulsive and willing to respond to in-store promotions, while Europeans traditionally tend to be less inclined to try something new.

However, these differences are often shaped more by what is offered in the marketplace than by innate differences among people. The opening up of eastern European markets after the fall of the Berlin Wall demonstrates this vividly. Many product variants which seemed self-explanatory in the West, such as shampoos for oily hair, required educational labelling in eastern European markets. Eastern European consumers also needed to be educated to make choices, not just buy anything on the shelf; buyers had to learn to accept that choosing one brand meant giving up another. Western brands carried a special attraction and so did product quality, after years of shoddy goods. At the same time, advertising was often less effective than word-of-mouth communication: commercials were often too similar to the official propaganda of the past. The sales of one well-established shampoo brand fell precipitously when a rumour was spread that it caused hair to fall out. Nevertheless, because of low media charges, television advertising remained a very efficient method of establishing brand recognition.

The differences in average tendencies between consumers in different countries are often obliterated by similarities between specific segments. Younger consumers tend to be more homogeneous across the globe, as do professionals with international jobs and people who travel frequently. It is thus possible to identify segments where behaviour in a number of different countries is quite similar. Furthermore, over time these behavioural differences undergo change and can make segments become more homogeneous. For example, with the increase in per capita incomes in many countries, one can discern similar behaviour among young families across the globe in their purchase and use of cameras, VCRs, cars and vacation travel. This development has made possible the development of globally standardized products, a development which has in turn reinforced the trend towards homogenization in these segments.

Increased affluence in many countries has also led to the emergence of several new leading markets for various products. A leading market is one where products featured advanced technology and where consumers are both sophisticated and demanding. In the 1960s the notion was that Western (especially US) technology and markets were ahead of the rest of the world, and that new innovations appeared in these markets first and then spread elsewhere; this was known as the product cycle theory (Vernon 1966). Later, however, new leading markets began to emerge; even in industries where US firms were leaders, the leading markets were often elsewhere. In products such as cosmetics, fashion and textiles, European markets are now more demanding than those in the USA, even though competition in the latter may be stronger. In industries such as consumer electronics and cars, the Japanese market demands greater quality and service than does the USA. Even in less lofty products such as diapers, detergents and soaps, the leading markets are not necessarily in the USA. Thus, even though firms such as Procter & Gamble and General Electric might be based in the USA, their top of the line products often derive from versions first marketed in other countries or regions.

This has not meant that so-called 'country of origin' effects are eliminated, however. Opinion is divided as to the degree to which consumers are influenced by a product's 'made in' label. Some marketing practitioners tend to downplay the importance of country of origin, arguing that customers will look for quality and value regardless of the country in which a product has been made. However, most research suggests that country of origin plays an important role in consumer perception. Direct surveys of customers suggest that even as people look for quality and value, country of origin plays an important role in helping them judge these attributes. Country of origin is an indirect clue to product quality because countries differ in production sophistication and capability. However, over time, if Third World countries develop manufacturing skills and the ability to produce high-quality goods – often with the assistance of multinational firms that have located plants there – then consumers may come to attach different meanings to a particular country of origin label. In the meantime, buyers tend to err on the side of caution and prefer products made in well-established producer countries.

Competition

It is important to analyse competition in local markets in some depth, and not simply assume that conditions at home will be replicated abroad. Domestic competitors might have a loyal following, and might also have exclusive access to distribution outlets and promotional media; in fact, the chief reason why some local competitors have not already ventured abroad themselves is that they have acquired monopolistic advantages in the home market which cannot be replicated abroad. This involves not only obvious cases such as the telecommunications industry and government procurement, but also includes examples such as Kao, the leading detergent maker in Japan, which controls its own wholesale system; American Airlines, which derives competitive advantage from its reservation system in the USA, and the independent *parfumerie* chains in Germany whose channel control helps limit the distribution of personal-care products through department stores and mass-distribution outlets. Although these firms may not be globally competitive, they are very strong in their home markets.

There may also be other foreign entrants, including global companies which may be competitors in other countries as well. Here it is important to recognize that competitors' strategic objectives may differ between markets. While competitors may decide not to contest a challenge to their market share in a small country market, they are apt to respond more vigorously in larger and leading markets. Another important question is whether a foreign competitor has global capabilities which match or even outstrip a potential entrant. For example, introducing a promising new product in a local market might provide a premature signal to global competitors, who then become first movers in other country markets. Kao learned this lesson the hard way when its successful condensed detergent brand, Attack, was pre-empted in many global markets by Procter & Gamble. P&G analysed Kao's new detergent in Japan, identified the key chemical processes and initiated production of condensed detergents under its own existing brands. Since these brands (Tide, Cheer, Ariel and others) already were well known and distributed in many countries, Kao lost the opportunity to be the first mover in the global arena.

Regulatory obstacles

There are also regulatory differences between country markets which often serve to inhibit entry by foreign firms. Some regulations favour domestic producers, such as the *Reinheitsgebot* in Germany, which stipulates that any beer sold has to be brewed without preservatives, effectively barring non-local beers from entry. Regulations can also limit the applicability of a firm's usual marketing techniques; restrictions on television advertising in Scandinavia have meant that American consumer goods manufacturers, which usually rely on this method of communication, have not had the same success as elsewhere. Similarly, marketing managers accustomed to relying on heavy in-store promotional outlays, will adapt uneasily to an environment where in-store promotions are limited by regulation, as is the case in most European countries.

2 Product decisions and segmentation

Companies which use independent agents such as trading companies or manufacturer's representatives to manage their exports are likely to have only limited control over the marketing of their goods and services in export markets. Products and services are unlikely to be substantially adapted to local conditions, as adaptation requires knowledge of local preferences and sufficient volume to justify changes. However, some form of localization will almost always be necessary if the product is to be successful.

Localization and adaptation

Localization represents the minimum level of product or service adaptation necessary for marketing in foreign markets. Examples include changes in electric voltage from 120 to 220, the addition of a third brake light to cars sold in the USA (homologation) and the translation of instruction manuals into local languages. Because localization necessarily involves specific country knowledge, the changes are often made by the importer rather than the manufacturer or producer. Car dealers routinely rewire imported cars, just as electronics distributors change the station bands on imported radios and employees at the Asian factories of Nike help design wider shoes to fit their own markets.

While localization is necessary in order for the customer to be able to use the product, *adaptation* aims to provide a competitive advantage over other brands in the target segment's evoked set of brands. Roughly speaking, localization does not provide a reason for buying a brand; it merely ensures that the brand is not rejected out of hand. Adaptation, on the other hand, suggests that the product is adapted to customer preferences, giving the individual a positive reason for choice. Offering Coca-Cola in smaller bottles in Japan to accommodate vending machine requirements is localization: changing the recipe of the drink to include less sugar is adaptation.

A good example which illustrates the issues raised by adaptation and localization is Euro Disney. When the Walt Disney corporation decided to open a European version of the Disneyland amusement park outside Paris, it established a joint venture with European investors. The aim was to spread the financial risk and to help localize the park. The basic themes of the park were to remain the same as in similar parks in the USA and Japan, although different languages would be accommodated and restaurant menus would be changed slightly for the European palate. These changes represented localization rather than adaptation.

However, the standard policy created difficulties. For example, the strict dress code for employees – including 'appropriate undergarments' for women and short fingernails – was considered as an invasion of privacy by the mainly French staff. Further, visitors to the park spoke a variety of languages including English, French, Spanish and German, and it was difficult to ensure that visitors found a guide who could speak the appropriate language. As for the catering, while Americans tend to be casual about their lunch, for many Europeans it is the main meal and needs to be served on time. For the French in particular, wine is an important element of meals, and Euro Disney soon had to relax its policy of not allowing alcohol on the premises.

Thus, while all indicators suggested that the Disney theme park concept was a globally acceptable product, and while the standard version had been very successful in Japan, Euro Disney did not attract as many visitors as predicted during its first year of operation. The park lost $900 million in the first year, and although attendance did increase with the end of the prevailing recession, financial problems continued. Further adaptation of the formula was necessary in order to recover lost goodwill.

Pros and cons of standardization

The benefits to the company of standardization of internationally marketed products and services are many. Larger volumes mean scale and scope economies in manufacturing and purchasing; investments in plant capacity and in improved product design are thus more easily justified. Training of sales personnel and dealers can be leveraged over larger volumes, and after-sales service can be more thorough. Creative ideas in advertising and product design can be applied more effectively, and coordination of product launch and new advertising campaigns are facilitated. Standardized packaging is also common, and has been helped by the emergence of similar measurement systems in various countries and the acceptance of multi-language labelling. Expanding on the effective use of a globally recognized brand name, Kodak has developed a stylized and characteristic yellow box for its films; its Japanese competitor Fuji has similarly standardized its green packaging around the world, with a slightly modified logo. An interesting example is Unilever's fabric-softener, sold under the brand name Snuggle in the USA, which features a globally uniform package, colouring scheme and symbol (a teddy bear, signifying softness) but uses a different brand name in every country (Yip 1992: 102–3).

With product standardization, costs come down, quality can be improved and the firm can offer better value to the customer. The potential buyer has to weigh the gain in value against the fact that, as mentioned above, the product is not uniquely designed for his or her use. The problem is not usually the lack of uniqueness itself, with many other people having the same identical product; indeed for some products (such as computers) high levels of standardization are a plus since this leads to increased compatibility with other products. However, the standardized product might not offer the particular features a customer wants. For example, a German driver might want a car with a five-speed transmission when only a four-speed model is available. A university student may want to record a short news programme from television only to find that all blank videotapes are of 120 minutes duration. The globally standardized product is often not quite what an individual consumer in a particular country wants.

This disadvantage of standardized products is precisely what creates advantage for locally adapted products. Strong global products can change preferences and attract a following, as has happened in the beer market where global competitors such as Budweiser, Heineken and Carlsberg have made inroads in many foreign markets. However, the most successful global competitors are those that have coupled their strong brand names and lower costs with flexible manufacturing techniques. Flexible manufacturing involves designing product variants which use a common 'platform' base, but whose particular features are adapted to local preferences. Using robots and programmable machines in manufacturing, these firms are able to keep manufacturing costs relatively low while producing a wide variety of product versions. Flexible manufacturing is responsible for the product proliferation in product categories as diverse as watches, cars, detergents, pens, microchips and ice cream.

Multi-domestic versus global markets

A distinction is commonly made between global markets and multi-domestic markets. The latter are markets which show distinctive differences between countries: food, drink, clothes and entertainment are common examples. Global markets, by contrast, are those where consumers all over the world have similar needs and wants. Consumer durables – cars, cameras, consumer electronics – often fall into this category. Generally speaking, multi-domestic markets tend to be those where consumption and product use are intimately tied to cultural factors.

This distinction can be misleading, since it suggests that products in multi-domestic markets must be adapted to local preferences. This is not always the appropriate conclusion. Cultural characteristics are sometimes related to historical conditions which no longer hold. Products marketed to the independent Western woman, such as sports apparel, have made great inroads in Japan as social conditions change. Preferences do not stay unchanged forever. 'Americans will always want big cars' was a common refrain in the 1960s, but is not true today. In particular, when markets open up and new products appear, local favourites are often seen for what they are, provincial tastes formed by special conditions. Thus, the belief among some European housewives that only a boiling wash can get the clothes clean vanished when new detergents appeared on the market. Casual fashion is becoming a global industry (see GLOBALIZATION), and diets are no longer limited by geographical boundaries.

The underlying process is quite simple. As trade barriers are lowered, products particular to individual companies are becoming available elsewhere. Over time, and with effective promotion, local markets will determine whether these new alternatives are superior to local offerings. There is no reason to assume that existing local preferences will completely change to accommodate the new alternatives; rather, there will be a maturing of the consumer sophistication and a development of differentiated tastes, culminating in a demand for increased variety. Consumers will be more interested in trying various options, and will also develop a taste for different brands on different occasions. Market segmentation will become necessary not only to determine individual buyers' lifestyles and usage levels, but also occasion and situational patterns. The market will offer more choices than before, and the consumer will try more alternatives than before (Douglas and Wind 1986).

It is thus too simplistic to define a market in terms of whether it is multi-domestic or global. Even in multi-domestic markets there are segments which are similar across countries and which thus support standardized (but localized) products; the success of global fast food chains is a case in point. At the same time, in global markets such as the car industry, adapted products may still appeal to niches in various country markets, in particular to consumers who are particularly loyal to special brands or who are offered customized features and service.

3 Price and positioning

Market pricing

The price of the product helps to position it in a manner attractive to the customer. The analysis on which foreign pricing decisions are based is similar to that carried out in home markets, and should focus on what price prospective buyers will find acceptable. Given an assessment of what the potential customer can afford, based where possible on market research data on income and price elasticities, the actual price can then be altered according to competitive pressures and marginal cost considerations. In addition, the possibility of short-term introductory price reductions which do not influence the basic positioning should be considered; an example of such a reduction is the strategy adopted by Kentucky Fried Chicken, whose entry into the Japanese market was spearheaded by an introductory period of low prices for buckets of chicken.

There is nothing intrinsically international about such a pricing approach; it is essentially the same approach as used in the home market, although the prices themselves may not be the same. Competitive pressures may be higher at home, marginal costs may be lower abroad because of scale returns or the foreign positioning might be high-end instead of low-end, all factors which will affect the final price. However, as will be seen below, the international dimension often dominates these traditional marketing considerations. Setting prices in foreign markets is often an entirely different process from that in the home market.

Tariffs and dumping

The most obvious pricing complications in cross-border business stem from trade barriers, especially tariffs. Customs duty on products will tend to raise prices on imported goods, as will transportation costs and the necessary use of storage facilities. The middlemen used to effect ownership transfer charge fees, and localization requirements cost money. Nevertheless, the consequent price escalation might be contained by company policy, the firm deciding to absorb tariff charges, keeping prices constant. Also, the firm may price according to marginal rather than average costs. Japanese entries into Western markets are often accomplished using marginal cost pricing, leading to lower prices abroad than at home.

The transfer cost to a subsidiary or independent importer overseas may in fact be lower than that to distributors at home. This is referred to as dumping. Dumping practices are illegal under the General Agreement on Tariffs and Trade (GATT), and are prosecuted actively by countries such as the USA whose large and lucrative market induces foreign firms to attempt to gain market share by any possible means. The practice of dumping continues, however, partly because prosecuting these cases takes a long time and partly because there is serious disagreement about the validity of pricing on the margin.

Another pricing complication arises from the fact that many shipments across borders are intra-company transfers; for example, a Northern Telecom plant in Canada may send goods to its subsidiary in Singapore. In such cases the landed cost for the product can be manipulated to show higher or lower profits for the importing subsidiary. The US Internal Revenue Service has argued that some Japanese subsidiaries in the USA are overcharged as their headquarters attempt to shift earnings back to Japan, thus avoiding paying US taxes. Whether or not this is correct, the example shows the complexities of pricing abroad. Subsidiaries can be accused of dumping when prices are too low and of avoiding taxes when costs are too high.

Exchange rates and countertrade

Prices in overseas markets also reflect to a greater or lesser extent variations in floating exchange rates. While the introductory price of a product may position it attractively for the foreign target segment, an unfavourable change in the exchange rate may make a price increase necessary unless the company is prepared to accept a loss in its home currency (see FOREIGN EXCHANGE RISK, MANAGEMENT OF). In 1993 the rise of the yen forced Japanese exporters to raise dollar prices, leading to loss of market share in the USA. In 1985, however, a similar rise did not translate into higher prices; in that instance Japanese manufacturers were able to streamline their operations and cut costs.

In Third World countries which lack hard currency to pay for imports – especially capital goods – there has been a shift towards countertrade, the payment for imports 'in kind'. Several forms of countertrade have emerged as less developed countries attempt to speed up their growth from a small industrial base. One refinement of simple barter is the counterpurchase or parallel barter agreement, where separate purchase contracts in a hard currency are signed but most of the payments are cancelled against goods exchanged. There is also the buy-back agreement, where a manufacturing investment is made from a hard currency nation and paid off as the goods produced by the factory are exported abroad.

There are also arrangements where the exact barter is left to be determined at a future date. These consist of drawing rights to the seller in goods produced, not hard currency. Using various clearing arrangements, these contracts can sometimes also be sold to another party. When the exact value of the drawing rights is uncertain, perhaps because of economic or political problems in the host country, the discount for such switch-trading can sometimes be very steep. A sophisticated version of clearing arrangements is the use of swaps of debts, where a secondary market is used by companies to exchange receivables in various countries.

In defence-related industries it has become common to use offsets. Purchases of military aircraft by a friendly nation, for example, are often combined with the sub-contracting of component parts to a manufacturer in the buying country, or by investments in related industries.

These bartering arrangements, although useful in enabling trade without hard currency, can be problematic for the company which then has to market its counterpurchase elsewhere. From a pricing viewpoint, it is also very difficult for the local marketing manager to determine the actual price of the product being traded.

Global customers and grey trade

While the international dimensions discussed so far tend to make a product's price in any given country unrelated to its price in other country markets, there is also a strong force in favour of more uniform prices across the globe. This force is the emergence of global customers.

In the period immediately after the second world war, most multinational companies (see MULTINATIONAL CORPORATIONS) treated their subsidiaries as independent operations, with transfer prices set at arms length (that is, local market) levels. Gradually, however, as manufacturing was rationalized globally, the benefits of global sourcing became apparent. More recently, as the benefits of globally coordinated competitive strategies have become clear, global coordination has extended from manufacturing into all company operations. The global company is now a global customer to its suppliers.

The pricing implications of globalization are that the prices of a company's products can no longer be widely different in different countries. This affects not only industrial components sold to global producers, but also consumer goods. If a camera is cheaper in Hong Kong than in Germany, given the existing exchange rates, there will be an arbitrage opportunity for an entrepreneur who will arrange for shipment of cameras to Europe from Hong Kong. This shipment need not be made by the producing firm, but can be carried out by independent foreign trade middlemen. The producing company can attempt to block such shipments – and camera makers do, by using different model numbers and limited service guarantees – but where the price differences are sufficient, such barriers will not be effective.

Partly because uniform global pricing is almost impossible with floating exchange rates, many companies have opted to price their product in one denomination only, often the US dollar. This means of course that ultimate prices in local markets may be drastically different. This has led to the 'grey trade' phenomenon, which by 1995 had reached huge proportions. For example, at one point Honda cars were cheaper in Belgium than in the UK; British buyers could then travel to Brussels and purchase Hondas – for delivery in England, and with the steering wheel changed to the right side – at no extra charge thanks to existing European Union (EU; see EUROPEAN UNION) regulations (such distortions are eliminated in the new EU statutes). Similarly, Japanese travelling to New York can often be seen buying video-cameras and compact discs (made in Japan) to bring back home. Canadians close to the border make shopping trips to the USA (as Europeans have started to do as well) in order to shop for the products and brands sold at higher prices at home.

An especially virulent form of grey trade is the trade in counterfeit products or 'knock-offs'. These are products with the same or similar designs and features as the original item, but produced by unauthorized manufacturers, often in Third World countries (Asia in particular). Counterfeit products are sold through regular channels or off-price outlets, where they may be presented as the authentic article but at a substantially reduced price. The growth in knock-offs is a consequence of multinationals locating plants in countries with low wages, and in the process transferring manufacturing skills to the local labour force. In garments, for example, the local manufacturer can often produce more than the ordered quota, or resell the design to another local manufacturer. Using computer technology, it is now possible to design exact copies from a real product, right down to the brand label. Manufacturers are attempting to stop the production and trade in knock-offs but, given

the opening of markets and the spread of technology, trade in low-priced counterfeit is likely to increase even further in the future.

In conclusion, the pricing decision in foreign markets is rarely an optimal one from a marketing manager's viewpoint. There are simply too many factors outside the manager's control that influence the actual price. This also means, of course, that a foreign entrant whose main competitive advantage in its own home market is price is in a very difficult position. This is a major reason why companies need to be doubly sure that they have a sustainable advantage (a differentiated product or service) to offer in a foreign market; this is also why many companies decide that the only way to compete effectively is to establish manufacturing operations directly in the market country.

4 Establishing distribution

Initial entry

Choosing channels of distribution in a foreign market is usually carried out in conjunction with the choice of mode of entry. When an exporter selects an agent and a distributor, the channels are automatically chosen as well. When a licensee is contracted, the channels of distribution are usually those already operated by the licensee. If a sales subsidiary is established, its first task is usually to secure distribution outlets.

The need for immediate decisions to be made about distribution is unfortunately coupled with a difficulty in reversing commitments. While prices can be changed, advertising can be shifted and products can be adapted, changing distribution channels in a foreign market is difficult, time-consuming and often costly. If the chosen channel does not perform effectively, it is not easy to find alternatives; and even if these are found, a poor performance record may mean that potential new channel members are unwilling to cooperate. In addition, the existing distributor will not usually give up without compensation or a legal suit. The product will lose momentum, and the brand image may be tarnished.

There are many instances of such failures, several of which relate to the recently emerged Japanese multinationals. Sony, for example, had to take its first US distributor to court in order to gain the rights to import its own television sets, and Chrysler's contract to sell Mitsubishi cars in the USA in the end forced Mitsubishi to establish a parallel dealer network (see DAIMLER CHRYSLER; MITSUBISHI HEAVY INDUSTRIES, LTD). Microsoft had to make a large payment to ASCII Ltd, its distributor in Japan, in order to create its own distribution system there. When Canon withdrew its camera distribution in the USA from Bell & Howell in the early 1970s, it also had to pay a large settlement fee.

Channel choice

The choice of channels of distribution is of course intimately related to where target customers make their purchases. If the clientele for a consumer durable is upmarket, the products may need to be sold in department stores. If it is marketing a food or drink product with mass appeal, the firm may wish to distribute to supermarkets or convenience stores. These considerations are the same in foreign markets as at home; the difference is that in overseas markets the firm may not have the power to get into the stores or onto the shelves.

While distribution in some countries such as the USA is on the whole highly rationalized and economically efficient, this is not the case in many other countries. In these cases, distribution systems are often based on monopolistic regulations of fair trade which limit local store penetration, allow price fixing and uphold territorial sales restrictions. A channel member holding a distributor's licence can exert considerable power and extract additional fees from manufacturers. Not surprisingly, such distribution systems are inefficient, with middlemen capturing what amount to monopoly rents. Licences are passed on through generations, the system becomes ossified, old friendships become paramount and new firms have difficulty in effecting entry. The Japanese market is a particularly difficult entry challenge for these reasons.

Where in-store information and after-sales service are important, firms frequently develop their own distribution system. Manufacturers thus develop their own channel networks in many countries; the car industry is a particularly notable example of this phenomenon, but electronics manufacturers in Europe and Japan often support dealers who sell their brands exclusively. Kao, the detergent manufacturer, has its own distribution centres in Japan, a key competitive advantage in the home market which unfortunately is difficult to transfer abroad. Honda established its own motorcycle outlets in the USA after the company observed the low levels of service offered by existing dealers and, after privatization, AT&T opened up its own retail centres in the USA (see AT&T CORPORATION).

In other products, producing companies have helped create alternative channels. The success of Swatch was helped by its global entry through department stores and mass merchandisers rather than speciality stores. Electrolux vacuum cleaners, denied access through manufacturer-controlled outlets in Japan, created its own door-to-door sales force. Jordan, the Norwegian toothbrush manufacturer, was instrumental in augmenting drugstore channels with supermarkets in Europe. Innovative packaging techniques have helped soft drink manufacturers gain access to previously closed distribution channels in many countries.

Many examples illustrating the importance and complexity of new channels of distribution come from the newly democratized countries of eastern Europe. Grocery stores are now slowly being transformed from the traditional system of service across the counter to the self-service system used by Western supermarkets. However, self-service requires more modern methods of packaging food products and dry goods, and of re-stocking shelves and price marking. The larger volumes necessary for efficient operations also require storage facilities and reliable suppliers who can transport large quantities rapidly. Not surprisingly, consumers unaccustomed to seeing products on the shelf and afraid that no more shipments will come sometimes take all available packages.

In these newly democratized countries, the burdens on the existing weak infrastructure have made disaster stories common and channel development has become a top priority among manufacturers. Unilever initially had to rely on the old state-run system of trucking and storage in Poland, and the company's ice cream often reached the stores half-melted. Subsequently Unilever has spent much time and money on setting up a wholesale and transportation system covering all the eastern European countries. Procter & Gamble now ships its Russian-destined detergents and shampoos by sea from factories in western Europe to St Petersburg in order to avoid the delays affecting road traffic on the Russian border. The lack of infrastructure in eastern Europe has also generally meant that, outside the major cities, there are large areas with a demand for, but no access to Western products.

The most striking innovation in distribution channels internationally is perhaps the growth of franchising. In particular, US-based companies in service industries (fast food, hotels, convenience stores) have been instrumental in transforming many distribution systems in foreign markets. Although to many locals these US incursions might seem threatening to traditional culture, the increased efficiency of the delivery systems and the opportunities created for local entrepreneurs seem to outweigh the drawbacks.

The lesson here is that the buying pattern of the target segment has to be imaginatively assessed before the appropriate channel choice can be made. As in the case of identifying the consumption gap, an understanding of current purchasing habits is only the start of the analysis. With domestic competitors often in monopolistic control of some channels, the firm needs to carefully evaluate the possibility of using – and perhaps helping to create – alternative channels. As in the case of foreign market entry, the premium is on local knowledge and connections with the right network. Before committing resources in distribution in a foreign market, the firm needs to observe at first hand the behaviour of customers in the marketplace.

5 Global communication

Technological advances in telecommunications and satellite broadcasting have made it possible to communicate instantaneously across the globe. The new technology has transformed the way organizations are administered, how purchasing is coordinated and where manufacturing is done. In marketing, it affects all communications with the customer, from person-to-person sales negotiations to large-scale global advertising campaigns.

Global brand names

At first glance, it would seem that differences in languages would render global mass communication impossible. However, the use of commonly recognized symbols makes it possible to communicate across nations and cultures. For marketers, the most important such symbol is the global brand name.

A well-recognized brand name with a clear and positive image is an asset in any market. Buyers associate the brand with added value and accept the assurance of quality that the name conveys, thus simplifying their choice process. The promotion of the brand by the manufacturer involves an investment which leads to an increase in brand value or 'equity'.

The global brand provides additional benefits to the manufacturer. Global customers are able to recognize and buy the brand anywhere, and entry into new foreign markets is facilitated as both potential channel operators and customers will be familiar with the brand. The effective reach of global media can be capitalized upon. Finally, there is a special cachet attached to global brands: since they can be recognized everywhere, buyers can derive added value everywhere.

One thing a global brand does not do, however, is suppress the country of origin effect. On the contrary, most global brands have definite home countries, regardless of where the products are actually manufactured. Pepsi-Cola bottled in Russia is still American (although the recent marketing of imported American products is forcing Pepsi in Russia to defend against the perception that it is a low-quality 'local' product). Toyota cars built in the USA are still Japanese, and Benetton sweaters knitted in Japan are still Italian. Global brands are not attractive because they have no identifiable nationality; rather, the successful global brands are those that embody the very qualities for which their home country is famous.

The power of global branding helps explain why products which are not perfectly adapted to a local market can still succeed. A standardized product with a strong global name will attract customers because of the extra cachet associated with the brand; while the product may be wrongly positioned in relation to the existing preferences of local buyers, the global brand name compensates for this deficiency. Japanese beer drinkers who do not like American beer may still order a Budweiser; Europeans who do not think much of American designers might still buy a Ralph Lauren sweater, and Americans who understand the value of a Korean-made television set may still opt to buy a Sony (made in the USA but still Japanese). The power of a global brand name thus derives partly from its ability to compensate for less than perfect targeting of customer preferences.

The global brand name associated with a standardized (localized) product is also a powerful driver of changing customer preferences. When combined with the increasing speed of new product proliferation, global brands help increase the speed of the product life cycle, and increase the acceptance of new product features. For the consumer, buying a product with new features involves a certain amount of risk. The product may not perform reliably and after-sales service is uncertain. The globally recognized brand serves as a guarantee to consumers that new models will function well and be serviced as the need arises; for its part, the company will fulfil this guarantee as it needs to protect the value of the brand and its brand equity.

Global advertising

Global brands are commonly established through the use of global advertising. There are two components to global advertising: the use of prototype ads, commercials and copy whose basic message stays unchanged across countries, and the use of global media such as satellite television and international editions of magazines and newspapers which make it possible to reach the same target segments in each country.

The typical prototype campaign starts with the development of a common message and slogan and the creation of the visual elements of the advertisement (see ADVERTISING STRATEGY, INTERNATIONAL). This creative work is typically carried out at the company's global or regional headquarters, with the aid of an advertising agency with offices around the world. After input from field offices of the advertising agency and company subsidiaries abroad, the usual practice is to develop one or more versions of the advertisement with a unifying theme. This material is sent to the local subsidiary and representatives along with an explanation of the strategic logic and implementation guidelines. The local manager, often in collaboration with the branch office of the advertising agency, will then modify the advertisements where deemed necessary. Unless the proposed changes are exceptional, the modified advertising will then be scheduled in local media.

In most cases, television advertisements intended for a global market are shot without voiceovers and with limited text. The verbal message and the slogan are however indicated, and local creative work is thus limited to the dubbing of the voiceover in the appropriate language and accompanying minor changes in the text, in effect a localization of the communication. Actors who appear in the commercials are often chosen to represent a general type of character; when celebrities are used, they need to be globally recognized. A Hollywood film actor such as Clint Eastwood is more likely to appear than a television star such as Johnny Carson. European advertisements sometimes feature actors from the USA because they are not identified with a particular European country.

It should be noted that global advertising will not always be the preferred alternative even among companies with global products and brand names. In 1990, the US-based company Colgate-Palmolive shifted from a global to a country-by-country advertising strategy. The reason was not that the global advertisements were not effective; through global advertising, the Colgate toothpaste brand had increased its world market share to more than 40 per cent. However, the company found that it needed to localize its strategy in order to introduce other products into specific countries. Colgate had been very successful in the UK and French markets with Actibrush, a plaque-fighting mouth rinse, and wanted to introduce the brand elsewhere to protect its first-mover advantage. Its Palmolive brand, number two in the world body care market, was also targeted for an expanded product line in the USA, and its new anti-plaque toothpaste formula had been very successful in the five countries entered so far and needed to be introduced into other countries. The new products were expected to increase worldwide sales by 10 per cent annually.

The shift to local advertising was made because the company had different strategic needs in different countries. However, the decision to leave advertising execution to local subsidiaries did not mean that other aspects of marketing were also localized; the products themselves would continue to be standardized within the confines of local regulations and, according to a company spokesman, the sales increases would come partly through powerful global distribution (Freeman 1990).

Sales promotion

In-store sales promotion is a very important marketing tool, particularly in North American markets. Special offers and large discounts are often used by smaller firms or new entrants to divert customers away from large and well-established brands; in response, national and global brands are forced to use similar promotional tactics in order to retain customers.

In other markets, sales promotion activities tend to be more limited. In-store factors are still important in the choice process, partly because of the product information possessed by sales clerks. The relatively inefficient distribution system in countries such as Japan and France compensates to some extent by providing better customer advice. While productivity in the typical US store is judged on the basis of dollar sales per employee or per square foot floor space (putting pressure on sales clerks to make sales more quickly and increase merchandise turnover), the family-owned shops in many countries allow the clerks to develop product knowledge and give customer information. This also explains the lower reliance on mass media advertising for consumer information in these countries.

Sales promotion activities are also often constrained by local regulation in various countries. Money-off coupons are not allowed in many European countries, for example, since the retail chains refuse to handle redemptions. Contests and special events are also tightly regulated in many countries. Such rules sometimes seem absurd to outsiders: when IKEA, the Swedish furniture store, launched a promotion in Germany which included a free breakfast for all first-day visitors, the local trade association complained that according to law a breakfast had to include eggs and IKEA's offer did not. When IKEA claimed to be Swedish, the trade association then filed a complaint because some of the furniture on sale in IKEA stores was not made in Sweden.

In general, marketers who are used to relying heavily on sales promotion activities to push their product through distribution channels have to be careful to ensure that their intended tactics are acceptable to the trade. When Procter & Gamble first introduced its detergent brand Cheer into Japan, the firm designed an introductory campaign focused on money-off coupons and two-for-one product offers. The campaign failed for two reasons: the Japanese consumers were unaccustomed to coupons, and the capacity of small Japanese supermarkets to handle a large number of detergent packages was too limited. A more successful introduction was made later with the help of free home samples and smaller package sizes in the stores.

Because of the importance of in-store advice in some foreign markets, local marketers do well to pay attention to the training and support of sales clerks. With the increasing level of competition in many markets and the accompanying need to provide higher levels of customer satisfaction, this may be a good strategy even in countries where sales clerks traditionally offer less value. An illustration of this principle can be found in the success of Japanese car makers in North American markets; a major factor behind their strong sales is the attention paid to dealer training and support.

Personal selling

Personal selling is naturally a marketing technique which largely remains localized. In selling, it is important that the salesperson is a fluent speaker of the local language, understands the culture and the people of the country and is well versed in how to do business in that country. Most effective salespeople will be natives of the country in question. For the expatriate manager, finding and hiring the best people is not easy without the help of a local assistant; one of the major criteria for a good local agent or representative is the ability to recruit top salespeople (see HUMAN RESOURCE MANAGEMENT, INTERNATIONAL). In many countries in eastern Europe and Latin America, the task is made easier by the fact that working for a foreign firm is prestigious; quite the opposite is true in Japan, for example, where there is still some social stigma attached to working for a foreign company.

Because of the increase in the number of global customers, however, there is also an increase in global account selling. Global accounts require the creation of an organizational unit, usually at corporate headquarters, which coordinates sales to multinational customers. This unit then works with local sales managers in various countries to coordinate orders, shipments and deliveries. Headquarters, local subsidiaries and global customers become members of a network which needs to be developed and sustained. The task is demanding, as the local manager must give up some authority, but coordination makes it possible to provide much better service to the customer at lower cost to the firm. Large service companies such as Citibank (banking), Marriott (hotels) and McCann-

Erickson (advertising) have successfully introduced global account management structures.

6 Coordinating global marketing

Global marketing (see INTERNATIONAL MARKETING) means more than standardized products and prototype advertising. It involves the coordination of various marketing activities within country markets in order to capture synergies such as sharing competitive information and creating a global service network. Firms that strive for global synergies usually find that not all activities or countries can be brought into a globally standardized strategy; at least some of the implementation and execution elements of the various marketing activities have to be left at the country level, if for no other reason than to keep the local representatives motivated.

The agent problem

When coordinating the global firm's marketing in different countries, it is important to understand the relationship between the home country or regional headquarters and the company's agent in each local market. In cases where the firm has established a wholly owned subsidiary, in sales and perhaps in manufacturing, the local marketing decision maker may possibly be an expatriate or local manager. Where the firm is represented by an agent and distributor or by a licensee, marketing decisions will often be made by independent individuals over whom headquarters has no direct control.

The advantages of using expatriate managers are the ease of communication with headquarters and the manager's ability to comprehend more easily the firm's global situation. Knowledge of local conditions might be weak, however. On the other hand, local managers or independent representatives might know local conditions well but have little understanding of global strategy and little ability to communicate with headquarters. In most companies, the solution is to use two marketing decision makers, with the aim of creating a global localization approach. In this approach, one manager, possibly an expatriate or a manager at a home or regional base, represents headquarters; a second, locally hired, provides knowledge and experience of the local market. Needless to say, this approach can easily lead to conflict between global and local interests.

Two aspects of this type of relationship need to be considered in the context of marketing decision making. First, there is the degree to which any marketing programme can be optimized for the local market: when should a globally standardized programme be imposed on the local market, even if this results in a less than perfect fit with market needs? This question has been discussed at length above. Second, there is the question of how headquarters should direct and coordinate activities in the local market: how can standardized programmes, which are advantageous for the firm as a whole, be imposed on local managers without a loss of motivation in the subsidiary, or alternatively, how can independent decision makers be motivated to give their best effort in marketing the company's products?

The solution in most companies is first to ensure that local decision makers are directly involved in developing the global strategy. This will help in formulating a superior global strategy; the evidence is that where local managers perceive the globalization process as equitable across all countries, the acceptance of that strategy and the motivation to make it work are increased (Kim and Mauborgne 1993). Second, some successful companies try to create organizational structures that allow various country managers to become leaders in some products or marketing activities; for example, one local subsidiary may be given lead responsibility for developing a new global product or for creating a new advertising prototype. Companies that have tried this approach include IBM, Erickson, Honda, Honeywell and Procter & Gamble. Although such spreading of a company's competence needs to be carefully structured in order to yield maximum benefits, it also consistently helps to motivate local management.

Local objectives

The difficulties involved in managing local subsidiaries are often increased by the fact that corporate strategic objectives do not always result in the creation of a free-standing profit centre in each country market. Headquarters may regard market entry as a way of securing scale returns in manufacturing without adapting the product. The goal of entry may be to attack a competitor in his or her home base, and products are accordingly positioned head-on against competitor products; or the main intent may be simply to learn from operations in a leading market without attempting any significant penetration. Alternatively the local market may be regarded as a cash cow, with funds siphoned off to cross-subsidize operations elsewhere, undercutting any attempt by the local manager to build a loyal brand following.

These policies can also create difficulties for domestic brand managers, but the problem is greater in overseas operations. So long as multinationals operated using independent country units, local marketing was simply marketing in another country. With the new emphasis on global localization, however, country managers face a more difficult situation. Lack of familiarity with local conditions and the difficulty of credible communication often combine to make local demands go unheeded at headquarters. Accordingly, while a global company may seem a formidable competitor in local markets, the fact is that it takes considerable managerial skill to leverage the global advantages effectively.

Finally, it is useful to remember that the marketing manager who has done an excellent job in one type of market might not do as well in another country. Successful management styles differ between Japan, North America and Europe, and among European countries. This variance is often ascribed to cultural differences, but the requirements of the market are also important. As the task of marketing differs given the maturity stage of the product, so the capabilities of a company's marketers need to fit with the market requirements. For example, Western consumer goods marketers who are used to relying on detailed and timely store sales data might have trouble adapting to a situation where such data are not available and where hands-on experience serves as the principal guide.

7 Conclusion

The world trade accords negotiated under GATT and its successor the World Trade Organization (WTO; see WORLD TRADE ORGANIZATION) and the consequent lowering of trade barriers are continuing to reinforce the trend towards the globalization of international marketing. Global communications, the spread of technology and the rise of Asia and the newly democratized countries of eastern Europe are all factors pointing in the same direction; recessionary forces may occasionally slow the globalization movement, but they are unlikely to halt it altogether.

It is also clear, however, that local competitors who can satisfy smaller market niches will continue to find room to survive. While the emergence of integrated blocs such as the EU has led to a consolidation of local producers, there will still be a demand for more customized offerings. Not only will some consumers still prefer the old and unique products, but buyers of global brand name products will also buy local brands for special occasions and for variety. With increasing affluence, consumers will find it possible to frequent globally franchised fast food outlets as well as the finer local restaurants; they will appreciate the convenience of a Toyota while also spending weekends polishing an old MG; they will be happy to try an inexpensive Chilean wine and order an expensive French Chardonnay for a special occasion.

In the new democracies and in developing countries, this vision still seems far away. As global companies enter these markets, local variants are shown to offer much lower quality at uncompetitive prices. Customers without money to buy the new Western products will feel disappointed. One of the challenges for international marketers in the future is to determine how the promises of material welfare embodied in marketing activities can be delivered to these new markets. It is to be hoped that the competitiveness of local

entrepreneurs and increases in disposable incomes will be sufficient to counter these actual and potential frustrations.

In advanced country markets, the recent emphasis on customer satisfaction and relationship marketing suggests why smaller niche players will be able to survive. Offering personal attention and good after-sales service can create customer satisfaction even when the product has no competitive advantages. Relationship marketing stresses the need to see the transactions with a customer as a long-term commitment; rather than assuming that the customer should become loyal to the seller's brand, it is now believed that the manufacturer should be loyal to the customer, a loyalty which is easier to sustain when both seller and buyer are in direct contact. Such relationships have long been common in high context cultures such as Japan, where they contribute to the difficulty faced by new entrants when attempting to break into existing distribution networks; they are also becoming prevalent among some successful Western firms. As the various foreign markets approach maturity, one would expect these factors to gain in importance, offering opportunities for local players.

In sum total, provided trade barriers remain low and assuming that the new democracies can create viable economies, the outlook in international marketing is very positive. The trend is towards a coexistence of two seemingly contradictory phenomena: strong global products and brands in the core of the markets on the one hand, and strong local products and brands in niches defined by usage occasion and consumers seeking variety on the other.

JOHNY K. JOHANSSON
GEORGETOWN UNIVERSITY

Further reading

(References cited in the text marked *)

Buzzell, R.D., Quelch, J.A., and Bartlett, C.A. (1992) *Global Marketing Management: Cases and Readings*, 2nd edn, Reading, MA: Addison-Wesley. (An updated collection of some classic cases and *Harvard Business Review* articles.)

Czinkota, M.R. and Ronkainen, I.A. (1993) *International Marketing*, 3rd edn, New York: Dryden. (A leading undergraduate text, especially strong on export entry, government policies and grey trade.)

* Douglas, S. and Wind, Y. (1986) 'The myth of globalization', *Columbia Journal of World Business* 23 (1): 19–30. (An instructive alternative view of product standardization which shows its limits.)

* Freeman, L. (1990) 'Colgate axes global ads; thinks local', *Advertising Age* 26 November: 1, 59. (Shows how the balance between global and local ads can change over time.)

Hassan, S.S. and Blackwell, R.D. (1994) *Global Marketing: Perspectives and Cases*, New York: Dryden. (A collection of original articles on current issues, especially strong in consumer behaviour and advertising.)

* Johanson, J. and Vahlne, J.E. (1977) 'The internationalization process of the firm: a model of knowledge development and increasing foreign market commitments', *Journal of International Business Studies* 8 (2): 23–32. (The seminal statement of the process of internationalization of domestic firms.)

Johansson, J.K. and Thorelli, H.B. (1985) 'International product positioning', *Journal of International Business Studies* 16 (3): 57–75. (An empirical article which demonstrates how country of origin effects lead to misperceived product positions.)

Kashani, K. (1992) *Managing Global Marketing: Cases and Text*, Boston, MA: PWS-KENT. (An excellent collection of local marketing cases, including several covering European companies. Very limited text.)

* Kim, W.C. and Mauborgne, R.A. (1993) 'Making global strategies work', *Sloan Management Review* 34 (1): 11–27. (An empirical study of what makes local subsidiaries accept global strategies.)

Levitt, T. (1983) 'The globalization of markets', *Harvard Business Review* May–June: 92–102. (A classic article which re-ignited the debate over standardization and globalization; reprinted in Buzzell *et al.* 1992.)

Papadopoulos, N. and Heslop, L.A. (eds) (1993) *Product–Country Images*, New York: International Business Press. (A compilation of original articles by leading academics, with a good overview of country of origin effects.)

Saeed, S. (1987) 'Pricing in marketing strategies of US and foreign-based companies', *Journal of Business Research* 15 (2): 17–30. (A good analysis of the practical difficulties and adopted solutions of multinational pricing.)

* Vernon, R. (1966) 'International investment and international trade in the product cycle', *Quarterly Journal of Economics* 80 (2): 190–207. (The original description of product cycle theory, showing the relationship between technology transfer and foreign market development.)

* Yip, G. (1992) *Total Global Strategy*, Englewood Cliffs, NJ: Prentice Hall. (Covers all aspects of globalization, including good examples of global marketing management.)

See also: ADVERTISING STRATEGY, INTERNATIONAL; AT&T CORPORATION; CULTURE, CROSS-NATIONAL; DAIMLER CHRYSLER; EUROPEAN UNION; EXPORTING; FOREIGN EXCHANGE RISK, MANAGEMENT OF; FOREIGN MARKET ENTRY STRATEGIES; GLOBALIZATION; HUMAN RESOURCE MANAGEMENT, INTERNATIONAL; INTERNATIONAL MARKETING; INTERNATIONAL TRADE AND FOREIGN DIRECT INVESTMENT; MARKETING, CULTURAL DIFFERENCES IN; MITSUBISHI HEAVY INDUSTRIES, LTD; MULTINATIONAL CORPORATIONS; WORLD TRADE ORAGNIZATION

Related topics in the IEBM: BRANDS; CHANNEL MANAGEMENT; GENERAL AGREEMENT ON TARIFFS AND TRADE; MARKET STRUCTURE AND CONDUCT; MARKETING; MARKETING ENVIRONMENT; MARKETING RESEARCH; ORGANIZATION STRUCTURE; PRICING ISSUES IN MARKETING; PRODUCT POLICY CONCEPTS IN MARKETING; RELATIONSHIP MARKETING; SALES PROMOTION; SEGMENTATION; TELECOMMUNICATIONS; TOTAL QUALITY MANAGEMENT

Multinational corporations

Overview

Multinational corporations (MNCs), alternatively known as multinational enterprises, international corporations or transnational corporations, are corporations owning and controlling production or other value-adding facilities in several countries. More generally, the term is used to refer to global chains of affiliated companies managed and controlled from a headquarters located in a specific country. The global expansion of an MNC is secured with foreign direct investment (FDI), which is defined as investment made abroad to secure a controlling interest in an enterprise. MNCs are important actors in the world economy, controlling large proportions of global output, international trade and the global pool of technology. Since the mid-1980s their importance in the world economy has risen dramatically with cross-border economic integration being pursued in different regions, due to the opening up of new opportunities and an improved investment climate in many host countries or regions.

1 Importance of multinationals in the world economy

Because of the large scale of their operations, multinational corporations (MNCs) account for a rather disproportionate share of the world's output and dominate a number of industries and services globally with a presence in most market economies. Companies such as Philips, Ford, Toyota, Unilever, GlaxoWellcome, Bosch, Sony, Nestlé, Singer, IBM, Coca-Cola and Holiday Inn (see COCA-COLA COMPANY; INTERNATIONAL BUSINESS MACHINES CORPORATION; UNILEVER), among many others, are household names in most countries. Multinational corporations account for nearly one-quarter of world output; between one-third and one-half of world trade takes place between affiliated companies or within MNCs. Since knowledge capital is central to the process of creation of MNCs, as will be shown later, their control over the global pool of technology is even more complete. About three-quarters of global patents are estimated to be under the control of multinational corporations.

Foreign direct investment (FDI) and other forms of MNC participation in the world economy are seen as channels of international transfer of productive resources such as capital, organizational and managerial skills, production and marketing technology, other intangible assets such as rights to use brand or trade names of parent, access to cheaper sources of raw materials and other inputs to the host country. Hence, MNCs are considered to be capable of fostering development and industrialization in their host countries. A large number of countries attempt to attract MNC investment through a variety of incentives and other policies (see GLOBALIZATION; INTERNATIONAL TRADE AND FOREIGN DIRECT INVESTMENT).

Although a number of MNCs came into being in the nineteenth century, FDI and other cross-border activities by corporations became an important phenomenon only in the post-Second World War period. In the 1960s and 1970s, however, excessive involvement of MNCs was resisted in many developing countries because of fears of neo-colonialism, as most MNCs originated in erstwhile colonial countries. The MNCs also wielded enormous economic and political influence due to their gigantic scale of operations and their market power. Hence, governments evolved policies to regulate MNCs and even nationalized their operations when it was deemed necessary. In the 1980s, however, the policy environment has become increasingly favourable to MNCs following liberalization of the foreign direct investment policies of a large number of countries.

2 Motivations and organizational forms

In terms of motivations, MNC operations abroad or FDI can be broadly classified into four types (Dunning 1993), depending on the nature of the investment being undertaken:

1 natural resource-seeking investments;
2 market-seeking investments;
3 efficiency-seeking investments;
4 strategic-asset seeking investments.

Natural resource-seeking investments are those made by MNCs abroad in order to seek privileged access to supplies of natural resources and raw materials or to exploit an abundance of certain raw materials in a particular country. Examples include plantation and mining investments in resource-rich developing countries, such as investments in tea and coffee plantations, iron ore and bauxite mining in India, rubber plantations in Liberia and Malaysia or copper mining in Chile and Zambia. However, investment in natural resources can also be made in industrialized countries such as Australia and Canada.

Market-seeking investments are defined as investments orientated towards developing or entering domestic markets in certain countries. These may include investments undertaken either to obviate host country tariff and non-tariff barriers, or investments aimed at precluding rivals or potential rivals from gaining new markets. These investments generally take the form of horizontal foreign direct investment and are by far the most common type of FDI.

Efficiency-seeking investments include investments made by MNCs to rationalize production globally according to factor costs in order to maintain their competitiveness. These investments result in a globally integrated production system where plants participating in rationalization across the world are integrated vertically. Finally, strategic asset-seeking investments include investments made abroad to acquire strategic assets such as brand or trade names, proprietary technology or market access. The acquisition of ICL in the UK by the Japanese firm Fujitsu, for example, aimed to improve Fujitsu's access to the European computer market.

The operations of multinational corporations abroad can take a variety of organizational forms. They can cover anything from a majority-owned subsidiary operation to taking a minority but controlling stake in an enterprise. Investment could also either be a greenfield investment or involve acquisition of an existing unit abroad. Finally, investment could take the form of a joint venture with a local enterprise, or be an independent or sole venture by the MNC.

3 The theory of internationalization of firms

The theory of the international operations of firms explains how a national firm evolves into a multinational enterprise. Hymer (1960) made the first attempt to understand the transition of a national firm into a multinational one. Previously, FDI flows were treated like any other international flows of resources, such as portfolio investments, and were thought to be driven by international factor price differentials. Hymer used the tenets of industrial organization approaches in his attempt to provide a theoretical basis for the overseas operations of national firms. Subsequently, this stream of theorizing has been enriched by the contributions of Kindleberger (1969), Caves (1982), Buckley and Casson (1976) and Dunning (1979), among others.

According to Hymer, a firm operating abroad must possess advantages that can more than offset the handicaps faced in an alien environment and cover the ensuing greater risks. These advantages are sometimes referred to as monopolistic advantages, and emanate from the ownership of proprietary assets possessed by firms such as brand goodwill, technology, managerial and marketing skills and access to cheaper sources of capital and raw materials. These advantages are first exploited abroad through exports from the country of origin. In later stages, local production is undertaken when locational factors begin to emerge that make production more profitable than exporting. The latter include factors such as tariffs and quantitative restrictions imposed on imports by host countries, communication and transport costs and inter-country differences in input/factor prices and productivity.

When undertaking local production, firms can choose further between foreign direct investment and 'arm's-length licensing' contracts under which production is undertaken by other, unrelated firms in the host country. In other words, a firm can exploit the revenue productivity of its intangible assets or ownership advantages, for example, knowledge, technology or brand names through FDI or internally within the firm, or it can choose to license these assets. The choice between FDI and licensing is usually determined by the transaction or governance costs involved in setting up licensing contracts. The higher the transaction costs, the higher the incentive to internalize the transaction and thus the greater the likelihood of FDI being chosen as a mode of foreign production. Transaction costs are generally high for market transactions of most intangible assets because of market failures arising from their nature as public goods, difficulty in making a convincing disclosure and buyer uncertainty, problems with the codification of knowledge and the risk of dissipation of brand goodwill. In practice, however, smaller firms lacking experience and resources in managing operations abroad may prefer to license their intangible assets. In summary, FDI takes place when ownership, locational and internalization (OLI) advantages are present. Dunning (1979) has woven these three preconditions for FDI to take place into a coherent framework referred to as the OLI or eclectic paradigm (see INTERNATIONAL TRADE AND FOREIGN DIRECT INVESTMENT).

The ownership of firm-specific intangible assets or knowledge capital which may be in the form of technology, expertise, brand name goodwill and marketing skills is therefore a prerequisite for the foreign operations of a firm. MNCs are therefore important in sectors which are intensive in their use of knowledge capital. MNCs are generally characterized by: (1) high levels of expenditure on R&D (2) a large proportion of professional and technical employees in their workforce; (3) new and technically more complex products; and (4) high levels of product differentiation or advertising. The importance of intangible assets for MNCs means that their market valuation greatly exceeds the value of their tangible assets such as plant and machinery.

4 Patterns in multinational corporation activity

The United Nations Conference on Trade and Development (UNCTAD) in Geneva estimated in the mid-1990s that there were about 44,000 MNCs in existence, controlling over 280,000 affiliates around the world. Over 80 per cent of these MNCs were based in the developed or industrialized countries. The largest few hundred MNCs accounted for the bulk of total assets, sales revenue and number of foreign affiliates; the largest 100 (excluding those in banking and finance) controlled US$4.2 trillion worth of global assets in 1995, of which about $1.7 trillion were held outside their home countries (UNCTAD 1997). Nearly all of these 100 largest MNCs were based in industrialized countries. The USA was the single most important country of origin, with 30 of the top 100 companies; 39 companies originated in the European Union (EU), Japan accounted for 18 and the remaining 13 originated in Switzerland, Sweden, Canada, Finland, Norway, Australia or New Zealand, and one each in South Korean and Venezuela. In terms of sectoral distribution of foreign assets of the top 100 MNCs, the automotive sector leads, with 21 per cent, followed by petroleum and mining (18 per cent), electonics (16 per cent), chemicals and pharmaceutical (13 per cent), and food and beverages (8 per cent). Details of the largest fifteen multinational corporations are shown in Table 1.

Trends in FDI flows reveal emerging patterns in the cross-border activities of MNCs. The scale of annual FDI flows rose dramatically in the second half of the 1980s. Compared to an annual average of US$55 billion, during the first half of the 1980s, global FDI flows averaged US$174 billion a year in the second half, peaking at US$209 billion in 1990. In the first two years of the 1990s the level of FDI declined, but then rose again in subsequent years. In 1996 the UN and International Monetary Fund estimated the flow of FDI at US$350 billion.

Among the factors that contributed to a rapid rise in FDI flows in the late 1980s was the cross-national economic integration among EU member states, which led to a sharp rise in FDI outflows from a few European countries towards other regional partners. The constant hardening of the yen

following the Plaza Accord in 1985 eroded the competitiveness of Japanese corporations, prompting them to locate production abroad. Japanese corporations also located production in EU countries to overcome increasing protectionist barriers and to exploit the benefits of regional integration by becoming insiders. Developing countries around the world have liberalized their investment codes in an effort to attract greater volumes of FDI as part of their structural adjustment programmes, and economic reforms in central and eastern Europe opened up completely new markets for FDI. Finally, the newly industrializing countries of east Asia emerged as significant outward investors in the late 1980s.

The decline in the magnitude of FDI flows in the early 1990s can be explained in terms of completion of restructuring of EU businesses in anticipation of the Single European Market, and the recession in

Table 1 Top 15 largest MNCs in terms of foreign assets (Figures are for 1995, US$ billion)

MNC	Country	Industry	Foreign assets	Total assets	Foreign sales
1 Shell, Royal Dutch	UK/The Netherlands	Oil, gas, coal and rel. services	79.7	117.6	80.6
2 Ford Motor Company	US	Automative	69.2	238.5	41.9
3 General Electric	US	Electronics	69.2	228.0	17.1
4 Exxon Corporation	US	Oil, gas, coal and rel. services	66.7	91.3	96.9
5 General Motors	US	Automative	54.1	217.1	47.8
6 Volkswagen AG	Germany	Automative	49.8	58.7	37.4
7 IBM	US	Computers	41.7	80.3	45.1
8 Toyota Motor Corporation	Japan	Automative	36.0	118.2	50.4
9 Nestlé SA	Switzerland	Food	33.2	38.2	47.8
10 Mitsubishi Corporation	Japan	Diversified	....	79.3	51.0
11 Bayer AG	Germany	Chemicals	28.1	31.3	19.7
12 ABB Asea Brown Boveri	Switzerland	Electrical equipment	27.2	32.1	29.4
13 Nissan Motor	Japan	Automative	26.9	63.0	24.9
14 Elf Aquitaine	France	Oil, gas, coal and rel. services	26.9	49.4	27.8
15 Mobil Corporation	US	Oil, gas, coal and rel. services	26.0	42.1	48.4

Source: UNCTAD (1997) *World Investment Report* 1997.

major industrial countries including Japan. The subsequent recovery from recession contributed in turn to a gradual recovery of global FDI flows (see ECONOMIC INTEGRATION, INTERNATIONAL).

The industrialized countries accounted for nearly 98 per cent of all FDI outflows in the early 1990s. Their share has declined slightly since, but still over 95 per cent of all FDI outflows originate in industrialized countries. The rest comes from a few newly industrialized countries largely in east Asia, such as South Korea, Taiwan, Hong Kong and Singapore. Several enterprises in these countries have accumulated the technological and managerial capability to expand overseas and become multinational in their own right. Here again, the impetus towards overseas production has come from rising wages, hardening of home country currencies and increasing protectionist tendencies in industrialized countries such as the EU member states.

The industrialized countries also receive the bulk of FDI inflows. In the early 1980s, nearly three-quarters of all FDI inflows were received by industrialized countries. In the late 1980s, coinciding with the rapid rise in FDI volume, the concentration of FDI among industrialized countries grew further, so that they received 85 per cent of global FDI inflows in 1990. Again, this was partly a result of heavy concentration of FDI inflows in the EU countries in the wake of the restructuring sparked off by the creation of the Single Market. The 1990s, however, have seen developing countries assume increasing importance in the distribution of FDI, with their share rising to 39 per cent in 1994. The inter-country distribution of FDI inflows has been highly uneven; just ten developing countries – China, Singapore, Argentina, Mexico, Malaysia, Indonesia, Thailand, Hong Kong, Taiwan and Nigeria – accounted for nearly 81 per cent of all developing country FDI inflows in 1994.

5 Future prospects

The current trends towards liberalization of restrictions on FDI, cross-national economic integration in different regions and liberalization of international trade in services suggest that MNCs will continue to grow in importance in the coming years. MNCs are, however, restructuring and constantly adapting themselves to the changing economic environment. The MNCs of the future may therefore be significantly different in terms of organizational structure from those of today.

Restructuring is changing the face of corporations on many fronts. For instance, the introduction of new organizational and manufacturing techniques such as lean manufacturing, just-in-time production and computer-integrated flexible manufacturing systems is shifting emphasis away from economies of scale and mass production. There is also a trend away from vertical integration towards concentration on core businesses and contracting out everything else in order to maintain competitiveness. Because of high tariffs and non-tariff barriers that insulated national markets in the past, MNC operations in different host countries had been organized as miniature replicas of themselves. With the increasing deregulation of trade worldwide and the formation of free trade areas in different regions, MNCs are now restructuring their national operations in a more productive manner than the 'multi-domestic' style of the past. In the EU, for example, MNCs are rationalizing their operations on a pan-European basis. This restructuring takes the form of an international division of labour where one plant is responsible for the production of one or more items for the entire region. The other plants similarly concentrate on other items for the entire regional market.

Another important trend is the increasing formation of strategic alliances and joint ventures by MNCs to complement their intangible asset bundles with those of others. These alliances are becoming an increasingly important form of inter-MNC cooperation, especially in emerging core technology industries such as microelectronics, information technology and biotechnology.

NAGESH KUMAR
THE UNITED NATIONS UNIVERSITY INSTITUTE
FOR NEW TECHNOLOGIES

Further reading

(References cited in the text marked *)

* Buckley, P.J. and Casson, M. (1976) *The Future of Multinational Enterprise*, London: Macmillan. (This book was among the first to theorize the conditions for internalization of transactions of intangible assets within MNCs.)

* Caves, R.E. (1982) *Multinational Enterprise and Economic Analysis*, Cambridge: Cambridge University Press. (This book provides a useful survey of the theoretical and empirical literature on the subject.)

Dicken, P. (1992) *Global Shift: The Internationalization of Economic Activity*, London: Paul Chapman Publishing. (This book usefully analyses trends in production, international trade and MNC activities globally and in select industries to understand the extent and patterns of internationalization of economic activity.)

* Dunning, J.H. (1979) 'Explaining changing patterns of international production', *Oxford Bulletin of Economics and Statistics* 41: 269–96. (Theoretical account of the preconditions for FDI.)

* Dunning, J.H. (1993) *Multinational Enterprises and the Global Economy*, Wokingham: Addison-Wesley. (This book provides a comprehensive and up-to-date perspective on the literature on different aspects of MNC activity in the global economy.)

The Economist (1995) 'Big is back: a survey of multinationals', 24 June: 1–23. (This survey examines emerging patterns in organizational styles and other trends in MNC activity.)

* Hymer, S.H. (1976) *The International Operations of National Firms: A Study of Direct Foreign Investment*, Cambridge, MA: MIT Press. (This PhD dissertation made the first attempt to analyse the evolution of national firms into multinational corporations using an industrial organization theory approach.)

Julius, D. (1990) *Global Companies and Public Policy: The Growing Challenge of Foreign Direct Investment*, London: Royal Institute of International Affairs. (This book highlights the increasing importance of MNCs in the global economy and the challenge this puts before policy makers.)

* Kindleberger, C.P. (1969) *American Business Abroad: Six Lectures on Direct Investment*, New Haven, CT: Yale University Press. (A clear exposition of the subject.)

Kumar, N. (1994) *Multinational Enterprises and Industrial Organisation: The Case of India*, New Delhi: Sage Publications. (This book applies economic theory and statistical techniques to understand and evaluate the implications of MNC investments for a developing economy such as India.)

Kumar, N., with J. Dunning, R. Lipsey, J. Agarwal and S. Urata (1998) *Globalization, Foreign Direct Investment and Technology Transfers: Impacts on and Prospects for Developing Countries*, London and New York: Routledge. (Discusses emerging patterns in the overseas activity of MNCs originating from major industrialized and emerging source countries, and examines the implications of these trends for developing countries and for policy.)

* United Nations Conference on Trade and Development (1997) *World Investment Report 1997*, Geneva: United Nations. (This, one in a series of annual reports, is an important source of statistics and analyses of current trends in the activities of MNCs worldwide.)

See also: COCA-COLA COMPANY; ECONOMIC INTEGRATION, INTERNATIONAL; GLOBALIZATION; HUMAN RESOURCE MANAGEMENT, INTERNATIONAL; INTERNATIONAL BUSINESS, FUTURE TRENDS; INTERNATIONAL BUSINESS MACHINES CORPORATION; INTERNATIONAL OPERATIONS; INTERNATIONAL TRADE AND FOREIGN DIRECT INVESTMENT; MULTINATIONAL CORPORATIONS, ORGANIZATION STRUCTURES IN; UNILEVER

Related topics in the IEBM: INTERNATIONAL BUSINESS ELITES; JUST-IN-TIME PHILOSOPHIES; MANUFACTURING SYSTEMS, DESIGN OF; MULTINATIONAL CORPORATIONS, HISTORY OF; TRANSFER PRICING

Multinational corporations, organization structures in

Overview

To engineer artfully an organization that configures globally dispersed resources to meet the mandates of multinational operations is the frontier of international management. While most international managers find it easier to decide what to do, the point of innovation has shifted to devising a structure of such clarity that the intricate organizational task of mediating worldwide integration versus local differentiation becomes straightforward. The shifting frontier of international business develops this assertion. The unfolding transition from the industrial to information era is transforming wealth creation in the multinational corporation (MNC) from a specialized division of sequential functions to a 'boundaryless' conception of synchronized business processes. The enormity of this transition is radically redefining the principles of organization in the MNC. Simply put, the bureaucracy of a vertically configured MNC, the mode of the industrial era, is surrendering to the entrepreneurialism of the horizontally configured network in the information era.

This entry develops this transition by profiling the past conventions, present practices and future principles of structure in the MNC. Interweaving these elements with emerging environmental imperatives and strategic canons of international business highlights the magnitude and trends of organizational change in the MNC. Simply put, the force of

change is converting the maxim of 'think global, act local' to 'think global, coordinate regionally, act local'. This entry clarifies the causes, correlates and consequences of this conversion. Throughout this explanation, we discuss how executives have, are, and probably will organize the MNC.

1 What is structure?

Weber (1947) theorized that managers designed a structure to control the firm's activities by specifying the vertical hierarchy, formal procedures and division of labour. March and Simon (1958) saw organization as the 'pattern of relationships and behaviours that change slowly' and thus provide clarity and stability. Similarly, Thompson (1967) defined structure as the map of relationships that lets the firm orchestrate specialized experts. Perrow (1967) expressed a more behavioural view, proposing that 'organizations are multi-purpose tools for shaping the world as one wishes it to be shaped. They provide the means for imposing one's definition of the proper affairs of men upon other men'. Lastly, Ranson *et al.* (1980) reason that structure is a 'complex medium of control . . . the framework of rules, roles and authority relations that seeks to facilitate prescribed purposes by differentially enabling certain kinds of conduct, conferring support for forms of commitment, as well as constraining and obligating those who reject the claims entailed by the framework'.

More precisely, structure delineates the verticality of the chain of command, breadth of communication, extent of dyadic relationships and relative prominence of functional, product and/or market responsibilities. The traditional pyramidal hierarchy of boxes and titles emphasizes differences in authority. The existence of differentiated departments shows how a firm coordinates pools of specialized labour. Structure also specifies who reports to whom and who is responsible for what. By doing so, structure outlines how managers will direct, coordinate and integrate individual behaviour and harness it to the firm's strategy. The number of 'boxes' in a structure outlines the firm's division of work among managers of differing degrees of specialization.

Structure serves many particular functions in the multinational corporation (MNC) (see MULTINATIONAL CORPORATIONS). It integrates units that are differentiated by functional, product or market responsibilities; it outlines which tasks require local specialization or global standardization; it sets the protocols of supervision and socialization that empower managers at headquarters to coordinate subordinates posted throughout the world; it arranges the relationships and responsibilities of geographically dispersed plants and culturally diverse employees so that differentiated operations meet universal standards; it reduces the costs of integration by eliminating duplication; it delineates the boundaries of accountability between headquarters, regional branch offices and local operating units; it decrees linkages between functions, markets and products that exploit the economies of common governance; it speeds transfer and diffusion of innovations among subsidiaries; finally, it outlines a coherent division of specialized labour that preserves a unified course of worldwide action.

Influencing executives' decisions on these and similar matters is the historic principle of organization in the MNC: balancing global integration with local differentiation. This dichotomy can be expressed in many ways, such as efficiency versus effectiveness, standardization versus customization, centralization versus decentralization, or even science versus art. Irrespective of the terms used, the dilemma is the same. Ensuring that workers in the MNC work with a unity of purpose requires setting points and policies of integration. If ignored, then the MNC forgoes the advantages of global reach that allow it to compete against better positioned national rivals. However, the complexity of the MNC's tasks means the same persons cannot do all the tasks. Similarly, the diversity of local conditions and preferences means the same policies cannot regulate all tasks. Consequently, the MNC must differentiate parts of its organization, permitting units, whether they are functional, product or geographic, to tailor their own practices and policies, whether professionally, technically or nationally, to the unique demands of their workplace. In the zero-sum context of integration versus differentiation, the MNC's goal is preserving the flexibility to differentiate operations when necessary, while maintaining forms of integration to exploit the opportunities of multinational economies of scale, scope and geographical diversification. In practice, MNCs have adopted a variety of slogans to express their logic of resolution; current favourites include 'think global, act local' or 'the art of being local worldwide' (see GLOBALIZATION).

2 Traditional structures in multinational corporations

In theory, all organizations have tendencies that we can trace to a functional, divisional, matrix or hybrid structure.

Functional

A functional structure, as depicted in Figure 1, is the ideal way to organize work when the MNC's products share a common technology and competitive pressures make high quality and low cost the standards of excellence. The clarity of a functional organization lets managers maximize scale economies. The precise division of work and utmost specialization of tasks lets workers stress functional optimization. A functional structure compels integrating specialized activities at the corporate level, thereby letting the MNC realize cross-functional synergies. A weakness of a functional structure is its inability to respond to environmental changes that require coordination between departments. A vibrant marketplace reveals the risks of the extreme verticality of a functional structure. Dynamism broadens the scope of pertinent data quicker than the many layers of a functional hierarchy can process it. Eventual overload leads to slow, reactive decision making.

For instance, consider the organizational saga of the Caterpillar Tractor Company (see CATERPILLAR INC.). For over forty years, Caterpillar – the leader in the earth moving equipment industry – used a functional structure to manage operations ranging the world. Management believed this straightforward format encouraged easy and informal communication and preserved the clarity of roles and relationships. Reinforcing this belief were Caterpillar's improving performances from the early 1940s until 1981. In 1982, the virtues of its functional structure became vices. Fierce assault by its Japanese rival, Komatsu, highlighted Caterpillar's organizational inflexibility. By 1985, the relentless siege had taken its toll. Amid the rubble of record losses – $953 million since 1982 – Caterpillar's management had no choice but to question its long-standing structure and more profoundly, its presumption that superior returns resulted from an ingenious mix of bigger plants and higher-tech equipment. Following unprecedented labour turmoil and plant closures, by the mid-1980s Caterpillar's management embraced the creed that organizational innovations made an economic difference. Quickly, management transformed Caterpillar's functionally dominated hierarchy into an organization marked by flexibility, focus and innovation. Caterpillar adopted unprecedented structural formats that supplemented historic functions with business

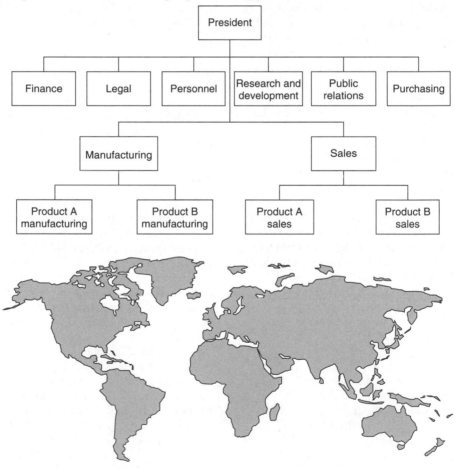

Figure 1 Structure by business function

and market-based units. Did the transformation work? In terms of practical outcomes, the rethinking of the division of labour, for instance, re-engineered the manufacture of a grader axle from the previous process of 276 stops across four buildings to two stops completed in a single cell. This and similar innovations enabled Caterpillar to report record income of $616 million in 1988. Even more dramatically, the transformation of Caterpillar from a superior manufacturer of high-quality goods to an innovative organization as well so changed the standards of success that in 1992 Komatsu, the global trendsetter just seven years

earlier, shocked analysts by announcing its planned exit from the earth moving industry through gradual diversification. While perhaps extreme, this example is not exceptional. Developments in other industries, such as automobile, power generation, electronics and food-processing, spin similar morals.

Divisional

Whereas executives organize a functional structure in terms of inputs, they use a divisional structure to organize it according to outputs. Each division in a company may be responsible for a different set of products or

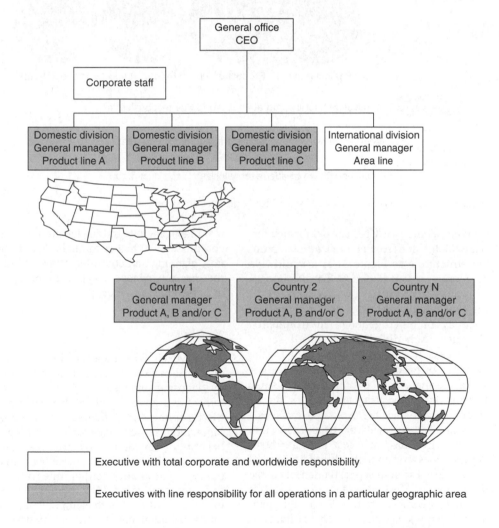

Executive with total corporate and worldwide responsibility

Executives with line responsibility for all operations in a particular geographic area

Figure 2 A multidivisional structure by domestic product divisions and an international division

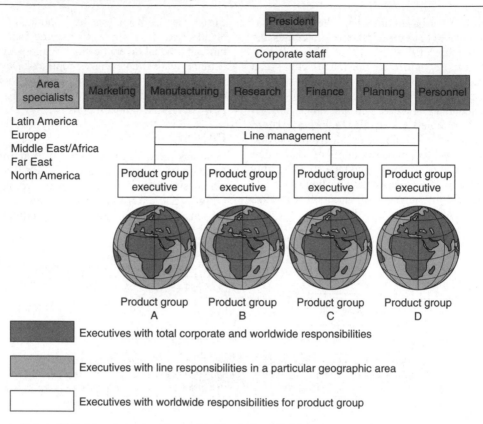

Latin America
Europe
Middle East/Africa
Far East
North America

Executives with total corporate and worldwide responsibilities

Executives with line responsibilities in a particular geographic area

Executives with worldwide responsibilities for product group

Figure 3 A multidivisional structure by worldwide product divisions

markets; as such, an MNC can opt for an international division (see Figure 2), a global product structure (see Figure 3) or a worldwide area structure (see Figure 4). The advantages of a division structure are its capacity to respond quickly to changes, and preserve consistency in heterogeneous environments. Because each division has a full set of resources, it can respond swiftly to the demands of products or markets. Also, divisional formats spur decentralization since there are fewer levels that must review, reconsider and ratify data before someone makes a decision. The segmentation of an MNC into discrete divisions, in effect separate businesses, does frustrate its ability to exploit economies of scale or scope. If unchecked, the diseconomies of a division structure can erode an MNC's competitiveness. Typically, managers in a divisional structure try to offset this disadvantage through extensive methods of manufacturing integration and administrative coordination. Whether through shared logistics, planning and control systems or budget routines, top management tries to seize points of cross-division synergy.

Matrix

Some MNCs face a special dilemma. They operate in markets where demand is jointly set by opposing dimensions, for example, customers and government in pharmaceuticals. MNCs in this bind often see organizational innovation as simultaneously attaining the benefits of functional and divisional structures through a matrix format. Rather than formally subordinating either integration or differentiation, these MNCs use a matrix to gain the benefits of both, and prevent prematurely excluding one. However, a matrix confuses the unity of command by imposing a

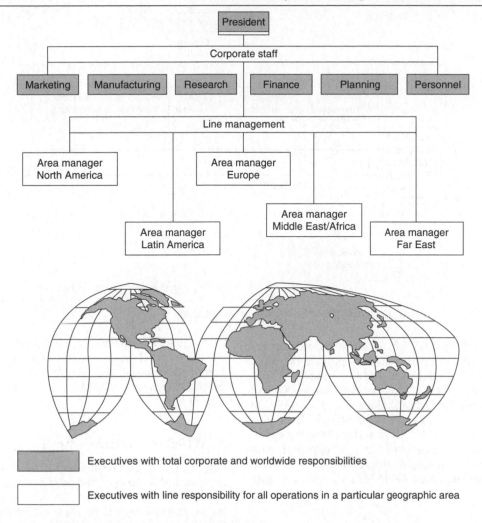

Figure 4 A multidivisional structure by geographic areas

dual hierarchy – for example, one that combines function and area – and that then purportedly coordinates across the particular demands of both dimensions. No matter how horizontal the matrix makes communications, it leaves intact the vertical hierarchy. As Figure 5 shows, it is confusing just to diagram the contemporaneous notion of dual command. This task, as many MNCs have conceded, pales in comparison to making the matrix work.

Many courageous firms have surrendered to the complexity of the matrix structure. Perhaps the swansong for this format was the recent experience of ABB, an MNC comprised of 5,200 profit centres operating in 65 businesses in 140 countries, that employed 214,000 people and had revenues of $30 billion in 1993. Preserving order in the face of such engineered chaos required an elaborate matrix of communication and control among the twelve members of the executive committee, the sixty plus business leaders, hundreds of country managers, and tens of thousands of workers. CEO Percy Barnevik (see BARNEVIK, P.) had earlier stated that ABB's matrix positioned it to develop deep local roots without sacrificing the economies of its global

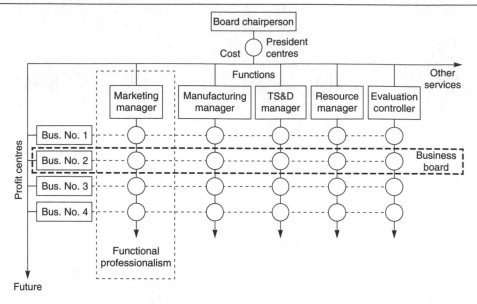

Figure 5 A matrix structure by function and product orientations

reach. Indeed, Mr Barnevik argued that the matrix enabled ABB to 'optimize our businesses globally and maximize performance in every country' (Asea Brown Boveri, Harvard Business School, Case no. 9-129-39). In August of 1993, ABB became the latest on a long list of MNCs to surrender to the operational drawbacks of a matrix. Shortly after reporting sluggish first-half earnings, ABB announced a $500 million charge to revamp its structure.

Hybrid

In reality, the organizational charts of few MNCs neatly mimic a functional, divisional or matrix structure. This oddity leads us to the final generic format – the hybrid structure. Some MNCs combine various characteristics of different structures in an idiosyncratic way under the assumption that the resulting amalgam benefits from each's virtues but neutralizes their peculiar vices. So, as we see with Caterpillar's structure in Figure 6, management has outlined a division of work that has functional, area and product dimensions. Again, some may point out that since a hybrid structure suggests a matrix, why does an MNC not opt for the purity of a matrix?

Unquestionably, this choice has tempted the management of many MNCs. As ABB's experience showed, the complications of a dual hierarchy eventually dissuaded or dashed their dreams.

3 Which structure when?

Few, if any, MNCs have the luxury to follow a set sequence towards a predetermined organizational format. Indeed, two MNCs executing the same strategy in the same industry are likely to end up with dissimilar structures. Historically, however, as firms expanded internationally, they followed a common strategy of structure. The first major structure for the internationalizing firm was an international division. Usually prompting this adaptation was high growth in the volume of international transactions that soon exceeded the processing capacity of a functional structure. An international division offered ways to decide better the appropriate degree of differentiation and devise ways to gain new opportunities of integration. Eventually, the success, scale and scope of foreign operations became so overwhelming that it changed the orientation of a firm's structure from 'domestic and international' to global.

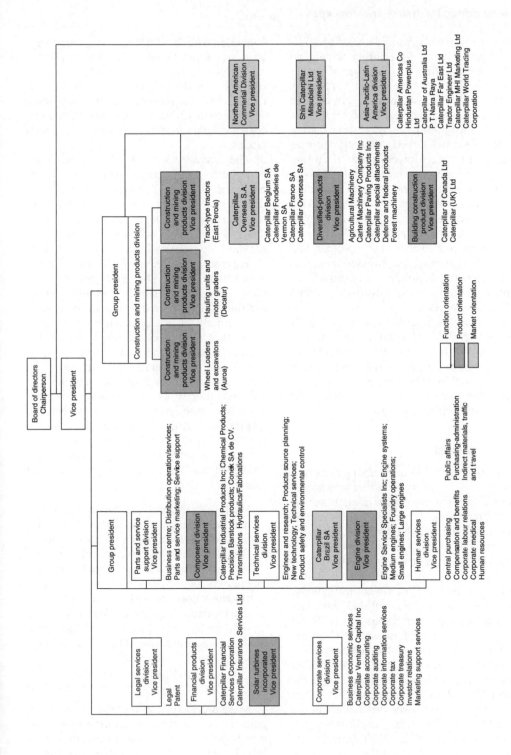

Figure 6 Caterpillar Inc. corporate organization chart as of November 1992

Despite resistance from historically dominant domestic units, firms often abandoned the international division in favour of a more global structure with either product or area divisions. An MNC's strategy largely decided the choice. Companies that opted for an area structure, such as 3M, tended to have mature product lines that served common end-user markets, emphasized lowering manufacturing costs by combining routine technologies with long production runs, and stressed marketing effectiveness. MNCs that chose a worldwide product structure, such as Procter & Gamble (see PROCTER & GAMBLE CO.), made products through new and unrelated technologies, had dissimilar consumers, and stressed manufacturing efficiency. In isolated cases some firms adopted global functional forms or global holding companies.

In essence, the unique structures of MNCs make 'which structure when' more rhetorical than not. While the historical conduct of MNCs suggests a developmental sequence in their structural evolution, its predictability is speculative. Instead, there are several paths that have dissimilar stages and outcomes.

4 It depends . . .

In principle, the differences among the structures of MNCs express each firm's vision of how to resolve the dilemma of integration versus differentiation. In practice, these differences reflect the unique internal and external environments of the firm. Simply put, the MNC's choice of structure 'depends' on how its executives plan to cope with the contingencies created by the firm's size, technology, scale, resources, environment and other factors. For instance, our discussion of 'what structure when' showed that an MNC's strategy influences it choice of structure. Nestlé, for instance, employs 199,021 people but bases 192,079 outside Switzerland, while the Boston Consulting Group (BCG) has 525 employees of which over three quarters are stationed in the USA. Thus, Nestlé uses a geographic structure while BCG experiments with a hybrid form. From a different angle, the complexity of NEC's (see NEC CORPORATION) and Caterpillar's organizations compared with those of BCG and Nestlé suggests that sophisticated technologies prompt intricate structures. Conversely, Nestlé's emphasis on developing global brands tailored to national markets – it produces some 200 different varieties of its Nescafé soluble coffee – helps to explain its choice of area divisions.

The uniqueness of an MNC's attributes contributes only a partial explanation of its choice of structure. The influence of internal dimensions is largely subordinate to that of the external environment. True in any context, this assertion takes on greater consequence for the MNC given that its operations span varied markets. Referencing the law of 'requisite variety' from cybernetics develops this point. This law mandates that any system, such as an MNC, must develop sufficient variety internally if it is to cope with variety externally. If it fails to do so, gaps appear that eventually make a robust organization obsolete. As such, the characteristics at play in the MNC's environment, and especially the way they relentlessly change, continually challenge the capacity of its structure to balance integration and differentiation. Jack Welch (see WELCH, J.), CEO of General Electric (GE; see GENERAL ELECTRIC CO.), articulates the linkage of requisite variety and organizational change:

> We [GE] had constructed over the years a management apparatus that was right for its time, the toast of the business schools. Divisions, strategic business units, groups, sectors, all were designed to make meticulous, calculated decisions and move them smoothly forward and upward. This system produced highly polished work. It was right for the 1970s, a growing handicap in the 1980s, and it would have been a ticket to the boneyard in the 1990s.
> (GE: Harvard Business School Case no. 9-381–248)

More precisely, consider the organization outcomes of the three principle waves of international expansion in the twentieth century (see Figure 7). The first wave was that of European firms expanding abroad in the inter-war period. Nationalistic trade policies

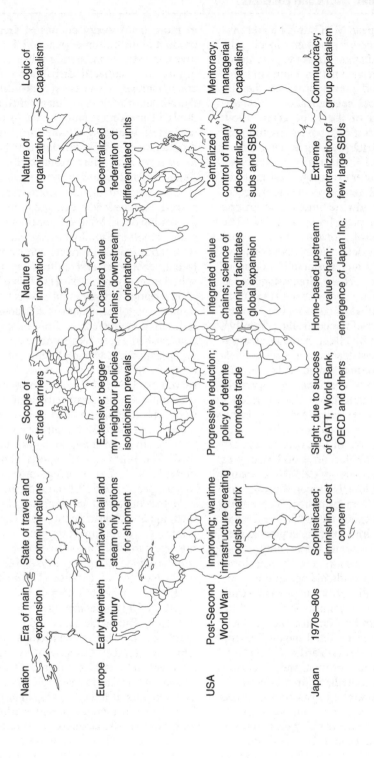

Nation	Era of main expansion	State of travel and communications	Scope of trade barriers	Nature of innovation	Nature of organization	Logic of capitalism
Europe	Early twentieth century	Primitave; mail and steam only options for shipment	Extensive; begger my neighbour policies isolationism prevails	Localized value chains; downstream orientation	Decentralized federation of differentiated units	
USA	Post-Second World War	Improving; wartime infrastructure creating logistics matrix	Progressive reduction; policy of detente promotes trade	Integrated value chains; science of planning facilitates global expansion	Centralized control of many decentralized subs and SBUs	Meritoracy; managerial capatalism
Japan	1970s–80s	Sophisticated; diminishing cost concern	Slight; due to success of GATT, World Bank, OECD and others	Home-based upstream value chain; emergence of Japan Inc.	Extreme centralization of few, large SBUs	Commuocracy; group capatalism

Figure 7 The interplay of environment, technology, strategic innovation and organization

compelled European MNCs to gain and preserve market access by building local, self-contained subsidiaries. Extreme differences in consumer tastes led national units to tailor products and marketing approaches, thereby emphasizing local specialization of downstream activities of the value chain. Slow steamship transport and postal communication coupled with the growing resource autonomy of local subsidiaries curbed headquarters' power to manage these units directly. Local differentiation thus took precedence over worldwide integration in the structure of the typical European MNC. The doctrine of control, however, took its cue from logistic barriers, family ownership of European MNCs and aristocratic norms of European society. These circumstances led European MNCs to rely on personal relationships as the method of control. They posted abroad a member of the controlling 'family', whether decided by blood, heritage or training, to create consistency in visions and values between home and abroad, and ensure the financial probity of decentralized, often remote, national organizations. The prevalence of this form of organization led to the Euro-specific 'mother–daughter' structure.

The second wave of international expansion, following the Second World War, was defined by the activities of US MNCs. Spared the destruction levelled upon Europe and Asia, benefiting from the political supremacy of the USA, and endowed with a world eager for goods, US firms had an unprecedented window of international opportunity. Also, the era of jet-transport and international direct-dial made worldwide operations more manageable. Finally, efforts to prevent a third world war inspired commissioning institutions – that is, United Nations, World Bank, International Monetary Fund and the General Agreement on Trade and Tariffs (GATT) – to sponsor worldwide growth and liberalize trade. US firms capitalized on this environment through the strategy of integrating mass production with mass distribution. They invested in high-volume manufacturing units in nations dispersed around the world. For example, as of the mid-1970s, IBM's manufacturing configuration included over fifty plants

in more than twenty countries. Getting the product to the customer pushed US MNCs to invest in national marketing subsidiaries with highly differentiated distribution facilities and personnel. In its heyday, IBM distributed the output of their many plants through hundreds of marketing units based in over 150 countries. Managing the union of integrated production with differentiated distribution led to progressive internationalization of the functional and multidivisional structure.

Internationalizing their domestic structure placed unprecedented demands upon the organization of US MNCs. Coordinating tens of plants supplying hundreds of specialized units with thousands of products across many political, economic and cultural systems resulted in an explosion of data. This tidal wave soon swamped incremental efforts to internationalize historically domestic structures. Coordinating the increasing flow of specialized data pushed executives to develop elaborate organization charts and planning and control systems. In 1977, for example, Vernon observed that US MNCs 'could be counted on to use unusually elaborate tables of organizational job descriptions and operating procedures, and to feel uncomfortable in the presence of more ambiguous systems of control'. The profusion of reports and memos pushed US MNCs to hire legions of managers to sort, process and distribute them. Incidentally, the concurrent development of scientific techniques of management – that is, portfolio planning, linear programming – changed management from a job to a profession and soon provided the *raison d'être* of the Master of Business Administration (MBA) degree.

The third wave of international expansion was that of Japanese firms (see MANAGEMENT IN JAPAN). Facing the exact opposite environment that had earlier challenged European firms, the typical Japanese MNC adopted a structure that was the antithesis of that used by European MNCs. Remarkable liberalization of international trade, notably that overseen by GATT, guaranteed foreign market access and lower tariffs. Japanese firms thus had the unprecedented option to remain at home, construct modern plants of tremendous scale, tap a homogeneous workforce, and use exports rather than local production to serve foreign consumers. Later developments moderated Japanese firms' degrees of freedom – that is, the Voluntary Export Agreement between the US and Japanese auto-makers in the early 1980s – but these policies were uncommon. More potentially daunting to integration, however, was the long held notion that consumer preferences are differentiated by national culture. Japanese MNCs rejected this notion, believing and repeatedly proving that a high quality, low cost product denationalizes consumers' preferences. The final hurdle to full integration – the economics of transportation and communication – became less important as new technologies reduced the marginal cost of each. So, given an environment that encouraged and rewarded extreme integration along with the extraordinary linkage of high quality and low cost, Japanese MNCs disregarded strategic and organizational differentiation for the Holy Grail of integration. A casual glance at most Japanese firms' structure highlights these developments. Implementing integration led to centralized structures that emphasized efficiency in all actions; thus functional organizations with an extreme degree of specialization and precisely defined division of work prevail.

5 The dawn of the 'fourth wave'

Other entries in the encyclopedia detail the specifics of environmental and strategic change in the global market (see GLOBAL STRATEGIC PLANNING). They shrewdly pinpoint the connection of an MNC's strategies to forces such as the consolidation of the global village, growing breadth and depth of linkages among political, economic and cultural dimensions, and the redrawing of the geography of capitalism following the liberation of 3 billion customers in China, India, Indonesia, South America, eastern Europe and the former USSR. The influence of these events on the nature of organization innovation is undeniable. These and other changes are creating radically new ways to conceive of the division of labour in the MNC. Simply put, this revolution is ushering in the 'fourth wave' of organization in an MNC. The ascendancy

of the information economy is converting wealth creation in the MNC from securing natural resources and physical labour to developing knowledge, accumulating intellectual capital and engineering its distribution. Indeed, the ramifications of the digitized revolution to organizational innovation evoke those unleashed by its predecessor, the industrial revolution, on the conception and division of work.

Quantum advances in computer and telecommunication technology are transforming the fabric of the market. For the MNCs, information technologies are redefining the economics of creating, sorting, storing and shipping knowledge, and as such, the economics of organization. Hierarchies, whether functional, divisional, matrix or hybrid, use tremendous resources to keep the specialized scheme of boxes, layers and levels from spiralling out of control. For instance, the vertical structures of Figures 1–5 require legions of managers to administer the flood of memos that track the performance of far-flung units. This bureaucracy, by demanding exhaustive documentation, preserves the unity of command in the MNC. The engine of the information era – computers – transposes this equation. Coordinating specialized activities is information intensive. Computers continually improve the efficiency and effectiveness of coordination. As the costs of computers and communication drop, the specialized bureaucracy of the vertical hierarchy loses its comparative advantage in coordinating the dispersed units of the MNC.

The low start-up and ever diminishing marginal costs of information technology, versus the requisite large-scale plant, equipment and staff of the industrial era, reduce the entry and mobility barriers of international competition. Consider, for instance, the time-line of innovation. The historic duration of product life cycles made periodic design brilliance sufficient to sustain an MNC's competitiveness. The emerging global market, however, makes advantage a function of continuous upgrading, or put it another way, perpetual innovation. New products, no matter how complicated, can be developed much more quickly. Powerful computer design systems replace with a click of a mouse days of laborious work done on hundreds of blackboards. 'Visual engineering' on video screens, for example, is helping Ford Motor Company reduce the time it takes to test physical prototypes from months in the industrial era to eight hours via computer simulations in the information era. Visual engineering, CAD/CAM and similar systems can reduce manufacturing costs by up to 75 per cent, reduce engineering changes by 70 per cent, cut product development time by 30 to 70 per cent, and slash time to market by 20 to 90 per cent. Furthermore, cross-border research programmes, global standardization and benchmarking speed the flow of products to market. Finally, artificial intelligence software, particularly expert systems, better shepherd product design and delivery. Given competitive standards, an MNC has no choice other than to develop swiftly, test and launch innovative products simultaneously across markets. The piecemeal country-by-country product releases of the past are now too expensive and too helpful to rivals.

The division of labour under systems of perpetual innovation imposes stiff organizational requirements. An MNC needs a structure that allows it to develop effectively and distribute efficiently a stream of innovations faster than rivals can imitate or surpass them. The looming challenges and opportunities of the 'fourth wave' are setting unprecedented standards of organization innovation. Plainly put, an MNC must develop a structure that can integrate activities so that it gains available scale and scope economies while simultaneously responding to the diversity of preferences of product and geographic markets through differentiated units. Essentially, the MNC must move from conceiving activity in terms of sequential value chain functions to a synchrony of business processes. Markets now deliver premium returns less to MNCs who plan carefully and act deliberately than to those that quickly respond to changing circumstances. In effect, environmental trends are reaffirming the adage that 'time is money'. The expanding power of computers and telecommunications compels and enables re-engineering the division of labour in an MNC

in unprecedented formats. The agile organization that drives rapid product development, flexible production systems, and fluid marketing transitions is ushering in an era where entrepreneurialism prevails over bureaucracy.

The specifics of this passage to our conception of organization in the MNC are revolutionary. Percy Barnevik, CEO of ABB, provides a measure of the scale of change, explaining that structure in the MNC must somehow resolve the dilemma of simultaneously being 'global and local, big and small, radically decentralized with centralized reporting and control' (*Harvard Business Review*, March–April 1991: 95). As hard as this task sounds in theory, the experiences of MNCs suggest that it is infinitely harder in practice. Consider the ordeals of Philips, IBM and Matsushita. After investing over 100 years of time and talent into building an organization envied for its local responsiveness, Philips has been in a decade-long struggle to integrate its differentiated units. IBM is rethinking its purpose, moving from obsolescent excellence in marrying mass production and mass distribution to devise a structure that engenders entrepreneurialism. Finally, following decades of success through integration, Matsushita is seeking ways to decentralize decision making from its monolithic headquarters to wanting subsidiaries. The search for the structural Grail has led these MNCs, once heralded for their organization prowess, to fire thousands of workers and helplessly watch investors shave billions off their market valuation.

Structure in the fourth wave

Executives of many MNCs are literally riding the so-called 'reorganization merry-go-round'. They experiment with various patterns of boxes, lines and layers, believing that a new and improved scheme will turbo-charge their organization. They draw and redraw charts that create high-power and high-profile teams to whip around the process, re-engineer information systems to generate more reports faster, and streamline the chain of command to reduce bureaucracy. Despite Herculean efforts, the clarity of their structures deteriorates and the spectre of the Tower of Babel looms larger.

Thwarting the efforts of many firms is the monistic disposition of their existing structures. An MNC's choice of a functional, divisional or hybrid structure makes functions, products or markets predominant. As we saw in Caterpillar's structure in Figure 6, subordinated dimensions are added if and where needed. In practice, the choice of the primary, secondary and tertiary orientation followed from the MNC's strategy and environment. More philosophically, the MNC's choice flowed from the doctrine that it cannot emphasize two or three dimensions simultaneously. The functions of a monistic structure – vertical scheme of roles, relations and routines, explicit hierarchy of authority, unity of command and control – require that resources, information and decisions travel clearly marked paths between superiors and subordinates. In stable environments, the resulting coherence of actions in, say, a product structure, offsets the expense of the corresponding inefficiencies in subordinated functional and market units. However, in dynamic environments, where information technology makes functions, products and markets indivisible, a monistic command and control structure makes divisional inefficiencies unendurable. Consequently, a monistic structure cannot cultivate the organizational capacities – entrepreneurialism, multidisciplinarian perspectives and pluralism – that the emerging environment requires. Additionally, turbocharging a monistic format by simply overlaying pluralistic devices tends to convert its strengths into weaknesses: rules degenerate into suggestions, relationships lapse into alliances, routines become arbitrary and the chain of command ruptures.

If an MNC is to resolve the evolving integration–differentiation dilemma by simultaneously managing functional, product and area matters, its organizational mentality must shift from one of a monistic hierarchy of vertical control to a pluralistic heterarchy of horizontal governance. The axis of orientation for an MNC's structure in the industrial era was vertical. The information era dictates rotating the axis until it becomes horizontal. Suggested designations for the logic of structure in the fourth wave include the time-based, total quality management, business-process redesign, horizontal, re-engineered, post-

1. *Organize around process, not functions.* Instead of creating a structure around functions or departments, build the company around its three to five core processes with specific performance goals. Appoint a manager or team as the 'owner' of each core process.

2. *Flatten the organizational hierarchy.* To reduce supervision, combine fragmented tasks, eliminate work that fails to add value and cut the activities within each process to a minimum.

3. *Use multidisciplinary teams to manage everything.* Make diverse teams the main building blocks of organization. Limit supervisory roles by making the team manage itself. Use as few teams as possible to perform an entire process. Hold it accountable for measurable performance goals.

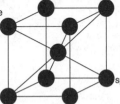

4. *Let customers drive performance.* Make appreciation or profitability – the primary Profits will come and stock will rise if the customers' satisfaction – not stock driver and measure of performances. customers are satisfied.

5. *Reward team performance.* Change team performance, not just individual develop multiple skills rather than it with empowerment and compensation. the appraisal and pay systems to reward performance. Encourage staffers to specialized knowledge. Reward them for

6. *Maximize suppliers and customer contact.* Bring employees into direct, regular contact with suppliers and customers. Add suppliers and customer representatives as members of in-house teams when they can be of service.

7. *Revamp employee systems.* Question the conventional methods of training, appraisal, pay and budgeting to support the new structure and link it to external benchmark like customer satisfaction. Resist the temptation to spoon-feed sanitized information on a 'need-to-know' basis.

Figure 8 Design principles of the network structure

industrial, cluster, self-designing, heterarchy and information-based organization. Notwithstanding distinctions, these ideas fall under the conceptual umbrella of the network structure.

6 The network structure

In some MNCs the network denotes informal, *ad hoc* ties among executives – that is, floating teams that span functions, businesses and products. In others, the network alludes to the joint ventures that comprise its web of external relationships. Finally, in some firms, the network evokes images of re-engineered information processing. Semantics aside, the network has general properties and design principles (see Figure 8).

The task of the network is direct: to enable executives to retain local flexibility while optimizing global scale without forfeiting speed, facility or breadth of perspective in fast-changing markets. To do so requires relentlessly decentralizing responsibility, authority and accountability as far into the MNC as possible and then connecting the resulting plurality of local, regional and global units so that each unit can apply leverage to peripheral and core competencies. The network dismisses the bureaucratic tendency of an MNC's breadth and depth to slow decisions. The network re-engineers an MNC so its size does not sacrifice the speed, flexibility and self-

confidence of an entrepreneurial unit. The network allows dynamic, small units to tap bits of specialized information, wherever they exist in the MNC. The network recasts the distribution of power so that these units have the authority to use this data to act quickly without necessarily consulting superiors. Rather than giving workers forms to fill to feed the bureaucracy, the network encourages defining clear tasks, clean accountability and maximum degree of freedom. Decomposing the levels of bureaucracy into cells of entrepreneurialism – ABB, for example, has over 5,200 separate profit centres that average just fifty employees apiece – ruthlessly decentralizes authority to the lowest possible level, thereby moving decisions as near as possible to the market. Rather than managing to avoid disasters, as is the bias in a monistic structure, the network gives managers the licence for creative improvisation based on solid standards.

The chart of a network is dramatically unlike that of a traditional structure (see Figure 9). The architecture of a network is no longer defined by a vertical hierarchy with multiple levels, specialized tasks and explicit chain of command, but a flat, horizontal heterarchy that has few formal levels, broad spans of control, diffused responsibility, elaborate linkages and a tacit chain of command. The network is not a new layer of bureaucracy. Instead, it eliminates the specialized

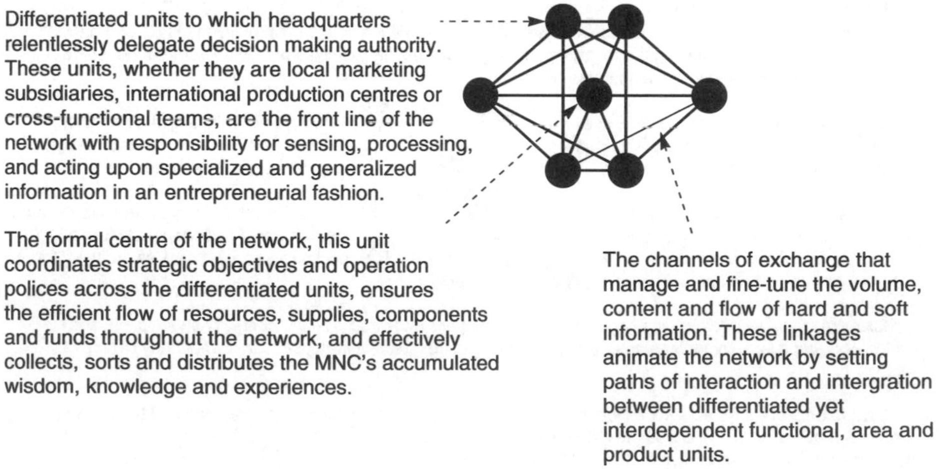

Differentiated units to which headquarters relentlessly delegate decision making authority. These units, whether they are local marketing subsidiaries, international production centres or cross-functional teams, are the front line of the network with responsibility for sensing, processing, and acting upon specialized and generalized information in an entrepreneurial fashion.

The formal centre of the network, this unit coordinates strategic objectives and operation polices across the differentiated units, ensures the efficient flow of resources, supplies, components and funds throughout the network, and effectively collects, sorts and distributes the MNC's accumulated wisdom, knowledge and experiences.

The channels of exchange that manage and fine-tune the volume, content and flow of hard and soft information. These linkages animate the network by setting paths of interaction and intergration between differentiated yet interdependent functional, area and product units.

Figure 9 A simple conceptualization of the network structure

departmental boundaries of the vertical hierarchy. Nor is the network a subversive means to wrest authority from weak units of the MNC. Rather, it identifies and elicits disagreements between functions, business units and product groups, and provides paths to resolve the dilemma created by their competing calls for integration or differentiation.

The network blurs both internal and external boundaries. Internally, moving from the benevolent fascism of a monistic structure to the vibrant pluralism of a network de-emphasizes rigid hierarchial channels in favour of cross-unit connections. In traditional structures, executives knew precisely where manufacturing 'ended' and marketing 'began'; in the network, these sequential terms are abandoned in favour of the synchronicity of business process management. Externally, the MNC's long-sacred boundaries are blurring, as formal ties with suppliers, buyers and rivals become more the norm than the exception. Value-added partnerships with vendors and customers, alliances with rivals, and other unprecedented relationships are obscuring which activities fall under whose authority. Collaboration with external players, many of whom are direct competitors, moves points of the value chain from 'at our own discretion' to real time interaction with partners stationed around the world. The arrival of real time decision making as the benchmark penalizes conferring with headquarters. Executives straddling the boundary of the firm must command the specialized knowledge and general perspective to act with authority.

The lifeblood of the network: information

The network's virtues – flexibility and fluidity of small units – are manifest in entrepreneurial profit centres. These centres' quasi-autonomous status imposes stiff communication standards. The tendency of a network's blueprint to change often reduces the usefulness of monistic command and control techniques. The solution to this dilemma is plain: share information swiftly and thoroughly among members of the network. Information must flow freely across functions,

products and businesses, moving effortlessly from where developed to where needed. The nature of data distribution influences the speed and accuracy of decision making in the network. Especially in the MNC, where the barriers of distance, language, culture and time distort information flows, real time collection and distribution of data is vital. Giving members of the network the same data simultaneously reduces the temptation for manipulation and the potential for distortion. Democratic data distribution pre-empts the odds of distracting personal conflicts or damaging turf battles over 'who gets what information when and why'. Instead, the network converts this logic to 'what do we know and what do we do', thereby shifting executives' attention from the selectivity or secrecy of the data flow to the clarity and substance of decision making.

Information technology is the means to collect and distribute hard data in the network in real time. Interconnecting the network's units are small bits of hard data transmitted at high baud rates that measure the latest planning, budget and performance outcomes. Hard data, always a powerful tool of control, takes on a broad mission in the network. Monitoring critical indicators of their profit centre, national market and global market updates executives on their absolute and relative performance. Reporting and analysing critical indicators enriches their perspective by making managers articulate the linkages between their unit and the network. Rigorous data management makes visible the invisible hand of the network, a vital discipline to check its entrepreneurial bent. For example, ABB manages the data demands of its sprawling network through 'Abacus', a centralized reporting system that collects performance data on the company's 5,200 profit centres, compares them with budgets and forecasts, converts them into dollars to enable cross-border analyses, and consolidates or breaks them down by segment, country and local company. Managers thus have the option to aggregate and desegregate data by business segments, national markets and companies within countries. No longer do they wait for a call from concerned superiors. A manager can quickly find out to the day, week or month how their unit's performance ranks with any other ABB profit centre in the world.

The diffusion of information, accountability and power is redefining the role of MNC's headquarters. The image of headquarters – long seen as the career capstone in the vertical structure – changes in the network. Centralized control requires a specialized bureaucracy that frustrates entrepreneurialism. Ensuring a flexible network requires a minimum of headquarters staff to disturb, or as some say disrupt, the activities of the profit centres. Rather than careful deliberations, the role of headquarters in the network is improving the efficiency of data exchange and ensuring the effectiveness of decision making. To do so means laying waste to the traditionally high head counts at headquarters. The radical changes inspired by ABB's adoption of a network dramatize this transition. Upon defining the tasks, units and connections of their network, top management reduced headquarters staff for the four business groups from 800 to 100 in Switzerland, 900 to 88 in the USA, 1,600 to 100 in Germany, and 880 to 25 in Finland. As Percy Barnevik, CEO of ABB, explained, installing a network empowers a CEO to go 'into any traditionally centralized corporation and cut its headquarter staff by 90 per cent in one year' (*International Management* September 1992: 82).

Reducing head counts is also changing the physical shape of headquarters. In the vertical MNCs, housing large staffs required towering skyscrapers or sprawling corporate campuses. Now, falling staff levels along with computer and telecommunication advances are 'redefining an MNC's headquarters into a suite of rooms in an office park near an international airport – a communication centre where many of the web's threads intersect' (Reich 1991). For instance, beginning in 1959, DuPont Europe (see E.I. DU PONT DE NEMOURS AND CO.) ran its continental operations from several buildings scattered throughout Geneva. In 1988, DuPont combined these units in a new office overlooking the airport and plugged in more than two computers for every employee. Remarkable changes happened after the move. Originally, executives'

anticipation of continuing staff increases led them to advise the architect 'the bigger the better'. Also, DuPont was then a centralized organization whose functional division of labour required a large, specialized bureaucracy. As such, Don Linsenmann, managing director of Lycra Europe, explained that Du-Pont Europe built a larger than needed complex that in hindsight had too many individual offices and too few conference rooms. Du-Pont's ongoing transformation into the 'most flexible, aggressive, responsive, and youngest 200-year-old company in the world' (declaration from the 1992 Annual Report of the Du-Pont Corporation) rests on rotating horizontally the axis of its organization. Installing a network has led to staff reductions and prompted DuPont Europe already to lease two floors of its complex to the United Nations.

If we were focusing on the monistic structure, we would halt our analysis of the role of information at the concept of hard data. In the realm of vertical hierarchies and militaristic chains of command, hard data sets the 'pulse' of information exchange. Unquestionably, analytical content is vital as the network processes more and more data. Accelerating the information metabolism of the network, however, raises the temperature of the organization. The risk that frenetic exchange of increasing volumes of hard data overwhelms the network's processing capacity requires complementary information. Searching for complements turns our attention to the software side of the network, notably knowledge conveyed through 'soft data'. More precisely, the network requires developing professional trust and empathy that enable executives to raze vertical boundaries. Doing so allows managers from function, market and product groups to see the MNC through various viewpoints and understand more intuitively the challenges, constraints and concerns of their counterparts in the network. Although some may counter that hard data more than meets this mission, efficient processing does not guarantee effective perception; hard data provides neither static nor dynamic cues thus depriving users of social context information. The vestiges of long-standing departmental boundaries fan the cynicism of malfunctioning groups which, if unattended, erodes the personal commitment needed to integrate the network. More challenging for the MNC is the puzzle of a multicultural workforce. Mixing nationalities brings to the forefront differing cultural attitudes on the 'right' way to do business. Hoping that the righteousness of hard data solves this jigsaw runs the risk of a network corroded by cultural misperceptions. Soft data, by letting managers deal openly with cultural diversity, boost the odds of useful exchanges between managers of different nationalities (see CULTURE, CROSS-NATIONAL).

In a world free of the dimensions of time and distance, an MNC would regulate the temperature of the network via direct communication among managers. In reality, mobilizing tens, hundreds or thousands of managers who are spread over thousands of miles to convene in order to converse is an ambition that may be met, at best, quarterly. For instance, 3M Europe only convenes the ten to fifteen members of each of its roughly fifty European Management Action Teams three or four times each year. Competitive rivalry does not forgive the rationalization that the network cannot work if people cannot meet. Multinational executives are jumping this hurdle by modernizing the simple technique of telephoning. Audio and video conference calls, person-to-person calls, voice-mail, and electronic-mail create a powerful medium of interface that allows executives to deal better with hard data by exchanging soft data. While seemingly modest devices, telecommunications build trust and camaraderie among members of the network.

Interestingly, the crucial role of soft data is leading non-US or UK MNCs to set English as their official language. The usefulness of interpersonal interaction in a network depends on removing the psychological barriers that some languages unavoidably elicit, which stifle communication. For instance, Leonardo Vannotti, executive board member of ABB, explained his firm's decision to abandon German for English by noting that 'German is a very structured language and when speaking it, it is difficult to be informal, which is an absolute necessity for a group trying to foster a multinational culture' (Arbose 1988: 30).

The role of people in the network

Looking at Figure 9 may prompt some readers to wonder what happened to the vast 'middle' of traditional organization structures. Simply put, the network has no such middle. The legions of mid-level managers who gathered, processed and transmitted information between specialized subordinates and generalist superiors paralysed the network. The entrepreneurialism of the network coupled with information technology culminates in a structure with neither justification nor need for many mid-level managers. In the USA, at least, this has proven true with force: the American Management Association reported that, while middle managers arc about 5 per cent of the workforce, they accounted for 22 per cent of layoffs in 1992.

While the initial focus is on middle-managers, soon no level will be sacred. Re-engineering the MNC into a network of small, quasi-autonomous nodes exposes those levels that frustrate decision making. The network inspires an ultimately simple solution: eliminate levels from the top, middle and bottom of the organization. Already many MNCs have reduced the number of levels by 25 to 50 per cent. General Motors (see GENERAL MOTORS CORPORATION) has eliminated nine of its twenty-eight levels and has no plans to stop. Its rival Toyota has dropped from over twenty to eleven layers. In consumer electronics, Matsushita is eliminating an entire level of senior management between the president's office and the product divisions; it is also rationalizing dozens of vaguely defined product operations into ten basic lines, each with more accountability and authority, and consolidating the company's twenty-seven research laboratories into two. In consumer products, Procter & Gamble's redesign of the way it develops, manufactures, distributes, prices, markets and sells products eliminated three levels of its management structure. Jack Welch, CEO of GE, has reduced GE's structure from nine to four layers in moving towards his ambition of one layer. Additionally, he is passionate about preventing their resurrection: 'We used to have things like department managers, section managers, subsection managers, unit managers, supervisors. We're driving those titles out. . . . We used to go from the CEO to sectors, to groups, to businesses. We now go from the CEO to businesses. Nothing else. There is nothing else. Zero' (GE, Harvard Business School, case no. 9-381-248).

Who will then staff the network? Unlike the vertical hierarchy's need for people who were focused, precise and analytical, the network's tasks require people who are adaptable, intuitive, and can symbolically process reams of diverse information. Drucker warns that the peculiar tasks of the network mean that 'being an educated person no longer is adequate' (Drucker 1991: 88–97) in becoming or performing as an executive. The tasks of the network require flexible individuals who can operate in multicultural environments and use a Zen-like synthesis of the science and art of management in devising innovations, taking risks, developing teams, and motivating workers. The era of the professional manager is surrendering to the age of the 'technopreneur'. Knowledge workers who integrate technological proficiency, functional expertise and soft skills will get the corporate jobs of tomorrow. More precisely, Percy Barnevik noted that ABB's executive recruitment 'sought people capable of becoming superstars . . . . tough skinned individuals, who were fast on their feet, had good technical and commercial backgrounds, and had demonstrated the ability to lead others. . . . It is essential that we have managers who are open and generous and capable of thinking in group terms' (Arbose 1988: 27). In effect, staffing the network will be 'change agents', with multiple competencies rather than narrow specialities.

Teams today, here tomorrow

The unprecedented tasks of the network do create points of vulnerability: two stand out. Excessive attention to eliminating elements of the vertical hierarchy can lead managers to misconstrue their role in a newly adopted horizontal network. Often, managers surmise that diluting the formal functional, area or product boundaries of the vertical structure eliminates differences of authority, talent or perspective as sources of friction. The exact opposite happens in the network. Deleting the management-by-memo tendency of a bureaucracy makes disagreement more visible. The network's performance, however, depends on sustaining creative tension among divergent but complementary skills and viewpoints. The increased uncertainty of tasks, roles and outcomes of work boosts the odds of personal clashes precisely because the network pushes executives to rely on eye-to-eye or voice-to-voice resolution.

The extreme decentralization in a network sets the managers of subsidiaries as decision makers. If unattended, regional and local managers may act contrary to pan-MNC goals. Indeed, the absence of a well-specified structure gives managers the latitude to subvert roles and amplify rules to realize personal agendas. Increasing the likelihood of subversion are units whose resources make them powerful entities in their own right. For example, ABB's German subsidiary has over 35,000 employees and generates nearly a third of the total company revenues of $30 billion. The endemic ambiguity of a network gives ABB Germany the opening, if it so wanted, to treat the core as less than the centre of integration and more as the means to achieve its ends.

A network must build the capacity to resolve conflicts between the goals and strategies of members and lessen any ambiguity over the locus of responsibility. The urgency of resolving tension between differentiated tasks with the need for an integrative vision explains why multidisciplinary teams are the preferred form of integration in the network. Teams enhance an MNC's capacity to integrate information directly across differentiated units without sending it to the core for review, as such teams force decision making down at least another level. Teams provide a low cost high impact mechanism to unite people with different yet complementary skills. For the MNCs, teams provide a way to mix executives of different nationalities without worry of formal dominance by a particular country. Teams can transform the complexity of differing economic, political and cultural conditions into a point of innovation; linking diverse units stimulates learning and diffuses ideas. Teams help executives learn the network's norms and rules, thereby obviating the need for formal procedure and direct supervision. Finally, contrary to popular fears, teams do not preclude individual opportunity. Teams blossom wherever boundaries inhibit the entrepreneurialism of the network.

Limits to the network

Many managers are understandably reluctant to conceive of structure in ways that radically differ from vertical formats. When called to adopt the network, executives are being called to abandon the decades-old idea of structure as a precise statement of rank, power and rules, in favour of the new-age notion of structure as a blend of mutual understanding and shared responsibility. Going from 'command and control' to 'propose and encourage' requires a leap of faith many dread making. For example, in the midst of Caterpillar's mid-1980s reorganization, one executive remarked that:

> Short of replacing a couple of generations of managers, we'll never be able to make such a dramatic change in our management style and values. Despite our historic claim that people are our number one asset, we always promoted the guys who could kick butt and get the product out the door. Now we want to introduce new technology and emphasize employee involvement. Well we planted an oak and got an oak. It's too late to wish it was an elm.
> (Caterpillar Tractor Co., Harvard Business School, Case no. 9-385-276

MNCs use several approaches to inspire executives. A fortunate few begin with a clean slate; their only constraint is imagination. Most MNCs face a tougher campaign, reorganizing in the face of the firm's heritage of administrative precedents. The complexity of reorganizing thousands of workers strewn about the globe typically leads executives

back to the maps shown in Figures 1–5 in search of incremental ways to rotate the axis of their structure. Turbo-charge, not transformation, becomes the point of innovation.

Executives tinker with the scheme of the hierarchy, depth and breadth of control, or make-up of cross-departmental teams. A common response is an MNC trumpeting a newly-formed team with the charter to operate horizontally. The rest of the structure is unchanged in the hope that this pseudo-network inspires emulation by the rank and file. In effect, the day-to-day routine remains vertically organized; employees look not to each other but up to their boss. There may be general awareness of the firm's transition to a network, but often this fades into the background of getting through the day, the month and the quarter. Simply put, thwarting turbo-charging is the virtuous vice of verticality: segmenting specialized people doing specialized jobs. Year upon year of vertical specialization culminates in a phenomenon called 'chimneys' by Ford Motor Company, 'functional silos' by McDonnell Douglas, and towers, foxholes or bunkers by others. Whatever the idiom, the outcome is constant: managers forfeit the vision to see from their department to the firm, the confidence to question authority and the courage to take chances.

Unless executives directly assault these boundaries, vertical mentalities ransack the network. Regrettably, the difficulty in defining these boundaries pales in comparison to changing them. Edwin Artzt, CEO of Procter & Gamble, notes that 'the hardest thing for a company is to change its thinking'. To do so, he adds, means that the firms 'have to have rules that give us intellectual permission to make changes' (Saporito 1994). In effect, large MNCs face the task of making a rule to make rule-breaking acceptable. MNCs' actions propose that transforming the hierarchy into a heterarchy depends on redefining the concepts of management through unprecedented methods. Jack Welch, for example, launched 'Work-Out' to begin installing a network in GE. Work-Out assembles a cross-section of fifty to one hundred employees for two to three day meetings during which the group candidly discusses the usefulness of prevailing rules of administration and proposes superior management practices. It is still uncertain whether group therapy will convert specialists who have spent their careers climbing the ladder of success. However, Work-Out is redefining the relationship between boss and worker and improving the 'speed, simplicity and self-confidence' of GE's emerging network.

Apart from chimneys, there are general concerns that inevitably limit an MNC's use of the network. The mechanics of time bound the network's functional potential. The typical MNC's operations span many time zones. Despite tremendous progress in information technology, the relativity of time precludes the network's objective: real time decision making. Scott Bihl, a director of General Motors European Coordination Centre, noted that 'When the European operation was handled from New York, problems arose because of the six-hour time lag. Working in Europe you had a two-hour window in which you could transmit information to New York. The New York people could rarely spin a decision in two hours. . . consequently you couldn't do things in one day; it was a two-day process at best' (*Euromoney*, February 1988). Also, there are only so many practical time slots in which managers can talk to counterparts. More often than not, one manager is anxious to go home while the other is just arriving at work. True, calls may be forwarded, however, the state of some technologies, such as video conferencing, delays this eventuality. Armstrong World Industries' adoption of global conference calls, for example, soon tested practical limits. The span of its network across the USA, Europe and the Pacific made 7 a.m. Pennsylvania time the most convenient time for the bi-monthly conference call.

Perhaps the ultimate boundary on an MNC's network is the typical manager's finite cognitive capacity to perceive and process hard and soft data. The network explodes the number of pertinent points of hard data. For instance, ABB's 5,200 profit centres create a data matrix of imposing arithmetic size and mind-boggling exponential scale. No matter how quickly computers create, sort,

store and ship data or how small telecommunications shrink the world, the bounded rationality of managers constrains the practical density of a network. Compounding limits on cognition is the persistence of psychic distance in international business. A manager's socialization in a particular cognitive cluster – that is, Anglo, Arab, Germanic, Confucian – imbues them with a unique 'cognitive map' of the principles of management (see CULTURE, CROSS-NATIONAL). The same bit of data may be perceived and acted upon differently by members of the same network due to each manager's particular cognitive map. Arguably, movement toward the global village, by converging management principles toward a single standard, reduces psychic distance. However, the recent addition of three billion 'capitalists' from decidedly non-Western markets prolongs the process. Also, the global village may be more than a little mythical. Nationalism, or tribalism as some prophesize, is influenced by, but ultimately immune to, globalization. As a marker for this state of affairs, consider that the world's population speaks over 6,000 languages and thousands more dialects. Even within Europe, a highly integrated market, the Indo-European language family has forty-six classes. Although information technology is shrinking the physical dimensions of the world, its influence on the cognitive maps of multinational operations is, at best, generational.

The combination of the relativity of time, bounded rationality, and psychic distance restricts the practical scale of a network in the MNC. Consider, for example, the valiant efforts of ABB's top management. When first designed, the global matrix meant that every three weeks the members of the executive committee met for a full day at a different site in the world. CEO Percy Barnevik estimated he was on the road 200 days a year but wryly noted that 'I travel a lot, but I'm normally in my office two days a week – Saturday and Sunday' (Asea Brown Boveri, Harvard Business School, case no. 9-192-139: 5). Such demands erode the vitality of the network. Most, if not all, international executives would testify that ceaseless time zone changes, long flight time, and day upon day away from home exact a heavy toll. Moreover, the network intensifies this toll. Its emphasis on interpersonal skills and cultural sensitivity leaves no room for the agitation or exhaustion that are the handmaidens of international travel.

7 Conclusion

We saw earlier that MNCs often used a plurality of dimensions to design an ostensibly monistic structure. Only in theory does the pure form of a structure exist. Reality tends towards entropy, and structure in the MNC tends towards hybrid forms. Therefore, most MNCs experiment with the network, seeking horizontal traits – that is, cross-functional teams, Work-Out, information technology – that can be melded onto the hierarchy. In effect, the present task is designing a vertical network.

Consider ABB's choice. Abacus kept tight rein on hard data but the global scope of the matrix inundated managers with a tidal wave of soft data. So, commencing 1 October 1993 ABB adopted regional divisions, integrating differentiated national units into Europe, the Americas or Asia-Pacific. ABB also consolidated industrial product segments, streamlining six segments to four. Within the segments, the sixty-five global business areas were cut to fifty. For the record, analysts projected these changes would reduce ABB's profits by 37 per cent in 1993 but would more than double them in 1994.

The careful reader might presume ABB's apparent return to a more traditional area division structure signifies the impracticality of a network. Instead, the re-engineered network of ABB, along with similar actions by other MNCs, suggests that the mandate of the network organization in the fourth wave is shifting from *think global, act local* to *think globally, coordinate regionally, act locally*. Mechanically, hard data will create global consciousness, soft data will honour regional parameters, and entrepreneurial profit centres will provide the local touch. In effect, MNCs are adjusting the presently unrealistic ambitions of the global network. Factors that wreck

the global network that the MNC can change – such as chimneys – are being demolished. However, those factors that limit the global network that the MNC cannot so easily change – time, bounded rationality, psychic distance – endorse adaptations like regional networks.

In a larger sense, some may say that ABB's experience reinforces other MNCs' suspicion of the network. This, in turn, reinforces their preference to turbo-charge the vertical structure. In practice, this is the favoured transition method. In principle, however, this will eventually prove to be a ruinous plan. A turbo-charged structure ultimately falls victim to the fatal flaw of the matrix structure: it leaves intact the command and control philosophy of the vertical hierarchy. Biasing the axis of the organization towards the horizontal is inevitably a poor substitute to full rotation. The environmental, technological and strategic forces that are ushering in the fourth wave have hit critical mass. If, as we expect, MNCs that transform rather than turbo-charge produce more, higher value output with fewer workers, then other MNCs will have no option other than imitation. Already evidence suggests as much. A study of 367 large companies by Brynjolfsson and Hitt (1993) found that the higher the investment in computers and telecommunications, the better the firm's performance. Indeed, the average gross annual return on investment in information technology was 81 per cent for manufacturing and service companies together. As this relationship clarifies – it took two decades to reap the full benefits of investment in electricity, the trigger of the Industrial Revolution, in terms of the productivity of the new division of labour in newly electrified factories – MNCs structured horizontally will ruthlessly challenge the competitiveness of rivals who remain vertically organized.

More precisely, we see the latter moving from leery believers to faithful disciples. Conversion, perhaps long avoided, will ultimately follow as their financial performance erodes under the competitive challenges of the early adopters of the network. Edwin Artz, CEO of Procter & Gamble, for instance, explained that his company's long insular culture, resistant to any rotation of its historic vertical axis, is now moving horizontally. Compelling this change was the cognitive fallout of Procter & Gamble's deteriorating performance, or as Mr Artzt noted, 'We have a much better view of our own mortality and that is a great reliever of arrogance' (Saporito 1994). Organizationally, Procter & Gamble's new found modesty led to stressing a regional network over its traditional country-by-country structure. Already, executives report that the regional network presently handles twice the business the company is now doing with the same number of staff. Boosting Procter & Gamble's information metabolism through additional information technology and further re-engineering of the management process, executives expect, will enable it to do more with less.

MNCs experiment with many forms of structures. So too will they experiment with many forms of the network. We discussed that the appropriate format depends on external and internal conditions. The previous waves of environmental, technological and strategic change affirmed that the prevailing standard of organization innovation is not timeless. In the short term, firms emulate successful counterparts. As more MNCs adopt the revolutionary innovativeness of the network, they will dilute the competitive edge it confers. In the longer term, relentless change will relentlessly create functional, product or area contingencies that exceed the network's capabilities. It is conceivable that in a few years, more stable conditions will let some MNCs cycle back to the vertical hierarchy. Then again, it is entirely possible that circumstances will permit structures whose forms are presently inconceivable. The current quest of the Eastman Kodak Company (see EASTMAN KODAK CO.) provides an inkling of this improbability. It spun-off Eastman Chemical Co., a $3.5 billion unit, as a stand-alone company on 1 January 1994.

The first order of business for the new company was reorganizing the vertical structure into a network. President Ernest Deavenport, Jr explained the design logic with an unprecedented metaphor: 'Our organization chart is now called the pizza chart because it

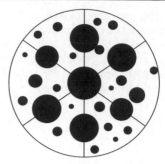

Figure 10 The pizza structure of Eastman Chemical Co.

looks likes a pizza with a lot of pepperoni sitting on it. We did it in a circle to show that everyone is equal in the organization. No one dominates the other. The white space inside the circles is more important than the lines'. Making the 'pizza' work meant replacing several of the company's senior vice-presidents in charge of key business functions with self-directed work teams. Mr Deavenport explained that the move 'was the most dramatic change in the company's seventy year history... it makes people take off their organizational hats and put on their team hats. It gives people a much broader perspective and forces decision making down at least another level' (Byrne 1993). Even further away from prevailing concepts of structure is the possibility of a world of networked one-person companies. A global consortium of experts, united to design the next product generation, exchange information and specifications over the Internet. When a snag happens, an information broker electronically locates someone with the requisite knowledge and connects them to the team. Upon completing its mission, the 'organization' disbands. Set free, cyber-executives will prepare for the next 'union', honing skills and scanning markets.

Admittedly, notions of one-person companies seem rather far-fetched; but five years ago, the concept of a 'pizza' structure was just as ludicrous. As the fallout of the information era spirals with the predictability of chaos theory, the only limitation of our conception of organization may be our imagination. Already, the leaders of MNCs are tackling this barrier. Work-Out was the initial step for GE to purge decades of the 'right way' to manage. Not content to stand still, Jack Welch, CEO of GE, coined a new term to describe the ultimate principle of the network: *boundarylessness*. More precisely, in GE's 1990 annual report, Jack Welch described this logic as follows:

> Our dream for the 1990s is a boundaryless company. . .where we knock down the walls that separate us from each other on the inside and from our key constituents on the outside. The demands of global markets and rivals mean that GE must remove the barriers among traditional functions, recognize no distinctions between domestic and international operations, and ignore or erase group labels such as management, salaried or hourly, which get in the way of people working together.
>
> (GE Annual Report 1990)

As unpredictable as the precise trigger of organization change in the MNC – faltering performance, competitive vulnerability, visionary executives, a new-found sense of humility or simply a leap of faith – is the certainty of the outcome. Executives will return to the blackboard, or more appropriately, the computer, to design a structure that works. This reading has tried to create a perspective on this fascinating process by helping aspiring and practising executives to appreciate past, understand present, and contemplate future points of innovation in organizing the MNC.

DANIEL SULLIVAN
UNIVERSITY OF DELAWARE

Further reading

(References cited in the text marked *)

* Arbose, J. (1988) 'ABB: the new energy powerhouse', *International Management* June: 24–30. (A practical overview of ABB, concentrating on the development of a global organization prototype.)

Bartlett, C. and Ghoshal, S. (1989) *Managing Across Borders. The Transnational Solution*, Cambridge, MA: Harvard Business School Press. (An exhaustive evaluation of strategic trends and organizational tendencies in the MNC.)

* Brynjolfsson, E. and Hitt, L. (1993) 'Is information systems spending productive? New evidence and new results', *Proceedings of the International Conferences on Information Systems* December: 47–64. (Empirical support that information technology enables fewer workers to produce more, higher valued output.)

* Byrne (1993) 'The horizontal corporation', *Business Week* December 20.

Caves, R. (1982) *Multinational Enterprise and Economic Analysis*, Cambridge: Cambridge University Press. (A rigorous conceptualization of the MNC that uses economics to set the parameters and guide the logic of analysis.)

Charan, R. (1991) 'How networks reshape organizations – for results', *Harvard Business Review* September–October: 104–15. (An interesting profile of the network organization based on illustrative experiences in leading enterprises.)

Davis, S. (1979) *Managing and Organizing Multinational Corporations*, New York: Pergamon Press. (A superior overview of the theoretical characteristics of vertical structures in the MNC.)

* Drucker, P. (1991) 'The world's work', *Harvard Business Review* July–August: 88–97.

* March, J. and Simon, H. (1958) *Organizations*, New York: Wiley. (A timeless study of the principles and properties of organizations.)

* Joyce, Romy (1992) 'Global hero', *International Management* September: 82.

* Perrow, C. (1967) *Complex Organizations: A Critical Essay*, Glenview, IL: Scott Foreseman. (An interpretation of structure that emphasizes behavioural attributes and tendencies.)

* Ranson, S., Hinings, B. and Greenwood, R. (1980) 'The structuring of organizational structures', *Administrative Science Quarterly* 25 (1): 1–17. (A theoretical analysis that offers a sophisticated interpretation of structure and its associations.)

* Reich, R. (1991) 'Who is them?', *Harvard Business Review* March–April: 77–88. (A sketch of the internationalization of the global economy and the practices of US MNCs.)

* Saporito, B. (1994) 'Behind the tumult at P&G', *Fortune* March 7.

* Thompson, J. (1967) *Organization in Action*, New York: McGraw-Hill. (A pioneering study of organization that explains complexity quite simply.)

Tichy, N. and Charan, R. (1990) 'Speed, simplicity, self-confidence: an interview with Jack Welch', *Harvard Business Review* September–October: 112–20. (A profile of Jack Welch's philosophy of revolution at GE.)

* Vernon, R. (1977) *Storm over the Multinationals*, Cambridge, MA: Harvard University Press. (A path-breaking study of the rise and spread of multinational operations.)
* Weber, M. (1947) *The Theory of Social and Economic Organization*, New York: The Free Press. (The touchstone of subsequent studies of organizational structure.)

See also: BARNEVIK, P.; CATERPILLAR INC; CULTURE, CROSS-NATIONAL; EASTMAN KODAK CO.; E.I. DU PONT DE NEMOURS AND CO.; GENERAL ELECTRIC CO.; GLOBAL STRATEGIC PLANNING; GLOBALIZATION; MANAGEMENT IN JAPAN; MULTINATIONAL CORPORATIONS; NEC CORPORATION; ORGANIZATION CULTURE; PROCTER & GAMBLE CO.; WELCH, J.

Related topics in the IEBM: CHANDLER, A.D.; CULTURE; DIVERSITY; ECONOMIES OF DEVELOPING COUNTRIES; ENTREPRENEURSHIP; GENERAL AGREEMENT ON TARIFFS AND TRADE; INNOVATION AND CHANGE; INTERNATIONAL BUSINESS ELITES; MANAGEMENT IN SWITZERLAND; MANUFACTURING STRATEGY; NETWORKS AND ORGANIZATIONS; ORGANIZATION BEHAVIOUR; ORGANIZATION STRUCTURE; ORGANIZATIONAL EVOLUTION; ORGANIZATIONAL INFORMATION AND KNOWLEDGE; ORGANIZATIONAL PERFORMANCE; SIMON, H.A.; THOMPSON, J.D.; WEBER, M.; WILLIAMSON, O.E.

Non-tariff barriers

Overview

Historically, goods in international trade have been subjected to tariffs, that is, taxes on imports. Those paying tariffs to foreign governments would therefore raise prices to cover this additional cost. In turn, consumers would be less inclined to buy imported goods because of their higher prices, reducing their effective demand. In this way, tariffs have long served as barriers to international trade.

Over the decades since the Second World War, however, most states have systematically and jointly agreed to reduce tariffs to historically low levels, and international trade has skyrocketed in volume to reach unprecedented levels today. Simultaneously, however, a variety of non-tariff barriers (NTBs) has sprung up to impede international trade flows. Six categories of NTBs are discussed: strategic goods restrictions; currency devaluations; national standards; voluntary export restraints; domestic subsidies and government procurement rules.

Even as types of trade barriers have proliferated, international commerce has become much more complex in form; cross-border commodity trade is now joined by burgeoning trade in services, and by huge volumes of foreign direct investment and other capital flows. Accordingly, firms have had to develop strategies by which to cope not only with NTBs to trade, but with various barriers to direct foreign investment as well. After a review of non-tariff barriers to both trade and foreign direct investment, the matter of corporate responses will be addressed.

1 The growth of trade under GATT

In the wake of the Second World War, most of the industrialized countries were forced to rebuild their economies and societies on the ashes of destruction. One part of the rebuilding strategy was to reverse the international trade policies of the disastrous 1930s (see INTERNATIONAL TRADE AND FOREIGN DIRECT INVESTMENT). By the end of the war, it was generally agreed that the Great Depression had been considerably worsened by exorbitant tariffs that countries had placed on imports in the misguided, neo-mercantilist hope that this would protect the jobs of those who still had work domestically. In fact, such protectionist policies had the opposite effect as high tariff barriers caused unemployment to soar in export sectors.

Led by the USA and Great Britain, the plan for the post-war trading system was to suppress tariffs and quotas as barriers to international trade and, in addition, to rid the trading system of privileged trade relations among small subsets of countries. To achieve these liberal ends, the General Agreement on Tariffs and Trade (GATT) with general membership was established in 1947 as an oversight institution. The GATT, its administrative apparatus renamed the World Trade Organization (WTO; see WORLD TRADE ORGANIZATION) as of 1995, has been in place ever since.

In order to join the GATT, a country is required to agree to abide by a set of rules. The most important trade rule is the most-favoured nation principle, by which each member pledges to assess identical tariffs on the imports from all other members. Similarly, members are not to impose quantitative limits (quotas) on imports nor to sell goods abroad at unfairly low prices (dumping).

The GATT was quickly joined by virtually all the major economies in the world, with the notable exceptions of the centrally planned (that is, communist) ones. In subsequent decades, membership has grown to about 125 countries representing more than 85 per cent of annual global production, and a still larger share of total world trade. Moreover, in successive rounds of multilateral negotiation, the GATT countries have lowered the average tariff on dutiable goods from some 40 per cent in the late 1940s to less than 4 per cent by the mid-1990s. Meanwhile, world trade volumes have mushroomed – from barely US$60 billion in 1950 to more than $3,100 billion in 1990 – and this trade is credited as a major engine of growth in the capitalist industrial societies over the last five decades.

2 Non-tariff barriers to trade

As tariffs on almost all goods have come down to modest levels, there has been a corresponding rise in non-tariff barriers to trade among GATT countries. They are generally disliked by economists because, unlike tariffs, they are not 'transparent'. That is, the effects of these barriers are difficult to estimate, although it is believed that their collective impact has come to be about ten times greater than that of tariffs themselves. Consider that NTBs on imports into the USA – historically the most open of GATT markets worldwide – doubled in the 1980s to affect some 25 per cent of all goods. The non-transparency of NTBs also renders them, once in place, all the more difficult to negotiate away as reciprocated trade concessions.

NTBs take many forms. Moreover, some of them exist for purposes other than to impede foreign trade and thus do so only incidentally. Most NTBs fall into one of six major categories.

Strategic goods

Explicitly exempted from GATT rules are national restrictions on goods that qualify as 'strategic' because of their vital military applications or implications. In a country where weapons are produced, for example, the government is allowed to restrict competing imports and otherwise subsidize its own producers. Similarly, a GATT member can also regulate weapons exports lest they fall into the wrong hands.

Although all states are sympathetic to the strategic goods exemption from GATT, it has always raised difficult trade issues. Concerns focus on the definitional boundaries of the category, but their implications are hardly marginal. Public quarrels between the USA and the European Union, for example, pit NATO allies against one another with respect to commercial aircraft exports. This is a huge industry in which Boeing (USA), McDonnell Douglas (USA) and Airbus Industrie (Europe) are the leaders. Airbus is owned by the governments of Britain, Germany, France and Spain, and its products are developed in concert with various private firms. Thus, its products are publicly subsidized. Boeing and McDonnell Douglas, on the other hand, are privately held. Yet the two US firms have long been subsidized by their hefty military contracts with the US government to produce military planes and missiles that incorporate technologies with civilian applications. Moreover, US military contracts guarantee a profit margin which itself can be seen as a subsidy for the civilian side of these firms' operations.

Another dimension of the issue has arisen as the sophistication of defence technology has increased, in parallel with civilian technology; the line between 'strategic' and civilian (that is, both capital and consumer) goods has become considerably more blurred than in decades past. A prime example are today's advanced microprocessors, the 'brains' of a computer, which are quickly growing more versatile and therefore often have dual-use potential. In other words, such chips might equally well be put to military or non-military purpose, guiding either a missile or a welding robot to target. The quandary for a government is whether it should attempt to limit such exports on strategic grounds, even as the larger volume markets may be in overseas, non-military applications that are thereby foreclosed to the home firm, implying losses in both employment and tax revenues, if not also in incentives for continuing advances in future technologies.

Two examples of the further blurring of the meaning of 'strategic' goods come from the USA, the world's largest arms producer. In 1993, the newly elected Clinton administration announced a policy reversal that would allow the sale of a supercomputer to the government of China. In a very low-volume industry, this represented a highly significant sale for a US firm. More to the point, Washington was continuing to nurture more cordial diplomatic relations with Beijing. However, it also put into the hands of a traditional adversary a computer of sufficient power to design not only an entire automobile but a complete advanced weapons system.

Then, from the White House came news in 1994 of a new government programme to subsidize US manufacturers of flat panel display screens, an industry in which Japanese companies are overwhelmingly dominant. These are the displays already widely employed in laptop computers, and their application is projected to spread quickly to cockpit and radar screens, medical imaging and television receivers. Justification for US government intervention is, once again, that reliance on foreign suppliers could jeopardize national security. Because of the versatility of some core hi-tech products, the strategic goods category is very likely to continue to be a source of political contention for the foreseeable future.

Currency devaluation

In international currency markets, the governments of the world's largest economies have only a quite limited capacity to manipulate the value of their national currencies (see FOREIGN EXCHANGE RISK, MANAGEMENT OF; INTERNATIONAL PAYMENTS). At the other end of the spectrum, poorer countries likewise do not have sufficient reserves to allow them to buy and sell large quantities of various currencies in order to influence their own currencies' exchange rates. However, unlike the wealthier states, they do have the ability to devalue their currency unilaterally. However it may be achieved – and indeed it may only occur inadvertently, for that matter – the devaluation of a country's currency relative to

others' has the effect of raising the price of imports while lowering to others the price of its exports. To raise the price of imports is to raise a barrier to their domestic consumption or, in other words, to raise a non-tariff barrier to trade.

National standards

Countries routinely impose standards on categories of traded products, both goods and services. For example, cross-border shipments of foods are subject to inspections to certify cleanliness, accurate labelling and freedom from pesticide contamination. Physicians, lawyers, accountants and other specialized practitioners must be licensed as competent. Electronic devices must be adequately insulated for user safety. Automobiles must often meet both safety and emissions standards set by one or another government. In short, many standards exist for purposes such as health, safety and other dimensions of consumer protection. Yet additional standards are historical accidents. Thread sizes for screws and other fasteners vary from country to country, for example, as do the concentrations of chemicals and the voltage in wiring. Ordinarily, none of the standards mentioned here is adopted with the intent to affect trade flows whatsoever, but affect trade they clearly do.

National standards have the effect of requiring a producer to prepare versions of its product that will satisfy differing standards in different national markets where sales are to occur. These standards thus demand that the producer either make multiple versions of the product tailored to the requirements of different markets or, in some instances, make one version of the product that satisfies even the most stringent of standards it might face somewhere. Either way, the producer must assume higher costs than it would if there were only one standard worldwide.

National standards also raise transaction costs. Overseas products (or providers) must be inspected and certified before goods can be released into the market. This procedure is often routine and simple. On the other hand, even truck drivers moving goods across national borders in the European Community complained, before 1993, of four- and six-hour delays for paperwork as commonplace, literally doubling their delivery times. Foreign auto producers have for many years alleged ulterior, protectionist motives behind the Japanese practice of elaborately inspecting every imported automobile at the port of entry, an inspection billed to the producer.

Voluntary export restraints

As indicated above, the GATT generally disallows the use of quotas. By the late 1950s, member states were beginning to employ voluntary export restraints (VERs) as a legally distinct but functionally identical mechanism to create a quantitative barrier to imports. The legalistic difference between a quota and a VER is that the former is imposed by the state that wants to shield its domestic producers from foreign competitors. By contrast, a VER is imposed by a state on its home firms' exports, an export restraint that is not in truth 'voluntary' but instead results from diplomatic pressure from abroad by those who are constrained by the GATT treaty not to use a quota.

Two of the most widely publicized VERs exist in automobile trade and, in both cases, it is the Japanese government that has 'voluntarily' limited the exports of its home firms. The first of these dates back to 1981, when Tokyo yielded to pressure from Washington by setting a level of 1.68 million units on annual Japanese car exports to the USA (then about 21 per cent of the US market, a level only slightly below the most recent sales figures). Although that VER was scheduled to expire after thirty-six months, it has subsequently been renewed on a continuing basis and is still in effect with only negligible quantitative adjustments in subsequent years.

The second VER in autos is the 1992 agreement by which the Japanese agreed to restrict auto exports to 11 per cent of the European Union market for the duration of the 1990s. In both instances, these VERs have led Japanese automakers to circumvent the trade barrier by direct foreign investment in overseas 'transplants' where vehicles are

assembled within the protected North American and European markets. More to the point, these VERs resulted from diplomatic pressure on the Japanese government to rein in their highly successful auto firms.

However, a state is not always sufficiently influential to convince another 'voluntarily' to reduce its exports. Thus, in 1977 the government of France declared that Japanese auto sales were growing at an alarming rate. Japanese market penetration in France, said the government, was quite high enough having already reached the astounding level of 3 per cent! As a variant on a true VER, the French resorted to another tactic to freeze the Japanese market share. Immediately following the official statement of alarm, the French refused to supply sufficient customs personnel to process the offloading of Japanese auto shipments beyond a rate that would satisfy precisely 3 per cent of monthly new car sales. In turn, the Japanese auto firms quickly learned not to waste resources on futile efforts to overcome this barrier. Thus, for the intervening fifteen years until the reforms of the Single Europe plan came into effect, Japanese autos comprised exactly 3 per cent of the French market.

Domestic subsidies

Among NTBs, and in addition to the strategic goods category, among the least transparent barriers are many of the types of government subsidies provided to home firms. One rationale for subsidy is to promote high value-added industries. Another is to support 'linkage' industries, so called because they are viewed as providers of ingredients to other industries. Thus might steel or semiconductors be supported. Still an additional reason for subsidies can be found in assistance given to industries with prospects for rapid growth.

Moreover, all the major industrial countries have some form of government loan programme from which overseas purchasers can borrow in order to pay for imports from their respective lenders. The US Export–Import Bank and its counterparts in all the other major industrial countries provide low-interest loans to overseas borrowers in order to finance the lenders' exports. One study (Fleisig and Hill 1984) of these practices indicated that about 10 per cent of US exports are subsidized in this way, while the figure rises to as much as 45 per cent for Japan, France and Great Britain.

In 1987–8, the Reagan administration initiated an annual subsidy for Sematech, a newly created US research and development consortium among US-owned computer firms for which the government would pay half the annual $400 million budget. In fact, Sematech is in the business of refining the process by which microprocessors are manufactured and the government's subsidy is channelled through the Department of Defense on the grounds that microprocessors are strategically crucial and so, therefore, is US leadership in their production. The alternative, after all, is to be reliant on foreign suppliers. Nevertheless, the industry subsidy clearly gives advantage to US firms in a linkage industry and in competition for overseas civilian markets.

Of course, official assistance can also disadvantage foreign competitors in the home market. Western European farmers, for example, are very heavily subsidized on the basis of production alone; in some recent years, more than half the European Union's entire budget has been devoted to agricultural subsidy costs. This comes at the obvious expense of more efficient farmers in Australasia, the Americas and elsewhere, whose abundant and much less amply subsidized goods are largely shut out of the EU market. In fact, the EU additionally underwrites a separate fund to support exports of European farm goods at the further expense of those same more efficient producers in other parts of the world.

Still different are domestic subsidies as provided by the Japanese *keiretsu* structure (see *KEIRETSU*). A *keiretsu* is a very large group of firms featuring cross-shareholdings, interlocking directorates, and typically organized around a central bank and trading company. There are a number of these groups in Japan. Because each firm within a *keiretsu* has a direct financial interest in buying its supplies from others in its own group, imports are discouraged. More germane at the moment, however, is the additional fact that a failing Japanese firm within a *keiretsu* will be subsidized by other members of the group because of their financial interests as shareholders. This not only guards against bankruptcy, but indeed it allows certain firms to sustain long-term losses in pursuit of global market share with little risk of collapse.

Government procurement rules

National governments, and even local governments, often have more or less explicit restrictions against the public purchase of foreign-produced goods and services. In some instances, such restrictions even extend to foreign-owned subsidiaries located locally. In addition to the more straightforward category of strategic goods purchases, noted above, injunctions to purchase only from domestic producers can in principle be applied to any type of product. Because government purchasing in many societies represents as much as 15 or 20 per cent of aggregate demand, this form of NTB can seriously undermine foreign trade.

One case illustrates that such an NTB need not even be explicit. In the USA, the County of Los Angeles opened public bidding in 1991 for a light rail transit line. Some months later, a committee of the county's Transit Commission announced that it would be recommending to the full Commission that the Sumitomo Corporation of Japan – rather than its US competitor, Morrison Knudsen – be awarded the contract. Californians, in the grip of recession and entering an election year, reacted bitterly to the prospect that yet more jobs would be denied to US workers whose tax dollars would instead go to Japan. A furore ensued, inflamed by local and state politicians' calls for procurement rules that would prohibit foreign firms' participation. Explicit laws to this effect were never passed, but the Transportation Commission nevertheless eventually reversed itself and reopened the bidding process early the following year. By 1993, the matter was resolved. A consortium of US and German firms, headed by Siemens, won the major contract by virtue of incorporating much US content in the production. Sumitomo was meanwhile granted only a small fraction of the project. Californians were then more satisfied. Unsurprisingly, many Japanese were not.

3 Barriers to foreign direct investment

As alluded to earlier, international trade issues increasingly intersect with foreign direct investment (FDI) activities (see GLOBALIZATION). For example, it is estimated that at least 50 per cent of all US foreign trade is between subsidiaries of single firms rather than between independent entities. Moreover, as already suggested by the case of Japanese automobiles, barriers to trade can stimulate FDI as an alternative means of foreign market penetration.

For a variety of reasons, then, FDI has grown at an accelerating rate since the Second World War. The accumulated stock of direct investment stood at $67 billion in 1960, but grew to $1,500 billion by 1989. Indeed, it has come to grow much faster than foreign trade in more recent years. Thus, new FDI grew from $22 billion in 1975 to $196 billion in 1989. Whereas the global economy expanded at a 2.8 per cent annual rate in the 1980s, world trade expanded at a 4.1 per cent rate yearly. FDI expansion, however, outpaced them both with an annual growth averaging fully 13.9 per cent (United Nations Centre on Transnational Corporations 1988, 1991). Indeed, the intimate relationships that have developed between trade and foreign investment are reflected in GATT's recent addition of trade-related investment measures (TRIMs) to the obligations of its members. Thus, no discussion of non-tariff barriers dares exclude barriers to foreign direct investment. Consider two important types of FDI barriers.

Equity restrictions

It is unsurprising that foreign investors are not allowed to purchase large shares of militarily strategic industries. Ordinarily, this prohibition is explicit in national law, but the case of the Shah of Iran's overseas investment in a major aerospace firm makes the point clear. Even in the USA, where the foreign investment climate is especially liberal, the Shah's purchase of some 12 per cent of McDonnell Douglas in the mid-1970s proved – although legal – to be politically intolerable. Public outcry led the Nixon administration to implore the Shah to sell off most of his shares, and he quickly did so.

Nowhere is non-military FDI more carefully controlled than in Japan. Since the 1960s, the government has taken several steps to liberalize foreign investors' access to the economy. Nevertheless, many core industries remain closed to foreign investment that might threaten to allow managerial control to fall into foreign hands. FDI is allowed, but only within limits that restrict foreigners to benignly minority shareholder status.

The principal agent of this restriction today is the *keiretsu*, the form of business group noted earlier (see *KEIRETSU*). Chrysler, Ford and General Motors, for example, are allowed only minority shares of ownership of Mitsubishi, Mazda and Isuzu, respectively. Indeed, each of these US firms was required as a condition of purchase to pledge never to attempt to gain shareholder control of its Japanese partner, a condition imposed by the banks and other leading firms in each *keiretsu*.

Nor does Germany provide so liberal an investment climate as is often supposed. A 1991 article in the *New York Times* described 'fortress Germany' as follows:

> Although less pervasive than in Japan, protectionism in Germany is often just as deep-rooted and effective. The telecommunication, banking, insurance, electrical utility, and chemical industries, for example, operate as virtual cartels. It is almost impossible for a foreign company to enter those markets without a German partner. Other barriers include restrictive laws, massive Government subsidies, and the rigid protocols of a clannish, old boy network that dominates the economy.
>
> (Thurow 1993: 79–80)

Local content requirements

Independently of equity limitations, firms investing abroad may well encounter local content requirements. They may be required to ensure that local inputs reach a minimally satisfactory percentage figure (routinely 50 per cent or greater) in order to be allowed by the host to invest in that country. Such statutory requirements are quite common in Europe and have more recently spread elsewhere. Indeed, in broader form, local content requirements are frequently folded into *performance requirements*, particularly in developing countries. In this form, they are supplemented by specific additional activities required of foreign firms. For example, the foreign investor might also be required to assist in the provision of housing, medical care and schooling for the families of local employees. In addition, the number of indigenous employees – and the rate of their professional advancement – may be specified among the items the firm is required to perform.

4 Corporate responses

Even as the rules of trade and foreign direct investment have evolved in recent decades, so too have firms changed. Corporate behaviour has responded to changing policy climates and, additionally, to opportunities (and competition) afforded by new technologies. Thus, many firms have now 'globalized' operations by dividing their various labours, from design to financing to production to marketing, across not only national borders but across whole continents. Such change is possible only because new technologies of 'the information age' have expanded the available markets, suppliers and business partners for a wide variety of products from toothpaste to banking (see GLOBAL STRATEGIC ALLIANCES). Thus have firms seized greater opportunities to mix traditional mechanisms for penetrating foreign markets such as exporting, production abroad and licensing of production rights to other firms overseas.

Sometimes the process is impelled by the opportunity to exploit greater economies of scale, as in the global sourcing of automobile parts common to several models. In other instances, the impetus has instead been to seize upon what have been called 'economies of scope'. This term refers to 'a global perspective [that] allows firms both to spot

opportunities faster than others and to build networks of supply that combine the strengths of various locations and so further reduce total supply costs' (Stopford and Strange 1991: 77). It is in this fashion that Kodak and Fuji can market new camera film products simultaneously in all their major markets rather than running the risk of sequential market entries that would dangerously expose their product to a competitor's earlier arrival. And, in their quest for global economies of scale and/or scope, firms are increasingly inclined to develop strategic partnerships with suppliers, customers and competitors, driven by the growing value of local knowledge and the accelerating costs of needed new technologies.

It may thus appear that the globalization process is driven only by market forces. In fact, however, the phenomenon is many times a reaction to policies of governments. For example, foreign business partners may be acquired in Japan in order to have access to (government sanctioned) *keiretsu* or in Europe to ensure either high local content or low-cost information in a complex regional market setting. More positive from an investment perspective are versions of the offshore assembly law that many industrialized states have by now adopted. These laws permit firms to export components to another country for assembly and then re-import with the inducement that they will owe the re-import tariff only for the offshore value added to the assembled product. Many developing countries have meanwhile created export processing zones for said offshore assembly activities and relaxed their earlier restrictions on the repatriation of profits. In short, both protective and welcoming government policies can stimulate globalization.

Moreover, the western European movement towards economic integration has to some extent been mirrored in the more recent regionalization of the North American market (via the North American Free Trade Agreement, NAFTA) and that which is promised for the Pacific Rim (via the Asia-Pacific Economic Cooperation group). Indeed, both the western European and North American agreements have moved aggressively towards the goal of eliminating non-tariff barriers among their members.

For its part, the GATT concluded its most recent (Uruguay) round of multilateral trade negotiations in 1994. This agreement made major substantive strides by incorporating new protocols for trade in services, intellectual property and agricultural goods. It also has established a much more decisive set of dispute settlement processes. Moreover, like the EU and NAFTA, the GATT is attempting to translate NTBs into more transparent tariff form, albeit less successfully than in those regional efforts.

In summary, these and many other laws and practices pertinent to taxation, financing, tariffs and non-tariff barriers have thereby facilitated the globalization process in the private sector. However, one must remember that these changes in government policy and the structure and behaviour of firms are not moving in lock step down the path of liberalization and market convenience. In truth, firms continue to encounter an uneven and ever-shifting business landscape that includes a profusion of non-tariff barriers to trade and foreign investment, and they must tailor their business strategies accordingly.

NEIL R. RICHARDSON
UNIVERSITY OF WISCONSIN–MADISON

Further reading

(References cited in the text marked *)

* Fleisig, H. and Hill, C. (1984) 'The benefits and costs of official export credit programs', in R.E. Baldwin and A.O. Krueger (eds), *The Structure and Evolution of Recent US Trade Policy*, Chicago, IL: University of Chicago Press. (A technical assessment of the US Export–Import Bank and similar programmes.)

Prestowitz, C.V., Jr (1988) *Trading Places: How We Are Giving Our Future to Japan and How To Reclaim It*, New York: Basic Books. (Develops the thesis that Japan is economically illiberal and suggests what the USA must do.)

Reich, R. (1991) *The Work of Nations: Preparing Ourselves for 21st Century Capitalism*, New York: Alfred A. Knopf. (Highly readable portrayal of mobility of multinational firms and analysis of a preferred national responsive strategy.)

Rugman, A. and Verbeke, A. (1990) *Global Corporate Strategy and Trade Policy*, London: Routledge. (An analytical presentation of corporate strategies appropriate to competing in the USA, Europe and Japan.)

* Stopford, J. and Strange, S. with J.S. Henley (1991) *Rival States, Rival Firms: Competition for World Market Shares*, Cambridge: Cambridge University Press. (An examination of contending pressures on firms and states in their bargaining relationships.)

* Thurow, L. (1993) *Head to Head: The Coming Economic Battle Among Japan, Europe, and America*, New York: William Morrow. (Advances the thesis that one industrial centre will write the global rules for the twenty-first century.)

* United Nations Centre on Transnational Corporations (1988) *Transnational Corporations in World Development*, New York: United Nations. (Provides much data and some analyses on multinational corporate investment behaviour.)

* United Nations Centre on Transnational Corporations (1991) *World Investment Report: The Triad in Foreign Direct Investment*, New York: United Nations. (Provides data and some analysis of multinational corporate investment by US, European and Japanese companies.)

United States, Office of the US Trade Representative (1994) *Final Act Embodying the Results of the Uruguay Round of Multilateral Trade Negotiations*, Version 15 of December 1993, Washington, DC: Office of the US Trade Representative. (Text of the act by which the USA interpreted the latest GATT revisions.)

Winhan, G.R. (1986) *International Trade and the Tokyo Round Negotiation*, Princeton, NJ: Princeton University Press. (Considers GATT's 'Tokyo Round' with emphasis on the enumeration of non-tariff barriers.)

See also: ECONOMIC INTEGRATION, INTERNATIONAL; FOREIGN EXCHANGE RISK, MANAGEMENT OF; GLOBALIZATION; GLOBAL STRATEGIC ALLIANCES; INTERNATIONAL PAYMENTS; INTERNATIONAL TRADE AND FOREIGN DIRECT INVESTMENT; *KEIRETSU*; NORTH AMERICAN FREE TRADE AGREEMENT; WORLD TRADE ORGANIZATION

Related topics in the IEBM: GENERAL AGREEMENT ON TARIFFS AND TRADE; TRANSACTION COST ECONOMICS

North American Free-Trade Agreement (NAFTA)

1 Trade-related measures
2 Investment-related measures
3 Unresolved issues: deepening and broadening

Overview

The North American Free-Trade Agreement (NAFTA) is a complex international agreement between Canada, the United States of America, and Mexico. It provides a set of rules and the institutional framework to govern both the trade and investment relationships of the three countries. It also provides a mechanism for the accession of new members and introduces new dispute settlement procedures (for both trade and investment disputes) not seen previously in international economic agreements.

The key trade-related provisions of NAFTA are the elimination of all tariffs between the member countries (over three timelines) and the introduction of new rules of origin to determine the tariff-free status of certain products such as vehicles and apparel. The key investment-related measure of NAFTA is the introduction of the principle of national treatment, which prohibits discrimination in the application of laws involving parties from the member states, except in certain sectors where the discriminatory laws are listed as derogations from the principle of national treatment. These trade and investment measures will now be discussed in more detail.

1 Trade-related measures

In the North American Free-Trade Agreement (NAFTA), the three member states agreed, without exception, to abolish tariffs on all goods traded between them. Because of these tariff abolitions, NAFTA is a classical 'free-trade area' and this satisfied the requirements of the General Agreement on Tariffs and Trade (GATT) for substantial trade liberalization. The tariffs are to be abolished, by sectors according to the GATT harmonized tariff schedules, in three categories:

Category A: Tariffs abolished immediately upon the implementation of NAFTA on 1 January 1994
Category B: Five equal cuts of 20 per cent a year over a five-year period, starting 1 January 1994
Category C: Ten equal tariff cuts of 10 per cent a year over a ten-year period, starting 1 January 1994.

For a few sectors a 'C-' category was introduced whereby tariffs will be cut over a fifteen-year period. Examples of Category A goods include computer parts and most advanced manufactured products; Category B includes many food products; and Category C includes pharmaceuticals, footwear, textiles and apparel.

The NAFTA tariff negotiations were mainly between Mexico and the USA and between Mexico and Canada. There were no tariff negotiations between Canada and the USA under NAFTA since the tariff schedules already negotiated over the 1986–8 period for the Canada–USA Free-Trade Agreement (FTA) were carried over into NAFTA without any changes. The business leaders of the three member countries were closely consulted about the tariff category in which they wished their businesses to be included and the final classifications matched these business requests almost exactly. This has an important implication since those sectors more fearful of the adjustment costs of NAFTA usually were placed in Category C, giving them a ten-year period to adjust to trade liberalization. This period of the tariff phase-out gives business leaders the time to make new investment decisions. Thus, the long phase-outs in themselves provide a type of adjustment assistance, which was determined by the input and the requirements of the business sectors themselves. In addition, some of the previously more vulnerable sectors, such as vehicles and textiles, received new protection in the form of rules of origin. The rules of origin are paper trails required by customs authorities to authorize duty-free access of the final traded product. Such access may be denied if the product contains too many inputs (and labour value) from outside the NAFTA membership. The rules of origin follow complex formulas, the ultimate effect of which is to deny duty-free access to the US market of any vehicle and apparel product manufactured in Mexico which has any significant component or input from non-NAFTA countries.

2 Investment-related measures

NAFTA incorporates the principle of national treatment for foreign direct investment (FDI) for the three partners. Before NAFTA, both Canada and Mexico imposed discriminatory measures on FDI. In Canada, the Foreign Investment Review Agency, from 1974–85, screened FDI to assess 'net benefit' to the Canadian economy. In Mexico, FDI had to be a minority in any enterprise until the mid-1980s. While the USA had no such formal agencies to prevent FDI, it has been using an informal review and monitoring system for over fifteen years. The Committee on Foreign Investment in the United States (CFIUS) continues to have an informal screening role and its powers are periodically increased by the Congress.

NAFTA will affect the North American investment regime through two types of provision. The first type deals explicitly with FDI issues. These appear in the following chapters: in chapter 11 of the Agreement, which outlines the basic rules for the treatment of FDI and for the resolution of disputes between investors and states; in chapters 12 and 14, which deal with investment issues related to the provision of services and financial services, respectively; and in chapter 17 on intellectual property rights. The second type of provision in NAFTA which will affect the North American investment regime consists of investment-related trade measures. These include the rules of origin and measures related to duty drawback and deferral.

While NAFTA was a step forward in establishing national treatment, for portfolio investment as well as FDI, it took half a step back by exempting many key sectors from this discipline. For example, in the annexes to NAFTA are listed fifty US laws as reservations from NAFTA. For Canada, the number is forty-eight, for Mexico, eighty-nine. Examples of exempted sectors are the US transportation sector, Canadian cultural industries and the Mexican energy sector. Furthermore, subnational levels of government have two years from 1 January 1994 to list additional state or provincial reservations. Besides the FDI reservations, the NAFTA also has restrictive rules of origin for vehicles and textiles that effectively discriminate against 'outsiders' and protect the 'insider' multinational enterprises (MNEs) of the three member states. These developments will make it harder to break down 'triad power' as NAFTA helps North American MNEs, in these protected sectors, at the expense of European and Japanese competitors.

Viewed in this light, NAFTA is a mixed deal with these strong elements of protection offsetting the tariff cuts and related moves towards freer trade. It is a regional free-trade agreement, of benefit to insiders, not outsiders. The reason that NAFTA is a somewhat flawed agreement is due to the lobbying process, by which MNEs took part in the negotiations. In all three countries the business sector was not just consulted; it wrote the agenda for NAFTA. The capture of the trade negotiating process by MNEs, especially US MNEs, is a troublesome trend as several sectors are inefficient besides US vehicles and US textiles. Agreements like NAFTA, and the latest GATT round, freeze these inefficiencies in place and prevent global competition (see MULTINATIONAL CORPORATIONS).

3 Unresolved issues: deepening and broadening

There are several unresolved issues in NAFTA which will lead to the ongoing development of its institutional fabric, for example, through the work and decisions of bureaucracies and committees established by NAFTA. Prominent amongst these are the new environmental and labour commissions set up after the text of NAFTA was negotiated in order to win approval in the US Congress. Of these two new bureaucracies, the labour and healthcare one is basically an agency to appease US labour interests concerned about potential job losses to Mexico. Labour adjustment is funded by the US government and the healthcare commission will probably have much less business than anticipated since the economic impact of NAFTA on US employment is largely neutral. The environmental commission is potentially much more important as it will seek to increase environmental standards and enforcement in Mexico through a series of cases and reports which will probably influence public opinion. However, it has no power to enforce its decisions, so its role is also somewhat limited.

There are over a dozen official committees established by NAFTA to work towards a deepening of the agreement, such as in the vehicle sector and in financial services. Here the most important new institutional provisions revolve around the caseloads of the binational panels which can be established to review chapter 19 appeals of anti-dumping (AD) and countervailing duty (CVD) laws. In the Canada–USA Free-Trade Agreement there were fifty such cases of AD and CVD over the 1989–93 period and this precedent of the review of unfair trade law decisions has been continued in NAFTA. There are also binational panels established under chapter 20 to review any other disputes under NAFTA. Finally, there are new dispute settlement mechanisms for investors. In all these areas there is the potential for NAFTA to be deepened towards more of a customs union than a free-trade area.

In terms of broadening NAFTA, there is an accession clause whereby each of the three members countries must approve entry. In November 1994, the three countries agreed to negotiate the entry of Chile to NAFTA. However, in 1997 the US Congress refused to delegate 'fast track' negotiating authority to President Clinton, so the accession of Chile was stalled. There is no immediate prospect of any of the Latin American countries joining NAFTA; if any countries do apply for membership in NAFTA, the approval process could take several years.

In conclusion, there is much more work to be done in terms of improving the institutional fabric of NAFTA by a deepening process than there is in terms of the very limited broadening possibilities. It appears that NAFTA, although limited to its three member countries, could become a very useful model, especially in terms of its investment provisions, for the Asia Pacific regional trade agreement and for a potential one across the Atlantic.

ALAN M. RUGMAN
UNIVERSITY OF OXFORD

Further reading

Baer, M.D. and Weintraub, S. (eds) (1994) *The NAFTA Debate: Grappling with Unconventional Trade Issues*, Boulder, CO: Lynne Rienner. (Eight essays by political scientists and economists from the three countries on the economic, social and political dimensions of NAFTA.)

Fatemi, K. and Salvatore, D. (eds) (1994) *The North American Free Trade Agreement*, Oxford: Pergamon Press. (Twenty essays by academics on NAFTA's economic and managerial implications.)

Globerman, S. and Walker, M (eds) (1993) *Assessing NAFTA: A Trinational Analysis*, Vancouver, BC: Fraser Institute. (Twelve excellent essays provide the best single assessment of the text of NAFTA and its implications for the sectors such as vehicles, energy, agriculture, textiles and financial services.)

Hart, M. (with B. Dymond and C. Robertson) (1994) *Decision at Midnight: Inside the Canada–US Free Trade Negotiations*, Vancouver, BC: University of British Columbia Press. (An 'inside' account of the detailed negotiations for the Free-Trade Agreement, which is the model for NAFTA.)

Hufbauer, G.C. and Schott, J.J. (1993) *NAFTA: An Assessment*, Washington, DC: Institute for International Economics. (An assessment, from a US perspective, of the good and bad points in NAFTA.)

Lipsey, R., Schwanen, D. and Wonnacott, R. (1994) *The NAFTA: What's In, What's Out, What's Next?*, Toronto, Ont: CD Howe Institute. (An assessment, from a Canadian perspective, of the good and bad points in NAFTA.)

North American Free Trade Agreement (1992). (Copies of the 2,000-page text of the Agreement are available from the governments of Canada and the USA, and the Government of the United Mexican States. Also available on computer disc.)

Rugman, A.M. (1990) *Multinationals and Canada–United States Free Trade*, Columbia, SC: University of South Carolina Press. (Analysis of the impact of the Free-Trade Agreement on multinational enterprises, including surveys of their strategies for adjustment.)

Rugman, A.M. (ed.) (1994) *Foreign Investment and NAFTA*, Columbia, SC: University of South Carolina Press. (Thirteen chapters by experts analysing new foreign investment provisions of NAFTA, from the viewpoint of the three members and also 'outsiders', and with a focus on sectors such as energy and forest products.)

Rugman, A.M. and Anderson, A. (1987) *Administered Protection in America*, London: Routledge. (A classic analysis of the capture, by US protectionist interests, of the administrative process of countervail and anti-dumping procedures.)

Rugman, A.M. and Gestrin, M. (1993a) 'The investment provisions of NAFTA', in S. Globerman and M. Walker (eds), *Assessing NAFTA: A Trinational Analysis*, Vancouver, BC: Fraser Institute. (A short and incisive analysis of the legal reservations from the national treatment provisions of NAFTA.)

Rugman, A.M. and Gestrin, M. (1993b) 'The strategic response of multinational enterprises to NAFTA', *Columbia Journal of World Business* 28 (4) (Winter 1993): 18–29. (Analysis of how multinational firms respond to NAFTA.)

Warner, M. and Rugman, A.M. (1994) 'Competitiveness: an emerging strategy of discrimination in US antitrust and R&D policy?', *Law and Policy in International Business* 25 (April): 945–82. (Discussion of the ways in which the US Congress can still discriminate against Canadian and Mexican firms over technology subsidies, despite NAFTA.)

See also: INTERNATIONAL BUSINESS, FUTURE TRENDS; INTERNATIONAL TRADE AND FOREIGN DIRECT INVESTMENT; MULTINATIONAL CORPORATIONS

Related topics in the IEBM: GENERAL AGREEMENT ON TARIFFS AND TRADE; MANAGEMENT IN LATIN AMERICA; MANAGEMENT IN MEXICO; MANAGEMENT IN NORTH AMERICA

Organization culture

Overview

The concept of 'organization culture' has become popular since the early 1980s. There is no consensus about its definition but most authors will agree that it is something holistic, historically determined, related to the things anthropologists study, socially constructed, soft and difficult to change. It is something an organization has, but can also be seen as something an organization is.

Organization cultures should be distinguished from national cultures. Cultures manifest themselves, from superficial to deep, in symbols, heroes, rituals and values. National cultures differ mostly on the values level; organization cultures at the levels of symbols, heroes and rituals, together labelled 'practices'.

Differences in national cultures have been studied for over fifty countries. They show five independent dimensions of values: power distance; individualism versus collectivism; masculinity versus femininity; uncertainty avoidance; and long-term versus short-term orientation. National culture differences are reflected in solutions to organization problems in different countries, but also in the validity of management theories in these countries. Different national cultures have different preferred ways of structuring organizations and different patterns of employee motivation. For example, they limit the options for performance appraisal, management by objectives, strategic management and humanization of work.

Research into organization cultures identified six independent dimensions of practices: process-orientated versus results-orientated; job-orientated versus employee-orientated; professional versus parochial; open systems versus closed systems; tightly versus loosely controlled; and pragmatic versus normative. The position of an organization on these dimensions is determined in part by the business or industry the organization is in. Scores on the dimensions are also related to a number of other 'hard' characteristics of the organizations. These lead to conclusions about how organization cultures can be and cannot be managed.

Managing international business means handling both national and organization culture differences at the same time. Organization cultures are somewhat manageable while national cultures are given facts for management; common organization cultures across borders are what keeps multinationals together.

1 The concept of organization culture

The term 'organization culture' (in the USA generally 'organizational culture') became popular in the English language around 1980 (Pettigrew 1979; Schein 1985). In the management literature the term '*corporate* culture' is common (Deal and Kennedy 1982). An earlier concept, in use since the 1950s, is 'organization climate'. The difference between 'culture' and 'climate' is a matter of definition; there is no consensus in the literature. 'Culture' tends to be treated as a long-range, stable characteristic of an organization and 'climate' as a shorter range, more changeable characteristic.

Since the early 1980s an extensive literature has developed on organization culture which has also spread to other language areas. 'Culture' has become a fad, among managers, among consultants and among academics, with somewhat different concerns. An important role in its popularization was played by a book by Peters and Waterman (1982), *In Search of Excellence*. The authors claimed that excellent US companies were characterized by strong, dominant, coherent cultures in which 'people way down the line know what they are supposed to do in most situations because the handful of guiding values is crystal clear' (1982: 76).

Because of the faddish nature of the concept, the literature on organization culture consists of a remarkable collection of pep talks, war stories and some insightful in-depth case studies. Systematic research is rare; Peters and Waterman's study of 'excellent companies', for example, does not meet academic standards.

Nevertheless, organization culture has proven to be more than just a fad. It has gained its place in organization theory. Organization(al)/corporate culture has acquired a status similar to structure, strategy and control.

There is no consensus about its definition, but most authors will probably agree that the organization(al)/corporate culture concept refers to something that is:

1 holistic (describing a whole which is more than the sum of its parts);
2 historically determined (reflecting the history of the organization);
3 related to the things anthropologists study (like rituals and symbols);
4 socially constructed (created and preserved by the group of people who together form the organization);
5 soft (although Peters and Waterman assure their readers that 'soft is hard');
6 difficult to change (although authors disagree on how difficult).

All of these characteristics of organizations had been separately recognized in the literature of the previous decades; what is new about organization culture is their integration into one single concept.

A distinction can be made between authors who see organization culture as something an organization *has*, and those who see it as something an organization *is* (Smircich 1983). The former leads to an analytical approach and a concern with change. It predominates among managers and management consultants. The latter supports a synthetic approach and a concern with understanding and is almost exclusively found among pure academics. Discussion here is from the first perspective (has), while accepting some insights from the second – especially that culture should be treated as an integrated whole.

2 Organization cultures and national cultures

The organization culture literature has been influenced by reports of differences among national cultures that affect organizations and management, sometimes labelled 'comparative management' (Farmer and Richman 1965; Haire *et al.* 1966; Negandhi and Prasad 1971; Lammers and Hickson 1979; Hofstede 1980). The evident competitive success of Japanese organizations in the 1960s and 1970s led to a recognition that national culture mattered (Ouchi 1981; Pascale and Athos 1981).

'Culture' in general has been defined as: 'the collective programming of the mind which distinguishes the members of one group or category of people from another' (Hofstede 1991: 5). Consequently 'organization culture' can be defined as: 'the collective programming of the mind which distinguishes the members of one organization from another'. Next to organization and national cultures, one can distinguish occupational cultures, business cultures, gender cultures, age group cultures (like youth culture), and so on. However, the use of the word culture, for all these categories, does not mean that they are identical phenomena. For different kinds of social systems, their cultures may well be of a different nature. This is particularly the case for organization cultures versus national cultures, if only because membership of an organization is usually partial and voluntary while 'membership' of a nation is permanent and involuntary.

Culture as collective programming of the mind manifests itself in several ways (see CULTURE, CROSS-NATIONAL). From the many terms used to describe manifestations of culture the following four together cover the total concept rather neatly: symbols, heroes, rituals and values. These can be imagined as the skins of an onion, symbols representing the most superficial and values the deepest manifestations of culture, with heroes and rituals in between.

Symbols are words, gestures, pictures or objects which carry a particular meaning only recognized as such by those who share the culture. The words in a language or jargon belong to this category, as do dress, hairstyle, Coca-Cola, flags and status symbols. New symbols are easily developed and old ones disappear; symbols from one cultural group are regularly copied by others. This is why symbols represent the outer, most superficial layer of culture.

Heroes are persons, alive or dead, real or imaginary, who possess characteristics which are highly prized in a culture, and thus serve as models for behaviour. Founders of companies often become cultural heroes. In this age of television outward appearances have become more important in the choice of heroes than ever before.

Rituals are collective activities, technically superfluous to reach desired ends but which within a culture are considered socially essential: thus, they are carried out for their own sake. Ways of greeting and paying respect to others and social and religious ceremonies are examples. Business and political meetings organized for seemingly rational reasons often serve mainly ritual purposes, like allowing the leaders to assert themselves.

Symbols, heroes and rituals together can be labelled '*practices*'. As such they are visible to an outside observer; their cultural meaning, however, is invisible and lies precisely and only in the way these practices are interpreted by insiders.

The core of culture is formed by *values*. Values are broad tendencies to prefer certain states of affairs over others. Values are feelings with a plus and a minus side. They deal with:

- evil versus good
- dirty versus clean
- ugly versus beautiful
- unnatural versus natural
- abnormal versus normal
- paradoxical versus logical
- irrational versus rational

Values are among the first things children learn – not consciously, but implicitly. Development psychologists believe that by the age of ten most children have their basic value system firmly in place, and after that age changes are difficult to obtain. Because they were acquired so early in our lives, many values remain unconscious to those who hold them. Therefore they cannot be discussed, nor can they be directly observed by outsiders. They can only be inferred from the way people act under various circumstances.

Two large research projects, one into national (Hofstede *et al.* 1990) and one into organization culture (Hofstede 1991) differences showed that national cultures differ mostly at the level of values, while organization cultures differ mostly at the level of the more superficial practices: symbols, heroes and rituals.

Figure 1 illustrates the different mixes of values and practices for the national and the organization levels of culture, as well as for gender, (social) class, occupation and business. These differences can be explained by the different places of socialization (learning) for values and for practices; these have been listed at the right side of the diagram. Values are acquired in one's early youth, mainly in the family and in the neighbourhood and later at school. The two characteristics present at birth are gender and nationality. By the time a child is ten years old most of its basic values have been programmed into its mind. The school as a socializing place relates to the student's future occupation. Organization cultures are only learned through socialization at

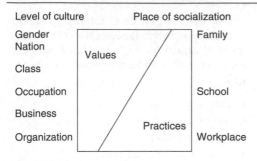

Figure 1 The mix of values and practices in culture for different social systems

the workplace, which most people enter as adults – that is, with the bulk of their values firmly in place. A business culture level (like the culture of banking or of tourism) is placed somewhere between occupation and organization.

Figure 1 illustrates that national cultures and organization cultures are phenomena of a different order. Using the same term 'cultures' for both can be misleading.

In the popular management literature organization cultures have often been presented as a matter of values (see for example Peters and Waterman 1982). The confusion arises because this literature does not distinguish between the values of the founders and leaders and those of the ordinary employees. Founders and leaders create the symbols, the heroes and the rituals that constitute the daily practices of the organization's members. Members do not have to adapt their personal values to the organization's needs. A work organization, as a rule, is not a 'total institution' like a prison or a mental hospital.

Members' values depend primarily on criteria other than membership in the organization: examples are gender, nationality, class and occupation. The way these values enter the organization is through the hiring process: an organization recruits people of a certain gender, nationality, class, education or age. Their subsequent socialization in the organization is a matter of learning the practices: symbols, heroes and rituals. Personnel officers who pre-select the people to be hired play an important role in maintaining an organization's values (for better or for worse).

The fact that organization cultures are composed of practices rather than values makes them *somewhat* manageable: they can be managed by changing the practices. The values of employees, once hired, can hardly be changed by an employer, because they were acquired when the employees were children. Sometimes an employer can activate latent values which employees possess but were not allowed to show earlier, like a desire for initiative and creativity, by allowing practices which previously were forbidden.

3 Dimensions of national cultures

The large research project into national culture differences referred to took place across subsidiaries of a multinational corporation (IBM) in sixty-four countries. Subsequent studies covered students in ten and twenty-three countries, respectively, and elites in nineteen countries (Hofstede 1991; Hofstede and Bond 1988; Hoppe 1990). These studies together identified five independent dimensions of national culture differences:

1 *Power distance*, that is the extent to which the less powerful members of organizations and institutions (like the family) accept and expect that power is distributed unequally. This represents inequality (more versus less), but defined from below, not from above. It suggests that a society's level of inequality is endorsed by the followers as much as by the leaders. Power and inequality, of course, are fundamental facts of any society and anybody with some international experience will be aware that 'all societies are unequal, but some are more unequal than others'.

Figure 2 lists some of the differences in the workplace between small and large power distance cultures. The statements refer to extremes; actual situations may be found anywhere in between the extremes. People's behaviour in the work situation is strongly affected by their previous experiences in the family and in the school: the expectations and fears about the boss are projections of the experiences with the father – or mother – and the teachers. In order to understand superiors,

Small power distance societies	Large power distance societies
Hierarchy means an inequality of roles, established for convenience	Hierarchy means existential inequality
Subordinates expect to be consulted	Subordinates expect to be told what to do
Ideal boss is resourceful democrat	Ideal boss is benevolent autocrat (good father)
Collectivist societies	**Individualist societies**
Value standards differ for in-group and out-groups: *particularism*	Same value standards apply to all: *universalism*
Other people are seen as members of their group	Other people seen as potential resources
Relationship prevails over task	Task prevails over relationship
Moral model of employer–employee relationship	Calculative model of employer–employee relationship
Feminine societies	**Masculine societies**
Assertiveness ridiculed	Assertiveness appreciated
Undersell yourself	Oversell yourself
Stress on life quality	Stress on careers
Intuition	Decisiveness
Weak uncertainty avoidance societies	**Strong uncertainty avoidance societies**
Dislike of rules – written or unwritten	Emotional need for rules – written or unwritten
Less formalization and standardization	More formalization and standardization
Tolerance of deviant persons and ideas	Intolerance of deviant persons and ideas

Figure 2 Consequences for the workplace of differences in national cultures

colleagues and subordinates in another country we have to know something about families and schools in that country.

2 *Individualism* on the one side versus its opposite, *collectivism*, that is the degree to which individuals are integrated into groups. On the individualist side we find societies in which the ties between individuals are loose: everyone is expected to look after him/herself and his/her immediate family. On the collectivist side we find societies in which people from birth onwards are integrated into strong, cohesive in-groups, often extended families (with uncles, aunts and grandparents) which continue protecting them in exchange for unquestioning loyalty. The word 'collectivism' in this sense has no political meaning: it refers to the group, not to the state. Again, the issue addressed by this dimension is an extremely

fundamental one, regarding all societies in the world.

Figure 2 also shows some differences in the workplace between collectivist and individualist cultures; most real cultures will be somewhere in between these extremes. The words 'particularism' and 'universalism' are common sociological categories. Particularism is a way of thinking in which the standards for the way a person should be treated depend on the group or category to which this person belongs. Universalism is a way of thinking in which the standards for the way a person should be treated are the same for everybody.

3 *Masculinity* versus its opposite, *femininity*, refers to the distribution of roles between the sexes which is another fundamental issue for any society to which a range of solutions are found. The IBM studies revealed that

women's values differ less among societies than men's values and that men's values from one country to another contain a dimension from very assertive and competitive and maximally different from women's values on the one side, to modest and caring and similar to women's values on the other. The assertive pole has been called 'masculine' and the modest, caring pole 'feminine'. The women in feminine countries have the same modest, caring values as the men; in the masculine countries they are somewhat assertive and competitive, but not as much as the men, so that these countries show a gap between men's values and women's values. Figure 2 also lists some of the differences at the work place between feminine and masculine cultures.

4 *Uncertainty avoidance* deals with a society's tolerance for uncertainty and ambiguity; it ultimately refers to man's search for Truth. It indicates to what extent a culture programmes its members to feel either uncomfortable or comfortable in unstructured situations. Unstructured situations are novel, unknown, surprising, different from usual. Uncertainty avoiding cultures try to minimize the possibility of such situations by strict laws and rules, safety and security measures, and on the philosophical and religious level by a belief in absolute Truth; 'there can only be one Truth and we have it'. People in uncertainty avoiding countries are also more emotional and are motivated by inner nervous energy. The opposite type, uncertainty accepting cultures, are more tolerant of opinions different from what they are used to; they try to have as few rules as possible, and on the philosophical and religious level they are relativist and allow many currents to flow side by side. People within these cultures are more phlegmatic and contemplative and are not expected by their environment to express emotions. Figure 2 lists some of the differences in the workplace between weak and strong uncertainty avoidance cultures.

5 *Long-term orientation* versus *short-term orientation*, the fifth dimension, was found in a study among students in twenty-three countries around the world, using a questionnaire designed by Chinese scholars (Hofstede and Bond 1988). It can be said to deal with Virtue regardless of Truth. Values associated with long-term orientation are thrift and perseverance; values associated with short-term orientation are respect for tradition, fulfilment of social obligations and protection of one's 'face'. Both the positive and negative rated values of this dimension are found in the teachings of Confucius, the most influential Chinese philosopher who lived around 500 BC; however, the dimension also applies to countries without a Confucian heritage. There has been insufficient research as yet on the implications of differences along this dimension to allow composing a table of differences like those for the other four dimensions given in Figure 2.

Scores on the first four dimensions were obtained for fifty countries and three regions on the basis of the IBM study, and on the fifth dimension for twenty-three countries on the basis of student data collected by Bond. For score values see Hofstede (1991). Power distance scores are high for Latin, Asian and African countries and smaller for Germanic countries. Individualism prevails in developed and western countries, while collectivism prevails in less developed and eastern countries; Japan takes a middle position on this dimension. Masculinity is high in Japan, in some European countries like Germany, Austria and Switzerland, and moderately high in English-speaking countries; it is low in Nordic countries and in The Netherlands and moderately low in some Latin and Asian countries like France, Spain and Thailand. Uncertainty avoidance scores are higher in Latin countries, in Japan and in German-speaking countries, and lower in English-speaking, Nordic, and Chinese culture countries. A long-term orientation is mostly found in east Asian countries, in particular in China, Hong Kong, Taiwan, Japan and South Korea.

The grouping of country scores points to some of the roots of cultural differences. These should be sought in the common history of similarly scoring countries. All Latin countries, for example, score relatively high on both power distance and uncertainty avoidance. Latin countries (those today speaking a

Romance language, namely Spanish, Portuguese, French or Italian) have inherited at least part of their civilization from the Roman empire. The Roman empire in its days was characterized by the existence of a central authority in Rome and a system of law applicable to citizens anywhere. This established in its citizens' minds the value complex which we still recognize today: centralization fostered large power distance and a stress on laws fostered strong uncertainty avoidance. The Chinese empire also knew centralization, but it lacked a fixed system of laws, being governed by men rather than by laws. In present-day countries once under Chinese rule, the mind-set fostered by the empire is reflected in large power distance but medium to weak uncertainty avoidance. The Germanic part of Europe, including the UK, never succeeded in establishing an enduring common central authority and countries which inherited its civilizations show smaller power distance. Assumptions about historical roots of cultural differences always remain speculative but in the given examples they are quite plausible. In other cases they remain hidden.

The country scores on the five dimensions are statistically correlated with a multitude of other data about the countries. For example, power distance is correlated with the use of violence in domestic politics and with income inequality in a country. Individualism is correlated with national wealth (per capita gross national product) and with mobility between social classes from one generation to the next. Masculinity is correlated negatively with the share of their gross national product that governments of the wealthy countries spend on development assistance to the Third World. Uncertainty avoidance is associated with Roman Catholicism and with the legal obligation in developed countries for citizens to carry identity cards. Long-term orientation is correlated with national economic growth during the past twenty-five years, showing that what led to the economic success of the east Asian economies in this period is their populations' cultural stress on the future-orientated values of thrift and perseverance.

4 National cultures and the functioning of organizations

Organization structure

The national culture of a country affects its parents and its children, teachers and students, labour union leaders and members, politicians and citizens, journalists and readers, managers and subordinates. Therefore management practices in a country are culturally dependent, and what works in one country does not necessarily work in another. Not only the managers and subordinates are human and children of their culture: also the management teachers, the people who wrote and still write theories and create management concepts, are human and constrained by the cultural environment in which they grew up and which they know. Such theories and concepts cannot without further proof be applied in another country; if they are applicable at all, it is often only after considerable adaptation.

The structuring of organizations is primarily influenced by the two dimensions of power distance and uncertainty avoidance. This is because organizing always demands the answering of two questions: (1) who should have the power to decide what?; and (2) what rules or procedures will be followed to attain the desired ends? The answer to the first question is influenced by cultural norms of power distance; the answer to the second question, by cultural norms about uncertainty avoidance. Individualism and masculinity affect primarily the functioning of the people within the organizations. Long-term orientation affects the economic performance of organizations.

Research into the *formal* structures of organizations carried out by British researchers from the University of Aston in Birmingham in the 1960s and early 1970s (the 'Aston studies': Pugh and Hickson 1976) already concluded that the two major dimensions along which structures of organizations differ are 'concentration of authority' and 'structuring of activities'. The first is affected by power distance, the second by uncertainty avoidance. Power distance and uncertainty avoidance indices measure the *informal*, subjective mental programming of the people within a country. The fact that these vary systematically between countries explains why the formal structures of organizations also vary: formal structures serve to meet informal cultural needs.

Differences in implicit models of organizations were proven for the case of France, Germany and the UK by a study among INSEAD (Institut européen d'administration) business students in Fontainebleau, France (Hofstede 1991: 140–3). In dealing with a case study of organizational conflict French students, coming from a country with large power distance and strong uncertainty avoidance, treated the organization like a 'pyramid of people' and advocated measures to concentrate the authority and also structure the activities. Germans, coming from a country with strong uncertainty avoidance but small power distance, treated the organization as a 'well-oiled machine' and wanted to structure the activities without concentrating the authority. British students with a national culture characterized by small power distance and weak uncertainty avoidance treated the organization as a 'village market' and advocated neither concentrating authority nor structuring activities but developing the managers' negotiation skills. Each of these models dealt with the same case study. All things being equal, French organizations do concentrate authority more, German organizations do prefer more structure and people in British organizations do believe more in resolving problems *ad hoc* (Maurice *et al.* 1980). A fourth combination, large power distance with weak uncertainty avoidance, is found in Asia and Africa and leads to an implicit model of an organization as an (extended) 'family', in which the owner–manager is the omnipotent (grand)father.

Mintzberg (1983) has provided a well-known typology of organization structures. Organizations in general contain up to five distinct parts – an operating core; a strategic apex; a middle line; a technostructure; and support staff – and they use one or more of five mechanisms for coordinating activities – mutual adjustment; direct supervision; standardization of work processes; standardization of outputs; and standardization of skills.

Most organizations show one of five typical configurations: (1) the simple structure, in which the key part is the strategic apex and the coordinating mechanism is direct supervision; (2) the machine bureaucracy, in which the key part is the technostructure and the coordinating mechanism is standardization of work processes; (3) the professional bureaucracy, in which the key part is the operating core and the coordinating mechanism is standardization of skills; (4) the divisionalized form, in which the key part is the middle line and the coordinating mechanism is standardization of outputs; and (5) the adhocracy, in which the key part is the support staff and the coordinating mechanism is mutual adjustment.

Mintzberg did not account for national culture in his typology but the link between the five configurations and the quadrants of the power distance × uncertainty avoidance matrix is easy to make. The adhocracy corresponds with the village market implicit organization model; the professional bureaucracy with the well-oiled machine model; the full (machine) bureaucracy with the pyramid model; and the simple structure with the family model. The divisionalized form, meanwhile, takes a middle position on both culture dimensions, containing elements of all four models. All things being equal, organizers in a particular country will favour a particular configuration because it fits their implicit mental model of what an organization should be.

Motivation

The power distance × uncertainty avoidance mix also affects the motivation of employees within an organization. Herzberg *et al.* (1959) argued that the work situation contains elements with a positive motivation potential (the real motivators) and elements with a negative potential (the hygiene factors). The motivators were the work itself, achievement, recognition, responsibility and advancement. These are often labelled 'intrinsic' elements of the job. The hygiene factors, which had to be present in order to prevent demotivation but which could not motivate by themselves, were company policy and administration, supervision, salary and working conditions. These are the 'extrinsic' elements of the job. Herzberg assumed this distinction to be a universal characteristic of human motivation. According to him it is the job content which makes people act, not the job context.

Long before Herzberg the issue of human motivation was raised by Sigmund Freud (1856–1939), one of the founding fathers of present-day psychology. According to Freud we are impelled to act by unconscious forces inside us which he calls our 'id'. Our conscious conception of ourselves, our 'ego' tries to control these forces. The ego in its turn is influenced by an inner pilot, again unconscious, our 'superego'. The superego criticizes the thoughts and acts of the ego and causes feelings of guilt and anxiety when the ego is felt to be giving in to the id. The superego is developed in the young child, primarily by the influence of the parents.

Freud was an Austrian and he conceived his ideas in the Austrian intellectual environment of his day. Austria in the power distance × uncertainty avoidance matrix takes an extreme position: small power distance but strong uncertainty avoidance. The latter stands for a strong psychological need for rules; the former for psychological independence from a flesh-and-blood boss to enforce these rules. The superego can be interpreted as an interiorized boss/father, who controls the individual through self-imposed guilt feelings. In Austria and other small power distance, strong uncertainty avoidance countries like Germany, rules as part of what Herzberg called 'company policy and administration' should not be seen as 'hygiene'; they can be real motivators.

In a similar way, when power distances are large supervision should not be seen as a hygiene factor. In large power distance countries dependence on more powerful people is a basic need which can be a real motivator. When, in addition, uncertainty avoidance is strong, as in most Latin countries, the motivator is the boss in the sense of the formally appointed superior. When uncertainty avoidance is weaker, as in Asian and African countries, the motivator should rather be labelled the master. The master differs from the boss in that the power of the former is based on tradition and charisma more than on formal position.

A cultural analysis thus shows that Herzberg's theory of motivation is culturally constrained; like all management theories it reflects the culture of the environment in which its author grew up and carried out research. The same holds for another US theory of motivation: Maslow's (1970) 'hierarchy of human needs'. In Maslow's hierarchy self-actualization is seen as the supreme need. However, this assumes an individualist culture in which the self prevails over the group. In collectivist cultures harmony with the group will rather be the supreme need. Maslow also ranks esteem over 'belongingness'. This assumes a masculine culture; in feminine cultures belongingness will prevail over esteem as a motivator.

A third culturally constrained motivation theory is McClelland's (1961) 'achievement motive'. McClelland predicted that countries for which he found a stronger achievement motive would show faster economic growth. This prediction did not come true. Hofstede (1980: 170–1) showed that McClelland's achievement motive corresponds to weak uncertainty avoidance plus strong masculinity; a combination found in all English-speaking countries. However, in the years following McClelland's study some stronger uncertainty avoidance countries like Japan and Germany grew faster economically than the English-speaking countries. McClelland had presented a culture pattern specific to his home society (the USA) as a universal norm.

Performance appraisal and management by objectives

Performance appraisal systems are recommended in the North American and western European management literature. They assume that employees' performance will be improved if the employees receive direct feedback about what their superior thinks of them, which may well be the case in individualist cultures. However, in collectivist countries such direct feedback destroys the harmony which is expected to govern inter-personal relationships. It may cause irreparable damage to the employee's 'face' and ruin his or her loyalty to the organization. In such cultures, including all east Asian and Third World countries, feedback instead should be given indirectly, for example through the withdrawing of a favour, or via an intermediary person trusted by both superior and employee.

Management by objectives as a management technique was developed in the USA. Under a system of management by objectives subordinates have to negotiate about their objectives with their superiors. The system therefore assumes a cultural environment in which issues can be settled by negotiation rather than by authority and rules, which means a medium to low power distance and a not too high uncertainty avoidance. In a large power distance environment subordinates and superiors will be unable to function in the ways the system prescribes. In a stronger uncertainty avoidance environment the system needs a more elaborate formal structure with norms and examples; this is the case in Germany.

Strategic management

Strategic management as a concept was also developed in the USA. It assumes a weak uncertainty avoidance environment in which deviant strategic ideas are encouraged. Although it is taught in countries with a stronger uncertainty avoidance, like Germany or France, its recommendations are followed there only rarely, because in these cultures it is seen as the role of top managers to remain involved in daily operations (Horovitz 1980).

Humanization of work

This is a general term for a number of approaches in different countries which try to make work more interesting and rewarding for the people who carry it out. In the USA, which is a masculine and individualist society, the prevailing form of humanization of work has been 'job enrichment': giving individual tasks more intrinsic content. In Sweden which is feminine and less individualist, the prevailing form has been the forming of semi-autonomous work groups, in which members exchange tasks and help each other. In Germany and German-speaking Switzerland the introduction of flexible working hours has been a popular way of adapting the job to the worker. Flexible working hours however have never become as common in other countries; their popularity in German-speaking countries can be understood by the combination of a small power distance (acceptance of responsibility by the worker) with a relatively strong uncertainty avoidance (internalization of rules).

5 National cultures: convergence or divergence?

Do national cultures in the modern world become more similar? The evidence cited is usually taken from the level of practices: people dress the same, buy the same products and use the same fashionable words (symbols), they see the same TV shows and movies (heroes), they perform the same sports and leisure activities (rituals). These rather superficial manifestations of culture are sometimes mistaken for all there is; the deeper, underlying level of values, which moreover determine the meaning to people of their practices, is overlooked.

Value differences between nations described by authors centuries ago are still present today, in spite of continued close contacts. Studies at the values level continue to show impressive differences among nations; after the IBM studies from around 1970 (Hofstede 1980) this was also the case for the European Value Systems Study (Harding and Phillips 1986; Ester *et al.* 1993). The only convergence is on the dimension of individualism, with countries that have become richer moving towards greater individualism. But even here pre-existing differences between countries survive. On average the Japanese have become richer than Americans and there is evidence of an increase in individualism in Japan, but traditional elements of Japanese collectivism survive as well. Because the process of organizing is affected by national cultural values, the nationality component in the structure and functioning of organizations is unlikely to disappear for decades or even centuries to come. International organizations will continue to have to take this component into account.

6 Dimensions of organization cultures

A research project similar to the IBM studies but focusing on organization rather than national cultures was carried out by IRIC (the Institute for Research on Intercultural Cooperation, The Netherlands) in the 1980s (Hofstede *et al.* 1990). Qualitative and quantitative data were collected for twenty work organizations or parts of organizations in The Netherlands and Denmark. The units studied varied from a toy manufacturing company to two municipal police corps. As mentioned above, this study found large differences among units in practices (symbols, heroes, rituals) but only modest differences in values, beyond those due to such basic facts as nationality, education, gender and age group.

Six independent dimensions permit description of the larger part of the variety in organization practices. These six dimensions can be used as a framework to describe organization cultures, but their research base in twenty units from two countries is too narrow to consider them universally valid. For describing organization cultures in other countries and/or in other types of organizations additional dimensions may be necessary or some of the six may be less useful. The six dimensions of organization cultures, discussed below, are listed in Figure 3, together with some of the ways in which they manifest themselves.

1 *Process-orientated versus results-orientated cultures*. The former are dominated by technical and bureaucratic routines, the latter by a common concern for outcomes. This dimension is associated with a culture's degree of homogeneity: in results-orientated units, everybody perceives their practices in about the same way; in process-orientated

units, there are vast differences in perception among different levels and parts of the unit. The degree of homogeneity of a culture is a measure of its 'strength': the study confirmed that strong cultures are more results-orientated than weak ones, and vice versa (Peters and Waterman 1982)

2 *Job-orientated versus employee-orientated cultures*. The former assume responsibility for the employees' job performance only, nothing more; employee-orientated cultures assume a broad responsibility for their members' well-being. At the level of individual managers the distinction between job orientation and employee orientation has been popularized by Blake and Mouton's Managerial Grid (1964). The IRIC study shows that job versus employee orientation is part of a culture and not (only) a choice for an individual manager. A unit's position on this dimension seems to be largely the result of historical factors, like the philosophy of its founder(s) and the presence or absence in its recent history of economic crises with collective layoffs.

3 *Professional versus parochial cultures*. In the former the (usually highly educated) members identify primarily with their profession; in the latter the members derive their identity from the organization for which they work. Sociology has long known this dimension as 'local' versus 'cosmopolitan', the contrast between an internal and an external frame of reference.

4 *Open systems versus closed systems cultures*. This dimension refers to the common style of internal and external communication and to the ease with which outsiders and newcomers are admitted. This dimension is the only one of the six for which there is a systematic difference between Danish and Dutch units. It seems that organizational openness is a societal characteristic of Denmark more than of The Netherlands. This shows that organization cultures also contain elements that reflect national culture differences.

5 *Tightly versus loosely controlled cultures*. This dimension deals with the degree of formality and punctuality within the organization. It is partly a function of the unit's technology: banks and pharmaceutical com-

1 Process-orientated	Results-orientated
People avoid taking risks	Comfortable in unfamiliar situations
People spend little effort	People spend maximal effort
Each day is the same	Each day presents new challenges
2 Job-orientated	**Employee-orientated**
Pressure for getting job done	Attention to personal problems
Important decisions by individuals	Important decisions by groups
Organization only interested in work people do	Organization concerned with welfare of employees and their families
3 Professional	**Parochial**
Think years ahead	Do not think far ahead
Employees' private life is considered their business	Norms of organization cover behaviour on job and at home
Only competence plays a role in recruiting	Family, social class and school play a role in recruiting
4 Open system	**Closed system**
Organization and people transparent to newcomers and outsiders	Organization and people closed and secretive, even to insiders
Almost anyone fits into the organization	Only very special people fit into the organization
New employees need only a few days to feel at home	New employees need more than a year to feel at home
5 Tight control	**Loose control**
Everybody cost-conscious	Nobody cost-conscious
Meeting times kept punctually	Meeting times only kept approximately
Lots of jokes about job and organization	Always serious about job and organization
6 Pragmatic	**Normative**
Emphasis on meeting needs of customers	Emphasis on correctly following procedures
Results more important than procedures	Correct procedures more important than results
Pragmatic not dogmatic in matters of ethics	High standard of ethics, even at expense of results

Figure 3 Manifestations at the workplace of different organization cultures

panies can be expected to show tight control, research laboratories and advertising agencies loose control. However, even when possessing the same technology, units still differ on this dimension.

6 *Pragmatic versus normative cultures.* This last dimension describes the prevailing way (flexible or rigid) of dealing with the environment, in particular with customers. Units selling services are likely to be found towards the pragmatic (flexible) side; units involved in the application of legal rules towards the normative (rigid) side. This dimension measures the degree of 'customer orientation', which is a popular topic in the management literature.

7 Determinants of organization cultures

Inspection of the scoring profiles of the twenty units on the six dimensions shows that dimensions 1, 3, 5 and 6 (process versus results, professional versus parochial, tight versus loose and pragmatic versus normative) are affected by the type of work the organization does and by the type of market in which it operates. In fact, these four dimensions partly reflect the *business* or *industry culture*. In Figure 1 it was located between the occupational and the organizational level because a given industry employs specific occupations and also maintains specific organizational practices, both for logical or traditional reasons. On dimension 1 most manufacturing and large office units scored process-orientated; research and development and service units scored more results-orientated. On dimension 3 units with a traditional technology scored parochial; high-tech units scored professional. On dimension 5 units delivering precision or risky products or services (such as pharmaceuticals or money transactions) scored tight, those with innovative or unpredictable activities scored loose. Surprisingly the two municipal police corps studied scored on the loose side: the work of a policeman is unpredictable and police personnel have considerable discretion in the way they carry out their task. On dimension 6 service units and those operating in competitive markets scored pragmatic; units involved in the implementation of laws and those operating under a monopoly scored normative.

While the task and market environment thus affect dimension scores, the IRIC study also identified distinctive elements in each organization's culture, even compared to other organizations in the same industry. These represent competitive advantages or disadvantages.

The remaining two dimensions, 2 and 4 (job versus employee and open versus closed), seem to be less constrained by task and market but rather based on historical factors like the philosophy of the founder(s) and recent crises. In the case of dimension 4, as shown above, the national cultural environment was proved to play an important role.

Although organization cultures are primarily composed of practices, they do have a modest values component. The organizations in the IRIC study differed somewhat on three clusters of values. The first resembles the cross-national dimension of uncertainty avoidance. A cross-organizational uncertainty avoidance measure is correlated with dimension 4 (open versus closed), with weak uncertainty avoidance obviously on the side of an open communication climate. A second cluster of cross-organizational values bears some resemblance to power distance. It is correlated with dimension 1 (process versus results orientated), larger power distances being

associated with process orientation and smaller ones with results orientation.

Clusters of cross-organizational value differences associated with individualism and masculinity were not found in the IRIC study. Questions which in the cross-national study composed the individualism and masculinity dimensions formed a different configuration in the cross-organizational study labelled 'work centrality' (strong or weak): namely, the importance of work in one's total life pattern. It was correlated with dimension 3: professional versus parochial. Obviously work centrality is stronger in professional organization cultures. In parochial cultures people do not take their work problems home with them.

For the other three dimensions, 2, 5 and 6, no link with values was found at all. These dimensions merely describe practices to which people have been socialized without their basic values being involved.

In the cross-national IBM study the country scores on the five dimensions were statistically correlated with a multitude of other data about the countries. The IRIC cross-organizational study included a similar 'validation' of the dimensions against external data. This time, of course, the data used consisted of information about the organizational units obtained in other ways and from other sources.

Besides interviews and an employee survey the IRIC study included the collection of quantifiable data about the units as wholes. Examples of such information (labelled 'structural data') are total employee strength, budget composition, economic results and the ages of key managers.

There was a strong correlation between the scores on dimension 1 (process versus results orientation) and the balance of labour versus material cost in the operating budget. Labour-intensive organizations (holding the number of employees constant) scored more results-orientated, while material-intensive organizations scored more process-orientated. Results-orientated units had lower absenteeism. They also had flatter structures (larger spans of control) and less specialization and formalization. Also, in results-orientated units union membership tended to be lower.

The strongest correlation with dimension 2 (job versus employee orientation) was with the way the organizational unit was controlled from above. If the top manager was evaluated on profits and other financial performance measures the members scored the unit culture as job-orientated; if they were evaluated on performance versus a budget members scored the unit culture as employee-orientated. Where the top manager stated they allowed controversial news to be published in the employee journal members felt the unit to be more employee-orientated. Job orientation was also correlated with the employees' average seniority and age and negatively with the education level of the top management team.

On dimension 3 (professional versus parochial) organizational units with a traditional technology tended to score parochial; high-tech units scored professional. The strongest correlations of this dimension were with various measures of size: larger organizations fostered more professional cultures. Professional cultures had less labour union membership. Their managers had a higher level of education and age. Their organization structures showed more specialization. An interesting correlation was with the way the top managers claimed to spend their time. In the units with a professional culture the top managers spent a larger share of their time in meetings and person-to-person discussions. Finally, the privately owned organizations studied tended to score more professional than the public ones.

Dimension 4 (open versus closed systems) was responsible for the single strongest correlation with external data; that between the percentage of women among the employees and the openness of the communication climate. The percentage of women among managers and the presence of at least one woman in the top management team were also correlated with openness. Openness was negatively associated with formalization and positively with higher average seniority of employees.

The strongest correlation on dimension 5 (tight versus loose control) was with an item in the self-reported time budget of the top managers where they affirmed spending a relatively large part of their time reading and writing reports and memos from inside the organization, control was tighter. Also, material-intensive units had more tightly controlled cultures. In units in which the number of employees had recently increased control was felt to be looser; where the number of employees had been reduced control was perceived as tighter. Finally, absenteeism among employees was lower where control was perceived to be less tight. Absenteeism is evidently one way of escaping from the pressure of a tight control system.

For dimension 6 (pragmatic versus normative) only one meaningful correlation with external data was found: privately owned organizations in the sample were more pragmatic, public units (such as the police corps) more normative.

Missing from the list of external data correlated with culture are measures of the organizations' performance. This does not mean that culture is not related to performance, only that it is extremely difficult to find valid yardsticks for comparing performance across different organizations.

8 Individual perceptions of organization cultures

Different individuals within the same organization will not necessarily perceive the culture of their organization in the same way. Hofstede, Bond and Luk (1993) re-analysed the data of Hofstede *et al.*'s Organization Culture study. This time, they focused on the variance of answers within the organizations studied. They did this by deducting from every individual's answer on a question the mean score of that question for the organizational unit. Thus, they only retained the within-unit variance, eliminating the between-unit variance that had been the basis of the dimensions of organizational culture found. After elimination of the between-unit variance, the data from the individuals within the twenty units were combined into one matrix of within-unit variance.

Study of this matrix showed that individuals within-unit showed large differences in values, but smaller differences in (perceptions of) organizational practices. This is the opposite of what was found at the between-organizational level. It is obvious, because value differences rest in differences of individual personality, whereas perceptions of practices are still based on the same objective practices.

A further (factor-) analysis of the individual answers showed that individual answers varied along six dimensions

1 integration (in the organization)
2 active involvement
3 orderliness
4 need for achievement
5 machismo
6 authoritarianism

The first five correspond closely to the five basic dimensions of personality ('the Big Five') recognized by modern personality theory: Neuroticism (with a negative sign), Extraversion, Conscientiousness, Openness, and Agreeableness (again with a negative sign). The sixth reminds us of the 'Authoritarian Personality' studies by Adorno *et al.* (1950).

In conclusion, differences among individuals in their perceptions of the culture of their organizations were shown to be a matter of the individual's personality. Agreeable individuals perceive the organizations as agreeable; conscientious individuals perceive the organizations as conscientious, etc.

9 Managing (with) organization cultures

In spite of their relatively superficial nature, organization cultures are hard to change because they have developed into collective habits. Changing them is a top management task which cannot be delegated. Some kind of culture assessment by an independent party is usually necessary, which includes the identification of different sub-cultures which may need quite different approaches. The top management's major strategic choice is either to accept and optimally use the existing culture or to try to change it. If an attempt at change is made it should be preceded by a cost–benefit analysis. A particular concern is whether the manpower necessary for a culture change is available.

Turning around an organization culture demands visible leadership which appeals to the employees' feelings as much as to their intellect. The leader or leaders should assure themselves of sufficient support from key persons at different levels in the organization. Subsequently, they can change the practices by adapting the organization's structure (its functions, departments, locations and tasks) matching tasks with employee talents. After the structure, controls may have to be changed, based on a decision on what aspects of the work have to be coordinated – how and by whom at what level. At the same time it is usually necessary to change certain personnel policies relating to recruitment, training and promotion. Finally, turning around a culture is a lengthy process. It takes sustained attention from top management, persistence for several years, and new culture assessments to see whether the intended changes have, in reality, been attained, as well as what other changes occurred in the meantime.

In the case of mergers and acquisitions a diagnosis is needed for identifying the potential areas of culture conflict between partners. Decisions on mergers are traditionally made from a financial point of view only: mergers are part of a big money power game and seen as a defence against (real or imaginary) threats by competitors. Those making the decision rarely imagine the operating problems which arise inside the newly formed hybrid organizations. A diagnosis of the cultures involved should be input when deciding whether or not to merge and after the decision has been made; it should also be input when planning for managing the post-merger integration so as to minimize friction losses and preserve unique cultural capital.

The six dimensions discussed above describe the culture of an organization, but they are not prescriptive: no position on one of the six dimensions is intrinsically good or bad. Peters and Waterman (1982) have presented eight maxims as norms for excellence. The results of the IRIC study suggest that what is good or bad depends in each case on where one wants the organization to go, and a cultural feature that is an asset for one purpose is unavoidably a liability for another. Labelling positions on the dimension scales as more or less desirable is a matter of strategic choice, and this will vary from one organization to another. In particular, the popular stress on customer orientation (becoming more pragmatic on dimension 6) is highly relevant for organizations engaged in services and the manufacturing of custom-made quality products, but it may be unnecessary or even harmful for, for example, the manufacturing of standard products in a competitive price market.

10 Managing culture differences in multinationals

Most multinational corporations do not only operate in different countries but also in different lines of business or at least in different product/market divisions. Different business lines and/or divisions often have different organization cultures. By offering common practices strong cross-national organization cultures within a business line or division can bridge national differences in values among organization members. Common practices, not common values, are what keep multinationals together.

Like all organizations multinationals are held together by people. The best structure at a given moment depends primarily on the availability of suitable people. Two roles are particularly crucial: country business unit managers who form the link between the culture of the business unit and the corporate culture which is usually heavily affected by the nationality of origin of the corporation; and 'corporate diplomats', home country or other nationals impregnated with the corporate culture, multilingual, from various occupational backgrounds and experienced in living and functioning in various foreign cultures. They are essential to make multinational structures work, either as liaison persons in the various head offices or as temporary managers for new ventures.

The availability of suitable people at the right moment is the main task of multinational personnel management. This means the timely recruiting of future managerial talent from different nationalities and career moves through planned transfers where these people will absorb the corporate culture. Multinational personnel departments have to find

their way between uniformity and diversity in personnel policies. Too much uniformity is unwarranted because people's mental programmes are not uniform. It leads to corporate-wide policies being imposed on subsidiaries where they will not work (or only receive lip service from obedient but puzzled locals). On the other side, the assumption that everybody is different and that people in subsidiaries therefore always know best and should be allowed to go their own ways is unwarranted also. In this case an opportunity is lost to build a corporate culture with unique features which keep the organization together and provide it with a distinct and competitive psychological advantage.

Mergers and takeovers within countries have a dubious success record, but cross-national ventures are even less likely to succeed. They have to bridge both national and organization culture gaps. Even more than in the case of national ventures, they call for a cultural map of the prospective partner as an input into the decision making on whether to merge or not.

Structure should follow culture: the purpose of an organization structure is the coordination of activities. For the design of the structure of a multinational, multi-business corporation, three questions have to be aswered for each business unit (a business unit represents one business line in one country). The three questions are: (1) which of the unit's inputs and outputs should be coordinated from elsewhere in the corporation?; (2) where and at what level should the coordination take place?; and (3) how tight or loose should the coordination be? In every case there is a basic choice between coordination along geographical lines and coordination along business lines. The decisive factor is whether business know-how or national cultural know-how is more crucial for the success of the operation.

Matrix structures are a possible solution but they are costly, often meaning a doubling of the management ranks, and their actual functioning may raise more problems than it resolves. A single structural principle (geographic or business) is unlikely to fit for an entire corporation. Joint ventures further complicate the structuring problem. The optimal solution is nearly always a patchwork structure that in some cases follows business and in others geographical lines. This may lack beauty, but it does follow the needs of markets and business unit cultures. Variety within the environment in which a corporation operates should be matched with appropriate internal variety. Optimal solutions will also change over time, so that the periodic reshufflings which any large organization knows should be seen as functional.

GEERT HOFSTEDE
INSTITUTE FOR RESEARCH ON
INTERCULTURAL COOPERATION,
MAASTRICHT AND TILBURG
UNIVERSITY OF LIMBURG

Further reading

(References cited in the text marked *)

* Blake, R.R. and Mouton, J.S. (1964) *The Managerial Grid*, Houston, TX: Gulf. (A classic US management theory arguing that the behaviour of individual managers can be classified along two independent dimensions: concern for people and concern for production.)

Czarniawska-Joerges, B. and Guillet de Monthoux, P. (1994) *Good Novels, Better Management: Reading Organizational Realities*, Chur: Harwood Academic Publishers. (Descriptions and analyses of famous nineteenth- and early twentieth-century novels from nine countries, considered as case studies of management.)

* Deal, T.E. and Kennedy, A.A. (1982) *Corporate Cultures: The Rites and Rituals of Corporate Life*, Reading, MA: Addison-Wesley. (An introduction to the subject, demonstrating how anthropological concepts can be used in the study of organizations.)

* Ester, P., Halman, L. and De Moor, R. (1993) *The Individualizing Society: Value Change in Europe and North America*, Tilburg: Tilburg University Press. (Results of a series of surveys measuring personal values among the populations of twenty-two countries.)

* Farmer, R.N. and Richman, B.M. (1965) *Comparative Management and Economic Progress*, Homewood, IL: Irwin. (A pioneer book on comparative management, now dated.)

Frost, P.J., Moore, L.F., Louis, M.R., Lundberg, C.C. and Martin, J. (eds) (1985) *Organizational Culture*, Beverly Hills, CA: Sage Publications.

(A collection of twenty-two readings, inspired by academic rather than practical interest.)

Frost, P.J., Moore, L.F., Louis, M.R., Lundberg, C.C. and Martin, J. (eds) (1991) *Reframing Organizational Culture*, Newbury Park, CA: Sage Publications. (Another collection of readings, even more esoteric than the previous one, which focuses more on the persons studying the organizations than on the organizations themselves.)

* Haire, M., Ghiselli, E.E. and Porter, L.W. (1966) *Managerial Thinking: An International Study*, New York: Wiley. (First international survey study of values in organizations.)

* Harding, S. and Phillips, D. (1986) *Contrasting Values in Western Europe*, London: Macmillan. (An earlier report on the survey study also covered by Ester *et al.*, see above.)

* Herzberg, F., Mausner, B. and Snyderman, B.B. (1959) *The Motivation to Work*, New York: Wiley. (A well-known American management theory distinguishing 'motivators' from 'hygiene factors'.)

* Hofstede, G. (1980) *Culture's Consequences: International Differences in Work-related Values*, Beverly Hills, CA: Sage Publications. (The first presentation of the first four dimensions of national culture across forty countries, written for a scholarly readership and with extensive validation against data from other sources.)

Hofstede, G. (ed.) (1986) *Organizational culture and control*, special issue of *Journal of Management Studies* 23 (3). (Links two central concepts in management: five papers on the relationship of culture with information, control and meaning; two on empirical studies of organization culture.)

* Hofstede, G. (1991) *Cultures and Organizations: Software of the Mind*, London: McGraw-Hill. (A popular overview of the author's and related research; deals with national as well as organization cultures. Translated into Chinese, Danish, Dutch, Finnish, French, German, Japanese, Korean, Norwegian and Swedish.)

* Hofstede, G. and Bond, M.H. (1988) 'The Confucius connection: from cultural roots to economic growth', *Organizational Dynamics* 16 (4): 4–21. (Using the results of the Chinese Values Survey, introduces the fifth dimension of national culture differences and argues that it explains national economic growth over the past twenty-five years.)

* Hofstede, G., Neuijen, B., Ohayv, D.D. and Sanders, G. (1990) 'Measuring organizational cultures', *Administrative Science Quarterly* 35: 286–316. (An account of the results of the IRIC

survey of organization cultures across twenty units in Denmark and Holland.)

* Hoppe, M.H. (1990) 'A comparative study of country elites', PhD thesis, University of North Carolina at Chapel Hill. (A replication of the Hofstede survey with elites from nineteen countries.)

* Horovitz, J.H. (1980) *Top Management Control in Europe*, London: Macmillan. (A comparison between the UK, France and Germany.)

Jaques, E. (1951) *The Changing Culture of a Factory*, London: Tavistock Publications. (A classic; the story of social change at the Glacier Metal Company in London.)

* Lammers, C.J. and Hickson, D.J. (1979) *Organizations Alike and Unlike: International and Inter-institutional Studies in the Sociology of Organizations*, London: Routledge & Kegan Paul. (A sociological overview of the relationship between societies and their institutions.)

* McClelland, D.C. (1961) *The Achieving Society*, Princeton, NJ: Van Nostrand Reinhold. (A US theory arguing that the strength of the 'need for achievement' is the determining factor in the economic development of societies.)

* Maslow, A.H. (1970) *Motivation and Personality*, 2nd edn, New York: Harper & Row. (The popular US theory of motivation, arguing that needs can be ordered in a pyramid.)

* Maurice, M., Sorge, A. and Warner, M. (1980) 'Societal differences in organizing manufacturing units: a comparison of France, West Germany and Great Britain', *Organization Studies* 1: 59–86. (A three-nation study showing the relationship between the larger society and the way work is organized.)

* Mintzberg, H. (1983) *Structure in Fives: Designing Effective Organizations*, Englewood Cliffs, NJ: Prentice Hall. (A well-known North American theory distinguishing five typical ways of structuring organizations.)

* Negandhi, A.R. and Prasad, S.B. (1971) *Comparative Management*, New York: Appleton-Century-Crofts. (An early introduction to the field.)

* Ouchi, W.G. (1981) *Theory Z*, Reading, MA: Addison-Wesley. (Describes how US management can use Japanese methods.)

* Pascale, R.T. and Athos, A.G. (1981) *The Art of Japanese Management*, New York: Simon & Schuster. (Japanese management described for US readers.)

* Peters, T.J. and Waterman, R.H. (1982) *In Search of Excellence: Lessons from America's Best-Run Companies*, New York: Harper & Row.

(Best-selling missionary document prescribing eight maxims for companies to become excellent.)

* Pettigrew, A.M. (1979) 'On studying organizational cultures', *Administrative Science Quarterly* 24: 570–81. (Early introduction to the 'organization culture' concept.)

* Pugh, D.S. and Hickson, D.J. (1976) *Organizational Structure in its Context: The Aston Programme I*, London: Saxon House. (An overview of the 'Aston studies' on organization structure.)

* Schein, E.H. (1985) *Organizational Culture and Leadership*, San Francisco, CA: Jossey Bass. (A boardroom consultant's view of organization culture and change; thorough discussion of the concept of organization culture but surprisingly blind to the influences of nationality and industry.)

* Smircich, L. (1983) 'Concepts of culture and organizational analysis', *Organizational Culture*, a special issue of *Administrative Science Quarterly* 28: 339–58. (A clear guide in the conceptual jungle; the whole issue is recommended as an overview of the state of the art at that time.)

Weinshall, T.D. (ed.) (1993) *Societal Culture and Management*, Berlin: Walter de Gruyter. (Reader reprinting some of forty articles that appeared in the 1970s and 1980s.)

See also: BUSINESS STRATEGIES, EAST ASIAN; CULTURE, CROSS-NATIONAL; ECONOMIES OF EAST ASIA

Related topics in the IEBM: AGENCY, MARKETS AND HIERARCHIES; ASTON GROUP; BUSINESS SYSTEMS; COGNITION; CONTEXTS AND ENVIRONMENTS; COORDINATION AND CONTROL; FREUD, S.; HERZBERG, F.; LEADERSHIP; MCCLELLAND, D.C.; MANAGERIAL BEHAVIOUR; MASLOW, A.II.; MINTZBERG, H.; MOTIVATION AND SATISFACTION; ORGANIZATION BEHAVIOUR; ORGANIZATION BEHAVIOUR, HISTORY OF; ORGANIZATION DEVELOPMENT; ORGANIZATION PARADIGMS; ORGANIZATION STRUCTURE; ORGANIZATION TYPES; ORGANIZATIONAL CONVERGENCE; ORGANIZATIONAL PERFORMANCE; ORGANIZING, PROCESS OF; PERFORMANCE APPRAISAL; POWER; STRATEGY, CONCEPT OF GROUPS AND TEAMS

Political risk

Overview

Political risk is a general term referring to a variety of political and quasi-political (economic and social) threats to the ownership or operation of a foreign investment. Different types of political risks are identified and discussed. Arbitrary governmental seizure of private assets, terrorist destruction of plant and equipment and politically induced labour strikes are examples of different types of political risk.

The levels of political risk vary by project, even within the same country during a single timeframe. Characteristics of overseas investment that increase or decrease these inherent political risks are explained. A brief review of the history of political risk insurance is presented, as well as broad outlines of public and private insurance programmes designed to protect against political risk. Consulting and forecasting services are described, as are the difficulties of longer term political risk assessment.

1 Types of political risk

Political risks can be divided into the following categories: expropriation, contract repudiation, currency inconvertibility, war, embargo and civil commotion, war risks and micro-political risks. These will all be discussed individually.

Expropriation

Perhaps the most catastrophic type of political risk is expropriation. Even more than war, where it is most likely that only partial physical damage is done, expropriation often results in the total loss of a foreign investment (see FINANCIAL MANAGEMENT, INTERNATIONAL). To expropriate means to dispossess of ownership. Expropriation can occur under the laws of a legitimate government: for example, the expropriation of private land for public transportation. Expropriation can also be the new policy of a revolutionary regime. In Cuba, in 1959, for example, when Fidel Castro came to power, his new government expropriated (or seized or confiscated – we use these terms interchangeably) all foreign investment. Such expropriation by hostile regimes is often arbitrary, unexpected and carried out without adequate compensation.

Expropriation of investor assets by a host government need not be carried out by radical governmental action. More subtle types of expropriation are just as damaging as having local troops marching into a facility to seize its assets. Dispossession of ownership also includes the inability of a foreign investor to use the assets that have been assigned to the host country (see INTERNATIONAL BUSINESS, LEGAL DIMENSIONS OF).

A classic example of this more subtle form of government expropriation occurred in a west African country during the late 1970s. This African government approved the establishment of a shrimp farm by a small group of foreign investors miles down the coast from the capital city. The capital was also the only port in the country. Foreign funds were invested, the shrimp farm was established and was soon producing a profit. As this was a small business concern, the profit margin was dependent upon keeping down transportation costs between the shrimp farm and the capital/port.

As originally planned, the shrimps from the shrimp farm would be packed on ice and flown periodically to the capital city for further shipment to overseas markets. The aeroplane used was relatively small, in keeping with the modest size of the shrimp-farming operation. During these intra-country shipments, a representative of the host government, a local health inspector, would fly with the pilot and the shrimps from the shrimp farm to the capital city. These arrangements were agreed upon by the African government and by the foreign (US) investors.

The health inspector in question was a relatively small man. As such, his weight in the aeroplane did not greatly displace the shrimps being carried to the capital. However, once the shrimp farm was operational and showing a continuing profit, the African government reassigned the initial health inspector and insisted that a new health inspector be used on the flights. The new health inspector weighed over three hundred pounds. His weight in the aeroplane was such that the amount of shrimps that could be carried was insufficient to allow the shrimp farm to make a profit. Transportation costs were now unacceptably high. The investors petitioned the government for a lighter-weight health inspector. The government refused. The investors had no option other than to abandon their investment, which was then taken over by representatives of the African government.

This is a classic case of subtle or creeping expropriation. As a result of new host government regulations or decisions, the foreign investors are unable to operate their investment at a profit. Such governmental regulations can be new taxes that only apply to foreigners, health and safety requirements that do not apply to domestic enterprises or any number of other arbitrary obstacles that in effect deny the foreign investors the anticipated use of their invested assets.

Contract repudiation

A second type of political risk is contract repudiation by a host government agency. Much like expropriation, contract repudiation entails significant financial risk to the parties involved. Also like expropriation, contract repudiation risks can be subtle in their execution. As a political risk, contract repudiation means the politically motivated failure on the part of a host government to honour its contractual obligations. Most contract repudiations entail either sales contracts to, or construction projects in, the host country.

For example, Host Government A, in Latin America, contracts with a US construction firm, XYZ, to build a new water purification plant in the host country's capital city. A quarter of the contract cost is paid by Government A to XYZ at the inception of the project. Interim payments are made when various stages of the project are completed. A final payment is due upon completion of the water purification plant.

This contract can be repudiated in two ways. First, payments due for work completed may not be made by the contracting host government agency. If no payments are forthcoming, or even if they are delayed, this will result in a financial loss for the contracting party. Second, even after all payments are made for work completed, the host government can often arbitrarily draw down on performance guarantees posted by the contracting party. In many construction projects, the companies that are bidding to do the work must agree to put up, or post, an agreed amount of money with one of the host country's banks. Under the terms of the contract, if the work is not completed on time and to specifications, the contracting government has the right to draw down, or receive, the money previously posted. This acts as a penalty for non-performance. However, there is a political risk involved with this arrangement. The government can arbitrarily decree that work was not completed according to specifications. It can draw down the performance guarantee previously posted by the contracting party when it has no legitimate right or cause to do so.

As with expropriation, there are subtle ways in which a host government can politically repudiate a contract by purposefully derailing the underlying project. A major pipeline project in Latin America, for example, was nearly wrecked in the early 1980s by the host government's implicit non-compliance with its obligations under the applicable contract with the foreign (US) contractor. This non-compliance took the form of open-ended delays in providing essential domestic-content supplies and materials that were required for the project's completion. Project timetables could not be met.

There was a high probability of the host government drawing down the posted performance bond. Upon investigation of the reason for the delays, it was determined that a high military official in the host government was opposing the project's completion. When this military official was given a consulting fee for work on the project, the delays in the delivery of local-content supplies immediately ceased and the project then continued to completion with no further problems. Was this a case of political corruption? Perhaps, and perhaps not. Such an answer is beyond the scope of this discussion. It is undoubtedly an example of different ways of doing business in different parts of the world. It is also a classic example of how political considerations can lead to contract repudiation and project non-completion.

As mentioned above, contract repudiation can also take the form of non-payment of goods or services that have been delivered to the host government. This non-payment can result from changing political and economic conditions in the foreign country, in which the buyer, the host government, claims an inability to pay for previously purchased goods. The debt crisis of many Latin American and African countries during the 1980s would be an example of this reason for non-payment.

Alternatively, as is often the case following major political upheaval or revolution, while the new government that comes to power may be quite able to pay for goods or services, it may refuse to do so. The Iranian revolution is an example of this latter form of contract repudiation. The reasons for governmental non-payment under a contract repudiation are quite important when it comes to managing political risk, as will be discussed later in this entry.

Currency inconvertibility

Inconvertibility of local currency has traditionally been considered a political risk (see FOREIGN EXCHANGE RISK, MANAGEMENT OF).

It is frequently tied to economic risk, although it always remains a political decision as to who is paid in hard currency and who is not. During the international debt crisis of the 1980s, for example, hard currency was always available in debt-strapped host countries for those goods and services that were deemed vital to the host country's national interest. In Mexico, for example, following the imposition of rigid currency controls, funds were still available – often through informal, unpublicized arrangements – for hard currency payment of materials needed in the Mexican oil fields. Likewise, in one central African country, where other companies were waiting indefinitely for hard currency conversion of local profits, the local Pepsi-Cola franchise continued to be paid on a regular and timely basis.

While tied to economics, inconvertibility of local currency is often insured by governmental agencies as a political risk. Therefore, it is appropriate to discuss the risk of currency inconvertibility in this present context.

Investing in a host country, even without local political interference, can be a disastrous business decision if the investor is unable to convert local currency to hard currency (such as the US dollar, yen, sterling or similar currencies which are interchangeable and freely traded on the world financial markets). Furthermore, once this conversion has been completed, the investor must be able to repatriate such converted currency to their home country. No matter how profitable a foreign investment might be, if those profits cannot be taken out of the host country and returned to investors, the value and use of that foreign investment is severely restricted.

As with other types of political risk, inconvertibility can be either serious or temporary. Using the case of the Cuban revolution, prior to the overthrow of the Batista regime by Fidel Castro, Cuban pesos and US dollars were freely interchangeable. There existed exchange rates and readily available mechanisms for exchanging one currency for another. However, since the revolution Cuban pesos have not been exchangeable for US dollars in Cuba.

Those foreign (mostly US) investors with assets in Cuba prior to the revolution may have had enormous business profits from their Cuban operations. However, even if these US business interests had not been expropriated (which they were), once the new Cuban government decreed that Cuban pesos would not be converted to any Western currencies, those local profits would have become practically worthless.

A less serious form of inconvertibility is the temporary shortfall of hard currency in the host country. When the foreign (that is, German, UK, Japanese) investor presents their local profits to the host government to be exchanged (for marks, pounds, yen), in certain economic circumstances the host government would be willing to make the exchange for hard currencies but cannot do so. The host government may not have sufficient hard currency on hand to make the exchange. Or, whatever hard currency is available, the government is using for other purposes (such as the purchase of imports where the overseas seller demands hard currency as the prescribed form of payment).

This lesser type of inconvertibility generally takes the form of delays in the conversion and repatriation of hard currency. Currency is eventually converted, but the timing of the exchange is at the discretion of the host government. Inconvertibility delays can be months, sometimes even years. Clearly, these delays in moving profits or dividends out of a host country can have important business consequences. Nevertheless, it is a less serious problem than is the case with revolutionary regime change and total, permanent inconvertibility of local currency into a currency that the investor wants.

War, embargo and civil commotion

There are two other significant types of political risk to property. These are war and the threat of war. The threat of war often entails the imposition of a politically motivated embargo. We shall discuss this risk of embargo first.

When one country embargoes another country, the embargoing country cuts off the supply of goods and sometimes people to the country being embargoed. From a political risk standpoint, complete embargoes are most costly. Production supplies and equipment, when not adequately stockpiled, will be used up. Local business operations will grind to a halt. In such cases, an embargo can mean a significant business loss.

Fortunately, many embargoes can be waited out, especially when proper business planning of inventories has been initiated or when overseas-sourced production inputs are not vital for the local production process. Likewise, host country operations that are not under tight deadlines for the export of a product are less affected by embargoes than businesses with sensitive schedules.

An example of a complete embargo was the case when the UK blockaded Argentina during the Falkland Islands dispute. Ships sailing towards Argentina were interdicted by UK warships and forced to turn back. Likewise, ships could not leave Argentine ports without finding themselves in a war zone. Such total embargoes completely cut off all supplies going into or out of the embargoed country.

Some embargoes are specific: only certain goods or material are denied passage. Examples of such embargoes are the Cuban Missile Crisis in 1962 and the Persian Gulf War in 1992, when ships carrying military weapons to Cuba and Iraq were denied passage, respectively.

In the case of the UK embargo of Argentina, for example, a huge supply of tobacco from a US firm that had invested in Argentina was threatened in this way. (In this case, a large number of pack mules was hired by the US company in Argentina. The tobacco was loaded on the mules and transported overland to Brazil, then exported to waiting buyers from a Brazilian port. In this case the embargo was broken, but at a large additional cost to the US investor in Argentina.)

War risk

As can be seen by the above example, the risk of embargo is significantly lessened when alternative transportation routes are available.

However, in the case of outright war, the political risk is sudden and unavoidable.

Physical damage or destruction of plant and equipment, by whatever source or cause, is equally costly no matter how or why the damage is done. If a factory is burnt down by a disgruntled worker who has been passed over for promotion or if it is destroyed by a marauding band of soldiers, the result is the same: an investor's asset is turned into rubble.

However, in terms of *insurable* political risk, what is war and what is not war makes a momentous difference. Political risk insurance will be discussed in more detail below. At this point, it is sufficient to say that some governmental agencies, both national and international, will provide war insurance to private overseas investors. Even some private insurance sources, such as Lloyd's of London, provide war insurance for certain types of risks. Almost all other international property insurance *excludes* coverage for war, but provides insurance, in very specific insurance policy language, against 'strikes, riots and civil commotion'.

As a result of this insurance market segmentation, overseas investors must purchase property insurance from one insurer and political risk war insurance from another. When a loss occurs, it is often difficult to ascertain whether the loss was caused by war (covered under one policy) or by civil commotion (covered under a separate insurance policy). In other words, it is often difficult to ascertain when a specific action results from a political risk, and when it does not.

One such event occurred in Central America in the mid-1980s. A US-owned plant in this Central American country was temporarily seized by disgruntled locals, some of whom worked in the plant's facilities. While under control of these workers and their friends, a great deal of property damage was done. When the investor filed an insurance claim with its property carrier, arguing that the cause of loss was a local strike, the insurance company denied the claim on the basis that what had occurred was not a work strike, but a politically motivated act of local insurgents. The investor then filed a claim with its political risk insurer. The political risk insurer

likewise denied the claim, arguing that the cause of loss was a mere civil commotion which should have been paid for by the investor's property insurer.

Clearly, the answer to resolving this political risk problem is to purchase both property insurance and political risk insurance from the same insurer. Were this to be accomplished, the insurer would pay the claim under one of the two coverages, deciding for itself under which category (political risk or property) the claim should be handled. Unfortunately, such joint insurance is rarely, if ever, available from the same insurance carrier. The one exception to this separate coverage is Lloyd's of London, and then only for a limited class of risks.

Lloyd's historically provided property and war coverage on land-based properties. However, during the Spanish civil war in 1936–9, a substantial number of the properties so insured by various Lloyd's syndicates were destroyed. So many, in fact, that the losses almost bankrupted many of the syndicates. As a result, the members of Lloyd's agreed among themselves and passed what has come to be known as the 'Waterborne Agreement'. Under this agreement, all syndicates of Lloyd's promised that, in perpetuity, none of them would provide war insurance for properties or assets located on land (thus, the term 'waterborne' for what could be insured).

Today Lloyd's will provide war insurance, but only for ships at sea, that is, waterborne (including some in-port coverage extensions), and for aircraft. These two classes of property are the only major kinds of insurance exposures for which property insurance and war risk insurance can be purchased from the same insurer. In all other situations, the determination whether a property loss is due to war – or is the result of strikes, riots or civil commotion – can lead to considerable insurance problems. We shall return to insurance considerations of political risk later in this discussion.

Micro-political risks

There also exists a series of personal, or micro, political risks. 'Micro' because these risks threaten the individual, either singularly or in groups, as opposed to more 'macro' risks, usually against large and inanimate buildings, factories or equipment. Some political phenomena can affect both huge manufacturing complexes and single individuals at the same time. Being caught in a war zone, for example, where enemy artillery razes buildings, can also lead to personal injury or death.

However, when we speak of micro or personal political risks, we mean those dangers that apply strictly to individuals. Primarily, this refers to three situations: (1) politically motivated assassination; (2) political kidnap and consequent demands for ransom; and (3) instances of forced evacuation from potentially hostile areas.

Political assassination rarely occurs to foreign personnel in a host country. Assassination is an effective way to eliminate *local* political, judicial, bureaucratic and business elites. Historically, it has been a practice not only of governmental authorities (as with the Phoenix programme conducted by the USA and South Vietnamese against Viet Cong village leaders during the Vietnam war), but also a political tool by rebel forces themselves (for example, the frequent terrorist assassinations by the Shining Path rebels in Peru).

However, foreign business personnel rarely make a direct impact on local political infrastructure (see HUMAN RESOURCE MANAGEMENT, INTERNATIONAL). Instead, these targets are most valuable for the financial worth they represent to their families, corporations or country. To obtain that financial value, expatriates are kidnapped and held for ransom. This can occur in countries in which there is little other activity in the way of overt political unrest. Moreover, kidnappings can occur not only for political reasons, but simply because a band of criminals is out to make a quick profit. (As is the case with the example given above, it is sometimes difficult to distinguish economic labour strife from political risk-based revolutionary activity, and it is often hard to tell when kidnapping is a political risk and when it is not. Very often, pecuniary and political motives are intermixed.)

Ironically, political kidnappings are often the safest kind, from the perspective of the victim. There is a much greater chance of the hostage being returned unharmed by political activists when the ransom payments are made. Once the money has been raised for other anti-government activities, political kidnappers are thereafter reluctant to incur the political repercussions of actually killing their victims.

Kidnapping should be distinguished from outright assassination. If the revolutionary group is interested in making a political statement, they will kill their target in a public setting, for example by ambushing a car in which the victim is riding. On the other hand, once a kidnapping is accomplished, often a team of negotiators will be able to pay the requested ransom and then successfully retrieve the kidnap victim.

There are organizations which specialize in kidnapping negotiations. They will even deliver the ransom on behalf of the victim's family or corporation. Sometimes this ransom payment will be put forward by insurance companies. There are insurers who provide kidnap and ransom insurance. For prior payment of an insurance premium, the insurance company will provide an insurance policy and pay the kidnappers an insurance settlement. Kidnap and ransom insurance is somewhat controversial. In some countries (such as in the UK, for example) insurers are forbidden to offer this coverage. It is seen as contrary to public policy, in that by offering kidnap and ransom insurance, underwriters are encouraging more acts of kidnapping because the kidnappers realize the ransom will be quickly paid. There may be some merit to this argument. In the early 1980s, one insurance company that did offer kidnap and ransom insurance had its offices burgled. During this burglary the only items that were taken were the insurance files naming those individuals to whom kidnap and ransom policies had been issued.

The final major form of political risk deals not with the immediate threat of assassination or kidnap. Rather, it involves the evacuation of personnel from potential zones of political unrest. The classic example is the intermittent revival of rebel activity in southern Sudan. In the early 1980s, a series of rebel attacks were carried out against European oil exploration teams operating in this region of Africa. Lives were lost, equipment was destroyed. Although these hit-and-run attacks occurred sporadically and over a fairly widespread area of Sudan, US and European companies working in this region were forced to make contingency plans to pull out their employees on a moment's notice. Although there were no proximate signs of political danger, these companies had to pare down their operations and devote time and resources to emergency planning to safeguard the withdrawal options, if necessary, of their in-country personnel. In countries of potential unrest, such micropolitical risk planning is an important aspect of managerial responsibility.

2 What makes a foreign investment politically risky?

Even in a politically unstable country, not all assets and people face the same degree of political risk. In Chile, for example, when the Allende regime came to power, one of the first acts of the new government was selectively to expropriate foreign investment. One such expropriation was of the International Telephone and Telegraph (IT&T), a US-owned and operated telephone system. However, the Allende government did not expropriate the Sheraton hotel in Santiago, although the hotel was likewise owned by IT&T.

In this instance, the same foreign investor with two assets in a hostile country, a phone company and a major hotel, suffered expropriation of one of its investments while the other remained completely untouched. It was said that Allende's government objected to foreigners listening in on personal Chilean telephone calls, but that only Americans could run the Sheraton hotel in such a manner that it would guarantee soft beds, clean rooms and world-class meals to the communist and socialist foreign dignitaries who visited Chile's new socialist regime.

The factors which can contribute to the political risk vulnerability of a foreign investment are type of operation, lack of local employment, lack of local business participation, lack of overseas production inputs, and lack of specialized overseas markets. These will now be examined.

Type of operation

In a civil war or as the target of terrorist bombings, different types of foreign investments face different levels of threat of destruction. A US water exploration team in the Sahara Desert, for example, operated successfully in a region that was rife with civil strife. None of the warring parties had an interest in destroying the camp and its equipment, because any water that was discovered would have been a valuable asset to all factions.

Assets that are of value, or that are not objectionable to in-country political groups, in general have less political risk associated with them than projects that are clearly owned and operated for the benefit of foreign investors. A number of operational characteristics reduce a project's political risk. Perhaps the two most important are (1) the employment level of the project; and (2) the overseas reliance on both production inputs and foreign markets.

Lack of local employment

In-country projects or investments that employ a large number of local workers tend to be less threatened by political risk. In El Salvador, for example, during the 1980s, a US electronics instrument manufacturer continued to operate successfully throughout a period of intense civil war. While other companies, both local and foreign, suffered labour strikes, terrorist bombings and other political setbacks, this US electronics company was untouched. Primarily this was because of the company's hiring practices. The company hired as many local workers as it could from its own neighbourhood, so that the surrounding population had a stake in keeping the company running without political opposition. Moreover, when new jobs became available in the plant, preferential hiring was given to relatives of those locals who already worked there. In short, the community had a stake in the electronics manufacturer and rebel forces could not attack this installation without incurring the displeasure of the local populace.

In less politically unstable countries, this local hiring also buffers foreign investment from possible governmental intervention. A government will be reluctant to expropriate a foreign investment that employs many local workers if that government cannot continue to operate the facility at full or high employment. The Sheraton hotel in Santiago is a classic example of this fact.

Alternatively, projects involving a small workforce, especially large projects such as mining and petroleum operations, are by definition subject to high levels of expropriatory political risk. A small expatriate workforce engaged in highly mechanized mining of bauxite or copper, for example, can be easily replaced by local personnel once the relatively low-technology skills are learned by the appropriate governmental workers. (There are ways in which even these types of projects can offset some of their political risk. These techniques will be articulated later in this entry.)

Lack of local business participation and/or local borrowing

Involvement of the local workforce is only one method by which a foreign investor can tie itself to local political and business interests. In addition, a joint local partner with political connections, rather than a completely foreign-owned operation, has been shown to reduce the amount of political risk problems that such an investment faces.

Local borrowing, instead of financing from abroad, also significantly reduces political risk. Many international companies that are experienced in foreign investment provide as little equity as possible for their foreign operations. Instead, they fund local operations, as much as possible, through assumption of local debt.

This has two advantages. First, by providing local bankers with a stake in the local company's success (if the local loans are to be repaid), these bankers become advocates of the investment with the host country's government. Should problems arise that may lead to expropriation, these bankers can and do petition their government to find other solutions to existing investment problems. Second, by maximizing local borrowing in local currency, the political risk of inconvertibility is thereby lessened. Rather than needing to exchange local currency for hard currency to repay offshore loans, when such foreign exchange is not readily available in the country, the local investment can use its soft currency profits to repay domestic loans. Indeed, as happened in Brazil during the debt crisis of the early 1980s, many overseas investors with local Brazilian currency used these funds as collateral to take out even more domestic Brazilian loans to expand their local business operations.

The only exception to this value of local borrowing is when such local borrowing reduces the availability of local funds to indigenous businesses. Under these circumstances, political risk may be increased. Fortunately, in most situations, the host government is more than willing to increase overall local debt availability. However, such economic and local banking policies must be thoroughly checked by the overseas investor.

Lack of overseas production inputs

Unlike overseas financing (which increases a project's chances of expropriation) the use of essential offshore production inputs can reduce these political risks significantly. By production inputs we mean anything that is required to produce a product. Such inputs can be specialized components, such as a unique computer chip that is required in an instrumentation device, or personnel with unique skills or training.

Governments are reluctant to seize foreign investments (if they intend to continue operation of the facility under their own authority and control) in situations where important production inputs must be sourced from overseas. Once spare parts or vital personnel are no longer available to the project, the production process will eventually come to a halt. This, in turn, has a number of negative consequences for the expropriating government. Local workers become unemployed, and the seized facility no longer produces revenue nor generates local taxes.

This strategy of sourcing production inputs from abroad is perhaps the only significant protection against expropriation for large mining and petroleum investments. However, once spare parts are available from alternative friendly sources or are capable of being manufactured locally in the host country, then this protection disappears. Oil exploration, drilling and producing, for example, has become a fairly low-technology industry. This accounts for the frequent expropriation of such facilities in some developing, anti-Western countries.

A similar decision on the part of overseas investors to hold back production inputs and source them from abroad is to establish only a partial production plant in the host country. These incomplete components are then shipped back to the home country of the investor for final assembly. Expropriation of such a local facility, even if the work can be continued, has little or no foreign markets (other than the parent company of the expropriated facility) to sell these incomplete goods.

In the late 1970s, one such expropriation of a partial assembly plant occurred in Latin America. For domestic political reasons, the host government felt pressured by local interests to effect this expropriation. Once accomplished, however, the government realized the negative consequences of its actions. Negotiations were entered into by the expropriated investor and the host government. The government upheld the expropriation and kept ownership of the seized facility. The investors nevertheless were made whole. They were given a lucrative management contract to continue to run the facility (thus keeping open the channels for the input of overseas-sourced vital production inputs) and a profitable re-sale price was established for sales from the government-owned plant to the US parent company.

The hybrid nature of the expropriated facility, the result of prior effective political risk planning by the parent company, did not avoid the eventual expropriation. However, not only did it minimize the impact of this local political decision, it also allowed the overall multinational production process to proceed eventually at a profit.

Lack of specialized overseas markets

Another characteristic of a foreign investment that reduces its risk of expropriation is when this facility relies completely upon specialized overseas markets for sales. In the case of many industries (such as the production and refinement of petroleum products), there is a ready domestic market for the goods produced by the expropriated facility. In some situations, however, the specialized products cannot be used in the local economy.

Following the expropriation of a specialized commodity exporter in the 1970s, the parent company contacted all its buyers worldwide, who in the past had purchased that product from the parent company's expropriated investment. The company informed these buyers that if they purchased any goods from the expropriated facility, they would never do any business again with the parent company. The expropriating government was subsequently unable to find any buyers for this commodity. Tons of product came to port from the government-run facility, but there the product sat, denying the government any export revenue. As a result, the host government reversed its position and returned the expropriated assets to the rightful owner, who then returned to the local facility and operated it successfully and freely thereafter.

3 Insurance considerations in political risk

Many types of political risks are included as 'perils insured against' in different political risk insurance programmes. (The buyer does not purchase one policy for expropriation, another policy for war, and so forth.) However, the actual policy coverages offered – including coverage terms and conditions, limitations and exclusions – will vary widely. Therefore this present review will limit itself to general political risk insurance principles.

In the preceding discussion, war risk, as well as kidnap and ransom insurance, have already been mentioned. Political risk insurance is also available for the perils of expropriation, inconvertibility and (in limited cases) politically motivated contract repudiation. Overseas credit risk is generally available from export agencies of most industrialized governments. Event cancellation insurance may include protection against political perils. Personal lines insurance for expatriate employees of major international corporations sometimes also provides political risk coverage.

Sometimes the perils insured are specifically mentioned as insurable causes of loss. An expropriation policy, for example, will precisely define expropriation (for the purposes of the coverage grant) as the insured peril which will trigger the insurance payment. Other types of policies provide political risk insurance by way of not excluding it as a reason for denying the insurance claim. Event cancellation insurance is a prime example of how this latter form of coverage works.

Event cancellation insurance is a broad coverage offered to those groups and individuals with a financial stake in the production and holding of an event. A major television network, for example, may purchase the rights to broadcast a Winter Olympic Games or the soccer World Cup. The network in turn sells advertising time to be aired during these broadcasts. However, if the sporting event in question does not occur, the advertisers are refunded their money and the network's broadcast rights become worthless.

This scenario is a classic example of where this hypothetical network would purchase event cancellation insurance. If the sporting event does not occur or is significantly delayed, financial losses borne by the network would be reimbursed by the event cancellation insurance policy. However, the policy will most likely contain a number of exclusions. The insurers will agree to provide event cancellation coverage, but not where the event is cancelled due to bankruptcy of the event's sponsors. Other causes of cancellation may also be excluded: labour strife or similar reasons why the host site itself is not ready in time for the event (whether such labour unrest is political or not), local rioting or political turmoil in the host country or city, and so forth.

For many such types of insurance policies, the absence of political risk exclusions inherently provides political risk coverage. The same can be said for personal lines or accident policies issued to major corporations. Employees transferred or travelling overseas are often provided with personal lines and/or accident coverage. Their goods are protected from theft or destruction. Their medical expenses and/or emergency repatriation to out-of-country hospitals are picked up by an accident policy. Again, some such policies exclude property damage or injury due to political turmoil. Other policies do not contain such exclusions.

The more explicit coverage grants (such as expropriation insurance) are generally provided in their own political risk insurance policies. A few words are in order regarding the historical origin of these political risk coverages. Mention has been made of war insurance from Lloyd's during the years between the First and Second World Wars. Even before then, limited forms of political risk insurance were available. The Chubb Group of Insurance Companies (a large US insurer), for example, offered bombardment insurance to coastal residents of New York and New Jersey in 1898 in the event that the conflict of the Spanish-American War moved northwards from Cuba.

However, these early insurance programmes (including the Lloyd's war risk facility) were quite limited in scope. The major thrust of modern political risk insurance began only after the Second World War. During these post-war years, a key element of US foreign policy was to encourage US companies to expand and invest abroad. Global political stability could be achieved, so it was thought, if jobs and rising personal income were available to workers in poorer countries around the world. Poor people, hopeless people, in their bitterness turn to communism. Working people with a middle-class stake in their societies will embrace and defend not only the free-market system but democracy as well.

This thinking was embodied in the Marshall Plan, primarily designed to aid in the rebuilding of western Europe. A small part of the Marshall Plan included US governmental guarantees of political risk and inconvertibility protection for those eligible US corporations who would invest in less developed areas of the world. It was believed that US corporations who would not expand overseas, who would not create local indigenous jobs, might otherwise do so if such political risk insurance protection were available.

The programme was an enormous success. From these humble beginnings arose an independent, quasi-governmental agency, the Overseas Private Investment Corporation (OPIC), which operates under the foreign policy guidance of the US State Department and which continues to provide political risk insurance as well as risk financing for eligible US overseas investors.

OPIC has served as a model for the establishment and operation of similar governmental programmes in many industrialized countries. While such national schemes will not be discussed in detail, certain aspects of the OPIC programme which have been adopted by various other national agencies should be addressed in the context of more fundamental political risk considerations.

Perhaps the most important of these is the 'foreign government approval' (FGA) and the waiver of confidentiality that are required prior to the issue of the political risk insurance policy. In this regard, governmental political risk policies are radically different from their private sector counterparts.

OPIC is not alone in obtaining prior governmental approval from the country in which it is about to issue a political risk insurance policy. The World Bank's multilateral political risk insurance facility, discussed later, has adopted this OPIC provision in its entirety.

Informing the host government that a political risk insurance policy is being contemplated with that nation as the locale of the offered coverage has advantages and disadvantages. Clearly, from a purely political standpoint, there are sovereignty issues to be taken into account. Governments usually object to other governments making secret guarantees for actions that may be taken within the first government's sovereign boundaries. If,

however, the insuring government has asked for and obtained permission from the host government for the issue of such a policy, then in the event of subsequent problems covered by the political risk insurance, the existence of such a prior policy is not the cause of embarrassment to the host government.

A second advantage of obtaining some form of FGA is that by doing so the host government agrees at least implicitly to negotiate future problems under the policy in good faith. The project country's government is indeed a willing host, which is not the case when the prior existence of a political risk insurance policy is unknown to the host government.

Of course, in the event of regime change, an FGA is of little value to the insured or to the insurer. The new government can easily repudiate any agreements entered into by its predecessor. However, the prior government's approval of an FGA has historically been shown to be important in subsequent political risk insurance negotiations.

Private sector political risk insurers traditionally have not sought FGAs from host governments. One reason is because the government-to-government sovereignty issue does not arise in dealings between a host government and a private insurer. The insurer – and its insured – are simply conducting a form of business, and establishing a private business relationship – for operations within a given host country. Claims payments, when made, are made in the insurer's home country, or in the home country of the insured investor.

Private sector insurers also will not be conducting claims or other negotiations on a government-to-government level. Teams of claims negotiators may approach the host government to try to resolve a political risk dispute, but this does not carry with it the broader political and international diplomatic implications of government-to-government negotiations. Most importantly, without the political clout of an insuring government, private sector insurers would rather not have anyone who is not immediately involved in the insurance to know of its existence. Indeed, most private sector insurance policies include a confidentiality clause: revealing the existence of the insurance policy to unauthorized individuals or agencies results in cancellation of the policy's coverage.

There is some merit to these restrictions. Private sector insurers are not as politically powerful in host countries as insuring governmental agencies. Indeed, in most instances, the foreign investment (with its benefits to the local country's economy, as discussed above) has more political leverage than the political risk insurer. As a result, when political risk problems arise, the insured investment itself (or its parent company) takes the lead in interfacing with the host government. The political risk insurer does not become directly and explicitly involved. Instead, it offers its expertise and guidance in private sessions with the political risk policyholder.

Which type of political risk insurance is best for the insurance buyer? This is a difficult question to answer. Many multinational companies with investments in foreign countries do not want to chance the ill-will that might be generated if an FGA were applied for and the host government were told that the investing company felt a need to purchase political risk insurance for their operations in that country. Other investors are convinced that the overt weight of their home country government behind them puts them in a better position to conduct their business in potentially troubled parts of the world.

Government-sponsored political risk insurance is often less expensive than similar private sector insurance. There are a number of reasons why this is generally true. One such reason is the portfolio size problem private insurers face. Any type of insurance requires the insurer to spread its potential risks as widely as possible so that no one loss or series of losses can wipe out the capital base on which the insurance is built. A hypothetical insurance company that only provides earthquake insurance in Tokyo, for example, may make significant profits for any number of years. However, when a disaster occurs, making all the required claims payments would bankrupt the insurer.

In political risk insurance, this portfolio size problem is severe. Few insureds purchase war insurance, for example, for projects in Switzerland (no matter how inexpensive the cover may be). There are, at any one time, probably no more than two or three dozen countries around the world where political risk insurance is routinely requested. For insurers, this is tantamount to putting all their eggs in a very few baskets. In the event of a major political upheaval in even a single country, the insurance losses could be catastrophic. As a result, private sector insurers must charge slightly higher premium rates to prepare themselves financially to withstand the (inevitable) major losses.

Government agency insurers, however, have access to other sources of funds in the event of a political risk catastrophe. The insuring governments also have additional foreign policy objectives beyond those of the private sector insurers' financial bottom line. Governmental insurance invariably has the full-faith guarantees of the home country's treasury behind its political risk programme. In the event that a sudden wave of political risk losses wipes out the insurer's capital, funds can be borrowed from the national treasury for claims and for ongoing insurance operations. The availability of such emergency funds means that governmental insurance pricing can be set much closer to the anticipated break-even point of profitability.

Not only do government-sponsored political risk insurance programmes have better access to emergency funds, they are also better able to spend local currencies than their private sector counterparts. When a political risk insurer pays an inconvertibility claim, that insurance company pays the insured in hard currency (outside the jurisdiction of the locally blocked soft currency). The insurer also takes possession of the inconvertible (or blocked) local currency as part of their rights of subrogation. Private sector insurers must then try to convert, or more likely spend, the blocked currency they have received. However, private sector insurers are in the business of trying to make money, not spend it. Governments, however, are in exactly the opposite position: governments spend money, such as paying for local embassies and foreign aid allocations; they do not try to accumulate profits.

These operational differences in goals between governmental and private sector insurance programmes translate directly into differential premium rates. For inconvertibility insurance, private sector insurance rates are often five to ten times higher than the identical coverage purchased from a governmental insurer. Moreover, governmental programmes are also designed to increase the amount of trade with, and investment in, politically important countries (from a foreign policy standpoint) around the globe. Private sector insurers do not have similar goals. As a result, governmental insurance is not only generally more inexpensive, the insurance policies can be more attractive as well: they act as enticements for investing overseas. In many instances, government schemes will also offer low-cost project financing as well, and/or non-recourse loans that do not have to be repaid if the foreign-location project fails because of political risk losses.

The difference in policy-period terms (the non-cancellable duration of the insurance policy) between governmental and private sector programmes is a prime example of these underlying differences in political versus business orientation. The policy period that is offered by governmental programmes is generally longer (often up to twenty years of guaranteed coverage) than is the case for private sector insurance (which can guarantee coverage for as little as one, two or in some instances three years).

Insuring governments know that they will be involved in political affairs with countries around the globe twenty years from now. Private sector insurers know that during such an extended timeframe they may change their business orientation significantly. It is difficult to find any private corporation, insurance-related or not, that is willing to make such a long-term commitment.

Another source of differentials in premium rates between governmental and private sector insurers is the fact that for certain types of political risk losses, governmental insurers are in a unique claims settlement situation. Losses are fewer and host country compensation is greater and swifter.

This is especially true for the political risk peril of contract repudiation. In the event of significant contract repudiation losses, the governmental insurer can often turn to another agency of that same insuring government – and the offending country that has caused the contract repudiation loss may find itself as the subject of governmental retaliation ranging from a withdrawal of trade credits to outright seizure or freezing of assets. Private sector insurers obviously do not have such collateral political and economic power.

The preceding discussion is not meant to imply that government-sponsored political risk insurance is, in all instances, superior to its private sector counterpart – it is not. In some ways, private market-sourced political risk insurance is superior. There are many instances when a corporation's political risk exposure is very short-term and/or quite unusual. Because of their flexibility, private sector insurers can be more desirable.

Even more traditional overseas investments often do not need the extended years of guaranteed coverage offered by governmental insurance programmes. In many instances, the return on investment for overseas projects is such that within three or four years the initial capital outlay is totally recouped (in terms of income flows and a continuing stream of profits). After this financial hurdle is overcome, what is at risk is future opportunity costs. A major political risk loss would be financially discouraging, but not as disastrous as would be the case if such a loss were incurred early in the years of the given project.

Governmental insurers are also reluctant to escalate an investment dispute into a full-blown confrontation between itself and a host government. The differences in 'waiting periods' (an insurance policy term and condition) that are used by governmental insurers and private sector insurers is instructive in this regard. All expropriation insurance policies contain what is called a waiting period. This waiting period is the length of time an expropriatory event must continue before it is deemed a permanent expropriation and therefore subject to a valid insurance claim and payment. Historically, governmental expropriation policies have required a one-year waiting period. This gives the governmental insurer a full twelve months to work behind the scenes to try to resolve a potential expropriatory dispute between itself and the host government.

Private sector political risk insurers – in part because of competitive pressures among themselves, and in part because of a willingness to utilize their claims personnel, consultants and negotiators – will often offer waiting periods as short as nine or even six months. Furthermore, private sector insurers are subject to legal challenges through the courts on the part of political risk insurance purchasers if the interpretation of the policy and/or the handling of the political risk insurance claim does not meet with the insured's satisfaction. Few if any such recourses are available against governments and the political risk insurance programmes they sponsor.

Finally, as mentioned above, governmental insurers are constrained by a number of considerations – or processes that they must complete – before insurance coverage can be offered to applying buyers. Governmental programmes may be restricted and unavailable in certain countries that are politically out-of-favour with the insuring government. The necessary FGAs may take a long time to obtain. Investigations may be required or evidence must be made available, that the insured is a qualifying business entity for the purpose of obtaining the governmental insurance. In some instances, studies must be completed demonstrating that the overseas investment will not eliminate home-country jobs by exporting them to an overseas (host country) location as a part of the proposed overseas investment.

Multilateral political risk insurance

Of the governmental political risk insurers currently in operation, perhaps the most ambitious is the Multilateral Investment Guarantee Agency (MIGA), part of the World Bank Group. MIGA, founded in 1988, is actually owned by its member countries and membership is open to all the member countries of the World Bank. (Over 107 countries were full members of the MIGA programme at the end of 1993.) MIGA guarantees foreign investment against political risks in developing member countries and provides advisory services (through its Foreign Investment Advisory Service, or FIAS) to assist member countries in creating an attractive climate for private foreign investment. MIGA, as a worldwide organization, is in effect broader in scope and intent than any purely national political risk insurance programme. However, MIGA has adopted many of the insurance concepts first pioneered on the purely national level.

Under the MIGA programme, eligible countries where insurance will be offered are also members of a larger financial community (that is, the World Bank). Projects insured are part of the public record. MIGA is still in its infancy, but this added World Bank leverage should make its political risk insurance programme attractive to many potential investors.

MIGA offers the standard base coverages of insurance against currency inconvertibility, expropriation and war and civil disturbance. MIGA's standard policy term is fifteen years (non-cancellable), but in exceptional cases, it may be extended to twenty. As with many other national governmental programmes, MIGA requires that the insured project will have positive developmental effects and that it will be environmentally sound. Again, as with other national programmes, the decision-making timetable is not quick. Basic underwriting reviews can take up to four months before a decision is made whether or not to offer political risk insurance coverage. Extended evaluations can actually take years before insurance approval is given (or declined).

MIGA programmes, like most national political risk insurance programmes, also require that the projects to be insured are *new* investments since these programmes are designed to encourage investment, not to insure what is already at risk. MIGA's definition of 'new', however, can include the expansion, privatization or financial restructuring of existing operations.

MIGA works closely with other international and national entities. For example, on a project-by-project basis, MIGA has established reinsurance arrangements with OPIC, with the EDC (the Economic Development Corporation, Canada's equivalent to OPIC) and with Japan's Economic Investment Department (a branch of the Ministry of International Trade and Investment). These reinsurance agreements will be used for the possible transfer of blocked funds (should the need arise) following a political risk inconvertibility loss (or losses) on a major MIGA-insured risk.

4 Conclusion

In the bi-polar world of the four decades following the Second World War, it was thought that political risk assessment would be a relatively easy task: that of identifying communist bloc influences and/or nations afflicted with widespread and abject poverty. These variables were correlated highly with most forms of political risk. Countries such as Guatemala, Cuba, Chile, Nicaragua, Algeria and Libya shared certain political antecedents and common denominators. Until recently, there has been little appreciation of the inapplicability of anti-communist, bi-polar thinking in a newly emerging, multi-polar world.

The decline of Russian influence in eastern Europe has led to more not less political risk in that part of the world. Similarly, the rise of religious fundamentalism has led not only to sudden regime change in Iran but to possible anti-Western governmental instabilities in countries ranging all across northern Africa and central Asia. Tribal or ethnic concerns continue to plague many countries of central Africa and – where combined with economic poverty and long-standing traditions of egalitarian thinking – portend possible major political risk problems in areas such as southern Mexico. Recalcitrant local elites, unconstrained and unchannelled by concerted 'superpower' guidance, are also creating new examples of political risk in countries around the globe, from Haiti to Cambodia.

In a very subtle sense, the levels of political risk seem to be increasing, not decreasing, as the world moves towards the twenty-first century. With the decline of class-based economic (although not nationalistic) ideology, political risk assessment has likewise become even more difficult. Religious, ethnic, human rights, collective bargaining (labour organizing), trade protection, environmental, consumer and numerous other variables often complicate the process of political risk assessment.

As a result, political risk specialists are being forced to expand their analytical and assessment capabilities. Much more emphasis is being placed on non-official, non-governmental sources of political risk information. On-site visits to possible areas of future overseas investment continue to be a major component of consequent political risk analysis and decision making. But now, instead of relying too heavily upon local governmental data and embassy (or intelligence) briefings, teams of political risk specialists are walking the streets, reading the local newspapers, shopping in the marketplaces and talking with students, local religious leaders and/or other potentially disaffected political elements.

There is nothing that replaces the value of such on-site visits by knowledgeable political risk experts for short-term political risk diagnosis. However, a number of additional political risk forecasting tools are now being routinely applied to the task of forecasting future political developments.

For example, a number of firms now provide short-term political risk 'event data banks' to corporate clients in North America, Europe and Asia. The Ackerman Group, Kroll Information Services and Political Risk Services are but three of the more well-known political risk assessment firms. Kroll provides a 'Daily Intelligence Briefing' with annotated comments. Political Risk Services provides 'Weekly Business Risk Alerts' with each story providing a short-term analysis.

The Ackerman Group has a computerized online RISKNET database which is updated daily and can be accessed via computer by subscribers to the program. They also provide over 100 fax transmissions a year for clients who subscribe to the Enhanced Travel Reports. The Ackerman Group also provides security assistance ranging from expatriate training to actual bodyguards for key personnel, plant location and plant security reviews, hostage recoveries, host country business partner investigations and a variety of similar political risk services.

Effective as these and other services might be, they serve only a short-term (or sometimes an after-the-fact) function. Six months before Castro seized control in Cuba and six months before the Sandinista forces came to power in Nicaragua, even the US Government – perhaps the most extensive short-term political risk assessment facility of all time – had very little idea that these two events would come to pass. Indeed, reports now surfacing indicate that the US intelligence community had no idea the Berlin Wall was going to be erected until East German soldiers showed up with construction supplies and started building.

Quantitative long-term political risk forecasting suffers from the same problems encountered by almost all forms of social science research: a lack of quantitative precision in the underlying units of political risk data. Even with mathematical advances in the study of chaos, and even more recently in what has come to be known as 'catastrophe theory', these tools are difficult to apply to the often tenuous and uncertain political events (and to the different societal levels of analysis) with which a political risk specialist must contend. To date, the value of such quantitative breakthroughs, for political risk analysis, has been primarily heuristic.

On a more qualitative front, political risk 'scenario-building' and 'worst-case analyses' continue to be important components of an overall political risk assessment programme. Such analyses can take a variety of forms, from evacuation planning and plant security, all the way to pre-arranging bartering or international 'countertrade' facilities in the event such worst-case scenarios actually come to pass.

In short, accurate long-term political risk assessment and forecasting remains quite elusive. Political risk insurance is one extremely important aspect of political risk planning, in that it widens the margin for forecasting error. (Thus the emphasis on political risk insurance in the preceding discussion.) Once invested in

a country, however, other defensive or 'buffering' measures also increase the acceptable margin for political risk forecast error.

But beyond these basic precautions, long-term political risk forecasting must take into account a myriad of lessons from twentieth-century political history. The analyst's goal must be to continue to try to extrapolate these historical lessons – using a wide variety of assessment tools, none of which are highly accurate – onto the current fears, dreams, aspirations, desires and hopes that today seem to be continuously unleashed across the face of the planet. As we approach the complicated and fragmented multi-polar world of the twenty-first century, such political risk forecasting is no easy task.

ROBERT S. FRANK
R. SHELBY FRANK & ASSOCIATES

Further reading

Bertrand, K. (1990) 'Politics pushes to the marketing foreground', *Business Marketing* (March).

Brewer, T. (ed.) (1985) *Political Risks in International Business: New Directions for Research, Management, and Public Policy*, New York: Praeger.

Brewer, T., David, K. and Chen, L.W.C. (1986) *Investing in Developing Countries*, New York: Lexington Books. (A review of the process of planning for international investment, with special attention towards assessing political risk.)

Collins, P. (1981) *Living in Troubled Lands, Beating the Terrorist Threat Overseas*, Boulder, CO: Paladin Press.

Desta, A. (1985) 'Assessing political risk in less developed countries', *Journal of Business* 5 (4): 40–53.

Ghadar, F. and Moran, T.H. (eds) (1984) *Managing International Political Risk: New Dimensions*, Washington, DC: Ghadar & Associates. (Update of an earlier study (1983) that Ghadar and Moran co-authored with Stephen J. Kobrin.)

Kobrin, S. (1985) *Managing Political Risk Assessment – Strategic Response to Environmental Change*, Berkeley, CA: University of California Press.

Leiden, C. and Schmitt, K.M. (1968) *The Politics of Violence: Revolution in the Modern World*, Englewood Cliffs, NJ: Prentice Hall. (Still one of the best examinations of violence and the 'pre-revolutionary environment'. Case studies of selected revolutions are included.)

Lifton, R.J. (1968) *Revolutionary Immortality*, New York: Vintage/Random House. (A classic text in the psychology of revolutionary movements.)

Shapiro, A. (1981) 'Managing political risk: a policy approach', *Columbia Journal of World Business* (Fall): 63–8.

Shine, E. (1987) 'Detecting country risk', *Corporate Finance* (September): 50–6. (An analysis primarily as to how political risk affects bankers and corporate financial planning.)

Simon, J. (1982) 'Political risk assessment: past trends and future prospects', *Columbia Journal of World Business* (Fall): 62–71. (A somewhat dated but excellent introduction to the topic of political risk.)

West, G.T. (1994) 'Investment insurance: the quiet facilitator of private investment to Latin America', *Project Finance in Latin America*, 34–7.

Wilkinson, P. (1974) *Political Terrorism*, New York and Toronto: Wiley.

See also: FINANCIAL MANAGEMENT, INTERNATIONAL; FOREIGN EXCHANGE RISK, MANAGEMENT OF; GLOBALIZATION; HUMAN RESOURCE MANAGEMENT, INTERNATIONAL; INTERNATIONAL BUSINESS, LEGAL DIMENSIONS OF; INTERNATIONAL MARKETING; INTERNATIONAL TRADE AND FOREIGN DIRECT INVESTMENT

Related topics in the IEBM: COMMITMENT IN JAPAN; COUNTRY RISK ANALYSIS; INSURANCE; INTERNATIONAL BUSINESS ELITES; LAW, CONTRACT; MANAGEMENT IN AFRICA; MANAGEMENT IN LATIN AMERICA; MANAGEMENT IN PACIFIC ASIA; MANAGEMENT IN SWITZERLAND; MIGRANT MANAGERS; MILITARY MANAGEMENT

Political risk, assessment and management of

Overview

This article defines political risk as governmental takeovers of property, either with or without compensation, generally referred to as nationalization or expropriation; agitation that disrupts operations or causes damage to property or personnel; and restrictions that impede the company's ability to take certain actions. Most treatments of political risk focus strictly on consequences within foreign countries where a company has direct investments; however, we broaden political risk to include repercussions in a company's home country or third country because of political actions. For example, Iraq's invasion of Kuwait caused NRM-Steel's 1990 earnings to fall by about 20 per cent because of a political action taken in its home country – the US embargo of sales to Iraq. Accusations about Shell's political and environmental practices in Nigeria led to consumer pressures to boycott Shell in such third countries as South Africa.

We have also deviated from some other treatises on political risk by excluding exchange control from our definition. Although we acknowledge that the decision to limit capital outflows is a political one, we feel it falls within the domain of economic risk, much as does currency depreciation. In reality, the decision to allow a currency's value to depreciate is also a political one, and outflow restrictions and currency depreciation are alternatives for dealing with the same set of economic conditions. The subject of these economic conditions is simply too large to address here except to discuss briefly how political-risk service organizations combine economic and political-risk indicators in their indices.

While we attempt to isolate political risk from economic risk, we acknowledge that the two are often intertwined, i.e. adverse economic conditions may bring on political unrest that hampers operations, and poor political decisions may disrupt the economy. In fact, most companies group political and economic risk together when deciding what portion of resources to allocate to each country where they might operate (see FOREIGN EXCHANGE RISK, MANAGEMENT OF).

1 The effect of political risk

The subject of political risk is most commonly approached from the viewpoint of a company from an industrialized country that is considering a new venture in a developing country. However, we have already alluded to the fact that political risk may occur in industrialized as well as in developing countries, and in home countries as well as in host countries. Further, political risk occurs for existing ventures as well as new ones; therefore the assessment and management of political risk need to occur both before and after the establishment of foreign operations and to be a nearly continuous effort.

Political risk services tend to be directed toward the management of companies and to financial institutions, notably banks, that may lend money to companies; however, political risk considerations go well beyond companies and lenders because political risk affects individual and institutional investor positions. Equity markets, especially in the United States, are often driven by investors seeking short-term returns in share prices. Long-term profits and dividends are of less concern. Top management knows this well, and is compensated for success in short-run profits and the upward movement of related share prices. The Asian share-price depression of the late 1990s has led most analysts to conclude that the traditional longer-term investment horizon of Asian companies and investors will also be shortened in the future.

The investment climate of the 1990s is such that mutual funds and other institutions which own large blocks of corporate shares are actually on the boards of the companies they own. Mutual funds are owned by individuals who have little knowledge of the companies in their portfolios and generally are not concerned with the contents of their funds. All that matters to those investors is that their mutual funds return a large yield each year. Mutual funds are regularly ranked on performance, and these rankings appear in the financial press. If individuals are not satisfied with the ranking of their mutual funds they are likely to move money into competing funds. Thus there is competition among funds, and fund managers attempt to influence activities of the companies in which they invest. Because all risks threaten short-run profits, short-term objectives invite avoidance of any activities that have a potential not to work out. This invites conservatism by attempting to earn a predictable and acceptable profit. Still, top management knows that risk avoidance is accompanied by a risk of loss of opportunity, as depicted in Figure 1.

As an example, since the fall of communism in eastern Europe, markets have opened in countries previously closed. Furthermore, these countries, such as Poland, provide highly trained people who are available for production at relatively low wage rates. Of course, the present deficiency in individual purchasing power limits the short-term market potential and the inadequacies of infrastructure counteract short-term production cost advantages. Hence, many foreign companies going to eastern Europe will likely have to wait years before they can establish and remit a good return on investment. During that time, many companies may perceive that political risk is high because of uncertain future legislation and stability, especially if governments are unable to promote growth as quickly as their citizens expect.

At the same time, the risk from not investing looms. Competitors with longer-term investment horizons may gain first-in advantages by buying the best local companies and lining up the best suppliers, distributors and local partners. Given the more short-term investment horizon of US companies than of Japanese and European companies in general, some shifts may occur in long-term national competitiveness, depending on whether political conditions (for which there is present risk) actually occur or not.

The assessment of political risk is no longer needed just for companies and lenders. It is also needed by individuals and mutual funds so that they can invest comfortably. As a first step, they must understand the nature of disclosures companies make to them about political risk. Next they must be able to evaluate political risk.

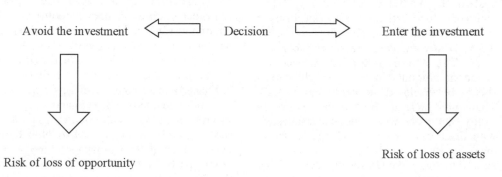

Figure 1 Risk avoidance and the loss of opportunity

503

2 What companies disclose in their annual reports

In the United States the reporting of foreign operations falls under the area of Segment Reporting, Financial Accounting Standard (FAS) 14. The standard requires that when an industry or geographic segment exceeds 10 per cent of sales or identifiable assets, certain information – such as sales, assets and operating profits – must be disclosed separately. Unfortunately this definition of segments allows companies to group many countries together so that individual investors cannot easily discern whether investments are located in a particularly troubled nation. For instance, a US company may simply show that 15 per cent of its sales and assets are abroad, without indicating whether they are all in Canada and western Europe or all in Cambodia and Vietnam. Even regional segmentation obscures information, i.e. how much of the European regional operations are in Switzerland versus Ukraine. Further, the 10 per cent rule for reporting segments is rarely met by an investment in a single troubled country, even though 100 per cent of that investment may be lost quickly because of political conditions, such as war damage or the freezing of assets in response to animosity between the home and host countries.

The International Accounting Standards Committee (IASC) is a body of national accounting standards setters. Its goal is to harmonize financial reporting across nations, and it overhauled its standard on Segment Reporting (IAS 14) in 1997. During the process of revision the IASC discussed requiring companies to report segments by categories of risk and reward levels. Thus high-risk areas were put forward as separate reportable segments. The IASC even discussed whether investment amounts in every single nation should be disclosed, no matter how small. This would have required companies simply to list each place where they have invested, with the investment value alongside. However, the Revised IAS 14 requires reporting similar to that of the US standard, except that geographical areas must be reported. This allows companies to combine risky and non-

risky countries. The significance of Revised IAS 14 is that subsequent revision to national standards, such as any made by the US Financial Accounting Standards Board (FASB), will be fairly minimal in the foreseeable future.

The second potential means by which companies can divulge political risk to shareholders is by disclosing in annual reports those contingent liabilities and losses that have a potential to occur. For example, in the United States, if at the date of financial statements a probable loss exists shortly and the amount of the loss can be estimated, companies are required actually to recognize the loss on the income statement, with a real liability for the company on the balance sheet. Companies often book lawsuits against them in advance of judgements when they know they will lose the suits. These are conspicuous warnings to shareholders that analysts easily see.

Most contingencies, however, are either less than likely to occur or difficult to measure. Thus they escape recognition on the balance sheet and income statement, and, instead, they are simply mentioned in footnotes at the end of the financial statements. The last category of contingencies is those which exist but have only a remote chance of occurring. Current US accounting requires no mention of these. Unfortunately for individual investors, most political risk losses either fall into the last category or, at best, require some mention as a footnote.

In a rather unscientific manner, we took a look at a few annual reports of multinational companies from around the world, as shown in Table 1. Only one of these reports (Alusuisse-Lonza) mentioned political risk, but only to say that, like other types of risks, it has the capacity to alter reported results. The report further stated that political risk could not be predicted at the time the report was published and the potential effects were therefore not included in the financial reports. From a US standpoint, the mention of political risk is purely voluntary. Akzo Nobel discussed at length how it managed foreign currency risk and foreign interest-rate risk, but this discussion can be linked only tangentially to political risk.

Table 1

Company	Home Country
ABB, 1996	Sweden/Switzerland
Akzo Nobel, 1995	Netherlands
Amcor, 1996	Australia
Alusuisse-Lonza, 1995	Switzerland
Ajinomoto, 1996	Japan
Bombardier, 1996	Canada
Italcementi, 1996	Italy
Lagardere, 1995	France
Kvaerner, 1996	Norway
Reynolds Metals, 1996	United States

In summary, companies publish very little financial information that informs shareholders of the potential political risks affecting them. Certainly, shareholders can usually find through supplementary research where a company operates; however, the amount of assets by country is much harder to determine. Still, where a company operates is a starting point for shareholders and their analysts to begin assessment of the political risk it faces. Only by being able to understand this risk can the shareholder then effectively communicate to top management the level of risk that is expected and tolerable.

3 What is at risk?

Of course, the assets of the multinational company are at risk. In addition, secondary losses arising from suits due to kidnapping and failure to complete contracts with outside customers can occur. Some insurance is available, especially for operations in developing economies. However, for the most part, insurance cannot cover these losses, particularly those arising from regulatory changes. Furthermore, it is sometimes difficult to prove that the causes of the losses are the insurable causes. Accordingly, it is reasonable to assume that exposure to loss can be quite high.

Although asset loss in a country can be total, asset takeover or property damage does not necessarily mean a full loss to investors. Most takeovers are preceded by a formal declaration of intent by the government and a subsequent legal process to determine compensation to the foreign investor. However, it is difficult to evaluate whether compensation is adequate. On the one hand, even if the investor is compensated for the full net book value or estimated market value of the assets, the investor may not be able to earn an equivalent return elsewhere. On the other hand, a compensation that is less than the book or market value may be misleading because the negotiated exit agreement may include additional benefits for the former investor, such as long-term purchase agreements on the output or management contracts.

The Chilean political decision to nationalize the ITT Telephone Company illustrates the difficulty of assessing how much is lost through a political occurrence. The Chilean Government offered about one-third of the book value of the properties, based on the argument that the equipment was run-down, causing customers to complain about the service. ITT countered that the book value understated the true value because a high return on assets had been earned and could be expected to continue in the future. The Government responded by saying that the return on assets was due to the rates charged to customers in the monopoly industry rather than to the equipment value. Each party proposed outside appraisal of the value, but each wanted to select appraisers and valuation criteria favourable to its position.

4 Assessment of political risk

Companies may analyse political risk with their own personnel, or they may rely on one or a combination of the many existing political risk services that are available. Both the companies themselves and the political risk services tend to look at similar indicators of political risk. Given the similarity, we discuss only a few of these services to demonstrate what so-called experts consider to be indications of political risk.

Most of the indices and services which follow are calculated or offered at least annually, with updates available with new information. Some are more frequent, such as Country Risk

Information Services, which has online availability. While many of these services calculate indices and rank countries, some do not. Information is available for the users to interpret, and since many of these services rely on similar or related information it is difficult to assess the track record for accuracy of one service compared to another.

Bank of America

Like many business analysis services, Bank of America's 'Country Outlook' and 'Country Risk Monitor' rely on a combination of economic, social, and political conditions. This is due to the difficulty of isolating economic risk from political risk, as one often causes the other. The 'Country Outlook' is a briefing or essay on a country by discussing its growth and employment, fiscal and monetary policies, trade and current account balances, capital and debt accounts, and some information on local markets and business conditions such as freedom and flexibility within the country. The 'Country Risk Monitor' assigns risk ratings and ranks countries on six economic constructs related to risks for multinationals, such as the ability to repay debts. Vital economic statistics are used to produce the ratings. Probably the most useful information to assess direct political risk is the description of current business conditions in the 'Country Outlook'.

Business Environment Risk Intelligence (BERI Index)

The BERI Index includes the following categories of country risk: political risk due to socio-political conditions, operating risk due to conditions which affect profits earned, and R Factor or risk to remittances of profit and repatriation of capital. Each of the three is forecast and the overall recommendation on a country is called the profit opportunity recommendation.

The political risk index (PRI) and the operating risk index (ORI) rely heavily on scores given by expert judges. The scores on factors are weighted by relative importance to the overall risk index. The PRI relies on political

scientists rather than business experts. The factors rated or judged are:

- fractionalization of the political system
- fractionalization of language, ethnicity and religion
- coercive measures in place to retain power
- mentality: corruption, nationalism, compromise and nepotism
- population density and wealth distribution
- ability for a radical left government to arise
- the amount of dependency on major hostile powers
- negative influences from regional politics
- conflict in society as evidenced by strikes, acts of civil disobedience, etc.
- instability such as guerrilla activity, wars and assassinations

The related operating risk index (ORI) uses experienced international business experts to judge:

- the degree to which nationals are favoured over guests
- the overall quality of the business climate

The latter includes measures of the political environment.

The R Factor measures both the willingness and ability of a country to allow repatriation of multinational corporate profits and capital. It is largely calculated through the use of economic statistics. A composite score is formed using all three indices.

Control Risk Information Services (CRIS)

This service is very much concerned with personal safety, such as whether employees and their families will be kidnapped or injured during insurrections or because of lawlessness. It relies on discussions with experts who have recent knowledge of events taking place in each country it surveys. It is concerned, among other matters, with the state of political parties, insurgencies, security in place and safety in airports. This information nicely complements the BERI Political Risk Index.

Political Risk Services Prince Model

The Prince Model is a forecast drawn from country specialists, government contacts, embassy officials and data from the International Monetary Fund (IMF) and government publications. One of the innovative aspects of this model is that clients can personalize it by altering the weighting of factors considered. Alternatively, they can use the preset weighting.

The specialists define the national characteristics of a country which they deem important. These are referred to as 'actors'. They then rate these actors on four constructs as to orientation or positive/negative nature towards the construct, certainty or consistency of this orientation, power or ability of the actor to have influence on the construct, and salience or relative importance of the actor relative to the other actors on the construct. Countries are then mapped and rated by their construct scores. The four constructs are:

- risk to regime stability
- likelihood of turmoil
- restriction on investment
- future restriction on trade

International Country Risk Guide (ICRG)

The ICRG rating includes five financial risk factors, six economic risk factors and thirteen political risk factors. Scores are calculated for each of the three composite risks as well as for a composite risk score. In addition, a narrative is included for each country. ICRG staff members compile data and weight them according to indicators that seem appropriate at the time. As with Political Risk Services PRI, clients can personalize the weights. Of the following political factors ICRG places the highest weights on the first four items:

- socioeconomic conditions
- economic planning
- government stability
- external conflict risk
- corruption

- involvement of the military in politics
- religion in politics
- degree of law and order
- ethnic tension
- political violence
- civil war threat
- party development
- bureaucracy quality

5 Summary of political risk services

Investors should probably use more than one of the above or other services to assess political risk, even though there is a great degree of overlap among services. By doing this they ensure comprehensive assessment. Moreover, the isolation of economic risk from political risk should be done carefully, as the two types of risk are very much intertwined. Finally, investors should assess political risk using their own criteria and knowledge. Internally, information is especially relevant for countries in which a company already has operations in place, because its management within those countries has experience in interpreting the consequences of political statements and events. It is also the most reliable source for determining micro versus macro risk and the means of dealing with changing political conditions. Internal company knowledge may augment the information from the political risk services, and a company should decide what factors are important for its specific situation. For example, a company's management within a given country may be so well connected to the political leadership that it can predict with some certainty how the government will respond to the conditions reported by a political risk service. Or the management may place either more or less weight than political risk services on ethnic tension because of the company's location within the country or its specific workforce composition.

6 Why companies operate in seemingly high political risk areas

Any cursory examination of political risk indicators alongside actual investment locations indicates that many companies are operating in areas that most political-risk assessment services consider high risk. For example, in the late 1980s and early 1990s Peru had high inflation, guerrilla warfare, political assassinations and a fall in industrial output; yet some foreign companies maintained their pre-existing Peruvian operations and others invested in Peru for the first time. This anomaly exemplifies the fact that there is no consensus as to what constitutes dangerous instability or how such instability can be predicted. It further illustrates differences in companies' perceptions of the effects of adverse political conditions on them. Basically, companies differ in perception of risk, tolerance of risk, perception of risk related to opportunity, and the portion of total assets and/or effort that must be put at risk. The following short discussion should depict these differences.

First, risk analysis depends largely on qualitative evaluation; thus it is understandable that two parties may view the same set of circumstances differently. This is analogous to the fact that not everyone bets on the favourite in a horse race. Companies respond to and act on an environment that their top managers have perceived and interpreted. For example, two US companies may attach very different probabilities to whether and how a government will control groups that are hostile to foreign investment. They may also attach different probabilities to their ability to deal with a given situation. (Methods of dealing with political risk are summarized below.) The attachment of the probabilities may be the result of a thorough analysis or simply a superficial conclusion based on impressions of a country or of the company's ability to handle the risk. In this respect, there seems to be some evidence that increased familiarity with a region reduces the perceived political risk of the region. For example, in a 1995 survey US companies perceived the Middle East to be much riskier than did UK companies; however, UK companies viewed Latin America as significantly more risky than did US companies. The difference was attributed to the higher proportionate presence of US and UK companies in Latin America and the Middle East, respectively (Dalby 1995).

Second, companies and their decision-makers have different tolerances of risk. For example, risk-taking behaviour sets entrepreneurial organizations apart from others; therefore it is logical that some companies will endure political risk that is unacceptable to others. There are, of course, anecdotes of positive outcomes from extremes in risk tolerance or risk aversion. However, the longer-term effect of extreme risk tolerance or aversion is apt to be an expensive failure. It is difficult to examine political risk tolerance in isolation from competitive risk. For example, a company may enter a country that it perceives to have high political risk simply because it considers the competitive risk of not entering to be even higher. In other words, if both company A and B enter a country and are later affected adversely by political conditions, neither one has suffered relative to the other. But if A shuns the market and B enters without adverse consequences, B will be better off than A. This potential outcome may spur A to enter a market that it perceives to have high political risk. Examples of such behaviour are often noted in oligopoly industries and where there are substantial first-in advantages.

Third, any decision on the comparative use of resources is dependent on the relationship between the expected returns and risks. Just as there are different qualitative assessments of risk, so there are differences in qualitative assessments of expected returns. For example, comparative economic growth is a major consideration when deciding how to allocate resources among countries; however, economists' projections of growth often vary substantially. Thus one company may forgo a project because it believes the lowest estimate; whereas the second party may move forward because it believes a higher estimate. Further, one company's perceived ability to exploit opportunities in a given market may be higher than the other's because of the relative fit of its products and operating methods. In addition, the investments already in place (or lack of them) may also influence the locations to which a company may feasibly go. For example, the French-headquartered company CFP has been criticized for concentrating its crude-oil exploration in countries that are unpopular politically, such as Libya and Iraq; however, as a relative late entrant into the globally integrated oil industry, CFP found that its competitors had already locked up available concessions in the less politically risky countries. Similarly, if a company is faced with saturated markets in countries with low political risk, its opportunities of expanding in its familiar product lines within those markets are apt to be low. In such a case a company may opt for an option with a higher return but higher political risk by shifting emphasis from the areas with low return but low political risk.

Fourth, the portion of assets that must be put at risk is also a factor. For example, two companies may assess the same risk and opportunities for a $1 million project in Kazakhstan; however, for a company with assets of $100 billion the portion of assets to be put at risk is far smaller than for a second company which has assets of only $100 million. Behavioural differences in this situation may thus be based on what can be lost, rather than on what can be gained. In other words, the larger company's performance will not be significantly altered if the project fails, but the smaller company's performance will be. This behaviour is akin to the buying of a lottery ticket, i.e. having a willingness to gamble on possible big payoffs with a low probability, provided one puts an insignificant portion of resources at risk.

7 Risk and the investing shareholder

The above discussion highlights the decision process for company managers, who act as agents for shareholders. Given that shareholders have scant knowledge of companies' dependence on different countries – much less the political risk of each of these countries – these managers may or may not be acting

according to shareholders' tolerance of political risk. If shareholders had more information about companies' international operations – for example by requiring them to list the value of investments by country – shareholders could factor in their own risk assessments and tolerances when deciding what stocks to buy, hold and sell. In such a scenario it is logical that individual investors would differ substantially from each other for the same reasons that companies differ in the geographical composition of their operations. In other words, some individuals may shun a company making a big commitment in the Democratic Republic of the Congo, whereas other individuals may be drawn to that company because, for example, they do not perceive the risk to be high in relation to opportunity, or because they are more willing to accept a high degree of risk. Presumably, if shareholders had more information they would reflect this information in their decisions on whether to buy, sell or hold shares in particular companies. If these decisions were not counterbalanced they would cause changes in share price. In turn, company decision-makers would be likely to alter their actions in order to satisfy the risk–return preferences of prospective shareholders.

8 Dealing with political risk

Not all types of political risk can be managed the same way. For example, lobbying may be effective to prevent the enactment of operational restrictions, but it has no bearing on insurrections that disrupt production or sales. A plant security programme (such as the posting of armed guards) may prevent property damage, but it will not avert the passage of unfavourable legislation. Further, companies may face tradeoffs among types of political risk. For example, tobacco companies have recently faced a high political risk from changes in operational restrictions in most industrialized countries, while simultaneously facing very low risks from either governmental takeovers or disruptive agitation in these same countries. The opposite has been true in some of the developing countries where they operate. Given these diversities, it is obvious that different types of political risk must be assessed and acted upon differently within each country.

Another complication comes about because political risk changes over time. A country with a high degree of risk may later have low risk, or vice versa. The political-risk-assessment process and the actions to deal with the risk must therefore be dynamic. This situation is complicated by the fact that a company may have different options before entering markets than it has after placing a large value of fairly immobile assets within those markets. For example, most types of political risk insurance must be contracted before making an investment. Further, a company's options are apt to be fewer when political risk is widely perceived to be high than when it is widely perceived to be low. For example, *ceteris paribus* it is harder to find good buyers for facilities in a country where political risk is widely perceived to be high than in those where the risk is perceived to be low. Given the variety and dynamics of risk situations, along with companies' differences in risk tolerance and assessment, there are a myriad risk-management combinations. The following discussion highlights the major approaches.

Altering expected risk versus return

Companies seldom have enough resources to take advantage of all alternatives available to them. If political risk is deemed to be too high relative to expected returns, companies commonly avoid entering a market altogether. Or they may simply require a higher expected return to motivate them to enter such a market. In addition, companies may decrease risk by such means as insuring against certain political events, engaging in security measures or building helpful allies. These allies may be any stakeholders who would benefit more from the company's success than from its failure in the market. These include suppliers, customers, employees and even groups that depend on the company's tax payments or altruistic actions. However, any such risk-reduction actions incur costs that reduce expected revenues. Therefore a company should enter a country

only if the expectations of risk and return are sufficiently favourable after expenses are incurred to reduce political risk.

The above highlights assessment prior to entering a market; however, situations may change after a company has made an investment. If the company anticipates such a change before the market does, then it may be able to recoup its investment and pre-empt the losses that it foresees. For example, the company may disinvest by selling to another company, which is either less informed about emerging political conditions or has, for whatever reason, a lower micro risk than the company wishing to disinvest. Or the company may be able to engage in a harvesting strategy whereby it remits maximum funds to the parent and attains an adequate return over the life of its investment before liquidating it.

But companies seldom have such inside information about the future political environment. Therefore by the time they see the consequences of, for example, a possible civil war in Lebanon, other companies see the same conditions and anticipate similar consequences. As knowledge about deteriorating political conditions becomes more widespread the market values of facilities in the country fall. Further, a deteriorating political situation is usually accompanied by capital flight as companies and individuals try to convert funds to place them within countries with more secure political conditions and currencies. The capital flight may per force lead to barriers on asset remissions, thus impeding the use of a harvesting strategy. At that point the company may accept losses by leaving the market, or it may attempt to wait out a situation in anticipation (or hope) that the situation will improve. The company must consider the costs of staying versus leaving. For example, during the early 1990s several foreign investors, including Occidental Petroleum and Email and Elders, wanted to take losses and leave the Chinese market; however, the Chinese Government imposed departure costs and restrictions on them that both delayed their disinvestments and made them more expensive. Exit costs are high in many countries because of mandated severance pay to employees, which consumes a high portion of the assets companies have invested. There is no clear-cut way of determining whether to leave a politically risky environment or to stay there. One need only look at companies' diverse approaches to political risk during South African apartheid (both from pressure abroad and from a deteriorating internal situation) to see that companies react very differently to the same set of circumstances. Further, some seem to have gained and some seem to have lost by exiting South Africa relative to other companies that waited out the situation.

Choosing locations within countries

The risk analysis services examine indicators for choosing countries as a whole, and this tends to mask regional and local differences within countries. Further, there is anecdotal evidence that many investors not only overlook differences within countries, but sometimes conclude that all the countries within a region, such as all those within Africa or Central America, have similar political risk. Such conclusions may suboptimize performance. For example, Costa Rica is located between Nicaragua and Panama but has had a very different political environment over the past two decades than its neighbours. Within countries, as well, rules and regulations have often differed by region; so have unrest that damages or upsets operations. For example, a Mitsui-led group entered into an Iranian joint venture, which was the largest foreign investment by Japanese interests. Losses for Mitsui came about not because of property seizure or changes in regulations, but because of the invasion by Iraq. If the venture had been located farther from the Iraqi border Mitsui would probably not have suffered losses. Another example concerns the break-up of Yugoslavia. Although investments throughout were left to operate in a much smaller market after the break-up than before, other political effects varied substantially by region, e.g. no property damage or business disruption in Slovenia, but significant ones in Bosnia-Herzegovina. The point of this discussion is that investors should not simply assume that political risk is the same throughout a country or region. By looking at differences within, investors may evaluate risk more accurately, and the risk for their operational location may be higher or lower than indicated by the situation for a country or region as a whole.

Unbundling of resources

Simply, the unbundling of resources involves setting an operational structure so that there are alternative means, other than dividends, of moving financial assets out of a country. For example, a company may sell goods and services from the parent to the subsidiary and/or vice versa, thus creating payables and receivables, for which settlement may be early or late, in order to locate funds in safer havens in a timely manner. The company may also loan funds to its subsidiary rather than placing all capital transfers in the form of equity, thereby creating the possibility of moving funds as interest or as loan amortization. The unbundling of resources is an area usually associated with the economic risk of being unable to remit sufficient profits; however, it relates to political risk because of a possible desire to transfer assets if a political environment deteriorates. This is also an alternative that must be addressed primarily when initiating entry into a country, rather than later. The purposes are twofold: to create options when some asset-transfer routes are blocked and to develop routes for which a government will give priority if foreign exchange is in short supply.

Using collaborative arrangements

One way to minimize loss from political occurrences is to minimize the base of assets located abroad. Doing this may dictate collaborative arrangements, such as joint ownership or licensing, so that the asset base is shared by others. This move also might reduce political risk because a government may be less willing to move against a shared operation for fear of encountering opposition from more than one company. This is especially true if the companies are headquartered in different countries and the companies seek assistance with their home governments to intervene in conflict situations, for example by threatening to cease foreign aid payments or to impose very specific trade sanctions if foreign investors are treated unfairly. For example, the government of India backed down on proposed restrictions on PepsiCo after the US Government threatened such trade sanctions. This type of intervention is usually successful because it deals with a very limited and specific agenda, the outcome of which is highly predictable. However, overall trade embargoes aimed at getting countries to alter their political systems or alliances have seldom been successful. If the partnership is with a local company the partner may run interference with the host government in terms of heading off unfavourable legislation. This may be particularly important if the foreign investor is precluded either by law or adverse publicity from participating in local politics. Another way to spread risk is to place operations in a number of different countries. This strategy reduces the chance that all foreign assets will be simultaneously subject to such adversity as political unrest. Finally, the minimization of the use of one's own assets permits a more rapid dispersion of operations among countries.

Building allies

Much of political risk is micro, i.e. takeovers of foreign companies may be selective, and protests that disrupt operations may be targeted only at some foreign companies. There is much evidence that companies perceived to be operating in a socially responsive manner are less apt to face adverse political situations than are other companies. One way to improve the perception is to satisfy stakeholders, who may benefit more by the company's presence than its absence. In other words, companies should work to increase the number of supporters and dampen potential criticism. This sometimes leads to social functions to build local support, such as Citibank's reforestation programme in the Philippines and Dow Chemical's financing of a kindergarten in Chile. Opinion surveys of such interested parties as customers and workers can be conducted to allay misconceptions and anticipate criticism, thereby heading off potentially more damaging accusations. Many MNEs use advocacy publicity at home and abroad in an aggressive effort to win support for their international activities. Such publicity may take the form of newspaper and magazine ads, and reports showing the positive effects a company's activities have had on home- and host-country societies. For example, GM (see GENERAL MOTORS CORPORATION) publishes a public-interest report to highlight its international involvement in such activities as AIDS education, Earth Day celebration and environmental clean-up.

An MNE may also foster local participation both to reduce the image of foreignness and to develop local proponents whose personal objectives may be fulfilled by the company's continued operations. However, if local participation is carried to an extreme it can result in the host country's becoming less dependent on the foreign company. Thus the company's strategy might be to hold out some resources so that it remains needed. These resources could include new technologies or access to markets abroad.

We wish to note that the above approaches are useful only as means of preventing micro political risks. If public opinion is against foreign private ownership in general, all foreign companies lose out. If civil insurrections are widespread, companies may lose assets regardless of the local allies they have developed. For example, during the long civil war in Lebanon foreign investment was not a target of political agitation; however, Holiday Inn lost business because of the fall in tourism. It also had its facility damaged because it was in the line of fire between east and west Beirut.

9 Conclusion

Although expropriation and nationalization of property occurred frequently in the 1970s and 1980s, it has been negligible in recent years. The reasons for the change include a growing need by developing countries for private capital as government-to-government assistance has diminished, the need to utilize MNEs' organizational infrastructures to move resources and finished products internationally in increasingly open economies, and the desire of many countries to privatize companies that pragmatically can be bought only by MNEs. In spite of this change, companies continue to worry sufficiently about takeovers so that many still seek insurance against them. For example, OPIC (Overseas Private Investment Corporation) recently provided large political risk coverage for Edison Mission Energy in Indonesia and for US West in Russia. Their worry may be well founded because historically there have been wide swings in host-country attitudes towards private ownership, especially foreign ownership. The present welcoming of foreign investment could easily be reversed, particularly if governments feel their own constituencies are not receiving a just share of global economic benefits. For example, Sri Lanka has passed legislation to allow the renationalization of privatized companies where new owners fail to manage them successfully, and the Socialist Party in France has indicated that it might renationalize certain companies when it is in power. In an interesting 1997 variation, Zimbabwe's head of government threatened to re-expropriate farms that were expropriated by colonial powers nearly a century ago so that they can be distributed to black farmers.

As the takeover of assets has decreased in recent years, civil unrest has become the dominant political risk. In reality, the consequences of civil unrest have always been more dire than those of expropriation. In the former case the assets may be destroyed. Further, employees may lose their lives. In the latter case the assets merely change ownership; thus there are possibilities for negotiations so that the former owners may receive at least some compensation. By the mid-1990s there was ethnic unrest in the form of violence or strong separatist movements in about one-third of nations. Further, terrorism has infiltrated many countries. The results can include the loss or damage of property, the disruption of operations and the dissolution of some present countries, such as occurred with the former Soviet Union, Czechoslovakia and Yugoslavia. Such dissolution is a political risk in that the size of the domestic market diminishes.

Changes in rules and regulations continue to be a risk. For example, three US companies reached agreement with the state of Maharastra in India to build a $2.8 billion power plant (the largest foreign investment in India), in which Enron would own 80 per cent and Bechtel enterprises and General Electric (see GENERAL ELECTRIC COMPANY) would each own 10 per cent. After investing $300 million, the Government halted further work but agreed to renegotiate the agreement. The companies lost about $250,000 per day during the renegotiations and finally agreed to use more Indian naphtha rather than Qataran natural gas to generate electricity; to allow the state of Maharastra to own 30 per cent of the facility; to reduce Enron's ownership to 50 per cent; and to reduce the price of power by 22.2 per cent.

An emerging change in rules and regulations is one in which potential home-country changes are sometimes riskier than those in foreign countries. A case in point is tobacco regulation in many tobacco companies' home countries. This is a case of a changing political attitude towards the industry, which has caused negative domestic economic consequences for tobacco companies and has spurred them to place a relatively greater emphasis on their business in developing countries. This has complicated the risk-management process. First, companies must evaluate one political risk against another, such as whether to move to a country with a higher risk from civil disorder but a lower risk from changing regulations concerning such operating conditions as what is required to protect the physical environment and to improve labour conditions. Second, companies must consider what operating in a particular country might mean in terms of increased political risks within their home- or third-country markets. As global communications have become more instant and widespread, stakeholder groups in one country have become more aware of occurrences in other countries, especially the practices of multinational companies. Therefore, companies' unpopular practices abroad or location in an unpopular country may lead to boycotts or trade embargoes that limit their operating practices. For example, PepsiCo withdrew from Myanmar because of concern that the poor Myanmar human rights record would affect sales in other countries.

As the importance of different types of political risk continues to evolve, companies will need to find additional means of evaluating and managing that risk. Information on conditions that may harbinger political risk is certainly becoming more plentiful. Further, it is reaching potential users more rapidly. The problem is in how to analyse the information. Clearly, there is a need to improve the modelling of political conditions, and their likely and actual effect on companies' operations. As countries continue to vie for investment, the perception of their political risk will be a major factor in determining where companies will locate the bulk of their activities; thus it is likely that countries will try to improve their political situations so that companies will see a relative improvement in their political situations – relative over time and in relationship to other countries. Concomitantly, economic interdependence is likely to bring more cooperation among countries to improve the safety of international companies' assets, for example through more extensive insurance programmes.

JOHN D. DANIELS
JAMES A. SCHWEIKART
UNIVERSITY OF RICHMOND

Further reading

(References cited in the text marked *)

Banker, Pravin (1983) 'You're the best judge of foreign risks', *Harvard Business Review* 61(2): 157–65. (Explores why companies differ in their acceptance of risk.)

Brewer, Thomas L. (1987) 'International investment dispute settlement procedures: the evolving regime for foreign direct investment', *Law and Policy in International Business* 26(12): 633–572, (Discusses the changing settlements for expropriation and nationalization).

Coplin, W. and O'Leary, M. (1994) *The Handbook of Country and Political Risk Analysis*, Syracuse, NY: Political Risk Services. (Discusses in detail the methods used by the available services analysing country risk.)

* Dalby, Stewart (1995) 'Political worries hit investors', *Financial Times*, 18 December: 4. (Compares UK and US perceptions of political risk in specific countries and regions.)

Geist, Michael A. (1995) 'Towards a general agreement on the regulation of foreign direct investment', *Law & Policy in International Business* 26(3), spring: 673–717. (Examines the various arguments against MNE activities that may lead to their greater regulation.)

Howell, Llewellyn D. and Chaddick, Brad (1994) 'Model of political risk for foreign investment and trade', *Columbia Journal of World Business* fall: 71–91. (Compares many political risk services.)

* IASC (1997) *International Accounting Standard No. 14 (Revised): Reporting Financial Information by Segment*, London: International Accounting Standards Committee. (Details the international requirements for financial reporting of significant industry and geographical divisions of businesses.)

Mascarenhas, Briance (1982) 'Coping with uncertainty in international business', *Journal of International Business Studies* 13(2): 87–98. (Presents a model for determining the level of political risk a company should accept.)

Nigh, Douglas (1985) 'The effect of political events on United States direct foreign investment: a pooled time-series cross sectional analysis', *Journal of International Business Studies* 16(1): 1–17. (Analyses time lags and country differences for similar political risk indicators.)

Pro Invest (1997) special issue of *Transnationals* 9(2–3), November: 1–12. (Summarizes a conference dealing with such questions as how countries can reduce perceived risk and why investors choose one country over another.)

Sealy, T. (1996) *International Country Risk Guide*, Syracuse, NY: Political Risk Services. (Discusses some of the services used in country risk analysis.)

FASB (1976) *Statement of Financial Accounting Standards No. 14: Financial Reporting for Segment of a Business Enterprise*, Norwalk, CT: Financial Accounting Standards Board. (Details the US requirements for financial reporting of significant industry and geographical divisions of businesses.)

See also: FOREIGN EXCHANGE RISK, MANAGEMENT OF; GENERAL ELECTRIC COMPANY; GENERAL MOTORS CORPORATION; POLITICAL RISK

Securities markets, international

1 Types of international securities market
2 Conclusion

Overview

Until the 1960s, there was no such thing as the international securities market. Securities markets were based in a single country and virtually all primary market new issues and secondary market transactions were undertaken by companies, investment institutions and individuals resident in that country. In consequence, securities firms (except those in London) dealt only in domestic securities and were unlikely to have overseas branches or subsidiaries.

From the investor's point of view, an obvious reason for this 'stay close to home' philosophy was that up-to-date information about a company or country, which is critical in assessing the trade-off between risk and potential return, was generally difficult to obtain in the case of overseas securities. In addition, cross-border settlement of securities transactions was complex and expensive. From the point of view of companies as issuers of securities, there was little need to consider issuing securities outside the home market or selling domestic securities to foreigners, since most firms had few overseas operations and what operations there were could easily be financed on the domestic market or through banks.

Governments gave no special consideration to selling bonds to foreign investors since there was no reason to believe that this would reduce the cost of government funding. Indeed, it was more likely to raise it since enticing foreigners into a distant market where information was slow to reach them would require the payment of a premium return. For securities firms, there was little reason to consider overseas branches or subsidiaries since their customers undertook so little overseas business. To the extent that they did, this could be undertaken through commission sharing agreements with, for example, overseas stockbrokers.

The change during the 1970s and 1980s from a domestic perspective on the part of issuers, investors and securities houses, to a global cross-border perspective, arose for a number of reasons. Companies became more multinational in their operations, and consequently investors started to appreciate the advantages of global diversification. Telecommunications systems improved and costs fell; screen-based systems were developed to disseminate information globally. Computing power also fell in cost and allowed easy analysis of information. At the same time, rising government deficits (particularly in the USA) could only be financed at an acceptable cost by widening the investor base to include foreign investors, while the gradual worldwide abolition of exchange controls facilitated cross-border transactions.

By the beginning of the 1990s, there had developed an international financial mechanism comprising internationally oriented investors, global securities houses and market mechanisms facilitating cross-border securities transactions. By the year 2000, it is likely that this mechanism will be greatly refined and will be the major source of funding for international companies, governments and quasi-government bodies.

1 Types of international securities market

A securities market is a market in which existing securities are exchanged between those who currently hold them and wish to sell, and those who wish to hold them and therefore want to buy. The two essential features of a securities market are price discovery (the process by which supply and demand are matched to determine the price of the transaction) and settlement (the process by which cash is exchanged for securities).

There are three types of international securities market. The first, traditionally known as the Eurobond market, but now also known as the international securities market, has always been international in the sense that it has no domestic base. The second has developed through the 1980s and has involved the internationalization of what have been traditionally domestic markets, the markets for bonds and equities. The third, derivatives markets, only came into existence in Europe in the 1980s and has developed alongside the underlying money, foreign exchange, bond and equity markets.

Eurobond market

The first international securities market to develop was the so-called Eurobond market. It came into existence in the early 1960s and has now become the world's largest international market in securities. Eurobond issues are defined as debt securities issued in a currency which is not that of the country in which the issue is arranged, and which are distributed by an international syndicate of banks and securities houses. Eurobonds now also include bonds issued in domestic currencies but issued to international investors in a standardized 'Eurobond' form. While the first issue (a US dollar issue for Autostrade arranged by the London investment bank Warburg) came out in 1963, it was not until 1968 that something that could truly be called a market came into existence.

The primary market is based in the City of London and a high proportion of secondary market dealers are also in London with others in most European financial centres and in the Middle and Far East. In addition there is a limited amount of secondary market activity in New York. The market is not based on an exchange but on price screens provided by Reuters, Telerate, Bloomberg and other information service providers and through transactions undertaken on the telephone. A high proportion of investors in this market traditionally operated through Switzerland, using the large Swiss banks for discretionary or non-discretionary fund management. In addition, the Eurobond market was traditionally used by individuals throughout Europe as an anonymous, withholding tax-free investment market. Today, however, the market is largely institutional and is used by investment funds based in all the world's major financial centres.

The factor which drove the market to expand sharply in the late 1960s and early 1970s was the prohibition by the US Congress of domestic fund raising for overseas investment by US multinationals. The intended purpose of the ban was to improve the US balance of payments, though in practice the balance of payments continued to worsen despite the measure. To overcome this prohibition, US multinationals wishing to finance factories in Europe and elsewhere arranged to raise funds in Europe. The denomination of these issues was almost entirely US dollar. In addition, however, there were Deutschmark, sterling, yen and other currency issues. Today these currencies are, in total, as important as the US dollar. Originally securities issues were generally either fixed rate bond issues with a life to maturity of 10–15 years or bonds convertible into the equity of the company at a later date. Today, there is a wide range of complex securities available to investors. In addition, in order to match better the needs of investors and borrowers, the proceeds from fixed rate bond issues are now frequently converted into floating rate liabilities through the use of interest rate swaps, in order to provide the issuer with liabilities the cost of which is linked to short-term interest rates rather than to long-term bond rates.

Today the market is larger than any other securities market in the world except for those in government bonds in the USA, Germany and Japan. Although it is not an exchange market and instead operates over-the-counter (that is, by telephone between dealers), it is a market that is regulated by a self-regulatory body, the International Securities Market Association (ISMA), with a membership of over 850 banks and securities houses worldwide and sets the rules by which international transactions are undertaken. The head office of ISMA is in Zurich, the computer facilities through which trade reporting is undertaken are in London, and the education and training arm is at the ISMA Centre at the University of Reading in England.

A global infrastructure has also been developed to facilitate trade settlement. The facilities are provided by two organizations, Cedel (based in Luxembourg) and Euroclear (based in Brussels). These organizations, in addition, provide for the safe-keeping of securities in depositories worldwide. It is the existence of a single rule book used worldwide and a single settlement system that allows the Eurobond market to function smoothly, efficiently and cheaply as a cross-border market. In contrast, domestic markets traditionally have each had their own idiosyncratic transaction rules and settlement systems, making cross-border transactions and international portfolio management much more difficult and expensive.

In the market's early years the major issuers of Eurobonds were US companies, but in later years the market started to be used by multinationals from all of the major countries. Over time, however, much of the issuing has come to be undertaken by governments, quasi-government bodies, supranational bodies such as the World Bank, and by commercial banks. The securities issued in this market provide investors in the major countries with the opportunity to acquire attractively priced securities denominated in different currencies that trade freely across borders, without the imposition of withholding tax and which can all be held in a single depository.

Government debt markets

Traditionally, government debt was purchased only by investors in the country of issue. However, as international investors became used to the concept of holding foreign currency denominated debt in their portfolios as a result of the growth of the Eurobond market, their attention increasingly turned to the large volumes of government debt available in domestic markets. The US Treasury market was the first to attract international interest, if only because of the huge growth in its size as a result of the tax cutting and consequent deficit

financing needs arising from President Reagan's policies in the late 1970s and early 1980s. Investor interest, especially in the surplus countries such as Japan, developed in this market because of the greater liquidity that was offered in comparison with the Eurobond market. This liquidity allowed institutional investors, speculating on currency developments as well as market developments, to transact easily and quickly on a large scale. For overseas official investors (such as central banks), the US Treasury market was attractive because it provided a 'credit risk-free' investment market in a currency which was the primary global transactions and investment medium. It was also, of course, the currency that was purchased by central banks when they intervened in the currency markets to try to slow down the depreciation of the dollar.

During the 1980s, not only did the supply of Treasury securities increase, but much better information on what was happening in the market became available outside of the USA. By the 1980s, information systems had become well developed with firms such as Reuters, and also bond brokers, providing information on prices in New York to dealers worldwide at the same time as they were available in New York. As international investors became accustomed to trading US Treasury debt, they then became more willing to consider German government debt, in particular the so-called 'Bunds' or Federal Republic Obligations. They also started to invest in Japanese, UK, French and Spanish government bonds, as these markets also began to deregulate and internationalize and adapt to the needs of international investors.

As the volume of demand for US and other treasury securities increased, it became economic to develop markets in these securities based in London to service international investor needs. US government securities, for example, are actively traded in London before the US market opens later in the day London time, and then in conjunction with New York when that market opens. Equally, London securities houses actively trade the government bonds of all the major European countries and provide their market making services in conjunction with the domestic market. These services are used not only by international investors, but also by large domestic investors who believe that they may obtain a better service from an international securities firm in London than from a domestic broker.

Domestic equity markets operating internationally

The Eurobond market came into existence in order to satisfy fixed income market needs in a world where domestic restrictions limited the transactions that issuers and investors might undertake. The gradual phasing out of these restrictions during the 1980s, combined with technological developments in communications and computing, has now given equity investors the ability to undertake cross-border transactions with almost the same ease as domestic transactions. While the ability to undertake such transactions does not in itself generate the need for them, a principal factor encouraging a global perspective among the institutional investment community worldwide, in both bond and equity markets, was the increasing acceptance of the benefits to the risk/return profile of a portfolio that could arise from international diversification.

Internationalization of domestic markets has occurred in both the primary market and secondary sectors. Through the 1980s and more particularly in the 1990s, the concept of the Euroequity has been developed. This is a primary market security issue undertaken through the auspices of a domestic equity market but syndicated internationally. Privatization issues in Europe have been particularly frequent examples of such Euroequity issues. These have used the international syndication model developed in the Eurobond market for debt issues but adapted to the peculiarities of equity issues undertaken under the rules of a domestic stock exchange.

On the secondary market front, there has been a different development. While in the 1970s, large companies often cross-listed their shares on different exchanges, in practice such listings were relatively meaningless, since there were very few transactions in foreign shares on domestic exchanges. In the 1980s, however, the London Stock Exchange developed an unlisted market in the shares of companies listed outside the UK. This market, known as Stock Exchange Automated Quotation International (SEAQI), has, since its inception, taken a considerable proportion of the total volume of share dealing in shares of international companies not quoted in London. There were two reasons why it could do this. First, the London market had dealers willing to quote in large size and, if necessary, take a position in a share in order to facilitate a customer trade. In contrast, most European exchanges were order-driven and had few facilities for dealer intervention. Second, most European exchanges, which had throughout their history been monopolies, had very restrictive rules and poor technology that made large institutional cross-border transactions quite difficult. As a result London was very successful throughout the 1980s in this business. It was also successful in providing a market in the European time zone in shares whose domestic exchange was in the USA or Japan.

In the 1990s, the shape of the European market in cross-border international share transactions has begun to change quite dramatically, towards a pattern that is likely to be fully in place by the millennium (see ECONOMIC INTEGRATION, INTERNATIONAL). Domestic exchanges throughout Europe have mostly de-regulated, as London did in 1986. They have also installed new technology to compete more effectively with that available in London. Most important is the likely impact of the Investment Services Directive (ISD) of the European Union. This Directive which came into effect in January 1996, requires that stock exchanges and other markets in the European Economic Area allow securities brokers and dealers with offices outside the domestic market to operate on that market with the same rights and responsibilities as domestic firms. As securities houses and stockbroking firms become increasingly international, it is likely that they will use this permission to deal directly on the domestic exchange of a country when they wish to transact on behalf of a client anywhere in the world.

Derivatives exchanges

At the same time as international diversification became both technically feasible and seemingly logically attractive to institutional investors, markets of all types started to become more volatile. In particular, in the 1980s, as a consequence of the Reagan/Thatcher monetary experiments that commenced in 1979, interest rates and exchange rates became highly volatile. This in turn increased the need for hedging mechanisms for investors who simply wanted a foreign market risk and not the concomitant currency or interest rate risk.

The need for a hedging mechanism to offset such risks has been satisfied over the 1980s, by the extraordinarily rapid growth of derivatives exchanges. These markets originated in Chicago, but in the early 1980s the London International Financial Futures Exchange (LIFFE) was inaugurated. This market, which views itself as the principal 'international' futures and options exchange in Europe, provides hedging services to investors and corporate issuers worldwide.

Derivatives exchanges provide futures and options contracts based on underlying (cash) instruments such as treasury bills, dollar/Deutschmark exchange rate, equity indices, US government bonds and also individual equities. The contracts can be purchased by investors based anywhere in the world. Increasingly, however, because of the difficulty overseas investors in distant time zones have in dealing out of their time zone, exchanges have started to link together on a worldwide basis to create 'fungible' contracts, that is ones which can, for example, be opened in one market and closed in another in a different time zone. It is likely that over time, more contracts will be created that are totally fungible, that is, the two exchanges in different time zones will have an agreement to trade what is, in effect, the same contract.

2 Conclusion

It is sometimes thought that the principal outcome of the globalization of securities markets is simply that investors can hold better diversified portfolios than they could with purely domestic assets (see GLOBALIZATION). If this were so, the only benefit to society would be a better spread of economic risk worldwide and a better trade-off between risk and return. Much more significant, however, is the political impact of the international securities markets. Now that the major developed countries have abolished exchange controls, investors in those countries are free to invest their savings where they choose. An overview of the scale of transactions is provided in Table 1. Under exchange control and before the advent of global markets, savings were, in effect, trapped within a country giving corporate and government borrowers a monopoly on domestic savings. In the case of corporations, returns to investors could be relatively low (provided most companies followed such a policy) since overseas options for investors were very limited. In the case of governments, inflationary policies and budget deficits of a size which today would be viewed as unacceptable by international investors, are much harder to follow. Today, governments following policies which international investors believe may have an unfavourable impact on their wealth, have to pay a premium in the market to finance their deficits. International investors are also very likely to ensure that no country is able to maintain an exchange rate which is not justified by the economic circumstances. When the UK, for example, was forced to leave the European Exchange Rate Mechanism in 1993, the pressure pushing down sterling arose because of the freedom of both UK and foreign investors to move out of sterling and into other assets such as Deutschmark bonds.

The internationalization of financial markets has also democratized them (see HUMAN RESOURCE MANAGEMENT, INTERNATIONAL; INTERNATIONAL BUSINESS, FUTURE TRENDS). When markets were domestic, highly regulated and not expanding rapidly, it was possible to survive without a high level of knowledge and skill. The additional complexity of today's international market has increased the need for highly trained personnel and opened up careers in financial markets to a much wider range of people.

Table 1 Borrowing on the international capital markets 1984–1994 - flows $bn

	1984	1985	1986	1987	1988	1989	1990	1991	1992	1993	1994
Bonds	111.5	169.1	227.1	180.8	227.1	255.7	229.9	297.6	333.7	481	428.6
Equities		2.7	11.7	18.2	7.7	8.1	7.3	23.4	23.5	40.7	45
Syndicated bonds	57	43	52.4	91.7	125.5	121.1	124.5	116	117.9	136.7	236.2
Committed back-up facilities	28.8	42.9	29.3	31.2	16.6	8.4	7	7.7	6.7	8.2	4.9
A Total securities and committed facilities	197.3	257.7	320.5	321.9	376.9	393.3	368.7	455.8	481.8	666.6	714.7
Euro-commercial paper programmes		12.6	59	55.8	57.1	54.1	48.3	35.9	28.9	38.4	30.8
Medium-term euro-note programmes		10.6	8.6	15.2	19.5	19.1	17.9	44.3	99	113.6	222.1
B Total uncommitted borrowing facilities		23.2	67.6	71	76.6	73.2	66.2	80.2	127.9	152	252.9
Grand total (A and B)	297.3	280.9	388.1	392.9	435.3	466.5	434.9	536	609.7	818.6	967.6

Source: OECD Financial Market Trends

New technology has also allowed new entrants to the industry, to challenge the monopoly traditionally held by domestic exchanges. Not only does each stock exchange now have to compete for business in its 'own' shares with other exchanges around the world, in addition, new market mechanisms are coming into being to offer similar secondary market services but at a lower cost than traditional exchanges.

An example of such an exchange is Tradepoint2 which is an electronic (order driven) market that was given a license to operate as an exchange by the UK Treasury, in June 1995. Another example is the Arizona Stock Exchange which offers a so-called 'periodic auction' in US stocks. These new competitors to traditional exchanges are likely to hasten the development of a secondary market in international equities, very similar in nature to the Eurobond market. The outcome will be to make it much easier for individual, as well as institutional investors, to undertake cross-border transactions. The ultimate outcome of all the technological developments in markets and the ever growing desire by investors to be able to transact in overseas securities as easily as domestic, will be the creation, by the turn of the century, of a single, truly international, capital (new issue) and (secondary) securities market, supplying the needs of issuers and investors worldwide at the lowest possible cost.

BRIAN SCOTT-QUINN
UNIVERSITY OF READING

Further reading

(References cited in the text marked *)

Bowe, M. (1988) *Eurobonds*, Homewood, IL: Irwin. (Provides practical information on the markets to help potential users and students of the market.)

Gallant, P. (1988) *The Eurobond Market*, Hemel Hempstead: Woodhead Faulkner. (Outlines the history and evolution of the products used in the market and describes how new issues are launched.)

ISMA *ISMA Quarterly Comment*, Zurich: ISMA. (Provides current insight into features of the international securities market.)

ISSA/ISMA *The Euromarkets*, Zurich: ISMA. (Glossary of terms used in the Euromarkets and the main features of the market.)

McLean, S. (1993) *The European Bond Markets*, Cambridge: Probus. (Overview and analysis for money managers and traders covering nineteen countries.)

* Organization for Economic Cooperation and Development *Financial Market Trends*, Paris: OECD. (Quarterly publication containing useful statistical data.)

Scott-Quinn, B. (1990) *Investment Banking: Theory and Practice*, London: Euromoney Books. (Practical guide covering all areas of investment banking from new issues to mergers and acquisitions and money markets.)

Walmsley, J. (1991) *Global Investing: Eurobonds and Alternatives*, Basingstoke: Macmillan. (Outline of how the global markets have evolved from foreign exchange to Eurobonds.)

See also: ECONOMIC INTEGRATION, INTERNATIONAL; FINANCIAL MANAGEMENT, INTERNATIONAL; GLOBALIZATION; HUMAN RESOURCE MANAGEMENT, INTERNATIONAL; INTERNATIONAL BUSINESS, FUTURE TRENDS

Related topics in the IEBM: FINANCIAL MARKETS, INTERNATIONAL; INFORMATION REVOLUTION

Taxation, international

1 Avoiding double taxation
2 Exempting or deferring taxes
3 Pricing transactions between related entities
4 Remitting profits
5 Transferring employees
6 Conclusion

Overview

Tax systems generally can be classified as either global or territorial; these differ most notably in the manner in which they treat resident entities. Countries with global systems tax the worldwide income of their resident entities. An overwhelming majority of nations have global tax systems, including Australia, Canada, Germany, Italy, Japan, the United Kingdom and the United States. In contrast, a territorial system generally taxes resident entities only on profit arising from sources within the country's borders. Territorial systems include those in Costa Rica, France, Guatemala, Malaysia, Panama, Singapore, South Africa, Uruguay and Venezuela.

The definition of a resident entity varies among countries. For example, the United States considers any corporation incorporated in the United States to be a resident entity; where the corporation does business or conducts its management activities is irrelevant. As an objective definition of residence, incorporation situs provides a measure of certainty to both taxpayers and governments. Most other countries define resident entities solely on the basis of central management or on the combined basis of central management and incorporation situs. For example, Portugal defines a resident entity as one that has its head office there or is effectively managed from Portugal. A resident entity in Germany is one managed and controlled from within Germany or incorporated under German law. Countries generally operationalize the place of management in terms of the location of the head office, the place where board meetings occur or some similar criterion.

All tax systems, whether global or territorial, limit the taxation of non-resident entities. Generally, a non-resident entity that conducts business in a country through a fixed facility or dependent agent (hereafter permanent establishment, or PE) is taxable at the same tax rates applicable to resident entities, but only on income attributable to the PE. In contrast, the investment income of non-resident entities from sources within a country is subject to a withholding tax (such as 30 per cent) on the gross earnings (i.e. no deductions are allowed). Global and territorial systems typically do not tax non-resident entities on business profits in the absence of a PE. Also, investment income is usually exempt unless sourced within the country.

This entry identifies tax issues that many multinational companies face and suggests possible tax-minimization strategies (see MULTINATIONAL CORPORATIONS). To the extent possible, multinationals seek to avoid double taxation and take advantage of opportunities to exempt or defer income recognition. Often, these strategies are implemented through adopting appropriate transfer pricing and profit remittance practices. Multinationals also must be concerned about the tax liabilities of individuals who are transferred across national borders since corporate policy generally calls for employee reimbursement of any additional tax incurred.

1 Avoiding double taxation

Since the tax systems in any two countries differ (sometimes drastically), the multinational corporation (MNC) is often exposed to the possibility that more than one country will claim jurisdiction to tax the same income stream (see MULTINATIONAL CORPORATIONS). This double taxation can arise in three general ways. First, two countries may claim jurisdiction over the same entity under their internal definitions of residence. For example, country A may assert its right to tax an entity because it is incorporated in country A, while country B may claim jurisdiction over the entity because its head office is in country B. Second, under overlapping source of income rules, two countries may assert their separate rights to tax the profit from a single transaction. Third, one country may claim jurisdiction to tax the party earning the income (i.e. as a resident entity), while another country may claim jurisdiction over the specific transaction generating the income. This latter type of double taxation is the most common and the most difficult to eliminate.

Without some effective remedy, double taxation can greatly increase the cost of doing business abroad, and may curtail international business and investment activities. A primary objective of international tax policy and planning is to mitigate the impact of double taxation.

Unilateral methods

Countries can take unilateral measures to reduce instances of double taxation. Most nations with territorial systems depend primarily on the exemption method. Under their internal laws they simply exempt income arising beyond their borders. For example, France does not generally tax the profits of resident entities derived from a branch (or PE) in another country. In theory, a PE in another country subjects business profits attributable to the PE to foreign taxation; thus France decides not to tax the profits a second time. A major advantage of the territorial system is that investors are able to determine their after-tax returns from foreign activities simply by reference to the host country's laws. A disadvantage is that losses incurred abroad through foreign branch operations, which often characterize the start-up years, may not be currently deductible against domestic profits. Because this disadvantage can curtail foreign investment, France departs from pure territorial principles and allows foreign branch losses to be deducted if authorization is obtained from the French Ministry of Economics and Finance. If a resident entity obtains such permission it must include the branch's operating loss (or profit) in its own tax return.

Some global systems use the exemption method too (e.g. in the Netherlands), but most rely primarily on a foreign-tax credit mechanism to reduce double taxation. In brief, a country with a global tax system taxes the worldwide income of resident entities but allows a credit for any foreign income tax paid on the same income. For example, assume a US corporation has 600 of domestic income and 400 of income from a PE in Germany. Both the United States and Germany consider the 400 income to be under their respective jurisdictions. Thus both countries tax the income, but the United States allows taxes paid to Germany as a credit on the resident corporation's US tax return. As in this example, the home (rather than the host) country is the jurisdiction that generally provides tax credit relief.

In addition to a credit for direct taxes paid, many countries allow an indirect or deemed-paid credit for foreign income taxes that a foreign subsidiary pays. The purpose of an indirect credit is to achieve some parity between operating abroad through a foreign branch and a foreign subsidiary. Since a foreign branch is not a separate entity from its domestic company, the income tax the branch pays is allowed as a credit in the home country. In contrast, a foreign subsidiary is a separate legal entity from its parent company. Absent an indirect credit, the domestic company receives no double-taxation relief from foreign income taxes paid by its foreign subsidiary. Thus an indirect credit is allowed in order to achieve some measure of equity. A dividend triggers the indirect credit mechanism. Generally, the percentage of the foreign subsidiary's earnings and profits paid as a dividend to its parent is the percentage of the foreign subsidiary's foreign income-tax payments that is allowed as an indirect credit to the parent company.

Assume a company residing in country A has a wholly owned subsidiary in country B. After the first year the subsidiary accumulates before-tax profits of 140, out of which it pays

40 in foreign tax. Thus its earnings and profits are 100. Then the subsidiary pays a dividend of 70 to its parent company out of its net earnings. Under these facts, the parent company is entitled to an indirect credit of 28 in the home country (i.e. 70/100 × 40).

Calculation of the indirect credit often is very complex, especially when income is earned in one year and dividends from those earnings are paid several years later. For this reason, some countries only allow a foreign-tax credit for taxes an entity pays directly. Nonetheless, an indirect credit might be permitted in these countries if granted through a treaty.

Most countries granting a foreign-tax credit limit the credit to the domestic tax paid on foreign income. In other words, no credit is generally allowed against the domestic tax paid on domestic income. As a rough rule of thumb, the effect of any limitation is that the worldwide effective tax rate (ETR) on a given income item is the greater of the ETRs in the two countries imposing their taxes (before considering any credit). Assume an entity's home country has a global tax system that uses a foreign-tax credit to relieve double taxation and limits the credit as noted above. The home country imposes a 30 per cent ETR. Income of the entity subject to a foreign ETR of 40 per cent pays an overall ETR of 40 per cent (i.e. the higher of the two ETRs). If, instead, the foreign ETR is assumed to be 25 per cent, the overall ETR is 30 per cent once the profits are remitted to the home country.

Most countries permit any foreign tax that cannot be credited because of this limit to be carried over to other taxable years. For example, the United States allows excess credits to be carried back to the two previous years and, if all the excess credits do not result in a refund, forward to the next five years. In contrast, Japan effectively allows a three-year carryback and a three-year carryforward, and Norway permits a ten-year carryforward.

Bilateral methods

Income-tax treaties provide bilateral means of mitigating the effects of double taxation. Some countries have extensive networks of treaties. For example, Canada, Denmark, Finland, Germany, Italy, the Netherlands, Norway and Sweden each have more than fifty income-tax treaties in force. The French and United Kingdom income-tax treaty networks are two of the most impressive in terms of sheer numbers, at approximately ninety each.

Treaties reduce double taxation through common rules that both countries agree to follow. For example, a given entity might be considered a resident under the internal laws of two or more nations (i.e. dual resident status). Perhaps the entity is a resident of one country because it is incorporated there, while it is considered a resident of the other country because management activities occur there. Treaties with most member nations of the Organization for Economic Cooperation and Development (OECD) usually dictate that the entity resides only in the country from which it is effectively managed. In the case of treaties with the United States, however, only the country where the entity is created can claim it as a resident. To a lesser degree, treaties may resolve double-tax problems in which two countries claim jurisdiction over the same transaction through common source of income rules.

Treaties often use the exemption method to prevent double taxation of certain types of income from occurring. The exemption method limits the ability of the host country to impose its tax on certain income streams. For example, income from transporting people or cargo between two treaty countries is generally taxable only in the home country. Also, treaties normally preclude the host country from taxing business profits unless the profits are attributable to a PE in the host country. In the absence of a PE the treaty exempts the business earnings from host-country tax. Thus, mere export sales between treaty countries generally result in no tax liability to the host country (see EXPORTING).

2 Exempting or deferring taxes

Establishing a subsidiary in a no-tax or low-tax foreign jurisdiction can often result in significant tax advantages. The advantages can range from the complete exemption of part or all of the subsidiary's profits to a long-term deferral of taxation in the home country until profits are remitted.

Tax holidays and tax sparing

Developing countries sometimes offer tax holidays to attract foreign investment (see ECONOMICS OF DEVELOPING COUNTRIES). Tax holidays exempt foreign investors who engage in specified activities from taxation over a specified period of time. In some cases the tax holiday is part of the country's domestic law and is available to all foreign investors. At other times tax holidays are separately negotiated ad hoc agreements with foreign investors.

Assume a developing country normally imposes a 25 per cent tax rate on business profits. However, it is willing to allow complete exemption from income taxation to foreign investors that establish manufacturing operations in a region with high unemployment. The tax holiday is guaranteed for ten years. A foreign investor from a global-system country decides to invest and earns 100 the first year. The global-system tax rate, payable to the home country, is a flat 40 per cent.

If the developing country had not granted the tax holiday the foreign investor would have paid a 25 foreign tax. The home-country tax would have been 40 less 25 foreign-tax credit, or 15. Thus the total tax on the 100 profit would have been 40 (i.e. 25 +15). How did the tax holiday benefit this investor? Under the tax holiday the investor pays no tax to the developing country. However, the tax to the home country is 40; no foreign-tax credit is allowed in the home country since no foreign income tax was paid. Thus the tax holiday provides no net tax benefit to the foreign investor. Whether or not the tax holiday is granted, the result in each case is that the investor pays 40 in taxes. No incentive to invest in the developing country results. Even worse, the effect of the tax holiday is simply to shift tax revenues from the developing country to the developed country. In effect, the

developed country, not the investor, is the beneficiary of the tax holiday.

To ensure that tax holidays accomplish their intended aim of attracting foreign capital, treaties between developed and developing countries often provide for a tax-sparing credit. Tax sparing allows the investor to claim a foreign-tax credit in the home country as if no tax holiday existed. In the example above, the tax holiday would exempt the foreign investor from host-country tax. In the home country the investor would pay a tax of 40 less 25 tax-sparing credit. In effect, the investor is assumed to pay tax to the developing country even though no tax is actually paid. Thus the tax-holiday incentive accomplishes its intended purpose. Although many developing countries routinely include tax-sparing clauses in their treaties, the United States does not as a matter of policy. This might explain why the United States has concluded fewer income-tax treaties with developing countries than have several of the European nations.

Subsidiaries in tax havens

Establishing controlled foreign subsidiaries in low-tax jurisdictions or tax havens can often lead to long-term tax deferrals in the home country. The longer the tax deferral, the greater the present-value benefits. Some tax havens, such as the Cayman Islands and Vanuatu, either impose no general income tax or impose relatively low taxes. Other tax havens, such as Liberia and Costa Rica, impose low or no taxes on specified activities even though their general income tax rates are relatively high.

Assume the multinational establishes a controlled foreign corporation in a no-tax haven (see MULTINATIONAL CORPORATIONS). The foreign subsidiary carries on international business and becomes very profitable but is careful not to remit any of its profits to the parent company in the home country. Absent some anti-deferral legislation in the home country, the subsidiary can accumulate large amounts of earnings that neither the host nor the home country taxes. Assuming a 10 per cent cost of capital, every 100 of home country tax deferred for ten years costs only 39 in present-value terms.

Many developed countries have laws that curtail tax-haven activities such as the one described above. The United States' so-called Subpart F legislation, which is similar to anti-haven laws in several other countries, identifies certain types of transactions for which tax deferral is disallowed. For example, a controlled foreign subsidiary that purchases goods for resale from its US parent, engages in no manufacturing activities in the country where it is created and sells to customers outside the country of incorporation results in 'tainted' income. A good business reason for the subsidiary to be established where it is does not seem to exist. The presumption is that the foreign location was selected for tax-haven activities or to obtain a long-term tax deferral. Income from these transactions is treated as a constructive dividend to the US parent company. The constructive dividend results in current taxation of the foreign profits and thus precludes a tax deferral.

As noted above, the US Subpart F approach is to identify certain transactions that suggest tax-haven activities. In contrast, the method that some countries use is to identify 'tax-haven subsidiaries' and end tax deferrals on all profits through such companies. Japan generally defines a tax-haven subsidiary as one that is subject to a foreign ETR of 25 per cent or less. Similar legislation in South Korea defines a tax-haven subsidiary as any company whose main or head office is located in a country that imposes an ETR not greater than 15 per cent. Other countries, such as Austria, currently have no anti-haven tax rules.

3 Pricing transactions between related entities

Unless they are prevented in some way, cross-border transactions between related or controlled entities provide almost unlimited opportunities to shift income from high-tax to low-tax jurisdictions through price manipulations. For example, assume that a manufacturer produces an item at a cost of 60 and sells it abroad for 100, resulting in a 40 profit per unit exported. The problem is that the country

where the manufacturer resides imposes a 50 per cent tax rate on the profit. To reduce the tax bite a related sales company is established in a no-tax country. Thereafter the manufacturer sells each unit of its product to the newly created sales company for 66. The sales company performs nominal tasks, such as labelling, and resells the product to ultimate consumers at 100 each. Absent some restrictions on pricing, this arrangement reduces the tax on each unit sold from 20 (i.e. 40 profit taxed at 50 per cent) to 3 (i.e. 6 profit taxed at 50 per cent). The remaining 34 of profit on each unit sold is captured in the sales company's country, which imposes no tax. Though this example involves the sale of tangible goods, similar pricing schemes can be developed for the use of tangible assets (rents), sales or transfers of intangible assets (royalties), loans or advances of money (interest), and performance of administrative or oversight services (management fees).

To prevent such abuses most countries allow their tax authorities to reallocate or reapportion income, deductions, credits or other allowances among related or controlled entities if necessary clearly to reflect income or prevent tax evasion. In effect, these anti-abuse provisions require that affiliated or related entities price transactions among them at arm's length. In other words, entities are expected to determine the prices applicable to similar transactions between *unrelated* parties and to charge those prices on transactions with related entities. In some countries, such as Mexico and the United States, the taxpayer has the burden of proof in transfer pricing disputes. Other countries, such as Denmark, place the burden of proof squarely on the taxing authority. Also, very stiff penalties apply to transfer prices that are substantially out of line in some countries, such as the United States.

Arm's-length pricing is the standard under many tax systems. However, the operational definition of arm's-length pricing varies from one country to the next. As a result, countries do not always arrive at the same transfer price for a particular transaction. In some cases, more than 100 per cent of the profit from a transaction may be taxed. Assume that a company in country A sells goods costing 80 to an affiliate in country B for 90. The affiliate, in turn, sells the goods to a consumer residing in country B for 100. If country A accepts 90 as the correct transfer price between the related parties, the company in country A has a profit of 10. If country B adjusts the transfer price down to 85 the affiliate's subsequent sale in country B results in a profit of 15. Though the total profit on the sale is only 20 (i.e. 100 less 80), countries A and B together are taxing profit of 25 (i.e. 10 plus 15). In this situation the two companies might request that the taxing authorities in the two countries try to arrive at a common transfer price. This procedure, known as invoking competent authorities, is a common method for resolving instances of double taxation and often is allowed through treaty.

To curb controversies proactively some countries, such as the United States, now permit advance pricing agreements. Taxpayers that wish to use these procedures can disclose their pricing methodology in advance of a dispute. The government examines the methodology and, if it is acceptable, reaches a contractual agreement with the taxpayer to the effect that such methodology will not be questioned. Such agreements can save both the taxpayer and the government countless hours and high litigation costs.

4 Remitting profits

Foreign subsidiaries can remit profits to the home country in several different ways. Earnings can be remitted through dividends. Alternatively, contractual arrangements may allow some earnings to be remitted as interest, royalties, rents or management fees. Deciding on the best remittance method or combination of methods requires careful analysis of at least two factors.

First, some remittances result in tax deductions, while others do not. Dividends are distributions of earnings and profits rather than expenses of doing business. Thus dividends are not deductible. In contrast, interest, rents and royalties are considered to be deductible business expenses in most countries, and thus might be the preferred method for remitting profits. Management fees are often also

deductible if determined according to arm's-length standards.

Second, many host countries impose withholding taxes on remittances that vary depending on the remittance method. For example, Italy generally withholds a tax of 32.4 per cent on dividends and 15 per cent on interest paid to non-residents. Italy's withholding tax on royalties is normally 21 per cent. If the recipient resides in a treaty country, however, the applicable withholding rates are often lower. Italy withholds only 15 per cent on dividends, 10 per cent on interest and 10 per cent on royalties paid to New Zealand residents.

The thin capitalization rules in some countries restrict the amount of debt in a company's capital structure. Thus the amount of profit that can be remitted as interest vis-à-vis dividends may be limited. Many countries, for example Canada and Japan, have adopted the general rule that debt cannot be more than three times the amount of equity. Some countries with thin capitalization restrictions, such as Luxembourg and the United States, do not have an explicitly stated ratio of debt to equity. Other countries, such as Belgium, Denmark and Norway, have no thin capitalization rules at present.

At times, profits can be remitted to the home country with a smaller withholding tax if a less direct route is taken. Assume a company in country A owns a subsidiary in country C. Dividends from country C to country A are subject to a 30 per cent withholding tax since there is no tax treaty in force between these countries. One possible solution is to interpose a holding company. That is, the company in country A owns an intermediate holding company in country B, which, in turn, owns the subsidiary in country C. If treaties exist between A and B and between B and C, the total withholding tax might be reduced. For example, the treaty between B and C might exempt dividends entirely, while the treaty between A and B might impose only a 10 per cent withholding tax. Using a holding company in this fashion to build a 'treaty bridge' between two countries without a treaty is called treaty shopping. Many income-tax treaties disallow or restrict treaty shopping. Also, international tax planners sometimes have differing opinions about whether a given instance of treaty shopping is ethical, especially when a significant non-tax business reason for the intermediate holding company is unclear (see INTERNATIONAL BUSINESS ETHICS).

5 Transferring employees

Ventures into the international market often involve the transfer of individuals across national borders (see HUMAN RESOURCE MANAGEMENT, INTERNATIONAL). Managers and technicians from the home country may be needed in the start-up phase of offshore manufacturing. Individuals from the target company may need training that can best be obtained in the country where the business has been conducted for several years already. Foreign sales operations usually require that some sales people be available on location to promote products or to take orders. A subsidiary's board of directors may include one or more directors who reside in the country where the parent company is located. In each case the transferred employee or board member is potentially subject to double taxation, once in the host and once in the home country. Many multinationals reimburse employees for all or part of any double tax resulting from foreign transfers (see MULTINATIONAL CORPORATIONS).

Treaty exemptions

Income-tax treaties normally contain a commercial traveller article that, when satisfied, eliminates host-country taxation of an employee's income. To qualify for exemption employees must generally limit their presence in the host country to 183 days during the year and receive their compensation from an entity that does not reside in the host country. Also, a PE in the host country usually cannot deduct the compensation without forfeiting the exemption. More lenient exemption rules generally apply to employees of ships or aircraft involved in international transportation.

Apprentices and trainees that are temporarily present in a treaty country for full-time training are usually exempt from their compensation if two conditions are met. First, an entity or party outside the host country must pay the compensation. Second, the purpose of the payment must be for the individual's maintenance or training. Some treaties specify that the exemption is limited to a specified time, such as one year from the date of transfer.

Some income-tax treaties explicitly address which countries can tax director fees. In those cases treaties allow the host country to tax any portion of such fees for services rendered in that country. Income from services rendered in a director's home country is generally not taxable in the host country.

Totalization agreements

Tax planning for cross-border transfers of individuals often focuses on ways of mitigating the impact of double income taxation. However, double social-security taxation is possible also. As with increased income-tax liabilities, multinationals often bear all or part of the cost of the double social-security taxes that transferred employees incur.

Totalization agreements exist between some nations that exempt transferred employees from the host country's social-security taxes during temporary visits. In most agreements five years or less is considered temporary. In the absence of a totalization agreement the host country can impose its social-security taxes on any individual who becomes a resident. Double taxation results if the home country also continues to cover the individual during his or her term abroad. For example, the United States continues to impose social-security tax on all US employees who work abroad for American employers.

Totalization agreements are not as widespread as income tax treaties. For example, Norway and the United States have only eighteen and seventeen agreements in force, respectively.

6 Conclusion

Multinationals engaged in international business or investment activities are potentially subject to taxation in both their home and host countries (see MULTINATIONAL CORPORATIONS). The primary objective in international tax planning is to avoid double taxation as far as possible. The internal laws of some countries reduce or eliminate double tax on certain types of income. Income-tax treaties and other international agreements are also helpful in reducing host-country taxation.

Once this primary objective is achieved multinationals can turn their attention to other goals. Tax holidays in some countries and the possibility of tax deferrals in tax havens can be the means of reducing a multinational's worldwide ETR. However, many developed countries have anti-haven domestic laws that curtail long-term tax deferrals. Transfer pricing and remittance policies can also be used to reduce worldwide income taxes in many cases.

Over the next several years international tax advisers expect to see an increased number of tax treaties signed and ratified. The treaty activity should be particularly heavy with the 'newly independent' nations of the former Soviet Union and countries in the Pacific rim and, perhaps, South America. To develop economically these countries must negotiate income-tax treaties so they can attract foreign capital. At the same time, the potential new markets in these areas are very attractive to developed countries. Thus both developing and developed countries are highly motivated to conclude new tax treaties that promote and encourage international commerce.

Transfer pricing laws in many countries have undergone considerable changes in the past few years. Controversies involving transfer pricing issues will continue to plague both taxpayers and taxing authorities. Also, disputes between governments on appropriate arm's-length standards are likely to erupt as each country seeks to ensure it obtains its fair share of tax revenues. An alternative to the arm's-length approach that has gained some momentum in recent years is the unitary or formulary apportionment method. This method uses a prespecified formula to apportion worldwide income among affiliated companies. If widely adopted, this formulary approach may replace the heavy dependence on arm's-length pricing some day, but probably not in the near future.

ERNEST R. LARKINS
GEORGIA STATE UNIVERSITY

Further reading

Arnold, Brian J. and McIntyre, Michael J. (1995) *International Tax Primer*, The Hague: Kluwer Law International. (Provides a terrific overview of international tax systems that is simple to read.)

Coopers & Lybrand (1998) *International Tax Summaries*, New York: John Wiley & Sons. (Presents tax-system summaries for more than 100 countries in a uniform way.)

Deloitte Touche Tohmatsu International (1997) *International Tax and Business Guide*, New York: Deloitte. (Multiple-volume set that summarizes foreign tax systems and other international tax topics.)

Diamond, Walter H. (1997) *Foreign Tax and Trade Briefs*, Albany, NY: Matthew Bender. (Loose-leaf service that summarizes the tax systems of many countries and also provides trade information.)

Diamond, Walter H. and Diamond, Dorothy B. (1997) *Tax Havens of the World*, Albany, NY: Matthew Bender. (Nicely arranged loose-leaf service covering all major tax havens in a readable format.)

Doernberg, Richard L. (1997) *International Taxation in a Nut Shell*, 3rd edition, St Paul, MN: West Publishing. (Gives a lay introduction to the international aspects of the US tax system.)

Dogart, Caroline (1997) *Tax Havens and Their Uses*, London: Economist Intelligence Unit. (Gives an introduction to low-tax jurisdictions around the world and how to take advantage of them.)

Larkins, Ernest R. (1991) 'Multinationals and their quest for the good tax haven: taxes are but one, albeit an important, consideration', *International Lawyer* 25, summer: 471. (Examines tax and non-tax factors that cause various tax havens to be popular.)

Ogley, Adrian (1992) 'Tax systems and their interaction', *Tax Planning International Review*: 3. (Provides an easy-to-read conceptual overview of principles common to many tax systems.)

Tretiak, Philip L. (1993) 'Tax planning for U.S. multinationals', *International Tax Journal* 19, winter: 67. (Focuses on fundamental tax planning ideas for US companies engaged in international business.)

See also: EXPORTING; HUMAN RESOURCE MANAGEMENT, INTERNATIONAL; INTERNATIONAL BUSINESS ETHICS; MULTINATIONAL CORPORATIONS

Related topics in the IEBM: BUSINESS ETHICS; CAPITAL, COST OF; CAPITAL STRUCTURE; DIVIDEND POLICY; ECONOMICS OF DEVELOPING COUNTRIES; TRAINING; TRANSFER PRICING

Technology strategy, international

Overview

Technological change as a response to outside environmental forces has in the past to a large degree determined the fate of individuals, organizations and nation states. Today more than ever before, the key to survival hinges on the ability to capitalize on the opportunities of technological change and implementation. The present is a very exciting time for both the understanding and the practice of management and technology; there is a growing awareness that the success of organizations is directly dependent on the effective management of technology in order to create competitive advantage.

The management of technology has as its goal the improvement of the products and the productive capability of an organization. There are a number of models of technology management, but none are considered to be universally applicable. There are different international perspectives on the management of technology; within the Triad (Europe, with Germany at the core, Asia, with Japan at the core and North America, with the USA at the core), there are different approaches to the value of management or technology activities. One important cause of these differences is differing emphases on technology in higher education within the various regions; for example, more than 25 per cent of all US university students take some type of business degree, while over 50 per cent of students in Japan and Germany take technical degrees. This fact alone may result in different approaches to the management of technology.

There are also different concepts of the role of technology within the organization. Technology is not the sole domain of the research and development personnel of an organization. Successful business use of technology requires strategic decisions concerning factors such as innovation, knowledge, time, value-added costs, strategic alliances as well as other functional areas such as marketing, production and finance.

Understanding the relative contributions of several different models of technology, and how these models relate to one another, can lead to a greater appreciation of the importance of the management of technology. This entry looks at three of these models and assesses their relative emphases and values.

1 Technology and strategic function

Value chain model

The research on which this entry is based chose two strands of theory in its approach to the international management of technology: the value chain and strategic alliance frameworks introduced by Porter (1985), and the concept of the Triad, first developed by Ohmae (1980) (see GLOBAL STRATEGIC ALLIANCES). These two approaches allow the subject to be approached simultaneously from both an international and a strategic perspective.

The two key categories in the value chain model are the internal (value chain) organizational activities and their integration. According to Porter, each organization is a collection of nine generic and discrete activities which add to or detract from the organization's total value. Porter goes on to divide these value chain activities into two broad groups which are called *primary activities* and *support activities*.

Primary activities are those involved in the physical creation of a product or service that can be sold in the international marketplace. Porter uses five typical organization functions in his model; to this can now be added a sixth, internationalization, based on European research. The six primary or 'functional' activities are:

1 inbound logistics;
2 production or operations;
3 outbound logistics;
4 marketing and sales;
5 service;
6 internationalization.

The four support or 'secondary' activities are:

1 infrastructure, which encompasses ownership and activities such as management, organizing, controlling, accounting, legal and strategic planning;
2 technological development, which encompasses innovation, product design and research and development activities;
3 human resource management, including the recruiting, training, organizing and development of personnel;
4 procurement, which is defined as obtaining the necessary organizational inputs.

In an international or transnational organization, strategy often involves making management decisions on how to spread the activities listed above among countries (see GLOBALIZATION; MULTINATIONAL CORPORATIONS). Coordination is also required so that activities in different countries are integrated with each other. In making these decisions, management faces an array of strategic options. Factors such as economies of scale, product/market life cycles, competitive advantages and disadvantages, joint venture policies and foreign direct investment policies are all important. Porter (1980, 1985) also suggests that an organization must make the key strategic decision of whether to emphasize price, focus or differentiation as a means of gaining competitive advantage in the world marketplace.

Against this background of Porter's very normative descriptive theory of strategic organizational behaviour, we applied the framework of a situational hypothesis in testing whether 'triad' organizations actually used the nine or ten activity value chain along with a goal involving margins (profit) or some type of modification of Porter's work. External coordination allows a firm to react to a dynamic world of shifting competitive advantages, and also gives the organization the flexibility of responding to suppliers, buyers, competitors and new innovations. Porter's modified strategic alliance model is shown below. It is modified as follows.

1 The traditional state of the art, which is one of the five elements of competition according to Porter, is replaced by a value chain involving the firm in question.
2 The other elements of competition are included as value chains.
3 'New technology' is used to replace Porter's concept of 'substitutes'.
4 The addition of international (regional and global level) competition adds a third dimension to the model. The first dimension involves the value chain model of the firm which includes the nine or ten internal generic activities. The second dimension involves national competition with (local) suppliers, customers, competitors and new technology. The final dimension involves the above mentioned four competitive forces on an international/global scale. We will continue with the theoretical analysis of strategic alliances in the Triad section of this paper. The revised three dimensional model is shown in Figure 1.
5 Government is a difficult dimension to introduce into the model since it permeates at all levels and affects all actors. We have placed it at the top of the model on this assumption.
6 New technology is often used in the recent literature instead of substitutes.

The above modifications and changes are generally in line with the 'improvements' that have been made to Porter's work since 1985. It is beyond the scope of this entry to treat these in detail. Essentially, our cases from Asia, Europe and North America have pushed

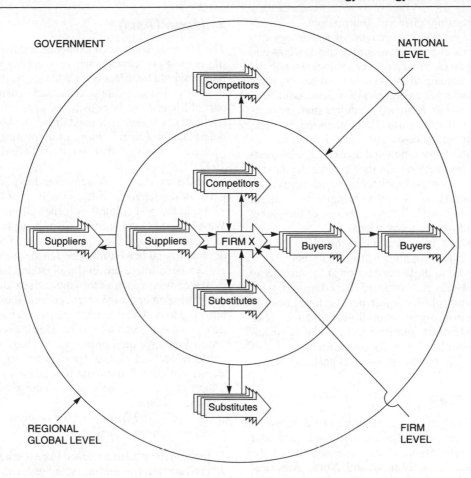

Figure 1 A global model of competitive elements for the firm

us in the situational (contingency theory or divergency theory are two of the most common terms used here) direction of explanation rather than the 'one best way' (convergency theory or universal explanation are the terms used).

The role of education

Education, particularly higher education at a university level, plays a major role in management performance and hence in organizational performance. Thus the structure, purpose and content of education have an influence on the management of technology and on business performance. Regional and cultural differences in education emphasis can be seen to have an important impact on technology strategy.

Education can be included in the model if one uses the casual logic of education impacting on individual management behaviour, which in turn impacts on organizational behaviour:

EDUCATION
  → INDIVIDUAL MANAGEMENT
        BEHAVIOUR
  → ORGANIZATION PERFORMANCE

However, one may also reject the idea that one universal model of the management of technology exists, or can be developed.

Presenting different international perspectives on the management of technology improves our understanding of the concepts and processes involved. Technology is not the sole domain of the research and development personnel of an organization. Successful business use of technology requires strategic decisions about innovation, knowledge, time, value-added costs and strategic alliances, as well as other functional areas such as marketing, production and finance. Bridging the cultural gap between different departments in an organization, as well as bridging the cultural gaps between different regions of the globe, are of central interest here.

Since education is a complex and all-encompassing theme, the focus here is restricted to higher education at the university level. It is also assumed that education plays a major role in management performance and hence in organizational performance. Thus the structure, purpose and content of education have an influence on the management of technology and on business performance.

The Triad

The aim of the research was to develop an aggregate model of international behaviour for each of the three main regions of the Triad, Asia, Europe and North America. Within these regions the bias is towards Japan, Germany and the USA, since these are the major countries representing the three regions. The research was founded on a number of case studies (60 in Europe, 15 in the USA and 10 in Japan over the period 1990–97), mostly of large international firms. An earlier study of smaller European firms has also been conducted (Joynt 1991). The cases were completed by executives in Europe and the USA after taking part in masters programmes in management. The structured action research task they were given was to develop a value chain and key strategic alliance for their organization. Each executive was required to survey the organization decided upon (Joynt 1991); the cases averaged 15–20 pages for each organization. Japanese executives participated in the US sample.

2 Japan (Asia)

The Japanese concept of existence and thinking is built on harmony where everything in nature should be balanced (see MANAGEMENT IN JAPAN). Business and work are an essential part of life and can be considered as an 'art of life' and not as an 'art of capitalism'. As such, behaviour in a firm is more of a vocation, a lifelong task and a fulfilment of life (Törnvall 1992).

At the same time, Western ideas have been a part of the Japanese culture for the past 400 years. In the past cultural influences from the West have widened individualism in the form of freedom, scepticism, private religion and organizational behaviour. The Japanese have always been interested in the West and have used techniques such as copying and scanning to absorb elements of Western culture. It is interesting to note that many Japanese management concepts such as quality and low-cost production have their origins in the West; the works of authors such as Drucker on organization structure, Deming on productivity and Thorsrud on group work have found a wide audience in Japan.

Törnvall (1992), in a study of over 300 Japanese students, found that:

1 most of the students wanted to be teachers, civil servants or engineers and technicians (the profession which appeared lowest on the list of desired jobs was 'inventor');
2 schoolwork is believed to help develop the student into a harmonious person with perseverance and duty;
3 hard work is a Japanese tradition;
4 the Japanese attitude towards work comes from tradition and not from philosophies such as Confucianism, Shintoism or Buddhism;
5 a professional worker follows traditions and has long-term training.

The typical Porter value chain for a Japanese firm includes the activities of logistics and procurement, which upon further investigation can be seen to be part of the overall production activity. Human resource management is also not considered as a separate activity but is integrated with other management activity in all parts of the firm. In conclusion, the Japanese firms studied tended to emphasize fewer generic activities than Porter's US-orientated model would suggest.

In generating a model involving key strategic alliances, the network relationships with suppliers were possibly the most important. This has always been a trademark for Japanese firms. The alliances also differed remarkably from their counterparts in Europe and the USA in that they were 'soft' long-term alliances, rather than 'hard' short-term alliances. As an example, just-in-time (JIT) alliances with suppliers often require a physical long-term plant location commitment by key suppliers in order to have the necessary time requirements. Cutting lot sizes, reducing inventory holding points and eliminating work-in-progress inventories as well as quick reactions to new technology were all advantages gained by Japanese firms through using softer relationships with suppliers.

A 'soft' relationship often involves higher degrees of flexibility as well as an intention of understanding the total production process on the part of both the firm and the supplier. Flexible low prices and high quality are also an essential part of the soft relationship. Finally, the 'soft' relationship usually involves a time framework of years rather than the normal one-year contract with suppliers that is subject to bidding and renewal at the end of each year.

The network or benchmarking activities concerning competitors are part of a long tradition for Japanese firms as well. Initially called 'copying', the language has changed in recent years to 'scanning', since many Japanese organizations are on the threshold of new products. The Japanese accomplish the scanning of competitors through a variety of activities such as reading trade journals, attending exhibits and visiting competitors directly. These 'benchmarking' strategies are perhaps one of the most popular new trends by Western firms in their attempts to match good Japanese management practices.

The most interesting element in our analysis of Japanese firms has to do with the management of technology. The process can be called the management of 'incremental technology'. This incremental aspect is the key to the main difference between the Western and the Eastern approaches to innovation. In the West the new idea, the new product and invention are often key objectives in the technological process; in the East, the key objectives are rather to improve, make small changes and make incremental changes to an existing product.

Car manufacture provides a good example. Japanese firms tend to locate their research and development (R&D) functions (technology) close to production, and closer to the customer. The function then becomes a 'broker' arrangement where the customer's ideas are acted upon and implemented in an incremental fashion. One can argue that most of the changes to a car are made by customer reactions, and invention is no longer the key element in the technological process. True, a new electric motor or new materials may be invented in the future, but in terms of frequency, the small incremental change, often initiated by customer feedback, is more important in both the long and the short run. Indeed, Figure 2 might almost include the customer as part of the system of strategic alliances, except that in reality there is both an internal and an external process which can best be described rather than illustrated in a model.

In conclusion, Japanese management has a flexible attitude to the management of technological development, and it is not felt that there is any need to wait until the next new model before making small changes to the product. Relationships with customers do not necessarily involve marketing only, and a close scrutiny of customer feedback is carried out in order to make incremental changes to products.

3 Germany (Europe)

While the USA has 950,000 people employed in research, Europe is not far behind with some 580,000 and Japan has approximately 435,000. During the fifty years prior to 1990, Europeans won 86 Nobel Prizes, compared with 143 for US researchers and 5 for

The typical Asian firm (Firm J) consists of a value chain with activities of production, technology, infrastructure and marketing. The strongest strategic alliances involve those with suppliers both at the national and international/global levels as well as competitors particularly at the international/global level.

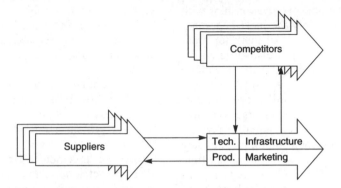

Figure 2 A scanning model for Japan

Japanese researchers. The twelve European Union (EU) countries spend 2 per cent of their combined GNP, while the USA and Japan spend around 2.9 per cent (*The Economist* 1993) on applied research.

In Germany there has long been a close relationship between management and engineering (see MANAGEMENT IN GERMANY). Prior to the First World War, Germany had introduced a special degree in *Wirtschafts-Ingenieur* (economics and engineering) with classes in both disciplines. Until recently there has been no MBA degree offered in Germany, but a high degree of managers in any large firm have doctorates. Praxis is important, but as Locke (1985: 182) points out through the eyes of a personnel manager 'the manager needs to know how decisions are made in the firm' and how planning processes are done, but the skill dimension is the province of the firm.

It is difficult to generalize from Germany to Europe for many reasons, yet it is also important to realize that the countries of Europe are converging as members in the EU. The EU goals which were set during the 1980s with the launch of programmes such as JET, Eureka, Esprit and Race include the following:

1 the development of home-grown expertise, especially in generic activities involving clean manufacturing techniques;
2 the achievement of economies of scale in R&D;
3 integration of firms in various countries;
4 to encourage equal ratios of spending for R&D in all countries.

Perhaps the most important trend in the EU has to do with the introduction of accepted standards across borders within Europe. This is eliminating a great deal of unnecessary product duplication. A manager from Belgium formerly required three different mobile telephones to communicate with company units in Belgium, The Netherlands and Germany; a single standard means that only one telephone will be needed. At an even simpler level, standardization of electrical appliances means that in the future travellers will not have to buy an adapter in order to be able to use their shavers in the morning when travelling from country to country. At the company level, a welding firm will be able to manufacture to about twenty standards, as opposed to the thousands of different standards that exist in the USA and Japan. The economies of scale resulting from making twenty products instead of thousands of thousands will give European firms a considerable competitive edge within Europe (Figure 2).

Another impulse towards technological development involves the European Space Agency (ESA), which manages the Ariane space project. The agency has six major goals, which have both technological and political aspects:

1 the encouragement of space science as a new scientific discipline;
2 the use of space technology on earth through such means as cartography and weather prediction;
3 improving telecommunications;
4 developing applications from new technology in fields such as pharmacy, fluid dynamics and chemistry;
5 profit (Ariane presently has over sixty satellite orders);
6 the political impact of a large European space project.

It is close to impossible to model the 'typical' European firm using a value chain with its associated external networks with strategic alliances. What is important is the concentration by firms on making the EU work at the economic, if not the political, level. The progress made on standards and economies of scale in the management of technology inspires most firms towards a better future. There is a danger, however, of a Europe which concentrates so hard on becoming unified that it forgets the outside world.

Education has played an important role in the development of the management of technology in Germany as well as in the creation of management culture in general (Locke 1985). Since the mid-nineteenth century, German universities have stressed the importance of scientific research. This research imperative in turn requires a specific approach to the nature of knowledge, which is tested constantly through scientific investigative processes and deepened, changed and perfected. *Wissenschaft* implies that all fields of knowledge are subject to systematic, disciplined research and development; this applies not only to the natural sciences (*Naturwissenschaften*) but also art, history and the humanities (*Geisteswissenschaften*).

Our model for Europe is very general at this time as the EU is in its infancy. The model suggests a heavy concentration on the region of Europe suggesting that international/global networks may be secondary firm strategies for the European firm at this time.

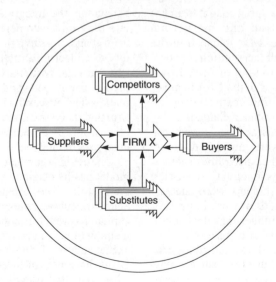

Figure 3 A regional model for Europe

Initially, students of engineering and business attended technical schools, but by 1890 students were allowed to acquire doctorates, the first engineering doctorates in the world and the technical schools were placed on the same level as universities. The first higher business education schools (*Handelshochschulen*) were established around 1900, and by 1920 it was possible to acquire a full range of graduate degrees in business economics. Schmalenbach and Nicklisch were well known writers in this era. Locke (1985) quotes from a Vienna Congress on Commercial Education in 1910:

> One could clearly see how the business schools in German speaking regions had begun to develop into teaching and research institutions and how the Latin countries with their very different academic goals, strived more and more to copy and to hold fast, to routine business practice.
>
> (Locke 1985: 170)

German business schools reached full maturity before 1940; by 1958, in that year alone 24,000 students received economics degrees in West Germany, and 6,200 received doctorates. Firms were studied as an integrated, multi-faced discipline in which the functional and institutional disciplines were for the most part submerged, with accounting overshadowing the others. Accounting sought to amalgamate the production and marketing function. The result was a flexible instrument of managerial control; accounting science could be applied to any kind of firm. However, following advances in the USA in areas such as marketing and finance, the university reforms in the 1960s produced changes in the curricula. Operations research and human resource management were introduced, along with elements from other disciplines such as law, sociology and psychology. Case studies were introduced and students were encouraged to undertake periods of work in firms.

In conclusion, the model for education – management behaviour – firm performance is very weak at this time; the technical aspects work with the model but other aspects may not, as the educational system has not concentrated on leaving these as a responsibility for firms. However, if we use the German model, one can see the impact that a technically oriented business education has had on the firm. It remains to be seen if this will eventually be the situation for all of Europe. Management culture in Germany, including the management of technology, has been strongly affected by the emphasis on science in education.

4 The United States of America (North America)

The most important value chain activity in the North American analysis is marketing, and the most important strategic alliance is between the firm and the customer (Figure 4). One language is spoken by the majority of the population in one of the largest regions in the world, so the above result is not surprising. However, the relationship between the customer and the firm can be taken to a further phase, the integration of the university or research centre that serves as an information gathering unit for all firms in the same customer branch. We found this to be true in about half of the US international firms studied.

While benchmarking has become a popular management technique in the USA, where firms look to competitors for 'best practices' behaviour, the integration of the university into the firm–customer relationship allows a neutral and objective third party the opportunity to collect information on new products, new markets, cost analysis, customer trends, market share trends and other valuable information. This research is often financed by the firm and its competitors working together, in other words by an entire manufacturing or industry segment.

One could argue that the present American model has its origins in the start-up firms of the past that were often formed by entrepreneurs from universities and funded by venture capital. However, in the recent past entrepreneurs without an academic background, such as Steven Jobs of Apple and Mitchell Kapor of Lotus, have not followed this mode (Kenney 1988). The tradition of relationships between universities and business that has served the

USA well in the past, has worked less well in more recent years. The dean of the business school at Carnegie Mellon University complained that while US firms were not willing to finance research projects at his school, Japanese firms proved more than willing.

The university–firm relationship has a long tradition in the area of technology in the USA. However, there may now be a shift in the balance from an innovation/entrepreneurial start-up role for the university, to one of assistance in marketing and information gathering. If the new role of assisting in marketing is replacing the old role of assistance with technology, there is a possibility that Asian researchers may step into the old role; the Carnegie example suggests that this may already be happening.

Universities in the USA grant close to one million degrees each year. Over 25 per cent of those are in business, 10 per cent are in the social sciences, 9.5 per cent are in education, 9 per cent are in engineering and 6 per cent are in health. Further down the list is psychology, the study of the individual, with 4.5 per cent, which is high in comparison with other countries. The USA has ranked very low in testing youth on the basics of knowledge such as reading, writing and mathematics, and there is a great deal of concern about quality at the lower levels of education. The USA has,

The American model suggests that the strongest value chain behaviour is marketing and the key strategic alliance is with the customer. Using the traditional university–firm linkage, one finds that many groups of firms are using the university to analyse the trends in the firm–customer relationship in detail.

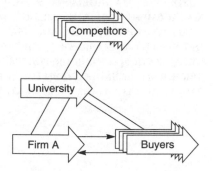

Figure 4 A marketing model for the USA

however, some of the best universities in the world. Many of these have a very high foreign student ratio at the graduate level, as it is difficult for many Americans to compete. The USA with its large English-speaking population is one of the largest markets in the world, and the business school curriculum reflects this. This is also reflected in firm behaviour.

5 Conclusions

In conclusion, it can be suggested that one should study the Japanese techniques for the upstream management of technology and production, analyse the Europeans concerning the advances made on standardization, and concentrate on the USA for the management of the marketing information function.

Competitive and comparative analysis is the name of the new game. While this entry has illustrated that the US model relies on a marketing emphasis, the key organization activities for the models of Europe and Japan suggest that upstream activities associated with the management of technology are more important. The models presented need more development and refinement, but the process of technology, the work done in any organization, emerges as a key competitive factor in this comparative analysis using the three largest trading nations (the Triad) as a focus. The issue is perhaps best summed up by Robert Reich, one of the leading writers and researchers in the area of technological strategy:

> Technology literacy is fundamental. The emerging global economy requires people at all levels who understand technology, design engineering and manufacturing engineering, energy, production and so on.
>
> (*Directors* 1991: 16)

PAT JOYNT
HENLEY MANAGEMENT COLLEGE, UK
BODØ GRADUATE SCHOOL OF BUSINESS,
NORWAY

Note
An earlier version of this chapter was published in the 1993 annual Proceedings of the European International Business Association, editor Vitor Corado Simêes.

Further reading

(References cited in the text marked *)

Campbell, A. and Warner, M. (1992) *New Technology, Skills and Management: Human Resources in the Market Economy*, London: Routledge. (A look at the relationship between technology and training in modern management.)

* *Directors* (1991) 'A conversation with Bob Reich' (Fall): 16. (Interview with a leading US thinker on technology and strategy.)

Drucker, P. F. (1991) 'The new productivity challenge', *Harvard Business Review* (November–December): 69–79. (Work on the relationship between technology and performance by a leading management thinker.)

* *The Economist* (1993) 'Europe's technology policy', 9 January. (Short article on technology strategy in Europe.)

* Joynt, P. (1991) 'International dimensions of managing technology', *Journal of General Management* 16 (3): 73–84. (Longer look at different international aspects of technology management and strategy.)

Joynt, P. (1993) 'International strategy: a study of Norwegian firms', in P.J. Buckley and P. Ghauri (eds), *The Internationalization of the Firm: A Reader*, London: Academic Press. (A look at Norwegian firms, which exhibit some distinctive national characteristics, in international operations.)

Joynt, P. and Warner, M. (eds) (1996) *Managing Cultures: Issues and Perspectives*, International Thomson Business Press, London. (Important an useful work on cross-cultural management.)

* Kenney, M. (1988) *Biotechnology: The University-Industrial Complex*, London: Yale University Press. (A study of the role of education in new technology, focusing in this case on biotechnology.)

Larsen, N.M. and Joynt, P. (1994) 'High-speed management and organizational communication: time as a competitive advantage in global markets', in D.P. Cushman and S.S. King (eds), *High Speed Management and Organizational Communication in the 1990s: A Reader*, Albany, NY: State University of New York Press.

(A look at another aspect of technology management, that of the importance of time.)

* Locke, R. (1985) 'The relationship between educational and managerial cultures in Britain and West Germany', in P. Joynt and M. Warner (eds), *Managing Different Cultures*, Oslo: Universitetsförlaget. (Cross-cultural comparison between the UK and Germany.)

Lorange, P. and Roos, J. (1992) *Strategic Alliances: Formation, Implementation and Evolution*, Oxford: Blackwell. (Leading work on global strategic alliances.)

* Ohmae, K. (1980) *Triad Power: The Coming Shape of Global Competition*, New York: The Free Press. (Highly influential work which helped define the nature of global competition.)

* Porter, M. (1980) *Competitive Strategy: Techniques for Analyzing Industries and Competitors*, New York: The Free Press. (Textbook on the fundamentals of strategy.)

* Porter, M. (1985) *Competitive Advantage: Creating and Sustaining Superior Performance*, New York: The Free Press. (Another highly influential work by the leading US writer on strategy.)

* Törnvall, A. (1992) *Work in Japan: Proceedings from Workshop on Managing in Different Cultures*, Cergy-Pontoise: EIASM. (Useful cross-cultural comparison with Japan.)

See also: GLOBAL STRATEGIC ALLAINCES; GLOBALIZATION; MANAGEMENT IN GERMANY; MANAGEMENT IN JAPAN; MULTINATIONAL CORPORATIONS

Related topics in the IEBM: BENCHMARKING; DEMING, W.E.; DRUCKER, P.F.; INDUSTRIAL RELATIONS IN JAPAN; INNOVATION AND CHANGE; INNOVATION MANAGEMENT; INNOVATION AND TECHNOLOGICAL CHANGE; JAPANIZATION; JUST-IN-TIME PHILOSOPHIES; MANAGEMENT IN EUROPE; MANAGEMENT IN NORTH AMERICA; MANAGEMENT IN PACIFIC ASIA; MANUFACTURING STRATEGY; MARKETING; OHMAE, K.; ORGANIZATION BEHAVIOUR; PORTER, M.E.; REICH, R.M.; TECHNOLOGY DIFFUSION IN JAPAN; TECHNOLOGY AND ORGANIZATIONS

World Trade Organization (WTO)

Overview

The World Trade Organization (WTO) was established on 1 January 1995. It is the umbrella organization governing the international trading system. It oversees international trade arrangements and it provides the secretariat for the General Agreement on Tariffs and Trade (GATT), which has been based in Geneva since its inception in 1948. The GATT undertook eight 'rounds' of multilateral trade negotiations, which were successful in achieving major cuts in tariffs and (after the 1970s) some reductions in related non-tariff barriers to trade. The last GATT round, the Uruguay Round, took seven years, as its agenda had broadened to include trade in services, trade in intellectual property and a revised system of dispute-settlement mechanisms.

1 Origin

Contrary to popular belief, the WTO does not replace the GATT. An amended GATT remains as one of the legal pillars of the world's trade and, to a lesser extent, investment system. The other pillars were set up in the Uruguay Round's Marrakesh Agreement of 1994 and include the General Agreement on Trade in Services (GATS) and the Agreement on trade-related aspects of intellectual property rights (TRIPS). The membership of the WTO has increased from the seventy-six founding members of 1995 to 132 members (1998). Members include virtually all the developed and most of the developing countries. A notable non-member of the WTO is the People's Republic of China, whose entry has been blocked by the United States on the grounds that its economy is not open enough and that intellectual property rights (IPRs) are not sufficiently protected. The members of the WTO account for well over 90 per cent of the world's trade and virtually all of its investment.

The origins of the WTO can be traced back to the Atlantic Charter of 1941 developed by the then US president Franklin Roosevelt and the then British prime minister Winston Churchill. In order to counter US isolationism, the principle of the Atlantic Charter was for an international trading system with equal access to trade for all nations. This was seen as a complement to an effective world political forum, the United Nations (UN), established in 1946, with its permanent headquarters in New York City. The United States organized an international conference on trade and employment which resulted in the Havana Charter of 1948, in which it was proposed that the International Trade Organization (ITO) be established. Concurrently, twenty-three countries agreed to a set of tariff cuts and these were ratified by the GATT, which was set up as a transition arrangement to be subsumed under the ITO. However, the ITO was never ratified and the GATT continued for forty-seven years, until the WTO finally emerged in the last stages of the Uruguay Round to take on the powers originally designed for the ITO. The WTO now stands with the World Bank and the International Monetary Fund (IMF) as the third leg of the global economic system.

2 WTO principles

The WTO carries on the key GATT principle of non-discrimination, i.e. that any barrier to trade should be applied equally to all member countries. It also keeps the most-favoured nation (MFN) principle, i.e. that any liberalization measures, with some exceptions, should also be granted to all members. To understand what these principles mean it is fruitful to think of the WTO as a club whose membership rules require that all members receive the same treatment and that if one member rescinds a trade concession other affected members can retaliate by withdrawing their reciprocal concessions, or receive compensation to equivalent commercial effect. If trade disputes arise then they can be settled by the unified dispute-settlement mechanism of the WTO, which can ensure timely compliance, in contrast to the basically voluntary procedures of the GATT. Now decisions of a WTO dispute panel can no longer be blocked by the disputant party, as was possible under the GATT. Panel findings can be subject to review by an Appellate Body of the WTO. In addition, the publication of trade-policy reviews and the activities of the Trade Policy Review Body (which regularly monitors the trade policies of member countries) complement the WTO's dispute-settlement activities by contributing significantly to enhanced transparency.

There are four important exceptions to the key GATT principle of non-discrimination. First, developed countries can give tariff preference to developing countries. Second, countries entering into regional free-trade agreements do not need to extend the preferences negotiated in this context on an MFN basis. Third, a country can invoke temporary 'safeguard' protection of one of its industries suffering serious injury due to a surge of imports. Fourth, temporary quantitative restrictions can be invoked by a country with serious balance-of-payment problems. In the latter two cases, these measures are temporary exceptions to the member's commitment to the GATT and a public investigation has to be undertaken to allow for limited relief from GATT obligations.

Another important principle of the WTO which is a significant improvement on the GATT is the 'single undertaking'. WTO members must accept all of the obligations of the GATT, GATS, TRIPS and any other corollary agreements. This ends the 'free ride' of some developing countries under the old GATT, when they could receive the benefits of some trade concessions without having to join in and undertake their full obligations.

For most developed countries in North America and western Europe the single undertaking was already being made and the WTO meant few new obligations.

3 Analysis

The major tensions in the WTO relate to the issues of agriculture, trade in services and trade-related investment measures. None of these issues were included in the original mandate of the GATT, which dealt with trade in goods. Agriculture is a sector which most governments subsidize, and it was badly neglected in the GATT. One technical advance which helps to increase the transparency of subsidies is the calculation of producers' subsidy equivalents. As a result, in the Uruguay Round some progress was made towards the future reduction of the most egregious agricultural subsidies through a process of 'tarification', i.e. the translation of existing subsidies and other barriers to trade into tariff equivalents. Much work remains to be done in future rounds to liberalize agricultural trade.

Today services account for 70 per cent of the employment and value added in advanced industrialized countries, and also for at least half the world's trade and investment. The Uruguay Round started to address issues of trade in services with the establishment of GATS. Trade-related investment measures (TRIMS) were also considered and a substantive agreement that prohibits a number of investment requirements affecting cross-border trade in goods was reached, e.g. the TRIMS agreement restricted the imposition of export requirements on foreign investors. Future negotiations at the WTO (following on the last Uruguay Round of the GATT) will need to develop a deeper and more comprehensive set of rules for multinational investment than exists in TRIMS. These may well be based on the model of the North American Free-Trade Agreement (NAFTA; see NORTH AMERICAN FREE-TRADE AGREEMENT), using the national treatment principle as the basic logic. National treatment states that foreign investors should not be discriminated against, but receive the same treatment as domestic firms in the application of domestic laws.

The WTO round could build on a multinational agreement on investment (MAI) which was partially negotiated by the Paris-based Organization for Economic Cooperation and Development (OECD) over the 1995–8 period. Currently, investment issues are being discussed at the WTO in the context of the Working Group on the Relationship between Trade and Investment, established and given a two-year mandate at the 1996 ministerial meeting in Singapore. Another important Working Group established during the WTO Singapore meeting is that examining the interaction between trade and competition policy.

4 Conclusion

Over a fifty-year period the GATT has moved forwards to the extent that today's new constitution for international trade, embodied in the WTO, includes an even fuller agenda of policy issues than was envisaged by its pioneering founders. These issues include further reduction of tariffs; a set of rules for multinational investment and competition policy; and the development of increased linkages between trade and issues of social policy, such as the environment and labour policy. The hurdles to achieving these three sets of objectives are lowest for tariff cuts, higher for investment, and highest of all for environmental and other social issues.

ALAN M. RUGMAN
TEMPLETON COLLEGE
UNIVERSITY OF OXFORD

Further reading

Krueger, Anne O. (1998) *The WTO as an International Organization*, Chicago, IL: University of Chicago Press. (Leading US academics analyse the WTO as an institution and consider current policy issues.)

Ostry, S. (1997) *The Post-Cold War Trading System: Who's on First?*, Chicago, IL: University of Chicago Press. (Presents an analysis of the GATT and WTO by the world's leading scholar of international institutions.)

Qureshi, A.H. (1996) *The World Trade Organization: Implementing International Trade Norms*, Manchester: Manchester University Press; New York: St Martin's Press. (Explains the legal framework of the WTO, how it works in practice and presents an appendix which reprints key selected documents.)

Rugman, A.M. (1996) *Multinationals and Trade Policy: Volume 2 of the Selected Scientific Papers of Alan M. Rugman*, Cheltenham: Edward Elgar. (Contains research papers reporting tests of GATT-related dispute-settlement procedures on countervail and anti-dumping, and on trade in services.)

Schott, Jeffrey J. (1996) *WTO 2000: Setting the Course for World Trade*, Washington, DC: Institute for International Economics. (Discusses the challenges facing the WTO and the agenda for future trade negotiations.)

World Trade Organization (1995) *The Results of the Uruguay Round of Multilateral Trade Negotiations: The Legal Texts*, Geneva: WTO. (Presents the actual legal texts of the last GATT round.)

World Trade Organization (1996a) *Annual Report 1996: Special Topic: Trade and Foreign Direct Investment*, vol. I, Geneva: WTO.

World Trade Organization (1996b) *Singapore Ministerial Declaration*, Document WT/MIN/(96)/DEC/W, Geneva: WTO. (Presents the report of the first WTO ministerial meeting in December 1996, including the Working Groups on competition policy and on investment.)

World Trade Organization (1997) *Annual Report 1997: Special Topic: Trade and Competition Policy, Vol. I.* Geneva: WTO.

Further resources

http://www.wto.org

See also: ECONOMIC INTEGRATION, INTERNATIONAL; INTERNATIONAL BUSINESS, LEGAL DIMENSIONS OF; INTERNATIONAL TRADE AND FOREIGN DIRECT INVESTMENT; NORTH AMERICAN FREE-TRADE AGREEMENT.

Related topics in the IEBM: GENERAL AGREEMENT ON TARIFFS AND TRADE (GATT)

Country and regional focus

Business culture, Japanese

Overview

The business culture of Japan is viewed as being quite different from that of English-speaking countries, particularly that of the USA. However, there is some similarity with continental European countries like Germany, and it considerably resembles those of Korea, China and southeast Asian countries, the so-called Confucian cultural area. How deep are these differences or similarities?

Moreover, was business culture the main force in Japanese economic development in the post-war period? Or was it just one contributory factor? Familism, groupism, vertical and horizontal values, long-termism, ways of decision making and so on are often pointed out as some characteristics of the uniqueness of Japanese culture. Alongside these aspects, there are some regional cultural differences between the Kanto area and the Kansai area. With an eye to religious background, the main features of Japanese business culture will be examined.

1 Key features and their importance

It is very difficult to understand Japanese business culture as a whole (see MANAGEMENT IN JAPAN). Consequently, the interpretation of this topic might vary according to scholar. However, several factors characterizing Japanese business culture are well known: familism; vertical values; groupism; long-termism; certain ways of decision making (informal, personal and bottom-up, as seen in *nemawashi* and *ringi*) and business nationalism. These features constitute the essence of Japanese business culture. And behind them, there is the religious background of Shintoism, Buddhism and Confucianism, the three major religions in Japan. These three doctrines have been traditional pillars of Japanese thinking and have co-existed. Confucianism probably provides the main basis of business culture.

Viewed from a different angle, fundamental elements of Japanese culture also come from the notions of *mura* (village) and *ie* (house) which are based on Confucianism. These concepts are still of much use in understanding Japanese culture.

2 The religious background

Shinto, Buddhism and Confucianism are the main religions in Japan. Although Shinto is the oldest, and native, religion of Japan, its direct influence has been limited in the business world, particularly after the Second World War. However, in that it emphasizes worshipping ancestors, it provides the concept of *continuity* from the past which is a vital notion in Japanese culture. Buddhism is significant in general philosophy, but not very important in the business scene. Both religions tend to come to people's minds only when there is some ceremony like a wedding, funeral or the purification of a building site.

In contrast, Confucianism exerts substantial power over Japanese behaviour and provides the basic ethics for the business world, though it is arguable whether it is a religion or simply an ethos of everyday life. In Confucianism, the concept of *chu ko* (loyalty and filial piety) is crucially important. Loyalty to a lord and piety to parents formed the basic morals of Japanese people and *chu ko* is still appreciably valid as the ideology of the Japanese. In addition to this, *giri* (duty) is a cardinal yardstick for behaviour and the linchpin of human relations among the Japanese. These factors form the so-called vertical and horizontal values, such as familism and groupism.

3 Familism and the importance of vertical relationship

The concept of *ie* was pivotal in pre-war Japan. Business paternalism was intentionally introduced into the business world in the 1920s and 1930s in order to create a distinctive management style (see *KEIRETSU*). The parent (management) held the supreme position over workers, and workers were treated as children. Yet, after the war, Western-style democracy permeated Japan and paternalistic management declined. But familism (in other words, communitarian thinking) is still strong despite the rise of nuclear families.

Family consists of parents, brothers and sisters. Surprisingly, there is no precise word meaning brother or sister in Japanese. Instead the words *ani* (elder brother) and *ototo* (younger brother) are used. This means that the vertical relationship is crucial, and it is extended to friends and acquaintances. In such relations, the words, *senpai* (senior friend) and *kohai* (junior friend) are used very often, instead of just 'friends'. Likewise, *joshi* (senior) and *buka* (subordinate) are common words in companies. This kind of vertical relationship is also applied to inter-firm relations. A parent company, subsidiaries and sub-subsidiaries shape a network of companies, known as *keiretsu*.

In the pre-war period, *zaibatsu* (company groups based on family ties) was made up on a quasi-family principle (see *KEIRETSU*). Accordingly, *zaibatsu* families, such as Mitsui, Iwasaki and Sumitomo had overwhelming power over employees. In post-war Japan, *zaibatsu* transformed into horizontal *keiretsu*, which are based on cross-shareholding, and lost the hierarchical relationship which is central to familism, but the vertical *keiretsu* (parent–subsidiary network)

kept its vertical relationship. In comparison with the American horizontal structure, the conspicuous hallmark of Japanese business is the vertical nature of relationships among persons, between firms and within firms.

4 Groupism as a horizontal relation

Shudan-shugi, which puts the interest of the whole over individual interests, is the concept often put forward in Japan. It is usually translated as groupism, collectivism or communitarianism. Since collectivism is now associated with communism, communitarianism is an appropriate translation. Groupism is used to represent the horizontal values of *shudan-shugi*, while familism is used for vertical ones.

As contrasted with familism, which originates from the *ie* concept, groupism comes from the *mura* concept. While *ie* is based on a blood relationship, *mura* is a community. On account of division of labour and cooperative work, the *mura* had to restrict individuals' rights. In the Tokugawa era, *gonin gumi* (five-person teams) were established, using group responsibility. Responsibility was not burdened on the individual but on the group. This nurtured team spirit and teamwork, suppressing individual rights and wants. This spirit still is predominant in Japan today. Firms do not encourage competition among individuals but among groups. Group evaluation is not uncommon. The typical case is quality control circles, which are thriving in Japan. Although the method of quality control was imported from the USA, quality control circles were invented and prospered in Japan. The traditional team spirit considerably contributed to this development.

Another example of horizontal *shudan-shugi* is the collusive relationship in trade associations. In Japan, cartels based on trade associations are material: if a firm becomes a member of a cartel or trade association, it can enjoy a variety of benefits in information and restraint of overproduction. It becomes an insider, discriminating against others as outsiders. As a consequence, some amount of exclusivity will result. Groupism is seen in almost every dimension of Japanese business; in teams of firms, trade associations and *keiretsu*. While intra-group competition is discouraged, inter-group competition is vehement.

The well-known ubiquity of company-based unions in Japan is understood as the other instance of groupism: it attaches significance to companies, not to the solidarity of the working class. In groupism, a special stress is put on *wa* (harmony) which is a vital notion for keeping order within a group. *Wa* is very frequently preached and encouraged to every member of a company.

5 Reality of groupism

Although groupism is important in Japan, it is misleading to interpret it simply as dedication to the group at the sacrifice of individual interest. It is quite often said that the Japanese 'salary-man' works very hard for his company, even offering *sabisu zangyo* (unpaid overtime). But in reality, Japanese 'salary-men' principally work for their own promotion, not for the company. Promotion is the prime objective, so that it is wrong to understand groupism as contrasting to individualism.

Without doubt, the old saying *messhi hoko* (serving public interests at the sacrifice of private interests) is out of date. Even if it is mentioned as an ideal, *messhi hoko* is not *honne* (real intentions) but *tatemae* (official stance). In essence, *shudan-shugi* is thus not very different from Western-style individualism.

6 Long-termism, or time-continuity

Ie or familism, brought the concept of survival to business. In Japanese business, the survival of *ie* or firms is of supreme importance and the maintenance of employment is crucial too because employees are members of *ie*. Business strategy must be decided and executed in the light of the goal of survival. From this emphasis, long-termism emerged. In making strategy decisions, long-term views became the first thing to be considered and short-term profits became secondary. On occasion, this led to conservatism hesitant to innovation and investment, so as to avert risk of bankruptcy.

However, after the Meiji Restoration in 1868, especially after the Second World War, the market environment changed drastically. Demand grew rapidly and technological innovation accelerated. For the purpose of mere survival, enlargement of firms became inevitable. Long-term growth as a business goal was viewed as having primary importance. This long-term growth policy gave rise to a low dividend–payout ratio and a high debt–equity ratio which was caused by the heavy reliance on bank finance.

Japanese firms prefer long-term contracts and trust between business partners, which is another feature of long-termism. Advantages of long-term contracts in reducing transaction costs are theoretically pointed out by some business economists.

To give an example of the workings of trust, Toyota Automobile did not buy steel from Kawasaki Steel for thirty-five years because Kawasaki had stopped supplying sheet steel to Toyota in 1955 when the latter suffered a serious financial crisis (see TOYODA FAMILY). It was, in fact, hardly surprising that Kawasaki should stop the supply of steel, since Toyota had been unable to pay. However, after recovering from the crisis, Toyota took its revenge; although it bought steel from all other major steel companies, it boycotted Kawasaki Steel until 1990. This reveals the kind of trust and human responsiveness that the Japanese are looking for in partners. This sort of trust can be seen in most transactions in Japan.

7 Consensual, informal, personal and participating decision making

Wa (harmony) is considered to be the most important touchstone in groups. *Wa* requires internal homogeneity and the exclusion of heretics; this is enabled by the fact that Japanese society consists of relatively homogeneous cohorts. In meetings, consensual decision making is pursued in most cases. Decision making by votes or macho-style management is not welcomed. This attitude derives from *wa*: the spirit of groupism and also from the objective condition of homogeneity which includes racial and religious uniformity.

Participation in decision making is another facet of Japanese cultural behaviour. Bottom-up decision making is a typical case. In comparison with top-down decision making and its implementation, bottom-up decision making characteristically has the features of slower decisions and faster implementation. Bottom-up decision making has merits and demerits, but it is suited to consensual decision. The representative example is the *ringi* system which is the decision-making process in which proposals are drafted at lower levels and are passed along the line of authority upward with each line superior attaching his seal of approval or adding some change on the *ringi-sho* (documents for *ringi*). As the *ringi* system is a consensual decision, all who put seals on the *ringi-sho* have responsibility jointly. As a result, the responsibility of each person becomes ambiguous since responsibility is dispersed. But it should be noted that the *ringi* system is mainly used for routine decision making, not for strategy.

Bottom-up decision making also serves to activate rank and file worker participation in management, even if the level of such participation is quite low. It can raise the morale of employees. Quality control circles and suggestion systems are examples of participating in decision making.

Informal decision making is another Japanese characteristic. A typical measure is *nemawashi* which means to secure informal consent from the people concerned prior to a formal decision. This is of utmost importance in doing business in Japan. Not only to business partners and suppliers, but also to bureaucrats, *nemawashi* is indispensable. If one would like to have any agreement in meetings, *nemawashi* is crucial for the people concerned. People who did not have *nemawashi* may be upset and object to the proposal, even if they are in favour of it. But even in Japan *nemawashi* has the slightly negative connotation of under-the-table transactions, because of its smack of secrecy and unfairness. This kind of informal decision making goes with personal communication rather than with formal structures. On the whole, people tend to depend on the human nexus, especially with regard to secret and key information.

Associated with bottom-up decision making, Japanese firms have relatively decentralized decision-making structures. This results in information-sharing among management and employees, which improves employees' morale.

Confucian respect for education results in importance attaching to training both in-house and in the public mind. Systematic on-the-job training is ubiquitous in large firms. Closely linked with this, *genba-shugi* (respect for on-site experience) is a dominant philosophy among management and employees. Even university graduates must experience on-site working. Engineers from top-level universities must spend a few years on the shop floor before entering research institutes, while white-collar workers who graduated from universities spend a few months in factories. This experience necessarily generates an egalitarian mind. Even a factory manager wears the same uniform as rank and file workers. From the viewpoint of familism and groupism, a uniform is of use in strengthening the feeling of unity; and likewise the company song.

Genba-shugi has some advantages for increasing productivity and improving the quality of products, for example, in trying to perfect 'zero defect' in the manufacturing process, not in an inspection department. The 'zero defect' movement developed keenly in the 1960s and 1970s. Whereas the American philosophy regarding defects is that inspectors should check finished products, the Japanese philosophy is that defects must be found and mended in the process. Related to this, Japanese workers' philosophy is that the defect ratio must always come nearer to zero, while the American one is that a certain standard, for example, 90 per cent will be reasonable, considering costs. Although Japanese perfectionism might be too costly, it can eventually win customers' trust.

8 Regional difference: Kansai culture versus Kanto culture

If one looks into Japanese culture in more detail, a substantial regional difference will be noticed. The Kansai area (the western part of Japan, including Osaka, Kyoto and Kobe) has a unique culture, which is pushy, aggressive, shrewd, talkative and business-orientated. Kansai is quite often contrasted to Kanto (the central area including Tokyo and Yokohama). Although most companies have their head offices in Tokyo, Kansai has yielded a number of first-rank firms. A top firm in each industry tends to be occupied by Kansai firms, such as Nissei in life insurance, Matsushita in electronics, Sumitomo and Sanwa in banking, NEC in computers and semi-conductors, Nomura in securities, Daiei in supermarkets, Kyocera in ceramics and Seibu in hotels and retail shops. Kansai firms are renowned or notorious for hard work and the Kansai way of business (*Kansai shoho*). The business climate is quite different from the Kanto area, which is comparatively less hard-working. It is fair to say that the Kansai way of management is the essence of Japanese-style management.

The *omikoshi* style of management (named after the portable Shinto shrine, carried by a group of men), the typical bottom-up management, is deemed to be suited to the Japanese situation. In this style, surprisingly, strong leadership is not preferred. The head who controls business closely and directly is not an ideal manager, but managers who delegate most of the work and responsibility to subordinates are respected. It is believed that this is the ideal type for top executives in Japan. However, by and large, in Kansai-style firms, top-down management of the American type is seen frequently. Considering the importance of Kansai firms, the top-down management style might be more important than is usually thought.

9 Business nationalism: government versus business

Business nationalism appeared in the early Meiji era, when Japan as a nation–state emerged under the pressure of foreign major powers, although the original idea relates to the concept, *ko to shi* (public and private). Traditionally, 'public' ranked above 'private'. Private profit was not regarded as beneficial; instead, public service had higher prestige. Private firms, however, devised the logic to overcome this handicap. Through business activity, they pointed out, private firms can contribute to the nation. Even if this was a superficial stance, business firms had to adopt it.

Both government and business thought that making Japan rich was the pressing task and both must cooperate for that purpose. As a consequence, industrial and foreign commercial policy was given priority, to increase economic wealth. Though in the pre-war period the target was import substitution of industrial goods by dispelling foreign goods from the domestic market, export became the focal goal of such policies in the post-war period.

From the nationalistic standpoint, cooperation between government and business was underlined in order to strengthen international competitiveness (see GLOBALIZATION). But once Japanese economic success was achieved, business nationalism began to weaken.

10 Conclusion

Japanese business culture puts its stress on human resources, depending on groupism and familism, in a word, *shudan-shugi* (communitarianism). Its features are shown in several distinctive words, such as *chu ko*, *wa*, *omikoshi*, *nemawashi*, *ringi* and *ko to shi*. The culture is particularly fit for the manufacturing process, stimulating incremental innovations like *kaizen* (continuous improvement), quality control and the zero defect movement. It is doubtful, however, whether this kind of communitarian culture is suited to radical innovation, a factor increasingly seems to gain in importance.

Also, how much this type of culture contributed to Japan's economic development is an open question, though part of its contribution is clear. Furthermore, it is true that the Confucian areas like Korea, Singapore and others have developed spectacularly in recent decades, but then non-Confucian countries like India are also starting to grow. Cultural influence over economic development may be limited, and culture itself is changing fast.

ETSUO ABE

MEIJI UNIVERSITY

Further reading

Benedict, R. (1974) *The Chrysanthemum and the Sword: Patterns of Japanese Culture*, New York: New American Library. (The classical analysis of haji (shame) in Japanese society.)

Clark, R. (1979) *The Japanese Company*, New Haven, CT: Yale University Press. (Anthropological study on Japanese companies, based on empirical research.)

Hall, E.T. and Hall, M. (1987) *Hidden Differences: Doing Business with the Japanese*, Garden City, NY: Anchor Press. (Explains about Japanese mentality and how to do business in Japan.)

Hamaguchi, E. (1985) 'A contextual model of the Japanese: toward a methodical innovation in Japan studies', *Journal of Japanese Studies* 11 (2): 289–321. (Stresses the importance of contextualism in understanding Japanese culture.)

Hampden-Turner, C. and Trompenaars, F. (1993) *The Seven Cultures of Capitalism* London: Piatkus. (Interesting interpretation of the business cultures of Japan, the UK, Germany, the USA and others.)

Hayashi, S. (1988) *Culture and Management in Japan*, Tokyo: University of Tokyo Press. (A unique analysis of business culture by a Japanese scholar, including some debatable points.)

Hazama, H. (1974) *Nihonteki keiei* (Japanese management), Tokyo: Nihon Keizai Shinbunsha.

(Analysis of positive and negative sides of communitarianism in Japan.)

Hofstede, G. (1991) *Cultures and Organizations: Software of the Mind*, New York: McGraw-Hill. (Comprehensive study on the business culture of over fifty countries, using the statistical method.)

Kumon, S. (1992) 'Japan as a network society', in S. Kumon and H. Rosovsky (eds), *The Political Economy of Japan*, vol. 3, *Cultural and Social Dynamics*, Stanford, CA: Stanford University Press. (Emphasizes the 'contextualist' culture in contrast to individualist culture.)

Murakami, Y., Kumon, S. and Sato, S. (1979) *Bunmei to shiteno ie shakai* (The ie Society as a Civilization), Tokyo: Chuo Koron Sha. (A very comprehensive study on ie organization and culture.)

Nakane, C. (1970) *Japanese Society*, Berkeley, CA: University of California Press. (Explanation of vertical relationship in Japanese society.)

See also: BUSINESS CULTURE, NORTH AMERICAN; BUSINESS CULTURES, EUROPEAN; BUSINESS STRATEGIES, EAST ASIAN; ECONOMY OF JAPAN; GLOBALIZATION; *KEIRETSU*; MANAGEMENT IN JAPAN; TOYODA FAMILY

Related topics in the IEBM: BUSINESS HISTORY, JAPANESE; BUSINESS STRATEGY, JAPANESE; DEMING, W.E.; DECISION-MAKING; FUKUZAWA, Y.; GROUPS AND TEAMS; INDUSTRIAL DEMOCRACY; INDUSTRIAL RELATIONS IN JAPAN; ISHIKAWA, K.; JAPANIZATION; JURAN, J.M.; MANAGEMENT EDUCATION IN ASIA; MANAGEMENT EDUCATION IN JAPAN; MANAGEMENT IN PACIFIC ASIA; OHMAE, K.; ORGANIZATION BEHAVIOUR; SHIBUSAWA, EIICHI; SUN TZU; TOTAL QUALITY MANAGEMENT

Business culture, North American

Overview

During the last several decades there have been major changes in the environment in which business organizations function. New social and political roles have been defined for business in North America as an increasing amount of attention has been devoted to social and political issues such as equal employment opportunity, product safety and quality, pollution control, and workplace health and safety. These concerns have resulted in a proliferation of new laws and regulations and public policies that restrict or redirect business activities that are seen to affect society in an adverse manner. The long-term effect of these laws and policies are a dramatic change in the 'rules of the game' by which business organizations are expected to operate. Thus the business institution has been reshaped to meet these new responsibilities and is continually changing to respond to new social issues.

North American business organizations in the 1990s are impacted by faster communication and knowledge acquisition, growing worldwide population, increasing interdependence and competition on limited resources, diversifying political and religious ideologies, constant transitions of power, global ecological distress, and the changing roles of gender, race, age and culture.

1 The changing environment of business

For the past couple of decades, management in North America has been impacted by changing social values, traditions and behaviour. Thus the business community has taken a pro-active and anticipatory role in responding to societal considerations. The American business community has devoted more resources, funds, human resources, and considerable time to business environment problems: equal employment opportunities, diversity in management, product quality and safety, ethical issues with respect to business practices, pollution control, workplace health and safety and domestic and international public policy issues.

Social and political concerns are now being addressed throughout the business organization. Most business decisions now require explicit consideration of influences emanating from outside the organization, and the key external factors of concern to the organization are increasingly social and political as well as economic. These factors greatly complicate the management task. There are many more external constituencies and stakeholders that have an impact on corporate activities and exercise considerable influence on its behaviour.

Basic to this change in the values and ideologies that society has held for some time, the corporation has come to be viewed as a socio-political institution as well as an economic institution and has been made to respond to a wide range of issues of concern to various societal groups. Ideologies that are supportive of free enterprise have been adapted to allow for more government intervention to pursue these values. These changes in values and ideologies have enormous implications for the role that business is expected to play in society (Buchholz 1994).

2 Developments

As a result of the vast social and public policy changes in the USA in the 1960s and 1970s the business institutions underwent major changes whereby social and ethical responsibilities were added to their traditional economic responsibilities. These new expectations of society with regard to business institutions were defined by Frederick (1960):

> Social responsibility demands that business does more than perform its traditional economic functions. Production and distribution should enhance the total socioeconomic welfare of the country and resources should be utilized for broad social ends and not simply for the narrowly circumscribed interests of private persons and firms.
>
> (Frederick 1960: 60)

Managers have been significantly affected by the changing roles of business in society. They have had to incorporate the social, political and public policy considerations into their decision making in the local, domestic and international arenas. According to Steiner (1983):

> Top managers of corporations spend a preponderant part of their time dealing with environmental problems. These include addressing social concerns of society, complying with new social legislations, communicating with legislators and government executives concerning new proposed laws and regulations, meeting with various self-interest groups concerning their demands and/or grievances, and administering their organizations in such a way as to respond to new attitudes of people working in the organization. This is in sharp contrast to the top executives of the major corporations twenty years ago whose attention and decision making was focused almost wholly on economic and technical considerations. The increased attention of top management time to social and political questions results, of course, in different allocations of time of lower-level managers than in the past. They too are spending more of their time on social and political issues and are being measured more and more on their performance in these areas.
>
> (Steiner 1983: 21)

The modern manager of the 1990s must, therefore, not only possess administrative and human resource skills, but also develop sensitivity skills, acculturation and a global awareness of public policies and societal concerns. This perspective is reflected in *The Public Affairs Handbook* (Nagelschmidt 1982). The corporation is no longer seen as a single-purpose economic institution devoted solely to developing and marketing products and services. By virtue of its size, resources and impact on society, the corporation has also become deeply involved in the accomplishment of a number of societal tasks, from clean water to culture, and is clearly expected to be more broadly committed to such nonbusiness concerns in the future. Today's business enterprise is critically affected by such matters as consumer and environmental protection, occupational health and safety, full financial disclosure, the political process at all levels, and the quality of life in the communities in which they are located and do business (Nagelschmidt 1982).

3 Corporate governance and social responsibility

Corporate trends in the 1990s in the areas of social responsibility and corporate governance in the USA include changing models of corporate governance from the traditional model that is dominant in the USA which is based on property rights. According to this model, shareholders control the corporation and are the major factors in the governance process. They supply the capital the corporation needs and therefore own the property of the corporation and have certain legal rights to see that this property is used to further their interests. The ownership of property legitimizes the shareholders' theoretical control over the use of corporate resources (Buchholz 1994).

The stakeholder model can be defined as any group or individual who has an impact on the corporation or who is in turn affected by its actions. Stakeholders include employees, customers, suppliers, stockholders, banks, environmentalist, government and other groups who can help or hurt the corporation. The participation of these various stakeholder groups in the governance process will assure that a wide range of interests are taken into account in the corporate decision making. The legitimacy of this model stems from the interest the various stakeholders have in corporate activities and decisions (Buchholz 1994).

Control of the modern corporation in the USA in the 1990s is constantly changing. The models of Corporate America now include: stockholders and management; family control; changing control due to takeovers and buyouts; institutional shared ownership (financial institutions' own substantial blocks of stock in many corporations, and employee-owned companies), ESOPs (employee stock-ownership plans) – employees form a stock ownership trust which borrows money from banks or insurance companies. This money is used to purchase newly issued stock of the company, and foreign control (where several key American corporations are being controlled by foreign ownership). Foreign direct investment in the USA has increased 400 per cent in a decade.

Reform of corporate governance includes: increased disclosure whereby corporations are more responsive to stockholders' interests, activist shareholders (a movement which began in the 1960s as shareholders interested in pursuing social goals found a way to be heard at annual meetings), and 'relationship investing' which began in 1993 as a system of long-term relationships between corporations and their management. Within this system, investors become expert in the workings of their portfolio companies and give management opinions and feedback about corporate policy (Buchholz 1994).

4 The future and conclusions

The changing business institution has demanded new road maps to managing change in business organizations. The changes surrounding the business communities are not merely trends but the workings of large, unruly forces: the globalization of markets, the spread of information technology and computer networks, the dismantling of hierarchy, the structure that has essentially organized work since the mid-nineteenth century. Growing up around these is a new

information age economy, whose fundamental sources of wealth are knowledge and communication rather than natural resources and physical labour.

In a historic convergence, not one but four business revolutions are upon us:

1 globalization. Once it meant forays abroad from a strongly defended home market; now, as the boundaries to commerce open up, new rivals are coming after your home market just as hard as you are going after theirs (see GLOBALIZATION).
2 the increasing use of computers, which are transforming work and learning.
3 changes in management, as the fall of hierarchy frees the men and women from their office, their boss and their boss's boss.
4 the information economy. Commerce now travels on the electronic highway, and wealth is the product of knowledge assets more than of natural resources.

Managing in the changing business environment requires an interdisciplinary knowledge of changing values, norms, public policies, environmental management concerns, equal employment opportunities, diversity management, ethical constraints and concerns, health and safety issues, union concerns, disaster planning and crisis communication, and development of corporate strategies and initiatives for the future. Hamel and Prahalad (1994) pose the important question as to what should drive a company's agenda; its competitors' view of the future, or its own.

Managing change in business organizations in the 1990s demands an understanding of the following industry trends. The major trends include: globalization, technological innovation and changing social and political standards, regulations and norms. Corporate organizations adapt to organizational changes through teamwork and networking. Training is required to help organizations and people adapt to change. The skills needed for managing change are: project management, people management and decision making. Interpersonal skills needed for managing change in dynamic business organizations are: group dynamics, team building, leadership, listening, coaching, diversity management and ethics.

Sherman (1993) provides seven steps to being the best company in the 1990s: (1) determine the world standard; (2) use process mapping; (3) communicate with employees as if your life depended on it; (4) distinguish what needs to be done from how hard it is to do it; (5) set stretch targets; (6) never stop; and (7) pay attention to your inner self.

JANE H. IVES
UNIVERSITY OF MASSACHUSETTS
BOSTON

Further reading

(References cited in the text marked *)

* Buchholz, R.A. (1994) *Business Environment and Public Policy*, Englewood Cliffs, NJ: Prentice Hall. (A text on the social and public policy issues impacting the business community.)
* Frederick, W.C. (1960) 'The growing concern over business responsibility', *California Management Review* 2 (4). (This article focuses on business and corporate responsibility.)
* Hamel, G. and Prahalad, C.K. (1994) *Competing for the Future*, Cambridge, MA: Harvard Business School Press. (Focus on corporate advantage building, and creating competitive business organizations for the future.)
Lodge, G.C. (1974) 'Business and the changing society', *Harvard Business Review* 52 (March–April): 59–72. (Article on changing business attitudes and changing societal norms.)
Nader, R. and Green, M.J. (1973) *Corporate Power in America*, New York: Grossman Publishers. (Consumer activist focus on corporate America.)
* Nagelschmidt, J. (1982) *The Public Affairs Handbook*, New York: Amacom. (Handbook on corporate public relations.)
* Sherman, S. (1993) 'How will we live with tumult?', *Fortune Magazine*: 123. (A contemporary analysis of new business trends.)
Sethi, P. (1990) *Up Against the Corporate Wall: Modern Corporations and Social Issues of the Nineties*, Englewood Cliffs, NJ: Prentice Hall. (Focus on the business and social issues of the 1990s.)
* Steiner, G. (1983) *The New CEO*, New York: The Free Press. (Study of the role of the chief executive officer in changing times by a leading social scientist and thinker.)
Sturdivart, F. and Vernon-Wortzel, H. (1990) *Business and Society: A Managerial Approach*, Homewood, IL: Irwin. (Text on business and society issues.)
Unseem, M. (1993) *Executive Defense: Shareholders, Power and Corporate Reorganization*, Cambridge, MA: Harvard University Press. (Book on business organizations and their stakeholders.)
Vogel, D. (1978) *Lobbying the Corporation: Citizen Challenges to Business Authority*, New York: Basic Books. (Lobbying organizations, constituency groups and their relationship to business organizations.)

See also: GLOBALIZATION

Related topics in the IEBM: BUSINESS AND SOCIETY; BUSINESS ETHICS; CORPORATE GOVERNANCE; ENVIRONMENTAL MANAGEMENT; MANAGEMENT EDUCATION IN NORTH AMERICA; MANAGEMENT IN NORTH AMERICA; TRADE UNIONS

Business cultures, European

Overview

Most of the countries in Europe, or at least in western Europe, are mature trading and manufacturing nations. As a result, each nation possesses its own unique business culture which has emerged over decades or even centuries. It is thus not feasible, within the scope of this entry, to depict all these business cultures in adequate detail. Attention therefore focuses on key aspects of the business cultures in three major economies of the European Union – the UK, Germany and France.

The three business cultures are compared and contrasted in terms of the relationships between business and government, business and the economy, business and finance, and business and the trade unions. Fascinating insights arise from a study of these relationships which give lie to the contention that there exists in Europe one common business culture.

1 Introduction

Many attempts have been made to define the term 'culture' but general agreement has not been forthcoming among anthropologists, sociologists, economists and linguists. Two schools of thought have emerged, however (see CULTURE, CROSS-NATIONAL). One perceives culture as a set of values, beliefs, attitudes and norms, as mental products; the other envisages culture as a whole way of life shared by a people, embracing their interpersonal relationships and behaviours as well as their rationalizations (Thompson et al. 1990). For present purposes, the latter, more comprehensive interpretation of culture is preferable.

When the concept of culture is applied to business the results of the 1970s IBM study still dominate thinking, especially in Europe. The work was carried out among some 100,000 IBM employees in over 50 different countries and defines business culture as 'learned assumptions and beliefs, attitudes and values shared by members of a group' (Hofstede 1980: 16).

Hofstede's study contrasts with that of certain US commentators, and in particular with context theory (Hall 1976). In a low-context business culture, information is contained in words of precise and unambiguous meaning, whereas in a high-context culture meaning is conveyed through less direct verbal and non-verbal codes. Thus culture is communication and communication is culture.

An attempt was made by the present contributor to arrive at a more pragmatic definition of business culture and its determinants (Randlesome et al. 1993). The concept of business culture is perceived as embracing the attitudes, values and norms which underpin commercial activities and help to shape the behaviour of companies in a given country. It is further postulated that the business culture of any country grows out of its business environment, past and present. The business environment itself is described as taking in the relationship between business and government, business and the economy, business and finance, business and trade unions, etc.

The three major business cultures in Europe are discussed below. They are listed in a particular sequence, in line with the claim, in the 1990s, by the president of one of France's leading insurance companies, that with the virtual demise of Marxism as an economic system what the world is left with are various forms of capitalism (Albert 1991). One of the ways in which the different types of capitalism can be differentiated is by way of their degree of 'hardness' or 'softness'. Adopting this approach, the UK will be discussed first as representing the 'hardest' of the major business cultures in Europe, followed by Germany and finally France.

2 The business culture in the United Kingdom

Although Britain was the first nation in the world to reach the Industrial Revolution, the business culture in the UK is dominated by considerations of trading rather than manufacturing or agriculture. Napoleon Bonaparte's jibe about 'a nation of shopkeepers' contains more than a grain of truth over two centuries later. However, the business culture in the UK evidences a large capacity for rapid change which is possibly unsurpassed by any other country in Europe.

The foundation of the British Empire in the sixteenth century, the rise of the East India Company and the establishment of a stock exchange in London in the subsequent century all fuelled the trading instincts of the British people. Shareholder interests began to prevail, with all their concomitant effects, such as the overwhelming importance of the bottom line and short-termism.

Given such an economic history, it is not surprising that the economic philosophy which most British governments since the eighteenth century have espoused, with a few notable exceptions, is that of a free market economy. This philosophy, which found its theoretical underpinning in the works of Adam Smith, contrasts starkly with the convictions of most of the UK's partners in the European Union (EU). Moving away from agriculture as the principal source of economic activity much later in history than the UK, they all adopted more protectionist economic tenets, or 'softer' forms of capitalism. This fundamental clash of philosophies goes some way to explain periodic British criticisms within the EU of an 'uneven playing field'.

Towards the end of the twentieth century the British concept of the free market economy found its expression in what came to be known as 'Thatcherism', so called after Margaret Thatcher, Conservative Prime Minister from May 1979 to November 1990. Thatcherism was based on an economic philosophy of free enterprise, unfettered competition and minimal state intervention.

One of the most radical policies implemented by the Conservatives under Margaret Thatcher was privatization; namely, the sale of state-owned companies to the private sector. Just as the sales of local council-owned houses to occupiers were used to foster a nation of property owners, privatization was favoured as the method to create a share-owning democracy. Among the public-sector companies sold in the 1980s were British Telecom, British Gas, British Petroleum and British Steel. By the turn of the decade over 42 per cent of nationalized industries, or roughly 6 per cent of the gross domestic product (GDP), had been transferred to the private sector.

In the 1990s the twelve electricity distribution companies in England and Wales and the two generating companies were privatized, followed by the Scottish power companies. The regional water boards in England and Wales were also sold on the open market. Although the privatizations of British Telecom, British Gas, and the water and electricity supplies were heavily criticized because private monopolies had replaced public monopolies, this wave of privatizations was without parallel at the time in any other business culture in Europe.

Although the sales of former nationalized companies brought brisk business to the traders in the City of London, in the early 1980s manufacturing industry began to feel disadvantaged. Whereas the index of industrial production registered a record 107.1 in 1979, it had plunged to 96.6 by 1981 as two million jobs were lost. The Conservatives' non-interventionist policies combined with a worldwide recession to thrust manufacturing industry into deep gloom by 1983, when the UK registered a deficit in manufactured goods for the first time since the Industrial Revolution. In the recession of the early 1980s some of the most illustrious companies in British industry went into liquidation or were taken over – a development which would not have been permitted by any government in any other country in western Europe.

This massive shake-up in manufacturing industry was followed in the mid- and late 1980s by a rise in productivity, and with it competitiveness. Productivity increased by an average 5–6 per cent per annum from 1980–8, faster than in any other developed industrial economy, including Japan. It is generally recognized that manufacturing industry went into the 1990s much leaner and fitter, if not actually large enough to satisfy domestic demand.

However, widespread neglect of the special needs of manufacturing – a benign government attitude, greater investment in research and development (R&D), a longer-term perspective – remains a disturbing feature of the business culture which looks set to continue well beyond the 1990s. Although the cultural hostility to manufacturing is slightly weaker than it was in the 1980s, it is still sufficiently pronounced to register as a continuing cause for concern.

As has already been indicated, the City of London exercises a major influence on business culture in the UK. It appears to enjoy most-favoured status with right-of-centre politicians, attracts the so-called 'brightest and best' that the country produces and rewards these people well. More international deposit and lending business is carried out in London than in New York or Tokyo, and more than in the rest of the EU put together, while the stock exchange in the UK is three times larger than in Germany and four times larger than in France.

The pre-eminence of the stock exchange within the business culture in the UK was cemented by a major development in the 1980s – the 'Big Bang' of 27 October 1986. This particular piece of reform was appropriate, first because it was in line with the existing government philosophy of deregulation throughout the economy, or letting market forces hold full sway. Second, it was convenient because the City needed to adapt to new trading systems elsewhere if it was to remain a global player and exploit to the full its position between the time zones of Tokyo and New York.

One effect of Big Bang was to induce a rush of mergers and acquisitions as banks and other financial initiations bought into traditional jobbing or brokering firms. Another was to create such a demand for staff in the City that recruits were sometimes welcomed not only with inflated salaries but also with 'golden hellos'. Within a year sanity was restored by an even larger explosion – the Crash of 19 October 1987, after which stock market values initially recovered only slowly.

Although the City of London, the British emblem of shareholder-driven capitalism, continues to exert a fatal fascination within the business culture, its status as Europe's premier financial centre is threatened by Frankfurt-am-Main (see below). It may be argued, however, that a diminution of the City's influence on business in the UK is not necessarily detrimental.

A further determinant of business culture in any country in Europe lies in the relationship between business and the trade unions. It is in this area that the business culture in the UK has changed most radically over the final two decades of the twentieth century.

In the late 1970s newspapers and magazines the world over were far from complimentary about the trade unions in the UK. An Australian newspaper coined the phrase 'British disease' to depict industrial strife. *L'Espresso* even referred to the British unions as 'a sovereign power'. Many employers felt restricted by fear of action by militant trade-union leaders and intransigent shop stewards. However, by 1989 management had regained the freedom to manage, and the will and incentive to do so; by 1991 the number of days lost through industrial disputes was at its lowest for over a century.

This turnaround in industrial relations was brought about by a series of Conservative government reforms. The clue to the success of these reforms lies in the fact that a step-by-step approach was adopted to what were perceived to be imbalances in the relationship between business and the trade unions. A large part of what could have been interpreted as 'union-bashing legislation', such as was attempted in the early 1970s, might have failed because the unions could have mustered all their opposition to a single piece of legislation. However, the unions found it impossible to mobilize, demobilize and remobilize against a series of measures.

The Employment Acts of 1980, 1982, 1984, 1988 and 1990, respectively, made secondary picketing illegal; reformed the legal liabilities of trade unions and trade-union officials; introduced secret ballots for union officials; gave members the specific right to prevent their union from calling for industrial action without first holding a secret ballot; and eliminated all legal protection for the 'closed shop'.

Towards the end of the millennium the trade unions had embraced the 'new realism' of industrial relations and were concentrating their lobbying efforts in Brussels and on the European Community Charter of Fundamental Social Rights. Their efforts were, however, frustrated when, of the twelve member states constituting the EU at the time, the British government was the only one to opt out of the Social Chapter of the Maastricht Treaty on Political Union. This omission was rectified in 1997 when 'new' Labour returned to power after eighteen years in opposition. In 1998 the new government published a White Paper on *Fairness at Work* laying out its proposals for cooperation between business and the unions. Its stance on union recognition, an election pledge, was widely viewed as a sign that Labour was unlikely to diverge greatly from the Conservatives' support for business.

Alone in Europe the business culture in the UK at the end of the millennium continues to be dominated by the philosophy of the free market economy and all that flows from this – fierce competition, short-termism and, above all, a capacity to change quickly and radically – as indeed it has over the final two decades of the twentieth century.

3 The business culture in Germany

Germany was not only a latecomer as a nation-state, but the individual German states themselves were also latecomers to the Industrial Revolution. After unification under Bismarck's Prussia in 1871 the German Chancellor began in earnest his efforts to compete with the premier economic power in the world at the time – the UK. To do so he imposed protectionist economic measures throughout Germany similar to those which had characterized Prussia since the time of Frederick the Great. Vestiges of this protectionism remain today, as do other traditional elements of the German business culture, such as the predominance of technology, long-termism and a resistance to change.

The business culture in Germany in the 1990s still reflects the division of the country, from 1945 to 1990, into a social market economy in the west and a command economy in the east. However, since the western philosophy is prevalent, the western economy dominant and the western culture ever more pervasive, the focus will rest on the former.

The official economic policy which all post-war federal governments in West Germany claim to have espoused, to a greater or lesser extent, is that of the social market economy – not a free market economy as in the UK. All federal chancellors, from Adenauer to Helmut Kohl, have struggled to strike a balance between the dictates of the market and the needs of society, although Kohl tried, at the outset of his chancellorship in 1982, to define the task by advocating 'as much market as possible, as much state [intervention] as necessary'. Kohl's attempts to introduce more market in his first government were faltering at best.

A start was made on a federal privatization plan in 1984 with the sale of part of the government's holding in VEBA, a conglomerate. In 1985 a plan for further sales of federal-held assets in thirteen companies was tabled, but a year later it was decided to proceed with the sale of only five companies. In 1986 VIAG, another federal-dominated conglomerate, offered 40 per cent of its shares to the public and was partly privatized. However, the real prizes remained unprivatized because of opposition from the individual German states; the federal government retained 75 per cent of Lufthansa, the national carrier, and 20 per cent of Volkswagen.

Under Kohl's second government federal privatizations were more successful, but not on the same scale as in the UK. The Federal Government sold its remaining shares in

VEBA in 1987; 24.9 per cent of its holding in DVKB, a bank, in 1988; and, in the same year, the rest of its interest in VIAG. Later, the Federal Government stake in Volkswagen was finally disposed of and its share of Lufthansa cut to 55 per cent. By the end of Chancellor Kohl's second government the Federal State had, primarily through smaller privatizations, reduced the number of companies in which it had direct holdings from the 808 it inherited in 1982 to 132. Large parts of West German industry still remained under Federal Government influence and control, however.

It is ironic to note that privatizations progressed only haltingly in West Germany for almost a decade, yet when confronted with the overwhelming problems of the failed East German economy in 1990 mass privatization was Kohl's only answer. Between 1990 and 1995 some 15,000 companies of all sizes were transferred to the private sector but approximately 500, mostly large, companies remained unsold – a continuing burden on both the Federal State and to the individual states in eastern Germany.

One aspect of business culture shared with equal enthusiasm by Germans in both the west and east is that of *Technik* (the art and science of making useful artefacts). Manufacturing thus looms large in the culture, to such an extent that it accounts for some 38 per cent of GDP, as compared to 23 per cent in the UK and 29 per cent in France. Moreover, manufacturing is so deeply entrenched in the business culture that services represent a Cinderella sector; anyone not involved, either directly or indirectly, in making goods is widely deemed not to be doing a proper job. Manufacturing is also supported by large Federal Government spending on R&D and by the long-termist attitudes of the German private commercial banks (see below).

High value-added products, high technology and technical innovation are forthcoming in Germany, and not only from the large manufacturing companies, many of which are household names throughout the world. The likes of Daimler-Benz (now Daimler Chrysler), Siemens, Hoechst and Thyssen are, at the least, European leaders in their individual sectors of manufacturing industry, but they are also supported by a myriad of *Mittelstand* (medium-sized and small) companies, which frequently act as preferred suppliers and form the backbone of German industry.

In contrast to their larger brethren, many of these *Mittelstand* companies are virtually unknown and have in fact been identified as 'hidden champions'. They are hidden because many of their products are subsumed in larger end-products or in the manufacturing process itself. Examples are companies making sunroofs for cars, calico for bookbinding, or labelling machines for bottles or cans. They are champions because they command world market shares of between 70 and 80 per cent and are represented in all industrialized countries. They thrive on their technical excellence and quality customer service in their market segments.

Manufacturing companies – large, medium-sized and small – have been supported both indirectly and directly by the German banking fraternity. First, the Deutsche Bundesbank (German Federal Bank) has been the most successful central bank in the world in controlling inflation over the last four decades of the millennium. Low inflation has thus provided a background of stability against which manufacturing companies have been able to produce, invest, plan and train for the long term.

Second, the private commercial banks, Deutsche Bank, Dresdner Bank and Commerzbank (the Big Three), have made their own unique contributions to long-termism, which is such a feature of the business culture in Germany. They have maintained the closest of ties with manufacturing companies by actually purchasing large packages of equity holdings. These major shareholdings entitle the Big Three to seats on the supervisory boards of the big manufacturing companies. They are thus privy to all that is happening inside these companies, act as their 'house bank' and look after their general well-being. There has not been a single hostile takeover in Germany since the end of the Second World War and strategic German companies have not been allowed to collapse or be sold to foreign interests.

The success of the German financial sector, from the Bundesbank downwards, has put Frankfurt in a position to challenge London as Europe's premier financial centre. Indeed, this success has been honoured by the EU, with Frankfurt having been chosen as the location for the European Monetary Institute (EMI), the forerunner of the European Central Bank (ECB). Yet the German equity market is relatively small, the country's financial institutions are far from innovative and the financial trading culture is not so well established as in the UK.

One facet of the German business culture that is well established is a post-war history of consensus and non-confrontation between employers and trade unions. There have been no references in Germany to 'the two sides of industry', let alone 'them and us'. Indeed, *Sozialpartner* is the collective term used to denote both employers and trade unions.

The degree of relative harmony which has been witnessed in German industrial relations is due in part to the fact that, after the Second World War, trade unions and employers' organizations, both of which had been banned under the Nazis, were able to reshape themselves. The trade unions set up one union per industry and the employers organized themselves accordingly.

Yet smooth industrial relations cannot be ascribed purely to forms of organization, no matter how good. A further contributory factor in the case of Germany has been the search for industrial democracy. Works councils have been recognized as one of the negotiating counterparts of employers since 1920. The country has known parity co-determination – an equal number of representatives on the supervisory boards of companies – in the coal, iron and steel industries since 1951. Similarly, parity co-determination has been established in major and larger medium-sized companies since 1976. Even the most sceptical of employers would admit that this drive towards industrial democracy has made a positive contribution to the prosperity of companies and employees alike.

Towards the end of the millennium it would appear that the business culture in Germany is replete with the values that make for success – a social market economy with no precipitate dashes for privatization except in dire emergencies; a large wealth-creating manufacturing base; and a caring, sharing, long-term-thinking banking system. These are, however, ideal values for a slowly changing world. Yet in a period of discontinuous change, of shorter product life cycles and rapid commoditization of products – conditions frequently forecast for the next millennium – a question mark must hang over the culture's ability to adapt adequately to rapidly changing circumstances.

4 The business culture in France

It was during the reign of Louis XIV, the seventeenth-century French king, that the overriding control of the State on business culture was first established. In fact, Louis XIV's controller-general of finances, Jean-Baptiste Colbert, gave his name to *colbertisme*, a term implying that the State knows best and thus directs or controls business. Hence the influence of the State in modern France has stretched beyond economics and into the very heart of the business culture. Yet this culture is changing, away from the all-pervasive hand of the State.

The relationship between the State and business became formalized in post-war France with the introduction of the planned economy. Planning was deemed to be the most logical solution to the country's problems of industrial backwardness and reconstruction. Indeed, so deep was the conviction of the French that the country's salvation lay in the planned economy – not the free market economy as in the UK or the social market economy as in Germany – that the 10th Plan (1988–92) was arrived at before the system was (half-)abandoned.

One of the last overt manifestations of the planned economy was witnessed between 1981 and 1986, when the Socialist Government nationalized vast swathes of industry. Among the manufacturing companies nationalized were CGE, Thomson (both electronics and telecommunications companies), Usinor, Sacilor (steel companies), and Saint-Gobain (glass and building materials). The French

State also procured majority financial stakes in Bull (information technology), Matra (weapons, electronics) and Dassault (military aircraft). At its zenith in this period the nationalized sector was responsible for some 16 per cent of GDP, 25 per cent of employment, 23 per cent of total value added and 31 per cent of exports. Also, 90 per cent of bank deposits and insurance policies were in the hands of nationalized financial institutions.

A change of government in 1986 brought about a volte-face in the relationship between State and business. The right-wing policies pursued by Jacques Chirac owed much to the liberal economics being pursued in the UK by Margaret Thatcher. In 1986 the original privatization programme contained a list of some sixty-five companies due for public sale. Among the companies privatized were Saint-Gobain, CGE and Matra, together with Sogenal, Société Générale and Paribas (all three of them banks). When the privatizations came to a halt in 1988, due to impending presidential elections and the aftershocks of the Crash, one-third of the programme had been completed.

François Mitterrand, in his 1988 presidential campaign, advocated a '*ni-ni*' policy (neither nationalization nor privatization). Although several partial privatizations followed where the State retained 51 per cent of the shares, it was widely felt that by 1988 the limits of French liberal economic thinking had been reached.

Lacking both the deep-seated trading culture of the British and the engineering culture of the Germans, France's traditional area of economic activity has been agriculture. Indeed, France is still the major food producer in the EU and acquires large earnings from exporting food products such as cereals, alcohol and dairy products. Exports of wine, even to California, are substantial. These successes are due in the main, however, to upstream activities. For example, it is surprising that France's food-processing industry is not more fully developed: of the top 100 food-processing companies in the world, only seven are French. The result is that France often exports the agricultural commodities but then has to re-import the finished produce.

Although France's traditional weakness in capital goods has disappeared over the final decades of the twentieth century, in part as a result of the policy of promoting 'national champions' up to 1986, the country has never succeeded in achieving world dominance in any one sector of industry. Rhône-Poulenc, France's largest chemicals company, achieves only half the turnover of Hoechst, BASF or Bayer.

Even in the high-technology sector of aerospace, one of the stars of the French economy (number one in Europe, number three in the world), France faces formidable international competition. Ariane, the rocket launcher, competes with its NASA counterparts; Dassault, the military aircraft maker, faces Lockheed in the USA and British Aerospace; and Aérospatiale, one of the lead partners in the Airbus consortium, is under pressure from the likes of Boeing.

While French flair in the luxury goods niche is legendary, with such names as Vuitton, Hermès and Yves St-Laurent, the consumer goods sector as a whole represents one of the country's weaknesses. French companies in consumer electronics, household goods and textiles have failed to make a significant impact internationally. Instead, import penetration has risen since the 1970s, despite protectionist efforts, such as the Multi-Fibre Arrangement, to erect barriers against developing countries.

It was not until the mid-1980s that the business culture in France began to be enriched by a more committed banking system. This period coincided with success for the Banque de France (the central bank) and with the privatization of three of the major commercial banks referred to above. It also saw major changes in the way in which French companies are capitalized.

France's membership of the European Monetary System (EMS) started to bear fruit in 1986 when the Banque de France succeeded in bringing inflation down to 2.1 per cent, one of the country's lowest rates since the Second World War. It did so by pursuing the so-called *franc-fort* (strong franc or Frankfurt) policy, shadowing German interest rates, which are, of course, fixed in Frankfurt.

Although this policy resulted in higher interest rates in France than in Germany, with a concomitant rise in unemployment, it did at least furnish a stable base for the economy.

The privatizations of Sogenal, Société Générale and Paribas were similarly deemed to be successful, not only for the revenue which they raised for the French Treasury but also because these banks at least were able to come closer to their corporate customers. Although French banks traditionally lent directly to companies, they have suffered from a reputation for being remote, even aloof. This relationship changed radically in the case of the privatized banks.

It was in part through the efforts of these three banks in the process of disintermediation (less direct bank financing and more financing through capital markets) that widespread concern at the low equity base of many French companies was dissipated. With the aid of the banks, French companies switched gradually to increasing equity and reducing debt. As a result the Paris Bourse was 25 per cent larger at the end of the 1980s than it had been at the start of the decade.

While the contribution of the banking sector to the business culture in the final years of the millennium is rated a success, that of the trade unions has been disappointingly small. A unionization rate of 20 per cent was recorded in the early 1980s but this had fallen to below 10 per cent in the 1990s.

The bodies representing workers in France are organized in confederations and have no umbrella organizations such as the Trades Union Congress (TUC) in the UK or the Deutscher Gewerkschaftsbund (DGB) in Germany. Each confederation thus comprises separate trade unions which represent different industrial sectors. The Confédération Générale du Travail (CGT) is particularly strong in the metal, building and chemical industries. Its leaders are members of the Communist Party. The Confédération Française Démocratique du Travail (CFDT) is still committed to workers' control. It maintains strong Socialist allegiances. The Force Ouvrière (FO) is the most moderate of the three, yet is, like the others, completely opposed to the capitalist ethos.

The reasons for the diminution of the unions' influence are a lack of cohesion in their efforts to represent their members and too close an identification with radical, left-wing political parties. They are also out of touch with an increasingly affluent working population which is more willing to accept a 'harder' degree of capitalism.

5 Conclusion

The business cultures in the UK, Germany and France, different as they are, represent only a sample of the rich variety of national cultures extant in Europe. Despite the European Single Market, the same attitudes, values, norms and behaviours are not shared by all the business people operating within Europe. Both the serious student of business cultures in Europe and the manager striving to do business across Europe must therefore attempt to achieve cultural fluency in all the countries with which he or she comes into contact. Whether business cultures in Europe will converge in the future or whether European business will continue to enjoy diversity in unity is a question that is as yet unresolved. It will probably remain so for the foreseeable future.

COLLIN C. RANDLESOME
CRANFIELD SCHOOL OF MANAGEMENT

Further reading

(References cited in the text marked *)

* Albert, M. (1991) *Capitalisme contre capitalisme*, Paris: Éditions du Seuil. (An analysis of the different gradations of capitalism in the world's economies.)

Gordon, C. (1995) *The Business Culture in France*, Oxford: Butterworth Heinemann. (An analysis of the French business culture according to its determinants from the business environment.)

* Hall, E.T. (1976) *Beyond Culture*, New York: Anchor Press. (A comparison of low-context and high-context cultures in terms of clarity of information exchange.)

* Hofstede, G. (1980) *Culture's Consequences: International Differences in Work-related Values*, Beverly Hills, CA: Sage Publications. (A depiction of four dimensions of culture for any given country: the power distance relationship;

individualism versus collectivism; masculinity and femininity; and uncertainty avoidance.)

Randlesome, C. (1994) *The Business Culture in Germany*, Oxford: Butterworth Heinemann. (An analysis of the German business culture according to its determinants from the business environment.)

* Randlesome, C. (ed.), Brierley, W., Bruton, K., Gordon, C. and King, P. (1993) *Business Cultures in Europe*, 2nd edn, Oxford: Butterworth Heinemann. (An analysis of the German, French, Italian, British, Spanish and Dutch business cultures according to their determinants from the business environment.)

* Thompson, M., Ellis, R. and Wildavsky, A. (1990) *Cultural Theory*, Boulder, CO: Westview Press. (A typology of five ways of life – egalitarianism, fatalism, individualism, hierarchy and autonomy – serving as an analytical tool in the examination of people, culture and politics.)

See also: CULTURE, CROSS-NATIONAL; ECONOMIC INTEGRATION, INTERNATIONAL; MANAGEMENT IN FRANCE; MANAGEMENT IN GERMANY; MANAGEMENT IN THE UNITED KINGDOM

Related topics in the IEBM: CULTURE, MANAGEMENT OF; ECONOMIC SYSTEMS, COMPARATIVE; HOFSTEDE, G.; HUMAN RESOURCE MANAGEMENT; HUMAN RESOURCE MANAGEMENT IN EUROPE; INDUSTRIAL RELATIONS IN EUROPE; ORGANIZATION BEHAVIOUR; PRIVATIZATION AND REGULATION; SMITH, A.; TRADE UNIONS

Business strategies, east Asian

Overview

In recent decades, many countries in east Asia have experienced some of the world's highest economic growth rates. Despite the financial crises that erupted among several Asian economies in late 1997, leading to speculations among some about an Asian economic "meltdown", many believe that the restructuring required to deal with the crises can indeed contribute to further growth in these countries. Investors from the industrialized west continue to express confidence in the economic future of these countries. In order to take advantage of the economic opportunities in this region and to cooperate and compete effectively with east Asians, it is imperative to understand the mind-set which lies behind their business dealings. This mind-set influences both approaches to competition and cooperation, and the formulation and execution of business strategies.

In general, business people from Japan, Korea, China, Hong Kong and Taiwan tend to draw their inspiration in the formulation and execution of business strategies from several ancient works, widely disseminated and read in east Asia but little known in the West. These works include Sun Tzu's *The Art of War* and Miyamoto Musashi's *The Book of Five Rings*, which are known to some extent in the West, and the lesser-known *The Three Kingdoms* and *The Thirty-Six Stratagems*. A synopsis of each of these four works is presented below.

This entry examines the important themes which underlie these works and analyses how they affect east Asia's overall approach to business cooperation and the formulation, reformulation and implementation of general business strategies.

1 Sources of east Asian strategy

The Art of War

The Art of War (or *Bingfa*) was purportedly written by Sun Tzu (also spelt Sun Zi), a Chinese military strategist who lived some 2,500 years ago. Sun Tzu identified six major components to success in military warfare. These are (1) the moral cause; (2) leadership; (3) temporal conditions, including the four seasons and the changes in weather, wind and tidal conditions; (4) the terrain; (5) organization and discipline; and (6) use of espionage.

The Book of Five Rings

Miyamoto Musashi, a samurai in the late sixteenth to early seventeenth century, purportedly wrote a book entitled *The Book of Five Rings*. In his later life, Musashi became a devoted student of Zen philosophy and sought to unravel the relationship between swordsmanship and Zen. Zen is not a religion in the Judaeo-Christian tradition; rather it is a way of life. In the book, Musashi contemplates his path of enlightenment and identifies several major tenets to success: (1) to grasp relationships between matters and to view situations from multiple perspectives; (2) to seek knowledge and information; (3) to be patient; (4) to train and discipline oneself; (5) to disguise one's emotions and true intentions; (6) to possess flexibility; (7) to use diversion as an attack strategy; (8) to divide and conquer; and (9) to assess the terrain.

The Three Kingdoms

The Three Kingdoms (or *Romance of the Three Kingdoms*), was written by fourteenth-century Chinese novelist, Lo Kuan-chung. It is a semi-fictional historical account of the struggle for power among the leaders of three fiefdoms for the control of China after the collapse of the Han dynasty (206 BC–AD 220), China's longest-running and mightiest dynasty. The novel details the intrigues, strategies, ploys and alliances used by the leaders of these three kingdoms and their advisors to gain control over China.

The Thirty-Six Stratagems

The Thirty-Six Stratagems is based on principles contained in *The Book of Changes* (or *I Ching*) and military strategies contained in twenty-four volumes of Chinese historical chronicles and literary classics, including *The Three Kingdoms*. Each stratagem has widespread applicability in military and non-military settings, including business and interpersonal relationships.

2 Principles guiding the east Asian approach to business

Based on a comprehensive analysis of these significant writings, there appear to be twelve common themes or principles which underlie the knowledge advanced in these collective works. They are listed in detail below.

The importance of strategies

According to Sun Tzu, the highest form of victory is to conquer by strategy. To wage a protracted war against one's adversaries, even if it culminates in a final victory, is costly and inefficient, whereas a brilliantly conceived strategy that can accomplish the same objective is both swift and efficient. From the east Asian perspective, there is a hierarchical ordering of preferred methods (from most to least desired) to gain the upper hand in any type of confrontation:

1 the formulation of a brilliant strategy to deal a swift and fatal blow to one's adversary/competitor;
2 resorting to diplomatic means (such as negotiations, mutual discussions and intermediaries) to resolve a confrontation;

3 resorting to non-diplomatic means (such as open warfare or litigation) to resolve a confrontation;
4 besieging a fortified city, that is, to wage war against a well-established opponent.

The significance assigned to strategy formulation has resulted in the east Asian disposition to engage in 'mind games', that is, to ferret out the hidden message in any type of communication (written, verbal or silent), and, subsequently, to formulate a strategy to counteract the perceived message sent by the other party. In the West, there is usually a negative connotation associated with 'game playing'. In China and east Asia, by contrast, game playing is considered to be an asset. Consequently, Westerners who seek to do business with east Asians have to be aware of this tendency and should try to fathom the hidden message or meaning associated with certain actions by their east Asian partners.

Transforming an adversary's strength into weakness

Sun Tzu's *Bingfa* calls for exhausting one's opponent through false alarms so that when it comes time for the real battle, they will be drained. This is the stratagem of 'relax while the enemy exhausts himself'. Several other stratagems also address this theme. One of these stratagems was entitled 'chain together the enemy's warships'. In *The Three Kingdoms*, two opposing armies were preparing for a battle on water. The troops from the fiefdom in the north were far stronger but were prone to motion sickness. At the advice of their strategist, the warships in their fleet were chained together to provide greater stability. The opposing side, however, took advantage of this situation and changes in wind directions (temporal conditions) and set the warships on fire. The chains, while providing greater stability against the tide and wind (therefore, a strength), became a liability because it was difficult to disengage the ships in the fleet once a vessel caught fire.

Of course, transforming an adversary/competitor's strength into a weakness can also be used in reverse, namely, to transform one's own weakness into a strength. For example, from the ruins of the Second World War, Japan was able to rebuild the country by importing technology from the West, and thus leapfrog the process of technological development, to establish a modern industrial base from which it could compete with the USA.

The moral of this principle is that one should not be complacent about one's strength nor abject over one's liabilities since fortunes or misfortunes can be reversed. East Asian philosophy believes that all events occur in cyclical patterns, whereas the West tends to perceive matters in discrete phases. The themes of non-complacency, reversal of fortunes, saving over spending and contradictions pervade the east Asian approach to business and are echoed through the other principles discussed below.

Engaging in deception to gain a strategic advantage

Many of the stratagems entail the use of some deceptive tactics or devices, such as creating an illusion that an attack will be launched from the east when the real offensive is to occur from the west, and pretending to be greater than one really is or have more than one really has, as exemplified by the stratagem 'deck the tree with bogus blossoms'.

In the West, because of the Judaeo-Christian influence, deception is considered as immoral and wrong. In east Asia, however, where there is no indigenous religion akin to Judaism or Christianity, deception has a neutral connotation, and should be engaged in if it brings about a greater good. From the east Asian perspective, the 'greater good' embraces the nation-state, the clan (that is, geographic region from which one's ancestors originate), the extended family, the nucleus family, the corporation for which one works and oneself. The hierarchical ordering of the aforementioned entities, in terms of importance, do vary across east Asian countries, however.

Three stratagems, 'pretend to be a pig in order to eat the tiger', 'play dumb while remaining smart', and 'inflict injury on oneself to win the enemy's trust', have specific implications for Westerners who seek to do business in east Asia. All three stratagems call for the aggressor to play the fool, including self-infliction of physical injury, so that the other party can become complacent. Through arrogance and complacency, when the opponent lets his guard down, the aggressor can launch an attack and thus emerge victorious.

Understanding contradictions

A principal tenet of Taoism, a major school of thought in China with worldwide followers, is the *yin/yang* principle which, on the one hand, emphasizes the contradictions and opposites inherent in all matters, and, on the other, stresses the unity of opposites. *Yin* represents the passive, negative, dark and female elements; *yang* represents the active, positive, bright and male elements. While opposites, *yin* and *yang* must co-exist before there can be life, and in order for life to continue. Following the principles of contradiction and duality, a perceived weakness can become a strength and vice versa.

An understanding of the contradictions and duality inherent in all matters can thus be put to one's advantage. An illustration of this principle is the oak tree versus a blade of grass. An oak tree is strong and mighty while a blade of grass is small and fragile. However, in a storm, the oak tree may collapse under the force of the wind, whereas the blade of grass can yield to the blowing wind and hence stand firm under such adverse conditions.

Compromise

Confucius preached the importance of moderation in all undertakings, and Musashi advocated the adoption of a 'middle-of-the-road' attitude. In other words, east Asian philosophy is guided by the premise that in order to attain the desired outcome, one has to compromise. At least three of the thirty-six stratagems call for the need for compromise and for baiting one's opponent with a small gain in order to obtain a greater prize. Consequently, gift-giving, lavish entertainment and the use of bribes to facilitate a desired outcome are common practice in east Asian societies.

Striving for total victory

While emphasizing compromise, east Asian philosophy also stresses the need to strive for total victory. Two of the thirty-six stratagems address this principle. 'Shut the door to catch the thief' and 'pull the ladder after the ascent' are strategies to cut off all escape routes for one's opponents/competitors so that they cannot regain strength and thus resurface as a threat in the future.

There are two important implications associated with this principle. First, do not be complacent or careless during good times; and second, think about the long-term consequences/implications of one's actions.

Taking advantage of misfortunes of an adversary/competitor

Since east Asians believe that fortunes and misfortunes occur in cyclical patterns, one should make the best use of what one has for the moment. Consequently, if an adversary/competitor is down, try to seize that opportunity to eliminate the former altogether, so that it cannot be a potential threat at a later time.

East Asian philosophy essentially espouses a pragmatic approach to life. The Chinese, in particular, emphasize pragmatism more than their counterparts in Japan and Korea (see ECONOMIES OF EAST ASIA). This Chinese emphasis on pragmatism has led to the formulation of the last, but considered by many to be the most important, of the thirty-six stratagems: 'run away'. When faced with imminent defeat, the Chinese believe it is best to escape from the situation rather than commit suicide or be killed. With escape, there is always a chance of regaining one's strength and former position. The Japanese, however, believe that to face death is the brave thing to do. Some people have attributed this difference in attitude between the Chinese and Japanese to the size (land mass) and natural resource endowment of the respective countries. In the case of China, the extensive land mass and vast natural resources have led its people to believe that there is always the opportunity of escape and regaining strength; hence, escape is preferred. In the case of Japan, however, the limited land mass and absence of natural resources have fostered a mentality among its people that since there is no escape, death is preferred.

Flexibility

According to Sun Tzu, one must 'know when to fight and when not to fight . . . . The laws of military operations are like water . . . . Consequently, just as water ceaselessly changes its flow, there are no constant methods of directing military operations'. In other words, it is important to maintain flexibility and adapt to changing conditions and fortunes.

This emphasis on flexibility accounts, in part, for the east Asian perspective of written legal contracts as organic documents which can be altered as the circumstances change.

Gathering intelligence and information

Both Sun Tzu and Miyamoto Musashi strongly emphasized the importance of gathering information and intelligence about one's opponents/competitors in order to gain the upper hand in a confrontation. Such information can be obtained through a variety of sources, including the use of spies. In the business context, industrial espionage has become common practice. Other means of information gathering include entering into alliances with local partners, and the employment of local nationals. The principle of gathering intelligence also involves the intentional spreading of erroneous information to one's opponents/competitors to contaminate their plans and foil their decision-making efforts.

In the east Asian context, knowledge entails not only the gathering of technical information but also intelligence about the key players. An accurate assessment about human nature can only be made after an extended period of time, however. Consequently, a lot of attention is directed towards developing relationships with business counterparts to discover their true intentions.

Grasping the interdependent relationships among matters/situations

The *yin/yang* principle outlined earlier emphasizes the duality and contradictions inherent in all matters. Since such duality and contradictions may not always be apparent, it is important to try to unravel such relationships so that they can be put to good use. The use of spiral and non-linear logic is common in east Asia.

Patience

Experienced Westerners who have had successful dealings in east Asia will readily concede that patience is a major requisite to success in conducting business in that region of the world. Several factors have accounted for the relatively slow pace at which actions occur in east Asia. First, the east Asians like to focus on the long-term implications of actions. Second, they assign importance to developing and nurturing human relationships. Finally, they believe that everything occurs in cyclical patterns. Hence, one should wait for the opportune time.

Avoiding strong emotions

Confucius cautioned against taking extreme positions on all matters. Sun Tzu warned that a military commander should never fly into a rage. Since strong emotions can confuse or distort logical thinking and action, this principle can be used against one's opponents/competitors to bring about their downfall. Two stratagems specifically address this principle. The first is entitled 'provoke strong emotions', and the second 'use a woman to ensnare a man', which explains why women and other forms of sensual entertainment are used often in Japan and Korea to enhance the chances of attaining desired outcome in business transactions.

Again, there are differences across countries as far as public display of emotions are concerned. In Japan, for example, it is considered to be bad form for a widow to cry incessantly during her husband's funeral, whereas in Korea, the converse would be true if a person did not cry loudly at even a distant cousin's funeral.

3 Conclusion

These twelve underlying themes identified and briefly explained here can be manifested in munificent ways. Each can be used in isolation, in the reverse, and/or combined with one or several others to produce an almost infinite array of stratagems.

While business people from Japan, Korea, China, Hong Kong and Taiwan may derive their inspiration from a common source, there can be important differences in how these are interpreted and applied in specific situations. Reference was made to two of these differences: escape versus death and public display of emotions. These cross-country differences are further compounded by foreign religious influences, education at universities abroad, overseas travel and social and business contacts with foreigners. Consequently, while it is erroneous to assume that east Asians are just like Westerners, it is equally fallacious to stereotype them as a homogeneous group.

ROSALIE L. TUNG
SIMON FRASER UNIVERSITY

Note

This is an abridged version of R.L. Tung (1994) 'Strategic management thought in east Asia', *Organizational Dynamics* (Spring): 5565. Reprinted with permission.

Further reading

Chan, M.W.L. and Chen, B.F. (1989) *Sunzi on the Art of War and its General Application to Business*, Shanghai: Fudan University Press. (A translation and interpretation of Sun Tzu's *The Art of War* and its applications to present-day business strategies.)

Chu, C.N. (1988) *The Chinese Mind Game*, Beaverton, OR: AMC Publishing. (An analysis of the Chinese mind-set and how it affects interactions with non-Chinese.)

Hall, E.T. and Hall, M.R. (1987) *Hidden Differences: Doing Business with the Japanese*, Garden City, NY: Anchor Press. (An analysis of the differences between Americans and Japanese and the implications of these for US/Japanese economic cooperative agreements.)

Kang, T.W. (1989) *Is Korea the Next Japan?*, New York: The Free Press. (An analysis of Korea's economic and sociocultural environments and how they influence business practices.)

Tung, R.L. (1991) 'Handshakes across the sea: cross-cultural negotiating for business success', *Organizational Dynamics* 14 (3): 3040. (A survey of US/Korean joint ventures and an analysis of the factors that led to successful collaboration.)

Yeung, I.Y.M. and Tung, R.L. (1996) 'Achieving business success in Confucian societies: The impact of *guanxi* connections', *Organizational Dynamics* 24(3): 54-65. (An explanation of how and why interpersonaal connections play a key role in east and southeast Asian business dealings.)

Yuan, G. (1991) *Lure the Tiger out of the Mountains: The Thirty-Six Stratagems of Ancient China*, New York: Simon & Schuster. (A translation and interpretation of *The Thirty-Six Stratagems* and its applications to present-day business strategies.)

See also: ECONOMIES OF EAST ASIA; MANAGEMENT IN CHINA; MANAGEMENT IN JAPAN; MANAGEMENT IN SOUTH KOREA

Related topics in the IEBM: BUSINESS STRATEGY, JAPANESE; MANAGEMENT EDUCATION IN ASIA; MANAGEMENT EDUCATION IN CHINA; MANAGEMENT EDUCATION IN JAPAN; MANAGEMENT IN HONG KONG; MANAGEMENT IN PACIFIC ASIA; MANAGEMENT IN SINGAPORE; MANAGEMENT IN TAIWAN; STRATEGY; SUN TZU

Chaebols

1 Characteristics
2 History
3 Strategy and management
4 Ownership and governance structure
5 Evaluation
6 Conclusion

Overview

'*Chaebol*' refers to an individual or his or her family clan that has management control over a cluster of Korea's major business firms that are highly diversified in various industries. '*Chaebol* firms' and '*chaebol* group' would therefore indicate the firms and the group that the *chaebol* controls.

As of the end of 1997 the Korean Government officially recognized the thirty largest *chaebol* groups. The total value added by the largest thirty *chaebol* groups accounted for about 15 per cent of nominal gross national product (GNP) in the fiscal year 1996 and 37 per cent of the value added in manufacturing industries. Their annual sales and total assets in the same year were 42 per cent and 47 per cent, respectively, of the total. Five per cent of Korea's total working population were employed by the thirty largest *chaebol* groups.

In terms of 1996 sales volume, Hyundai Group (see CHUNG FAMILY OF HYUNDAI GROUP) ranked number one, with $68 billion, followed by Samsung (see LEE FAMILY OF SAMSUNG GROUP), with $60 billion, LG (see KOO FAMILY OF LG GROUP), with $47 billion, Daewoo (see KIM FAMILY OF DAEWOO GROUP), with $38 billion, and Sunkyong, with $27 billion.

Chaebols have played a central role in the Korean economy by accumulating the critical mass of capital needed for industrializing the national economy, and, more recently, in enhancing national competitiveness in the global marketplace. Domestically, however, *chaebols* have been a target of social criticism because of their monopoly on scarce capital and human resources, ruthless takeovers of small to medium-sized companies and collusion with the Government.

In the wake of the foreign-exchange crisis which started in November 1997 and the change of government to President Kim Daejung in February 1998, *chaebols* were under pressure to restructure. Specific action programmes were implemented, including consolidation of overdiversified business domains, reduction of huge debt-to-equity ratios and abolition of cross-subsidization practices among the affiliated firms.

1 Characteristics

Chaebols have the following three characteristics (Cho 1997): first, a *chaebol* is an individual or his or her family clan. Second, a *chaebol* controls a group of major business firms that are highly diversified in various industries. Third, a *chaebol* owes its growth to government support via the government-driven industrialization policies of the 1970s and the 1980s.

Each *chaebol* group consists of many affiliate firms. Each affiliate firm is an independent, self-standing entity in legal terms. In practice, it is managed as a business unit or a division within a *chaebol* group. The *chaebol* is typically the largest shareholder, but not always. When the *chaebol* is not the largest shareholder he or she can still control the firms by means of 'cross share-holding'.

The *chaebol* controls and coordinates the affiliate firms by having specialist staff reporting directly to him or her. A *chaebol* group is similar to a conglomerate as both are diversified in a variety of business fields. Yet a *chaebol* group is different from a conglomerate in terms of its legal structure: a *chaebol* group is composed of multiple affiliate firms that are legally independent, while a conglomerate is legally one firm. A *chaebol* group is similar to a Japanese *keiretsu* as affiliate firms are interdependent with other affiliate firms. Yet a *chaebol* group is different from a *keiretsu* in terms of family control: a *chaebol* group is invariably controlled by a single individual or his or her family; a *keiretsu* is typically run by professional managers.

2 History

Chaebols were formed and/or emerged during the period of industrialization of the Korean economy in the 1960s through to the 1980s. In this period *chaebols* started or moved to various so-called 'strategic industries' that were needed by the Korean Government in its attempt to industrialize the nation. To attract investment by *chaebols* the Government provided them with direct and indirect guidance and support in the form of loan guarantees, restriction of new entries into the industry and protection of local markets.

Chaebol groups rapidly grew in size, in part based on their own hard work, shrewd business practices, and highly disciplined labour and managerial forces, and in part based on government initiatives and subsidies. Due to the lack of initial capital and the relative ease of securing foreign loans backed up by the government, *chaebol* firms started their operations with high debt-to-equity ratios, often reaching 1000 per cent or more.

Instead of improving the financial structure with the monopolistic profits that they had made in the domestic market, *chaebol* firms diversified into new business fields. This practice of diversifying into new fields in spite of high debt burdens, at least in the short term, allowed *chaebols* better returns because of the protected nature of the domestic market that they moved in.

In each new field *chaebol* firms invested heavily in manufacturing facilities to strengthen their competitiveness in process technology, which enabled them to capture a significant share in the international market. In essence, the competitiveness that *chaebol* firms maintained was in effect that of the Korean economy, as the products of Hyundai, Samsung, LG, Daewoo and SK became household brands in the international market.

Chaebols, despite their contributions to the national economy, came to a pivotal situation in the mid-1990s. Three basic pillars of *chaebol* groups' competitiveness crumbled. First, protected local markets were no longer available after Korea joined the World Trade Organization (WTO; see WORLD TRADE ORGANIZATION) in 1995 and the Organization for Economic Cooperation and Development (OECD) in 1996, depriving Korean firms of the previously enjoyed monopolistic profits of which *chaebol* firms had been the primary beneficiaries. Second, the implicit back-up of the Korean Government for loans was gone. The Government would instead limit its policy choice to non-interventionist measures. Finally, non-*chaebol*, specialist firms increased the competitive pressure on *chaebol* firms based on their comparative advantage in differentiation, which appealed to a new breed of consumers.

Chaebol groups were urged to make drastic structural and behavioural transformations to enhance their competitiveness in the midst of major changes in the technological and competitive environment. No less pressurizing was the severe social criticism of the *chaebols*' lack of social legitimacy due to their government-linked growth, non-democratic and inefficient management by a family, and illegal ways of inheriting property.

3 Strategy and management

The business domain of a typical *chaebol* group is widely diversified, from manufacturing to retailing and wholesaling, financial services and mass media. *Chaebols* have a presence in every industry except for agriculture, fisheries and public utilities, which are a government monopoly.

The Korean Government used to have virtual control of all the major industries. Yet *chaebol* firms with easy access to the Government could easily enter undeveloped industries. *Chaebol* firms were able to meet the rising need for capital and human resources with their reputation and implicit *chaebol* back-up. When Korea was emerging from the underdeveloped stage of its economy towards a developing one, such diversifying activities of *chaebol* firms had positive effects through vertical or horizontal diversification by moving their managerial capabilities away from non-competitive fields to dynamic and advanced ones.

However, most *chaebol* groups failed to develop their own unique core competence. Instead, they came to have a fragile financial structure as a consequence of continuing diversification through debt financing by cross-payment guarantee. Worse, some *chaebol* groups sacrificed their competitive businesses to cross-subsidize new businesses. At the end of 1996 the average debt-to-equity ratio of the thirty largest *chaebol* groups was 450 per cent.

4 Ownership and governance structure

The *chaebol*, i.e. usually the founder and his family clan, controls affiliate firms by maintaining a large proportion of shares in a few leading affiliate firms. The leading affiliate firms hold shares in other affiliate firms. In this way the *chaebol* can effectively control the group with a relatively small total proportion of the shares. Within each *chaebol* group there is a central planning and coordinating office, which works closely with the chief executive officer (CEO) to monitor and control affiliate companies in a more effective way.

The power and role of professional managers in charge of affiliate companies vary according to the characteristics of the *chaebol* or the relative importance of the companies within the *chaebol* group. Irrespective of the professional managers' power, the *chaebol* has an absolute power in the management of the *chaebol* group, and this power is in principle passed on to the eldest son.

5 Evaluation

Chaebol groups played a major role in the industrialization of the Korean economy. In particular, the entrepreneurs who founded *chaebol* firms were the engines of the industrial revolution in Korea. *Chaebol* firms have grown into global players in such business

fields as semiconductors, the automotive industry and shipbuilding.

Despite the contributions of *chaebol* firms, the *chaebol* system itself has come under fierce criticism from society at large. The focus of the criticism was the enormous wealth that *chaebol* firms have amassed, with the far-reaching implication of a movement against unfair practices of accumulating wealth by virtue of monopolistic profits accrued from government-protected domestic markets, and succession of management control between family members in illegal and unethical ways.

6 Conclusion

As Korean society became more affluent and democratic, and the economy bigger and more competitive, *chaebol* firms were expected not only to be economically efficient but also to conform to society's expectations. In the wake of the foreign-exchange crisis of November 1997 and the change in government leadership in February 1998, *chaebol* firms faced two options for transformation, either voluntary or forced.

DONG-SUNG CHO
SEOUL NATIONAL UNIVERSITY

Further reading

Cho, Dong-sung (1997) *Hankook Chaebol* [Korean *chaebols*], Maeil Business Daily Press. (Presents an historical analysis of Korean *chaebol* groups' formation processes, quantitative analysis of their magnitude and impact on the Korean economy, case analysis of four major *chaebol* groups, a description of the Korean Government's *chaebol* policies, Korean society's feelings about *chaebol* activities and a projection of the future of *chaebols*.)

Choi, Sung-No (1995/1996/1997) *HanKook-eui Daekumo Kieopjipdan* [The Korean big business groups], Jayu Kieop Centre. (Presents a quantitative analysis of Korean *chaebol* groups from the point of view of the national economy.)

Chung, Byung-geol and Yang, Young-sik (1992) *Hankook-chaebol-boomoon-eui kyungje-boonseok* [An economic analysis of the Korean *chaebol* sector], Korea Development Institute. (Gives a critical analysis of the diversification strategies of Korean *chaebol* groups, their ownership structure and the concentration of economic power from the point of view of the national economy.)

Jungang-ilbo Daily (1996) 'Jaekye-reul umjiki-neun saram-deul' [People that move financial circles]. (Gives a detailed description of the top-management profile in Korea's thirty largest *chaebol* groups.)

Lee, Kyu-eok and Lee, Sung-soon (1985) *Kiup-kyulhap-kwa kyungjeryuk-jipjoong* [Corporate merger and concentration of economic power], Korea Development Institute. (Presents a critical analysis of the concentration of economic power within the Korean economy and the resulting problems.)

Yim, Wung-ki (1988) *Kieop-soyukujo-wa jabon-sijang-baljeon* [Corporate ownership structure and capital market development), Korea Investors Services. (Presents a quantitative analysis of the ownership structure of Korean *chaebol* groups, their impact on, and problems associated with, the capital market.)

See also: CHUNG FAMILY OF HYUNDAI GROUP; KIM FAMILY OF DAEWOO GROUP; KOO FAMILY OF LG GROUP; LEE FAMILY OF SAMSUNG GROUP; WORLD TRADE ORGANIZATION

Economics of developing countries

Overview

The economics of developing countries are concerned with those major theories and policies that may bring economic growth and prosperity to poor countries in the world economy. Since the emergence of the idea of developing countries, in the period since 1945, the means to achieve economic growth has been subject to changing fashions in economic theory and policy practice. The experience of economic development in the world economy has been mixed, with sub-Saharan Africa having had a poor economic growth performance since the 1960s, while southeast Asia has recorded high and sustained rates of economic growth. The multilateral economic institutions, namely the International Monetary Fund, the World Bank and the General Agreement on Tariffs and Trade (GATT), have promoted policies to encourage free trade in the world economy, while the Food and Agricultural Organization, the United Nations Conference on Trade and Development and the European Union have promoted policies to intervene in markets, either by the nation-state or by agreements among nation-states, to achieve particular economic and social objectives in addition to economic growth. The economics of developing countries is concerned with the selection of appropriate trade policy or policies to promote growth and development.

Free trade has not been universally considered as the best policy for primary commodity producing countries, largely because of the decline in the terms of trade and the perceived bias of the trading system in favour of the rich and industrialized countries. Policies to promote industrialization through import substitution and state intervention through economic planning, in most developing economies resulted in inward-looking strategies which did not provide the basis for lasting and sustained economic growth. The combination of import protection of industry and state intervention in the economy often resulted in unsustainable inflation and the collapse of economic growth. The combination of the protection of industry through import substitution policies and direct state intervention in the economy either resulted in economic stagnation, as in sub-Saharan Africa, or unsustained inflation and economic collapse, as in South America. In southeast Asia, however, state intervention in the economy to promote industrialization and economic growth through the outward-looking strategies of selling manufactures on world markets, provided the basis for the sustained and lasting growth of the economies known as the Asian Tigers.

Economic aid, or the transfer of resources from rich to poor countries, while contributing to the social and economic welfare of some developing countries, has not universally proved to be as effective a means of promoting growth and development when compared with trade. Agricultural growth, while having increased in both the developed and the developing countries, has not meant that hunger and malnutrition has been eradicated in the world. The growth of the world population, particularly among poor countries, taken together with increasing environmental degradation, poverty and food insecurity, suggest that the economics of developing countries will continue to cause concern that economic growth, stability and prosperity eludes so many of the poor countries in the world.

1 Introduction

In the world economy, countries are grouped into different categories according to their relative prosperity or poverty. This economic condition is measured by the proxy of per capita income, which is the gross national product (GNP) divided by the population of the nation-state concerned. Per capita income, expressed in dollar terms, provides a very approximate measure of relative prosperity or poverty. In 1989 Mozambique had a per capita income of 80 dollars, whereas Switzerland had some 29,880 dollars per capita. The average annual growth rate between 1965 and 1990 of countries ranged between Botswana growing by some 8.5 per cent and Kuwait by some –4.0 per cent.

The categorization of countries as being either rich or poor, is too general a classification and docs not sufficiently allow for the explanation of the factors that have contributed to their relative prosperity or relative poverty. The economics of developing countries is concerned with explaining the underlying factors, both the economic theory and policy, that have contributed, or not, to the economic progress of nation-states.

The causes of economic growth are as central a concern in the 1990s as they were in 1776 when the economist Adam Smith first published his famous *Wealth of Nations*, where he explored and explained the process of growth and the distribution of wealth among nation-states. Explaining the processes of economic growth and the distribution of income is still today the essential purpose of the economics of developing countries.

The economics of developing countries have provided a forum for alternative views as to what is the most appropriate means to achieve the eradication of poverty and provide the basis for sustained economic growth and prosperity. Developing countries as a category, came into being during the period of decolonialization and the Cold War struggle of economic ideas (and political frameworks) was very much a part of economic policy debates. These policy debates have preoccupied development specialists over the last fifty years (Bauer 1991; Lal 1983).

Poor countries have been variously described in the last fifty years as backward, low income, underdeveloped, Third World, peripheral (as in metropolitan, peripheral areas), South (as in North/South) or as low- and middle-income developing countries, and fashions with regard to economic theory and policy that may alleviate conditions of poverty and provide the basis for sustained economic growth have been the central concern of development economics, or the economics of developing countries, since the period of the 1940s (Brandt 1980). During the 1980s countries in the world economy were categorized into low-income, medium- and high-income countries, and in the 1990s former medium-income developing countries were considered as emergent market economies with prospects for foreign private capital investment obtaining a higher rate of return than in the rich countries. Former Soviet bloc eastern European economies are referred to as transitional economies. International multilateral economic institutions have played a central part in the ideas and thinking on the economic development of poor countries.

The economics of developing countries have been concerned with recurrent themes, *inter alia*:

1 the measurement of poverty and the meaning of development, including the importance of population growth;
2 what are the appropriate macroeconomic, microeconomic, international trade and payments policies to achieve economic growth on a regular and continuing basis;
3 the provision of economic aid from rich countries to contribute to the well-being and growth of poor countries and policies to promote the redistribution of wealth on a global scale.

The economics of developing countries have been concerned with identifying the appropriate policies for sustained economic growth and the alleviation of poverty. Since the idea of developing countries emerged in the immediate post-war period, there has not been a consensus among development economists as to what are the appropriate economic policies for the transformation of poor countries into prosperous ones. The idea that the economic policies pursued by developing countries, as opposed to developed countries, has a separate body of theory and practice, has been a recurrent theme and concern for most of the last fifty years. Economic policy recommendations towards poor countries, were inextricably interwoven with the politics of the Cold War period, where the role of the State as the agent for progress and prosperity contrasted sharply with the alternative view that unrestrained free trade and free markets would provide the basis for lasting growth and economic development.

At the heart of all major policy debates on the process of economic development lies a sharp contrast between arguments that propose the State as the agent of economic change and those that propose free markets and free enterprise as a superior agent for change. The issues are often contrasted by policies which emphasize redistribution of resources for purposes of social planning and political objectives such as equity. Improving the distribution of income and direct poverty alleviation is considered to have a direct trade-off with allocative efficiency and economic growth. Free market economics has an implicit theory of distribution (known as trickle-down) that emphasizes the primacy of economic efficiency and growth over redistribution of wealth as the means of providing economic development. The free market theory of distribution argues for economic growth as the means to improving the distribution of income in an economy and, for that matter, for the distribution of income in the world economy taken as a whole. As an economy grows, so more people will be drawn into the growth process and prosperity will spread. Interventionist theories (or structuralist theories as they are sometimes known) consider direct intervention by the State into the economy for the purposes of improving the distribution of income in favour of the poor as a more appropriate means to overcome poverty and economic backwardness. Interventionist policies are justified on the grounds of the failure of markets due to the existence of monopoly, externalities such as pollution or instabilities (adverse prices or terms of trade)

inherent in the market system, taken together with bottlenecks (such as a shortage of capital) that prevent sustained growth and therefore an improving distribution of income in favour of the poor. The State is considered as the agent of economic change for overcoming the failures or excesses of the free market system, and it is believed that state planning can provide a framework for allocative and distributive justice that will simultaneously achieve both equity and growth.

There is, of course, a middle ground between the market and the State, where in the economics of developing countries pro-market theorists concede that on issues of poverty alleviation the poor can be targeted directly, provided that the cost of government programmes does not undermine economic efficiency and economic growth. The State has played a direct role in formulating investment and economic growth policies in the Asian Tigers or Dragon economies (South Korea, Taiwan, Hong Kong, Singapore) but within the context of promoting trade. These economies have had exceptionally high rates of sustained economic growth since the 1960s until the present time. Over the last five decades free market economics have gradually come to dominate the economic policy framework for the developing countries and particularly since 1989 with the emergence of the eastern European countries (transitional economies) in the post-Cold War capitalist world economy. The promotion of free market economic ideas and policy frameworks has largely been the concern of three multilateral economic institutions which were established in the 1940s.

2 International economic institutions and the economics of developing countries

The ending of the Second World War saw a rethinking of the framework for international economic policy which would provide a guide for the capitalist economies and their conduct of international economic relations during the Cold War period (1950–89) (see INTERNATIONAL TRADE AND FOREIGN

DIRECT INVESTMENT). The conduct of economic policy between the First and Second World Wars had resulted in worldwide protectionism, depression and the collapse of world trade and economic growth, policies which in turn had contributed to the war itself. The economic order which emerged during the immediate post-war period was designed to provide the basis for world economic growth and prosperity. To this end the principles on which it rested were those of the nineteenth-century liberal economic tradition which had emphasized the centrality of the doctrine of free trade and the importance of the adherence to comparative advantage in the conduct of economic policy on the world economy. Nations should compete with each other on the basis of their costs of production and their economic efficiency and the State should provide a minimalist role in terms of its intervention in economic affairs. The role of the State should be to uphold law and order, national security and not to engage in direct economic activity, although this minimalist view was somewhat moderated by Keynesian ideas on macroeconomic management during the 1950s and 1960s. The shortage of capital and the non-convertibility of the currency of many nation-states provided a rationale for the giving of economic support by way of economic aid from rich to poor countries (Lewis 1978).

Multilateral institutions were established to oversee the conduct of economic policy in four key areas: international finance and payments; investment and development; international trade policy; and international agricultural and food policy.

The International Monetary Fund

The International Monetary Fund (IMF) was established together with the International Bank for Reconstruction and Development (IBRD), or the World Bank as it has come to be known, at Bretton Woods in New Hampshire, USA, in 1944. Both these international agencies are based in Washington, DC. The IMF had originally been conceived as a world monetary authority and was to operate in the world economy as a world central bank with powers analogous to a central bank in a nation state. The IMF does not, in fact, act as a world central bank, but more as a coordinator of exchange rate, monetary and related policy issues among its members. The IMF has been concerned to promote international monetary cooperation, to aid the expansion and balanced growth of trade, to promote exchange rate stability, to assist in the establishment of a multilateral system of payments, and to give confidence to members by making its resources temporarily available to decrease the intensity and duration of balance of payments disequilibria. There are currently 179 member countries of the IMF. The role of the IMF has evolved over the last half century with a particular emphasis upon providing policy advice and short-term financial support to developing countries. The general policy framework in which the IMF support is given is known as conditionality, whereby countries are entitled to financial support conditional on liberalizing their economy and adopting economic policy measures that will address their underlying economic problems. These problems are invariably related to the rate of inflation, overvalued exchange rates, budgetary deficits and balance of payments deficits. Members of the IMF can draw upon their subscription to membership of the fund and in addition there are financial facilities of varying degrees of 'conditionality' in terms of repayment. Drawing from the IMF beyond the quota system entitlement involves financial penalties that approximate free market rates of interest and stricter terms of repayment. The IMF economic policy framework nearly always emphasizes monetary contraction; devaluation, either implicit or explicit; the redirection of government intervention in the price system or the promotion of privatization; internal financial reform and the raising of interest rates; external liberalization, through the reduction of barriers to trade and the freezing of wage demands with a view to cutting inflationary pressure. IMF policy draws heavily upon orthodox neo-classical economic theory and policy.

The World Bank

The World Bank as a sister institution to the IMF was concerned with providing loans on both a grant and concessional basis for the reconstruction of war-torn Europe and as such operated as a development fund rather than as a bank. While the IMF has been largely concerned with short-run to medium-term monetary, financial and balance of payments problems in developing countries, the World Bank has focused its policy on the medium- to long-run issues concerning project investment and appraisal and sectoral development. The World Bank specialized in project development, infrastructure and the identification of both projects and programmes to promote economic growth and development in recipient developing countries. Cost–benefit analysis became a major tool for the identification of appropriate projects during the period from the late 1960s until the 1980s. While cost–benefit analysis still provides a major means to identifying and evaluating appropriate projects, the Bank has gradually shifted its policy from an almost exclusive microeconomic emphasis to that of a both a micro- and macroeconomic framework (known at first as programme lending). The Bank's approach to lending is known as structural adjustment policy.

Structural adjustment lending is concerned with identifying investment in projects, programmes and general budgetary support for the promotion of sustainable economic growth in developing countries in receipt of World Bank funds. The World Bank group includes the original organization (the IBRD) and three other specialist lending agencies. World Bank funds are given on a concessional basis to developing countries which, in due course, repay these monies to the Bank. World Bank lending is undertaken by the group of four institutions: the IBRD which makes market-rate loans and offers training and technical advice; the IDA (International Development Association), established 1960, which provides interest-free loans, training and technical advice; the IFC (International Finance Corporation), established 1956, mobilizes capital for private ventures; and the

MIGA (Multilateral Investment Guarantee Agency), established 1986, insures foreign direct investment against political risk and provides advisory services to help countries attract private foreign investment.

It was increasingly recognized that the policy framework of both the IMF and the World Bank overlapped and a developing country that failed to meet IMF conditionality would not receive IBRD structural adjustment funding. The policy overlap of the sister institutions required a greater coordination, if contradictory policy advice and support was to be avoided. To this end IMF and World Bank policies are complementary and not separate from their common purpose of promoting sustained economic growth through liberalized trade in the world economy. Periodically calls are made for the unification of both organizations. This has hitherto been rejected, although both organizations are increasing their levels of joint work and cooperation on the framing of development policies. The lines between their respective areas of policy advice and development funding are becoming blurred.

The General Agreement on Tariffs and Trade/World Trade Organization

The General Agreement on Tariffs and Trade (GATT) was established in Geneva to supervise the development of a world system of free trade. Since 1947 signatories to the GATT have increased to include all countries in the world economy, with the exception of China which now seeks to become a member. Unlike the IMF and the World Bank, the GATT has a legal framework for its trade policy which is binding on its membership. Free trade is promoted by the GATT through its legal framework and by periodic trade negotiations among its members, known as 'trade rounds'. Each trade round has considered both the rules on trade as well as specific types and categories of trade. Free trade has been gradually extended and deepened over the last half century, from the deepening of trade in industrial products to the extending of new areas such as the inclusion of agricultural trade policy in the Uruguay round. The GATT trade negotiations of the Kennedy round of 1967, the Tokyo round of 1979 and the recently completed Uruguay round 1994, have reduced the level of protection in the world economy and thus have contributed to world economic growth. The GATT has been superseded by a new World Trade Organization (WTO; see WORLD TRADE ORGANIZATION) in 1995. Over the last half century the GATT has successively widened its scope and the principles of free trade have extended over a wider range of products and services and world trade as a whole is freer today than it was in the immediate post-war period (Meerhaeghe 1974).

Food and Agricultural Organization

The Food and Agricultural Organization of the United Nations became operational in Rome in 1945 and was to be concerned with policies to alleviate world hunger and poverty. Its advocacy of policies to intervene in world agricultural trade and promote agricultural commodity stabilization schemes was considered to be incompatible with the principles of free trade and consequently its role was limited and has largely been confined to that of gathering data and technical information on aspects of world agriculture. Issues of world hunger and poverty have seen the proliferation of world food agencies (all Rome based). In addition to the FAO (proposed in 1943 at Hot Springs), the World Food Programme (WFP) was established in 1961 to use food aid to promote economic and social development in the Third World; the world food crisis of 1972–4 saw the establishment of the World Food Council (WFC) and the International Fund for Agricultural Development was established in 1977 to improve the lives of the rural poor, the thirteenth UN Agency (Talbot 1990).

The economics of developing countries have been influenced by the ideas and thinking of the free trade multilateral institutions of the IMF, GATT and the World Bank, as well as by the more interventionist thinking of the FAO and the three other Rome food and agricultural agencies. The earlier focus of the GATT in the 1950s and 1960s saw many

agriculturally and primary commodity based developing countries excluded from the benefits of trade negotiations that were concerned with industrial products. Partly as a result of this exclusion, the United Nations Conference on Trade and Development (UNCTAD) (1964) urged policies for intervention in commodities to offset the adverse effect of a decline in their terms of trade. Prices of commodities (other than energy products) are near their lowest levels in real terms this century (see Figure 1). The trend in these commodity prices has been downward over most of the past ninety-five years. The UNCTAD proposals argued for an extension of commodity agreements and arrangements on the lines of the Wheat Trade Convention of 1933, the International Sugar Agreement of 1937, the International Coffee Agreement of 1957 and the International Tin Agreement of 1934. The agreements had sought to stabilize production and output by various means, such as buffer stocks, production quotas and price agreements in order to regulate trade and offset any deterioration in the terms of trade of producer countries and to smooth the variability of prices that many commodities were liable to experience. The UNCTAD proposal culminated in a scheme for a multicommodity fund to intervene in international commodity trade in the late 1970s. The period of the 1970s saw considerable instability in world commodity markets with the world

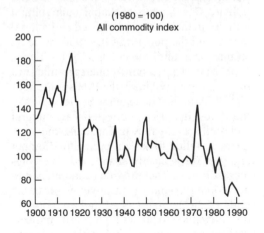

(1980 = 100)
All commodity index

Figure 1

food crisis and the formation of the Organization of Petroleum Exporting Countries (OPEC) and its successful but temporary quadrupling of the price of oil. The policy options of developing countries in response to the secular deterioration of their terms of trade is either to adopt measures in a vain attempt to offset this decline or to diversify their economies.

In addition to multilateral institutions, the economic policy prescriptions, concessions and finance of the bilateral aid agencies have played a major part in the formulation of the policy and the economics of many developing countries. The USA particularly, through its influence upon the Bretton Woods Agencies, the GATT and the Organization for Economic Cooperation and Development (OECD), was the dominant bilateral country in the formulation of economic policy towards developing countries and in the provision of economic assistance towards their economic development. The communist bloc influenced the formulation of economic policies in many developing countries through its advocacy of 'economic planning' in the form of state ownership and control of industry and agriculture. Heavy industrialization was a favoured but unsuccessful policy prescription. The collectivization of agriculture in the Soviet bloc and in communist China, as well as attempts made in developing countries, proved, with experience, to be unsuccessful, and agricultural output invariably fell as a consequence of these policies. The failures of Stalinist agricultural policies in the 1930s undermined agricultural output and the policies of the 1950s were on similar lines until the collapse of the Berlin Wall. Maoist agricultural policies resulted in a major famine in China in the 1960s as the policies of Stalin had done in the Soviet Union in the 1930s. In Africa a collectivist agricultural and rural social policy in Tanzania, known as Ujamaa, failed to sustain agricultural output and was subsequently abandoned. The communist bloc did not provide economic aid to developing countries on anything near the scale of the capitalist West. Indeed, communist aid tended to favour high-profile projects such as the Aswan Dam in Egypt or the provision of military aid to its client states. Military aid was also provided by the West to bolster regimes in the developing world, particularly those countries that were on Cold War frontiers such as South Korea.

The United States Agency for International Development (USAID) and its allied agencies provided aid to developing countries. Economic aid was considered an essential transfer to poor countries to underpin the process of economic growth and development. The USA was the major aid donor during the 1950s and 1960s although other rich countries had their own bilateral aid programmes. In the 1960s the Pearson Commission (established by the IBRD) reported recommendations to the United Nations that rich countries should endeavour to allocate 1 per cent of their GNP per annum to poor countries in the form of economic aid. Apart from the Scandinavian countries and the Netherlands, who have accepted this aid target, other rich countries have not reached as much as 1 per cent of their GNP in their aid contributions (Brandt 1980).

European Union

During the 1960s the European Community (now the European Union (EU); see EUROPEAN UNION), developed its own distinctive aid and trade policies towards the developing world. The European Union trade policies towards developing countries are under the Lome Conventions, of which there have been four. Each Lome agreement runs for a five-year period and each new agreement is renegotiated with the ACP (Africa, Caribbean and Pacific) countries. Members of Lome were essentially former colonies of the European Union countries. The EU has established preferential trade access to ACP countries through the Generalized System of Preferences (GSP). The USA has also introduced a generalized system of preferences in its sphere of influence (in response to the EU initiative), an agreement with South American countries known as the Punta del Este agreement (see ECONOMIC INTEGRATION, INTERNATIONAL).

European Aid Policies are operated through the European Development Bank (EDB) and the European Bank for

Reconstruction and Development (EBRD), the latter having been established to assist the new transition economies of Eastern Europe. The EBRD also has funding from the USA and other non-EU rich countries. Its development lending is limited to help the former Soviet bloc economies to transform their institutions and economy to free market policies. EBRD lending policy is constrained, in so far as almost half of its funds must be directed to the private sector. EU trade policies towards developing countries are unified into a single policy but European aid policies coexist with the bilateral aid policies of member states.

These various international institutions, by a combination of resources and policy prescriptions, have had a major influence on the economics of developing countries during the Cold War era and are likely to continue to do so. The emphasis now is on channelling multilateral funding to private sector development as witnessed by the changes in policy of the IBRD and the introduction of the EBRD policy emphasis upon encouraging the private sector. Since 1989 the economics of developing countries have highlighted the role of the private sector in policy changes, particularly within the multilateral institutions. Policy is being increasingly formulated to facilitate private sector development, the government sector is receiving policy advice to liberalize, and development funds are being directed to promote these objectives. In theory, as markets fill the role as providers of capital for development, then the need for multilateral development agencies will lessen, if not entirely disappear.

Over the last fifty years and particularly since 1989, free-trade and free-market policies are in the ascendant, and these policy prescriptions are likely to be reinforced by increased economic growth in the world economy. They are also likely to be moderated if global economic prospects go awry. The global depression of the 1930s set the economic agenda for most of the twentieth century in so far as post-Second World War economic policy has sought to undo the policies of the inter-war period.

3 Trade and aid policy issues (1945–89)

In the period when the classical doctrine of free trade was being enshrined at Bretton Woods as a fundamental doctrine for the post-war economic order and as an operating principle for the new international institutions, doubts were being expressed as to whether free trade would be beneficial to poor countries taken as a whole (see INTERNATIONAL TRADE AND FOREIGN DIRECT INVESTMENT). Those countries emerging from colonialism had an economic structure that had been established to provide raw materials for their colonial masters. Their economies were highly specialized in the production of primary commodities, which were subject to wide fluctuations in price on world markets. This specialization provided commodity price instability to emergent developing countries and undermined their prospects for economic growth and development. The collapse of commodity markets in the 1930s had seen the introduction of marketing boards with monopoly powers to purchase commodities and to try to stabilize commodity prices. The marketing boards also used buffer stock as part of their stabilization policy. In West Africa the newly independent countries, for example, inherited these boards which had accumulated considerable funds which in turn were to be applied for the general development of the new states. The colonial legacy had left behind economic institutions that did not operate on the basis of free trade, and indeed these marketing boards taxed producers to raise general revenues. The result of these revenue raising policies had a profound effect on the pattern of production of primary commodities. In West Africa the monopoly commodity boards' taxation policy resulted in a supply response from producers that either caused the output of commodities to decrease, or led producers to find, through smuggling, alternative markets, usually in neighbouring countries. The marketing boards, in their internal price policies and taxation policy, eventually undermined their own production base which in turn resulted in a revenue crisis for the state concerned.

The dependence of developing countries upon primary commodities, in addition to providing a rationale for monopoly policies within countries, resulted in attempts by the developing countries themselves to cartelize commodity trade through producer agreements and the regulation of trade. Free-trade policy was being challenged as the first best policy for developing countries through the terms-of-trade hypothesis.

The terms of trade

Studies by Han Singer and Raul Prebisch in the late 1940s suggest that the trading system was not neutral towards the prospects for primary producing countries. These studies indicated that the terms of trade worked against the interests of poor countries and in favour of rich countries. The Singer–Prebisch hypothesis (or the terms-of-trade hypothesis) provided a powerful argument for interventionist policies in international trade through direct intervention in trade policy itself to correct the bias towards rich countries in favour of poor countries (Meier and Seers 1984). The fall in commodity prices meant that commodity-dependent countries found that increases in their productivity resulted in lower prices and lower government revenues. These lower revenues in turn made development financing more difficult, and in times of commodity-price instability revenues were unpredictable. The benefits of primary commodity productivity were being passed on to rich countries in lower prices and not being retained by the poor countries. The terms-of-trade hypothesis and the non-neutrality of the international trading system provided the basis, in the 1960s and 1970s, for the development of dependency theories which argued that the economic order of the post-war world was a continuation of the exploitative nature of international trade that had been central to the colonial system of economics which had shaped the nineteenth and early twentieth centuries. Trade according to this school had become a mechanism for the extraction of profit from the poor countries to the rich.

Allied to this view of the exploitative nature of the trade system itself, was a further view that multinational corporations (MNCs) were the institutional mechanism for the expropriation of profits from developing countries (see MULTINATIONAL CORPORATIONS). MNCs were said to practise 'transfer pricing', which was the charging of prices not according to costs and profits but for the purpose of concealing their profitability and overcoming developing country government policy to retain profits in the country of origin.

The Singer–Prebisch hypothesis also provided an additional argument for economic aid from rich countries to poor countries. The terms-of-trade hypothesis proves to be a resilient idea and provides an alternative theoretical focus, or an exception for many, to the doctrine of free trade. The bias of the trading system is not considered by all economists (or multilateral institutions) as having been proven and over the last fifty years numerous studies have tried to refine the hypothesis or refute it. The decline in the terms of trade suggests for IMF analysts that the economy concerned should diversify to other economic activities and not to put in place policies to resist the decline. In addition to the terms-of-trade hypothesis, trade pessimism also saw the re-emergence of the Infant Industry or Infant Economy argument for protectionism. Classic free-trade theory and its modern refinements such as the Heckscher–Ohlin theory, saw trade as the engine of economic growth, and free trade as the means to establish the fastest rate of growth for the world economy as a whole since free trade provided both static and dynamic gains to a country engaged in it. Since the nineteenth century, when John Stuart Mill argued that countries which did not have industries but wished to establish them, it had been considered reasonable to protect the fledgling industry as a parent would an infant, until such time as the child could take care of itself. Mill had provided an argument for a limited period of protection of new industries or new economics. The infant industry argument lent itself to justify tariff barriers (or quotas) or producer subsidies in developing countries where import substitution policies were being established as some poor countries sought to industrialize. Producer subsidies were considered as less pernicious than tariffs and less damaging to trade. The weakness of the infant industry or economy argument is that once protectionism has been established it becomes difficult to know when it will give way to free trade – indeed it may become endemic to an economy. Rich countries protect their older industries (senile industries) on the basis of a similar argument to that of the infant industry argument – once protectionism is established it can be difficult removing it.

Import substitution and industrialization policies

Import substitution policies stressed industrialization as a means to rapid economic growth and development, since the rate of productivity increase in industry was higher than that possible in agriculture. Economic development that embraced industry would produce higher and faster growth than agriculture alone. Policies to promote industrialization as a means of faster economic development were also influenced by the Cold War. The Soviet Union had followed a policy of promoting heavy industry in the form of capital goods. The planning system in the Soviet Union was considered, at that time, as being superior for the purpose of creating heavy industry. The idea of state planning or the command economy gained considerable support during the first three decades of the Cold War, with the Soviet model being considered in countries such as India. The Chinese model, emanating from the cultural revolution, of small-scale production as in the case of iron, proved to be a fiasco. In India the Mahalanobis plan for industrialization, in which heavy industry was to be promoted by the State through state investment and forced savings, was adopted. This policy was not successful.

Economic planning

Economic planning was considered as the essential framework, with the State guiding the economy to economic growth and prosperity. National plans were produced and planning periods became the norm for many developing countries. Five-year development plans were produced in the hope that economic aid would be forthcoming from rich donors, but these plans more often than not were wish-lists and could not and did not achieve their targets. State planning did not provide a panacea for underdevelopment, but provided a justification for the direct intervention of government into economic activity which, in most developing countries, government was singularly ill equipped to carry out successfully. Where government operated industry directly the results were not usually efficient, although countries such as South Korea did successfully operate import substitution policies under the guidance of the State (see MANAGEMENT IN SOUTH KOREA). In this case the State set industrialization priorities for the private sector and backed them with state resources.

Throughout the 1970s and 1980s the failures of economic policy in many developing countries were becoming apparent with low growth, high unemployment and increasing poverty. State intervention into economic policy was coming to be seen not only as an inappropriate means to promote economic growth but also as positively harmful to growth. The policy failures of economic planning were being characterized as government failure rather than market failure. Government intervention had produced rent-seeking behaviour on the part of entrepreneurs and businessmen. State intervention in the economy through excessive regulation (such as import and export licences) had caused business to spend increasing time, effort and money on overcoming these impediments to growth. Rent-seeking activity was therefore positively unproductive and contributed to low economic growth. The role of the State in the direct conduct of economic planning, including direct ownership and control of business, was not a success.

Economic aid

Economic aid from rich countries to poor countries had emerged at the end of the Second World War when the USA had provided economic assistance for the restructuring of the economies of Europe under the Marshall

Plan. This aid was short term but substantial and allowed Europe to overcome shortages and bottlenecks which had resulted from the devastation of war, and put these countries on the path to reconstruction and economic recovery. The success of the Marshall Plan indicated that transfers from government to government in the form of grants and concessional loans could enable economic recovery and economic growth. While under the Bretton Wood system economic growth was to be achieved by the promotion of free markets, private foreign investment and the expansion of world trade, it was also recognized that this was unlikely to happen spontaneously in the dollar shortages of the 1950s, and therefore transfers of resources would be beneficial to both donors and recipients of those transfers. Economic aid would help to pump prime the economies of the newly emerging developing countries.

The Cold War had a particular influence upon policies of the aid donor countries. Development countries receiving economic aid, more often than not received it on the basis of the foreign policy concerns of the donor rather than on the intrinsic needs of the recipient economy. Economic aid was not given on the basis of need or of strictly economic criteria, but often for purposes of global foreign policy which were determined by the Cold War.

Economic aid from rich countries to poor countries became a prominent feature of the economics of developing countries during the Cold War period. The lack of convertibility of the currency of most developing countries and their balance of payments difficulties provided an impediment to the growth of international trade. To some degree, the transfers from donors alleviated these currency and convertibility bottlenecks.

Transfers of economic aid from rich to poor countries took a number of forms. Tied aid was transfers given to specific projects and programmes in developing countries, the donor specifying the aid either in kind or in terms of the donor currency. Military aid, technical aid and commodity aid (food aid) are highly tied and the sourcing for tied aid was invariably the donor country. While tied aid may provide benefits to the recipient, it also provided benefits to the donor. The industries in donor countries producing military equipment, or the farmers producing food surplus to effective demand, or the construction companies building a dam, all benefited from aid programmes. The aid programmes of most donor countries were strongly supported by vested interests within the donor country.

Transfers of freely convertible untied aid were less frequently given than tied aid. It has been suggested that tied aid would allow the donors to account for the way that the aid is used in the recipient country, as often it is more difficult to account for untied financial aid. However, aid switching or fungibility would be possible. If the recipient country had already allocated resources in its development budget for a project or programme that the aid could meet, the resources could be used for alternative purposes. Since the giving of economic aid was predominantly a government-to-government activity, this encouraged the public sector rather than the private sector. Multilateral economic aid also consisted of transfers and support for the government sector.

Tied aid did not allow developing countries to look for the lowest cost available on world markets for their economic projects and was therefore potentially less efficient than financial transfers. Aid in general also encouraged government economic activity over that of private enterprise. The effects of economic aid on the development of poor countries was a mixed picture; in the cases of some countries aid had provided benefits to both donor and recipient, and in others it had not. By the late 1970s, the effectiveness of aid was being called into question.

The 1970s were a watershed in terms of policy prescriptions from the rich countries to the poor. The efficacy of economic aid was being called into question by both donors and recipients alike. Third World countries through UNCTAD and the example of OPEC were advocating policies for direct intervention in the world trading system to transfer greater resources for their economic and social development. Calls were made for a new international economic order (NIEO) to benefit poorer countries, and the rich countries (the

North) and the poor countries (the South) sought different remedies for economic development. The Brandt Commission published a report that emphasized the need for greater transfers of economic aid and greater intervention in the world economy to assist the South. The recommendations of the Brandt Commission Report (1980) and those of the UNCTAD integrated commodity proposals were not acceptable to the rich countries who did not support these.

The economics of developing countries during the 1980s through the Bretton Woods institutions re-emphasized the primacy of free markets, private foreign investment and the growth of international trade. Both the IMF and the World Bank promoted and funded policies that provide a framework for macroeconomic stabilization that is dependent upon conditionality and structural adjustment within developing countries. These policies stress the importance of privatization, 'getting the prices right', financial reform, particularly with regard to exchange rate policy, and monetary and interest rate policy as the basis of sound and stable growth. The distribution of income was to be left almost entirely to market forces, through the process of trickle-down. However, dire poverty could be exceptionally considered by government, provided market forces were not thwarted and the programmes and policies adopted were targeted to the specific needs of those poor who would be unable to benefit from growth. Welfare programmes should focus upon those poor who would be excluded from economic prosperity and expenditure would be specific to their needs but not general budget welfare expenditure. The emergence of the eastern European economies has reinforced their view that economic development is dependent on free markets and free trade. The macroeconomic stabilization policies of the Bretton Woods institutions are designed to enhance economic growth and stability within a free-market, free-trade world economy.

Asian Tigers

The experience of the Asian Tigers or Dragons (South Korea, Taiwan, Hong Kong and Singapore) during the 1970s and 1980s was considered to be a model for economic growth and prosperity (see MANAGEMENT IN SOUTH KOREA). These economies had consistently grown at an annual rate well in excess of 8 per cent per annum and continue to grow at amongst the highest rates of economic growth in the world economy. These Tiger economies prospered by developing their manufacturing industries exporting for world markets. Although the experience of each of these economies is unique, they did have a number of factors in common. The economies were relatively open economies dependent upon world markets for their growth. They all have high rates of savings and investment and government has encouraged industry by cooperation with private investment. The State in these countries has facilitated investment and growth and these economies have adjusted to export objectives as primary objectives of economic policy. While these economies have depended on world markets for their growth, both Taiwan and South Korea have developed an industrial organization on conglomerates. These organizations (*chaebols*) are similar to Japanese industrial organizations although not the same. The South Korean *chaebols* are active participants in the formulation of government economic policy on a regular basis. While South Korean economic policy is market orientated, it is not free from government supervision and indeed support. South Korea is often cited as a model of *laissez-faire* economics and the benefits of such a framework for policy are held up as an example. However, the role of the State as a promoter of South Korean policy was interventionist in so far as industrial and trade policy was state determined. These hyper-growth Asian economies or NICs (newly industrialized countries) have evolved an economic policy formula that may not be easily replicated in other parts of the world. Their largely Confucian cultural heritage (and the homogeneous nature of their society) may account for a large part of their success, rather than the application of market principles on their own.

Food and agriculture

The economics of developing countries have been influenced by changing fashions in economic policy as well as by poverty, hunger and malnutrition (Foster 1992). In spite of the growth of the world economy and the emergence of many developing countries on to a path of sustained economic growth, the persistence of poverty in many low-income countries has prompted policies from rich countries to alleviate these problems. Food aid has been given from the rich countries, most notably the USA, Canada, Japan and the European Union, as well as from the World Food Programme of the United Nations, to over 100 developing countries. This form of development assistance has proved to be controversial, since it is a form of aid that has the capacity to displace agricultural markets, both those of the recipient of the aid and of third-party agricultural producers. Food aid as emergency aid to meet famine, drought and dislocation of economies from civil war forms a small part of the total food commodity aid that is given. Its contribution to recipient economies takes the form of general economic aid since many food aid programmes allow the sale of the aid on their internal market, thus providing government revenues and foreign exchange savings. The sale of food aid may displace local producers of similar foodstuffs if the pricing policy in the country concerned is set below the cost of production.

The FAO and the EU advocate policies for the instigation of national food plans in developing countries with reserves of food stocks to offset any shortfall in supply that might result from higher world food prices or drought. The holding of food stocks is very costly and it also requires the intervention of a government agency to manage these stocks. The Bretton Woods institutions do not favour this approach to the food problem in developing countries, since it involves state intervention in markets. Their preferred options for a food security policy is one based on government holding financial reserves for the import of food, should that be necessary.

The problem of food shortages and food insecurity in many developing countries is regarded by many development economists as being unlikely to be solved by market mechanisms alone. The Theory of Entitlements provides a framework for the understanding of hunger and famine within a social and institutional setting that suggests public or state action to deal with food shortages (Dreze and Sen 1989).

Agricultural productivity has increased remarkably in the world economy since the Second World War. Agricultural production in the developed world underwent a massive increase in output and with it the growth of agricultural trade. This fact explains why world population growth has increased, outwitting the Malthusian spectre. The productivity increase in the developed world was due to government intervention to support agriculture, particularly prices and trade, as well as the introduction of new technology in the form of fertilizers, hybrid seeds and mechanization. In the developing world the introduction of improved seed varieties and fertilizers has contributed to a remarkable increase in output which has come to be known as the Green Revolution. The Green Revolution was a major initiative of the Ford and Rockefeller research institutes over many years and has undoubtedly contributed to an increase in the world food supply. These productivity increases are, however, unlikely to balance against the absolute increase in world population.

The emergence of the environment as an issue in the economics of developing countries has focused on urbanization, poverty, food insecurity and population policies. The Brundtland Report (1987) highlighted these issues and suggested policy prescriptions which involved the direct involvement of the State and international actions to alleviate these problems.

The UN population conference in 1994 recommended an explicit population policy to limit the growth of world population through contraception and family planning. Religious groups have reluctantly accepted these proposals but their response is unlikely to promote such policies. The UN population conference in 1967 had advocated economic development as the best population policy since economic growth is usually accompanied by smaller family sizes.

The economics of developing countries have been influenced by the Cold War and this has taken the general form of policy recommendations that have advocated free markets or state planning and intervention to achieve economic growth and welfare. Developing economies, particularly the NICs, have shown that high rates of economic growth and industrialization can provide the basis for economic prosperity and welfare. The State has provided the framework for economic activity in many developing countries, including some of the NICs. The replication of a country's economic performance by another country may not always be successful since there are unique factors in the situation of each country. It is not possible for all the countries of the world economy to industrialize and therefore different policy prescriptions will apply to different country circumstances (North 1990).

The emergence of the transitional economies of eastern Europe and the emergent markets in the world economy – together with growing environmental concerns, not least the rapid growth of world population – suggest that the economics of developing countries are likely to be a continuing focus for policy prescriptions that oscillate between free-market and state solutions. Trade, technology, institutions and the environment, as well as continuing poverty and hunger, are likely to determine the economics of developing countries.

JOHN CATHIE
UNIVERSITY OF CAMBRIDGE

Further reading

(References cited in the text marked *)

* Bauer, P.T. (1991) *The Development Frontier*, Hemel Hempstead: Harvester Wheatsheaf. (Collection of essays on development economic issues with a pro-free-market emphasis.)
* Brandt, W. (1980) *North–South: A Programme for Survival. Report of the Independent Commission on International Development Issues*, London: Pan. (Covers a wide range of development issues which in the event were not acted upon in terms of recommendations to the rich countries.)
* Brundtland Report (1987) *Our Common Future, World Commission on Environment and Development*, Oxford: Oxford University Press. (An excellent report which looks at the range of environmental problems in the Third World and offers proposals for tackling them.)
* Dreze, J. and Sen, A.K. (1989) *Hunger and Public Action*, Oxford: Clarendon Press. (Comprehensive analysis of hunger and famine in developing countries; gives an indication of policy options.)
* Foster, P. (1992) *The World Food Problem: Tackling the Causes of Undernutrition in the Third World*, London: Adamantine Press. (Comprehensive textbook analysis of the problems of world hunger.)
* *IMF Survey* (1994) 'Adjustment, not resistance, the key to dealing with low commodity prices', October, occasional paper no. 112, Washington, DC: IMF. (Regular publication of IMF.)
* Lal, D. (1983) *The Poverty of 'Development Economics'*, Hobart paperback 16, London: Institute of Economic Affairs. (A very readable polemic against 'unorthodox theories' of development.)
* Lewis, W.A. (1978) *The Evolution of the International Economic Order*, Princeton, NJ: Princeton University Press. (Classic short essays on trade and aid policy in the Third World.)
* Meerhaeghe, M.A.G., van (1974) *International Economic Institutions*, 2nd edn, London: Longman. (Good account of the origins of the IMF, World Bank, GATT and commodity agreements, the EU and OECD.)
* Meier, G.M. and Seers, D. (eds) (1984) *Pioneers in Development*, New York: Oxford University Press. (Excellent collection of essays by major contributors to development economics. Very readable and comprehensive.)
* North, D. (1990) *Institutions, Institutional Change and Economic Performance*, Cambridge: Cambridge University Press. (Classic work on economic growth and institutions.)
* Smith, A. (1776) *Wealth of Nations*, Harmondsworth: Penguin, 1976. (Systematic analysis of the causes of economic growth and prosperity that remains influential today.)
* Talbot, R.B. (1990) *The Four World Food Agencies in Rome*, Ames, IA: Iowa State University Press (Good factual account of Rome food and agricultural agencies.)

See also: ECONOMIC INTEGRATION, INTERNATIONAL; EUROPEAN UNION; GLOBALIZA-

TION; INTERNATIONAL TRADE AND FOREIGN DIRECT INVESTMENT; MANAGEMENT IN SOUTH KOREA; MULTINATIONAL CORPORATIONS; MULTINATIONAL CORPORATIONS, ORGANIZATION STRUCTURES IN; WORLD TRADE ORGANIZATION

Related topics in the IEBM: BUSINESS CYCLES; FINANCE, INTERNATIONAL; GENERAL AGREEMENT ON TARIFFS AND TRADE; GLOBALIZATION AND CORPORATE NATIONALITY; GOVERNMENT, INDUSTRY AND THE PUBLIC SECTOR; INDUSTRIAL STRATEGY; MANAGEMENT IN HONG KONG; MANAGEMENT IN PACIFIC ASIA; MANAGEMENT IN SINGAPORE; MANAGEMENT IN TAIWAN; MILL, J.S.; MULTINATIONAL CORPORATIONS, HISTORY OF; SMITH, A.

Economies of east Asia

Overview

The economies of east Asia have established a remarkable record of high and sustained growth. In addition to the immense economy of Japan, they consist of South Korea, Taiwan, Hong Kong and Singapore (known together as Asia's newly industrializing economies, or the Asian NIEs), Indonesia, Malaysia, the Philippines and Thailand (which, together with Singapore, are founding members of the Association of South-East Asian Nations, or ASEAN), and China.

The pattern of economic development in post-war east Asia has been likened to a flock of wild geese flying in formation. The development process began in Japan, rippling out to the Asian NIEs and later to the ASEAN economies and China. Traditionally these economies have depended heavily on the USA for trade and investment but the trend towards intra-regional economic interdependence has accelerated since the Plaza Accord in 1985. The end of the Cold War has also helped promote the integration of the socialist countries (China, Vietnam, Laos, Cambodia, Burma, Mongolia, North Korea and Far East Russia) into the regional economy. While strengthening ties among the east Asian economies has until now been achieved mainly through the initiative of the private sector, multilateral economic cooperation at the government level is also gaining momentum. All these favourable factors notwithstanding, the east Asian economies suffered a major setback in mid-1997 when a currency crisis started in Thailand and spread to the rest of the region.

1 The flying-geese pattern of economic development

East Asia has been the most dynamic part of the world economy throughout the post-war period. Through trade and investment, the wave of industrialization that spread from Japan to Asia's newly industrializing economies (NIEs) in the 1960s is now spreading to the Association of South-East Asian Nations (ASEAN; see ASSOCIATION OF SOUTH-EAST ASIAN NATIONS) and China. Economic growth in the Asian NIEs has averaged over 8 per cent a year in the last three decades, despite two oil crises in the 1970s and sluggish world demand in the first half of the 1980s and the early 1990s. Economic growth in the ASEAN countries, which had lagged far behind that in the Asian NIEs, has picked up since the mid-1980s thanks to the rapid increase in foreign direct investment. Economic growth in China has also accelerated since the late 1970s, when the government shifted to an open-door policy that promotes foreign investment and exports (see BUSINESS STRATEGIES, EAST ASIAN).

The expansion of the dynamism of the east Asian economies from Japan to the Asian NIEs, and then further to ASEAN and China has come to be known as the 'flying-geese pattern'. Countries specialize in the export of products in which they enjoy a comparative advantage commensurate with their levels of economic development; at the same time they seek to upgrade their industrial structures by augmenting their endowment of capital and technology. By promoting the relocation of industries from the more advanced nations to the less developed ones, foreign direct investment plays a dominant role in this process (see INTERNATIONAL TRADE AND FOREIGN DIRECT INVESTMENT).

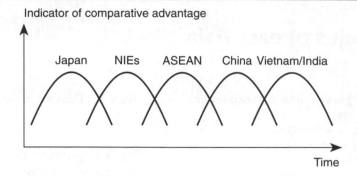

Figure 1 'Flying geese' pattern of economic development
Note: For a particular industry, for example, textiles

The flying-geese pattern can be illustrated by looking at the long-term trend in the shift of industries across national borders (Figure 1). The centre of the textile industry in east Asia, for example, has shifted from Japan to the Asian NIEs and on to ASEAN and China, a process reflecting the descending order of the level of economic development. The life cycles of the textile industry in Japan, the Asian NIEs, ASEAN and China can be depicted as a set of overlapping inverted V-shaped curves (which look like wild geese flying in formation, hence the name of the pattern) (see MAN-AGEMENT IN JAPAN). In this way, declining industries in more advanced countries are reborn as emerging industries in countries catching up from behind; the dynamism of the region is thereby sustained.

2 Expanding new frontiers

Through the removal of the political barriers separating socialist countries and market economies, the global trend towards *détente* has helped make cooperation across national borders possible in east Asia also. The collapse of communist regimes in eastern Europe and the Soviet Union, in particular, has had an immense impact on the socialist countries in this Asian sub-region. The failure of Soviet-style socialism as a model of economic development contrasts sharply with the success of the Asian NIEs and ASEAN nations, which have fundamentally relied on the market in their organization of economic activity. With the dominance of

ideology waning and aid from the former Soviet Union terminated, the time is ripe for the socialist countries in east Asia to reconsider their development strategy. An obvious alternative is to open their doors further to the outside world in order to take advantage of the dynamism in neighbouring countries.

During the 1960s, at the height of the Cold War, the famous domino theory predicted that if Vietnam were to fall to communism the rest of southeast Asia would follow. Ironically, the reverse is now taking place, with the transition to a market economy gathering pace in the socialist countries in the region. Prompted by the rapid dismantling of barriers separating the two sides, China and Vietnam are fast emerging as new economic frontiers of east Asia. The spread of economic dynamism from the Asian NIEs and ASEAN countries to the socialist countries in the region is consistent with the flying-geese pattern mentioned earlier. Propelled by the energy accumulated over decades in the form of immense unexploited business opportunities, the geese are flying even faster and farther than before.

The expansion of east Asia's new frontiers is creating economic zones encompassing countries with different economic and political systems and at various stages of economic development. In addition to the 'South China Economic Zone' centring around Hong Kong, concepts of regional cooperation at more embryonic stages have emerged. They include the 'Northeast Asia Economic Zone' (comprising Japan, the Korean Peninsula, northern

China and the Russian Far East) and other various 'growth triangles' to be formed among the ASEAN countries. These interlocking economic zones form a corridor linking fast-growing economies from the north to the south along the western Pacific Rim.

China has become east Asia's largest new frontier. With a population of 1.2 billion and its economy growing at nearly 10 per cent a year since converting to an open-door policy in the late 1970s, China is emerging as a regional, if not global, economic power (see MANAGEMENT IN CHINA). This is particularly true in instances where China is broadly interpreted to include Hong Kong and Taiwan. Integration among the three economies has now reached a point where they have come to be known as Greater China or the Chinese Economic Area. The World Bank estimates that the gross domestic product of Greater China, adjusted for the difference in purchasing power, has now surpassed that of Japan and will surpass that of the USA by the year 2002, to make Greater China the number one economic power.

China's transformation to a market economy and its opening to the world are having a major effect on neighbouring countries. First, China can now present itself as a model to follow for other socialist countries in the region, and thereby help to accelerate the reverse-domino phenomenon. Vietnam's open-door policy is a good example. Second, the Asian NIEs, which are more developed than China, should benefit from expanding investment and trade ties with China. This is particularly true for Hong Kong and Taiwan. Third, the smooth transition of Hong Kong to Chinese sovereignty has been facilitated by the virtual economic integration of China and Hong Kong. Indeed, Hong Kong is expected to play an even larger role as the gateway to China. Fourth, China is competing vigorously with the ASEAN countries, not only for export markets but also for foreign direct investment. In fact, the expansion of foreign direct investment flows to China since 1992 might have been at the expense of the ASEAN countries.

3 Deepening intra-regional interdependence

While thus far the economic growth rate of the east Asian countries has depended on the industrial countries, especially the USA, the ability to generate demand from within the region has increased, thanks to rising intra-regional trade and investment. Until the mid-1980s, trade in east Asia had been dominated by exports across the Pacific, a pattern of trade flow that has changed dramatically since the Plaza Accord among the G5 countries in 1985, which resulted in a sharp appreciation of the yen against the dollar. With east Asia growing at twice the speed of the USA and trade friction between the two sides of the Pacific escalating, intra-regional trade among east Asian countries has increased sharply, while the relative importance of the USA as an export market for these countries has declined. Reflecting the rising level of intra-regional trade, the Asian NIEs, ASEAN and China together now hold a larger share of world trade than the USA and house all top-three container ports of the world, namely Hong Kong, Singapore and Taiwan's Kaohsiung.

In addition to the market-size factor, rising intra-regional investment has also contributed to the recent surge in intra-regional trade. In east Asia, Japan has replaced the USA as the largest source of foreign direct investment, while the Asian NIEs have also become major investors in China and the ASEAN countries. Currency appreciation in Japan and the Asian NIEs since the 1985 Plaza Accord has prompted their companies to move production facilities overseas. Overall, the investment objective of Japanese companies has been shifting from using the region as an export base to using it as a production base serving local markets; as a result, the focus has shifted from the Asian NIEs and the ASEAN countries to China. Japanese investment in east Asia has been led by the electronics companies: headquarters in Japan are specializing in high value-added products and research and development, while subsidiaries in east Asian countries are taking over the manufacturing of standardized products.

Not only is Japan playing a more and more important role in the east Asian economies, but Japan's own economic fortune now hinges more and more on the performance of its Asian neighbours. During the post-war and Cold War periods, Japan became highly dependent on the USA not only for its defence but also for export markets and the technology that has supported the Japanese economic miracle. With the fading of the Cold War and the US hegemony, the re-Asianization of the Japanese economy has gathered pace. This trend has been accelerated by rising trade friction with the USA (push factor) and hypergrowth in the east Asian economies (pull factor). The growing importance of east Asia for Japan has become apparent in trade and investment flows (see INTERNATIONAL TRADE AND FOREIGN DIRECT INVESTMENT). Indeed, east Asia has replaced the USA as Japan's most important export market and the largest source of its trade surplus. It is only a matter of time before east Asia replaces the USA as the most important destination for Japanese investment.

4 Strengthening multilateral cooperation at government level

While economic integration in east Asia so far has been achieved mainly through the initiative of the private sector, multilateral economic cooperation at the government level, with a focus on ASEAN and Asia-Pacific Economic Cooperation (APEC), is also gaining momentum.

ASEAN has remained the symbol of regional economic cooperation. ASEAN was established in 1967 between Indonesia, Malaysia, the Philippines, Singapore and Thailand to foster regional economic and political cooperation. Brunei became the sixth member in 1984. Vietnam joined in 1996, and Laos and Myanmar followed in 1997. Up to now ASEAN has played an important role in political cooperation, but has yet to achieve significant results in the sphere of economic cooperation. To cope with the rising tide of regionalism and to halt the shift of direct investment to the new competitors such as China, Latin America and eastern European countries, ASEAN has decided to establish an ASEAN Free Trade Area (AFTA). By liberalizing trade in the region, AFTA should encourage a more horizontal division of labour in manufactured goods by making it more attractive for multinationals to build production networks across national borders.

A major barrier to economic cooperation has been the relatively low degree of complementarity in economic structures among ASEAN members. This can be solved by extending membership to countries at different stages of economic development. With the socialist countries of Indochina as members there should be more diversity in economic structures within ASEAN. Other schemes along this line include promoting economic cooperation among all countries in east Asia, for example by forming an East Asian Economic Caucus (EAEC), as proposed by Malaysia's prime minister, Mahathir bin Mohamad. In addition to increasing east Asian countries' bargaining power in international negotiations, the EAEC aims to exploit complementarity through economic cooperation by coupling those countries at a low stage of development, such as China and Vietnam, with the economically advanced countries, such as Japan and the NIEs. The EAEC, however, does not include countries on the other side of the Pacific as its potential members. This has prompted the USA to criticize the proposal as counter-productive and racist. In the absence of US support, Japan has hesitated to take the lead in realizing this proposal.

Meanwhile, the APEC forum is emerging as the dominant force of economic cooperation in the Pacific region. Its members now include all the major players on both sides of the Pacific. Since the first ministerial meeting in 1989, APEC's role has centred on the promotion of dialogue and cooperative sectoral projects to deal with the major problems affecting the region's economy; trade and investment liberalization has recently also become an important item on the agenda. At the 1994 APEC summit, held in Jakarta, the participating countries reached a consensus on a two-speed schedule, stipulating that the liberalization of trade and investment be completed by 2010 for the advanced member countries and by 2020 for the developing member countries.

5 The Asian currency crisis

The performance of the east Asian economies, however, was adversely affected by the currency crisis that infected the whole region in mid-1997. Escalating speculation on the baht forced Thailand to abandon the basket peg exchange-rate system and shift to a managed float regime on 2 July 1997. This was accompanied by a sharp devaluation of the Thai baht and contagion on the currencies of neighbouring countries. One after another, Thailand, Indonesia and South Korea had to seek financial support from the International Monetary Fund (IMF). Sharp currency depreciation aggravated the bad-debt problem facing east Asian banks, which in turn found it difficult to raise funds in international capital markets. The resulting credit crunch problem, together with austerity measures implemented to reduce trade deficits, sharply depressed economic growth in the region.

The currency crisis took place against a background of a sharp depreciation of the yen since mid-1995, growing competition with China in international markets, and massive capital flows into and subsequently out of the region. A rigid exchange-rate system and premature capital-market opening constrained Asian governments' ability to cope with this rapidly changing international environment. The following lessons should therefore be learnt from the crisis. First, pegging to the dollar may no longer be consistent with macroeconomic stability in the Asian countries and more attention should be paid to stability against the currencies of major competitors, such as the Japanese yen and the Chinese yuan. Second, a developing country should not liberalize capital-account transactions at too early a stage when banks' risk appraisal is inadequate and monetary control is difficult. Third, to prevent the occurrence of similar crises in the future Asian countries should maintain sound economic fundamentals, including a healthy level of foreign-exchange reserves. Finally, further international cooperation among monetary authorities is needed to contain the contagion effect.

The currency crisis in Asia has cast doubt over the sustainability of the east Asian miracle. However, there are good reasons to remain optimistic about the region's economic future. While short-term economic growth largely depends on demand-side factors, long-term growth is determined mainly by supply-side considerations. Although a period of adjustment is inevitable following the crisis, if Asian countries take the appropriate steps to address the structural problems facing them, high economic growth can still be achieved in the longer term. This is because the basic factors contributing to the Asian miracle – high savings rates, heavy investment in human resources and the market-friendly stance of economic policy – are not likely to change with the crisis.

C.H. KWAN
NOMURA RESEARCH INSTITUTE, TOKYO

Further reading

Abegglen, J.C. (1994) *Sea Change: Pacific Asia as the New World Industrial Center*, New York: Free Press. (An analysis of the emergence of Pacific Asia as an industrial power and the implications for business strategies of multinationals.)

Asian Development Bank *Asian Development Outlook*, Hong Kong: Oxford University Press. (Regular updates of macroeconomic performance of Asian countries, published annually.)

Bergsten, C.F. and Noland, M. (eds) (1993) *Pacific Dynamism and the International Economic System*, Washington, DC: Institute for International Economics. (A collection of papers on economic integration in Asia from a global perspective.)

Far Eastern Economic Review, Hong Kong: Dow Jones & Co. (Comprehensive and in-depth analysis of current political and economic issues in Asia, published weekly.)

Garnaut, R. and Drysdale, P. (eds) (1993) *Asia Pacific Regionalism: Reading in International Economic Relations*, Canberra: The Australia–Japan Research Centre. (Collection of papers on Asia-Pacific economic regionalism and its impact on the international economic system.)

Gibney, F. (1992) *The Pacific Century: America and Asia in a Changing World*, New York:

Scribner. (A historical account of the development of east Asia and ramifications for today's world.)

Krugman, P. (1994) 'The myth of Asia's miracle', *Foreign Affairs* (November/December). (Controversial paper casting doubt over the sustainability of the east Asian miracle.)

Kwan, C.H. (1994) *Economic Interdependence in the Asia-Pacific Region: Towards a Yen Bloc*, New York: Routledge. (An analysis of macroeconomic issues of the east Asian economies viewed from a regional perspective.)

Overholt, W.H. (1993) *The Rise of China: How Economic Reform is Creating a New Superpower*, New York: W.W. Norton & Co. Inc. (A political-economic analysis of China's open-door policy and economic reform and their implications for the global economy.)

World Bank (1993) *The East Asian Miracle*, New York: Oxford University Press. (A comparative study of economic growth and public policy in east Asia.)

See also: ASSOCIATION OF SOUTH-EAST ASIAN ECONOMIES; BUSINESS CULTURE, JAPANESE; BUSINESS STRATEGIES, EAST ASIAN; INTERNATIONAL TRADE AND FOREIGN DIRECT INVESTMENT; MANAGEMENT IN CHINA; MANAGEMENT IN JAPAN; MANAGEMENT IN SOUTH KOREA

Related topics in the IEBM: BUSINESS STRATEGY, JAPANESE; ECONOMIES OF DEVELOPING COUNTRIES; MANAGEMENT IN HONG KONG; MANAGEMENT IN MALAYSIA; MANAGEMENT IN PACIFIC ASIA; MANAGEMENT IN SINGAPORE; MANAGEMENT IN TAIWAN; MANAGEMENT IN THAILAND

Economy of Japan

Overview

Since the end of the Second World War, the Japanese economy has sustained a high rate of economic growth, and by 1990 its per capita income surpassed that of the USA. Factors that contributed to the success of the Japanese economy – especially the role of the government, the role of business groups, and the relationship between management and labour – have been the focus of many articles and books.

The period before the first oil crisis of 1973 is commonly known as the period of high-speed economic growth. During this period Japan maintained a high investment/gross domestic product ratio, while domestic saving levels were also sufficient for high investment to be made possible without the accumulation of foreign debts. Improvement in human capital, developed through a solid education and on-the-job training, was also an important factor for growth.

Industrial policy, in common terminology, is a wide-ranging combination of policies that influence the level and composition of industrial investment and production. In Japan it is generally interpreted as the nurturing of specific industries through subsidized (policy) loans from the development bank: for example, in the 1950s and 1960s, the coal, steel, shipbuilding and petrochemicals industries. Imports were strictly controlled until the early 1960s, and raw materials and intermediate goods, as opposed to consumption goods, were favoured.

Japanese monetary and fiscal policy was flexible but prudent enough to produce high growth without excessive inflation (except in 1974–6). During the 1950s and 1960s, monetary policy maintained a fixed exchange rate. However, in 1974, in order to control inflation, tight monetary policy was introduced. Inflation was quickly reduced, at the cost of a sharp decline in output. After 1975, monetary policy focused on keeping the inflation rate low.

Fiscal policy was fairly conservative in the 1950s and 1960s. The budget was essentially balanced every year until 1965, when government construction bonds (for infrastructure projects) were issued. Pure deficit-financing bonds have been issued as of 1975. Government deficits grew rapidly in the second half of the 1970s, but fiscal austerity during the 1980s reduced the issue of deficit-financing bonds to zero by 1990. However, the slump in the first half of the 1990s, forced the government to issue new deficit-financing bonds.

Economic institutions and structural configuration are important in evaluating performance. Some critics argue that Japanese institutions and business practices are unique among the industrial countries, although close examination has revealed similarities with the USA and Europe. Various forms of loose relationships between corporations (*keiretsu*) have been of particular interest to researchers.

The yen has appreciated with respect to the US dollar since 1971. In mid-1994, the yen became 100 to one dollar, and then in the spring of 1995, the value reached 80 yen per dollar. In less than a quarter of a century, the value of the yen against the dollar more than quadrupled (less than one quarter of 360 yen now purchases one dollar). Even with this appreciation of the yen, Japan has maintained large external surpluses throughout the 1980s and 1990s, except for brief periods immediately after the two oil crises.

The Japanese economy in the second half of the 1980s was known as the bubble period – sharp increases in asset prices, such as stock prices and land prices. In many places land prices tripled or quadrupled over a few years. However, asset prices declined in the first half of the 1990s, and by 1995, price levels had returned to pre-bubble levels. This had various consequences, including the appearance of a large number of non-performing loans among the commercial banks.

1   High economic growth, 1950–71

Economic growth

The Japanese economy experienced high economic growth from the beginning of the 1950s up to the first oil crisis in 1973, average economic growth rates exceeding 10 per cent. Before 1973, a reduction of growth to around a 3 per cent annual rate, a level which was considered to be reasonable in other industrial countries, was judged as a recession. Strong growth was mainly driven by a strong demand from investment and exports on the aggregate demand side, made possible by increasing productive capacity on the aggregate supply side. The ratio of investment to gross domestic product (GDP) had been fluctuating at around 20 per cent, a level considerably higher than other industrialized countries. The quality of the labour force was improved by increasing levels of education and by extensive on-the-job training. However, empirical studies tend to find that rapid growth in Japan can been mainly attributed to the rapid accumulation of capital and fast technological progress. About half the growth cannot be explained by labour or capital contribution and is thus attributable to technological progress and better usage of existing resources (see MANAGEMENT IN JAPAN).

The Japanese household savings rate has been the highest among the OECD (Organization for Economic Cooperation and Development) countries. The savings rate increased from about 15 per cent in the mid-1950s to above 20 per cent in the beginning of the 1970s. The high savings rate during this period helped to keep investment high because capital had to be found domestically. Since then, the household saving rate in Japan has been declining, now standing at around 15 per cent. In the USA, in contrast, savings rates have been about 5 per cent, and those in Europe about 8 per cent in the UK and France, 12 per cent in Germany and 18 per cent in Italy.

Economic growth was so successful it became a 'motto' of economic policies in the 1960s. In 1960, the then Prime Minister Ikeda initiated a ten-year economic plan for 'income-doubling', a strong policy of support for high economic growth: for example, infrastructure investment in highways, bullet trains and industrial ports increased sharply. Although many critics were sceptical about the possibility of doubling national income in ten years (that is, an average of 7 per cent growth for ten years), the Japanese economy in fact achieved this goal even quicker.

Macroeconomic policy

During the period from 1949, when the value of the yen was fixed at 360 yen per dollar, to 1971, when the Bretton Woods regime collapsed, Japan tended to run trade deficits when an economic boom occurred. When trade deficits occur, the central bank must intervene to buy or sell foreign exchange at the fixed rate. With capital flow restricted in the 1950s and 1960s, trade surpluses meant an increase in foreign reserves and trade deficits a decrease. Hence, monetary restraint was applied whenever the trade account deficit persisted. Japanese macroeconomic policy was thus operating under the constraint of the fixed exchange rate system.

Japan was running chronic current account deficits in the 1950s and 1960s. Business booms during this period tended to rapidly increase imports, thus sending the trade balance into deficit and drawing down foreign reserves. In order to maintain the fixed exchange rate, the monetary authorities had to tighten policy to stop a boom. Towards the end of the 1960s, even during the boom, trade balances did not turn to deficits. Japanese trade surpluses and refusal, along with Germany, to appreciate its currency within the Bretton Woods system, played a part in the demise of the system in 1971.

Although the decade of 'income-doubling' was regarded as a success, there was a brief period of trouble in the middle. The year 1965 was regarded as a severe recession. The growth rate suddenly dropped to 5 per cent from an average of 10 per cent growth for the decade. Financial troubles (a large securities firm came close to bankruptcy) magnified the trouble. This was the year in which the government decided to issue the so-called 'construction bonds' to supplement revenue, and continue spending on infrastructure. Prior to this, fiscal policy had been conservative, in the sense that the budget was balanced every year without issuing long-term government bonds.

Industrial policy

Some economists regard industrial policy, in addition to prudent macroeconomic policy, as responsible for Japan's success in economic growth and development. According to the conventional view, industrial policy encouraged 'sunrise' industries – industries that would flourish in the coming years. The theory is as follows. When an industry is in an 'infant' stage, it is better to nurture domestic firms through protection by limiting entry to the industry or by maintaining high tariffs: domestic firms thus capture domestic markets. The Ministry of International Trade and Industry (MITI) carefully monitor demand and supply projections and approve the expansion of capacity so that profit margins are guaranteed. New facilities are often helped by low interest-rate loans through the Development Bank. By taking advantage of scale economies and profits, the protected industries will quickly reach a stage that is internationally competitive in producing quality goods with at cost efficient prices. Firms are then encouraged to export. Export subsidies, for example in the form of export insurance, are provided. By expanding

markets to other countries, the firms continue to grow. How many industries fit this traditional mould is debatable. Steel and coal were designated as priority industries in the late 1940s. Later, in the 1950s and 1960s, shipbuilding, petrochemicals, oil-refining and aluminium were encouraged.

Steel and shipbuilding seem to be the success stories of such a policy, Japan becoming one of the leading countries in these industries in the 1980s. However, not all industries designated as important in industrial policy succeeded. The coal industry became a 'sunset' industry, soon after oil replaced coal for various uses and cheap coal became available on international markets. The aluminium industry was hampered from the beginning by the high electricity costs in Japan. More interesting cases are the motor and electronics industries, which succeeded without the benefit of an advantageous industrial policy. Although cars and televisions had been protected by relatively high tariffs in the 1950s, they did not any receive any overt subsidies or particularly favourable entry restrictions. Indeed, when the MITI tried to merge some automobile companies in the early 1960s in order to achieve 'scale economies' by limiting competition, it was opposed by the motor industries. The MITI thus failed in its attempt to follow a traditional-style industrial policy. Now, a few decades later, most of the automobile companies (Toyota, Nissan, Honda, Subaru and Isuzu) have become winners in the world markets.

The Japanese electronics industry – from radio to black-and-white televisions, to colour televisions, to video recorders and finally to computers – is also one of the most important players in the world market. Sony, Matsushita (Panasonic) and Toshiba are household names in many countries. However, Sony and Matsushita each basically grew from a shop owned by a single individual to the status of a multinational company in a few decades, without the help of subsidized loans or entry restrictions. Hence, economists are divided in assessing the benefits and costs of industrial policy. Proponents cite industries with successful results; and sceptics cite examples of failure.

For better or worse, industrial policy was practised in the 1950s and 1960s. Since foreign exchange was scarce, import licences could work as a policy tool. Capital was scarce and a large pool of money in postal savings could be used as funds for policy (subsidized) loans. In the 1970s, however, the environment changed, with the scope for industrial policy becoming extremely limited in the 1980s.

2 The oil shock and its aftermath, 1971–5

The eventful five years from 1971 to 1975 brought many changes to Japan. The fixed exchange rate regime yielded to the floating exchange rate regime. This meant that the guide to monetary policy had to be changed. Oil prices quadrupled in a matter of several months from October 1973. Industrial policy, which had promoted heavy and chemical industries, needed a new direction. The Japanese economy, after high economic growth for twenty years, was at a crossroads.

On 15 August 1971, the dollar convertibility to gold was suspended and the dollar was unilaterally depreciated against major currencies, including the yen. This fundamental change in the foreign exchange regime was considered to be a surprise by many policy makers in Japan. In December, in an effort to return to the fixed exchange rate system, the Smithsonian agreement was struck, introducing a new parity (308 yen per dollar, an appreciation of 17 per cent from the Bretton Woods parity). In the spring of 1973, after the transition period, the yen and the European currencies became free floating.

In 1972, monetary policy was considerably relaxed, partly to prevent further yen appreciation (from the Smithsonian rate). Some policy makers thought even inflation should be tolerated in order to stop yen appreciation. Another reason for easy monetary policy was the initiative by Mr Tanaka (who became Prime Minister in July 1972) to 'reconstruct' Japan, which included large public works programmes to build bullet-train and highway networks. Inflation pressure built up in the first half of 1973. By summer of 1973, the inflation rate crept up to more than 10 per cent.

The first oil crisis occurred in October 1973. The oil crisis brought severe inflation and recession, a combination called 'stagflation'. The oil embargo from OPEC (Organization of Petroleum Exporting Countries) in October 1973 and subsequent sharp increases in oil prices threw industrial economies into chaos. The Japanese economy was hardest hit. In 1974, inflation reached an annual rate of around 30 per cent and real GDP growth rate was negative. In order to fight inflation and inflationary expectation, monetary policy was dramatically tightened in 1974. Although growth was halted, inflation continued feeding itself through inflationary expectation. Inflation did not fall below 10 per cent until late 1975, or below 5 per cent until 1978.

3 Stable economic growth, 1975–85

In retrospect, a trend growth rate shifted sharply downwards at around the time of the oil crisis, 1973–4. The average growth rate from 1974 to 1990 was about 4 per cent, less than half that of the preceding fifteen years. A major reason for this reduction was the fact that the technological gap between the West and Japan narrowed, so that Japan could not simply import technology to produce competitive goods, but needed to spend more on research and development. As shipbuilding, steel and cars became the leading industries in output and exports, it became difficult to expand on the previous scale. Rapid industrialization also brought pollution in the 1960s. Social consciousness concerning the environment was raised as a result of several highly publicized pollution cases. Anti-pollution investment had to be increased throughout the 1970s.

A severe recession followed the first oil crisis, but only a mild recession followed the second oil crisis.

Monetary policy

After the economy shifted to a floating exchange rate system, a shortage of foreign reserves was no longer a concern for monetary policy. Monetary policy was freed from the obligation to preserve the fixed exchange rate. However, rapid yen appreciation became a major concern because of its adverse effect on export industries. The monetary authorities viewed the inflation experience of 1973–5 as a major policy failure. The Bank of Japan thus started to look for a better indicator, or intermediate target, for monetary policy. This was the monetary aggregate (M2), which has been emphasized since 1978, when its forecasts were first regularly announced.

In fact, the Bank of Japan successfully reduced the monetary growth rate gradually from the mid-1970s to 1987. As the rate was lowered, the inflation rate was also lowered. Whether this fact is proof of a successful implementation of monetarism is a matter of debate. Some researchers believe that monetary policy in the floating (post-1973) period reacted to the exchange rate: yen appreciation prompts intervention (selling yen, buying dollars) which, without sterilization, results in an expanding domestic money supply, which in turn lowers interest rates.

Fiscal policy

Deficit-financing bonds (that is, bonds to fill the fiscal deficits rather than for construction projects) were first issued in 1975, as an exception to the fiscal law, in order to combat the severe recession of 1974. The amount of deficit bonds increased quickly from 1975 to 1980. By 1980, the proportion of debt financing in Japan was one of the largest among the OECD countries. From 1980 to 1990, new issues of debt-financing bonds were gradually curtailed, finally reaching zero in 1990.

In general, budget sizes can be shown to have responded to business cycles; namely, recession prompted the government to form a bigger budget, even within the fiscal year, through supplementary budgets. In this sense, there is some evidence that fiscal policy was conducted to stabilize the economy.

The Japanese fiscal authority has more than just tax revenues with which to determine resource allocations. The Fiscal Investment and Loan Programme (FILP) is a Ministry of Finance administered programme, mainly funded by postal savings, which is loaned out to finance and subsidize public works and other government investment projects. It can be viewed as a capital budget. There are several special accounts which are financed by FILP, subsidized by general accounts (tax money) and/or funded by user fees.

Major national tax revenues were previously taken from personal income tax and corporate tax. Consumption tax, which is the name for a Japanese version of value added tax, was introduced in 1989. A uniform rate of 3 per cent is imposed on the value added at each stage of distribution. With the introduction of consumption tax, some selected excise taxes and transportation taxes were eliminated.

4 A bubble economy and a burst bubble, 1985–95

Stock prices and land prices soared in the second half of the 1980s. Stock prices (measured in Nikkei 225) tripled in the four years from 1985 to 1989, while land prices (measured in residential land in six large cities) more than doubled in the four years from 1986 to 1990. Consumer and wholesale price indices remained stable. However, any euphoria in the market disappeared in the 1990s, when prices declined sharply. Stock prices plummeted from a peak of about 39,000 at the end of 1989 to 15,000 in August 1992, while the stock market lost more than 60 per cent of its value in two and half years. Land prices also started to decline from 1990. Compared to the peak of 1990, the typical land price in Tokyo fell by half in a few years.

Although several explanations have been offered for asset price increases in the second half of the 1980s (lower interest rates and rosy expectation of renewed growth), 'selffulfilling' expectation played an important role. Price/earning ratios increased sharply, so that price increases were justified only by further price increases. The term for this in the finance literature is a 'bubble', so the economy in this period has been dubbed a 'bubble economy'. It was only a matter of time before the bubble would burst.

One of the consequences of the bubble and its bursting was that many suffered substantial loss in their balance sheets. In particular, real estate companies and developers suffered from bad assets, for which they could not find buyers or use in development projects. Many failed to make interest payments to banks, with the result that banks' balance sheets deteriorated with non-performing loans. In 1993 and 1994, bank lending failed to grow. Several banks essentially failed and were absorbed by other banks.

5 Industrial organization

Japanese industries are said to have a unique structure, the so-called *keiretsu* (company network), characterized by long-term business relationships, personal exchange, lending and borrowing on favourable terms and cross-share holdings. There are two kinds of *keiretsu*; horizontal (across different industries) and vertical (parts suppliers and a manufacturer, or a manufacturer and distributors). Both are characterized by long-term business relationships and cross-share holdings (see *KEIRETSU*).

The Big Six enterprise group – Mitsubishi, Mitsui, Sumitomo, Ikkan (Dai-ichi-Kangyo), Fuyo and Sanwa – are the most prominent, traditional, horizontal *keiretsu* groups. Each group, with a large bank at the core, contains manufacturing firms in different industries and some service-sector firms. The firms are linked through informal financial and trading arrangements. For example, the Mitsubishi group is most often defined by participation in the 'Presidents' club of Mitsubishi. There are twenty-nine firms in the group (as of October 1993), including financial institutions (Mitsubishi Bank, Mitsubishi Trust, Meiji Life, Tokyo Marine and Fire), trading companies (Mitsubishi Corp.), shipbuilding and other heavy manufacturing companies (Mitsubishi Heavy Industries) and automobile companies (Mitsubishi Motors).

The Mitsubishi Bank holds about 4 to 5 per cent of the equities of most of the Mitsubishi group companies. In return, Mitsubishi group firms combined hold a quarter of Mitsubishi Bank's equities. Other pairs of Mitsubishi companies also hold equity shares each other. Although only a few Mitsubishi companies are majority-owned by other Mitsubishi companies, about a quarter of total Mitsubishi firms' total equities are held by other firms in the group. In addition to cross-holding of equity shares, Mitsubishi manufacturing firms tend to borrow more from the Mitsubishi financial institutions than from other financial institutions.

Each group tries to extend and diversify its sectoral spans. Hence, all six groups end up having big banks, insurance companies, trading firms and major manufacturing corporations. Horizontal *keiretsu* rarely act in an oligopolistic manner, competing fiercely with each other.

There are several theories concerning the role of the horizontal *keiretsu*. One theory emphasizes the bank's role in monitoring management's effort. A bank can monitor management's effort through lending screening and by planting board members in the management team. Another theory limits the positive role of banks when a company becomes financially weak. Since a bank holds both equities and lending, it can act without conflict of interests as a source of (secured) loans and (unsecured) equities. Other researchers think that across-industry grouping is good for synergy – promoting externalities among different industries. Synergy produced by linking different firms is, however, difficult to quantify.

A typical vertical *keiretsu* group is formed by a manufacturer and its various parts suppliers. A vertical *keiretsu* can also be formed through a distribution channel, from a manufacturer to wholesale agents, to retailers. For example, Toyota has a group of parts suppliers – many small-scale family businesses and a few large stock-exchange-listed companies – with which Toyota cooperates in developing specifications in advance of mass production. Suppliers are chosen after product samples have been through various quality control tests.

Quality control is a major positive aspect of vertical *keiretsu*, and is made possible by the long-term relationship between the various organizations. Trust, reputation and long-term commitment play an important role. The 'lean production system', cutting down the level of inventory and asking the parts suppliers for just-in-time delivery, became a hallmark of Japanese production systems. The manufacturer values these efforts by parts suppliers, and rewards them with a implicit guarantee of continuing orders for many years.

Product distribution channels are sometimes controlled by manufacturers. A network of dedicated distributors may often be created to deal only with a particular brand. For example, Matsushita (Panasonic) stores deal exclusively with Matsushita products, and Sony stores likewise deal only with Sony products.

6 Labour relations

It is striking that Japan has maintained a very low unemployment rate over the last thirty-five years. The unemployment rate was between 1 and 2 per cent in the 1950s and 1960s, and between 2 and 3 per cent since the mid-1970s. This performance is attributed to many institutional features in the labour market as well as a strong macroeconomic performance.

One such feature is the conventional stereotyped description of the Japanese labour market. Japanese workers, under the commitment of 'lifetime employment' at one company, accept any job assignments, and the seniority wage structure ensures that compensations are skewed towards the later stage of life. Unions cooperate with management. Stable employment and compensation make it possible to achieve high productivity increase and low unemployment.

However, this stereotyped view needs to be examined carefully. First, lifetime employment is limited to workers in large-size firms and comprises only about 30 per cent of the total number of male workers. The rest of the workers change jobs frequently, and go in and out of the labour market. Second, even for those who hold lifetime jobs, annual total compensation and working hours are quite flexible. Lifetime earnings vary across individuals of the same worker group, reflecting merit and overtime. Third, the relationship between labour unions and management became more cooperative only after the 1970s. In the 1950s and 1960s, some unions were quite confrontational, reflecting the political–ideological divide in Japan at the time.

7 Is Japan unique?

Between the mid-1980s and mid-1990s, trade conflicts between the USA and Japan became increasingly bitter. The USA complained that the Japanese markets were not open to foreign goods (in particular US goods), and pressed for measures to guarantee 'market access'. Many officials in the US government, in particular United States Trade Representatives (USTR) have argued that the Japanese economy is unique in that, compared with other industrial countries, manufactured goods imports into Japan are low, as is direct investment. The USA demanded, with varying degrees of success, increased imports into Japan of semiconductors, supercomputers, satellites and cars. US proponents of the cause argued that the Japanese markets are structurally closed to foreign goods and capital, citing *keiretsu* and labour practices as examples. As Japan is regarded as unique, US critics argued, a unique approach to the problem, such as demanding 'measurable results' of market shares, can be justified. Thus, the semiconductor agreement had a foreign products' market share of 20 per cent in Japan as its target. The Japanese government became increasingly resistant to demands for numerical targets, as typified by the semiconductor agreement, partly because they were used as a basis for sanctions and partly because of the realization that Japanese 'uniqueness' is not necessarily a barrier to foreign goods and services but a sign of efficient business relationships.

Defenders of the Japanese argued that the current account position of one country is a reflection of saving and investment, and that the current account deficits of the USA were primarily a result of domestic economic performance, especially the low savings rate. A particularly bitter dispute over the access to the motor and auto parts markets in Japan, negotiated from July 1993 to June 1995, highlighted the nature of the conflict. Japan argued that the principal reason that US and other foreign car makers had not penetrated the market was that they did not produce cars fit for Japan's narrow roads and left-hand-drive system, nor for its consumer tastes, while the USA believed that there was a structural barrier.

The issue highlights the question of whether Japan's economy is in some way unique, in terms of both production and demand. As this entry has shown, Japan's economy developed under some unusual circumstances, and has also been strongly affected by the business culture and environment of Japan (see BUSINESS CULTURE, JAPANESE). The misunderstandings between Japan and its Western trading partners stem at least in part from the highly different economic circumstances which each of them face.

TAKATOSHI ITO
HITOTSUBASHI UNIVERSITY
INTERNATIONAL MONETARY FUND

Further reading

Ito, T. (1992) *Japanese Economy*, Cambridge, MA: MIT Press. (General introduction to the Japanese economy. Designed to be an undergraduate textbook, with full references to advanced studies. Easy to understand analyses of economic phenomena.)

Komiya, R., Okuno, M. and Suzumura, K. (1988) *The Industrial Policy of Japan*, San Diego, CA: Academic Press. (Comprehensive study on industrial policy, theory and practices.)

Kosai, Y. (1986) *The Era of High-Speed Growth*, Tokyo: University of Tokyo Press. (Focus on the Japanese economy up to the first oil crisis.)

Nakamura, T. (1995) *The Postwar Japanese Economy*, 2nd edn, Tokyo: University of Tokyo Press. (Good overview and description of the post-war macroeconomic situation.)

Yamamura, K. and Yasuba, Y. (eds) (1987) *The Political Economy of Japan*, vol. 1, Stanford, CT: Stanford University Press. (Collection of papers on selected topics. Knowledge of intermediate economics required.)

See also: BUSINESS CULTURE, JAPANESE; *KEIRETSU*; MANAGEMENT IN JAPAN

Related topics in the IEBM: ACCOUNTING IN JAPAN; BANKING IN JAPAN; BUSINESS HISTORY, JAPANESE; BUSINESS STRATEGY, JAPANESE; COMMITMENT IN JAPAN; ENVIRONMENTAL MANAGEMENT; FINANCIAL MARKETS, JAPANESE; INDUSTRIAL RELATIONS IN JAPAN; JAPANIZATION; MANAGEMENT EDUCATION IN JAPAN; MANAGEMENT IN JAPAN; MANAGEMENT IN PACIFIC ASIA; TECHNOLOGY DIFFUSION IN JAPAN; TOTAL QUALITY MANAGEMENT

Keiretsu

1 Historical background
2 Structure
3 The relevance of *keiretsu*
4 The future

Overview

The Japanese management system has developed in the twentieth century based on three pillars – state-led growth, industry–finance links and industry structure. The last of these three pillars, industry structure, developed around large conglomerate forms of business organization, known as *zaibatsu*. Since 1945 they have become better known as *keiretsu*.

The *keiretsu* member companies act as mutual support groups, providing markets and financial support for one another. They have been of interest to western practitioners as an alternative form of business organization to that prevalent in Anglo-Saxon capitalism. Recently, they have become central to a political debate on the nature of free trade and competition. There has also been speculation as to the future of these forms of business organization as the Japanese economy matures and internationalizes, and as it has stagnated domestically.

1 Historical background

The large Japanese business groupings, *keiretsu*, have their origins in the nineteenth century (Kikkawa 1995; Whitehill 1991). In particular, they developed as Japan underwent industrial revolution after 1868. An understanding of this industrialization process is necessary in order to place these industrial groupings in context. In 1868, after the death of the Tokagawa emperor, members of the leading class created a strong central government through the restoration of the Meiji line. In order to protect Japan from western military incursions it became apparent that Japan would need to militarize via industrial strength. Japanese industrialization took a different form from that of Anglo-Saxon capitalism, in which the State played a secondary role to capitalist barons. Instead, the State initiated a path of key-industry development (railways, mining and ship-building), using imported western ideas and technology gained from extensive 'learning missions' to the USA, the UK and Germany.

During the same period the social structure of Japan underwent rapid change. The Shoguns and Samurai, the former elite, lost power to the emerging merchant classes, who had previously been at the bottom of the social strata. In the 1880s these merchant classes were co-opted by the political elite, who took advantage of the State divesting itself of its holdings in the key industries. The new owners were elite merchant families who bought at extremely low prices. These families were to become the centres of vast industrial combines known as *zaibatsu*, of which four dominated – Sumitomo, Yasuda, Mitsui and Mitsubishi (see MITSUBISHI HEAVY INDUSTRIES LTD; MITSUI AND CO., LTD).

This arrangement was to have two long-term implications for Japanese capitalism, and for business structures and systems in particular (see MANAGEMENT IN JAPAN). First, there were close personal links between political and business elites, resulting in a patronage system which favoured the established organizations. Second, these industrial combines, which represented oligopolistic power, were tolerated and even encouraged as a source of competitive strength, once again shoring up the established system. This situation was in contrast to that in the West, where there was strong resistance to the idea of cartels.

The *zaibatsu* provided the engine for pre-war Japanese industrial growth. In the late 1930s, despite some resistance, the *zaibatsu* became involved in Japan's military–industrial complex. As a result, in the 1940s they came under considerable scrutiny from the US occupation forces, because of both their close links with the military and the concentration of economic and industrial power in the cartels. The occupation forces ordered them to disband and their leaders were barred from participating in industry.

By the 1950s, however, the former *zaibatsu* had begun to re-emerge (Yamamura and Yasuda 1987), albeit in a somewhat diluted form. The USA acquiesced to this for two reasons: in the hope that Japan would be a close ally in the Cold War and due to US reliance upon Japanese companies to supply US military in the Korean War.

Three of the four pre-war *zaibatsu* re-emerged: Mitsubishi, Mitsui and Sumitomo. These were to form the core of the enterprise form known as the *keiretsu*. The nature of the enterprise groupings had changed, however (Aoki 1987). The strong family control over the enterprises had shifted to new managers with different loyalties, an occurrence described by Aoki as 'a managerial revolution from above'.

In addition to these former *zaibatsu*, new types of enterprise were emerging. First were the groups centred around the large city banks, of which three were prominent – Samwa, Daiichi Kangyo and Fuji. To give an indication of the power of these groups, in the 1980s they controlled 60 per cent of Japan's total assets (Abbeglen and Stalk 1985). Another group emerged around the new companies which appeared in the 1950s. These included Toyota, Honda, Matsushita, Sony, Canon and Seiko (see MATSUSHITA, K.; MORITA, A.; TOYODA FAMILY).

Today these three groups – the former *zaibatsu*, the bank-based groups and the newly established groups – are known collectively as *keiretsu* (Dore and Whittaker 1994). They usually take one of three forms, as indicated below.

2 Structure

Horizontal *keiretsu*

The horizontal *keiretsu* is the form most often taken by the former *zaibatsu* and the bank-based organizations. Each group consists of between twenty and fifty member companies, including industrial and commercial firms: Mitsubishi, for example, comprises some twenty-nine companies, including Mitsubishi Bank, Mitsubishi Electric, Mitsubishi Motor, Asahi Glass, Kirin Beer and NYK Shipping. These groupings are unique in that there is no holding company nor any controlling stock interests (these were prohibited by monopoly laws). As Whitehill notes: 'These groups are loose federations of independent companies bound together over a long period of time because of mutual interests and the many benefits of mutual cooperation' (1991: 96).

While there is no overall controlling interest *per se*, there are considerable cross-holdings between member companies; 38 per cent in the case of Mitsubishi (Dawkins 1994). There is also a fairly high degree of inter-group sales (14 per cent at Mitsubishi). Coordination is achieved through information sharing at monthly meetings of member companies' presidents and top officials. Member companies also favour other *keiretsu* members: Mitsubishi Electric, for example, is Mitsubishi Motor's second biggest supplier. Patronage tends to depend on pricing structure and quality.

Organizations belonging to the bank-based group have their capital needs met by the bank with which they are linked. Historically, this has proven crucial in terms of the high debt–equity ratio typically found in Japanese companies. It has also enabled Japanese firms to take a long-term view with regard to investment decisions.

Vertical (or 'supplier') *keiretsu*

The second organizational form is the vertical (or supplier) *keiretsu*. These consist of one major company surrounded by a complex constellation of small and medium-sized affiliate and associate companies. The latter are usually subsidiaries of, or subcontractors to, the parent company. The parent company may thus hold a financial interest in the smaller company or the relationship may exist because the smaller firm is a major supplier to the parent. In either case the relationship is a long-term collaborative one, such as has been the hallmark of stable and efficient buyer–supplier relationships in Japan. The relationship is historically specific, developing in the 1950s when Japan experienced a shortage of key components and skilled workers. Such an arrangement tied in suppliers to major Japanese manufacturing companies and was (and is) particularly prevalent in the motor and electronics industries (Cusumano 1985; Imai 1994).

The buyer–supplier relationship is of mutual benefit to both parties. For the smaller organization, there is a guaranteed stable market and technology transfer from the parent group. The parent organization benefits from a long-term relationship with a dedicated supplier providing quality components.

The benefits to the parent organization go beyond this, however. There are considerable cost savings from contracting out work: wage rates are considerably lower in small firms and small-firm workers do not receive the benefits of core large-firm workers, such as lifetime employment and seniority wage systems. In this sense the large firms use the smaller firms as a buffer against cyclical changes in product demand. The large firms also use the small firms as an extended internal labour market. Workers are often 'seconded' from the large to smaller firms at times of low demand, transferred permanently and typically retired at 55–60 years of age.

Distribution *keiretsu*

The third, and perhaps least known, form of *keiretsu* is the distribution *keiretsu* (Flath 1994; Sheard 1994). They are known as such because the distribution division plays a key role in the expansion of the overall group, and structurally they are similar to the supplier *keiretsu*. However, whereas the supplier *keiretsu* are concerned with upstream activities, distribution *keiretsu* focus on downstream activities. Less attention has been paid to the distribution *keiretsu* due to this similarity in form, the supplier *keiretsu* having been analysed in detail in the just-in-time literature, as well as in the new institutional economics.

The distribution *keiretsu* consist of a parent firm and a set of firms comprising its distribution network, affiliated dealer and chain-store networks. Shimotani's (1995) study of Matsushita Electric's distribution *keiretsu* is illustrative of this type of organization (see MATSUSHITA, K.). Initiated as a response to intense domestic competition between Japanese electronics producers, the distribution *keiretsu* have become less powerful since the 1970s due to the growth of independent large-scale stores. However, while this form of *keiretsu* has been neglected in comparison to the horizontal and vertical supplier *keiretsu*, it has been an important focus for trade disputes (as will be illustrated later).

3 The relevance of *keiretsu*

Keiretsu have been of interest to academics, practitioners and policy-makers for various reasons. At a policy level these business organizations have been central in debates about competition policy in international trade. They were, for example, at the centre of the agenda in the US–Japan Structural Adjustment Talks from 1989: first, because the *keiretsu* are anti-competitive in that they facilitate cartels and restrictive practices (the main reason for the abolition of the *zaibatsu* in the 1950s); second, because the horizontal *keiretsu* are immune to hostile bids and less prone to bankruptcy than comparable US- or UK-owned firms.

The existence of cartels is not the only issue of interest: market access must also be considered. The nature of links between member companies of the horizontal *keiretsu*, and between parent companies, subsidiaries, suppliers and distributors in the vertical *keiretsu* is said to limit the access of competitors, particularly foreign ones. It is not coincidental, for example, that US motor manufacturers (and component suppliers) have been especially critical of vertical production *keiretsu*. Similarly, Western finished goods are said to be prohibited from entry into the Japanese market because of the links between manufacturers, distributors and retailers in vertical distribution *keiretsu*.

A second area of interest in these business organizations is the field of industrial organization and policy. In the field of economics – particularly the new institutional economics – there is growing interest in the groups as lying somewhere between the traditional notions of markets and hierarchies. In particular, *keiretsu* are of interest because of the industrial partnership that exists in Japan between the state bureaucracy, in the form of the Ministry of Trade and Industry (MITI), the government and industry (both the *keiretsu* and their management associations, Zaikai and Keidanren). The close links between industrial capital and finance capital are also of interest, engendering long-term partnerships, in contrast to the short-termism of Anglo-Saxon capitalism (Dore 1986).

Another field of interest is in the realm of production organization. Vertical production *keiretsu* have been the focus of considerable attention for their buyer–supplier links and, in particular, their links to just-in-time and total quality management. Such close links between the parent group and the subsidiaries, affiliates and suppliers have led to long-term partnership arrangements between the parties, resulting in lower prices, enhanced quality and a greater degree of technology transfer (Sako 1992; Whittaker 1997).

4 The future

In common with many other features of the Japanese management system, the *keiretsu* system is historically specific. There are now indications of a weakening of ties. For the most part this is a response to the globalization of markets, the emergence of Japan as a high-factor-cost country and the subsequent internationalization of the Japanese economy (see GLOBALIZATION).

The trend towards company individualism has manifested itself in a variety of ways. First, the larger Japanese groupings are entering into a series of joint ventures and strategic alliances with western groups, particularly in the fields of high-technology electronics (semiconductors and computers) and

aerospace. Second, there has been a decline in the size of cross-share holdings, particularly in the manufacturing sector.

The third major change has been in patterns of purchasing, as a response both to internationalization and the high value of the yen. There are indications that overseas operations, for example, are more likely to buy from foreign-owned companies and from Japanese-owned non-*keiretsu* members. Japanese-based producers are also purchasing from non-Japanese, often Asian, suppliers because of cost factors. Japanese supplier companies, meanwhile, are loosening their ties with the parent company, even where there is an ownership stake. This has the advantage for the supplier of broadening the scope to amortize research and development costs. This is particularly pronounced in the motor industry. Consequently, the strict hierarchies that exist in vertical *keiretsu* are being blurred.

The *keiretsu*, however, remain a strong and integral part of the Japanese system. Despite slow growth and recession in Japan in the 1990s following the bursting of the 'bubble boom', they have remained essentially intact as a form of corporate governance. Moreover, the associated personnel practices have also remained intact. However, their links with the other two members of the 'iron triangle' (the bureaucracy and the political elite) have been eroded as the power of the two other groups has waned, heralding the demise of 'Japan Inc.' (Berggren and Nomura 1997).

Keiretsu, therefore, encapsulate both continuity and gradual change in the Japanese system. Two developments in the 1990s pose further challenges. First, the east Asian economic crisis poses a threat as east Asia is the prime Japanese export market, as it has been a focus for Japanese production and due to heavy Japanese bank lending in the region. Second, the crisis of the Japanese domestic system potentially poses an even greater longer-term threat to the Japanese domestic economy, and hence to the *keiretsu*.

JONATHAN MORRIS
CARDIFF UNIVERSITY

Further reading

(References cited in the text marked *)

* Abbeglen, J.C. and Stalk, G. (1985) *Kaisha: The Japanese Corporation*, New York: Basic Books. (Excellent introduction to the development and functions of the modern Japanese corporation.)
* Aoki, M. (1987) 'The formation of Japanese management 1945–65', in K. Yamamura and Y. Yasuda (eds) *The Political Economy of Japan*, vol. 1, *The Domestic Transformation*, Stanford, CA: Stanford University Press. (This study provides an account of the development of the Japanese system in the post-Second World War era.)
* Berggren, C. and Nomura, M. (1997) *The Resilience of Corporate Japan: New Competitive Strategies and Personnel Practices*, London: Paul Chapman Publishing.
* Cusumano, M. (1985) *The Japanese Automobile Industry: Technology and Management at Nissan and Toyota*, Cambridge, MA: Harvard University Press. (A study of the development of the two major Japanese automobile producers.)
* Dawkins, W. (1994) 'Loosening of the corporate web', *Financial Times*, 11 November: 15. (Contemporary data on changes in Japan's industrial structure.)
* Dore, R. (1986) *Flexible Rigidities: Industrial Policy and Structural Adjustment in the Japanese Economy 1971–80*, Stanford, CA: Stanford University Press. (Analysis of industrial and economic policy in Japan in the 1970s.)
* Dore, R. and Whittaker, M. (1994) 'Introduction', in K. Imai and R. Komiya (eds) *Business Enterprise in Japan*, Cambridge, MA: MIT Press. (Good definitional source for the main forms of business enterprise in Japan.)
* Flath, D. (1994) 'Keiretsu shareholding ties: antitrust issues', *Contemporary Economic Policy* 12: 24–36. (Empirical study and analysis of *keiretsu* trading issues.)
* Imai, K. (1994) 'Enterprise groups', in K. Imai and R. Komiya (eds) *Business Enterprise in Japan*, Cambridge, MA: MIT Press. (Outline of the development of the main Japanese corporate groupings.)
* Kikkawa, T. (1995) 'Kigyo Shudan: the formation and function of enterprise groups', *Business History* 37(2): 44–53. (Outline of the development of the main Japanese corporate groupings.)
* Sako, M. (1992) *Prices, Quality and Trust: Interfirm Relationships in Britain and Japan*, Cambridge: Cambridge University Press. (Historical and contemporary analysis of the development of inter-organizational links in Japan.)
* Sheard, P. (1994) *Keiretsu, Competition and Market Access*, discussion paper 94–17, Osaka: Faculty of Economics, Osaka University. (Good summary of the trade issues posed by the *keiretsu*.)
* Shimotani, M. (1995) 'The formation of distribution keiretsu: the case of Matsushita Electric', *Business History* 37(2): 54–69. (Case study of the development and characteristics of a distribution *keiretsu*.)
* Whitehill, A. (1991) *Japanese Management: Tradition and Transition*, London: Routledge. (Useful introduction to the contemporary Japanese management system.)
* Whittaker, D.H. (1997) *Small Firms in the Japanese Economy*, Cambridge: Cambridge University Press.
* Yamamura, K. and Yasuda, Y. (eds) (1987) *The Political Economy of Japan*, vol. 1, *The Domestic Transformation*, Stanford, CA: Stanford University Press. (Provides an economic history of change in Japanese business in the twentieth century.)

See also: BUSINESS CULTURE, JAPANESE; ECONOMY OF JAPAN; GLOBALIZATION; MANAGEMENT IN JAPAN; MATSUSHITA, K.

Related topics in the IEBM: BANKING IN JAPAN; BUSINESS HISTORY, JAPANESE; FUKUZAWA, Y.; INDUSTRIAL ECONOMICS; INDUSTRIAL STRATEGY; JAPANIZATION; TECHNOLOGY DIFFUSION IN JAPAN; TOTAL QUALITY MANAGEMENT

Management in China

1 Chinese traditions in management
2 The evolution of Chinese management systems
3 Chinese management practices
4 Future trends

Overview

Chinese management has its roots in ancient thinking and practices, especially with regard to values, performance evaluation, personnel selection, quality control and project management. It is characterized by teamwork, orientation around relationships and multi-level regulations. Public ownership is the mainstay of the economy, although four types of ownership exist: state-owned, collective, joint venture and private.

Historically, China has tested several models of management system, from 'three-men management', through 'one-man management' and 'director responsibility under Communist Party committee leadership' to the 'director responsibility' system. Approaching the twenty-first century, under the programme of economic reform instigated in the early 1990s China is moving towards a more decentralized, market-orientated, innovative and international stage, with a resultant need for changes in management.

1 Chinese traditions in management

The development and practices of Chinese management have been heavily influenced by the cultural traditions of the country. Many ideas regarding the work ethic, performance evaluation, personnel selection, accounting, systems management, production and quality control have been applied for centuries in Chinese work and business situations. Their origins are described below.

The influence of ancient Chinese philosophy

Early Chinese management was influenced by several ancient Chinese philosophies including Confucianism, Taoism, Buddhism and Legalism. Confucius (551–479 BC), who most affected thinking on administrative behaviour during later periods, emphasized that benevolence should be regarded as the highest ideal of morality and as the basis of administrative power. Taoism denied the hierarchical administrative system and showed less social responsibility, while Buddhism emphasized equality, kindness and commitment. Han Fei, a Legalist representative around 230 BC, noted four management principles: (1) management by standards and rules; (2) management by strategy planning and the control of personnel; (3) established practices for responsibility and authority within organizations; and (4) prevention of usurpation using ruthless means (Laaksonen 1988; Bond 1986).

Financial and accounting management

In China the concept of accounting originated with the Chou Dynasty around 1027–800 BC. It consisted of 'counting' – the daily checking of expenses and income – and 'summing' – the comprehensive periodic evaluation of the economic situation. The formal Chinese accounting system was established around 475–221 BC and functioned primarily as a performance evaluation system, with indicators for promotion and demotion. During the T'ang Dynasty (AD 618–907) the formal Chinese auditing system was set up. By the time of the Song Dynasty there existed comprehensive volumes of accounting records listing and analysing economic data.

Personnel management and performance evaluation

According to the *Rites of the Chou Dynasty* (Yang 1984), a classic of ancient Chinese literature, the first Chinese bureaucratic system was formulated as early as 1200–1100 BC with management responsibilities for 360 positions in six categories of official rank. In the *Art of War*, an ancient Chinese military text, Sun Tzu stressed the principle of 'understanding counterparts for every success', advocating the importance of understanding the characteristics of subordinates, tasks and situations in management (Griffith 1963). Then, around AD 587 China established the world's first comprehensive national system of personnel examination and selection, the imperial examination systems, for the civil service, a system which lasted over 1300 years. The emphasis was on multi-level screening, public recruiting and competitive selection, with examinations on both basic knowledge and problem-solving abilities. With examinations at three levels – county, provincial and state – the system included essays, oral exams and performance texts. During the Ming and Ch'ing Dynasties (1368–1900), the personnel examination system became more complicated, incorporating four aspects of assessment: ability; morality; performance; and seniority (Wang 1993).

Production and systems management

In ancient China mass movement was the primary means of organizing and managing large projects such as the building of the Great Wall, which involved more than 300,000 labourers (306–214 BC), and the opening of the Great Canal, which involved nearly one million people (AD 585). Prior to this Mo introduced the idea of labour division (about 468–376 BC), while more recently Dong tried to reduce unnecessary time lags in order to shorten the production process and raise work efficiency (around 1279–1368). Another well-known example of Chinese ancient systems management was the implementation of the Dujiang Dam project during 306–251 BC.

Development of management structure

The current pattern of management structure in China can be traced back to the 'three-men management system' in the factories of revolutionary areas in the 1930s. It consisted of the director, the Communist Party secretary and a worker representative. In the 1940s this system was replaced by the 'factory committee meeting' attended by the director, party secretary, trade union leader, technician and worker representatives. After the founding of the People's Republic of China in 1949 the Soviet 'one-man management system' became the major Chinese management model, lasting until the early 1960s. Under this system the director had almost total power in the management field. However, this structure was inconsistent with the Chinese tradition of group approach as well as the leadership of the Communist Party in industries. Thus, in the 1960s it changed to the 'director responsibility under Communist Party committee leadership', in which party organization, management team and trade union were together responsible for management tasks but the party played a more important role (Wang 1993). During the Cultural Revolution (1966–76) the 'revolutionary committee' and ideological indoctrination formed a kind of management in most organizations. Political norms and egalitarianism were dominant (Laaksonen 1988).

In 1978 China began a new era. Economic reform and an open policy were introduced and a new system of management, 'director responsibility', was adopted. The latter is now a major part of the Chinese management structure. The reforms have meant great changes in areas such as reward systems, responsibility contract systems, personnel management, teamwork, leadership, managerial decision making, joint-venture management, technological innovation and organization structure. There is a new emphasis on work efficiency, individual and team responsibility, work competition and democratic management which has forced management to modify existing organizational strategies and structures.

2 The evolution of Chinese management systems

Reform stages

Nationwide decentralization and the introduction of participative managerial decision making have enhanced the new organizational structure of Chinese enterprises. The reform of the management systems took place over four stages:

1 The *experimental stage* (1979–83), decentralizing some management power to enterprises.
2 The *expansion stage* (1983–5), trying out various management responsibility systems in some large and medium-sized enterprises and handing over to enterprises decision-making power in areas such as production, sales, pricing of non-quota products, disposal of assets, organization, personnel selection and staffing and monetary incentives.
3 The *management systems reform stage* (1986–91), implementing management responsibility contract systems in about 90 per cent of large and medium-sized enterprises.
4 The *management structure transformation stage* (1992–6), implementing the 1992 state regulations on changing the management mechanism and the 1993 'Communist Party decision on establishing a socialist market-economy structure', namely to delegate fully various managerial decision-making powers and responsibilities of state-owned enterprises in areas including import and export, investment, after-tax profit distribution, joint venture, merging, recruitment and wage systems.
5 The *strategic reorganization stage* (1997–), emphasizing strategic restructuring and reorganization in Chinese management. Efforts are being made to convert large and medium-sized state-owned enterprises into shareholding corporations according to the requirements of 'clearly established ownership, well defined power and responsibility, separation of enterprise from administration, and scientific management'. The main management reform

initiatives include separating management power from ownership, and reorganizing enterprises into shareholding and contracting, and grouping with trans-regional, inter-trade, cross-ownership and transnational operations. The focus of management development is also shifted to the internationalization of management practices and systems changes, e.g. the development of international joint ventures, the implementation of corporate strategies and the adaptation of cross-cultural businesses.

These reforms have resulted in significant increases in output values, profits and taxes. Specific management reform initiatives have included separating management power from ownership and splitting management into shareholding, contracting and internationalizing functions.

The Chinese trade union and workers' congresses have participated more actively in democratic management. Focus has shifted from the daily interests of the workers (housing, bonuses and benefits) to higher level participation in management selection, production planning, investment evaluation and upholding the legitimate rights and interests of the workers and staff.

In line with the latter, another important event has been the formalization of the legal system of Chinese management, with the Enterprise Law (1988), Joint Venture Law (1979, 1990) and Labour Law (1993). Included in the enterprise law is a clear definition of the three organizational systems in Chinese management: (1) the Communist Party; (2) the management responsibility system; and (3) trade union and workers' congress.

Ownership structure

Economic reform has resulted in a new ownership structure within China. While public ownership is still the mainstay of the national economy, many enterprises are under mixed ownership. Four types of ownership exist:

1 *state-owned*, where the properties belong to the State and management is undergoing transition from the state planning system to

the market system; this is the case for the majority of enterprises;

2 *collective*, where the properties belong to a collective of workers and management is relatively autonomous, as in township enterprises;

3 *joint venture*, enterprises co-owned by Chinese and foreign partners and managed by the 'general manager responsibility system under the board of directors';

4 *private*, only a very small proportion of enterprises.

3 Chinese management practices

Socialist management principle

Chinese management is formally based on a top-down command structure with multi-level regulations. In reality, however, the management system operates on an informal basis through personal contact, loyalty and obligation (Child and Lockett 1990). The most influential management principle is the 'two-way participation, one reform and three-in-one combination', which developed from a popular nationwide management practice of the 1960s. 'Two-way participation' represents the participation of workers in top management and cadres (managers and supervisors) in daily shop floor operations. 'One reform' is to change unreasonable management regulations and improve management systems. 'Three-in-one combination' is to encourage cadres, technicians and workers to work together closely in technical innovations and management. This nationwide practice was successful in enhancing efficiency and morale and became the main part of the constitution of the Anshan Iron and Steel Company, a socialist management principle stressing the importance of mass mobilization, participation and Communist Party leadership in management and production.

Team management

A dominant principal in Chinese management is the team approach, including group decision making, group reward, group responsibility and team management through the 'excellent group evaluation campaign' and 'optimization through re-grouping'. The team approach has been especially effective in the field of quality management, which is characterized as 'expert–worker joint quality control'. In relation to this approach, good interpersonal relationships within teams is emphasized as crucial to a successful management. Linking individual interests with group and organizational interests has been greatly encouraged to facilitate higher organizational commitment and effectiveness. Loyalty is further encouraged via the provision by organizations of housing, medical care, children's daycare and services for retired employees.

Human resource management

The Chinese labour system is undergoing reforms to allow enterprises more power over recruitment and placement. The labour contract system was introduced throughout the country as a solution to the problem of the 'three guarantees as iron' (guaranteed job assignment, pay irrespective of performance and tenure). In addition, labour markets have been established with some form of unemployment insurance plans. Within enterprises, since 1978 various kinds of reward systems have been implemented as a supplement to the fixed and structured wage system. Most of these include multi-bonuses and are linked to an enterprise's economic efficiency. Finally, in late 1993 China began implementing a new civil service system nationwide.

Vocational training has also been established throughout China, greatly raising the skills and competence level of the Chinese workforce. The nationwide management educational programmes running since the early 1980s have trained millions of managers and supervisors for large and medium-sized enterprises. The Chinese State Economic Commission and respective ministries of industries now require managers to take short training programmes on general management and organizational behaviour (Pieper 1990). Distance learning and on-the-job training are also major strategies for managers and workers, with the Chinese Enterprise Management Association setting up a network of 'business school' type programmes, in consultation with international schools, to train top managers (Warner 1987).

Leadership and managerial decision making

Since 1984 leadership assessment has been a growth area in China. Assessment centres are now used to select top managers with the aid of group simulation tasks. Analysis of jobs has shown seven categories of management functions in Chinese enterprises: administration; ideological work; production; technical work; marketing; welfare; and personnel. Other research has revealed a three-dimensional structure to Chinese leadership: performance; maintenance; and morality (namely, honesty, integrity and organizational commitment) (Xu 1987).

The study of scientific and democratic procedures for organizational decision making was another major growth area during the mid-1980s, surveys reporting the positive effects of participative decision making upon management effectiveness (Wang 1989b). Research also revealed different patterns and strategies of organizational decision making and influence–power sharing within management, dependent upon the type of management system and decision tasks (Wang and Heller 1993).

Organizational development and technology management

Since 1978 a series of organizational reforms have taken place and four 'special economic and development zones' including fourteen coastal cities have been opened up to foreign investment and joint ventures. By 1993 there were more than 140,000 joint ventures in China, giving them a significant role in Chinese management (Campbell and Henley 1990).

In relation to organizational change, innovation and the transfer of technology is of great importance within Chinese enterprises, especially with regard to new management information systems. Wang (1989a) formulated a theory of human–computer interface hierarchy from studies on systems development. This theory views computing skills or expertise, system link or networking and participation as three facets of an interface hierarchy among people, the computer system and an organization, interaction among which influences the effectiveness of technological innovations. On the basis of action research among Chinese enterprises Wang (1992) also formulated three strategies for organizational reform and technology transfer: (1) personnel strategy, which focuses upon the quality of skills, knowledge, expertise, attitudes and motivation; (2) system strategy, which deals with the reform of organizational structure, regrouping, vertical and lateral coordination, communication channels and management networks; and (3) participation strategy, which emphasizes participative management styles, joint planning and user involvement for better management transparency and a more democratic management climate. These strategies have been applied to the transformation of management both in state-owned companies and joint ventures.

4 Future trends

Holistic management

As Chinese management undergoes systematic reform, there has been a significant move towards holistic means of coordinating subsystems of management. Chen (1988) adopted the concept of macroergonomics as a broader framework and called for holistic management to integrate individual and organizational functions, short-term interests and long-term potentials, and material incentives and moral development. The holistic approach has also been used to integrate culture, organizational reform and management principles.

Towards a socialist market economy

The Chinese Communist Party's decision in 1993 to establish a socialist market-economy structure and the 15th National Congress of the Communist Party of China in 1997 have the clear goal of establishing a modern enterprise system with Chinese characteristics. This goal has several implications for China. Managing international joint ventures has become a major issue in management reform, with a resultant need to introduce management expertise from outside, to enhance organizational culture, to improve investment and the business environment, and to facilitate organizational development. To establish the socialist market economy and maintain sustained, rapid and sound development, a strategic reorganization of state-owned enterprises is under way by managing large enterprises through competitive grouping and downsizing while invigorating the small ones by way of reorganization, association, merger, leasing, contract operation and joint-stock partnership. Other future needs include clearly defined property-rights relationships, independent management with full responsibility, market-based production and management, effective leadership and organizational systems, a viable wage increase, increased teamwork and an adaptive macro-regulative government system.

ZHONG-MING WANG
HANGZHOU UNIVERSITY

Further reading

(References cited in the text marked *)

* Bond, M.H. (ed.) (1986) *The Psychology of the Chinese People*, Hong Kong: Oxford University Press. (An important collection of psychology literature about Chinese people, mainly in Hong Kong and Taiwan.)

* Campbell, N. and Henley, J.S. (eds) (1990) *Joint Ventures and Industrial Change in China*, vol. 1, part B, in N. Campbell (ed.), *Advances in Chinese Industrial Studies*, London: JAI Press Inc. (One of a comprehensive series on Chinese industrial studies by both Chinese and overseas scholars.)

* Chen, L. (1988) 'Macro-ergonomics in industrial modernization', *Chinese Journal of Applied Psychology* 3 (1): 1–4. (Argues in favour of a holistic approach to reform which would help integrate the various sub-systems of management.)

* Child, J. and Lockett, M. (1990) *Reform Policy and the Chinese Enterprise*, vol. 1, part A, in N. Campbell (ed.), *Advances in Chinese Industrial Studies*, London: JAI Press Inc. (Another book in the useful series on Chinese industrial studies.)

* Engholm, C. (1989) *The China Venture: America's Corporate Encounter with the People's Republic of China*, Glenview, IL: Scott, Foresman and Co. (A book chronicling the successes and failures of pioneering firms while offering specific and practical advice on doing business in China.)

* Griffith, S.B. (1963) *Sun Tzu's The Art of War*, trans. and intro., London: Oxford University Press. (One of the most important and classic texts in ancient Chinese literature on military management, especially strategic management.)

* Laaksonen, O. (1988) *Management in China During and After Mao in Enterprises, Government and Party*, Berlin: Walter de Gruyter. (The most comprehensive English text on Chinese management throughout history. Excellent discussions based upon empirical research in enterprises and government.)

* Pieper, R. (ed.) (1990) *Human Resource Management: An International Comparison*, Berlin: Walter de Gruyter. (A collection of papers from an international conference on human resource management.)

* Simon, D.F. and Rehn, D. (1988) *Technological Innovation in China: The Case of the Shanghai Semiconductor Industry*, Cambridge, MA: Bellinger Publishing. (A critical evaluation of the technological innovation in China's computer and electronic industry based on in-depth field work and interviews with officials and managers in Shanghai.)

Stewart, S. and N. Campbell (1994) *Advances in Chinese Industrial Studies*, vol. 4, *Joint Ventures in the People's Republic of China*, London: JAI Press Inc. (Proceedings of the Conference on Joint Ventures in the PRC held in Hong Kong in 1992.)

* Wang, Z.M. (1989a) 'Human–computer interface hierarchy model and strategies in systems development', *Ergonomics* 32 (11): 1391–400. (A confirmatory factor model on human–computer system interaction and decision strategies in organizational settings in Chinese companies.)

* Wang, Z.M. (1989b) 'Participation and skill utilization in organizational decision making in Chinese enterprises', in B.J. Fallon, H.P. Pfister and J. Brebner (eds), *Advances in Industrial*

Organizational Psychology, Amsterdam: Elsevier. (A research report on decision making and industrial relations from a British Council supported project.)

* Wang, Z.M. (1992) 'Managerial psychological strategies for Sino-foreign joint-ventures', *Journal of Managerial Psychology* 7 (3): 10–16. (A recent research report on field surveys on managerial issues in joint ventures in China.)

* Wang, Z.M. (1993) 'Culture, economic reform and the role of industrial and organizational psychology in China', in M.D. Dunnette and L.M. Hough (eds), *Handbook of Industrial and Organizational Psychology*, vol. 4, 2nd edn, Palo Alto, CA: Consulting Psychologists Press, Inc. (A summary of the historical development and recent research in Chinese industrial and organizational psychology in relation to the economic reform in China.)

* Wang, Z.M. and Heller, F.A. (1993) 'Patterns of power distribution in managerial decision making in Chinese and British industrial organizations', *International Journal of Human Resources Management*, 4 (1): 113–28. (A research report on decision making and power in industrial organizations from a British Council supported project.)

* Warner, M. (ed.) (1987) *Management Reforms in China*, London: Frances Pinter. (A collection of critical surveys on China's attempts to modernize its economy by reforming its industrial management systems.)

* Xu, L.C. (1987) 'Recent development in organizational psychology in China', in B. Bass (ed.), *Advances in Organizational Psychology: An International Review*, London: Sage Publications. (A general review of research and applications in organizational psychology in China.)

* Yang, D.N. (1984) 'Management thought in ancient China', in *Chinese Encyclopedia of Enterprise Management*, Beijing: Enterprise Management Press (in Chinese). (A historical review of the main management literature and ideas in ancient China.)

See also: CULTURE, CROSS NATIONAL

Related topics in the IEBM: GROUPS AND TEAMS; FINANCIAL ACCOUNTING; HUMAN RESOURCE MANAGEMENT; MANAGEMENT EDUCATION IN ASIA; MANAGEMENT EDUCATION IN CHINA; MANAGEMENT IN PACIFIC ASIA; PERSONNEL MANAGEMENT; PROJECT MANAGEMENT; RECRUITMENT AND SELECTION; SUN TZU; TEAMS IN MANUFACTURING

Management in France

Overview

France is often perceived as a nation of contrasts and exceptions. Despite (or perhaps because of) the long shadow cast by her history and traditions, the French are perpetually engaged in a process of modernization. Innovative ideas, new technologies, brash new departures in architecture, all are welcomed yet translated into a characteristically French idiom. France as a country leans towards long-term planning (as witnessed by the five-year economic plans of the 1950s and 1960s which survive in the regional planning process and the strategic emphasis on telecommunications, nuclear energy and aerospace) yet French managers are adaptable, willing to accept change and have a reputation for rapid, improvised solutions. Moreover, the French are markedly individualistic yet have a strong tendency to centralize decision making.

A view frequently held by the French business world maintains that the role of the centralized state in coordinating and directing economic growth and development – so-called *dirigisme* – has been crucial to the post-war success which has transformed France from an economic backwater into a leading industrial nation, whose gross domestic product (GDP) per capita is the seventh highest in the world and the third highest in Europe. France is often seen as the home of protectionism and interventionist industrial policy. Indeed, the state–industry partnership has produced excellent results in select fields such as high-speed trains, Concorde, Airbus and Ariane. However, although this interpretation highlights a traditional French preference for institutional solutions promising order and logic rather than the vagaries of market mechanisms, it exaggerates the power of the French state *per se*. A specific management style for both the economy and firms can be seen but is the result of an extensive intermeshing of the political, administrative and business domains. Such a style allows solutions which may be seen as characteristically French and which have few parallels around the globe. This entry will develop this argument by considering the education of managers, the composition of the business community, management culture, industrial relations and attitudes to international trade.

1 Background, education and training of managers

Business and political elites interpenetrate to a larger extent in France than in comparable nations due to the nature of the educational system and the pattern of career tracks to top office. The breeding ground of French managers is the *grandes écoles* of which the most prestigious are the École Polytechnique and the École Nationale d'Administration (ENA) but the category also includes the many business schools proper (*écoles supérieures de commerce*) found in Paris and the provinces. The *grandes écoles* recruit on merit, using a competitive entrance examination, but studies have shown that access is skewed towards the middle and upper classes. As a result their graduates display considerable sociological homogeneity and have highly developed social skills (much prized in French business) as well as considerable intellectual prowess: a potent combination of factors which favour elitist outlooks. Originally the *grandes écoles* were established to produce the most talented engineers and administrators to work within the civil service for the general good of the nation. Over time, however, the graduates of these institutions have been drawn to the private sector, resulting in a tight coupling between the education and training provided by and for the state and career opportunities in management at large. Thus, in 1994 over one-third of France's fifty largest companies had as chief executive officer (CEO) a graduate of a single institution, the École Polytechnique: these included Total (oil), Usinor (steel), Pechiney (aluminium), Saint-Gobain (glass, construction materials), Rhône-Poulenc (chemicals), Alcatel-Alsthom (energy, rail), France-Télécom (telecommunications), Compagnie Générale des Eaux (water, sewage disposal), Axa (insurance), Paribas, Suez, Caisse des Dépots, Banque Nationale de Paris and Crédit Lyonnais (all finance).

This coupling of state-sponsored training and the private sector is particularly marked in the influence of those key providers of professional talent known as the *grands corps* – notably the Corps des Mines, Corps des Ponts et Chaussées and the Inspection des Finances – which have become springboards for top managers. From the start of their careers, members of the *grands corps* are given challenging posts which foster leadership qualities. They represent a pool from which major French corporations are eager to recruit what they consider to be the *crème de la crème* due to their combination of social pedigree, intellectual distinction, understanding of the levers of state, high-level contacts and early managerial experience. Their length of time in a civil service post varies between a minimal two or three years to several decades. Leaving the public for the private sector is common practice and is known as *pantouflage*. Its importance was indicated by Bauer and Bertin-Mourot (1987), who discovered that of the top twenty-four French industrial enterprises, seventeen had former civil servants as CEOs. Despite several phases of privatization, in the 1990s over one-third of the bosses of the largest 200 firms were members of a *grand corps* and had frequently held high state office (Bauer and Bertin-Mourot 1996). Thus the interpenetration of administrative and business elites is stark at the highest levels of France's biggest companies, but the *grands corps* have extensively colonized intermediate levels too.

2 The French business community

It is frequent in France to merge the concepts of the firm and its owner, the right to manage and the fact of ownership into a single category. Business literature in France habitually focuses on *patrons* (owners or 'bosses'), rather than on 'managers'. This is largely because in France the family business (which erases the distinction between the manager and the owner) has traditionally been predominant. It still remains so, although three significantly different subgroups of *patrons* can be discerned.

First, the category of inheritor figures prominently. Although the dynastic element may be diluted or disguised by the recruitment of professionals to senior office, the majority stake in many major French firms is still family-owned: examples include Peugeot (cars, etc.), Michelin (tyres), Rothschild (banking), L'Oréal (cosmetics), Bouygues (construction), LVMH (luxury goods), Carrefour and Casino (distribution). In the early 1990s almost one-third of the 200 largest French enterprises still had as majority shareholders a single individual or family (Dupuy *et al.* 1995). Clearly family capitalism in France is alive and well.

Conversely, large firms having a widely dispersed share ownership are rarer than in the USA or the UK. Where institutions do have a stake in the capital of family firms, these are usually banks, with the family seeking to retain majority ownership and managerial control. The phenomenon of pension funds holding large stakes is rare. For these structural reasons company takeovers are infrequent in France, as are boardroom revolutions (creating consequences which will be discussed below). The negative feature of the stability of family dynasties is that they limit top appointments made on merit alone since firms in which outstanding managers can rise to the very top by dint solely of professional competence are few in number. This does not exclude professionalism however, since the dynastic heir will usually benefit from a high-powered *grande école* qualification (as described above) as well as inside-track business experience. Consequently, the figure of the *patron* as a professional manager with no family ties to the firm emerged significantly later in France than in the USA or the UK and is still less prominent. But the number of professional managers in France has increased dramatically. Between 1954 and 1975 the number of *cadres supérieurs* increased by over 1 million and that of *cadres moyens* by over 1.6 million: broadly speaking, these groups correspond to British supervisory and managerial grades (see MANAGEMENT IN THE UNITED KINGDOM). (The term *cadre* corresponds to a legal rank in French, whereas 'manager' corresponds to a function in English.) Undoubtedly, the development of the professional category of *cadres* has renewed management practices in France. Yet just over one-third of the 200 largest French enterprises had a widely dispersed body of shareholders in the early 1990s and thus were run entirely by professional management (Dupuy *et al.* 1995). Family ownership and the continued influence of the state remain central features. The incompleteness of the 'managerial revolution' is a distinguishing trait of French capitalism.

Setting up a company is undoubtedly the fastest route to becoming a *patron*. As in the UK the 1960s ideology of 'big is beautiful' limited company start-ups, but entrepreneurship as a mass phenomenon reappeared in the 1980s, with around 20,000 small firms being formed each year during most of the decade. However the revamped image of the entrepreneur has only been accompanied in part by an understanding of the fragility of the small firm sector. Entrepreneurs and company founders do represent an important source of renewal of the business community, but a lasting change in the composition of the business community depends on a buoyant economic environment for company founders and on greater opportunities for professional managers. In both respects, conditions declined at the start of the 1990s with recession cutting

start-ups, increasing company closures and creating the new phenomenon of redundancies and unemployment for *cadres*. A few 'self-made men' do figure in the ranks of France's most prominent business leaders but, unlike the USA, they have lacked widespread respect as a societal role model.

Due to these various factors, France's *patrons* form a fairly small, often tightly-knit personal network. Interlocking directorates, where a relatively small number of directors sit on a large number of boards, have long been commonplace. The privatization process of leading firms such as Saint-Gobain, Paribas, Société Générale, Rhône-Poulenc and UAP has paradoxically reinforced this phenomenon since the right-wing governments of 1986–8 and from 1993–7 ensured, through an elaborate mechanism of company crossholdings, that a small number of prominent businessmen sat on large number of boards. Yet with little interference from the board of directors, with shareholder meetings almost never using their power of sanctions and with takeovers rare, French chief executives are often free to do as they will. These features, together with the high level of homogeneity in social, educational and professional backgrounds already indicated, point to the existence of a very particular management culture.

3 French management culture

Here culture is used in the sense of patterns of thought, expression and behaviour which are both meaningful in themselves and sources of systematic differences between societies and social groups. In an insightful phrase, Crozier (1964: 7) described culture as a 'design for living'. Such a design clearly exists within the French business world, not only at the superficial level of a love of style (expressed in extended gastronomic lunches, high-tech business suites, etc.) but also in terms of business practices and relationships.

Large social distances have resulted in a tendency towards 'top-down' management styles. Senior management sees itself as qualitatively different from middle management, the *cadres*. Yet *cadre* status itself carries prestige. Barsoux and Lawrence (1991) compared being named *cadre* to passing an intelligence test. French *cadres* see themselves as the brains of their firms – with considerable justification given their usually high qualifications. Employees and workers have been considered as belonging to different groups again.

French intellectual style has reinforced the tendency towards directive and divisive styles of management. The rejection through much of this century of participation and compromise in the workplace was conditioned by the French predilection for Cartesian rationality and a preference for working from *a priori* principles involving neat demarcations and dichotomies. From believing that logical arguments admitted only one conclusion, it is a short step to insisting that there is only 'one best way' to solve any problem. The *patron*, by virtue of his *grande école* education emphasizing abstract and mathematical reasoning, has been inclined to think that only he could find the 'right' answers.

Due to this perceived intellectual superiority and high social position, giving orders became second nature to business leaders. A command structure was part of their outlook. Its roots can be traced to the educational system. As noted, the École Polytechnique is probably France's top *grande école* but it started life in 1794 as a military academy and has preserved its military ethos. *Polytechniciens* have a uniform and they take part in military parades. True to the traditions of a warrior caste, the École Polytechnique was all male until the start of the 1970s. These various factors have served to foster autocratic tendencies within French management rather than participative management.

The archetypal organizational form ensuing from these tendencies may be termed the 'full bureaucracy' (Hofstede 1991: 152), understood as a rule-based system, with clear competencies attached to positions and standardized work procedures. The symbol of this organizational form is the steep pyramid, created by elitism, centralization of authority, hierarchical controls and with power centralized at its peak. The tendency to create

hierarchies is illustrated by the fact that French plants often have more hierarchical levels than elsewhere in the world. Hierarchical differences are accompanied by significant status and salary differentials. Yet the functioning of this system manifests considerably more subtleties than this preliminary analysis allows. Alongside the familiar centralizing tendencies exist strong aspirations towards individual autonomy. The attempt to reconcile these aspirations with the dependence relations implicit in a command structure gives French organizations their considerable complexity.

In a classic study, Crozier (1964) identified the four key elements of command and personal relationships in two French bureaucracies as: (1) impersonal rules; (2) centralization of decisions; (3) strata isolation; and (4) the development of parallel power relationships. He found that these social structures were formed of paradoxical components. Authority was centralized, yet the top managers lacked discretionary power. Employees formed subgroups, affording themselves protection, yet were individualistic and even isolated within them. He perceived causal links between the isolation of the individual, the lack of collective spirit and the limited ability of the French to form bottom-up organizations. Crozier summarized the consequences of those historical processes as 'individual isolation and lack of constructive cooperative activities on the one side, strata isolation and lack of communication between people of different rank on the other' (1964: 218). He termed the net result as 'negative solidarity': a group hostility towards hierarchical superiors which aims not towards a new collective order but to creating a space for individual autonomy.

The reconciliation of individual freedom with a rule-governed system was achieved not by a mobilizing consensus nor even by formal authorization (as is sometimes supposed) but by a sophisticated pincer mechanism. The individual had scope to exercise independent powers at each stratum but real authority was sandwiched between official rules and unofficial social pressures. At any rank, rules preserve the individual's prerogatives from arbitrary interference from above, thus ensuring a high degree of autonomy. At the same time, peer group pressure from below counters tendencies towards abuse of power, for each rank is aware of its own rights and knows the extent of the prerogatives of other ranks. The inequalities of rank are accepted because the rule of reason has eliminated arbitrary power. Because the rights of the individual are respected and because servile subjugation is not exacted, contradictory pressures can be contained in one system. In conclusion, Crozier emphasized that although senior managers ostensibly had great powers, their real power was limited by the resistance of lower strata. Only exceptional circumstances allowed them to use their theoretical powers. Crozier modified the conventional thesis of militaristic command structures, since these were tempered by the existence of competing power bases.

A complementary explanation for the distinctive mix of French characteristics has been offered by Hofstede (1980, 1991), who has aimed to trace 'culture's consequences' by revealing contrasts between national populations (see CULTURE, CROSS-NATIONAL; ORGANIZATION CULTURE). In order for meaningful comparisons to emerge, this necessitated comparing as large a number of nations as possible. Thus his work is not specifically about France but covers France in an illuminating manner. Hofstede traced national cultures along four dimensions: power distance; uncertainty avoidance; individualism; and masculinity. With power distance, he constructed a scale measuring the continuum of styles of exercising authority in organizations, running from the pole of autocratic procedures to the pole of participative management. On this scale France was distinctive in having the highest power distance rating of any European nation, indicating that authority tended to be centralized and that individuals who exercised it did so in an autocratic way. Subordinates did not expect or seek to be consulted on decision making, thereby demonstrating a dependency reaction towards their superiors.

By uncertainty avoidance Hofstede understood reactions towards the unpredictability of the future and the risks it holds. Some populations are more relaxed, some more anxious about the open-endedness of the future. With the uncertainty avoidance index, populations that sought to minimize or avoid risk were placed at the high end of the scale. This was the case for France.

Because Hofstede used individualism in its ordinary meaning, no special commentary on the term is required. However, he did add the clarification that his individualism index measured *non-dependence on the organization. On this index the score of French respondents was again relatively high.*

The masculinity scale derived from the tendency noted across a range of human communities to socialize men towards assertiveness, self-reliance and achievement while socializing women towards nurturing and caring for others. The scale measured the relative importance of 'achievement' in terms of recognition, promotion and pay. Conversely, it measured the relative (un)importance of personal relations, cooperative behaviour and security at work. The French had a medium to low score on this scale, indicating a tendency towards a 'feminine' outlook.

In France high uncertainty avoidance occurs simultaneously with great power distance. France shares this characteristic with other Latin countries and, interestingly, Japan. Although hierarchical structures are a basic fact of most societies (as are their cognates: inequalities in the distribution of strength, power and wealth), Hofstede pointed out that their connotations vary markedly. In cultures characterized by high power distance, superiors are considered to be existentially different to subordinates. This contrasts with low power distance countries – such as the USA – where superiors are considered to be basically the same as their subordinates and with whom they may even exchange positions.

In France the possibility of trading places is much reduced by class structures and by the elitist education system. These features create the unconscious assumption that individuals towards the top of the social and organizational pyramid are intrinsically different, and that the distance between ranks is insuperable.

Pyramid culture is reflected in management style. High power distance nations are characterized by centralized, autocratic or paternalistic decision making. By their actions (if not always their words), the French express preference for an enlightened despot or father-figure as ideal manager.

Inequalities produce latent conflicts between the powerful and the disempowered, but the choice of the road to reform varies with culture. In high power distance countries, change is usually achieved by the dethroning of powerful persons and their replacement with another set of powerful persons, whereas in low power distance countries change can be effected by a redistribution of power or a change of system. Hofstede's picture of the consequences of high power distance accords well with the French polity and with certain French business practices. In French companies, the Président-Directeur Général can exercise autocratic, personalized power, sometimes for life. Neither the spectacular falls from grace in 1993 of Jean-Yves Haberer at Crédit Lyonnais, Bernard Attali at Air France and Jean-Michel Bloch-Lainé at Banque Worms, nor the practice of incoming governments to replace heads of nationalized firms with more amenable candidates, should be misinterpreted as signs of a new trend towards greater accountability: rather these examples illustrate the French tendency towards rotating people, not overhauling structures.

The individualism of the French has often been noted. Connotations of individualism include seeking autonomy, variety, status and pleasure for self. Making one's own decisions is crucial, and usually involves critically distancing oneself from organizations and institutions, both emotionally and intellectually. Thus, the relationship between individualists and organizations does not involve a moral commitment, but is primarily calculative. The individual accepts the goals of the group only insofar as they coincide with a personal agenda. Two further consequences follow. One, the individual's sense of distance from the organization results in a sharp division between the workplace and private life. And two, there is an emphasis on personal initiative and on the leadership ideal. However, the combination of a high individualism rating with great power distance is distinctive and highlights a paradoxical trait of the French. To quote a phrase by Hofstede, the French were frequently 'dependent individualists' (Hofstede 1980: 221). Thus they preferred clear lines of authority and a single 'boss' and were dependent on their superior's judgement, goodwill and favour. But dependence can leave room for individual autonomy. In delegating decision making upwards, the individual shrugs off personal responsibility and unloads the uncertainties inherent in making choices. This also leaves subordinates free to distance themselves from a superior's decisions, unlike consultative modes of policy making which implicate all concerned. Thus a large power distance does not necessarily arise from the superior taking two steps back from the subordinate. In some contexts, the power distance grows from each party taking a step back from the other. For Hofstede the combination of large power distance and high uncertainty avoidance meant that the French were among those nations who looked to powerful people and strong institutions to resolve uncertainties.

This distinctiveness is rooted in contradictions within French society generally. On the one hand there is the drive to conformity, the acceptance of long-standing traditions, of elitist and hierarchical institutions. On the other are tendencies towards individual self-expression, rebellion against authority, revolutionary idealism and radical egalitarianism. Historically, major social and political crises have resulted from the conflict between these contradictory tendencies. But the cost of crisis is usually exorbitant: other solutions to social and cultural dysfunctions are required. The analyses of Crozier and Hofstede throw light on how the ingrained tensions of French society are diffused and (usually) defused at the workplace.

4 Industrial relations

A key problem within the French system of high power distance, large numbers of hierarchical levels and high structuring of activities is the difficulty of managing industrial relations. The French habitually refer to employees, *patrons* and the state as *partenaires sociaux* but, despite the rhetoric, the partnership has rarely been based on consensus. Industrial 'democracy' is an alien concept for many French employers and trade unionists alike: each are more accustomed to conflict than agreement. The personalistic and absolute view of authority have largely ruled out compromise and power sharing.

Unions were long considered illegitimate by employers and even when accepted as partners in dialogue were treated with suspicion due to the extent to which political ideologies have shaped the French trade union movement. Of the five main unions, the two largest (the Confédération Générale du Travail and the Confédération Française Démocratique du Travail) were in the past associated with 'revolutionary' aims. However, the smaller 'reformist' unions (the Confédération Française des Travailleurs Chrétiens, Force Ouvrière and the Confédération Générale des Cadres) have enjoyed less political and industrial influence. In consequence, industrial relations have been marked by an oscillation between stalemate and violent protest, with the government periodically induced to arbitrate. Ironically, in the wake of the massive 1968 demonstrations it was the government which promoted the peak employers' confederation in France – the Conseil National du Patronat Français – to the status of a negotiator in a national industrial relations settlement, where previously it had no such role.

Viewed over the long term, the sedimentation of cultural change in industrial relations has been slow but nevertheless significant. The end of the Second World War saw the rehabilitation of unions at a time when firms were debilitated in both ideological and material terms, the result of collaboration between key industrialists and the Nazi occupiers and the devastation of war. By the mid-1980s firms had been rehabilitated while unions were debilitated, ideologically in that extreme Left positions had lost credibility and materially in that union membership was at a European low of less than 10 per cent of the workforce. This turnaround in their mutual positions dissipated the violent antagonism

between the two partners. By the start of the 1990s, apparently little remained of the old, class war model of industrial relations. This evolution indicates a significant degree of modernization in French industrial relations. However, there is still a fine line between industrial and political solutions, as illustrated by government intervention in the Air France dispute of 1993 and the Jospin government's proposals in 1998 for a '35-hour week', aimed at reducing chronic levels of unemployment.

5 Towards a new internationalism

Modernization is evident too in attitudes towards world trade. France has often been taxed with protectionism, even chauvinism, due to a concern with national greatness and a partiality for sabre-rattling – the 1993 GATT talks being a case in point. Yet in practice French managers have grown increasingly international in outlook and France is now the fourth largest exporter in the world.

The interest of the French business community in the European Single Market programme has been sufficient to nonplus many observers from across the Channel (see ECONOMIC INTEGRATION, INTERNATIONAL). Surveys of managers in both large and small firms discovered levels of enthusiasm for '1993' that were far higher in France than elsewhere (Barsoux and Lawrence 1991). A number of factors explain this enthusiasm. First, French business people looked on 1993, the year the Single Market 'officially' opened, as a historical landmark, as confirmation of France's historical integration into Europe. They have been keen to cast off the protectionism that historically constituted French policy, the poor reputation it gave France abroad and the inadequate market adaptation that went with it at home. The French believe that their country will be the new crossroads of Europe, linking Germany to the UK via the Channel Tunnel and uniting south and north Europe by various high-speed rail and motorway links. Second, the Single Market presents an opportunity to reinforce French competitiveness by greater internationalization; the aim is to build a strong France in a united Europe. Third, the

French business community saw the Single Market programme as a means of reinforcing pressure on the French government to undertake a number of reforms for which it has long lobbied, in particular an overhaul of the tax and social security systems – France has the highest tax burden of all the G7 countries. The idea of European Union (EU) tax harmonization, particularly on VAT, was welcomed. Fourth, company owners have increasingly disapproved of government intervention in business by subsidies or nationalization, which they consider expensive and ineffective. With EU policy on competition growing firmer and vigilance in Brussels towards market distortions caused by government intervention increasing, French opponents of interventionism have found new allies. In brief, the popularity of the Single Market is related both to the long-term struggle of major sections of the French business community to shake off what it considers to be the dead hand of the state and to the continued search for larger markets abroad. The commitment of French business and political elites to European integration places France at the forefront of the drive towards monetary union (see ECONOMIC INTEGRATION, INTERNATIONAL).

Problems do remain. The danger of a preoccupation with Europe might be to lose sight of the need to accelerate France's adaptation to a world economic order by sustained geographical diversification. A common criticism of French firms has been the failure to adjust to the specific needs of foreign markets, relying on opportunistic selling rather than on sustained marketing, and a lack of permanent distribution networks and after-sales facilities. Indeed, despite vociferous enthusiasm since the 1960s for US-style marketing, the emphasis has consistently been on the supply-side of the equation. French technology policy has put engineering prowess first (itself a reflection of the State–*grande école*–industry nexus), leaving consumer marketing skills greatly underdeveloped. Yet if areas of weakness persist – especially in consumer electronics – strengths should not be underestimated. French expertise in large-scale projects – road and rail construction, water and sewage systems, etc. – has allowed significant penetration of markets around the world. Unlike the USA and the UK, France in the 1990s enjoyed record trade surpluses.

6 Conclusions

From being an apparently state-led, inward-looking country, France has nearly completed the transition to a market-driven, open economy. Secular French aversion to competition seems to have been overcome, as evidenced by the increased clarity and rigour of the 1986 ordinance on anti-competitive practices and its beneficial effects on the business climate. Thus the complacency and parochialism traditionally associated with the narrow sociological base of the French business elite presents fewer economic dangers than in the past. This is not to deny the wider social problems which exist, particularly the growing inequalities of income distribution and consistently high levels of unemployment (over 10 per cent in the 1990s). On the other hand, the effects of the world recession of 1992–3 were short and shallow in France but deep and prolonged in countries such as the USA and UK. Economic expansion has been maintained in the late 1990s. These positive signs suggest that the French management model will continue to figure prominently in world business.

JOSEPH SZARKA
UNIVERSITY OF BATH

Further reading

(References cited in the text marked *)

* Barsoux, J.-P. and Lawrence, P. (1991) 'The making of a French manager', *Harvard Business Review* (July–August): 58–67. (Valuable introduction to the training and mentality of French managers.)

Barsoux, J.-L. and Lawrence, P. (1997) *French Management: Elitism in Action*, London: Cassell. (Wide-ranging study of the content and style of French management practice.)

* Bauer, M. and Bertin-Mourot, B. (1987) *Les 200. Comment devient-on un grand patron?*, Paris: Éditions du Seuil. (Revealing analysis of the career paths to top office trodden by the CEOs of France's top companies.)

* Bauer, M. and Bertin-Mourot, B. (1996) *Vers un modèle européen de dirigeants?*, Paris: Abacus. (Updates their analysis of CEO career paths in France and extends it to Britain and Germany.)

* Crozier, M. (1964) *The Bureaucratic Phenomenon*, Chicago: University of Chicago Press. (Sociological study revealing the specificity of French forms of bureaucracy and bureaucratic behaviour.)

* Dupuy, C., Cancel, S. and Morin, F. (1995) 'Vingt ans de capitalisme à la française', *Alternatives économiques* 127 (May): 28–34. (Surveys patterns of ownership in France's largest firms.)

Hall, E.T. and Hall, M. R. (1989) *Understanding Cultural Differences: Keys to Success in West Germany, France and the United States*, Yarmouth, ME: Intercultural Press. (Successful conversion of anthropological analyses of psychology and behaviour into practical advice for managers.)

Hampden-Turner, C. and Trompenaars, F. (1993) *Seven Cultures of Capitalism: Value Systems for Creating Wealth in Britain, the United States, Germany, France, Japan, Sweden and the Netherlands*, London: Piatkus Books. (Argues that differences in international competitiveness and wealth-creating potential flow from national management cultures.)

* Hofstede, G. (1980) *Culture's Consequences: International Differences in Work-Related Values*, London: Sage Publications. (Seminal work based on his original survey of IBM employees.)

* Hofstede, G. (1991) *Cultures and Organizations: Software of the Mind*, London: McGraw-Hill. (Cross-national analysis of management culture based on an extensive database of questionnaire responses, external data from international literature searches as well as considerable and rich insight.)

Szarka, J. (1992) *Business in France. An Introduction to the Economic and Social Context*, London: Pitman. (Surveys the contexts and conduct of French business and has detailed bibliographies.)

Szarka, J. (1998) 'French business in the Mitterrand years: the continuity of change', in M. Maclean (ed.) *The Mitterand Years: Legacy and Evaluation*, London: Routledge. (Analyses developments in French business from 1981 to 1995.)

See also: BUSINESS CULTURES, EUROPEAN; CULTURE, CROSS-NATIONAL; ECONOMIC INTEGRATION, INTERNATIONAL; MANAGEMENT IN GERMANY; MANAGEMENT IN THE UNITED KINGDOM; ORGANIZATION CULTURE

Related topics in the IEBM: BUREAUCRACY; CAREERS; CROZIER, M.; GENERAL AGREEMENT ON TARIFFS AND TRADE; HOFSTEDE, G.; HUMAN RESOURCE MANAGEMENT IN EUROPE; INDUSTRIAL DEMOCRACY; INDUSTRIAL RELATIONS IN EUROPE; INDUSTRIAL STRATEGY; INTERNATIONAL BUSINESS ELITES; MANAGEMENT DEVELOPMENT; ORGANIZATIONAL CONTEXTS AND ENVIRONMENTS; PRIVATIZATION AND REGULATION; TRADE UNIONS

Management in Germany

Overview

Irrespective of whether the word is used to focus on structures for designing performance-oriented achievement processes based on the division of labour (organizational aspects) or on action concepts for performing tasks involved in such achievement processes (functional aspects), management is always the attempt or the result of the attempt to reconcile, in the employment of resources, the cultural guidelines of both individual and collective action with the requirements of an actual or potential market. The content and form of management emanate from strategies whose visionary core and concrete basic conditions cannot be separated from the cultural environment in which the actors are embedded and to which they feel more or less committed.

When determining the peculiarities of German management it is important – in view of a tendency towards standardization of managerial action strongly influenced by the requirements of worldwide competition – to investigate the cultural or environmental characteristics in which management in Germany has its roots and which constitute its general basis.

The cultural environment as well as the cultural experiences of the past in particular influence to a large extent management structures and processes because they provide the actors, in the form of implied basic assumptions and moral concepts, with a corridor for the detection and assessment of alternatives to managerial action. At the same time managerial action shows with reference to its national implications an important influential factor for the cultural development of the country, so that a close correlation between management and culture can be spoken of.

As a result of the greatly increased worldwide economic integration (globalization) which has taken place over the last decades, the question arises, on the one hand, as to the possibility of a standardization of managerial action as well as that of cultural development (theory of convergence), and on the other hand as to the significance of the existence and continuance of the management characteristics which are peculiar to the country concerned.

The characteristics of German management can be determined by an examination of the cultural or environmental characteristics in which management in Germany is rooted, and which constitute its basic conditions. It is appropriate to consider the problem from five viewpoints which are interrelated:

1 the *economic and ethical basis*;
2 the *legal framework* limiting individual and collective decision areas;
3 the *qualification structure* of the decision makers;
4 the *organizational structure* of management;
5 the *conceptual view* for managerial action and the functional management area as based upon the specific conditions.

These perspectives influence managerial action in Germany with regard to, for example:

- the identification of priorities, which are often oriented towards the technological standards of product development and the production process (as opposed to a stronger orientation towards customer requirements shown by American companies) and where the question of customer service, in comparison to other countries (at least until now) has been of little importance;

- the planning timeframe, which tends to be oriented towards medium and long-term planning (as opposed to American companies, which tend to favour short-term planning considerations); in this context mention can also be made of the stereotype of the German 'obsession' with planning;

- risk orientation, which is marked by an inclination towards safety and the avoidance of risk (as opposed to the more pragmatic approach of American companies, which are more willing to accept risk);

- conflict resolution, and in particular in relation to conflicts between the interests of the company and those of the employees; the 'democratic culture of discussion' which developed in the post-war years, and which without doubt proved in the past to be an important locational factor, had a positive effect on the political stability and 'social peace'.

I The economic and ethical roots of management in Germany

The essential roots of German managerial thinking and action are the normative principles of Protestant and Catholic social doctrine, on the one hand, and Max Weber's analyses and tentative theories, purporting to be objective, on the form of (socially) 'efficient' organizational structures, on the other hand. Both have an impact on the interpretation of the concept of the 'social market economy' which evolved during the period of German reconstruction after the Second World War.

With regard to the religious influences on German managerial thinking, Catholic orientation mixed with the forms of Protestantism (Lutheranism, Calvinism), so that diverse structures of awareness and lifestyle emerged. The significance of these influences for the

basic models of society, organization and individualism can be clearly seen in the social Utopia of the Catholic social doctrine, the Protestant ethic and its form of Calvinism, together with their respective normative principles.

The Catholic social doctrine had its beginnings in the nineteenth century and can be considered as a theological systematization of social norms and structures. The major principles of the *Catholic social system* are:

1 The principle of *human dignity* which says that man must be the end of all social institutions;
2 the principle of *solidarity* which emphasizes a basic common responsibility of people for each other, both at the level of the individual and of the group;
3 the principle of *subsidiarity* which attempts to link one's own responsibility in terms of the right and obligation to handle one's own affairs independently with solidarity;
4 the principle of the *inviolability of property* and lately, in the wake of the encyclical '*Centesimus Annus*' of 1991;
5 the principle of *efficiently supplying the population while recognizing self-interest* as the driving force of competition.

In essence therefore the Catholic social doctrine comprises a critical stance against a 'secular' oriented state. A social policy, the focal point of which is the demand for the respect of human rights, social justice and harmony, belongs to society's most important goals, from which even 'economic forces' cannot escape.

Even if the characteristic strength of the Catholic social doctrine has diminished generally in Germany today, and in particular in German management, it is nevertheless perceptible, in the form of a Christian ethic of responsibility, as a counter principle to that of the purely capital-oriented principle of profit increase, for the shaping of management awareness. With the aim of a juxtaposition of capital and work, the Catholic social doctrine shows, especially in its most recent encyclicals, the possibilities for the implementation of a limited capitalistic economic system in the form of the 'social market economy'. The chances for the development of a democratic, egalitarian, liberal and solidarity-oriented social and political community, which are inherent in the German economic system, is one of its most important potentials for the future.

In contrast to Catholicism, Protestantism opposes the omnipotence of the church as an institution, and supports a Protestant devoutness for secular institutions, in particular the state, as well as a strengthening of subjectivity and autonomy, in other words, an individualial's personal freedom in thought and belief. In the centre of Protestantism stands the replacement of the external guidance by means of religious institutions, by a person's internal guidance, which is oriented toward the word of God alone. The key phrases, inwardness, personality, subjectivity and autonomy have stood therefore since the eighteenth century in the centre of the anthropological discussion in Protestant Germany. The model of the associated lifestyle accordingly comprised of specific orientation values such as independence, responsibility, conscientiousness, freedom of thought, a willingness to criticize, and tolerance.

This Protestant ideal of a devout member of the educated classes, also promotes, in particular through the stipulation of an inner asceticism and the connected self-discipline, an efficient and economic lifestyle. Consequently the Protestant ideal combines with a productive cultural development, which seeks to achieve a higher value over and above a strict, rationalized, anti-hedonistic lifestyle, and manifests itself in the form of efficient self-management. The devout Protestant member of the educated classes does not therefore live from day to day without any plan, but follows – using modern terminology – a rational time management, with its indispensable virtues of punctuality and accuracy.

It consequently becomes clear, that the complete canon on orientation values (devotedness, honour, honesty, objectivity, servitude, self-discipline), which are described as the 'Prussian sense of duty', is religiously anchored in Protestant roots. Although in the course of the changes in social values which have occurred since the 1970s, a tendency

towards a loss of significance of the Prussian values of duty and acceptance can be noted, their influence on the systems, methods and instruments of management to be found in Germany nevertheless remains significant.

It has become obvious from discussions on changing values and their impact for economics that the success of enterprises also depends, last but not least, on the degree of synergy between ways of thinking characterized by values such as duty and acceptance and others where the emphasis is on free development of personality. The outcome of changes, for instance in the sense of the philosophies of Lean Management Business Reengineering or Total Quality Management, will greatly depend on this.

The connection between the Protestant principles of lifestyle, and their significance in the economic context became the subject of a fundamental discussion as a result of Max Weber's famous 1904 study *Die protestantische Ethik und der Geist des Kapitalismus* (*The Protestant Ethic and the Spirit of Capitalism*), and which extended over all of the historical cultural sciences. Weber thereby justified the clear experience that was obvious around 1900, that the Protestant parts of the German Empire and the Protestant countries of Europe were superior to Catholics in economic respects, by showing that the economically relevant rationalization process of Protestant devoutness, and in particular the inner asceticism and self-discipline had the effect of promoting capitalism. This was also confirmed by McClelland (1961) in his study about the effect of religion on the key requirement of 'strival for performance' which was identified by him, where he showed, that Protestant countries showed a higher level of productivity in relation to the Catholic countries studied. The reason for this can be seen in the close correlation between life's religious and economic principles:

He who lived unhealthily, and as a result became indebted and bankrupt, was not only treated as an economic failure, but was also excluded as a sinner, who had brought about his own downfall. Success which was achieved through modesty, thrift, performance, rationality and efficiently strood for a sign of merciful acceptance by God in the sphere of Protestant devoutness.

(Graf, 1997, p. 566).

The openness of Protestantism towards the ideology of integration of the middle-class society must however also be critically looked at. Protestantism runs the risk, through the devaluation of religious institutions, of elevating the state to the church, and of combining political activity with excessive moral requirements. The Protestant ethic of a 'fundamental attitude', in other words, acting from conviction by way of one's attitude and individual morality, which had priority over the institution-oriented 'ethic of responsibility' supported National Socialism which arose in the twentieth century. The Protestant personality is therefore, because it relies on itself, more at risk and more delicate; it is more of a contradiction in terms and more torn than that of the institution-defined Catholic personality. The negature experiences of National Socialism, from today's point of view, can be seen as the reason for a widespread scepticism towards an incorrectly handled integration ideology, which can also be encountered at management level, and which is therefore of considerable importance in relation to the implementation of comprehensive management conceptions.

The connections between Protestantism and the modern age, the changed political cultures and the change in values of German society can be seen to be more stringent and decisive than those which occur with Catholicism. The political culture of Germany, which has a decisive influence on the basic conditions of German management, has on the one side been shaped over the centuries by a militaristic and feudalistic orientation towards authority, and on the other side by a Protestant theology, which supported this political culture by its religious stance (Greiffenhagen, 1993).

Through the connection between religion and culture, above all through devoutness and education, the early Protestant liberalism in Germany formed a specific German cultural ideal, which constituted a basis of authorization for a 'special way' of social and political development, and thereby for the prevailing attitudes of managerial action in Germany. Protestantism and its ethical fundamental principles form in essence the foundation of the 'social market economy', which developed in the period of reconstruction following the end of the Second World War.

The pioneers of the regulative basis (competitive and social system) of this economic concept, which is closely linked to the former Minister of Economics and later Federal Chancellor Ludwig Erhard, were the members of the socalled *Freiburger Kreis* (1942/1943) – a circle within the resistance movement against National Socialism which included in addition to distinguished Protestant theologians (e.g. Otto Dibehus) also renowned economists (e.g. Walter Eucken). Since the 1980s, *Protestant theology* has intensified its economic and ethical commitment which dates back to the nineteenth century and was strongly influenced by Adam Smith in the beginning. This commitment is reflected, among others, in a memorandum on 'Public Interest and Self Interest' and had a particular impact on the incorporation of ecological problems in the economic decision process.

The legal framework for economic action in the Federal Republic of Germany and changes to it provide the basis for the stabilization and development of the concept of the social market economy.

2 The legal framework and its constraints on managerial decision-making in German enterprises

The complexity and turbulence involved in controlling free-market processes require all industrial nations to develop a sophisticated legal framework. Of particular importance for management in Germany is its labour and social legislation and the principle of the right to free collective bargaining; there are significant differences compared to other countries as far as employee codetermination is concerned.

Free collective bargaining and management action

Managerial decision-making is considerably restricted in its scope by labour costs. Over the last few years German labour costs have always been the highest in the world which has had a deeply adverse effect on the competitiveness of the German economy in international markets (see GLOBALIZATION). In addition to the level of labour costs, German industry is particularly burdened by a rigid pay system which, as a result of the collective agreement system in effect in Germany, is scarcely adaptable to productivity development.

Article 9, paragraph 3 of the German Basic Law guarantees the right to form associations to safeguard and improve working and economic conditions independently of governmental control, and provides the basis for the system of collective agreement negotiations. Thus, unions and management decide autonomously on the distribution of the national product.

The Collective Agreements Act of 1949 regulates collective bargaining in Germany. Bargaining partners are the trade unions as the employees' representatives and the employers' associations or individual companies. Trade unions and employers' associations are organized according to their branch of industry; i.e. they act for all employees and all companies belonging to a particular branch of industry independent of their size or production structure.

The more the conclusion of a collective agreement relies on the economic situation of high-yielding companies, the more difficult the situation becomes for the low-yielding companies in the same branch of industry. In the past, this phenomenon has paved the way in many cases for processes of concentration, and especially smaller companies which cannot pass on increased labour costs in the form of price increases were squeezed out of the market. Since the opposition of trade unions means that companies cannot react to cost

pressure from the market by reducing labour costs, staff are frequently laid off as a last resort, even if this is to the detriment of the company's potential. Particularly during economic crises, therefore, high demands are put upon German management to offset the necessity of cost reductions against the need to maintain the company's real-asset values. The protection guaranteed by labour and social law, which requires that layoffs are 'socially acceptable', adds to this problem.

Provisions of labour and social law

General

The provisions of labour and social law in Germany which limit and govern management action have their roots in the middle of the last century when the conviction grew that working life in capitalist industrial societies is characterized by fundamental conflicts of interests between employees and employers and that it is the task of government to reconcile these conflicts by appropriate regulations while simultaneously maintaining a maximum of contractual freedom in order to guarantee economic stability and productivity in the interest of both parties. This is a major task of labour law while social law attempts to mitigate risks resulting from the weaker position of the employee during the conclusion and termination of employment contracts or deficits with respect to his financial basis, equality of opportunity and free development of his personality with a view to ensuring relative justice. In the course of time, a social network emerged which provides considerable security for employees and their families while burdening German companies with the highest benefit costs in the world. These high employee benefit costs are a major reason for the high labour costs in Germany.

German labour law has its roots in the following authorities:

1 The *constitution of the Federal Republic of Germany* and the fundamental rights established therein;
2 a variety of *laws and acts* supplemented by interpretive *judicial decisions;*

3 *provisions of the collective agreements* concluded between unions and management;

4 *company agreements* negotiated between employer and works council in a company;

5 *provisions* established by the *contract of employment* and standards resulting from company practice, the equality of treatment principle or the employer's right to give instructions.

The situation in Germany is specifically characterized by the set of rules of the collective labour law which deals with the origins, organization and tasks of associations under labour law, that is to say trade unions, employers' associations and company staff, and their interrelations. The Works Constitution Act of 1972 (as well as the Employees' Representation Act of 1974 for the public sector, and the Acts relating to employee participation of 1951 and 1976 (MontanMitbG 1951, MitbG 1976) are of special importance in the practice of company management.

Works constitution law

The purpose of the Works Constitution Act is to apply democratic principles to cooperation in a company and to convey to the employee the feeling that he is not a mere factor of production or the target of employer's instructions. This Act aims to implement the partnership idea contained in the concept of the social market economy. Consequently, it supports the principle of counterbalance which can work properly only if both sides are willing to cooperate for the joint benefit despite conflicting interests. A major requirement of this Act is therefore 'trustful cooperation' as defined in section 2.

The Works Constitution Act also contains provisions relating to the individual employee's rights, such as the right to access to his personal file, although his direct participation is limited to a few matters within narrowly defined areas. A participation occurs however largely indirectly in the form of a representation of interests through internal or external representatives. Within the company itself, the employees' interests are represented by the *works council*, whose members are elected

by all employees according to democratic election principles. The Works Constitution Act provides the works council with a great number of participation rights, ranging from the right to obtain information to the right to be heard or be consulted and even to enforceable codetermination rights. In the latter case the employer requires the approval of the works council in order to implement an intended measure, and which thereby ensures an equal participation in the decision-making process. In particular social and personnel but also economic matters as well as the layout of the work place, the flow of work and the work environment are subject to these participation rights.

These broad participation rights laid down in the Works Constitution Act have an impact both on the freedom of action of management as an institution and on the individual superior, for example in relation to the transfer of subordinates, the organization of working hours and so on. This situation requires an appropriate cooperative environment and tends to decentralize the process of balancing economic and social interests down to the level of the individual superior. The ability to handle this cooperation or even conflict management is an important key to success, particularly in crisis situations which necessitate a high degree of adaptability.

The right of co-determination at managerial level

Even the Works Constitution Act of 1952 provided for a codetermination of employees' representatives not only in personnel and social matters but also in economic planning and decision processes at company level. This meant in practice that employees' representatives obtained seats and voting rights in the supervisory boards which appoint the members of the managing board and supervise the management of the company. The basic idea behind this approach was, in addition to sociopolitical objectives, to safeguard jobs by exercising an influence on company policy.

The right of codetermination as established by the Works Constitution Act was considerably extended by the *Codetermination Law* of 1976. This Law bears close resemblance to a law which had been passed in 1951 for the iron, steel and mining industries and requires that the supervisory boards of companies with more than 2000 employees be constituted by an equal number of representatives from the shareholders and the employees. The chairman of the supervisory board, who is elected by the shareholders, has a second vote in cases of conflict (equality of votes). This second vote would adversely affect the environment of cooperation required for the application of the Works Constitution Act, and for this reason it has only been exercised very rarely in the past. Codetermination at managerial level subjects management guidelines to a political negotiation process on the one hand and attaches greater significance to control by the employees' representatives on the other. This requires a high degree of social competence and political sensibility on the part of decision makers in management. It predudes partiality in favour of the shareholders' side. Both the contents and the nature of management policy in Germany are therefore determined in such a way that the internal company decision makers must take into consideration the reactions of the affected employees.

3 Management action and management qualification

A description of management in Germany as an action process requires an institutional differentiation appropriately relating to the various management levels and reference to the qualification structure on which the action is based.

Management levels

The bearers of management functions differ as to their hierarchical position, their frequently associated status as superior or the right to give binding instructions to others, the degree of decision-making power and their actual control over the company which need not necessarily be coupled to their hierarchical position. In the following, these criteria shall be looked at in relation to top, middle and lower management. In addition to the members of the supreme management

organizations in Germany, top management also includes executive personnel, while the chiefs of special areas and the holders of staff positions usually belong to middle management and those who are at the boundary of management positions and operative employees form the lower management. A typical example of the latter is the foreman. Of course, such general distinctions cannot delineate the areas sharply, and in any case the situation of each individual case must be considered.

The *foremen or masters* as representatives of *lower management* hold a traditionally strong position where the criterion of actual influence is concerned, in particular in German trade and industry (Zündorf 1987). Their management function has undergone a profound change in the last 30 to 40 years, and is currently likely to undergo another radical change. The companies' growth in the 1960s and in particular the emergence of electronic data processing have reduced the scope of functions at the master level, primarily with respect to planning responsibilities. Convinced they were creating a higher degree of professionalism and thus also greater economic efficiency, companies attached these functions to specific management departments (planning departments, operations scheduling, etc.). However, this trend towards reducing the functions of the master was compensated for by the fact that the master became important as a disturbance handler due to the increasing complexity and a resultant susceptibility of technical production. A successful performance of this function requires a high technical competence and functional authority. As a result, masters frequently became key figures in the necessary mediation process between formal and informal organization. Often their attitude is determined by the effort to maintain loyalty in the working group rather than by the achievement of abstract efficiency standards. It is to be expected that some of the management functions will shift back from middle management to the master level in the course of the emerging reorganization towards leaner structures.

The functions of *middle management* in the German economy expanded strongly in the course of the above-mentioned growth process and the adoption of computerized planning and control. The traditional task at this level is to translate the company's objectives and policy decisions into practical programmes and concrete performance targets and to control their implementation (Staehle 1989). The large number of newly established management positions was a strong incentive, in particular for aspiring young people, and therefore pressure was exerted on the training system to satisfy the needs of the economy by providing appropriate qualifications (see below). A generally career-oriented attitude and the concurrence of qualification patterns differing in form and content at this management level potentially create considerable conflict which puts high demands on the leadership abilities of superiors. The tendency towards leaner organizations intensifies this potential for conflict because it necessarily involves career disappointments unless adequate alternatives can be provided.

The task of *top management* is to formulate the company's policy and objectives and to establish the necessary conditions for middle management to be able to translate these into action programmes. In this respect the executives play an important role in Germany.

The *executives* regard themselves as a specific interest group between two fronts, namely the shareholders or their representatives and the employees (Welge 1992). They see themselves therefore neither as employees in the classical sense nor as employers. This creates problems, in particular for the election of the works council and of the employees' representatives on the supervisory board. The 1988 amendment to the Works Constitution Act attempts to solve these problems by exempting the executives from this Act, which requires a sufficiently precise definition of their status, and by establishing parallel to the works council an executives' representative body which also delegates a representative to the supervisory board. Thus the executives are recognized by law as an community of interest groups.

The executives are the pool from which the members of a company's executive organs are normally selected. Therefore their qualification requirements differ only slightly from those of the members of the managing board. They are derived from the various roles which characterize the activities of top managers. In this context, the results of a study conducted by Mintzberg in 1973 can also be regarded as typical for German managers (Mintzberg 1973; Schirmer 1992). The following roles can therefore be identified, which can in principle describe the actions of every manager:

1 Interpersonal Roles	2 Informational Roles	3 Decision Roles
a) Figurehead	a) Monitor	a) Entrepreneur
b) Leader	b) Disseminator	b) Disturbance handler
c) Liaison	c) Spokesperson	c) Resource allocator
		d) Negotiator

As a result of their specific legal framework, the roles of managers which refer to the navigation of socio-functional working relationships take on a particular significance. It is quite obvious that the significance of the individual roles depends on both the hierarchical level and the functional area of the managers which has a considerable impact on the role pattern as empirical studies have shown (Strehl 1987; Ramme 1989). In addition, a major impact on the roles of top managers stems from the level of internationalization of a company or its activities and the economic situation. The qualification level required of managers rises correspondingly. An empirical study conducted by Poensgen has shown that the training level of members of the managing board rises with increasing company size and technological dynamics while advancement tends to slow down (average appointment age: 46 years). Often a career is helped by a doctorate (Poensgen 1982; Poensgen/Lukas 1982).

The qualification background of managers

The qualification of managers tends to determine how they play the various management roles. The aims of education and training are therefore of special significance, since they shape not only the qualification process itself, but also have a lasting effect on the behaviour of those subject to the education and training. The structure of the German university system today in particular is still influenced by the educational ideals of Wilhelm von Humboldt. These basically unattainable human ideals have in all probability a close correlation with the often repeated notion of the German search for perfection.

The sophisticated German education system offers a great variety of educational opportunities to suit one's own interests and needs which differ in duration, content and formal requirements. As a rule, however, specific educational paths can be assigned to the various management levels.

The great majority of German managers have either an engineering or technical, or an economic or commercial background. Due to the great variety of engineering and technical courses on offer and the many differences between them depending on the branch of industry for which they prepare their students, only education in the field of economics will be looked at here.

Qualification background for management in Germany

Traditionally, the so-called *dual education system* plays an important role in vocational qualifications in Germany, and in the past the vast majority of people starting out in working life have benefited from this education. Having completed secondary school, they begin a three-year appentriceship during which they receive practical training on the job and theoretical training provided by the vocational schools. The apprenticeship is completed by an examination and entitles those who pass to take up the job of a skilled worker or commercial employee. The vast majority of the members of lower management have this training background. This standard qualification may be followed up by attending a technical or commercial college.

The growing number of jobs available in middle management since about the 1960s, their greater attractiveness for ambitious young people and the widespread conviction

– fostered by business practice – that a higher formal qualification offers better career opportunities resulted in a reorientation process away from apprenticeship towards university education, and which was seen as an educational expansion.

In 1993 the number of young people in Germany attending university equalled for the first time those in the dual education system. With reference to the most recent statistics, this trend appears to be confirmed. At the beginning of 1997, there were approximately 1.6 million young people involved in company apprenticeships, whilst approximately 1.8 million students were registered at German universities for the Winter Semester 1997/98.

But Germany still lags behind its neighbours in this development: while 27 per cent (in 1996 the figure was 30 per cent) of the 1991/1992 age group in Germany left secondary school having passed their , '*Abitur*' (final school-leaving examination which is a requirement for university entrance), the corresponding figure was 30 per cent for Great Britain, 48 per cent for Italy and even 60 per cent for France. Just under one out of four in France and only one out of three in Great Britain starting working life have completed an apprenticeship. Whether this is beneficial to the respective economic system obviously depends on the type and quality of alternative educational opportunities.

The university system in Germany is represented on the one hand by the traditional *universities* and on the other by the *degree-granting colleges of higher education* (*Fachhochschulen*) which have experienced an upswing since the 1960s. To meet the requirements of the economy, these colleges were to offer courses of a higher technical standard than the dual system, close to the level of the universities but with a distinct emphasis on the practical side. The education provided at these degree-granting colleges of higher education therefore became the normal educational path for entering middle management with opportunities for advancement to top management.

In addition to experience, a university degree in a technical, engineering or economic discipline continues by and large to be the standard qualification required for entering top management.

Education in business management in Germany

In Germany the science of business management as a central scientific discipline for the training of managers is not characterized by a uniform paradigm, i.e. at the various universities, there are different opinions on the subject matter, the objectives or the research methods to be applied in this discipline. Since the 1970s the so-called *decision-oriented or managerial approach* has become prevalent which is more or less a synthesis of traditional German research approaches and those of American management science whose influence has been obvious since the early 1970s.

Traditional German business management thinking was unmistakably influenced by the works of Eugen Schmalenbach (1873–1955), Heinrich Nicklisch (1876–1946) and Wilhelm Rieger (1878–1946) in the first half of the twentieth century (Stein 1993). These three economists held very different opinions.

Schmalenbach, who has strongly influenced the development of accounting and company finance, emphasized the formulation of a practical scientific concept, which understood business management as an artistic or technological discipline and focused the idea of economic efficiency. The primary objective of economic action is not profit but rather a maximum contribution to satisfy the demands of the community. Profit – and the entrepreneur Schmalenbach is well aware of its great significance – has only an instrumental function.

Nicklisch pursues the community idea even more rigorously, in that he formulated it as a normative integration ideology. A business is for him a social entity which should be guided by the idea of a business community which, in turn, means that the interests of the people working in the business must come to the fore. The basic idea of this concept is to meet the needs of the working man by developing standards for economic action. The current ecological discussion is based on the same community idea as found in Nicklisch's

concept, and the conviction, that economic action should not be left to the 'free interplay of forces', but must be regulated by guidelines which are derived from basic ethical principles. The discussion as to company culture is also essentially made up of the question as to a normative framework acting as a binding element for the company employees, and shows therefore basic similarities with Nicklisch's thoughts.

The central idea of the theory developed by *Rieger,* who similarly to Schmalenbach was primarily concerned with accounting and financing problems, is the maximization of profitability in terms of the ratio of profit to invested capital. For him, there is no other motivation for entrepreneurial action than profit. His goal is to investigate and explain empirical business management phenomena in order to derive a theory of capitalist enterprises'. He rejects the formulation of recommendations for organizing company activities. The main assumptions formulated by him relating to the employer and his behaviour are of a typically idealistic nature, so that his academic findings lack certain academic features and thereby the criticism can be made of a distinct gulf between 'theory' and 'practice'.

Building first and foremost on Rieger's methodological principles, *Erich Gutenberg* developed a comprehensive theoretical concept after the Second World War which assumed the neo-classical approach to economics, and which centred on the economic analysis of the production process (1951). According to Gutenberg the task of management is to establish a combination of production factors which benefits profitability and economic efficiency. In addition to the resources (engines, buildings, etc.) and the raw materials and supplies, these factors of production also indude the operative work of the employees. Thus, human behaviour in an enterprise is reduced to mechanistic aspects in an attempt to develop a comprehensive economic theory. Thereafter Gutenberg expanded further the fundamental basic principles of business management identified by him with his reports relating to 'Sales' (1955) and 'Finances' (1968). This theory was used as a basis in the mid-1960s for the above-mentioned managerial or decision-oriented approach which was essentially shaped by Edmund Heinen.

Heinen's reflections centre around the managerial decision processes on the basis of a realistic image of human decision behaviour which deliberately dissociates itself from the *homo oeconomicus*. He links the methodical approach of Gutenberg with both the ideas of Nicklisch and the findings of neighbouring social sciences, thus selecting an approach similar to that of March and Simon in the USA. Heinen questions the unambiguity of business objectives and the logic behind the ways and means to attain these. He replaces the profit objective with a system of objectives which is derived from the usually competing individual objectives of the decision-makers and which is characterized neither by operationality nor consistency, and instead of logical decisions based on mathematic models he makes use of psychological decision-making behaviour. This requires the opening up of the, 'economic' discipline business management towards the neighbouring social sciences, which necessarily tends to dilute the notion of the 'economical'. Heinen's behavioural and managerial approach is obviously flexible enough to integrate, for instance, the principle of general systems theory as developed in the German linguistic area, in particular by the St. Gallen school of thought (for example Ulrich; Malik; Probst), and it is particularly suited to the socio-cultural situation which characterizes practical management action in Germany. Therefore, it is not surprising that this approach has been accepted as the prevailing paradigm and strongly influenced practical management concepts.

Present-day business management in Germany is characterized by a high level of specialization in specific areas, which, of itself, emphasizes the necessity for a common, binding framework. In this context, present day business management can be split into two directions, both of which have implications for management:

- a behaviour-oriented direction, which follow in the footsteps of Heinen, and in par-

ticular his integration approach to the social sciences theory, and

- an economic-rationalistic direction, which is marked by microeconomic theories as well as the (neo-)institutional economic approaches of the property rights theory and the principal agent theory, which have gained interest in the past few years, as well as the transaction costs approach.

As a result of the differences in their starting positions, it would seem that a reciprocal fertilization, or a joining together of the different schools under a common roof is almost impossible, so that a basic paradigmatic dispute can be spoken of.

4 Management concepts and management tasks

The socio-cultural environment described above for management action in Germany and in particular the principle of 'trustful cooperation' between employer and employee which is anchored in the Works Constitution Act necessitate a basic orientation towards gaining and safeguarding acceptance. Therefore, purely economy-oriented management concepts in the classical sense of short-term profit maximization would be doomed to failure because of the opposition to be expected from the employees representatives. In the present environment *management concepts* can only be successful if they are designed to reconcile interests and, for all practical purposes, indude all the parties concerned. This however does not at all mean that management in Germany always takes the form of equality in the area of the consideration of interests, or that there is an authentic participation by the employees. Weighting of these two aspects rather evolves from negotiations or conflict resolution processes which, however, must be anticipated early.

The performance of concrete management tasks must also be seen against this background. In their essence, such tasks do not differ from those of managers in other countries who are exposed to keen worldwide competition. After all, it is always important:

- to develop and stabilize those segments which are of vital importance for sustaining the business,
- to integrate strategy, structure and culture in order to set the stage for a successful management of change and, closely connected to that, to ensure the necessary reconciliation of interests, and
- to control the value added process.

It cannot however be overlooked, that the concrete conversion of these fields of function will be influenced by specific cultural conditions.

The *process of developing and stabilizing segments important for sustaining the business* must consider the competition situation and thus also the unfavourable cost structure due to the high labour costs of German companies at the international level. This forces management to place great emphasis on quality and to instigate and promote product and process innovations in conjunction with intensive efforts to reduce costs. In this respect, management can rely on a relatively high qualification level of the employees. Special attention should be given, therefore, to the development of incentive systems to stimulate performance and innovation and also to the flexibility of working time. In view of the development and preservation of fields of business, and in particular in the international dimension, neglecting an orientation towards service in Germany has shown itself to be a central problem. The future success of German businesses depends to a greater degree on the extent to which the traditionally predominant orientation towards technology can be replaced by a stronger customer orientation within a framework of innovative procedures. As a result, an important area of personnel development emerges. Moreover, a central management task is the promotion and support of an increased readiness to take risks, for example by the formation of corresponding incentives.

The *integration of strategy, structure and culture* must consider both the market requirements necessitating the ability to react in a flexible manner and the expectations of employees with regard to content and conditions

of work. The latter are characterized in Germany, too, by certain shifts in the work-related system of values. The values of duty and acceptance prevailing among the gainfully employed in the post-war period have been replaced in the last 20 years by values more closely associated with self-development and a hedonist way of life.

The changing of values in Germany, which can be viewed in the emergence of a movement away from an authoritarian state's patterns of thought and behaviour to that of the greater penetration of a society with democratic principles, manifests itself in particular in a pluralization of lifestyles, and situations, which in total contribute towards the lasting procedure of an individualization of German society. Management in Germany will thereby not be able to escape the necessity for the consideration of individual characteristics. This trend, which above all is reflected in the requirements of customers and employees for individual treatment, can be taken into account through conceptual innovations, such as in the form of individualized or differential management approaches. The considerations as to the influence of values of management has led on the one hand to an intensive discussion about the necessities and possibilities of a company management culture, and on the other hand has had an effect on concrete management practice, particularly with respect to the division of labour and coordination but also management strategies for routine conflicts. This touches on the control of the value added process.

As a result of increasingly fierce competition and the high degree of export dependency, the German economy is forced to seek new structures and mechanisms *to control the value added process.* It is becoming more and more evident that the hierarchic control typical of German companies lacks flexibility and is too expensive. As a consequence, new ways of integrating elements of self-control are being sought in order to vest more planning and control authority in the working groups. In this context it is also to be expected, that the relationship between employer and employee will increasingly be regulated by temporary contracts of manufacture as opposed to long-term contracts of employment. The principle of welfare support as an essential element of the classical employment contract, which is of such importance especially in light of the economic ethic in Germany, will therefore be done away with to a greater extent. Pursuant to the principles of self-responsibility and self-determination, the employee will therefore be more involved in the risks run by the company. This has a profound influence on management structures and management processes and is therefore opposed by those whose power and status might be reduced by such changes. But on the other hand pressure from the market necessitates new structures and processes. The traditional long-term orientation of German management therefore stands in direct contrast to the ever increasing speed of movement of products and markets and thereby the net product processes. The greatest challenge to German management in the near future, but also to management in all other Western industrial countries and the countries of Eastern Europe in the process of change, will be the development of concepts and the implementation of programmes for the successful management of change, which manage to balance out the ambivalence between stability and change and which constructively include cultural characteristics.

RAINER MARR
UNIVERSITÄT DER BUNDESWEHR MÜNCHEN

Further reading

(References cited in the text marked *)

Graf, F.W. (1997) 'Protestantismus II' (Protestantism II) in Müller, G. *Theologische Realenzyklopädie*, 27: 551–80

Greiffenhagen, M. and S. (1993) *Ein schwieriges Vaterland–Zur politischen Kultur im vereinigten Deutschland* (A Difficult Fatherland: On Political Culture in a United Germany), Munich.

Gutenberg, E. (1958) *Einführung in die Betriebswirtschaftslehre* (Introduction to Business Administration Studies), Wiesbaden: Gabler.

Heinen, E. (1982) *Einführung in die Betriebswirtschaftslehre* (Introduction to Business Administration Studies), 8th edn, Wiesbaden: Gabler.

Heinen, E. (ed.) (1991) *Industriebetriebslehre – Entscheidungen im Industriebetrieb* (Industrial Business Studies – Decision Making in the Industrial Enterprise), 9th edn, Wiesbaden: Gabler.

Marr, R. (1979) *Personalwirtschaft – ein konfliktorientierter Ansatz* (Personnel Management – an Approach to Conflict), Landsberg: Moderne Industrie.

* Mintzberg, H. (1973) *The Nature of Managerial Work*, Englewood Cliffs, NJ: Prentice Hall.

Nicklisch, H. (1922) *Wirtschaftliche Betriebslehre* (Economic Business Studies), 5th edn, Stuttgart: Poeschel.

* Poensgen, O.H. (1982) 'Der Weg in den Vorstand' (How to get into the managing board of directors), *Die Betriebswirtschaft* 42 (1): 32.

* Poensgen, O.H. and Lukas, A. (1982) 'Fluktuation, Amtszeit und weitere Karriere von Vorstandsmitgliedern' (Turnover, tenure and further career for members of the managing board of directors), *Die Betriebswirtschaft* 42 (2): 177–95.

* Ramme, I. (1989) *Die Arbeit von Führungskräften* (The Work of Executives), PhD thesis, Dortmund: Dortmund University.

Rieger, W. (1984) *Einführung in die Privatwirtschaftslehre* (Introduction to the Private Sector), 3rd edn, Erlangen: Palm & Enke.

Schmalenbach, E. (1911) 'Dir Privatwirtschaftslehre als Kunstlehre' in *Zeitshcrift für handelswissenschaftliche Forschung* 6: 304–16 also in *Zeitschrift für betriebswirtschaftliche Forschung* 1970, 22: 490–98

Schmalenbach, E. (1949) *Einführung in die Betriebswirtschaftslehre* (Introduction to Business Administration), Tübingen.

Schanz, G. (1997) 'Wissenschaftsprogramme–Orientierungsrahmen und Bezugspunkte betriebswirtschaftlichen Forschens und Denkens' in *Das Wirtschaftstudium*, 1997(11): 554–61

Schirmer, F. (1992) *Arbeitsverhalten von Managern* (Managerial Behaviour), Wiesbaden: Gabler.

Schneider, D. (1997) 'Geschicte der Betriebswirtschaftslehre' (History of Business Administration) in *Das Wirtschaftsstudium* 1997(10): 490–500

* Staehle, W.H. (1989) *Funktionen des Managements* (The Functions of Management), Berne: Haupt.

* Stein, J.H. von (1993) 'Betriebswirtschaftslehre, Gegenstand der' (Business administration), in

W. Wittmann, W. Kern, R. Köhler, H.–U. Küpper and K. Wysocki (eds), *Handwörterbuch der Betriebswirtschaft* (Dictionary of Business Administration), Stuttgart: Poeschel.

* Strehl, F. (1987) 'Arbeitsrollen der Führungskräfte (nach Mintzberg)' (The functions of executive managers (according to Mintzberg)), in A. Kieser, G. Reber and R. Wunderer (eds), *Handwörterbuch der Führung* (Dictionary of Leadership), Stuttgart: Poeschel.

Ulrich, H. (1970) *Die Unternehmung als produktives, soziales System: Grundlagen der allgemeinen Unternehmungslehre* (Enterprise as a Productive and Social System: Basics of General Entrepreneurship), Berne: Haupt.

* Welge, M.K. (1992) 'Führungskräfte' (Executives), in E. Gaugler and W. Weber (eds), *Handwörterbuch des Personalwesens* (Dictionary of Personnel Management), Stuttgart: Poeschel.

See also: GLOBALIZATION; MANAGEMENT IN FRANCE

Related topics in the IEBM: COLLECTIVE BARGAINING; COMPETITIVE STRATEGIES, DEVELOPMENT OF; HUMAN RESOURCE MANAGEMENT IN EUROPE; INDUSTRIAL DEMOCRACY; INDUSTRIAL RELATIONS IN EUROPE; MANAGEMENT IN EUROPE; MANAGEMENT IN SWITZERLAND; MANAGERIAL BEHAVIOUR; MARCH, J.G. AND CYERT, R.M.; ORGANIZATION STRUCTURE; PRODUCTIVITY; SCHMALENBACH, E.; TRADE UNIONS; TRAINING; TRAINING, ECONOMICS OF; WEBER, M.

Management in Italy

Overview

A number of factors exist which distinguish Italian management from its counterparts in northern Europe and North America. Italian managers tend to view their organizations as 'families', with corresponding authority relationships. They have a preference for personal rather than work-specific relationships, and their ability to innovate, adapt and operate flexibly is well developed. Italian managers are also considered to be less formally trained than some of their international counterparts although Italian companies have achieved considerable success in the post-war period, with design and styling underpinning the success of Italian products and services.

Within Italy itself differences also exist. Italian management reflects the historical and regional diversity which has had a significant influence on business culture in Italy. This comprises a number of contrasts: the economic and cultural divide between northern and southern Italy; the persistence of a large public sector of industry operating alongside privately owned organizations; and the economic influence of large domestic multinationals and the relatively large number of small companies.

These differences help give Italian management a distinct flavour of its own. However, this is currently under threat as Italian business and management undergo a period of substantial flux, the result of social and political trends and the rising impact of European and international developments.

1 Historical context

Since 1945 Italy, one of the G7 group of nations, has developed into one of the world's most developed industrial economies. Italian managers in both large multinational corporations (see GLOBALIZATION; MULTINATIONAL CORPORATIONS) and small businesses can now lay claim to many achievements: 'Made in Italy' is a concept of economic significance, especially in relation to the design and style of products while engineering strengths are also evident in the construction of the rail and motorway networks down the mountainous backbone of the Italian peninsula and the road tunnel under Mont Blanc. This economic success has been achieved using a style of management particular to Italy, the nature of which can only be understood in the context of Italy's historical development.

The unification of Italy as an independent state was achieved only in the latter half of the nineteenth century. Until then the Italian peninsula had been divided between a number of states, the majority of which had foreign rulers: the Austrian Habsburgs in Lombardy and Venetia, the Spanish Bourbons in southern Italy and Sicily and the House of Savoy in Piedmont and Sardinia, together with the Pope in the Papal States, were the major dynasties controlling Italy. Unification under the House of Savoy, however, failed to gain a general consensus and the new state continued to be regarded by large sections of the population as a foreign body which had been imposed upon them. Many Italians still retain this feeling of detachment from the State and its representatives and continue to give primary allegiance to the locality in which they were born. Considerable diversity thus persists between Italians from different regions.

Occupation by the various foreign powers also resulted in differing stages of regional economic development which can still be seen today, particularly in the disparity between the advanced north and less developed south.

Economic development in the north has been in general similar to that of northern Europe, although most of Italy's industry was concentrated in the northwest until the 1960s. The south and Sicily on the other hand have continued to bear the imprint of feudalism, and the nascent industries of these areas tended to stagnate and wither after unification. Here economic development has been slow, in part conditioned by cultural attitudes not conducive to entrepreneurial activity. While in the north professional role models have been engineers and architects, in the south they have been lawyers, teachers or government officials. The distinction between north and south has often been portrayed as different ways of achieving personal aims; in the former through the accumulation of wealth, in the latter through the acquisition of power, authority, prestige and fame.

Until the early 1960s Italy stayed predominantly an agricultural society. With the 'economic miracle' and the process of industrialization, many people moved out of agriculture and became small entrepreneurs, bringing with them the traditional attitudes of a largely agricultural society – in particular, self-reliance, resourcefulness and adaptability.

Italian industry has always had to contend with strong foreign competition and has relied in varying degrees on the support of the State. The Fascist government took a number of companies into state ownership in the 1930s, and the Italian state has subsequently played a leading role in economic development, particularly in the more depressed areas of the south and the islands.

Periods of occupation by foreign powers, widespread periods of uncertainty and a lack of trust in state institutions led many Italians to regard the family as their main refuge and security. The family consequently gained a high degree of psychological and economic significance and many Italians continue to give their primary allegiance to the family rather than to the Law or the State. This strong allegiance to the family has tended to undermine the development of civic attitudes and behaviours and the rule of law (for example, tax evasion is frequent).

While Italy's fragmented historical development has resulted in continuing widespread disparities, the country's artistic heritage has acted as a kind of unifying factor. The physical presence of the past is everywhere. Even in small towns and villages buildings and monuments bear testimony to the achievements of Italian culture. Italians are very preoccupied with the appearance and impact of persons and objects, and a concern for the aesthetic dimension is a major aspect of many products and services offered by Italian companies.

2 Types of company

Italian companies fall into three broad categories:

1 a small number of large private sector companies such as Fiat, Pirelli and Olivetti;
2 a number of state-owned holding companies, for example, the Institute for Economic Reconstruction (IRI) which includes companies such as the national airline, Alitalia, and RAI, the national broadcasting corporation;
3 a great number of small businesses.

Italy's large private sector companies appear to dominate the economic landscape, although Italy has relatively fewer large companies than, for example, the UK or France. The State, however, is a major employer, not only because of public administration, education and the armed forces but because of the extent of the state-owned sector of industry: IRI, the largest of the holding companies, employed around 350,000 people in 1994. Since 1992, however, successive governments have supported a policy of modernizing the country. This policy has included making state-owned companies more efficient and privatizing them. This process, even though protracted, is reducing the number of state employees in industry.

Italy's economic structure is notable for the relative paucity of medium-sized firms and the extent of its small firm sector. Small firms have been a feature of traditional activities such as agriculture and the craft industries and have persisted in retailing, giving Italy one of the highest densities of retail outlets in western Europe. These outlets comprise large numbers of small family-run shops and bars which in comparison to other major European countries are only slowly ceding ground to supermarkets and hypermarkets.

The small firm sector has achieved considerable success and attention since the 1970s and has been held up frequently as a model of economic development. Small firms (the majority employing less than twenty people) have been particularly successful in a number of areas including fashion goods, ceramic tiles and furniture. Castronovo (1980) describes the rise of the small industry sector and links it to a number of developments in the Italian economy and society. While many Italians were moved to set up small businesses because of the decline of agriculture, a driving force in the setting up of new business has been the desire of the company's founder to be independent and successful.

The establishment of new companies was given fresh impetus by the response of large companies to the industrial troubles of the late 1960s, in particular the 'hot autumn' of 1969. Large companies succeeded in developing strategies to counteract the increasing demands of their workforces. These included cutting the number of employees, raising capital intensity and introducing labour-saving processes such as automation and robots. As a result employment in large companies declined. At the same time employment in small companies (11–500 employees) and very small companies (10 or less employees) expanded considerably. Consequently these firms came to employ more than three million people compared to one and a quarter million in large companies.

The decline in employment opportunities in large companies forced many workers to seek alternative sources of employment, generally at a lower level of pay. Larger companies stimulated the development of alternative sources of employment by contracting out increasing proportions of their operations, especially those requiring low levels of specialist skills. These were now carried out by small businesses which could perform them more cheaply because of lower wage costs. There

was thus a substantial increase in the volume of economic activity carried out in small firms and even in domestic households.

Small businesses also had the advantage that in general they were excluded from many of the legal obligations imposed on larger firms and were not involved in national wage negotiations. Small businesses were therefore frequently able to pay lower wages because employees also had one or more other sources of income. The small business sector is thus closely associated with the 'hidden' economy which is reckoned to account for at least 30 per cent of Italy's gross domestic product.

In northern Italy, small firms became the major employers in the traditional industrial areas of the northwest and created what has become known as the 'Third Italy'. Small firms also set the pace in developing industries in northeast and central Italy. Venetia is particularly noted for the production of white goods such as refrigerators and washing machines. Emilia-Romagna has become Italy's Silicon Valley, with a large number of firms developing and producing microprocessor systems and technologies. At the same time traditional firms based on local agricultural production have continued to prosper.

In many respects the small companies have become the motor of the Italian economy, even though this sector comprises a mixture of traditional and more advanced activities. In general small companies have demonstrated great dynamism and vitality, initiative and specialized skills, adaptability and flexibility. They have also spread the ideas and practices of industrial culture more widely throughout Italy. The south of Italy has not been excluded from such developments and has also experienced an increase in industrial activity. Developments, however, have been far more limited, numerically and in terms of scope. The level of industrial development and the establishment of new businesses have been much lower than in the north and centre and in general have been linked to the agricultural sector. Furthermore, certain regions of the south seem not to have contributed at all to the establishment of new industrial firms.

A key factor of this success has been unity: rather than the small firm standing alone, it is a component in an overall system. The system comprises a group of companies in a specific geographical area that specialize in various aspects of the total production process (for example, the components, the final product and the machinery required to manufacture the product or its components). The firms are often supported by a network of local public organizations such as trade associations, chambers of commerce, local banks and local and regional governments. Companies both cooperate and compete. They exchange ideas and expertise but compete for customers and orders. Positive responses to customer demand result in upstream developments and innovations which help to ensure the overall viability of the system. Because of local concentration, information and new developments are speedily disseminated. The small size of firms allows a high level of responsiveness. Firms that collapse are also speedily replaced.

Porter (1990) uses a number of examples from Italian industry to illustrate his model of national competitive advantage. Porter uses the Italian ceramic tile industry as a prime example, with Italian companies producing around 30 per cent of world output and accounting for about 60 per cent of world exports in 1987. Although a traditional industry, it has boomed only since the Second World War. Production of ceramic tiles is concentrated in the area of Sassuolo, a small town in Emilia-Romagna, and hundreds of small firms are involved in the industry, both producing tiles and the related products and equipment. Domestic demand initially encouraged the expansion of the industry. Firms could be set up with relatively little capital and there was a supply of trained workers and engineers (Emilia-Romagna was home to Italy's luxury sports car industry).

The industry went through a period of intensive technological development in order to eliminate dependence on imported raw materials and the relationship between tile manufacturers and equipment manufacturers became very close. As a consequence of this relationship equipment manufacturers also became major exporters. Geographic concentration in and around Sassuolo facilitated the exchange of views and the adoption of new techniques and practices. This close interrelationship also benefited a broad spectrum of related industries supplying materials and services to the tile manufacturers.

Because of the large number of companies involved and their close geographical proximity there was also a high degree of competition as it was difficult to conceal new developments. This proved a further spur to innovation. In spite of the intense personal rivalry between companies, the companies formed an industry association and a research and development centre. According to Porter, the continuing success of the industry will depend on the capacity of its members to pursue dynamism and change.

Not all small firms are part of such a system and many play a more traditional supporting role, supplying parts and services to larger companies. The existence of a broad web of small firms allows large firms to contract out many activities. In some cases (such as the fashion industry) the work is carried out by domestic households which can undertake the work at an even lower cost. Benetton, for example, is reputed to subcontract around 80 per cent of its activities to outside operators.

One characteristic which applies to both small and large private sector firms is family ownership. While family ownership is typical of small firms in general, large private companies are predominantly owned and run by members of the families which founded them, for example, the Agnellis (Fiat), Pirellis and Benettons. Members of the family, in addition to owning a majority of the shares, will frequently hold senior positions. The company will also be structured in such a way that it deflects the attention of outsiders and limits the risk of takeover. Even when the company's shares are publicly quoted, the number of shares available for purchase tends to be small as the majority are held by family members.

3 Managerial characteristics

In seeking to generalize about the characteristics of Italian managers, it is important to bear in mind the difference between privately owned and state-owned companies. In many respects managers in state-owned companies share the attitudes and behaviours of government officials as well as the benefits. State-owned companies have tended to be run according to party political agendas. Their aims and objectives have also differed from those of companies in the private sector. State-owned companies suffer from many of the deficiencies of state organizations. Many people are attracted by the job security which employment in a state organization affords.

Because of the size of the sector, public sector managers are of considerable importance. Many public sector managers, particularly senior managers, have traditionally been political appointees, with key appointments shared out between the members of the ruling coalition. The majority of the appointees have traditionally come from the ranks of the Christian Democratic Party which dominated post-war Italian politics until 1994. However, in the 1980s there was an increase in public sector managers appointed from the Socialist camp.

Public sector managers have often been accused of managerial ineffectiveness because of the public sector's inefficiency and indebtedness. While it would be wrong to dismiss all public sector managers as purely political appointees, the public sector has had difficulty in shaking off the accusation of partiality when it comes to appointments and conducting business. Furthermore, some public sector managers argue that they hold a philosophy distinct from the sole pursuit of profit (which is implied for the private sector) and are motivated by Christian and Socialist values such as social justice and assisting those in need in addition to striving to achieve economic goals. They often see themselves as guardians of economic activities which would not necessarily appeal to the private sector. However, there has frequently been tension between managers' identification of what is required in a strictly business sense and the broader political demands of the party which has appointed them (Galli 1989). In any case, with increasing pressure for privatization public sector managers are having to behave more

and more like managers in privately owned companies.

In private sector companies there are some formal differences in the characteristics of managers. For example, entry to managerial grades in large organizations is almost exclusively restricted to graduates (hence the prevalence of titles such as *dottore* and *ingegnere*). In smaller companies managerial positions are more likely to be occupied because of family or close personal ties. Nevertheless, irrespective of company size, there is a large degree of consistency in the way Italian managers (who are almost exclusively male) relate to their organizations and the tasks they have to perform.

A major study of the top Italian industrial companies and their managers, conducted by Milan's Bocconi University (Magrino 1989) provides systematic information on managers in Italy's main companies. Middle managers accounted for 6.7 per cent and senior managers for 2.7 per cent of the total workforce.

The study also confirmed some general aspects of the activities of Italian companies, for example, the high degree of specialization (just over 70 per cent of firms had one core activity), the reliance on sub-contracting (75 per cent of firms contracted out some of their operations, with 30 per cent of firms sub-contracting more than one-fifth) and the extent of export sales (just over half of the firms sold more than one-fifth of their output abroad, with a quarter selling more than half).

The overwhelming majority of managers in the sample were graduates (70 per cent of all managers and 93 per cent of senior managers). Almost three-quarters of managers had studied technical and scientific courses, with the remainder divided almost evenly between economics and arts subjects. The average age of managers was forty-eight and on average each manager had worked for eighteen years. Sixty per cent of managers had worked all their lives for the same company and just over half had always worked in the same functional area such as production or sales. Relatively few managers had worked in more than one industry and even fewer overseas. However, a distinguishing feature of top managers was that a quarter had postgraduate training (the majority abroad) and greater experience of working in different industries and countries. Most top managers had worked either in technical or commercial functions. Managers were generally promoted internally (around one-half), with small companies more likely to recruit managers from outside (38 per cent of managers) than large companies (26 per cent).

Education and training have been the subject of debate for many years in Italy. State provision has frequently been criticized for its inappropriateness to the needs of a modern society and for the high wastage of human and economic resources. Italy has one of the highest student populations in Europe, but relatively few graduates. Exposure to international competition has raised the profile of training in large companies although smaller companies devote little time and few resources to training. However, the results of the Bocconi survey were generally positive. Ninety per cent of firms offered training to their employees. Seventy-two per cent of middle managers had received training and on average each manager had received almost six days of training during the year.

The analogy of the traditional family can be usefully applied in order to understand the organization and functioning of Italian companies. The head of the company is the key decision maker and power tends to be exercised in an autocratic way. Hierarchy and status play an important role but are determined less by formal position than by personal standing, authority and relationship to senior decision makers. Power and authority are shared along personal linkages rather than through formal organizational relationships. Power is thus strongly based on personal ties, although this is expected to be complemented by the appropriate knowledge and skills. Superiors are expected to deserve the positions they hold and to be able to provide their subordinates with the knowledge and information they require.

As in a traditional family the organization expects personal loyalty from its members and in its turn offers support which often extends beyond the workplace. All in all, there is a strong identification with the company and between the individuals working within it. Italian companies thus tend to function as closely knit organizations and there is a strong drive to maintain consensus. Even though decision making is predominantly autocratic, key decision makers will seek to ensure that decisions are widely accepted. Conversely, criticism of individuals within the company is commonly regarded as criticism of all the managers of the organization.

This preference for personal relationships also extends to dealings with representatives of other organizations. Decisions on orders and contracts are influenced by the personal rapport between the parties involved. People believe that formal criteria (such as legal conditions and contracts) play a secondary role to the mutual understanding and respect between individuals. The building of viable interpersonal relationships is seen as an essential pre-condition of conducting business.

The family dimension of Italian companies is counterbalanced by the individualism of Italian managers. Within the context of autocratic decision making and overt consensus, individual managers may behave in an individualistic and competitive way as they strive to make their mark and score points off company colleagues. This is often reflected in the apparent disorganization of Italian companies and, at the extreme, when it occurs within the senior group, this individualism can result in major dissension and crisis for the organization.

Because of the way in which power and authority is organized and distributed, Italian managers tend to be strong on interpersonal skills such as negotiating, building alliances and exploiting personal and political contacts. On the other hand, they are considered less effective in a range of more formal skills. The predominance of interpersonal relationships is said to militate against the effective implementation of formal organizational structures. Italian managers, moreover, appear more effective at responding to situations than in planning for them. Their ability to respond quickly has enabled them to capitalize on many opportunities. However, there is limited investment in research and as a consequence there have been few inventions and patents. Strategic planning is also interpreted in a restricted way; there is often great euphoria that projects are completed on time (even if the implementation has been a catalogue of mini disasters).

A different view and interpretation is put forward by the authors of the Bocconi survey. Managers had a clear understanding of strategic aims, the main three mentioned being product development, increased market share and long-term profit maximization. Companies were also engaged in a broad range of strategies to achieve these aims, including acquisitions and joint ventures intended to gain control of material or knowledge resources.

With regard to organizational structure, the majority of firms in the survey had a functional structure. Forty per cent of large firms (but only 20 per cent of firms defined as 'excellent' because of their performance by the authors of the Bocconi survey) had a divisional structure. This possibly reflects the concentration of power in Italian companies and the prevalence of traditional autocratic management methods. Many companies also utilized various control mechanisms, including regular meetings and reports, to monitor the performance of the company and of managers and other subordinates. The quality of the mechanisms was variable and companies with what was considered above average performance had strategic planning and monitoring systems that were more developed than in the sample firms in general.

The survey did identify a particular weakness of Italian management in the human resource area. Over one-third of the firms had no formalized personnel systems or, if they had them, did not implement them. Nevertheless, almost 60 per cent of firms awarded personal bonuses to their middle managers. The authors of the survey interpret this as part of an Italian model of management in which companies are reluctant to specify and formalize aims and procedures in order to retain maximum flexibility, in particular with regard to their human resources. Human resources are socialized and developed more through cultural conditioning and the informal personal network than through formal personnel instruments such as appraisals and incentives.

Researchers into comparative management have painted a generally consistent picture of management and business culture in Italy (see BUSINESS CULTURES, EUROPEAN). According to Trompenaars (1993) Italians tend to be particularist, that is, they regard personal relationships as more important than formal arrangements such as laws and contracts. This is supported by a diffuse, high-context culture which stresses personal loyalty and honour. Situations are evaluated according to one's involvement with individuals rather than according to objective criteria. The degree of emotional identification is high and emotions are generally openly displayed. Emotions are also exploited to gain advantages, and Italians are skilled at reading others' emotions and intentions in non-verbal forms of communication. Allied with this is a great concern for losing face. Status and authority are generally ascribed to individuals and there is a great respect for hierarchy. Individuals act as members of a group and decisions taken in isolation generally carry little weight.

This view of Italian business culture is supported by Mole, who categorizes Italian business organizations as organic with marked group leadership. Mole defines an organic organization as 'a social organism growing out of the needs and relationships of its members' (Mole 1993: 165). Hofstede (1980), in his comparative study of work-related values, identified an Italian propensity towards hierarchy and autocracy, with subordinates dependent on their superiors. Italians attach great importance to expert opinion, qualifications and detailed rules and procedures as these all tend to reduce uncertainty. However, where regulations become excessive, as in the state bureaucracy, individuals will seek to circumvent them. Hofstede also sees Italy as a country with a high concern for material success. Managers expect to be assertive and to compete with their colleagues.

The one criterion on which Hofstede appears to differ with Trompenaars and Mole is on the work value he denotes as individualism, on which Italians score very highly. Italian management is very much concerned with the management of individuals, with the attainment of personal power and prestige. This ought to conflict with the notion of Italian companies as families, with the stress on interpersonal relations, but does not. In order to succeed as individuals Italian managers need the support of friends, colleagues and subordinates to make the system work for them.

4 Change

The characteristics of Italian management have been strongly influenced by factors arising from the course of Italian history and these are likely to persist. In the recent past, however, a number of trends have begun to influence the way Italian managers think and behave.

The US model of management has influenced a number of Italian managers who admire the achievements of US companies or have even been employed by them. US influence is also visible in the expansion of business schools in Italy and in the number of managers with MBAs. It is thus likely that the deficit in formal management skills will be reduced.

Progress towards European economic integration, the establishment of a Single European Market and the general process of internationalization have opened Italy's relatively protected markets to European and other competitors (see ECONOMIC INTEGRATION, INTERNATIONAL). Italian managers will need to enhance their organizational skills and become more pro-active if they are not to lose out. Managers in state-owned companies will be particularly affected as barriers are removed, monopolies are broken up and companies are privatized.

Finally, Italy itself is changing as the influences of an agricultural society decline. This is heralding a shift from particularist family values to a demand for impartial civic modes of behaviour. Nevertheless, even though the traditional family is under threat as Italy has one of the lowest birth rates in Europe, there is little evidence that the family as the bedrock

of Italian society is in decline. However, family businesses are unlikely on their own to be able to provide the financial resources needed for survival in the more competitive markets of the future.

VINCENT EDWARDS
BUCKINGHAMSHIRE CHILTERNS UNIVERSITY

Further reading

(References cited in the text marked *)

Barzini, L. (1966) *The Italians*, London: Hamish Hamilton. (Classic work on the Italians.)

Brierley, W. (1993) 'The business culture in Italy', in C. Randlesome *et al.* (eds), *Business Cultures in Europe*, 2nd edn, Oxford: Butterworth Heinemann. (Provides much useful information on Italian business.)

* Castronovo, V. (1980) *L'industria italiana dall'ottocento a oggi*, Milan: Mondadori. (Reviews the evolution of Italian industry from the nineteenth century.)

Celli, P. (1997) *L'illusione manageriale*, Laterza. (Presents a critique of contemporary Italian management, indicting it, among other things, for being detached from society and lacking vision.)

Gagliardi, P. and Turner, B. (1993) 'Aspects of Italian management', in D. Hickson (ed.), *Management in Western Europe*, Berlin: Walter de Gruyter; also available in Hickson, D. (ed.) (1997) *Exploring Management Across the World: Selected Readings*, Harmondsworth: Penguin. (Possibly the only work in English dealing exclusively with Italian management; focuses in particular on the context within which managers work.)

* Galli, G. (1989) *Manager*, Milan: Rusconi. (Based on interviews with senior managers, this book explores the various attitudes and philosophies of Italian managers.)

Haycraft, J. (1987) *Italian Labyrinth*, Harmondsworth: Penguin. (Gives a broad portrayal of life and society in Italy. Covers topics such as the family, business and the general diversity of Italy.)

Hofmann, P. (1990) *That Fine Italian Hand*, New York: Henry Holt & Co. Inc. (The author gives a broad portrayal of life and society in Italy, covering topics such as the role of the family, small business and the general diversity of Italy.)

* Hofstede, G. (1980) *Culture's Consequences: International Differences in Work-related Values*, Beverly Hills, CA: Sage Publications.

(Seminal work on the impact of national cultures on work-related values.)

Hofstede, G. (1991) *Cultures and Organizations: Software of the Mind*, Maidenhead: McGraw-Hill. (Deals primarily with national cultural differences, including illustrations from Italian life.)

* Magrino, F. (1989) 'La svolta dei mille', *Il Mondo* 1 May: 92–5. (Reports the results of the Bocconi survey of Italian managers.)

* Mole, J. (1993) *Mind Your Manners – Culture Clash in the Single European Market*, London: Industrial Society Press. (Investigates the different cultures of the European Union, providing good insights into Italian management and business culture.)

* Porter, M. (1990) *The Competitive Advantage of Nations*, New York: The Free Press. (Italy is one of the nations investigated by Porter and the work contains an analysis of the Italian ceramic tile industry.)

'Survey: Italy' (1997) *Economist*, 8 November. (A comprehensive survey of the Italian economy.)

* Trompenaars, F. (1993) *Riding the Waves of Culture*, London: Nicholas Brealey. (This is primarily comparative, covering a range of different cultures. In so doing it provides good insights into Italian management and business culture.)

Vidal, F. (1990) *Le management à l'italienne*, Paris: Inter Editions. (Deals comprehensively with management in Italy; stresses in particular strengths in design and the intellectual dimension of senior management.)

See also: BUSINESS CULTURES, EUROPEAN; GLOBALIZATION; MULTINATIONAL CORPORATIONS

Related topics in the IEBM: BUSINESS SCHOOLS; COLLECTIVE BARGAINING; CORPORATISM; ENTREPRENEURSHIP; FLEXIBILITY; HUMAN RESOURCE MANAGEMENT IN EUROPE; INDUSTRIAL AND LABOUR RELATIONS; INDUSTRIAL RELATIONS IN EUROPE; INDUSTRIAL STRATEGY; MANAGEMENT IN EUROPE; MANAGEMENT IN NORTH AMERICA; PORTER, M.E.; POWER; PUBLIC SECTOR MANAGEMENT; SMALL BUSINESS FINANCE; SMALL BUSINESS STRATEGY

Management in Japan

Overview

There are several theories about the origin of Japanese management, some tracing it back to the pre-industrialization era of the Shogunate. Such theories naturally stress its cultural aspects. However, if one considers that foreign interest in Japanese management was triggered by the miraculous growth of the Japanese economy in the 1960s, any explanation becomes more complex. It is necessary also to take into account more systematic factors brought about by the democratization of Japan after the Second World War. Taking a more long-term view, it is also necessary to consider the impact that Japanese management has had upon the management systems of other countries since the 1970s.

1 Formation of consensus: the *ringi* system

Management practice in Japan is based around consensus formation within organizations. The system that has developed to facilitate such a decision-making process is known as the *ringi* system, and is outlined in Figure 1.

The figure shows two decision makers, D(A) and D(B), who are members of an organization. Their jobs, denoted by J(A) and J(B), are independent of each other. In other words, D(A) and D(B) do not have to talk or coordinate decisions with one another before

carrying out their jobs. As Simon (1945) explains, the two decision makers have two decision premises: one factual and one based on value. If one accepts the assumption that Japanese people are culturally homogeneous, the two value premises of D(A) and D(B), being cultural in nature and based on factors such as belief, taste and given codes of conduct, can be taken to be identical. In such a case the only condition required for D(A) and D(B) to reach consensus is the same set of factual premises (denoted by F(A) + F(B)). To meet this condition D(A) gives F(A), a set of factual information such as data, figures and files, to D(B). Likewise D(B) gives F(B) to D(A).

Such information sharing (process 1 and process 2 in Figure 1) in order to reach agreement among organizational members is not unique to Japanese organizations. What does make the *ringi* system unique, however, is the information handling shown by processes 3 and 4 in Figure 1. These processes represent

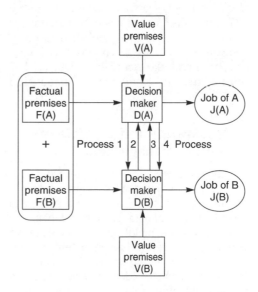

Figure 1 Decision making in Japanese organizations: the *Ringi* system

the means by which one obtains agreement from the other. As their jobs, J(A) and J(B), do not overlap, agreement does not mean coordination. It is instead a form of moral support based on the sentiment: 'If I were you, I would do the same'. Without such a moral endorsement, members of organizations in Japan are reluctant to take any action.

Concerning organizational activities, however, it is unrealistic to assume that any job is independent from any other, in any sense. This is particularly true of a section or a department in a business organization where jobs overlap and depend upon each other. If a company is working on a large-scale project almost all jobs there are interrelated. In such a situation management by agreement is obviously better than management by disagreement, and the degree of mutual dependency produces various combinations of moral support and coordination.

The *ringi* system incorporates the whole process and mechanism of those organizational behaviours aimed at group and organizational consensus. The formal document used under the *ringi* system is the *ringi sho*. On the *sho* (literally document or paper), those managers concerned and who have offered support affix their seals. Thus, the *ringi sho* is a symbol of group consensus. Since the 1970s the *ringi* system has been regarded as feudalistic and has been abolished in many companies. What has been abolished, however, is simply the use of the *ringi sho*. The spirit of it is still living, and is embodied in *nemawashi*.

2 *Nemawashi* and the role of middle management

Nemawashi means root binding or extending the roots of a tree deeply enough into the ground to let it stand solidly. As a concept, it is an integral part of management in Japan.

In *nemawashi*, middle management plays a very important role as liaison or 'linking pin' (Likert 1961) at the crossroads of various information channels. Ideally, when carrying out this role middle management is not only a transmitter but also a translator of information. Figure 2 illustrates the concept, where

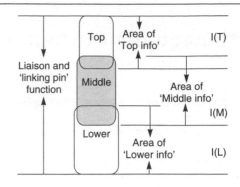

Figure 2 The role of middle management

I(T) represents the information set belonging to top management, I(M) middle management and I(L) lower management.

To play such a part successfully, middle management must know 'what's what' and 'who's who' in the organization. 'Lifetime employment' and the personnel rotation system of Japanese companies have contributed greatly to this. A typical case of *nemawashi* is described by Sasaki (1990) as follows.

In a section of a department middle management presents an idea for a new sales campaign. The *kacho*, or section chief, therefore calls a meeting of the section. Through discussion of the campaign the section members judge that they will need the overall support of the firm. The *kacho* reports to the *bucho*, or department head, and consults with him/her. The *bucho* agrees that the campaign is a good idea. It is at this point that the time-consuming activity of raising a general consensus begins. By this point a local section consensus has been reached. The next move is to seek a wider agreement within the department. Once this has been achieved, an overall consensus within the firm is sought. As part of the information exchange process the *bucho* may arrange meetings with other departments concerned. Each department sends one *bucho*, one *kacho* and perhaps two *kakaricho*, or sub-section chiefs. If there are four departments involved, in all between ten and sixteen members will attend the meeting. If the opinions of specialists from the shop floor are needed, engineers or sometimes foremen will be invited. The initiator and his colleagues, under the leadership of the *kacho*, liaise (formally and informally) between sections and departments, preparing the necessary documents and materials. Such prior coordination is vital if the *ringi* system is to be effective.

It is only after the department has attained an informal agreement from all of the other departments concerned that the formal procedure begins. This is the circulation of a formal document of request, the *ringi sho*, for approval or authorization of the proposal. All of the managers concerned affix their seals to it as a sign of agreement. (In Japan seals are used for signing documents instead of a signature). The number of seals is often as many as ten or twelve. In order for the document to be circulated the details of the plan are completed by the members of the original section. Finally, the *ringi sho* is sent to the top decision-making body for formal authorization and the final 'go-ahead'.

3 Gravity of information

Although middle management plays a vital role as the link between top and lower management, each sector possesses its own information, and thus power. Any corporate decision is a function of $I(T)$, $I(M)$, and $I(L)$ as shown in Figure 2, and the degree of influence each has is defined by the importance of the information possessed. This concept can be stated as 'gravity of information'.

With the end of Second World War came a sudden influx of new information on US management styles. In those Japanese companies in which respect for seniority was deeply rooted, it was easier for the younger management – essentially middle or lower management – to digest the new knowledge, and thus to acquire greater influence via the gravity of information only they possessed.

Management Training Programme (MTP), a version of the Supervisor Training Programme of the US Far East Air Force, was one such innovation. Others included Training within industry (TWI) and quality control methods. The new methods were implemented in quick succession. These efforts matched well with the democratization movement promoted by the American Occupation Authority. The formation of labour unions, which was legally permitted for the first time in the history of Japan, reinforced this social trend. It would be valid to say the democratic industrialization and spiritual modernization of Japan progressed only after the war.

As stated above, these new social and organizational settings meant greater importance for middle and lower management, increasing the gravity of the information they possessed and conferring substantial decision-making power at their level. This increase in power can be demonstrated using a quality circle as an example.

A quality circle

After the Second World War, Japanese industries improved product quality from 'cheap and bad' to 'cheap but good'. The move was forced by necessity, and was essential if Japan were to survive in a global economy. Quality may be divided into two spheres; originality and reliability. In the immediate post-war period, with the Japanese economy undergoing major reconstruction, it was too early for Japanese industries to produce the former. Accordingly they began efforts to produce the latter through mass production factories, into which had just been introduced US production techniques such as statistical quality control (SQC) and industrial engineering. SQC played an important role in the sphere of reliability especially on the software side, and industrial engineering did the same for the hardware side. Toyota's *kanban* system, for example, is a refined extension of industrial engineering.

In the case of SQC, when used to measure the quality of reliability, gravity of information, as derived from factual premises, facts and data, was located on and near to the shop floors. To produce reliability in the mass production factories the standardization of production processes was vital. Because a substantial part of the factual premises for these processes lay with the workers, worker participation became essential. Unfortunately, at the time the level of general education of these workers was not of a sufficiently high standard to warrant participation. According to Ishikawa (1985), it was this need that triggered the massive re-education of workers (from general education to quality control methods) at the hands of individual companies.

Other major changes were also taking place. Lifetime employment, previously only enjoyed by management, was now extended to the workers. Following this, the status differentiation between management and labour began to dissolve, and the title 'worker' was changed to 'operator'.

Another change came with the formation of labour unions. As part of the drive for a 'one company, one union' system, membership was opened up to include managers up to the middle management level. It was hoped that having both managers and operators together as members would form a strong bond and foster feelings of solidarity within the company. This idea was further reinforced by a newly created bonus system in the form of a share in profits.

As a result of these innovations, managers and operators naturally started to identify. There was a strong feeling of team spirit, of fighting for common goals. More importantly, identification of common goals meant a convergence of values, the values on which decisions would be based. As time passed workers gradually progressed from operators to decision makers who could statistically analyse and handle data.

4 The P–D–C–A cycle

After the Second World War, the P–D–C–A cycle or the cycle of control (or management, as of recently) was born in Japan. Derived from the basic concepts and methods of quality control introduced by William Edwards Deming and other US advisors, the acronym represents P for 'plan', D for 'do', C for 'check' and A for 'act'. In the biggest cycle, which is a company cycle, top management make company plans; these plans are broken down into department and section plans; according to these plans, 'dos' or implementations are undertaken (in case of production this is done by so-called workers); statistical

checks are carried out and, in the light of any defects, analyses made of meaningful cause-and-effect relations for the defects; corrective actions are then taken.

For a P–D–C–A cycle to function, continuous flows of data and knowledge of the factual premises on which a process is based are vital. In addition, everyone contributing to the data flow has to send information in understandable forms to the receivers and to transmit it with due understanding.

Use of the P–D–C–A cycle initiated further unexpected change among workers, who amended the model to create a cycle of their own within – the quality circle. Re-educated workers or operators started to carry out checks or inspection personally, in addition to their own tasks. Then they advanced proposals for corrective action and for permission to correct actions in their own domain in person. Some well-educated operators even started to make plans for their own tasks. Thus the role of these workers changed from slaves of machines to masters of them. Although standardization is essential in order to make products with reliable qualities, historically such a process has meant monotonous jobs for workers and a loss of the capacity for decision making. Under the P–D–C–A cycle workers retain this capacity, in that they have the authority to design and make standardizations by themselves.

Figure 3 illustrates the P–D–C–A cycle/quality circle at work. The larger cycle represents the company cycle, the smaller one in D the workers' cycle, or quality circle. This P–D(p–d–c–a)–C–A cycle as a symbol represents total quality control (TQC), where the quality cycle is a harmonious part of the TQC system. Managers and workers are qualitatively the same. Both are decision makers. In point of fact, the leader of a quality circle is usually the foreman, and the supervisor above has to play the role of the facilitator.

Both the supervisor and the foreman are the 'linking pin', which is located on the overlap between management and labour. Thus, as Kondo, who conceptualizes this New P–D–C–A cycle, TQC including a quality circle is not based on 'them and us' but on 'us' (Kondo 1988).

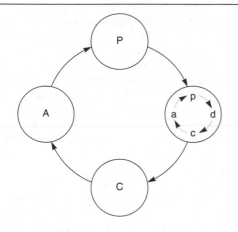

Figure 3 The P-D-C-A cycle/quality circle

5 Homogeneity: the convergence of value premises

Many regard cultural homogeneity as the factor governing management in Japan (see ORGANIZATION CULTURE). However, a cross-sectional study of the world reveals cultural homogeneity everywhere. A static existence determined by cultural homogeneity is not the primary factor contributing to the uniqueness of Japanese management practices. This uniqueness, although a result of homogeneity, is caused by the convergence of value premises, forced together by the communalities of lifetime employment, the co-membership of managers and workers in one union, the *ringi* system and personal acquaintances among members expedited by the rotation system.

Moreover, this convergence is intentionally accelerated. For example, the most important expected effect of the first in-company seminar for newcomers is not to let them learn about individual jobs but to let them utilize the seminar as an opportunity to socialize. Organized camping trips, drinking and sports within a company are all intended to facilitate increasing affectionate identification between members. In particular, drinking is so common that the Japanese invented a new English word 'nommunication', an integration of *nomu*, (literally 'drink' in Japanese) and

'communication'. This new word is being used more and more throughout the world, especially by quality control managers. In Japanese organizations it carries great weight. When recruiting new members character and personality are considered vital as participation in nommunication is intended to continue until retirement.

6 The quality of decisions

The quality of an organizational decision, Q(Y), is a function of the quality of the individual decisions made by members of the organization, Q(X), and the quality of the transformation of those decisions into an organizational decision, Q(P) (see Figure 4). To improve organizational performance, one must improve Q(Y), and to do this, one must improve Q(X) or Q(P) or both. In Japanese organizations attempts to improve Q(X) usually consist of the internal re-education of existing members of the company. Due to lifetime employment it is extremely rare of them to try and improve organizational performance by obtaining better human resources from external markets.

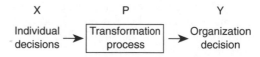

Figure 4 Decision quality model

To improve Q(X) is easier than to improve Q(P). In order to improve Q(P) one must improve the quality of human relations among managers, among workers and between managers and workers. Information necessary for decision making flows more smoothly through networking between organizational members with good relations than between those without.

Japanese companies have placed relatively more importance on Q(P) than Q(X). Convergence of value premises has contributed to improving Q(P), and thus Q(Y). When existing human resources are judged incapable of carrying out a job the first measure taken is training and education. If this fails, then job rotation is instigated to try to make better matches between organizational members and jobs.

7 Pros and cons

Vague responsibility and lack of individual leadership

The collection of seals to show agreement on the *ringi sho* is a symbol of group responsibility, which is common to all decision making in Japanese society. The moral support of the *ringi* system and the 'understanding' of *nemawashi* are contained within a 'responsive responsibility' which manifests when a decision taken brings failure. The concept is embodied in the phrase: 'You did not disagree when the plan was shown'.

This inability to apportion responsibility results in a vicious circle. It is safer for individual members to make accountability vaguer than to claim clear individual responsibility. For this reason, when a manager has to have a critical meeting with, say a counterpart manager of a foreign company, he takes several other managers to minimize personal risk. The drawback of such a system is that Japanese managers have been robbed of a spirit of individual leadership.

Slow decision making, quick implementation

Decisions which require group consensus naturally take time. Thus, time-wise, efficiency levels in Japan are relatively low. It has often been said of the Japanese that they lose the first chance of profit in the market and that they stick to the safety-first rule to gain second best. However, a study by Drucker (1971) sheds light on an important aspect of Japanese decision making. Drucker's points can be summarized as in Figure 5.

In Figure 5, W stands for the West and J for Japan, d stands for decision, i for implementation and t for time. In the West, organizational decisions are made more on an individual basis and thus take less time than in Japan. However, in Japan decisions are based on organizational agreement and consensus, and accordingly at the implementation stage no objections are raised. In the West, at implementation stage, individual decisions tend to meet with disagreement and talks for organizational agreement have to take place. As a result, the implementation time of Japanese companies can be shorter than that of Western companies, and accordingly the whole processing time of the former (t_3) can be shorter than that of the latter (t_4).

The process of management includes not only the decision-making process but also the implementation process. It is meaningless to measure the efficiency of making decisions simply by the making of a decision. Implementation must be taken into account. Profits are not achieved by decisions but by actions and implementation.

This conceptualization of Drucker's explains well the behaviour of Japanese companies during the growth period, when they did not have to be a market leader in the world economy but could settle for the position of second best. However in the 1990s, because of the appreciated value of the yen and subsequent bursting of the bubbles, the Japanese economy has plunged into an era of crises nationally and internationally. Faced with this situation, Japanese management may well fail due to lack of the individual leadership required for quick decisions, and of specialist creativity.

Participative decision making

For any management system, MBO, or management by objective, is important. However, problems arise when a superior who does not know much about the jobs of his subordinates sets objectives for them. In this case it is

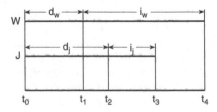

Figure 5 Decisions for implementation

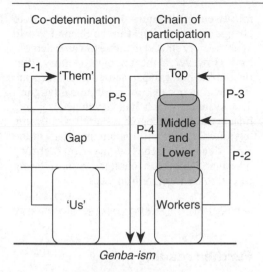

Figure 6 Two types of participation

essential that the subordinates work with their superior to set out their objectives. Instead of MBO, there should be MOO, or management *of* objective.

Figure 6 illustrates two types of participation. The first is the ideologically institutionalized co-determination system developed especially in Germany and Sweden after the Second World War. Representatives of labour (usually union representatives) participate in the board by sitting there as equal decision makers, with 50–50 voting rights shared within the management. In this system, however, the 'them and us' gap still exists. The two sides, management and labour, may be equal in making corporate decisions, but on the shopfloor workers participation in making decisions about their jobs is not guaranteed.

The second type of participation is typical of that developed in Japan after the second world war. Most representative of this type is the quality circle, where workers or operators participate (P-2) in not only checking but also in taking corrective actions and even planning their own tasks (the P–C–A–D cycle). To define the form in simple terms, it is the participation of labour in middle management (although it is not ideologically designed to extend this right to the decision areas of the board).

Another extension of participation is also to be found under the *ringi* system, where middle management participate (P-3) in board-level decisions. Known as *nemawashi*, this can take two forms: vertical and horizontal. Talks between quality circle leaders and supervisors or engineers are viewed as vertical *nemawashi*.

With both of these types of participation there exists a continuous flow of information. And to achieve such continuity, the liaison role of middle management is vital. They must know the aims and desires of lower management and workers as well as those of top management. To convey top management policies to lower echelon members they have to understand the value premises of top management. In order to make decisions to answer questions from the top they need factual premises from the shop floor. For this reason they have 'harmonious' talks with workers and often work alongside them to dig out new facts. This is the participation of middle management in labour (P-4).

In Japanese management, and especially in the fields of TQC or TQM (total quality management), this kind of management participation is also made at the top management level. It is known as 'top management audit' (P-5). In order to make a decision, for example, to invest in a new production line to make better quality products, it is preferable even for very top management to have actual contact with the shop floor than to just hear about things. This philosophy is called *Genba-ism*, with *Genba* meaning shop floor or workplace in Japanese. When top management in Japan is unsure of what decision to make, they often keep to the rule 'return to *Genba*'. Top management audit is another form of management participation in labour.

By using such systems, Japanese management permits two-way participation. Although industrial democracy *per se* does not exist, the boundary between labour and management as the decision makers is more vague than in the West.

8 Conclusion

After the Second World War, the strength of company culture as a binding factor in Japanese organizations became increasingly powerful (see ORGANIZATION CULTURE). This was particularly true for the larger companies. The new organizational homogeneity, coupled with cultural homogeneity, gave a centripetal and cohesive nature to such cultures. Under the *ringi* system and the influence of *nemawashi*, the value premises of company members have accelerated in their convergence towards an identical organizational value.

This organizational value has resulted in strong decision codes for members of a company, who thus reject anything or anyone different. Although the *ringi* system and the reliance on the formation of consensus dominates Japanese business practices, these have not been extended to include foreign managers or workers of subsidiaries in foreign countries. It is not only due to language difficulties experienced by Japanese managers; company culture also plays a part. There is often conflict between a domestic unit and a foreign unit.

This cultural and organizational problem is not limited to the international operation of Japanese companies. It is found even with a merger of two Japanese companies. For the Japanese, fusion and real integration of two different cultures is not complete until the existing members of the two organizations have left. Until that time any department of the new company effectively retains two departments within it – one from each company.

On a global scale such problems of integration are even more marked. Thus, a merger with a foreign company is the last thing which a Japanese company would consider. Much progress would need to be made before the mutual lack of understanding could be overcome, but, as Drucker (1995) asserts, in the recent trend of changes in the world economy Japanese companies are not given much time for that.

In the mid-nineteenth century Japan was forced to change by foreign pressures. As a result a new civilization and new technologies flowed in to enlighten the nation. And in the mid-twentieth century Japan was forced to change again by defeat in the Second World War. Society started to move towards democracy. However, at the turn of the century, after the bubble burst, Japan started to disintegrate from within because of 'institutional fatigue'. The systems which had developed Japan's businesses and economy started to become dysfunctional. It will remain uncertain in the first decade of the twenty-first century whether Japan can change without being forced to by foreign influences.

NAOTO SASAKI
TOKOHAGAKUEN HAMAMATSU UNIVERSITY

Further reading

(References cited in the text marked *)

Chatterjee, B. (1990) *Japanese Management: Maruti and the Indian Experience*, New Delhi: Sterling Publishers. (Compact but deep analysis of the cultural aspect of Japanese management for practices in India.)

* Drucker, P. (1971) 'What we can learn from Japanese management', *Harvard Business Review* (March–April): 11–23. (A pioneering work which divided decisions for the sake of decision and for the sake of implementation.)

* Drucker, P. (1995) *Managing in a Time of Great Change*, Stoneham, MA: Butterworth Heinemann. (New insights for the growing power of Asian economies and their impact on the world economy.)

Fukuda, K.J. (1988) *Japanese-Style Management Transferred: The Experience of East Asia*, London: Routledge. (Analytical and systematic international comparison of Japanese management with other Asian management.)

Guest, D. and Knight, K. (eds) (1979) *Putting Participation into Practice*, Farnborough: Gower. (A clear description to divide participation at plant level and participation at company level.)

Hirschmeier, J. and Yui, T. (1975) *The Development of Japanese Business*, London: Allen & Unwin. (Detailed description of businesses and managers before the Second World War.)

* Ishikawa, K. trans D.J. Lu (1985) *What is Total Quality Control?: The Japanese Way*, Englewood Cliffs, NJ: Prentice Hall. (Good translation of Ishikawa's book on the development of quality control systems in Japan.)

* Kondo, Y. (1988) *Quality in Japan, Juran's Quality Control Handbook*, New York: McGraw-

Hill. (A compact explanation with insights into how Japanese quality control systems were developed.)

* Likert, R. (1961) *New Pattern of Management*, New York: McGraw-Hill. (One of the classics of industrial psychology for organization theories.)

* Sasaki, N. (1990) *Management and Industrial Structure in Japan*, Oxford: Pergamon Press. (Behavioural science approach to the *ringi* system in Japanese organizations and industries.)

* Simon, H.A. (1945) *Administrative Behaviour*, New York: Macmillan. (A pioneering work showing how behavioural sciences can be used for organizational decision making.)

See also: BUSINESS CULTURE, JAPANESE; BUSINESS STRATEGIES, EAST ASIAN; MANAGEMENT IN GERMANY; ORGANIZATION CULTURE

Related topics in the IEBM: BUSINESS HISTORY, JAPANESE; BUSINESS STRATEGY, JAPANESE; COMMITMENT IN JAPAN; COMMUNICATION; DEMING, W.E.; DRUCKER, P.F.; GROUPS AND TEAMS; INDUSTRIAL DEMOCRACY; INDUSTRIAL RELATIONS IN JAPAN; ISHIKAWA, K.; JAPANIZATION; JURAN, J.M.; MANAGEMENT EDUCATION IN JAPAN; MANAGEMENT IN EUROPE; MANAGEMENT IN NORTH AMERICA; MANAGEMENT IN PACIFIC ASIA; MANAGEMENT IN SCANDINAVIA; MANAGERIAL BEHAVIOUR; OHMAE, K.; ORGANIZATION BEHAVIOUR; SIMON, H.A.; TEAMS IN MANUFACTURING; TOTAL QUALITY MANAGEMENT; TRADE UNIONS

Management in South Korea

1 Organizational structure
2 Managerial processes
3 Human resource management
4 Competitive strategies
5 Trends in management in South Korea

Overview

Over the past few decades and until recently South Korea has enjoyed spectacular economic success. This can be traced to a number of factors, one of which is the competitiveness of Korean companies. The Korean management system has three major sources of influence. The first is Confucianism, which was the state philosophy of Korea for more than 500 years, beginning with the Yi Dynasty in 1392 and ending in 1910 when Korea was annexed by Japan. The profound influence of Confucianism on the values, attitudes and behavioural patterns of Koreans has apparently spilled over into the Korean management system. The second and third sources, Japanese and US influences, are more recent. Korea was a Japanese colony from 1910 to 1945; after the Second World War, influences from the USA outweighed those from Japan until 1965, when Korean–Japanese relations were normalized. Since then, many Korean companies have developed close business ties with both nations. The USA is seen as a key market for exports, while Japan is relied upon as a source of intermediary products needed to manufacture those exports.

Based on these sources of influence and Korea's own historical traditions and experiences, Korean companies have developed their own management system, sometimes known as 'K-type management', that includes top-down decision making, paternalistic leadership, clan management, *inhwa* (harmony-oriented cultural values), flexible lifetime employment, personal loyalty, compensation based on seniority and merit rating, high mobility of workers and expansion through conglomeration. In spite of various inherent problems and a constant pressure for change, the Korean management system has maintained its own uniqueness. This entry will focus on the organizational structure of Korean companies, their common managerial processes, their competitive corporate strategies and trends towards development and change.

1 Organizational structure

Organizational structure is an important aspect of the Korean management system. Structure in Korean terms refers to relatively stable relationships between individuals and sub-units within a given organization. In many ways, organizational structure reflects the management values of Korean culture.

Formal structure

Korean companies are often characterized by a high degree of centralization and formalization. Authority is concentrated in senior levels of managerial hierarchies, with major decisions (especially financial decisions) entailing *kyul-jae*, a formal approval from top levels of management that involves taking many *chops* (personal stamps of approval). The Samsung group in the past used a process of twenty-one *chops*, needing several months to get a project approved; upon taking over the group in 1987, Kun Hee Lee demanded that the number be cut to three (Paisley 1993). The hierarchic structure starts with the chairman, followed by the president, vice president (*busajang*), senior managing director (*junmu*), managing director (*sangmu*), department manager (*bujang*), section manager (*kwajang*) and so on down to the foreman and workers. Korean structures tend to be much more top-down and authoritarian than their counterparts in Japan, for example.

Korean companies usually have a 'tall' hierarchical structure of organization. One outstanding organizational feature of Korean companies is that they normally do not employ personal staff, with the exception of assistants for the group chairman. Other executives tend to be supported by deputies and assistants in line positions rather than as personal staff. This increases the layers of vertical hierarchies conducive to a centralized and tall organizational structure. Another outstanding feature of Korean companies is that their vertical and hierarchical control is supported by strong functional control from staff departments such as planning, finance and personnel. Korean companies attach great importance to functional specialization, allowing the planning and finance departments to exercise functional control under the leadership of the chief executive. Many *chaebols* (large industrial groups; see *CHAEBOLS*) have a planning and coordination office under the group chairman, that is responsible for allocating major internal resources within the group (Aguilar and Cho 1984). Therefore, many Korean companies have a combined organizational structure placing a vertical concentration of decision-making power at the senior levels of management and a horizontal concentration of functional control in staff departments.

In contrast to the centralized organizational structure and formalized functions, individual jobs are not clearly structured in many Korean companies and do not usually have clear-cut job descriptions. The responsibilities of the individual employees tend to be decided by the supervisor according to the needs of the occasion. Although poorly defined job descriptions can bring about low efficiency from ill-distributed workloads and work redundancy, the managers may also enjoy a high degree of flexibility when adjusting to changing conditions. When the high degree of centralization and formalization is combined with poorly defined work assignments, then it can be seen that the individual manager's ability to obtain the support of others is crucial to work performance.

Generally speaking, the organizational performance of Korean companies is closely related to how effectively the company can overcome the centralized and formalized structure. This can be achieved in a number of ways. Many companies depend heavily on autonomous or temporary organizations such as task teams or special committees. Others take advantage of informal interaction. Highly successful Korean companies tend to use fewer top executives and staff personnel in order to increase delegation of authority while decreasing central control (Lee 1989). Task forces and informal interactions help overcome departmental divisions and enhance organizational flexibility. Authority delegation helps simplify the organizational structure.

Informal structure

The concentration of authority results partly from the fact that ownership and management are not separated in most Korean companies. The owner and family actively participate in the management of most companies, and family and clan members dominate the management structure, as is shown in Table 1. Many Koreans are part of an extended clan or *chiban*, based on blood relationships, that provides broad-based security for family members; the larger the *chiban*, the greater the security for individual members (Song 1990). Business leaders are expected to take care not only of their own immediate family members but also of other relatives. This relationship based on kinship is called *hyul-yun* (literally meaning 'blood related').

Professional executives and managers also form an important power group in Korean companies (see Table 1). In some Korean companies the career managers, who have been promoted during their extended service with the company, can also exert powerful influence on company management through the creation of personal networks within the company and foster them over the years. Many of these managers are initially recruited through open competition from an elite group (*gong-chae*); most Korean companies have been using the *gong-chae* system since the early 1990s. With the passage of time, internally

Table 1 Backgrounds of *chaebol* executives

	The founder and family members	Professional career managers	Others	Total
Hyundai	7	42	8	57
Samsung	2	28	11	41
LG	7	26	11	44
Daewoo	2	25	25	52
Sungung	3	21	2	26
Sangyong	2	11	8	21
Hankuk Hwayak	1	9	11	21
Total	24	162	0	0

Source: Chang 1988

promoted career executives and managers will grow in number and power.

Common geographical and educational ties also play a strong role in the formation of management and power groups. It is common practice for owners to bring their friends from school and their home town into management. In some Korean companies, top management positions are predominantly filled by those who are from the same geographical area, such as Seoul, the south-western province of Honam, or the south-eastern province of Yeongnam. In other Korean companies, graduates from elite universities such as Seoul National or Yonsei dominate top management. In the past, a graduate with a 'K-S mark' (a degree from Kyunggi High School and Seoul National University) automatically enjoyed a better chance of getting into top management. The relationship with the owner based on geographical ties is called *ji-yun* (region-related) while the relationship with the owner based on school ties is called *hahk-yun* (school-related). Both *ji-yun* and *hahk-yun* tend to constitute a very strong factor in informal relationships, giving common identities, backgrounds and a sense of belonging.

Hyul-yun, or blood relationship, promotes career managers internally while *ji-yun* and *hahk-yun* are important not only in senior-level power group formation but also in the formation of informal cliques or groups at all levels within a Korean company. All three relationships affect the power structure and informal groupings. Family ownership based on *hyul-yun* has been the most important factor affecting the power structure of Korean companies whose ownership and management are not separated. While the power of internally promoted career managers has been increasing with continued management professionalization, power based on *hyul-yun* remains predominant in Korean companies. *Ji-yun* and *hahk-yun* also significantly influence informal groupings and social interactions with these companies.

2 Managerial processes

Leadership and decision making

Owing to the strong influence of family traditions, there is a tendency for Korean corporate leaders, especially founders, to manage on the basis of principles governing the family or clan system. In the traditional Korean family, the father is the unquestioned and respected head. If he wishes, he can wield almost absolute power. The traditional Korean father also has full responsibility to feed the family and decide the future of the children. One legacy of such a family tradition for business leadership in Korean companies is the strong authoritarian style of superiors in the managerial process. A top-down decision-making style is fairly typical among Korean companies; usually, 80 per cent of the authority lies in the upper management level, with middle or lower management having a very limited authority (Lee and Yoo 1987a). Authoritarian leadership has been a well-accepted managerial norm under the centralized structure of Korean companies, the passive attitude of the subordinates being further conducive to this authoritarian style. The traditional decision-making style has been used more to diffuse responsibility than to reach consensus (De Mente 1991).

Nevertheless, the authoritarian style is not despotic. Corporate leadership in Korean companies is also heavily influenced by a key value of Korean behaviour, *inhwa* (harmony), which is similar to the Japanese *wa*. However, *inhwa* does not emphasize the group element as in *wa*; it emphasizes harmony between unequals in rank, power and prestige (Alston 1989). Korean managers cherish good relations with their subordinates and try to keep the needs and feelings of their subordinates in mind. Another aspect of *inhwa* is that each party has a responsibility to support the other.

This aspect of harmony is evidenced in the decision-making patterns of Korean managers, who try to maintain good relationships with subordinates even if this sometimes means they have to compromise group performance. Korean managers tend to make decisions with the consultation of subordinates. The Korean process of informal consensus formation, *sajeonhyupui*, is similar to that found in Japan (Song 1990), but Korean subordinates are usually reluctant to express their opinions (see MANAGEMENT IN JAPAN). Subsequently, managers are often expected to understand the feelings of their subordinates before making appropriate decisions. Managers maintain various interactions on an informal basis with the subordinates as an important way to achieve a harmony-oriented leadership that is based on mutual trust and benevolent authoritarianism.

Motivation

Koreans are highly motivated workers and are well known for being willing to work long hours. The motivation of Korean employees is influenced by traditional values as well as realistic needs. The key Confucian values of diligence and harmony have contributed to a relatively strong work ethic. The instinct for survival has also been an important driving force among Koreans, who have been haunted by instability and poverty throughout most of their recent history. A strong work ethic and harmony have become the most cherished values of Korean employees.

While the specific motivations of Korean employees vary depending on the size of the company and the level of seniority, high wages and job security tend to be the most important motivational factors. According to a study conducted in 1984 by the Korean Chamber of Commerce and Industry, executives of large companies tended to cite an 'environment for voluntary participation' as the most effective incentive, while the Chief Executive Officers (CEOs) of small companies regarded the management-by-objectives system as the best way to heighten the spirit of workers. It was also reported that employees aged over sixty cited wages as the most important incentive for hard work, while new management staff aged under thirty viewed 'environment for voluntary participation' as the most effective means of motivating employees and promoting productivity (Kim and Kim 1989).

As a group, Korean employees tend to put a somewhat stronger emphasis on extrinsic factors (such as wages, working conditions and job security) than on intrinsic factors (such as creativity and a sense of achievement) for high motivation (Lee 1989). Moreover, the need for a sense of achievement and recognition tends to be satisfied within the framework of the harmony of a given group. Since harmony is a dominant value in interpersonal relationships within a group, external factors tend to be even more important motivating factors to Korean employees. Nevertheless, the trend is for more Korean companies to shift their emphasis to intrinsic motivating factors such as *changjo* (creativity), achievement and recognition.

Communication

One outstanding feature of organizational communication in Korean businesses is that formal communication is mainly handled through vertical hierarchies (Lee 1989). The organizational communication process depends heavily on hierarchical relations, which are determined by a combination of factors ranging from formal authority and informal social status to length of employment and age. In the vertical communication process, superiors are expected to give directives while subordinates are expected to understand and implement those directives. The superiors tend to prefer to issue general directives as opposed to specific and detailed instructions; and subordinates prefer using their own judgement rather than asking superiors for explanations in event of the latter's directives not being clear-cut or detailed.

Another notable feature of communication in Korean companies is that employees usually attach much greater importance to upward formal communication on horizontal interdepartmental lines. This may have resulted from the high centralization of authority in Korean companies. The strictly hierarchical structures of Korean companies tend to determine the nature of vertical and horizontal communication. For employees, vertical communication is more work-related than horizontal communication, and thus more important. Poor horizontal communication between vertically structured departments has become a major barrier to efficient organizational performance in many large Korean companies (De Mente 1991).

The preference of superiors to communicate in general terms, combined with a relatively large power distance, comprises a major source of misunderstanding in Korean companies. It is very important for subordinates to develop the ability to decipher the intentions of the superior from general directives. Good personal relations with superiors tend to help overcome hierarchical barriers to communication; blood relationships as well as school and regional ties may further enhance mutual understanding and trust, thereby contributing to more straightforward communication. Those who share good lines of communication often tend to develop an informal management clique within the company.

Many Korean employees are not good at open communication in formal meetings and have difficulty in airing their views, especially opposing ones. An openly different opinion may embarrass or antagonize one's superior, or provoke a colleague. Besides, Koreans are not culturally encouraged to share information openly with others except within close personal relationships. However, many Koreans are very good at informal communications, especially on a one-to-one basis with a superior. Sophisticated superiors will constantly make opportunities for such communication to be available; they may for example invite subordinates to dinner at their home or at a restaurant. Subordinates can also visit their superiors at home for private talks. The use of informal occasions or settings for open communication is very important for mutual understanding and trust between superiors and employees.

3 Human resource management

Korea has a large pool of well-educated human resources. About 98 per cent of the population is literate; more than 80 per cent of Korean teenagers finish high school studies and most high school graduates attend colleges or professional training schools. Human resource management priorities in Korea include recruiting the best candidates, operating on-the-job training programmes and instituting reward and appraisal systems.

Recruiting and training

In a general survey (Shin 1985), it was found that most large Korean corporations classify employees into three categories: core (top management), basic (permanent employees) and temporary. Most Korean companies hire employees through a combination of reference checks, tests of knowledge, common sense and proficiency in English, personal interviews and physical examinations. New college graduates or experienced professionals are preferred. Large companies recruit twice a year, in June and November, and prefer to recruit their management trainees from reputable universities such as Seoul National University, Yonsei University and Korean University. Mid-sized and small Korean companies recruit once a year. Recruitment is very competitive.

Once new employees have been recruited, the elite groups tend to be assigned to such core departments as planning and finance after an in-house training programme lasting 7–10 days. Korean companies place great emphasis on employee development, which is normally conducted through in-house training programmes; many large *chaebols* have their own employee training centres and set aside as much as 5 per cent of regular work hours for formal training. The emphasis on employee development is in conformity with traditional Korean cultural values that attach great importance to education. Traditional Korean society was ruled by the *yangban* or educated class; the greatest ambition of the promising sons of *yangban* families was to pass the civil service examination and attain a high rank in government.

Reward and promotion system

The reward and promotion systems in Korean companies are traditionally based on social seniority, but performance is becoming an increasingly important factor (Lee 1989). Korean companies have gradually combined social seniority with performance in distributing their rewards; wages may be based on seniority but bonuses are often based on performance. Generally speaking, high-growth companies tend to attach greater emphasis to performance than do low-growth companies.

Promotion is regarded as extremely important to both employees and employers. In many Korean companies, top management is actively engaged in promotion decisions. Promotion is based on a number of criteria that can include seniority, performance,

personality, family ties, school and region. Many Korean companies consider not only performance but also job attitude and special ability. Many managers are unwilling to give their employees too negative an evaluation; *inhwa* emphasizes the importance of harmony among individuals who are not equal in prestige, rank and power, and superiors are required to care for the well-being of their subordinates. A negative evaluation may undermine harmonious relations. Another Korean value, *koenchanayo* (which can be loosely translated as 'that's good enough'), also hampers critical evaluation as it urges tolerance and appreciation of people's efforts. According to this tradition, one should not be excessively harsh in assessing someone else's sincere efforts.

Severance and retirement

Layoffs are a common practice in Korean companies. Whenever they encounter a business downturn, they feel free to lay off employees at all levels. Korean employees also change jobs fairly freely, although many do work in the same company until retirement; while Korean employees normally attach great importance to their companies, they would not normally feel embarrassed at accepting better offers from other companies. Skilled employees tend to change jobs more often than do the unskilled. As the concept of loyalty in Korea is often based on individual relationships, the loyalty of Korean employees is often devoted to a particular superior (Song 1990); consequently when managers change companies they often bring many of their subordinates with them.

Korean companies do not have a uniform retirement age, though many require their employees to retire at fifty-five to sixty (see MANAGEMENT IN JAPAN). Retirement age is also determined by rank and senior executives and managers tend to have an extended retirement age. Korean companies do not make a distinction between resignation and retirement when calculating severance pay; most companies set aside one month's salary per year for severance or retirement (Chang 1988), while some companies will add an additional two or even three months per year when calculating the total length of service.

Trade unions

After the Korean War, US-style labour legislation was enacted, guaranteeing workers' rights to organize and bargain collectively. However, these rights never emerged in practice. The government-dominated Federation of Korean Trade Unions helped employers to control workers. In 1960, workers joined radical students in overthrowing the government of Syngman Rhee.

Through the 1960s and 1970s the government of Park Chung Hee followed a policy of growth first and distribution later, and suppressed the labour movement. The Special Act on National Security of 1971 required workers to obtain government approval prior to any labour confrontation; this law was lifted in 1981 but new restrictions were then imposed. Industry-wide national unions were banned in 1980 and replaced with 'enterprise unions' that were controlled by labour–management councils, and were required to meet on a quarterly basis to coordinate conflicts between productivity and welfare. These councils tended to favour the interests of management, as many labour representatives were appointed by the government.

The political reforms of 1987 removed government intervention in labour relations and granted workers the right to unionize. Industry-based national unions were allowed to be established, and the newly amended Trade Union Act ensured protection from unfair labour practices and allowed workers to organize, negotiate and take collective action. Trade unions grew and began actively seeking wage increases and improved working conditions. However, the subsequent strength of the unions and the existence of powerful labour laws made it virtually impossible to sack workers or make them redundant. To cope with the economic downturn and ensuing recession changes to these laws were proposed such that corporations would have the ability to introduce redundancies. Initially this led to a series of general strikes instigated by the unions in a bid to preserve their dominance.

However, renegotiated changes to the laws were finally introduced in February 1998.

4 Competitive strategies

Manufacturing development strategies

In the early period of development, many Korean companies followed the strategy of choosing the growth/maturity stages of products (Hahn 1989), taking advantage of governmental policies promoting import substitution. Apart from the cement and fertilizer industries which were very important for Korean reconstruction and agricultural development, most manufacturing was concentrated in the labour-intensive light industrial sectors. Selecting products in the growth/maturity stage decreased the risks for Korean companies, while from the government's perspective the development of labour-intensive and consumer product industries provided employment for the large pool of unskilled workers and conserved badly needed foreign currency. Protected by governmental industrial policies, Korean manufacturing companies developed quickly into strong competitors in international markets.

There have been two basic types of technology transfer into Korea. The large intermediate goods manufacturers in sectors such as chemicals, cement and fertilizer adopted an apprenticing policy and relied heavily on foreign assistance in the form of turnkey plants, consultants and licensing. On-the-job training under the direction of foreign suppliers and off-the-job training at foreign sites provided Korean engineers and technicians with the basics of production expertise. Small manufacturing companies, that lacked the financial resources to negotiate with suppliers of foreign technology, upgraded their products and production technologies through reverse engineering of locally available foreign products (Kim and Kim 1989). This informal approach was prevalent in the early period of technology transfer; Korean Steel Pipe, for example, successfully duplicated and improved the Japanese model through imitation.

Other commonly used manufacturing strategies were concerned with the project implementation process, during which many Korean companies tried to minimize the total project completion period. There are a number of competitive advantages to be gained thus: cash flow can be generated much earlier, interest and overhead costs can be reduced significantly, and huge profits and market share can be achieved by early entry into growth markets. Samsung, for example, completed its first 64K DRAM chip manufacturing facility in just six months, as compared to an average of eighteen months for a similar project in the USA (Hahn 1989).

Diversification strategies

Diversification strategies are important for growth in any business. In Korea, large business groups, or *chaebols*, have been pursuing diversification strategies for the last three decades; in fact, diversification strategies have been widely advocated by the Korean government as part of the national economic policy. The Korean government has also favoured the development of world-class large business that can compete successfully in the international market (see GLOBALIZATION; INTERNATIONAL TRADE AND FOREIGN DIRECT INVESTMENT). With the support of government, the *chaebols* have successfully implemented an 'octopus arm' diversification strategy and expanded their role in the Korean economy. Major *chaebols* such as Samsung, Hyundai, Lucky-Goldstar (now the LG Group) and Daewoo have become mainstays of the economy. Diversification has also been facilitated by strong Korean entrepreneurship; many Korean business leaders have an

attitude of 'get the order first and figure out how to do it later' (Kang 1989: 67).

Generally speaking, diversification can be classified into seven categories: single, vertical, dominant-constrained, dominant-linked, related-constrained, related-linked and unrelated. The largest *chaebols* have tended to follow a strategy of unrelated product diversification. Samsung, for example, entered into sugar and wood textiles in the 1950s, electronics, fertilizer and paper production in the 1960s, construction, electronics components, heavy industry, synthetic textiles, petrochemicals and shipbuilding in the 1970s, and aircraft, bioengineering and semiconductors in the 1980s. Smaller companies generally pursue a strategy related to a single or dominant product structure. Medium-sized companies tend to fit in between these two extremes, typically following a strategy of related product diversification. The latter seems to be the most important strategy followed in terms of numbers, but, given that the ten largest *chaebols* own more than 200 companies, it can be seen that unrelated product diversification has been an important strategy and has greatly facilitated the rapid growth of Korean business (see Table 2).

However unrestrained diversification has in part been responsible for the problems that the *chaebols* now find themselves in. Companies diversified at the expense of improving their financial stability by using profits from one enterprise to fund new markets. Therefore all areas of the corporations had high debt to equity ratios including their highly profitable sectors. With no core industries and a high degree of cross-subsidization the *chaebols* found themselves under immense pressure

Table 2 Growth strategies of *chaebols*

Business group	Single	Dominant	Related	Unrelated	Total
10 largest (213)	0	1 (10%)	1 (10%)	8 (80%)	10
11–20 largest (123)	0	2 (20%)	3 (30%)	5 (50%)	10
21–50 largest (206)	0	9 (30%)	14 (47%)	7 (23%)	30
51–108 largest (248)	12 (21%)	21 (36%)	19 (36%)	6 (10%)	58
108 largest (788)	12 (11%)	33 (31%)	37 (34%)	26 (34%)	108

Source: Chung (1989), based on Jung (1987); reprinted with permission of Greenwood Publishing Group, Westport, CJ, Copyright 1989

from new smaller specialist firms who werre able to compete because of their comparative advantage. The largest conglomerates have had to make massive cuts in overseas investments and reverse the national trend by refocusing and concentrating on core businesses.

The types and degrees of diversification strategies vary substantially from industry to industry, mirroring the differences in their nature. Vertical diversification for example is most often used by manufacturers in textile and garment industries because a continuous supply of raw materials and market outlets is critical to the maintenance of a company's competitive edge. A related-constrained strategy is more prevalent among companies in the food and beverage industries, which tend to produce goods closely related to each other in terms of the use of raw materials and distribution channels. In the metal and non-metal manufacturing industries, dominant-constrained strategies seem to be popular as they enable management to focus on a few dominant product lines while using the same organizational resources.

5 Trends in management in South Korea

The business environment in South Korea is undergoing rapid change. Traditional managerial values and organizational systems are under growing pressure to change accordingly. In many companies changes have already taken place; examples include shifts from seniority-based reward systems to more balanced systems combining seniority and performance, a shift from strict family control to an increased role for career managers, a move from over-centralized functional control to decentralized horizontal cooperation, a shift of cultural emphasis from *inhwa* to the encouragement of *changjo*, and a shift in emphasis from non-material rewards to a balance of the material and the non-material.

There are also signs of a shift in attitude by the Korean government towards the *chaebols*, particularly over the issue of ownership. By the mid-1990s, levels of ownership by founding families and their associates

ranged from 61.3 per cent at Hyundai to 39 per cent at the LG Group; the official maximum is 40 per cent. The government wants these 'insider' shareholdings reduced to 25 per cent. *Chaebols* that comply with this wish will then be allowed to further expand and diversify.

Several *chaebols* have announced plans for change. The Samsung Group, for example, is now trying to change its top-heavy and often unwieldy management structure that often hinders productivity and competition; chairman Kun Hee Lee hopes to graft modern Western management practices on to the group's Confucian hierarchy and give more autonomy to middle and lower management (Paisley 1993). In early 1995 Hyundai announced it would reduce the number of its subsidiaries from 50 to 23 through mergers and sell-offs. Daewoo also plans to decentralize, turning the subsidiaries loose to be run more freely by their chairpersons. LG plans to give subsidiaries more independence and to reduce insider holdings to approximately 24 per cent within two years.

With the continued internationalization of Korean companies, the trend towards professionalization will increase in strength. However, Korean management will continue to maintain its uniqueness, based on the country's general cultural and social environment.

MIN CHEN
THUNDERBIRD – THE AMERICAN GRADUATE
SCHOOL OF INTERNATIONAL MANAGEMENT

Further reading

(References cited in the text marked *)

* Aguilar, F. and Cho, D.S. (1984) 'Daewoo Group', Harvard Business School Cases 385–014, Cambridge, MA: Harvard Business School Press. (Pioneering case study on Korean *chaebol*, very informative on the early development of Daewoo.)
* Alston, J.P. (1989) '*Wa, guanxi* and *inhwa*: managerial principles in Japan, China and Korea', *Business Horizons*, March–April: 26–31. (Concise cultural introduction to the differences and similarities of the three related cultural values: *Wa* (Japanese), *Guanxi* (Chinese), and *Inhwa* (Korean).)

* Chang, C.S. (1988) '*Chaebol*: the South Korean conglomerates', *Business Horizons* 31 (2): 26–31. (General introduction to large Korean business conglomerates, *chaebol*, covering their organizational structure, cultural values and historical evolution.)

Chang, C.S. (1989) 'Human resource management', in K.H. Chung and H.C. Lee (eds), *Korean Managerial Dynamics*, New York: Praeger. (Intensive discussion on various aspects of Korean human resource management.)

Chung, K.H. and Lee, H.C. (1989) *Korean Managerial Dynamics*, New York: Praeger. (This is so far the most comprehensive edited volume on Korean management.)

* De Mente, B. (1991) *Korean Etiquette and Ethics in Business*, Lincolnwood, IL: NTC Publications. (Well-written cultural handbook on how to do business in Korea.)

* Hahn, C.K. (1989) 'Korean manufacturing strategy', in K.H. Chung and H.C. Lee (eds), *Korean Managerial Dynamics*, New York: Praeger. (Explains the major strategies that Korean manufacturing companies have used in their period of rapid growth.)

Jung, K.H. (1987) *Growth Strategy and Management Structure of Korean Business*, Seoul: Korean Chamber of Commerce and Industry. (Provides one of the most authoritative explanations on the growth and management of Korean businesses during the first three decades.)

* Kang, T.W. (1989) *Is Korea the Next Japan?*, New York: The Free Press. (Very informative book on Korea's overall competitiveness, written in a straightforward and simple style.)

* Kim, D.K. and Kim, C.W. (1989) 'Korean value systems and managerial practices', in K.H. Chung and H.C. Lee (eds), *Korean Managerial Dynamics*, New York: Praeger. (Good conceptual discussion on the influence of the Korean cultural value system on managerial practices.)

* Lee, H.K. (1989) 'Managerial characteristics of Korean firms', in K.H. Chung and H.C. Lee (eds), *Korean Managerial Dynamics*, New York: Praeger. (Detailed discussion on unique Korean managerial features, using a cultural approach.)

* Lee, S.M. and Yoo, S. (1987a) 'Management style and practice of Korean *chaebols*', *California Management Review* 29 (4): 95–110. (Short, simple but very interesting discussion on the management style and practices of large Korean business conglomerates.)

Lee, S.M. and Yoo, S. (1987b) 'The K-type management: a driving force of Korean prosperity', *Management International Review* 27 (4): 67–8. (There are many similarities between this article and their earlier one, although this article tries to develop a conceptual framework for the understanding of Korean management style and practices.)

* Paisley, E. (1993) 'Innovate, not imitate', *Far Eastern Economic Review* 13 May: 64–9. (Updated, journalistic description of recent reforms among *chaebol*, especially the Samsung Group.)

* Shin, Y. (1985) *Characteristics and Problems in Korean Enterprise*, Seoul: Seoul National University Press. (Good critique of Korean management style and practices by a Korean scholar.)

* Song, B. (1990) *The Rise of the Korean Economy*, New York: Oxford University Press. (Concise but interesting introduction to the economic miracle of Korea for those who know little about the country.)

See also: BUSINESS STRATEGIES, EAST ASIAN; *CHAEBOLS*; HUMAN RESOURCE MANAGEMENT, INTERNATIONAL; INTERNATIONAL TRADE AND FOREIGN DIRECT INVESTMENT; *KEIRETSU*; MANAGEMENT IN CHINA; MANAGEMENT IN JAPAN

Related topics in the IEBM: BUSINESS STRATEGY, JAPANESE; COLLECTIVE BARGAINING; COMMUNICATION; DECISION-MAKING; DOWNSIZING; HERZBERG, F.; HUMAN RESOURCE MANAGEMENT; INDUSTRIAL AND LABOUR RELATIONS; INDUSTRIAL STRATEGY; MANAGEMENT IN PACIFIC ASIA; MASLOW, A.H.; MOTIVATION AND SATISFACTION; ORGANIZATION STRUCTURE; ORGANIZATIONAL PERFORMANCE; PERFORMANCE APPRAISAL; TRAINING

Management in the United Kingdom

Overview

Changes in the economic and occupational orders of the modern-day UK have led to increasing proportions of workers in managerial and professional positions. Although it is difficult to define precisely the nature of the managerial role, definitions of managers taken from occupational censuses suggest that they comprise more than two million of the workforce. This is certainly the case if the two broad categories incorporating managers in central and local government and in large-scale commercial and industrial enterprises are included with those engaged in smaller establishments. There have been a wide range of studies in the UK covering different aspects of the managerial role and, as a consequence, there is an increasingly clear picture of the dominant characteristics of managerial attitudes and behaviour. Indeed, much is now known about patterns of share ownership among managers in the UK, industrial relations experience, job satisfaction and motivation, and views on the role of government and the enterprise culture. Moreover, specific aspects of managerial behaviour with respect to issues such as careers, training and education have increasingly been targeted as areas of particular focus.

Here, the intention is to delineate various aspects of the managerial role and of related managerial experiences in the UK. The entry begins with an analysis of the historical context, in which early debates on the separation of ownership from control and the concomitant emergence of a 'separate' and 'specialist' management function are assessed. This is followed by accounts of the social position, social origins and education of managers, together with issues of managerial careers with special reference to gender. Following this, details of the range and types of managerial work and related aspects of job satisfaction are then discussed. Issues of professionalism and training are then assessed, after which managerial attitudes towards industrial relations and employee participation are evaluated. There is then a review of public and private sector similarities and differences in the nature of managerial roles and behaviour. Discussion then focuses upon future prospects and identifies five key issues for special consideration: the corporate state and the enterprise culture; professionalism and management development; ownership, control and competing interests; the employment relationship; and the increasing internationalism of management. The special importance of British managers in shaping the future of the country's organizations and society is forcefully stressed as an overall conclusion.

1 Historical context

The rise of managers as an occupational group in the UK during the nineteenth and twentieth centuries is usually attributed to the growth in size and complexity of industry, (facilitated by the emergence of the joint stock company), coupled with the expanding administrative activities of the State. Typically, this overall development has been analysed in terms of the separation of ownership from control at the top of the business enterprise: managers are understood to occupy the controlling positions, but have little or no involvement in the ownership of enterprises (which has passed increasingly to institutional shareholders).

However, early theories about the relationship between ownership and control can be classified into two contrasting perspectives. The first argues that a separation of ownership from control has taken place at the top of the modern corporation and that, accompanying this development, a new type of manager who is essentially non-propertied, technically proficient and professional has replaced the old-style entrepreneur or owner-manager. The second asserts that this change has been overstated and that, even where it has occurred, management still tends to pursue policies in which the interests of business ownership are to the fore. Essentially, the so-called '*managerialists*' argued that a separation of ownership from control has taken place; these include such writers as Berle (1960), Burnham (1941) and Galbraith (1967). Berle contended that as companies grew in size the proportion of voting stock held by the largest individual shareholders declined, and thus there was a progressive movement from owner to management control in the enterprise. Moreover, Berle argued that this process would gradually bring about changes in business behaviour and ideology since whereas the old-style owner-manager pursued policies which maximized shareholder interests, the 'new' managers would ensure that the interests of all stakeholders in the enterprise would be accommodated – employees, consumers and the public at large as well as the owners. Burnham and Galbraith diagnosed similar trends to Berle but put forward somewhat different interpretations. Burnham considered that managers would ultimately pursue their own vested self-interests and that, particularly in the public sector, they would use their indispensable positions in the decision-making processes of organizations to ensure the dominance of managerial rather than ownership priorities. Galbraith on the other hand viewed power as shifting from ownership to a more broadly based *technostructure* consisting not only of managers but also of professionals, specialists and other key personnel within the enterprise.

The second perspective argues from an opposite view to claim that, for a number of reasons, ownership or large shareholder interests continue to be the dominant force in modern corporations despite the emergence of a specialist management function (Nichols 1969). First, devices such as non-voting shares and the difficulties in organizing large numbers of small shareholders means that the larger shareholders can effectively exercise corporate control, even with a minority of total shares. Second, even though top managers may hold a relatively small percentage of the total shareholdings issued, on an individual basis they are often sufficient to encourage managers to pursue policies which favour corporate ownership. Third, similarities in background, attitudes and values between owners and senior managers ensure that both groups subscribe to the primacy of large shareholder interests. Finally, and perhaps most important of all, external market pressures ensure that in the long run managers must pursue profit-orientated policies to the advantage of owners rather than others among the enterprise's stakeholders. This arises not least because of the risk of predatorial takeover by competitor companies if different policies are pursued (Nichols 1969).

In the UK the most influential early empirical work on these issues was conducted by P. Sargent Florence. In an early study, *The Logic of British and American Industry* (1953), he concluded that the managerial revolution had not proceeded as far as had previously been supposed. However, evolutionary trends along lines consistent with the arguments of the 'managerialist' thinkers were identified in a later work, *The Ownership, Control and Success of Large Companies* (1961). First, he found an inverse relationship between size of company (in assets) and the percentage of ordinary shares owned by the board. The percentages of director shareholding by size of company were, for smaller companies, 2.9 per cent; medium size, 2.1 per cent; and very large companies, 1.5 per cent. Second, for the same size ranges, the proportion of directors among the twenty largest shareholders was 30 per cent, 21 per cent and 16 per cent, respectively. Third, Sargent Florence found that the median percentage of directors' ordinary holdings in the very large companies had fallen from 2.8 per cent in the year 1936 to only 1.5 per cent in

1951 (see Nichols (1969) for a review of these data). However, as his critics have argued, the amount of wealth owned by directors and senior managers may still be considerable, and for the reason stated above, it is unlikely that they will pursue policies in any way detrimental to ownership interests. On the contrary, in the UK the propensity towards 'short-termism', associated with the renowned tendency to reward ownership interests particularly favourably, has been viewed as explaining in part the relatively poor long-term investment performance of British companies.

During the 1980s, in the UK there have been major changes in patterns of ownership. However, and as a consequence, the issue of ownership–control has become increasingly prominent in discussions on the role of the manager. For much of the twentieth century the growing scale and complexity of industry, coupled with public ownership of the means of production and distribution, appeared to have occasioned a significant degree of formal separation of ownership from control at the top of the business enterprise. Managers had come to occupy positions of control and, outside family firms, any participation in ownership was seen to be largely irrelevant for the managerial role. However, from the 1980s onwards, phenomena as diverse as the upsurge of entrepreneurialism, restructuring and privatization, profit-sharing and share ownership schemes and management buyouts have reflected a radical change. Indeed, the prospects of a substantial change in patterns of ownership (with capital being widely, if very unequally, distributed among modern working populations) have become more likely than at any stage since the rise of industry itself. The origins of these changes are complex but five are particularly worthy of mention:

1 Dislocations in political economies of the post-1970s brought about by 'oil shocks', turbulent currency movements, inflation, high unemployment and worldwide economic recessions.
2 A transformation in ascendant ideologies and values in which entrepreneurship and new forms of ownership have been sought as counterpoints to the traditional capitalist firm, the managerially dominated corporation and the impersonal state bureaucracy.
3 Legislative changes (reflecting these ascendant values) that have given a fiscal stimulus to profit sharing and share ownership and to similar departures, some of which have applied directly to managers; for example, executive share option schemes.
4 New technologies that have placed a heavy premium on the retention and the redeployment of core workforces (including managerial personnel) who require expensive retraining.
5 Large-scale organizational transformations brought about by increasing international competition and the processes of globalization.

Moreover, these developments appear to have impacted substantially on managers; an inference which is certainly reasonable on the basis of Institute of Management studies of managers in the UK, 1980 and 1990 (see Mansfield *et al.* 1981 and Mansfield and Poole 1991 for a comparison of data from the two studies). Taking direct shareholdings by managers first of all, in the 1980 study, unless attention is restricted to private sector board members, the evidence by and large supports the thesis that a separation of ownership from control has taken place in the modern business enterprise. However, it is clear that for managers in the 1980s the incentives to hold shares have had an appreciable effect on behaviour in this regard and, in consequence, this earlier conclusion now requires reappraisal.

In 1980 78.1 per cent of manager respondents did not own shares in the companies in which they were employed, leaving a balance of approximately one-fifth who had a direct financial stake in their enterprises. By 1990, although only a minority of managers overall owned shares in their companies, the pattern had altered considerably (64.2 per cent of respondents reported that they did not own shares in their employing organizations, leaving a balance of 35.8 per cent as owner-managers). However, if one concentrates on managers in publicly quoted firms, the majority (52.5 per cent) are now owner-managers. Moreover, although there are no direct data to compare with the situation in 1980, the 1990 findings are that most managers own shares (indeed, 64.4 per cent of managers possess shares in companies other than their own. Hence, it is clear that the bulk of British managers are now shareholders.

Of course, it is also important to know which of the various 'stakeholder' interests are endorsed by modern managers. In the Institute of Management surveys, the following groups' interests were identified: owners and shareholders; managers; other employee groups; consumers; suppliers; and the public at large. And there has, over time, been an increase in the percentage of managers who consider that owners' or shareholders' interests should be promoted by their organizations (81.8 per cent in 1990; 77.5 per cent in 1980). If anything, therefore, there is a greater degree of commitment to ownership interests in the 1990s than in 1980, a situation which is not surprising given the increased number of managers who are currently owners of shares in their companies. But what is of particular interest is the apparently paradoxical commitment to consumer interests. In 1980, these were a significant concern for managers. Indeed, at that time 73.3 per cent considered that consumer interests should be promoted by their firms. By 1990 the relevant figure had risen to 84 per cent. Consumers rather than owners now have what the classical economists referred to as 'sovereignty'. In other words, according to managers, they comprise the most important single interest group among the various stakeholders in the modern corporation. The dominance of markets and market issues (alongside ownership) for managers are thus worth stressing, together with the growing significance of organization cultures – with their emphasis upon 'close to the customer' values – for management behaviour.

2 Social position, social origins and education

The position of managers in the system of social stratification in the UK has also been an issue of debate. According to one view, the main dimensions of stratification may be understood in terms of the ownership of the means of production, the purchase of the labour power of others and the sale of one's own labour power. On these assumptions, managers do not own the means of production (except in a limited way) or formally employ labour, but they are distinctive in that they control and supervise labour power (see Wright and Perrone 1977). Moreover, for Goldthorpe (1980), managers are a principal example of 'third parties' within modern capitalist societies brought about by the growth of joint stock companies and the increasing size of 'industrial plant and commercial enterprise'. More specifically, in most occupational structures, managers are broadly classified in either Class I or Class II categories. Incumbents of Class I have relatively high incomes, a wide range of discretion and considerable autonomy of freedom from the control of others and encompass 'all higher grade professionals, self employed or salaried; higher grade administrators and officials in central and local government and in public and private enterprises (including company directors); managers in large industrial establishments; and large proprietors'. Incumbents of the Class II category are typically seen to carry 'staff' status and conditions of employment but are subject to control from above (despite some degree of discretion and authority). Encompassed in this category are 'lower grade professionals and higher grade technicians; lower grade administrators and officials; managers in small businesses and industrial establishments and in the services; and supervisors of non-manual employees' (Goldthorpe 1980: 39–40).

Similar occupational categories have been used to assess changes in patterns of recruitment into management over time. Indeed, the Registrar General's Occupational Classification has five categories running from professional and administrative to unskilled manual and the early studies in the UK revealed a strong propensity for managers to be recruited from Category III families; that is, clerical and skilled manual occupations. Thus, in a study by Clements (1958), 55 per cent of managers were found to have fathers whose social origins were of this kind while in a study by Clark (1966) the percentage was 43.6. Indeed, in an investigation by Leggatt (1970) the relevant percentage figure was found to be as high as 62 per cent. Later studies using the Institute of Management (then British Institute of Management) as a sampling frame revealed a slightly different pattern, with the largest groupings being drawn from either Category II (which includes middle managers) or Category III (Mansfield and Poole 1991). In the 1980 study, the relevant percentages were 32.2 per cent and 28.4 per cent and, in the 1990 study, 29.4 per cent and 29.5 per cent respectively for these two categories. It is of course difficult to make comparisons over time, given the different samples involved, but there does seem to be evidence that managers have been increasingly recruited from a broader spectrum of occupational backgrounds than in the past. This reflects in part the changing employment structure of British society, but it may also be a result of managerial positions having gained in terms of pay and prestige compared with other occupations during the post-war era.

In terms of educational qualifications it is, of course, frequently claimed that British managers are relatively poorly qualified compared to their counterparts in other countries. Unlike many other occupational groups there are no specific academic or professional qualifications required to become a manager, although specific jobs or particular employers may impose their own requirements. Under these circumstances it is to be expected that a wide range of educational experience will be found among them. However, given the relatively prestigious and highly paid status of managers, it is also the case that they are relatively well educated compared to the norm of British society. From the surveys carried out for the Institute of Management, the majority of British managers have been educated at grammar or technical schools with a sizeable

(but declining) percentage drawn from the independent sector. The overwhelming majority of managers have also undertaken some form of full-time or part-time further or higher education, including more than 30 per cent who have attended university. In addition, the 1990 survey shows that nearly 30 per cent of the sample have been educated at polytechnics (the 'new' universities) while only a very small proportion attended Oxford or Cambridge. Overall, it is clear that managers in the UK are significantly better educated than the population as a whole, but equally it is evident that they are not as well educated as members of the learned professions where almost 100 per cent are graduates. It also has to be recognized that the percentage of graduates in any particular age group has risen steadily in British society over a lengthy period and this will explain in part any apparent improvements in the educational accomplishments of British managers.

3 Careers

Career progression is another important aspect of the experiences of managers in the UK. Nicholson and West (1988) have characterized managerial careers in terms of a transition cycle comprising four stages: (1) preparation; (2) encounter; (3) adjustment; and (4) stabilization. Career development programmes are typical for managers in large bureaucratically-administered enterprises, particularly those in the public sector. They involve a planned progression up career ladders to help managers acquire the necessary experience for future jobs. Thus, job changes are driven by much more than simply the personal needs and desires of managers, although this is in part because the coupled forces of organizational hierarchy and human ageing cause a continuous process of managerial succession. However, the introduction of new technology, the redesign of jobs, intra-organizational transfers and the recruitment or shedding of personnel can all create uncertainties about career changes as well as less predictable career paths.

Over time there has almost certainly been an increase in inter-firm mobility among

British managers, even though this may be contrary to many human resource management philosophies which view long-term commitment to the firm as essential. On human resource management assumptions, all employees (including managers) are viewed as assets and hence commitment to the organization is carefully nurtured. It is for this reason that distinctive career ladders for the personal development of managers are designed. In the context of the UK in the 1990s, however, there is far more employment insecurity, changes of career, organizational restructuring and de-layering, all of which creates unpredictable job moves (Arnold 1997). Of particular interest is that, in an early study by Clements (1958), 34 per cent of managers were found to have been employed in a single firm, whereas Mansfield and Poole (1991) found this to be the case for only 11.6 per cent. Nevertheless, the dominant type of job change continues to be *in-spiralling* (movement within a single firm), although men with low domestic responsibilities and women with dependent children have the highest rate of movement between employers (Nicholson and West 1988).

Gender is a significant factor in British management, with few women reaching senior organizational positions. Indeed, although roughly 42 per cent of employees in the UK are female, only 7 per cent of senior managers are women. Successful women in management include so-called 'late starters', professionals, 'go-getters', entrepreneurs and the 'unconventional' (White *et al.* 1992). Moreover, other aspects of successful careers for women are the importance of an early challenge, a wealth of experience, prospects for movement, mentoring and the handling of power and politics. None the less, the overwhelming pattern is for women still to experience considerable gender problems associated with identity, social position and prescribed roles which substantially inhibit their career progress (Scase and Goffee 1990).

4 Managerial work

As a result of the increased complexity of organizations and industry, British managers, like mangers in other countries, are engaged in a wide variety of disparate functions. The most common category is that of general management; but other areas include sales and marketing; finance and accounting; personnel, training and industrial relations; production; research and development; engineering and maintenance; strategic management; and information technology management. Arguably, in the UK there is a stronger emphasis on financial management than in other nations such as Germany, where production management is accorded a greater priority.

The modal category for managerial salaries in the early 1990s was between £20,000 and £30,000 per annum. Managerial salaries appear to have increased over the years and are substantially above those of other occupational groups in British society. This is particularly the case for those in senior managerial positions. On the other hand, employment is less secure because of uncertain economic conditions, mergers and acquisitions, and corporate de-layering (involving a substantial loss of those in middle-management positions). There are also more managers in the UK in commerce and service industries rather than in manufacturing; and a substantial number of British managers now work for overseas rather than British-owned companies.

British managers appear to work long hours. In the Institute of Management study (Mansfield and Poole 1991), 40.6 per cent claimed to work for more than fifty hours per week. Indeed, given that in an earlier study by Stewart (1976) an average working week of forty-two hours was recorded, it appears that managers in the UK are working increasingly hard. As far as job satisfaction is concerned, the job characteristics identified by Maslow (1954) have been used to study this. Managers have been asked to assess the characteristics of their work in terms of the extent to which it provides scope for various material and psychological rewards. These include: opportunities for independent thought and action; security; scope for feelings of self-esteem; pay; opportunities for personal growth and development; the opportunity to develop close friendships; and promotion opportunities. Accordingly, it is possible to assess the extent to which managers consider such characteristics *are* present in their jobs or *should* be present, and the importance which they attach to any given characteristic. Essentially, managers in the UK rank opportunities for independent thought and action, scope for feelings of self-esteem, pay and security relatively highly in terms of the characteristics which they deem to be present in their jobs. Overwhelmingly, too, they rate opportunities for independent thought and action as the most important characteristic to them in their work and strongly emphasize that this should be present in their jobs (Mansfield and Poole 1991). Given the difficult economic conditions and the continuous changes with which they have to cope, British managers appear to be more satisfied with their work than might have been expected. The areas of greatest concern appear to be possibilities for promotion, opportunities for personal growth and development, pay, security and scope for feelings of self-esteem.

5 Professionalism and training

The development of professionalism has been an important aspect of the general changes in the manager's role over the years. Indeed, the growth of bodies such as the Institute of Management may be viewed as a part of the process of evolution in which a concern over professional standards and conduct of behaviour has increased. However, for managers the issue of professionalism has always been somewhat ambiguous. This is because the classic model of professionalism emphasizes the role and function of the professional body as a means of control over membership of the body. But managers are likely to have, primarily, an organizational-based identity and to be in control over specialists (including various professionals) who carry out the work process. From the Institute of Management study conducted in 1990, it is clear that the majority of British managers consider themselves to be professionals (62.7 per cent). Even though the characteristics of the sample may bias the responses towards professionalism to some extent, it is notable that 89.1 per

cent claimed that the Institute of Management should promote and enforce standards of training for managers; 69.8 per cent endorsed the provision of courses and/or material or issues of importance to members and 75.4 per cent supported the enforcement of professional standards in management. Moreover, one of the main characteristics of professionalism is the establishment of professional norms (usually enshrined in a 'code of ethics'). In this respect, it is interesting that 76.9 per cent of the 1990 sample of managers endorsed this as an aim of the Institute of Management.

In the 1980s and 1990s in the UK a great deal of interest has focused upon the quality of management education and the related concerns over training and development. Various studies have indicated that managers in the UK still receive less training than their contemporaries in competitor nations and also that delivery is less systematic (Handy *et al.* 1987; Constable and McCormick 1987). Against this background, in 1987 the Council for Management Education and Development (CMED) launched the Management Charter Initiative in 1987. A proposal in this initiative was to establish a coherent set of management qualifications and to set up a Chartered Institute of Managers. However, this has been the subject of considerable controversy among employers, training providers and professional institutes and associations. Even so, it is clear that British managers strongly endorse developments in training and management education and view these as important aids to management performance. A study by Warr conducted in 1991 found that 82 per cent of managers undertook some training in work time in that year (the median number of training days being five) (Warr 1993). Moreover, a formal management training policy was found to exist in 68 per cent of organizations in the sample.

In the 1990 Institute of Management survey, 87.8 per cent of managers 'agreed' or 'strongly agreed' with the statement that management development and training were important in helping them to do their job well and 86.3 per cent endorsed the statement that training is important in aiding them to develop as managers. In addition, 73.6 per cent of managers had heard of the Management Charter Initiative and the overwhelming majority supported its essential aims. In short, despite a concern over trends in training and management development in the UK, there does seem to be considerable support for major improvements in these respects (see Poole and Jenkins 1996; Storey *et al.* 1997). Indeed, the expenditure of a typical British company on management development would typically be far more than for technical and manual grades of employee.

6 Industrial relations and employee participation

Managing of the employment relationship is a major feature of the manager's role in the UK. Broadly speaking, it is possible to classify the overall approaches of UK managers into *pluralist* and *unitarist* approaches. Pluralism recognizes a coalition of diverse individual and group interests in the firm and is broadly associated with the recognition of trade unionism. Unitarism focuses on a unified authority structure in the firm and emphasizes common policies and objectives within an overall organizational identity. In the 1970s it was assumed that pluralism and so-called constitutional management (in which pay and conditions of work are regulated by collective bargaining and conducted through the medium of recognized trade unions) would become increasingly ascendant. But these predictions were to be largely falsified by the events of the 1980s and 1990s. As a result of changes in labour and product markets, governments fostering market-orientated strategies and the introduction of labour legislation which circumscribed the role of trade unions, managements increasingly found themselves in a position to choose between diverse sets of industrial policies and objectives. Thus, in the UK the following developments have occurred:

1 the re-emergence of 'macho' or authoritarian styles of management in industries with highly competitive product markets and subject to substantial rationalization;

2 an increasing interest in 'paternal' industrial relations styles as a consequence of the enormous success of Japanese companies in world markets and direct Japanese investment in the UK;

3 a growing concern for employee involvement and direct forms of employee participation in expanding industries where skilled and educated workers remain scarce and where technological change is particularly rapid;

4 a decline in constitutional management outside the public sector and manufacturing industry occasioned by (a) the reduction of 'corporatist' economic management by the State and (b) the appreciable weakening of trade unions, reflected in a significant loss of union membership;

5 the growth of hybrid styles of industrial relations management (such as consultative–paternal) which incorporates elements of more than one industrial relations style.

These and other changes have reflected movements in the political, economic and legal environment that have impacted upon the competitive strategies that managers pursue and, in turn, on their industrial relations attitudes and behaviour. Market conditions and the firms' financial performance are reflected in the extent to which corporate-level managers involve themselves in industrial relations. Firms with unfavourable demand conditions are likely to seek greater control over pay settlements by increased intervention, whereas 'organizational slack' and local autonomy are more likely to occur where competition in the product market is relatively weak. The growth in company size is also reflected in divisionalized structures, with financial decentralization (in terms of profit accountability) spreading down to enterprise level or below.

Changes in the wider environment and in competitive strategies tend to reinforce managerial commitments to a free-enterprise system and to unitarism rather than pluralism in industrial relations. And of course, power and influence in industrial relations has shifted substantially, to the detriment of organized labour. Union membership fell by over three million in the 1980s from the peak of 1979 and remained strongest in job grades and employment sectors that were in decline (manufacturing and the public sector). The 1980s also witnessed a decline in shop steward power and the rise of the so-called 'new realism', with labour movement solidarity giving way to an enterprise consciousness among certain trade unions (MacInnes 1987).

The manager's experiences of industrial relations has thus changed in major respects in the UK and is reflected in attitudes to trade unionism, personal commitments to collective representation, experience of collective bargaining, and employee participation and involvement.

Insofar as attitudes towards trade unions are concerned, on the basis of the Institute of Management surveys, it is clear that there is now less hostility to trade unions than was once the case. In 1980 82.1 per cent of managers considered that unions in the UK had too much power, a figure which fell to 31.7 per cent in 1990. In 1980 just over half of managers (52.9 per cent) considered that trade unions were more powerful than management; a figure which fell to 14.1 per cent in 1990. And although at both times the majority of respondents agreed with the statement that trade unions were not acting in the country's economic interests, those strongly agreeing with the view declined from 40.4 per cent to 11.4 per cent between 1980 and 1990 (Mansfield and Poole 1991). On the other hand, the willingness of managers to recognize trade unions for collective bargaining purposes has declined. In terms of personal commitments to collective representation, managers appear to be increasingly individualistic in approach. Again on the basis of the Institute of Management surveys, whereas in 1980 only 32.8 per cent of managers felt that no kind of collective representation was relevant to them, this figure rose to 43.2 per cent in 1990. Moreover, union affiliation has also featured prominently in the analysis of the managerial role. Broadly speaking, union membership increased dramatically in the 1970s (and not just in the UK). However, following the decline of the corporatist state and the increasing autonomy of managers and enterprises experienced in the 1980s and 1990s, the extent of managerial collectivism has declined.

Theoretical interpretations of managerial unionism (and other modes of managerial collectivism) include: (1) the systematic listing of co-terminous factors; (2) the industrial relations focus on recognition policies; (3) sociological analyses based on the study of adaptations in market, work and status situations; (4) 'radical analysis' by industrial relations specialists and sociologists focusing on the labour process; and (5) social action models emphasizing managers' orientations and perceptions. Thus, the issues which have been seen as encouraging managerial unionism include economic pressures, fear of exclusion from national-level consultations/negotiations and fears over job security. Conversely, fear of loss of promotion, of losing the trust of employers and senior managers, and the inappropriateness of trade unionism for managers' needs (for example, opposing philosophies and policies) have been seen as discouraging membership. However, the most potent forces appear to be presence and recognition of a trade union at the manager's level, commitment to collective rather than industrial representation of interests by the managers themselves and employment in the public rather than the private sector (see Poole *et al.* 1983).

In any event, union membership among managers has declined in the 1980s and into the 1990s. On the basis of the Institute of Management studies, it is apparent that three-quarters of managers (75.4 per cent) now have no collective representation of their interests. Moreover, less than 20 per cent of managers in the early 1990s were trade union members compared with nearly a quarter at the beginning of the 1980s (Mansfield and Poole 1991). The period since 1980 has also witnessed a major shift in employer approaches towards regulating the employment relationship via collectivism and collective bargaining. Where collective regulation still exists, bargaining structures have become increasingly decentralized to the level of the firm. From the Institute of Management surveys it would appear that there has been a decline in managers experiencing formal collective bargaining (20 per cent in 1980; 17.4 per cent in 1990). Informal meetings with union representatives appear to have declined appreciably: 48.5 per cent of managers in 1980 were engaged in these types of practice, compared with only 31.3 per cent in 1990. But managers' handling of individual grievances brought by union representatives has declined far less sharply (42.2 per cent in 1980, 38.2 per cent in 1990). Indeed, it is clear that the formal aspects of industrial relations have changed less than the informal procedures. The decline in trade union power appears to have enabled managers in the UK increasingly to deal with individual employees rather than having to discuss issues first of all with a trade union representative.

Turning to employee involvement and employee participation, there have been many interesting developments in the UK since the 1980s. For a period, in the 1970s, the Bullock proposals on Industrial Democracy appeared to herald a major change to the board levels of the UK, with trade union representation appearing at this level. However, these proposals are no longer on the political agenda and although a series of European initiatives on company law, disclosure of information and, more latterly, the Social Charter became increasingly important, the focus of attention has been on employee involvement and on profit-sharing and employee shareholding schemes. Managers in a large number of firms have introduced various types of direct employee involvement (such as two-way communications and quality circles) while eschewing board-level practices. Above all, managers in the UK have encouraged the growth of profit-sharing and employee shareholding schemes. Indeed, a wide range of schemes may be identified in the UK, with over half of workplaces employing more than twenty-five employees having at least one such scheme. The most prevalent are those with profit-related payments and bonuses, but Inland Revenue approved profit-sharing schemes, 'save-as-you-earn' schemes and executive share option schemes are also common developments. Between 1979 and 1992

in the UK, 1,015 general profit-sharing schemes were approved by the Inland Revenue under the auspices of the 1978 Finance Act. Between 1980 and 1992, 1,058 share option schemes under the provisions of the Finance Act of 1980 were approved. Finally, no less than 5,089 discretionary share option schemes under the provisions of the 1984 Finance Act received the Inland Revenue seal of approval by 1992.

7 Public and private sectors

The emergence of joint stock companies in the private sector and the rise of governmental activities (furthering the growth of large-scale public enterprises) have been the main forces underpinning a sizeable increase in the number of British managers over the years. However, it is also the case that the experiences of managers in these two sectors are different, even though recent developments may be indicative of a greater degree of convergence than was once evident. Essentially, public sector managers have been more constrained – in comparison with their private sector colleagues (in terms of autonomy and freedom to develop new products and services) – to act on the basis of a market logic and to take strategic decisions without reference to overall governmental policy. Differences in respect of industrial relations are particularly noteworthy. First of all, attitudes towards trade unionism tend to be less hostile in the public sector and union density is higher. Managers in the public sector are also more likely themselves to want some collective representation of their own interests and, indeed, about half of British public sector managers belong to trade unions (Mansfield and Poole 1991). Collective bargaining is typically more centralized in the public sector. Although direct experience of collective bargaining does not differ greatly between public and private sectors, managers in the public sector are far more likely to deal with individual grievances brought by union representatives (in the 1990 Institute of Management survey, the respective percentages were 61.4 and 32.2).

Reflecting differences in managerial autonomy, managers in the private sector are typically more satisfied than those in the public sector, with opportunities for promotion, personal growth and development, self-esteem and independent thought and action. However, as a result of major changes in the public sector (including privatization, contracting out of services and a far greater market logic being developed), corresponding adaptations in the manager's role are occurring. For instance, in the health sector there is more organized and ever-increasing 'purchaser power'. Indeed, the emphasis on the purchaser/contractor has developed alongside the spawning of measures and indicators of relative performance (for example, league tables for schools). The upshot has been increasing pressure on public sector managers to adapt to a rapidly changing environment which is radically different from that previously encountered in traditional, bureaucratically-administered organizations.

8 Future prospects

The political and economic framework of the UK has changed substantially since the 1980s. Government intervention has been largely displaced by a belief in the virtues of the market economy. Entrepreneurism and the enterprise culture have become ascendant themes, while privatization programmes have reduced the state sector. Prices and incomes policies have been formally abandoned and replaced by practices such as profit sharing and profit-related pay. Trade unions have been substantially weakened by the exigencies of the early 1980s recession, the rise of the service sector and adverse legislation. Industrial democracy is no longer on the political agenda, replaced by developments such as worker involvement through employee shareholding and by shop-floor level developments in quality circles and similar ventures. All of these far-reaching changes have impacted appreciably on the role of the manager.

Whether or not these developments will continue is debatable, but five ascendant themes for the future of British management merit attention at this juncture: (1) the corporatist state and the enterprise culture; (2) professionalism and management development; (3) ownership, control and competing interests; (4) the employment relationship; and (5) internationalization.

The corporate state and the enterprise culture

In the UK over the past decade there has been a major attempt to 'roll back' the powers of the State and to replace the neo-corporatism of the 1970s with the market economy. However, British managers have never been very corporatist in outlook. They have tended to support strong state intervention in the sphere of industrial relations and there is some support for the control of foreign enterprises in the UK. However, they are against the statutory control of prices, wages and salaries; and few wish to see extensive import controls on the subsidization of exports. There is also strong opposition to the increasing powers of government ministers and to the principle of state monopolies (see Mansfield and Poole 1991). Indeed, rather than corporatism, they are far more likely to support an enterprise culture, reducing the regulatory powers of government, encouraging share ownership, reducing monopolies and encouraging competition. Looking to the future, it can be anticipated that there will be a continued underpinning of the enterprise culture by British managers even though certain types of state intervention in specific areas of interest to managers may well be encouraged.

Professionalism and management development

Arguably no issue is likely to affect the role of managers more in the future than the concern over professionalism and management development. The view expressed by, among others, Handy et al. (1987) and Constable and McCormick (1987) has been that British managers are less well trained than their competitors and that their experiences in this area are, by and large, less systematic. The Management Charter Initiative has been particularly symptomatic of the concern over management development more generally. However, the professional commitments of British managers appear to remain strong and are likely to increase in the future. Strong support for management development as an important company responsibility, for corporate support for management development, for the encouragement of continuous self-development, and for all members of the organization to obtain recognized qualifications is likely to continue (see Mansfield and Poole 1991). The attention devoted to these issues in the media and in management circles may have had a dramatic effect on managers' attitudes to their own training and development and to that of their colleagues. Managers themselves appear to be willing to invest more of their own time and resources in their attempts to obtain competence. This is encouraging for the prospects of an increasingly professional, well-educated and well-trained management emerging in the twenty-first century, even though the advance may not be sufficient to close the gap entirely with competitor nations.

Ownership, control and competing interests

One of the main developments in the UK in recent years has been the popular notion of a property-owning democracy in which the role of the State in economic management is reduced. This is in sharp contrast to the corporatist economic and political policies of the 1960s and 1970s, which relied heavily on state intervention and a substantial public sector. Moreover, economic restructuring and the privatization of state assets have encouraged managers and employees to take equity stakes in their firms and to endorse the ideals of a 'free' market economy in which the role of the consumer is paramount. Partly as a result, there has been a substantial increase in the number of managers who own stocks and shares, and particularly in those who own shares in the companies in which they work. Indeed, as we have seen, if one excludes managers in the public sector and in voluntary organizations, the majority of managers who are eligible to do so now appear to have a stake

in the ownership of the firms in which they are employed. The development of executive share ownership schemes, in particular, was an important part of this process in the 1980s. Accordingly, the formal separation of ownership from control at the top of business concerns has been substantially reduced over the last decade, a trend which may well continue.

With respect to managers' perceptions of whose interests should be most predominant within their own employing organizations, these are fairly comprehensive. However, in line with changes in ownership, it is scarcely surprising that owners' and shareholders' interests are a dominant concern. None the less, as has also been seen, in recognition of the importance of markets and the interests of customers, consumers have often replaced owners and shareholders as the single most important group whose interests managers should most actively pursue (Mansfield and Poole 1991). The focus on the market economy is thus clearly evident and, given the increasing measure of multi-party support for this proposition, there is every reason to suppose that such concerns will continue to predominate in the future.

The employment relationship

The reform of industrial reform and the curtailment of trade union activities have also affected managers in the UK. Above all, Thatcher era policies have adversely affected trade unions in a number of ways:

Legislation limited the way unions could act and they were no longer consulted by government nor their agreement or cooperation on economic policy sought. The harshness of the new economic regime slashed revenues in manufacturing leading to a collapse of profits, record bankruptcies and a fall of about one-third in employment in established firms. This produced a very hostile climate for unions in the workplace. In the public sector, unions also faced job losses and a hostile government and usually a new hostile management . . . . Finally unemployment, which rose by more than two million, weakened unions directly by reducing their membership and income and indirectly by threatening their workplace bargaining power. The unions suffered a series of severe defeats: particularly that of the miners, barely ten years after they could claim to have brought down a Conservative government. The unions were powerless to resist the government's challenge, much of which was popular with their own members.

(MacInnes 1987: 3)

Managers at enterprise level have been the principal beneficiaries of these changes. It is, then, scarcely surprising there has been a decline in the direct experience of managers of formal collective bargaining and a substantial reduction in informal meetings with union representatives. The vast majority of managers now view themselves more powerful than trade unions. However, in part as a result, managers are now far less likely than at the beginning of the 1980s to consider that trade unions are not acting in the country's economic interests.

Notwithstanding public and private sector differences, managers are now also far less likely to wish for collective representation of their own interests through managerial unions. Indeed, the percentage of managers belonging to trade unions has undoubtedly fallen. But does this involve a long-term change in patterns of employment relationships or merely a reaction to alterations in the wider environment? There can be no certain answer, but unless there are dramatic changes in the political environment of the 1990s, it would appear to be most unlikely that there will be any appreciable endorsement of collectivism by British managers in the medium term. It is also likely that, in the employment relationship, human resource management policies on the one hand and the non-union firm on the other will feature increasingly prominently.

accelerated by substantial investment into the UK by Japanese, US and German companies. The majority of large firms in the UK are multinational in any case and this brings in its wake problems of formulating adequate human resource policies and the tendency to create substantial numbers of expatriate managers. The early classification of staffing policies in the multinational firm distinguished between ethnocentric, polycentric and geocentric types. Moreover, the tendency towards ethnocentricism is greater than is sometimes supposed, although firms may adapt different staffing policies over time and the patterns in reality are complex. In any event, it is likely that global tendencies will increasingly affect the dominant modes of operation of British companies and, hence, the behaviour of managers themselves. British managers in the future are likely not only to be increasingly aware of overseas developments but to have substantial 'foreign' experiences, either from their own overseas assignments or from the impact domestically of the policies of particular multinational enterprises.

Finally, the conclusion must be that the attitudes and behaviours of managers are likely to become increasingly ascendant in shaping the future condition of British organizations and wider society. Accompanying the relative decline in influence of the State and trade unions, managers have become progressively more dominant in the UK and, for better or worse, it is the strategic choices made by them that are likely to fashion powerfully the destinies of the majority of the British people. What is even more certain, structural changes in the economy are creating greater demands for those with administrative and managerial skills.

MICHAEL POOLE
CARDIFF BUSINESS SCHOOL

RICHARD SCASE
UNIVERSITY OF KENT AT CANTERBURY

Internationalization

Along with other countries, the increasing globalization of business has impacted substantially upon managers in the United Kingdom (see GLOBALIZATION). This has been

Further reading

(References cited in the text marked *)

* Arnold, J. (1997) *Managing Careers into the 21st Century*, London: Paul Chapman. (Details

changes in careers and the implications for management.)

* Berle, A.A. (1960) *Power Without Property*, New York: Harper & Brace. (Classic argument for the separation of ownership from control, with managers occupying the controlling positions in the modern enterprise.)

* Burnham, J. (1941) *The Managerial Revolution*, New York: Day. (Argues, like Berle, for a separation of ownership from control but focuses particularly on the rise of management in the public sector.)

* Clark, D.G. (1966) *The Industrial Manager: His Background and Career Pattern*, London: Business Publications. (One of the early studies of managers in the UK which is essentially empirical in compass.)

* Clements, R.V. (1958) *Managers: A Study of their Careers in Industry*, London: Allen & Unwin. (Another very early study of managers in the UK which is essentially an empirical contribution.)

* Constable, J. and McCormick, R. (1987) *The Making of British Managers*, London: British Institute of Management and Confederation of British Industry. (Along with Handy *et al.* (1987), a key report on the low levels of training and education of British managers and one of the spurs to subsequent reforms.)

* Galbraith, J.K. (1967) *The New Industrial State*, Boston, MA: Houghton Mifflin. (Argues for the growth of a technostructure (rather broader in compass than management *per se*) as the key controlling force in modern industry.)

* Goldthorpe, J.H. (1980) *Social Mobility and Class Structure in Britain*, Oxford: Oxford University Press. (A key text locating managers in terms of their position in the social stratification system of British society.)

* Handy, C., Gow, I., Gordon, C., Randlesome, C. and Maloney, M. (1987) *The Making of Managers*, London: National Economic Development Office. (A key report tracing the need for greater training provision for managers in the UK.)

* Leggatt, T. (1970) 'Managers in industry: their background and education', *Sociological Review* 26 (4): 807–25. (Examines the social origins and educational experiences of British managers based on a large size of sample.)

  Legge, K. (1995) Human Resource Management: Rhetorics and Realities, London: Macmillan. (A valuable, critical text on human resource management in the UK.)

* MacInnes, J. (1987) *Thatcherism at Work*, Milton Keynes: Open University Press. (Deals with the effects of the Thatcher years and the consequences for management power in the workplace.)

* Mansfield, R. and Poole M. (1991) *British Management in the Thatcher Years*, London: Institute of Management. (This is a longitudinal analysis of managers' attitudes and reported behaviour based on a comparison of fellows and members of the Institute of Management in 1980 and 1990.)

* Mansfield, R., Poole, M., Blyton, P. and Frost, P.E. (1981) *The British Manager in Profile*, London: British Institute of Management. (A national, formative study of managerial attitudes and behaviour in the UK.)

* Maslow, A.H. (1954) *Motivation and Personality*, New York: Harper & Row. (A classic study on motivation which has been applied to managers in several countries.)

* Nichols, T. (1969) *Ownership, Control and Ideology*, London: Allen & Unwin. (An excellent review of the ownership–control debate which is highly critical in approach and compass.)

* Nicholson, N. and West, M. (1988) *Managerial Job Change: Men and Women in Transition*, Cambridge: Cambridge University Press. (A valuable, theoretically informed, empirical analysis of managerial careers focusing on sociopsychological concepts and ideas.)

* Poole, M. and Jenkins, G. (1996) *Back to the Line?*, London: Institute of Management. (Presents the results of a survey of managers' attitudes to human resource management issues, including material on training and development.)

* Poole, M., Mansfield, R., Frost, P. and Blyton, P. (1983) 'Why managers join unions: evidence from Britain', *Industrial Relations* 22 (3): 426–44. (Seeks to examine the factors affecting the propensity of managers in the UK to join unions based on systematic data analysis.)

* Sargent Florence, P. (1953) *The Logic of British and American Industry: A Realistic Analysis of Economic Structure and Government*, London: Routledge & Kegan Paul. (An early empirical study suggesting that the notion of separation of ownership from control was not wholly supported by the evidence.)

* Sargent Florence, P. (1961) *The Ownership, Control and Success of Large Companies*, London: Sweet & Maxwell. (Argues that an evolutionary trend along the lines predicted by the 'managerialist' thinkers has been occurring.)

* Scase, R. and Goffee, R. (1990) 'Women in management: towards a research agenda', *International Journal of Human Resource Management* 1 (1): 107–25. (Isolates various

studies of women managers and identifies ten major areas in a research agenda for the future.)

* Stewart, R. (1976) *Contrasts in Management*, Macmillan. (A valuable contribution on the nature of managerial work in the UK based on careful empirical observations.)

* Storey, J., Edwards, P. and Sisson, K. (1997) *Managers in the Making*, London: Sage. (A comparative analysis of managers in Britain and Japan focusing on careers and development.)

* Warr, P. (1993) *Training for Managers*, London: Institute of Management. (A detailed empirical study of training provision and attitudes to training among British managers based on an Institute of Management sample.)

* White, B., Cox, C. and Cooper, G. (1992) *Women's Career Development: A Study of High Flyers*, Oxford: Blackwell. (Examines the factors accounting for the career development of women and some of the obstacles to this (not least in management).)

* Wright, E.O. and Perrone, L. (1977) 'Marxist class categories and income inequalities', *American Sociological Review* 42: 32–55. (Seeks to develop sophisticated analytical categories of relevance for understanding the position of managers in the social stratification system of society.)

See also: BUSINESS CULTURES, EUROPEAN; GLOBALIZATION

Related topics in the IEBM: BIG BUSINESS AND CORPORATE CONTROL; BUSINESS SCHOOLS; CAREERS; CORPORATISM; EXECUTIVE TRAINING; HUMAN RESOURCE MANAGEMENT; HUMAN RESOURCE MANAGEMENT IN EUROPE; INDUSTRIAL AND LABOUR RELATIONS; INDUSTRIAL RELATIONS IN EUROPE; MANAGEMENT DEVELOPMENT; MANAGEMENT IN EUROPE; SHORT-TERMISM

Profiles of leading companies

Airbus Industrie

Overview

Airbus Industrie (Airbus) is one of the leading aircraft manufacturers in the world. Airbus was established in 1970 and has annual revenues of $9.6 billion (1997). Airbus shares its production with many partners around the world. Around 100,000 people worldwide are engaged in Airbus Industrie's operations, 32,000 of whom are directly involved in the manufacture of Airbus aircraft. Airbus Industrie is a consortium of four European aerospace companies: Aérospatiale of France (37.9 per cent), Daimler-Benz Aerospace Airbus of Germany (37.9 per cent) (see DAIMLER-CHRYSLER), British Aerospace (20 per cent) and CASA of Spain (4.2 per cent). Its headquarters is located near the city of Toulouse in southwest France and has a staff of 2700 of thirty-three different nationalities.

1 Brief history

In 1970 Airbus Industrie was established to build a twin-engine short-range wide-body aircraft. While European aircraft manufacturers had made a number of innovations in aircraft manufacturing – including the development of the turbojet engine, the first commercial jet aircraft, and the first supersonic airliner – they had less than a 10 per cent share of the world's aircraft market. Individual aircraft manufacturers in Europe were unable to compete against the size and resources of established aircraft manufacturers in the United States. To compete, a multinational consortium, Airbus Industrie, was formed. Airbus Industrie was established as a *groupement d'intérêt économique*, the French term for a grouping of economic interests.

Under French law, the legal entity enabled its member firms to focus efficiently on a group project within a consortium framework. By 1995 Airbus had captured approximately 35 per cent of the world's aircraft market, and it hopes to increase its share to 50 per cent in the future.

2 Innovation and significant contribution

The consortium is one of the first major multinational collaborative arrangements in the world. It provides an outstanding example of how entities from different nations can set aside cultural differences to work together to accomplish a common objective, namely to develop an aircraft industry that could compete effectively against major US commercial aircraft manufacturers. The Airbus family comprises three different groups: 124–185-seat single-aisle A319/A320/A321; 220–266-seat wide-body A300/A310; and 263–350-seat wide-body A330/A340. From its inception, Airbus has followed one basic philosophy, namely to 'develop aircraft that fill market needs, design them with the requirements of airline users in mind, and apply the best technology to produce the most comfortable and economic airplanes available'. According to the company, these factors have contributed enormously to the consortium's success.

Airbus has one of the most efficient and flexible production systems in the world. Approximately 96 per cent of the aircraft are made in plants operated by its partner firms. Aircraft parts are manufactured throughout Europe, with final assembly in France and Germany. The consortium has been cited as an outstanding example of cooperative production in the manufacturing industry.

3 Challenges and opportunities

Airbus was formed to help increase the market share of European aircraft manufacturers through the sharing of development costs and cooperative efforts. At the beginning, each participating company had to meet the challenges of setting aside national pride and working hard to overcome difficulties posed by different languages, cultures, and systems of weights and measures. The founders saw a need to fill a market niche overlooked by the major US aircraft manufacturers (SEE BOEING), namely short- to medium-range aircraft with a capacity of 250–300 seats and which can operate economically. To expand its market share further in the decades ahead, the consortium must lower production costs and solve other management challenges, such as establishing a higher profile in industry and transforming itself from a joint venture to a single company.

Airbus has more than 1500 suppliers in twenty-seven countries. It has also entered into cooperative agreements with other aerospace industries in nineteen countries. Its major suppliers in the world include General Electric (see GENERAL ELECTRIC COMPANY), Honeywell, Westinghouse, and Allied Signal in the United States; Kawasaki Heavy Industry and Sumitomo Precision Products in Japan; Korean Air Aerospace Division in South Korea; and Hindustan Aeronautics in India. The challenge is how to work effectively with these various suppliers. Since many of these suppliers are leaders in their respective industries, there are tremendous opportunities for Airbus to grow and diversify further.

ROSALIE L. TUNG AND MOHI AHMED
SIMON FRASER UNIVERSITY

Further reading

Guyon, J. (1998) 'Airbus: the sole competitor', *Fortune* 137, 12 January: 102. (Discusses the transformation of Airbus management.)

McGuire, S. (1997) *Airbus Industrie: Conflict and Cooperation in US–EC Trade Relations*, New York: St Martin's Press. (Presents US–EC economic relationship, with special emphasis on Airbus.)

Spain, P.J. and Talbot, J.R. (eds) (1995) 'Airbus Industrie', *Hoover's Handbook of World Business 1995–1996*. Austin: The Reference Press, Inc. (Gives a general overview of the company.)

Thorton, D.W. (1995) *Airbus Industrie: The Politics of an International Industrial Collaboration*, New York: St Martin's Press. (Gives an overview of the consortium.)

Further resources

http://www.airbus.com

See also: BOEING COMPANY; DAIMLER-CHRYSLER; GENERAL ELECTRIC COMPANY; GLOBAL STRATEGIC ALLIANCES; MANAGEMENT IN FRANCE; MANAGEMENT IN GERMANY

American Express Company

Overview

American Express Company is one of the largest companies providing diversified financial, travel and business services. At present the major businesses of the company range from travel-related services (including credit card, traveller's cheques and travel planning) to financial services (including financial planning, property/casualty insurance and banking services). Established in 1850, the American Express Company now provides services in more than 130 countries and has regional management operations in more than fifteen countries. The company employs about 72,000 people (1997) worldwide and its revenues exceeded $17 billion in 1996. The corporate headquarters of the company is located in New York City.

1 Brief history

The history of the American Express Company dates back to the 1830s. During that period, along with the growth in population and migration to America's heartland, business expanded around the United States. There was a growing need to move goods faster and more safely over vast distances. At that time the company offered to transport goods with speed and safety, and assumed responsibility for damage and loss. In the early years the company carried all kinds of financial instruments for banks, including cash, securities and gold. Later this became a major part of the company's business. In that era rail was the primary means of transportation and communication for American commerce. In 1950 the American Express Company was formed by a merger of two competitors, Wells & Company and Butterfield, Wasson & Company. Soon thereafter it also merged with yet another competitor, Livingston, Fargo & Company. In the early years, even though the company went through battles in its management after the mergers, the company continued to expand.

In 1918 the US government wanted to nationalize express companies. Through negotiations with the government, however, American Express executives were able to keep the company in the private sector, but the company emerged with only 40 per cent of the stock, at a cost of about $11 million. In late 1918 the company began to expand its business. In the 1940s the company entered into international business. The company introduced the American Express credit card in 1958. The company continued to grow from 1960 through the 1980s and became one of the best-known financial services organizations in the world. As the overall business environment changed significantly in the early 1990s, the company needed an entirely new strategy. According to Peter Grossman, a long-time observer of American Express and its businesses, 'the history of the company was dependent not on structure or theory of management, but on its people.'

2 Innovation and significant contributions

The American Express Company itself was formed around the concept of service innovation. Since its beginning, the company has introduced innovative services for individual and corporate customers, and made significant contributions to the industry by providing high-quality services and gaining trust. The company seeks to provide the best services to its customers by making them easier to access while maintaining a high level of security. The company has developed several services for its card members, such as membership rewards and special offers. In addition, it has specially designed business services (e.g. small business services, merchant services and corporate purchasing card), individual and corporate travel services, and financial services (e.g. financial advisers, online investment, educational loan programme, etc.). American Express has set the standard in the travel service industry.

Significant advances in information and communication technologies (ICTs) have facilitated the growth of electronic commerce (e-commerce) throughout the world, thus enabling the buying and selling of products and services over the Internet and the World Wide Web. As a result, virtual global shopping has become a reality, enabling people to shop without leaving home. However, security remains a primary concern. American Express has now implemented state-of-the-art security systems such as SSL (Secure Socket Layer) and SET (Secure Electronic Transaction Protocol), developed in conjunction with partners such as Microsoft, IBM (see INTERNATIONAL BUSINESS MACHINES), Netscape and GTE.

3 Challenges and opportunities

Up to the 1980s the American Express Company was more focused on the quality of its services. As customers have become more cost-conscious and value-oriented, competition in the industry has become more intense. In addition, significant developments have been made in ICTs. In response to these developments the company has introduced new services, including the provision of high-quality, secure and timely services in the emerging e-commerce, and integrated marketing. This was done in partnership with other organizations, such as Microsoft, GTE, Hewlett Packard and Mercantec.

ROSALIE L. TUNG AND MOHI AHMED
SIMON FRASER UNIVERSITY

Further reading

Friedman, J. and Meehan, J. (1992) *House of Cards: Inside the Troubled Empire of American Express*, New York: G.P. Putnam's Sons. (Introduces the historical background and challenges of American Express.)

Grossman, P.Z. (1987) *American Express: The Unofficial History of the People Who Built the Great Financial Empire*, New York: Crown Publishers Inc. (Profiles the history of the company and people who contributed to building American Express.)

Hoover, G., Campbell, A. and Spain, P.J. (eds) (1995) 'American Express Company', *Hoover's Handbook of American Business*, Austin: The Reference Press Inc. (Gives a general overview of the company.)

Murphy, I.P. (1997) 'Amex looks beyond satisfaction, sees growth', *Marketing News* 31(10), 12 May: 6, 22. (Discusses customer satisfaction research and quality-control strategies at American Express (Amex).)

Nathans, L. and Landler, M. (1992) 'Less-than-fantastic plastic', *Business Week*, 9 November: 100–1. (Identifies challenges facing Amex.)

Nishimoto, L. (1996) 'American Express, Microsoft team up for travel', *InfoWorld* 18(32), 5 August: 40. (Discusses partnership between Microsoft and American Express.)

Further resources

http://www.americanexpress.com

See also: AT&T CORPORATION; GATES, BILL; GLOBAL STRATEGIC ALLIANCES; INTERNATIONAL BUSINESS MACHINES

AT&T Corporation

Overview

AT&T Corporation is one of the world's leading providers of communication services, with annual revenues exceeding $74 billion (1996). The company currently offers long-distance services to almost every country and territory in the world. It has operations, joint ventures and alliances in more than thirty countries, and employs more than 130,000 people worldwide. AT&T provides state-of-the-art communications networks, long-distance and wireless services, online services, access to home entertainment and local telephone services as well. The company also offers consulting, outsourcing, systems integration, customer-care services for larger businesses and manages one of the largest credit card programmes in the world. The corporate headquarters of AT&T is located in New York City.

1 Brief history

AT&T Corporation, formerly the American Telephone and Telegraph Company, was established in 1885 in New York as a wholly owned subsidiary of the American Bell Telephone Company to manage and expand the long-distance businesses of the company and its licensees. In 1899 American Bell sold all of its assets (except AT&T stock) to its subsidiary, AT&T, and as a result AT&T emerged as the parent company in Bell Systems, assuming the holding company functions previously exercised by American Bell Telephone Company.

In the early 1900s the Western Electric Company, a subsidiary of AT&T, manufactured equipment to meet the needs of the world's telephone companies. A subsidiary of Western Electric, International Western Electric Company, had expanded its operations to London, Paris, Vienna, Milan, St Petersburg, Tokyo, Montreal, Berlin, Antwerp and Buenos Aires by 1914. In 1925 International Telephone and Telegraph Company (ITT) was formed and the International Western Electric Company was sold to ITT.

Until 1984 AT&T was the parent company of the Bell Systems. During the period of 1984–96 AT&T was an integrated provider of communication services, products, network equipment and computer systems. In 1991 AT&T merged with NCR. This gave AT&T the ability to meet its customer needs for networked computing. In 1993, through the acquisition of McCaw Cellular, AT&T was able to provide services in the fast-growing cellular services market. The continuous change in the industry and customers needs shaped AT&T's evolution as an integrated telecommunication and information services and equipment manufacturing company.

On 20 September 1995 AT&T announced a major corporate reorganization and was split into three companies: AT&T, Lucent Technologies and NCR Corporation. Lucent became an independent systems and technology company on 1 October 1996; NCR Corporation became an independent computer business company on 31 December 1996; and AT&T became a communications services provider company. Currently, AT&T consists of Consumer Markets Division (CMD), Business Markets Division (BMD), AT&T Solutions, AT&T Wireless Services, AT&T Local Services Division, AT&T Universal Card Services, Network and Computing Services, and the AT&T Labs.

2 Innovation and significant contribution

Over the years AT&T Labs has developed new technologies, products and services to support the company's customers. According to AT&T, more than two patents are filed every business day to help shape the future of communications. AT&T's continuous efforts in product innovation have made significant contributions to the telecommunications industry around the world. In 1915 AT&T engineers experimentally transmitted the first human voice across the Atlantic Ocean via radio. In 1927 the company inaugurated the first commercial transatlantic telephone service using two-way radio. Through direct radio links, AT&T expanded its services to other countries as well. AT&T developed cellular wireless communication technology, communications satellite, commercial ISDN long-distance network service and optical digital processors, which have changed the way people communicate today. AT&T Labs engages in R&D in networking, speech- and image-processing, computer science, communications systems, and a wide spectrum of new communications services concepts, technology development and implementation.

AT&T serves both large and small businesses, and government customers around the world with a wide range of advanced long-distance, local, wireless, video, data and Internet services. The company has also helped multinational corporations identify and realize through the power of networking new sources of value that link business, strategy, people, processes, organizations, structures and technology together. AT&T's leading digital PCS (personal communications service) provides a powerful combination of voice, messaging and paging communications in a single hand-held wireless device. The company's Wireless Services is also a global leader in aviation communication. AT&T has received the Malcolm Baldridge National Quality Award on three occasions (twice in 1992 for the manufacturing and service categories, and again in 1994 in the service category).

3 Challenges and opportunities

One of the major challenges for AT&T is to create and provide enhanced tailor-made services to its customers around the world. To increase its opportunities and compete in the emerging digital age and electronic commerce, AT&T has to make continuous efforts to provide state-of-the-art Internet and wireless communications, and an infrastructure that will allow the company to provide the best services to its customers. According to AT&T, the company has made efforts to integrate life-cycle environmental, health and safety considerations into its business decisions and activities in order to be recognized by the global community as a world-class company that contributes to human health as well as the global environment through innovation.

ROSALIE L. TUNG AND MOHI AHMED
SIMON FRASER UNIVERSITY

Further reading

Danielian, N.R. (1974) *AT&T: The Story of Industrial Conquest*, New York: Arno Press. (Provides a detailed case study of AT&T showing how scientific research can have a major impact on industrial development, employment and the earning of monopoly profits.)

Hamblen, M. (1998) 'AT&T makes comeback', *Computerworld* 32(3), 19 January: 114. (Gives financial analysts' perspectives on the company's financial direction.)

Hoover, G., Campbell, A. and Spain, P.J. (eds) (1995) 'AT&T Corporation', *Hoover's Handbook of American Business*, Austin: The Reference Press, Inc. (Gives a general overview of the company.)

Kanter, R.M. (1995) *World Class: Thriving Locally in the Global Economy*, New York: Simon & Schuster. (Provides guidelines on how companies can become globally competitive in their respective industries.)

Kleinfield, S. (1981) *The Biggest Company on Earth: A Profile of AT&T*, New York: Holt, Rinehart & Winston. (Gives an overview of AT&T.)

Quinn, J.B. (1992) *Intelligent Enterprise: A Knowledge and Service Based Paradigm for Industry*, New York: Free Press. (Discusses the management of knowledge-based service companies, including AT&T Bell Laboratories.)

Further resources
http://www.att.com

See also: AMERICAN EXPRESS COMPANY;
GLOBAL STRATEGIC ALLIANCES

The Bank of Tokyo-Mitsubishi Ltd (BTM)

1 **Brief history**
2 **Innovation and significant contributions**
3 **Challenges and opportunities**

Overview

The Bank of Tokyo-Mitsubishi Ltd (BTM) is one of the world's largest financial organizations. The organization was formed on 1 April 1996 by a merger of the Mitsubishi Bank Limited (MBL) and the Bank of Tokyo Limited (BOT). BTM now has 326 branches, twenty-eight sub-branches and two agencies in Japan, and about 400 facilities in major financial and commercial centres around the world. The group operates in more than twenty-eight countries and employs about 19,300 people worldwide. The revenues of BTM exceeded $46 billion in 1996. The corporate headquarters of BTM is located in Tokyo, Japan.

1 Brief history

The origin of BTM can be traced back to the 1880s. The founder of the Mitsubishi industrial group, Yataro Iwasaki, established the Mitsubishi Exchange Office, a money exchange house, in 1880. The Exchange Office was succeeded by the Banking Division of the Mitsubishi Group. In 1919 the MBL was established and took over the Banking Division of the group. In subsequent years MBL continued to expand its businesses around Japan and overseas through a series of mergers and acquisitions. MBL was the main bank for the Mitsubishi group companies.

BOT was established in 1946. The bank was the successor of a special foreign-exchange bank, the Yokohama Specie Bank Limited (YSB), established in 1880. YSB had international banking networks including the United States, Europe, Africa and Asia. After World War II BOT was the only Japanese bank that was authorized by the Japanese Ministry of Finance (MOF) to establish offices abroad and to engage in foreign exchange and international finance. Thus until recently the global network of BOT was more diversified than that of any other Japanese bank. After the merger of MBL and BOT, BTM became the world's largest financial organization, with assets in excess of $696 billion.

Japanese financial institutions are experiencing a severe business environment as a result of a downturn in the country's economy as well as structural reform plans, referred to as the 'Big Bang', in Japan. As a leading financial institution, BTM is also undergoing major structural reforms, the principal ones being a reduction in the number of directors and their pay, suspension of basic wage-rate increases and staff reduction, reduction in the number of domestic and foreign branches, sale of idle properties and reduction in general expenses, i.e. non-personnel expenditure.

2 Innovation and significant contributions

BTM's diversified global network and broad range of innovative financial products and services have made it a unique global financial group. The group is capable of providing total services to its customers around the world. Its innovative services in structured finance, corporate advisory and investment advisory services are also well recognized. The group's business activities include commercial banking, corporate banking, project finance, foreign exchange to housing mortgages, estate planning and real-estate management services.

The group's efforts to increase customer satisfaction and establish a reputation for reliability with global communities are significant. BTM has identified three pillars which guide its operations: 'Corporate Value' (customer satisfaction, preserving one's own integrity and contributing to the global community), 'Guiding Principles' (ensuring customer satisfaction, developing the skills and knowledge necessary to respond to challenges, maintaining professional ethics, and acting with responsibility and pride) and 'Corporate Objectives' (building a solid domestic management base to provide quality and diversified financial services in Japan and overseas, and acquiring a reputation for reliability among customers, employees, shareholders and communities).

3 Challenges and opportunities

As BTM was formed by a merger of two Japanese giant financial institutions with very different corporate cultures, a major challenge for the organization is to integrate the two systems to improve efficiency. While the merger has combined the former MBL's huge domestic branch networks with the extended international networks of BOT, the challenge now confronting BTM pertains to its internal management. Besides, BTM also has to contend with the challenges arising from Japanese economic turmoil and the restructuring programmes of the Japanese government.

To meet these challenges and to take advantage of new opportunities, BTM has implemented risk-management systems, advanced management information systems and efficient management practices. The group has taken measures to respond to rapid technological changes in information and telecommunications, globalization and social transformations worldwide. To meet the challenges in the fast-changing global marketplace and to increase its opportunities in the emerging electronic commerce (e-commerce), BTM has to improve its speed of delivery and enhance its strategic partnerships with other organizations.

ROSALIE L. TUNG AND MOHI AHMED
SIMON FRASER UNIVERSITY

Further reading

Economist (1997) 'And it finally came to tears', *Economist* 345(8045), 29 November: 77–9. (Discusses changes in Japan's financial system.)

Smith, C. (1996) 'The bashful giant', *Institutional Investor* 30(11), November: 133–6. (Discusses the challenges facing BTM.)

Further resources
http://www.btm.co.jp

See also: ECONOMY OF JAPAN; FOREIGN EXCHANGE RISK, MANAGEMENT OF; *KEIRETSU*; ORGANIZATION CULTURE

The Boeing Company

1 **Brief history**
2 **Innovation and significant contributions**
3 **Challenges and opportunities**

Overview

The Boeing Company, McDonnell Douglas and North American, as one company, constitute the world's largest manufacturer of commercial aircraft. In 1997 the company received orders totalling $42.8 billion. These orders came from fifty-two customers around the world and constitutes almost two-thirds of the global market share. Boeing has its headquarters in Seattle, Washington, USA. The company's three major business segments are commercial aircraft, space systems and defence systems. Boeing is now the largest builder of military aircraft in the world, as well as the principal supplier of goods and services to the Pentagon and the National Aeronautics and Space Administration (NASA). The corporate vision of the group is 'people working together as one global company for aerospace leadership'.

1 Brief history

Shortly after the Wright brothers' famous flight, William Boeing assembled his first seaplane and established the Boeing B&W Seaplane Company in 1916. In the 1930s and 1940s Boeing manufactured bombers and aircraft for commercial transport. In 1954 the company developed the first prototype of 707, which ultimately revolutionized air travel around the world. In 1967 McDonnell Douglas was formed by a merger of two separate companies, McDonnell and Douglas. The merged company continued to manufacture commercial aircraft, combat aircraft and space vehicles. McDonnell Douglas introduced the DC-3, which became so popular that 90 per cent of the world's air travellers

flew on them. North American Aviation Inc. was first established in 1928. In the beginning the company focused its business primarily on small, single-engine aircraft to avoid competing with the manufacturers of large, multi-engine aircraft. During the late 1930s the company also began to make military aircraft. According to the company, between the years 1939–67 the company built more military aircraft than any other aircraft manufacturer in the United States.

McDonnell Douglas developed Mercury and Gemini, the manned space flights in the early 1960s. In 1968 Boeing introduced its jumbo jet, the 747, to meet the growing demand for air travel, and McDonnell Douglas developed the F-4 Phantom II fighter aircraft. The business interests of Boeing, McDonnell Douglas and North American began to intersect in the 1960s when they became partners in the NASA Apollo Program, followed by the International Space Station. The three companies finally merged in December 1996 to become the new Boeing. A prime motive for the merger was to compete more effectively with rivals.

2 Innovation and significant contributions

Boeing has made significant efforts toward system integration, customer satisfaction and continuous quality improvement and innovation. Boeing's knowledge and skills in designing, building, marketing and servicing of aircraft for decades has made it a truly global company. To reduce cost and to spread the commercial and economic risks associated with the design and manufacture of new aircraft, in the 1980s Boeing entered into co-production programmes with other entities around the world, including Alitalia of Italy and the Civil Transport Development Corporation of Japan. These collaborative efforts, particularly the one with Japan, have been decried by some in the United States as 'Faustian deals'. Some believe that, while Boeing may derive short-term economic benefits from such cooperative endeavours, in the long term it may compromise the US's superiority in the aerospace industry.

According to Boeing, the development of the new Boeing 737 family and the new 767-400ER in response to customer demand was key to the company's position as market leader in 1997. In that year Boeing delivered 375 jetliners compared with Airbus's 182 (see AIRBUS). Customer demand has also led to the expansion of the 767 family and the development of Boeing 777. The latter is the first aircraft to be designed from start to finish using computers.

3 Challenges and opportunities

Two major challenges lie ahead for Boeing. These include competition from Airbus and the financial crisis in Asia. Airbus, a European consortium which is heavily subsidized by the governments of France, Germany, Spain and the UK, has made significant inroads into the commercial aeroplane market around the world. Boeing has to deal effectively with this growing competition. Because of the economic growth in the Asia-Pacific region between 1960 and the mid-1990s, Asian countries have emerged as major purchasers of commercial aircraft. However, the financial crisis that began in late 1997 may lead to the cancellation of some orders.

According to the company, the long-term challenge for Boeing is to build a large-scale system that can integrate aeroplanes, space stations and launch vehicles. Success in such integration will create new opportunities for Boeing in the future. To maintain its competitive edge and to increase opportunities, Boeing must continue to integrate its systems, increase productivity in its manufacturing plants, reduce costs and respond effectively to the needs of its customers all over the world.

ROSALIE L. TUNG AND MOHI AHMED
SIMON FRASER UNIVERSITY

Further reading

Henkoff, R. (1998) 'Boeing's big problem', *Fortune* 137(1), 12 January: 96–103. (Discusses the challenges confronting Boeing's manufacturing systems.)

Rodgers, E. (1996) *Flying High: The Story of Boeing and the Rise of the Jetliner Industry*, New York: Atlantic Monthly Press. (Gives a historical account of Boeing and the jetliner industry.)

Further resources
http://www.boeing.com

See also: AIRBUS INDUSTRIE; GLOBAL STRATEGIC ALLIANCES

Caterpillar Inc.

1 **Brief history**
2 **Innovation and significant contributions**
3 **Challenges and opportunities**

Overview

Caterpillar Inc. is one of the world's largest manufacturers of construction and mining equipment, natural gas engines and industrial gas turbines, and is a leading global supplier of diesel engines. Its major businesses include construction, mining and agricultural machinery, engines and financial services. The company's revenues exceeded $16 billion in 1996. With a network of 192 dealers, the company supplies its products and services to customers in nearly 200 countries and employs around 57,026 people worldwide (1996). The corporate headquarters of Caterpillar Inc. is located in Peoria, Illinois.

1 Brief history

The history of Caterpillar dates back to the late nineteenth century, when Daniel Best and Benjamin Holt tried to make steam tractors for farming. Prior to establishing Caterpillar in 1925, Best and Holt pioneered track-type tractors and petrol-powered tractor engines. After that they continued to make innovations in energy-efficient tractors. In 1931 the first Diesel Sixty Tractor was manufactured, and the company continued to expand its product line to include motor graders, blade graders, elevating graders, terracers and electric generator sets.

During World War II there was an increased demand for track-type tractors, motor graders, generator sets and a special engine for the M4 tanks. In 1950 the company established Caterpillar Tractor Co. Ltd in Great Britain. This was the company's first operation abroad and helped the company gain useful knowledge in managing foreign exchange,

tariffs and import controls, and in providing better customer services around the world. The company continued to establish more manufacturing plants in strategic regions around the world, such as Great Britain, Belgium, Germany, Brazil and Australia. In 1963 Caterpillar and Mitsubishi Heavy Industries Ltd (see MITSUBISHI HEAVY INDUSTRIES LTD)formed one of the first joint ventures, Caterpillar Mitsubishi Ltd, in Japan and two years later began manufacturing in their new plant in the Tokyo area. The joint venture was renamed Shin Caterpillar Mitsubishi Ltd in 1987, and became one of the most enduring and successful US–Japanese joint ventures.

Since the 1970s Caterpillar has continued to introduce a broad range of new products, and in 1981 the company established Caterpillar Financial Services Corporation to provide financing options to its customers around the world. In 1989 Caterpillar also established a Building Construction Products Division to serve its customers in the construction industry, and continued to improve its management and expand around the globe. Caterpillar currently has thirty-two manufacturing plants in the United States and a total of twenty-nine in Australia, Belgium, Brazil, China, France, Germany, Hungary, India, Indonesia, Italy, Japan, Mexico, Poland, Russia and the United Kingdom.

Caterpillar's growth between 1950 and 1980 can be attributed in large part to investments in infrastructure around the world. In 1981 the company reported its highest sales and profits ever. However, shortly after this record performance things began to unravel. Part of the problem was a 'sense of invulnerability . . . that sometimes bordered on arrogance' stemming from its 'virtually unchallenged success' in more than half a century. Management was overcentralized in corporate head offices which had an ethnocentric outlook (Bartlett and Ehrlich 1989).

This situation was further exacerbated by two major developments in the early 1980s. In 1982, during the global recession, the US dollar was close to its all-time high. This made US products very expensive in the global marketplace. Furthermore, Caterpillar had to contend with a 205-day strike by members of the United Auto Workers (UAW). Komatsu, a Japanese competitor, took advantage of the situation, rapidly expanding its share of the world market to 25 per cent by 1984, double its share six years earlier. Caterpillar responded successfully to Komatsu's challenge by closing plants, downsizing, sourcing for parts and components from around the world, and reducing inventory. Through massive restructuring, the company was able to accomplish a strategic turnaround, so much so that in the early 1990s Komatsu, which had posed such a formidable challenge to Caterpillar just a few years earlier, announced that it was quitting the earth-moving equipment market altogether.

2 Innovation and significant contributions

Caterpillar's continuous efforts in product and service innovation have made significant contributions to the industrial equipment industry throughout the world. Caterpillar construction machines are now used in building, maintaining and rebuilding much of the world's infrastructure – highways, dams, airports and commercial buildings. Caterpillar machines were used to build the Hoover Dam and the Chunnel under the English Channel, to put out fires in the oil fields of Kuwait and to tear down the Berlin Wall.

The company's famous brand engines are used to power ships and boats, locomotives, highway trucks, and construction, mining and agricultural machines. The engines are also used in offshore drilling rigs and huge mines in remote mountain ranges. Their engines are also used to supply power to hospitals, factories, airports and office buildings in case of emergencies. The company's financial services provide assistance to customers worldwide to buy its products. In addition,

Caterpillar Insurance Services Inc. offers insurance coverage to its customers and dealers throughout the world.

3 Challenges and opportunities

The major challenges confronting Caterpillar are to make continuous innovations; to design, manufacture and supply quality products to its customers around the world; and to sustain growth in a slowing global market. The company seeks to build closer relationships with its customers worldwide so as to provide better products and services.

ROSALIE L. TUNG AND MOHI AHMED
SIMON FRASER UNIVERSITY

Further reading

(References cited in the text marked *)

* Bartlett, C.A. and Ehrlich, S. (1989) *Caterpillar Inc.: George Schaefer Takes Charge*, Boston, MA: Harvard Business School.
Elstrom, P. (1997) 'This cat keeps on purring: despite labor woes, Caterpillar's plans are paying off', *Business Week*, 20 January: 82–4. (Discusses product development at Caterpillar.)
Eric, S. (1994) 'Working to delight the internal customer', *Work Study* 43(6), September–October: 27–9. (Examines departmental support teams and their activities.)
Fites, D.V. (1996) 'Make your dealers your partners', *Harvard Business Review* 74(2), March–April: 84–90. (Examines Caterpillar's relationship with its dealers.)
Hendricks, J.A., Defreitas, D.G. and Walker, D.K. (1996) 'Changing performance measures at Caterpillar', *Management Accounting* 78(6), December: 18–24. (Discusses performance measurement at Caterpillar.)
Hoover, G., Campbell, A. and Spain, P.J. (eds) (1995) 'Caterpillar Inc.', *Hoover's Handbook of American Business*, Austin: The Reference Press, Inc. (Gives a general overview of the company.)
Weimer, D. (1998) 'A new cat on the hot seat', *Business Week*, 9 March: 56–61.

Further resources
http://www.caterpillar.com

See also: FOREIGN EXCHANGE RISK, MANAGEMENT OF; GLOBAL STRATEGIC ALLIANCES;

MITSUBISHI HEAVY INDUSTRIES LTD;
MULTI-NATIONAL CORPORATIONS, OR-
GANIZATION STRUCTURES IN

The Coca-Cola Company

Overview

The Coca-Cola Company is one of the world's largest beverage companies. The company manufactures and sells syrups, concentrates and beverage bases for Coca-Cola and the company's flagship brand products worldwide. As a global leader in the soft drinks industry, the Coca-Cola Company operates in more than 195 countries and employs about 30,000 people worldwide. The company's operations consist of five geographical groups: the North American Group (the United States and Canada), the Latin American Group (Central and South America), the Middle and Far East Group (the Middle East, India, China, Japan and Australia), the Greater Europe Group (most parts of Western Europe and parts of Eastern and Central Europe) and the African Group (47 countries in sub-Saharan Africa). The corporate headquarters of the Coca-Cola Company is located in Atlanta, Georgia. The revenues of the company exceeded $18 billion in 1996.

1 Brief history

The Coca-Cola Company was established in 1892 in Atlanta, Georgia, but the history of the company began in 1886 with the invention of a syrup by John S. Pemberton, a pharmacist. The inventor's bookkeeper, Frank M. Robinson, named the syrup Coca-Cola. While the formula for the syrup remains one of the world's best kept secrets, it is believed that the formula contained cocaine in the early years. Later, cocaine was removed from its formulation. Coke was first bottled in 1894. Within a very short time the drink became very popular and captured a significant share of the soft

drinks market in the United States. The product is now one of the world's most popular non-alcoholic beverages.

Since the beginning, the company's advertising slogans (e.g. 1905: 'Coca-Cola revives and sustains'; 1927: 'Around the corner from everywhere'; 1963: 'Things go better with Coke'; 1996: 'Always Coca-Cola') have been very popular around the world. The company changes its slogan every few years. Since the company became a sponsor of the 1928 Summer Olympic Games in Amsterdam it has continued to expand its presence around the world. According to Coca-Cola, 'the Company takes pride in being a worldwide business that is always local', i.e. it offers standardized global products which are adapted to local tastes.

With few exceptions, its bottling plants are locally owned and operated by independent local business people. Local bottling companies provide capital for facilities, machinery, bottles and the distribution of products. The Coca-Cola Company supplies the concentrates and beverage bases to the local bottling companies, and provides some management assistance to the local companies to facilitate growth in profits. In some cases the Coca-Cola Company also shares its expertise in plant design, manufacturing, quality control, marketing and training in some areas. The company's juice business unit, formerly known as Coca-Cola Foods, is now called The Minute Maid Company. The Minute Maid Company is located in Houston, Texas, and is the world's leading marketer of juice drinks. The company's key competitors are PepsiCo, Dr Pepper/7Up and Seagram.

2 Innovation and significant contributions

The company began with the invention of a syrup named Coca-Cola. In the first year the company sold about six drinks per day; now it sells 834 million drinks per day throughout the world. The company's effective advertising slogans, its region-based product development and marketing activities have made its products very popular worldwide. For example, the company has introduced a carbonated soft drink, Smart, specifically designed for young Chinese consumers. The product was the first carbonated beverage introduced into China by an international beverage company. It has been very well received in China. The company has introduced Ciel, a new 'brand' water, in Mexico and new packaging graphics for Fanta in Thailand. Now Fanta is one of the fastest-growing soft drinks in Thailand.

The Coca-Cola company's innovation in marketing, distribution, quality control, development of human resources and adaptability to change have made significant contributions to the beverage industry. The company and its bottling partners have made efforts to solve environmental problems for more than twenty years. To reduce solid waste, all of its packaging is recyclable.

3 Challenges and opportunities

Sustaining its products and businesses throughout the globe by encouraging creativity in its human resources, strategy and brands is the major challenge for the Coca-Cola Company. The company is now making efforts to meet the challenges by maintaining the quality and value of its products; introducing new products; and maintaining and improving effective and efficient distribution systems, customer satisfaction, human resources innovation and management of assets. In this way, the company hopes to maintain its global leadership in the beverage industry.

ROSALIE L. TUNG AND MOHI AHMED
SIMON FRASER UNIVERSITY

Further reading

Fisher, A. (1997) 'The world's most admired companies', *Fortune* 136(8), 27 October: 220–8. (Profiles the world's most admired companies, including Coca-Cola.)

Hoover, G., Campbell, A. and Spain, P.J. (eds) (1995) 'The Coca-Cola Company', *Hoover's Handbook of American Business*, Austin: The Reference Press, Inc. (Gives a general overview of the company.)

Kishi, M. and Russell, D. (1996) *Successful Gaijin in Japan: How Foreign Companies are Making it in Japan*, Lincolnwood: NTC Business Books. (Profiles several successful foreign companies in the Japanese market, including Coca-Cola.)

Lorge, S. (1997) 'Coca-Cola', *Sales & Marketing Management* 149(11), October: 62–3. (Discusses Coca-Cola's sales structure.)

O'Reilly, B. (1997) 'The Secrets of America's Most Admired Corporations: New Ideas, New Products' *Fortune* 135(4), 3 March: 60–4. (Presents the management style, innovation and corporate culture of several of the most innovative US firms, including Coca-Cola.)

Sfiligoj, E. (1998) 'The Pepsi challenge', *Beverage World* 117(1652), 15 January: 98–101. (Identifies the challenges facing Coca-Cola.)

Further resources
http://www. cocacola.com

See also: ADVERTISING STRATEGY, INTERNATIONAL; INTERNATIONAL MARKETING; MARKETING MANAGEMENT, INTERNATIONAL

Corning Incorporated

Overview

Corning Incorporated (Corning) is one of the world's major manufacturers of diversified products and services. Its major products and services include optical fibre, cable, high-performance glass, components for television, electronic displays for communication and communication-related industries, advanced materials for the scientific, life sciences and environmental markets, and consumer products. The company values 'quality, integrity, performance, leadership, innovation, independence, and the individuals'. These values, in turn, contribute to the overall success of the company. Corning operates fifty affiliates in sixteen countries and employs about 20,000 people worldwide. The headquarters of the company is located in Corning, New York. The 1996 revenues of Corning exceeded $4 billion.

1 Brief history

The history of Corning began in 1851 when Armory Houghton started a business in Cambridge, Massachusetts. In 1854 he founded the Union Glass Company in Somerville, Massachusetts. Houghton later sold his interest in Union Glass and bought the Brooklyn, New York, based Flint Glass Company. In 1868 the company was relocated to Corning, New York, and renamed Corning Flint Glass Company. In 1875 the company was incorporated as Corning Glass Works. After its initial contact with the inventor Thomas Edison in 1880, the company began to produce the first blank (the glass part of a lightbulb) for incandescent lamps. From its beginning, the company has established a tradition of technological innovation. In 1989 the company changed its name to Corning Incorporated.

2 Innovation and significant contributions

In 1908 Corning established its first research laboratory, one of the earliest in the United States. In 1909 it began to produce heat-resistant glass for railway lanterns. Corning continued to innovate. Some of its major innovations are new glasses with X-radiation shielding and ultraviolet absorbing compositions (1916); the world's largest piece of glass, cast for the 200-inch telescope mirror on Palomer Mountain in California (1934); photochromatic spectacle lenses (1968); spacecraft windows, fibre optics, computer memories and integrated circuits (1969); and fibre for use in transmitting voice, video and data signals with laser beams (1971).

In 1984 a total quality management system was introduced and the Quality Institute was established. In 1991 Corning collaborated with Mitsubishi Electric Corporation of Tokyo to manufacture the world's largest mirror blank for Japan National Large Telescope on Mount Mauna Kea in Hawaii. In 1991 the company was selected as one of the major suppliers for Japan's Nippon Telephone and Telegraph's (NTT) Track III high-count optical-fibre cable development project in Japan. According to Corning, as a result of this project the company will install cabled fibre in every Japanese home and business by 2015. In 1993 Corning was selected by AT&T (see AT&T CORPORATION) as the supplier of fibre-optic couplers for the next generation of undersea telecommunications system.

MCI Communications Corporation also collaborated with Corning to use dispersion-shifted optical fibre throughout the United States. Corning is the first optical-fibre manufacturer to sign a long-term supply agreement with several Russian cable manufacturers. In 1994 Corning was awarded the National Medal of Technology by the US President. The company's telecommunications products division won the Malcolm Baldridge National Quality Award in 1995.

3 Challenges and opportunities

Continuous improvement and better understanding and anticipation of customer needs are some of the major challenges for Corning. According to the company, to meet its challenges and to create new opportunities Corning has identified eight areas which it seeks to improve upon. The first five dimensions relate to how the company runs its businesses and the subsequent three pertain to how the company works. The areas are:

1 customer focus (anticipate and respond to customer needs);
2 result-oriented (customers keeps the company focused);
3 forward looking (perspectives on sustaining competitive advantage);
4 entrepreneurial (anticipate market need and promote ideas to market);
5 rigorous (clear communication and disciplined processes);
6 open (foster continuous learning);
7 engaging (involvement with customers for better solutions);
8 enabling (enable people to share information and involve the right people to make the correct decisions).

ROSALIE L. TUNG AND MOHI AHMED
SIMON FRASER UNIVERSITY

Further reading

Ackerman, R. (1997) 'After reengineering', *Executive Excellence* 14(5), May: 9. (Presents the views of Roger Ackerman, Corning's chairman, on why the company is successful.)

Hideo, F. (1992) 'History of optical fiber cable R&D in Japan', *Japan 21st*, 37(3), March: 53–6. (Discusses Japanese perspectives on R&D in optical-fibre communications systems and profiles key players in this sector, including Corning Inc.)

Hoover, G., Campbell, A. and Spain, P.J. (eds) (1995) 'Corning Incorporated', *Hoover's Handbook of American Business*, Austin: The Reference Press, Inc. (Gives a general overview of the company.)

LaPlante, A. and Alter, A.E. (1994) 'Corning Inc.: the stage-gate innovation process', *Computer World* 28(44), 31 October: 81. (Traces Corning's experiences in using the state-gate innovation decision method.)

Stoner, J. and Werner, F. (1994) *Managing Finance for Quality: Bottom-line Results from Top-level Commitment*, Milwaukee: ASQC Quality Press. (Discusses quality management at Corning, with a focus on finance.)

Further resources

http://www.corning.com

See also: AT&T CORPORATION; GLOBAL STRATEGIC ALLIANCES

Daimler Chrysler

Overview

Daimler-Benz AG is one of the world's largest transportation and services groups. The group offers products and services encompassing various modes of transportation on land and sea, and in the air and outer space. Daimler-Benz has twenty-three business units, which fall into four major divisions: Passenger Cars, Commercial Vehicles, Aerospace and Services. Other industrial business units of Daimler-Benz are rail systems, micro-electronics and diesel engines. The group's principal profit-generating unit is Mercedes-Benz, manufacturer of luxury cars. The annual revenues of Daimler-Benz exceeded $71 billion in 1996. The group has operations in fifty countries and employs about 290,000 people worldwide. The corporate headquarters of the group is located in Stuttgart, Germany.

In May 1998 Daimler-Benz merged with Chrysler, the largest industrial merger in the world, with annual revenues around $130 billion.

1 Brief history

Daimler-Benz was established in 1926 through a merger of two German companies, one established by Gottlieb Daimler and the other by Karl Benz. The group's history dates back to the 1880s, when the two founders were doing business separately. In 1883 Benz & Co. was established and started car manufacturing. In 1890 Daimler Engine was incorporated; it started manufacturing motorcycles and began the sale of motor engines to French car manufacturers. The businesses of both companies were severely affected by World

War I. After the merger of Daimler and Benz in 1926, the new company began to recover. During World War II the company started to manufacture military vehicles and aeroplane engines, but most of its factories were destroyed during the war.

During the post-war recovery period in the 1950s there was a heavy demand for cars and trucks in Germany and this created opportunities for Daimler-Benz. In the 1970s sales of its luxury cars continued to grow and brought benefits to the rest of the group. Growing competition in the automobile industry forced the group to diversify and make efforts toward sustainable innovation. During the 1980s the group expanded its businesses, and in 1993 the group established its first Mercedes factory in the United States to manufacture fuel-efficient and less expensive cars. The group has made continuous efforts to innovate and further diversify its business through the development of new products and services.

In May 1998 Daimler-Benz merged with Chrysler to form the world's fifth largest car company (after GM, Ford, Toyota and the VW Group). The group will be managed by two bosses, Jürgen Schrempp from Daimler-Benz and Robert Eaton from Chrysler, from two headquarters, Stuttgart (Germany) and Michigan (USA). Daimler Chrysler will be owned 53 per cent by the largest industrial firm in Germany and 47 per cent by the third largest automobile manufacturer in the United States.

2 Innovation and significant contributions

Daimler-Benz's contributions to the industry are significant. The group promotes innovation throughout its management, including the analysis of social trends, the monitoring of innovative global technologies and the adoption of sustainable technology strategies in all of its product segments. The Research and

Technology unit of Daimler-Benz supports the development of technology strategies, secure integrated innovation and technology management through networks and knowledge-based cooperation with its business units to compete in the rapidly changing global marketplace. According to the group, the Research and Technology unit is the nerve centre for technological innovations in the group.

In 1997 Daimler-Benz introduced emission-free fuel-cell city buses powered by hydrogen. The group is currently developing a new electric car, the NECAR 3. To come up with new product innovations, besides relying on in-house efforts, Daimler-Benz also collaborates with partners around the globe. For example, the group has entered into a partnership with Ballard Power Systems Inc. (Canada) and Ford Motor Co. (US) to facilitate the development of fuel-cell technology for use in energy-efficient cars.

Daimler-Benz has also developed a prototype passenger car equipped with state-of-the-art communication systems which will allow Internet access on the road. According to the group, it should be able to mass produce this car by the twenty-first century. Mercedes-Benz has entered into a joint venture with Swatch AG to manufacture Smart, a sporty little car, another trend-setting effort in the industry. The Smart car is designed specifically for use in the city and is environmentally friendly. The Smart project represents the first of the group's efforts to collaborate with firms in completely different industries to compete and adapt to the changing global business environment. This is an example of the strategies of 'co-evolution' and 'collaborative advantage' espoused by the group. The group has also developed a road-side assistance programme and other services for its Mercedes-Benz customers by using satellite communication systems. The group is focused on quality products and services and sustainable innovation.

3 Challenges and opportunities

The major challenges confronting the group are rapid technological change and increased competition in the automobile industry, continuous advances in information and communication technologies (ICTs), and growing concerns with sustainability. The group has tried to increase opportunities by taking advantage of ICTs and innovative technologies developed by the group and other firms around the world. It also seeks to become more competitive through strategic alignment of individual divisions and related subsidiaries to take advantage of opportunities as they arise.

According to Maryann Kellyer, an American car analyst, the merger of Daimler and Chrylser will pose formidable challenges, principal of which is the difference in corporate cultures of the two companies. 'When it comes to the cultures of these two companies, how they think and act and what drives their decisions, they're oil and water' (Kellyer 1998: 62). Another issue pertains to the future of Daimler's businesses in other sectors, such as aerospace and services. The question is how these other sectors will fit into the mission of a car company.

ROSALIE L. TUNG AND MOHI AHMED
SIMON FRASER UNIVERSITY

Further reading

(References cited in the text marked *)

Chalsma, J. (1994) '1994 Mercedes-Benz E420: easy to get used to', *Machine Design* 66(2), 24 January: 124–5, Cleveland, OH. (Compares Mercedes Benz E-420 series to its Japanese competition.)

Economist (1996) 'Selling fuel cells', *Economist* 339(7967), 25 May: 86. (Discusses trends in the automobile industry, including electric vehicles.)

Heller, R. (1997) *In Search of European Excellence: The 10 Key Strategies of Europe's Top Companies*, London: Harper Collins Business. (Presents the key strategies of major European companies.)

* Kellyer, M. (1998) 'A new kind of car company', *Economist*, 9 May: 61–2.

Spain, P.J. and Talbot J.R. (eds) (1995) 'Daimler-Benz Aktiengesellschaft', *Hoover's Handbook of World Business 1995–1996*, Austin: The Reference Press, Inc. (Gives a general overview of the company.)

Templeman, J., Woodruff, D. and Reed, S. (1992) 'Downshift at Daimler', *Business Week*, 16 November: 88–90. (Identifies the challenges facing Daimler-Benz.)

Further resources

http://www.daimlerbenz.com

See also: CULTURE, CROSS-NATIONAL; GENERAL MOTORS CORPORATION; GLOBAL STRATEGIC ALLIANCES; ORGANIZATION CULTURE; TOYODA FAMILY

Dentsu Inc.

1 **Brief history**
2 **Innovation and significant contributions**
3 **Challenges and opportunities**

Overview

Dentsu Inc. is one of the world's largest advertising companies. The firm employs 5629 people and had revenues in excess of $1.3 billion in 1996. With its headquarters in Tokyo, Japan, Dentsu has offices in thirty-five countries. The slogan of the company is 'communications excellence'. It began operations as a news telegraph service and advertising firm. Later Dentsu expanded its activities to encompass nearly every aspect of creative communication. The major services offered by Dentsu are creative market development, market research, strategic planning, sales promotion, event promotion, corporate communication and media/digital advertising.

1 Brief history

In 1901 Dentsu Inc. was founded by Hoshiro Mitsunaga. It began as a news telegraph service and advertising firm in Tokyo and later evolved into a leader in the communications industry. In 1986 Dentsu redefined its role as a full-service communications company and implemented a new management philosophy to accomplish this mission. This new management philosophy has guided its corporate objectives, the qualifications it seeks in its employees (communication, planning, creative and production capabilities) and ten principles governing work. According to the company, the ten principles are:

1 Initiate projects on one's own instead of waiting for work to be assigned.
2 Take an active, not passive, role in all one's endeavours.
3 Search for large and complex challenges.

4 Welcome difficult assignments.
5 Complete a task once it is started, i.e. never give up.
6 Lead and set an example for one's fellow workers.
7 Set goals for oneself to ensure a constant sense of purpose.
8 Move with confidence.
9 At all times challenge oneself to think creatively and find new solutions.
10 Since confrontation is inevitable in the course of progress, when confrontation arises do not shy away from it.

This management philosophy was put forward by Hideo Yoshida, Dentsu's fourth president, to inspire its employees to attain the corporate slogan. These guidelines have helped Dentsu grow to become one of the largest advertising companies in the world (see ADVERTISING STRATEGY, INTERNATIONAL).

2 Innovation and significant contributions

Dentsu has broadened the domain of the traditional advertising firm from one of providing mass-media services to encompass total communication. This has opened new opportunities for the company and other firms in the industry. The firm has also contributed towards the enrichment of people's lives by enhancing communication. It has also tried to stimulate creative talent, which is so important in the advertising industry, by providing an environment where employees are free to develop their own ideas.

Dentsu has begun efforts to create solutions for the emerging digital network era, and has won numerous national and international awards for its innovative advertisements.

3 Challenges and opportunities

Of the top fifteen advertising companies in the world in 1996, only eight are publicly owned. In 2001 Dentsu will make the transition from private to public ownership. This change is designed to help the firm meet the challenges of expanding its global presence in order to take advantage of increasing opportunities around the world. Initially, the company will focus on Asia-Pacific. To facilitate this development, it has established education exchange projects with China and Korea.

Emerging digital technologies have created challenges as well as new opportunities for marketing and advertising companies such as Dentsu. The increase in multimedia use, Internet advertising, cable-television systems and satellite broadcasting are some issues that these firms have to contend with in the years ahead.

ROSALIE L. TUNG AND MOHI AHMED
SIMON FRASER UNIVERSITY

Further reading

Japan 1998 Marketing and Advertising Yearbook, Dentsu Inc. (Gives a detailed overview of the company.)

Rehak, R. (1996) *Greener Marketing & Advertising: The Key to Market Success*, Dentsu Inc. Japan. (Discusses the advertising industry's growing concern with environmental issues.)

Further resources

http://www.dentsu.co.jp

See also: ADVERTISING STRATEGY, INTERNATIONAL; MARKETING MANAGEMENT, INTERNATIONAL

E.I. du Pont de Nemours and Company (DuPont)

1 Brief history
2 Innovation and significant contributions
3 Challenges and opportunities

Overview

DuPont is one of the oldest industrial enterprises in the world. DuPont operates in approximately seventy countries and employs 97,000 people around the globe. About 35 per cent of DuPont's employees work outside the United States. In 1996 the company had revenues in excess of $39 billion. DuPont has 175 manufacturing and processing facilities worldwide – 140 chemicals and speciality plants, eight petroleum refineries and twenty-seven natural-gas processing plants. Its major products are chemicals, fibres, plastics, films, petroleum, healthcare products, biotechnology and composite materials.

1 Brief history

The company was established by a French immigrant to the US, Eleuthère Irenée du Pont de Nemours, in 1802 near Wilmington, Delaware. The company started its business in gunpowder production in 1804. In 1805 it exported its first products to Spain. Since the early 1900s DuPont has grown into a diversified chemical company specializing in synthetics. In the 1930s, with the invention and commercialization of nylon, DuPont expanded its range of products and business activities.

In 1958 DuPont began its major overseas expansion. During the 1950s and 1960s the company established subsidiaries in Europe, Latin America and the Asia-Pacific region. In the 1970s DuPont placed more emphasis on marketing and continued to grow through

diversification. In 1981 DuPont purchased Conoco, a fully integrated oil, gas and coal company with operations around the world. Since the 1980s DuPont has continued its international expansion to serve local customers around the world. In 1993 DuPont acquired ICI's nylon business and ICI acquired DuPont's acrylic business. This transaction further strengthened DuPont's position in the global nylon business. In 1993–4, DuPont formed an alliance with Asahi of Japan to expand its nylon business in Asia.

2 Innovation and significant contributions

Starting with product innovation, DuPont has continued to create new products through R&D efforts. DuPont established one of the first industrial research laboratory in the United States. Its innovation in the area of synthetic materials has formed the basis of its global businesses. DuPont has made pioneering efforts to investigate the impact of chlorofluorocarbons (CFCs) on the atmosphere and introduced the first substitute compounds to replace CFC-based refrigerants. DuPont also played a leading role in establishing the Montreal Protocol to phase out CFC production. As a result, Charles J. Pedersen, a chemist at DuPont, was awarded the Nobel Prize in Chemistry.

DuPont considers its major strengths to lie in science and technology, commitment to safety, concern for people, a sense of community, an emphasis on personal and corporate integrity, a focus on the future and willingness to change. Every year DuPont spends over $1 billion on R&D. DuPont believes that the most important contributions can be made through collaboration with other companies. As a result, it has entered into collaborative R&D and joint-venture arrangements with several entities around the world, including Harvard University, Merck, Conoco and Asahi of Japan.

3 Challenges and opportunities

In the last decade of the twentieth century increasing attention has been paid to industrial ecology, which focuses on the interaction of industry and society with the global environment. To meet this challenge, companies have to reconsider their manufacturing strategies and come up with viable alternatives. DuPont, along with other large firms such as AT&T (see AT&T CORPORATION) and General Motors (see GENERAL MOTORS CORPORATION), has made efforts to improve material and energy flows in its products and processes, and to implement sustainable manufacturing strategies to optimize the total materials cycle (i.e. from virgin material to finished material, product, waste products and disposals). While they pose challenges, such efforts can also create opportunities to develop new businesses, as the move towards industrial ecology fosters a cultural change within companies as well the communities they serve. According to DuPont, throughout the company's history many of its major contributions to the market have come through collaboration with other entities. DuPont will continue to collaborate on R&D efforts with other firms.

ROSALIE L. TUNG AND MOHI AHMED
SIMON FRASER UNIVERSITY

Further reading

Barnes, P. (1998) 'Industrial ecology', *Business and Economic Review* 44(2), January–March: 21–4. (Discusses industrial ecology issues and efforts undertaken by DuPont and other major companies in this regard.)

Cheape, C.W. (1995) *Strictly Business: Walter Carpenter at DuPont and General Motors*, Baltimore, MD: Johns Hopkins University Press. (A biographical account of Walter Carpenter, a former DuPont top executive.)

Colby, G. (1984) *DuPont Dynasty*, New Jersey: Lyle Stuart Inc. (Gives a detailed historical background of the company.)

Freeburn, C. (1997) 'DuPont keeps top spot', *Chemical Week* 159(48), 17 December: 20. (Discusses trends in the chemical industry.)

Kanter, R.M., Kao, J. and Wiersema, F. (eds) (1997) *Innovation: Breakthrough Thinking at 3M, DuPont, GE, Pfizer, and Rubbermaid*, New York: Harper Business. (Presents perspectives on innovations at several leading companies, including DuPont.)

Further resources

http://www.dupont.com

See also: AT&T CORPORATION; GENERAL MOTORS CORPORATION; GLOBAL STRATEGIC ALLIANCES; TECHNOLOGY STRATEGY, INTERNATIONAL

Eastman Kodak Company (Kodak)

1 **Brief history**
2 **Innovation and significant contributions**
3 **Challenges and opportunities**

Overview

Eastman Kodak is one of the world's largest manufacturers of imaging products and services. Kodak had revenues in excess of $15 billion in 1996 and in the same year employed 94,800 people worldwide, including 53,400 in the US. Kodak has nine business units: Business Imaging Systems, Consumer Imaging, Commercial and Government Systems, Global Customer Service and Support, Digital and Applied Imaging, Health Imaging, Professional Motion Imaging, Office Imaging and Kodak Professional. The company's products and services are now available in more than 150 countries. The corporate headquarters of the company is located in Rochester, New York.

1 Brief history

The history of Kodak dates back to the 1880s. George Eastman established the Eastman Dry Plate and Film Company in 1884. Eastman espoused four basic business principles (mass production at low cost, international distribution, extensive advertising and a focus on customers) and adopted three major policies ('foster growth and development through continuing research; reinvest profits to build and extend the business; and treat employees in a fair, and self-respecting way'). The company's success is closely linked to these principles and policies. Since the early years, Eastman has made efforts to mass produce at low cost.

In 1888 the name Kodak was first registered as a trademark. According to Eastman Kodak, K was George Eastman's favourite letter. Eastman tried to make words that began and ended with K and the word Kodak came out. The first Kodak camera was sold to the market with the slogan 'You push the button – we do the rest'. That marked the beginning of snapshot photography. By 1896 Kodak had manufactured its 100,000th camera, and the company continued to innovate and develop imaging systems.

To sell abroad, Eastman established a sales office in London only five years after the establishment of the Eastman Dry Plate and Film Company in New York. In 1889 the Eastman Photographic Materials Company Ltd was established in London, England, to distribute Kodak products in overseas markets. In 1892 the company became the Eastman Kodak Company of New York, and in the early 1900s several other distribution outlets were established in France, Germany, Italy and other European countries. Now the company has manufacturing operations in Canada, Mexico, Brazil, France, Germany, Australia, the UK and the US, but its products are marketed by subsidiary companies in more than 150 countries.

2 Innovation and significant contributions

Kodak's innovation started with the photographic dry plates for photographers invented by George Eastman. He also became one of the first American industrialists to employ a full-time research scientist to support the commercialization of a flexible, transparent film base. Since its beginning in the late 1880s, Kodak has continued to innovate in the area of imaging products.

The company's breakthrough development of Kodak T-Grain technology has contributed to the further improvement of its major imaging products. Hybrid Imaging, Kodak photo CD and Digital Imaging are some of the company's other recent major innovations. In 1995 the US Environmental

Protection Agency (EPA) gave Kodak an Environmental Champion award for voluntary efforts to reduce air emissions of seventeen targeted chemicals. Kodak has undertaken R&D efforts to reduce the emission of ozone-depleting chlorofluorocarbons (CFCs) as well.

Kodak has succeeded in making photography a popular leisure activity for millions of people around the world. According to Kodak, 'in 1996, people [would] take some 65 billion pictures, most with cameras that owe their basic design to Eastman's first roll-film models'. Kodak is also the world leader in medical laser imaging.

3 Challenges and opportunities

Eastman Kodak has led the imaging market for more than a century. Its major challenge now is to remain competitive in the emerging digital era. The new digital technology also poses tremendous opportunities for Kodak. To compete in the changing global marketplace Kodak is now making efforts to improve its customer focus, reduce costs and increase collaboration with other organizations. Some of the collaborative ventures include its efforts with IBM (see INTERNATIONAL BUSINESS MACHINES CORPORATION) to develop digital imaging, with Microsoft to develop co-brand software to market digital images and with Kinko's to market photo CDs. Through continuous innovation and collaboration with other organizations, Kodak

expects to remain in the forefront of the world's imaging business.

ROSALIE L. TUNG AND MOHI AHMED
SIMON FRASER UNIVERSITY

Further reading

Champy, J. (1997) 'What makes you so special', *Sales and Marketing Management* 149(12), November: 24–6. (Identifies the marketing strategies of some innovative firms, including Kodak.)

Hoover, G., Campbell, A. and Spain, P.J. (eds) (1995) 'Eastman Kodak Company', *Hoover's Handbook of American Business*, Austin: The Reference Press, Inc. (Gives a general overview of the company.)

Maremont, M. (1995) 'Kodak's new focus: an inside look at George Fisher's strategy', *Business Week*, 30 January: 62–8. (Presents the perspectives on strategy of George Fisher, Kodak's CEO.)

Smith, G. (1997) 'What Kodak is developing in digital photography', *Business Week*, 7 July: 108–9. (Discusses Kodak's strategy for the digital era.)

Swasy, A. (1997) *Changing Focus: Kodak and the Battle to Save a Great American Company*, New York: Times Books. (Identifies the challenges confronting Kodak.)

Further resources

http://www.kodak.com

See also: GATES, BILL; GLOBAL STRATEGIC ALLIANCES; INTERNATIONAL BUSINESS MACHINES CORPORATION

General Electric Company (GE)

Overview

General Electric (GE) is one of the world's largest diversified manufacturing, technology and services companies, with revenues of more than $79 billion (1996). The company operates in over 100 countries around the world, including 250 manufacturing plants in twenty-six different countries, and employs about 239,000 people worldwide. The company's major products and services include aircraft engines, appliances, capital services, electrical distribution and control, information services, lighting, medical systems, industrial control systems, broadcasting and communications services, plastics, power systems, transportation systems and support operations (including GE supply, investments and corporate R&D Center). The company has its corporate headquarters in Fairfield, Connecticut.

1 Brief history

In 1892, as a result of a merger of the Edison General Electric Company and the Thomas–Houston Electric Company, General Electric Company was established in New York. In 1895 GE built the world's largest electric locomotives (90 tons) and transformers (800 kw), and GE controlled 97 per cent of the lamp business in the United States in 1905. In 1919 GE organized the Radio Corporation of America (RCA). In 1932 RCA became an independent company, but it was re-acquired by GE in 1986.

During the early 1940s, to meet wartime needs, GE manufactured and tested the first US jet engines and 400 plastic aircraft parts. In 1946 it began to study power generation

from nuclear energy. From the 1950s to the 1970s GE expanded the range of its products and services. The range covers automatic washing machines; the world's first jet engine, with which an aircraft can fly at twice the speed of sound; earth-oriented meteorological satellites, which can supply scientific data on atmospheric and environmental conditions; computer tomography (CT) scanners; and the world's largest nuclear power plant.

In 1919 International General Electric Company was formed, but foreign revenue accounted for only 10 per cent of its total revenues in 1953. In 1970 international revenue accounted for only 16 per cent of GE's total revenues, and the company had more than 100,000 employees outside the US. At that time the company had 129 affiliated companies, manufacturing products in twenty-three countries and serving markets in 150 countries through 350 distributors. Since the mid-1980s GE has increased the number of joint ventures with foreign firms to gain technical and/or marketing advantages around the world. In 1996 GE had 250 manufacturing plants and employed 131,000 people outside the US; it derived 40 per cent of its revenue from abroad.

2 Innovation and significant contributions

Prior to the merger of Thomas–Houston and Edison Electric Light Company to establish GE, Thomas A. Edison's vision was to establish a company that would light a nation by producing all components of electrical power stations and electric lamps. Since the beginning, the company had the vision of making continuous innovations. GE established a research laboratory in 1900, the first industrial R&D lab in the United States. Its corporate R&D Center is currently one of the world's largest and most diversified industrial laboratories, providing international trade support, market development, licensing and investment information to GE's various businesses around the world.

GE's contribution goes far beyond the innovation of new products and services – its business management concepts are well recognized around the world. At the company's Management Development Institute at Crotonville, New York – dubbed 'the Harvard of corporate America' – GE executives engage in a continuous debate on the management issues confronting the company in a changing business environment. GE was the first company to establish such an institute, in 1956. GE's CEO John F. Welch, Jr (Jack Welch), has established several examples of best practice in managing an organization in a changing global business environment. Welch pioneered the #1 or #2 strategy of 'fix/close/sell'. According to Tichy and Sherman (1993), 'Jack Welch divided GE businesses which met the requirements of being #1 or #2 globally into three strategic circles: core manufacturing; technology-intensive, and services, and any businesses outside these circles would have to be made more competitive or be closed or sold.' 'the human engine', 'shared values', 'boundaryless organization', 'reward systems' and 'walk the talk' are other significant business/management concepts that have been pioneered by GE and which have been emulated by companies around the world (see WELCH, JACK). GE has been selected by *Fortune* magazine as one of the ten most admired companies in the US and is the third most profitable company in the world, after Royal Dutch/Shell (see ROYAL DUTCH/SHELL GROUP) and Exxon.

3 Challenges and opportunities

Most of GE's products and services are known worldwide. The company competes with Siemens (see SIEMENS AG), Hitachi and ABB (Asea Brown Boveri) around the globe. The company seeks to expand its market share in India, China, Mexico and other emerging markets in the Asia-Pacific region. To meet the challenges of increasing business opportunities around the world, GE has focused on different products and services for each

country to meet local demands. For example, GE focuses on jet engines and capital in China, medical systems in India and power systems in Mexico.

ROSALIE L. TUNG AND MOHI AHMED
SIMON FRASER UNIVERSITY

Further reading

(References cited in the text marked *)

Burton, J. (1997) 'The stars that make Jack shine', *Chief Executive*, September: 24–31. (Profiles twelve GE executives, including its CEO, Jack Welch.)

Curran, J. (1997) 'GE Capital: Jack Welch's secret weapon', *Fortune* 136(9), 10 November: 116–34. (Tells the inside story of GE Capital and its contribution to the success of GE.)

Fisher, A. (1997) 'The world's most admired companies', *Fortune* 136(8), 27 October: 220–8. (Gives an overview of several world-class companies.)

Hoover, G., Campbell, A., and Spain, P.J. (eds) (1995) 'General Electric Company', *Hoover's Handbook of American Business*, Austin: The Reference Press, Inc. (Gives a general overview of the company.)

Nash, J.C. (1989) *From Tank Town to High Tech: The Clash of Community and Industrial Cycles*, New York: State University of New York Press. (Provides a historical background of GE, with a special focus on the company's linkage to American society at large.)

Slater, R. (1993) *The New GE: How Jack Welch Revived an American Institution*, Homewood, IL: Business One Irwin. (An examination of how Jack Welch brought significant change to GE and created the new GE.)

Smart, T., Engardio, P. and Smith, G. (1993) 'GE's brave new world: Welch sees the future, its China, India, Mexico', *Business Week*, 8 November: 64–70. (Outlines GE's efforts in expanding its businesses in the emerging marketplace.)

Stewart, T.A. (1998) 'America's most admired companies', *Fortune*, 2 March: 70–82.

* Tichy, N.M. and Sherman, S. (1993) *Control Your Destiny or Someone Else Will: How Jack Welch is Making General Electric the World's Most Competitive Corporation*, New York: Currency Doubleday. (Tells the inside story of the transformation of GE and gives the views of the company's CEO, Jack Welch.)

Further resources
http://www.ge.com

See also: GLOBAL STRATEGIC ALLIANCES; IN-
TERNATIONAL TECHNOLOGY TRANSFER;
ROYAL DUTCH/SHELL GROUP; SIEMENS AG;
WELCH, JACK

General Motors Corporation (GM)

Overview

The world's largest industrial corporation, General Motors (GM), is a full-line vehicle manufacturer. Established in 1908, GM has a presence in more than 190 countries. The company employs over 647,000 people worldwide and its revenues exceeded $168 billion in 1996. The General Motor Corporation is made up of General Motors North American Operations, Delphi Automotive Systems, General Motors International Operations, General Motors Acceptance Corporation, Hughes Electronics Corporation, General Motors Locomotive Group and Allison Transmission. Its corporate headquarters is located in Detroit, Michigan.

1 Brief history

GM was founded in 1908. In 1920 it completed the GM building, and in 1924 it began to assemble vehicles in Denmark, in its first assembly facilities outside the United States. Alfred P. Sloan (see SLOAN, ALFRED P.), who was the president of GM during the period 1923–37, implemented innovative management systems which are still considered to be management guidelines for many modern high-technology industries. Sloan, along with Pierre Du Pont of DuPont Chemicals (see E.I. DU PONT DE NEMOURS AND COMPANY), was credited with 'applying the principles of decentralization and the use of staff services in senior management' to large-scale manufacturing companies in the private sector. Sloan was also 'responsible for influential developments in consumer marketing, for innovations in the use of specialist expertise in management, and for numerous developments in ways of obtaining, presenting and using data needed by decision makers' (Glover 1996: 4481). On January 11 1940 the company manufactured its 25 millionth car. During World War II it continued to expand its products and adopted innovations.

In 1978 GM established the Cancer Research Foundation, and in 1981 it opened its European assembly plant in Saragossa, Spain, one of GM's largest overseas expansion projects. In 1985 GM established a Medical Committee for Automotive Safety and developed the crash dummy to measure forces exerted during side impacts as a part of its safety-related R&D programme. In 1997 GM introduced fourteen new models, the biggest launch in the company's history.

2 Innovation and significant contribution

Since its beginning, GM has made significant contributions to the automobile industry. Its many innovations include the electric headlamp for automobiles (1908), the electric self-starter (1911) and the all-steel body (1912). In 1924 GM opened the first automotive proving-ground test facility, and it introduced shatter-resistant safety glass in 1926. GM set the industry standard by introducing the column-mounted gearshift in 1938 and curved glass windscreens in 1949. GM also introduced power steering and automatic windscreen wipers as standard equipment for automobiles.

GM established the world's first safety test laboratory in 1955 and conducted atmospheric R&D. The company shares its findings with industry and government. GM's guidance and navigation system, for example, contributed to the Apollo II mission. GM introduced the first airbags in 1974. In 1988 GM won the Car of the Year award, and in 1990 it introduced a nearly pollution-free gas-electric-powered vehicle. Its electric vehicles were also a significant contribution to the automobile industry.

3 Challenges and opportunities

GM's major challenges include the need to make continuous improvements in productivity, to shorten product development time, to reduce costs and to increase market share around the world. According to GM, the firm is now making efforts to increase opportunities in the global marketplace through a coordinated approach. Since 1984 GM has established a joint venture with Toyota as New United Motor Manufacturing Inc. (NUMMI) in Fremont, California. Through the joint venture, GM seeks to learn from Toyota with regard to reducing time and costs in production. The joint venture allowed Toyota, on the other hand, an opportunity to apply its production systems in an American work environment. The NUMMI joint venture has proved to be very successful.

Continuous efforts in R&D for environment-friendly automobiles and social marketing will create further business opportunities for GM in the future.

ROSALIE L. TUNG AND MOHI AHMED
SIMON FRASER UNIVERSITY

Further reading

(References cited in the text marked *)

* Glover, I. (1996) 'Alfred P. Sloan', in M. Warner (ed.) *International Encyclopedia of Business and Management*, London: International Thompson Press. (Gives a biographical account of Alfred P. Sloan.)

Hoover, G., Campbell, A. and Spain, P.J. (eds) (1995) 'General Motors Corporation', *Hoover's Handbook of American Business*, Austin: The Reference Press, Inc. (Gives a general overview of the company.)

Kanter, R.M. (1989) *When Giants Learn to Dance*, New York: Simon & Schuster. (Offers guidelines on how large companies can engage successfully in collaborative agreements with other entities.)

Kerwin, K. (1993) 'Can Jack Smith fix GM?', *Business Week*, November: 126–35. (Discusses the challenges facing GM.)

Sullivan, T. (1996) 'GM shifts direction to gain global clout', *Marketing Week* 19(34), 15 November: 20–1. (Discusses corporate re-engineering at GM.)

Taylor, A. (1997) 'GM: time to get in gear', *Fortune* 135(8), 28 April: 94–102. (Discusses the challenges that lie ahead for GM.)

Womack, J.P., Jones, D.T. and Roos, D. (1990) *The Machine that Changed the World: Based on the Massachusetts Institute of Technology 5 Million Dollar 5 Year Study on the Future of the Automobile*, New York: Rawson Associates. (Provides some guidelines for auto manufacturing and production management systems.)

Further resources

http://www.gm.com

See also: E.I. DU PONT DE NEMOURS AND COMPANY; FOREIGN MARKET ENTRY STRATEGIES, GLOBAL STRATEGIC ALLIANCES; INTERNATIONAL TECHNOLOGY TRANSFER; SLOAN, ALFRED P.; TOYODA FAMILY

The Gillette Company (Gillette)

Overview

Gillette is the world leader in the blades and razors business. The company is also a major producer of toiletries, writing instruments and alkaline batteries. The company manufactures its products in sixty-four facilities in over twenty-seven countries and sells its products throughout the globe. In 1996 Gillette's revenues exceeded $9 billion. The company employs 31,000 people worldwide, with more than 75 per cent of them working outside the United States. The corporate headquarters of Gillette is located in Boston, Massachusetts.

1 Brief history

The history of Gillette dates back to 1895, when King C. Gillette developed the idea of disposable razor blades while shaving at home with a conventional razor. In 1901 William Nickerson of the Massachusetts Institute of Technology (MIT) joined Gillette to develop safety razors and formed the American Safety Razor Company in Boston. It first marketed the safety razor in 1903, and sold only fifty-one sets in the first year. By 1904, however, more than 90,844 sets had been sold. The company established its first overseas operation in London in 1905 and within thirteen years of the formation of the American Safety Razor Company its products were sold in eight countries. The company continued expansion through new product innovation and effective marketing of its products.

In the late 1940s the company started to diversify its business. In the 1950s Gillette adopted its current name. During the 1960s and 1970s Gillette further diversified its

product lines. In 1967 Gillette acquired Braun, manufacturer of electric shavers and appliances. In 1984 Gillette expanded into dental products by acquiring Oral-B. In the early 1990s the company introduced the Gillette series, a line of men's shaving and skin products. In 1993 the Oral-B unit established a joint venture in Shanghai, China. At present the major business areas of Gillette are personal care products (blades, razors, oral care products and toiletries), stationery products (writing instruments and correction products) and small electrical appliances (small household appliances and batteries).

2 Innovation and significant contribution

Since the beginning, Gillette has made important innovations and expanded its business around the world. The company's strategically integrated international manufacturing, R&D, marketing and distribution systems have made significant contributions to the industry by establishing best management practices for global companies. Gillette's efforts to standardize products and services for the world market, its strategies on production, worldwide sourcing and management from any location, and coordinated international business activities have established the company as a leading world-class corporation.

Besides being the world leader in blades and razors, Gillette has many other products which are very successful around the world. For example, Braun is the number one marketer of electric shavers in Germany, other parts of Europe, North America and Japan. Oral-B is one of the major brand toothbrushes in the world. Duracell alkaline batteries are among the most popular batteries in the world. Each of Gillette's businesses has its own R&D facility. The company also has three corporate research laboratories, in Boston, Washington, DC, and Reading (in the UK).

3 Challenges and opportunities

Continuous product innovation and improvement of existing products, reduction of manufacturing costs and expansion to international markets (including the emerging markets in Asia, Eastern Europe and Latin America) are some of the major challenges confronting Gillette. To further increase its presence in the global marketplace Gillette must launch all its major products simultaneously in its markets around the world. To increase productivity of its global business activities it must implement state-of-the-art information and communication technologies (ICTs).

ROSALIE L. TUNG AND MOHI AHMED
SIMON FRASER UNIVERSITY

Further reading

Chakravarty, S.N. (1991) 'We had to change the playing fields', *Forbes* 147(3), 4 February: 82–4. (Discusses how Gillette manages change and integrates its marketing and product development.)

Higgins, R.B. (1996) *The Search for Corporate Strategic Credibility: Concepts and Cases in Global Strategy Communication*, London: Quorum Books. (Examines how Gillette manages stockholder communications.)

Hoover, G., Campbell, A. and Spain, P.J. (eds) (1995) 'The Gillette Company', *Hoover's Handbook of American Business*, Austin: The Reference Press, Inc. (Gives a general overview of the company.)

Kanter, R.M. (1995) *World Class: Thriving Locally in the Global Economy*, New York: Simon & Schuster. (Examines how companies can become competitive globally in their respective industries.)

Symonds, W. (1998) 'Gillette's edge: the secret of a great innovation machine? Never relax', *Business Week*, 19 January: 70–7. (Provides the historical background of Gillette's innovations and a discussion of the company's future plans as well as challenges.)

See also: FOREIGN MARKET ENTRY STRATEGIES; GLOBAL STRATEGIC ALLIANCES

International Business Machines Corporation (IBM)

1 **Brief history**
2 **Innovation and significant contributions**
3 **Challenges and opportunities**

Overview

IBM is one of the world's leading providers of information technology and services. The company's two primary missions are to lead in the creation, development and manufacturing of the most advanced information technologies, and to translate those technologies into value for its customers. IBM designs, develops and manufactures computer systems, including software, networking systems, storage devices and microelectronics. In 1996 the revenues of the company exceeded $79.9 billion. The company operates in most countries around the globe and employed about 222,000 people worldwide in 1994. IBM has its headquarters in Armonk, New York.

1 Brief history

In 1911 IBM was first incorporated in New York as the Computing-Tabulating-Recording Company. The company's history, however, can be traced back to 1890, when the United States was receiving waves of immigrants. To meet the needs of measuring population the US Census Bureau sponsored a contest to find the most efficient means of tabulating census data. The contest was won by German immigrant and Census Bureau statistician, Herman Hollerith. Hollerith formed the Punch Card Tabulating Machine Co. in 1896. In 1911 Hollerith's company merged with Computing Scale Co. of America and International Time Recording Co. to form the Computing-Tabulating-Recording (C-T-R) Co. The company manufactured and sold products ranging from commercial scales and industrial time recorders to meat and cheese slicers, tabulators and punch cards.

In the beginning the company operated in New York City only. Within a short period of time, however, it quickly expanded its offices and plants to other parts of New York State, Washington, DC, Ohio, Michigan and Toronto, Canada. In 1914 Thomas J. Watson joined the company and became the president of the company within eleven months. Under his leadership the company continued to expand its products and services. At that time the company focused on producing large-scale custom-built tabulating solutions for businesses. Within ten years Watson had expanded the company's business operations to Europe, South America, Asia and Australia, and in 1924 the company was renamed International Business Machines Corporation (IBM) to reflect the firm's worldwide expansion.

IBM refers to the decades between 1939 and 1963 as the 'Era of Innovation'. During this period the company's product line expanded significantly. During World War II IBM made its first steps towards the development of computers. In 1944 IBM developed the automatic-sequence-controlled calculator, the first machine that could automatically execute long computations. In 1952 the company introduced the IBM 701, its first large computer based on the vacuum tube. This machine was used in business for billing, payroll and inventory control. Between 1960 and the 1980s IBM introduced the system/360 computer, which used interchangeable software and equipment. In 1969 IBM changed its way of selling products; instead of selling hardware, software and services in packages, the company began to sell the components separately, while remaining as the world's leader in the hardware and software industries.

In 1981 IBM introduced personal computers (PCs) for small businesses, schools and homes. For the first time, IBM collaborated with Intel and Microsoft to produce PCs (see GATES, BILL). In 1985 IBM introduced local area networks (LANs), which permitted PC users to exchange information and share printers and files within a building or complex. IBM established a foundation for network computing and numerous applications of PCs. In 1993 Louis V. Gerstner, Jr, a former executive at American Express (see AMERICAN EXPRESS COMPANY), Nabisco and McKinsey & Co., joined IBM as CEO. Gerstner emphasized the need to provide integrated solutions for the company's customers. He also decided to keep the company together instead of splitting it into separate independent companies. Today IBM's strength lies in its combined expertise in solutions, services, products and technologies.

2 Innovation and significant contribution

IBM has changed the way people work, live and interact today, and has made significant contributions to the industry by revolutionizing the way in which business is conducted. IBM's recent innovations range from the DRAM memory chip, semiconductors, display technology, storage technology, design automation, computer architecture and software to computer networks, user interfaces and multimedia. Five IBM researchers have received Nobel prizes for their contributions to science and technology. The company's research division headquarters is located in New York, and the company has several other key sites in San Jose, California; Austin, Texas; Beijing, China; Haifa, Israel; Yorktown Heights, New York; Tokyo, Japan; and Zurich, Switzerland.

IBM has received the first edition of worldwide ISO 14001 registration, which covers all the company's global manufacturing and hardware development operations across all its business units. IBM has received the Best of the Best Award from the US Environmental Protection Agency (EPA) for its contributions to stratospheric ozone protection, and the Environmental Excellence Award from the US and Japan for contributions to environmental protection and product design.

3 Challenges and opportunities

To respond to challenges in the rapidly changing computer industry, IBM has expanded its collaboration with other firms around the world. For example, IBM has begun collaboration with Netscape, Oracle and Sun Microsystems to promote a standards-based approach in the information-communication industry. IBM's leadership in the area of electronic commerce will likely give it a competitive edge in the future.

The goal to bring integrated solutions to its global customers may bring further benefits for IBM. The company's continuous and coordinated efforts in innovation and marketing to provide information and communication technologies, products and services at the right time in the right markets may further contribute to the company's success in the future.

ROSALIE L. TUNG AND MOHI AHMED
SIMON FRASER UNIVERSITY

Further reading

Arnst, C., Verity, J.W. and Rebello, K. (1993) 'Rethinking IBM', *Business Week*, 2 October: 86–97. (Presents the major challenges to IBM.)

Cortese, A. (1995) 'The View From IBM', *Business Week*, 30 October: 142–8. (Provides an inside look at the network-centric computing at IBM.)

Hoover, G., Campbell, A. and Spain, P.J. (eds) (1995) 'International Business Machines', *Hoover's Handbook of American Business*, Austin: The Reference Press, Inc. (Gives a general overview of the company.)

Jones, P. and Kahaner, L. (1995) *Say It & Live It*, New York: Currency Doubleday. (Presents the mission statements of fifty corporations.)

Kanter, R.M. (1989) *When Giants Learn to Dance*, New York: Simon & Schuster. (Offers guidelines on how large companies can collaborate effectively with other entities.)

Kanter, R.M. (1995) *World Class: Thriving Locally in the Global Economy*, New York: Simon & Schuster. (Discusses how companies can become globally competitive in their respective industries.)

Mills, D.Q. and Friesen, G.B. (1996) *Broken Promises: An Unconventional View of What Went Wrong at IBM*, Boston, MA: Harvard Business School Press. (Provides an historical background of the challenges confronting IBM.)

Further resources

http://www.ibm.com

See also: AMERICAN EXPRESS COMPANY; FOREIGN MARKET ENTRY STRATEGIES; GATES, BILL; GLOBAL STRATEGIC ALLIANCES; INTERNATIONAL TECHNOLGY TRANSFER

The Michelin Group (Michelin)

Overview

Michelin is one of the largest manufacturers of rubber and plastic products in the world. The company's major businesses are tyres and travel publications. Michelin makes tyres for all types of vehicles, including bicycles, motor-cycles, automobiles, trucks, buses, subways, trains, aeroplanes and the space shuttle. Michelin's revenues reached $14 billion in 1996. The group employs more than 119,000 people and has operations in over 170 countries in the world. Michelin has seventy-four manufacturing facilities in seventeen countries on all continents – forty-four in Europe, twenty in North America, six in Asia, two in Africa and two in South America. It operates six rubber plantations in Africa (Nigeria) and South America (Brazil). Every day Michelin produces more than 770,000 tyres, 46,500 wheels, 4 million kilometres of wire, and 60,000 tourist maps and guides.

1 Brief history

Michelin was established in 1889 in Clermont-Ferrand, France. From 1906 the company expanded its business abroad and diversified into other businesses. Between 1946 and 1954 Michelin developed the radial tyre, a revolutionary innovation in the industry. Between 1955 and 1969 the company established fifteen factories in various locations. In the 1970s Michelin expanded its operations into North America.

Michelin's radial tyre was used in the Mirage III E planes in 1981, and in 1983 was used in Airbus A300 planes (see AIRBUS IN-DUSTRIE). Since then Michelin has continued to increase its supply of tyres to aeroplanes. In the late 1980s Michelin entered the Asia-Pacific region. In 1988 Michelin expanded into Japan and Thailand, and in 1989 moved into Malaysia. In 1989 Michelin acquired the B.F. Goodrich tyre-manufacturing operations, which make aircraft tyres. In 1995 it established a joint venture with the Shenyang Tyre Factory in China.

2 Innovation and significant contributions

Michelin is a global leader in the tyre industry. It made significant contributions to the industry by developing the radial-ply tyre in the mid-1950s and ecological tyres in the early 1990s. The company has continued to make innovations, both product- and process-related, including improved communication with its customers worldwide. In 1991 Michelin introduced the XH4 tyres for passenger cars in the United States, with a road-life guarantee of 80,000 miles (130,000 km).

In 1994 Michelin tyres were selected for use in Boeing's 777 planes (see THE BOEING COMPANY) and in 1995 the space shuttle landed on Michelin tyres. Michelin operates R&D centres in Europe, the US and Japan. These facilities seek to make innovations in both product and process. The R&D centres are equipped with a Cray supercomputer – Michelin is the first manufacturer in the world to utilize such technology in its R&D facilities.

3 Challenges and opportunities

With operations in so many countries around the world, a major challenge is effective communication with its customers worldwide. The firm has now developed an extranet for its independent tyre dealers. In the US, for example, Michelin has already established Bib Net, which links it with all its dealers. Dealers can check inventory, order tyres and handle claims processing through the net.

In the early 1990s, due to severe competition in the tyre market and a decline in the size of the market, Michelin incurred a large amount of debt. In 1996 the company changed this condition by reorganizing its decision-making processes and restructuring its management to improve financial performance.

ROSALIE L. TUNG AND MOHI AHMED

SIMON FRASER UNIVERSITY

Further reading

Economist (1997*)* 'Michelin gets a grip', *Economist* 342(8006), 1 March: 63–4. (Tells how Michelin improved its profit margins through restructuring.)

Spain, P.J. and Talbot J.R. (eds) (1995) 'Michelin', *Hoover's Handbook of World Business 1995–96*, Austin: The Reference Press, Inc. (Gives a general overview of the company.)

Wreden, N. (1997) 'Good deal for Michelin dealers', *InformationWeek* 653, 20 October: 98–100. (Presents Michelin's implementation of an extranet for its dealers in the US.)

Further resources

http://www.michelin.com

See also: AIRBUS INDUSTRIE; THE BOEING COMPANY; FOREIGN MARKET ENTRY STRATEGIES; GLOBAL STRATEGIC ALLIANCES

Minnesota Mining and Manufacturing Company (3M)

Overview

Minnesota Mining and Manufacturing Company (3M) is one of the most innovative global companies, with revenues of about $14 billion in 1996. It employs 74,000 people worldwide, 39,000 of whom work in the US. The company started out in a small town in Minnesota in 1902. It now operates in more than sixty countries, with manufacturing operations in forty-two international locations and laboratories in twenty-two locations around the world. 3M's business units fall into one of two major sectors: industrial and consumer sector (automotive and chemical markets, electronic/electrical and communications, consumer and office, industrial markets) and the life science sector (dental, medical, pharmaceuticals, traffic and safety, diaper closures, commercial graphics, advertising markets). According to the company, its key strengths lie in 'market leadership', 'technological innovation', 'customer focus', 'global reach' and 'employee initiatives to advance the lives and businesses of its customers and provide an attractive return for shareholders'. 3M seeks to become the most innovative firm and the preferred supplier in these two business sectors.

1 Brief history

3M was established in Minnesota, near the Lake Superior town of Two Harbors. It began in mining, but as the mineral deposits proved to be of little value the company quickly turned its focus to sandpaper products and, in the process, moved its business to the Duluth area. In 1910 the company relocated to St Paul, and grew through technical and marketing innovations.

In 1925 a young lab assistant at 3M invented masking tape, the first of many Scotch-brand pressure-sensitive tapes. In the 1940s 3M also produced defence materials for the US military for use in World War II. In the 1950s 3M introduced the thermo-fax copying process, Scotchgard fabric protector, videotape and many other electro-mechanical products. Between the 1960s and 1980s 3M continued to expand through other innovations, such as Post-it Notes in the 1980s and liquid-display films in the 1990s. Since the early 1990s the company's annual revenue has reached the $14 billion mark, 30 per cent of which comes from product innovations introduced in the preceding four years.

2 Innovation and significant contributions

At 3M innovation is key. 3M provides an example of how continuous innovation can contribute to the continued growth of a company. 3M operates in more than thirty technology platforms spanning virtually all disciplines of science. 3M has received numerous awards for its innovations, including the National Medal of Technology in 1995, the highest honour bestowed by the President of the United States for technological achievement. In 1997 3M's dental products unit received the Malcolm Baldridge National Quality Award in recognition of its achievements in quality and business performance.

3M conducts R&D at three levels. The first level is the division laboratories, where scientists work closely with the company's customers to come up with developments that support existing product lines and technologies. At the second level scientists in the sector laboratories try to anticipate technologies that will serve the market in the next five to ten years. At the third level, the corporate research laboratory, scientists try to predict what will be needed in the market ten to fifteen years hence. Besides in-house technical innovation, 3M has formed alliances with its customers and suppliers, including PSI Telecom, Hoechst Marion Roussel and Catholic Materials Management Alliances.

3 Challenges and opportunities

3M serves a diverse group of markets ranging from consumer products to construction/maintenance, automotive, office products, telecommunications and transportation. The company has made efforts to meet the challenges of market leadership, technological innovation, customer satisfaction and global reach. These can be daunting challenges since the company operates in such a diverse range of products and markets. In the past 3M's approach has been to offer integrated solutions by providing technologies, products and services to its customers. It is likely that 3M will continue with this approach, which has enabled it to remain in the forefront of its industry for such a long

time. Continuous innovation has been a cornerstone of 3M's success in the global marketplace. As the concern for ecological and economic efficiency continues to grow, companies such as 3M must come up with ecologically efficient products and services.

ROSALIE L. TUNG AND MOHI AHMED
SIMON FRASER UNIVERSITY

Further reading

Business America (1997) 'Four US companies are named winners of the Malcolm Baldridge Quality Award', *Business America* 118(11), November: 33–4.

Hoover, G., Campbell, A. and Spain, P.J. (eds) (1995) 'Minnesota Mining and Manufacturing', *Hoover's Handbook of American Business*, Austin: The Reference Press, Inc. (Gives a general overview of the company.)

Kanter, R.M., Kao, J. and Wiersema, F. (eds) (1997) *Innovation: Breakthrough Thinking at 3M, DuPont, GE, Pfizer, and Rubbermaid*, New York: Harper Business. (Presents perspectives on innovations at several leading companies, including 3M.)

Further resources
http://www.mmm.com

See also: GLOBAL STRATEGIC ALLIANCES; INTERNATIONAL TECHNOLOGY TRANSFER

Mitsubishi Heavy Industries Ltd (MHI)

1 **Brief history**
2 **Innovation and significant contributions**
3 **Challenges and opportunities**

Overview

Mitsubishi Heavy Industries Ltd (MHI) is one of the world's largest manufacturers of industrial equipment, facilities and services. The range of the company's business operations covers shipbuilding, steel structures, power systems, nuclear power plants, machinery for industrial and general use, aerospace systems, and air-conditioning and refrigeration systems. MHI offers over 700 industrial products for use on land and sea, and in the air and outer space. In 1997 the annual revenues of the company exceeded $25 billion, of which roughly 29 per cent was from international markets. The company employs about 67,000 people worldwide (1996). The corporate headquarters is located in Tokyo, Japan.

1 Brief history

The company's history can be traced back to 1884. The founder of Mitsubishi Group, Yataro Iwasaki, leased a government-owned shipyard in Nagasaki, Japan, and started a shipbuilding business, which was later converted into Mitsubishi Shipbuilding Co. Ltd and subsequently renamed Mitsubishi Heavy Industries Ltd (MHI) in 1934. The company became Japan's largest private firm before World War II. After the war, at the insistence of the Allied Occupation forces, the Economic Decentralization Act was enacted in Japan. The objective was to dissolve the powerful Japanese *Zaibatsu* (see *KEIRETSU*), giant corporate circles. As a result, MHI was divided into three separate entities: West Japan Heavy Industries Ltd, Central Japan Heavy Industries Ltd and East Japan Heavy Industries Ltd. In 1964, to integrate

management and technological expertise, the company was consolidated and once again re-established as Mitsubishi Heavy Industries Ltd (MHI). In 1970 the automobile unit of MHI became independent and began manufacturing and marketing automobiles as the Mitsubishi Motors Corporation.

Since the late 1980s the company has expanded its business abroad and has continued to grow rapidly. The company's business activities are now divided into four major segments: machinery and plants; aerospace systems; shipbuilding and steel structures; and others. The largest revenues are generated by the machinery and plants division ($17 billion in 1997). MHI has constructed several plants throughout the world, such as the Sea Water Desalination Plant in Saudi Arabia, the Methanol Plant in Venezuela, the Propylene Plant in Malaysia, the Polythene Plant in China and the Natural Gas Treatment Plant in Japan.

2 Innovation and significant contributions

MHI has made significant contributions to the industry through its continuous innovations. The experience and technologies accumulated by the company for more than a century have contributed to its extensive manufacturing capabilities, comprehensive engineering, procurement, fabrication, construction and overall project management services throughout the world. According to the company, MHI is now capable of providing its clients with a wide range of high-quality technology, products and services; undertaking large-scale projects; making extensive use of its own manufacturing and fabrication facilities; organizing a diversified project team drawn from its large pool of professionals; providing high-quality services in specialized fields by consulting with its numerous R&D centres;

and executing a project with solid financial backing.

Recently MHI introduced the world's fastest paper-making and printing machines and highest-temperature (1500 degree Celsius) gas turbines. MHI's R&D activities are conducted through the combined efforts of the advanced research centre and five other R&D centres. Product development is undertaken primarily by eleven research promotion offices within these R&D centres. These are divided into shipbuilding and steel structures, thermal power plants, environment-related equipment, etc. These research promotion offices also provide relevant technologies and materials, assist with development that integrates related technology fields and strive to achieve efficient management that utilizes MHI's comprehensive capabilities. Recently MHI established a Comprehensive Recycling Technologies R&D Center, including an Industrial Waste Incineration Plant, Refuse-Derived Fuel (RDF), Plant Melting and Gasification Plant, Waste-Plastic Liquefaction Plant and Resources Recycling Plant.

3 Challenges and opportunities

Since the early 1990s, to meet the challenges of remaining competitive and to increase opportunities in the changing global marketplace MHI has sought to expand its international collaboration with other firms. Some of the major international partners of MHI include Flour Daniel Inc., Westinghouse, ABB, Bombardier Aerospace Group and Caterpillar (see CATERPILLAR). To contribute to sustainable development, MHI has engaged in R&D efforts to develop environment-friendly technologies and products through its newly established R&D centres.

ROSALIE L. TUNG AND MOHI AHMED
SIMON FRASER UNIVERSITY

Further reading

Engineering Advancement Association of Japan (1994) 'Mitsubishi Heavy Industries, Ltd.', *Engineering Advancement Association of Japan Directory*. (Gives an outline of the company's business.)

Mishima, Y. (1989) *The Mitsubishi: Its Challenge and Strategy*, translated by E. Yamaguchi, London: JAI Press. (Presents the challenges and strategies of the company.)

Spain P.J. and Talbot, J.R. (eds) (1995) 'Mitsubishi Group', *Hoover's Handbook of World Business 1995–96*, Austin: The Reference Press, Inc. (Gives a general overview of the company.)

Further resources

http://www.mhi.co.jp

See also: CATERPILLAR; FOREIGN MARKET ENTRY STRATEGIES; GLOBAL STRATEGIC ALLIANCES; INTERNATIONAL TECHNOLOGY TRANSFER; *KEIRETSU*

Mitsui & Co. Ltd (Mitsui)

1 **Brief history**
2 **Innovation and significant contributions**
3 **Challenges and opportunities**

Overview

Mitsui & Co. Ltd (Mitsui) is the world's largest general trading company. The revenues of the company exceeded $132 billion in 1997. It has investments in nearly 1200 enterprises and has 900 subsidiaries throughout the world. The company employs about 41,000 people worldwide. Mitsui's business revolves around the facilitation of the international trade-related needs of its clients, the creation of new trade flows (such as the promotion of information and communication technologies (ICTs) in Japan), and investment in new enterprises and industries around the world through its extensive network of information, human, financial and other resources. Mitsui's industrial and products portfolio ranges from iron and steel to non-ferrous metals, property development and service management, machinery, electronics and information, chemicals, energy, foodstuffs, textiles, general merchandise and transportation logistics.

1 Brief history

Mitsui was established in 1876, but its history dates back to the 1680s. Since the 1880s Mitsui has established branch offices in Shanghai, Paris, New York and London. In the beginning Mitsui mainly exported rice and coal. During the 1880s Mitsui played a leading role in Japan's modernization and the country's opening up to international trade and commerce. Mitsui imported modern equipment from around the world for the Japanese cotton-spinning industry. This allowed the textile industry to flourish in Japan, so much so that by 1897 Japan had become a major exporter of cotton yarn. Since the early 1900s Mitsui has focused on the machinery and chemical industries, and contributed to the development of Japan's industrial structure and its shipbuilding industry.

After Japan's defeat in World War II, Mitsui had to dissolve itself into 200 companies on the insistence of the Allied Occupation forces. The objective of the Economic Decentralization Act after the war was to disband the powerful *Zaibatsu* (see *KEIRETSU*), giant corporate circles or industrial conglomerates which had played a major role in the Japanese war effort. In 1959 the companies were reunited again and started to grow significantly. Since the 1980s Mitsui has continued to expand its businesses further by entering the information and communication industries, and the area of satellite communications for business purposes. The company is now the world's most diversified general trading company, with operations in more than ninety countries.

2 Innovation and significant contributions

Since the beginning the company has made significant contributions to facilitating international trade and investment and technology exchange around the globe. During the period of rapid economic growth in the 1960s, by sourcing raw materials and advanced technologies from all over the world and exporting Japan's manufactured products, Mitsui contributed significantly to the development of Japan as a major economic power in the global arena. The core competencies of the company are in the provision of innovative services in transactions (acting as intermediary between buyers and sellers or exporters and importers), market information (providing its customers with the right information at the right time), credit supervision (risk-sharing in trade transactions), financing and transportation logistics (providing efficient and economical transportation of goods). Mitsui's roles as distributor of goods and services, transfer agent of technology, investor, project organizer, market and resource developer, well-informed consultant and business partner, and go-between in third-party trade have contributed to the company's success as well as the development of industries in both Japan and other countries.

With the emergence of Japanese multinational companies which carried out their own imports, exports and foreign investment, some predicted the demise of the general trading companies. Mitsui's timely and strategic expansion into new business proved to such critics that general trading companies can indeed continue to succeed in the changed world of global competition. Since the late 1980s Mitsui has placed heavy emphasis on ICTs. Mitsui combined its information- and telecommunications-related business units into a single operating group in 1994 and launched its first satellite in 1995. By implementing state-of-the-art ICTs, Mitsui has expanded its business in the emerging era of the digital economy and enhanced the efficiency of its distribution systems worldwide. Since the mid 1990s Mitsui has continued to make strategic investments in all aspects of multimedia, including terminals (interface with users), information delivery systems (media and networks) and contents (software).

3 Challenges and opportunities

The major challenges for Mitsui lie in the provision of timely information and integrated services to its customers. Through active participation in the information and telecommunications industries, Mitsui has played an important role in facilitating society's transition to the era of advanced information. Another major challenge is the maintenance of environmental quality. The company's concern with growth as well as environmental quality has led Mitsui to develop products and services that are environmentally friendly.

ROSALIE L. TUNG AND MOHI AHMED
SIMON FRASER UNIVERSITY

Further reading

Hunter, D. (1996) 'Japanese trading houses focus on investment and trade', *Chemical Week* 158(49), 18 December: 49–51. (Profiles the nine giant Japanese trading companies' business in chemicals.)

Roberts, J.G. (1973) *Mitsui: Three Centuries of Japanese Business*, New York: Weatherhill. (Presents the historical background of the Mitsui Group.)

Spain P.J. and Talbot, J.R. (eds) (1995) 'Mitsui Group', *Hoover's Handbook of World Business 1995–96*, Austin: The Reference Press, Inc. (Gives a general overview of the company.)

Taketoshi, Y. (1996) 'Sogo Shosha hoping to take the lead in multimedia', *Tokyo Business Today* 64(1), January: 20–4. (Highlights the role of Japanese giant trading companies in the multimedia business.)

Further resources
http://www.mitsui.co.jp

See also: ECONOMY OF JAPAN; EXPORTING; FOREIGN MARKET ENTRY STRATEGIES; INTERNATIONAL TECHNOLOGY TRANSFER; INTERNATIONAL TRADE AND FOREIGN DIRECT INVESTMENT; *KEIRETSU*

Motorola Inc.

Overview

Motorola is one of the world's leading companies in the area of wireless communication, semiconductors, advanced electronics systems, components and services. The company's operations are highly decentralized. It has six sectors and one group: Semiconductor Products Sector; Cellular Subscriber Sector; Cellular Networks and Space Sector; Land Mobile Products Sector; Messaging, Information and Media Sector; Automotive, Energy and Components Sector; and Motorola Computer Group. In 1996 the annual revenues of Motorola exceeded $27 billion, of which 58 per cent came from overseas. Motorola now maintains manufacturing, sales and services throughout the world and employs more than 139,000 people worldwide. The corporate headquarters of the company is located in Schaumburg, Illinois.

1 Brief history

The history of Motorola dates back to 1928, when Paul V. Galvin established the Galvin Manufacturing Corporation in Chicago. The major product of the company was the battery eliminator, a device to allow radios to operate directly from household electricity instead of batteries. In the 1930s the company commercialized car radios under the brand name Motorola, a new word suggesting sound in motion, and the product was very successful. In 1947 the company changed its name to Motorola Inc.

In the 1940s Motorola continued to expand and became a leader in military, space and commercial communication. In the 1950s the company built its first semiconductor facility and continued to grow in consumer electronics as well. In the 1960s Motorola started to expand its businesses into international markets and shifted its business focus away from consumer electronics. In the late 1980s the company became the major supplier of cellular telephones. Since the early 1990s Motorola has become the prime contractor for the satellite-based global communication system, and a major manufacturer and distributor of semiconductors, integrated circuits (including microprocessors) and digital signal processors. Since its beginning the company has come up with new product innovations and expanded its business activities.

2 Innovation and significant contribution

Motorola has made significant contributions in the area of wireless communication, semiconductors, and advanced electronics systems and services. The company states that Motorola 'enable[s] people to do the things they want to do'. Motorola's Semiconductor Products Sector designs, produces and distributes a wide range of semiconductors and integrated circuits, including microprocessors, digital signal processors, memories and sensors. The company's Cellular Subscriber Sector designs, manufactures and distributes the full range of wireless telephone products for the global market. Its Cellular Network and Space Sector designs, manufactures and distributes wireless telephone systems, and satellite communication for commercial and government customers.

Motorola's Land Mobile Products Sector designs, manufactures and distributes analog and digital two-way radio products, and systems for worldwide applications and wide-area communication. Its Messaging, Information and Media Sector designs, manufactures and distributes a variety of messaging products, including pages and paging systems, wireless data communications products, infrastructure equipment and systems. Its Automotive Energy and Components Sector designs, manufactures and distributes a broad range of electronic components, modules and integrated electronic systems, and products for automotive, industrial, transportation and communication markets. The Motorola Computer Group designs, manufactures and distributes system platform products for computers.

Motorola is widely recognized as a leader in total quality management (TQM). In 1988 the company received the Malcolm Baldridge National Quality Award for its company-wide TQM activities. Motorola collaborates with other organizations around the world. For example, it collaborates with Apple Computer to make the Power PC.

3 Challenges and opportunities

Improvements in the product innovation process, refocusing of investments in the areas of core competencies, customer satisfaction, and the design, manufacture and distribution of high-quality products at reduced costs are some of the major challenges confronting Motorola. To meet these challenges and to increase opportunities in the global marketplace, Motorola strives to engage in continuous innovation and improvement of marketing activities.

ROSALIE L. TUNG AND MOHI AHMED
SIMON FRASER UNIVERSITY

Further reading

Coy, P. and Stodhill, R. (1996) 'Is Motorola a bit too patient', *Business Week*, 5 February: 150–1. (Presents some key challenges facing Motorola.)

Engardio, P. (1993) 'Motorola in China: a great leap forward', *Business Week*, 17 May: 58–9. (Discusses Motorola's business expansion in China.)

Hoover, G., Campbell, A. and Spain P.J. (eds) 'Motorola, Inc.', *Hoover's Handbook of American Business*, Austin: The Reference Press, Inc. (Gives a general overview of the company.)

Jones, P. and Kahaner, L. (1995) *Say It & Live It*, New York: Currency Doubleday. (Presents the mission statements of fifty corporations.)

Krysten, J. (1997) 'Satellites: critical to the new global Telecommunications network', *Business America* 118(7), July: 13–15. (Discusses new global telecommunications networks via satellites.)

Further resources
http://www.mot.com

See also: GLOBAL STRATEGIC ALLIANCES

NEC Corporation

Overview

NEC is one of the world's leading manufacturers and suppliers of computers and industrial electronic systems, communication systems and equipment, and electronic devices. The company now operates in more than twenty-nine countries. It has sixty-one plants in Japan and fifty-two plants overseas. NEC employs more than 151,000 people worldwide. The revenues of the company exceeded $43.9 billion in 1996. According to the company, 'NEC strives through C&C (the integration of computers and communications) to help advance societies worldwide toward deepened mutual understanding and the fulfilment of human potential'. The corporate headquarters of NEC Corporation is located in Tokyo, Japan.

1 Brief history

The history of NEC dates back to 1899, when Nippon Electric Company Limited (renamed NEC Corporation in 1983) was formed in Japan as a joint venture with Western Electric Company of Illinois (renamed Western Electric Company Inc. and now AT&T Technologies Inc. (see AT&T CORPORATION)). The company's first overseas sales office was established in Seoul, Korea, in 1908, and its first overseas joint venture was formed in Beijing, China, with China Electric Co. in 1917. International Western Electric Company (IWE) was established in 1918 to manage the international business operations of Western Electric and NEC.

In 1925 IWE and NEC were sold to International Telephone and Telegraph Corporation (ITT) and renamed International Standard Electric Corporation (ISE). In 1932 NEC started its affiliation with the Sumitomo Group of Japan when the latter acquired a substantial share of NEC's stocks (see KEIRETSU). The Sumitomo Group eventually acquired the business from ISE. Since the early 1950s NEC has become one of the major suppliers for Nippon Telegraph and Telephone (NTT) of Japan.

In 1963 Nippon Electric New York Inc. (now NEC America Inc.), was established as the company's first overseas marketing subsidiary after World War II. In 1968 NEC established its first overseas manufacturing subsidiary, NEC de Mexico, in Mexico. In 1977 the company embarked on its slogan C&C, the vision for integrated computer and communications, at INTELCOM 77. In the 1980s NEC further expanded its global presence by establishing a manufacturing plant for digital communications equipment in Japan, a semiconductor plant in Scotland and a mass-production plant for colour television sets in the United States. In 1992 NEC launched Solution 21, a concept for providing integrated systems and services to its customers. In 1996 NEC shipped the 15 millionth unit of its PC-9800 series of personal computers.

2 Innovation and significant contributions

NEC has made significant contributions to the communications and computers industry through innovation. Since 1939 NEC has engaged in research and development efforts. The company started R&D on transistors in 1950 and on computers in 1954. Since the announcement of the company's C&C vision NEC has continued its R&D efforts in the fields of communication and computers.

Along with in-house R&D activities, NEC has engaged in collaborative R&D with other organizations. For example, NEC collaborated with NTT in 1956 to develop an electronic switching system (ESS) and supplied Japan's first commercial central office ESS. In 1986 NEC announced the world's first prototype 4Mbit DRAM, and within seven years it developed the world's first prototype 256Mbit DRAM (1993). Marketing of the latter product began in 1996. In 1991 NEC announced its Customized Network Platform (CNP), a new communications network architecture that offers network solutions. In 1994 the company produced the world's fastest supercomputer, the SX-4 series. In 1997 NEC made the world's first prototype 4Gbit DRAM, and in 1997 its semiconductor group received its first Japan Quality Award.

3 Challenges and opportunities

The communications and computers industry is changing very rapidly. To remain competitive and to create new opportunities in the industry, firms have to innovate on all fronts of their business activities. Some of the major challenges confronting NEC include ways to reduce product development time and cost, increase customer satisfaction, engage in continuous in-house and collaborative R&D efforts to develop new innovative products, and compete effectively in the rapidly changing global marketplace. NEC seeks to meet these challenges through its 'strategic architecture' – a vision or blueprint for new functionality, integration of existing and new competencies, and the establishment of interactions with customers – and through continuous learning and development by means of in-house R&D, strategic information exchange and collaboration with other organizations around the world.

ROSALIE L. TUNG AND MOHI AHMED
SIMON FRASER UNIVERSITY

Further reading

Engineering Advancement Association of Japan (1994) 'NEC Corporation', *Engineering Advancement Association of Japan Directory*. (Gives a general overview of the company.)

Gloster, P. and Leung, J. (1996) 'Innovators spearhead global drive by techno giants', *Asian Business* 32(5), May: 28–34. (Discusses NEC's re-engineering of research capabilities to compete in the rapidly changing global marketplace.)

Hamel, G. and Prahalad, C.K. (1994) *Competing for the Future*, Boston, MA: Harvard Business School Press. (Gives some guidelines on how companies can prepare to compete in the future marketplace; also introduces NEC's C&C concept.)

Kirkpatrick, D. (1996) 'Your next PC may be Japanese', *Fortune* 134(8), 28 October: 140–8. (Presents the international marketing strategies of the five largest Japanese electronics companies: NEC, Fujitsu, Hitachi, Sony and Toshiba.)

Nigel, C. and Burton, F. (eds) (1994) *Japanese Multinationals: Strategies and Management in the Global Kaisha*, London: Routledge. (Gives a general overview of Japanese multinational companies and their management challenges.)

Spain, P.J. and Talbot, J.R. (eds) (1995) 'NEC Corporation', *Hoover's Handbook of World Business 1995–96*, Austin: The Reference Press. Inc. (Gives a general overview of the company.)

Further resources

http://www.nec-global.com

See also: AT&T CORPORATION; FOREIGN MARKET ENTRY STRATEGIES; GLOBAL STRATEGIC ALLIANCES; *KEIRETSU*

Nippon Steel Corporation

Overview

Nippon Steel is one of the world's largest steel producers. With the decline in demand for steel in the late 1980s, the company started to diversify its businesses. Now Nippon Steel and its subsidiaries operate in seven major industry segments: steel producing and fabrication; engineering and construction; chemicals, non-ferrous metals and ceramics; electronics and information/communications and semiconductors; real estate; transportation; and services and others. The revenues of the company exceeded $27 billion in 1996. The company employs about 88,000 people worldwide and its corporate headquarters is located in Tokyo, Japan.

1 Brief history

The Nippon Steel Corporation was established in 1970, but the history of the company dates back to 1886. According to the company, steel production was started at Kamaishi, Japan, in 1886. In 1901 the Japanese government-owned Yawata Steel Works was established in Kyushu prefecture in Japan. In 1934 Japan Iron & Steel Co. Ltd was established by merging Yawata Steel Works and many other steel manufacturers. After the merger the company continued to grow. Under the Economic Decentralization Act after the war, the company was ordered to dissolve into two separate entities, the Yawata Iron & Steel Co. Ltd and Fuji Iron & Steel Co. Ltd.

In 1955 Yawata Steel established Hikari Works, and in 1967 Fuji Steel established Nagoya Works. In 1970 Yawata Steel and Fuji Steel once again merged, to form the present-day Nippon Steel Corporation. In 1971 the company established its Oita Works. In the 1980s Nippon Steel began to diversify its businesses, and in 1987 the company started its full-scale multiple-business operations. In 1988 Nippon Steel established Space World Inc. to undertake the management and construction of a theme park called Space World in Kyushu, Japan. In the late 1980s the company started to expand its presence in the Asia-Pacific region (including Malaysia, Thailand, Indonesia, Hong Kong and China). In 1993 Nippon Steel established its Semiconductor Division as part of its efforts to diversify its businesses further.

2 Innovation and significant contributions

Through continuous innovation, cost advantage and large-volume production capabilities, the company has continued to grow and beat its competition in the global marketplace. Since the late 1980s, however, due to sluggish sales in steel and sharp fluctuations in international exchange rates, the company has started to restructure its organizations and diversify its businesses. In 1996 Nippon Steel implemented a new strategy designed to respond to market trends under an integrated system which includes products, manufacturing and R&D. Along with overall business system integration, the company has also achieved cost reduction, primarily for the steel market in Japan.

Nippon Steel has established a Research and Engineering (R&E) Center in 1991 to come up with innovations. According to the company, the main priority is research themes that focus on significant contributions to its users' and social needs, and which enhance the quality and cost competitiveness of the company's products and services. Nippon Steel also encourages 'research on timely issues that accurately grasp the needs of steelmaking, engineering and the various new business divisions, and creation of innovative seeds that yield competitive capabilities able to overwhelm the competition'. The company has set an example of how to manage businesses in a changing business environment.

3 Challenges and opportunities

A major challenge for Nippon Steel is to compete with South Korea's Pohang Iron & Steel Co. (POSCO), which is already selling steel to Japanese car makers (e.g. Mitsubishi Motors and Honda) and which is poised to take leadership in the steel industry through cost competitiveness. To meet this challenge and to increase opportunities in the changing global marketplace, Nippon Steel has increased its R&D activities and entered into partnership with external organizations. For basic technology, Nippon Steel is promoting collaboration with universities.

To increase opportunities in the high-growth markets of information and communications, Nippon Steel has collaborated with international organizations such as Oracle Corporation, Electronic Data Systems Corporation, Nihon Sun Microsystems and Summit Systems Inc. Nippon Steel has implemented a medium-term business plan for fiscal years 1997–99. According to the company, the plan is aimed at strengthening the health of each business division and further reorganization of the company through consolidated management of all member companies of the Nippon Steel Group.

ROSALIE L. TUNG AND MOHI AHMED
SIMON FRASER UNIVERSITY

Further reading

Berry, B. (1996) 'World steel: competing strategies in metallics, melting, and casting', *Iron Age New Steel* 12(4), April: 74–8. (Highlights R&D, market strategy and strategic planning in the large steel manufacturers, including Nippon Steel.)

Economist (1996) 'Why Japan is losing its metal', *Economist* 340(7975), 20 July: 56–8. (Discusses Pohang Iron & Steel's challenges to Nippon Steel.)

Engineering Advancement Association of Japan (1994) 'Nippon Steel Corporation', *Engineering Advancement Association of Japan Directory*. (Provides an outline of the company.)

Forbes (1997) 'Nippon Steel', *Forbes* 159(1), 13 January: 30. (Describes the R&D activities at Nippon Steel.)

Spain, P.J. and Talbot, J.R. (eds) (1995) 'Nippon Steel Corporation', *Hoover's Handbook of World Business 1995–96*, Austin: The Reference Press, Inc. (Gives a general overview of the company.)

Wall Street & Technology (1996) 'Summit teams with Nippon Steel', *Wall Street & Technology* 14(8), August: 16. (Discusses Nippon Steel's collaboration with Summit Systems Inc.)

Further resources

http://www.nsc.co.jp

See also: ECONOMY OF JAPAN; GLOBAL STRATEGIC ALLIANCES; GLOBAL STRATEGIC PLANNING; INTERNATIONAL TRADE AND FOREIGN DIRECT INVESTMENT

Nortel (Northern Telecom)

1 **Brief history**
2 **Innovation and significant contributions**
3 **Challenges and opportunities**

Overview

Nortel (Northern Telecom) is a leading provider of digital network technology and solutions around the world, with 1996 revenues of $12.85 billion (of which 63 per cent was from the US and Canada, and 37 per cent from other countries). The firm employs approximately 68,000 people worldwide. Bell Canada Enterprises Inc. (BCE Inc.), Canada's largest telecommunications company, owns 51.25 per cent of Northern Telecom. The corporate headquarters of Nortel is located in Brampton, Ontario, Canada. Nortel's corporate mission is to deliver market leadership through customer satisfaction, superior value and product excellence.

1 Brief history

Since the late nineteenth century Nortel has evolved from a small Canadian telephone equipment supplier to a major provider of solutions for a global network. After the invention of the telephone in 1874 by Alexander Graham Bell, the Bell Telephone Company of Canada was founded. The manufacturing branch of the Bell Telephone Company of Canada was incorporated as a separate company and named the Northern Electric and Manufacturing Company Limited in 1895. In 1899 the Bell Telephone Company of Canada purchased a Montreal wire and cable factory known as the Imperial Wire & Cable Company Limited. In 1914 the two companies merged to form the Northern Electric Company Limited – 44 per cent of it was owned by Western Electric, a manufacturing subsidiary of AT&T Company (see AT&T CORPORATION) in the United States, and the remainder was owned by Bell of Canada. In 1976 Northern Electric changed its name to Northern Telecom Limited.

By the 1980s it had become the world's leading supplier of digital telecommunications equipment. In 1983 Northern Telecom entered the Chinese and Japanese markets, and it formed Northern Telecom Pacific in 1985. In 1987 Northern Telecom shipped its first DMS-10 digital switching systems to Nippon Telegraph and Telephone (NTT) in Japan and created NT Meridian SA in France. In 1994 it opened new plants in Mexico and China. In 1995 Northern Telecom celebrated its 100th anniversary and adopted a new corporate identity, Nortel. The legal name remained Northern Telecom, however.

2 Innovation and significant contributions

In 1957 Nortel began independent R&D activities. In 1959 R&D laboratories were established in Ottawa, Ontario. In 1971 Northern Electric and Bell Canada merged their R&D activities to form BNR (Bell-Northern Research). BNR developed an electronic switching system called the E-thing. The success of this innovative digital switch system resulted in very rapid growth of the firm in the 1980s, including international expansion to the Caribbean, Europe and the Pacific Rim.

Since 1993 the firm has contributed to the development of digital networks around the globe by responding to the needs of emerging global multimedia markets. Nortel has a staff of 17,000 R&D professionals, support staff and partners in seventeen R&D sites in North America, fourteen in Europe and the Middle East, and eight in the Asia-Pacific region. Nortel's ability to design, build and integrate a wireless enterprise, public carrier and broadband networks for information, education, entertainment and commerce has contributed to the creation of a world of networks and state-of-the-art telecommunications around the globe.

Nortel has earned international recognition for its innovation and market leadership in the telecommunications industry. It has invested heavily in R&D and has received numerous awards, including the Industry Information Technology Award from the US federal government, an environmental award from the UK, an award as Canada's leading R&D spender ($2.6 billion in 1996) and the Business Excellence Award from the Canada–Israel Chamber of Commerce. In addition, *Industry Week* selected Nortel as one of the 100 best-managed companies in 1997.

3 Challenges and opportunities

The emergence of digital networks has created new challenges and opportunities. Nortel's major businesses are in broadband networks (40 per cent of 1995 revenues), enterprise networks (30 per cent), public carrier networks (15 per cent), wireless networks (10 per cent) and others (5 per cent). The projected market size for global telecommunications equipment is $270 billion by 1999. To capture a larger share of the market and to continue leadership in the industry, Nortel is making continuous efforts to innovate and integrate its R&D efforts with its marketing and manufacturing activities around the world.

ROSALIE L.TUNG AND MOHI AHMED
SIMON FRASER UNIVERSITY

Further reading

Hoover, G., Campbell, A. and Spain, P.J. (eds) (1995) 'Northern Telecom Limited', *Hoover's Handbook of American Business*, Austin: The Reference Press, Inc. (Gives a general overview of the company.)

Newman, P.C. (1995) *Northern Telecom, Past, Present, Future*, Northern Telecom Limited. (Gives the historical background and tells the inside story of Northern Telecom.)

Nortel (Northern Telecom) (1997) *Northern Telecom: The Anatomy of a Transformation (1985–1995)*, Northern Telecom. (Outlines how Nortel transformed itself in the global telecommunication industry.)

Further resources

http://www.nortel.com

See also: AT&T CORPORATION; FOREIGN MARKET ENTRY STRATEGIES; INTERNATIONAL TECHNOLOGY TRANSFER

Novartis AG

1 **Brief history**
2 **Innovation and significant contributions**
3 **Challenges and opportunities**

Overview

Novartis was established in 1996 as a result of the merger of two giant enterprises, Ciba and Sandoz. Novartis is the world's leading company in the field of life sciences and the largest company in the pharmaceutical industry. In 1996 the company's revenues exceeded $29 billion. According to Novartis, the company's name came from the Latin term *novae artes*, which means 'new arts' or 'new skills', and the company's motto is 'New Skills in the Science of Life'. The core business units of Novartis are healthcare (pharmaceuticals, generics, consumer health, CIBA vision), agribusiness (crop protection, animal health and seeds) and nutrition (infant and baby nutrition, medical nutrition and health nutrition). The healthcare unit operates 126 affiliates in sixty-three countries; the agribusiness unit operates 116 affiliates in fifty countries; and the nutrition unit operates thirty-three affiliates in twenty-nine countries. Novartis employs about 116,000 people worldwide and its headquarters is located in Basel, Switzerland.

1 Brief history

Novartis was established in 1996 following the merger of Ciba and Sandoz. The history of both companies dates back to more than two centuries ago. In 1758 Johann Rudolf Geigy-Gemuseus began trading in all kinds of materials (chemical, dyes and drugs) in Basel. Before the merger in 1996, Sandoz, Ciba and Geigy had set up the Interessengemeinschaft Basel (Basler IG), an agreement which was disbanded in 1950. In 1970 Ciba-Geigy was formed as a result of the merger of Ciba and

Geigy. In 1992 it was renamed Ciba. In 1886 a chemical company called Kern & Sandoz was established in Basel. It entered into pharmaceutical research in 1917. Later it expanded its business around the world. Sandoz established its first overseas subsidiary in England in 1919 and entered Latin America between 1941 and 1957. In 1960 Sandoz established its first subsidiary in Japan, and in 1964 the company established its first research centre outside Switzerland, in East Hanover, New Jersey. Ciba established a special biotechnology unit in 1980 and Ciba vision in 1987. After continuous transformations and growth, Ciba and Sandoz merged to create Novartis. The motives behind the merger were to remain competitive in the rapidly changing marketplace and to reduce the cost of operating in Switzerland.

2 Innovation and significant contributions

The mission of Novartis is to utilize 'scientific research, imagination, and new technologies to provide ever greater benefits for humankind'. The company seeks to innovate to serve its customers' needs in healthcare, agriculture and nutrition. Even prior to the merger, both Ciba and Sandoz were leading companies in the industry. Ciba's major products were pharmaceutical products, formulated pesticides, dyestuffs and pigments, synthetic resins and plastics, photographic equipment, materials and chemicals, and spectacles and lenses. The major products of Sandoz were miscellaneous chemical products for industrial use, pharmaceutical products, infant and dietetic foods, and textile raw materials.

Both Ciba and Sandoz have introduced several major breakthroughs in the life sciences. Calcium-Sandoz, for example, the foundation of modern-day calcium therapy, was developed by Sandoz. A Geigy researcher received a Nobel prize in 1948 for his discovery of DDT for use as an insecticide. In 1963 Sandoz began large-scale production of antibiotics and other substances developed on the basis of biotechnology. In 1977 the company began the production of anti-allergy drugs. In 1980 Ciba established a special biotechnology unit, and it continued to make efforts in R&D. Since the merger in 1996, the company has continued to innovate in its various business units: healthcare, agribusiness and nutrition.

The company has established the Novartis Foundation for Sustainable Development, which focuses on strengthening the development capacities of the developing countries; supporting the self-help efforts of the most deprived people in developing countries; developing and implementing innovative strategies for improving the effectiveness of programmes and projects; and researching and teaching in development policy issues. As the world's leading life sciences company, Novartis is now trying to introduce new products within a shorter period of time.

3 Challenges and opportunities

Novartis currently has about ninety projects under development and expects to introduce about seventeen new products by the turn of the century. This will create new opportunities for the company. According to the company, the goal of Novartis is not only to 'expand the horizons of science, but also [to] expand the horizons of life through science'. To avoid duplication of R&D efforts, the company realizes that it is important for its research activities to be comprehensively documented. To meet these objectives, Novartis has established a globally active group responsible for document management using state-of-the-art information and communication technologies.

ROSALIE L. TUNG AND MOHI AHMED
SIMON FRASER UNIVERSITY

Further reading

Financial Post Daily (1996) 'Sandoz–Ciba merger hailed as world's biggest', Financial Post Daily 9(21), 8 March: 5. (Discusses the merger of Ciba-Geigy AG and Sandoz AG.)

Henkel, N. (1997) 'Novartis creates global access to documents', Document World 2(6), November–December: 51. (Documents Novartis's efforts to avoid duplication in R&D efforts.)

Further resources

http://www.novartis.com

See also: FOREIGN MARKET ENTRY STRATEGIES

The Proctor & Gamble Company (P&G)

Overview

Proctor & Gamble (P&G) is one of the world's largest manufacturers of consumer products. In 1996 the total revenues of P&G exceeded $35 billion. Its major products are in personal care (soap and cosmetics), laundry and cleaning, and food and beverages. P&G was the first company in the world to hire full-time professionals to study consumer needs to facilitate new product development. P&G was established in 1837 as a result of a merger between a candle-maker (William Proctor) and a soap manufacturer (James Gamble). With its headquarters in Cincinnati, Ohio, the company employs 103,000 people and has operations in seventy countries. P&G products are sold in over 140 countries around the world.

1 Brief history

From 12 April 1837 William Proctor and James Gamble produced and sold soap and candles. Twenty-two years later P&G sales reached $1 million and the company employed eighty people. In 1886 P&G started production at the Ivorydale factory, a facility recognized for its progressive approach towards creating a pleasant work environment for its employees.

In 1887 P&G established a profit-sharing programme for its employees. This policy has contributed, in part, to the success of the company. In 1915 P&G built its first manufacturing plant in Canada, the first of many manufacturing facilities to be established outside the United States. P&G established a market research department to analyse consumer preferences and buying habits, the first of its kind in the world.

In 1930 P&G established its first overseas subsidiary, in England, and it built a manufacturing company in the Philippines in 1935. In 1937 P&G celebrated its 100th birthday with revenues of $230 million. In the late 1940s P&G set up an overseas division to manage its growing international business activities. In 1973 P&G began operations in Japan. In the early 1990s P&G introduced its new corporate logo and expanded to Eastern Europe (Hungary, Poland and Russia).

In 1993, for the first time in the company's history, more than 50 per cent of the company's revenue was derived from outside the United States. Since 1995 P&G has managed its business under two broad divisions: the US and international. All regional reports are directed to a single chief operating officer, however. This strategic coordination at the very top has contributed to the company's global competitiveness.

2 Innovation and significant contribution

P&G is well regarded in the industry for its innovations and efforts to analyse consumer needs. P&G has done a good job in meeting the needs of consumers around the world, including adaptation to the needs of individual markets (see MARKETING MANAGEMENT, INTERNATIONAL). Every year the company spends about $1.5 billion on R&D and files about 20,000 patent applications. According to P&G, 'innovation is a global network of insight and discovery' and 'innovation is the ability to combine fresh consumer insights with deep technology understanding'. Over the years P&G has made many innovations, including the creation of a pleasant work environment and a profit-sharing programme, the establishment of one of the earliest product research laboratories in the manufacturing industry, the establishment of a market research department for studying consumer preferences and buying habits, the discovery of detergent technology, and development of the first detergent shampoo and the first fluoride toothpaste.

In 1990 P&G won the International Du-Pont Packaging Awards for being the first manufacturer to package with 100 per cent recyclable plastics. P&G has also received the World Environment Center Gold Medal for International Corporate Environmental Achievement. In 1994 the US Department of Labor presented P&G with the Opportunity 2000 Award in recognition of its commitment to equal employment opportunities and creating a diverse workforce. P&G values diversity among its employees as the company makes products for diverse consumers around the world. In 1995 P&G received the National Medal of Technology, the highest award in the United States for achievement in technological innovation.

3 Challenges and opportunities

A major challenge for P&G is to maintain its market share in a fast-changing environment by delivering the highest-quality products at the most affordable price to its consumers worldwide. Localized operations and continuous study of consumer needs around the world have helped the company to sustain its global competitiveness. In 1993 the company started an initiative to improve organizational effectiveness and cost competitiveness in the global marketplace. This initiative has contributed to the company's continuing success.

ROSALIE L. TUNG AND MOHI AHMED
SIMON FRASER UNIVERSITY

Further reading

Galuszka P. (1997) 'Where P&G's brawn doesn't help much', *Business Week*, 10 November: 112–14. (Presents the challenges facing P&G's pharmaceuticals business.)

Hoover, G., Campbell, A. and Spain, P.J. (eds) (1995) 'The Proctor & Gamble Company', *Hoover's Handbook of American Business*, Austin: The Reference Press, Inc. (Gives a general overview of the company.)

Kishi M. and Russell D. (1996) 'Becoming a household name: Proctor & Gamble', *Successful Gaijin in Japan: How Foreign Companies are Making it in Japan*, Lincolnwood: NTC Business Books. (Details the success story of P&G in Japan.)

O'Reilly, B. (1997) 'The secrets of America's most admired corporations: new ideas, new products', *Fortune* 135(4), 4 March: 60–4. (Discusses P&G's innovative capabilities.)

Schisgall, O. (1981) *Eyes on Tomorrow: The Evolution of Proctor & Gamble*, Chicago, IL: J.G. Ferguson Publishing. (Provides the historical background of the company and its many innovations.)

Further resources
http://www.pg.com

See also: FOREIGN MARKET ENTRY STRATEGIES; INTERNATIONAL MARKETING; MARKETING MANAGEMENT, INTERNATIONAL; MULTI-NATIONAL CORPORATIONS, ORGANIZATION STRUCTURE IN

Royal Dutch/Shell Group

1 Brief history
2 Innovation and significant
   contributions
3 Challenges and opportunities

Overview

The Royal Dutch/Shell Transport and Trading Group, commonly known as Shell, is one of the world's largest and most profitable companies. The group employs more than 100,000 people in over 120 countries and its revenues exceeded $128 billion in 1996. Two parent companies, Royal Dutch Petroleum and Shell Transport and Trading, own the group in the proportion of 60 per cent and 40 per cent, respectively.

1 Brief history

In 1833 Marcus Samuel started a small shop in London's East End selling seashells. The company soon developed into an export–import business. Marcus Samuel, Jr, the founder's son, expanded into the oil-export business because he saw the huge opportunities there. At that time Standard Oil in America had a monopoly in the oil business, so Marcus Samuel, Jr, had to compete on the basis of lower price. During the 1890s a Dutch company (NV Koninklijke Nederlandsche Maatschapppijtot Exoplotatie van Petroleum-bronnen in Nederlandsch-indi) was engaged in the oilfield development business and built its own tanker fleet to compete with Marcus Samuel's company. However, both companies soon realized that they could do better by working together; consequently, they merged to form the Asiatic Petroleum Company in 1903. The partnership worked very well and four years later, in 1907, extended its operations worldwide with the creation of the Royal Dutch/Shell Group of companies. The two parent companies retained their separate businesses, however.

The group continued to grow into a giant multinational company, with its major businesses in the exploration and production of oil products, chemicals, gas and coal. The group is now extending into a fifth core business, renewables, which brings together the group's activities in solar energy, biomass and forestry. The most important and risky part of the group's business is in the exploration and extraction of raw materials, which are then converted into oil products, gas and coal. Some of the specialized outputs from the crude-oil refineries are subsequently converted into plastic and industrial materials. In the 1990s the firm has sought to expand its share in the fast-growing renewables market.

2 Innovation and significant contributions

The group perceives the continuous development of technology (primarily communication technology), globalization and trade liberalization as important forces that will shape the demand patterns and expectations of stakeholders around the world (see INTERNATIONAL TRADE AND FOREIGN DIRECT INVESTMENT). To meet these challenges Shell uses 'scenario building' as an important management tool. Since the early 1970s Shell has used scenario building to help the company prepare for sudden changes, and to create a common culture and language throughout its disparate operations around the world. In the late 1990s Shell adopted the following two scenarios: 'Just do it' and 'Da Wo' Big me. In the first scenario it seeks to take advantage of the latest innovations in technology to implement new ways of doing business and solve problems; and in the second it seeks to develop relationships through the building of trust and mutual obligations. Besides sustaining its profitability, the group seeks to improve the working conditions of its employees by paying greater attention to employee safety and the comfort of its workers. In addition, the group seeks better to address the issue of global environmental protection.

Shell undertakes R&D to develop and implement new technology that can contribute to increased profits, improved safety and productivity, protect the environment through lower emissions or better use of resources, reduce capital expenditure and develop new materials (for example synthetic materials) that have new applications. The group has twelve main research and technology development centres, which are located in the Netherlands, the UK, the US, France, Belgium, Germany, Japan and Singapore.

The Royal Dutch/Shell Group is truly an international company and a remarkable example of a long-term corporate partnership between two companies from two countries. The group has also established other examples of inter-firm collaboration around the world (e.g. collaboration with GTE and collaboration with professional firms: legal, tax, human resources, planning, finances and investment services). Shell's timely and scenario-based strategic decisions have made it one of the world's most profitable companies.

3 Challenges and opportunities

The group focuses its corporate vision on 'wealth creation', 'customer satisfaction' and 'responsiveness to changing needs and expectations in the outside world'. The group is fairly decentralized and most of its companies operate locally in different countries. To coordinate its global operations, however, strategic decision and business support functions are performed by some 300 people in the UK, the Netherlands and Belgium. The ultimate decision-makers in the group are the directors of the two parent companies. Development of human resources is one of the group's top priorities. The company needs people who have the ability to get things done and who are interested in cross-cultural team-building. Shell has several extensive training programmes to develop these skills (see COMMUNCIATION, CROSS-CULTURAL).

Like other companies, Shell faces new challenges arising from the changes in technology, globalization and trade liberalization. To meet these new challenges and to expand its business activities Shell needs the right people and the right technology at the right time. To sustain its competitiveness in the rapidly changing global marketplace the group must pay adequate attention to the issue of environmental protection.

ROSALIE L. TUNG AND MOHI AHMED
SIMON FRASER UNIVERSITY

Further reading

Gerreston, F.C. (1957) *History of the Royal Dutch*, vols 1–4, translated from the Dutch *Geschiedenis der Koninklinjke*, The Hague: Leiden. (Gives the detailed historical background of the Royal Dutch.)

Guyon, J. (1997) 'The world's most profitable company', *Fortune*, 4 August: 120–5. (Identifies major challenges and the diversification of the group.)

Schwartz, P. (1996) *The Art of the Long View*, New York: Doubleday. (Examines scenario planning in the Royal Dutch/Shell group.)

Spain, P.J. and Talbot, J.R. (eds) (1995) 'Royal Dutch/Shell Group', *Hoover's Handbook of World Business 1995–96*, Austin: The Reference Press, Inc. (Gives a general overview of the company.)

Further resources
http://www.shell.com

See also: COMMUNICATION, CROSS-CULTURAL; GLOBAL STRATEGIC ALLIANCES; INTERNATIONAL TRADE AND FOREIGN DIRECT INVESTMENT

Shimizu Corporation

Overview

Shimizu Corporation (Shimizu) is one of the world's largest and technologically most innovative architectural/engineering/construction (A/E/C) firms. The firm's major activities cover project planning, design, construction, operation, maintenance and R&D. Shimizu operates in more than forty-six countries and employs about 16,000 people. The annual sales of the firm have been declining since the mid-1990s, however, due to the downturn in the Japanese economy and severe competition in the industry – the revenues of Shimizu were about $14 billion in 1996.

1 Brief history

In 1804 the firm was founded by Kisuke Shimizu in Kanda-cho, Edo (present-day Tokyo). In 1915 the company was transformed from a private to a publicly traded corporation and was renamed Shimizu Gumi. In 1948 the firm changed its name again to Shimizu Construction Co. Ltd. In 1950 the firm started its first international business operation in Pakistan. In the subsequent twenty years Shimizu expanded to almost all parts of the globe. In 1987 the firm was again renamed the Shimizu Corporation. In the late 1980s the firm expanded its business activities from international property development to international financial sectors around the world.

2 Innovation and significant contributions

Shimizu is renowned worldwide for its R&D activities, which range from underground to super-high-rise buildings and space stations in outer space. Since 1944 the firm has engaged in extensive R&D activities. These efforts increased dramatically with the establishment of the Institute of Technology, the first R&D centre in the A/E/C industry in the world. Shimizu has made substantial contributions to the international A/E/C industry by developing and implementing the world's first computer-integrated automated construction system for high-rise buildings (the SMART system). This system allowed the company to transform the whole image of the construction sector. Shimizu has received the Nova award in the United States, the Japan Science and Technology Federation Ishikawa Award and the Nikkei BP Awards in Japan for the SMART system. Through the SMART system, which also implements state-of-the-art robotics systems, Shimizu has been able to reduce construction time and waste materials by more than 30 per cent over the industry's standard.

Shimizu has built the world's largest underground LNG (liquefied natural gas) tanks and was recently awarded one of the world's largest building projects in Shanghai, China. It is also engaged in R&D projects on environmental protection. In collaboration with several leading organizations, such as NASA and Bell, Shimizu is involved in designing and developing future space station projects for use in outer space. It has expanded its technological capabilities by participating in the IMS (Intelligent Manufacturing Systems) consortium. Shimizu also collaborates with several domestic and international R&D institutions, such as the Massachusetts Institute of Technology (MIT), Harvard, Stanford, the University of California-Berkeley, the University of Texas at Austin, the National Research Council, the National Science Foundation, Karlsruhe University (Germany) and Reading University (UK).

Shimizu has been held up as a model of an innovative and future-oriented A/E/C firm.

The major strengths of the company lie in technological innovation in very diversified fields and its rapid commercialization of innovations. In general, very few A/E/C firms around the world engage in in-house R&D efforts in such diversified areas such as those undertaken by Shimizu. The firm has also entered into many strategic alliances with partners around the world. This has enabled it to expand rapidly in the international arena.

3 Challenges and opportunities

The company, which once concentrated its operations in the domestic market, has now expanded its international business activities to more than forty-six countries. To compete effectively in the changing global marketplace, the firm is now reorganizing its overall corporate structure by integrating its business and innovative capabilities. In the A/E/C industry, since R&D tends to support business activities indirectly the return on investment in R&D is not always clear. To remain competitive in the industry Shimizu is now making efforts to increase its innovative capabilities by means of several internal reorganizations. Shimizu is also making R&D efforts in information and communication technologies (ICTs) to take advantage of the emerging digital network-based business and to design and build state-of-the-art facilities that will facilitate electronic commerce activities in the twenty-first century.

ROSALIE L. TUNG AND MOHI AHMED
SIMON FRASER UNIVERSITY

Further reading

CERF Report (1996) *Creating the 21st Century Through Innovation, #96–5016.E*, Washington, DC: Civil Engineering Research Foundation. (Examines the research agenda for sustainable development in relation to the A/E/C industry; also presents the perspectives of Shimizu's R&D executives on international collaboration for sustainable development.)

Miyanohara, Kuiaki (1989) *Strategy for Construction Industry in the 21st Century*, Japan Management Association. (Provides an overview of the construction industry and Shimizu Corporation.)

Tulacz, G., Reina, P. and Normile, D. (1995) 'Going global, construction – untangling global confusion', *ENR*, 28 August: 29–42. (Examines the globalization of the construction industry and Shimizu's role in the global market.)

Further resources
http://www.shimz.co.jp/English

See also: ECONOMY OF JAPAN; FOREIGN MARKET ENTRY STRATEGIES; GLOBAL STRATEGIC ALLIANCES; INTERNATIONAL TECHNOLOGY TRANSFER

Siemens AG

1 Brief history
2 Innovation and significant
contributions
3 Challenges and opportunities

Overview

Siemens is one of the world's largest electrical engineering and electronics companies, with 1996 revenues totalling $63 billion. Siemens's businesses are in eight sectors: communication, transportation, information technology, lighting, health, energy, industry and trade, and electronic components. In 1966 Siemens & Halske AG, Siemens-Schuckertwerke AG and Siemens-Reiniger-Werke AG were consolidated to form Siemens AG. The company now operates in 193 countries and employs 379,000 people worldwide.

1 Brief history

In 1847 Telegraphen-Bauanstalt Siemens & Halske (Siemens & Halske Telegraph Construction Enterprise) was established by Werner Siemens, Johann Siemens and Georg Halske. In 1848 Siemens & Halske began construction of the first long-distance telegraph line in Europe, stretching from Berlin to Frankfurt. This was completed in 1849. In 1853 the company began construction of the Russian state telegraph network and continued to expand its business throughout Europe. In 1918 it developed the long-distance radio transmitter. In 1934 the company built the first Moscow Metro (subway line) in the then Soviet Union and expanded into the heavy electrical engineering business throughout Europe.

In 1951 it developed semiconductor compounds; this marked the beginning of semiconductor engineering. In 1977 Siemens and Corning Glass established Siecor Optical Cable Inc. to manufacture and distribute fibre-optic cables. Corning Glass supplied optical fibres in the US, while Siemens provided the expertise necessary to install the fibres in the cables (see CORNING INCORPORATED).

At the end of 1983 the company decided to continue with the production of memory chips and introduced a private communication system called Hicom. In 1984 the system met the world standard for ISDN (Integrated Services Digital Network) and the telecommunications network of the future. In addition to voice, the system can also transmit text, images and data over existing two-wire telephone lines. In 1985 this innovative communications technology was installed in Munich. During the period 1987–96 Siemens continued to make efforts to restructure and change its corporate culture, with the goal of achieving a stronger global presence and market share.

2 Innovation and significant contributions

To sustain growth over 150 years Siemens has invested heavily in R&D. As a result it has come up with many significant innovations in the fields of electronics and electrical engineering. According to the company, most of the world's state-of-the-art technologies in the area of electronics and electrical engineering have links of one form or another with Siemens. The company's technology was used to connect the first direct transatlantic cable from Ireland to the US (1874), in the first electric train (1879), the first electrified elevator (1880), the first electric street lighting (1888), the first-patented X-ray tube (1896), the first recording telegraph for transmission of images (1933), the first electron microscope (1939), the first real-time ultrasound diagnostic system (1965) and the first 256-megabit memory chip (1995). The 256-megabit memory chip was developed in collaboration with IBM (see INTERNATIONAL BUSINESS MACHINES CORPORATION) and Toshiba.

3 Challenges and opportunities

In 1997 Siemens announced its mission to become one of the most competitive firms in the world in the field of electrical and electronics engineering. It seeks to accomplish this by increasing productivity, new product innovations and changing its corporate culture to become more adaptable to the changing business environment. The latter includes the recruitment and development of a cadre of internationally oriented management personnel and mobile employees, and the implementation of new promotion and compensation programmes (see ORGANIZATION CULTURE). Major challenges include the need to increase the speed of its innovation and to respond more rapidly to the needs of the market. To meet these new challenges and take advantage of opportunities in the future, Siemens is now testing a programme called TOP (Time Optimized Process or Turn On Power), which is designed to optimize business processes to increase productivity, promote innovation and foster growth through cultural change. To maintain and increase its future competitiveness, Siemens must sustain innovation which accommodates ecological concerns.

ROSALIE L. TUNG AND MOHI AHMED
SIMON FRASER UNIVERSITY

Further reading

Feldenkirchen, W. (1992) *Werner von Siemens: Inventor and International Entrepreneur*, Columbus, Ohio: Ohio State University Press. (Gives a historical overview of the company.)

Spain, P.J. and Talbot, J.R. (eds) (1995) 'Siemens AG', *Hoover's Handbook of World Business 1995–96*, Austin: the Reference Press, Inc. (Gives a general overview of the company.)

Teresko, J. (1997) 'Managing innovation for 150 years', *Industry Week* 246(23), 15 December: 101–5. (Highlights how Siemens' management of innovation has contributed to the firm's success.)

Further resources
http://www.siemens.de/

See also: CORNING INCORPORATED; GLOBAL STRATEGIC ALLIANCES; INTERNATIONAL BUSINESS MACHINES CORPORATION; INTERNATIONAL TECHNOLOGY TRANSFER; ORGANIZATION CULTURE

Unilever

Overview

Unilever is one of the world's largest producers of personal care and food products. The company was formed by a merger of Dutch Margarine Union and British soap-makers Lever Brothers in 1929. The company has headquarters in both London, England, and Rotterdam, the Netherlands. Unilever now produces hundreds of items, ranging from cosmetics/perfume (Calvin Klein, Elizabeth Arden) to foods (Lipton, Country Crock), personal care products (Vaseline, Timotei) and soap/laundry products (Sunlight, Dove, Lux). The company operates all over the world and employs about 300,000 people worldwide. The revenues of Unilever exceeded $52 billion in 1996.

1 Brief history

The history of Unilever dates back to 1885. William Lever established a soap-manufacturing company in the UK with his brothers and named the company Lever Brothers in 1885. Their product, Sunlight, the world's first packaged soap, was very successful. Fifteen years after the product's launch in the UK Lever Brothers started selling the soap in Europe, Australia, South Africa and the United States. As the company needed a large quantity of vegetable oil to produce soap, it established plantations and trading companies throughout the world to source raw materials and to distribute its products.

Two butter-makers, Jurgens and Van den Berghs, formed Margarine Union in 1927. The Dutch Margarine Union merged with Lever Brothers of United Kingdom in 1929 to form Unilever. For tax purposes, two separate entities were established, one in London and another in Rotterdam (see TAXATION, INTERNATIONAL). While Unilever lost out to Proctor & Gamble in the United States, it continued to enjoy success with its products in the rest of the world. Unilever has continued to diversify its product line and acquire other companies around the world. In 1991 Unilever acquired twenty-seven businesses worldwide. These have contributed to the expansion of the company's products and services. Unilever is now a global leader in the area of deodorants, fragrances, personal care, margarine, tea-based beverages and ice-cream products.

2 Innovation and significant contributions

Unilever's success lies in its ability to understand local consumers and in the process come up with new product innovations and ways of marketing to meet their needs (see MARKETING MANAGEMENT, INTERNATIONAL). The company has innovation centres in strategic locations around the world. These centres have created new opportunities for the company. For example, Unilever has innovation centres for hair care-related products in Japan, France, Argentina and India; and innovation centres for ice cream in France, Germany, India, the UK and the United States. Unilever considers sustainable development to be critical to the company's continued success. The company is engaged in continuous R&D to produce new products.

Unilever has made contributions to the industry by introducing high-quality products and through its management concepts (e.g. regional focus; giving priority to developing and emerging markets; focusing on competitive cost and innovative products to improve profitability). Many global companies are now learning from the experiences of Unilever in doing business in the changing marketplace. The company states: 'Unilever provides basic products which are the first purchases when economies start to develop; it provides low-unit-cost priced convenience products which are the most in demand when incomes begin to rise; and its provides more sophisticated products which satisfy growing aspirations. Providing the right product at the right time is the key to successful introductions.' A case in point is Unilever's operations in Mexico. Several years ago its deodorants business there was insignificant; now it leads the market.

3 Challenges and opportunities

According to Unilever, the company's long-term success 'requires a total commitment to exceptional standards of performance and productivity, to working together effectively and to a willingness to embrace new ideas and learn continuously'. The company's continuous efforts to do business with the right products at the right time in the right places will create more opportunities and bring continued success to the company.

ROSALIE L. TUNG AND MOHI AHMED
SIMON FRASER UNIVERSITY

Further reading

Dwyer P. (1994) 'Unilever's struggle for growth: under fierce pressure in Europe and the U.S., it's grabbing a bigger share in emerging markets', *Business Week*, 4 July: 54–6. (Discusses how Unilever is gaining an advantage in emerging markets.)

Reader, W.J. (1980) *Fifty Years of Unilever, 1930–80*, London: Heinemann. (Gives the history of the company during the period 1930–80.)

Spain, P.J. and Talbot, J.R. (eds) (1995) 'Unilever', *Hoover's Handbook of World Business 1995–96*, Austin: The Reference Press, Inc. (Gives a general overview of the company.)

Wilson, J.F. (1995) *British Business History, 1720–1994*, Manchester: Manchester University Press. (Gives a detailed historical background of businesses in Britain.)

Further resources

http://www.unilever.com

See also: GLOBAL STRATEGIC ALLIANCES; FOREIGN MARKET ENTRY STRATEGIES; INTERNATIONAL MARKETING; INTERNATIONAL TRADE AND FOREIGN DIRECT INVESTMENT; MARKETING MANAGEMENT, INTERNATIONAL; TAXATION, INTERNATIONAL

Wal-Mart Stores Inc.

Overview

Wal-Mart Stores Inc. is one of the world's largest general merchandisers. The Wal-Mart stores consist of roughly forty departments ranging from apparel for women, men, girls, boys and infants to paper products, sporting goods, pharmaceuticals, personal care and healthcare products, food, toys, car supplies, small appliances, electronics, hardware, furniture and garden supplies. The annual revenues of the company exceeded $106 billion in 1996 and more than 675,000 people work for the firm. The corporate headquarters of the Wal-Mart Stores Inc. is located in Bentonville, Arkansas.

1 Brief history

The founder of Wal-Mart, Sam Walton, opened the first large-scale variety store, Wal-Mart Discount City, in 1962. In 1969 Sam Walton incorporated his firm as Wal-Mart Inc. and established a general headquarters and a distribution facility in Bentonville, Arkansas. By 1970 the company had established thirty-two outlets (eighteen Wal-Mart discount and fourteen variety stores) in four states, with net revenues reaching $31 million. In 1970 the firm changed its name to Wal-Mart Stores Inc. By 1980 there were 279 Wal-Mart Stores in eleven states, with net revenues exceeding $1 billion. During the 1980s Wal-Mart continued to expand. In 1983 Sam Walton opened Sam's Club, a membership warehouse club, to further expand the businesses.

In 1985 the firm inaugurated a Buy American programme and Sam Walton became one of the richest people in the United States, with a fortune of $2.8 billion. At that time the firm had 1114 stores, with $6.4 billion in annual revenues. By 1990 Wal-Mart had a total of 1531 stores in twenty-nine states, with net revenues totalling $25.8 billion. In 1992 Wal-Mart entered into a joint venture with CIFRA, Mexico's largest retailer, to develop and expand its businesses in Mexico as a part of its international expansion effort. In 1995 the firm entered into Hong Kong and Chinese markets by establishing joint-venture operations with local organizations. By 1995 the firm had more than 1990 stores, with revenues reaching $82.5 billion. By 1997 Wal Mart had 2744 stores in the United States, 136 stores in Canada, 145 stores in Mexico, eleven stores in Puerto Rico, five stores in Brazil, six stores in Argentina, two stores in Indonesia and two stores in China.

The firm's Supercenters concept, which combines groceries and general merchandise in a one-stop shopping facility, has become very popular around the world. The firm's small-town origins, strategic location of stores in the area of small communities, where local merchants were its principal rivals, and strategic absorption of businesses for miles around the stores contributed to the success of Wal-Mart.

2 Innovation and significant contributions

Wal-Mart has succeeded in establishing a reputation for its low-cost merchandising and high-quality customer services, including quick-response merchandise supply and innovative supply-chain management systems. The firm's RetailLink private network for sharing inventory and sales data with merchandise suppliers represents one of the most innovative implementations of information technologies (IT) in the general merchandisers industry. Wal-Mart's 'data warehousing' and 'data mining' have contributed to the firm's competitive edge in the retail industry. The firm's state-of-the-art IT system allows each store to customize the merchandise collection to match the needs of the community it serves. Wal-Mart also seeks to contribute to the communities in which it is located through fundraising activities for local children's hospitals, by educating the public about recycling and other environmental topics, and by awarding industrial development grants each year to towns and cities which foster the development of the local economy.

3 Challenges and opportunities

Cutting costs, reducing out-of-stock items and ensuring the efficient distribution of goods to its stores in international locations are the major challenges confronting Wal-Mart. The firm has tried to meet these challenges through strategic expansion in international locations, establishment of partnerships with its suppliers around the world and implementation of one-stop shopping concepts in the international marketplace. Strategic expansion and continuous innovation of the firm's distribution system and effective management of the supply chain in the emerging era of electronic commerce (e-commerce) will bring further success to the firm.

ROSALIE L. TUNG AND MOHI AHMED
SIMON FRASER UNIVERSITY

Further reading

Hoover, G., Campbell, A., and Spain, P.J. (eds) (1995) 'Wal-Mart Stores, Inc.', *Hoover's Handbook of American Business*, Austin: The Reference Press, Inc. (Gives a general overview of the company.)

Vance, S.S. and Scott, R.V. (1994) *Wal-Mart: A History of Sam Walton's Retail Phenomenon*, New York: Twayne Publishers. (Presents the perspective of Sam Walton.)

Wilder, C. (1997) 'Chief of the year: Wal-Mart CIO Randy Mott innovates for his company's and customers' good', *Information Week* 662, 22 December: 42–8. (Discusses implementation of IT at Wal-Mart's distribution centres.)

Zellner, W., Shepard, L., Katz, I. and Lindorff, D. (1997) 'Wal-Mart spoken here', *Business Week*, 23 June: 138–44. (Discusses the international expansion strategies of Wal-Mart.)

Further resources
http://www.wal-mart.com

See also: FOREIGN MARKET ENTRY STRATEGIES; GLOBAL STRATEGIC ALLIANCES, INTERNATIONAL MARKETING; MARKETING MANAGEMENT, INTERNATIONAL

The Walt Disney Company

Overview

The Walt Disney Company, together with its subsidiaries (Disney, in short), is one of the world's most diversified entertainment business organizations. Disney's major business segments consist of 'Creative Contents (consumer products operations, filmed entertainment activities not related to broadcasting, etc.)', 'Broadcasting (ABC television and radio networks, etc.)', and 'Theme Parks & Resorts (Disneyland Parks, Walt Disney World Resort in Florida, etc.)'. The company produces animated motion pictures, books and magazines, videos, computer-game software and live animation. The company distributes its products primarily through its own sales and marketing channels around the world. The company employs about 85,000 people worldwide and had annual revenues in excess of $18 billion in 1996. The corporate headquarters of the company is located in Burbank, California.

1 Brief history

The history of the Walt Disney Company dates back to 1919, when Walter E. Disney met Ub Iwerk while they were working together at a small studio that created animated commercials for use in local theatres in Kansas City. After learning about animation, Walt began creating his own cartoons and made short films called 'Laugh-O-Grams'. In 1922 Walt incorporated Laugh-O-Grams, but the company went bankrupt within a year of establishment. Walt moved to California in 1923 and began a short-film production business. The studio started to produce animated films and continued to expand. In 1955 Disney Land was opened at Anaheim, California. After Walt Disney's death in 1966 his brother Roy became the chairman of the company. In 1971 Disney World was opened in Florida.

Since 1984, under the leadership of Michael D. Eisner, Disney has continued to expand its business significantly. According to the company, the expansion includes international film distribution; television and radio broadcasting; ownership of cable systems and television stations, newspapers, magazines and book publishing; Disney stores; live theatrical entertainment; home-video production; interactive computer programs and games; online computer programs; ownership of professional sports teams; partnership with a telephone company; Disney regional entertainment; and Disney Cruise Line.

2 Innovation and significant contributions

The founder of the company, Walt Disney, established a standard for innovation and creativity throughout the entertainment industry. The company has made significant contributions to the entertainment industry by fostering creative talent. Since creativity is crucial to success in the industry, the company runs a professional development programme at its Disney Institute. The programme trains participants in how a world-class organization deals with real-world issues, in providing ideas for new strategies, and teaches knowledge and skills for new ways of doing business in the rapidly changing global marketplace. The company has shown that creativity is key to success in the entertainment business. Its leadership in this area has contributed to the development of the entertainment business. Disney was selected by *Fortune* magazine as one of the ten most admired companies in the US in 1998.

3 Challenges and opportunities

A major challenge for the Disney company is to maintain its leadership in the entertainment business in a world characterized by the globalization of the news media, products and services, extended deregulation of international telecommunication services, rapid technological change and increasing competition in the entertainment business. To compete with its emerging rivals (e.g. Universal Studios and Sony) (see MORITA, AKIO) and to increase opportunities in the global marketplace, the company has continued to diversify its businesses and make investments in new projects, such as building new theme parks and hotels.

ROSALIE L. TUNG AND MOHI AHMED
SIMON FRASER UNIVERSITY

Further reading

Flower, J. (1991) *Prince of the Magic Kingdom: Michael Eisner and the Re-making of Disney*, New York: J. Wiley. (Gives an overview of Disney's CEO, Michael D. Eisner, and a history of the Walt Disney Company, its productions as well as its reorganization.)

Grover, R. and DeGeorge, G. (1998) 'Theme-park shootout: a host of new competitors has Disney building like crazy', *Business Week*, 6 April: 66–7. (Explains how competition is shaping the business of Disney.)

Hoover, G., Campbell, A. and Spain, P.J. (eds) (1995) 'The Walt Disney Company', *Hoover's Handbook of American Business*, Austin: The Reference Press, Inc. (Gives a general overview of the company.)

O'Neal, M., Baker, S. and Grover, R. (1995) 'Disney's kingdom: as seismic shifts shake the media biz, Eisner lands on top – for now', *Business Week*, August 14: 30–4. (Discusses Disney's takeover of the ABC network.)

Stewart, T.A. (1998) 'America's most admired companies', *Fortune*, 2 March: 70–82.

Further resources

http://www.disney.com

See also: GLOBAL STRATEGIC ALLIANCES; FOREIGN MARKET ENTRY STRATEGIES; INTERNATIONAL MARKETING; INTERNATIONAL TRADE AND FOREIGN DIRECT INVESTMENT; MORITA, AKIO

Waste Management Inc.

Overview

Waste Management Inc. is one of the world's leading providers of comprehensive waste management and related services. The company provides services to commercial, industrial, municipal and residential customers, as well as to other waste management service companies. The company operates in more than twenty-three countries, and provides solid and hazardous waste management services through its subsidiaries. The revenues of the company exceeded $9 billion in 1996. The number of employees totals more than 60,000 (1996). The corporate headquarters of the company is located in Oak Brook, Illinois.

1 Brief history

While Waste Management Inc. was established in 1971, its origin dates back to 1894. In the early years the company was a small family-owned company. In 1978 the company expanded abroad. During the 1980s a specialist hazardous waste subsidiary, Chemical Waste Management, was also established. In 1993 it created WMX Technologies Inc. as the parent company, with a group structure under it. In 1997 the company reverted to its former name, Waste Management Inc.

The company's 'reduce, reuse, recycle' approach allows its customers to benefit from expert consultation on how to handle waste materials. The company provides on-time collection services by a fleet of professional drivers for solid waste collection, transportation and disposal. These services are locally based and are available to commercial, industrial and residential customers. The company offers technical knowledge and regulatory expertise for industrial and hazardous waste identification, treatment, recovery and disposal, including the provision of special procedures to help customers reduce risks. In addition, Waste Management offers other services including construction-site services such as roll-off containers and special/outdoor-event services. The company has continued to expand its network of waste management services.

In late 1997 Waste Management Inc. acquired Wheelabrator Technologies Inc., which provides a wide range of environmental products and services in North America through its three subsidiaries: Wheelabrator Environmental Systems Inc. (WESI), Wheelabrator Bio Gro Division (Bio Gro) and Wheelabrator Air Pollution Control Inc. (WAPC). Another subsidiary of the company, Waste Management International PLC, provides a wide range of solid and hazardous waste management services overseas. These services include collection, transportation, storage, treatment, recycling and disposal of waste. Waste Management International also operates a waste-to-energy facility, develops and operates water and waste-water treatment facilities, and other environmental services, along with fifty-six landfills for solid and hazardous waste, eighty transfer stations and twenty-six treatment facilities.

2 Innovation and significant contributions

As global concern for sustainability increases, Waste Management Inc. continues to innovate and make significant contributions in waste management technologies and services. The company's efforts toward reducing environmental pollution through the management of solid and hazardous waste have contributed to a cleaner and safer environment. These efforts include waste reduction, recycling, treatment and disposal, conserving nature and natural resources through biodiversity, sustainable use of natural resources and wise use of energy. The company has taken a leadership role in R&D and implementation of technologies for integrated waste management, public education and participation in environmental organizations.

3 Challenges and opportunities

To serve customers better and to meet the challenges of reducing environmental pollution the company has restructured its organization, implemented cost-control programmes which are projected to save $100 million annually (5–10 per cent procurement savings by 2001) and adopted a new fleet management strategy to modernize collection and to reduce maintenance costs. The company is continuously making efforts to diversify its services in order to increase its market opportunities around the world.

ROSALIE L. TUNG AND MOHI AHMED
SIMON FRASER UNIVERSITY

Further reading

Chakravarty, S.N. (1993) 'Dean Buntrock's green machine', *Forbes* 152(3), 2 August: 96–9. (Discusses the major businesses of Waste Management Inc.)

Ellis, J.E. (1994) 'Cleaning up after Waste Management', *Business Week*, 24 January: 99–102. (Examines restructuring, diversification, and international growth at WMX.)

Melcher, R.A. (1996) 'Back to the nitty-gritty: trash kind WMX is tossing out its acquisition strategy', *Business Week*, 17 June: 76–80. (Focuses on competition in the environmental services industry and the strategies of WMX in this regard.)

Rick, M. (1997) 'WMX: back to Waste Management', *Chemical Week* 159(6), 12 February: 40. (Provides an overview of WMX's reorganization to compete in the changing global marketplace.)

Further resources

http://www.wastemanagement.com

See also: FOREIGN MARKET ENTRY STRATEGIES

Xerox Corporation

Overview

Xerox, which name is synonymous with photocopying, is a global company with revenues in excess of $17 billion in 1996. Xerox was founded in 1906 in Rochester, New York, as the Haloid Company and renamed Xerox Corporation in 1961. Xerox produces and sells copiers, printers, scanners, fax machines, document management software, and associated products and services in about 130 countries around the world. About one-third of Xerox revenues come from digital products. The company employs about 86,700 people worldwide, including 46,000 in the United States (1996). Its corporate headquarters is located in Stamford, Connecticut.

1 Brief history

The Haloid Company, which manufactures and sells photographic paper, was founded in Rochester, New York, in 1906. In 1938 Chester Carlson invented the first xerographic image in his lab in New York. Haloid acquired the licence to Carlson's basic xerographic patents and introduced the first xerographic copier, the Model A, in 1949. In 1953 Haloid established its Canadian sales subsidiary, the first subsidiary outside of the United States. In 1956 Rank Xerox Limited was established as a joint venture between the Haloid Company and the Rank Organization PLC. In 1958 the Haloid Company changed its name to Haloid Xerox Inc., and the company was renamed again, as Xerox Corporation, in 1961.

In 1962 Fuji Xerox Co. Ltd was established as a joint venture between Rank Xerox

Ltd and Fuji Photo Film Co. Ltd of Japan. In 1965 Rank Xerox opened a manufacturing plant in the Netherlands. In 1969 Xerox Corporation acquired a majority interest (51.2 per cent) in Rank Xerox. In the same year Xerox moved its corporate headquarters from Rochester, New York, to Stamford, Connecticut. In 1975 Xerox ceased manufacturing and selling mainframe computers. During the 1970s Xerox's market share dropped tremendously as a result of severe competition in the global marketplace. Its major competitors include Canon, Sharp, Toshiba, Siemens (see SIEMENS AG), Kodak (see EASTMAN KODAK COMPANY) and Hewlett-Packard. The company has successfully responded to this challenge by adopting a strategy known as 'leadership through quality'. Through reduced cost, higher quality, participatory management and benchmarking, Xerox was able to recapture much of its lost market share.

In 1991 Xerox and Fuji Xerox established Xerox International Partners to market its printers in the global market. After significant corporate restructuring, Xerox announced its corporate identity as 'The Document Company, Xerox', in 1994. The company continued to expand its products and services around the globe.

2 Innovation and significant contributions

Since the beginning, Xerox has made important innovations and contributions in the area of document processing. Xerography, the laser printer, Ethernet networking, bit mapping and the graphical user interface are examples of major technological innovations by Xerox – all these innovations have revolutionized the way people work. To many people, the word 'xerox' is synonymous with 'photocopying'. In 1970 Xerox established the Xerox Palo Alto Research Center in Palo

Alto, California, which provided a focal point for its R&D efforts. In 1989 Xerox Business Products and Systems received the Malcolm Baldridge National Quality Award. The company has continued to receive awards for quality from around the world.

Xerox uses only recyclable and recycled thermoplastics and metals, and has adopted designs in its products to facilitate assembly and disassembly for cleaning, testing and re-use of parts. In 1992 Xerox received the Gold Medal for International Corporate Environmental Achievement from the World Environment Centre and the Environmental Achievement Award from National Wildlife Federation.

Its joint venture with Fuji Photo, in addition to being one of the earliest joint ventures between an American and a Japanese entity, has been cited as an example of a highly successful cross-national collaborative agreement. In fact, the joint venture itself has made major innovations, which were, in turn, introduced into the parent companies.

3 Challenges and opportunities

To continue to innovate and expand, Xerox has entered into collaborative arrangements with other entities around the world. In 1987 Xerox established technology alliances with Sun Microsystems Inc. In 1992 Xerox entered into an agreement with Apple Computer to market Apple-brand supplies for Apple printers; and in 1993 Xerox formed a partnership with Microsoft (see GATES, BILL) to integrate personal computers and document processing products. In 1995 Xerox began partnerships with the American Foundation for the Blind to donate Reading Edge machines to blind people, and in the same year Xerox established a subsidiary, Xerox (China) Limited, to manage existing Xerox manufacturing and marketing operations in China. To increase opportunities in China, Xerox also established its first Document Technology Center in Beijing in 1996.

Linking technology and market is one of the major challenges facing Xerox. To remain one of the most innovative and competitive firms around the world and further develop opportunities in the competitive global marketplace, Xerox must make continuous advances in digital technologies and cost reduction, and must broaden its products and services distribution networks throughout the world.

ROSALIE L. TUNG AND MOHI AHMED
SIMON FRASER UNIVERSITY

Further reading

Hoover, G., Campbell, A. and Spain, P.J. (eds) (1995) 'Xerox Corporation', *Hoover's Handbook of American Business*, Austin: The Reference Press, Inc. (Gives a general overview of the company.)

Jones, P. and Kahaner, L. (1995) *Say It & Live It: 50 Corporate Mission Statements That Hit the Mark*, New York: Currency Doubleday. (Presents the mission statements of fifty companies, including Xerox's.)

Kiely, T. (1994) 'Innovation congregations', *Technology Review* 97(3): 54 (MIT, Cambridge). (Discusses Xerox's approach to encourage innovation and experiments among its employees.)

Rosenbloom, R.S. and Spencer, W.J. (eds) (1996) *Engines of Innovation: U.S. Industrial Research at the End of an Era*, Boston, MA: Harvard Business School Press. (Focuses on R&D and change management at Xerox.)

Smart, T. (1993) 'Can Xerox duplicate its glory days', *Business Week*, 4 October: 56–8. (Discusses the challenges facing Xerox in the areas of technology, products and markets.)

Smart, T. (1997) 'Out to make Xerox print more money', *Business Week*, 11 August: 81–2. (Outlines the mission of Xerox's president, ex-IBM CFO Richard Thoman, to create a new Xerox.)

Smith, D.K. and Alexander, R.C. (1988) *Fumbling the Future: How Xerox Invented, Then Ignored, the First Personal Computer*, New York: William Morrow & Company. (Gives an insight to Xerox's change management process.)

Xerox Quality Solutions (1993) *A World of Quality: The Timeless Passport*, Milwaukee, WI: ASQC Quality Press. (Examines TQM principles, practices and their importance at Xerox.)

Further resources

Http://www.xerox.com

See also: EASTMAN KODAK COMPANY; FOR-
EIGN MARKET ENTRY STRATEGIES; GATES,
BILL; GLOBAL STRATEGIC ALLIANCES; IN-
TERNATIONAL TECHNOLOGY TRANSFER;
MULTI-NATIONAL CORPORATIONS, OR-
GANIZATION STRUTURES IN; SIEMENS AG

Biographies

Barnevik, Percy (1941–)

Personal background

- born 13 February 1941 in Simrishamn, Sweden
- graduated from Gothenburg School of Economics
- MBA from Stanford University in 1964
- when young he worked for his father's small print shop in Sweden
- from 1966 to 1969 worked for the Johnson Group in data processing (Datema AB)
- joined Sandvik AB in 1969 and served as group controller until 1975
- in 1975 became president of Sandvik AB's American subsidiary
- from 1979 to 1980 was executive vice-president of the parent company Sandvik AB
- became president and chief executive officer (CEO) of Asea in 1980, and in 1983 also became chairman of the board of Sandvik AB
- after the merger of Brown Boveri (BBC) and Asea in 1988, was appointed president and CEO of Asea Brown Boveri Ltd (ABB) Zurich and made chairman of the board of Sandvik AB
- in October 1996, at age 55, announced that he would step down as president and CEO of ABB
- in April 1997 accepted the position of chairman of the giant Swedish holding company Investor, whose holdings include Saab, Electrolux and Ericsson; in addition, remains chairman of ABB, a company which Investor includes among its portfolio of investments
- chairman of the boards of Skanska AG and Sandvik, and also serves on the boards of E.I. Du Pont de Nemours & Cie. (see E.I. DU PONT DE NEMOURS AND COMPANY), Providentia and General Motors (see GENERAL MOTORS CORPORATION)
- the first non-American to serve on General Motors' board of directors
- in 1991 was selected Manager of the Year by the Union de la Presse Économique et Financière Européene
- in 1995 received the Emerging Markets CEO of the Year Award from ING Bank and International Media Partners
- in 1996 became the first non-American to receive the Bernhard H. Falk Award from the National Electrical Manufacturers' Association of America (NEMA); in presenting this award 'NEMA recognizes Barnevik's innovative inspirational leadership in the electroindustry and his role as a chief architect of a global company that recognizes no national borders and vigilantly protects the spirit of entrepreneurship' (http://www.abb.ch (1996b))
- in 1997 received the European Leadership Award from Stanford University

1 Introduction

Barnevik has been described as charismatic and as a workaholic known for working twenty-hour days (Kennedy, 1996). '[S]ome in the Swedish and European business establishments ... have found Barnevik's flamboyance and outspokenness grating' (Reed and Sains 1996). He has been described as 'A hard-nosed manager with scant regard for fancy management theories' (Kennedy 1996). Barnevik says, 'what really gives me the greatest satisfaction is seeing young people whom I have promoted succeed' (de Vries 1998). He also says that he is motivated by the desire to create a better world by creating employment opportunities and improving environmental conditions (de Vries 1998). He credits his experiences in his father's small printing business (fifteen employees) with teaching him the importance of customer service and flat management structures (Greenhouse 1988; Kennedy 1996).

2 Main contribution

In 1987 Percy Barnevik masterminded the merger of Asea and Brown Boveri, the largest in European history. At ABB Barnevik 'created what many consider the model stateless company' (Reed 1997). 'Years of drastic restructuring under Barnevik are paying off in steady growth' (Reed and Sains 1996). After becoming CEO of ABB, Barnevik led the company in just four years to huge increases in earnings (×6) and stock value (×12). According to Barnevik, 'ABB has come together by merging 50 companies with 100 years of tradition in a number of different countries' (*Business Week* 1993).

'There is very little precedent for the ABB kind of setup in its ability to rapidly integrate local and global operations' (Cohen 1992). At ABB Barnevik established their famous set of global profit centres. Under this system 'accountabilities are broken down to 5,000 small profit centres operating within 1,000 companies – typically 40 people in each profit centre, focused on specific products and dealing directly with customers' (Kennedy 1996).

'Barnevik has consistently advocated better terms of trade for developing countries as part of the global integration process and viewed ABB's investments in emerging markets over the long term' (*Business Wire* 1995). He left ABB as CEO with the feeling that he had accomplished most of what he had set out to do (Reed and Sains 1996).

3 Evaluation

There was evidence that he was fatigued at the time of his departure from ABB as president and CEO: 'All the big acquisitions, the 70-to-80 hour weeks, have been a tremendous strain' (Reed and Sains 1996). There are few, however, who would argue that Barnevik's leadership at ABB has not made a difference. Largely thanks to him, 'ABB has stood apart from many other multinationals in its emphasis on the human side of production, with a strong multi-domestic structure enabling local managers to work within local business conditions and cultural traditions' (*Business Wire* 1995).

He also has a reputation as a brutal 'downsizer'. He uses what he calls the 30–30–30 approach to downsizing. Under this approach 10% or fewer of the workers keep their existing jobs, i.e. in theory 30% are laid-off, 30% are transferred to existing operating units and 30% are moved to positions in newly formed companies designed to service ABB on a competitive basis. The impact of this approach is dramatic. For example, in Finland the head office staff was cut to 28 from 880 employees; in Germany personnel were reduced to 100 from 1800, and at the former Brown Boveri headquarters in Switzerland only 200 employees remain out of 4000 (Cohen 1992).

Perhaps most notable is Barnevik's persistent and aggressive approach to management: 'Barnevik emphasizes that he will "relentlessly push for higher targets and instill a mentality of continuous change." He prefers to fix problem companies but thinks if that's not possible they should be dumped' (Reed 1997). His leadership style has provided a new model for other business executives to consider and he has influenced current thinking regarding organizational structure in a global economy (de Vries 1998). Barnevik and ABB are discussed in management classes and frequently cited in strategic management textbooks. According to Barnevik, 'It all comes down to the same idea: you have to move things down to people, empower them, stimulate them, take away this layer of bureaucratic management' (Kennedy 1996).

Given his past record, it is likely that he will use a very aggressive management style at Investor: 'Barnevik's ambitions for Investor are even more far-reaching than those he had for ABB ... He envisions it adding major ventures in the U.S., emerging markets, and perhaps Eastern Europe' (Reed 1997). However, Barnevik is not saying what these ventures might be.

STEPHEN J. HAVLOVIC
SIMON FRASER UNIVERSITY

Further reading

(References cited in the text marked *)

* *Business Week* (1993) 'Mr. Barnevik, aren't you happy now?', 27 September: 128. (Presents an exclusive interview with Percy Barnevik, who discusses the changes he initiated at ABB.)
* *Business Wire* (1995) 'Percy Barnevik named "Emerging Markets CEO of the Year"', 10 October. (News release.)
* Cohen, Roger (1992) 'The very model of efficiency', *New York Times*, Section D, 2 March: 1. (Reviews the downsizing and globalization of operations at ABB.)
* de Vries, Manfred F.R. Kets (1998) 'Charisma in action: the transformational abilities of Virgin's Richard Branson and ABB's Percy Barnevik', *Organizational Dynamics*: 7–21. (Presents interviews with Branson and Barnevik.)
* Greenhouse, Steven (1988) 'The emerging European elite', *New York Times*, Section 3, 17 July: 1. (Presents executive profiles of Barnevik–ABB, Gomez–Thomson Group and Scharp–Electrolux AB.)
* Kennedy, Carol (1996) 'ABB's sun rises in the east', *Director* 50(2), September: 40–4. (Examines Barnevik's approach to management.)
Peterson, Thane (1996) 'More moves at GM', *Business Week*, 16 December: 44. (Discusses appointments to General Motor's board.)
* Reed, Stanley (1997) 'New company, same ambition: build a global giant', *Business Week*, 12 May: 60. (Examines Barnevik's acceptance of the position as chairman of Investor.)
* Reed, Stanley and Sains, Ariane (1996) 'Percy Barnevik passes the baton', *Business Week*, 28 October: 66. (Discusses Barnevik's early retirement and accomplishments as CEO of ABB.)
Wallace, Charles (1997) 'Percy Barnevik gets a shot', *Fortune*, 9 June: 166. (Discusses the challenges and opportunities facing Barnevik at Investor.)
Who's Who Edition European Business and Industry (1992) 'Percy Nils Barnevik'. (Provides a brief career and educational profile.)

Further resources

http://www.abb.ch (1996a) 'GM board appointment'. (ABB corporate communications announcement.)
* http://www.abb.ch (1996b) 'Bernhard H. Falk Award'. (ABB corporate communications announcement.)
http://www.abb.ch (1997) 'Percy Barnevik'. (Provides a career summary.)

See also: E.I. DU PONT DE NEMOURS AND COMPANY; GENERAL MOTORS CORPORATION

Related topics in the IEBM: CORPORATE STRATEGIC CHANGE; DOWNSIZING; MANUFACTURING STRATEGY

Boonstra, Cornelis (1938–)

Personal background

- born 7 January 1938 in Leeuwarden, the Netherlands
- joined Unilever in 1955 as a junior representative and worked in a variety of functions, including assistant sales manager
- in 1962 became a sales manager for Zuivel Handel Maatschappij, a dairy foods producer, which became SRV
- promoted to President of SRV in 1966
- joined Intradal, a Sara Lee Corporation subsidiary, in 1974 as general manager, and in 1978 became president and chief executive officer (CEO)
- in 1983 promoted to coordinator of European activities of Sara Lee Corporation, and made a board member and deputy chairman of Douwe Egberts, a Sara Lee subsidiary, which later became Sara Lee/DE
- became chairman of the board of management of Sara Lee/DE in 1984 and senior vice-president of Sara Lee Corporation in 1986
- in 1988 promoted to executive vice-president and director of Sara Lee Corporation, and in July 1993 appointed president and chief operating officer (COO) of Sara Lee Corporation in Chicago
- on 31 December 1993 retired for personal reasons at age 55 after only six months on the job
- in July 1994 joined Philips Electronics NV as a member of the board of management and as executive vice-president responsible for the Asia-Pacific region
- from July 1994 to April 1995 was also president and CEO of Philips Lighting Holding BV
- on 1 October 1996 became president and chairman of the board of management of Philips Electronics NV
- became chairman of the supervisory board of Eindhoven Technical University in 1997

1 Introduction

'A high school dropout with no technical expertise, Boonstra established himself as a gifted marketer of consumer products' (Wallace and Prochniak 1997). He worked his way up through the ranks of the Sara Lee Corporation, but after his appointment as president and COO of Sara Lee Corporation in 1993 he retired for personal reasons. 'A rigorous travel schedule, including short-stay visits to Europe, where Sara Lee is rapidly expanding, is a factor some analysts said contributed to Mr. Boonstra's decision. Others said Mr. Boonstra wanted to be closer with his family at its residence in the Bahamas' (*New York Times* 1994). Rumours circulated that his wife decided not to live in Chicago and that this may have been a factor in his decision to take early retirement. His position as president and COO of Sara Lee Corporation would remain vacant for three years after his sudden departure. Boonstra has received a number of honours, including an Honorary Doctorate of Law from the University of Rochester in 1992 and appointment as an Officer in the Dutch Order of Orange Nassau in 1993.

2 Main contribution

Cornelis (Cor) Boonstra was instrumental in Sara Lee establishing a strong presence in Europe, which accounts for over a quarter of their sales revenue (Ryan 1993). At the time of Boonstra's departure from Sara Lee Corporation, chairman and CEO John H. Bryan stated: 'Mr. Boonstra leaves a very important legacy to the corporation. Over the past two decades he has been one of the major figures in the development of our international presence' (*PR Newswire* 1994). Sara Lee Corporation had annual sales of $14.6 billion when Boonstra announced his decision to leave the firm (*PR Newswire* 1994).

Shortly after his arrival at Philips 'Chairman Cor Boonstra decided on Shock Therapy. On October 28 [1997], he announced that Philips headquarters would move to energetic Amsterdam. ... Since he took the helm of the troubled company one year ago, ... [Cor] has sold off dozens of money-losing or underperforming businesses [e.g. Grundig, cable operations, car navigation systems] and brought every division into the black' (Edmondson 1997). He has formed joint ventures with Marantz and Lucent Technologies Inc. in order to advance Philips in established technologies such as cellular telephones (Edmondson, 1997).

Boonstra is 'the first CEO in Philips' 106-year history who didn't rise through the ranks' (Edmondson 1997). After taking office he set specific performance targets for management: 'Managers of business units have been told that their jobs will be at risk unless they make returns of at least 24% on the net assets they manage. Shareholders have been promised a similar level of profitability' (*Economist* 1997). He has made improvements in shareholder value a top priority (Wallace and Prochniak 1997).

3 Evaluation

At the end of 1997 Philips had 264,685 employees, sales of $39.2 billion, and the outlook for 1998 appeared relatively strong (*Business Wire* 1998). 'Boonstra's first-year performance has been impressive. He has cut 6,000 jobs in consumer electronics, moved more production from Western Europe to Asia and Eastern Europe, and implemented a global purchasing strategy. He has sold off underperforming businesses ... and net income from operations was up 133% over the year before, to $966 million' (Edmondson 1997). His downsizing and streamlining of operations at Philips are consistent with the policies of other firms competing in intense global markets.

Despite his financial achievements at Philips, not everyone approves of Boonstra's management style: 'His ruthless elimination of the old guard has already earned him a nickname, "Corleone", with an alarming Mafia flavour. Victims include his predecessor, Jan "The Butcher" Timmer, himself no pushover' (*Economist* 1997). This assessment is surprising given that he has ruled out wholesale layoffs as a means of quickly restructuring Philips. Boonstra has stated: 'I disagree with the approach that for the whole Philips organization you take off 25% of the individuals. ...It's a rough approach that doesn't serve our shareholder value' (Wallace and Prochniak 1997). A number of observers see cost-cutting in combination with reducing the management layers as Boonstra's most important contribution to Philips.

One Philips' senior executive sums up Boonstra's performance by simply saying, '"He has the guts" to change Philips' (Edmondson 1997). Standard & Poor's Credit Wire improved Philips rating in August 1997 after revising its outlook for Philips from negative to stable, based on significant improvements over the previous ten months: 'The ratings also reflect Philips' position as a diversified global electronics group, coupled with a reasonable and rapidly improving, financial profile' (*Business Wire* 1997). The changes at Philips reflect more than administrative and procedural adjustments: 'There are also signs of a profound philosophical change that reflects the company's move from an engineer-dominated business to a marketing-driven one' (Wallace and Prochniak 1997). It was also his marketing successes that he was best known for at Sara Lee.

STEPHEN J. HAVLOVIC
SIMON FRASER UNIVERSITY

Further reading

(References cited in the text marked *)

Business Wire (1997) 'Philips' outlook revised to stable', 29 August. (News release.)

* *Business Wire* (1998) 'The Philips Group in 1997', 12 February. (News release.)
* *Economist* (1997) 'Consumer electronics: the dimmest bulb of all', 7 June: 69. (Discusses the ability of Boonstra to reverse the crisis at Philips.)
* Edmondson, Gail (1997) 'Ultimatum at Philips', *Business Week*, 17 November: 134. (Reviews major changes at Philips initiated by Boonstra.)
  Millman, Nancy (1997) 'Sara Lee succession seen in expected job changes', *Chicago Tribune*, Business Section, 27 March: 3. (Gives an announcement regarding the replacement for Boonstra at Sara Lee.)
* *New York Times* (1994) 'Retirement at Sara Lee', Section D, 5 January: 13. (Announces Boonstra's sudden retirement.)
* *PR Newswire* (1994) 'Sara Lee Corporation announces retirement of Cornelis Boonstra', 4 January. (News release.)
* Ryan, Nancy (1993) 'New Sara Lee president guided Europe growth', *Chicago Tribune*, Business Section, 14 April: 4. (Announcement of Boonstra's promotion at Sara Lee.)
* Wallace, Charles P. and Prochniak, Andrea L. (1997) 'Can he fix Philips?', *Fortune*, 31 March: 98. (Examines the challenges facing Boonstra at Philips.)
  Who's Who Edition European Business and Industry (1992) 'Cornelis Boonstra'. (Gives a brief overview of his professional career.)

Related topics in the IEBM: CORPORATE STRATEGIC CHANGE; DOWNSIZING;

Bronfman, Edgar Jr (1955–)

1 Introduction
2 Main contribution
3 Evaluation

Medical Center, the Solomon R. Guggenheim Foundation and WNET

Personal background

- born May 1955 in New York City, to Edgar Bronfman, Sr, and Ann Loeb Bronfman, one of seven children
- belongs to a wealthy family which established the Seagram Company Ltd and continues to own a large portion (135.7 million shares or 36.4%)
- moved to London in the early 1970s to work in films
- returned to the US in 1975 and continued to work in the entertainment business
- joined Seagram in 1982, serving as assistant to the Office of President of the Seagram Company Ltd and Joseph E. Seagram & Sons Inc.
- during 1983–84 was managing director of Seagram Europe, based in London
- from 1984 to 1988 was president of the House of Seagram, the production and marketing operation for Seagram distilled products in the US
- elected to the board of directors of the Montreal-based Seagram Company Ltd in May 1988
- in August 1988, at age 33, became executive vice-president of Joseph E. Seagram & Sons Inc., the US subsidiary of the Seagram Company Ltd
- became president and chief operating officer (COO) of Seagram Company Ltd in 1989
- in May 1994 was recommended by his father as chief executive officer (CEO) of Seagram Company Ltd, and duly succeeded him a few days later
- member of a number of boards, including the Wharton School of Business, the New York Public Library, New York University

1 Introduction

The Seagram Company was founded by Edgar Bronfman, Jr's grandfather Samuel Bronfman in 1924 in Canada and established a US subsidiary in 1933 (Collins 1994). Seagram sells its brands in more than 150 countries (*Business Wire* 1994a). 'At age 14, [Edgar, Jr] persuaded his father to invest in a movie and spent the summer on the set' (Cuff 1989). After his parents separated in the early 1970s he moved to London to work with film producer David Puttnam. Edgar, Jr never attended college. In 1973 he produced his first film *The Blockhouse* and began a song writing career, sometimes using the alias Junior Miles. His song with Bruce Roberts, 'Whisper in the Dark' was recorded by Dionne Warwick.

Edgar, Jr, did not return to the United States until 1975, when his older brother Samuel was kidnapped and held for ransom. He then married actress Sherry Brewer and continued to work in the entertainment business: 'he spent several years in Hollywood, reading screenplays and working for the producer David Puttnam, who later became president of Columbia Pictures' (Landler 1995). In 1982 he produced a Hollywood film called *The Border* starring Jack Nicholson and Valerie Perrine. Throughout the 1970s he did not get along well with his father Edgar, Sr. Oddly enough, it was the premier of *The Border* in New York which reunited him with his father and led to his joining Seagram in 1982.

His son Ben was born in 1982. He later divorced Sherry Brewer, and in 1993 married Clarissa Alcock. Edgar Bronfman, Jr, lives in New York City with Clarissa and his four children. In 1994, at age 39, he became CEO of the Seagram Company Ltd. His appointment made him the third generation of the

Bronfman family to manage the company (Collins 1994). Edgar Bronfman, Jr, has been described as a 'hands-on executive' (Bates 1995). His father and uncle believe he is the family member with the best ability to guide the company into the next century.

2 Main contribution

For the 1995 fiscal year, the year after which Edgar Bronfman, Jr, was appointed CEO, Seagram's pre-tax earnings were $1.14 billion (Landler 1995).

As CEO Edgar, Jr, expanded Seagram's interests from beverages and distilled spirits by entering the entertainment business with the purchase (80 per cent) of MCA for $5.7 billion (Bates 1995). He received some criticism at the time for this diversification. For instance, Landler (1995) reported that 'The 39-year-old former film producer is also apparently transforming Seagram from a reliable generator of earnings into a company that will depend heavily on the vagaries of Hollywood'. Edgar, Jr, had been instrumental in earlier expansions such as the 1988 purchase of Tropicana for $1.2 billion and a $2 billion investment (14.9 per cent) in Time-Warner (Landler 1995).

In October 1997 he agreed to merge Seagram's Universal Studios TV and cable operations with the Home Shopping Network Inc. (HSN), operated by long-time friend Barry Diller. Under the agreement Seagram can increase its 45 per cent ownership in HSN when Diller retires or exits (Grover 1997). At the 1997 Seagram Company Ltd annual meeting in Montreal Edgar, Jr, said 'Seagram entered into a "landmark" agreement to combine Universal's television assets with those of HSN, Inc. into a new company, USA Networks, Inc. He indicated the transaction 'lays the groundwork for achieving the kind of major position in television that Universal must have to survive and prosper in this increasingly vertically integrated world' (Seagram Company Ltd 1997).

3 Evaluation

'Citing his accomplishments as President, they [his father Edgar, Sr, and his uncle Charles] said Mr. Bronfman has recast Seagram into a global competitor with a focus on premium brands' (*Business Wire* 1994b). Edgar, Jr's decision to move Seagram into films and music was based on his belief in the future growth potential of the entertainment sector. He believes that the liquor industry will continue to see a shrinking market place. A combination of stricter government regulations on alcohol consumption and increased consumer health consciousness has led Edgar, Jr, to this conclusion (Landler 1995).

According to Thomas Pirko, president of Bevmark Inc., 'a lot of people, in some cases grudgingly perhaps, have come to see Edgar Bronfman Jr. as being a lot more capable than once thought' (Cuff 1989). Edgar, Jr, initiated Seagram's diversification strategies, first from a liquor distributor to a beverage distributor, and then leading the company into the entertainment business. Today Seagram Company Ltd employs 30,000 people worldwide and 'operates in two global business segments: beverages and entertainment' (Seagram Company Ltd 1997). At Seagram's annual meeting in November 1997 Edgar, Jr, reported strong earnings on revenues of $2.9 billion in the first fiscal quarter suggesting that his diversification strategy may well be on target (Seagram Company Ltd 1997).

STEPHEN J. HAVLOVIC
SIMON FRASER UNIVERSITY

Further reading

(References cited in the text marked *)

* Bates, James (1995) 'Company town: star attraction; Bronfman seems bent on making the artists happy', *Los Angeles Times*, Business Section D, 11 July: 1. (Discusses the installation of a new management team at MCA.)
* *Business Wire* (1994a) 'Edgar Bronfman, Jr. tells Seagram shareholders company is poised to meet new challenges', 1 June. (News release.)
  Business Wire (1994b) 'Seagram appoints Edgar Bronfman, Jr. as chief executive officer', 1 June. (News release.)

Celebrity Biographies (1998) 'Edgar Bronfman, Jr.', Baseline II Inc. (Gives details of the milestones and a brief biography.)

* Collins, Glenn (1994) 'Family shift is expected for Seagram', *New York Times*, Section D, 19 May: 5. (Announces Edgar, Jr, as heir apparent at Seagram.)

* Cuff, Daniel F. (1989) 'Edgar Bronfman Jr. promoted at Seagram', *New York Times*, Section D, 20 February: 3. (Discusses Edgar, Jr's promotion to CEO.)

Forbes (1996) 'The Forbes four hundred'. (Gives a brief biography of Edgar Bronfman, Sr.)

* Grover, Ronald (1997) 'It's prime time for Barry', *Business Week*, 3 November: 37. (Reviews the agreement to merge Seagram's TV and cable operations with HSN.)

Hicks, Jonathan P. (1988) 'Edgar Bronfman Jr. advances at Seagram', *New York Times*, Section D, 3 August: 4. (Announces Edgar, Jr's selection as Seagram's CEO.)

Jones, Tim (1994) 'Seagram exec douses rumours of a bid for Time Warner', *Chicago Tribune*, Business Section, 2 June: 3. (Announces, on Edgar, Jr's first day as CEO, that he will end a Time Warner takeover bid.)

* Landler, Mark (1995) 'Seagram heads for Hollywood', *New York Times*, Section D, 7 April: 3. (Examines Seagram's diversification strategy.)

PR Newswire (1988) 'Edgar Bronfman Jr. elected to Seagram board', 26 May. (News release.)

Reuter Business Report (1994) 'Seagram says Edgar Bronfman, Sr. to resign as CEO', 30 May. (News release.)

* Seagram Company Ltd (1997) 'Edgar Bronfman, Jr. tells shareholders Seagram is a "reenergized" company', http://www.seagram.com. (News release.)

Further resources:

http://www.seagram.com (Provides a biographical information sheet.)

Related topics in the IEBM: CORPORATE STRATEGIC CHANGE

Browne, E. John P. (1948–)

1 Introduction
2 Main contribution
3 Evaluation

Personal background

- graduated with a BSc in Physics from Cambridge University and an MBA from Stanford University
- joined British Petroleum (BP) in 1966 at the age of 18 as a university apprentice
- from 1969 to 1983 he held a variety of exploration and production positions in Anchorage, New York, San Francisco, London and Canada
- became group treasurer and chief executive of BP Finance International in 1984
- promoted in 1986 to executive vice-president and chief financial officer of the Standard Oil Production Company based in Cleveland, Ohio
- after the BP and Standard Oil of Ohio merger he was made chief executive officer (CEO) of the Standard Oil Operation
- transferred to London in 1989 and was named managing director and CEO of BP Exploration
- became a member of the board of BP in 1991
- replaced his mentor David Simon as group chief executive of British Petroleum Plc (BP) in 1995
- appointed to the SmithKline Beecham board of directors in June 1996
- joined the Intel Corporation Board in January 1997
- non-executive Director of Redland Plc and a trustee of the British Museum
- serves as chairman of the Stanford University Advisory Board, and is a fellow of the Royal Academy of Engineering and the Institute of Mining and Metallurgy

1 Introduction

John Browne is unmarried and is an only child. His father worked for British Petroleum in the Middle East and his mother was from Transylvania (Farrand 1995). 'He is fond of opera, the ballet, and pre-Colombian art' (Salpukas 1994).

John Browne has been described by his colleagues as a 'no-nonsense, focused executive' (Salpukas 1994). He has a reputation as an 'insatiable worker' and is said 'to wield commanding influence over the company's [BP] direction' (Donovan 1994). Others have characterized him as 'a shy, unassuming man'. The investment community has labelled him 'the shy genius' (Farrand 1995). Browne is the kind of person who never accepts that something cannot be done and who is always asking if there is a better way or if someone might have a better idea (Prokesch 1997). He does not believe in hierarchies and structures that hamper a free exchange of ideas and knowledge. His egalitarian beliefs are revealed when he says, 'It may sound like fantasy, but I truly consider myself only the first among equals in the top management team' (Prokesch 1997).

2 Main contribution

When in charge of BP's North Sea Forties Field in the early 1980s Browne raised $537 million by selling smaller exploration firms small pieces of the field. From this 'he won almost legendary status in the company as the man who made BP a windfall profit of $320 million' (Farrand 1995). As chief executive of BP Finance International, Browne is credited with essentially building BP's in-house bank 'from scratch'.

During his time in BP's Exploration and Production Division 'he somehow combined an oilman's adventurous instinct to hunt for oil and recover it with the desk bound number-crunching acumen of an accountant.

He cut BP Exploration's exposure from 30 countries to 10, halved the work force to 7,000 and slashed costs' (Farrand 1995). During this period BP's costs for finding oil dropped from $5 per barrel to $2, and development costs were halved.

At the time John Browne took over as CEO of British Petroleum Co. Plc (BP) the firm employed 60,000 employees, operated in seventy countries and had returned to prosperity (Farrand 1995). He has served as a member of a management team which has streamlined the BP organization: 'Today BP is the most profitable of the major oil companies. Its debt, which had grown as a result of acquisition, unrestrained capital spending, and the buy back of a big block of shares from the Kuwaiti government, has been slashed to $7 billion from a 1992 peak of $16 billion' (Prokesch 1997). Browne attributes much of the success to empowering people. In an interview with Steven Prokesch (1997) he stated: 'For people to learn how to deliver performance and grow BP, we had to make them feel that, individually and collectively, they could control the destiny of our businesses.'

'Browne believes that for BP to thrive, so must the communities in which it does business. To make that happen, Browne has insisted that the economic and social health of the villages, towns, and cities in which BP does business be a matter of central concern to the company's board of Directors' (Garten 1998). For example, BP has donated computer technology to prevent flooding in Vietnam, reforested areas around the Black Sea destroyed by fire, provided solar-powered refrigerators in Zambia to store anti-malaria vaccines and helped the development of small businesses in Soweto in South Africa (Garten 1998).

John Browne has been instrumental in forming a partnership with Sidanco to expand British Petroleum's (BP) portfolio into Russia and to markets in China and the Far East. He was instrumental in forming an alliance with Mobil Oil which merged its European fuel and lubricant operations: 'As part of the deal, all 3,300 Mobil filling stations in European countries from Gibraltar to Ukraine will be re-flagged as BP stations and operated by the British giant' (Reed and McWilliams 1997). This is expected to yield up to $500 million per year in savings (Prokesch 1997).

He is also active in leading BP in the development and marketing of solar power. 'The company has spent $160 million developing solar energy and has 10% of the world's solar-power market' (Arnst et al. 1997). BP will provide a solar-powered Olympic Village at the 2000 Summer Games in Australia.

Under his leadership BP has taken a position of strong environmental leadership. Browne states: 'Our goal is not just to clean up damage but to create no damage at all in the first place' (Fisher and Kahn 1997). In essence, he feels that what is good for the environment is good for business. In May 1997, during a speech in Berlin, 'BP Chief Executive John Browne asked the international community to work together to address global climate change issues' (Gottschalk 1997).

In 1997 John Browne became the first recipient of the Petroleum Executive of the Year Award, given by the Energy Intelligence Group. 'Browne's vision was cited as one of the main reasons for his selection. ... This award is particularly noteworthy in that both the nominations and selections were made by Browne's peers in the industry' (*Oil Daily* 1997).

3 Evaluation

John Browne has distinguished himself by being innovative and solving complex problems (Farrand 1995). Perhaps most noteworthy is that he has made significant contributions as both a financial executive (e.g. CEO BP Finance International) and a technical executive (e.g. CEO BP Exploration). At the time of John Browne's promotion, a London-based analyst commented: 'It's been a long time since they've had a real oil person in charge' (Walsh 1995). John Browne has transformed BP into one of the most profitable oil producers in the world (Farrand 1995). In 1996 BP's profits increased by 31 per cent, to $4.1 billion (Reed and McWilliams 1997).

A portion of the improvement has been the result of Browne leading BP into oil rich territories in unstable and/or dangerous environments, e.g. Algeria, Columbia and the Shetland Islands: 'In politically unstable areas, some of Browne's gambles may not pay off. For now, though, he seems bent on pushing the envelope in the oil business' (Reed and McWilliams 1997). Browne's philosophy has been that you must enter into dangerous territories to find new deposits of oil with high yields, i.e. explore where your competitors have not been willing to take the risks.

'[T]he most admired company in Britain, British Petroleum, also ranks No. 1 among its compatriots in environmental responsibility' (Fisher and Kahn 1997). It is rare and noteworthy to find a company which is recognized for both its profitability and concern for the environment. John Browne has demonstrated his belief that top management must stimulate, not control, the organization (Prokesch 1997). He believes in meetings with individuals rather than 'town-hall-style meetings', which he feels are ineffective (Prokesch 1997).

STEPHEN J. HAVLOVIC
SIMON FRASER UNIVERSITY

Further reading

(References cited in the text marked *)

* Arnst, Catherine, Reed, Stanley, McWilliams, Gary and Weimer, De'Ann (1997) 'When green begets green', *Business Week*, 10 November: 98. (Examines Browne's activities, which support both aggressive oil exploration and environmental protection.)

Business Wire (1997) 'Intel elects John Browne to its board of directors', 27 January. (News release.)

* Donovan, Patrick (1994) 'Shuffle at the top of BP's board', *Guardian* (London), 30 November. (News release.)

* Farrand, Tim (1995) 'John Browne takes over at British Petroleum', *Reuters Business Report*, 2 July. (Gives a personal profile and assessment of Browne.)

* Fisher, Anne and Kahn, Jeremy (1997) 'The world's most admired companies', *Fortune*, 27 October: 220. (Gives a review of BP and other successful firms.)

* Garten, Jeffery E. (1998) 'Globalism doesn't have to be cruel', *Business Week*, 9 February: 26. (Reviews Browne's belief in supporting communities where you conduct business.)

* Gottschalk, Arthur (1997) 'BP takes 1st step to cut greenhouse gas emissions', *Journal of Commerce*, 1 October: 12A. (Reviews Browne's historic speech in Berlin.)

* *Oil Daily* (1997) 'Browne receives EIG award', *Oil Daily* 47(225), 25 November: 8.

PR Newswire (1996) 'Browne appointed to Smith-Kline Beecham board of directors', 20 June. (News release.)

* Prokesch, Steven E. (1997) 'Unleashing the power of learning: an interview with British Petroleum's John Browne', *Harvard Business Review*, September: 147. (Provides an exclusive interview.)

* Reed, Stanley and McWilliams, Gary (1997) 'BP: a well-oiled machine', *Business Week*, 26 May: 80. (Reviews Browne's achievements at BP.)

* Salpukas, Agis (1994) 'Chief to turn over B.P. reins to supporter', *New York Times*, Section D, 30 November: 3. (Announcement of Browne's promotion to Chairman.)

* Walsh, Campion (1995) 'New BP head poised to send upstream success rippling downstream to keep profits buoyant', *Oil Daily* 45(125): 1. (Reviews John Browne's promotion.)

Related topics in the IEBM: CORPORATE STRATEGIC CHANGE

Chung family of Hyundai Group

1 Biographical data
2 Main contribution
3 Conclusion

Summary

It would be impossible to think of Hyundai Group without Chung Ju-yung, founder and honorary chairman of the group. Since Chung Ju-yung established a small construction company in 1947, he has grown the business into a widely diversified business group with combined revenues in 1996 of $77 billion, in just over half a century.

Hyundai Group has earnt worldwide recognition, especially in construction, car manufacturing, shipbuilding and, most recently, semiconductors. Hyundai Corporation and Hyundai Motor were ranked 109th and 278th, with revenues of $27.3 billion and $14.5 billion, respectively, in *Fortune*'s Global 500 in 1997.

Hyundai Group's culture has stemmed mostly from Chung Ju-yung. Fast growth and an overseas orientation, heavy-industry focus and aggressive entry strategy into new fields such as shipbuilding and electronics, in a massive way, were manifestations of Chung's unyielding entrepreneurship.

1 Biographical data

Chung Ju-yung (1915–)

The founder of the Hyundai Group, Chung Ju-yung was born in 1915, the eldest son of a farmer in a small rural town. As a teenager, Chung left his hometown empty-handed, with only his hopes and dreams for the future. With savings from construction sites where he had worked as a manual labourer, he opened a small motor repair shop in Seoul. The shop became very successful.

In 1947 Chung established Hyundai Engineering & Construction Company, the cornerstone of the Hyundai Group. Even in the midst of the Korean War, Chung never lost his drive for success. He was able to rise above the occasion by being highly creative and bold, and made Hyundai Engineering & Construction Company the best construction company in Korea in terms of size and quality of work.

Chung started Hyundai Motor Company in 1967, making Korea the sixteenth country in the world to mass produce cars. In the same year Hyundai also won the biggest overseas construction contract, worth $1 billion, for the construction of the Jubail Industrial Harbour in Saudi Arabia, creating a launchpad for the Korean economic takeoff that was in large part fuelled by the so-called 'oil money'.

Chung established Hyundai Shipbuilding Company in 1973. The company took significant strides forward by winning two major contracts for shipbuilding even before it had started to construct the shipyards. For the very first time in the world, the dedication ceremony of a shipyard and the christening of the first vessel constructed on site were celebrated simultaneously.

His orientation towards overseas markets came from his conviction that competing inside the poor country of Korea would not bring success, so it was essential to go abroad to get rich. In line with this conviction, he started Hyundai Corporation, a general trading company, in 1977. Hyundai Corporation became the largest general trading company in Korea in terms of export quantities. The general trading company affiliated to the group plays the role of an international arm of the group.

Chung made another heavy investment in electronics in 1983. Instead of the conventional approach of other Korean firms, who were moving into home electronics, he chose to focus on computers.

At the start of the 1990s Chung extended Hyundai Group's domain into more technologically advanced businesses. Semiconductors, especially DRAM chips, were developed during this period, and added to Hyundai's list of the most profitable businesses in 1994 and 1995. In 1998 Chung was appointed chief executive officer (CEO) of Hyundai Construction Co. Ltd, the flagship company of the group.

The second-generation Chungs

In 1996 Chung Mong-koo (born 1938), the second son of Chung Ju-yung (Chung Ju-yung's eldest son was killed in a traffic accident), took over the chairmanship from his uncle Chung Se-yung, who had governed the group since Chung Ju-yung's semi-retirement in 1987.

In 1998 Chung Mong-hun (born 1948), the fifth of Chung Ju-yung's eight sons, also became chairman of the group, establishing dual leadership with his elder brother.

Chung Mong-joon (born 1951), the sixth son of Chung Ju-yung and an adviser to Hyundai Heavy Industries Company, the biggest shipbuilder in the world, has chosen to pursue a political career by becoming a representative in the National Assembly.

2 Main contribution

Chung Ju-yung

Chung had also assumed pivotal roles in business organizations and other public committees in Korean society. He served as chairman of the Federation of Korean Industries and many other organizations. As the former chairman of the Korean Amateur Sports Association, he headed the task force which brought the 1988 Olympics to Seoul.

His pioneering spirit and boldness were revealed once again when he became the first Korean businessman to be officially invited by both Moscow and Pyongyang, North Korea, for prospective investment. Chung was the very first Korean civilian to establish business relations with communist nations.

In January 1992 Chung took on the great challenge of creating a new political party and

running for the presidential election. However, he was unsuccessful.

The second-generation Chungs

Chung Mong-koo managed the group in the name of 'value management' for customers, employees and society at large.

Having succeeded in establishing Hyundai Electronics Company as one of the major producers of semiconductors, Chung Mong-hun is generally regarded as the shrewdest and most entrepreneurial among the brothers.

Chung Mong-joon is widely considered a future political leader. He is playing a key role in co-hosting with Japan the 2002 World Cup Finals, which he successfully bid for as chairman of the Korea Football Association.

Hyundai Group

Hyundai Group has typically tapped into businesses which were new to Korea and developed them to world standards. In particular, Chung drove the export and economic development of the 1970s and 1980s by entering into heavy machinery, shipbuilding and automotive industries. Hyundai Group was one of the major players in the process of the 'Korean industrial revolution'.

Chung Ju-yung has presented himself with exceptional entrepreneurship. He is reportedly the most respected Korean entrepreneur and is looked up to as the so-called 'president' of the Korean economy, the most influential person in the economic arena in Korea.

Although it has been successful so far, Hyundai has yet to meet the challenge of upgrading of its technological edge to become a global player. Hyundai Group has capitalized on cost advantage, not yet catching up with the quality level of the world's leading companies. Hyundai Motors, for example, has stayed still in terms of its quality level, with a reduced share of the US market. Diversification into a variety of industries, which had been beneficial in the period of high growth, became detrimental as the markets of these industries stagnated. President Kim Dae-jung's mandate for major *chaebol* (see CHAEBOLS) groups to improve financial structures and

consolidate over-diversified business structures will put further pressure on Hyundai
Group in its attempt to maintain leadership in
diverse industries.

3 Conclusion

Chung Ju-yung, with unyielding entrepreneurship, has built the Hyundai Group of
companies as major international forces to be
reckoned with, leaving an indelible mark in
the history of Korean economic development.

Nevertheless, there is a question whether
Hyundai Group may remain integrated or not
in the post-Chung Ju-yung period. The
group's businesses are currently under the
control of Chung's sons and nephews, and
may be divided up accordingly. If this scenario takes place, Hyundai Group will be split
into several much smaller groups of firms. Alternatively, however, Hyundai Group may
choose to conform to the expectation of the
government by consolidating its business domain with deeper technological bases.

DONG-SUNG CHO
SEOUL NATIONAL UNIVERSITY

Further reading

Chung Ju-yung (1986) *Ee Achim-edo Seoleim-eul
Anko* [This morning, with the leaps in my
heart], Seoul: Samsung Press. (Chung's memoirs.)
Chung Ju-yung (1992) *Shiryun-eun Isseo-do
shilpae-neun eopda* [There are ordeals, but
there are no failures], Seoul: Jesam-kihoek.
(Chung's autobiography, with a focus on his
business philosophy and lifestyle.)
Chung Ju-yung (1997) *Hankook-kyungje Iyagi*
[The story of the Korean economy], Ulsan: Ulsan University Press. (Chung's views on the development process of the Korean economy and
its future prospects.)
Chung Ju-yung (1998) *Iddang-e taeeo-naseo*
[Born to This Land], Seoul: Sol Press. (Chung's
memoirs.)
Department of Corporate Culture, Hyundai Group
(1997) *Hyundai Osipnyunsa* [Fifty years of
Hyundai], Seoul: Keumkang Kihoek. (Fifty-
year history of Hyundai Group.)
Hyundai Group (1997a) *Building a Better Future*.
(Details the future business strategies of Hyundai Group by industrial sector.)
Hyundai Group (1997b) *Hyundai 97 Handbook –
50th Anniversary Issue of the Group Foundation*. (Describes Hyundai Group's business
structure and profiles affiliate companies, business plans, etc.)

See also: *CHAEBOLS*

Gates, Bill (1955–)

1 Introduction
2 Main contribution
3 Evaluation

Personal background

- born 28 October 1955 in Seattle, Washington
- with a school friend he founded Traf-O-Data, which analysed vehicle traffic data for Seattle area communities; in 1969, when he was 14 years old, Traf-O-Data had revenues of $20,000
- was let off school so that he could work as a full-time computer programmer
- attended Harvard from 1973 to 1975, then dropped out to found Microsoft Corporation
- member of the board of Icos Corporation
- founded Corbis Corporation, which is developing one of the world's largest digital archives of art and photography

1 Introduction

William Henry Gates III was born to William, Jr, a successful Seattle attorney, and the late Mary, a school teacher, University of Washington regent and chairwoman of the United Way International. Bill has an older sister Kristianne and a younger sister Libby (Rosen 1993; Andrews, 1994).

As a child Gates was gifted in mathematics (Rosen 1993; http://www.microsoft.com 1997). At the age of 13 he became interested in computer programming while attending Lakeside School. He wrote a computer program for class scheduling which was implemented by the school. The following year, Gates and his schoolmate Paul Allen cofounded Traf-O-Data, which analysed vehicle traffic data for Seattle area communities. When Gates was 14 years old (1969) Traf-O-Data had revenues of $20,000 (Contemporary Newsmakers 1988;

Rosen 1993; Forbes 1997; http://www.microsoft.com 1997). 'During the last half of his senior year in high school, Gates got permission to forgo classes in favor of working ... as a full-time, $30,000-a-year computer programmer at TRW' (Zuckerman 1990). Gates scored a perfect 800 score on the mathematics portion Scholastic Aptitude Test (SAT) for college admission. After high school he attended Harvard from 1973 to 1975, but then dropped out to pursue his entrepreneurial desires by cofounding Microsoft Corporation with Allen (Contemporary Newsmakers 1988; Chiu and Gallo 1991).

On New Year's Day in 1994 Gates married Melinda French on the Hawaiian Island of Lanai. He met Melinda in 1987 at a Microsoft company picnic (Ellis 1994). In April 1996 their daughter Jennifer Katharine was born (Forbes 1997). The Gates's mansion is a $35-million Bellevue, Washington, waterfront home which has 42,000 square feet and features a 26-car garage, a movie theatre and digital artwork (Ellis 1994; Fortune 1997; Zuckerman 1990).

Gates is a member of the board of Icos Corporation. He also founded Corbis Corporation, which is developing one of the world's largest digital archives of art and photography (http://www.microsoft.com 1997). Gates has established a non-profit foundation, which is administered by his father, which mainly supports education, population control, and the United Way (Gabriel 1996). When the foundation announced that it would be giving computers to 8500 libraries in the US and Canada, the executive director of the American Library Association said: 'Bill Gates is becoming the 21st century's Andrew Carnegie' (Smith 1997).

2 Main contribution

Bill Gates and Paul Allen were excited about the invention of the Altair 8800 microcomputer. Allen convinced Gates to help him write a computer operating system for the new computer. They enjoyed the challenge of creating a system from paper specifications only: 'The two worked nonstop for six weeks to devise an operating system for it [Altair 8800] (Chiu and Gallo 1991). After it worked perfectly they sold a license for the operating system to the manufacturer. Perhaps it was at this point that Bill realized that '[t]he biggest money-makers were going to be operating-system languages and application software' (Rosen 1993). He decided to drop out of Harvard to write and create software with Allen for a market that they believed would be insatiable.

In 1975, at the age of 19, Gates cofounded Microsoft Corporation with Allen (Rosen 1993). They were guided by a belief that the personal computer would be a valuable tool on every office desktop and in every home' (http://www.microsoft.com 1997). The company set up operations in Albuquerque, New Mexico, but in 1979 moved to Bellevue, Washington (Andrews 1994).

The big break came for Microsoft when IBM (see INTERNATIONAL BUSINESS MACHINES CORPORATION) travelled to Redmond, Washington, for a confidential meeting with Gates to discuss the development of an operating system for the new microcomputer IBM was developing. He initially turned IBM's offer down, but then remembered having seen an operating system that could work with the IBM Personal Computer (PC). He purchased the operating system known as QDOS (Quick and Dirty Operating System) for $50,000 and, after making some modifications, sold the licence for MS-DOS to IBM for $125,000. Since Microsoft maintained ownership of MS-DOS, Gates had strategically placed the firm to capitalize on the growth in the marketplace (Rosen 1993; *Forbes* 1997).

In addition to developing operating systems, Microsoft produces application software such as MS-Word and MS-Excel, which run on its own operating systems as well as that of its main competitor, Apple Inc. This strategy has allowed Microsoft to gain a large market share in both the operating systems

and applications portions of the business (Rosen 1993).

Thinking ahead, Gates developed MS-Windows and unveiled it to IBM in 1987. Initially IBM was not inclined to go with Microsoft's new system as the company wanted to develop its own, but Gates was able to convince top management that his firm was two years ahead of IBM and better in touch with customers' needs. This last point got their attention and Gates signed a second major deal with IBM. 'By early 1993, Windows was selling at the rate of one million copies a month' (Rosen 1993).

Gates has also made significant contributions to the 'hardware' side of the business. During the 1980s Gates was among the first to pursue the development and application of CD-ROM technology for the PC. He continues to believe that accessing large volumes of text, music or visual files will eventually almost replace 'hard copy'. He was also involved in the development of the first portable computer, which sold as the Radio Shack model 100, NEC PC-8200 and Olivetti M-10 (*Contemporary Newsmakers* 1988; Gates *et al.* 1995).

In 1995 Gates co-authored *The Road Ahead*, which included a CD-ROM interactive disk and quickly became number one on the *New York Times*'s bestseller list (*Forbes* 1997; http://www.microsoft.com 1997), According to Gates, 'The information highway will have significant effects on all of our lives in the years to come' (Gates *et al.* 1995). An updated version of the book came out in 1996, and this places even more emphasis on the Internet: 'As he acknowledges, he was late to grasp the significance of the Internet's explosive growth, and the book has been rewritten to give it prominence' (Gabriel 1996). Microsoft now publishes an online magazine called *Slate*, and in conjunction with NBC has established a cable news channel (CNBC) along with a world wide web (WWW) news service called MSNBC (*Forbes* 1997).

The guidance and leadership provided by Bill Gates is a large factor in Microsoft being the world's leading provider of software for personal computers. Microsoft has experienced exponential growth. In 1980 the company employed 40 people and by 1983 it had 450 employees; the firm expanded to 5000 employees in 1990, and in 1996 Microsoft had more than 20,000 employees in 48 countries. Microsoft's sales revenues were $8.6 billion in 1996 (Wittner 1983; Zuckerman 1990; http://www.microsoft.com 1997).

3 Evaluation

It has been said that '[h]is technical acuity distinguishes him, perhaps more than any other C.E.O. in America, as a corporate leader who understands every subtlety of his company's products' (Rosen 1993). This may be a result of his staying involved in all phases of the business: 'Gates is actively involved in key management and strategic decisions at Microsoft, and plays and important role in the technical development of new products. A significant portion of his time is devoted to meeting with customers and staying in contact with Microsoft employees around the world through e-mail' (http://www.microsoft.com 1997). Gates's work schedule is long (75 hours per week), and includes most week nights and at least one day on the weekend (Wittner 1983; Chiu and Gallo 1991).

When Microsoft Corporation went public in March 1986 the price per share started at $21 and soared to $35.50, instantly making Bill Gates a multimillionaire (*Contemporary Newsmakers* 1988; Rosen 1993). By the age of 30 Bill Gates was a billionaire (*Economist* 1990). In 1996 Microsoft Corporation shares climbed 74 per cent (Gabriel 1996). The continued success of Microsoft has made Bill Gates the richest man in the world (*Forbes* 1997). Gates's wealth from his Microsoft stock alone was said to be $38.13 billion in October 1997 (Schofield and Smithers 1997).

Both Gates and Microsoft have critics and legal battles continue. In 1992 Gates and Microsoft won a critical legal case when a federal judge ruled that MS-Windows had not infringed the copyrights of Apple Inc.'s operating system (Rosen 1993). In 1995 the company was not as fortunate and Gates announced that 'the Microsoft Corporation was abandoning its planned $2 billion purchase of Intuit Inc., because of the Justice

Department's antitrust challenge to the deal' (Lohr 1995). Microsoft has continued to be criticized because of its marketplace dominance (Schofield and Smithers 1997). In November 1997 Ralph Nadar organized a conference which brought together critics of Microsoft's dominance in PC software. Meanwhile 'Gates defended his company ... He criticized the Justice Department's action ... forcing Microsoft to remove Internet Explorer, its Web Browser, from its Windows 95 operating system, and recommending the company be fined $1 million per day until it does' (Tran 1997). The Federal Government and Attorney-Generals from more than 20 states filed anti-trust lawsuits against Microsoft during the Spring of 1998. Testifying before a US Senate Committee on 3 March 1998 Bill Gates stated that 'Microsoft does not have monopoly power in the business of developing and licensing computer operating systems' (Lawsky 1998b). The Justice Department and the Federal Courts continue to investigate and hear anti-trust complaints against Microsoft, e.g. Caldera Inc., Netscape Communications Corp., Sun Microsystems Inc. (*Reuters* 1998; Lawsky 1998a).

Gates was initially sceptical about the Internet, but by 1995 had changed his mind and had become a believer (*Forbes* 1997). However, his aggressive approach to catching up with software for Internet applications was what created and fuelled the recent rounds of criticism and legal battles. In a 1995 speech 'Gates announced that every Microsoft division would be refocused to develop products for the internet market' (Gabriel 1996).

Bill Gates has demonstrated that he has not only the aptitude to build a large corporation but also the skill to lead and manage a world-class enterprise. *Fortune* magazine selected Microsoft as one of 'America's 10 most admired companies'. The primary reason for the selection was that '[i]n its 12 years of being publicly traded, there's never been a bad time to buy Microsoft' (*Fortune* 1998). In 1996 alone, the stock went up by 56 per cent.

Microsoft's success can in part be attributed to Gates's ability to keep the corporation 'nimble and quick' despite its large size. In addition to avoiding the bureaucratic layers that usually come with organizational size, Gates has been able to create an organizational culture at Microsoft which is both professional and relaxed. He designed the organization headquarters to feel more like a university 'campus' than a corporate facility. This approach has helped to motivate employees and to produce low turnover rates (*Contemporary Newsmakers* 1988; Rosen 1993).

STEPHEN J. HAVLOVIC
SIMON FRASER UNIVERSITY

Further reading

(References cited in the text marked *)

* Andrews, Paul (1994) 'Mary Gates dies', *Seattle Times*, 10 June: A1. (Obituary of Mary Gates.)
* Chiu, Tony and Gallo, Nick (1991) 'If people complain that we have become a nation of followers, they probably haven't met these one-of-a-kind wizards', *People*, 24 October: 72. (Takes a personal look at Gates and his successes at Microsoft.)
* *Contemporary Newsmakers* (1988) 'William H. Gates III'. (Gives personal and professional biographical information.)
* *Economist* (1990) 'Microsoft', *Economist*, 24 March: 72. (Gives an analysis of Microsoft's performance and Gates's ability to lead the company.)
* Ellis, David (1994) 'Love bytes', *People*, 17 January: 42. (Reviews the Hawaiian wedding of Bill Gates and Melinda French.)
* *Forbes Magazine* (1997) 'Forbes 400 richest people in America'.
* *Fortune* (1997) 'Fortune 500' Special issue.
* Gabriel, Trip (1996) 'Catching up with: Bill Gates', *New York Times*, Section C, 28 November: 1. (Profiles Gates during his visit to New York for the release of the paperback version of his book *The Road Ahead*.)
* Gates, Bill, Myhrvold, Nathan and Rinearson, Peter (1995) *The Road Ahead*, Viking. (Reviews the evolution of the PC and discusses future PC

applications as well as the impact of computer technology.)
* Lawsky, David (1998a) 'Microsoft's Gates to testify before Senate', *Reuters*, 14 February. (News release.)
* Lawsky, David (1998b) 'Gates says Microsoft has no monopoly', *Reuters*, 3 March. (News release.)
* Lohr, Steve (1995) 'Gates, the pragmatist, walked away', *New York Times*, Section D, 22 May: 1. (Examines Gates's decision not to pursue the purchase of Intuit Inc.)
* Markoff, John (1992) 'Armistice for Apple and Microsoft', *New York Times*, Section D, 16 July: 1. (Reports an exclusive interview with John Sculley and Bill Gates.)
* *Reuters* (1998) 'Caldera wins a round', *Reuters*, 10 February. (News release.)
* Rosen, Isaac (1993) 'Bill Gates', *Newsmakers*, issue 4. (Gives professional biographical information.)
* Schofield, Jack and Smithers, Rebecca (1997) 'Microsoft and schools: Windows of opportunity', *Guardian* (London), Guardian Features Page Section, 7 October: 15. (Reviews Bill Gates, Microsoft and his assistance in connecting British Schools to the Internet.)
* Smith, Alex Duval (1997) 'Bill Gates donates $200M to put libraries online', *Guardian* (London), Guardian Home Page Section, 25 June: 3. (News release.)
* Tran, Mark (1997) 'Computing on the Net', *Guardian* (London), Guardian OnLine Page Section, 13 November: 4. (Announces a conference for consumer activists against Bill Gates and Microsoft.)
* Wittner, Dale (1993) 'William Gates', *People*, 26 December: 36. (Profiles the 25 Most Intriguing People of 1993.)
* Zuckerman, Ed (1990) 'William Gates III', *People*, 20 August: 91. (Reviews Gates and his business accomplishments.)

Further resources
* http://www.microsoft.com (1997) 'Bill Gates' web page'.

See also: INTERNATIONAL BUSINESS MACHINES CORPORATION

Kim of Daewoo Group

Summary

From its birth in 1967, Daewoo grew rapidly as a textile exporter, later branching out into such diverse industries as trading, heavy machinery, finance, construction, automobile, shipbuilding and home electronics, becoming one of the four major *chaebol* (see *CHAEBOLS*) groups in Korea. Daewoo group's total revenues of $65.1 billion in 1996 placed it twenty-fourth in *Fortune*'s Global 500.

Daewoo means 'the great universe'. At the same time, the second syllable, 'woo', came from the first syllable of the name of its founder, Kim Woo-Choong, who has devoted most of his life to Daewoo Group. Likewise, Daewoo Group without Kim Woo-Choong is almost unthinkable, as major decisions in the group cannot be made without his presence.

1 Biographical data

Kim Woo-Choong (1936–) was born in Taegu, Korea, to university-educated parents. His father devoted his entire life to education, while his mother, a devout Christian, always emphasized the Puritan work ethic to her children.

Hardship began for him during the Korean War, when his father and an elder brother were abducted by North Korean troops. At the age of 14 Kim had to support his mother and four siblings by selling newspapers at local markets.

He attended Kyunggi Senior High School and graduated with a BA in economics from Yonsei University in 1960. Kim began his business career at Hansung Industrial Co. Ltd, then a major textile manufacturer, where he was responsible for exporting products as well as expanding overseas markets.

2 Main contribution

In 1967, with only four other members, Kim launched Daewoo Industrial Co. Ltd, a textile-export company, with $10,000 of capital. The other founding members included Lee Woo-Bock, who was Kim's classmate at Kyunggi Senior High School, Yoon Young-Suk, who was junior to Kim by two years at the school, a typist and a business associate who allegedly contributed part of the capital needed.

This company grew in exports from $580,000 in 1967 to $40 million in 1972. In that year the company was awarded the Order of Industrial Service Merit, Gold Tower, by the Korean government as the second-largest exporter.

In 1973 Daewoo Industrial went public as the first company on the Korean stock exchange to offer stocks at a premium. With the capital secured from profits and stock offerings, Kim began to acquire financially distressed companies in financial services (1973), apparel manufacturing (1973), heavy machinery (1976), shipbuilding (1978) and construction (1984).

In 1976 Kim acquired the loss making Hankook Machinery Ltd and turned it around within a year of the takeover. In 1978 he acquired the Okpo Shipyard, which at the time had twice the asset value of the Daewoo group. This acquisition laid the foundation for Kim's corporate empire as well as establishing his name as a salvager of ailing companies.

By 1978 Daewoo had become the biggest exporter and the fourth-largest *chaebol* group in Korea. Consumer electronics and telecommunications were added to the group's business portfolio in 1983. Daewoo Telecom's 16-bit personal computer Model D became a popular choice in the US market under the Leading Edge brand.

Daewoo's expansion into the emerging markets during the 1970s and the 1980s paved the way for the initiation of diplomatic relations between Korea and Sudan, Libya, Iran, China and Russia. Daewoo established Korea's first commercial office in Eastern Europe in East Berlin in 1988, followed by offices in Prague in 1989 and Moscow in 1990, while a refrigerator plant was dedicated in China in 1988. In 1989 Daewoo formed the first Korean–Chinese joint venture to produce colour-picture tubes. Throughout the 1990s Daewoo continued its leading role in building economic relations with Poland, Ukraine, Romania, Uzbekistan, Vietnam and North Korea.

Overseas automobile investments were the core of Daewoo's globalization and growth strategy in the 1990s. Faced with stiff competition in the saturated domestic market, Kim took charge of the business and led a series of overseas automobile investments in Poland, Uzbekistan, Ukraine, Romania, India, China, Vietnam and the Czech Republic.

During this time another series was initiated in electronics, telecommunications and financial services as Daewoo began overseas electronics manufacturing operations and mobile communication services, while establishing local banks and financial institutions in eighteen nations. At the end of 1997 Daewoo had invested $3.6 billion in more than 400 overseas projects. In 1998 Daewoo had 320,000 employees and 590 business sites around the globe.

3 Conclusion

Kim Woo-Choong continues to exercise hands-on leadership on key strategic issues for the thirty-two affiliated companies of Daewoo Group. His entrepreneurial spirit, long hours of work – typically 110 hours a week and 280 days of travel a year – business insights and visionary leadership have made him a prominent role model for younger Koreans. His autobiography, *It's a Big World and There's Lots to Be Done*, published in 1989, sold 1.36 million copies in Korea. The book has been published in twenty-two languages, including the English translation, *Every Street is Paved with Gold* (Kim 1997).

Kim is widely recognized as a master of deal-making with an unrivalled talent for marketing and sales. However, his intuitive understanding of international economy and finance and his ability to create diverse sources of funding have been the core competence of Daewoo Group as it has actively pursued diversification. At the age of 61 Kim does not show any sign of giving up the hard work, and is due to assume the chairmanship of the Federation of Korean Industries in 1999.

In recent years the overstretched business portfolios of major *chaebol* groups have become a cause of public concern, especially after the Korean financial crisis. President Kim Dae-Jung has been mandating major *chaebol* groups to improve their financial structures and consolidate their overdiversified business structures. Daewoo Group seems to be responding positively to these external pressures with its campaign for a Global Management Plan.

DONG-SUNG CHO
SEOUL NATIONAL UNIVERSITY

Further reading

(References cited in the text marked *)

Asiaweek (1997) 'Daewoo driving to the world', *Asiaweek*, 21 March. (Describes Daewoo Group's investment overseas.)

Asian Wall Street Journal (1997) 'Daewoo believes it's ready to focus on major markets', *Asian Wall Street Journal*, 4 March. (Describes Daewoo Group's investment overseas.)

Daewoo (1997) *Daewoo Fact Book*, Daewoo Group. (Gives details of Daewoo Group's business structure, affiliated companies and major investment plans.)

Far Eastern Economic Review (1997) 'Daewoo's world', *Far Eastern Economic Review*, 1 May. (Describes Daewoo Group's investment overseas.)

Financial Times (1996) 'Passport for Uzbeks to Daewooistan', *Financial Times*, 27 September. (Describes Daewoo Group's investment activities in Uzbekistan.)

Industry Week (1997) 'Daewoo chairman Kim Woo-Choong gambles his company on global expansion', *Industry Week*, 23 June. (Analyses Daewoo Group's global strategy.)

International Herald Tribune (1997) 'Daewoo: a leader in Eastern Europe', *International Herald*

Tribune, 1 September. (Analyses Daewoo Group's investment strategy in East European countries.)

* Kim Woo-choong (1997) *Every Street is Paved with Gold*, New York: Willam Morrow. (Profiles Kim's business philosophy and management style in running Daewoo Group.)

New York Times (1996) 'Daewoo in big bet on Polish car plant', *New York Times*, 24 July. (Describes Daewoo Group's investment in the automobile industry in Poland.)

See also: *CHAEBOLS*

Knight, Philip (1938–)

Personal background

- born 24 February 1938 in Portland, Oregon, to William W. and Lota (Hatfield) Knight
- became a University of Oregon track star under coach Bill Bowerman
- received a BBA from Oregon in 1959
- from 1959 to 1960 served in the US Army, where he attained the rank of first lieutenant
- earnt his MBA from Stanford University in 1962
- in 1962 cofounded Blue Ribbon Sports with Coach Bowerman to import running shoes from Japan
- during the early years of the company he worked as a certified public accountant (CPA) with Price Waterhouse LLP and Coopers & Lybrand accounting firms, and taught accounting as an assistant professor at Portland State University
- in 1968 Bluc Ribbon Sports was incorporated in Oregon as Nike Ltd, the name of the Greek mythological goddess of victory
- currently the chairman and chief executive officer (CEO) of Nike Inc.
- trustee of Reed College and also serves on a number of other boards and advisory committees, including Metheus Corporation, PacifiCorp, National Council on US–China Trade, Asian Business Council and the Stanford University Graduate School
- named the Oregon Business Man of the Year in 1982

1 Introduction

Knight grew up in Portland, where his father published the *Oregon Journal*, a former competitor of the *Oregonian*. It is said that his father was both loving and domineering. Knight's nickname was 'Buck', and he was too small to play contact sports but excelled at track. As a young man, Knight went to work for the *Oregonian* after his father refused to hire him for the summer at the *Oregon Journal*. Legend has it that 'he worked the night shift tabulating sports scores and every morning ran home the full seven miles' (Hauser 1992).

It was during his time at Stanford that he conceived the idea and wrote a paper on starting a shoe company which marketed high-quality athletic shoes using inexpensive Asian labour (*Forbes*, 1996; *Newsmakers*, 1994; Hauser, 1992; *Contemporary Newsmakers*, 1985). When he graduated, in 1962, he founded Blue Ribbons Sports with his former athletics coach, Bill Bowerman. The company was incorporated as Nike Ltd in 1968.

Knight was president of the corporation until 1983, when Robert Woodell was named president and CEO. After Nike did not perform well under Woodell, Knight returned as president in 1984. In 1990 he again passed along the presidency to Richard Donahue, but this time he remained an active and involved CEO (*Daily News Record* 1983; Low 1984; *Daily News Record* 1990).

Knight has been described as 'reclusive, formal, a bit odd'. He is said to have a non-glamorous lifestyle, with the exception of several luxury sports cars, e.g. a black Lamborghini and a red Ferrari (Hauser 1992). He met his wife Penny (Penelope Parks) at Portland State in 1967, when she was a student and he an accounting professor. They were married in September 1968. They now have two grown sons, Matthew and Travis (*Newsmakers* 1994).

Knight is an avid runner (30 miles per week) and plays a competitive game of tennis. The couple enjoy animals and have a variety of pets, including dogs, ferrets, horses and a cat. They live in a hilltop home located on 5 acres near the Nike headquarters in Beaverton, Oregon. Knight is a scholar of Asian history and business. He is said to be fiercely competitive and even has the Nike 'swoosh' logo tattooed on his left calf (*Forbes* 1996; Hauser 1992).

Philip remains Oregon's only billionaire (*Forbes* 1996). In 1993 he was named the *Sporting News'* 'most powerful' person of the year (*Newsmakers* 1994).

2 Main contribution

Philip Knight formed a partnership with his former track coach Bill Bowerman and created what has become the 'world's most successful sporting-goods company' (Hauser 1992). 'Together they determined that American shoes were inferior in style and quality, too heavy, and too easily damaged' (*Newsmakers* 1994). In 1962 he visited the Onitsuka shoe company in Kobe, Japan, where he passed himself off as a shoe importer and spontaneously created Blue Ribbon Sports (Hauser 1992). The company matured as the exclusive US distributor of Onitsuka Tiger shoes in the 1960s and in 1968 became Nike Inc. (*Business Wire* 1984; *Contemporary Newsmakers* 1985; Nike Inc. 1997b). In the early 1970s Knight and cofounder Bowerman were in a dispute with Onitsuka over its decision to end the exclusive Tiger import agreement. It was at this juncture that Knight and Bowerman decided to manufacture their own shoes in Asia (*Contemporary Newsmakers* 1985). In 1971 Knight paid a Portland State student $35 to create a logo for the Nike shoes and she designed the 'swoosh' (http://www.nike.com 1998). 'They shipped their first batch of Nikes ... emblazoned with the now familiar "swoosh" emblem, to the United States just in time for the 1972 Olympic track trials in Eugene, Oregon' (*Contemporary Newsmakers* 1985).

Nike has consistently created high-quality and ingenious products: 'By the mid-70s Nike was at the cutting edge of workout shoe technology' (*Newsmakers* 1994). Thomas Clark has stated that 'One of the reasons why Nike has been successful is that Phil [Knight] had his eye on the horizon instead of on the bottom line' (Hamburg and Hill 1994). The Nike corporate culture rewards teamwork and utilizes a collaborative management style. According to Knight, '[m]aking the most of a changing marketplace has always been one of Nike's greatest strengths' (*PR Newswire* 1994).

In 1980 the company went public (Hauser 1992). One of the few mistakes in Knight's success story occurred in the early 1980s when Nike did not recognize that aerobics was more than a temporary fad. This allowed upstart Reebok to corner the market for aerobic exercise shoes. However, Nike quickly recovered and gained market share after Knight returned as president in 1984 (*Newsmakers* 1994).

'In 1990 Knight opened his $147 million Nike World Campus headquarters, complete with three restaurants for employees, a jogging track, a discount dry cleaner and a daycare center' (Hauser 1992). By 1990 sales for Nike Inc. were in excess of $2 billion (*Daily News Record* 1990).

During the 1990s Knight led Nike into the global marketplace. In addition to athletic footwear and apparel, Nike also produces dress and casual shoes through its Cole Haan subsidiary, and licensed headwear through its Sports Specialties subsidiary (*PR Newswire* 1994). By the end of fiscal year 1997 Nike's total annual revenue exceeded $9 billion (Nike Inc. 1997a).

Knight's aggressive marketing has established new approaches which have been noteworthy and often controversial. 'Nike slogans – Bo Knows, It's Gotta Be the Shoes, and especially Just Do It – have entered the pop-culture lexicon' (*Newsmakers* 1994). The marketing strategy has involved endorsement of their products by well-known athletes (e.g. Michael Jordan, Chicago Bulls; Reggie White, Green Bay Packers; Tiger Woods, Professional Golf Association) and sports teams (e.g. Brazil's national soccer team, American universities).

3 Evaluation

Under the leadership of Philip Knight, Blue Ribbon Sports and its successor Nike Inc. have experienced exponential growth. 'Knight was an early believer in jogging, but even he never envisioned the speed and vastness of the nation's conversion to the pastime in the mid-1970s, nor could he imagine that the "jogging look" would become so fashionable that non-athletes would sport Nikes by the million' (*Contemporary Newsmakers* 1985). Knight's success has, however, not come without considerable controversy regarding Nike's manufacturing strategies and operations. Part of Knight's business strategy has been to manufacture Nike shoes by using low-wage Asian contract labour. In 1997 subcontractors employed almost 500,000 Asian workers in countries such as Korea, Vietnam and China to manufacture Nike shoes (http://www.nike.com). The company claims that this approach is required to offer competitively priced high-quality shoes.

There are numerous groups who resent and protest against Philip Knight and Nike. Some of these groups have organized boycotts (e.g. PUSH) against Nike's products (Daley 1990). Ricky Hendon stated that 'Nike does not provide jobs that many Americans need, and they are even more insensitive to the black community' (Rudd 1990). Nike has been accused of violating human rights and running sweatshops (Tran 1997). The boycotts and accusations appear to have got Nike's attention, as a contractor labour code and independent auditing procedures have been initiated to improve and monitor working conditions (http://www.nike.com 1998). In a few cases subcontractors have lost their contracts (e.g. Korea) because of failing to comply with new minimum-wage or workplace standards imposed by Nike (Tran 1997).

In fiscal year 1997 Nike achieved its best performance to date, with a 42 per cent increase in revenues from the previous year, to $9.19 billion (Nike Inc. 1997a). It will prove difficult for Nike to repeat this performance in 1998, with the Asian economic crisis and sales off by 20 per cent in the second quarter (*Seattle Times* 1998). Adidas has also managed to re-emerge as an aggressive competitor. While analysts and competitors suggest that Nike will have a difficult time increasing its global market share (e.g. Himelstein 1997), given Knight's past record and the company's aggressive marketing style he will likely prove otherwise.

STEPHEN J. HAVLOVIC
SIMON FRASER UNIVERSITY

Further reading

(References cited in the text marked *)

* *Business Wire* (March 14 1984) 'Pacific-power; directors declare dividends, elect new board member, approve company name change'.
* *Contemporary Newsmakers* (1985) 'Philip H. Knight'. (Gives personal and professional biographical information.)
* *Daily News Record* (1983) 'Woodell president of Nike', *Daily News Record* 13, 16 June: 7. (News release.)
* *Daily News Record* (1990) 'Donahue joining Nike as president', *Daily News Record* 20, 19 June: 4. (News release.)
* Daley, Steve (1990) 'PUSH, Nike talk, but boycott still on', *Chicago Tribune*, Business Section, 25 August: 1. (Discusses the boycott facing Nike.)
* *Forbes* (1996) 'The Forbes four hundred – Philip Hampson Knight'. (Gives biographical information.)
* Hamburg, Ken and Hill, Jim (1994) 'Nike official promoted to no. 2 job', *Oregonian*, Business Section, 15 February. (News release.)
* Hauser, Susan (1992) 'Must be the shoes', *People*, 4 May: 139. (Takes a personal look at Knight and the business he built.)
* Himelstein, Linda (1997) 'The swoosh heard "round the world"', *Business Week*, 12 May: 76. (Provides an in-depth examination of Nike's marketing tactics.)
* Low, Kathleen (1984) 'Knight again takes Nike reins', *Footwear News* 40, 24 September: 1. (Discusses Knight's decision to return as president.)
* *Newsmakers* (1994) 'Philip Knight', *Newsmakers*, issue 4. (Provides personal and professional biographical information.)
* Nike Inc. (1997a) *Annual Report*.
* Nike Inc. (1997b) *10-K*.
* *PR Newswire* (1994) 'Nike names Dr. Thomas E. Clarke president-elect Richard K. Donahue to

become vice chairman', *PR Newswire*, 14 February. (News release.)

* Rudd, David C. (1990) 'Supporters try to widen Nike boycott', *Chicago Tribune*, Chicagoland Section, 20 August: 3. (Reviews the Nike boycott.)

* *Seattle Times* (1998) 'Nike's chief financial officer Robert Falcone resigns', *Seattle Times*, Business Digest, 9 January: C4. (News release.)

Strasser, J.B. and Becklund, Laurie (1991) *Swoosh: The Unauthorized Story of Nike and the Men Who Played There*, Harcourt Brace Jovanovich Inc. (Presents a biography which Philip Knight claims does not represent the true story.)

* Tran, Mark (1997) 'Nike boots out clothing firms', *Guardian* (London), Guardian City Page: 23 September: 17. (Announces that Nike is cracking down on contractors.)

Further resources

* http://www.nike.com (1998) 'Frequently asked questions'.

Koo family of LG Group

1 Biographical data
2 Main contribution
3 Conclusion

Summary

Starting in 1947 with a chemical business, LG Group has grown into a cluster of companies in electronics, telecommunications, semiconductors, securities and oil refining. Its total annual revenues of $73 billion in 1996 put the group among the four largest *chaebols* (see *CHAEBOLS*) in Korea. Its affiliated companies, LG International and LG Electronics, were ranked 216th and 270th in *Fortune*'s Global 500 in 1997, with revenues of $17.3 billion and $14.8 billion.

Unlike other *chaebols* in Korea, LG Group has been forged as a coalition of two families, Koos and Huhs. The Koo family has occupied the chairmanship for three generations: Koo In-hwoi, the founder, Koo Cha-kyung, his son, then Koo Bon-moo, the grandson. Due to the partnership of the two families, however, the group has nurtured a unique corporate culture based on 'In-hwa' (harmony among people).

1 Biographical data

Koo In-hwoi (1907–1970)

Koo In-hwoi, the founder of the LG Group, was born into a conservative family. He took care of family matters until 1947 when he started his first business in Pusan, the second-largest city on the south-east coast of Korea. He manufactured cosmetics and had huge success with facial creams. In 1951 he entered into plastics to manufacture cases to contain cosmetics. The plastics business induced him in 1958 to move into the home electronics industry, which required such components as plastic fans and chassis, and into the telecommunications industry, which also required plastic components such as telephone shells. In each move Koo marked the start of a domestic industry in Korea. Koo made successive entries into new businesses, including the cable industry in 1962 and oil refining in 1967.

He died at the age of 63, and the management of the group was passed to his eldest son, Koo Cha-kyung.

Koo Cha-Kyung (1925–)

Koo learnt the trade from his father and worked his way up to the position of manager. Later, in the 1970s and 1980s he diversified and concentrated on R&D. In 1995 he reorganized the groups diversified businesses to get rid of the rigidity imposed by centralization, and in the same year he handed over the group chairmanship to his eldest son, Koo Bon-moo.

Koo Bon-moo (1945–)

On graduating from Ashland College, Ohio, US, Koo Bon-moo joined LG Chemical as manager in 1975. He became group chairman in 1995. In 1998 Koo assumed the positions of chairman and chief executive officer (CEO) of LG Chemical and LG Electronics as a part of the broad-based corporate restructuring.

2 Main contribution

Koo In-hwoi

Koo In-hwoi placed high priority on the human side of management in running companies. He once said that good employees and good customers make a good company. This emphasis on the human aspect has become a key criterion in every strategic move of the group, whether diversification into new business fields or investment abroad.

Koo Cha-Kyung

Koo Jr had on-the-job training from his father as he helped him with sales of facial cosmetics. Koo also believed that corporate activities are performed and governed by the people, and that the ultimate goal of the firm is to contribute to the general welfare of the people. It was in this vein that he set a rule for all family members, even his sons, to compete from the lowest level to become a manager.

He diversified the group's business domain into securities, machinery, construction, finance and semiconductors through either internal development or acquisition. LG Group's growth in the 1970s and 1980s, which was less than that of its arch rivals Samsung and Hyundai, proved his conservative inclination. Instead, Koo focused on R&D until the middle of the 1980s, when he started a management innovation programme to make a leap as a global company in the twenty-first century.

In 1995 he reorganized LG Group's highly diversified businesses into twenty-one autonomous business culture units and announced the LG Group Management Constitution, which laid out the future vision of the company. Special emphasis was put on autonomous management. Koo, recognizing the inefficiency of the highly centralized organization as the group grew in both scale and scope, put professional managers in firm control of each business. He also carried out a Corporate Identity (CI) project to present the group with a clear and integrated identity across the world.

Koo Bon-moo

Since his inauguration as the group chairman, he has initiated drastic changes not only in the business structure but also in the LG culture. Instead of the traditional low-profile attitude, Koo Bon-moo has exercised strong leadership by solidifying the group image under the slogan of globalization.

LG Group

With a careful balance between conservatism and commitment to technological leadership, LG Group has developed a unique model that many Korean firms have emulated, making substantial contributions to the growth of the Korean economy. LG group has also developed a unique human-centred corporate culture based on traditional Korean values. Based on 'In-hwa', LG Group has built mutual trust between employees and management. In the 1990s the group applied the same human-centred principle to creating a new vision that called for customers as king. As a result, LG Group is widely considered by college graduates to be one of the best companies to work for. Because of the rather extensive involvement of Koo and Huh families in the management of group firms, however, the group offers limited opportunities for professional managers.

LG Group, like all the other major *chaebol* groups in Korea, is facing pressure from the government of President Kim Dae-jung to restructure its business portfolio and to improve its financial structure. With its emphasis on human harmony, which can also be applied to the group's harmony with the surrounding society, LG Group seems to be poised to accommodate the changes mandated by the government.

3 Conclusion

Although it is not as visible as the founding families in other major *chaebol* groups in Korea, the Koo family has guided the group through the ebb and tide of the Korean economy with its balanced approach to conservatism and technological leadership. It is no surprise that LG Group is generally considered in Korea to be the group to watch in the twenty-first century. The Koo family has itself practised 'In-hwa' (human harmony): the family has harmoniously run the group together with the Huh family, with whom it co-founded the group in 1947. Worth evaluating also is the harmony which the Koo family has shown in the succession of chairmanship. Not the tiniest incident took place among family members regarding the inheritance of sizeable fortunes.

DONG-SUNG CHO
SEOUL NATIONAL UNIVERSITY

Further reading

Business Korea (1996) 'New challenges for Korean conglomerates', February. (Analyses the challenges that Korean *chaebols* are facing.)

Financial Times (1997) 'A Korea change', 8 August. (Describes the development of the Korean economy and the evolution and tasks of the Korean *chaebol*.)

Koo Cha-kyung (1993) *Crisis, Customers and Change: A Vision for Excellence*, Seoul: Lucky Ltd. (Presents anecdotes that illustrate the business philosophy and management style of Koo Cha-kyung.)

LG Group (1997) *LG Oshipnyun-sa: 1947–1997* [The fifty-year history of LG: 1947–1997], Seoul: LG Group. (Tells the fifty-year history of LG Group, with a detailed description of its formation and development.)

See also: *CHAEBOLS*

Kroc, Ray (1902–1984)

Personal background

- born 5 October 1902 in Oak Park, Illinois
- served in the Red Cross in the First World War
- began selling paper cups for Lily-Tulip and, after a time as a professional pianist, returned to his job as a salesman
- in 1941 obtained franchise rights for the Prince Castle Multi-Mixer and created the Prince Castle Sales Division; to pursue this business venture he borrowed money and paid Lily-Tulip for the time remaining on his work contract
- in 1954 he met the McDonald brothers and made an agreement with them to franchise their restaurant
- opened his first McDonald's restaurant in Des Plaines, Illinois in 1955
- opened the 100th McDonald's restaurant in 1958
- in 1961 paid the McDonald brothers $2.7 million for exclusive ownership of the name, trademarks, copyrights, formulas and the golden arches
- McDonald's Corporation went public in 1965
- ran the business until 1968, after which he served as chairman
- established the Kroc Foundation in 1969 to help find cures for arthritis, diabetes and multiple sclerosis
- in 1972 gave away $7.5 million in McDonald's Corporation stock to charities and individuals
- received many awards, including the Horatio Alger Award in 1972 and the Outstanding Chicagoan of Today in 1975

1 Introduction

Kroc was the son of Bohemian immigrants, Louis and Rose Kroc. He was the eldest of three children. His father worked for Western Union in Chicago, and his mother was a housewife who played the piano for pleasure and extra income.

Kroc loved music and as a child enjoyed playing the piano (Boas and Chain 1976). As a boy he was known to his family as 'Danny Dreamer' for his continuous daydreaming (Kroc and Anderson 1977; Steele 1983). During the First World War, at the age of 16, he left school and joined the Red Cross. He was assigned to France, where he drove an ambulance. He was later reassigned as a piano player and performed at officer's parties (Boas and Chain 1976).

After the war he worked briefly in Chicago as a stockbroker, and then began to play piano in local orchestras. By 1922 he was married to his first wife Ethel (Fleming). After marrying he began selling paper cups for Lily-Tulip (Fishwick 1983). Shortly after the birth of his daughter Marilyn in 1924, Ray returned to playing the piano as a second job on the radio with the newly formed WGES. In 1925 Ray moved the family to Florida, where he sold real estate, but by 1926 he was broke and moved back to Chicago, where he resumed selling paper cups for Lily-Tulip. In 1941 Ray obtained franchise rights for the Prince Castle Multi-Mixer and created the Prince Castle Sales Division (Fishwick 1983). In order to pursue this business venture he borrowed money and paid Lily-Tulip for the time remaining on his work contract ($85,000). It was during the subsequent sales calls that he became familiar with inefficient kitchens and poor-quality food (Boas and Chain 1976).

In 1954, at the age of 52, after receiving a large order for multi-mixers from a San Bernardino hamburger stand, he met the McDonald brothers. 'Ray Kroc showed up there one day after deciding that he wanted a first hand look at an operation that found it necessary to make forty-eight milkshakes at the same time' (Boas and Chain 1976). He was amazed by the sight of so many customers flocking to the 'golden arches'. After several hours of observing the long lines, Kroc became convinced that this restaurant would work anywhere in the world. He was particularly impressed by the speed, simplicity, efficiency, quality and value of the operation. Kroc studied the operation for several days and estimated that this one restaurant was doing $250,000 per year in sales. Ray sold the McDonald brothers on the idea of franchising their restaurant and promised to send them payments to supplement the earnings from their successful restaurant (Boas and Chain 1976). The franchising agreement gave Kroc nationwide rights for ten years. He paid the two McDonald brothers 0.5 per cent of sales and they did not permit him to charge franchisees more than 1.9 per cent of sales (Emerson 1990). In April 1955 Kroc opened his first McDonald's restaurant in Des Plaines, Illinois (http://www.mcdonalds.com 1998). He would quickly become a leader and role model in establishing business franchises.

For a while Kroc continued to sell multi-mixers along with McDonald's franchises (Boas and Chain 1976). In the mid-1950s he approached his suppliers for a loan to help him through a financial crisis caused by building eight restaurants on sites without clear property titles. At that time his net worth was $90,000. Kroc figured correctly that his suppliers had the most to gain or suffer and they came to his rescue (*Institutional Distribution* 1985; Fishwick 1983).

By 1958 Ray had opened the 100th McDonald's restaurant. In 1961 Ray borrowed money to pay Dick and Mac McDonald $2.7 million for exclusive ownership of the name, trademarks, copyrights, formulas and the golden arches (Kroc and Anderson 1977). By 1962 McDonald's system-wide sales were $76.2 million. In 1965 McDonald's Corporation went public (Fishwick 1983). Kroc continued to run the business until 1968, when he appointed Fred Turner as president of McDonald's Corporation. While Kroc continued to serve as chairman, he played a less

active role, and maintained homes in Chicago and Florida, as well as a ranch in California. In 1972 he purchased the San Diego Padres and seemed to enjoy being the team owner during his 'retirement' (Kroc and Anderson 1977).

Kroc has been criticized 'for the cavalier manner in which he disposed of two wives as he clawed up the sides of the mountain of success' (Steele 1983). He separated and later divorced his first wife Ellen after falling in love in the late 1950s with Joni (Joan Beverly Smith). After the younger Joni decided not to divorce her husband to marry him, he moved to California, where he met John Wayne's secretary Jane Dobbins Green in 1963. After dating for only two weeks, they were married and moved into a home in Beverly Hills. Five years later Joni changed her mind and decided to divorce her husband to marry Kroc. According to Kroc, 'as fond as I was of Jane, the more I thought about being away from Joni ... the more impossible it became' (Kroc and Anderson 1977). He immediately pursued a divorce, and Joni and Ray were married at his ranch in Southern California on 8 March 1969 (Kroc and Anderson 1977; *Forbes* 1996).

In 1969 the Kroc Foundation was established to help find cures for arthritis, diabetes and multiple sclerosis (Boas and Chain 1976; King 1983). In 1972, on his 70th birthday, Kroc gave away $7.5 million in McDonald's Corporation stock to charities and individuals (Boas & Chain, 1976; Kroc & Anderson, 1977).

The Kroc family is not active in running McDonald's corporation. However, Joni remains on the *Forbes* four hundred list of wealthiest Americans, with her inheritance listed at $1.7 billion (1996).

2 Main contribution

Ray Kroc went from being a Chicago milkshake-machine salesman to founding McDonald's Corporation, which became the world's largest fast-food operation (*Forbes* 1996; Emerson 1990). System-wide sales totalled $31.8 billion in fiscal year 1996, and by April 1997 McDonald's Corporation had more than 21,000 restaurants in over 100 countries. Approximately

85 percent of these restaurants are owned and operated by franchisees (http://www.mcdonalds.com 1998).

Kroc is credited with improving the original production line devised by the McDonald brothers by using standardization, volume and profit as main objectives (Boas and Chain 1976). 'Inspired by F.W. Woolworth's idea of selling commodities at low fixed prices, Kroc applied Henry Ford's lessons of the assembly line and of efficiency studies to "strip down" the process of receiving, cooking, warming or freezing, packing, and serving to their barest possible components' (King 1983). Kroc initiated and developed strong internal quality and training standards, including Hamburger University, a state of the art training facility for restaurant management (http://www.mcdonalds.com 1998). From the 1950s Kroc insisted on quality, service and cleanliness in his restaurants, and later add value to form the McDonald's QSCV standard (Boas and Chain 1976; King 1983).

In addition to being a pioneer in fast-food and limited-menu concepts, Kroc also was among the first to develop one-stop purchasing among multi-unit operators (*Institutional Distribution* 1985). 'Through this diffused system of highly recognizable icons and architecture which function as havens of security and certainty under their golden arches, McDonald's has created an entire network of reassuring predictability. It provides a definite "known," for both travelers and for local patrons, in an uncertain cosmos' (King 1983). The relative cost of a meal at McDonald's has even been adopted as an informal measure of a country's cost of living, i.e. the McDonald's index.

Kroc, with the guidance of Harry Sonneborn, created Franchise Realty Corporation, which leases property from its owners and then sublets the property to McDonald's franchisees (Fitzell 1983; Emerson 1990). This has allowed McDonald's Corporation to make significant profits as a landlord above the sales commission obtained from franchises. In addition, by using this process to build his fast-food business, Kroc established major real-estate holdings for the corporation (Morgenstern 1992).

Kroc initiated McDonald's philosophy of community service. This is reflected in the Kroc Foundation and in Ronald McDonald House Charities (http://www.mcdonalds.com). Today Ronald McDonald Houses provide overnight accommodation across the US and Canada for families of children who are hospital patients. These houses receive funding from the Kroc Foundation, as well as from McDonald's franchise owners and operators (McCarthy 1985).

3 Evaluation

Kroc has been noted for his farsightedness and for hiring the best talent to guide the corporation (Fitzell 1983). 'Ray Kroc ... predicted in 1955 that the "Hamburger Science" of McDonald's was a system that could be reduced to a formula that would govern all aspects of the operation and could be taught to unskilled people with impunity' (King and King 1983).

Some claim that McDonald's changed world dining expectations by establishing service, price, quality and cleanliness benchmarks (King 1983). McDonald's has established and maintains strict quality and operating standards. Kroc set the standards himself, and created a research and evaluation lab (Fitzell 1983).

While Kroc was very generous with his charitable contributions, he refused to give money to colleges and universities. According to him, 'Our colleges are crowded with young people who are learning a lot about liberal arts and little about earning a living' (Kroc and Anderson 1977). However, when it came to causes he believed in, Ray was a very generous philanthropist. The Kroc Foundation and Ronald McDonald Houses continue to fund medical research and to provide assistance to families with sick children.

STEPHEN J. HAVLOVIC
SIMON FRASER UNIVERSITY

Further reading

* Boas, Max and Chain, Steve (1977) *Big Mac: The Unauthorized Story of McDonald's,* New York:

New American Library Inc. (A behind the scenes exposé.)

* Emerson, Robert L. (1990) *The New Economics of Fast Food*, New York: Van Nostrand Reinhold. (Provides a thorough examination of the fast-food industry.)

* Fishwick, Marshall (1983) 'Introduction', *Ronald Revisited: The World of Ronald McDonald*, Bowling Green, OH: BGU Popular Press. (Provides an introduction to Ray Kroc and McDonald's Corporation.)

* Fitzell, Phillip (1983) 'The man who sold the first McDonald's hamburger', *Ronald Revisited: The World of Ronald McDonald*, Bowling Green, OH: BGU Popular Press. (Takes a look at the early years of the corporation and the practices established by Ray Kroc.)

* Forbes (1996) 'The Forbes four hundred'. (Lists the wealthiest Americans.)

Indonesian Commercial Newsletter (1995) 'Indonesia has the potential to develop the franchise business', 11 September. (Discusses franchising opportunities in Indonesia.)

* *Institutional Distribution* (1985) 'Systems distributors; foodservice distribution: the evolution of an industry', *Institutional Distribution* 21: 235. (Provides an in-depth look at food distribution in the fast-food industry.)

* King, Margaret J. (1983) 'Empires of popular culture: McDonald's and Disney', *Ronald Revisited: The World of Ronald McDonald*, Bowling Green, OH: BGU Popular Press. (Discusses the business standards established by Ray Kroc and McDonald's Corporation and their impact on society.)

* King, Sarah Sanderson and King, Michael J. (1983) 'Hamburger University', *Ronald Revisited: The World of Ronald McDonald*, Bowling Green, OH: BGU Popular Press. (Takes a look at a school established for training McDonald's managers and maintaining quality and efficiency standards.)

* Kroc, Ray and Anderson, Robert (1977) *Grinding It Out: The Making of McDonald's,* Chicago, IL: H. Regnery. (Autobiography.)

* McCarthy, Peggy (1985) 'New home for kin of ailing youngsters', *New York Times,* Section 11CN, 5 May: 16. (Announces the opening of the New Haven Ronald McDonald House and discusses the assistance these houses provide to families with sick children.)

* Morgenstern, Henry (1992) 'Big Mac comes to Israel', *Israel Business Today*, 6(305), 27 November: 15. (Takes a look at how McDonalds made a successful entry into the Israeli market.)

* Steele, Michael R. (1983) 'What can we learn from Ronald?', *Ronald Revisited: The World of Ronald McDonald,* Bowling Green, OH: BGU Popular Press. (Reviews Ray Kroc and the institutions he left behind.)

Further resources

* http://www.mcdonalds.com (1998) (Provides McDonald's Corporation information.)

Lee family of Samsung Group

Summary

Samsung, which means 'three stars', is widely considered the most representative of the Korean *chaebol* (see *CHAEBOLS*) groups. Samsung Group has grown with the industrialization and globalization of the Korean economy. Samsung has been at the forefront of Korean economic growth for a long time and has exerted one of the most profound influences on it.

Founded in 1938 by Lee Byung-chull, who was succeeded by his third son, Lee Kun-hee, in 1987, Samsung Group is one of the most diversified of all *chaebol* groups, with its presence in electronics, semiconductors, textiles, heavy machinery, shipbuilding, construction, trading, insurance and retail business. Samsung Group's 260,000 employees worldwide and annual revenues of $92.7 billion in 1996 made it one of the biggest *chaebol* groups in Korea. Its affiliated companies Samsung Corporation, Samsung Electronics and Samsung Life Insurance were ranked 71st, 124th and 212th in *Fortune*'s Global 500 in 1997, with revenues of $34.3 billion, $24.7 billion and $17.5 billion, respectively.

1 Biographical data

Lee Byung-chull (1911–1987)

Lee Byung-chull was born in Uiryong, Kyungsang-namdo, in 1911 as Korea came under the power of Japanese colonialists. Lee spent his younger years attending traditional Korean schools, then went to Waseda University in Tokyo, Japan.

Lee's journey into business began in 1938 at the age of 27, when he founded Samsung Co. to specialize in the processing and export of rice. Based on this commercial capital, he established Samsung Moolsan Co., the mother company of Samsung Group, in 1948.

During the 1950s and 1960s Lee concentrated on import-substitutive goods such as sugar and woollen fibre. Based on these daily necessities, Samsung became the first and largest *chaebol* in Korea as early as the 1960s.

In the 1970s Lee shifted focus to machinery, engineering and construction in line with the change in the Korean government's policy towards the heavy-industrial sectors. In the 1980s Lee moved into the defence and aerospace industries. In the meantime Samsung Electronics developed into a global player in a wide range of businesses, including consumer electronics, industrial electronics, computers, telecommunications and core parts including semiconductors.

The last and perhaps the most successful decision made by Lee Byung-chull was the large-scale manufacture of semiconductors through Samsung Electronics Co. in the early 1980s. Samsung Electronics soon became the world's largest supplier of leading-edge products, and semiconductors became the most profitable component of the group's extensive portfolio of businesses. Following its successful production of 256 K-DRAM chips, Samsung developed 1 M-DRAM chips for mass production in 1985 and showed to the world Korea's potential for high-tech industry.

Lee Kun-hee (1942–)

Lee Kun-hee, the third son of Lee Byung-chull took over the chairmanship of Samsung group in 1987. (His two elder brothers had left Samsung Group and started their own businesses, due in part to a difference of opinion with their father.) Lee also brought a dramatically different personal style to his job. He separated a number of affiliated companies, including Shinsegae Department Store, Cheil

Sugar, Saehan Video and Hansol Paper, from Samsung Group by sharing them among his brothers and sisters. Instead, he concentrated investment in four major sectors: electronics, engineering, chemicals and finance. Nevertheless, his 1992 decision to move into the automotive industry as a means of coping with Samsung's arch rival Hyundai has been draining the group financially.

2 Main contribution

Lee Byung-chull

Even though he did not complete his studies at Waseda University, Lee has conducted his businesses with a distinct philosophy and a rigorous discipline that have become a model for other Korean companies. Lee's philosophy could be summed up as 'service to the nation through business', while his discipline called for a capable workforce based on rationality. As Korean society can be characterized as one guided by human contact and emotional elements, Lee's adherence to rationality became the most important ingredient of the firm.

Lee's vision for the future took him beyond the realm and boundaries of ordinary business tycoons. He devoted himself to preserving the nation's cultural heritage by establishing the Ho-Am Art Museum, the largest private museum in Asia.

By 1987, when Lee Byung-chull died, Samsung's business portfolio reflected Korean gross national product (GNP) – chemical, trading, mass media, heavy industry, construction, electronics, insurance, department stores, hotels and so on.

Lee Kun-hee

Having been educated at Waseda University and George Washington University, Lee Kun-hee emphasized innovative management and globalization.

Samsung Group

The history of Korea's economic development cannot be traced without tracing the history of Samsung Group. The Samsung group of companies has made substantial contributions to Korea as the first and one of the largest *chaebol* groups from the 1950s to the 1990s. Entering into the manufacturing of import-substitutive sugar and woollen fibre products in the 1950s and then export-oriented home electronics and machinery products in the 1960s and the 1970s, Samsung grew in parallel with the evolution of the Korean government's trade-related policies. In the 1980s Samsung laid the foundations for chemicals and semiconductors through massive capital investment in R&D and plant facilities.

Samsung is characterized by its emphasis on 'First-ism'. This emphasis is translated into market leadership in each industry Samsung participates in. It also implies the group's role as a leading force in the economic development of the nation by possessing leading-edge technologies. Most importantly, this emphasis is translated into recruiting only the best and brightest among the university graduates and grooming them as the most capable managers through its extensive and rigorous in-house training programmes.

3 Conclusion

Samsung has achieved remarkable success in the Korean market, as the Samsung brand has become synonymous with quality. The power of Samsung is embedded into Koreans' lives. Samsung's domestic success, however, will not enable it to become a real force to be reckoned with in the global market, in spite of its aggressive investment and extensive operations in global markets.

The future of Samsung Motors, which is still unclear, will largely determine the fate of Samsung Group as a whole. The mandates on *chaebol* restructuring as declared by President Kim Dae-jung will put pressure on Samsung Group's attempt to maintain diversity in its business portfolio. Given the symbolic importance of Samsung in Korea, the success of the government's policy on *chaebols* will be dependent on Samsung's restructuring plans, as yet unannounced.

DONG-SUNG CHO
SEOUL NATIONAL UNIVERSITY

Further reading

Business Week (1994) 'Samsung: a management revolution', *Business Week*, 28 February. (Describes Samsung Group's overall effort on management innovation.)

Fortune (1993) 'How Samsung grows so fast', *Fortune*, 3 May. (Presents the major characteristics of Samsung Group's growth strategy.)

Joongang-ilbo (1997) 'Leebyungchull-hoejang Shipjooki: Hoam-sasang Jae-jomyung' ['The 10 years after Chairman Lee Byung-chull's death'], 19 November. (Presents recollections on the late Lee Byung-chull by his friends and acquaintances.)

Samsung Group (1996) *Samsung Annual Report*.

Samsung Group (1997a) *Samsung Press Information*, Samsung Press. (A collection of newspaper clippings featuring Samsung Group.)

Samsung Group (1997b) *Samsung's New Management*, Samsung Group. (An internal document which gives a detailed explanation of the true meaning of 'Samsung's new management' and its strategic implications.)

See also: *CHAEBOLS*

Li Ka-Shing (1928–)

Personal background

- born 1928 in the fishing village of Chaoz-hou, Guangdong (Southern China), the eldest son of a school teacher, but the family moved to Hong Kong in 1939, after the outbreak of the Second World War, and Li started to work at the age of 14
- started a plastic factory in 1945, focusing on making plastic toys and small household utensils
- during late 1950s and early 1960s specialized in producing plastic flowers for export to Europe and the United States, and was called the 'king of plastic flowers'
- in 1958 bought his first piece of land and built a twelve-storey factory
- with a decline in the demand for plastic products in the late 1960s, Li gradually moved into real-estate development, buying a lot of land at low prices during 1967, when Hong Kong was experiencing riots and social instability due to the influences of the Cultural Revolution in China.
- in 1972 Cheung Kong (Holdings) was publicly listed on the stock exchange, perfect timing because Hong Kong's first stock-market and property-market boom began at this time
- in 1979 Li bought a 22.4 per cent share in Hutchison Whampoa, a British firm, from Hong Kong and Shanghai Banking Corporation, making it the only Chinese group which had a controlling interest in a British firm
- at the same time, started to invest in China by engaging in joint ventures with Chinese firms
- in 1986 bought 23 per cent of Hong Kong Electric through Hutchison Whampoa from Jardines, another British *hong* (trading conglomerate)
- the Li group also moved into the international arena: Hutchison Whampoa purchased 50 per cent of Husky Oil in Canada; engaged in the real-estate development of the Expo site in Vancouver; invested in the UK by taking a 5 per cent share in the Pearson Group and the Cable & Wireless Group in 1987
- in 1988 Hutchison Whampoa and Proctor & Gamble (P&G) (see PROCTOR & GAMBLE COMPANY) entered into a joint venture with a mainland Chinese enterprise to build a P&G plant in Guangzhou, China
- in 1989 received the CBE (Commander of the British Empire) medal from the United Kingdom for his contributions to Britain
- in 1990 Li's empire extended into the hi-tech communication sector – in Hong Kong, a satellite television company, StarTV, and Hutchison Telecom for paging services were formed; the Asian market was also covered, especially Singapore
- in 1990 the US market was started through a partnership with Gordon Investment in junk bonds business (though this failed), and by pursuing real-estate development in California and New York
- in 1991 Li increased his involvement in the British paging and cellular-phone market by purchasing Microtel
- with the opening of the Chinese economy, major projects in China were undertaken, such as container ports and power-generation plants in Shanghai and Guangdong
- appointed to the Draft Committee of Basic Law and the Preparatory Committee of Hong Kong Special Administrative Region by the Chinese government, to facilitate the return of Hong Kong to China
- in 1997, when the handover took place, a new company, Cheung Kong Infrastruc-

ture, owned by Hutchison Whampoa, was created for infrastructure business development in China, and Cheung Kong Holdings became the parent of Hutchison Whampoa

1 Introduction

Li Ka-Shing, often referred to as 'superman Li' by Hong Kong people, started his empire with a tiny investment in the plastic flower business in the 1950s. Li was able to turn the initial investments into multi-billion multinational corporations. As the first Chinese to control a British *hong*, Li changed the competitive landscape in Hong Kong from the late 1970s through the network of two key holding companies, Cheung Kong (literally, Yangtze river) and Hutchison Whampoa in Hong Kong. Li has built a $60-billion business empire, with a personal interest estimated at over $16 billion in these two companies alone.

He is perceived as a businessman with a traditional Chinese culture but with Western management skills. His business philosophy is characterized by many traditional Chinese cultural attributes, such as face-giving, mean (adopting a middle-of-the-road approach by avoiding extremes), reciprocity and trust. His ability to identify and pursue business opportunities strategically all over the world is a critical success factor in his empire.

2 Major contribution

There is no doubt that Li Ka-Shing is a symbol of the Hong Kong Chinese businessman. He started with nothing and is now chairman of a multinational group, with a personal net worth of over $16 billion (already much discounted with the decline of the stock market in Hong Kong in late 1997 and 1998). His two flagships, Cheung Kong and Hutchison Whampoa, represent his business kingdom, which has penetrated into many major industries, such as real-estate development, container ports, oil and energy, electricity, finances, hotels, retailing, telecommunications and supermarkets. Li's investments are now all over the world, with China as the major area for development in the near future.

He was highly acclaimed by many individuals because he was the first in Hong Kong to take control over British companies. He had close relationships with many high-level Chinese officials, including Deng Xiaoping, Jiang Zemin and Li Peng. His redevelopment project of properties in central Beijing near Tiananmen Square – including the relocation of McDonald's, which had signed a long-term lease with the city – reflected his status in the eyes of Beijing leaders. Nicknamed 'superman' by many local Hong Kong people, he is seen as someone who can change things. He has often been cited as a businessman with Chinese cultural attributes blended with Western management skills.

Business philosophy

Li Ka-Shing has used a lot of traditional Chinese thinking in his business dealings. For example, he has a philosophy of giving room to others, i.e. not pressuring and cornering somebody so as to maximize one's own interest. He once said that it was not wise to earn the last cent from your partner. In his property investment, for example, he seldom overplayed the selling price. He preferred a speedy turnover rather than maximizing profits.

As a Chinese, he advocates the need to develop gradually through stability, not through drastic changes. Even in some major business decisions which might involve big changes the implementation was well paced. In addition, he recognizes the need to be diligent, trustworthy and to engage in continuous learning in order to succeed. By diligence he meant hard work, and he himself worked long hours. For example, in the initial ten years of Cheung Kong, he worked sixteen hours a day, seven days a week. he believes this is the key to success in life – one must invest in order to receive a good return.

Trustworthiness is the second success factor and goes beyond keeping to contractual agreements. His aim is to establish long-term relationships, rather than simply transactional relationships. In order to move forward one needs new knowledge, which he believes to be the drive for new development.

Business development

Li Ka-Shing has a mind that is both analytical and intuitive. For example, he was often very informal in making important decisions. His business partners say that Li can be trusted on the basis of a handshake alone. Since he loves to play golf, a number of business deals were made on the golf course. For instance, he decided to buy an office property from a Japanese at a consideration of $250 million some years ago. The deal was made after a two-hour game of golf with the seller.

Though Li is described as thinking and behaving with a Chinese mentality, he maintains the Western analytical style as well. He relies a lot on information and data analysis. In addition, in the early days of development, especially in Hutchison Whampoa, he had a number of Westerners in the top management team. Some of these top management people are still in his business empire.

He is also famous for his strategic mind in identifying business opportunities. This was evidenced by his interest in real-estate development. When people were leaving Hong Kong in 1967 he bought an important land bank for future development. He understood well that land supply was a scarce commodity on this small island of 6.5 million people. Several large projects in the late 1980s and early 1990s (Laguna City, South Horizons and Tin Shui Wai) were developed during a period of uncertainty. These prime sites turned out to be the major source of property income for the group.

He also knew how to cultivate business opportunities. In 1979, when China had just announced the desire to open up its economy, he started his courtship with China immediately. He initiated a partnership with Chinese and American interests to invest in a $200-million cement plant in Hong Kong. He joined a hotel consortium project in Guangzhou consisting of Hong Kong, Chinese, American and European interests. He was invited for a meeting with the leaders Deng Xiaoping and Zhao Zhiyang in May 1982. This was an important *guanxi* (connection) that facilitated his move to China. His status in the eyes of the Chinese government was reflected by the award of the contract to build the Foreign Ministry Office complex in Hong Kong SAR (Special Administrative Region).

3 Evaluation

Li Ka-Shing understood how to succeed in business in Chinese societies. He recognized the need to be an honest and trustworthy person in order to make long-term business deals. His ability to nurture *guanxi* and interpersonal relationships was critical in his business development. He was able to integrate and apply the analytical and strategic concepts of the West in building up his empire.

His multi-business empire competed with major British *hongs* and multinationals. Many other Chinese firms were very specialized. The closest was Wharf and Wheelock (a British *hong* taken over by Sir Y.K. Pao, now managed by his son-in-law Peter Woo), the performance of which was not as remarkable as that of Cheung Kong and Hutchison Whampoa. Li Ka-Shing's business was a good example of globalization by an Asian firm. For those wishing to know how Asian firms were able to compete in the global economy, the expansion of Li's group with diversified business was clearly a prime case to study.

Similarly to many family business owners, Li also had the succession problem. However, with his long-term vision and a Chinese mentality, Li prepared the road for his two sons to move into his empire. He had two sons, Victor and Richard, both of whom graduated from Stanford. The elder son, Victor, graduated with degrees in civil and structural engineering, returned to Hong Kong in 1985 and worked for Hutchison Whampoa. The second son, Richard, is a graduate in computer engineering and economics. Unlike his elder brother, he worked in Toronto for an investment bank for three years before returning to Hong Kong. He was also involved in his father's business for a while, but later chose to work in his own business. Recently, Li told the press that he would step down as chairman and hand over to Victor very soon. As Victor has been with the group for a long time, and has established his connections and reputation, the transition should be smooth.

Because of the handover, and with quick and widespread economic reform in China, Li Ka-Shing has every confidence in China. He also understood his strategic role in China, and thus China became the focus of the development of his empire. Nevertheless, with the currency crisis in Asia in 1997, how Li will seize the opportunities to turn the Asian crisis into an Asian miracle again is a great challenge to him before his retirement.

CHUNG-MING LAU
CHINESE UNIVERSITY OF HONG KONG

Further reading

Chan, A.B. (1996) *Li Ka-shing: Hong Kong's Elusive Billionaire*, Toronto: Macmillan. (A book-length biography in English which documents Li's life and business development.)

Emerson, T. (1997) 'The Midas touch', *Newsweek*, 10 November: 26–7. (A special report on Li and his companies after the stock market crash in 1997.)

Lam, C. (1996) *Li Ka Shing*, Hong Kong: Notable Publishing. (A Chinese biography of Li which is regarded as the most comprehensive.)

Leung, J. (1997) 'Face to face with Taipan Li', *Asian Business*, March: 25–31. (An exclusive interview with Li, who talked about the existing position and the future of his business.)

Lui, C.W. (1992) *Great Entrepreneurs in Hong Kong,* Hong Kong: Ming Pao Publishing. (A Chinese book on Hong Kong's entrepreneurs which gives very good information.)

See also: BUSINESS STRATEGIES, EAST ASIAN; CULTURE, CROSS-NATIONAL; GLOBALIZATION; PROCTOR & GAMBLE COMPANY

Related topics in the IEBM: LEADERSHIP; MANAGEMENT IN HONG KONG

Matsushita, Konosuke (1894–1989)

Personal background

- born 27 November 1894 in Japan at Aza Sendanno-ki, Wasamura, Kaiso-gun, Wakayama Prefecture into an impoverished farm family
- father lost home and farmlands in rice market speculation, 1899
- left school, aged 9, to take an apprenticeship in a *hibachi* (charcoal grill) shop
- joined Osaka Electric Light company as an interior wiring assistant in 1910
- opened a small electrical fixture shop in Osaka in 1918
- invented bullet-shaped, battery-operated bicycle lamps in 1923
- his home electrical appliance plant becomes the Matsushita Electrical Industrial Company, 1932
- founded Peace and Happiness through Prosperity (PHP) Institute, 1946
- first visits to the USA and Europe in 1951
- established contractual ties with Philips, 1952
- resigned as chairman of Matsushita Electric in 1973 and took up post of executive advisor
- died of pneumonia, aged 94, on 27 April 1989

Major works

Quest for Prosperity: The Life of a Japanese Industrialist (1988)

Summary

Konosuke Matsushita (1894–1989) is famed for two major contributions to the development of Japanese business and management – for the founding, development and direction of Matsushita Denki Sangyo (Matsushita Electric Industrial Company), which has become one of the world's largest consumer electronics companies, and for a stream of writings and reflections which contributed to philosophies of management. His business career had relatively humble beginnings in inter-war Japan, but blossomed in the post-war recovery, and Matsushita Electric Company's market shares in 'the three treasures' (washing machines, refrigerators and televisions) made it synonymous with the mass production, mass consumption and rising living standards of Japan's high-growth years. Konosuke Matsushita was closely identified with many of the features of business organization and management which underpinned this prosperity and he championed a humanistic philosophy of business and management in his writings and practice. Thus he is widely seen as the patriarch of the Japanese consumer electronics industry and a 'god of business management'.

1 Biographical data

Konosuke Matsushita was born in Wakayama Prefecture in 1894, the youngest of three boys and five girls in a comfortable landlord family which drew its income from tenant farmers. His carefree early childhood was interrupted by loss of the family farmlands and home after his father's unsuccessful speculation on the rice market in 1898. The move to a cramped town apartment and the family vulnerabilities and vicissitudes were compounded by the young Matsushita's own frail health and the deaths of the three oldest children (including the two brothers) by 1901 from infectious ailments. So, at the age of 9, Konosuke Matsushita left school and boarded a train to take an apprenticeship in a *hibachi* (charcoal stove) maker's shop, followed by an apprenticeship in a newly fashionable bicycle shop, which introduced him to lathes and repair work. At the age of 15, the fascination of electricity, seen in the trains of Osaka, beckoned him to join the Osaka Electric Light Company as a wiring assistant.

Still troubled by his own poor health but emboldened by his promotion to inspector, the 23-year-old Matsushita decided to form his own business, the Matsushita Electric Company, which manufactured electric sockets. In 1918, he started a business manufacturing electrical fixtures in a two-room apartment with less than ¥100 capital. In the early 1920s, he diversified his activities by developing a new battery-powered bicycle lamp to replace the candle lamps which had been vulnerable to even the slightest winds.

During the depression of 1929 stock lay unsold in warehouses, but the company weathered the storm when Matsushita determined that he would not lay off employees but allow them to work half time on full pay, and urge employees, relatives and friends to sell the company's goods (Matsushita 1984: 129). Despite recession, the company made steady progress and Matsushita selected 5 May (Boys' Day) 1932 as the official founding day to re-launch the company with its corporate mission to society. The fifth day of the fifth month had historic significance as one of the traditional seasonal festivals in the 'Tokugawa period' (1600-1868) and usually celebrated as 'boys' day' until it was designated children's day in 1948. As 'boys' day', it was customary to hang long streamers from house poles depicting the carp to celebrate the courage and bravery of the fish in its swim (and the courage of young males in life). Thus, it seemed an auspicious day to launch the new beginning for the Matsushita Electric company. The company song *'Ai to Hikari to Yume de'* (With Love and Light and Dream), introduced in 1933, was another of Matsushita's innovations designed to build the corporate spirit of the company.

As the militarist governments took direct control over the economy in the late 1930s, the Matsushita Electric Company was increasingly mobilized for state purposes and drawn into war production. While Konosuke Matsushita later commented that companies had little option but to comply at the time, the company's commitment reaped the advantages of domestic prosperity and the widening markets in Korea, Taiwan and Manchuria.

The end of the Second World War marked a bleak period for Matsushita and his company. His earlier involvement in industrial production earned the family a citation as a *zaibatsu* family and the company was marked for dissolution. The *zaibatsu* were financial and industrial combines that operated as units under the control of families through holding companies used as the command centres for the group. They limited shareholding, controlled the appointment of officers and used a variety of additional measures to maintain control. Because they came to assume a dominant position in the Japanese economy after the turn of the century, the US Occupation authorities determined that the *zaibatsu* should be dissolved to democratize the economy and prevent the re-emergence of Japanese militarism. Yet in the middle of the turbulence of a wage demand pursued vigorously by the company union, the union and employees paused to deliver 15,000 signatures on a petition to 'save the linchpin' of the company. Surprised to learn that this was a labour union petition to retain and not remove a company president, the administration relented. The family was removed from the list, Konosuke Matsushita remained head of the enterprise, and the company was not broken down.

Finally freed from Allied Occupation restrictions, Matsushita made visits to the USA and Europe in 1951 and determined that the USA would become a major market for the company. But Matsushita personally selected the European company, Philips, for close links and technology licence arrangements in 1952. By 1953, the company was proving its product lines in Japan with the successful introduction of washing machines, televisions and refrigerators, with vacuum cleaners added in 1954. By 1957, the company had moved into high-quality FM radio receivers and developed a colour television receiver in 1958. Successful domestic sales provided a springboard for an ambitious international strategy, independent from the trading companies which dominated the trading system in Japan. Matsushita was one of the first companies to take advantage of low labour costs and stable dollar relations for overseas production in the less-developed countries of East Asia.

The 1970s were marked by the battle between JVC (in which Matsushita had a 50 per cent shareholding since the early 1950s) and its allies against Sony over the standard for the video cassette recorder (VCR). Matsushita had been developing a system, but on hearing of a superior 'VHS' system being developed in JVC, Akio Tanii (Head of Matsushita VCR development) argued for a delay in order to refine the JVC VHS system. This delay in launching a Matsushita company product until it could be based on the new JVC VHS system meant that Sony, determined not to share its technology, could enjoy a one-year monopoly in the market for its 'Betamax' system. Yet Konosuke Matsushita argued rightly that Sony had insufficient production capacity and the JVC-Matsushita allies were able to enter the marketplace and establish VHS as the industry standard through their production and marketing strengths.

Konosuke Matsushita remained head of the company until 1973 when he retired from direct management, but he retained considerable influence as a special adviser. He devoted much of his time in retirement to writing on business philosophy. He died in 1989 aged 94. His estate was recorded at ¥244.9 billion, the highest figure in Japan's history (Rafferty 1995: 186).

2 Main contribution

Matsushita learned from the biography of Henry Ford the importance of broadening demand by mass production and lowering the product price (Matsushita 1984: 21). Within his company, he broadened and developed the mass-production ideas into strategies which became the epitome of Japanese management. Yet to achieve this position, Matsushita had to adopt and develop many novel business practices unfamiliar to the traditions of the larger companies such as the *zaibatsu* and trading companies.

He set the company in its place in society with a quasi-religious mission: 'The real mission of Matsushita Electric is to produce an inexhaustible supply of goods, thus creating peace and prosperity throughout the land' (Matsushita 1984: 22). His promotion of a 'good' fit' between company strategy and structure and the culture of the wider society have attracted much admiration (Pascale and Athos 1982). In the midst of the uncertainties of 1946, Matsushita established the Peace and Happiness through Prosperity (PHP) Institute, as a response to the war. Later, it became a vehicle for publishing his homilies on management and for training. In 1980, he added the Matsushita School of Government and Management, the aim of which was to develop leaders for Japan in the 1980s and 1990s.

In 1933, The Matsushita Electric Company was among the pioneers in adopting a divisional management structure in order to clarify the achievements and responsibilities of the various divisions and in order to give a better idea of company strengths and weaknesses (Matsushita 1988: 223–4; Suzuki 1991: 305–8). The centrifugal tendencies of divisionalization were countered by linking methods in successive programmes of divisionalization (Pascale and Athos 1982: 33). Further innovatory organizational features in a Japanese company were the five-year business plan and profit centres, both introduced by Matsushita.

Matsushita set great store by effective distribution, going directly to retailers to create a strong system of single-channel retail outlets, and reinforcing relationships with trade financing (Pascale and Athos 1982: 30). Success in this field enabled the increase in market shares which financed the cost cutting and the virtuous circle of a consumer goods company aiming at mass consumption through mass production.

Eager to re-establish the company as quickly as possible after the relaxation of constraints, Matsushita was an early adopter of assembly line production, which he observed in Toyota's car production in 1951–2 (Matsushita 1992: 146–7). He directed his managers to visit Toyota and learn from their practice (see TOYODA FAMILY).

The advantages of 'just-in-time' production and low stock holdings were borne in on Konosuke Matsushita when he reviewed the level of losses through excess stockholding in company plants after a large earthquake struck Niigata on the Sea of Japan coast in 1964 (Matsushita 1984: 98–9). Yet Matsushita himself had already developed an important ingredient of the just-in-time system in the 1930s by building strong relations with suppliers, surprising suppliers with visits and advice to secure the cost-cutting which Matsushita sought.

Good industrial relations were an important feature stressed and secured by Matsushita. His determination to maintain stable employment in the depression and the support of the company union against the occupation directives were two examples of the rapport with employees. The Matsushita enterprise union was one of the biggest members of the industrial union federation, the Japanese Federation of Electrical Machine Workers' Unions (*Denki Roren*). The Federation has supported the Social Democratic Party. Through these links, Matsushita was able to sustain a cooperative rather than a conflictual model of union-management relations. Against the background of declining unionism in most industrial countries, Matsushita still supported labour unions and thought that the Japanese enterprise union could serve as a model in developing countries (Matsushita 1989: 76–8; Whitehill 1991: 247–8).

The successful battle with Sony over the VHS standard demonstrated the importance of a comprehensive approach to innovation and the need to ally technical virtuosity to marketing and production strengths.

3 Evaluation

As a major industrialist featuring in Japan's post-war economic success, Matsushita promoted many of the features of organization and management now thought to be distinctive of Japanese business. Moreover, he added a philosophy of business which emphasized the interdependence of the various stakeholders in the enterprise – customers, employees and suppliers.

Matsushita's character revealed in his home-spun writings has been likened to that of 'a kindly, but elderly clergyman of the conservative school' (Rafferty 1995: 187). He conceded that he made little mention of his wife and family in his writings, but asked for his readers' understanding as he was a man of the nineteenth century (Matsushita 1988: ix).

Konosuke Matsushita founded and developed a major company in spite of his lack of family connections and advantages. It has grown from his small workshop into a giant multinational corporate group with over 200,000 employees, more than 100 subsidiaries and plants, and aggregate annual sales of US$35 billion. Despite a lack of formal education, he both managed the company and was an influence on a much wider audience through his writings: these were remarkable achievements. Today, the debate is whether the framework which he built has become a cage inhibiting further development and whether the company can adapt to changing business conditions in the 1990s. Throughout the long years under his personal direction the company built a reputation based on following the technical innovations of rivals with superior production engineering and marketing. The relatively low level of research and development (R&D) spending has raised questions about the company's ability to secure the more creative individuals and relationships thought necessary for the 1990s.

4 Conclusion

In the mid-1980s, Tanii, the new president, concluded that the traditional consumer electronics markets were saturated. He urged entry into new markets, but feared difficulties in attracting the most able engineers to advance the company's R&D effort, and complained that the company's 600 subsidiaries and group companies were weakly harnessed to pull in the new directions. One signal policy revision was directed toward achieving a new relationship with the network of 25,000 corner stores, which had served Matsushita well in the past but were now threatened by discount stores. However, Tanii resigned in 1993, taking responsibility for increasing difficulties such as widely publicized refrigerator faults, a financial scandal and sluggish company performance. Underlying these difficulties were problematic relations with the Matsushita family and Tanii's attempt to fashion a new style and structure for the company. Chairman Masaharu Matsushita, son-in-law of the founder, was a strong critic of the scheme (Rafferty 1995: 189). The new president, Morishita, abandoned the Tanii plans and put in place new proposals to renew the company, taking care to show the continuities with Konosuke Matsushita:

> Our basic philosophy of the company inherited from our founder has not changed at all. We must contribute to society and contribute to the well-being of people, and this is immutable and we will follow it eternally. But our founder was a very flexible person, very innovative. I shall be as innovative as he was. Times are changing and the society and economy are changing rapidly, so we must change to meet new challenges.
>
> (Rafferty 1995: 202)

KEVIN MCCORMICK
UNIVERSITY OF SUSSEX

Further reading

(References cited in the text marked *)

Gould, R. (1970) *The Matsushita Phenomenon*, Tokyo: Diamond Sha (The Diamond Publishing Company). (This study attempts to explain the success of the Matsushita Electric Industrial Company through an examination of the influence of Konosuke Matsushita's personal business philosophy and rested on secondary materials and interviews with Konosuke Matsushita.)

Kono, T. (1984) *Strategy and Structure of Japanese Enterprises*, London: Macmillan. (This study gives a view of similarities and differences among some of the major Japanese companies in their development of strategy and structure.)

* Matsushita, K. (1984) *Not for Bread Alone: A Business Ethos, a Management Ethic*, Tokyo: PHP Institute. (This volume draws on four books written in Japanese by Konosuke Matsushita between 1973 and 1980. It contains the short essays 'Earthquake shakeup' and 'Clear the warehouses'.)

* Matsushita, K. (1988) *Quest for Prosperity: The Life of a Japanese Industrialist*, Tokyo: PHP Institute.

* Matsushita, K. (1989) *As I See It*, Tokyo: PHP Institute. (This collection of fifty-six essays comes from Matsushita's column in the monthly magazine *PHP Intersect* over the years 1985 to 1989. They include 'Labour and management: Yin and Yang', a 1988 essay in which he praised labour unions and their enterprise form.)

Matsushita, K. (1991) *Velvet Glove: Iron Fist*, Tokyo: PHP Institute. (Originally published in Japanese in 1973 as *Shidosha no Joken: Jinshin no myomi ni omou* (Prerequisites of Leadership: The Secrets of Charisma).)

* Matsushita, K. (1992) *People Before Products*, Tokyo: PHP Institute. (Contains material from two books written in Japanese, *Jinjimagekyo: watashi no mikata sodatekata* (My approach to Personnel Management) and *Oriori no ki-Jinsey de deatta hitotachi (Accounts of Memorable Encounters).)*

Matsushita, K. (1993) *A Piece of the Action*, Tokyo: PHP Institute. (This volume is based on *Shain kokoroecho* (Precepts for Employees) (1981) and *Jinsei kokoroecho* (Precepts of Life) (1984).)

* Pascale, R. T. and Athos, A. G. (1982) *The Art of Japanese Management*, Harmondsworth: Penguin. (This study looks closely at the management system – strategy, organizational structure, financial controls, etc. – in the Matsushita Electric Company.)

* Rafferty, K. I. (1995) *Inside Japan's Power Houses: The Culture, Mystique and Future of Japan's Greatest Corporations*, London: Weidenfeld & Nicolson. (This volume reviews the history and future prospects of several major Japanese corporations including the Matsushita Electric Company.)

* Suzuki, Y. (1991) *Japanese Management Structures, 1920–80*, Basingstoke: Macmillan. (This book examines the organization structure of the 100 largest Japanese industrial companies over the period since 1920, and includes Matsushita.)

* Whitehill, A. (1991) *Japanese Management: Tradition and Transition*, London: Routledge. (This overview of Japanese management provides a context for studying aspects of

805

Matsushita's contributions to the development of his company and management in Japan.)

See also: GLOBALIZATION; *KEIRETSU*; MANAGEMENT IN JAPAN; MORITA, A.; TOYODA FAMILY

Related topics in the IEBM: BUSINESS HISTORY, JAPANESE; ECONOMY OF JAPAN; FORD, H.; INDUSTRIAL RELATIONS IN JAPAN; JAPANIZATION; JUST-IN-TIME PHILOSOPHIES; MANAGEMENT EDUCATION IN JAPAN; TOTAL QUALITY MANAGEMENT

Maucher, Helmut (1927–)

Personal background

- born 9 December 1927 in Eisenharz, Germany, and grew up on a Bavarian farm
- drafted into the Wehrmacht during the close of the Second World War
- joined Nestlé as a business apprentice in 1948
- graduate of the University of Frankfurt, where he studied economics and business administration while working part time at Nestlé
- has completed postgraduate courses at IMEDE, Lausanne
- in charge of Findus from 1964 to 1969
- re-recruited by Nestlé in 1972
- in 1975 became president and chief executive officer (CEO) of the Nestlé Gruppe Deutschland
- in 1980 became executive vice-president and a member of the Executive Committee of Nestlé SA
- in 1981 became president and CEO of Nestlé SA
- in 1990 became chairman and CEO of Nestlé SA, Vevey
- in 1995 was asked to stay on as chairman until 2000, but vacated the position of CEO in 1997
- vice-chairman of the board of CS Holding, Zurich and Crédit Suisse, Zurich; also a member of the following boards of directors: Henkel KGAA, Düsseldorf; Zurich Versicherungsgesellschaft, Zurich; and Allianz Insurance, Munich
- serves on the International Council of Morgan Bank, New York
- *Financial World* CEO of the Year in Europe in 1992; in 1995 received the Appeal of Conscience Award 'for his leadership in advancing international cooperation through his contribution to free trade and the global economy' (*PR Newswire* 1995)
- in 1997 he was President of International Chamber of Commerce (ICC)

1 Introduction

Helmut Maucher finished high school after serving in the Wehrmacht during the Second World War. He is married and has three sons. For relaxation he enjoys playing the violin and golfing (Tagliabue 1984; Tully 1987).

Maucher is fluent in his native German and English, and since moving to Switzerland has learnt French, which is required at 'the Nestlé headquarters ... with meetings often conducted in all three languages at once' (Tagliabue 1984).

In 1964 Nestlé placed Maucher in charge of Findus, which produced frozen foods. He restored this operation to profitability, but became so disgruntled when Nestlé sold Findus to its rival Unilever that he quit the company in 1969. However, Nestlé recruited him back in 1972 to deal with problems between corporate staff and the staff at a Bavarian milk producer Nestlé had acquired. In 1975, after successfully handling his assignment, he became president and CEO of the Nestlé Gruppe Deutschland (Tagliabue 1984). He was transferred to Switzerland in 1980 and promoted to executive vice-president and made a member of the Executive Committee of Nestlé SA. Then in 1981 he was promoted again to president and CEO of Nestlé SA. In 1990 he was made both Chairman and CEO of Nestlé SA, Vevey. The Directors requested in 1995 that Maucher stay on as chairman of Nestlé SA until the year 2000. He vacated the position of CEO in June 1997 to give a younger person a chance to gain some experience while he was still chairman (http://www.nestle.com 1998).

Maucher built his career on the basis of solving difficult problems. He is known to have a remarkable memory and an eye for detail. One colleague described him thus: 'He's a tough guy, but personable. Someone who gets things done, but in a gentle, humane way' (Tagliabue 1984). He is known for his management philosophy of 'management by provocation' (Queenan 1994). It is also said that he 'has a sociable manner that puts visitors at ease' (Tagliabue 1984).

2 Main contribution

On his arrival in Switzerland in 1980 Maucher began divesting Nestlé of non-strategic and non-profitable businesses. As CEO of Nestlé in the early 1980s, he effectively dealt with a boycott of Nestlé products caused by the company's marketing of formula baby's milk in developing countries. During his tenure as CEO Nestlé made a series of significant acquisitions, including Carnation in 1985, USA; Buitoni-Perugina in 1988, Italy; Rowntree, GB; and Perrier in 1992, France (http://www.nestle.com 1998). In September 1984 Maucher 'stunned the business world with his rapid-fire move to acquire the Carnation Company' by putting together a deal which at that time was 'the largest non-oil merger in American corporate history' (Tagliabue 1984).

During the 1980s Maucher transformed Nestlé from an overcentralized, inefficient corporation into a global leader (Greenhouse 1989). In the mid-1980s he assumed 'direct-line' responsibility for Nestlé's North American operations: 'Mr. Maucher eliminated the four-man executive committee that formerly ran the company worldwide. He replaced it with seven senior V.P.s who ... report to him' (Parry 1986). It is well known that he did away with lengthy business plans and reports: 'He required that they [regional managers] send in a one-page monthly summary of their activities. ... Only if he spots signs of trouble, does he intervene' (Tully 1987).

Maucher has positioned Nestlé for increased sales in emerging markets in Asia, and in Central and Eastern Europe: 'We are working to produce and sell in every country where it is possible' (*East Europe Agriculture & Food* 1996). He has established an aggressive goal of double-digit annual growth for Nestlé through to the year 2000 (Reier 1992).

Record sales in 1996 and 1997 suggest that he may very well achieve his goal (Shields 1997).

Maucher's text *Leadership in Action* (Maucher 1994) offers his views on managing a global corporation and strategies for achieving success in a competitive marketplace. As president of the Paris-based International Chamber of Commerce (ICC), Helmut has worked hard to have the ICC recognized as 'the voice of global business' (Barnard 1997).

3 Evaluation

'Mr. Maucher continuously indulges his habit of poking into details, a custom that he maintains accounts for much of his, and Nestlé's success' (Tagliabue 1984). As a manager at Nestlé, he is credited with decentralizing decision-making and improving communication: 'Through his one-man crusade, he has changed the psyche of this 200,000 employee company from conservative and risk-averse to aggressive and risk-taking' (Greenhouse 1989).

His decentralization of decision-making has allowed Nestlé to offer products which effectively meet local customer preference (Greenhouse 1989). 'In 1993, 12 years after Maucher took the helm at the world's largest food company, the Swiss food titan achieved sales of $38 billion. ...during that time, Nestlé's stock price rose at an annual rate of more than 15%, beating the S&P 500' (Queenan 1994).

Maucher has stated his concern for the environment and Nestlé's responsibility in waste management. He says 'we at Nestlé have always been concerned regarding environmental problems' (http://www.nestle.com 1998). He has tried to put systems in place at Nestlé which protect the environment where their raw materials are grown and to reduce the waste associated with product packaging (http://www.nestle.com 1998).

STEPHEN J. HAVLOVIC
SIMON FRASER UNIVERSITY

Further reading

(References cited in the text marked *)

* Barnard, Bruce (1997) 'Business group wants special role in WTO', *Journal of Commerce*, 5 March: 3A. (Takes a look at Maucher's role as president of the ICC.)
* *East Europe Agriculture & Food* (1996) 'Nestlé expecting strong market growth in E. Europe', *East Europe Agriculture & Food*, July: 32. (Announces intentions to expand in emerging markets.)
* Greenhouse, Steven (1989) 'Nestlé's time to swagger', *New York Times*, Section 3, 1 January: 1. (Reviews Maucher's influence on Nestlé.)
* Maucher, Helmut (1994) *Leadership in Action: Tough-minded Strategies From the Global Giant*, New York: McGraw-Hill. (Provides a view of being CEO of a large multinational corporation and offers management strategies.)
* Parry, John (1986) 'Nestlé beefs up in No. America', *Advertising Age*, 12 May: 69. (Announcement of realignment of Nestlé management responsibilities.)
* *PR Newswire* (1995) 'Helmut O. Maucher, chairman and CEO of Nestlé to receive Appeal of Conscience Award', *PR Newswire*, 15 October. (News release.)
* Queenan, Joe (1994) 'Balancing the books: slash-and-burn CEO tells all', *Barron's* 74(39), 26 September: 58. (Reviews Maucher's book on management strategy.)
* Reier, Sharon (1992) 'Helmut Maucher', *Financial World*, 13 October: 42. (Announces CEO of the Year award.)
* Shields, Michael (1997) 'Nestlé sees good 1997 profit growth', *Reuter European Business Report*, 6 May. (Reviews recent financial performance.)
* Tagliabue, John (1984) 'After a buying spree, can he move the company ahead?', *New York Times*, Section 3, 9 December: 6. (Reviews Nestlé's rapid expansion, including the purchase of Carnation.)
* Tully, Shawn (1987) 'Helmut Maucher', *Fortune*, 3 August: 44. (Gives a profile of Maucher.)
* *Who's Who Edition European Business & Industry* (1992) 'Helmut Oswald Maucher'. (Provides professional biographical information.)

Further resources

* http://www.nestle.com (1998) (Internal documents and news releases.)

Related topics in the IEBM: CORPORATE STRATEGIC CHANGE

Morita, Akio (1921–)

Personal background

- born 26 January 1921 in Nagoya, the eldest son of a wealthy *sake*-brewing family
- studied physics at Osaka Imperial University
- wartime service in the Imperial Japanese Navy as a technical officer
- joined Masaru Ibuka in Tokyo Tsushin Kogyo (Tokyo Telecommunications Engineering Company) (TTK) in 1946
- first international success when TTK began mass production of the world's smallest transistor radio in 1955
- TTK renamed Sony Corporation in 1958
- became president of Sony Corporation in 1971 and chairman in 1976
- awarded the Albert Medal by the Royal Society of Arts and Manufactures in the UK in 1982
- Sony acquired CBS Records in 1987
- Sony acquired Columbia Pictures Entertainment Group from Coca-Cola in 1989
- knighted for services to Anglo-Japanese relations in 1992
- retired as chairman due to ill health at the age of 73 in 1994

Major works

Made in Japan: Akio Morita and Sony (with E.M. Reingold and M. Shimomura) (1987)

Summary

The name of Akio Morita has become almost synonymous with the Sony Corporation, one of the foremost brand names in consumer electronics. The company has become renowned worldwide for a flood of innovative products, including the transistor radio, the Trinitron television tube and screen, the Betamax video cassette recorder and the Walkman portable cassette player. Morita will always be remembered as the 'product champion' for the development of the Walkman cassette recorder. His success as co-founder and chairman of Sony in post-1945 Japan has marked him out as one of the outstanding businessmen of his generation. Ibuka and Morita determined to develop a company based on innovation. While Ibuka (the engineer) focused on the technical side, Morita (the physicist) gave much attention to marketing. They made innovations in managerial style, too, to try to create an organizational structure and culture to foster innovation. Morita coined terms such as 'global localization' to characterize his company's approach to overseas operations. In addition to his prominent role in representative business organizations such as the Keidanren, his excellent command of the English language, his forthright manner and his readiness to engage with a variety of audiences and media enabled him to play a wide role in the dissemination of business philosophies and in the representation of Japanese industry in overseas relations.

1 Biographical data

Akio Morita was born in 1921 into a rich and privileged *sake*-brewing family which traced its history back over fifteen generations (Morita *et al.* 1987: 4–5, 9). Morita's early determination to overturn tradition and strike out on his own path was evident in his decision to become an engineer rather than follow in the family footsteps as eldest son and take charge of one of Japan's oldest brewing businesses. His own father had given up his business studies course at Keio University to discharge his duty as eldest son and rescue the business from a decline triggered by one or two generations of aesthetic Morita art collectors. Yet Morita evaded his father's preferred course of economics and entered Osaka Imperial University to study physics under Professor Tsunesaburo Asada, an outstanding applied physicist.

By 1940 Asada was engaged on research work for the Imperial Japanese Navy and the young Morita helped with projects. Through this connection Morita gained a commission as a technical officer. On graduation he was assigned to the navy to work on thermal guidance weapons and night-vision gun sights. Here he met a brilliant electronics engineer, Masaru Ibuka, whose amplifier was critical to work on submarine detection. Thirteen years older than Morita, Ibuka was to become a friend, colleague, partner and co-founder of the Sony Corporation.

At the end of the war Ibuka, with seven of his former colleagues, formed a small company, Tokyo Tsushin Kenkyusho (Tokyo Telecommunications Laboratory), to make short-wave radio adapters in a gutted department store in downtown Tokyo. Morita became a part-time employee of Ibuka's company and a part-time teacher at the Tokyo Institute of Technology (TIT). However, he took the opportunity of the purge of former military personnel from teaching to leave TIT and also negotiated his release from obligations to the Morita family business. By 1946 he was free to join Ibuka in a new company, Tokyo Tsushin Kogyo (Tokyo Telecommunications Engineering Company, abbreviated as TTK). The blessing of the Morita family was made evident in a series of loans to the fledgling company.

Morita and Ibuka had an initial vision for an innovative company: 'a clever company that would make new high technology products in ingenious ways' (Morita *et al.* 1987: 50). Yet the basic survival of the company rested on supplying new motors and magnetic pickups for the growing interest in popular music recordings in occupied Japan. An opportunity for innovation arose with Ibuka's inspection of an American tape recorder (and the need to adopt a paper tape as an alternative to magnetic tape). Despite the technical virtuosity of the product, disappointing sales led

Morita to the realization that they would need to identify, educate and even create a market for a product that was new to Japan. Using demonstrations in law courts on how to solve the shortage of stenographers, as well as visits to schools, Morita worked successfully to secure a market.

Morita was impressed by a music student's detailed and constructive criticism of the sound quality of the tape recorder and invited the student, Norio Ohga, to join the company as a consultant on the development of a new tape recorder. Meanwhile, Ibuka was exploring the potential for a small valveless radio using the transistor developed by the Bell Laboratories of the Western Electric Company in the USA. TTK began mass production of the radios in 1955. Morita learnt from his first trip to the USA that the company was unlikely to excite interest in this potentially huge market, and so Morita and Ibuka renamed their TTK radio company Sony, derived from the Latin word *sonus* (meaning 'sound'), an appropriate name for a company preoccupied with audio technology.

The celebration of Sony's fifteenth anniversary in May 1961 brought Morita into sharp conflict with the labour union. Morita saw the original union as left-dominated and considered that it was using the celebration as a bargaining chip in its demand for a union shop. Resisting this demand as an infringement of individual liberties, Morita outflanked the union demonstration planned for the anniversary celebration by donning a morning coat at the headquarters building, thus giving the impression that that was where the celebration would take place; meanwhile Ibuka addressed guests, including the prime minister, Ikeda, at another venue. Subsequently, Morita went on the offensive by responding positively to the formation of a rival union by engineering staff. Nearly three decades later, Morita observed that the Sony parent company had two unions, one of which still caused occasional difficulty, but a majority of the employees were non-unionized (Morita *et al.* 1987: 141–3).

Motivated by Ibuka's complaints about the headphones of recorders, Morita set a specification for Sony engineers which led to the development of the Walkman. Morita set the engineers to strip out the recording features of a tape recorder, to lighten the resulting playback-only machine, to produce light-weight headphones and to achieve a target price within the budget range of a teenager. In the face of scepticism from engineers and salesmen, Morita persisted and added that the project time-scale should be six, rather than twelve, months. The Walkman machine that appeared in 1979 has become the stuff of legend in terms of its impact on sales and lifestyles.

In 1989 Morita's co-authorship, with an ebullient right-of-centre politician, of a book entitled *The Japan That Can Say 'No'* (Ishihara and Morita 1989) brought sharply mixed reactions. Washington policy makers tended to focus on the more strident notes of co-author, Shintaro Ishihara – for example, his claim that Japan could tip the balance of strategic power by selling semiconductors to the USSR. Although some Japanese thought that Japan should re-examine its national interests in the post-cold-war era, Morita was deeply embarrassed by the affair and refused permission for his own contributions to be included in the US edition (Ishihara 1991). Morita's own strictures had been directed at American society, which he believed had come to devalue manufacturing, and at American management, which had often abandoned high-quality manufacturing in favour of making money by manipulating financial markets. However, the more nationalistic overtones of his co-author were a liability for Morita, who was prominent as a constructive spokesperson in trade-friction talks, and also for Sony, with its large presence in the US market.

Morita achieved even greater prominence in the USA through the Sony Corporation's purchase of the US cultural icons CBS Records and Columbia Pictures, and by 1990 he had arrived in *Fortune*'s list of 'The Year's Twenty-five Most Fascinating People'. This followed a rather different kind of recognition accorded him by the UK in 1982, when the Royal Society of Arts and Manufactures presented him with the Albert Medal 'for outstanding contributions to technological innovation and management, industrial design, industrial relations and video systems, and the growth of world trade relations'. In 1992 Queen Elizabeth II granted Morita an honorary knighthood in recognition of his contributions to Anglo-Japanese relations.

During the speculation between the July elections in 1993 and the formation of the new Japanese cabinet, Morita, despite being politically unattached, was widely tipped for the post of minister in the Ministry of International Trade and Industry. However, the possibility of Morita's further participation in public life was cut short by a stroke in 1993. Morita announced his retirement as the Sony chairman in November 1994 after a disappointingly slow recovery.

2 Main contribution

Some commentators emphasize that Morita was not the creator of new technology but someone with the vision and skill to package it and create markets. Such commentaries should not underestimate the importance of his own technical background in appreciating new technology or in motivating teams of engineers to achieve technological breakthroughs.

Morita built Sony's reputation for high-quality technology through a firm insistence on controlling the distribution of company products (Morita 1986: 98–102). The company's forerunner, TTK, avoided using the traditional trading companies, despite their familiarity with the USA, on the grounds that they were unfamiliar with TTK products and did not necessarily share the TTK business philosophy. In the mid-1950s, the Bulova company offered to purchase a large order of radios, provided that they carried the Bulova name, but Morita refused to put another company's name on a TTK product. In 1959 Morita determined that Sony's first transistorized television set should not be discounted or marketed cheaply and risk damage to its image. Although this strategy of tight control over the technology proved successful in the early years, it came into serious difficulties with the development of the video recorder and the market failure of Sony's Betamax system. If Sony had been willing to share its technology it might have built an alliance to secure sufficient market share to withstand the arrival of JVC and its allies with the VHS system.

Morita commented that he and his colleagues had little formal business training, and much of their activity was developed through experience. As managers of an innovative company, they did relatively little market research but pinned their efforts on refining their product development and then educating and communicating with the public.

Few companies have matched the track record for innovative products of the Sony Corporation. The company has kept faith with the original vision of Morita and Ibuka of a company where teamwork and creativity could flourish. Yet it has been a demanding strategy. Sony has poured much greater resources into research and development (R&D) than its rivals; for example, the annual R&D budget as a proportion of sales has often been double that of a company such as Matsushita. Moreover, Sony has had to keep on innovating as the rivals have moved into the Sony slipstream with effective manufacturing capabilities and cheaper versions of Sony innovations. The profit record comparisons suggest that the followers often make a better return for their shareholders (Rafferty 1995).

Under Morita's leadership Sony has not been innovative in technology alone. Morita has tried to secure organizational structures which motivate engineers, and, even with a company of 6000 employees in 1965, Sony had not established a formal organizational structure (Suzuki 1991: 312). However, by 1970 Sony had adopted a divisional structure, which was further developed into a division headquarters structure through the 1970s. In 1970 Sony became the first Japanese company to appear on the New York Stock Exchange and the first to raise capital in the USA. The company has pioneered new business practices and developments in human resource management. In the early years, because of rapid growth and technology intensiveness, Sony breached the tradition of 'lifetime employment' by attracting experienced staff from other companies (Kono 1984: 31). As Sony became established as a larger company itself, it was less easy to play the maverick with vigorous mid-career recruitment. Yet even in the 1990s Sony is still regarded as an innovative company and watched as a key to new developments in personnel policy in Japan, for example in its policies and practices for graduate recruitment.

Morita coined the term 'global localization' to describe the Sony Corporation's strategy in response to global competition as a combination of local management style and marketing with an overall corporate philosophy and a high standard of technology. With over 70 per cent of its sales outside Japan and an increasing proportion of its manufacturing overseas, Sony has built a network of factories to serve each of its main markets. By 1991, 475 of the 500 overseas subsidiaries were headed by non-Japanese staff, whereas in 1994 only thirteen of Matsushita's 158 subsidiaries were headed by a person who was not Japanese (Rafferty 1995: 197; Kono 1984: 164). Regional managers have been given considerable scope for investment and product decisions, and senior managers from the worldwide subsidiaries hold a twice-yearly policy meeting to facilitate more rapid responses to market changes and new product launches. Thus Morita's concept has become a guide for policy and practice.

Morita's retirement meant not only the loss of a colourful chairman for the Sony Corporation, but the loss to public life of the chair elect of the Keidanren, the very influential Japan Federation of Economic Organizations. Throughout the 1980s, Morita had acted as an important mediator in trade negotiations – someone who could urge Americans to put their house in order and strengthen their manufacturing industry while telling the Japanese to reduce their working hours and simplify distribution systems (Morita 1992b).

3 Evaluation

The Walkman has become one of the most successful products of the century, frequently appearing in popular listings of the top-ten technological innovations and so successful that rival companies have adopted the name

Walkman as a generic term for portable cassette players. By 1993, over 100 million Walkmans had been sold worldwide. The outstanding success of this one product could mean that Akio Morita figures more in the public imagination as 'Mr Walkman' than as the founder and chairman of a major electronics company or as an international industrialist.

From its early years Morita's company had a strong international outlook. This orientation was driven partly by its constrained situation in Japan, where Matsushita had built a huge network of over 20,000 retail outlets which sold mainly Matsushita products. By 1965 over half Sony's sales were to overseas markets, especially to North America. Morita's personal commitment to an international orientation was signalled by the move of his family to the USA in the 1960s and the education of his children in Europe. His keen advocacy of Japanese staff going out beyond the Japanese community in overseas locations was reflected in his decision to locate the German subsidiary away from the Japanese community in Düsseldorf.

Morita has conceded that a creative company is likely to make mistakes, and he has admitted his responsibility in the Betamax débâcle, in that he failed to build alliances and share technology. The $3.4 billion takeover of Columbia Pictures in 1989 has remained controversial. Many argue that the financial and management problems of the acquisition have illustrated the wide gulf between US and Japanese business practice, even in Japan's most westernized company.

Succession can be a major problem bequeathed by any charismatic leader to an organization. Yet Sony has continued to select presidents who have broken the anticipated organizational mould, reflecting a determination to develop along new paths and select leaders fit to grapple with novel problems. Ohga, the musician and opera singer who became president in 1982, was Morita's direct nominee. Nobuyuki Idei, who became president in 1995 (as Ohga moved to chairman), moved from head of Sony's product design strategy, past several more senior frontrunner candidates, to become president. With a

background in politics and economics, his strengths are said to lie in his understanding of both the hardware and the software aspects of Sony's business. Having passed its fiftieth anniversary in 1996, Sony is no longer the small entrepreneurial company that was led by the charismatic Morita. Yet the vision of its founders remains a powerful talisman for a company with one of the most famous brand names in the world.

4 Conclusion

Morita has sometimes been regarded as a maverick, applauded for his courage and outspoken views, and contrasted with the massed ranks of more reticent and self-effacing Japanese businessmen. Some even comment on the non-Japanese conduct of Morita and Sony. Yet Morita has served as an exemplar for a post-war generation in Japanese business. Morita *et al.*'s book *Made in Japan* (1987) carries the subtext 'self-made', for it describes the growth of a company whose founders, lacking substantial advantage, but with skill and technological resourcefulness in the post-war era, anticipated and responded to worldwide consumer demand. Moreover, the name Morita has always carried a strong sense of tradition because of the link with the 300-year-old family business which prepared such staples of the Japanese diet as *sake*, soy sauce and *miso* paste. His own public role in Japan and overseas has written a family tradition of public service in a modern idiom: 'Being in a business so central to the life of the community (*sake* brewing), the Morita family has taken a position of civic leadership as well' (Morita *et al.* 1987: 4–5).

KEVIN MCCORMICK
UNIVERSITY OF SUSSEX

Further reading

(References cited in the text marked *)

Buruma, I. (1996) 'We Japanese', *The Missionary and the Libertine: Love and War in East and West*, London and Boston, MA: Faber & Faber. (This chapter discusses national identities and makes a critical assessment of the role of Morita as an international businessman projecting images of Japan and the Japanese.)

Du Gay, P. *et al.* (1997) *Doing Cultural Studies: The Story of the Sony Walkman*, Sage Publications in association with the Open University. (This introductory text on culture, identity and media uses the example of the Sony Walkman as a cultural artefact; therefore the author offers a critique of both the technical and cultural aspects of the development of the Sony Walkman, including the representation of it as the product of inspired individuals, as the result of a unique organization and as a happy accident at work.)

* Ishihara, S. (1991) *The Japan that Can Say 'No'*, New York: Simon & Schuster. (This English-language version of the book was published without Morita's contribution. Its bold assertion of Japan's capacity to influence relations between the superpowers struck some sensitive nerves among its US readers.)

* Ishihara, S. and Morita, A. (1989) *'No' to ieru Nippon* [The Japan that can say 'no'], Tokyo: Kobunsha. (This controversial book sold more than 1 million copies in 1989 and 1990; Morita gave an account of industrial relations in Japan as essentially cooperative and a contributory factor to Japan's post-war economic development, and outlined his view of the shortcomings of American management.)

* Kono, T. (1984) *Strategy and Structure of Japanese Enterprises*, London: Macmillan. (This account of strategy and structure among Japanese companies gives particular insights into the multinational aspects of management and organization in Sony Corporation.)

* Morita, A. (1986) 'When Sony was an up-and-comer', *Forbes* 138(7): 98–102. (This paper offers insights into the early years of the Sony Corporation.)

Morita, A. (1992a) 'Partnering for competitiveness: the role of Japanese business', *Harvard Business Review* 70(3): 76–83. (This paper discusses the international role of Japanese corporations.)

* Morita, A. (1992b) 'Nihon-gata Keiei ga Abunai' [The crisis of Japanese management], *Bungei Shunju* 2. (A paper which stirred controversy in Japan because Morita pointed to some of the downside of Japanese management and organization, with their long working hours and the pressure for conformity.)

* Morita, A., Reingold, E.M. and Shimomura, M. (1987) *Made in Japan: Akio Morita and Sony*, London: Collins. (This autobiography covers the development of Morita and Sony, and the context of Japan's post-war development.)

Pascale, R.T. and Athos, A.G. (1982) *The Art of Japanese Management*, Harmondsworth: Penguin. (This study of Japanese management is based on a close analysis of Konosuke Matsushita and the Matsushita Electric Company; comparisons with Morita and Sony are often made.)

* Rafferty, K.I. (1995) *Inside Japan's Power Houses: The Culture, Mystique and Future of Japan's Greatest Corporations*, London: Weidenfeld & Nicolson. (This study of some major corporations provides illustrative comparisons of strategies and performance between the Sony Corporation and the Matsushita Electric Company.)

* Suzuki, Y. (1991) *Japanese Management Structures, 1920–80*, Basingstoke: Macmillan. (This study gives an account of the adoption of the divisional organizational form in the Sony Corporation.)

Whitehill, A. (1991) *Japanese Management: Tradition and Transition*, London: Routledge. (This overview of Japanese management provides a context for Morita's own distinctive approach to management.)

See also: MANAGEMENT IN JAPAN

Murdoch, Rupert (1931–)

Personal background

- born 11 March 1931 in Melbourne, Victoria, Australia, to Sir Keith and Dame Elisabeth Joy (Greene) Murdoch
- in 1952 graduated from Oxford University, where he studied political science and economics
- has received many awards, including Companion of the Order of Australia (1984); First Class, Commander of the White Rose Award (1985); and Papal Knighthood (1998)
- worked briefly as a junior sub-editor on the *Daily Express* in London
- in 1954 returned to Australia to run two small newspapers (*News* and *Sunday Mail*) which he inherited from his father
- moved to the USA in 1974 and became a naturalized citizen in 1985
- News Corp. Ltd valued at $20 billion in 1995
- Rupert Murdoch is chairman and chief executive officer (CEO) of News Corp. Ltd and Chairman of Fox Inc.

1 Introduction

Murdoch 'was known as an indifferent student who disliked authority' when he studied at Oxford University (Dowd 1985). His publishing career began in London, where he worked briefly for the *Daily Express*, but he returned to Australia in 1954 to run two small newspapers inherited from his father, a newspaper publisher. He restored these papers to profitability and in 1956 made his first expansion when he purchased a newspaper in Perth, Australia. Murdoch would go on to expand his media empire to England and then the United States. He has essentially never stopped expanding the company since 1956.

In 1974 he moved to the United States. In 1985, in order to comply with regulations which specify that TV stations can only be owned by Americans, Murdoch became a naturalized US citizen (*Newsmakers* 1988).

In 1995 his News Corp. Ltd empire was valued at approximately $20 billion and included newspapers and magazines; book publishers; television network, stations and cable operations; a movie studio; and other holdings. Many of his publications and companies are famous names, such as *TV Guide*, *The Times* (London), Fox Television Network, 20th Century Fox Film Corp. and British Sky Broadcasting (BSkyB) (Dowd 1985; *Newsmakers* 1988; *Reuter Business Report* 1995).

Murdoch has been married twice. He married his first wife Patricia Booker in 1956 and they had a daughter, Prudence. The couple were divorced in 1965. He married Anna Maria Torv in 1967 and they have three children: Elisabeth, Lachlan and James (*Newsmakers* 1988). Rupert and Anna separated in Spring 1998.

The heir to the Murdoch media empire will be his eldest son Lachlan, but Murdoch has no plans of stepping down soon from his positions as chairman and CEO at News Corp. Ltd. His other children, Elizabeth and James, are also active in the business (Bates 1997). Little is known about the management skills of Lachlan and his siblings as Murdoch dominates in all major decisions.

Murdoch enjoys swimming, tennis, jogging, and skiing (Dowd 1985; *Contemporary Theatre ...* 1988). 'He has been called a complex and intelligent man who often surprises people with his charm and wit' (Dowd 1985).

2 Main contribution

Beginning in the 1980s, Murdoch began diversifying away from newspapers and towards electronic media, which he believes are poised for long-term growth (Cohen 1990). His extensive acquisitions brought News Corp. Ltd close to bankruptcy in 1990.

Murdoch spent 'two-years refinancing News Corp.'s $7.6-billion debt' (Lippman 1992). Once again he prevailed and his media empire essentially remained intact, although he has sold off most of his US magazines and some newspapers in order to reduce his debt load (Kurtz 1993). Throughout the financial crisis Murdoch remained steadfast in not jeopardizing family control by selling off any of the 45 per cent of voting stock controlled by the Murdoch family (Feder 1990).

Murdoch claims that 'Money is not the motivating force. ... What I enjoy is running the business' (Cohen 1990). In 1992, when Barry Diller quit as Chairman of Fox Inc., Murdoch stepped in as chairman and has since run the daily activities at Fox (Weinraub 1992). Murdoch works twelve-hour days, arriving at his office at Fox by 6.30 a.m. He spends his first three hours on the telephone with his companies around the globe (Lippman 1992; Weinraub 1992). During 1997 Murdoch lobbied key Congressmen to bring about changes in US law on local television broadcasts. Had he been successful this would have enabled 'Sky to be the first satellite broadcaster to offer subscribers local stations as well as hundreds of other channels (Grant 1997).

3 Evaluation

It has been noted that 'Little escapes his attention, no matter how mundane' (Lippman 1992). He enjoys being involved in the details, but finds it difficult to accept that he cannot be involved in all the decisions because his company spans the globe. Murdoch is also known for his ability to make fast decisions. 'His belief is anything can be done, so just do it. He doesn't understand failure' (Lippman 1992). He has consistently proved to analysts that he can exceed expectations (Carter 1996).

'Murdoch built the News Corporation into a global media powerhouse from virtually nothing' (*Celebrity Biographies* 1998). However, he has many critics, including politicians and journalists. In a 1977 speech to news publishers he came down on his critics, stating: 'A press that fails to interest the whole community is one that will ultimately become a house organ of the elite engaged in an increasingly private conversation with a dwindling club' (*Newsmakers* 1988). Even his critics agree he is resourceful.

It has been claimed that 'Rupert Murdoch is Britain's most powerful non-Briton' (Darnton 1995). Critics charge that he has influenced British election outcomes and destabilized the monarchy (Darnton 1995). He also wields considerable power outside Britain. In 1995 *Vanity Fair* magazine 'named Rupert Murdoch as the world's most powerful man in what it calls the "New Establishment," linking entertainment, information and technology' (*Reuter Business Report* 1995). Despite such recognition it was pointed out by Anderson (1997) that 'The only place News Corp. has yet to succeed is on the Internet, where Murdoch has dabbled, buying and then closing Delphi Internet Services Corp.'

He runs his media empire with a modest number of people, and remains active and in control of day-to-day operations. '[H]e has proven that he is willing to risk everything to achieve his goals' (*Celebrity Biographies* 1998). Murdoch hopes to challenge the TV news operations of CNN (Lippman 1992), but to date this goal has proved illusive. His attempts to establish Fox News as a major competitor to CNN have so far been unsuccessful. Murdoch believes that not purchasing CNN when he had the chance in the mid-1980s was his biggest mistake (Lippman 1992).

STEPHEN J. HAVLOVIC
SIMON FRASER UNIVERSITY

Further reading

(References cited in the text marked *)

* Anderson, Howard (1997) 'The man who would be media king', *Upside* 9(8), September: 110. (Reviews Murdoch's ambitions and media holdings.)
* Bates, James (1997) 'Company town', *Los Angeles Times*, Business Section, 10 December: 9. (Announces that Murdoch's son Lachlan is the eventual successor of the Murdoch media empire.)
* Carter, Bill (1996) 'The media business', *New York Times*, Section A, 31 January: 1. (Announces 24-hour news service.)

* *Celebrity Biographies* (1998) 'Murdoch, Rupert'. (Provides personal and professional biographical information.)
* Cohen, Roger (1990) 'Rupert Murdoch's biggest gamble', *New York Times*, Section 6, 21 October: 31. (Discusses the difficulties of expanding into television and entertainment businesses.)
* *Contemporary Theatre, Film, and Television* (1988) 'Rupert Murdoch', vol. 5. (Provides personal and professional biographical information.)

Craig, David Cobb (1998) 'Passages', *People*, 19 January: 72. (Announces Murdoch's papal knighthood.)

* Darnton, John (1995) 'Murdoch and Laborite: Britain's new odd couple', *New York Times*, Section A, 21 July: 2. (Discusses Murdoch's influence in Britain.)
* Dowd, Maureen (1985) 'Man in the news', *New York Times*, Section D, 7 May: 10. (Takes a look at the personal life of Rupert Murdoch and his media empire.)
* Feder, Barnaby J. (1990) 'Murdoch's time of reckoning', *New York Times*, Section D, 20 December: 1. (Reviews Murdoch's financial crisis and refinancing of News Corp.'s debt.)

Forbes (1996) 'The Forbes four hundred – Keith Rupert Murdoch', *Forbes*. (Provides biographical information.)

* Grant, Peter (1997) 'Murdoch can't sway lawmakers', *Daily News* (New York), Business Section, 10 April: 72. (Discusses Murdoch's attempt to change the law to allow satellite broadcasts of local stations.)
* Kurtz, Howard (1993) 'The post's man rings twice', *Washington Post*, Style Section, 29 March: D1. (Discusses Murdoch's values and repurchasing of the *New York Post*.)
* Lippman, John (1992) 'Taking the wheel at Fox', *Los Angeles Times*, Business Section, 9 August: 1. (Examines how Murdoch runs Fox Inc. and News Corp.)
* *Newsmakers* (1988) 'Rupert Murdoch'. (Gives a personal biographical summary.)
* *Reuter Business Report* (1995) 'Rupert Murdoch named leader of information superhighway', 5 September. (News release.)

Shawcross, William (1997) *Murdoch: The Making of a Media Empire* (revised edition), Touchtone Books. (Biography of Rupert Murdoch.)

* Weinraub, Bernard (1992) 'Rupert Murdoch, in Hollywood, learns the value of "no"', *New York Times*, Section C, 21 July: 11. (Takes a look at Murdoch's life as Chairman of Fox Inc.)

Roddick, Anita (1942–)

Personal background

- born 23 October 1942 in Littlehampton, England, to Gilda de Vita and Henry Perilli
- attended Maude Allen Secondary Modern for Girls in 1954
- attended Newton Park College of Higher Education, Bath, in 1961
- married T. Gordon Roddick in 1970 and has two daughters, Justine and Samantha
- taught at Maude Allen Secondary School
- worked at the International Herald Tribune in Paris and the Women's Department of the International Labour Organisation in Geneva
- started a restaurant and hotel with T. Gordon Roddick in Littlehampton
- opened the first Body Shop in Brighton in 1976 and has expanded to over 1500 shops (as of July 1997)
- currently co-chairperson of Body Shop Intl
- Gordon Roddick currently serves as chairman of the board and has been crucial in leading the company through its explosive growth

Major works

Body and Soul: Profits with Principles (1991)
An Entrepreneur's Journey (1997)
Numerous chapters in edited volumes, including World Business Academy *Perspectives*

1 Introduction

People all over the world associate the name Anita Roddick with entrepreneurship. Applied to Roddick, the label has many meanings. It means the founder of the Body Shop – a successful publicly traded retail operation that manufactures and sells cosmetics and hair and skin-care products in over 1500 shops, in twenty-four different languages and forty-seven markets around the world. It also means a maverick who has reinvented what it means to be a successful business person and has zealously challenged the notion that business is just about making profits. The commercial success of the Body Shop has demonstrated that companies can make profits and have a positive impact on the world.

Soon after the founding of her first shop in Brighton in 1976, Anita and Gordon Roddick looked for ways to run her business as a force for social good. Over the years, the Body Shop has led the way in corporate social responsibility, breaking ground in corporate environmentalism, animal rights and protection, fair trading practices and corporate social campaigning. For instance, the Body Shop's 15 per cent stake in the Bryn Titli wind farm in Wales offsets about 25 per cent of its electricity consumption at its three main manufacturing sites in the UK. The company was built on the practice of developing products that create trading opportunities for people in developing economies and has established trading relations with twenty-three community-based groups from developing societies. These relationships have resulted in innovative products for the Body Shop and economic opportunities for targeted communities.

The company has also been an outspoken champion of animal rights, leading the way with its ban on animal testing. From the company's early beginnings, Roddick has experimented with ways to use the retail shop as a forum for public awareness campaigns and citizen participation, such as voter registration. The company and its employees have taken on a range of social campaigns, ranging from women's rights and domestic violence to the condition of Romanian orphans and the rights of the Ogani tribe of Africa against the practices of a multinational oil company that is exploiting the land and livelihood of the tribe. Roddick has become a symbol of corporate social responsibility and a passionate spokesperson for many of these campaigns.

Led by the Roddicks, the Body Shop has challenged the commercial practices and social consequences of the beauty and cosmetic industries, charging the industries with creating images that girls and women cannot live up to, and with making promises that the industry cannot fulfil. Rather than playing on the fragile self-esteem of women and girls, the Body Shop has attempted to build a brand image around helping people care for and feel good with who they are and what they look like. A recent campaign that was published by the Body Shop and distributed as an insert in a respected British newspaper ('The Body and Self Esteem', *Full Voice*, Issue 1) displayed vivid images created by the beauty industry and details of the ways in which these images undermine women's self-esteem. The Body Shop's 1997-8 brand campaign 'Love Your Body' offers a social alternative by emphasizing in its marketing the importance of making the most of one's actual body, age and facial features, rather than trying to change these to fit idealized images.

In many ways, Roddick has been an icon for business women and female entrepreneurs. Not only is she a spokesperson and a campaigner for numerous women's causes, but her corporate staff is comprised primarily of women, although the proportion of women at senior levels drops off precipitously. This drop is of great concern to Roddick, and this was part of her motivation to enter into a long-term experimental project on creating gender equality in her company. In 1996 she opened the doors of her company to the scrutiny and experimentation of a team of US- and UK-based researchers funded by the Ford Foundation. This longitudinal action-research project has been attempting to locate processes of change that will eradicate the subtle, but deeply ingrained, cultural processes that continue to perpetuate gender inequalities. Her persistence with this experimental work

affirms Roddick's leadership in and commitment to gender equality. She is committed to helping her organisation become a corporate exemplar in the area of gender equality.

2 Main contribution

Most commentators would readily agree that Anita Roddick has been a charismatic leader of the corporate social responsibility movement. She has pushed the limits of what business can be and how it can conduct its activities. As a child of the 1960s, her vision has helped others of her own generation to reconcile their commitment to social justice and their desires to achieve material success. Her legacy will undoubtedly have an impact on business for years to come.

The importance of Roddick's leadership extends far beyond the boundaries of her business. As a passionate and charismatic spokesperson, she has inspired other business people to seek a broader, socially oriented mission. A number of organizations throughout the world have been formed to bring together business people with socially based missions and to help business people reflect on the social implications of their practices. These include the Social Venture Network, Students for Responsible Business, Business for Social Responsibility and the World Business Academy. Roddick serves on the board of some of these organizations, is regularly a speaker at the conferences and has been cited consistently as a leader of this 'movement'.

The desire to disseminate the mission and methods of socially responsible business practice inspired Anita and Gordon Roddick to found and support an educational institution devoted to this objective. In the mid-1990s the New Academy of Business was founded to offer a curriculum on socially responsible business practice for business people and students. As of 1996 the Academy had a number of programmes, including a graduate degree programme offered in partnership with the University of Bath.

3 Evaluation

A number of critics have suggested that Roddick makes claims about socially responsible practice beyond what she has been able to achieve in her own company. Some have charged Roddick with exaggerating the company's achievements in the areas of environmentalism, animal rights, women's rights and even fair trading practice. Some accuse her of being a radical and of breaking the rules of business.

Roddick has readily admitted that she has refused to follow the rules of business. For the company's first seventeen years it had no marketing department and refused to pay for advertising, yet the Body Shop is one of the most widely recognized brands in the world, according to Interbrand, a leading brand consultancy. Some attribute this success to the visibility, charisma and passion of Roddick, while others suggest that it is due to the market niche the company has established throughout the world.

Although her passion, flamboyance and visionary rhetoric may make Roddick vulnerable to charges that she has not lived up to her claims, her vision and her passion have inspired thousands of people throughout the world. The rhetoric of revolutionary leaders is always ahead of their reality. That is in part what makes them leaders. Few can doubt that Roddick has been a leader. She has provided inspiration for those who want to see a broader role for business in the world, who want business to be run with heart as well as mind, and who want compassion and justice to drive decisions at least as much as profitability.

Hopefully, Roddick will continue to push the boundaries of what is possible for business and at the same time work to make her company an exemplar of her visions.

For her leadership, Roddick has been awarded numerous awards and honorary degrees, including Honorary LLDs at Nottingham (1990), New England College (1991) and Victoria (1995), and an Honorary DBA at Kingston (1996), as well as others. She has been awarded the Veuve Clicquot Business Woman of the Year Award (1984), National Association of Women Business Owners Award and Business Leader of the Year Award (1992), Mexican Environmental Achiever Award (1993), National Audubon Society Medal (1993), Botwinick Prize in Business Ethics (1994), Hunter College Campus Schools, American Dream Award (1996) and UNEP Women Leaders in Action Award (1997), among others.

4 Conclusion

Anita Roddick is and has been a role model and leader to women and men throughout the world. As a successful entrepreneur, charismatic leader of socially responsible business, (com)passionate political activist, and tireless champion of civil rights and women's self-esteem, she has inspired millions of people throughout the world through her legacy and vision. Given the prominence of Roddick as a spokesperson for her company and her role as the company's creative beacon, some wonder what will happen to the company's unique brand when she retires. Since neither of her daughters has been active in the organization, there is speculation about succession. Fortunately, Roddick shows no sign of slowing down.

DEBRA MEYERSON
STANFORD UNIVERSITY

Further reading

The Body Shop (1997) *The Entrepreneurs Journey*. (Brochure that describes the development and mission of the Body Shop as articulated by Roddick.)

Liebig, J. (1994) *Merchants of Vision*, San Francisco, CA: Berrett-Koehler Publishers. (Provides profiles of innovators in business who have tried to link business objectives to socially oriented missions.)

Renesch, J. (1991) *New Traditions in Business: Spirit and Leadership in the 21rst Century*, San Francisco, CA: New Leaders Press. (Anthology that includes works by fifteen scholars who trace the impact of the transition of the role of business in society.)

Roddick, A. (1991) *Body and Soul: Profits with Principles – the Amazing Success Story of Anita Roddick and the Body Shop*, New York: Crown Publishers. (Autobiography of Anita Roddick, tracing her life and journey in founding and expanding the Body Shop.)

Roddick, A. (1997) 'Anita Roddick's column', *Independent on Sunday*. (Regular feature columns written by Roddick on various topics.)

The Salim group

Summary

The Salim Group is Indonesia's largest conglomerate. It is also one of the most diversified. There are more than 400 affiliated
companies and they employ at least 135,000
people. Group assets amounted to more than
$14 billion in June 1997. Increasingly, the
group is expanding offshore. At least 35 per
cent of the group's revenue now comes from
overseas. The group has large operations in
Hong Kong and Singapore, and, through
these, operates in China, the rest of South-
East Asia and Australia. Liem Sioe Liong
(Sudono Salim), Djuhar Sutanto (Liem Oen
Kian), Ibrahim Risjad and Sudwikatmono
jointly own the Salim Group but the leading
figure is Liem Sioe Liong, with whom the
group is synonymous. Day-to-day management increasingly is in the hands of one of
Liem's sons, Anthony Salim.

1 Introduction

Liem Sioe Liong was born in 1916 near
Fuqing, in China's Fujian Province. He left
China for Indonesia in 1938, where, together
with his brother Liem Sioe Hie, he joined an
uncle's peanut-oil business in Kudus, central
Java. From these humble beginnings he rose
to become one of South-East Asia's wealthiest business people. His loose and highly
diversified business interests form the Salim
Group.

2 Biographical data

Little is known about Liem's early years. He
was the second son of peasant parents in
China. He is believed to have married in
China, but his wife remained there when he
emigrated to central Java in 1938. He married
again after his arrival in Java. He is believed to
have only elementary schooling, and is a practising Buddhist who donates to Buddhist tem-
ples in Jakarta. Also, many Salim Group
buildings reflect the principals of *feng shui*, or
Chinese geomancy, in their designs, which is
a testament to Liem's beliefs. Importantly, he
is a native speaker of the Chinese Hokchia
dialect, a dialect he shares with several other
prominent overseas Chinese businessmen.
Like many first-generation overseas Chinese
entrepreneurs, he is personally very frugal and
maintains a vegetarian diet and a daily exercise routine. Chinese clan and dialect associations are banned in Indonesia, but Liem is an
honorary lifetime chairman of the Singapore
Futsing Association.

3 Main contribution

Liem supplied the fledgling Indonesian
army's Diponegoro division in central Java
with food, medicines and military supplies
during Indonesia's struggle for Independence
(1945–1949). The then quartermaster of the
division was Soeharto (commonly spelt
Suharto in the West), until recently president
of Indonesia. Soeharto held the position
throughout most of the 1950s. The relationship between Liem and Soeharto endured and
is one of the more important factors in the
Salim Group's phenomenal success. In the
years immediately after Independence, Liem
concentrated on agricultural commodities
trading, as well as textiles manufacturing and
importing.

In 1968 Liem's company, PT Mega, and
one other company jointly were designated by
ministerial decree as the exclusive importers
of cloves. The Government set the clove import and selling price, but both companies
were guaranteed a 5 per cent commission.

Cloves are an essential ingredient in Indonesia's famous kretek cigarettes, and Liem's share in the clove import monopoly netted him the capital he needed to expand and diversify his business interests. Earnings from monopolistic rents have been a constant feature of the Salim Group's history.

In 1969 Liem and Djuhar Sutanto established PT Bogasari Flour Mill, which the Government permitted a virtual monopoly over the domestic milling of wheat flour. The Salim Group's control of flour milling allowed it to become the world's largest producer of instant noodles, as potential competitors in noodles found they were unable to secure independent and reliable sources of flour. The noodle interests were the basis for PT Indofood Sukses Makmur, what is today Indonesia's largest food manufacturer.

Clove, flour and noodle profits allowed Liem to start Indocement in 1973. Since its inception Indocement has had a close relationship with the Indonesian Government. By the mid-1980s Indocement had over-expanded and it was effectively bailed out by the Government, which bought into the company, providing a much-needed capital infusion. Today Indocement is the largest cement manufacturer in Indonesia.

Liem's closeness to the Government was again underscored in 1989, when another Salim Group unit was in trouble and the Government helped out once more. The group's 40 per cent share in the loss-making PT Cold Rolling Mill Indonesia Utama was acquired by the Government and now is a fully owned unit within the state-owned PT Krakatau Steel.

The Group's foray into banking has ultimately proved very successful. Liem founded Bank Central Asia (BCA) in 1957. It did not experience any significant capital growth for many years. In 1973 it was a one-branch bank unable to trade in foreign exchange. However, in 1975 fellow Indonesian Chinese Mochtar Riady was appointed president, having been enticed with a 17.5 per cent shareholding. Riady immediately set about increasing BCA's net worth, largely by injecting the profits from other group members to increase the bank's capital base. The branch network was expanded; new clients were solicited and cultivated; lending at rates lower than other private banks expanded the loan portfolio; and permission to trade in foreign exchange was successfully sought. Today BCA is the largest private bank in Indonesia and has more branches across Indonesia than any other bank. The Salim Group owns the majority of equity in BCA, but Soeharto's oldest son Sigit Harjojudanto has a 16 per cent stake and his eldest daughter Siti Hardijanti Rukmana holds a 14 per cent stake. BCA's links to the Soeharto family saw it become a target during riots in 1998 and a subsequent run on deposits.

During the 1990s the group made new forays in Indonesia into chemicals (it now is Indonesia's sole producer of the detergent ingredient alkylbenzene, which again underlines the group's strategy of seeking out monopolies), office-tower development, hotels, industrial estates, telecommunications, television, insurance, car assembly, infrastructure development, fast food, supermarkets, logging, coal mining, palm oil, sugar refining and fisheries. In fact, there are few sectors in Indonesia in which the group is not involved.

The group has made deft use of the stock market, raising billions of dollars to fund further expansion, but also to enrich the majority shareholders. Assets that are privately held by Liem and his family and associates are routinely sold to the publicly listed members of the group. Five of the group's Indonesian subsidiaries were listed on the Jakarta stock exchange at the end of 1997.

Structure and management

The Salim Group in Indonesia has attempted to modernize its corporate structure. Greater use has been made of holding companies and there has been an attempt to group formerly disparate companies into divisions.

A Salim Group board of directors was set up in 1990 to control the group's interests. The board consists of Liem (chairman of the Salim Group), Andree Halim (vice-chairman of the Salim Group and Liem's second son;

the family name is Halim, not Salim, but many Chinese Indonesians are flexible with their Indonesian aliases), Anthony Salim (group president and chief executive officer (CEO)) and several non-family directors.

Formally, there are eleven divisions under the board of directors, each of which has a steering committee to determine basic policy and a division management committee to supervise day-to-day operations. A division is composed of a number of subdivisions, under which sit the individual companies. Ten divisions are concerned largely with overseeing the group's Indonesian interests, and an international division oversees the group's growing overseas interests.

However, it is not clear to what degree this structure is actually adhered to. The group retains the vestiges of a large family-run enterprise. It remains easier to define the group by common ownership rather than through any formal corporate structure.

The group's expansion offshore

More than 35 per cent of the Salim Group's revenues are sourced from outside Indonesia. Its largest holdings abroad are in Hong Kong and Singapore, although group operations now are spread across dozens of countries. The Salim Group often cooperates with various companies that are linked to the Singapore Government – with which it has good relations – particularly in ventures in Singapore, China and Indonesia.

The Salim Group's Hong Kong operations began in earnest with the acquisition of Hong Kong-based Shanghai Land Ltd in the early 1980s. It transformed the company into the First Pacific Group, which today is listed on the stock exchange of Hong Kong, operates in more than fifty countries, with total assets of around $8.5 billion, and has in excess of 53,000 employees. First Pacific now is among Hong Kong's ten largest companies by sales. A team of highly trained expatriate professionals manages it. The principal affiliates of First Pacific include Hong Kong-based property manager First Pacific Davies, Thailand-based distributor Berli Jucker Co. Ltd, Hong Kong-based First Pacific Bank and the

Philippines-based holding company Metro Pacific. In 1995 Metro Pacific led a consortium that paid $1.6 billion for a 214-hectare site adjacent to Manila's central business district. The consortium will develop the site as an integrated office and residential area. In late 1997 First Pacific Davies announced plans to open 100 fitness centres around Asia, representing an estimated investment of $400 million. In early 1998 the First Pacific announced that it intended to sell its principal asset, a 40 per cent stake in the Netherlands-based distribution company Hagemeyer (which alone has worldwide sales of more than $4.5 billion). The sale was forced by Asia's financial crisis and the group's need to reduce its US-dollar debts. Some of the remaining proceeds are likely to be used by First Pacific to buy assets from the Salim Group. Diversification rather than consolidation remains a driving motivation at First Pacific Group.

The Kabila Mandiri Persada (KMP) Group holds Salim's Singapore-based interests. KMP's major asset is a controlling interest in the publicly traded United Industrial Corporation (UIC) Ltd. UIC in turn controls another public company, Singapore Land, which is one of Singapore's largest holders of commercial real estate. In this, Liem cooperates with Wee Cho Yaw, another senior South-East Asian Chinese entrepreneur, who also is the chairman of United Overseas Bank, one of Singapore's largest banks. Other UIC subsidiaries are involved in information technology, travel services, shipping, detergents production, printing and packaging. Other KMP subsidiaries include the Singapore franchise for the fast-food chain Kentucky Fried Chicken (KFC).

4 Evaluation

Salim Group and its Hong Kong and Singapore offshoots defy the conventional management wisdom that it is best to focus on core competencies. Instead, the group is forever diversifying. Its diverse and unwieldy structure can survive only while its operations face few competitors. In a world of more open markets the group will need to adjust its practices if it is to remain intact and prosper.

Another uncertainty for the group relates to politics. Much of its position in Indonesia has been achieved through favours bestowed due to the close relationship between Liem Sioe Liong and Soeharto. It remains to be seen whether the privileges granted will remain after Soeharto's fall from power. Also, another threat has been the Asian financial crisis of 1997–8. Cronyism of the type suggested by the Liem–Soeharto relationship was pinpointed as one the causes of the crisis. Consequently, such practices are under threat by financial markets and austerity measures imposed by the International Monetary Fund (IMF). The group's dependence on Liem Sioe Liong's connections and its insufficient separation between ownership and management pose serious risks for the future. This was borne out in late 1997 when false reports of Liem's death led to a major run on several branches of BCA, which caused the bank to lose deposits worth millions of dollars.

5 Conclusion

While the Salim Group has several owners, it is closely identified with Liem Sioe Liong. Liem and the Salim Group demonstrate many characteristics typical of first-generation overseas Chinese entrepreneurs. The cross-border networks of these entrepreneurs have allowed them to access opportunities and capital quickly. In turn, this has allowed them to dominate many of the South-East Asian economics in which they reside. In Indonesia, for example, the ethnic Chinese comprise no more than 4 per cent of the population but are believed to own as much as 70 per cent of the non-land private capital. The Salim Group has established itself as an important conglomerate across Asia, although the focus of much of its activities remains in Indonesia. Management and structural weaknesses, as well as political risk, mean its future prospects are uncertain. If the group is able to modernize sufficiently – by introducing more professional management, greater transparency in its decision-making and more distinct boundaries between individual subsidiaries – it should evolve into an important multinational in years to come.

MICHAEL BACKMAN
AEMC FELLOW

Further reading

Backman, Michael (1998) *Asian Eclipse*, Singapore: John Wiley & Sons. (Provides a detailed account of corporate governance issues as they relate to the Salim Group as well as the group's role in the overseas Chinese community.)

Ch'ng, D.C.L. (1993) *The Overseas Chinese Entrepreneurs in East Asia: Background, Business Practices and International Networks*, Melbourne: Committee for the Economic Development of Australia (CEDA). (Provides basic information on the Salim Group and other overseas Chinese-owned companies in East Asia.)

Cragg, C. (1995) *The New Taipans*, London: Century Ltd. (Provides a brief account of Liem Sioe Liong's business activities.)

East Asia Analytical Unit (1995) *Overseas Chinese Business Networks in Asia*, Canberra: Department of Foreign Affairs and Trade. (Provides a detailed account of the origins and development of the Salim Group, as well as a biographical account of Liem Sioe Liong and his social, ancestral and business relationships with other important overseas Chinese business people; also contains a chart that shows the structure of the Salim Group, and another that shows the group's joint ventures and cross-shareholdings with other Indonesian conglomerates.)

Institute for Economic and Financial Research (1997) *Indonesian Capital Market Directory 1997*, Jakarta: Jakarta Stock Exchange. (Provides summaries and financial information for those Salim Group subsidiaries listed on the Jakarta stock exchange.)

Pusat Data Business Indonesia (1997) *Conglomeration Indonesia*, vol. 3, Jakarta: Pusat Data Business Indonesia. (Gives an account of the Salim Group's development and presents a list of each known Salim Group subsidiary and affiliate.)

Sato, Y. (1993) 'The Salim Group in Indonesia: the development and behaviour of the largest conglomerate in Southeast Asia', *Developing Economies* 31(4): 408–41. (Summarizes the early development of the Salim Group in great detail and with excellent analysis.)

Schwarz, A. (1994) *A Nation in Waiting: Indonesia in the 1990s*, Sydney: Allen & Unwin. (Deals particularly with Liem Sioe Liong's reliance on President Soeharto, and vice versa.)

Suryadinata, L. (1988) 'Chinese economic elites in Indonesia: a preliminary study', in J.W. Cushman and Wang Gungwu (eds), *Changing Identities of the Southeast Asian Chinese since World War II*, Hong Kong: Hong Kong University Press. (Provides an account of Liem Sioe Liong's early days in business.)

See also: BUSINESS STRATEGIES, EAST ASIAN; POLITICAL RISK

Related topics in the IEBM: BIG BUSINESS AND CORPORATE CONTROL; ENTREPRENEURSHIP; MANAGEMENT IN INDONESIA

Sloan, Alfred Pritchard, Jr (1875–1966)

Personal background

- born 23 May 1875 in New Haven, Connecticut
- eldest of four sons of a New Haven tea, coffee and cigar wholesaler and retailer
- grew up in Brooklyn, New York, from the age of ten
- graduated with degree in electrical engineering from Massachusetts Institute of Technology in 1895
- began career with Hyatt Roller Bearing Company, New Jersey, in 1895, becoming its president at the age of twenty-six
- after Hyatt was acquired by General Motors (GM) he became vice president and a member of its executive committee in 1918, then its operating vice president in 1920, then its president and chief executive officer in 1923
- reorganized GM from an untidy group of largely separate businesses into a widely emulated model of rational organization
- divided GM into five different divisions, each with its make of car in a different price range
- decentralized production while centralizing administration
- built up GM to surpass Ford's car sales in the USA in the late 1920s, and to become the largest company in the world
- funded several charities named after him, a centre for the advanced study of engineering and the prestigious Sloan School of Management at the Massachusetts Institute of Technology

Major works

Adventures of a White Collar Man (with B. Sparkes) (1941)
My Years with General Motors (1964)

Summary

Alfred P. Sloan, Jr (1875–1966) was an administrative genius who, with Henry Ford, brought the modern car industry into being. His successes followed Ford's with the Model T Ford, which was becoming increasingly obsolescent as General Motors (GM) began developing a wider range of cars. His very successful reorganization and development of GM along federal lines and evolving elaborate decentralization was and is imitated all over the world. Sloan used cost accounting, market analysis and internal competition as strong frameworks for a philosophy and style of management which was relatively fair, open, informal and democratic. Sloan joined GM in 1918 and retired in 1956, and was its chief executive officer from 1923 to 1946. Sloan's flexible and innovative approach to very large-scale organization and management was extremely successful, but elements of complacency and fear of change were apparent in GM by the 1960s. Habits of undue emphasis on economy and rather stereotyped approaches to marketing, as well as decreasing emphasis on technical innovation, combined with foreign competition to give the company problems from the 1970s onwards. Nevertheless most of the main elements of Sloan's philosophy are still widely praised for their administrative, economic, moral, political, psychological and social logic.

1 Introduction

Sloan is generally recognized as an organizational genius and, to a lesser extent, a marketing genius, who unified the efforts of a varied group of car manufacturing companies into the world's largest and most successful maker of cars. His achievements brought the car industry to its early maturity and were massively influential on other companies and in other sectors, and on the understanding and study of management.

The principles of decentralization and of the use of staff services in senior management developed under Sloan were not new but he and Pierre Du Pont (of Du Pont Chemicals), his helper and collaborator, applied and elaborated them extensively in large-scale private sector manufacturing for the first time. He was also responsible for influential developments in consumer marketing, for innovations in the use of specialist expertise in management, and for numerous developments in ways of obtaining, presenting and using data needed by decision makers.

The above achievements of Sloan have been built upon, but not genuinely superseded in spite of criticisms based on their somewhat inward-looking character. They were inward-looking in so far as they were strongly focused on GM's internal or immediate commercial concerns, and because GM faced little seriously effective competition during the 1920s, when its mould was made. They were sometimes described as being important building blocks for a democratic capitalist social order and then criticized for their narrowness, for the failure of GM executives to think beyond the corporation's relations with its suppliers, dealers and customers to its role in the wider society. However, Sloan's emphasis on fairness, on cooperation and competition used creatively in management, and on decision making based on rational discussion of facts, all within a very large, diverse, widespread and productive organization, continues to point the way forward for students and practitioners of management, industry and business, and of their roles in society.

2 Biographical data

Alfred P. Sloan, Jr was born into a middle-class business and professional family in New Haven, Connecticut on 23 May 1875. The family moved to Brooklyn in New York City when he was ten, and in 1895 he graduated from the Massachusetts Institute of Technology with a degree in electrical engineering. In the same year he began work for the Hyatt Roller Bearing Company of Harrison, New Jersey, which made tapered roller bearings, as a $10 per week draughtsman. After a short while Sloan left Hyatt to work for a firm which made one of the first electrical refrigerators, but after two years he returned to Hyatt, which was about to go out of business. However, the company was loaned $5,000 by Sloan's father and some friends while Sloan and a young bookkeeper, Peter Steenstrup, tried to change its fortunes. Steenstrup looked after Hyatt's finances and Sloan looked after design, engineering, production and sales, learning much about business management and something about mass production in the process. The latter occurred because when Sloan took Hyatt over the car industry was the main buyer of its products, and its demands were constantly growing and changing. Two particular lessons concerned the ever-growing precision of the parts used in cars, and the demand for price concessions from major buyers, which impressed on Sloan the need to look continually for lower costs and better methods, and thus the full value of systematic accounting, research and planning.

In 1916 the first major architect of General Motors, William C. Durant, then of the currently forming United Motors, suggested that Hyatt be sold to it. After some thought Sloan saw that because the future of Hyatt lay with large mass producers like Ford and GM, it was dependent on mass production and could only be profitable as long as it was selling to mass producers. Because Ford and GM were both capable of making their own roller bearings, the Durant proposal was accepted. Sloan became president of United Motors, which GM bought in 1918, when he also became a vice president of GM. At the same time the General Motors Company became the General Motors Corporation. This ended Chevrolet control of GM with Chevrolet remaining a major part of the new corporation. William C. Durant, the founder of GM, had foreseen, around 1900, the brilliant prospects for big vertically integrated companies making a variety of cars. GM was first founded in 1908 from Buick, Cadillac, Oakland (to become Pontiac) and Oldsmobile. Durant made two attempts to buy Ford at a time when Ford's great successes were imminent or starting, with Ford's responses making it hard to believe that he was doing any more than flirting with the idea of joining the corporation which was to overtake his company to become the USA's and the world's number one car producer from the mid-1920s onwards.

Durant had a whirlwind approach to business growth. He joined forces with Louis Chevrolet in 1911 to produce, around 1915, a popular car to challenge the rise of Ford's all-conquering Model T. Durant had lost control of GM and he began to try to recover it with the help of the Du Pont family which was making a great deal of money manufacturing chemicals during the First World War and which saw a potentially very good investment in the motor industry. The bankers' trust that controlled GM expired in 1916 and Durant returned to power, along with the Chevrolet company as the tail wagging the GM dog.

During the First World War and for most of the following decade until 1928, Ford's enormous success with the Model T swept almost all before it. Most cars apart from the Model T, however, were becoming more complicated and expensive to make, and newcomers to the industry found survival increasingly difficult. The First World War had given a big impetus to the mass production of motor vehicles. In 1919 Ford produced about 50 per cent and GM about 20 per cent of the cars made in the USA and the prospects for the industry seemed very bright. However the depression of 1920–1 began with most car manufacturers over-extended and led to major reorganizations in the industry which had long-term effects on its future structure. In 1919 the General Motors Acceptance Corporation was founded to help dealers with the finance of loans to customers and with handling used car sales. Dealers were thus supported through difficult periods by what was a very forward-looking measure for its time. However, while Durant was a very dynamic salesman and promoter with considerable energy, integrity and

managerial ability, his management of so large and complex an organization as GM tended to be too single-handed and impulsive.

Unlike Walter Chrysler, then head of Buick, Sloan did not quarrel with Durant about the effects of the latter's style of management. However Sloan reacted to it by producing a plan for the reorganization of GM which Durant approved but then did nothing to implement. The plan offered decentralization and delegation of authority to counteract the administrative chaos of Durant's approach to management. In 1920 Sloan saw how GM needed to cut its prices from wartime to peacetime levels. The ever-optimistic Durant could not see this and feared that price-cutting could put at risk his attempts to support GM on the stock market. Sloan saw this as an example of Durant's overemphasis on financing operations through the stock market and relative neglect of more mundane but important matters.

Sloan took a month's leave of absence in Europe to consider his future, as he could foresee ruin for GM. When he returned it was to find Durant gone. The Du Pont company had bought Durant's GM shares and paid off his obligations, and secured his resignation from the presidency of GM. Sloan and other executives got Pierre Du Pont to take over as president of GM to reassure the public about the company's basic soundness. Sloan became executive vice president and put his reorganization plan into effect.

By 1921 Ford was manufacturing about 60 per cent of all the motor vehicles made in the USA, whereas GM, which had just survived a near disaster, depended on two of its five models, Buick and Cadillac, for most of its sales. However, during the 1920s it replaced Ford as the industry's leading company. This was partly due to Henry Ford's idealization of the Model T and the assembly line. Ford mistook them for the culmination of car production, rather than as very important steps in its progress. The Model T of 1908 continued to sell on the basis of its low price for most of the 1920s, at a time when the rising affluence it was bringing into being was making price less and less important in the US public's buyer behaviour. Ford's failings combined with the success of Sloan's plan to engineer a sea change in the industry's structure.

Sloan's structural plan clearly distinguished GM's central planning and policy-making bodies from its operating divisions, which were autonomous, self-contained and competing within GM's general policy framework. This was a clear separation of staff and line functions. Following his experiences with Durant, but also by employing his own clear logic, Sloan recognized that no one person could ever manage a corporation of GM's size effectively. Careful analysis of relevant facts was needed as a basis for group judgement. While lines of authority were defined clearly, authority was nevertheless decentralized as much as possible. Managers at all levels were encouraged and empowered to make decisions. Each of GM's companies became an operating division under an executive with almost complete responsibility for its management. The services of the staff functions like financial and sales policy and research were available to all the constituent operating divisions but without direct authority over them.

All of GM's operations were covered by Sloan's changes. Thus Sloan spent a great deal of time visiting dealers in what was increasingly changing into a buyers' market. Mechanisms for managing the dealer relationship and giving financial support to dealers were developed way beyond those used by Ford. Sloan also built up an efficient and co-operative team at the top of GM. William S. Knudsen was in charge of the ailing Chevrolet Division and he made it Ford's main challenger. GM also introduced the annual model change, a sales technique designed to fight the ageing Model T and to encourage the growth of second-hand car sales. Knudsen became GM's production genius, the equivalent of Ford's Charlie Sorensen, and he eventually became Sloan's successor. GM developed an increasingly sophisticated range of cars at moderate prices. In 1927 the production of Ford's Model T ended and Chevrolet became the industry leader in terms of sales, a position which it generally retained for many years, even if Ford's Model A, first sold late in 1928, outsold Chevrolet in its first year.

In the 1930s the US car industry's three main firms, GM, Ford and Chrysler, all suffered but were never threatened with extinction. Chrysler survived by technical innovation and, especially, careful financial management. Ford was very badly managed but too big to go under. GM came through safely by efficient management and good financial planning, and expanded successfully into new areas, such as aircraft and diesel engines. Sloan resigned from the presidency of GM in 1937, remaining chairman of the board. When he stood down GM made over one-third of the world's output of motor vehicles, as well as aircraft engines, diesel locomotives and refrigerators. It had been the world's largest manufacturer of cars since 1925. Apart from the Chevrolet, the best-selling car in the USA, it also made the Cadillac and its La Salle version, the Oldsmobile, Pontiac and Buick, trucks and buses, and Opel cars in Germany and Vauxhall cars in the UK. It had grown into the biggest industrial concern of all time. The Du Pont Company owned nearly a quarter of its shares: otherwise GM's ownership was quite widely shared.

Sloan opposed trade unions in the USA in the 1920s and 1930s but accepted them as inevitable when Roosevelt was elected in 1936 along with the New Deal. Sloan was a businessman and engineer of his time and place in his suspicion and fear of trade unions and government intervention. On the other hand, he had strong and positive ideas on the contributions which business and industry made to society and his methodical and open-ended approach to management was far more than a matter of logically balancing centralization and decentralization.

Sloan was a very able selector of managers, a strong and effective advocate of research, and in some respects a marketing genius. Above all he was a great advocate and practitioner of teamwork, whose breadth of understanding and diplomacy had marked him out for the highest levels of management early in his career. He was a 'great empiricist, a complex personality and a tireless worker who made GM his all embracing interest. He let time, precision and an incisive appeal work for him' (Dale 1971: 86). He gave up being

GM's chief executive officer in 1946, and finally resigned from the chairmanship in 1956, while remaining an honorary chairman and working as a strategic consultant. He had endowed the Sloan Foundation in the late 1930s and supported such philanthropic societies as the Memorial Sloan–Kettering Cancer Center, New York City, and the Sloan School of Management and a centre for advanced engineering at the Massachusetts Institute of Technology. In 1964, two years before his death, he outlined his management policy in great detail in *My Years with General Motors*. He had written the ebullient *Adventures of a White Collar Man* with Boyden Sparkes in 1941.

3 Main contribution

Sloan's greatest contribution to the practice and understanding of management is most closely summarized by one word, which he and others often called an oversimplification: decentralization. Schnapp (1979) described how decision making at GM under Sloan was informal and collaborative and how the company did not have a formal strategic planning function like that of the Ford Motor Company. Decisions were made partly through a complicated but logical grouping of senior committees and partly in an arguably very *ad hoc* way, rather democratically and 'more effectively than other companies because of some basic values deeply embedded in the GM organization' (Schnapp 1979: 145). Most people who knew GM would inevitably think of Sloan on reading this.

In the early 1920s Sloan saw that the overwhelming need at GM was for coordination of product and financial policies and of the activities of its five largely independent divisions. He and his team foresaw significant market growth because of the development of closed body (all weather) car designs, of the USA's systems of paved highways, of the used car market and of bank financing of car purchases. GM needed a more coordinated and rational product policy and strong central control, too, over finance. An integrated business policy which minimized overlap and waste was vital. This implied central control

over all design, development, investment, location, production and promotional decisions. It meant genuine delegation of decision-making power to genuinely competing product divisions. Divisional management could, therefore, only be overridden by decisions taken at the highest level of GM, so that central staff functions had to use persuasion, and not coercion, to influence divisional managers.

The power to finance projects was separated from their originators and advocates. This meant that GM's top decision-making group, the executive committee, had to pass on proposals that it had approved itself to the corporate finance committee for its separate approval, before they could be submitted to the board of directors. The executive and finance committees were thus deliberately set up partly in opposition to each other.

Writing soon after the end of the Second World War, Drucker explained how Sloan had developed decentralization in GM to 'satisfy the basic requirements of institutional life' (1946: 41). These requirements included survival as an efficient entity, which demanded a policy that harmonized the divergent claims of administration and of specific tasks, which facilitated change and rejected expediency, and which provided a suitable framework for local action. Thus responsibility and power had to be distributed appropriately, policy formulation and operational planning had to be both undertaken and balanced, and considerable attention had to be paid to the selection and development of all kinds of staff, at all levels and for almost every purpose. In the 1930s and 1940s GM consisted of three major product groups: cars and trucks; accessories and spare parts (also refrigerators); and non-automotive (diesel and aircraft) engines. These businesses were organized in around thirty divisions, some very large, such as Chevrolet cars, and some small single plant ones with fewer than a thousand employees.

Each division was organized and managed as an autonomous business unit and the three largest were represented at the most senior level of GM by their own top managers. The others were represented at that level of GM by individuals drawn from product-based groups. As part of GM's central management and side by side with the product management organization, functional service staffs with their own vice presidents (manufacturing, engineering, sales, research, personnel, finance, public relations, legal affairs and so on) advised both divisional (line managers) and central management, liaised between the divisions, and formulated corporate policies. The line or manufacturing organization of GM was headed by the president and two executive vice presidents, and the staff one was headed by the chairman of the board of directors, who was also the chief executive officer of GM, and by the vice chairman of the board.

These five formed a team that worked with and through two major committees, the administration and policy ones. These two committees were the 'government' of GM, the 'central organ[s] of co-ordination, decision and control' (Drucker 1946: 43). They were the final courts of appeal for disagreements about policy in GM. All the most senior people in GM and representatives of its major shareholders belonged to them and they combined all sorts of experiences and backgrounds into one policy. They were kept fully informed about all general and staff and line issues and decisions facing GM and their role was to discuss and decide about them.

Numerous, much smaller sub-committees formed from these members dealt with mainly functional matters on a regular basis, feeding information and recommendations upwards to the two main committees. GM had up to 500 senior executives and 250,000 employees (double the latter number in the Second World War). Strong financial control had become one of the main ways of keeping divisional managements in line while encouraging them to have the prestige and to exercise the power of real bosses. Central management needed to know even minor details of divisional management but divisional managers needed to have real authority and standing, too. Drucker (1946: 47) called GM 'an essay in federalism', which successfully combined the highest levels of corporate unity with divisional autonomy and responsibility. Decentralization at GM under Sloan was far more than a

division of labour. It was a philosophy of management and a system of local self-government which extended down to include the level of first line supervision and externally to relations with business partners (especially car dealers).

The benefits of Sloan's system of decentralization appear to have included clear and reasonably quick decision making, a relative lack of internal conflict, an atmosphere of fairness, democracy and informality, a sense of management being a large-scale activity shared among many, a plentiful supply of experienced and able leaders, the early detection and timely resolution of problems and an absence of management by edict. Central policies were unified and coherent and set clear goals and gave clear guidance to divisions. Central management acted as the eyes and ears for the whole of GM, and it planned and governed the long-term future of the divisions. It obtained their capital and it handled many of their financial, legal and accounting tasks as well as most trade union negotiations and contracts. Central management's services staff also kept divisions up to date with developments in engineering, marketing, accounting and other specialist areas. Divisional managements were in complete charge of production and sales, almost all staffing, of engineering, investment planning, advertising, public relations, buying and relations with dealers and so on.

About 95 per cent of all division-level decisions were taken by divisional managers who were virtually in complete control of their own businesses. They operated a system of bonuses which gave them considerable independence within centrally determined limits designed to curb excesses of favouritism and spitefulness. There were many open and informal devices designed to maintain a two-way flow of information between the highest levels of central management and the lowest levels of the divisions' management. Twice a year, and at the GM headquarters in Detroit, between 200 and 300 senior managers from all over GM met, so as to ensure that all senior managers got to know something about the whole GM picture. Also, members of GM's central management regularly visited divisions for several days at a time.

GM's relations with car dealers were a further significant element in the decentralized approach. Dealers were often locally prominent businessmen who were none the less tied to GM and its fortunes. They had little control over their own costs, or over the price of cars or the manner of their sale. Also, while GM was mainly interested in dealers' new car sales, dealers got most of their profits from the sales of used ones. GM applied the philosophy of enlightened self-interest to support dealers through difficult times and to protect them against financial pressures from sales staff. GM established a Dealers Council in the mid-1930s, with nearly fifty members representing a geographical cross-section of GM's USA car dealers. It discussed such issues as the nature of GM's franchise, car design and advertising techniques. The less well-known Motor Holdings Division financially supported and encouraged about 300 good and improving dealers from the late 1930s onwards. GM– dealer relations typified GM's management policies through their emphasis on harmony, mutual self-interest and stability.

Managers at all levels were encouraged to criticize GM policies and practices. Criticisms were not penalized: they were taken seriously. Persuasion and rational arguments were used at virtually all times. However central management was the boss. There was a mixture of freedom and order; open management tended to ensure that issues, ideas, problems and decisions were discussed and decided upon thoroughly. Cost accounting and market analysis provided the necessary objective and impersonal background and framework for all this, with base pricing and competitive market standing respectively the main indices in use. Efficiency was thus measured, as well as debated thoroughly, with all measurements and discussions being related to production planning. The style of management mixed the informal and the impersonal and was based on the strong respect for facts which Sloan encouraged perhaps more than anything else.

When Sloan ceased to be GM's chief executive officer in 1946, he had used decentralization to manage and develop GM very effectively for a quarter of a century. Henry Ford II had just taken over his grandfather's ramshackle empire and was unashamedly copying GM's methods of organization. Sloan's methods were flexible and strongly entrenched enough to handle all but the most unusual and special problems which face very large companies. However, the experience of government control in the Second World War had shown how decentralization within GM could be threatened, not just by the centralizing tendencies of government contracts and demands, but also by other external forces such as *one* very big and powerful trade union or the US motor industry becoming a cartel.

Sloan's main contribution to the practice and understanding of business and management was to demonstrate how to balance the conflicting interests of the central and the local in a very large and diverse company. He also made a major contribution to the development of the car industry through his recognition of the growing, if structured, diversity of its market. His organizational methods and some of his other innovations were copied widely, notably by the General Electric Company as well as by Ford in the USA, by Imperial Chemical Industries in the UK, and in the USSR, Japan and western Europe.

4 Evaluation

From the 1930s to the 1960s many GM managers saw GM as something of a model for a capitalist society's industrial and social order. A very diverse and large enterprise had practised diversity through decentralization, using many different kinds of training, team building, internal representation of interests, decentralization within its constituent divisions, various forms of autonomous group working, and so on. GM's management under Sloan was a good compromise between efficiency and personal freedom and development. Performance was measured objectively and improved by a reasonable mixture of discussion, persuasion and coercion. Decentralization under Sloan meant respect for small scale and to some extent, implementation of the belief that small is beautiful. Certainly a significantly higher proportion of GM's top executives than might be expected tended to come from its smaller divisions.

During the years from when Sloan, after the Second World War, was largely part of GM's past, through that of his death in 1966 and until the 1970s and the rise of serious foreign competition, GM continued to prosper. From the 1960s until the 1980s at least, so-called liberal criticism of big US business grew louder and more strident. GM had been very effective at developing its expert management but since the 1920s it had also been more of a managed than a truly innovating company, and in almost every respect a domestic, US one rather than a true multinational, at least until long after 1945. By the 1970s it was no longer an unequivocal source of pride for most Americans, just as car ownership no longer symbolized their personal achievements. Decentralization had been a very positive thing, but GM and other large US organizations increasingly needed to work with the US and other governments, and with international agencies, and with each other, in an internationalizing and ever-more interdependent world.

There is a real if rather unfair sense, using hindsight, in which Sloan's policy of decentralization looks like one of insularity. In his book *My Years with General Motors* (1964) Sloan tells his story in a highly impersonal way, and focuses almost entirely on the internal management and organization of GM. By writing in such a way Sloan was clearly trying to set a strong example of his ideal of 'professionalism' in management. In one sense this was odd because Sloan was a very human and people-centred person. However, while he was very democratic in a typically demotic, ebullient and even slightly folksy American way, and while GM was a more or less unequivocal major success from the 1920s until the 1970s, it was increasingly under attack and out of touch with the views of many people from the 1960s onwards.

In many important respects GM was a prisoner of its own success. The affluence that it had played a big part in creating gave people the time and other resources to criticize the hands that were feeding them. Sloan appreciated business very well as a source of work, jobs, wealth, security and so on, but less well in terms of its wider roles as a source of power and influence, within communities and within society in general. He understood its economic, technical, psychological, commercial and financial aspects both imaginatively and in great detail, but at least as far as GM and his own work was concerned, his historical, political and sociological imagination was rather limited from a later twentieth-century vantage point. However, they were far from limited from the appropriate one, that of the early to mid-twentieth century, a far less affluent period in which the scale of international economic cooperation and interdependence was much smaller than it is now.

Sloan has long been a hero figure in GM as much for the atmosphere that he encouraged as anything else (Kanter 1985: 347). Dale described him as 'the great empiricist ... a complex personality and a tireless worker who made GM his all-embracing interest' (1971: 86). According to Kennedy (1941: 157, 158), Sloan was very much 'the type that does well with a big organization, provided that big organization is supplied for him'. He had been helped by being 'an accessory man, not an automobile man' in his big task of 'keeping peace among the various heads of the General Motors manufacturing divisions'. Until Sloan had the authority to do this, the very sound policy of each of the five car divisions being virtually independent was hampered by all attempts at control from head office. Sloan was very much a second-generation car industry leader, more of a team leader than an individualist, more pragmatic than romantic, more of a manager than an innovator.

Even so, Sloan's organization and management of GM was original in several respects through its very strong emphasis on facts, cooperation and 'system', in particular through the coordination and control of staff services. The line-staff distinction came from the military, and decentralization to partly autonomous sub-units had been practised by the Roman Catholic church for centuries when Sloan came to power in GM. But it was his dynamic combination of them in a commercial context (and that simultaneously taking place at du Pont Chemicals) which was new, along with the presentation and continued adaptation of his flexible 'framework of "decentralized operations and co-ordinated control"' (Dale 1971: 106), mainly through oral tradition among Sloan and other GM founder members, over several decades. Sloan and his team were also innovative in marketing policy: their aim to offer 'a car for every purse and purpose' (Chandler 1964: 16), to reach every sector of the market, effectively superseded Ford's concentration on one model. Regular developments in the performance and styling of GM's cars and energetic advertising helped the company to expand market share. Sloan's policy of financing both its car dealers and customers was also highly innovative in its day, and also the opposite of Ford's policies.

Sloan and GM's other top managers of the 1920s and 1930s had to innovate because their company, their industry and the scale of their operations were all new. As a consequence, and while most of their ideas have stood the test of time, some elements have a dated quality. Their early success probably helped to curtail consideration of alternatives and to engender a certain conservatism. This tendency was discussed by Rothschild at some length in her discussion of 'Sloanism, or GM's variety marketing' (1973: 37–40). She noted how the company focused on sales techniques in the 1930s, at the expense of technical innovation. GM stimulated and developed the cyclical trading of used cars as down payments on new ones, so that 'USA auto marketing became a worldwide model for the selling of expensive consumer goods, showing businesses how to create and nourish demand' (1973: 40). However, while the US car industry 'led the expansion of consumer demand at the end of the Second World War' (1973: 41), the increasingly saturated car market became more and more jaded.

On the technical side, the industry was no longer a new one and GM's investment levels had fallen from around 25 per cent of total sales value from 1918 to 1920, to about 4 per cent in the early 1970s. Capital investment was increasingly seen as a 'regrettable necessity' (Rothschild 1973: 49), not as an exciting adventure, as it was viewed previously. Marketing techniques and cost-cutting had increasingly been the main preoccupations of large USA car company head offices, at the expense of technical innovation. Also, ever-increasing 'Fordist regimentation' (1973: 33) of car production, aimed at cost-cutting, had long been alienating the workforce. Customers were often alienated, too, by the perpetual, generally marginal at best and expensively cosmetic at worst, upgrading of the product. For Rothschild (1973: 247), cars were the definitive US product, just as railways had been for the UK and as televisions and other electronic consumer goods were for Japan.

5 Conclusion

The main achievements of Sloan's work were: (1) the stabilization, restoration and very successful expansion of the fortunes of the major grouping of companies in a major industry; (2) the solution of many problems of very large-scale and diverse commercial management through elaborate and flexible systems of decentralization; (3) influential developments in techniques of consumer marketing; (4) the development of numerous techniques and structures for providing top managers with facts needed for making strategic policy and operational decisions; and (5) the dissemination of his experiences and achievements through example and informal education programmes, influencing management and organizational practices across the world.

Sloan's main achievement was to make the practice of management more sophisticated and to show how management could be a broadly responsible and socially benign activity. Affluence, the internationalization of production and markets, and foreign competition all eventually eroded Sloan's success at GM but others have continued to emulate and build on them for many years, both there and elsewhere.

IAN GLOVER
UNIVERSITY OF STIRLING

Further reading

(References cited in the text marked *)

Baughmar, J.P. (ed.) (1969) *The History of American Management: Selections from the Business History Review*, Englewood Cliffs, NJ: Prentice Hall. (Contains varied accounts of the development of US organizations and management which help to explain the influence of Sloan and GM in US industrial history.)

* Chandler, A.D., Jr (ed.) (1964) *Giant Enterprise: Ford, General Motors and the Automobile Industry: Sources and Readings*, New York: Harcourt, Brace and World. (Mainly consists of readings and discussions of their relevance, concerned with the development of GM and Ford from 1900 to the 1950s. Excellent on GM's innovations in management and marketing.)

* Dale, E. (1971) *The Great Organizers*, New York: McGraw-Hill. (On the development of systematic organization in US management: particularly stories on the contributions of Sloan and GM.)

* Drucker, P.F. (1946) *The Concept of the Corporation*, New York: John Day. (Considers the problems of large-scale capitalist organization and industry in the USA using GM under Sloan as its main source of evidence.)

* Kanter, R.M. (1985) *The Change Masters: Corporatist Entrepreneurs at Work*, Hemel Hempstead: Unwin. (Contains chapter on GM's problems of the 1970s and 1980s which includes a useful account of Sloan's legacy.)

* Kennedy, E.D. (1941) *The Coming of Age of Capitalism's Favourite Child*, New York: Reynal and Hitchcock. (Covers the period 1890 to 1940; rather descriptive but useful for understanding thc roles of Sloan and GM in the US car industry in the years when it was established.)

Kuhn, A. (1986) *GM Passes Ford, 1918–1938: Designing the General Motors Performance-Control System*, University Park, Pennsylvania: State University Press. (Excellent on Sloan's design of GM's structure, the prototype of the modern managerial bureaucracy.)

Rae, J.B. (1959) *American Automobile Manufacturers: The First Forty Years*, Philadelphia: Chilton. (Excellent, balanced account of the history of the industry's companies until the mid-1930s; contains many useful comparisons between GM and its rivals.)

Rae, J.B. (1965) *The American Automobile: A Brief History*, Chicago: University of Chicago Press. (Covers the industry from the 1890s to the 1960s; includes a balanced account of the roles of Sloan and GM.)

* Rothschild, E. (1973) *Paradise Lost: The Decline of the Auto-Industrial Age*, New York: Random House. (On the problems of the US car industry in the early to mid-1970s, facing public scepticism, market saturation and foreign competition; excellent on the growing conservatism of GM.)

* Schnapp, J.B. (1979) *Corporate Strategies of the Automotive Manufacturers*, Lexington, MA: D.C. Heath & Co. (Covers the strategies of four American, one German and three major Japanese car companies in the mid-late 1970s; GM and its history are compared usefully with the others.)

* Sloan, A.P., Jr (1964) *My Years with General Motors*, New York: Doubleday. (Impressively professional account of General Motors' story under Sloan, of the 'logic of management in relation to the events of the automobile industry' (p.xxiii).)

* Sloan, A.P., Jr and Sparkes, B. (1941) *Adventures of a White Collar Man*, New York: Books for Libraries. (Ebullient and endearing account of most of Sloan's life which offers much evidence of his integrity, enthusiasm, imagination and middle-class American folksiness.)

See also: GLOBALIZATION; MULTINATIONAL CORPORATIONS, ORGANIZATION STRUCTURE IN;

Related topics in the IEBM: ADVERTISING CAMPAIGNS; BIG BUSINESS AND CORPORATE CONTROL; CHANDLER, A.D.; CORPORATE STRATEGIC CHANGE; DECISION MAKING; DRUCKER, P.F.; ECONOMIC INTEGRATION, INTERNATIONAL; FORD, H.; GROUPS AND TEAMS; INDUSTRIAL AND LABOUR RELATIONS; LEADERSHIP; LOGISTICS IN MANUFACTURING MANAGEMENT AND OPERATIONS; MANAGEMENT IN NORTH AMERICA; MANAGERIAL BEHAVIOUR; MARKETING; MARKETING, FOUNDATIONS OF; MARKETING STRATEGY; ORGANIZATION BEHAVIOUR, HISTORY OF; ORGANIZATION STRUCTURE; PUBLIC RELATIONS; SCHUMACHER, E.F.; STRATEGIC CHOICE; STRATEGY AND BUYER–SUPPLIER RELATIONSHIPS; STRATEGY, CONCEPT OF; TRADE UNIONS; TAYLOR, F.W.; WILLIAMSON, O.E.

Soros, George (1930–)

1 Introduction
2 Main contribution
3 Evaluation

Personal background

- born 1930 in Budapest, Hungary, to Tivia-dor Soros, a Jewish lawyer who survived internment in Siberia from 1917 to 1921
- fled communist Hungary in 1947 when he was 17 and made his way to Paris; worked as a farm hand, house painter and railway porter
- began his studies in 1949 at the London School of Economics (LSE)
- graduated with a BS in Economics in 1952
- worked at the Singer and Friedlander merchant bank in London
- moved to New York in 1956; his parents followed him in 1957 and he supported them after their Coney Island coffee shop failed
- began as a Wall Street researcher and worked his way up to international money manager
- in 1963 became vice-president of Arnhold and S. Bleichroeder, specializing in foreign securities and investments
- in 1969 formed a business partnership with James B. Rogers, Jr, which became Soros Fund Management in 1973; Rogers left the business in 1981
- in 1973 became president of Soros Fund Management
- also chief investment adviser to Quantum Fund NV

Major works

The Alchemy of Finance (1987)
Underwriting Democracy (1991)
Soros on Soros: Ahead of the Curve (1995)

1 Introduction

The Soros family was Jewish and survived the Nazi regime in Budapest during the Second World War by using false names and identity papers. As a student at the LSE George Soros 'was influenced by the British philosopher Karl Popper, who argued that Communism and Fascism were philosophically linked and who championed the open, democratic system' (Hedges 1990).

Soros is active on a number of boards, including Fairchild Industries, Helsinki Watch, Americas Watch, the International League for Human Rights, the Brookings Council, and AIESEC (Cuff 1987; *PR Newswire* 1987). 'His philanthropies include the Open Society Inc., The Soros Foundation, the Fund for Reform and Opening of China, Inc. and the Glasnost Foundation Inc.' (*PR Newswire* 1987). He has received honorary doctoral degrees from the New School for Social Research, the University of Oxford, the Budapest University of Economics and Yale University. In addition, he was awarded the Laruea Honoris Causa by the University of Bologna for his global efforts to promote democratic societies (http://www.soros.com 1998).

Soros is 'an intellectual who could discuss finances in five languages while turning his clients' investments into fortunes' (Scardino 1987). He enjoys playing chess and philosophical debates. He has three children with his first wife, whom he broke up with in 1978 and divorced in 1981. His philanthropic activities began after his 1981 divorce. In 1983 he married Susan Weber, an art historian who is twenty-five years younger than him. The couple have two sons and maintain homes in Manhattan, Long Island and Bedford, New York, as well as London, England (Lycett 1993; Crowley 1994; Hawthorne *et al.* 1994; Smith 1996).

2 Main contribution

Soros spends 'two-thirds of his time and half of his annual income on promoting democracy abroad and a more tolerant society in the United States' (Miller 1997). In 1992 Soros contributed $100 million to support scientists and scientific research in Russia and the former Soviet countries. The donation was made by Soros in an attempt to slow the 'brain drain' which has occurred since the break-up of the Soviet Union and to create what he hopes will become the equivalent of the National Science Foundation in the United States (Southerland and Brown 1992). Also in 1992, Soros provided Bosnian civilians with $50 million to help alleviate their suffering (Miller 1997). 'Soros now runs foundations in 18 central and east European countries that support educational, cultural and economic activities' (Southerland and Brown 1992). His contributions have 'funded Oxford scholarships for Hungarian, Polish and Soviet students' (Hedges 1990). Worldwide, his philanthropic efforts in 1997 employed 1300 people in twenty-four countries coordinated by regional headquarters in New York and Budapest (Miller 1997).

In 1993 he was the highest-paid executive on Wall Street, earning $1.1 billion or more (*Chicago Tribune* 1994). 'For years he has been a hugely successful money manager and investor, but the $1 billion that he reportedly made in just a few days ... by betting against the British pound [1992] has turned him into a guru – and his investments are mimicked across the world' (Uchitelle 1993). He is, however, not immune to failures: 'George Soros lost $600 million on Feb. 14 [1994] when the yen took a jump he had bet against ... Soros' Quantum Group said the loss took almost 5% of the fund group's $12 billion in assets' (Joy 1994). However, $10,000 invested in Soros's Quantum Fund in 1969 was worth more than $21 million in 1994 (Crowley 1994). By 1996 the assets of Soros Fund Management were approximately $15 billion (*Reuters Financial Service* 1996).

Soros is an active author. In 1987 Soros published a book on his financial philosophies titled *The Alchemy of Finance*. In this book he explains his 'theory of reflexivity', which is based on his belief that stock prices are not based on facts but on the attitudes of investors.

3 Evaluation

According to *Institutional Investor Magazine*, George Soros is 'The World's Greatest Money Manager' (Cuff 1987). Soros also has his share of critics of his approach to both money management and philanthropy. There are some who claim that there is a conflict of interest when Soros invests in countries where he is giving money (Lycett 1993; Miller 1997). In terms of his philanthropy, 'Some say it is too impulsive and mercurial, too arrogant and micromanaged' (Miller 1997). According to Shawcross (1997), 'Soros deliberately courts controversy and publicity, trying to build a platform from which to propagate his views'.

In 1990 Soros stated that his biggest failure was in China, where his multimillion-dollar donations did not stimulate the democratic movement: 'The foundation itself [in China] had become an organ of the security police, ... I thought that I could apply the thinking that I used in Hungary, but the Chinese society has not reached that stage' (Hedges 1990).

He has not let that experience dampen his interest in helping emerging democracies around the globe. For example, in Russia alone, 'His foundation ... spent $25.8 million in 1994 printing textbooks, helping Russian journalists, helping libraries and carrying out other reforms' (Gordon 1995). Over the past decade Soros 'has spent more than a billion dollars promoting a free press and political pluralism abroad' (Miller 1997). He says, 'I never have regrets about having spent a lot of money trying to make things better' (Miller 1997). Soros considers himself to be more of a 'philosopher than a money manager' (Scardino 1987).

STEPHEN J. HAVLOVIC
SIMON FRASER UNIVERSITY

Further reading

(References cited in the text marked *)

* *Chicago Tribune* (1994) 'George Soros 1993's highest-paid Wall Street exec, at $1.1 billion', *Chicago Tribune*, Business Section, 16 June: 3. (Discusses the salaries of investment managers.)
* Crowley, Lyle (1994) 'George Soros', *New York Times*, Section 6, 3 April: 26. (Examines his philanthropy, business activities and personal life.)
* Cuff, Daniel F. (1987) 'Top fund manager overcame '81 loss', *New York Times*, Section D, 13 July: 2. (Reviews Soros's money management successes.)
* Gordon, Michael R. (1995) '"Cautiously pessimistic", but investing in Russia', *New York Times*, Section D, 22 December: 1. (Review of George's efforts to stimulate Russian democracy.)
* Hawthorne, Fran, Carroll, Michael, Conger, Lucy, Cooper, Wendy, Davis, Stephen, Muehring, Kevin, Peltz, Michael and Picker, Ida (1994) 'Why George Soros is Bedford-bound', *Institutional Investor*, April: 13. (Announces his new weekend estate.)
* Hedges, Chris (1990) 'Honoring investing that paid', *New York Times*, Section A, 15 October: 3. (Reviews Soros's investments to support emerging democracies.)
* Joy, Pattie (1994) 'Dow drop', *USA Today*, Money Section, 28 February: 1B. (Announces Soros's loss when he bet against the yen.)
* Lycett, Andrew (1993) 'Soros: Midas or Machiavelli?', *Accountancy* 112, July: 36–40. (Reviews Soros's business ventures and personal life.)
* Miller, Judith (1997) 'A promoter of democracy angers the authoritarians', *New York Times*, Section 1, 12 July: 1. (Examines conflicts between governments in former Soviet states and Soros's foundations.)
* *PR Newswire* (1987) 'Fairchild elects Soros to board', *PR Newswire*, 10 July. (News release.)
* *Reuters Financial Service* (1996) 'Vinik could team up with George Soros', *Reuters Financial Service*, 1 August. (News release.)
* Scardino, Albert (1987) 'Market turmoil', *New York Times*, Section D, 28 October: 1. (Analyses losses to Soros's Quantum Fund and his investment theories.)
* Shawcross, William (1997) 'Turning dollars into change', *Time Magazine* 150(9), 1 September. (Discusses Soros's philanthropy.)
* Smith, Dinitia (1996) 'At home with: Susan Soros', *New York Times*, Section C, 7 March: 1. (Interviews George's wife Susan.)
* Soros, George (1987) *The Alchemy of Finance*, Simon & Schuster. (Discusses his theory of the markets and finance.)
* Soros, George (1991) *Underwriting Democracy*, Free Press. (Gives his personal perspective on creating democratic societies.)
* Soros, George (1995) *Soros on Soros: Ahead of the Curve*, J. Wiley. (Presents his observations on life, politicians and philosophy.)
* Southerland, Dan and Brown, David (1992) 'Former Soviet Union to get science aid', *Washington Post*, Financial Section, 10 December: B11. (Discusses Soros's philanthropy and personal history.)
* Uchitelle, Louis (1993) 'Europe's currency crisis', *New York Times*, Section D, 2 August: 1. (Examines his influence and leadership as a money manager.)

Further resources

* http://www.soros.com (1998) 'About George Soros'. (Provides biographical information.)

Toyoda family

1 **Introduction**
2 **Biographical data**
3 **Main contributions**
4 **Evaluation**
5 **Conclusion**

Summary

There is no one 'great person' who bears the name Toyota in the same way as Henry Ford. The Toyota Motor Company, which in 1982 became Toyota Motor Co. Ltd. (TMC), was founded by the Toyoda family. The company took on the name Toyota after staging a contest to select a new name in 1936. TMC has become the most powerful Japanese car manufacturer and one of the world's largest manufacturers of motor vehicles, third in size after General Motors (GM) and Ford. The success of TMC has been associated with its production system, which has given TMC the reputation of being highly efficient and of

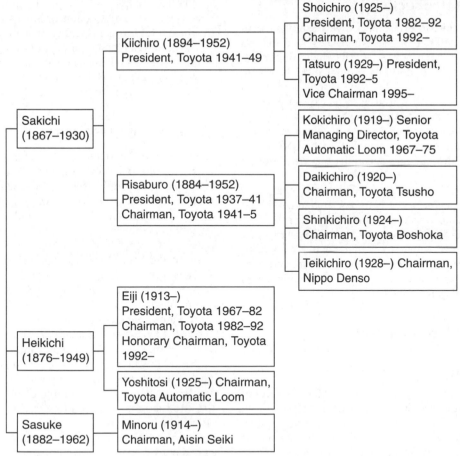

Figure 1 The Toyoda family: members in director positions with Toyota
Source: Adapted from Kamiya (1976: 100–1) and Cusumano (1985: 184) and personal

producing high quality cars and trucks. Much of TMC's success can be attributed to the achievements of the Toyoda family.

Personal background

See Figure 1 for details of the Toyoda family tree.

Major works

Toyota – Fifty Years in Motion: An Autobiography by the Chairman, Eiji Toyoda (1987)

Toyota, A History of the First Fifty Years (1988)

I Introduction

Toyota Motor Company was established in the summer of 1937, in 1952 it became the largest car producer , and it remains dominant. Since the mid-1980s, prompted by the rise in the value of the yen and of periodic tendencies towards protectionism in its export markets, the Toyota Motor Corporation (TMC) has made major investments in overseas manufacturing plants, including in the USA, Canada, the UK and Australia, but also in other countries.

In 1974 when most of the world's car companies were making losses, Toyota continued to make a modest profit. Competing manufacturers began making visits to Toyota to discover the key to that company's success. What they discovered was the Toyota production system which Toyota had continued to develop over forty years.

2 Biographical data

Sakichi Toyoda (1867–1930)

The founding father of the Toyota Group, Sakichi was born in Shizuoka Prefecture on 14 February 1867, the son of Ikichi Toyoda. As the first born, Sakichi was the *kacho*, or head of the household, and it was his duty to carry forward the obligations of his father and his trade as a carpenter. However, Sakichi was

not interested in carpentry and in 1885 he decided instead to become an inventor. Over the next thirty-five years Sakichi worked on improving weaving looms. In 1907 he became a partner in Toyoda's Loom Works, from which he resigned in 1910. He later started his own business, Toyoda Spinning and Weaving Company. In 1924, with the aid of his son Kiichiro, he developed a fully automatic loom and in 1926 Sakichi formed another company, Toyoda Automatic Loom Works. In 1929 he granted the patent rights of the automatic loom to the British firm Platt Brothers & Co. Ltd, for £100,000. He was awarded the Imperial Order of Merit, Japan's highest civilian honour, by the Emperor in 1927, and died on October 30 1930.

When the people of the Nagoya region laid Sakichi to rest, they honoured him as a man who made his dreams reality, who had embraced the challenges and opportunities of the Meiji Restoration, and who had helped lead his country into the modern world.

(Togo and Wartman 1993: 39)

Kiichiro Toyoda (1894–1952)

The founder of Toyota Motor Company, Kiichiro, was born in Shizuoka Prefecture in 1894, the eldest son of Sakichi Toyoda. He graduated in 1920 from Tokyo Imperial University as a mechanical engineer and joined his father's company, Toyoda Spinning and Weaving Company, in that same year. In 1930, at the bequest of his father, Kiichiro began work to produce cars. He began by sectioning off an area of the Toyoda Automatic Loom Works in which to disassemble and study a small engine. In September 1933, the directors of Toyoda Automatic Loom agreed to fund an automotive department and in September 1934 Kiichiro and his staff completed their first prototype engine, type A. The A1-type passenger car was completed in May 1935 and the first truck prototype was completed in August 1935.

The cost of the automotive department was a great burden on the Loom company and Kiichiro reasoned that the only way to become established in the market was to expand. With the board's approval, the acquisition of credit and the sales of shares, Toyota Motor Company was formally established in the summer of 1937. Kiichiro was Executive Vice President and in 1941 he became President of the company. But by 1950 the company was in turmoil as the entire workforce went on strike, protesting against a proposed reduction in employees. In an attempt to smooth labour relations, Kiichiro resigned from the company. He was due to return as president in 1952 to oversee the production of cars, but unfortunately he died of a cerebral haemorrhage on 27 March 1952.

Eiji Toyoda (1913–)

Eiji was born in Nagoya in 1913, the eldest son of Heikichi Toyoda, Sakichi Toyoda's brother. He graduated from Tokyo Imperial University, where he had studied mechanical engineering, and joined the Toyoda Automatic Loom Works in 1936 at the newly established car research lab. Eiji lodged with Kiichiro and his family and became an integral part of their household. He transferred to Toyota Motor Company in 1937.

In 1950 Toyota and Ford were beginning talks of a joint venture; part of the deal was to accept Toyota trainees at Ford's facilities, and Eiji Toyoda was the first person sent by Toyota. In 1951, he redesigned Toyota's plants to incorporate more advanced methods and machines. Eiji became president in 1967 and, in 1982, Chairman of the new Toyota Motor Corporation (TMC). In this same year Eiji began talks with General Motors (GM) about an important joint venture, New United Motor Manufacturing Incorporated (NUMMI), which would produce a Corolla-type car (a Toyota model) at a recently closed GM plant in Fremont, California. The project was widely hailed as a success, and demonstrated that the Toyota production system could be adapted to a Western context.

Dr Shoichiro Toyoda (1925–)

Shoichiro, the eldest son of Kiichiro, was born in 1925. He graduated from Nagoya University in 1949 with a degree in engineering and joined Toyota Motor Company in 1952. In 1955 he earned a doctorate in engineering at Tokyo University, with a thesis on fuel injection systems. He assumed the presidency of TMC Sales Co., Ltd in 1981. After its merger with Toyota Motor Company the following year, he became the President of the new Toyota Motor Corporation and, in 1992, Chairman of the Board. He presided over Toyota's becoming a global corporation. In May 1994 he became chairman of Keidanren (Japan Federation of Ecomonic Organizations), the most powerful organization in Japan.

3 Main contributions

TMC's success reflects the foresight and determination of the Toyoda family. Each of the above members contributed to the development of the Toyota philosophy.

Sakichi Toyoda

Having no formal educational qualifications, Sakichi learnt by trial and error; he believed that he could learn all that he needed to know by working on machines with his hands. Sakichi also recognized that industry in Japan had to advance in small steps and to fill niche markets not met by Western companies. He came to recognize the importance of constantly improving machines regardless of what the competition was doing. Sakichi believed that no process ever reached a point where it could not be improved; this policy of *kaizen* (continuous improvement) became part of his basic philosophy.

Despite much opposition, Sakichi was sure that cars would be a worthwhile product of the future. When he sold the patent rights to Toyoda's automatic loom, he told his son, Kiichiro Toyoda, that he was giving him £100,000, but there was one condition: Kiichiro had to use the money for research on car production. Kiichiro agreed.

Kiichiro Toyoda

Kiichiro took on Sakichi's legacy and formally established Toyota Motor Company. However, his contribution to the Toyota story did not stop there. Kiichiro realized that in order to compete with such powerful Western companies as Ford and GM, Toyota needed to invest in research and development. Hence, in 1936, he established a research lab in Tokyo. Japan differed from the USA in its lack of space and other resources. The US manufacturers could afford to stockpile parts and could build big warehouses. Kiichiro wanted to develop a Japanese production system that reflected the country's lack of space and resources, as well as the flexibility and versatility of its people, so he bought general-purpose machines rather than specialized machines. His plan was to adapt them and make them multi-purpose.

In the past the process of building cars had been 'learning by doing'. This had generated waste, which the Japanese could not afford. Kiichiro envisaged a system in which no component would be produced unless it was needed, hence eliminating the need for stock piles and waste. Therefore, in his factory, he hung a sign that read JUST IN TIME. He told the workers that no component for a car should be produced before it was needed: in other words components should be made just-in-time (JIT) (Togo and Wartman 1993: 79). The practices of *kaizen* and JIT became an important part of the Toyoda philosophy. However the philosophy was not developed fully until Taiichi Ohno joined the team.

Eiji Toyoda

In January 1951, Eiji Toyoda developed a five-year modernization plan. This plan involved the modernization of equipment and the transformation of production methods. Like Kiichiro and Sakichi before him, Eiji recognized that Toyota would have to do things differently from Western firms. Production would have to be streamlined; workers would have to search for continuous improvement and waste had to be minimized. Eiji employed Taiichi Ohno to implement these changes.

Ohno had begun his career with the Toyoda family in 1932 and was familiar with their philosophies. He introduced *kanban* cards (which keep track of stock), taught workers to understand *kaizen*, fully implemented the JIT system, rationalized the machinery and assembly lines, and introduced multi-skilling. Eiji was supportive of Ohno's work, and within two years Eiji had devised a radical new principle of factory operation. Whenever a problem developed in assembly, the production line was to be shut down, thus providing an incentive for a speedy and effective remedy.

By 1963 the JIT system had been instituted throughout the company and Toyota Motor Company began asking its suppliers to adopt the same system. It took Eiji Toyoda and Ohno more than twenty years to implement this set of ideas fully (including JIT) within the Toyota Motor Company supply chain.

Eiji also set another precedent. He decided that the future of the company depended on how well it built cars, even more than on how well it designed them. He proclaimed that production was the most important thing that happened at Toyota. The mission of designers and engineers was to enable the production staff to do their best. Accordingly, the status of assembly-line workers was elevated.

Shoichiro Toyoda

A novel production system had improved Toyota's efficiency and had enabled the company to put cars on the market at competitive prices. The quality, however, was still inadequate. Shoichiro Toyoda, then managing director of corporate planning, came to realize that the company was practising *kaizen* at too late a stage. Having to mend cars after they came on the market was damaging Toyota's reputation. In search of a means to improve quality, Shoichiro came across the work of Deming. Toyota had instituted some aspects of Deming's approach in the early 1950s. Shoichiro realized that for Toyota Motor Company to improve, two aspects of their quality process needed to change: first, it had to become more systematic, and second it had to be extended to every department. Therefore, Shoichiro implemented a quality programme throughout the company and in 1965 Toyota Motor Company won the coveted Deming Prize for quality.

Toyota Motor Company

Following the first 'oil crisis', by 1974 the international car industry was in a state of flux. Toyota was one of the few car manufacturers in the world that was consistently profitable. Competing manufacturers wanted to know how Toyota could be profitable in a bad market. Toyota was able to achieve extremely high levels of quality (few defects) and productivity in manufacturing (output per worker that was as much as two or three times higher than US or European plants in the late 1980s). Toyota was also able to achieve high levels of flexibility, producing relatively small batches of different models with little or no loss of productivity or quality. Accordingly, this Japanese style of manufacturing and product development has come to be studied and emulated around the world. By the mid-1990s the best US-owned car manufacturing plants appeared to have achieved relative parity with all but the most efficient Japanese plants.

Many believed that Toyota's most critical factor for success was its production system and underlying philosophies, sometimes known as 'Toyodaism'. The Toyota production system includes:

- JIT production
- minimal in-process inventories and efficient use of resources
- geographic concentration of assembly and parts production
- good communications
- elimination of waste
- manual demand-'pull' with *kanban* cards
- production levelling
- rapid set-up
- machinery and line rationalization
- work standardization
- foolproof automation devices
- multi-skilled workers
- high levels of sub-contracting
- selective use of automation
- continuous incremental process improvement (*kaizen*)
- teamwork

Since the publication of *The Machine that Changed the World* (Womack *et al.* 1990), Toyota's production system has also become known as 'lean production'. Lean production has been put forward as a model of 'best practice', which can be successfully implemented even in cultures very different from Japan, not merely in the car industry, but in other industries too.

4 Evaluation

The success of Toyota's production system has helped to transform Japan into one of the capitals of the automotive world and has also led to improved productivity and efficiency in Western manufacturing. For example, following a change to lean production at the GM–Toyota joint venture plant (NUMMI), performance in terms of quality, productivity and other indicators improved dramatically from one of the worst in the USA to one of the best. A typical body-stamping die-change time was reduced from twelve hours to less than ten minutes. Lean production involves significant differences from and advantages over Fordist and neo-Fordist mass-production factory regimes as illustrated in Table 1, and the key components of lean production can contribute to a major improvement in competitiveness (Shadur and Bamber 1994).

Nevertheless, as manufacturers around the world have tried to copy TMC's methods, there have inevitably been criticisms. Compared to Fordism, lean production systems place greater demands on managers and supervisory staff since they are responsible for managing a broader range of issues in their unit, such as human resource management, safety, absenteeism, and continuous improvement. There are also more demands on them to maintain extensive information systems for each work unit and optimize performance on each item they measure.

Critics argue that the pace of work in such Japanese production plants is frantic (for example, Kamata 1982; Williams *et al.* 1992). The JIT system creates pressures for operators to maintain production at a pre-set rate, and the demands of smaller batches and

Table 1 Critical differences between Fordism, neo-Fordism and lean production

	Fordism	*Neo-Fordism*	*Lean production*
Innovation	Wholly technocratic	Mostly technocratic	Technocratic/ continuous improvement
Quality control	Inspected in	Part inspected and built in	Built in
Operations management	Bulk supply	Bulk supply/JIT incipient	JIT
Throughput efficiency	Operational	Operational	Process
Approach to HR	Individual/plant	Individual/ some teams	Teams
Authority structure	Highly vertical	Vertical	Vertical/some decentralization
Information to workers	Minimal	Some provided	Extensive
Role of workers	Appendages of machines	Important part of production	Crucial part of production
Role of supervisory staff	Directive	Controlling/ organizing	Facilitating/ organizing/training
Company's role for union	Non-recognition	Adversarial	More cooperative

Source: Shadur and Bamber (1994)

shorter set-up times can lead to pressure on them to work harder. But advocates of Toyodaism hold that it requires people to work smarter, not necessarily harder. Others have argued that lean production uses labour as a buffer for a fragile production system, and that the workers have little real control over their job design. Such criticisms have led some authors to describe lean production as 'management by stress' (Parker and Slaughter 1988).

From the perspective typical of Toyota, however, such criticisms are merely seen to be a reminder that the lean notion itself should be subjected to continuous improvement. While US, European and other car makers continue to study and, at least in part, try to emulate Toyota's manufacturing and engineering practices, it has become apparent to many Japanese managers, policymakers and industry observers that the notion of 'continuous improvement' – continually pushing for gains in manufacturing and engineering efficiency – can precipitate new problems and has some practical limits. *Kaizen* continues at TMC, as Toyota and other Japanese car makers are exploring ways to modify their approaches.

5 Conclusion

The Toyota Motor Corporation had its beginnings in 1930 when Sakichi Toyoda gave his son Kiichiro Toyoda a grant to produce cars. Since its establishment, TMC has grown to be the world's third-largest car manufacturer, with plants in many countries. Toyodaism has been emulated around the world and has been widely advocated as a paragon of best practice. TMC and its production system continue to attract much international acclaim. In spite of the rise in the value of the yen and economic recessions, Toyota has remained competitive, as it continues to improve its production system.

GREG J. BAMBER
GRIFFITH UNIVERSITY
KELLIE CAUGHT
QUEENSLAND UNIVERSITY OF TECHNOLOGY

Further reading

(References cited in the text marked *)

Berggren, C. (1992) *Alternatives to Lean Production: Work Organisation in the Swedish Auto Industry*, Ithaca, NY: Cornell University Press. (Also published in London by Macmillan under the title *The Volvo Experience: Alternatives to Lean Production in the Swedish Auto Industry*; challenges the superiority of Toyodaism, arguing for a more human-centred approach, contrasting and comparing the Swedish and Japanese styles.)

Clark, K.B. and Fujimoro, T. (1991) *Product Development Performance: Strategy, Organization and Performance in the World Auto Industry*, Boston, MA: Harvard Business School Press. (Shows that Toyota and other Japanese companies develop products more quickly and efficiently than Western manufacturers.)

* Cusumano, M.A. (1985) *The Japanese Automobile Industry: Technology and Management at Nissan and Toyota*, Cambridge, MA: Harvard University Press. (Provides an account of the developments of Nissan and Toyota, contrasts their different systems and highlights ways in which Japanese manufacturing diverged from US and European practices.)

* Kamata, S. (1982) *Japan in the Passing Lane*, New York: Pantheon. (A radical journalist's critique of working life in a Toyota plant in Japan, based on participant observation.)

* Kamiya, S. (1976) *My Life with Toyota*, Nagoya: Toyota Motor Sales. (A personal history of Shotoro Kamiya, his life with Toyota and the Japanese automobile industry.)

Kimoto, S. (1991) *Quest for the Dawn*, Milwaukee, WI: Dougherty. (An insight into the origins of Toyota Motor Company, based on translations of diaries, memos and other documents written by Sakichi and Kiichiro Toyoda and their contemporaries.)

Kochen, T., Lansbury, K.D. and MacDuffie, J.P. (1997*) After Lean Production: Changing Employment Practices in the World Auto Industry*. Ithaca: Cornell University Press. (Research based on car assembly plants in eleven countries includes the way work is organized, how workeers and managers interact, the way in which worker representatives respond to lean production strategies and the nature of the adaptation and innovation process.)

Krafcik, J.F. (1988) 'Triumph of the lean production system', *Sloan Management Review* 30 (1): 41–52. (An account of the superiority of the Toyota production system which manufactures a wide range of models but maintains high degrees of quality and productivity as revealed by research of the International Motor Vehicle Program (IMVP), Massachusetts Institute of Technology.)

MacDuffie, J.P. and Frits, K.P. (1995) 'The international assembly plant study: update on round two findings', IMVP Research Briefing Meeting, Toronto, 5 June (mimeo, Wharton School, University of Pennsylvania and International Motor Vehicle Program (IMVP), Massachusetts Institute of Technology.) (A comparison of the findings of IMVP's surveys conducted in 1989 and 1993 which show general improvements in plant performance, but Japanese plants in Japan appeared to be the most productive in both surveys.)

Monden, Y. (1983) *The Toyota Production System*, Atlanta, GA: Industrial Engineering and Management Press. (An explanation of Toyodaism dating from before it was popularized by the IMVP's publications.)

* Parker, M. and Slaughter, J. (1988) 'Management by stress', *Technology Review* 91 (7): 37–44. (A critique of Toyodaism by two radical critics based in Detroit with the Labor Education and Research Project.)

* Shadur, M.A. and Bamber, G.J. (1994) 'Toward lean management? International transferability of Japanese management strategies to Australia', *The International Executive* 36 (3): 343–64. (Reports a study of an attempt to transplant Toyodaism to Australia.)

* Togo, Y. and Wartman, W. (1993) *Against All Odds: The Story of the Toyota Motor Corporation and the Family That Created It*, New York: St Martin's Press. (An account of the Toyoda family and the development of the Toyota Motor Corporation from 1867 to 1990.)

Toyoda, E. (1987) *Toyota – Fifty Years in Motion: An Autobiography by the Chairman, Eiji Toyoda*, New York: Kodansha International. (An account of the life of Eiji Toyoda, from birth to Chairman of Toyota.)

Toyota Motor Corporation (1988) *Toyota, A History of the First Fifty Years*, Japan: Toyota Motor Corporation. (An official synopsis of Toyota Motor Corporation's 50-year history, spanning 1937–87, with reference to Toyota's beginnings and the development of its management style.)

Toyota Motor Corporation (1995) *You ain't seen nuthin' yet!*, Japan: Toyota Motor Company. (Toyota Annual Report 1995: a review of operations, finances, Board of Directors and share information for the 1994–5 financial year.)

* Williams, K., Haslam, C., Williams, J. and Cutler, T., with Adcrost, A. and Sukhdev, J. (1992) 'Against lean production', *Economy and Society* 21 (3): 321–54. (A critique of the lean production system.)

* Womack, J.P., Jones, D.T. and Roos, D. (1990) *The Machine that Changed the World*, New York: Rawson/Macmillan. (Examines the differences between mass production and lean production in the automotive industry in Japan, North America and western Europe. Reports the results and implications of the International Motor Vehicle Program (IMVP) study.)

See also: MANAGEMENT IN JAPAN; SLOAN, A.P.;

Related topics in the IEBM: BUSINESS STRATEGY, JAPANESE; DEMING, W.E.; FORD, H.; INDUSTRIAL RELATIONS IN JAPAN; INVENTORY AND JUST-IN-TIME MODELS; ISHIKAWA, K.; JAPANIZATION; JURAN, J.M.; JUST-IN-TIME PHILOSOPHIES; OHNO, T.; PRODUCTIVITY; TEAMS IN MANUFACTURING; SHINGO, S.; TAYLOR, F.W.; TOTAL QUALITY MANAGEMENT

Turner, Ted (1938–)

Personal background

- born 19 November 1938 in Cincinnati, Ohio
- attended Brown University, but was expelled
- worked for his father's billboard business as general manager of Turner Advertising in the early 1960s and became president and chief executive officer (CEO) after his death
- in 1970 purchased an independent UHF television channel in Atlanta and renamed it WTBS
- founded the Turner Broadcasting System (TBS) in 1979
- in 1980 created the Cable News Network (CNN) and two years later added CNN Radio and Headline News
- in 1985 cofounded the Better World Society to promote world peace
- in 1985 purchased the MGM/UA Entertainment Co.
- in 1986 sold United Artists (UA) and the non-library portion of MGM and created the Turner Entertainment Company to oversee the libraries
- acquired the Hanna-Barbera animation studio in 1992
- in 1993 TBS purchased New Line Cinema and Castle Rock Entertainment
- merger with Time Warner in 1996

1 Introduction

Robert Edward Turner III was born on 19 November 1938 in Cincinnati, Ohio. His family moved to Savannah, Georgia, when he was 9 years old. His father was so busy and preoccupied with his work that Turner was largely raised by a family employee by the name of Jimmy Brown. According to Turner, 'my friendship with Jimmy Brown [an African American] has made me a great believer in equal rights and equality for all people' (Booker 1994). It was Brown who taught Turner to hunt, fish and sail.

Turner attended Brown University. While at Brown he was vice-president of the Debating Union and commodore of the Yacht Club. Unfortunately he was expelled from Brown University for violating visitation rules when he was caught with a woman in his room (Farhi 1996). When his father committed suicide, Turner was 24 years old and inherited his father's financially troubled billboard business. 'Against the advice of financial consultants, Turner canceled the sale of the business and then proceeded to restore it to success'. Seven years later he expanded the business into broadcasting with the purchase of an Atlanta TV station (renamed WTBS) (*Contemporary Theatre, Film and Television* 1988; *Celebrity Biographies* 1998)

He has been married three times and has five children. Robert Edward IV and Laura Lee are from his first marriage to Judy Nye. Rhett, Beauregard and Sarah Jean are from his marriage with Jane Smith, whom he wed in 1964. Turner and Jane Smith divorced after twenty years of marriage. In 1991 he married the actress Jane Fonda at Avalon, his plantation in Capps, Florida (*Contemporary Theatre, Film and Television* 1988; *Celebrity Biographies* 1998)

Turner was named Yachtsman of the Year four times, won the cherished America's Cup in 1977 and received the Fastnet Trophy for yachting in 1979. *Sales and Marketing* magazine named him Outstanding Entrepreneur of the Year in 1979. Turner received the President's Award from the National Cable TV Association in 1979. He was named International Communicator of the Year by sales and marketing executives in 1981. Ted was named *Time* magazine's Man of the Year in 1991, and inducted into the TV Hall of Fame in 1992 by the Academy of Television Arts and Sciences. The *Sporting News* named Ted Turner the 1993 Most Powerful Person in Sports. In 1995 he received the David Susskind Lifetime Achievement Award in Television (Elliott 1993; *Contemporary Theatre, Film and Television* 1988; *Celebrity Biographies* 1998).

He serves on several boards, including Better World Society (chairman), Atlanta Chapter of the National Association for the Advancement of Colored People (NAACP) and Martin Luther King Center for Nonviolent Change. His outspoken and aggressive style contributed to Turner being called the 'Mouth of the South' and 'Captain Outrageous'. On several occasions he has acted in movies, e.g. *Southern Voices, American Dream, Gettysburg* (*Contemporary Theatre, Film and Television* 1988; *Celebrity Biographies* 1998).

2 Main contribution

In the early 1960s Turner worked for his father's billboard business as general manager of Turner Advertising. After his father's death he became president and CEO of the company. In 1970 he entered broadcasting when he purchased an independent UHF television channel in Atlanta and renamed it WTBS. Since 1976 WTBS has been widely distributed by cable systems. He owns the Atlanta Braves baseball team (acquired in 1976) and Atlanta Hawks basketball team (acquired in 1977), and televises their games on WTBS. He founded the Turner Broadcasting System (TBS) in 1979. In 1980 Turner created the Cable News Network (CNN), the first 24-hour news network. Two years later he expanded his news coverage by adding CNN Radio and Headline News (*Contemporary Theatre, Film and Television* 1988; *Celebrity Biographies* 1998). In 1986 he created the CNN Center in Atlanta after purchasing the Omni International site.

In 1985 Turner purchased the MGM/UA Entertainment Co. for $1.5 billion. After purchasing MGM Turner was financially overextended and sold shares in TBS, reducing his ownership in the firm to 51 per cent. Turner agreed to allow the cable owners who had invested in his firm to approve all purchases over $2 million (Fabrikant 1989). In 1986 he sold UA and the non-library portion of MGM as he was primarily interested in the MGM film and TV libraries. He created the Turner Entertainment Company to oversee these libraries. Turner has been criticized for the colourization of classic black and white movies acquired from MGM. In 1987 he created a new cable network called Turner Network Television (TNT). He acquired the Hanna-Barbera animation studio in 1992, and the following year TBS purchased New Line Cinema and Castle Rock Entertainment. By 1994 Turner had six cable networks: CNN, TBS, TNT, Headline News, Cartoon Network and Turner Classic Movies (Hall 1994; *Contemporary Theatre, Film and Television* 1988; *Celebrity Biographies* 1998). Turner's merger with Time Warner in 1996 created the world's largest media and entertainment company (*Chicago Tribune* 1996). In 1996 Time Warner had combined revenues of $23.7 billion (Time Warner Corp. 1997).

After being frustrated by the absence of Soviet athletes during the 1984 Los Angeles Olympic Games, Turner organized and co-sponsored the 1986 Goodwill Games in Moscow (*Celebrity Biographies* 1998). He has been outspoken against gratuitous violence on TV and in films, and has tried to present family-style content on his entertainment networks (Hall 1994).

In 1985 Turner cofounded the Better World Society, an organization which promotes world peace. He continues to be active in the peace, environmental and population control movements (Green 1986; Farhi 1996). In a 1994 interview Turner stated: 'I'm planning right now to give half of what I have away. ... There are so many problems in the world that need addressing' (Hall 1994). Ted Turner has lived up to his promise and in 1997 pledged to donate a historic $1 billion to the United Nations (UN) to support the UN economic, environmental, social and humanitarian causes. 'Complementing the Turner pledge was the Turner promise – to encourage other leaders from the world of business and philanthropy to follow his lead in supporting UN causes' (*PR Newswire* 1997).

3 Evaluation

Turner is known for accomplishing in business what most have considered impossible. For example, 'He took an unknown, unheralded station that in nine years grew to 33 million viewers' (Cuff 1985). Turner attempted but failed to purchase the CBS (1985) and NBC (1993–4) television networks (Farhi 1996). This, however, did not necessarily reduce the impact he has had on the television industry.

It has been said that '[h]e is pushing television ... to its farthest frontiers' (*Contemporary Theatre, Film and Television* 1988). He was a leader in foreseeing consumer demand for news and creating the first global 24-hour news network. CNN has been available to viewers around the world since 1989 (Hall 1994). Turner has been credited with revolutionizing the broadcast industry by making it possible actually to see news in the making (Booker 1994). In 1991 'his Cable News Network presented the Gulf War, the Hill-Thomas hearings, the end of the Soviet Union, and the William K. Smith trial, all those great events, while they were happening' (Vecsey 1992).

Turner has made some enemies over the years. Perhaps most well known are his outspoken conflicts with his competitor Rupert Murdoch (see MURDOCH, RUPERT) of News Corporation Ltd. When Murdoch announced that Fox News would be challenging CNN, Turner called Murdoch 'the schlockmeister' and 'promised that CNN would "squash [Murdoch's new venture] like a bug"' (Farhi 1996). To date, after several false starts, Fox News has not successfully entered the market with CNN.

While Turner and the TBS board of directors made strategic decisions and purchases, he has allowed knowledgeable managers to make key operating decisions. For example, when it comes to the movies Turner admits he does not 'know a good script from a bad script' and allows qualified staff to make this type of decision (Hall 1994). As vice-chairman of Time Warner, he has a number of key executives (e.g. HBO, CNN, TBS) who report directly to him (*Reuters Financial Service* 1996). According to Gerald Levin, the chairman and CEO of Time Warner Inc. at the time of the merger, 'Assembling all of our cable programming assets under Ted's leadership will ensure the continued growth and development of these assets and maximize our ability to build and deliver value for our shareholders' (*PR Newswire* 1996).

Among his personal accomplishments is his battle with manic depression, which he has fought and overcome (*People* 1995). Turner does not have plans ever to retire, but has shifted more of his efforts towards philanthropy. He has said: 'I try to relax. But I end up doing a lot of work wherever I am, out in Montana or wherever' (Hall 1994).

STEPHEN J. HAVLOVIC
SIMON FRASER UNIVERSITY

Further reading

(References cited in the text marked *)

* Booker, Simeon (1994) 'TV's Ted Turner reveals black man served as his "second" father', *Jet*, 18 April: 33. (Takes a look at Jimmy Brown and his impact on Turner.)
* *Celebrity Biographies* (1998) 'Turner, Ted'. (Gives personal and professional biographical information.)
* *Chicago Tribune* (1996) 'Time Warner, Turner shareholders approve $7.5 billion merger', *Chicago Tribune*, News, 10 October: 1. (Announces merger.)
* *Contemporary Theatre, Film and Television* (1988) 'Ted Turner', vol. 5. (Gives personal and professional biographical information.)
* Cuff, Daniel F. (1985) 'The formidable Ted Turner', *New York Times*, Section D, 5 April: 1. (Takes a look at Turner's aggressive approach to business.)
* Elliott, Stuart (1993) 'Ted Turner earns top sports honor', *New York Times*, Section D, 27 December: 7. (Announces award.)
* Fabrikant, Geraldine (1989) 'Some promising signs for Turner's empire', *New York Times*, Section D, 23 January: 1. (Reviews how Turner refinanced his business empire.)
* Farhi, Paul (1996) 'Mogul wrestling: in the war between Murdoch and Turner, similarity breeds

contempt', *Washington Post*, Style, 18 November: C1. (Discusses and analyses the animosity between Turner and Murdoch.)

Goldberg, Robert and Goldberg, Gerald Jay (1995) *Citizen Turner: The Wild Rise of an American Tycoon*, Harcourt Brace & Co. (A biography of Ted Turner.)

* Green, Michelle (1986) 'Ted Turner stages his own Olympics – and tries to rescue the planet', *People*, 14 July: 62. (Takes a look at the Goodwill Games in Moscow and his personal life.)

* Hall, Jane (1994) 'We're listening Ted', *Los Angeles Times*, Calendar Section, 3 April: 9. (An exclusive interview with Ted Turner where he discusses his professional and personal lives.)

* *People* (1995) 'Ted Turner', *People*, 25 December: 87. (Turner was selected as one of the twenty-five most intriguing people of 1995.)

* *PR Newswire* (1996) 'Time Warner creates operating structure and management team for Cable Networks Group', *PR Newswire*, 17 September. (News release.)

* *PR Newswire* (1997) 'Ted Turner names Tim Wirth to oversee gift in support of UN causes', *PR Newswire*, 19 November. (News release.)

* *Reuters Financial Service* (1996) 'Time Warner <TWX.N>, Turner <TBSA.A> Team Together', *Reuters Financial Service*, 17 September. (News release.)

* Time Warner Corp. (1997) *1996 Annual Report*.

* Vecsey, George (1992) 'Sports of the Times', *New York Times*, Section B, 10 January: 11. (Profiles *Time* magazine's Man of the Year.)

See also: MURDOCH, RUPERT

Wachner, Linda (1946–)

1 Introduction
2 Main contribution
3 Evaluation

Personal background

- born 3 February 1946 in New York City
- received a BS degree in Economics and Business from the University of Buffalo in 1966
- hired as an assistant buyer for Associated Merchandise Corp. in 1966
- became an assistant buyer for Foley's from 1967 to 1968
- became a buyer for Macy's from 1968 to 1973
- married Seymour Applebaum in 1973; widowed in 1983
- hired by Warner, a division of Warnaco, in 1973
- became vice-president of advertising, Warner Division, Warnaco, in 1975
- appointed vice-president of corporate marketing, Caron International, from 1976 to 1978
- appointed president, Max Factor & Co., US Division, in 1978
- became president and chief operating officer (COO), Max Factor & Co., in 1980
- became president and chief executive officer (CEO), Max Factor & Co. Worldwide, in 1981
- was made managing director, Adler & Shaykin, from 1985 to 1986
- chairman and CEO, Warnaco Group Inc., from 1986
- chairman and CEO, Authentic Fitness Corporation, from 1991
- nominated America's Most Successful Businesswoman, by *Fortune* in 1992

- member of President Reagan's, Bush's and Clinton's Advisory Committee for Trade Policy and Negotiations

1 Introduction

Linda Wachner was born in 1946 to a fur salesman and homemaker. She was the second of two children. Her sister (now deceased) was eighteen years her senior. When Wachner was only 11 years of age she suffered a terrible accident. A boy at school pulled a chair out from underneath her. As a result, Wachner needed corrective spinal surgery and had to wear a head-to-knee body cast for over a year (Landrum 1994). She was virtually immobile during this time, never sure she would be able to walk again. Yet Wachner credits this tragedy as being pivotal to her future: 'The focus I have today comes from when I was sick. When you want to walk again, you learn how to focus on that with all your might, and you don't stop until you do it' (Caminiti 1992: 106). It was during this incapacitation that Wachner decided she would run her own company 'when she grew up' (Ingham and Feldman 1990). With both her father and uncle in the apparel business, the clothing industry was a logical choice for Wachner to realize her dream.

As a child, Wachner attended New York City public schools and graduated from high school at the age of 16. She attended the University of Buffalo and graduated with an undergraduate degree in business administration. Wachner spent her college holidays and summer vacations working in department stores. After graduating from college, Wachner worked as an 'assistant market representative' at Associated Merchandising Corporation in New York. A year later she landed a job as an assistant buyer at Foley's department store in Houston, where she was taught the business art of 'holy hours', created by the president of Foley's (Ingham and

Feldman 1990). 'Holy hours' refers to the lunch-hour rush, when all company personnel were required to talk with customers and salespeople to find out what was selling, why it was selling and what Foley should be selling. Wachner refined this management practice to fit her own style and has used it throughout her career (Ingham and Feldman 1990).

Macy's hired Wachner as a buyer when she was 22. She was one of the youngest buyers in the company's history (Ingham and Feldman 1990). She met her husband, Seymour Applebaum, during this period. Applebaum also worked in the fashion industry as an executive in a dressmaking company. Applebaum was approximately thirty-two years Wachner's senior and, in addition to being her husband, he served as her mentor.

At the age of 28 Wachner moved from the retailing segment of the fashion business to the manufacturing end and landed a job in advertising with Warner, the lingerie division of Warnaco. Within a year Wachner was promoted to vice-president and became the first female to serve in this role in Warnaco's 100-year history (Landrum 1994). Wachner was lauded for her marketing innovations in the lingerie business. She took lingerie merchandise out of its boxes and hung it up on hangers for customers to touch and feel. A slumping bra market was turned around by Wachner.

Wachner's mentor at Warnaco, Mary Wells, introduced her to David Mahoney, who hired Wachner in 1979 to serve as the president of the US Division of the cosmetics firm Max Factor (Landrum 1994). Wachner made the unprofitable division profitable in two years. She did this by cutting staff, severing production lines and by reducing a hefty promotion budget (Donahue 1987). Wachner's reward was to be put in charge of Max Factor's international division; she was equally successful there. Her approach to management, 'hard-nosed and no-thrills' (Landrum 1994: 364), did not make her many friends, but it did earn her a promotion in 1980 (over the heads of many men) to president and COO of the entire company. During Wachner's reign Max Factor introduced a new perfume, Le Jardin de Max Factor, and it was considered a runaway success (Caminiti 1992).

Wachner was put in charge of Max Factor when the company was losing money; she used mass firings to turn it around. She was criticized by many at the company for taking such a heartless approach. Wachner defended her actions: 'If you have to get a company turned around before it bleeds to death, you have to have a certain posture in the way you go about things. I'm tough, but I'm fair' (Donahue 1987: 80). David Mahoney, chief of Norton Simon, which owned Max Factor (and the individual responsible for recruiting Wachner), complimented Wachner's handling of the matter: 'Linda is a problem solver. If she gave you numbers for the business, you could go to bed at night and be able to sleep because you knew she'd make them' (Caminiti 1992: 107). According to Mahoney, Wachner '[m]ay have been hard to get along with, but most companies that are losing millions of dollars a year will find their CEOs hard to get along with' (Caminiti 1992: 107).

While at Max Factor, Wachner began her practice of requiring executives to carry and use spiral notebooks with the words 'Do It Now' on the cover. According to Wachner, 'These books contain my notes from meetings with managers ... They are my way of instilling a sense of immediacy into my people. If you see something in black and white, you tend not to put it on the back burner' (*Chief Executive* 1994: 42). However, not everyone at Max Factor was as much of a fan of these notebooks as Wachner was (Leinster 1986). At meetings Wachner would use the information recorded in the notebooks to question managers on what they had accomplished.

In 1983 Max Factor's parent Company, Simon, was taken over by Esmark. A year later Esmark was taken over by Beatrice. During this time Wachner tried to buy Max Factor but was turned down. She subsequently resigned from the company. Wachner then tried to purchase Revlon's cosmetic and perfume business via a leveraged buy-out. She gave her pitch when she became managing director of Adler & Shaykin, a leveraged buy-out firm. She did not succeed.

Wachner then set her sights on Warnaco, the company she had worked for many years before. She met with success. In 1986 she arranged a hostile takeover of this Fortune 500 company, the first woman in history ever to do so, for $485 million (Strom 1992). Furthermore, she risked $10 million of her own money in this venture (Landrum 1994).

2 Main contribution

When Wachner took the helm at Warnaco she began by meeting with employees and visited nearly all of the company's twenty-four plants (Taylor 1987). She discovered that the company ran the product brands (such as Olga, Chaps by Ralph Lauren, Fruit of the Loom) like autonomous organizations, paying more attention to manufacturing than marketing, with high overhead costs, overlapping functions and few checkpoints. As a result, she installed her own managers and reorganized the company into several divisions (Taylor 1987; Ingham and Feldman 1990: 722). As she has typically done, she focused on the bottom line: 'Our senior executives need to do three things: Get the product right, cut overhead, and maximize cash flow' (*Chief Executive* 1994: 40).

Wachner is a self-acknowledged workaholic who lacks a family outside her company; her mother, father, sister and husband have all died. She has no children and regrets this choice (Landrum 1994). Despite her own circumstances, Wachner recognizes the importance of family to her immediate staff. When it is necessary for them to work late, Wachner allows them to include childcare costs as an expense-account item (Donahue 1987). And working late is requested by Wachner. Wachner will call meetings that begin at 5 p.m. and run until midnight (Dumaine 1993: 41). Respect for time-zone differences when she makes international calls is not one of her noted strengths (Leinster 1986). Moreover, she is not always considerate about vacation time (Dumaine 1993). Wachner admits to a hard-nosed management style: 'I've yelled at people, and I'm not ashamed of it. We have to run this company efficiently and without a bunch of babies who say, 'Mommy

yelled at me today' (Dumaine 1993: 41). In 1997 Wachner was on a list of 'Insensitive Bosses'. A total of five bosses were on this list. The list was compiled by *Washington Post* reporter Sharon Walsh (1997), who surveyed management experts and executive searchers.

Warnaco went public in 1991. Wachner is credited with cutting Warnaco's expenses, 'increasing its market share, developing new markets and enhancing the value of the stock' (Strom 1992: 6). Wachner also serves as chairman and CEO of Authentic Fitness Corporation, a company formed in 1990 by a management and investor group, led by Wachner, to acquire the assets of the activewear division of Warnaco (Strom 1992). Authentic Fitness completed its initial public offering in June 1992.

Wachner is the only woman who owns a Fortune 500 industrial company (Dumaine 1993). She earns between $10 million and $16 million a year as the head of the Warnaco Group Inc. and Authentic Fitness Corporation (*New York* 1997: 74). Wachner, one of the richest women in America, has a net worth estimated at around $80 million (*New York Times* 1992).

3 Evaluation

Wachner has achieved great power and wealth in a business world that closes rather than opens doors for women. She has achieved many firsts and has left her mark on the fashion industry. Still, in many ways she is like most other high-level women; she has no family and appears to be quite 'masculine' in her personality attributes (Fagenson 1990, 1993). Wachner is also very much like the men at her level. Her orientation is very militaristic – high control, high concern for task accomplishment and low concern for people. Parting with tradition, she used the essence of a cutting-edge management approach long before it became popular – total quality management, although she knew it as the 'holy hours'.

It is interesting that a tragic childhood accident taught Wachner what she needed to succeed in the business world: focus and persistence. She clearly applied this lesson when she failed twice in her efforts to purchase her own company but succeeded in her third attempt. To succeed, Wachner benefited from the help of others, her mentors. Most individuals who succeed in the corporate world have secured them during their careers (Fagenson 1989).

All in all, Wachner has achieved the typical symbols of what the male world values – money, power and turf – and it has made her a happy and fulfilled person (Caminiti 1992; Donahue 1987).

ELLEN FAGENSON-ELAND
GEORGE MASON UNIVERSITY

Further reading

(References cited in text marked *)

* Caminiti, S. (1992) 'America's most successful businesswoman', *Fortune* 15(12), 15 June: 102–7. (Describes the career path of Linda Wachner.)
* *Chief Executive* (1994) 'Queen of cash flow', *Chief Executive* 91, January–February: 38–42. (Presents a rare interview with Wachner and displays her business acumen.)
* Donahue, C. (1987) 'Linda Wachner', *Ms.* 15(7), January: 78–100. (Presents Wachner's professional success as a woman and the contributions she has made as a woman in business.)
* Dumaine, B. (1993) 'The queen of impatience', *Fortune* 128(9), 18 October: 41. (Describes how Wachner views herself and how others view her.)
* Fagenson, E.A. (1989) 'The mentor advantage: perceived job/career experiences of proteges vs. non-proteges', *Journal of Organizational Behavior* 10: 309–20. (Examines the benefits of mentoring for high- and low-level organizational men and women.)
* Fagenson, E.A. (1990) 'Perceived masculine and feminine attributes examined as a function of individual's sex and level in the organizational

power hierarchy: a test of four theoretical perspectives', *Journal of Applied Psychology* 75: 204–11. (Looks at the personality characteristics of men and women at upper and lower organizational levels.)
* Fagenson, E.A. (1993) *Women in Management: Trends, Issues and Challenges in Managerial Diversity*, Newbury Park, CA: Sage Publications. (Examines the societal, organizational and personal factors that influence and, in turn, are influenced by women managers.)
* Ingham, J.N. and Feldman, L.B. (1990) *Contemporary American Business Leaders: A Biographical Dictionary*. (Profiles Linda Wachner and other leaders in the business community; includes many excerpts from the articles written about her.)
* Landrum, G. N. (1994) *Profiles of Female Genius: Thirteen Creative Women Who Changed the World*, NY: Prometheus Books. (Analyses Wachner's personal life and professional background, as well as her personality, disposition her life choices, and compares them to those of other famous women; an excellent resource.)
* Leinster, C. (1986) 'The would-be queen of Revlon's beauty business', *Fortune* 113(1), 6 January: 76–80. (Describes Wachner's efforts to become the CEO of Revlon.)
* *New York* (1997) 'Big Shots make the grade: from rags, riches', *New York* 30(4), 22–9 December: 68–77. (Gives Wachner's earnings.)
* Strom, S. (1992) 'Fashion Avenue's $100 million woman', *New York Times*, 17 May: 1–6. (Profiles the career of Linda Wachner.)
* Taylor, A. (1987) 'Linda Wachner: new outfit for a beauty queen', *Fortune* 115(1), 5 January: 56. (Describes how Wachner mastered the purchase of Warnaco.)
* Walsh, S. (1997) 'Era of the brutal boss may be giving way to a new sensitivity', *Washington Post*, 31 August: H1. (Describes sensitive and insensitive bosses.)

Related topics at the IEBM: ACQUISITIONS AND JOINT VENTRUES; MERGERS; WOMEN IN MANAGEMENT AND BUSINESS

Wang, Yung Ching (1917–)

Personal background

- born 18 January 1917 in Xindian, Taipei county, a northern region of Taiwan, the eldest son of a very poor tea farmer
- in 1931 worked as a clerk in a rice shop in Jiayi, a southern city of Taiwan, after leaving school
- in 1932 opened a rice shop with his father's help, borrowing money from relatives and friends
- in 1942 engaged in brick production, goose farming and the timber business after his rice business was forced to close by the Japanese government because of the Second World War
- in 1954 established Formosa Plastics Corporation, supported by the Taiwanese government and US aid
- in 1958 opened Nan-Ya Plastics Corporation in order to use the PVC produced by Formosa Plastics
- in 1964 established Ming-Chi Institute of Technology, a two-year college, and Formosa Chemicals & Fiber Corporation
- in 1976 established Chang Gung Memorial Hospital to commemorate his father
- in 1980 acquired a VCM (Vinylchloride Monomer) producer in Texas
- in 1982 acquired JM Plastic Tube Company in the US and its eight US subsidiaries
- in 1983 the group became the world's largest PVC producer and the PVC plastics-processing producer
- in 1984 the group entered the information industry by producing circuit boards
- in 1985 contributed US$4 million to the Taiwanese government to help establish an economic research institute
- in 1987 and 1988 established Chang Gung College of Medicine and Technology and Chang Gung Institute of Nursing
- in 1992 declared the intention of setting up a large petrochemical-processing complex in Fujian, China; the project was withdrawn in 1993 because of intervention by the Taiwanese government and, instead, a US$11 billion investment, the sixth Naphtha Cracking Project, was undertaken in Taiwan
- in 1993 published a book, *Grow Roots and Plough Deep* (in Chinese), a collection of speeches on his management philosophy, business and life experiences, and opinions towards social issues
- in 1995 announced the establishment of an electricity company in Fujian, China; ever since, the project has been a controversy and under slow construction
- in 1996 had a conflict with his eldest son, the strongest candidate as future head of the industrial group; his son left the group and started his own plastics-processing business in China
- stepped down from the position of chief executive officer (CEO) in 1997 to become chairman of Formosa Plastics Corporation

1 Introduction

Yung-Ching Wang is the chairman of Formosa Plastics Group. He has become a symbol of the rich, a management god and the toughest entrepreneur in Taiwan. He is also admired for being a self-made tycoon born to a very poor tea farmer. From early on, when he started his own rice business at the age of 16, he developed a unique management philosophy, continuously looking for the root of the problem and seeking constant improvement to become the best. This philosophy, combined with low-cost (large-scale) and vertical and horizontal integration strategies, and his strong character traits of frugality, perseverance, willingness to learn, toughness, energy, ambition and risk-taking have helped him build one of the best management systems and the largest enterprise group in Taiwan.

2 Main contribution

Wang's contributions may be divided into three areas: social responsibility, role model and management thinking. These are discussed below.

Social responsibility

The Formosa Plastics Group is the largest business group in Taiwan and has contributed significantly to Taiwan's economic growth, government tax revenue, exports and employment. In 1996 the group had a total capital of US$5.7 billion, total assets of US$18.8 billion, total operating revenues of US$10.9 billion and 56,184 employees worldwide. The group is composed of Formosa Plastics Corporation, Nan Ya Plastics Corporation, Formosa Plastics and Fiber Corporation, fourteen domestic affiliated companies, six overseas affiliated companies, Chang Gong Memorial Hospital, Chang Gung University and Ming-Chi Institute of Technology. In addition to establishing the hospital, college and university, the Wang has made various donations to charity organizations and social groups.

Role model

Wang is a self-made entrepreneur born to a very poor family. His business success is attributed to his strong character traits of frugality, perseverance, willingness to learn, toughness, energy, ambition, risk-taking and good management skills. As a role model, his life and business provide many stimulating lessons for others to emulate.

Management thinking

The management system built by Wang has contributed to the success of the Formosa Plastics Group. This management system is known as the Formosa Plastics Model and has the following characteristics:

1 Strategic vision: to build a petrochemical empire from oil refineries to plastic-processing manufacturing. This is the chairman's and the group's driving force.
2 Strategic action: characterized as being bold, large-scale, and in endless pursuit of cost reductions and rationalization.
3 Implementation:
- Strong leadership: Wang's self-discipline – frugality, perseverance, energy (he runs 5000 metres almost every day), attention to detail, zealous pursuit of cost reductions and rationalization (improvement), and the use of Japanese competitors as a benchmark – has a strong impact on how the system is implemented.
- High pressure management: for example, Wang often uses lunch meetings for project presentations, in which questions and criticisms are raised by the chairman. Sometimes the presenters are fired after their presentations.
- Training is emphasized, especially for mid-level supervisors.
- Extensive computerization has been implemented to reduce costs and increase efficiency.
- Effective organizational structure: a general administration group with around 200 experienced experts at headquarters to control and set up standards for procedures, process and unit costs for every unit in the whole system. This group has been called the 'Red Guard', a metaphor borrowed from the youth group used during the Cultural Revolution in China to indicate the pressure imposed from the top on the bottom.
- Relatively generous payments to excellent performers: this is an effective way of retaining talented managers while working in a high-pressure environment.

This management system has helped Wang achieve his strategic vision and build the largest enterprise in Taiwan.

3 Evaluation

The great success of the Formosa Plastics Group and the story of Wang will always be part of Taiwan's business history and will be remembered by many.

The Formosa Plastics Model is like a typical Japanese firm in that it pursues endless cost reductions, but it seems to lack the human factor well known in the Japanese model; instead, it has the cold transactional nature of many American firms, using rewards and punishment as tools to motivate employees. Formosa Plastics' organizational culture of high pressure, standardization and tight control may very well suit an industry that uses continuous-processing technology requiring tight control, and rigid standards and procedures. This inflexibility may not be suitable for an industry that needs frequently to adapt to continuous market changes – such as the electronics industry, in which market change, not low cost, is the focus. The Formosa Plastics Group has now entered the electronics industry in a joint venture with the Japanese company Komatsu Electronics to produce 8-inch silicon wafers. Whether this will be successful remains to be seen.

The petrochemical industry is a high-pollution industry. According to a 1987 survey conducted in Taiwan, the fact that the Formosa Plastics Group was only ranked sixth in social responsibility among forty manufacturers may indicate a problem for the group in the increasing public awareness of environmental protection in Taiwan. The problems could be overcome if the group used experiences of its US subsidiaries, which encountered and overcame a series of environmental challenges in the early 1990s. Furthermore, the rising glamour and importance of the electronics industry in the 1990s in the Taiwanese economy has shadowed traditional industries like the petrochemical industry in attracting highly talented employees and investors.

This change may be a real threat to the status of the group unless it is able to overcome its inertia, reorient its prior strategic commitment and avoid the Icarus paradox, the tendency to rely on the skills and capabilities that made the group successful. All these have to do with Wang himself, who has personalized the entire group. The organization is an imprint of Wang, a reflection of his strong personal characteristics. He still tightly controls the group even though he is over 80. The succession issue is of serious concern not only to the members in the group but also to the public. Powerful positions have increasingly been occupied by his relatives, especially the sons and daughters of Wang and his brother and sisters. Even though these relatives have been trained in US business schools and some high-ranking executive posts are filled with professionally seasoned managers, this situation has alarmed the public, which wonders whether the group will follow the same route as many Chinese family enterprises that have fallen apart after the death of the founder.

RYH-SONG YEH
THE CHINESE UNIVERSITY OF HONG KONG

Further reading

Formosa Plastics Group (1997) *1996 Annual Report*, Taipei, Taiwan. (Gives a brief description of the operations of each major unit in the Formosa Plastics Group and the progress of some investment projects.)

Guo, T. (1997) *The Driving History of Wang Yung Ching* (in Chinese), Taipei, Taiwan: Yuan Jin Publishing Co. (This updated biography of Wang Yung Ching was first published in 1985; it is the only biography available and, although it is not authorized, it is very well researched and documented.)

Liao, C.Z. (1987) *The Successful Story of Modern Entrepreneurs* (in Chinese), Taipei, Taiwan: Economic Daily News. (A reporter's view of the business practices of various Taiwanese entrepreneurs; the first chapter is about Wang's business practices.)

Richard, D. (1997) 'Formosa's harshest critics now laud pollution efforts', *Chemical Market Reporter* 252(17): 7, 19. (Reports on how various Formosa Plastics operations in the US overcame their previous image of being polluters.)

Wang, Y.C. (1989) *Wang Yung Ching on Chinese Management* (in Chinese), Taipei, Taiwan: Yuan Jin Publishing Co. (Summarizes various managerial issues discussed by Wang Yung Ching in speeches and on other occasions.)

* Wang, Y.C. (1997) *Grow Roots and Plough Deep* (in Chinese), Taipei, Taiwan: Yuan Jin Publishing Co. (A collection of Wang's speeches on his management philosophy, business and life experiences, and opinions towards societal issues.)

See also: BUSINESS STRATEGIES, EAST ASIAN

Related topics in the IEBM: ENTREPRENEURSHIP; MANAGEMENT IN TAIWAN

Welch, Jack (1935–)

Personal background

- born 19 November 1935 in Peabody, Massachusetts
- received his BS in Chemical Engineering from the University of Massachusetts in 1957
- earnt an MS (1958) and a PhD (1960) in Chemical Engineering from the University of Illinois
- engineer at the General Electric Company (GE) from 1960 to 1968
- general manager of the Worldwide Plastics Division from 1968 to 1971
- promoted to vice-president in 1972
- from 1973 to 1977 served as vice-president and chief executive of the Components and Materials Group
- served as senior vice-president of the Consumer Goods and Services Division from 1977 to 1979
- promoted to vice-chairman and executive officer in 1979
- appointed chairman and chief executive officer (CEO) of General Electric in 1981

1 Introduction

John Francis Welch, Jr (aka Jack), was born on 19 November 1935 in Peabody, Massachusetts, the only child of John Francis, Sr, and Grace Andrews Welch. His father was a railroad conductor on the Boston & Maine Railroad and spent a lot of time away from home. Welch was largely raised by his mother, who was said to have been both demanding and supportive of her son. She told him 'that his serious stammer was not a speech impediment, but the result of a hyperactive brain working too fast for his mouth' (Rosen 1993).

Welch grew up in a tough working-class neighbourhood where fights were common (Smart 1992). He was an aggressive and determined athlete who played neighbourhood sports (e.g. baseball, basketball) in an abandoned quarry named 'The Pit' (Harris 1986). 'Friends say Welch was an accomplished, if not natural, athlete who always pushed himself to the limit' (Harris 1986). College classmates remember his intense competitive spirit and how much he hated to lose, 'even in touch football' (Harris, 1986).

After finishing his graduate education, Welch joined the General Electric Company (GE; see GENERAL ELECTRIC COMPANY) where he worked his way up from the position of engineer. In 1981 he made history when he became the youngest person (at 45) to be appointed chairman and CEO of GE.

From 1959 to 1987 Welch was married to Carolyn Osburn. In April 1989 he married Jane Beasley. He has four children (Katherine, John, Anne and Mark) from his first marriage (Rosen 1993; Harris 1986).

In 1995, at the age of 59, Welch underwent elective triple bypass heart surgery to relieve arterial blockages. Following the surgery he ran GE from his home and a month later he was back on the job. He has plans to work until his 65th birthday in the year 2000 (Smart 1995).

2 Main contribution

'Within three years of his appointment as general manager of GE's worldwide plastics division, Welch turned the fledgling division into a $400 million-a-year powerhouse. Promotions followed rapid-fire' (Rosen 1993). Welch was nicknamed 'Neutron Jack' in the 1980s after his massive downsizing and restructuring had led to more than a 25 per cent reduction in employment at GE (Rosen 1993). 'Welch has trimmed GE's work force from 400,000 in 1981 to 220,000 today, has nearly doubled revenue from $26 billion a year and has transformed GE into truly a global corporation' (Swoboda 1994).

During Welch's tenure as chairman and CEO GE has bought and sold companies/divisions to bolster overall corporate performance. After taking over the top job at GE in 1981, Welch stated that any operating unit which was not ranked number one or two in terms of world market share would be sold (Swoboda 1994). He divided the company's divisions into 'winners' and 'losers', and gave those on the loser list one year to turn their operations into winners, i.e. number one or two globally (Rosen 1993). In 1988 Welch even sold GE's Consumer Electronics group to Thomson SA of France after he became convinced that the group would not be able to meet his high profitability standards (Stein 1989). History supports Welch's prediction, as Thomson's consumer electronics operations posted sizeable operating losses in the 1990s, including a 1991 write-off of $365 million (Levine 1991; *PR Newswire* 1997).

As part of his long-term strategy, Welch has led GE into new markets such as television (NBC and MSNBC) and established a new corporate intranet to improve significantly the utilization of information within GE (Smart 1996). In 1996, GE used the intranet and the Internet to match GE buyers with outside sellers for $1 billion worth of goods purchased electronically: 'The payoff ... is that GE can select from a broader base of suppliers as well as cut its purchasing costs' (Smart 1996).

During the 1990s Welch has attempted to create what he refers to as a 'boundaryless company'. According to Welch, 'A boundaryless company ... will remove the barriers among engineering, manufacturing, marketing, sales and customer service; it will recognize no distinctions between "domestic" and "foreign" operations. ... [It] will ignore or erase group labels such as "management", "salaried" or "hourly", which get in the way of people working together' (Swoboda 1994). He has implemented a strategy of worker participation and empowerment in the 1990s. 'The cornerstone of Welch's New Age management is the Work-Out, an intense [2–3-day] forum in which rank and file GE employees and managers brainstorm about ways to make production more efficient in factories and other facilities' (Rosen 1993).

Sticking to his vision, Welch is in the process of further restructuring GE in order to ensure the company's ability to compete after his planned retirement in the year 2000. As in the past, 'Plants and product lines may be closed or sold, wages cut, and work transferred to non-union plants and subcontractors both here and abroad' (Bernstein, Jackson and Byrne 1997).

3 Evaluation

'Welch's intense intellect and hard-charging style have earnt him a reputation as one of the country's toughest managers, as well as one of its emerging gurus of business management' (Lueck 1985). He is known for continually cutting costs and improving productivity throughout GE. There are also some signs that Jack is more sensitive than he is generally perceived to be. He resents the nickname 'Neutron Jack' and has stated that '[i]t was really painful for me and for the people [whose jobs were eliminated]' (Swoboda 1994). He believes that job security is provided only by the ability to compete effectively in a global marketplace. Welch loathes inefficient bureaucracies and continually strives to eliminate layers of management which he sees as impeding efficient decision-making. At GE Welch has reduced the management hierarchy from nine levels to as few as four (Byrne 1989). He believes that '[t]he role of a successful corporate leader ... is to create "shock" and then lead the company to recovery' (Swoboda 1994).

While Welch is often criticized for his harsh management style, he is frequently cited for his strategic leadership abilities. Many now believe that GE under the leadership of Jack Welch has been a trend-setting multinational corporation (MNC): 'Welch has been a pioneer of fundamental structural change in the American workplace' (Swoboda 1994). His influence has been further enlarged by his ability to mentor and nurture GE managers and executives who have gone on to lead other prominent organizations. For example, he has contributed to the development of CEOs such as Larry Bossidy of Allied Signal, Glen Hiner of Owens Corning, Jon Trani of Stanley Works, and Norm Blake of USF&G (Martin 1997; Reingold and Byrne 1997). Welch has also been invited to share his management philosophy with corporate executives at firms such as IBM (see INTERNATIONAL BUSINESS MACHINES CORPORATION) (Hammonds 1994).

Despite all of his successes, Welch is not immune to mistakes and failures. For example, 'GE did not pursue research into magnetic levitation technology for railroads ... even as it boosted its investment in the manufacturing of conventional locomotives, whose revival Welch had optimistically and incorrectly predicted' (Rosen 1993). Shortly after GE purchased the brokerage firm of Kidder Peabody in 1986, Welch was embarrassed by a government bond scandal within the brokerage (Hawthorne et al. 1994). Internal fraud with GE's military accounts in the 1980s was also difficult for Welch to accept (Rosen 1993; Lueck 1985).

These problems have not hindered Welch from positioning GE to continue to produce 25 per cent or greater annual returns on equity (Bernstein, Jackson and Byrne 1997). In the first quarter of 1998 GE had record earnings of $1.891 billion on revenues of $22.6 billion. 'It was the 22nd consecutive quarter that GE has delivered double-digit earnings growth from ongoing operations' (Hanley 1998). GE was listed by *Fortune* magazine as one of America's ten most admired companies and the most valuable, with market capitalization of $254 billion (Stewart 1998). Similarly, *Forbes* magazine (20 April 1998) named GE the most powerful corporation in the United States after its profits increased by 13 per cent in 1997, to $8.2 billion (Reuters 1998). GE is the third most profitable company in the world, after Shell and Exxon (Stewart 1998).

STEPHEN J. HAVLOVIC
SIMON FRASER UNIVERSITY

Further reading

(References cited in the text marked *)

* Bernstein, Aaron, Jackson, Susan and Byrne, John (1997) 'Jack cracks the whip again', *Business Week*, 13 December: 34.
* Byrne, John A. (1989) 'Is your company too big?', *Business Week*, 27 March: 84.
Hammonds, Keith H. (1994) 'Empty chairs in IBM's boardroom', *Business Week*, 7 March: 54.
* Hanley, John (1998) 'GE's higher Q1 hits target', Reuters, Business News, 8 April.
Harris, Marilyn A. (1986) 'He hated losing – even in touch football', *Business Week*, 30 June: 65.
* Hawthorne, Fran, Carroll, Michael, Conger, Lucy, Muehring, Funke, Jennifer, Makin, Claire, Kevin, Peltz, Michael and Picker, Ida (1994) 'GE draws a line in the sand at kidder', *Institutional Investor*, July: 13.
* Levine, Jonathan B. (1991) 'The heat on Alain Gomez', *Business Week*, 11 March: 66–7.
* Lueck, Thomas J. (1985) 'Why Jack Welch is changing G.E.', *New York Times*, Section 3, 5 May: 1.
* Martin, Justin (1997) 'Another GE veteran rides to the rescue', *Fortune*, 29 December: 282.
* *PR Newswire* (1997) 'Thomson & units ratings affirmed', *PR Newswire*, 3 June.
* Reingold, Jennifer and Byrne, John A. (1997) 'The top 20 heads to hunt', *Business Week*, 11 August: 69.
* Reuters (1998) 'GE is no. 1 on *Forbes* super 100 list', Business News.
* Rosen, Isaac (1993) 'Jack Welch', *Newsmakers 1993*, issue 4.
Slater, Robert I. (1993) *The New GE: How Jack Welch Revived an American Institution*, Homewood, IL: Business One Irwin. (Uses interviews with Jack Welch to interpret and explain organizational change and performance at GE.)
* Smart, Tim (1992) 'How Jack Welch brought GE to life', *Business Week*, 26 October: 13.
* Smart, Tim (1995) 'Who could replace Jack Welch?', *Business Week*, 29 May: 32.
* Smart, Tim (1996) 'Jack Welch's cyber-czar', *Business Week*, 5 August: 82.
* Stein, Charles (1989) 'Ex-GE executive hired to run Wang', *Boston Globe*, Economy Section, 24 August: 1.
* Stewart, Thomas A. (1998) 'America's most admired companies', *Fortune*, 2 March: 70–82.
* Swoboda, Frank (1994) 'Up against the walls', *Washington Post*, 27 February: H1.
Tichy, Noel M. and Sherman, Stratford (1993) *Control Your Destiny or Someone Else Will:*

How Jack Welch is Making General Electric the World's Most Competitive Corporation, New York: Doubleday. (Provides an 'inside' view of Jack Welch's leadership style and accomplishments at GE.)

See also: GENERAL ELECTRIC COMPANY; INTERNATIONAL BUSINESS MACHINES CORPORATION

Related topics in the IEBM: DOWNSIZING; MANUFACTURING STRATEGY

Yang, Jerry (1968–)

Personal background

- born 1968 in Taiwan
- graduated from Stanford University in 1990 with a BS and MS in Electrical Engineering
- PhD student at Stanford
- launched Yahoo! with David Filo in 1995
- appointed to board of directors of Metricom Inc. in 1996
- in 1996 Yahoo!'s initial public offering of stock was the second most profitable ever

1 Introduction

Jerry Yang was born in Taiwan in 1968. When he was 2 years old his father died. According to his mother, Lily, Jerry was precocious and started learning the Chinese alphabet by the age of 3. In 1978 Yang, his younger brother Ken and his mother moved to San Jose, California, where Yang became a straight-A student (Plummer and Harrison 1995).

He graduated from Stanford University in 1990, earning both Bachelor of Science and Master of Science degrees in Electrical Engineering. Yang then entered the PhD engineering programme at Stanford after determining that the job market was not robust. As recently as 1994 he was a PhD student at Stanford University. He described himself as 'quasi retired at age 23 ... playing a lot of golf' (Plummer and Harrison 1995). That lifestyle changed in April 1995 when Yang and David Filo launched Yahoo! as a business. Now they 'can barely find the time to sleep and eat' (Plummer and Harrison 1995). Yang does, however, manage enough time to have a girlfriend, Akiko (Plummer and Harrison 1995).

Co-founder David Filo's father used to call Yang and him 'Yahoos', and Yang has become known as the Chief Yahoo. Officially, Yahoo! stands for 'Yet Another Hierarchical Officious Oracle' (Plummer and Harrison 1995). According to Jerry, the exclamation mark is 'pure marketing hype' (Stross 1998). Yang appears to enjoy the press and public relations aspects of his job. Perhaps most notable was his meeting with the US vice-president, Al Gore, to discuss the future of the Internet (Wylie 1997). In June 1996 Metricom Inc. appointed Yang to its board of directors (*PR Newswire* 1996c).

Money does not seem to be an important motivator for Yang: 'To tell you the truth ... I don't even know how many shares I have. ... I mean I'm 28 – I don't need the money, I don't want the money, I don't want to pay taxes' (CNET 1997). He says he has made no major purchases and still flies in economy class when he travels. He has an easygoing image and has been pictured working in T-shirts, jeans and without shoes (Wylie 1997).

2 Main contribution

Yahoo! was created in 1995 when two Stanford PhD students, Jerry Yang and David Filo, created a directory of their favorite Web sites. 'As a lark, they decided to offer their combined list to other WEB wanderers – and now Yang and Filo are on the verge of becoming as well-known, say, as Hewlett and Packard' (Plummer and Harrison 1995). By December 1996 their business had grown into an Internet empire with 20 million 'page turns' per day. More people visit Yahoo! than America Online or Netscape (Stross 1998). In 1997, while its revenues were low ($67 million), it had a market capitalization of $2.8 billion, putting it in the same league as Estée Lauder, the cosmetics giant (Stross 1998). By November 1997 the company had 200 employees

(Wylie 1997). Yahoo! Inc. is located in the Silicon Valley of California.

Yang is able to describe metaphorically the business intensity that he and the other employees at Yahoo! face on a daily basis. He says: 'There's this huge, fast moving train called the Internet. And we're just half a mile ahead laying tracks to make sure it doesn't go off the cliff. It's felt like that since the very beginning' (CNET 1997). According to Yang, 'you never, ever want to compete with Microsoft. And even if they want to compete with you, you run away and do something else' (Wylie 1997). He sees his role at Yahoo! Inc. as one of influence, not control or dominance (CNET 1997).

From the beginning the strategy has been 'to make money through advertising and licensing fees from on-line services rather than charging for the service itself' (Plummer and Harrison 1995). The company has been developing a group of Yahoo! brand services, including Yahoo! Computing; Yahoo! Internet Life; Yahooligans – a web guide for kids; Yahoo! Japan; and Yahoo! Canada (*PR Newswire* 1996b). As of February 1998 Yahoo! offered its Internet directories in German, French, Japanese, Korean and three Nordic languages (Michelson 1998).

Yang spends his time primarily in business development. He has formed key partnerships in order to expand Yahoo! For example, he worked with Softbank to set-up Yahoo! Japan and with Ziff-Davis Publishing Company to establish the interactive magazine Yahoo! Internet Life (CNET 1997). Yang stated in early 1996 that 'Yahoo! Internet Life has already established a new standard for in-depth, insightful, comparative reviews of Web sites' (*PR Newswire* 1996a). Yahoo! Internet Life is the largest and fastest-growing consumer magazine dedicated to the Internet and maintains its own separate Web site (*PR Newswire* 1996d). Among the services offered by Yahoo! is a free e-mail service (http://www.yahoo.com).

In 1996 Proctor and Gamble (P&G; see PROCTOR & GAMBLE COMPANY) contracted Yahoo! as an interactive advertiser to promote its brands and to direct interested Internet users to P&G Web sites. 'Yahoo! has run interactive promotions with leading companies like Citibank, NBC, NFL, Disney Online [see WALT DISNEY COMPANY], Snapple and Southwest Airlines. The P&G program is the latest to demonstrate Yahoo!'s expertise and leadership in this area' (*PR Newswire* 1996c). In early 1998 Autoweb.com, an online car-buying service, coordinated a car giveaway with Yahoo! which gave 15 million Yahoo! users the opportunity to see Autoweb.com's promotion on Yahoo!'s home page (*Business Wire* 1998).

There is recent evidence to suggest that Yahoo! is beginning to take a more aggressive position in the marketplace: 'Yahoo! ... now aims to create communities on the net and compete with on-line service providers such as America Online as well as publishers' (Michelson 1998). In 1998 Yahoo! hopes not only to expand its search and directory service geographically, but to connect users online and to develop relationships with its users. In January 1998 Yahoo! entered into a marketing deal with MCI Telecommunications Corporation to provide 'a Yahoo! branded internet-access service' by the end of March 1998 (Stross 1998).

3 Evaluation

What started as a hobby has in a very brief period of time grown into an important and trend-setting corporation (Wylie 1997). Yang and Filo did not have previous business experience (CNET 1997), but they did have the skills successfully to develop 'a computerized index system that catalogs the Web' (Plummer and Harrison 1995). Yahoo! has hired Tim Koogle, a Stanford-educated engineer with nine years' experience at Motorola, as chief executive officer CEO (Stross 1998). It remains to be seen whether they have the management abilities necessary successfully to lead a rapidly expanding and highly competitive business.

According to Yang, 'Had we wanted to do it for money, we would have sold it very early on, because there was a lot of money dangling in front of us' (CNET 1997). Some key agreements early on were important. They received cash from a Menlo Park, California, venture capital firm, and Netscape lent them computers and Internet access lines in exchange for a Netscape advertisement that appeared whenever the Yahoo! Web site was accessed (Plummer and Harrison 1995).

Yang's official line is that '[w]e're intent on growing the business in the next couple of years. I think the profitability, for us, is accidental. We run a disciplined business and try to break even' (CNET 1997). In early 1996 Yahoo! made history when its initial public offering (IPO) of stock was the second most profitable ever (*PR Newswire* 1996c).

Jerry Yang has helped guide Yahoo! Inc. to respect simultaneously First Amendment free speech rights, the Communications Decency Act and the basic rights of advertisers. At the same time, Yahoo! has tried to be socially responsible by denying tobacco and hard alcohol manufacturers the right to advertise on Yahoo! sites (CNET 1997).

STEPHEN J. HAVLOVIC
SIMON FRASER UNIVERSITY

Further reading

(References cited in the text marked *)

* *Business Wire* (1998) 'Autoweb.com and Yahoo! partner to deliver biggest on-line promotion', *Business Wire*, 26 January. (News release.)
* CNET (1997) 'Yang: just for fun', *News.com – Newsmakers*. (An exclusive interview with Jerry Yang.)
* Michelson, Marcel (1998) 'Yahoo! to offer services, eyes Spain', *Reuters*, 10 February. (News release.)
* Plummer, William and Harrison, Laird (1995) 'The world at their fingertips', *People*, 4 December. (Takes a look at Jerry Yang and David Filo.)
* *PR Newswire* (1996a) 'Ziff-Davis names Barry Golson editor-in-chief of Yahoo! Internet Life', *PR Newswire*, 15 February. (News release.)
* *PR Newswire* (1996b) 'Yahoo and Proctor & Gamble develop interactive traffic building promotion', *PR Newswire*, 8 May. (News release.)
* *PR Newswire* (1996c) 'Metricom announces Yahoo! co-founder and the CEO of World-Net Access join its board of directors', *PR Newswire*, 25 June. (News release.)
* *PR Newswire* (1996d) 'Cybercolumnist John Motavalli "scoops" for Yahoo! Internet Life', *PR Newswire*, 7 October. (News release.)
* Stross, R.E. (1998) 'How Yahoo! won the search wars', *Fortune*, 2 March: 148–54. (Takes a look at Yahoo!'s growth and business performance.)
* Wylie, Margie (1997) 'Barefoot millionaire boys', *News.com – Newsmakers*, 10 November. (Reviews the business successes of Jerry Yang and David Filo.)

Further resources

* http://www.yahoo.com (Home of the Yahoo! World Wide Web directory.)

See also: PROCTOR & GAMBLE COMPANY; WALT DISNEY COMPANY

Related topics in the IEBM: INTERNET AND BUSINESS

Index